THE ATLANTIC WORLD

As the meeting point between Europe, colonial America, and Africa, the history of the Atlantic world is a constantly shifting arena, but one which has been a focus of huge and vibrant debate for many years. In over thirty chapters, all written by experts in the field, *The Atlantic World* takes up these debates and gathers together key, original scholarship to provide an authoritative survey of this increasingly popular area of world history.

The book takes a thematic approach to topics including exploration, migration, and cultural encounters. In the first chapters, scholars examine the interactions between groups which converged in the Atlantic world, such as slaves, European migrants, and Native Americans. The volume then considers questions such as finance, money, and commerce in the Atlantic world, as well as warfare, government, and religion. The collection closes with chapters examining how ideas circulated across and around the Atlantic and beyond. It presents the Atlantic as a shared space in which commodities and ideas were exchanged and traded, and examines the impact that these exchanges had on both people and places.

Including an introductory essay from the editors which defines the field, and lavishly illustrated with paintings, drawings, and maps this accessible volume is invaluable reading for all students and scholars of this broad sweep of world history.

D'Maris Coffman is a Leverhulme Trust Early Career Fellow and Director of the Centre for Financial History at Newnham College, University of Cambridge; **Adrian Leonard** is a post-doctoral researcher at the Centre for Financial History at Newnham College, University of Cambridge; and **William O'Reilly** is lecturer in Early Modern History at the University of Cambridge.

THE ROUTLEDGE WORLDS

THE CELTIC WORLD
Edited by Miranda Green

THE GREEK WORLD
Edited by Anton Powell

THE REFORMATION WORLD
Edited by Andrew Pettegree

THE EARLY CHRISTIAN WORLD
Edited by Philip F. Esler

THE ROMAN WORLD
Edited by John Wacher

THE MEDIEVAL WORLD
Edited by Peter Linehan and Janet L. Nelson

THE BIBLICAL WORLD
Edited by John Barton

THE HINDU WORLD
Edited by Sushil Mittal and Gene Thursby

THE ENLIGHTENMENT WORLD
Edited by Martin Fitzpatrick

THE WORLD OF POMPEII
Edited by Pedar W. Foss and John J. Dobbins

THE BABYLONIAN WORLD
Edited by Gwendolyn Leick

THE RENAISSANCE WORLD
Edited by John Jeffries Martin

THE EGYPTIAN WORLD
Edited by Toby Wilkinson

THE ISLAMIC WORLD
Edited by Andrew Rippin

THE VIKING WORLD
Edited by Stefan Brink and Neil Price

THE BYZANTINE WORLD
Edited by Paul Stephenson

THE ELIZABETHAN WORLD
Edited by Susan Doran and Norman Jones

THE WORLD OF THE AMERICAN WEST
Edited by Gordon Morris Bakken

THE OTTOMAN WORLD
Edited by Christine Woodhead

THE VICTORIAN WORLD
Edited by Martin Hewitt

THE ORTHODOX CHRISTIAN WORLD
Edited by Augustine Casiday

THE SUMERIAN WORLD
Edited by Harriet Crawford

THE ETRUSCAN WORLD
Edited by Jean MacIntosh Turfa

THE GOTHIC WORLD
Edited by Glennis Byron and Dale Townshend

THE WORLD OF THE REVOLUTIONARY AMERICAN REPUBLIC
Edited by Andrew Shankman

THE WORLD OF INDIGENOUS NORTH AMERICA
Edited by Robert Warrior

THE FIN-DE-SIÈCLE WORLD
Edited by Michael Saler

THE OCCULT WORLD
Edited by Christopher Partridge

Forthcoming:

THE MODERNIST WORLD
Allana Lindgren and Stephen Ross

THE BUDDHIST WORLD
John Powers

THE CRUSADER WORLD
Adrian Boas

THE POSTCOLONIAL WORLD
Jyotsna Singh and David Kim

THE WORLD OF FORMATIVE EUROPE
Edited by Martin Carver and Madeleine Hummler

THE ATLANTIC WORLD

Edited by

D'Maris Coffman, Adrian Leonard and William O'Reilly

LONDON AND NEW YORK

First published 2015
by Routledge
2 Park Square, Milton Park, Abingdon, Oxon OX14 4RN

and by Routledge
711 Third Avenue, New York, NY 10017

Routledge is an imprint of the Taylor & Francis Group, an informa business

© 2015 D'Maris Coffman, Adrian Leonard and William O'Reilly

The right of D'Maris Coffman, Adrian Leonard and William O'Reilly to be identified as the authors of the editorial material, and of the authors for their individual chapters, has been asserted in accordance with sections 77 and 78 of the Copyright, Designs and Patents Act 1988.

All rights reserved. No part of this book may be reprinted or reproduced or utilized in any form or by any electronic, mechanical, or other means, now known or hereafter invented, including photocopying and recording, or in any information storage or retrieval system, without permission in writing from the publishers.

Trademark notice: Product or corporate names may be trademarks or registered trademarks, and are used only for identification and explanation without intent to infringe.

British Library Cataloguing-in-Publication Data
A catalogue record for this book is available from the British Library

Library of Congress Cataloging-in-Publication Data
A catalog record for this book has been requested

ISBN: 978-0-415-46704-9 (hbk)
ISBN: 978-1-315-73921-2 (ebk)

Typeset in Sabon
by Saxon Graphics Ltd, Derby

Printed and bound in the United States of America by Publishers Graphics, LLC on sustainably sourced paper.

CONTENTS

List of Figures   *xi*

Acknowledgments   *xiii*

Notes on Contributors   *xiv*

1   The Atlantic World: Definition, Theory, and Boundaries   1
D'Maris Coffman and Adrian Leonard

PART I: ATLANTIC EXPLORATIONS   11

2   Animals in Atlantic North America to 1800   13
James Taylor Carson and Karim M. Tiro

3   Science and Ideology in the Spanish Atlantic   34
Sandra Rebok

4   Fish and Fisheries in the Atlantic World   55
David J. Starkey

PART II: THE MOVEMENT OF PEOPLES   77

5   Facing East from the South: Indigenous Americans in the Mostly
Iberian Atlantic World   79
Laura E. Matthew

6   Southern Africa and the Atlantic World   100
Gerald Groenewald

7   Emigration from the Habsburg Monarchy and Salzburg to the
New World, 1700–1848   117
William O'Reilly

vii

– Contents –

8	Seafaring communities, 1800–1850	131
	Brian Rouleau	

PART III: CULTURAL ENCOUNTERS — 149

9	Colour Prejudice in the French Atlantic World	151
	Mélanie Lamotte	
10	Atlantic Slaveries: Britons, Barbary, and the Atlantic World	172
	Catherine Styer	
11	Morocco and Atlantic History	187
	James A. O. C. Brown	
12	The Atlantic and Pacific Worlds	207
	Paul D'Arcy	
13	An Enslaved Enlightenment: Rethinking the Intellectual History of the French Atlantic	227
	Laurent Dubois	

PART IV: WARFARE AND GOVERNANCE — 243

14	Violence in the Atlantic World	245
	John Smolenski	
15	War and Warfare in the Atlantic World	264
	Geoffrey Plank	
16	Political Thinking, Military Power, and Arms Bearing in the British Atlantic World	281
	Charles R. Drummond, IV	
17	Atlantic Peripheries: Diplomacy, War, and Spanish–French Interactions in Hispaniola, 1660s–1690s	300
	Juan J. Ponce-Vázquez	

PART V: RELIGION — 319

18	Catholicism	321
	E. L. Devlin	
19	Protestantism in the Atlantic World	347
	Travis Glasson	
20	The Freest Country: Jews of the British Atlantic, ca. 1600–1800	364
	Natalie A. Zacek	
21	Islam and the Atlantic	376
	Denise A. Spellberg	

Contents

22 American Identity and English Catholicism in the Atlantic World 393
Maura Jane Farrelly

23 Navigating the Jewish Atlantic: The State of the Field and Opportunities
for New Research 413
Holly Snyder

PART VI: CREDIT, FINANCE, AND MONEY **439**

24 British Joint-Stock Companies and Atlantic Trading 441
Matthew David Mitchell

25 Speculating on the Atlantic World 457
Helen Paul

26 Paper Money, 1450–1850 471
Dror Goldberg

27 The Credit Crisis of 1772–73 in the Atlantic World 491
Paul Kosmetatos

PART VII: COMMERCE, CONSUMPTION, AND MERCANTILE NETWORKS **511**

28 Reassessing the Atlantic Contribution to British Marine Insurance 513
A. B. Leonard

29 The Economic World of the Early Dutch and English Atlantic 531
Edmond Smith

30 The Cultural History of Commerce in the Atlantic World 546
Jonathan Eacott

31 'To Catch the Public Taste': Interpreting American Consumers in
the Era of Atlantic Free Trade, 1783–1854 573
Joanna Cohen

PART VIII: THE CIRCULATION OF IDEAS **597**

32 'Excited Almost to Madness:' Slave Rebellions and Resistance in the
Atlantic World 599
Jeffrey A. Fortin

33 Economic Thought and State Practice in the Atlantic World:
The 'Phénomène Savary' in Context 618
D'Maris Coffman

34 The Classical Atlantic World 633
N. P. Cole

– Contents –

35 The Atlantic Enlightenment 650
William Max Nelson

Index 667

FIGURES

2.1 Mask with antlers, 1400–1600 (wood & bone), Mississippian culture
(c. 800–1500) 14
2.2 Florida Indians hunting deer while disguised under deerskins, from
'Americae Decima Pars' engraved by Theodor de Bry (1528–98) 1591 16
2.3 New Belgium Map, plate from 'Atlas Contractus' c. 1671 18
2.4 'A view of ye Industry of ye Beavers' from Herman Moll's New and
Exact Map, 1715 19
2.5 Pennsylvania Town and Country Man's Almanack 24
3.1 Las Casas 38
3.2 Emperor Carl V with Quevedo and Las Casas 39
3.3 Alejandro Malaspina 43
3.4 Indigenous man. From the Canadian Expedition of Alejandro
Malaspina (1789–94) 44
4.1 Dragging in the seine net 65
4.2 A naval architect's representation of an early fifteenth-century
English dogger 69
5.1 Tlaxcalteca and Spaniards fighting the Mexica Tenochca at Tenochtitlan 81
5.2 Frontispiece of a 1722 reprint of the second part of el Inca Garcilaso
de la Vega's *Commentarios reales*, originally published in 1617 87
6.1 A view of the Cape of Good Hope and a plan of the town of the
Cape of Good Hope and its environs, published 1795 (engraving) 101
8.1 John Archibald Woodside's painting, entitled: We Owe Allegiance to
No Crown 135
10.1 Barbary Pirates 175
10.2 Tripoli – stronghold of Barbary Pirates 176
11.1 Catalan Map of Europe and North Africa 188
12.1 Map of the Atlantic, Pacific and Indian Oceans 208
15.1 Pinasses, large French and English ships trading with the Americas 266
15.2 Slave traders in Gorés 270
16.1 The specter of the standing army in eighteenth-century America 285
17.1 Santo Domingo, 1671 301
17.2 Buccaneer in the West Indies, 1686 303

Figures

18.1 Virgin of Guadalupe	331
18.2 Inca Princess	333
19.1 Frontispiece and title page of the 1787 edition of the Book of Common Prayer into the Mohawk language	354
19.2 Engraved portrait of the Afro-Dutch minister Jacobus Capitein	356
21.1 The title page of Roger Williams' 'Bloudy Tenent' 1644	385
21.2 Ibrahima Abd al-Rahman, also known as the Prince of Slaves	388
22.1 Virginia, Maryland, Chesapeake Bay	396
22.2 Cecil Calvert, first Lord Baltimore	402
24.1 The several journals of the Court of Directors of the Company of Scotland Trading to Africa and the Indies	442
24.2 The South-Sea House in Bishops-gate Street, published according to Act of Parliament, for Stowe's Survey, 1754	443
24.3 Views of forts and castles along the Gold Coast, West Africa, about 1700	447
25.1 Trade label of the South Sea Company	458
25.2 'The Bubblers Bubbl'd' or 'The Devil Take the Hindmost', 1720	459
26.1 Bill of Exchange, 1690/1	475
26.2 Assignat (banknote) for 50 sols dated revolutionary year II (1793) of French Republic	482
27.1 Tobacco ships in America	494
28.1 The Corsini Papers	515
29.1 Hakluyt's Map of the New World 1587	532
29.2 New Belgium, plate from 'Atlas Contractus', c. 1671	540
30.1 Ralph Earl, *Elijah Boardman*, 1789	564
32.1 Slavery/West Indies	607
32.2 Black slaves working on a plantation and sugar factory	608
33.1 Frontispiece of 'Le Parfait Negociant' by Jacques Savary, Paris, 1665 (engraving)	620
33.2 The Great Financier, or British Economy for the Years 1763, 1764, 1765	626
33.3 An exciseman of the seventeenth century leads an attack on smugglers	628

PUBLISHERS' ACKNOWLEDGEMENTS

The publishers are grateful to the following for permission to reproduce copyright material: Alamy, Alan Hopper of the Maritime Historical Studies Centre, University of Hull, Baker Business Historical Collections – Kress Collection, Harvard University, Bridgeman Art Library, The Trustees of the British Museum, Denver Art Museum, Getty Images, John Carter Brown Library at Brown University, Library of Congress, Massachusetts Historical Society, Mary Evans Picture Library, National Maritime Museum, Greenwich, Scala Archives.

We would also like to thank the editors of *Wiener Zeitschrift zur Geschichte der Neuzeit* (5.Jg, 2005, Heft 1) for permission to reprint William O'Reilly's article, 'Emigration from the Habsburg Monarchy and Salzburg to the New World, 1700–1848' as Chapter 7, and to thank Routledge for permission to reprint Laurent Dubois' article, 'The Enslaved Enlightenment: rethinking the intellectual history of the French Atlantic' (*Social History*, Volume 31, Issue 1, 2006) as Chapter 13.

ACKNOWLEDGMENTS

The editors would like to thank Laura Pilsworth, Associate Editor of History at Routledge, Emily Kindleysides, then Assistant Editor, Geraldine Martin, Senior Production Editor, and Catherine Aitken and Paul Brotherston, Editorial Assistants, for their stalwart support of this volume through the vicissitudes of the past seven years. Catherine in particular worked tirelessly to shepherd the book through the critical final months. The recruitment of contributors proved a remarkably rewarding experience, and offered a rare opportunity to blend various methodological approaches and theoretical stances. As editors, we are pleased that so many of the original contributors remained onboard when the editorial team changed in August 2013 and are proud that the new contributors, numbering almost two dozen, went to such Herculean efforts to produce their own essays within only nine months.

Throughout the volume's lengthy birthing, there was some attrition with resulting oversights and omissions. We trust that those who rue the absence of an article on their favorite theme will at least discover new topics and new approaches within these covers.

Special thanks are due to Charles Drummond, Jaya Dalal, Lucia Novak, and Penelope Coffman for their indefatigable work as research assistants, copy editors, and proofreaders of the original submissions. Froma Zeitlin also deserves a warm thank you for ensuring the speedy delivery of a clean digital copy of one of the reprinted chapters for use by the optical character recognition software. Conversations with the contributors and with Mark Goldie, Jenny Mander, John Morrill, David Ormrod, and Julia Rudolph have produced both recommendations for contributing authors and new directions to explore. Any errors nevertheless remain our own.

Finally we would like to acknowledge our students, especially those at the University of Cambridge and the University of Pennsylvania, for their enthusiasm for the subject matter and for asking the very questions these essays are meant to answer. We hope that future generations will profit from their curiosity and from the vibrancy and rigor of this new generation of Atlantic scholarship.

CONTRIBUTORS

James A. O. C. Brown recently completed a Research Fellowship at the University of Cambridge funded by the Leverhulme Trust, exploring the development of political legitimacy in the medieval Maghrib and Islamic Spain, as part of which he contributed to a recent volume of the Proceedings of the British Academy, *The Articulation of Power in Medieval Iberia and the Maghrib* (2014). His other research has focused Morocco's relationship to the emergent modern world, particularly in his first book *Crossing The Strait: Morocco, Gibraltar and Great Britain in the 18th and 19th Centuries* (2012).

James Taylor Carson is Professor of History and Chair of Department at Queen's University in Kingston, Ontario, Canada. His work focuses broadly on the ethnohistory of North America's first peoples and he has authored *Searching for the Bright Path: The Mississippi Choctaws from Prehistory to Removal* (1999) and *Making an Atlantic World: Circles, Paths, and Stories from the Colonial South* (2007) as well as numerous articles and book chapters. He is currently working on a short book about how historians use racial language and categories to write United States' history.

D'Maris Coffman is a Leverhulme/Newton Trust Early Career Fellow in the History Faculty of the University of Cambridge and is the Director of the Centre for Financial History at Newnham College, where she remains a fellow. From October 2008 through September 2013, she was the Mary Bateson Research Fellow at Newnham. Her first monograph, *Excise Taxation and the Origins of the Public Debt*, was published in October 2013. Most of her current research focuses on the role of state finance in the development of capital markets in eighteenth- and nineteenth-century Europe and North America and on the consequences of the growth of the fiscal state for agricultural commodity markets.

Joanna Cohen is lecturer at Queen Mary University of London. Her research examines the intersections of consumer culture, political economy, and citizenship in nineteenth-century America. She is currently completing a book called *Luxurious Citizens: Consumption and Civic Belonging in Nineteenth Century America*. She

– Contributors –

has published articles in the *Journal of the Early Republic* and *The Winterthur Portfolio* and has appeared on the BBC Radio 3 program, *Freethinking*, as one of the AHRC New Generation Thinkers.

Nicholas Cole is a Senior Research Fellow in History at Pembroke College, Oxford. His research focuses on the political thought and governing institutions of the early American Republic. He has a particular interest in the utility of classical thought for the founding generation. He is currently working on a study of the understanding of Executive Power in the nineteenth century. *Thomas Jefferson, the Classical World, and Early America*, which he edited along with Peter Onuf, was published by the University of Virginia Press in 2011.

Paul D'Arcy is Associate Professor in the Department of Pacific and Asian History at the Australian National University. He teaches courses in Pacific history and environmental conflict in the Asia Pacific region. His current research focuses on Pacific and Southeast Asian indigenous maritime history, engagement and interactions between Asia and the Pacific, and regional perspectives on contemporary maritime resource management in the Pacific region. He is the author of *The People of the Sea: Environment, Identity and History in Oceania* (2006).

E. L. Devlin is a British Academy Postdoctoral Fellow at the Faculty of History, University of Cambridge, and a bye-fellow at Selwyn College. His research explores British diplomacy in the long eighteenth century, with a particular emphasis on cultural exchange, the public life of ambassadors, and the importance of extra-European affairs to Anglo-European relations. His first book is a study of British relations with Papal Rome in the late seventeenth century, and he is currently beginning a project investigating British responses to the baroque from the late sixteenth to the late eighteenth centuries.

Charles R. Drummond, IV, is the Postdoctoral fellow at the William P. Clements, Jr. Center for History, Strategy, and Statecraft at the University of Texas at Austin. He has recently completed his Ph.D. in history at Trinity College, Cambridge that explores debates over military power in the British Isles in the second half of the seventeenth century. From 2014 to 2015 he will be a post-doctoral fellow at the Clements Center at the University of Texas at Austin where he will be working on a monograph on the original meaning of the Second Amendment to the U.S. Constitution.

Laurent Dubois is Marcello Lotti Professor of Romance Studies and History at Duke University, where he is the Faculty Director of the Forum for Scholars and Publics. His most recent book is *Haiti: The Aftershocks of History* (2012) and he is currently completing a history of the banjo.

Jonathan Eacott is an Assistant Professor of History at the University of California, Riverside. His publications include, 'Making an Imperial Compromise: The Calico Acts, the Atlantic Colonies, and the Structure of the British Empire,' in the *William and Mary Quarterly*. His forthcoming book uncovers the vital importance of India in the development of the British Empire in the Atlantic and, later, the early American Republic.

– Contributors –

Maura Jane Farrelly is Associate Professor of American Studies and Director of the Journalism Program at Brandeis University. She holds a Ph.D. in history from Emory University, with an emphasis on religion and the colonial and early-American periods. Farrelly is the author of *Papist Patriots: The Making of an American Catholic Identity*, published by Oxford University Press. Before joining the faculty at Brandeis, she was a full-time journalist, working for Georgia Public Radio in Atlanta and the Voice of America in Washington, D.C., and New York. She has also freelanced for National Public Radio and the British Broadcasting Corporation.

Jeffrey Fortin is an Assistant Professor of History at Emmanuel College, Boston where he teaches courses on Atlantic and Early American history. His research focuses on race, migration, and identity formation during the Age of Revolution. He has published in *Atlantic Studies*, among other journals, and recently co-edited *Atlantic Biographies: Individuals and Peoples in the Atlantic World*, a collection of essays that use biography to interpret and analyze Atlantic history. Jeff is currently finishing a book-length biography of Paul Cuffe, the celebrated African-American sea captain, entrepreneur, and supporter of African colonization.

Travis Glasson is Associate Professor of History at Temple University and received his Ph.D. from Columbia University. He is the author of *Mastering Christianity: Missionary Anglicanism and Slavery in the Atlantic World* (2012) and his other publications include articles in the *William and Mary Quarterly* and the *Journal of British Studies*. He is currently at work on a project examining the experiences of neutrals around the British empire during the American Revolution.

Dror Goldberg is a senior lecturer in the Department of Management and Economics at The Open University of Israel. His research focuses on the history of money since the early modern period and the theory of money. He is currently writing a book entitled *How Americans Invented Modern Money, 1607–1692* for the University of Chicago Press.

Gerald Groenewald is an Associate Professor in the Department of Historical Studies at the University of Johannesburg. He has published widely on the social, economic, and cultural history of the Cape of Good Hope during the seventeenth and eighteenth centuries, including *Trials of Slavery* (2005).

Paul Kosmetatos is a retired structured products trader, who obtained his M.A. in Early Modern History at Kings College London before undertaking a Ph.D. at the University of Cambridge on the Credit Crisis of 1772/3. He has a forthcoming article in the *Financial History Review* on the winding up of the Ayr Bank. He won Best Graduate Student Paper at the British Society for Eighteenth-Century Studies in 2012.

Mélanie Lamotte is a Ph.D. student at the University of Cambridge. Her research focuses on color prejudice in the early modern French empire, especially in seventeenth- and eighteenth-century Guadeloupe, Louisiana, and Bourbon Island. Her thesis is entitled 'Colour prejudice in the early modern French empire, c. 1635–1767.' In 2013, she was a Fellow at the Kluge Center, Library of Congress.

– *Contributors* –

A. B. Leonard is a post-doctoral researcher at the Centre for Financial History, University of Cambridge, and Affiliated Lecturer at the University's Faculty of Economics. He has written widely on topics related to marine insurance and the Atlantic World. Current projects include a history of commercial insurance in London in the twentieth century, editing *Marine Insurance: International Development and Evolution*, co-editing *The Caribbean and the Atlantic World Economy: Circuits of Trade, Money and Knowledge, 1650–1914*, and curating a permanent exhibit about the history of Lloyd's, to be installed on the old insurance market's trading floor. Prior to returning to academia to receive Masters and Ph.D. degrees in Economic History from Cambridge, he worked as a writer and commentator on commercial insurance for publishers including the *Financial Times* and Reuters.

Laura Matthew is an Associate Professor of Latin American history at Marquette University. Her research focuses on Mesoamerican history and indigenous experiences of early Spanish colonialism in Guatemala. She is the co-editor with Michel Oudijk of *Indian Conquistadors: Indigenous Allies in the Conquest of Mesoamerica*, and author of *Memories of Conquest: Becoming Mexicano in Colonial Guatemala*, winner of the Howard F. Cline Prize and the Murdo MacLeod Prize. She is currently working on a book about indigenous trade and migration along the southern Pacific coast in the sixteenth century.

Matthew David Mitchell is an Assistant Professor of History at Sewanee: The University of the South. He has published on joint-stock companies and on British involvement in the Atlantic slave trade in such journals as *Enterprise and Society*, *Itinerario*, and *The Journal of the Historical Society*. He is currently at work on a book examining the transformation of British trade with Africa between 1697 and 1732.

William Max Nelson is Assistant Professor of History at the University of Toronto specializing in the history of the Enlightenment and the French Revolution. His research focuses on the ways that ideas about time, race, and biopolitics emerged in eighteenth-century France and the Atlantic world. He is the author of a forthcoming book on this topic and he recently co-edited a book with Suzanne Desan and Lynn Hunt, *The French Revolution in Global Perspective*.

William O'Reilly is University Lecturer at the History Faculty of the University of Cambridge. He has worked on a range of topics in early modern European and Atlantic history, and is particularly interested in the history of European migration, colonialism, and imperialism. His current research project, with the working title, *Surviving Empire: The Translation of Imperial Context in a Globalizing World, 1550–1800*, explores the inter-relationship of European imperialisms from the later sixteenth century to the French revolution. In 2006 Dr. O'Reilly was awarded a Philip Leverhulme Prize for his work in European and Atlantic History. In 2013, he was awarded a Philip Leverhulme Prize for excellence in teaching.

Helen Paul is a lecturer in Economics and Economic History at the University of Southampton. She is an economic historian focusing on the early modern period,

xvii

– Contributors –

especially the Financial Revolution and Atlantic trade. Her first book, *The South Sea Bubble: An Economic History of its Origins and Consequences*, is a revisionist account of the famous financial crash of 1720. She has published a number of book chapters about the fiscal-military or contractor state in Britain and its links to the Royal Navy. She is currently the chair of the Women's Committee of the Economic History Society.

Geoffrey Plank is Professor of Early Modern History at the University of East Anglia. He is the author of *John Woolman's Path to the Peaceable Kingdom: A Quaker in the British Empire, Rebellion and Savagery: The Jacobite Rising of 1745 and the British Empire*, and *An Unsettled Conquest: The British Campaign Against the Peoples of Acadia*.

Juan J. Ponce-Vázquez is a Visiting Assistant Professor at St. Lawrence University. His research focuses on the Spanish Caribbean societies during the seventeenth century. His current book project, entitled *At the Edge of Empire: Social and Political Defiance in Hispaniola, 1580–1697*, explores how the peoples of the Spanish colony of Santo Domingo transcended their marginal location and status within the Spanish colonial world and took advantage of the intense imperial competition that engulfed the Caribbean during the seventeenth century, with the arrival of Northern European settlers.

Sandra Rebok works for the Spanish National Research Council and is currently a Marie Curie Fellow at the Huntington Library (2013–2015). Her actual research project focuses on the networks of knowledge Alexander von Humboldt established within the United States and his impact on the development of sciences in this country. She has recently published a book on the relationship and intellectual exchange between Humboldt and Thomas Jefferson (University of Virginia Press, 2014). She has also curated several exhibitions in the field of history of science.

Brian Rouleau is an Assistant Professor of History at Texas A&M University. His first book, *With Sails Whitening Every Sea: Mariners and the Making of an American Maritime Empire*, focuses on encounters between U.S. sailors and peoples overseas during the nineteenth century. He has also published articles in *Diplomatic History*, the *Journal of the Early Republic*, and *Early American Studies*.

Edmond Smith is undertaking his Ph.D. at the University of Cambridge. His research focuses on the commercial communities of early modern Europe with a specific focus on the English East India Company. His thesis, 'Networks of the East India Company, 1600–1625,' will be completed in 2015. He has published articles on Anglo-Dutch relations, the role of naval power in Indian Ocean diplomacy and the distribution of practical information for investors in overseas commerce.

John Smolenski is Associate Professor of History at the University of California, Davis. His research focuses on culture and identity in the Atlantic world. He is the author of *Friends and Strangers: The Making of a Creole Culture in Colonial Pennsylvania* and the co-editor (with Thomas Humphrey) of *New World Orders: Violence, Sanction, and Authority in the Colonial Americas*. His current book, *Rethinking Creolization: Culture and Power in the Atlantic World*, is under contract with the University of Pennsylvania Press.

– *Contributors* –

Holly Snyder has been Curator of American Historical Collections at Brown University's John Hay Library since July 2004. Her research focuses on Jews in the colonial British Atlantic, and her articles have appeared in the journals *Rhode Island Jewish Historical Notes*, *The William & Mary Quarterly*, *Jewish History*, and *Early American Studies*, as well as in a number of scholarly compilations. She received her Ph.D. in American History from Brandeis University in 2000, and holds an M.S.L.S. and an M.A. degree in American History from The Catholic University of America.

Denise A. Spellberg is Professor of History and Middle Eastern Studies at the University of Texas at Austin. Her research focuses on Islamic civilization and the history of Islam in Europe and the United States. She is the recipient of the Carnegie Foundation Scholarship for her research on Islam in early America. Her most recent book is *Thomas Jefferson's Qur'an: Islam and the Founders* (2013).

David J. Starkey is Professor of Maritime History at the University of Hull, UK. He is Chair of the British Commission for Maritime History and editor-in-chief of the *International Journal of Maritime History*. He has written and co-edited works on various maritime themes, with *British Privateering Enterprise in the 18th Century* (1990), *Shipping Movements in the UK, 1871-1913* (1999), *England's Sea Fisheries* (2000), *Oceans Past* (2007) and *A History of the North Atlantic Fisheries* (2009, 2012) among his published works.

Catherine Styer earned her Ph.D. at the University of Pennsylvania. Her research focuses on race, gender, slavery, and empire in the early modern Atlantic world. She is currently completing a manuscript *Slaves to Empire*. Before returning to academia, she trained as a solicitor in London.

Karim M. Tiro is Professor of History at Xavier University. He is the author of *The People of the Standing Stone: The Oneida Nation from the Revolution through the Era of Removal* and co-editor of *Along the Hudson and Mohawk: The 1790 Journey of Count Paolo Andreani*. His essays have appeared in the *Journal of the Early Republic*, *American Indian Law Review*, and elsewhere.

Natalie Zacek is Senior Lecturer in American Studies at the University of Manchester. Her research focuses on the colonial and antebellum American South and the Caribbean, and she is currently at work on a study of the cultural meaning of horse-racing in nineteenth-century America. Her first monograph, *Settler Society in the English Leeward Islands, 1670–1776* (2010), won the Royal Historical Society's Gladstone Prize, and she has published articles in, amongst other journals, *Slavery and Abolition*, the *Journal of Peasant Studies*, and *History Compass*.

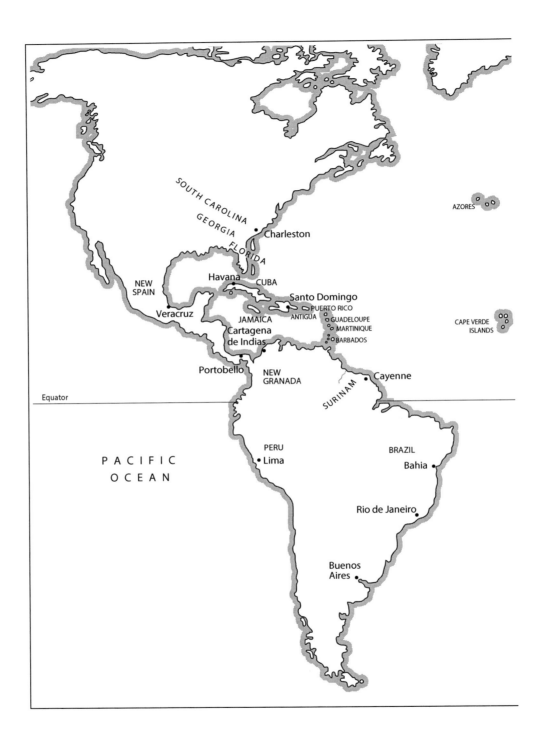

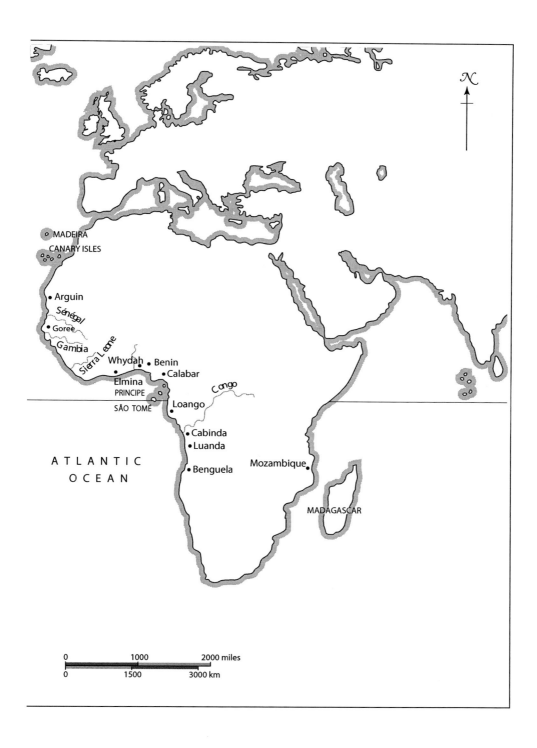

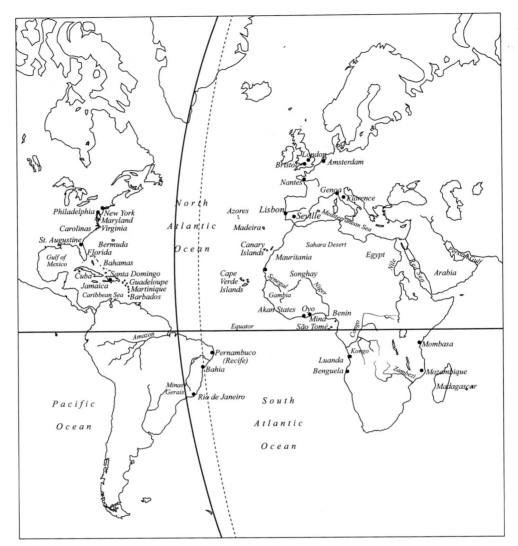

The Atlantic in the early colonial period

CHAPTER ONE

THE ATLANTIC WORLD
Definition, theory, and boundaries

——•◆•——

D'Maris Coffman and Adrian Leonard

What is meant by the term 'Atlantic World' and how has its usage evolved in the last thirty years? If 'Atlantic history' has entered its fourth decade, what is left of the intellectual project inaugurated in the 1980s by Bernard Bailyn at Harvard and Jack Greene at Johns Hopkins? How should the Braudelian ambitions of the *longue durée* of Atlantic regional history sit with postcolonial explorations of the African and Native American experiences, which are by their nature punctuated by political narratives?

Historians have traditionally defined 'Atlantic history' by the ocean itself and through the interactions among the continents that compose its basin: the Americas, Africa, and Europe. For over a decade, David Armitage's construction of three types of Atlantic history: circum-Atlantic, trans-Atlantic, and cis-Atlantic, have underpinned the debate. Circum-Atlantic history focused in this typology on the Atlantic as a geographical expression, while trans-Atlantic history was essentially comparative, and cis-Atlantic history (the ideal type) was contextualist, offering 'history of a place in relation to the wider Atlantic world' (Armitage, 2002, pp. 21–24). Although seldom acknowledged, such an approach contained within it a bias for particular flavors of intellectual history or micro-histories done by social and cultural historians, which had come to the fore in the intellectual climate of the 1990s. Older approaches still had some currency, though they often bore the stain of 'trans-Atlantic history.'

That has begun to change. Peter Coclanis has recently added a fourth category to Armitage's tripartite system: conjuncto-Atlantic history (Coclanis, 2009, p. 349). This approach links Atlantic studies with other historiographies, in order to gain further insights into broader historical experiences. It does so by exploring the interrelationships between, and impacts upon, ex-Atlantic regions, institutions, and peoples arising from the various political, social, and economic developments which occurred in the Atlantic region. This approach adopts Atlantic history as a field of the even newer discipline of world history, and seems for Coclanis to act as a justifying *raison d'être* for studies of the Atlantic world, helping to overcome what he has described as its 'limiting' explanatory power (2009, p. 338). (Indeed, if Armitage was correct in his 2002 declaration [p. 11] that 'we are all Atlanticists now,' then we are all world historians today.) There is much to be said for adopting Atlantic history to investigate bigger historiographical questions, maybe even to contribute to the resurgent grand-theory history which has returned to the discipline. Much recent work that is or could be classed as Atlantic history has made such contributions. That said, Coclanis's complaint could be made of any branch of history, yet the vast majority of the entries on publishers' swelling lists in all historical branches prove that it is possible to avoid antiquarianism, and to make a genuine contribution to historical understanding, without addressing the 'big questions' of history, or adopting a world history approach.

The extended Armitage assignment of types of Atlantic history has been augmented by several reflective assessments of the structure of the discipline. In their introduction to *Atlantic History: A Critical Appraisal* (2009), editors Jack Greene and Philip Morgan present and refute five 'objections' to the idea of Atlantic history, declaring it 'not necessarily a flawed, conceptually muddled subject.' They then offer a complex framework to avoid these perceived potential pitfalls. These prescriptions – to avoid the reductionism which lurks when looking for sharp similarities or differences in comparative Atlantic history; to look across borders; to focus sometimes on sectors; to consider the circulation of values and ideas; to consider the traditional questions of imperial history in the context of the Atlantic world; and to pay close attention to chronologies – have all been embraced by at least some Atlanticists since Greene and Morgan wrote (and had in many instances been considered much earlier). These are useful methodological guidelines, but they may also be constrictive. Recent works, such as Guy Chet's *The Ocean is a Wilderness: Atlantic Piracy and the Limits of State Authority, 1688–1856* (2014), have respected all of these guiding principles to a greater or lesser degree, but moved beyond them to consider broader questions in a way which follows the direction set out by Coclanis (in the case of Chet, to examine questions of the nature and reaches of sovereignty).

In assembling the chapters for this book, the editors have sought intentionally to eschew Atlantic history which follows a prescribed course. The Atlantic world, according to most chronological brackets adopted to define it, was distinctively early modern. As such, it was part of Europe's evolution to modernity, its great period of transition when new ideas were floated, new institutions built, and new approaches adopted. While the 'old world' was in the throes of this tumultuous change, it was simultaneously shrugging off the truths of scholasticism in a world now known to extend far beyond the knowledge of the ancients. Europeans were entering unknowns both at home and abroad. In this way the Atlantic could operate as an experimental space, a bolt-hole, and a wild west. This opens the door to an array of historical explorations which may extend or enlighten other historiographies of the early modern experience, or indeed may rest, freestanding, upon their own merits. Unconstrained historical research, work which is seen as Atlantic history by the researcher, or indeed by the consumers of the product, should therefore be a component of Atlantic history, regardless of its scope or focus. This may, of course, make Atlantic history something of a dog's breakfast, yet that in itself does not necessarily make it conceptually muddled, provided reductionism is avoided.

This goal is not always accomplished, of course. The danger exists in the study of Atlantic history – as in any field of historical enquiry – that one can give greater weight to events in one's own Atlantic world than they merit in a broader context. This happens often, such as the observation that Atlantic exploits 'involved the nation in expensive wars' (Kupperman, 2012, p. 96). In fact, for the most part, the

– CHAPTER I: *The Atlantic World* –

great, distinctively home-grown dynastic conflicts which were fundamental to the shaping of early modern Europe were played out in part in the Atlantic and other realms of European empires (as had never been possible before), but activities in these distant locations were not in and of themselves casual. Indeed, much of this rivalry was expressed not in the Atlantic, but in the eastern reaches of the British, Dutch, Portuguese, and Spanish empires. Thus, reductionism can be unwittingly accomplished with equal ease when some of the favorite subjects of Atlantic history, from economic integration to evangelization, are considered in an Atlantic context to the exclusion of important, related, and often modifying developments in other realms which had been opened to direct access by European navigation. Again, Coclanis would applaud such expansive consideration of broader histories.

Thus, this volume is not meant to serve as a handbook of Atlantic history as such. Those looking for one would be much better served by the recent publication of the *Oxford History of the Atlantic World* (Canny and Morgan, 2011) which offers a comprehensive view of the current state of play from within Atlantic history as an established discipline. Our volume on the 'Atlantic World' offers something radically different, and encapsulates an approach that does not fit neatly within historical schema. Our Atlantic World, as befits the *Routledge Worlds* series, reflects an ecumenical approach to the topic, one that seeks neither to compartmentalize nor to discipline practitioners, but rather to illustrate the methodological diversity of more recent 'post-Atlantic' approaches. Our authors consider not only traditional interactions amongst Africa, Europe, and the Americas, but also look to the Pacific, the Baltic region, the Cape Colony, and North Africa for evidence of commercial and cultural exchanges. Essays in this volume consider the natural world alongside that of a human-built environment, and make no clear distinctions between maritime and oceanic historical approaches. Many of the essays in this volume take up neglected themes, which were marginalized by traditional approaches to Atlantic history, but upon closer inspection should be central to the project. The history of Judaism and Islam in the Atlantic World is considered alongside more familiar accounts of Catholic and Protestant Christianity. Atlantic slavery is explored from all angles, including that of Europeans enslaved by Barbary piracy. Although the chapters are not deliberately arranged to highlight disagreements amongst authors, perceptive readers will detect them.

As two of the editors are financial historians by trade, the volume also explores the Atlantic experience of money and credit, and considers the integration of Atlantic financial and money markets with those in Europe in particular. Political economy is not divorced from histories of consumption and commerce, and mercantile practice is considered alongside state practice. The editors hope that the sheer scale and scope of this work will prove stimulating for students and established scholars alike.

STRUCTURE OF THE BOOK

Part I, entitled 'Atlantic Explorations,' examines the physical world as experienced both by indigenous peoples and by European settlers. In Chapter Two, James T. Carson and Karim M. Tiro offer a lyrical description of attitudes and beliefs of the native peoples towards the animal world as they experienced it, and show how those differed from those of European settlers. They describe a centuries-long process by which Palaeolithic land use patterns were rapidly replaced by Old World post-Neolithic farming practices, with predictable results for native flora, fauna, and peoples. Sandra Rebok's Chapter Three explores the Spanish encounter with the New World and considers how the discovery altered the European consciousness, informing not only science and humanistic scholarship, but also re-shaping ideology and religion. Her account concentrates on contemporary narratives of New World exploration, and considers the entire period from first contact in the fifteenth-century through to late nineteenth-century writers. In Chapter Four, David Starkey offers a compelling example of a new maritime history that goes beyond traditional treatments of oceangoing vessels to a wider explanation of the maritime economic sector, especially fish and fisheries, upon which so many livelihoods depended. His treatment considers simultaneously the social, economic, technological, institutional, and geographical influences upon those communities whose main employment came from the harvesting of food from the sea. Not only does his chapter introduce students to the Nordic Atlantic, so often neglected in other treatments, but also he connects these apparently regional economies to larger global networks.

If Part I frames the physical world for the reader, Part II considers the 'Movement of Peoples' through a multitude of often-neglected imperial frames. In Chapter Five, Laura Matthew explores the uneasy place of the history of the indigenous peoples of South and Central America in the historiography of the Iberian Atlantic world. The tragic destruction of the Mexica and Inca empires owed both to the fierce rivalries between them and the arrival of Europeans, but Matthew argues forcibly that the new arrivals were not only Spanish, but also French, Italian, English, Irish, and Dutch in origin. Her essay conveys both a sense for the sixteenth- and seventeenth-century experiences and for the fate of indigenous peoples in Iberia after the Bourbon succession and the Atlantic revolutions. Gerald Groenewald surveys rarely acknowledged connections between South Africa and the Southern Atlantic World in Chapter Six. As he acknowledges, part of the neglect of the pivotal role played by the Cape colony in the historiography was a result of the isolation of South African scholars in Apartheid. Over two decades later, the progress of re-integration remains a slow one, with the most attention paid to the slaving and whaling activities of the Dutch East Indian Company (VOC) in the seventeenth and early eighteenth centuries. Groenewald suggests additional possibilities for research, as the Cape colony served as a portal between the Atlantic and Indian oceans. William O'Reilly's Chapter Seven, a reprint of an article that appeared in *Wiener Zeitschrift zur Geschichte der Neuzeit* ten years ago, reminds readers of an equally overlooked corner of Atlantic history, namely that of emigration from Hapsburg lands to the New World in the eighteenth and early nineteenth centuries. O'Reilly explains that Protestants migrating for religious reasons could move to Magyar lands and that many did. Thus migration to the New World from the Empire occurred on a small scale, involving individuals, families or small groups. The one exception to what O'Reilly calls 'micro-migration' involved the Protestants of Salzburg, whose eighteenth-century experience he explores in detail. By the early nineteenth century, emigration controls were relaxed enough in practice (though not in theory) to permit mass emigration to the Americas. In Chapter Eight, Brian Rouleau investigates neglected early-nineteenth-century seafaring communities, finding them paradoxically playing a central role in the broader Atlantic experience. Rouleau reminds readers of the significance that complaints of seamen and their masters had for the American Revolutionaries, and considers the myths and realities of their 'radical republican' politics and the putatively loose morality of waterfronts. Seafaring communities resisted most reformist impulses, but ultimately oceangoing commerce, the vessels and their crews were transformed by the technological shift from sail to steam.

Part III explores a variety of 'Cultural Encounters,' echoing many of the themes in Part II while showcasing a variety of new methodological approaches and surprising source material available to the current generation of Atlantic historians. In Chapter Nine, Mélanie Lamotte looks at experiences of color prejudice in the French Atlantic using Guadeloupe as a case study. She argues that color prejudice existed from the outset of French colonization in the Caribbean. Lamotte considers how the legislation produced by the governmental élite in Guadeloupe and across the broader Caribbean and French Atlantic World contributed to the entrenchment of color prejudice. Drawing upon a wealth of under-explored sources, she also illustrates cases of fluidity across color lines in the social life of early modern Guadeloupe. Echoing many of the themes in Chapter Eight, Catherine Styer's treatment of Barbary slavery in Chapter Ten contextualizes the practice, which ultimately saw over twenty-five thousand captives put to work in North Africa as slaves. Contrary to popular histories of Barbary slavery (which romanticize it in comparison with New World slavery), Styer finds that the overwhelming majority of captured Britons died in captivity, often through over-work, starvation and violence. She argues that historiography which promotes the comparison of Barbary slavery to New World slavery does violence to our understanding of both phenomena, which can be better understood on their own terms. In Chapter Eleven, James Brown ponders the consequence of considering the place of Morocco in Atlantic historiography. In contrast to Styer, he de-emphasizes narratives of piracy in favor of considering the sultanate of Morocco as a state actor, in particular in the context of the struggle over Gibraltar as a gateway to the Atlantic. While Morocco remained firmly part of the 'Old World', Brown emphasizes that the European powers saw North Africa as part of the same imperial frame as the rest of their Atlantic empires. Modern historians have done otherwise at our peril, even as Brown's findings challenge the 'Atlantic paradigm' so prevalent in earlier generations of Atlantic historiography. Paul D'Arcy takes an even wider perspective in Chapter Twelve with his exploration of the implications of the emerging Pacific historiographies for Atlantic history. D'Arcy's essay will be especially useful to students as he helps his readers conceive of the complex physical and human geographies, the weather patterns and the enormous distances involved. Pacific Islanders left traces of their own pre-historic encounters with the indigenous peoples of the Atlantic world. These contacts continued into the colonial period and by the eighteenth century, they even travelled on western ships and settled in western colonies. In effect, Groenewald's case for the importance of considering Southern Africa in Chapter Six is mirrored by D'Arcy's survey of the significance of the Pacific context. This section closes with Chapter Thirteen, a reprint of an essay by Laurent Dubois which considers the importance of Michèle Duchet's *Anthropologie et histoire au siècle des lumières* (*Anthropology and History in the Century of the Enlightenment*) for our understanding of the intellectual history of the French Atlantic. This piece was chosen because universalist histories of the sort attempted by Duchet should be rendered comprehensible and made far more meaningful by the first four chapters in this section. Duchet's focus on the problems of colonial governance anticipates the theme of the next section.

In Part IV, the authors consider problems of 'Warfare and Governance' in the Atlantic context, beginning with the everyday realities of violence in Chapter Fourteen. Smolenski argues, somewhat controversially, that violence and preconceptions legitimizing its use served as a kind of 'perpetual motion machine of colonial domination' (Smolenski, p. 256). In constructing his narrative around this theme, he finds commonalities in the British, French, Spanish and Portuguese Atlantic experiences of race and slavery, and in the processes of conquest and colonization. Without seeking to supplant more traditional approaches, Smolenski's example suggests the possibilities of thematic approaches to comparative cultural histories of institutional practices. In Chapter Fifteen, Geoffrey Plank also looks at the role of violence in shaping four and a half centuries of the Atlantic experience, but mainly restricts his enquiry to warfare, particularly interstate warfare, in an attempt to give students a good grounding in the political narratives of conquest and colonization. In Chapter Sixteen, Charles Drummond turns instead to militias, and their places in the 'military vocabularies' of the British Atlantic. Disputes over where military power rested, in the legislature or the executive, which began during the English Civil Wars, continued through the Revolutionary period and the early American republic. Militias were contrasted foremost with standing armies. Drummond ultimately argues for a 'distributionist' approach to the Second Amendment of the American constitution in an effort to recapture the contemporary meaning. Chapter Seventeen concludes this section with Juan Ponce-Vazquez's exploration of Spanish and French interactions in seventeenth-century Hispaniola. His case study of conflict and cooperation in what he calls the 'Atlantic periphery' will help students understand how these conflicts played out in practice, while at the same time illuminating the often-neglected experiences of elites in the Spanish and French Caribbean settlements.

Part V consists of six essays exploring 'Religion' in the Atlantic World. Eoin Devlin offers a comprehensive overview in Chapter Eighteen of New World Catholicism, conveying a sense for the chronological sweep, the geographical reach, and the diversity of belief and practice in the Spanish and French overseas empires. Devlin contrasts the implications of the extension of the Gallican liberties of the French church with the more orthodox Spanish Catholicism. Travis Glasson's treatment of Protestantism in Chapter Nineteen considers the diversity of Protestant belief and practice, and considers tensions both between Catholics and Protestants and between different Protestant denominations. Some of these conflicts were an extension of European rivalries in the imperial frame, whereas others were born of competition for resources in the New World. Both these chapters also explore the indigenous experience of Christian missionary activity, evangelization and forced conversion. In Chapter Nineteen, Natalie Zacek considers the experience of New World Jewry in the British Atlantic, comparing the experience of Jews to those of Quakers and Huguenots. She finds that Jews were numerically small but economically significant, with strong networks reaching into the Iberian Atlantic world as well. While Jewish settlers may have been integrated into wider communities, few were assimilated, a finding she attributes partly to anti-Jewish sentiment and partly to the self-enclosed, communal tendencies of the emigrants themselves. Denise Spellberg's discussion of Islam in the Atlantic world focuses both on actual West African Muslim slave populations, on the one hand, and with attitudes contemporary Europeans had towards 'notional Muslims' or the possibilities of Islamic communities in the New World. In this wide-ranging piece, she reflects on rumors of those Muslim crewmembers who purportedly sailed with Columbus, on the meaning of 'Mohametan' in contemporary discourse, and on the origins of Jefferson's edition of the Qu'ran. Maura Jane Farrelly looks ahead to English Colonial Catholicism and its place in the formation of early American identity. Her essay serves to redress the scant attention paid to the experience of English Catholics when confronted with an explicitly latitudinarian, contractarian theory of government as embodied in the American constitution. Her treatment naturally focuses on Quebec and Maryland, where most Catholics lived, and conveys a sense of how the inhabitants of Maryland in particular dealt with the intense anti-Catholicism of the Protestant British state before the Revolution and with their ready embrace of the possibilities of independence from England thereafter. Holly Snyder ends this section with a polemical essay on the place of early modern Jewish history in wider trends of Atlantic historiography, arguing forcibly that the latter has been too 'Christocentric' whereas the former has shown a reluctance to confront the difficult issues of where Jewish peoples fit within early modern racial discourses. As she observes, the often fantastic eschatological constructs that governed the place of Africans and indigenous peoples within a Christian cosmology, and in turn provided rationales for their enslavement and extermination, were complicated by the presence of Jews in ancient Christian texts. She concludes that both scholars of Europe and of the Atlantic world would benefit from enlarging the field of vision not only to the Atlantic but also to Africa when exploring relations between Christians, Muslims, and Jews. The editors believe that the first five essays in this section, in very different ways, respond to the spirit of her plea, as do those offered by Catherine Styer and James Brown in Part III.

In Part VI, four authors consider different dimensions of 'Credit, Finance and Money' in the Atlantic context. In Chapter Twenty-four, Matthew Mitchell offers an overview of British joint stock companies and their roles in the Atlantic trade. Mitchell notes that they were chartered by the British state and highlights their importance as instruments of state policy. In his account, success depended on a subtle mix of political connections and the expertise of personnel, and he weighs the experiences of the Company of Royal Adventurers, the Royal Africa Company, the Hudson Bay Company, and the South Sea Company in turn. Mitchell concludes by noting their commercial success while acknowledging the roles of many of these companies in the expansion of the slave trade.

In her treatment of joint-stock companies in Chapter Twenty-five, Helen Paul focuses instead on the events of 1719/1720 and the role of the Atlantic trade in fuelling speculation in shares in the John Law's Mississippi Company and in the British South Sea Company. She argues forcefully for the significance of contemporary beliefs about the possibilities of Atlantic trade after the end of the War of Spanish Succession and the Great Northern War. Her account will be especially useful to students who want to understand how the Atlantic and Baltic trading systems overlapped, and why the early eighteenth century experienced a step-change in contemporary appreciation of the potential profits that such trade could bring. Dror Goldberg looks at both the real and mythological contributions of Atlantic trade to the development of paper money in Chapter Twenty-six. First, Goldberg emphasizes the expansion of the sheer volume of bills of exchange used to finance transatlantic trade as an advance upon their use in predominately intra-European trade in the preceding centuries. Second, he argues that interstate competition and with it military finance increased both the varieties and the volume of paper money. Finally, the Atlantic colonies themselves issued inconvertible paper money when confronted with the scarcity of precious metals with which to mint coin. Despite a variety of cautionary tales of the dangers of rapid inflation, the use of paper money in the Atlantic world continued more or less unabated. Paul Kosmetatos offers a case study in Chapter Twenty-seven of the Credit Crisis of 1772/3, which began with Alexander Fordyce's flight to the continent in June 1772 and rapidly spread to Scotland leading to the collapse of the Ayr Bank just over a fortnight later. Kosmetatos traces the transmission of the crisis to North America, and in doing so establishes the extent to which British Atlantic financial markets were integrated with those of the metropole. Tobacco merchants emerge as the vector of contagion as they were the most vulnerable to a generalized tightening of credit conditions. Ironically, the Glasgow tobacco merchants themselves were saved by the fact that most of their customers were French (an unintended consequence of the collapse of Law's scheme as described in Chapter Twenty-five) and paid in coin, rather than via the Dutch and English bills market described in the previous chapter.

Part VII looks in turn at 'Commerce, Consumption and Mercantile Networks' in the Atlantic world. In a polemical Chapter Twenty-eight, Adrian Leonard argues forcibly against Joseph Inikori's view that Atlantic trade catalyzed the development of the London insurance market. He shows that the institutional practices of the London market were developed well before the seventeenth century, and that any unique problems of insuring human cargoes contributed little to what institutional changes did occur. Atlantic warfare did increase demand for insurance; the London market turned out to be stable enough to accommodate it, while other European markets for marine insurance declined in importance. In Chapter Twenty-nine, Edmund Smith explores commercial relations between the Dutch and English Atlantic worlds. While many studies of Anglo-Dutch relations end with the loss of New Netherland to the English in 1673, Smith focuses on the first hundred years. As with Starkey in Chapter Four, Smith emphasizes the importance of the fishing industries as the primary mover of early commercial expansion by both the English and Dutch, which he regards as just as important as (and even a driver of) anti-Iberian foreign policies in the twin contexts of the Dutch Revolt and Spanish Armada. In Chapter Thirty, Jonathan Eacott considers the cultural history of Atlantic commerce in a globalized context. Although demand for Atlantic goods was scarce in Asian markets, demand for Asian goods was great in Atlantic ones. By the same token, demand for New World products was high in Europe, and over time New World markets for European goods eclipsed the importance of colonial possessions as sources of raw materials. The resulting economic warfare shaped not only ideas about political economy, but also labor practices and business forms. In Chapter Thirty-one, Joanna Cohen turns to the question of how ideas about public taste interacted with *laissez-faire* economic ideologies and free trade policies in the early American republic. On the whole, the Victorians deplored what they perceived as the crudeness of American tastes, especially their embrace of foreign goods. Cohen reveals the nationalist dimensions of debates over taste, and traces how American ideas about taste converged with notions of a democratic marketplace.

The eighth and final part explores 'The Circulation of Ideas' in the Atlantic world. In Chapter Thirty-two, Jeffrey Fortin explores slave rebellions and slave resistance. He traces these phenomena over a four-hundred year history and considers both the African and indigenous American experiences, but focuses most of his attention on the eighteenth century, especially the Revolutionary era. Not surprisingly, the Jacobin rhetoric of the French Revolution resonated in slave societies, but failed to find support from the French armies, who continued to suppress revolts brutally. If anything, there was a remarkable consistency in the way in which the French, British, Spanish and Portuguese empires worked to contain the spread of revolutionary ideas. In Chapter Thirty-three, D'Maris Coffman investigates the spread of mercantile policies and commercial practices through the publication of merchant manuals, of which Jacques Savary's *Le Parfait Négociant* is a paradigmatic example. Coffman employs the tools of historians of the book to explore the work's publication history, and argues that careful attention to the text of successive editions reflects both a cementing of European commercial rivalries and a concern with providing up-to-date guides to trading in the Atlantic and African contexts. In Chapter Thirty-four, Nicholas Cole examines the reception of classical texts in the Atlantic world. Just as the New World posed problems for European eschatology, the ancient world provided frameworks through which Europeans might understand their discoveries. Contemporary understandings of classical political thought have long since had a place in intellectual histories of the British Atlantic world, but these discussions are often narrow in scope and tend to ignore, for instance, the importance of classical rhetorical forms in favor of classical political thinking. Cole's survey suggests the value of a more rigorous, subtler approach to these discourses. The thirty-fifth and final chapter by William Nelson focuses attention on the idea of an 'Atlantic Enlightenment,' the use of which he defends against critics of the term. Nelson is particularly interested in Enlightenment discourses of racial differentiation, on the one hand, and natural rights and anti-slavery on the other. He explores how they might co-exist simultaneously. Nelson also sees the Atlantic context, somewhat more controversially, as a laboratory for political experimentation, as well as stimulant to developments in political economy and in radical politics. Nelson emphasizes what he calls 'intellectual reciprocity' between America and Europe, a metaphor which works equally well for the more mundane spheres of economic, social, and cultural exchange explored in this volume.

As editors, we hope that our readers have come away with an appreciation of the methodological pluralism that characterizes the new generation of Atlantic scholarship. In contrast with too much of the historiography of early modern Europe, which tends to magnify the differences between social and cultural history, between longer-term economic histories and contingent political narratives, and between confessional histories and histories of religious practice, Atlantic historiography tends to embrace an array of sources and approaches, organized instead around particular themes or problems, such as slavery or conquest. Atlantic historians have also been quicker to embrace interdisciplinary approaches drawn from geography and anthropology, while preserving a prominent place for written sources where they exist. This, in turn, has made Atlantic history especially receptive to work on consumption, taste, and material culture.

Economic history in the Atlantic context has also welcomed the work of financial historians, who focus on market microstructure, market intervention, and state policies rather than longer-term narratives of economic and social change. This spirit of ecumenism has also served to bridge traditional divisions amongst historians of political and economic thought, and between intellectual historians and historians of the book. If Atlantic History has lost some of its coherence in the aging process, this volume's editors hope that what has been gained in midlife is a genuine appreciation of new ideas and new approaches.

REFERENCES

Armitage, David, 'Three concepts of Atlantic history,' in Armitage, David and Michael J. Braddick (eds), *The British Atlantic World, 1500–1800* (Palgrave Macmillan, 2002), pp. 11–27.

Armitage, David, *The Ideological Origins of the British Empire* (Cambridge University Press, 2000).

Canny, Nicholas and Morgan, Philip (eds.), *The Oxford History of the Atlantic World* (Oxford University Press, 2011).

Chet, Guy, *The Ocean is a Wilderness: Atlantic Piracy and the Limits of State Authority, 1688–1856* (University of Massachusetts Press, 2014).

Coclanis, Peter A. 'Beyond Atlantic history,' in Greene, Jack P. and Morgan, Philip D., *Atlantic History: A Critical Appraisal* (Oxford University Press, 2009), pp. 337–356.

Elliott, J.H. *The Old World and the New, 1492–1650* (Cambridge University Press, 1970).

Greene, Jack and Morgan, Philip, *Atlantic History: A Critical Appraisal* (Oxford University Press, 2009).

Kupperman, Karen Ordahl, *The Atlantic in World History* (Oxford University Press, 2012).

Padgen, Anthony, *Lords of All the World: Ideologies of Empire in Spain, Britain and France, c. 1500–c. 1850* (Yale University Press, 1995).

PART I
ATLANTIC EXPLORATIONS

CHAPTER TWO

ANIMALS IN ATLANTIC NORTH AMERICA TO 1800

—·◆·—

James Taylor Carson and Karim M. Tiro

The Native peoples of North America historically believed that animals helped bring about the world as we know it. According to the Iroquois, for example, it was Muskrat who dived to the bottom of the waters to gather the mud that he spread on Turtle's back to make the world we inhabit today. Algonquian peoples who lived along the present-day Potomac River saw in the hares that scurried through the forest undergrowth reminders of Ahone who had once fashioned the earth in his forepaws. With help from the winds the Great Hare then populated the world with men and women before creating the fish, deer, and other beings that would feed and clothe those first people.[1]

The Europeans who first arrived in North America saw things otherwise. In their stories, it was a Father who first made the earth and then the animals and then the people. 'And the fear of you and the dread of you,' the Book of Genesis promised, 'shall be upon every beast of the earth, and upon every fowl of the air, upon all that moveth upon the earth, and upon all the fishes of the sea; into your hand are they delivered.' Men became as gods ruling the land just as He ruled them from the heavens such that those who possessed the power to control nature became 'civilized' while those who were a part of nature became 'savage.' The promise of such domain, however, came at a steep price. 'And surely your blood of your lives will I require,' the Father covenanted with his chosen children 'at the hand of every beast will I require it, and at the hand of man; at the hand of every man's brother will I require the life of man.'[2]

When they invaded North America, Europeans encountered a dynamic faunal ecology that had come into being around ten or eleven thousand years earlier. Under pressure from a warming climate and hungry humans, the giant mammals that had dominated life during the preceding Pleistocene Ice Age became extinct. The hunters who finished them off, however, unwittingly created a new animal world. Smaller mammals like white-tailed deer, mountain lions, raccoons, wolves, beavers, and opossums emerged from the shadows once cast by their massive cousins and, notwithstanding the ebbs and flows that characterize any ecosystem, such modest animals assumed a more important place in the landscape and the human diet.

Just three centuries after Christopher Columbus's landfall in the Caribbean in 1492 the post-Pleistocene faunal ecology of eastern North America had crashed and been replaced by a new one that drew together the domesticated and commensal creatures of Europe, Asia, and Africa with the remnant indigenous survivors of the invasion of America. We might think of this new animal world as 'creole,' given its multiple origins and hybrid implications. The word 'creole' suits what happened in eastern North America between 1492 and the end of the eighteenth century because of the creative if also often destructive changes that occurred and the hybrid faunal ecology that resulted from three centuries of colonization. Indeed, the term derives from the Spanish word *criollo* that named the American cattle that had evolved from Iberian types after they were let loose on the salt marshes of Hispaniola and the grasslands of Mexico.[3]

Figure 2.1 Mask with antlers, 1400–1600 (wood & bone),
Mississippian culture (c. 800–1500)
Private Collection/Photo © Dirk Bakker/Bridgeman Images

— CHAPTER 2: *Animals in Atlantic North America* —

Archaeologists have shown that although women's horticulture contributed the majority of calories to the diet of most First Peoples after AD 800, animals remained crucial to the survival of North America's Native populations, and none more so than the white-tailed deer. Women turned its skins into clothing while both men and women transformed its bones and antlers into scrapers, awls, flutes, and other tools. Turkey and bear were also important as were, depending on the weather, time of year, or other circumstances, squirrels, rabbits, beaver, waterfowl, mussels, turtles, and a variety of freshwater fishes. Oysters, crabs, and fish from salt marshes and ocean shores added to the richness of this living world.[4]

Such a world, however, was not 'natural' in the sense that it existed independently of the people who inhabited it. People set fires annually in late winter to clear forest undergrowth and to encourage first-growth grasses that attracted deer, turkeys, and other animals while it also wiped out the hordes of irritating chiggers, ticks, and fleas. The fires also consumed much of the acorns, nuts, and pine mast and so disadvantaged bears. To compensate, some people preserved bear grounds by selective weeding to enable hardwood trees, berry undergrowth, and grapevines and persimmon trees to flourish and provide everything an ursine could want.

Beyond the boundaries of human habitation plentiful layers of mast, nuts, and other forest foods attracted any number of animals. Massive canebrakes that wound, ribbon-like, along the rivers and creeks enabled rabbits, bison, bear, and deer to browse and prosper while ensuring that new stands of cane emerged from the nubby stumps they left behind. Beaver too made their mark on the land. The ponds they built diversified forest landscapes by sustaining a wide variety of marsh plants and fishes, and they also provided secure sources of water. People were the paramount predators but wolves, coyotes, and mountain lions also moved through the land and preyed primarily upon the deer herds that were rooted to their particular, perhaps even ancestral, territories.[5]

To talk of deer, bears, and rabbits, however, pinpoints animals we know today, collapses the distance between then and now, and distorts what they meant to the people who lived with them. To gain some sense of eastern North America's animal history, we must open the perspective of biology to the more obscure and contingent realm of cosmology, for what people believed about animals influenced everything they did. Native American women, for example, tended to make the pottery that people used to cook and store food and imprinted their creations with stylized snakes, owls, falcons, and frogs. Occasionally they mixed coiled serpents from the watery underworld with the crested heads of the birds that soared in the orderly sun's sky into one hybrid creature to express the frightful powers of creatures that fit no known categories. Priests, shamans, and chiefs used bright red cardinal feathers to invoke the sun, black crow feathers to conjure death, or owl skins and bones to access the darker powers of witchcraft. They used their powers to communicate with animal spirits and, at times, even transformed themselves into animals.[6] In such a world animals conveyed sacred powers, moral meanings, and existed as signposts to guide people through the mysteries of their lives.

While Native North Americans had domesticated dogs (and turkeys here and there), they had nothing resembling Europeans' close relationship with horses, cows, sheep, swine, and chickens. It had taken people in what today we call the Near East and east Asia about ten thousand years to perfect the Neolithic complex that came

Figure 2.2 Florida Indians hunting deer while disguised under deerskins, from 'Americae Decima Pars' engraved by Theodor de Bry (1528–98) 1591
Private Collection/Bridgeman Images

to characterize European agriculture. They began with beasts of least resistance: sheep and goats, gregarious animals that were submissive and who needed no specific territory in which to live. Then came other animals that possessed characteristics that suited them to cohabit with humans – hogs, cattle, and last, horses and chickens. Such animals evolved to depend on humans for their food, reproduction and safety and, in return, they conferred upon their masters ready supplies of meat, milk, cheese, butter, tallow, eggs, and leather, not to mention the power to build, to travel, and to conquer.[7]

The Neolithic Revolution reached Europe about seven thousand years ago and with it came one of its many unforeseen consequences: disease. Lethal viruses emerged in the dirty and overcrowded conditions that characterized the early farms, towns, and cities that arose on the backs of domesticated animals. Close proximity and poor sanitation enabled pathogens to jump species all the while becoming stronger and more adaptable. People astride horses, donkeys, and camels carried them farther and farther afield where the new germs decimated people who had had no prior exposure to such things as smallpox, measles, influenza, and plague.[8]

Native North Americans, by contrast, lived among, rather than with, animals. Epidemiologically, this distinction would prove devastating, since it meant they did not co-evolve with animal diseases. After Columbus's voyages successive epidemics of smallpox, measles, influenza, and other pathogens that had arisen from the domestication of animals sliced through eastern North America's indigenous population, reducing it from an estimated one million in 1492 to fewer than 200,000 by 1800. In the aftermath of the initial and most dramatic demographic collapse, remnant groups across eastern North America had to band together into new societies in order to survive.[9]

As people died or fled the epidemics, deer, bison, and other animals moved into their empty homes, fields, and towns as did Europeans. As time passed and colonial towns grew out from their original toeholds on the coast and expanded ever westward up rivers and down paths, the survivors and the invaders shared in all the complexity that accompanies human contact wherever it occurs. Indigenous hunters, for example, provided the newcomers with dried venison and fish, smoked bear and turkey while women offered maize porridge, squashes, and other garden crops. Such exchanges and interchanges caused colonial governors anxiety about the mixing of what they took to be 'savages' with their own 'civilized' people. But as colonial populations grew the invaders began to clear the forests, destroy animal habitats, and assert their own environmental sensibilities. Such steady pressure diminished deer, bear, beaver, and other animal populations and imperiled indigenous populations who, at the same time, were still struggling to recover from the original epidemics that had accompanied the invaders across the sea.[10]

Europeans regarded the early American faunal landscape with profound ambivalence. America's animals elicited a mix of sentiments that ranged from wonder, curiosity, and desire to fear and contempt. Coming from a continent where wild animals had been largely extirpated, Europeans were immediately struck by the abundance of fauna. Early depictions of North America, like John White's sixteenth-century paintings of present-day coastal North Carolina, highlighted the ample fish and fowl. Matthew Visscher filled empty spaces on his map of "New Belgium" with bears, rabbits, turkeys, beavers, and deer. For potential colonists and

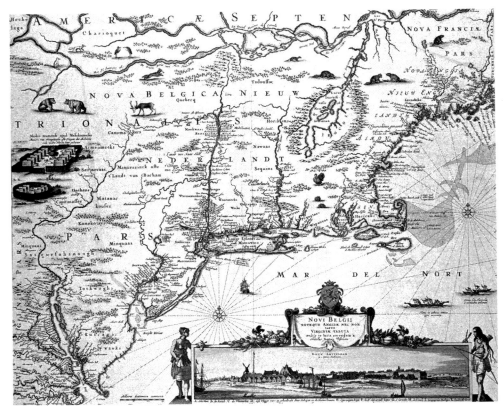

Figure 2.3 New Belgium, plate from 'Atlas Contractus' c. 1671 by Matthew Visscher
Private Collection/Bridgeman Images

the investors who backed colonial ventures, these images of animals represented food security and economic opportunity. Deer even lent the enterprise a whiff of gentility, since in Europe they were to be found mostly in game parks for the sporting pleasure of the aristocracy.

There were also animals that Europeans had never seen. *Circa* 1520, Pietro Martire d'Anghiera published his description of an opossum: 'a monstrous beaste with a snowte lyke a marmasette, eares lyke a batte, handes lyke a man, and feete lyke an ape, bearing her whelpes about with her in an outwarde bellye much lyke unto a greate bagge or purse.' In America, Europeans also reacquainted themselves with animals that had disappeared from their own countries. Beavers, once present throughout Europe, were now rarely to be found west of the Ural Mountains. Early descriptions of northern North America were replete with droll descriptions of the rodents. Beavers were praised for their ability to alter the landscape, and their lodges and dikes elicited comparisons to Venice.

By way of explanation, observers exaggerated the animals' social organization, and wrote of beaver architects and beaver republics. Europeans could not help but think that such strange creatures said something important about the place, although they were not exactly sure what.[11]

– CHAPTER 2: *Animals in Atlantic North America* –

Figure 2.4 'A view of ye Industry of ye Beavers'
from Herman Moll's New and Exact Map, 1715
Private Collection/© Look and Learn/Bridgeman Images

Such curiosity, however, soon gave way to commerce because the invaders needed products that they could sell in order to fund their costly trans-Atlantic enterprises. Animal skins and furs were among the first commodities that underwrote the European invasion of North America. The colder northern forests were home to many species of fur-bearing animals, including otter, bear, bobcat, mink, muskrat, fox, and marten. European furs having been largely depleted, these animals stimulated great interest. Sixteenth-century European fishermen, primarily Basques, quickly identified furs as a commodity they could obtain from the Indians and sell back home at a tidy profit, and none more so than the beaver.

The beaver's woolen underfur was superbly adapted to the manufacture of hat felt, and hats mattered deeply to Europeans as markers of prosperity and of identity. Whatever their particular shape or style, hats fabricated with beaver wool were uniquely capable of retaining their shape when wet. Thus, the fur-trade entrepôts of Québec and Beverwijck (Albany) emerged as the economic engines of New France and New Netherland. Dutch lawyer and administrator Adriaen van der Donck wrote in 1655 that 'The beaver is the main foundation and means why or through which this beautiful land was first occupied by people from Europe.' French- and Dutch-traded pelts made their way not just to Paris and Amsterdam, but to Russia, where the manufacture of fur hats was a specialty craft. The fur trade was less central to English colonization, but its economic potential was hardly lost on them. Puritans may have traversed the Atlantic for reasons unrelated to beaver, but they were also famously fond of their hats, and they knew what they were made from. Popular demand for durable and water-resistant headgear was such that England passed laws imposing penalties on those who sold items advertised as 'beaver' but that were in fact devoid of the animal.[12]

French, Dutch, and English merchants relied on Native trappers, and offered a variety of goods that Native communities desired. In 1636 one Montagnais chief observed with satisfaction, 'the Beaver does everything perfectly well, it makes kettles, hatchets, swords, knives, bread; in short, it makes everything.' Although the Montagnais chief's statement reverses common Eurocentric assumptions regarding Indian naïveté in the exchange of goods, the trade was already moving quickly beyond exotic foodstuffs and useful implements to ones that made life more dangerous. Specifically, European traders introduced firearms. As hunters ranged ever more widely, and competition for a limited supply of animals increased, so did conflict. By mid-century, guns were indispensable for self-defense. Still, a band or village could only use so many guns. After all other wants were satisfied, traders engaged another motivation for the hunt: alcohol. In the end, the Indians' ideological proscriptions against overhunting were nullified by their pressing need for weapons for self-defense, their communities' growing dependence upon European metalware and textiles, and their addiction to alcohol.

This vicious cycle of dependency drove Native trappers to decimate the beaver population across the Northeast several times over. Once the colony of New France was firmly established, it exported 20–30,000 beaver pelts every year. Beavers were particularly vulnerable, since their slow and sedentary ways made them relatively easy to kill. Although beavers might produce two to five offspring per year, this was not enough to counter the increasingly intense hunt, and there is evidence to suggest that the beaver were struck by epizootics as well. As early beaver-hunting areas failed, trappers went farther afield. The Hudson Bay Company was chartered in 1670; by 1800 – at which time North American harvests were in excess of a quarter-million beaver per annum – its trapping activities of necessity extended as far as the Canadian Rockies and Beaufort Sea. Since beavers altered local hydrology, the deaths of millions of them in turn led to declines in populations of birds, fish, and amphibians that thrived in the habitats the beavers had created.[13]

The southeast's warm climate meant that beaver pelts never achieved the thickness of their northern counterparts. Instead, deerskins emerged as the top trade item owing to European demand for soft gloves, book bindings, riding breeches, and early industrial belts. Estimates of the deerskin trade that financed the early southern colonies are difficult to quantify but some specific examples suggest catastrophe for the animals. In 1707, for example, 120,000 processed skins departed Charles Town,

South Carolina, in the holds of ships bound for England. In the mid-1700s Savannah exported between 100,000 and 150,000 annually while in the 1780s Choctaws traded about 100,000 skins annually, and the French and Spanish trading houses and ports accounted for untold tens of thousands as well. Hunters traded the skins for commodities such as cloth, metal tools, guns, ammunition, and alcohol, and as they invariably lapsed into debt in the rigged credit system they had to hunt more and more to cover their deepening losses. If we combine the deer killed in the skin trade with the numbers needed for domestic consumption, scholars' best estimates reckon that indigenous hunters probably took about one million deer a year from southeastern forests. Such over-hunting emptied the forests to such an extent that by the early 1800s, when the European market for furs and skins had coincidentally also dried up, what had been a way of life for indigenous peoples for centuries was no longer possible. As one Choctaw leader put it, 'We cannot expect to live any longer by hunting. Our game is gone.'[14]

But it was not hunting alone that altered eastern North America's post-Pleistocene faunal ecology. While the hunting of animals promised profits for skin traders and merchants, the great majority of trans-Atlantic migrants sought advancement by transforming the landscape to make it more hospitable to the animals and crops they were accustomed to raising and consuming back in Europe. The attendant habitat destruction was vast. Slowly but steadily, trees were cut down in order to clear land for planting, to supply lumber for building houses, to provide fuel for fires to keep them warm, and to build fences to either contain their livestock or keep them apart from their crops. Deforestation deprived native animals of shelter and sustenance, reduced the diversity of plant life, and ultimately raised temperatures and promoted soil runoff that silted rivers.[15]

Livestock were regarded as key sources of motive power, fertilizer, and food, so they were afforded considerable space on ships carrying European settlers to America. The first animals to arrive were spread among the 17 ships that comprised Christopher Columbus' second voyage to the Caribbean. In November, 1493, cats, dogs, pigs, cattle, horses, chicken, and goats arrived on Hispaniola along with 1500 men brought to establish control over the land. During the voyage disease had jumped from the pigs to everyone else and when they disembarked they introduced a lethal sickness to the indigenous Arawak people. The pigs and cattle turned loose on the island laid a foundation for the subsequent expansion of Spanish livestock throughout the region and on to the mainland through de Soto's expedition, the establishment of Spanish missions in Florida, and English raids during the War of the Spanish Succession.[16]

Further north, John Smith boasted of how in 1608–9 'Of three sowes in eighteene moneths, increased 60, and od Piggs. And neere 500 chickings brought up themselves without having any meat given them.' (Less fortuitously, the colonists' corn had been 'consumed with so many thousands of Rats that increased so fast, but there original was from the ships.') Governor Francis Wyatt proclaimed in 1623 that his colony's fortunes 'depends upon nothing more, then the plentifull increasing and preserving of all sorts of Beasts and birds of domesticall or tame nature.'[17] In the same spirit, John Winthrop made careful reckonings of cows as he oversaw immigration to Boston. In 1625, the Dutch West India Company sent more than one hundred 'stallions and mares, bulls and cows' as well as pigs and sheep to New Netherland.[18] Self-reproducing populations of cows, pigs, and horses had taken root in the colonies within about a quarter-century. By 1651, Rensselaerwijck boasted more than seven horses per farm. In 1682, Thomas Ashe wrote of South Carolina that 'The great encrease of their Cattle is rather to be admired than believed; not more than six or seven years past the Country was almost destitute of Cows, Hogs and Sheep, now they have many thousand head.'[19]

While most of these animals were kept for subsistence purposes, a modest trade in livestock developed among the mainland colonies, obviating the need to transport large numbers of animals across the Atlantic except to improve breeding stock, which was done only rarely. Mainland colonies also began to supply animals and animal products to West Indian colonies, a trade that grew throughout the colonial period. Caribbean sugar mills were turned by horses, and slaves needed meat for sustenance. New England provided both by 1650. The islands along its coast were proving ideal for grazing livestock since they could be easily cleared of predators and were convenient for shipping. The production of live animals, hides, and salt beef for the West Indian market was also an important element of the economy of South Carolina at its founding. The colony's early population benefitted from the presence of West Country Englishmen and enslaved Africans from Jamaica and the Spanish islands in the Caribbean whose past experiences with livestock in both their original homelands and in the Caribbean brought together English bullwhips with Spanish and Senegambian traditions of horse-mounted pastoralism and nightly penning to create a new way of raising cattle.[20]

European animals were themselves important agents of change, and they often acted independently of humans. Since labor was scarce in all the colonies, the practice of allowing animals to range freely was widespread. In 1705, New Jersey's royal governor, Lord Cornbury, stated that the 'woods are full of wild horses,' and such observations were commonplace.[21] Animals were least carefully tended and controlled in those areas where the opportunity cost was highest. Thus, tobacco-growing settlers in the Chesapeake were the least patient husbandmen. The self-reliant hog was the animal of choice in early Virginia, and sheep, cows, and even horses were initially rare. There was little need for draft animals so long as tobacco was cultivated by hoe. An English visitor in Virginia in 1700 observed that 'the Hogs run where they want and find their own Support in the Woods without any Care of the Owners.' The hogs apparently did well enough without them. As he described it, the swine 'swarm[ed] like vermin upon the Earth.'[22] Cattle, horses, pigs, and chickens acted as a kind of advance guard, seizing control of forests and grasslands in advance of the march of human conquest and dispossession. Animals exerted their own particular forms of invasion and destruction. Cattle, for example, required 15 to 20 acres each to subsist and, along with other livestock and swine, they devoured grasses and shrubs, pine and hardwood mast, and berries upon which the remnant stocks of deer, bear, and other native species relied. Roving herds also flattened canebrakes, trampled gardens, and uprooted forests such that they, along with settlers' axes and saws, contributed to widespread deforestation and soil erosion. Native plants and grasses also began to yield to hardier European plants that had co-evolved with the new herd animals. The seeds of such grasses came in the coats and dung of the invading domesticated species, or were planted by colonists to sustain their creatures. As native pasturage declined, farmers would have to devote significant acreage to hay, timothy, and other grasses to sustain their livestock.[23]

– CHAPTER 2: *Animals in Atlantic North America* –

By 1739, the roughly 40,000 people of New France occupied themselves with the upkeep of 26,000 sheep, 9,700 horses, 27,000 pigs, and 38,800 head of cattle. Due to the expense of feeding over the long winter, livestock were either released to roam the woods, stabled with insufficient food, or slaughtered. The cold climate likely accounts for the relative abundance of sheep which, due to their particularly high requirements for shelter and protection, had a more limited presence as one proceeded southward through all the Atlantic colonies. Kalm reported that the horses of New France were strong, but the cows and sheep were degenerated from their French stock.[24] Kalm, who visited the English colonies as well, made similar comments about the livestock there, and this assessment was echoed widely.

New Englanders lined their landscape with fences and walls to keep crops and animals separate, and many towns maintained a commons and hired young men to serve as communal herders. However, New Englanders proved slower to erect structures to protect the animals against winter. Most New England cattle were oxen used for draft and, like the region's horses, were unimpressive in stature. As farms were subdivided and soil fertility declined, the practice of cattle raising and penning grew more common and became more market-driven. Upland farmers sold cattle to their counterparts in the valleys, who fattened them to the greatest extent possible for sale in Boston and New York. The region continued to find a market for beef and small horses in the West Indies. Dairying intensified as well – a fact that was nowhere better exemplified by the 1200-pound 'mammoth cheese' sent to President Jefferson upon his inauguration by the people of Cheshire, Connecticut.

The upkeep of animals in the Middle Colonies had generally hewed more closely to European standards than elsewhere. This was partly because of closer attention to breeding from the outset on the part of Dutch farmers and William Penn and ongoing animal regulation in the form of marking and the collection of stray animals. The eighteenth-century influx of German immigrants, who excelled in cultivating meadows and building barns, also helped hold the line on deterioration. However, the feeding and labor demands of livestock upkeep placed an upper limit on the size of herds in the Middle Colonies. The key was the economic opportunity provided by the presence of larger, better-organized export and urban markets.[25]

Animals were present in all colonial cities, which teemed with a variety of creatures brought there to be slaughtered and consumed or shipped, or to reside there to supply food, transportation, sport, or companionship. The built landscape was modified to include facilities for killing and marketing animals, as well as sustaining populations of fowl, dairy animals, and horses. Household pets included cats, dogs, and exotic birds. Of course, some animals made their homes there of their own volition: rats and stray dogs became a particular problem as human settlements grew increasingly dense.

To the south and west of the Philadelphia hinterland, herding, fencing and housing of animals diminished as settlements were smaller and the demands of tobacco had absorbed colonists' energies. Even after the tobacco economy went into decline, the only animals that received careful tending were racing horses; hogs and all other horses continued to run wild. In the Shenandoah Valley, the Carolinas, and Georgia, wild Spanish cattle and stock imported from the Middle Colonies were mixed in a loose but effective system of occasional penning that allowed colonists to maximize the benefit of the free range while retaining some control over the animals. One

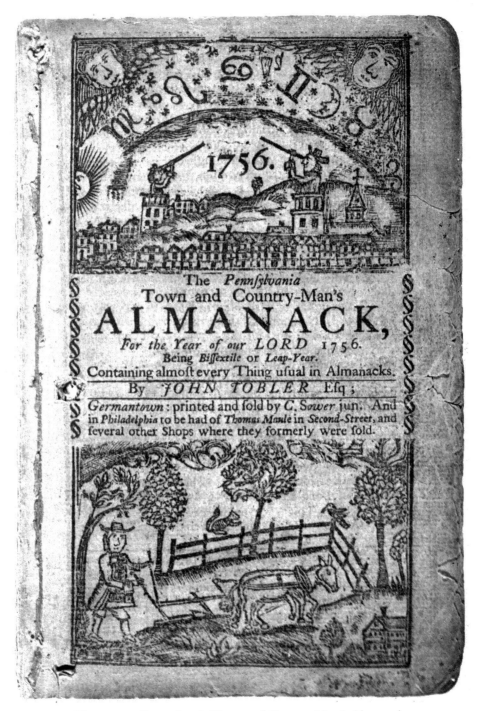

Figure 2.5 Pennsylvania Town and Country Man's Almanack
Encyclopaedia Britannica/UIG/Bridgeman Images

– CHAPTER 2: *Animals in Atlantic North America* –

account claimed it 'not an uncommon thing to see one man the master of from 300 to 1200, and even 2000 cows, bulls, oxen, and young cattle; hogs also in prodigious numbers.' This observation is significant not just in its description of the quantity of cattle, but the paucity of people involved. These ranches constituted the aggressive avant-garde of a colonial ecosystem that was literally chewing its way inland at an ever-quickening pace.[26]

Maintaining control over herds that ranged freely required a modicum of effort in the form of collecting, feeding, and neutering animals. Through a combination of the neglect of their owners and the animals' own initiative, many of these domesticates escaped human control and returned to some degree of wildness. This was particularly true in the South, where forage was available year-round, and the animals could withstand the cold. As early as 1560, Spanish swine introduced by explorers and missionaries ran wild in the southeast, and as they did so their genetic heritage as European wild boars re-emerged so that with each subsequent generation the tusks grew a little longer, the bristles a little more wiry, and the backs a little more ridged. Long-horned cattle and chickens followed into La Florida about sixty years later as part of the mission system that the Spanish erected to subjugate Native populations. To these were added the myriad domesticates introduced by the English in the seventeenth century. Although colonists erected enclosures, known as cowpens, to which cattle would be lured back nightly in order to ensure their safety and docility and to collect their dung, many creatures absconded.

The principal native animals that gained in this new faunal landscape were those that found themselves presented with a sudden abundance of food. Birds, such as bobolinks and crows, that ate seeds planted by colonial farmers, throve. For a time, so, too, did the top predators. Colonial domesticates were prey to wolves, bears, and pumas. However, the predators' victory would prove short-lived, as the colonists launched a sustained and unsparing counterattack with guns and traps on behalf of their beasts. That they enlisted Natives in the enterprise indicates the colonists' seriousness in this endeavor given that they were generally leery of armed Natives in the woods so close to their settlements. Predator populations were decimated, and they forced them to beat a steady retreat as the colonial ecosystem deprived them of both their accustomed forest habitat and their lives.[27]

Against a massive and implacable backdrop of awful loss of life, land, and liberty, native peoples benefitted somewhat from the increasing prevalence of relatively docile – hogs excepted – animals wandering in the woods. Native hunters regarded cattle, hogs, and horses as fair game and either took or killed and consumed them when they could. However, doing so did not compensate calorically for the foodstuffs that animals destroyed when they ravaged Native clambeds and fields of corn, beans, and squash. Nor did it compensate for the antagonism livestock-killing might provoke on the part of the animals' colonial owners and the colonists in general. As historian Virginia DeJohn Anderson has pointed out, livestock topped the list of irritants in quotidian relations between Indians and colonists. Divergent cultural perspectives on the proper relationship between humans and living animals reflected different understandings of property and nature. The struggle over animals was the struggle over land writ small.[28]

When Natives complained of animal trespasses, New England colonists initially offered compensation and attempted to control the animals by fencing them in, or by helping the Indians build fences around their fields. However, it was not long before unruly animals had surpassed the limits of New Englanders' willingness to bear the full cost of their livestock. Fencing strategies failed because fences were regularly defeated by rooting pigs, and ready access to wood diminished over time. English-style stone walls would have been more effective, but the additional investment of time and labor was unacceptable to the colonists. Ultimately, the Puritans acknowledged the justice of Native complaints but also defined the livestock in question as an important marker over their native neighbors. It was by virtue of animal husbandry itself that they felt entitled to eminent domain over Indian lands. In his *General Considerations for the Plantations in New England*, John Winthrop took up the objection, 'what warrant have we to take that land?' His answer was that the Indians' claim was inferior because they 'enclose no ground, neither have they cattle to maintain it.'[29]

In 1666, Patuxent Indians in Maryland asked the colony's leaders to grant them refuge from the plague of swine. They asserted, 'Your Hogs & Cattle injure Us. We Can fly no farther. Let us know where to live & how to be secured for the future from the Hogs & Cattle.'[30] But the Patuxents' complaints were scarcely heeded in the rough world that was the seventeenth-century Chesapeake, where an English servant could have two years added to his indenture for the theft of a hog. If harassment by livestock prompted the Indians to move, then the animals had served colonization well. Of course, resentful Natives oftentimes stole, killed, or mutilated livestock in retribution.[31]

Indeed, some colonists came to see opportunity in livestock conflicts. In 1640, the governor of New Netherland, Willem Kieft, purposefully escalated a dispute over the alleged killing of several Dutch hogs on Staten Island by Raritan Indians in order to subdue them decisively. This controversy festered and ultimately spiraled into a vicious war with Algonquians across the lower Hudson River Valley and Long Island, known as Kieft's War. Bacon's Rebellion in Virginia was more aptly named than we usually recognize, since it was sparked when some Indians took a colonist's hogs and the colonists took the Indians' lives in retribution. Thomas Ludwell, secretary of the colony of Virginia, asserted that the colonists who were 'the forwardest in the rebellion' had been those who settled near Indians and whose 'cattle and hoggs destroye[d] all the corn of the other Indians of the towne.' Bacon's Rebellion resulted in the death of a large number of Indians and the expropriation of those who survived them, although not as quickly or completely as Bacon's followers had hoped.[32]

As native fauna dwindled, Native peoples' traditional subsistence cycles were compromised and the trade in furs and skins declined. To survive they had to replace the lost meat and trade commodities and adopt the invaders' Neolithic complex if they were to regain the food, energy, and trade goods that they had lost. This included revising their relationship to animals to become, in a much more proximate way, masters rather than partners. With reluctance, they slowly turned to animal husbandry themselves. Swine and chickens were the first animals adopted, since they were least disruptive to seasonal patterns of movement and had reasonably close predecessors in dogs and turkeys.[33] Native women often took the lead in this enterprise, since their traditional roles were as the sustainers of life in the homes and fields that comprised the towns and villages of native North America. Native men eventually took up horse, hog, and cattle raising and, in so doing, retained the spatial mobility that had defined their earlier roles as woodland hunters. Animals under Native care were more generally supervised only casually, so they grew more scrawny, hardy, and ornery, and the growing herds of horses, cattle, and swine forced people to spread out and live on scattered ranches rather than in the closely packed villages that had been home to their grandparents. Native people also began to fence their crops to keep the browsers out, all of which had a tendency to inculcate notions of private property that had not been there before, just as the many brands burned on cattle's flanks and notches cut into pigs' ears bespoke a novel kind of ownership of living beings that, in the pre-contact past, would have been unthinkable.[34] But the unthinkable had, in fact, happened. Thousands of years before, hunters had triggered the creation of a new faunal environment in eastern North America when they and a changing climate drove mammoths and other large mammals into extinction. Such losses enabled a new order of smaller, more prolific mammals to flourish alongside the insects, fishes, and birds that had been there all along. Afterwards, the post-Pleistocene ecology ebbed and flowed as all ecologies do for millennia until the arrival of Europeans, their animals, and their diseases at the end of the fifteenth century. While it had taken people in Eurasia ten thousand years to domesticate animals, in eastern North America it took only a generation or two in any given place for Neolithic animal husbandry to devastate the post-Pleistocene ecology. After three centuries of ongoing colonization and colonial expansion, the faunal ecology had been thoroughly creolized.[35] The European invaders and their descendants cleared forests, drained swamps, and dispossessed entire nations of people to make way for livestock pastures, free ranges, and separate fields of corn, wheat, tobacco, and rice. Euro-American animal husbandry and agriculture did not, however, completely displace indigenous fauna nor did they constitute a wholesale replication of the western European pattern. Instead, a mix of the two emerged that, to be sure, bore all of the substantial scars that had followed the European invasion of North America.

As the three sets of European invaders – the people, the animals, and the diseases – moved into eastern North America they did mighty destructive work. Conquests and epidemics decimated towns, villages, and families, emptying the land of thousands of people and allowing other animal populations to flourish. With the rise of the commercial skin and peltry trades, the invasion's survivors took to the forests and fields to kill far more animals than their parents had to keep up with the demands of the Atlantic World's burgeoning economy and the spiral of economic dependency. For a nearly a century millions of animals fell annually and their furs, pelts, and skins voyaged across the seas back to the European metropoles until, at the end of the eighteenth century, market demand for the skins and furs collapsed along with the stocks of deer, beaver, and bear that had once so populated the landscapes of eastern North America. In the widowed forests, streams, and savannas, horses, cattle, and swine proliferated and claimed vast amounts of land and resources for their own subsistence. Through foraging and trampling, they devastated former ecosystems in ways that the invaders who introduced them could hardly have imagined. By feeding the invaders, powering their mills, pulling their ploughs, fertilizing their fields, running wild, and destroying habitat, not to mention helping to wreck Native Americans' former way of life, the animal invasion of eastern North America helped to create a new creole landscape that bespoke three centuries of struggle between two ancient faunal ecosystems, one domesticated the other not, for the life and land of one corner of the larger Atlantic World.

NOTES

The authors wish to thank Virginia DeJohn Anderson, James D. Rice, and Jack Stenger for their comments and criticisms.

1 Richter 1992: 8–11; Rice 2009: 1–2.
2 Hale 1993: 15; Pagden 1993: 6; Genesis 9: 5, King James Bible.
3 Domínguez 1986: 13; Klein 2000: xiii–xv.
4 Silver 1990: 30.
5 Silver 1990: 24–28, 31, 51, 61–62; Ethridge 2003: 38; Chapman and Feldhamer 1982: 98, 214, 269, 465, 507, 711; Krech 1999: 153–55; Braund 1993: 65; Pearson 2013: 129, 130, 133; Skabelund 2013: 804.
6 Williams and Elliott 1998: 1–5; Snow 1998: 63, 76–78; Milanich, Cordell, Knight, Kohler, and Sigler-Lavelle 1997 (1984): 41–42, 91–112, 176–77; Lankford 1987: 57, 62, 66–67, 106–7, 125; Krech 2012: 73–82; Bogan 1980: 48–49.
7 Aberth 2013: 141–48; Crosby 2004: 21–25.
8 Panno 2011: 29–30, 57–58; Crosby 2004: 12, 29–31; Zimmerman and Zimmerman 2003: 59–60, 156.
9 Crosby 1976: 289–99; Ubelaker 2006: 694–701.
10 White 1983: 10–11, 34; Bartram 1995: 60–164; Bossu 1962: 68–69, 146–47; Silver 1990: 186; Davis 2000: 53–55; Usner 1992: 27, 36.
11 Parrish 1997: 485; Sayre 1997: 219–47, esp. 228–30.
12 Quoted in Jacobs 2009: 109; Turgeon 1998: 585–610; Rich 1955; Carlos and Lewis 2010: 18.
13 Richards 2003: 511–13.
14 Krech 1999: 155, 160–63; Braund 1993: 69–72; Silver 1990: 99–100; White 1983: 85; Oatis 2004: 112–39; Carson 1999: 71, as quoted.
15 Haan 1981: 341–58.
16 Crosby 2004: 182; Cook 1998: 28–29.
17 Smith 1632: 86; quoted in Anderson 2002: 379.
18 Anderson 2004: 99; Jacobs 2009: 122.
19 Quoted in Haan 1981: 350.
20 Romani 1995: 52, 60; Anderson 2004: 244; Jordan 1993: 23–25, 55–68, 109–18; Otto 1986: 123–24; Otto 1987: 20–21.
21 Wacker and Clemens 1995: 65; Miquelon 1987: 202.
22 Anderson 2004: 110–16; quoted in Taylor 2001: 47.
23 Cronon 1983: 142; Bidwell and Falconer 1925: 105–6.
24 Miquelon 1987: 202–3; Kalm 1772: II:327–28.
25 Thompson 1942: 18–42; Russell 1982: 82–92; Garrison 1987: 3–8; Purvis 1995: 37–55; Bidwell and Falconer 1925: 105–6.
26 Thompson 1942: 44–63 (quote 63).
27 Coleman 2004: 52–65.
28 Anderson 1994: 606–8.
29 Anderson 2004: 192–95.
30 Quoted in Taylor 2001: 136.
31 Perdue 1995: 100; Anderson 2004: 236; Richard L. Haan 1981: 350–51;
32 Williams 1995: 253–55; Anderson 2004: 231; Washburn 1957: 135, 161 (quote); Rice 2012: 4–6, 123–25, 191.
33 Pavao-Zuckerman 2007: 5, 11; Hatley 1993: 161–62; Saunt 1999: 47–54; Adair, 1930: 241, 444–45; Bartram 1995: 227; Romans 1775: 16, 23–24, 62–63, 68, 92–94, 184, 326; Silver 1990: 110–12, 135, 149, 175–76, 179–80; Davis 2000: 46, 52, 68, 72, 77; Braund

– CHAPTER 2: *Animals in Atlantic North America* –

1993: 51, 58, 72, 157, 178; Anderson 2004: 119, 178–79; White 1983: 87–92, 100, 102; Ethridge 2003: 50, 159, 164–67.

34 Braund 1993: 75–76, 135; Anderson 2004: 112–14; Stewart 1996: 22, 55, 72–74; Bartram 1995: 53, 189; Otto 2002: 56, 60; Saunt 1999: 159–71; White 1983: 103–5, 109; Ethridge 2003: 137, 163–64, 182–83.

35 Vigne 2011: 178.

REFERENCES

Aberth, John (2013) *An environmental history of the Middle Ages: the crucible of nature*, London: Routledge.

Adair, James (1930) *Adair's history of the American Indians*, Samuel Cole Williams (ed), Johnson City, Tenn.: Watauga Press.

Anderson, Virginia DeJohn (1994) 'King Philip's herds: Indians, colonists, and the problem of livestock in early New England', *The William and Mary Quarterly* 51/4: 601–24.

——(2002) 'Animals into the wilderness: the development of livestock husbandry in the seventeenth-century Chesapeake', *The William and Mary Quarterly* 59/3: 377–408.

——(2004) *Creatures of empire: how domestic animals transformed early America*, Oxford: Oxford University Press.

Bartram, William (1995) *William Bartram on the Southeastern Indians*, Gregory A. Waselkov and Kathryn E. Holland Braund (eds), Lincoln: University of Nebraska Press.

Bidwell, Percy Wells and Falconer, John I. (1925) *History of agriculture in the northern United States, 1620–1860*, Washington: Carnegie Institution.

Blitz, John H. (1993) *Ancient chiefdoms of the Tombigbee*, Tuscaloosa: University of Alabama Press.

Bogan, Arthur Eugene (1980) 'A comparison of late prehistoric Dallas and Overhill Cherokee subsistence strategies in the Little Tennessee River Valley', PhD thesis, Knoxville: University of Tennessee.

Bossu, Jean-Bernard (1962) *Travels in the interior of North America, 1751–1762*, Seymour Feilor (ed and trans), Norman: University of Oklahoma Press.

Braund, Kathryn E. Holland (1993) *Deerskins & duffels: the Creek Indian trade with Anglo-America, 1685–1815*, Lincoln: University of Nebraska Press.

Carlos, Ann M. and Lewis, Frank D. (2010) *Commerce by a frozen sea: Native Americans and the European fur trade*, Philadelphia: University of Pennsylvania Press.

Carson, James Taylor (1999) *Searching for the bright path: the Mississippi Choctaws from prehistory to removal*, Lincoln: University of Nebraska Press.

Chapman, Joseph A. and Feldhamer, George A. (eds) (1982) *Wild mammals of North America: biology, management, and economics*, Baltimore: The Johns Hopkins University Press.

Coleman, Jon T. (2004) *Vicious: wolves and men in America*, New Haven: Yale University Press.

Cook, Noble David (1998) *Born to die: disease and New World conquest, 1492–1650*, New York: Cambridge University Press.

Cronon, William (1983) *Changes in the Land: Indians, Colonists, and the Ecology of New England*, New York: Hill and Wang.

Crosby, Alfred W. (1976) 'Virgin soil epidemics as a factor in the aboriginal depopulation in America', *The William and Mary Quarterly* 33/2: 289–99.

——(1994) *Germs, seeds, & animals: studies in ecological history*, Armonk, N.Y.: M. E. Sharpe.

——(2004) *Ecological imperialism: the biological expansion of Europe, 900–1400*, 2nd ed., New York: Cambridge University Press.

Davis, Donald Edward (2000) *Where there are mountains: an environmental history of the southern Appalachians*, Athens: University of Georgia Press.

Domínguez, Virginia R. (1986) *White by definition: social classification in Creole Louisiana*, New Brunswick: Rutgers University Press.

Ethridge, Robbie (2003) *Creek country: the Creek Indians and their world*, Chapel Hill: The University of North Carolina Press.

Fischer, John Ryan (2007) 'Cattle in Hawai'i: biological and cultural exchange', *Pacific Historical Review* 76/3: 347–72.

Galloway, Patricia (1994) 'Confederacy as a solution to chiefdom dissolution: historical evidence in the Choctaw case', in Charles Hudson and Carmen Chaves Tesser (eds), *The forgotten centuries: Indians and Europeans in the American South, 1521–1704*, Athens: University of Georgia Press.

——(1999) *Choctaw genesis, 1500–1700*, Lincoln: University of Nebraska Press.

Garrison, J. Ritchie (1987) 'Farm dynamics and regional exchange: the Connecticut Valley beef trade, 1670–1850', *Agricultural History* 61/3: 1–17.

Gifford-Gonzalez, Diane and Hanotte, Olivier (2011) 'Domesticating animals in Africa: implications of genetic and archaeological findings', *Journal of World Prehistory* 24/1: 1–23.

Gleach, Frederic W. (1997) *Powhatan's world and Colonial Virginia: a conflict of cultures*, Lincoln: University of Nebraska Press.

Haan, Richard L. (1981) 'The "trade do's not flourish as formerly": the ecological origins of the Yamassee War of 1715', *Ethnohistory* 28/4: 341–58.

Hale, John (1993) *The civilization of Europe in the Renaissance*, London: Fontana Press.

Hatley, M. Thomas (1993) *The dividing paths: Cherokees and South Carolinians through the era of Revolution*. New York: Oxford University Press.

Jacobs, Jaap (2009) *The colony of New Netherland: a Dutch settlement in seventeenth-century America*, Ithaca: Cornell University Press.

Jordan, Terry G. (1993) *North American cattle-ranching frontiers: origins, diffusion, and differentiation*, Albuquerque: University of New Mexico Press.

Kalm, Peter (1772) *Travels into North America*, London: T. Lowndes.

Klein, Sybil (2000) 'Introduction', in Sybil Klein (ed), *Creole: the history and legacy of Louisiana's free people of color*, Baton Rouge: Louisiana State University Press.

Knight, Vernon J. Jr. (1994) 'The formation of the Creeks', in Charles Hudson and Carmen Chaves Tesser (eds), *The forgotten centuries: Indians and Europeans in the American South, 1521–1704*, Athens: University of Georgia Press.

Krech, Shepard III (1999) *The ecological Indian: myth and history*, New York: W. W. Norton and Co.

——(2012) 'Indigenous ethnoornithology in the American South', in David M. Gordon and Shepard Krech III (eds), *Indigenous knowledge and the environment in Africa and North America*, Athens: Ohio University Press.

Lankford, George E. (ed) (1987) *Native American legends: Southeastern legends – tales from the Natchez, Caddo, Biloxi, Chickasaw, and other nations*, Little Rock, Ark.: August House.

Mainfort, Robert C. Jr. (1988) 'Middle Woodland ceremonialism at Pinson Mounds, Tennessee', *American Antiquity* 53/1: 158–73.

Melville, Elinor G. K. (1997) *A plague of sheep: environmental consequences of the conquest of Mexico*, Cambridge: Cambridge University Press.

Milanich, Jerald T., Cordell, Ann S., Knight, Vernon J. Jr., Kohler, Timothy A., and Sigler-Lavelle, Brenda J. (1997 [1984]), *Archaeology of northern Florida, A.D. 200–900: The McKeithen Weeden Island culture*, Gainesville: University Press of Florida.

Miquelon, Dale (1987) *New France, 1701–1744: a supplement to Europe*, Toronto: McClelland and Stewart.

Mooney, James (1992) *History, myths, and sacred formulas of the Cherokees*, Asheville, N.C.: Historical Images.

Mwacharo, J.M., Bjørnstad, G., Hern, J.L., and Hanotte, O. (2013) 'The history of African village chickens: an archaeological and molecular perspective', *African Archaeological Review* 30/1: 97–114.

Oatis, Steven J. (2004) *A colonial complex: South Carolina's frontiers in the era of the Yamassee War, 1680–1730*, Lincoln: University of Nebraska Press.

Otto, John Solomon (1986) 'The origins of cattle-ranching in colonial South Carolina, 1670–1715', *South Carolina Historical Magazine* 87/2: 117–24.

——(1987) 'Livestock-raising in early South Carolina, 1670–1700: prelude to the rice plantation economy', *Agricultural History* 61/4: 13–24.

——(2002) 'Cattle-grazing in the Southeastern United States, 1670–1949', in Mary J. Voss-Henninger (ed), *Animals in human histories: the mirror of nature and culture*, Rochester: University of Rochester.

Pagden, Anthony (1993) *European encounters with the New World: from Renaissance to romanticism*, New Haven: Yale University Press.

Panno, Joseph (2011) *Viruses: the origin and evolution of deadly pathogens*, New York: Facts on File.

Parrish, Susan Scott (1997) 'The female opossum and the nature of the New World', *The William and Mary Quarterly* 54/3: 475–514.

Pavao-Zuckerman, Barnet (2007) 'Deerskins and domesticates: Creek subsistence and economic strategies in the historic period', *American Antiquity* 72/1: 5–33.

Pearson, Chris (2013) 'Dogs, history, and agency', *History and Theory* 52/4: 128–45.

Perdue, Theda (1995) 'Women, men, and American Indian policy: the Cherokee response to "civilization"', in Nancy Shoemaker (ed), *Negotiators of change: historical perspectives, on Native American women*, New York: Routledge.

Pluckhahn, Thomas J. (2003) *Kolomoki: settlement, ceremony, and status in the Deep South, A.D. 350–750*, Tuscaloosa: University of Alabama Press.

Potter, Stephen R. (1993) *Commoners, tribute, and chiefs: the development of Algonquian culture in the Potomac Valley*, Charlottesville: University of Virginia Press.

Pyle, Gerald F. (1986) *The diffusion of influenza: patterns and paradigms*, Totowa, N.J.: Rowman & Littlefield Publishers.

Purvis, Thomas L. (1995) *Revolutionary America 1763 to 1800*, New York: Facts on File.

Rice, James D. (2009) *Nature and history in the Potomac country: from hunter-gatherers to the age of Jefferson*, Baltimore: The Johns Hopkins University Press.

——(2012) *Tales from a revolution: Bacon's Rebellion and the transformation of early America*, Oxford: Oxford University Press.

Rich, E. E. (1955) 'Russia and the colonial fur trade', *The Economic History Review* 7/3: 307–28.

Richards, John F. (2003) *The unending frontier: an environmental history of the early modern world*, Berkeley: University of California Press.

Richter, Daniel K. (1992) *The ordeal of the longhouse: the peoples of the Iroquois League in the era of European colonization*, Chapel Hill: The University of North Carolina Press.

Romani, Jr., Daniel A. (1995) 'The Pettaquamscut purchase of 1657/58 and the establishment of a commercial livestock industry in Rhode Island,' in *New England's Creatures: 1400–1900: Dublin seminar for New England folklife annual proceedings 1993*, Boston: Boston University Press.

Romans, Bernard (1775) *A concise natural history of east and west Florida*, New York: Bernard Romans.

Russell, Howard S. (1982) *A long, deep furrow: three centuries of farming in New England*, Hanover, N.H.: University Press of New England.

Saunt, Claudio (1999) *A new order of things: property, power, and the transformation of the Creek Indians, 1733–1816*, New York: Cambridge University Press.

Sayre, Gordon M. (1997) *Les sauvages américains: representations of Native Americans in French and English colonial literature*, Chapel Hill: The University of North Carolina Press.

Silver, Timothy (1990) *A new face on the countryside: Indians, colonists, and slaves in South Atlantic forests, 1500–1800*, Cambridge: Cambridge University Press.

Sioui, Georges E. (1992) *For an Amerindian autohistory: an essay on the foundations of a social ethic*, Montreal: McGill-Queen's University Press.

Skabelund, Aaron (2013) 'Animals and imperialism: recent historiographical trends', *History Compass* 11/10: 801–7.

Smith, John (1632) *The Generall Historie of Virginia*, London: Edward Blackmore.

Smith, Marvin T. (1987) *Archaeology of aboriginal culture change in the interior Southeast: depopulation during the early historic period*, Gainesville: University Press of Florida.

——(2000) *Coosa: the rise and fall of a Southeastern Mississippi chiefdom*, Gainesville: University Press of Florida.

Snow, Frankie (1998) 'Swift Creek design investigations: the Hartford case', in Mark Williams and Daniel T. Elliott (eds), *A world engraved: archaeology of the Swift Creek culture*, Tuscaloosa: University of Alabama Press.

Steadman, David W. (2001) 'A long-term history of terrestrial birds and mammals in the Chesapeake-Susquehanna watershed', in Philip D. Curtin, Grace S. Bush, and George W. Fischer (eds), *Discovering the Chesapeake: the history of a watershed*, Baltimore: The Johns Hopkins University Press.

Stewart, Mart A. (1996) *'What nature suffers to groe': life, labor, and landscape on the Georgia coast, 1680–1920*, Athens: University of Georgia Press.

Storey, Alice A., et al (2012) 'Investigating the global dispersal of chickens in prehistory using ancient mitochondrial DNA signatures', *PLoS ONE* 7/7: 1–11.

Taylor, Alan (2001) *American colonies: the settling of North America*, New York: Penguin.

Thompson, James Westfall (1942) *A history of livestock raising in the United States, 1607–1860*, Washington: United States Department of Agriculture.

Turgeon, Laurier (1998) 'French fishers, fur traders, and Amerindians during the sixteenth century: history and archaeology', *The William and Mary Quarterly* 55/4: 585–610.

Ubelaker, Douglas H. (2006) 'Population size, contact to nadir', in Douglas H. Ubelaker (ed), *Handbook of the North American Indians*, vol. 3: *Environment, origins, and population*, Washington: Smithsonian Institution Press.

Usner, Daniel H. Jr. (1992) *Indians, settlers, & slaves in a frontier exchange economy: the Lower Mississippi Valley before 1783*, Chapel Hill: University of North Carolina Press.

Vigne, Jean-Denis (2011) 'The origins of animal domestication and husbandry: a major change in the history of humanity and the biosphere', *Comptes Rendus Biologies* 334/3: 171–81.

Wacker, Peter O. and Clemens, Paul G. E. (1995) *Land use in early New Jersey: a historical geography*, Newark: New Jersey Historical Society.

Washburn, Wilcomb E. (1957) *The governor and the rebel: a history of Bacon's Rebellion in Virginia*, Chapel Hill: The University of North Carolina Press.

Welch, Paul D. (1991) *Moundville's economy*, Tuscaloosa: University of Alabama Press.

White, Richard (1983) *The roots of dependency: subsistence, environment, and social change among the Choctaws, Pawnees, and Navajos*, Lincoln: University of Nebraska.

Williams, James Homer (1995) 'Great doggs and mischievous cattle: domesticated animals and Indian-European relations in New Netherland and New York', *New York History* 76/3: 245–64.

Williams, Mark and Elliott, Daniel T. (1998) 'Swift Creek research: history and observations', in Mark Williams and Daniel T. Elliott (eds), *A world engraved: archaeology of the Swift Creek culture*, Tuscaloosa: University of Alabama Press.

Wood, Peter H. (1989) 'The changing population of the colonial South: an overview by race and region, 1685–1790', in Peter H. Wood, Gregory A. Waselkov, and M. Thomas Hatley (eds), *Powhatan's mantle: Indians in the colonial Southeast*, Lincoln: University of Nebraska Press.

Worth, John E. (1998) *Timucuan chiefdoms of Spanish Florida*, vol. 1: *Assimilation*, Gainesville: University Press of Florida.

Zimmerman, Barry E. and Zimmerman, David J. (2003) *Killer germs: microbes and diseases that threaten humanity*, revised ed., New York: Contemporary Books.

CHAPTER THREE

SCIENCE AND IDEOLOGY
IN THE SPANISH ATLANTIC

—·◆·—

Sandra Rebok

INTRODUCTION

Spain's encounter with the New World in the fifteenth century had a crucial impact on both sides of the Atlantic. One important aspect was its contribution to the progress in different fields of scientific knowledge through the then unknown nature and cultures of America. This process unleashed in the year 1492, and consisted in the beginning of the intellectual awareness of this part of the world, until then ignored by the European consciousness. The activities of Spanish royal officers, soldiers, merchants and missionaries constituted what can be considered an early scientific revolution, since the information collected in America questioned and in some aspects even contradicted the European classical scientific tradition.[1] Furthermore, it was indeed an innovative approach to validate the personal experience of a scholar as source of learning; this new empirical tradition emerging in America was opposed to the textually based scholastic and humanist tradition.[2] Nevertheless, evaluating the impact of the newly obtained scientific information about natural history, geography, ethnography and medicine of the New World, we have to keep in mind the fact that this knowledge was essential for controlling the acquired regions and for establishing the Spanish empire overseas. As a consequence, it cannot be seen disconnected from its colonial purpose; thus analyzing the history of Spanish scientific research undertaken in America and its contribution to early modern European knowledge includes also the study of colonial science in the frame of an imperial expansion.

During the last 500 years, in different historical epochs there were many approaches to the historiography of the scientific exploration of America. This essay does not focus on the much debated question of which approach can be considered scientific in a modern sense. Rather it departs more from the idea that scientific research is subject to evolution, that it is imbedded in ideological, political, philosophical and social currents and cannot be meaningfully analyzed in isolation from these factors. Two main aspects that have to be mentioned in this context are on one side the ideology, the actual discussions and philosophical currents which define the consciousness of the researchers and their way to approach the object of the study, modify the focus of their work and conduct the topic of their interest. On the other side, the political

– CHAPTER 3: *Science and ideology in the Spanish Atlantic* –

circumstances deciding which topics are to be investigated, which studies are actually to be published and which research fields should receive financial support.

My intention is to demonstrate the impact of these questions on the evolution of the Americanist anthropology in Spain. The definition of Americanism being used in the following study comprehends the knowledge and the research of the American, namely the entire environment which comprises the persons as well as the institutions dedicated to the study and interpretation of the American cultures, in their merely theoretic as well as practical aspects. In fact, the Americanism conceives a complete aggregation of disciplines and interests, united by the only but sufficient link of the American as a primarily geographic concept. Our focus of attention centers basically on the anthropological and ethnographic aspect – though, in certain moments, other aspects, such as the American archaeology for instance, will receive corresponding attention.

Spain was a pioneer in the discovery, as well as in the scientific investigation of the New Continent, therefore there exist strong historical, cultural and traditional links between both worlds on either side of the Atlantic. This also explains the extraordinary possibilities that Spain had in the research related to different human cultures, since the New World for a long time has been considered a singular laboratory for questions related to this field.

This study approaches the Americanism exclusively from the Spanish side, particularly taking into account its rather dynamic and variable character during the centuries. It is a study of the Spanish science in America from an inside view; due to the limitation of its extension, no comparisons to other nations can be established, nor can the critics from outside regarding the Spanish science, what is understood as *Leyenda Negra,* be included. For the same reasons, unfortunately, within the framework of this article, the American voices cannot be considered.

This historic process will be presented in its different phases in order to highlight the characteristic aspects of each period of time and to indicate the evident modifications undergone from one to the other. The focus of this essay is not to chronicle all Spanish activity undertaken in the field of Americanism, but rather to demonstrate the basic research interests and methods that characterize the studies undertaken in each epoch. Therefore, the scope of this contribution is based on the description of main theories and the scientists behind the projects conducted overseas as well as the modifications in the methods of work applied during the different phases.

PHASE OF CONTACT AND DISCOVERY: 1492–1600

A certain polemic debate arises when trying to find the most appropriate term for the historic occurrences of those times – was it a discovery, an encounter between two worlds or a culture clash? We can definitely say that in the year 1492 an encounter occurred between the *Old World*, bearer of the so-called western Christian culture, and the *New World*. There was an enormous richness in different cultures, situated in very distinct levels of development. Actually, since it was not a contact between equals, but a quite aggressive encounter, the term encounter becomes somewhat euphemistic. Looking at it this way, it could be more adequate to name it a violent *cultural clash*. Nevertheless, this paper adopts the point of view that there was indeed a discovery – the scientific discovery of America.

The first phase of the development of the Americanism can be considered from the point of view of a naturalist, since it is characterized by a marked predilection for the natural elements in its broadest understanding. When the Europeans encountered the *New World*, this put into question a large part of their existent knowledge or their acquired ideas about geography, biology, fauna, flora as well as the nature of the human being. Inevitably the richness of the American nature, regarding the variety in the flora, fauna as well as the different cultures, has been contemplated from the perspective of the *Old World* and compared with what had been known until then. A first attempt to classify the entirety of new knowledge – followed by the majority of the authors – was to divide it into two large categories: the *natural* (geography, flora and fauna) and the *moral* or *cultural* (the human being and its different cultural manifestations). The numerous Spaniards in this period of time who conducted studies or research projects in America had one general interest: getting to know the native societies. Nevertheless, behind this common aim, very different intentions became manifest. Basically, three groups with their particular approaches to the indigenous societies can be differentiated: the military, the missionaries and the royal officials. Whereas the soldiers were looking for information about these cultures for military reasons; the missionaries depended on knowledge about the native population in order to convert them to Christianity; and finally, the officials needed this information in order to be able to administer these societies in a more efficient way.

The group that provided us with most information and whose working methods were more similar to the tasks of a modern anthropologist is without doubt that of the missionaries. What were the interests and the motivation of these first chroniclers? Which aspects of the work of those scholars caught more attention? One of the first and main tasks of the missionaries was the study of the functioning and origin of the American religions. The majority of the missionaries who wrote about the autochthonous cultures recognized that it was imperative to know the principles of the indigenous religions before proceeding to the Christianization of the native population. Therefore, in this period, an elevated number of descriptions of the different religious systems were produced giving an account of their deities, sacred intermediaries, mystic formulations, festive rites or rites of transition, forms of religious organization, the different classes of priesthood or shamanism, as well as their ethical convictions, which were all integral parts of their religion or at least legitimized this way.[3]

Along with the interest in converting the indigenous population to Christianity, the linguistic work of the missionaries was carried out in parallel. At the beginning, the predominant intention was to teach Spanish in order to establish a better communication with the Indians, but due to the obtained experience, the missionaries saw that they had an easier access to the people by learning their language. As a consequence, many missionaries dedicated their time to the study of the native languages, annotating the obtained information and thus writing the first dictionaries.

Another important issue, the axis of the anthropological considerations of those times, was the functioning and the legitimacy of the native societies. The contemplation about this aspect has always been conditioned considerably by the Spanish policy towards the autochthonous population – their interest to obtain information, which could help to administer the new colonies. Thus, their efforts to understand the local form of government originated an elevated number of descriptions about the political and cultural systems of the indigenous societies. In addition, both the legitimacy of these societies as

— CHAPTER 3: *Science and ideology in the Spanish Atlantic* —

well as the much-debated question of the 'capability of the Indians' were discussed. Another topic of interest, generated in this context, was the process of acculturation of the indigenous population in the communities and the towns as a hybrid society.[4]

A part of these first studies had as a fundamental motive the defense of the Indians. There was an intellectual movement in the sixteenth and seventeenth century called *indigenist* or *criticist*, which criticized the Spanish behaviour during the colonization of America. The first to express their protest regarding the treatment of the native population in the public were the missionaries. A considerable number of them dedicated their time to write about the American cultures with the intention of finding arguments to defend them against the aggressions of the Spanish military as well as the *encomienda* system,[5] the slavery, the labour in the mines or other ways to dismantle the cultural order established prior to the arrival of the Spaniards.

Without doubt, the most famous representative of this group was the Dominican friar Bartolomé de Las Casas (1484–1566), whose treatises are today considered as indispensable indigenist writings. One of his lifetime concerns was to define with precision and clarity the cultural content of the American Indians. He considered them as a cultural unity, in disregard of the differences among the diverse cultures.[6] For Las Casas, the Indians were human beings equal to all in everything except their beliefs – a point of view that shocked his contemporaries – and it can be asserted that, though his language was not that of a modern anthropologist, his concepts in many aspects contain an approach well ahead of his time.

One common element in the writings of the first chroniclers in their descriptions of the curiosities of the *New World*, regarding nature as well as the indigenous cultures, was comparing them with the European knowledge of those times. On one hand this served to give a point of reference to the scholars and researchers for their studies and on the other hand, it made it easier for the readers to imagine from what they were reading.

Another subject that has been a constant issue in the Americanist bibliography was the question of the origin of the American Indian. Since the discovery, all type of speculations and theories were spread: apart from the most absurd and inept ones, there were also others which raised the question with a certain rigour based on rather scientific methods. Already in the first period of research in the *New World* this topic had been addressed in a more theoretical way, without direct implications in the practice of evangelization or of the functionaries of the colonial administration. This subject was of interest because it answered the question of how to connect the American population with the *Old World* – by using the comparative method between cultural features and institutions of the Euro-Afro-Asian and American cultures.[7]

Among the numerous scholars and authors of this epoch, the Franciscan missionary Bernardino de Sahagún (1499–1590) is especially noteworthy for his applied working methods and his decisively scientific approach and can be considered as one of the first anthropologists regarding the American cultures. His famous publication *Historia General de las Cosas de la Nueva España*, written between 1570 and 1580,[8] is appreciated as a veritable anthropological writing of the Aztec population in which he meticulously studies their cultural reality. Another person who influenced the thinking and approach of the chroniclers at the end of the sixteenth century was the Jesuit José de Acosta (1539–1600) whose paradigmatic opus *Historia natural y moral*

Figure 3.1 Bartolomé de las Casas
© Mary Evans Picture Library

– CHAPTER 3: *Science and ideology in the Spanish Atlantic* –

Figure 3.2 Emperor Carl V with Quevedo and Las Casas
© Mary Evans Picture Library

de las Indias was published for the first time in 1590.⁹ According to Alcina Franch, the treatment of the American reality by Acosta could also be qualified, in the more open sense of the word, as 'scientific' or 'systematic', since he analyzed the reality of the American continent as if it were a *natural history*, in which the climate, geography, fauna, flora and the human being had an equivalent value; though the latter was addressed in a special manner, as being the creator of culture and for holding moral values.¹⁰ Another of the primary natural history books of America in the sixteenth century was published by Gonzalo Fernández Oviedo (1478–1557), who in 1532 was officially appointed *cronista de Indias*,¹¹ having been assigned the task of writing the social and natural history of the Indies. Under the title *Historia general y natural de las Indias* his major work appeared between 1535 and 1547, which was based on his prior writing, *Sumario de la natural historia de las Indias* of 1526.¹² The main purpose of his natural history was practical and utilitarian – to identify the use of plants, animals, trees and fish for human purposes.¹³ It comprised two aspects of natural entities: the empirical description of single entities and their incorporation into a single framework for the understanding of this diversity. According to Oviedo's conception of the world, both hemispheres shared the same system of relations and the diversity of the natural phenomena was merely the product of diverse provinces and constellations.

Regarding the testimonies of these first chroniclers it has to be mentioned that there have been doubts and concerns about the authority and reliability of these early historical sources. Some scholars claimed they were based on Eurocentric misinterpretations, misleading testimonies or even imaginary elements associated with the *New World*. This raised the question – impossible to answer in the framework of this article[14] – regarding what point in time material to reconstruct historical processes should be considered as scientific in the more narrow sense.

In addition to these writings by early scholars there were other important sources for ethnological or ethnographical information, such as the *Leyes de Indias*, promulgated by Felipe II in 1567. This was a compendium of legal dispositions aimed to organize life in the Spanish colonies. Part of them were the so-called *Relaciones geográficas de Indias*,[15] which through detailed questionnaires gathered concrete information about the geographical, cultural, social and economic situation of the new territories as well as their inhabitants. Another way to glean information of anthropological interest was from the *Probanza de Méritos*, a system to accredit private or communal rights regarding the Crown, which usually included relevant data of the indigenous world. Also the *Casa de Contratación*, a government agency created in Seville in 1503, which attempted to control all Spanish exploration and colonization from the sixteenth to the eighteenth centuries, is an important resource in this context. Thanks to the many experts dedicated to produce information about the *New World*, it became a real chamber of knowledge regarding the navigation, cosmography and geography of America.[16]

Without doubt, what gives a unique and indispensable importance to the information collected in the first part of the sixteenth century was the fact that the cultures were still existent and almost without influence from the European world. Thus, valuable observations could be obtained and registered about an anthropological reality that was on its way to extinction as a sequel of the discovery and conquest.

To summarize, it can be asserted that this initial period of Spanish Americanism was characterized on one side by the lack of correct and exact data about the American reality, and on the other by the broad search for precise information considered necessary to clarify the mysteries of the *New World*.[17] Besides this scientific curiosity, the interest for the American continent derived mainly from the possibilities it offered for a future economic exploitation. In this phase also the study of the unknown cultures in its last instance was undertaken with the aim to use this information for a better and more profitable administration of the Spanish empire. Therefore, in this context anthropology in its initial stages can also be considered as a weapon of knowledge for the exploitation of the colonies.

PERIOD OF COMPILATION: 1600–1750

This period was a phase of revision and reorganization of the information obtained during the prior centuries. By then there were fewer unknown things to discover compared to earlier, and certain idea about the American cultures already existed. Therefore, the scholars of those days dedicated their time mainly to the lecture of the works of the first chroniclers in order to make compilations about what had already been investigated and to note the modifications that had been produced since then. In this context the works of the Jesuit scholar Francisco Javier Clavijero (1731–87) should be pointed out in particular.

– CHAPTER 3: *Science and ideology in the Spanish Atlantic* –

Another reason to study the already known data was to write the first historical books of certain regions of America in general. Therefore, the seventeenth century was very fruitful, the *New Continent* seemed now less mysterious than before and the acquired knowledge helped to see and understand its context. Some of these historians wrote exclusively from Spain, using these written sources, others combined them with their own research in America. One of the best known examples is the *Historia del Nuevo Mundo* written by the Jesuit scholar Bernabé Cobo (1582–1657).[18] This work, which remained incomplete, was conceived in three parts, the first one dealing with natural history and the other two with moral history, one about Peru and the other about New Spain.

Another example is the Franciscan historian Juan de Torquemada (1562–1624), who was chosen to be chronicler of the *Orden de San Francisco de Nueva España* to write a history of the Franciscan missionary work and to compile the most notable of the indigenous traditions. He produced several books, though he is basically known for his *Monarquía Indiana*, finished in the year 1613.[19] For this major undertaking he used several sources such as ancient pictographic codices or those produced at the moment of the conquest, Indian relations written mainly in Nahuatl in addition to oral information provided by the Indians themselves.[20] Finally, both Felipe Guamán Poma de Ayala and Martín de Murúa devoted their time to write the history of Peru, and should be mentioned in this context as well.

In addition to these revisions of the main publications of the eighteenth century, there was another anthropological interest, more of a philosophical orientation, which occupied the scholars: The polemic about the 'nature' of the Indians. Not only in Spain, but also later in other colonizing nations, this subject provoked many philosophical discourses about the 'good savage' or the 'bad savage'. The various American peoples evoked different images by the Spaniards and attracted more or less sympathies. For example, the Araucanos were associated with braveness and independence, and, the Patogones were rather described as miserable and 'animal-like' people.[21] The ethnic group that caused the most controversy were the Jíbaros whom the Spaniards saw as clear manifestations of the 'bad savage', due to their social anarchy, misanthropy as well as their religious indifference.[22] Particularly the last aspect was of considerable weight; therefore, it is not surprising that the Spaniards rejected the Jíbaros from their Catholic ideal.

Among the few concrete research projects undertaken in this period of time is the work of some missionaries. The publications of Jacinto de Carvajal (1648), who carried out expeditions along the rivers of Santo Domingo, Apúre and the Orinoco, described the geography as well as the fauna, flora and anthropology of the Llanos.[23] He developed large lists of ethnic groups with their more or less precise localization, along with excellent descriptions of their traditions, rituals and diverse habits.[24] In 1741 José Gumilla presented a book focused mainly on the missionary activity, in which he treated with the same passion aspects of the language, physical appearance and culture of the Indian groups living on both sides of the River Orinoco.[25] Another example is Miguel del Barco (1706–90), who described in his work *Historia natural y crónica de la antigua California* (1757) first the animals, then plants, mineralogy and finally the subjects of anthropological matters, particularly the indigenous languages and cultures of California. In the second, apparently added, part of his work, known as *crónica*, he addresses the Spanish activities in this region, particularly the missionary labour.[26]

These three cases belong to what can be considered 'late naturalism', a period of time which connected the discoveries of the sixteenth century with the so-called scientific travels of the eighteenth century. According to Alcina Franch, in the first half of the eighteenth century a confluence of two traditions can be observed: One is represented by the naturalism of the prior centuries, typical for the labour of the intellectuals of this period of time on the American continents, and the other more recent tradition of a rather scientific character, which proceeded from Europe and had a specific interest for the territories in the *New World*. This preference was in part political and always of an economical nature, since the incipient capitalism, which was to peak in the second half of this century, had at the same time a need for raw materials, places for experimentations with cultivations and, furthermore, markets for the expansion of Western Europe.[27]

With this focus and reference to the Spanish Americanism, the seventeenth century and the first part of the eighteenth can be considered as a period of transition, in which fewer new aspects were discovered, but where the bases were prepared for the future developments.

PERIOD OF THE GRAND SCIENTIFIC TRAVELS: 1750–1862

With the Enlightenment, from the second half of the eighteenth century an important project to modernize the country began. The ministers of the Spanish monarch Carlos III pretended to reform the *Antiguo Régimen* from inside the regime, and this was reflected in their opposition to the isolation of Spain, towards the Inquisition as well as the exaggerated privileges of the aristocracy, which were conceived as obstacles for the progress of the country.[28] Moreover, the enlightened Bourbons had a major cultural interest; among other ways this became evident in numerous scientific expeditions that were sent towards different regions of America.

These travels, encouraged and patronized by the Crown or by different institutions, caused a significant advancement in the knowledge about the *New World*, basically in the fields of botanical, geological, zoological or cultural questions. Several of these expeditions were called 'vaccination expeditions', and their aim was the protection of the indigenous population against diseases, for instance smallpox. It remained difficult to establish a clear category for these scientific expeditions, because even if the main focus were directed to a specific field, this did not diminish their interest for other collateral aspects or subjects of equal scientific value, such as anthropology or archaeology.

What can be asserted is that in this epoch there was no predilection for the human element, it was rather conceived as a part of the whole complex of natural sciences. The eighteenth century represented the rise of the biological and natural sciences, which explains why a significant number of the Spanish scientific expeditions of this period had a particular fondness for botanical and zoological questions. Important expeditions in a more anthropological context were those directed by Alejandro Malaspina and Guillermo Dupaix; thus their principal characteristics will be mentioned as representative examples.

The large expedition of Alessandro Malaspina (1754–1810), an Italian born nobleman and naval officer in Spanish service, and José Bustamante y Guerra (1759–1825) was undertaken along the American and the Asian coasts in the Pacific Oceanic during the years 1789 to 1794 and constituted one of the major economic, scientific and logistic efforts achieved by a European country during this fruitful period of time. The group of naturalists on this expedition had an intrinsic fondness for the topics related to geography and particularly the improvement of the cartography of the coasts along where this expedition sailed, as well as the fauna and flora of the regions visited. Regarding the more anthropological questions, it can be said that though they were not focusing on these matters in particular, from an ethnographical point of view the Malaspina expedition is considered one of the most important ones of its epoch. During its journey from south to north along the Pacific coast of America, numerous and valuable data about the various indigenous groups was collected, concerning the human beings themselves, their culture, instruments, clothing, ornaments, celebrations and funeral customs.

Figure 3.3   Alessandro Malaspina
© Mary Evans/Iberfoto

Figure 3.4 Nootha Indian, drawn during Malaspina's visit
to the Spanish outpost on Vancouver Island
© Mary Evans/J. Bedmar/Iberfoto

– CHAPTER 3: *Science and ideology in the Spanish Atlantic* –

Guillermo Dupaix (1750–1817), on the other hand, with his travels through Mexico between 1805 and 1808, became one of the pioneers of the archaeological sciences. The travels of Dupaix can be taken as the culmination of a posture of archaeological curiosity at the end of the eighteenth century, and on the other hand, as the first of a large series of what we have called 'archaeological travellers'.[29] He would compare his discoveries in Mexico constantly with what he had read about Egyptian, Greek and Roman artwork. Through this method, very soon he became aware of some deficiencies in the first archaeological questions of his time and this gradually evolved into methods that we could qualify as to some extent scientific.

Nevertheless, the veritably innovative aspect of his approach was his anthropological interest from the point of view of an archeologist, showing the link between the cultures he encountered with the constructors of the artwork he described. Meanwhile, during the entire nineteenth century and occasionally even at the beginning of the twentieth century, many archeologists did not get further than an esthetic or stylistic interpretation of the objects, or their pure classification. Dupaix – foreseeing what was going to be the real content of archeological science – explained that the major interest was not in the objects themselves, but in the fact that they were the evidence to understand their complex culture.

These scientific travels coincided with a new spirit in European society known as exoticism and defined as a certain fascination for foreign and distant cultures or ways of life. The enlightened Spanish nation again manifested its interest in the American cultures, although now from a different angle: a considerable number of publications around the idea of the 'good savage' came up, particularly dramas with a romantic–philosophical background. In these writings, the enlightened idea became apparent that it would have been better to civilize the Indians instead of destroying them as the conquerors had done.[30] This exoticism materialized in a certain passion for the curiosities brought from America by those travelers, and as a consequence, in gathering these rarities.

A crucial role in this context was played by the Spanish king Carlos III, as the art of collection reached its peak during his kingship.[31] Due to his special predilection for the objects coming from the *New World*, he instructed the colonies in America to collect samples of all types of material. Therefore, several expeditions were sent overseas with the aim to remit to the Peninsula all types of material that belonged to both the natural and the social sciences. In this context a number of expeditions can be highlighted: the expedition of Martín de Sessé y Lacasta and José Mariano Mociño in New Spain (1787–1803), the voyage of Hipólito Ruiz and Joseph Pavón through Peru and Chile (1777–88), the long experience of the Spanish botanist and physician José Celestino Mutis in Nueva Granada and furthermore the scientific exploration of Cuba conducted by the Count of Mopox (1796–1802) as well as Félix Azara's expedition through Mesoamerica (1781–1801).[32]

In order to display the numerous objects gathered at the most distant points of America, in the year 1771 the *Real Gabinete de Historia Natural* in Madrid was created, being officially opened in 1776 under the direction of the natural scientist Pedro Franco Dávila (1711–86).[33] This demonstrates that the ethnographic-anthropologic interest of this period of time had a very important museographic or collectionist component, since in the *Real Gabinete de Historia Natural* almost the same significance was given to the anthropological and archaeological collections as to the objects of a strictly natural sciences provenance. Besides these kinds of collections, Carlos III also expressed a notable fondness for American antiquities and he was considered the protecting spirit and first promoter of the archaeology in Spain – a role that was assumed and developed by his successor Carlos IV. Thanks to the effort of Carlos III, archaeology emerged as a scientific branch, with the first excavations carried out in the years 1785 and 1787 in the Maya ruins of Palenque, which had considerable significance as the beginning of the official study of ancient cultures. The eighteenth century was not only an important period for travellers and collectors, but as a consequence of these circumstances, the interest to classify the obtained material arose. The idea of the classification emerged from the necessity to sort the newly acquired plants in the botanical gardens and the collections in the cabinets and perhaps even more from the need to prepare and print catalogues of the obtained material.

In this context, the labour of Carl Linnaeus (1707–78) leading to the creation of a taxonomical system of universal value should be emphasized. This system permitted the natural scientists of the entire world to understand each other and enabled them to accumulate in a rational manner the acquired knowledge of the nature in a way which facilitated comparison of this information coming from very different places.[34]

Another decisive event that resulted from the arrival of an increased amount of information from the *New World* in those times, was the creation of the *Archivo General de Indias* in 1785 by the historian Juan Bautista Muñoz (1754–99) in Sevilla.[35] This archive was built to collect all types of documents such as unpublished travel reports of the sixteenth and seventeenth century, countless geographical surveys, various manuscripts on natural history as well as the entire official correspondence between Spain and its colonial territories in America. At the same time, Muñoz began working on his opus magnum *Historia del Nuevo Mundo*,[36] which included a compilation of numerous and relevant facts about the indigenous peoples of America. It constituted a clear replication from Spain's side to the work of William Robertson (1721–93) titled *The History of America,* published in 1777, which revealed the English point of view, and was sought to present the contribution of Spain to American natural history and geography.[37] Unfortunately, Muñoz was only able to finish the first volume, leaving behind countless preparative documents.[38]

In this manner, the travels of the eighteenth and the first years of the nineteenth century with all their corresponding consequences, directly or indirectly set the tone for the beginning of scientific Americanism in the second half of the nineteenth century. Nevertheless, there was a crucial event which ruptured this process for a considerable period of time: That event was the end of the Spanish rule in their American colonies as one of the results of its War of Independence against the French in the context of the European Napoleonic wars.[39] This major change emerged in most Hispanic territories at approximately the same time and provoked a radical cut in the relationship of the ancient colonies with their mother country. Until the beginning of the 1860s, Spain refused to admit this independence and still intended to recover its former American belongings. Therefore, from Spain's side there was also a loss of scientific interest in these territories and thus the expeditions and the research in these regions of the *New World* were suspended. Another consequence of the independence of the American countries was the end of the strict and exclusive politics established by the Spaniards for their colonies that prohibited scientific research conducted by other

European nations in these territories. The expeditions under the auspices of the Spanish Crown were then substituted by travels, missionary work or expeditions organized by other countries, mostly European. There were also progressively more and more North American initiatives. In this context we can discuss a certain 'rediscovery' of America as a result of the decline of the Spanish empire: scholars no longer had to rely upon the information given by Spanish authors, as they were now able to undertake their own studies according to their own questions and methodology.

Though until the year 1862 no research of relevance launched in America can be pointed out, there was certain progress in the anthropological sciences in Spain, which also had its impact on the theoretical development of the Spanish Americanism. The first anthropological publications of a general character appeared, for example, the philosophical-moral treatise of Vicente Adam entitled *Lecciones de Antropología ético político-religiosa*[40] or the work of Francisco Fabra y Soldevila with the title *Filosofía de la legislación natural, fundada en la Antropología*.[41]

A considerable number of these first enthusiasts of anthropology in the early nineteenth century were physicians. Their incentive for increasing their studies in this aspect was their desire to categorize the human being; which soon turned out to be one of the favourite discussion topics in the national *Ateneos*, the traditional forum for intellectual discussions.

In general it can be presumed that in the period of time described above, the interest for America was no longer inspired because of it being something magic, susceptible of numerous interpretations, but by the fact that it was now something more familiar, better known and conceivable for Europeans. In contrast to prior centuries, the base for manifestations of Americanism was rationalism. One consequence of this new spirit was the reestablishment and redefinition of the order of the world, by integrating the American cultures in the general history of mankind.

PHASE OF FORMATION: 1862–1936

Since the 1860s, Spain recognized the impossibility of recovering its colonies and this was manifested by a change of its policy towards these countries. As a consequence, new relations were established with these independent republics, though now under a different concept: no longer in the frame of the motherland–colony relationship, but as an encounter of equality between sovereign governments. The proof of this modified attitude was the dispatch of a new scientific expedition to America in 1862: the *Comisión Científica del Pacífico* (CCP), a Spanish scientific expedition to the Pacific,[42] under the leadership of Marcos Jiménez de la Espada (1831–98).[43] The idea for this project was born in 1860 due to the lack of material from the *New World* for the universities and museums; finally two years later, the departure of a naval squadron to the coast of South America was approved, organized by the Spanish government in order to include a commission of several scientists tasked to carry out an in-depth study of the geography, fauna, flora, etc. Among these specialists in different fields there was also the anthropologist Manuel Almagro y Vega, who was responsible for the research undertaken on the indigenous cultures, being the first Spanish anthropologist with this academic denomination conducting studies in America.[44]

Until their return in 1866 the participants of this project spent almost four years travelling through different countries of America, from time to time divided in smaller groups in order to work in a more effective way, studying in detail the reality of this world and collecting an elevated number of objects of the encountered material culture. These data and collections were sent to the Peninsula and there received by a special commission, in charge of cataloguing and arranging the collections until the return of the members of the expedition. Shortly after their return to Spain, this material was exposed to the public in the context of a major exhibition prepared in the *Real Jardín Botánico* of Madrid. Unfortunately, the political and economic problems that Spain had to face at this point in time deferred the study of this collection according to the planned manner. They were consigned to the *Museo Nacional de Ciencias Naturales*, from where they would be later on transferred to other places, such as the *Museo de América* and the *Museo Nacional de Etnología,* both located in the Spanish capital.

The *Comisión Científica del Pacífico* can be regarded as the decisive event for the development of the Spanish Americanism in the second half of the nineteenth century, since now the focus, under which America was studied, had changed: for the first time the New Continent was approached as an autonomous region. A new generation of researchers had been formed, who now saw America as completely independent and different from Spain, a territory where Spaniards were to be merely neutral observers.

Aside from this scientific exploration, there was only sparse Spanish activity in America in this period of time. Indeed this was the last large voyage to America undertaken by Spain and it took almost one century until another interdisciplinary project was accomplished; meanwhile the travelers and scientists from other countries showed a substantial eagerness to conduct their research in these regions.

Nevertheless, during the same years the institutionalization of anthropology in Spain progressed considerably through the creation of museums, anthropological societies, research laboratories or similar institutions.[45] A very important personality in this process was Pedro González Velasco, considered also as one of the first modern anthropologists in Spain.[46] In 1865 he created the *Sociedad Antropológica Española*, which edited two publications: the *Revista de Antropología* (1874), and the *Antropología moderna* (1883). In addition to this editorial activity, the Society promoted a favourable environment for teaching as well as for debate of contemporary scientific questions such as the evolutionist theory of Charles Darwin regarding the classification of the races and the variety as well as the origin of the human species.[47] Another merit of this institution was the study of the ethnographical problems using as their basis the extensive information of the scholars of the sixteenth and seventeenth century (Gómara, Fernández de Oviedo, Diaz de Castillo, Francisco de Xerez, Cieza de León, etc.).[48]

In 1867 the *Museo Arqueológico Nacional* was created, to which the historic collection – such as the antiquities and rarities of the *Museo Nacional de Ciencias Naturales,* the former *Real Gabinete de Historia Natural* – was transferred. The objects of American origin were there established in different categories, which were primarily comprised of archaeological and ethnographic objects, next to a smaller section of colonial art.[49]

Also, due to the personal initiative of González Velasco, in 1875 the *Museo Nacional de Etnología* was founded as the first museum with an anthropological character in Spain. During its history it has undergone different stages, having been renamed, changed its institutional situation and, as a consequence, its corresponding

– CHAPTER 3: *Science and ideology in the Spanish Atlantic* –

scientific conceptions as well. Nonetheless, this museum was not merely a place for the exposure of objects since it also collaborated closely with other scientific institutions. It was, for instance, the first director of this museum, Manuel Antón Ferrándiz, who implemented anthropological studies in the Spanish university in the year 1892. He started teaching in the laboratory that he created in the museum, where he inaugurated a free professorship in 1885. Finally in 1892 he established a chair of anthropology in the faculty for science of the *Universidad Central de Madrid*.[50]

By reason of the IV *International Americanist Congress* celebrated in 1881, an important exhibition of the objects coming from the *New World* was organized, this being the second one after the one exposed in the *Real Jardín Botánico*. Nevertheless, due to various difficulties and the limited knowledge acquired in those days about the ancient history of America, it was difficult to assign the objects to their corresponding cultures or ethnic groups, and the lack of geographic information precluded comparisons with already classified pieces in other museums.

Another significant event of that time related with the Americanist concerns, was the first official historic (and not religious) celebration of the discovery of America: the fourth centennial of 1892.[51] Dozens of chronicles were edited for the first time, several exhibitions were organized, besides important congresses and scientific meetings.[52] Also numerous Latin American countries participated in this commemoration with a huge number of objects, coming both from public property and from private collections. The reaction provoked in the Spanish society by this centennial reflects the different attitude of the people that existed in those days towards America. Besides the critical voices who pointed out the violence and injustice committed during the conquest of America, there were numerous defences of the civilizing work undertaken by Spain in the *New World*. Some were obsessed with the revitalization of the Spanish colonialization, and some maintained a rather nationalist position and in spite of the intellectual and political efforts to take up again the Americanist concerns on a new basis, they continued to see America basically as a problem and not as an assimilable cultural area.[53]

In the midst of this process of institutionalization of scientific Americanism there was also a decisive political development that produced a major change in the national self-consciousness of Spain: that was the independence of the last Spanish colonies, Cuba, Puerto Rico and the Philippines. As a consequence of this loss the Spanish society suffered a painful disinterest regarding America. The intellectuals and the writers of this country constituted what later would be called the *Generación del 98*, a critical movement that searched in society the causes of this colonial decadency in the midst of the epoch of major English and French imperialism.

One consequence of this political incidence was the duality of the scientific interest in America from 1898 onward: on one hand, rather from the left wing of society, there was a feeling of shame about what had happened in the former colonies and they preferred to forget about this experience, and on the other hand, people situated more in the right wing, continued to see America as something glorious, where the merits of Spain were to be highlighted. In the following years, and particularly with the beginning of World War I, this duality was intensified, which resulted in the fact that in Spain, until the end of the 1920s, there was no progress in the field of American anthropology.

Looking at this panorama of activities and problems relating to the development of anthropology and more precisely to the Americanism of the second half of the nineteenth century, the question about the contribution of this period of time to the approach towards this scientific branch emerges. It is certain that the years between 1868 and 1936 were the most unstable period in Spanish politics and that these circumstances naturally had their impact on the development of sciences in general – and even more on those concerning social aspects. This became evident in the inability to establish a scientific programme. Nonetheless, in spite of these difficulties, along these years the foundation was prepared for modern Spanish anthropology. The earlier mentioned ensemble of expeditions, travels, exhibits, congresses, creation of institutions, etc. facilitated the birth of anthropology as a modern science in the second half of the nineteenth century. The objects gathered in prior expeditions not only served to enrich the collections, but also they were now studied in detail in the newly established research centres of the museums and universities. This was the context in which scientific Americanism emerged, distinguishing itself from prior scientific travels through a more theoretic basis, in connection with concrete approaches to the problems as well as through different ideological currents.

FINAL CONSIDERATIONS

From its first contact with the western world the American continent became a magnificent scenario where under varying circumstances in different periods of time, Spain conducted important research projects and studies.[54] Due to the role this country played in the process of the conquest as well as the scientific discovery of the *New World*, Americanism in its anthropological or historical facets is an integral part of its own past and not a mere scientific or scholarly field as could be said for some other countries. Therefore, the history of Americanist anthropology in Spain should be studied depending on the changes, struggles and ideological comings and goings of the last 500 years. For these reasons, the present article demonstrates the connections between the particular approach of the research and the contemporary philosophical background in each period of time.

It can be asserted that numerous interesting anthropological studies in America were already conducted shortly after the conquest, in the sixteenth and seventeenth century. The motivation for those researchers to carry out their scientific activities might have been curiosity, ambition, ardour for adventures, love for the fellow human being or simply compliance with their duties, since many were devoted to the missionary work or employed in other ways for the conquering government. In any event, through their general observations and annotations, their interest in other societies, their study of the native languages (which led to the first dictionaries), and finally the fact that they lived long periods of time among the Indians, the basis for modern fieldwork was set.

The activities and the mentality of the Spanish traveler of the eighteenth century cannot be compared with the Americanist work undertaken by the writers of the sixteenth century. As already mentioned, these were basically travelers who spent only a short time with the populations they visited. What motivated them was more a general curiosity for the American world and less a particular interest for its cultures; rather, this was considered as another integral part of the foreign natural landscape, such as the minerals or the plants. Also in the cabinets of curiosities, the Indians were not of interest as representatives of their particular cultural heritage, but

– CHAPTER 3: Science and ideology in the Spanish Atlantic –

rather their belongings as well as their products were shown as rare objects, due to the collectionist eagerness that was predominant in that society.

From the second half of the nineteenth century and through the Comisión Científica al Pacífico, finally the interest for American cultures was resurrected, an interest that in a way shows similarities with that of the first naturalist of the sixteenth century, although, as a matter of course in the nineteenth century, according to the general tendencies of this epoch, there was less speculative background and more of a scientific approach.

In conclusion, it can be said that as a result of all these research projects and studies in the field of American anthropology from the time of the discovery until our days – independently of the concrete intentions of each epoch – the Spanish Americanism is based on a rich tradition. The historical conditions for this process were the encounter and establishment of connections between the two hemispheres of the world, studied in the scope of Atlantic History. From the sixteenth century, this country contributed considerably to the development of empirical practices. The Spanish Crown used the knowledge of natural history to create its Atlantic empire, and American ethnography and anthropology to control and administer these territories. In the process of establishing a long-distance empire, Spain provided a paradigmatic case to explore the relations between politics and knowledge[55] – and particularly the interconnection of both, as the case of the development of Spanish Americanism during the history shows. Thus, its contribution to the scientific exploration of the far side of the Atlantic was shaped by the experience of being pioneers in this endeavour; Spaniards writing the history of the *New World* with their unique approach, interest and conditions constitute a relevant branch of Atlantic History.

NOTES

This study has been undertaken under the framework and with financial aid of a research project HAR201021333-C03–02, financed by the *Ministerio de Economia y Competitividad* and within the activities aimed at the dissemination of science carried out at the *Vicepresidencia Adjunta de Cultura Científica* at the Spanish National Research Council in Madrid. Final research and modifications of the text were carried out in the frame of the Marie Curie Grant AHumScienceNet (FP7–PEOPLE–2012–10F), financed by the European Commission Research Executive Agency. It is a thoroughly revised and actualized version of a prior publication: S. Rebok, 'Americanismo, ciencia e ideología: La actividad americanista española a través de la historia', *Anales. Museo de América*, vol. 4, 1996, 79–105. The advice and help received from Félix Jímenez Villalba, subdirector at the Museo de América in Madrid, was of utmost importance in the preparation for the first Spanish version of this text.

1   Among the works that reflect on the Spanish Atlantic are: J. Cañizares-Esguerra, *Nature, Empire, and Nation: Explorations of the History of Science in the Iberian New World*, Stanford: Stanford University Press, 2006; A. Barrera-Osorio, *Experiencing Nature: the Spanish-American Empire and the Early Scientific Revolution*, Austin: University of Texas Press, 2006; Daniela Bleichmar, et al. (eds), *Science in the Spanish and Portuguese Empires, 1500–1800*, Stanford, California: Stanford University Press, 2009.

2   Barrera-Osorio, op.cit., p. 128.

3   M. M. Marzal, *Historia de la antropología indigenista: México y Perú*, Barcelona: Editorial Anthropos, 1993, p. 20.

4   Ibid., p. 21.

5 The *encomienda* system was a trusteeship labour system that was employed by the Spanish Crown on the native population during the colonization of the *New World*.

6 J. Alcina Franch, *El descubrimiento científico de América*, Barcelona: Editorial Anthropos, 1988, p. 41.

7 Marzal, op. cit., pp. 21–22.

8 B. de Sahagún, *Historia general de las cosas de la Nueva España*, Madrid: Alianza Editorial, D.L. 1988.

9 F. del Pino-Díaz (ed.), *Acosta, José de, Historia natural y moral de las Indias*, Madrid: CSIC, 2008.

10 Alcina Franch, op. cit., pp. 189–90.

11 Already in the year 1511 an official position had been created with the title *Cronista de Indias del Rey*, whose work can be compared with the one of a librarian in our days.

12 F. de Oviedo, Gonzalo, *Historia general y natural de las Indias, islas y tierra-firme del mar océanico*, Guadalajara: Ediciones Facsímiles Ponton, 2006.

13 A good analysis of Oviedo's work is found in: Barrera-Osorio, op. cit., pp. 104–12.

14 For more information please see Rebok, op. cit., pp. 101–3.

15 F. de Solano (ed.), *Cuestionarios para la formación de las Relaciones Geográficas de Indias. Siglos XVIXIX*, Madrid: CSIC, 1988; R. Álvarez Peláez, *La conquista de la naturaleza americana*, Madrid: CSIC, 1993, particularly pp. 99–246.

16 Barrera-Osorio, op. cit., particularly chapter 2, 'A Chamber of Knowledge: The Casa de la Contratación and its Emprical Methods'.

17 For more details on diverse campaigns to gather information see ibid., chapter 'Circuits of information. Reports from the New World'.

18 B. Cobo, *Historia del Nuevo Mundo*, Madrid, Atlas, 1943; B. Cobo, *History of the Inca Empire: an account of the Indians' customs and their origin together with a treatise on Inca legends, history, and social institutions*, Austin: University of Texas Press, 1979.

19 J. de Torquemada, *Monarquía indiana: de los veinte y un libros rituales y monarquía indiana, con el origen y guerras de los indios occidentales de sus poblazones, descubrimiento, conquista, conversión y otras cosas maravillosas de la mesma tierra*, Mexico: UNAM, 1975.

20 Alcina Franch, op. cit., p. 63.

21 J. A. Gonzalez Alcantud, 'América desde España: Entre el ideal heróico y el exotismo', *América: una reflexión antropológica*, Granada: Disputación provincial de Granada, 1992, p. 10.

22 Ibid., p. 9.

23 J. Caravajal, *Relación del descubrimiento del río Apure hasta su ingreso en el Orinoco*, Madrid: Edime, 1956.

24 Alcina Franch, op. cit, p. 192.

25 Idem; J. Gumilla, *El Orinoco ilustrado. Historia natural, civil, y geographica, de este gran rio, y de sus caudalosas vertientes (...)*, Madrid: M. Aguilar, 1945.

26 Ibid., p. 193. M. del Barco, *Historia natural y crónica de la antigua California*, Mexico: UNAM, 1973.

27 Alcina Franch, op. cit., p. 195.

28 M. Sellés, J. L. Peset and A. Lafuente, *Carlos III y la ciencia de la Ilustración*, Madrid, Alianza, 1988; L. Rodríguez Díaz, *Reforma e Ilustración en la España del siglo XVIII. Pedro Rodríguez Campomanes*, Madrid: Fundación Universitaria española, 1975.

29 Alcina Franch, op. cit., p. 223.

30 Gonzalez Alcantud, op. cit., p. 14.

31 See chapter 'Panorama histórico de las Ciencias Naturales en la España de finales del siglo XVIII', in: M. Á. Puig-Samper and S. Rebok, *Sentir y medir. Alexander von Humboldt en España*, Aranjuez: Doce Calles, 2007, pp. 19–46; Sellés, Peset and Lafuente, op. cit.

– CHAPTER 3: *Science and ideology in the Spanish Atlantic* –

32   M. Á. Puig-Samper, *Las expediciones científicas durante el siglo XVIII. Historia de la ciencia y de la técnica*, vol. 28, Madrid: Akal, 1991; A. González Bueno, *La expedición botánica al Virreinato del Perú (1777–1788)*, Barcelona: Lunwerg, 1988; J. A. Amaya, *Celestino Mutis y la Expedición Botánica*, Madrid: Debate, 1986; M. Frías Núñez, *Tras el Dorado Vegetal. José Celestino Mutis y la Real Expedición Botánica del Nuevo Reino de Granada*, Sevilla: Diputación de Sevilla, 1994; *Mutis al natural: ciencia y arte en el Nuevo Reino de Granada*, exhibition catalogue, Museo Nacional de Colombia, Dec. 2008–March 2009, Bogotá: Museo Nacional de Colombia, SEACEX, 2008; D. Higueras (ed.), *Cuba Ilustrada. La Real Comisión de Guantánamo*, Barcelona: Lunwerg, 1991; M. P. de San Pío Aladrén and M. Á. Puig-Samper (eds), *El águila y el Nopal. La expedición de Sessé y Mociño a Nueva España (1787–1803)*, Madrid: Lunwerg, 2000; A. R. Steele, *Flores para el Rey. La expedición de Ruiz y Pavón y la Flora del Perú (1777–1788)*, Barcelona: Serbal, 1982; M. Á. Puig-Samper and F. Pelayo, 'Las expediciones botánicas al Nuevo Mundo durante el siglo XVIII. Una aproximación histórico-bibliográfica', in D. Soto Arango, M. Á. Puig-Samper and L. C. Arboleda (eds), *La Ilustración en América Colonial*, Aranjuez: Doce Calles, 1995, pp. 55–65.

33   A. J. Barreiro, *El Museo Nacional de Ciencias Naturales*, Aranjuez: Doce Calles, 1992.

34   M. Á. Puig-Samper, 'Difusión e institucionalización del sistema linneano en España y América', in A. Lafuente, A. Elena and M. L. Ortega (eds), *Mundialización de la ciencia y cultura nacional*, Aranjuez: Doce Calles, 1993, pp. 349–59.

35   N. Bas Martín, *Juan Bautista Muñoz (1745–1799) y la fundación del Archivo General de Indias*, Valencia: Artes Gráficas Soler, 2000.

36   J. Bautista Muñoz, *Historia del Nuevo Mundo*, Madrid: Viuda de Ibarra, 1793.

37   W. Robertson, *The History of America*, 2 vols, London: A. Strahan, 1777. About the reception of this publication in Spain see: Cañizares-Esguerra op. cit., 2007, pp. 170–90.

38   For a good analysis about Muñoz's work, the creation of the archive and the difficulties he had to face publishing his *Historia del Nuevo Mundo* see ibidem, pp. 190–203.

39   Also known as the Peninsular War.

40   V. Adam, *Lecciones de antropología ético-político-religiosa: o sea, sobre el hombre considerado como ser sociable, religioso y moral*, Madrid: Imprenta Real, 1833.

41   F. Fabra y Soldevila, *Filosofía de la legislación natural, fundada en la antropología o en el conocimiento de la naturaleza del hombre y de sus relaciones con los demas seres*, Madrid: Imprenta del Colegio de SordoMudos, 1838.

42   M. Á. Puig-Samper, *Crónica de una expedición romántica al Nuevo Mundo: La Comisión Científica del Pacífico (1862–1866)*, Madrid: CSIC, 1988; R. Ryal Miller, *Por la ciencia y la gloria nacional: La expedición científica española a América (1863–66)*, Barcelona: Serbal, 1983.

43   L. López-Ocón Cabrera, *De viajero naturalista a historiador: Las actividades americanistas del científico español Marcos Jiménez de la Espada*. 2 vols, Madrid: Universidad Complutense, 1991; L. López-Ocón Cabrera and C. M. Pérez-Montes Salmerón (eds), *Marcos Jiménez de la Espada (1831–1898). Tras la senda de un explorador,* Madrid: CSIC, 2000.

44   M. Almagro, *Breve descripción de los viajes hechos en América por la Comisión Científica enviada por el Gobierno de S. M. C. durante los años de 1862 a 1866*, Madrid: M. Rivadeneyra, 1866.

45   M. Á. Puig-Samper and A. Galera, *La antropología española del siglo XIX*, Madrid: CSIC, 1983.

46   M. Á. Puig-Samper, 'Pedro González de Velasco. Creador del primer Museo Antropológico español', *Historia 16*, 78, 10/1982, 103–8.

47   About the darwinist polemic in Spain see M. Á. Puig-Samper, *Darwinismo y Antropología en el siglo XIX*, Madrid: Ediciones Akal, 1992, pp. 47–52.

48   C. Lisón Tolosana, *Antropología social en España*, Madrid: Siglo XXI, 1971, p. 108.

49 P. Cabello Carro, *Coleccionismo americano indígena en la España del siglo XVIII*, Madrid: Ediciones de Cultura Hispánica 1989, p. 37.

50 P. Romero de Tejada, *Un templo a la ciencia. Historia del Museo Nacional de Etnología*, Madrid: Ministerio de Cultura, 1992, pp. 17–18.

51 S. Bernabeu Albert, 'Los orígenes del Americanismo español contemporáneo: El IV centenario del descubrimiento de América (1892)', in P. Cagiao Vila and E. Rey Tristán (eds), *Aproximación al americanismo entre 1892 y 2004: proyectos, instituciones y fondos de investigación*, Santiago de Compostela: Servizo de Publicacións e Intercambio, 2006, pp. 13–31.

52 Ibid., pp. 24–25.

53 Gonzalez Alcantud, op. cit., p. 19.

54 For more information on the history of Spanish science see J. M. López-Piñero, *Ciencia y técnica en la sociedad española de los siglos XVI y XVII*, Barcelona: Labor, 1979; Álvarez Peláez, op. cit.; J. Vernet, *Historia de la Ciencia Española*, Barcelona: Alta Fulla, 1998; L. López-Ocón Cabrera, *Breve historia de la ciencia española*, Madrid: Alianza, 2003.

55 Barrera-Osorio, op. cit., p. 133.

CHAPTER FOUR

FISH AND FISHERIES
IN THE ATLANTIC WORLD

————·◆·————

David J. Starkey

Maritime historians might have ambivalent feelings concerning the assertion of two leading Atlantic historians that 'we need historical studies of all things maritime, from weather patterns to port cities, from sailors to winds and currents' (Greene and Morgan 2009: 12). On the one hand, they might be gratified to read that their specialist subject area is deemed to be of relevance to researchers in another field of enquiry. At the same time, they might be dismayed that their contributions to knowledge and understanding have seemingly made little impact, for Greene and Morgan's call for more work on 'the most obvious leading edge of the Atlantic world: the maritime sector' (Greene and Morgan 2009: 12) infers that research into the maritime dimension of the historical process is underdeveloped. This might well have been true in the early 1970s, when maritime history was generally regarded as a topic for 'hobbyists' (Broeze 1989). Since then, however, it has not only developed steadily as a recognizable sub-discipline, but also generated a substantial body of literature, elements of which bear directly on the human engagement with the ocean that gives Atlantic history its name (Broeze 1995).

Three of these elements are particularly relevant to this chapter. First, a technical approach has yielded a welter of evidence concerning the development of the vessels that have enabled people, cargoes, ideas, cultures and *modi operandi* to move around and across the Atlantic region since time immemorial. The fundamental historical significance of the practicalities of sea travel is the core theme of this literature, the most comprehensive and accessible work on this subject being the twelve-volume *Conway's History of the Ship* (Gardiner 1992–96). The second historiographical strand relates to the utilization by humans of the sea for purposes of transport, defence, resource extraction and recreation. Such functional divisions are broken down, in turn, into discrete industries, notably shipping, shipbuilding, port and fishing, as well as less clearly demarcated activities like oil and gas extraction, maritime defence, seaside tourism, marine recreation and the multifarious ancillary services that support the sea-reliant industries (Starkey 1997). In the context of this economic approach to the maritime past, a growing number of historical studies of the fisheries have been published in recent decades (Robinson 2011; Starkey and Heidbrink 2012: 16–20), including broad appraisals of the North Atlantic fisheries (Starkey et al. 2009; Starkey and Heidbrink 2012; Sicking and Abreu-Ferreira 2009) and more focused analyses of particular fisheries (Robinson 1996; Poulsen 2007; Poulsen 2008) and the fishing interests of regions and nations (Gray 1979; Vickers 1994; Coull 1996; Starkey et al. 2000; Thór 2002, 2003). Whereas the exploitation of a largely passive resource is key to the technical and socio-economic approaches, the interaction between human and natural factors in the historical process lies at the heart of a third element in the maritime literature. According to this environmental view, human activities have impacted upon the dynamic process of environmental change, while natural drivers have influenced the development of human societies (Bolster 2006, 2012; Poulsen 2007; Starkey et al. 2007; Poulsen 2008; Jackson et al. 2011).

This chapter draws upon these maritime perspectives to examine the place of fish and fisheries in the evolution of the Atlantic world. Attention is initially afforded to the physical characteristics of the North Atlantic, specifically the topographic, oceanographic and ecological factors that largely condition the marine ecosystems inhabited by fish and penetrated by humans. The second part focuses on the economic, social and cultural drivers that underpinned the capture, processing and consumption of fish by the societies that developed on the littorals and islands of the North Atlantic. The *modi operandi* by which free-living fish were commodified into a marketable product are the subject of the third section of the study. In the final part, the various ways in which fish and fisheries influenced the movement of people, cargoes, techniques and cultures around and across the North Atlantic are discussed. By charting these courses, this chapter offers a positive response to Jeffrey Bolster's charge that historians need to put the Atlantic into Atlantic history (Bolster 2008).

ENVIRONMENT AND ECOLOGY

Three broad factors have interacted to configure the waters, terrain and life forms that comprise, bound and inhabit the North Atlantic – an ocean realm that extends southwards from approximately 80°N in the Arctic to a hypothetical line connecting Cape Hatteras in North America to the Straits of Gibraltar that separate Europe from North Africa (this section is based on Starkey and Heidbrink 2012: 14–16). First, the topography of the region is fundamental to the character and distribution of its natural resources. This is evident in the physical interface between land and sea at the margins of the ocean. Here, the mountains and fjords that dominate the coastlines of Norway and Greenland contrast with the coastal dunes and marshlands of the Bay of Biscay, the sandy beaches, spits and lagoons of the Portuguese shoreline and the estuarial salt marshes that mark the littoral areas of the Gulf of Maine, Chesapeake Bay and Delaware Bay. It is also apparent in the shape of the islands that intrude upon the vast expanse of water that both divides and connects Europe and North America. The Faroes and Iceland, which break into three segments the submarine ridge that extends from Scotland to Greenland, exemplify the truly ancient lineage of such topographical features. When volcanic material poured through fissures in the Earth's crust some 50 million years ago, it solidified into a basalt plateau that has subsequently been sculpted by glacial, fluvial and coastal processes to form the 18 islands of the Faroese archipelago. Iceland is a product of volcanic activity that has persisted over the last 20 million years at the intersection of the Mid-Atlantic and Greenland–Scotland ridges, where lava has exuded and cooled to form a highly

– CHAPTER 4: *Fish and fisheries in the Atlantic World* –

distinctive and somewhat bleak terrain. Ridges are but one facet of the sea floor. Rather more significant from the perspectives of fish and fisheries are the shelves that were once part of the continental land masses, but were submerged when the end of the last Ice Age caused sea levels to rise. Varying in extent from a few to over 500 kilometres, these shelves comprise sandy slopes, irregular outcrops and deep trenches, such as the Devil's Hole, the Norwegian Deep and the Cap Breton Canyon. Elevated plateaux also occur on the shelves, with Dogger, Faroe, Grand, Burgeos, Stellwagen and Georges among the more notable of these 'Banks'.

The second factor is oceanography. Identifiable by the coherence of their salinity and temperature, numerous water masses flow across and around the varied topography of the North Atlantic. Perhaps the single most important influence is the relatively warm and saline North Atlantic Current (Gulf Stream), a body of water that moves from the Gulf of Mexico through the Caribbean and proceeds in a northeasterly direction across the ocean. In pursuing this course it collides and mixes with colder water flowing south from the Arctic Ocean, and is channelled by the land masses, depths and bottom gradients of the Atlantic. It has a differential bearing on the region. In the northwest Atlantic, for instance, it has a minimal influence, for the Labrador Current, fed by the cold waters of the Canadian and West Greenland Currents, flows southwards along the Labrador coast, its outer stream sweeping past eastern Newfoundland and across the Grand Banks. Around Iceland, the North Atlantic Current mixes with colder waters flowing from the north in a generally clockwise gyre, while it dominates the upper layers in the seas surrounding the Faroes. In the deeper water of the Greenland and Norwegian Seas, a complex system of horizontal and vertical exchange occurs, whereby the comparatively warm water of the North Atlantic Current flows in from the south in the upper layers and comparatively cold water from the north flows out through the deeper layers. In this ocean space, the North Atlantic Current separates into various discrete flows, some of which move south around the British Isles to form the predominant oceanographic influence in the Celtic and North Seas, and the waters off the west coast of the Iberian Peninsula.

The third broad factor is the relationship between living organisms and their environment – that is, the ecology – of the North Atlantic. Currents, sea temperatures, topographical features and wind systems interact to determine the precise mix of marine animals in the twelve large marine ecosystems – Barents Sea, Norwegian Shelf, North Sea, Celtic-Biscay Shelf, Iberian Coastal, Faroes Plateau, Iceland Shelf, East Greenland Shelf, West Greenland Shelf, Labrador-Newfoundland Shelf, Scotian Shelf, Northeast US Continental Shelf (LME 2009) – that occupy the region's continental shelves. Such environmental factors condition the abundance of phytoplankton, the microscopic cells that form the base of ocean life, and zooplankton, a very heterogeneous group that ranges in size from a few micrometres to several centimetres, with some species only existing as plankton in their juvenile stages, while others are planktonic through their whole life cycle. Plankton are consumed by fish and marine mammals, which in turn are eaten by predators – including humans – from further up the food chain. But as the productive capacity of any given water mass is highly variable and seasonal, plankton abundance and fish populations are by no means evenly distributed across the diverse waters of the North Atlantic. Some general patterns can be perceived. Whereas the biodiversity of marine life diminishes from the Equator to the North Pole, the abundance of individuals and tolerance to environmental variations normally increases. In the eastern reaches of the North Atlantic, for instance, approximately 700 species of fish have been identified in Ibero-Atlantic waters and the Bay of Biscay, while 230 species are known to inhabit the North Sea and 170 have been recorded on the Faroe Shelf. Further north, relatively few cold-water species predominate, a pattern that is replicated in the northwest Atlantic, although the prevalence of colder ocean currents means that the limits of these species extend much further to the south.

Amidst this diversity of marine life, two types of fish have attracted human predators. Pelagic species, such as herring, mackerel, sardine, pilchard and tuna, which have oily flesh and are rich in unsaturated fats, shoal in the upper layers of the sea. Although they are prevalent across the North Atlantic region, particular concentrations inhabit different ecosystems; for instance, while Atlanto-Scandian herring live in the northeast Atlantic, discrete stocks of herring inhabit the North Sea, the Barents Sea and the waters covering the Iceland shelf and the Northeast US Continental Shelf. Such fish are highly migratory and swim in vast numbers to spawn in favourable environmental conditions. Although this behaviour is generally predictable, there have been many instances when shoals have periodically 'appeared' or 'disappeared' in certain locations, the most striking example being the extraordinary concentrations of herring that gathered off the Swedish west coast during the so-called 'Bohuslän periods' of c. 1556–89 and c. 1752–1808 (Sendahl 2003: 189; Poulsen 2008: 50–53). The other set of species are bottom-swimming demersal fish such as cod, ling, pollock, hake, haddock, plaice and halibut, which are especially prolific in the northerly waters of the region. Often termed 'white fish' due to the colour of their comparatively dry flesh, these species do not shoal in the manner of herring, sardine and mackerel, and comprise individuals that are much larger on average than pelagic fish. Nevertheless, they migrate regularly in search of prey and waters that are conducive to reproduction, conditions that attract substantial congregations of cod off north Norway in the early spring, Iceland in June and July and in the inshore waters of New England and Newfoundland during the summer months. In stimulating the extractive efforts of human fishers, such natural congregations of fish have suffered high levels of mortality, which over the long term have affected the reproductive capabilities, migratory movements and abundance of some stocks of demersal and pelagic species (Rosenberg et al. 2005).

Environmental drivers further influence ecology through the strong positive correlations that exist between ocean currents, sea temperatures and climatic conditions. Sub-flows of the North Atlantic Current, for instance, serve to increase the surface temperature of the Norwegian and Barents Seas to levels that are 5–10°C higher than those prevailing in similar latitudes in the northern and southern hemispheres. Adjacent terrestrial areas are influenced by such exceptional marine conditions and therefore the coastal districts of Norway and Russia enjoy less severe winters and milder summers than the maritime regions of northeast North America, which are cooled by the Labrador Current. Human behaviour is shaped to some extent by such basic environmental factors, notably in respect to settlement patterns, the seasonal rhythm of life and the quest for naturally occurring sources of food. This is evident in the development of the fisheries in the northern reaches of the Atlantic World during the early modern era.

MOTIVES AND DRIVERS

Humans are not born with an innate desire to extract fish from their natural habitats. Fishing is therefore a product of the conscious decisions of people and societies to capture aquatic animals. In the 1450–1850 era, such a choice was sometimes exercised for recreational purposes, with angling for freshwater species emerging as a pastime during the fifteenth century. In England, this was signalled in 1496, when Dame Juliana Berners published her *Treatyse of Fysshynge with an Angle* – the first documentary indication that fishing had assumed a place alongside hawking and hunting in the leisure pursuits of gentlemen. Over the next century or so, sport fishing developed to such an extent that in 1653 Izaak Walton's *Compleat Angler*, which unequivocally cast fishing as a pleasurable diversion, appealed to a growing, largely well-to-do audience (Cowx 2002: 367). Throughout human history, however, the principal motive for taking fish from freshwater and saltwater environments has been to provide food for human consumption. With flesh that is rich in protein, calcium, unsaturated fats and vitamins A, B and D, fish also yield oil, fertilizer and other by-products.

In environmental settings where subsistence options were comparatively limited, fishing played a significant role in the lifeways of the human inhabitants. This was apparent in the far northern reaches of the Atlantic region, where indigenous peoples like the Beothuk and Mi'kmaq in northeast North America, the Greenlandic Inuit and the Sami of Fennoscandia were obliged to adapt to the fluctuating abundance and distribution of natural resources, both terrestrial and marine. During the early modern period, these adaptive strategies paralleled, connected with, or were absorbed by market-oriented forms of fishery emanating from the south and the east. Commercial fishing entails commodification, a process by which living aquatic animals are converted into food and other marketable goods. Although it had long been practised in freshwater and inland seas, it did not extend into the saltwater of the North Atlantic until the later stages of the first millennium. Archaeological analyses of fish bones found in various British locations indicate 'that the most important change in English fishing between AD 600 and 1600 occurred within a few decades of AD 1000 and involved large relative increases in catches of herring (*Clupea harengus*) and cod (*Gadus morhua*), many of which were probably distributed by trade' (Barrett et al. 2009: 33). The diets of western Europeans altered during this period, with freshwater species becoming less significant than fish caught at sea. This shift offered advantages to captors. Whereas fish might belong to landowners, monarchs and others who exercised riparian rights of ownership over inland – and sometimes coastal – waters (Woolgar 2000: 39; Amorim 2009a: 279–80; Amorim 2009b: 245–79), the 'high seas' and their inhabitants, which lay beyond what later became known as territorial limits, were less constrained by such proprietary rights (Barnes 2009: 165–220). Here, fishing transformed a free resource into private property that captors might choose to process into a product for marketing and sale. Such a prospect persuaded countless people over many centuries to risk their capital, labour power and lives in an effort to generate personal income and profit by harvesting food from the sea.

The scale and character of this commercial activity was governed by the interplay of a range of economic, political, socio-cultural, technological, institutional and environmental influences that varied in intensity and impact over time and space. Demand was generally the key determinant. At the societal level, this was broadly conditioned by the number, distribution and prosperity of prospective consumers. It is probable, for instance, that the expansion of the early medieval fish trade in northern Europe was driven by the increase in the continent's population from approximately 30 to 80 million between 1000 and the 1330s (Cipolla 1993: 96). Intensifying this demand-side pressure was urbanization, which stimulated commercial food production, including the supply of freshwater and marine fish, as inferred by evidence pertaining to fish consumption in Scandinavia, England, eastern Europe and the Netherlands (Nielssen 2009: 104–6; Woolgar 2000: 39–40; Van Dam 2009: 309–10). A similar pattern was apparent in the late fifteenth and sixteenth centuries, when the growth of Europe's population from 61.6 million in 1500 to 78 million in 1600 (De Vries 1984: table 3.6), coupled with the expansion of the majority of towns and cities, precipitated an increase in food production, with the extension of agriculture into common and marginal lands being mirrored, to some extent, by the extension of European fishing activity to the continental shelves that surround Iceland and lie adjacent to Newfoundland and New England. Separating these expansive phases, the Black Death of the 1340s and 1350s, which killed at least 25 million people – or one-third of Europe's population (Cipolla 1993: 96) – had a profoundly negative impact on the sea fisheries during the late fourteenth century. In a similar, though less pronounced, manner, the decline and slow recovery of Europe's population – from 78 million in 1600 to 74.6 million in 1650 to 81.4 million in 1700 (De Vries 1984: table 3.6) – was probably one of the causes of the stagnation apparent in many fisheries in the seventeenth and early eighteenth centuries.

Levels of demand were affected in various ways by the standard of living of the population. Whereas falling real incomes might increase demand for relatively cheap varieties of fish, greater relative affluence could have the opposite effect, as it sometimes allowed consumers to purchase comparatively expensive foodstuffs such as meat, fowl, 'luxury' freshwater fish species and fresh sea fish (Carmona and López Losa 2009: 262–63). Such consumption decisions were not simply made on the basis of personal preference, for food choices have deep cultural meanings, with local custom, social status and fashion, as well as market forces, explaining why over the long term the Portuguese came to prefer *bacalhau* (dried salted cod), while the Dutch generally opted for herring and the English developed a taste for fresh white fish. As Turgeon asserts in relation to the burgeoning desire of the French to eat Newfoundland cod during the sixteenth century:

> Eating gives agency to foods and to people. It represents a form of social action by the choice of foods eaten, by the people who eat them, by the manner in which they are prepared, by the place they are eaten and by the performance of eating itself.
>
> (Turgeon 2009: 34–35)

Religious belief further shaped the pattern of demand, for Christians were discouraged from eating meat on fast days, which in much of medieval Europe comprised three days per week, as well as the four weeks of Advent and the six weeks of Lent. Fish

– CHAPTER 4: *Fish and fisheries in the Atlantic World* –

consumption was permissible during these fasts, a concession that probably stimulated fishing activity, although abstainers might choose other alternatives to meat, such as eggs, cheese and butter (Woolgar 2000: 36–37; Van Dam 2009: 314–18). Fasting became less prevalent after the Reformation in the sixteenth century, which perhaps precipitated a contraction in the demand for fish, at least in Protestant countries. In England, for instance, the state passed legislation in 1548 and 1563 that was designed to revive fishing activity, and thereby train seafarers for naval service, by restoring Saturdays and Wednesdays as 'fish days' (Jackson 2000: 47). Nevertheless, notwithstanding the Reformation, stockfish from north Europe and saltfish from Newfoundland continued to sate the large Catholic markets of France, Iberia and the Mediterranean, while Dutch herring exports to the Baltic remained buoyant until well into the seventeenth century (Michell 1977: 177–78).

A range of inputs influenced the development of the early modern fisheries, with human resources the most important of the various factors of production. Labour was a vital ingredient, for muscle rather than mechanical power was largely used to haul sails, pull oars, cast nets and lines, cure catches and convey produce to market during the 1450–1850 period. While skill and experience were required to catch and process fish in viable commercial quantities, the seasonality of fisheries – as dictated by ecological and environmental factors – meant that many fishermen engaged in occupations other than fishing for parts of the year, with agricultural work the most common (Starkey 1992: 169–70; Nielssen 2009: 84–88; Thór 2009: 325–26). Merchants were likewise central to the production, processing and marketing facets of the fisheries. It was their initiative and capital that purchased and set forth carrying vessels to convey fishermen and gear to the fishing grounds and catches to curing facilities, which were often under their control. Credit was also advanced by merchants to enable fishermen to procure the necessary equipment and materials to engage in the fishery, with the season's catch normally serving as the in-kind repayment (Nielssen 2009: 85–86; Candow 2009a: 388–89). Among the resources supplied, facilitated or managed by mercantile creditors were two pre-requisites. First, in fisheries that deployed hook and line catching methods, such as the cod fisheries, bait production was a highly significant ancillary activity; indeed, in many coastal districts, it not only constituted an important occupation, but also a fishery in its own right (McKenzie 2007: 77–89; Payne 2010: 1–28). The second pre-requisite was salt. Essential to the curing branch of many fisheries, this basic but valuable commodity was conveyed to shore-based processing stations and shipped aboard vessels engaged in 'offshore' fisheries, wherein the fish were cured on deck and stored in barrels in the hold. Nations, regions or merchants with ready access to supplies of salt had an important cost advantage, with source areas like the Bay of Biscay and the Portuguese littoral assuming a significant role in the fisheries (Innis 1954: 48–51).

Technical change was generally piecemeal and incremental during the 1450–1850 period, although there were a number of important innovations, notably in the processing sector. While the development of a high-quality herring cure in the Netherlands underpinned the pre-eminence of the Dutch North Sea herring fishery during the early modern period, the eastwards diffusion of salting techniques from Newfoundland to Iceland and Norway enabled cod producers to sell dried salted cod (*klipfish*) as well as stockfish from the 1740s onwards (Nielssen 2009: 90; Thór

2009: 337–38). At the same time, the market for stockfish, especially the poorer quality varieties, improved when it was softened by mechanical rather than manual hammering in purpose-built mills that were increasingly prevalent in Germany from the early sixteenth century (Wubs-Mrozewicz 2009: 197–98). In Galicia, the introduction by Catalonians of pressing techniques during the late eighteenth century served to increase the productivity of the pilchard fisheries by rendering marketable a greater proportion of catches and generating fish oil (*sain*), a saleable by-product (Carmona and López Losa 2009: 263–64). There were fewer major innovations in the capture sector of the fisheries, although the introduction of decked sailing vessels (smacks) from the 1790s added a new dimension to the Icelandic fisheries (Thór 2009: 340–43), while in the early nineteenth century the replacement of handlines by longlines had a positive impact on the productivity of French fishermen on the Newfoundland banks (Candow 2009a: 395). Improvements in sea transport also facilitated the development of the fisheries, for vessels were necessary to convey fishermen and their gear to the fishing grounds, and to return catches to market. In this respect, the significant improvements in navigation, vessel design and propulsion that collectively constituted the 'first shipping revolution' in the fifteenth century not only allowed Columbus to cross the Atlantic, but also enabled early-modern fishermen to promote long-distance migratory fisheries (Gardiner and Unger 1994). Although a host of relatively minor incremental improvements in the size, efficiency and safety of vessels took place in the interim (Gardiner and Bosscher 1995), it was not until the nineteenth century that the 'second shipping revolution', in which wooden walls and sail power were gradually supplanted by metal hulls and steam propulsion, significantly altered the scope and scale of the sea fisheries.

Shipping was just one of numerous external factors that served to stimulate, facilitate or constrain the development of the fisheries. Shifts in the supply and price of other foodstuffs, including freshwater fish, were another exogenous force. In this respect, changes in the prices of grain and fish in northern Europe during the seventeenth century, which saw the relative value of fish decline sharply (Nielssen 2009: 86–87), perhaps explain the contraction in fishing activity that marked the period. Institutional factors also impinged on the workings of the market for fish. States and rulers occasionally offered bounties to encourage fishing activity, a notable example being the payment of 30–50 shillings per ton to English merchants who fitted out herring 'busses' from the 1740s (Jackson 2000: 52–53). In contrast, government policy might constrain the fish trade, as demonstrated by the establishment of state-controlled, monopolistic trading companies in Iceland, the Faroes and Greenland in 1602, 1709 and 1774 respectively by the Danish crown, the prohibition of fish exports in seventeenth-century Portugal and the erection of mercantilist trading and colonial frameworks, especially by Britain and France. Taxes levied on salt, landings and vessels added to the operational costs of fishermen (Jones 2000: 107–8), while the onset of maritime war generally led to losses of men, gear and vessels, either to state mobilization or enemy action, as was evident in the damage and disruption wrought upon the Netherlandish herring fleet during the wars of the 1400–1650 period (Sicking and Van Vliet 2009: 337–64), and in the frequent attacks on English fishing stations on Newfoundland by French forces, and *vice versa*, during the seventeenth and early eighteenth centuries (Candow 2009b: 424–26). Equally, war might yield advantages for fishermen through the forcible exclusion of rivals from fishing grounds or shore areas. The private sector also spawned institutions and interest groups. In the Dutch Republic, for instance, the North Sea herring fishery (*Grote Visserij*) was increasingly dominated by a *College* of merchants, which prescribed the onboard curing process, controlled the supply of labour and restricted the entry of merchants into the business (Poulsen 2008: 109–21). In Spain, maritime guilds not only managed the fisheries, but also regulated the work and remuneration of the fishermen (Carmona and López Losa 2009: 257–61), while in Portugal, brotherhoods (*confrarios*) of fishermen emerged in medieval times as members endeavoured to ensure that each enjoyed material and spiritual equality (Amorim 2009a: 283–84).

MODES AND ZONES

The multifarious factors that interacted to persuade people to capture fish and consume fish products gave rise to a range of fisheries in the North Atlantic region during the 1450–1850 period. Some of these were prosecuted in inland areas, where freshwater fish were caught for human consumption. In Labrador, for instance, the Innu used vegetal fibre nets to take trout under the ice (Keenlyside and Andreasen 2009: 378), while in Iceland the sagas relate how salmon – 'God's Gift' – helped to sustain the population (Pétursdóttir 1998: 54–71), and across Europe the appetites of the wealthier members of society were sated by pike, perch, trout and sturgeon taken by rod and line from ponds and rivers (Woolgar 2000: 44). In many places, the exploitation of naturally occurring fish was complemented – and often superseded – by the cultivation of fish stocks in purpose-built freshwater ponds, a practice that intensified in relatively densely populated, urbanized regions during the fourteenth and fifteenth centuries. In Brabant and Hainaut, for instance, ponds, reservoirs and even defensive ditches were developed by entrepreneurial property owners intent on generating profits from 'carp in the city'; that is, from the production and sale of a valued commodity in a growing market (Deligne 2009: 283–95).

Numerous commercial fisheries – each embracing catching, processing, distribution and marketing activities – were conducted concurrently or sequentially according to the seasons. They have been afforded various descriptors in the historical literature. Some authors have adopted political divisions to describe fisheries based in, and administered by, nation states – a parameter that for larger and more active fishing countries such as France, Spain and England included a range of discrete businesses. Other studies have focused on particular marine areas and species. Such approaches indicate, for instance, that North Sea herring was the object of relatively large-scale fishing efforts emanating from nine northwest European countries and regions – the Dutch Republic, Norway, Bohuslän, Scotland, England, 'German states', Denmark, Flanders and France (Poulsen 2008: 43–69) – while the cod stocks off Newfoundland were exploited during various epochs, and in various ways, by Basque, Portuguese, Spanish, French, English and North American fishermen (Innis 1954; Barkham 2009; Candow 2009b). Another descriptor commonly deployed relates to the productive resources utilized, with catching devices cast adjectivally to describe the trawl and line fisheries (Robinson 1996; Robinson 2000: 72–80), while the socio-economic status of fishers is also used to differentiate indigenous, subsistence, artisanal and commercial fisheries.

Appraisals of the North Atlantic fisheries over the long term are rendered problematical by such definitional complexities. Enumerating the fisheries, for example, depends upon which criteria are applied, with political divisions indicating that some twenty 'fishing nations' were active during the early modern era, while the broader criteria of nationality, principal catching area and target species suggest that at least fifty large-scale, recognizably discrete fisheries were prosecuted (Starkey et al. 2009). Even so, the many changes in political boundaries and regimes that occurred over time, as well as the regional variations in techniques, products and markets within seemingly 'national' fisheries, mean that such calculations lack precision. A clearer, more enlightening picture can be painted by considering the fisheries in terms of space and process. Although the catching branch of each fishery was prosecuted in the relatively shallow waters that cover the littoral areas and continental shelves of the North Atlantic region, the means of production and distribution were not necessarily based on the adjacent land masses and islands, while various *modi operandi* were practised afloat and ashore. Assessing the fisheries according to such variables reveals that four 'zonal modes' were current during the early modern era.

First, there were the shore fisheries. A diverse, ubiquitous facet of the coastal districts of the region, these activities entailed the capture of fish, and gathering of shellfish, by people working from the coast and banks of estuaries. This was not a seagoing, vessel-based business. Rather, the catching gear deployed along the region's shores ranged from large, sophisticated dams to spears, lines, nets and pots, the fish and shellfish they ensnared providing a significant – and often fresh – supplement to the diets of the captors and their communities (Kowaleski 2000: 23–25). Indigenous peoples engaged in such activity during the early modern era. In Labrador and Newfoundland, for instance, Europeans in the late fifteenth century encountered fishing practices dating back 4,000 years, when 'early maritime people possessed elaborate fishing and sea mammal hunting tools to exploit coastal and offshore marine resources', notably swordfish, walrus and seal (Keenlyside and Andreasen 2009: 376). In Greenland, Danish traders and government officials interacted with the hunting culture of the Inuit, who trailed seals, bears and other animals, deriving food, skins, oil and blubber from their prey. Mobility and an annual resort to winter, spring, summer and autumn settlements were the cornerstones of a highly seasonal hunting cycle, in which fish were not captured on a large scale, but served as a supplementary source of nourishment in certain times of the year, and as an emergency food in times of dearth (Keenlyside and Andreasen 2009: 383). A seasonal migratory pattern also prevailed in the northernmost parts of Norway, Finland, Sweden and Russia, where the Sami population adapted opportunistically to its natural and commercial environments. Here, fishing assumed its place alongside hunting, animal husbandry and, in ecologically favourable areas, grain cultivation in a semi-subsistence, semi-commercial adaptive strategy. Accordingly, 'when market demand failed and external supplies became scarce, the Sami were able to withdraw from the market and rely on other forms of sustaining life. But as long as the market mechanisms functioned, they were equally capable of using them to satisfy their needs' (Hansen 2009: 76).

Other shore fisheries were essentially market-oriented, with pelagic species the primary targets. Around the rim of the North Sea, for instance, shore fishing techniques were deployed in the herring fishery, with seine nets set from beaches in Norway, Sweden, Denmark, the Netherlands and England accounting for part of the salted herring output that constituted a highly significant facet of the region's commercial activity throughout the early modern era (Poulsen 2008: 72). The Bohuslän fishery was the most productive of these shore-based businesses, though only during the comparatively short periods when the herring shoals migrated regularly into coastal waters. In 1574–88, for example, exports of salted herring averaged almost 6,000 metric tonnes per year and reached a peak of just over 13,000 metric tons in 1585. When the herring next appeared in significant numbers from 1748 to 1808, Bohuslän became the single most important contributor to the North Sea herring catch, with over 30,000 tonnes of salted fish exported in the 1790s and early 1800s, as well as over 100,000 tonnes of train oil (Poulsen 2008: 51–53, 70–71). Further south and west, the Cornish pilchard fishery was partly conducted from the shore, with seine nets used to encircle the shoals when they ventured towards the low water mark on the county's many accessible beaches. Seining was dominated by 'men of substance, drawn from the local landowning gentry and merchant classes', with the fishermen working for a wage and a productivity bonus of a small proportion of the catch. Although the seining season rarely extended beyond eight weeks, the pilchard it generated formed a major item in the diets of local people as well as an export good that in the 1760s accounted for 60 per cent of British fish exports, most bound to markets in the Mediterranean (Pawlyn 2000: 85–87).

Figure 4.1 Dragging in the seine net
Reproduced from C.F. Drechsel, *Oversigt over vore Saltvandsfiskerier I Nordsøen og Farvandene indenfor Skagen*, Copenhagen 1890

In terms of operational area and curing technique, the inshore fisheries – the second zonal mode – were not far removed from the shore fisheries. Their catching effort, however, was largely expended in sailing vessels or rowing boats that conveyed fishermen to grounds that were rarely more than a few hours from the coast (Childs 2000: 19–22). Provisioned only for short voyages, and with limited carrying capacity, inshore fishing boats generally returned within two or three days of departure, ideally with an optimal quantity of fish – in Lowestoft, this was ten–twelve lasts, or 120,000–144,000 fish – that was fresh enough to process ashore (Butcher 2000: 57). Although distinct from the shore fisheries in that portable, as opposed to static, catching techniques were deployed, there were many similarities and overlaps between the two modes. With regard to the pelagic sector, the pilchard fisheries of southwest England boasted an inshore dimension, with self-employed boatmen driving pilchard shoals ashore amidst the darkness of summer nights (Pawlyn 2000: 85–86). Moreover, the inshore herring fisheries were prosecuted in the North Sea by fishermen taking herring in gill, seine and drift nets cast from a great variety of generally small, short-range craft (Haines 2000: 66–70; Poulsen 2008: 43–69). Such catches were landed on the adjacent coasts for salting, smoking or pickling in line with local practice and preference. Typically, shore and inshore catches were cured in the same facilities before despatch to local, inland or overseas markets.

The inshore mode dominated cod production in north Europe and the mid-Atlantic islands, with catches largely taken by men fishing in boats with handlines, rod and line, or, from the late eighteenth century, longlines. Many of the vessels utilized for inshore fishing were oar-powered, their names indicative of the manpower they required; accordingly, the Shetlanders set forth four-oared *fourerns*, while Faroese rowing boats ranged in size from the *fýramannafar*, propelled by four oarsmen to the *seksæringur*, which was worked by twelve men. Similar ranges of oared vessels were deployed in the inshore fisheries of Iceland, where the rowing boat was the mainstay of the fishing effort for nearly a millennium. In these Nordic areas, the fish were taken on baited lines and returned to shore, where they were beheaded, split, gutted and hung to dry on horizontal poles (*stokkr*), stone walls or gravel for weeks, or even months, depending upon the amount of dry weather. Temperatures fluctuating around 0°C for months at a time, with the aid of strong winds – climatic conditions that prevailed in north Norway and the mid-Atlantic islands – were essential for freeze-drying the catches. The dried cod – known as stockfish – yielded by this simple, low-cost process remained viable as a food product for between five and seven years, an attribute that rendered it a highly valued commodity throughout the medieval and early modern periods (Perdikaris and McGovern 2009: 63–65; Wubs-Mrozewicz 2009: 190–92; Thór 2009: 337–38). The inshore cod fishery possessed a migratory quality in that many fishermen travelled relatively short distances to live in temporary settlements while they engaged in inshore catching and processing activity for the duration of the fishing season. In Norway, for instance, fishermen annually moved north to work in the inshore waters and on the shore of the Lofoten Islands, a practice that spread further north to Finnmark from the fifteenth century. While large numbers of Icelanders walked for up to twelve days across their island to engage in seasonal inshore fishing activity off the southwest and west coasts, the 'haaf' fishery that emerged in the Shetlands during the seventeenth century also entailed seasonal migration, with fishermen travelling to the northern parts of the archipelago to live and work in rudimentary fishing stations for up to two

– CHAPTER 4: *Fish and fisheries in the Atlantic World* –

months during the summer. The finished product, moreover, was carried long distances to points of consumption, with Bergen serving as the mercantile hub of a trade that for centuries linked north Norwegian, Icelandic, Faroese and Shetland fishing grounds with markets in Scandinavia, the British Isles, central and southern Europe (Wubs-Mrozewicz 2009: 187–208).

Movements of labour and gear were the defining characteristics of the third zonal mode, the migratory fisheries prosecuted by Europeans in the inshore waters and coastal areas of northeast North America. This business resembled the inshore fisheries in that it was undertaken by fishermen working from small vessels close to the shore, where catches were returned for processing. But it differed from the inshore fisheries of north Europe and the mid-Atlantic islands in respect of spatial scale. This was a transoceanic activity in which fishermen, gear and other productive resources were shipped out and back across the Atlantic in spring and autumn, having been resident in temporary dwellings at the processing stations established on the shore for the duration of the summer fishing season. Likewise, in this truly 'international economy' (Innis 1954), their products were also conveyed across the ocean to markets in southern Europe and the Caribbean. A further contrast with the Nordic inshore fisheries lay in the product, for a different type of cured cod was produced in northeast North America. Here, fishermen in chaloupes, skiffs, dories or other forms of small boat caught cod by rod and line in the inshore waters of the Gulf of Maine and Newfoundland. Their catches were landed at shore processing stations – known as stages in Newfoundland – where they were beheaded, split and laid out to dry after receiving a light covering of salt (Candow 2009a: 392–94, 398–400). The final product was salted dried cod – or saltfish – which from the early sixteenth century assumed a prominent place in the growing array of staple goods that were traded and consumed in the emerging Atlantic World.

English merchants and fishermen, the majority based in southwest England and the Channel Islands, dominated the migratory inshore fisheries from the late sixteenth century to the 1790s. Down to the 1630s, they endeavoured to conduct a migratory fishery in New England, but the region's favourable resource endowments and comparatively benign climate enabled early settlers to develop economic activities – grain cultivation, timber production, handicraft manufacturing – that complemented the fisheries and gave migrants the option to over-winter and settle. Whereas an inshore fishery conducted by New England residents soon became a mainstay of the region's economy (Innis 1954: 70–81; Gray 2000: 96–100; Candow 2009a: 405–7), Newfoundland, with its narrow resource base and generally inhospitable climate, remained little more than a 'fishing ship moored on the banks' during the seventeenth and early eighteenth centuries. However, the migratory character of the fishery sowed the seeds of its own demise, for members of the transient workforce began to over-winter and survive by engaging in the inshore 'bye-boat' fishery. This was a slow process that commenced during a series of poor fishing seasons in the third quarter of the seventeenth century, but only gathered momentum from the 1730s, especially during the 1739–48, 1756–63, 1775–83 and 1793–1815 wars. As the inshore fishery grew symbiotically with the island's population, the merchants – despite persistently lobbying the English government to support the migratory fishery – adjusted their core business from production to servicing, from catching and curing cod to supplying island-based fishermen with credit and provisions, and distributing and selling their catches in transoceanic markets (Starkey 1992: 168–70; Candow 2009b: 426–38).

Whereas migratory fishing swiftly gave way to resident fisheries in New England, and eventually gave rise to permanent settlement in Newfoundland, the offshore fisheries – the fourth zonal mode – had few migratory ramifications, for it entailed transitory work that was undertaken afloat. Such activity might be termed 'industrial' in scale, scope and organization, for it was practised in comparatively large, capacious seagoing vessels that remained on the fishing grounds for relatively long periods. Distinguished by the curing process used, practitioners of this mode of production preserved their catches aboard ship, generally by packing the fish in barrels of salt and storing them in the hold before returning to port when fully laden. This process was deployed in the North Sea, with the *Grote Visserij*, as it later became known, emerging in the Netherlands in the fourteenth century and developing into the most productive strand of the multi-layered herring fishery from the late sixteenth century to the 1740s. Undertaken annually by fleets of 'busses', which preyed on the herring shoals as they proceeded south from Shetland waters in the late spring to the southern reaches of the North Sea in the autumn, this business was organized and regulated from the 1560s to 1857 by merchants belonging to the *College van de Grote Visserij*. Key to the viability of this industry were the co-ordination of the fishing effort, the barriers to entry imposed by the *College* and, most importantly, the consistently high quality of the herring produced through the regulated, systematic curing process conducted at sea and ashore – a product that rivals in England, Scotland and the German and Scandinavian states struggled to emulate. Responsible for approximately 75 per cent of the herring extracted from the North Sea during the seventeenth century (Poulsen 2008: 43–46, 70), the *Grote Visserij* was perceived as a highly profitable 'Golden Mountain', which accounted for an estimated 8.9 per cent of Holland's gross domestic product in the early sixteenth century – a figure that had declined to 0.3 per cent by 1807, due largely to the expansion of other sectors of the Netherlandish economy (Van Bochove 2009: 209–11).

Cod was also taken on a large scale by offshore enterprise. English fishermen, for instance, were extracting cod from Icelandic waters from the early fifteenth century to the 1680s. In the early stages of this business, catches were taken ashore and processed into stockfish in the manner of the Icelandic rowing boat fishery (Thór 2009: 343–44). During the early sixteenth century, however, deteriorating relations between English mercantile interests and Iceland's increasingly restrictive Danish rulers persuaded the fishermen to alter their *modus operandi* by salting their catches in a shipboard operation that only involved contact with the shores of the adjacent island during times of emergency. This was a seasonal activity, which commenced in March with the departure from East Anglian ports of fleets of 'doggers' – relatively large vessels of 30–100 tons burthen, with 20–40 strong crews – for Icelandic grounds, whence they returned with holds full of salted and barrelled cod in late August and September. While the English Icelandic fishery appears to have ceased by the 1690s – having peaked in the early 1630s, when some 160 vessels engaged in the fishery (Jones 2000: 106–10) – other Europeans continued to prosecute offshore fishing in Icelandic waters, notably the Dutch during the eighteenth century, with the French dominating the business for over a century from the 1780s (Thór 2009: 345–46). France's principal offshore interest, however, was the 'green' fishery conducted on the Newfoundland banks from the 1540s, or possibly earlier (Candow 2009b: 418). In terms of *modus operandi*, this business appears 'to have borrowed heavily from the Dutch North Sea

– CHAPTER 4: *Fish and fisheries in the Atlantic World* –

herring fishery in that cod, like herring, was caught on the high seas and salted aboard ship' (Candow 2009a: 394). Baited hooks on lines paid out by men standing in tapered barrels on platforms erected on the ship's sides was the catching method deployed, with the cod being treated, salted and barrelled afloat to yield a product that was conveyed directly to France in the fishing ship when her hold was full. Practice altered over time, the most significant variation being the development of 'bank' fishing by the French and the British off Newfoundland and by New Englanders on the Scotian Shelf. This was essentially a hybrid of inshore and offshore techniques, with fishing vessels returning to adjacent coasts at regular intervals to land salted or 'wet' catches for drying at shore stations on St Pierre, southeast Newfoundland and Nova Scotia (Candow 2009a: 394–401).

In the late eighteenth century, the fisheries, in common with other economic activities in the North Atlantic region, began to experience structural, technical and market changes on an unprecedented scale. The dismantling of state controls and monopolistic practices in Russia, Norway, Denmark and the mid-Atlantic islands liberalized fishing effort and marketing, leading to increasing output and product diversification (Lajus et al. 2009: 56–59; Nielssen 2009: 89–92; Thór 2009: 330, 340). In Newfoundland, the 'ancient' migratory fishery, which had reached its greatest extent by many measures in the late 1780s, collapsed, never to recover, during the wars that raged across the region over the following two decades (Starkey et al. 2000: 103–4). Further south, the New England fisheries were 'revolutionized' by the

Figure 4.2 A naval architect's representation of an early fifteenth-century English dogger
Used with kind permission of Alan Hopper, Maritime Historical Studies Centre, University of Hull

emergence in the 1830s of the mackerel fishery and, more especially, by the introduction of ice as a preservative in the inshore cod fishery, which eliminated the need for shore processing and facilitated the rapid growth of the fresh fish market (Candow 2009a: 401). A similar pattern was evident across the ocean, where fishermen from southwest England – perhaps displaced by the demise of the migratory fishery in Newfoundland – began deploying beam trawls in the North Sea to capture demersal species in the 1820s. Once the railways connected ports with the burgeoning urban districts of early industrial England in the 1840s (Robinson 2000: 73–76; Gerrish 2000: 112–18), white fish caught by sailing trawlers and delivered fresh to market – a new form of inshore fishery that grew and spread to other countries after 1850 – swiftly developed into the leading sector of the 'modern' North Atlantic fisheries.

YIELDS AND FLOWS

The scale of the early modern North Atlantic fisheries, both separately and in the aggregate, is difficult to measure due to the paucity, inconsistency and doubtful reliability of surviving sources of information. Nevertheless, numerous estimates of effort and catches are available. These reveal, for instance, that approximately 12,000 men were engaged in the French Newfoundland fishery during the late sixteenth century (Turgeon 2009: 37), while some 6,000 Englishmen travelled to work on Newfoundland in 1615 (Starkey and Haines 2001: 5), 9,000 Icelandic fishermen worked their island's inshore waters in 1770 (Thór 2009: 348), and around 14,000 humans preyed on the cod stocks off Lofoten in 1829 (Nielssen 2009: 91). Among the disparate figures that relate to output, it is apparent that in 1680 the North Sea yielded between 25,000 and 35,000 metric tonnes (mt) of herring (Poulsen 2008: 69–70), and the Newfoundland fisheries (English and French) produced a total of 185,280 mt of cured cod (Turgeon 1995: 106), whereas in 1770 the equivalent estimates stood at 40,000–60,000 mt of herring (Poulsen 2008: 69–70), and 260,232 mt of cod (Starkey and Haines 2001: 10). By the mid-nineteenth century, calculations suggest that production levels had reached 200,000 mt of North Sea herring (Poulsen 2008: 69–70), 322,000 mt of British Newfoundland cod (Starkey and Haines 2001: 10), 185,000 mt of New England cod (Candow 2009b), and 164,000 mt of Norwegian stockfish (Nielssen 2009: 111), with a further 64,000 mt of fish landed in Spain's Atlantic ports (Carmona and López Losa 2009: 275).

Effort and yields of the magnitude suggested by these snapshots were significant to the development of the Atlantic World. From a narrow business perspective, they generated wealth for investors of capital in the catching, processing and retailing sectors, income and employment for those whose labour was recruited to take, transport, cure and sell fish, and food that was consumed by populations across the region, in inland as well as coastal areas. Losses of vessels, crews, materiel and money might also accrue from this business, while opportunity costs and negative long-term impacts on fish stocks and marine habitats could ensue from the commodification of living marine resources. From a broader, deeper Atlantic perspective, the fisheries entailed the delivery of food from points of extraction to places of consumption by virtue of the movement of resources and goods around and across the ocean. In essence, they were supply chains, the links in which comprised flows of various types and amplitudes. Commodity flows involving the exchange of fish products for other

– CHAPTER 4: Fish and fisheries in the Atlantic World –

goods enabled societies on the fringes and islands of the Atlantic to exploit their comparative advantages. Norwegian, Faroese and Icelandic stockfish, for instance, was exchanged for textiles manufactured from English wool in Flemish towns, and grain from central Europe, while herring extracted from the North Sea by the Dutch paid for the primary and manufactured commodities they procured in all parts of their far-flung trading world, and the salted cod of the inshore, migratory inshore and offshore fisheries of northeast north America was conveyed to southern Europe and the Caribbean, where it was traded for wine, fruit, specie or rum (Pope 2004; Candow 2006). Fish was therefore one of the principal commodities in the commercial nexus that lay at the base of the Atlantic economy.

People travelled along the coasts and across the ocean in the quest to take fish. Some set forth specifically to find commercially viable stocks of fish, with voyages to the northwest Atlantic in the late fifteenth and early sixteenth centuries offering a prime example of the exploratory role that the fisheries might play. Countless numbers were shipped to the catching zones, with fishermen from the North Sea littoral, the British Isles and Iberia 'following the fish' to Shetland, Iceland, Newfoundland and New England, while Norwegians and Germans moved north to engage in the cod fisheries of Nordland and Finnmark. Some of these movements were short in terms of both distance and time; for instance, many agricultural workers in coastal districts across the region engaged in the fisheries on a seasonal basis, which might oblige them to live in comparatively rudimentary dwellings in marginal settlements for just a few weeks each year. In other settings, however, seasonal migrations were not only of longer duration, but were also a first step towards permanent settlement in places adjacent to the fishing grounds. The ways in which the extent and character of the fishing effort could shape migratory and settlement patterns are exemplified by Newfoundland's experience from 1500 through to the early nineteenth century. For much of this period, over-wintering was discouraged by the merchants who dominated the business, hazardous due to the island's harsh climate and limited resource base, and socially unappealing because of the virtual absence of women, families and civil institutions. But once the population of the island began to grow in the second quarter of the eighteenth century, the settlements that developed not only reflected the seasonality and commercial fluctuations of the fishery, but also the socio-cultural and political characteristics of the areas where the incoming residents originated – that is, southwest England and, from the early nineteenth century, Ireland (Handcock 1989: Pope 2004; Pope 2009).

Lifeways, cultures and *modi operandi* flowed in other directions, notably in the Nordic realm. This had been manifest in the Viking Age (c. 750–1100), when the farming–fishing dual economy practised by Scandinavians was transplanted to the places they settled, notably the Shetlands, Orkneys, Faroes and Iceland. Such diffusion of process and product had longstanding ramifications for such places:

> The long-term consequences of the pre-commercial Norse fish distribution network 'going global' were profound. The commonplace expertise of Nordic fisher-folk and Nordic chieftains in making and marketing dried fish, though an unworthy subject for sagas, may well be one of the most lasting legacies of the Viking era.
> (Perdikaris and McGovern 2009: 87)

Such deep-seated technical and cultural connections underpinned the emergence of important commercial ties between northern Europe and these Atlantic islands, with capital and mercantile expertise flowing westwards to procure the islanders' stockfish for despatch to the markets of Europe via entrepôts such as Bergen and Copenhagen (Thorleifsen 2009). The fisheries therefore served as a binding agent in the Nordic sphere of influence – the *Norgesvoldet* – that has shaped the political, economic and cultural development of the northern reaches of the Atlantic over the last millennium.

REFERENCES

Amorim, I. (2009a) 'Portuguese fisheries, c.1100–1830', in D.J. Starkey, J.Th. Thór and I. Heidbrink (eds) *A History of the North Atlantic Fisheries: Volume 1, From Early Times to the mid-Nineteenth Century*, Bremerhaven: Deutsches Schiffahrtsmuseum.

——(2009b) 'The evolution of Portuguese fisheries in the medieval and early modern period: a fiscal approach', in L. Sicking and D. Abreu-Ferreira (eds) *Beyond the Catch: Fisheries of the North Atlantic, the North Sea and the Baltic, 900–1850*, Leiden: Brill.

Barkham, M.M. (2009) 'The offshore and distant-water fisheries of the Spanish Basques, c.1500–1650', in D.J. Starkey, J.Th. Thór and I. Heidbrink (eds) *A History of the North Atlantic Fisheries: Volume 1, From Early Times to the mid-Nineteenth Century*, Bremerhaven: Deutsches Schiffahrtsmuseum.

Barnes, R. (2009) *Property Rights and Natural Resources*, Oxford: Hart.

Barrett, J.H., Locker, A.M. and Roberts, C.M. (2009) '"Dark Age economics" revisited: the English fish-bone evidence, 600–1600', in L. Sicking and D. Abreu-Ferreira (eds) *Beyond the Catch: Fisheries of the North Atlantic, the North Sea and the Baltic, 900–1850*, Leiden: Brill.

Bolster, W.J. (2006) 'Opportunities in marine environmental history', *Environmental History*, 11 (3): 567–97.

——(2008) 'Putting the ocean into Atlantic history: maritime communities and marine ecology in the northwest Atlantic, 1500–1800', *American Historical Review*, 113 (1): 19–47.

——(2012) *The Mortal Sea: Fishing the Atlantic in the Age of Sail*, Cambridge MA: Harvard University Press.

Broeze, F. (1989) 'From the periphery to the mainstream: the challenge of Australia's maritime history', *Great Circle*, 11 (1): 1–13.

——(1995) (ed.) *Maritime History at the Crossroads: A Critical Review of Recent Historiography*, St John's, Newfoundland: International Maritime Economic History Association.

Butcher, D (2000) 'The herring fisheries in the early modern period: Lowestoft as microcosm', in D.J. Starkey, C. Reid and N.R. Ashcroft (eds) *England's Sea Fisheries: The Commercial Sea Fisheries of England and Wales since 1300*, London: Chatham.

Candow, J.E. (2006) 'Salt fish and slavery', in D.J. Starkey and J.E. Candow (eds) *The North Atlantic Fisheries: Supply, Marketing and Consumption, 1560–1990*, Hull: North Atlantic Fisheries History Association.

——(2009a) 'The organization and conduct of European and domestic fisheries in northeast North America, 1502–1854', in D.J. Starkey, J.Th. Thór and I. Heidbrink (eds) *A History of the North Atlantic Fisheries: Volume 1, From Early Times to the mid-Nineteenth Century*, Bremerhaven: Deutsches Schiffahrtsmuseum.

——(2009b) 'Migrants and residents: the interplay between European and domestic fisheries in northeast North America, 1502–1854', in D.J. Starkey, J.Th. Thór and I. Heidbrink (eds) *A History of the North Atlantic Fisheries: Volume 1, From Early Times to the mid-Nineteenth Century*, Bremerhaven: Deutsches Schiffahrtsmuseum.

Carmona, J. and López Losa, E. (2009) 'Spain's Atlantic coast fisheries, c.1100–1880', in D.J. Starkey, J.Th. Thór and I. Heidbrink (eds) *A History of the North Atlantic Fisheries: Volume 1, From Early Times to the mid-Nineteenth Century*, Bremerhaven: Deutsches Schiffahrtsmuseum.

– CHAPTER 4: *Fish and fisheries in the Atlantic World* –

Childs, W.R. (2000) 'Fishing and fisheries in the Middle Ages: the eastern fisheries', in D.J. Starkey, C. Reid and N.R. Ashcroft (eds) *England's Sea Fisheries: The Commercial Sea Fisheries of England and Wales since 1300*, London: Chatham.

Cipolla, C.M. (1993, 3rd edn) *Before the Industrial Revolution: European Society and Economy*, London: Routledge.

Coull, J.R. (1996) *Scotland's Sea Fisheries: A Historical Geography*, Edinburgh: John Donald.

Cowx, I.G. (2002) 'Recreational fishing', in P.J.B. Hart and J.D. Reynolds (eds) *Handbook of Fish Biology and Fisheries: Volume 2, Fisheries*, Oxford: Blackwell.

Deligne, C. (2009) 'Carp in the city: fish-farming ponds and urban dynamics in Brabant and Hainaut, c.1100–1500', in L. Sicking and D. Abreu-Ferreira (eds) *Beyond the Catch: Fisheries of the North Atlantic, the North Sea and the Baltic, 900–1850*, Leiden: Brill.

De Vries, J. (1984) *European Urbanization 1500–1800*, London: Methuen.

Gardiner, R. (series ed.) (1992–96) *Conway's History of the Ship*, London: Conway Maritime Press (12 volumes).

Gardiner, R. and Unger, R. (eds) (1994) *Cogs, Caravels and Galleons: The Sailing Ship 1000–1650*, London: Conway Maritime Press.

Gardiner, R. and Bosscher, P. (eds) (1995) *The Heyday of Sail: The Merchant Sailing Ship, 1650–1830*, London: Conway Maritime Press.

Gerrish, M. (2000) 'Following the fish: nineteenth-century migration and the diffusion of trawling', in D.J. Starkey, C. Reid and N.R. Ashcroft (eds) *England's Sea Fisheries: The Commercial Sea Fisheries of England and Wales since 1300*, London: Chatham.

Gray, M. (1979) *The Fishing Industries of Scotland, 1790–1914*, Oxford: Aberdeen University Studies.

Gray, T. (2000) 'The distant-water fisheries of south west England in the early modern period: fisheries to the east and to the west', in D.J. Starkey, C. Reid and N.R. Ashcroft (eds) *England's Sea Fisheries: The Commercial Sea Fisheries of England and Wales since 1300*, London: Chatham.

Greene, J.P. and Morgan, P.D. (2009) *Atlantic History: A Critical Appraisal*, Oxford: Oxford University Press.

Haines, M. (2000) 'The herring fisheries, 1750–1900', in D.J. Starkey, C. Reid and N.R. Ashcroft (eds) *England's Sea Fisheries: The Commercial Sea Fisheries of England and Wales since 1300*, London: Chatham.

Handcock, W.G. (1989) *So Longe as There Comes No Women: Origins of English Settlement in Newfoundland*, St. John's, Newfoundland: Breakwater.

Hansen, L.I. (2009) 'Sami fishing in the pre-modern era: household sustenance and market relations', in D.J. Starkey, J.Th. Thór and I. Heidbrink (eds) *A History of the North Atlantic Fisheries: Volume 1, From Early Times to the mid-Nineteenth Century*, Bremerhaven: Deutsches Schiffahrtsmuseum.

Innis, H.A. (1954, 2nd edn) *The Cod Fisheries: The History of an International Economy*, Toronto: University of Toronto Press.

Jackson, G. (2000) 'State concern for the fisheries, 1485–1815', in D.J. Starkey, C. Reid and N.R. Ashcroft (eds) *England's Sea Fisheries: The Commercial Sea Fisheries of England and Wales since 1300*, London: Chatham.

Jackson, J.B.C., Alexander, K. and Sala, E. (2011) *Shifting Baselines: The Past and Future of Ocean Fisheries*, Washington DC: Island Press, 2011.

Jones, E. (2000) 'England's Icelandic fishery in the early modern period', in D.J. Starkey, C. Reid and N.R. Ashcroft (eds) *England's Sea Fisheries: The Commercial Sea Fisheries of England and Wales since 1300*, London: Chatham.

Keenlyside, D.L. and Andreasen, C. (2009) 'Indigenous fishing in northeast North America', in D.J. Starkey, J.Th. Thór and I. Heidbrink (eds) *A History of the North Atlantic Fisheries: Volume 1, From Early Times to the mid-Nineteenth Century*, Bremerhaven: Deutsches Schiffahrtsmuseum.

Kowaleski, M. (2000) 'Fishing and fisheries in the Middle Ages: the western fisheries', in D.J. Starkey, C. Reid and N.R. Ashcroft (eds) *England's Sea Fisheries: The Commercial Sea Fisheries of England and Wales since 1300*, London: Chatham.

Lajus, J., Kraikovski, A.V. and Yurchenko, A. (2009) 'The fisheries of the Russian north, c.1300–1850', in D.J. Starkey, J.Th. Thór and I. Heidbrink (eds) *A History of the North Atlantic Fisheries: Volume 1, From Early Times to the mid-Nineteenth Century*, Bremerhaven: Deutsches Schiffahrtsmuseum.

LME (2009) http://lme.edc.uri.edu. Accessed 23 June 2014.

McKenzie, M.G. (2007) 'Baiting our memories: the impact of offshore technology change on inshore species around Cape Cod, 1860–95', in D.J. Starkey, P. Holm and M. Barnard (eds) *Oceans Past: Management Insights from the History of Marine Animal Populations*, London, Earthscan.

Michell, A.R. (1977) 'The European fisheries in early modern history', in E.E. Rich and C.H. Wilson (eds) *The Cambridge Economic History of Europe: Volume 5, The Economic Organization of Early Modern Europe*, Cambridge: Cambridge University Press.

Nielssen, A.R. (2009) 'Norwegian fisheries, c.1100–1850', in D.J. Starkey, J.Th. Thór and I. Heidbrink (eds) *A History of the North Atlantic Fisheries: Volume 1, From Early Times to the mid-Nineteenth Century*, Bremerhaven: Deutsches Schiffahrtsmuseum.

Pawlyn, T. (2000) 'The South West pilchard, trawl and mackerel fisheries, 1770–1850', in D.J. Starkey, C. Reid and N.R. Ashcroft (eds) *England's Sea Fisheries: The Commercial Sea Fisheries of England and Wales since 1300*, London: Chatham.

Payne, B.J. (2010) *Fishing a Borderless Sea: Environmental Territorialism in the North Atlantic, 1818–1910*, East Lansing: Michigan State University Press.

Perdikaris, S. and McGovern, T.H. (2009) 'Viking Age economics and the origins of commercial cod fisheries in the North Atlantic', in L. Sicking and D. Abreu-Ferreira (eds) *Beyond the Catch: Fisheries of the North Atlantic, the North Sea and the Baltic, 900–1850*, Leiden: Brill.

Pétursdóttir, S.S. (1998) 'God's gift: salmon fishing in Iceland in the Middle Ages', in P. Holm and D.J. Starkey (eds) *North Atlantic Fisheries: Markets and Modernisation*, Esbjerg: North Atlantic Fisheries History Association.

Pope P. (2004) *Fish into Wine: The Newfoundland Plantation in the Seventeenth Century*, Chapel Hill: University of North Carolina Press.

Pope, P. (2009) 'Transformation of the maritime cultural landscape of Atlantic Canada by migratory European fishermen, 1500–1800', in L. Sicking and D. Abreu-Ferreira (eds) *Beyond the Catch: Fisheries of the North Atlantic, the North Sea and the Baltic, 900–1850*, Leiden: Brill.

Poulsen, B. (2008) *Dutch Herring: An Environmental History, c. 1600–1860*, Amsterdam: Askant.

Poulsen, R.T. (2007) *An Environmental History of North Sea Ling and Cod Fisheries, 1840–1914*, Esbjerg: Fiskeri-og Søfartsmuseet.

Robinson, R. (1996) *Trawling: The Rise and Fall of the British Trawl Fishery*, Exeter: University of Exeter Press.

——(2000) 'The line and trawl fisheries in the age of sail', in D.J. Starkey, C. Reid and N.R. Ashcroft (eds) *England's Sea Fisheries: The Commercial Sea Fisheries of England and Wales since 1300*, London: Chatham.

——(2011) 'Hook, line and sinker: fishing history – where have we been, where are we now and where are we going?' *Mariner's Mirror*, 97 (1): 167–79.

Rosenberg, A.A., Bolster, W.J., Alexander, K.E, Leavenworth, W.B., Cooper, A.B., and McKenzie, M.G. (2005) 'The history of ocean resources: modeling cod biomass using historical records', *Frontiers in Ecology and the Environment*, 3 (2): 78–84.

Sendahl, J. (2003) 'The Bohuslän herring fishery, c.1752–1808', in D.J. Starkey, P. Holm, J Th. Thór and B. Andersson (eds) *Politics and People in the North Atlantic Fisheries since 1485*, Hull: North Atlantic Fisheries History Association.

Sicking, L. and Abreu-Ferreira, D. (eds) (2009) *Beyond the Catch: Fisheries of the North Atlantic, the North Sea and the Baltic, 900–1850*, Leiden: Brill.

Sicking, L. and Van Vliet, A.P. (2009) '"Our Triumph of Holland": war, violence, and the herring fishery of the Low Countries, c.1400–1650', in L. Sicking and D. Abreu-Ferreira (eds) *Beyond the Catch: Fisheries of the North Atlantic, the North Sea and the Baltic, 900–1850*, Leiden: Brill.

Starkey, D.J. (1992) 'Devonians and the Newfoundland trade', in M. Duffy, S. Fisher, B. Greenhill, D.J. Starkey and J. Youings (eds) *The New Maritime History of Devon: Volume 1, From Early Times to the late Eighteenth* Century, London: Conway Maritime Press.

——(1997) 'Introduction', in D.J. Starkey and A.G. Jamieson (eds) *Exploiting the Sea: Aspects of Britain's Maritime Economy since 1870*, Exeter: University of Exeter Press.

Starkey, D.J., Reid, C. and Ashcroft, N.R. (eds) (2000) *England's Sea Fisheries: The Commercial Sea Fisheries of England and Wales since 1300*, London: Chatham.

Starkey, D.J. and Haines, M. (2001) 'The Newfoundland fisheries, c.1500–1900: a British perspective', in P. Holm, T.D. Smith and D.J. Starkey (eds) *The Exploited Seas: New Directions for Marine Environmental History*, St. John's, Newfoundland: International Maritime Economic History Association.

Starkey, D.J., Holm P. and Barnard M. (eds) (2007) *Oceans Past: Management Insights from the History of Marine Animal Populations*, London: Earthscan.

Starkey, D.J., Thór, J.Th. and Heidbrink, I. (eds) (2009) *A History of the North Atlantic Fisheries: Volume 1, From Early Times to the mid-Nineteenth Century*, Bremerhaven: Deutsches Schiffahrtsmuseum.

Starkey, D.J. and Heidbrink, I. (eds) (2012) *A History of the North Atlantic Fisheries: Volume 2, From the 1850s to the early Twenty-First Century*, Bremerhaven: Deutsches Schiffahrtsmuseum.

Thór, J.Th. (2002) *Sjósókn og sjávarfang: Saga sjávarútvegs á Íslandi I. bindi. Árabáta-og skútuöld*, Akureyri: Vélaöld.

——(2003) *Uppgangsár og barningsskeið: Saga sjávarútvegs á Íslandi II. bindi 1902–1939*, Akureyri: Vélaöld.

Thór, J.Th. (2009) 'Icelandic fisheries, c.900–1900', in D.J. Starkey, J.Th. Thór and I. Heidbrink (eds) *A History of the North Atlantic Fisheries: Volume 1, From Early Times to the mid-Nineteenth Century*, Bremerhaven: Deutsches Schiffahrtsmuseum.

Thorleifsen, D. (2009) 'The role of fishing in colonial Greenland', in D.J. Starkey, J.Th. Thór and I. Heidbrink (eds) *A History of the North Atlantic Fisheries: Volume 1, From Early Times to the mid-Nineteenth Century*, Bremerhaven: Deutsches Schiffahrtsmuseum.

Turgeon, L. (1995) 'Fluctuations in cod and whale stocks in the North Atlantic during the eighteenth century', in D. Vickers (ed.) *Marine Resources and Human Societies in the North Atlantic since 1500*, St. John's, Newfoundland: Institute of Social and Economic Research.

——(2009) 'Codfish, consumption and colonization: the creation of the French Atlantic world during the sixteenth century', in C.A. Williams (ed.) *Bridging the Early Modern Atlantic World: People, Products, and Practices on the Move*, Farnham: Ashgate.

Van Bochove, C. (2009) 'The "golden mountain": an economic analysis of Holland's early modern herring fisheries', in L. Sicking and D. Abreu-Ferreira (eds) *Beyond the Catch: Fisheries of the North Atlantic, the North Sea and the Baltic, 900–1850*, Leiden: Brill.

Van Dam, P.J.E.M. (2009) 'Fish for feast and fast: fish consumption in the Netherlands in the late middle ages', in L. Sicking and D. Abreu-Ferreira (eds) *Beyond the Catch: Fisheries of the North Atlantic, the North Sea and the Baltic, 900–1850*, Leiden: Brill.

Vickers, D. (1994) *Farmers and Fishermen: Two Centuries of Work in Essex County, Massachusetts, 1630–1850*, Chapel Hill: University of North Carolina Press.

Woolgar, C.M. (2000) '"Take this penance now, and afterwards the fare will improve": seafood and late medieval diet', in D.J. Starkey, C. Reid and N.R. Ashcroft (eds) *England's Sea Fisheries: The Commercial Sea Fisheries of England and Wales since 1300*, London: Chatham.

Wubs-Mrozewicz, J. (2009) 'Fish, stock and barrel: changes in the stockfish trade in northern Europe, c.1360–1560', in L. Sicking and D. Abreu-Ferreira (eds) *Beyond the Catch: Fisheries of the North Atlantic, the North Sea and the Baltic, 900–1850*, Leiden: Brill.

PART II
THE MOVEMENT OF PEOPLES

CHAPTER FIVE

FACING EAST FROM THE SOUTH
Indigenous Americans in the
mostly Iberian Atlantic World

———·◆·———

Laura E. Matthew

Where do Indigenous peoples of the Americas fit within the Atlantic World paradigm? It cannot be imagined without them. Like their counterparts in the North Atlantic, Natives in the mostly Iberian South Atlantic were prominent allies in European military conquests and active participants in an extraordinary cultural and intellectual exchange. Their lands and labour were essential to the wealth of new empires. Their agriculture helped trigger a demographic boom in Europe. Like Africans and to a lesser extent Europeans, Native Americans experienced dramatic relocation and dislocation in the South Atlantic during the early modern period. 'Indians, far from being marginal to the Atlantic experience, were, in fact, as central as Africans,' writes Jace Weaver, arguing for a Red Atlantic to parallel Paul Gilroy's Black one. 'Native resources, ideas, and peoples themselves traveled the Atlantic with regularity and became among the most basic defining components of Atlantic cultural exchange.'[1]

Yet as Paul Cohen has pointed out, there are good reasons for historians of the Indigenous peoples of the Americas to hold the Atlantic World at bay.[2] The dizzying sense of movement that so often characterizes Atlantic studies stands in stark contrast to Indigenous America's powerful sense of historical permanence: the 'we people here' that the Nahuas of central Mexico used to describe themselves in their own language rather than adopt the Spanish misnomer *indios*.[3] Indigenous Americans were and are the only members of the Atlantic World rooted in the hemisphere 'since time immemorial', as they often claimed in Spain's colonial-era courts. In the face of warfare, epidemic disease, and colonization, some Natives reconstituted their communities in relation to known geographies. Others proclaimed their indigeneity despite significant migrations.[4] And while some Natives were coastal peoples, continents rather than oceans constitute the centre of Indigenous American history. Natives did not cross the sea to the same degree as Europeans and Africans during the early modern period, and for Indigenous history the Pacific represents the shoreline of major civilizations rather than an even more remote outpost of Europe or Africa. To fold Indigenous history into the Atlantic World therefore runs the risk of academic cannibalism. Too often, Native America serves merely as a tragic backdrop to the main stories of Atlantic history thus far: the global rise of Europe and the African slave trade.

My answer to this dilemma is not to provide an overview of Indigenous history under European colonialism, an approach that evades the question of 'where Indigenous peoples fit'. Nor do I wish here to catalogue the ways in which Native America inevitably participated in the rhythms of the Atlantic world, though this approach – exemplified most recently by Weaver – has its merits.[5] Instead, I will explore three key themes of Atlantic World history that have mostly been developed from a European or African perspective: imperial warfare, transatlantic migration, and imagining the Other. What happens when we interrogate these themes from the perspective of Native America, in this case from the Caribbean and northern Mesoamerica to Patagonia? Do the themes still make sense? Are the histories they tell still Atlantic?

BEYOND CONQUEST: IMPERIAL WARFARE

Atlantic history tends to distinguish between the mostly Spanish, sixteenth-century military conquests of Native America and the violence incited by Dutch, French, and English challenges to the Iberian empire in the seventeenth and eighteenth centuries. There are good reasons to do so; the mutual shock of initial contact combined with the fall of such large, hierarchical polities as the Mexica and Inca empires would not be repeated.[6] From an Indigenous historical perspective, however, early conquest wars and later imperial rivalries are not so easily separated. Imperial rivalries within and amongst the Mexica and Inca sowed as much destruction as the European invaders, and were replicated on a sometimes smaller scale in nearly all successive encounters with Europeans. The sixteenth century was not uniquely Spanish or even Iberian; French, Italians, English, Irish and Dutch entered the South Atlantic and engaged Native Americans almost immediately. Militarized incursions into un-subjugated Native territory continued into the mid-nineteenth century and beyond. And like their European counterparts, Native leaders consistently confronted the perils and possibilities of the Atlantic World by adopting new methods of warfare to their advantage and exploiting tensions among strangers, from the sixteenth century onwards.

It has long been recognized that internal and imperial rivalries played a major role in the downfall of both the Mexica and the Inca empires. From 1519 to 1521, the Spanish served as crucial allies in what was essentially an uprising of massive proportions against the Mexica centred at Tenochtitlan. Yucatecan Maya initially attacked the Spanish expedition led by Hernando Cortés in 1519. But as Cortés traveled up the Gulf Coast he encountered informants eager to stoke his interest in Tenochtitlan with tales of great riches and abusive leadership. The independent *altepetl* (city state) of Tlaxcala, implacable enemy of the Mexica, attacked the Spanish as they approached Tlaxcalteca territory. At the point of doing away with the intruders, the Tlaxcalteca then proposed an alliance against the Mexica. The partnership was sealed by a joint massacre against the ancient altepetl of Cholula, bringing the pacified pilgrimage site into the alliance as well. Accompanied by thousands of Tlaxcalteca and Cholulteca warriors, the Spanish were escorted inside Tenochtitlan and received as guests. For six months, the strangeness of the situation and Moctezuma's clear concern provided Tlaxcala and its partners a perfect opportunity to destabilize the imperial city before being forcibly chased out in June 1520. During the following year the insurgent allies rebuilt their forces, incorporating disaffected altepetl subject to the Mexica. They attacked Tenochtitlan again in June 1521, with a new partner:

– CHAPTER 5: *Facing East from the South* –

Ixtlilxochitl of Texcoco, a breakaway member of the Mexica's own Triple Alliance. Weakened by siege and smallpox, Tenochtitlan fell in August of that year. As William Prescott put it in his epic, nineteenth-century Anglo-American history of the event, 'the Indian empire was in a manner conquered by Indians'.[7]

The Spanish conquistadors, despite being the natural heroes of their own letters and chronicles, reported that tens of thousands of Nahuas and others fought alongside and vastly outnumbered them in Mesoamerica. But seeing the conquest of Tenochtitlan from a Native perspective means more than simply acknowledging the extent to which Natives participated in the event. Historians have recently emphasized the Mesoamerican flavour of Hernando Cortés's and other Spanish conquistadors' *entradas* into Tenochtitlan and later, to the edges of the former Mexica empire.[8] Spaniards relied on Mesoamerican messengers, military and political intelligence, and knowledge of the region for cues regarding future campaigns. They went where the Mexica had gone, towards regions of significant wealth or production on the suggestion of Mesoamerican leaders who also gathered troops, coordinated supplies along the invasion routes, communicated with resistant towns, and colonized recently pacified areas based on their own past experience and strategic aims. The Mexica were key players in these early efforts, supported by their vast military infrastructure. Michel Oudijk and Matthew

Figure 5.1 Tlaxcalteca and Spaniards fighting the Mexica Tenochca at Tenochtitlan
© British Library Board. All Rights Reserved/Bridgeman Images

Restall deem the spread of joint Mesoamerican-Spanish forces extending from Peru to New Mexico 'precedented expansion', as defeated yet still powerful polities shifted alliances and were recruited for new campaigns in ways that would have seemed utterly familiar to Mesoamericans.[9] While Spaniards brought valuable new technologies, an element of unpredictability, and in some cases a desperate viciousness, 'Spanish' campaigns against Mesoamerican polities in the sixteenth century followed recognizably Mesoamerican patterns and goals and were fought mostly by Mesoamericans themselves, sometimes entirely independent of any Spanish participation or even awareness.

The Inca empire, too, was famously brought down as much by intra-imperial and regional rivalries as by Spanish attack. The death around 1528 of the Inca Huayna Capac, head of the four-cornered empire Tahuantinsuyu – possibly of smallpox, which arrived in Peru before the Spanish did – set off a fratricidal war of succession into which the Spaniards were inserted. One son, Atahuallpa, seized control of his father's armies in the north. Another son, Huascar, seized the capital city of Cuzco in the south and led a campaign against Atahuallpa that resulted in Huascar's defeat. After the famous, violent encounter between Atahuallpa and the Spanish conquistador Pizarro in November 1532 that led to Atahuallpa's capture, Atahuallpa ordered Huascar's execution in Cuzco from his *own* captivity in Cajamarca. Another son of Huayna Capac, Manco Inca, allied with the Spanish to take over Cuzco after Atahuallpa's execution by Pizarro. Manco Inca abandoned Cuzco to the Spanish in 1536. His sons maintained independent Inca rule in Vilcabamba for almost forty years, until the defeat of Tupac Amaru in 1572.[10] Meanwhile, other Andeans allied with the Spanish against the Inca. The Cañari of modern-day Ecuador and the Chachapoya of the regions north of Cuzco had only been subjugated by the Inca a half century earlier, and sided with Huascar against Atahuallpa. They remained loyal to the Spanish when Manco Inca later broke his own Inca-Spanish alliance, with varied results across their dispersed colonial-era settlements.[11] And in Cuzco, the new Spanish ally Paullu Inca carefully built his own political dynasty based on his increasingly sophisticated reading of Spanish ideas of lordship. Andeans gathered intelligence about and manipulated the Spanish as much as the other way around, and maintained particular, even triumphant, memories of the period.[12]

The historiographical prominence of these imperial defeats is what sets the early Spanish conquests apart, not any particular patterns of alliance and warfare. At the same time that the Spanish were fighting wars of conquest in Mexico and Peru, both Spaniards and Portuguese were making steady but less spectacular inroads into independent regions such as the Muisca territory of what would become the Kingdom of New Granada (Colombia), the Brazilian coast, and the Rio de la Plata area, with varying mixtures of violence and diplomacy.[13] Challenges to Iberian expansion arose almost immediately from English and French pirates threatening both the Atlantic and Pacific Coasts throughout the sixteenth century, and from English, German and Dutch explorations and settlements along the Atlantic coast beginning as early as the 1530s. In every instance, Natives resisted and aided Europeans according to their own strategic aims. Northeastern Brazil and Guyana, where no Native empire existed, is a case in point. Speakers of Karib, Awarak, and Tupi languages alternately fought, fled and allied with the Portuguese, English, Irish, French, Dutch and Scots who established trading posts along the Atlantic coast. The intruding Europeans depended on Native allies to protect them against each other, against hostile Native groups,

– CHAPTER 5: *Facing East from the South* –

and eventually against African slave revolts on sugar plantations. One Native lineage in the Darién peninsula, the Carrisolis, positioned themselves as the main point of contact between Spanish administrators and potential Native allies based on their descent from a Spaniard captured and adopted as a boy.[14] These Native-European alliances, however, depended on remuneration and were easily dissolved. Where Europeans saw treachery and betrayal by subjected Indians, Natives saw opportunities for trade and the maintenance of their autonomy. At the same time, European incursions led to new intra-Native alliances, conflicts and migrations, leading to wholly new tribal configurations still surviving in the Amazon today. In northeastern South America, as Neil Whitehead put it, 'tribes made states and states made tribes.'[15]

In the eighteenth and first half of the nineteenth centuries, the history of European invasion of the Americas looks much the same. Natives continued to resist and aid Europeans, to maintain their own polities, to suffer and survive epidemic disease, and to play European rivals off each other well beyond the early modern period, in ways that strongly echo the early conquest and colonial experience. In northern New Spain, the Comanches, Apaches, Kiowas, Caddos, Pawnees, Tonkawas, and other Native groups so thoroughly controlled their own and surrounding territories between 1750 and 1850 that they rendered European and Euro-American claims to land and power practically meaningless. Native trade and diplomacy purposefully pitted the French, British, and Spanish against each other in the eighteenth century, and the United States against Mexico in the nineteenth. At their height of territorial and political dominion the Comanches were so unassailable that Pekka Hämäläinen has classified their network of family alliances an empire akin to that of the Mongols. Like the sixteenth-century Natives of northeastern Brazil, the Comanches allied with U.S. agents only as long as they received remuneration (sometimes as ransom for stolen captives), and viewed offers of money as gifts between friends rather than indications of submission.[16] Like the Spanish-descended Carrisolis of Darién in the seventeenth century, Quanah Parker, the son of an Anglo captive woman and a Comanche man, would be the primary point of contact between his tribe and the U.S. government in the 1860s and 1870s though with a decidedly less friendly beginning and less assimilationist attitude. At the other end of the Iberian empire the newly christened Mapuche – in reality, like the Comanche, a shifting mix of alliances and kinship groups – also maintained their independence and control of substantial territory well beyond the beginnings of Chilean and Argentinian statehood. Once again, some chose to ally with invading powers while others resisted.[17] As had been true for the 'Chichimeca' at the fringes of the Mexica empire and the resistant Inca of Vilcabamba in the sixteenth century, only with concerted, violent repression and the continued pressure of European and Euro-American colonization – not only Spanish, Anglo-American, Chilean, and Argentinian, but also German, British, French, and Italian – would the Comanches in the north and the Mapuches in the south finally be subjugated.

In Atlantic history, imperial warfare almost always refers to conflicts between Europeans. It is temporally situated in the seventeenth and eighteenth centuries, and geographically near the water (on the ocean, in the Caribbean, along coastlines) or in imperial borderlands (which as Claudio Saunt has pointed out were also Native homelands).[18] But from a South Atlantic Native perspective, the term 'imperial warfare' also brings to mind the sixteenth-century Mexica and Inca whose own militarism and rivalries are impossible to disentangle from their experience of

83

European conquest. It alludes to the shifting Native alliances that characterized not only these early conflicts but many hundreds of smaller or less famous military encounters throughout the early modern period and across the American continents. It does not preclude the epic battles for Comanchería and Patagonia in the nineteenth century, or the 'rebellions' of Tupac Amaru in Peru and the Caste War of Yucatan. What seems most pertinent in all these military encounters is their inherent sense of instability and insecurity, which quickly hardened into a 'colonial normal' characterized by unequal power relations and enforced by violence.[19] Bernard Bailyn's characterization of the early Atlantic World as imperiled by 'authorized brutality without restraint' can be extended far beyond the sixteenth century.[20]

INDIANS IN UNEXPECTED PLACES:
TRANSATLANTIC MIGRATION

Transatlantic migration from east to west – whether voluntary or forced, European or African – has been a foundational topic of Atlantic Worlds research. Intra- and intercontinental migrations of Indigenous peoples constitute a rich vein of research for the history of Native America. But what about Natives who traveled from west to east? It is an indication of how intermittently this question has been asked that a recent surge of interest in the topic has rested firmly on the foundations of mid-twentieth century scholarship.

The largest numbers of Natives traveling to Europe in the sixteenth century were slaves and servants, many of them children who came primarily from the Caribbean in the earliest years of colonization. Slaving was a natural extension of Christian expansion during medieval times and intensified after the fall of Constantinople in 1453 and the progression of the Portuguese into the Azores and Madeira Islands and northwest Africa. Christopher Columbus and his associates brought a dozen or so Native slaves from the Caribbean to be shown and sold in their first journey back to Europe, in 1493. By 1495 slaving had become a formal enterprise, and Columbus famously brought some 500 Native captives to Iberia in four ships that year. In a pattern that would be repeated, some died on the journey while others became so ill that they were left in Andalucía while the little more than the half remaining were sent to Barcelona to be presented to the queen. Isabel I was apparently disturbed by the sight of these survivors, and suspended any future slaving until the legal question of the Indians' status as vassals of the Crown could be resolved. Columbus and others meanwhile continued to bring hundreds of Native captives to Iberia, whom they sold primarily in the markets of Seville and Lisbon.[21]

In 1500, queen Isabel declared the liberty of any Natives enslaved in Spain without proper paperwork. Contradictory royal statements in subsequent years allowed for the enslavement of 'cannibals' and the voluntary passage of Natives to Spain with authorization – rules that were bent or broken to continue the trade. Isabel I's request in her will that her husband clarify the proper treatment of the Crown's newest vassals in Spanish territory was followed by a royal council regarding policies of 'just war'. The rate of Native slaves being imported into Europe slowed, but did not stop. Slavers continued to bring Native captives from Spanish America to Lisbon, then sold them as 'Brazilians' or *indios de Calicut* since it was legal to buy Natives enslaved by the Portuguese. Other Natives – both newcomers and those already enslaved in the Iberian peninsula – were classified as '*moros*', '*loros*', or '*berberiscos*' (Muslims from north and west Africa) or as '*moriscos*' (Muslims from the peninsula), all of whose enslavement was also legal. Natives from Portuguese Brazil were increasingly labeled 'black' to distinguish them from illegally captured *indios* of the Spanish realms, though all indications are that the numbers of Natives who were transported from Brazil in Iberia in the sixteenth century also remained low due to their vulnerability to Old World diseases. (Disease also threatened *Brasilianen* Natives who fought as allies of the Dutch in Africa in the mid-seventeenth century; a majority died, mostly of yellow fever rather than battle wounds).[22] Esteban Mira Caballos has quantified 2,442 Natives brought to Spain between 1493–1550, over 80 percent of these from Hispaniola before 1502 but with significant surges from New Spain and northern South America between 1513–17 and 1528–32. While surely lower than the true total, the decreasing numbers and lack of documentary evidence of Native slaves being brought into Iberia en masse after 1550 suggest a tapering off in the trade towards the second half of the sixteenth century, in part due to the ban on Native slavery within Spanish realms instituted by the New Laws of 1542.[23]

What was life like for these Native American slaves in Iberia? If they had not already been, they were branded on the face, usually with the date of sale and name of owner, a practice prohibited in Spain in 1532 but still practiced in the 1550s. As was typical of Iberian slavery, they served as household slaves who worked for the clergy, court, merchants and artisans, sometimes learning new crafts and practicing them independently. Some had come to Iberia as paid servants traveling with their masters, but found themselves treated or even sold as slaves in the peninsula. Many lived a peripatetic life, moving from household to household and city to city. Some became homeless and/or beggars, to be mentioned in court cases and concerned complaints issued by city administrators. Natives were baptized in Spanish churches, and when they married, tended to marry other Natives or perhaps Mestizos. In the second half of the sixteenth century some petitioned the Council of the Indies in Spain for their freedom on the basis of having been illegally enslaved, or sometimes simply out of a desire to return to the Americas. Those whose petitions were successful were supposed to have their passage paid by the Crown, but records indicate that many ended up stranded in the port city of Seville, legally free but unable to afford the trip home.[24]

Although their mortality rates from the crossing were often high, things were not necessarily as bleak for '*criados*' – both Natives and Mestizos – who were adopted by Iberian clergy, conquistadors and administrators eager to train collaborators for their Christianizing mission and to demonstrate the exotic wonders of the New World. Cristobal Colón brought Natives captured in Hispaniola to Spain to be trained as interpreters in his first return voyage in 1493; in 1515–16 the archbishop of Seville received another such group to be trained as translators at the city's monastery of San Leandro, where the few who survived were seen playing their famous ball game.[25] In multiple trips beginning in 1519 Hernando Cortés brought Native performers to impress the Hapsburg court, servants and noble sons whom he intended to distribute amongst Spanish monasteries.[26] Beyond the dangers of mortal illness, crossing the Atlantic could mean both risk and refuge for these 'go-betweens'.[27] Fr. Calixto de San José Tupak Inka, for instance, was an Inca descendant and Mestizo who served the Franciscan order as an adopted servant (*donado*) in Peru. After a Native uprising attacked the Franciscan missions, in 1742 Fr. Calixto became the order's ambassador to the Inca nobility. In 1748 he traveled illegally to Spain with a fellow Franciscan to warn the Crown of the nobility's unrest, chasing down the king's carriage on the road towards a hunting expedition.[28] Fr. Calixto does not seem to have suffered in Spain for his boldness, professing as a Franciscan lay brother in 1751 and being aided by the Franciscans in acquiring license and money to return to Peru in 1753. Promptly, however, the viceroy of Peru accused him of sedition, dwelling on his Indianness and the 'natural inconstancy of his kind'.[29] Fr. Calixto was arrested, sent in chains back to Spain, and died there comfortably but confined to a Franciscan convent in Granada.

Mestizo children of Spanish fathers and Indigenous mothers were particularly liable to be sent to Spain in the first generations of European settlement of the Americas. Young Martín Cortés, son of Hernando Cortés and his Nahua translator and partner Malintzin, was only six years old when he traveled with his father to visit the Hapsburg court in 1529. He remained in Spain to be part of Prince Philip's retinue while his father went back to Mexico, and did not return until 1562.[30] The transatlantic experience of Mestizo children like Martín Cortés depended to a great extent on their father's wealth, status and personal concern for their wellbeing. Most were sent to the households of their Spanish father's relatives to be raised, sometimes by an abandoned but legal wife. Most were generally well provisioned as a matter of paternal responsibility and even love. As Jane Mangan has pointed out, European-born fathers who sent their children back to their European families were in a profound way sending them 'home'. But although these children's transatlantic experiences were generally not as traumatic as those of Indigenous slaves, they could nevertheless be difficult. Crossing the Atlantic meant forcible separation not only from their Indigenous families and culture but more painfully, from their mother – whose loss is often perceptible in bequests left many years later to children still in Spain who had never been seen again.[31]

These children might or might not be welcomed in their new homes. They often assimilated into Spanish society, but not all found that process easy or entirely desirable, as exemplified by one of the most famous cases of Mestizo transatlantic crossings: that of Gómez Suárez de Figueroa, or el Inca Garcilaso de la Vega. Born in 1539 to Spanish captain Sebastián Garcilaso de la Vega and the Inca princess Chimpu Ocllo (Isabel Suárez), Suárez de Figueroa was raised in a bicultural, bilingual household until age 10 when his father contracted marriage with a young Spanish woman and removed him from his mother's care. Upon his father's death in 1559, Suárez de Figueroa traveled to Spain to continue his education as his father's will had requested and for which he received a substantial sum of money. He presented himself to the Spanish court seeking favours befitting the rank of both his mother and his father, and was granted the required permission to return to Peru when his petitions were rejected. Gómez Suárez de Figueroa, however, did not go home. Instead, he settled in Montilla, Córdoba, and changed his name to Garcilaso de la Vega. He would never leave Europe, but spent the rest of his life writing histories of the New World as 'el Inca'.[32] An invented coat-of-arms in the frontispiece of his most ambitious work, the *Commentarios reales* (1609), combines references to his own and his father's military service to the Spanish Crown and Christianity with symbols of Inca rulership and dualistic philosophy.[33] Writing in Spain to a Spanish audience and largely as a Spaniard, Garcilaso nevertheless claimed the authority to write true history – and to point out the errors of such famous Spanish chroniclers as Francisco López de Gómara – based not only on extensive research but also on his childhood experience in Peru and perhaps most importantly, his Native heritage.[34]

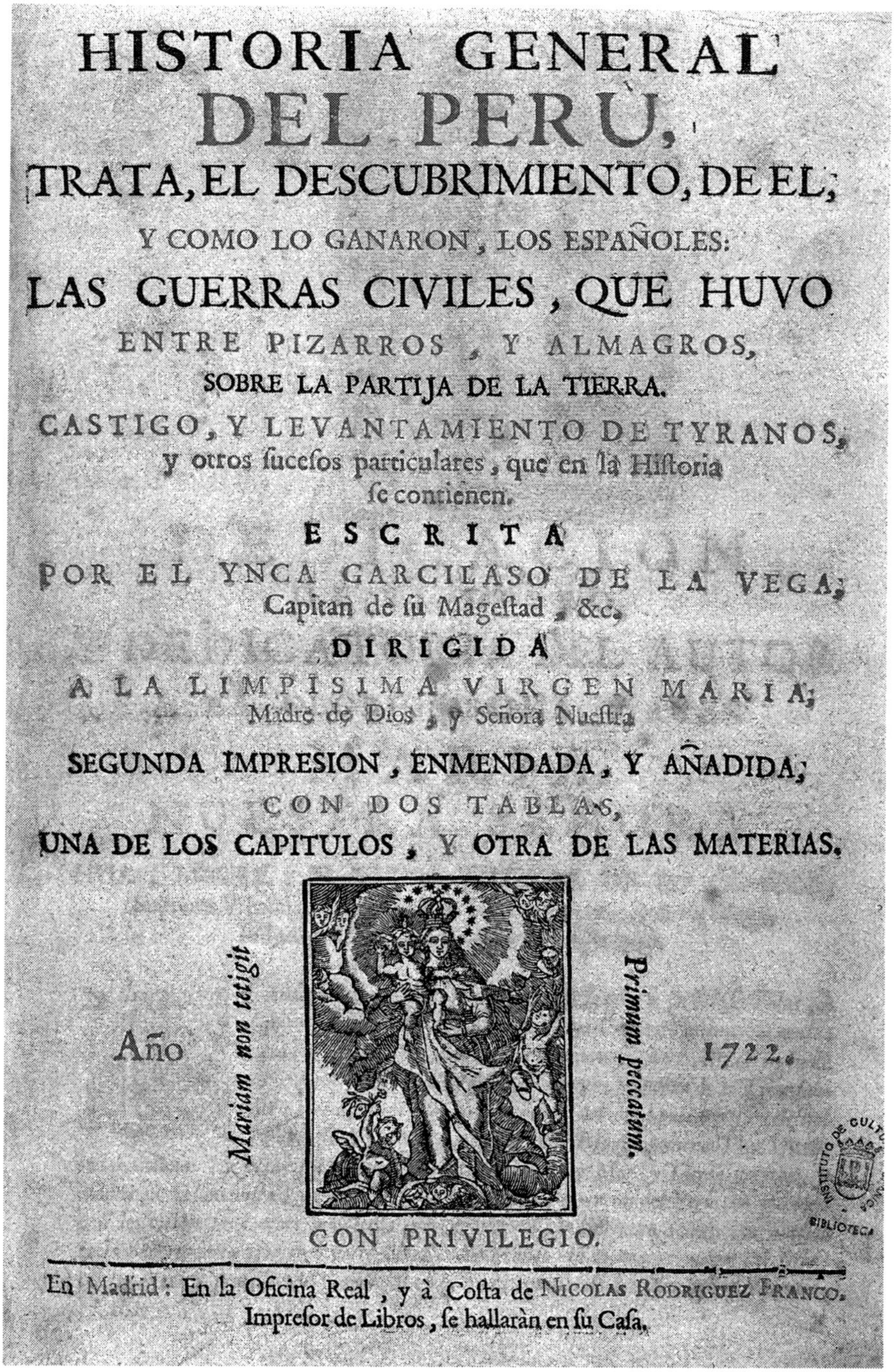

– CHAPTER 5: *Facing East from the South* –

HISTORIA GENERAL
DEL PERU,
TRATA, EL DESCUBRIMIENTO, DE EL;
Y COMO LO GANARON, LOS ESPAÑOLES:
LAS GUERRAS CIVILES, QUE HUVO
ENTRE PIZARROS, Y ALMAGROS,
SOBRE LA PARTIJA DE LA TIERRA.
CASTIGO, Y LEVANTAMIENTO DE TYRANOS,
y otros sucesos particulares, que en la Historia
se contienen.
ESCRITA
POR EL YNCA GARCILASO DE LA VEGA,
Capitan de su Magestad, &c.
DIRIGIDA
A LA LIMPISIMA VIRGEN MARIA,
Madre de Dios, y Señora Nuestra,

SEGUNDA IMPRESION, ENMENDADA, Y AÑADIDA;
CON DOS TABLAS,
UNA DE LOS CAPITULOS, Y OTRA DE LAS MATERIAS.

Mariam non tetigit.   *Primum peccatum.*

Año   1722.

CON PRIVILEGIO.

En Madrid: En la Oficina Real, y à Costa de NICOLAS RODRIGUEZ FRANCO,
Impresor de Libros, se hallaran en su Casa.

Figure 5.2 Frontispiece of a 1722 reprint of the second part of
el Inca Garcilaso de la Vega's *Commentarios reales*, originally published in 1617
© Iberfoto/Mary Evans Picture Library

Finally, Indigenous nobles from New Spain and Peru traveled to Iberia to petition the Spanish crown for individual or community privileges throughout the colonial period. Despite the Crown's official sanction against such Native transatlantic crossings, these Indigenous nobles traveled in style, were received with honour, and usually enjoyed the financial support of the Spanish Crown during their stay. The firstborn son of Moctezuma, don Martín Cortés Moctezuma Nezahualtecolotzin, arrived in Spain to request a coat of arms and restitution of lands in 1524, only three years after Tenochtitlan's defeat. In 1527, he returned to Spain accompanied by no less than forty nobles from Tenochtitlan, Texcoco, and Tlacopan (the old Triple Alliance), as well as Tlaxcala (the leaders of the insurgency against that alliance), Culhuacan, Chalco-Tlamanalco, Tlatelolco and Cempoala – all presumably seeking privileges and recognition. By 1532 don Martín had personally petitioned the king three times, had been the guest of the Dominicans at their Toledan convent of Santo Domingo de Talavera de la Reina and the Franciscans at their convent in Madrid, and had married a Spanish noblewoman who returned to Mexico with him.[35] The Tlaxcalteca nobility traveled to Spain in 1528–29 with their own agenda: to seek collective recognition as a province and city with the same legal status as any city in Spain, and thus protection from being given in *encomienda*.[36] Mesoamerican nobility, both Indigenous and Mestizo, would continue to petition the Crown directly throughout the sixteenth century and beyond. Indeed, some of the most famous images of the conquest period from a Native perspective were finished during one of these trips. Diego Muñoz Camargo of Tlaxcala, Mexico, was a Mestizo nobleman raised in a Spanish household in Mexico, but who had spent much of his adult life writing a laudatory history of Tlaxcala in prose and painting on behalf of that city's petitions for royal recognition. In 1583, Muñoz Camargo traveled with the Tlaxcalteca lord don Antonio de Guevara to Spain to deliver his work to the king, and completed one early version, now known as the *Relación geográfica* or *Descripción de la ciudad y provincia de Tlaxcala*, in Madrid before returning to Mexico.[37]

Andean noblemen and women also crossed the Atlantic. The case of doña Beatriz Clara Coya of Lima reminds us that some Indigenous women moved to Spain with their Spanish husbands; doña Beatriz received special permission to travel in exchange for a payment of 1000 pesos and the assurance that she was not being forced to leave her homeland.[38] Caciques and other descendants of Andean nobility often traveled to Spain illegally, and perhaps more persistently than Mesoamerican elites throughout the colonial period because the Inca policy of absorbing local elites produced a large number of Inca descendants. These Native supplicants petitioning on their own or their community's behalf were not looked upon favourably by the Council of the Indies, which encouraged the Crown to prohibit them for the 'inconveniences' they caused: risk of death for the petitioners, but also the cost and bother of supporting them during their stay in the peninsula for periods that in some cases lasted more than a decade, and the danger that they would remain in Spain indefinitely as 'vagabonds' or as potential subversives interested in restoring Inca power. José Carlos de la Puente Luna argues that Indigenous nobles from Peru learned quickly to manipulate both the Crown's desire to protect its 'poor and miserable' Native vassals and the Council's concerns over their presence in the peninsula. They were practically bribed to return home by grants of titles and generous funds tied to their departure.[39]

African and European transatlantic crossings are usually treated separately in the historiography of the Atlantic World, yet both help illuminate the Native experience.

Indigenous slaves who were captured, chained and transported in the holds of ships to be branded and sold in Portuguese and Spanish markets obviously had much in common with their African counterparts forcibly sent to the Americas. Their fate depended to a great extent on the qualities of the owners they acquired. They were unlikely to be united with family and neighbors on the other side of the ocean. Being relatively few in number, Indigenous slaves in Iberia also lacked the opportunities Africans had to build new diasporic communities or to maintain their traditions except, perhaps, in port cities like Seville.[40] But more so than their African counterparts, enslaved Natives could appeal to the Crown as vassals and victims with a reasonable expectation of positive results.

The experiences of free Natives who crossed the Atlantic, by contrast, are more comparable to those of Europeans. Their fortunes would to a large degree be based on patronage, class and connections. Middling sorts had the possibility to make a new life across the ocean and to gradually assimilate into their new milieu. At the level of the nobility and upper classes, however, the subjugation, segregation and even fear of Indigenous culture are apparent. Though they might stay in Iberia for a number of years, most Indigenous nobility returned to America and to their own communities, forming a parallel elite subordinate to Euroamerican *criollos*. Wealthy Mestizos and descendants of Indigenous nobility who assimilated into the Spanish ruling classes, meanwhile, might retain their social position and carefully celebrate the noble parts of their Indigenous heritage.[41] But on either side of the Atlantic, the elite to which they belonged – whether peninsular or *criollo* – was fundamentally European in character.

A STRANGE LIKENESS:
NATIVE IMAGINARIES OF THE EUROPEAN 'OTHER'

A great deal of scholarship has considered how early modern Europeans intellectually assimilated the Americas: from Edmundo O'Gorman's *The Invention of America* in 1961 and J.H. Elliott's *The Old World and the New* in 1970, to Anthony Pagden's *European Encounters with the New World* in 1993 and Karen Ordal Kupperman's *America in European Consciousness* in 1995, to Jorge Cañizares Esguerra's *How to Write the History of the New World* in 2001. Most recently, interest in this question has been keen within the history of science.[42] The Spanish, particularly those involved with Christian evangelization, were enthusiastic students of Indigenous history, language and customs. Other Europeans exhibited considerably less interest in Native intellectual or historical traditions until later in the early modern period. Indigenous peoples, on the other hand, had no choice but to rapidly size up their invaders – but their assessments are more elusive and require a reconsideration of the traditional sources of intellectual history.

The most direct and earliest representations of Europeans in the South Atlantic come from Native painters and scribes who were trained to write in Roman script by Catholic friars. In New Spain, the monumental *Florentine Codex* (1547–79) co-authored by Franciscan Fr. Bernardino de Sahagún and a team of mostly unnamed Natives describes central Mexican history and culture in both Nahuatl and Spanish, with illustrations. The Mexica Tlatelolca who were Sahagún's main partners in the creation of the Codex were ethnically related to the Mexica Tenochca of Tenochtitlan.

In Book Twelve describing the Spaniards' arrival and the battle for the city, the Tlatelolca scribes tend to blame the Tenochca for the empire's downfall. The challenges of reading for a Native perspective via colonial-era texts are exceptionally apparent here. Despite the unusual format of Nahuatl and Spanish versions side-by-side and the fact that the two versions differ in significant ways, it is impossible to untangle the mutual influences of the Codex's European and Native authors. James Lockhart wonders whether the anti-Tenochca bias so apparent in Book Twelve of the *Florentine Codex* may have actually been mitigated by Sahagún; likewise, the use of the loan word '*diablo*' (devil) to describe a preconquest indigenous deity would, Lockhart suggests, have been an entirely natural usage to these Christian-educated Nahua scribes.[43] Nevertheless, the *Florentine Codex* provides a distinctively Indigenous view of the conquest of Tenochtitlan. The Spaniards are impressive, at times ruthless, and particularly greedy when it comes to gold. The Tenochca are weak and pitiable; the Tlatelolca are brave and constant; the Tlaxcalteca are conniving and the Xochimilca are treacherous. In a story within the story the Spaniards are described to Moctezuma, who has not yet seen them:

> Their war gear was all iron. They clothed their bodies with iron, they put iron on their heads, their swords were iron, their bows were iron, and their shields and lances were iron...and they wrapped their bodies all over; only their faces could be seen, very white. Their faces were the color of limestone and their hair yellow-reddish, though some had black hair...and their dogs were huge creatures, with their ears folded over and their jowls dragging. They had burning eyes like coals, yellow and fiery. They had thin, gaunt flanks with the rib lines showing; they were very tall. They did not keep quiet, they went about panting, with their tongues hanging down. They had spots like a jaguar's...

Of these terrible dogs the parallel Spanish text merely states: 'They also told him [Moctezuma]...of the dogs they brought along and how they were, and of the ferocity they showed and what color they were.'[44]

The *Florentine Codex* seems to confirm the popular idea that Moctezuma and other Natives initially took the Spanish to be gods. Much ink has been spilled on this theme, mostly to discredit it as a Spanish fantasy, mourn it as a retrospective rationalization of the defeated, or ridicule it as a Eurocentric misunderstanding of what the Nahuatl term for 'god' signified.[45] A deeper consideration of Native epistemologies is needed to get much beyond these conclusions, much as literary scholar Gonzalo Lamana has attempted to do for Peru. According to the 1557 account of Juan de Betanzos, a Spaniard who married an Inca noblewoman and gathered testimony from her relatives, the Spaniards were quickly labeled 'gods' with certain characteristics that could be analyzed via Andean schemas. Messengers reported to Atahualpa that the strangers from the sea did not eat raw meat (i.e. human flesh), and thus had not arrived to conquer. They seemed to consume gold and silver. They looked strange, and their clothes did not indicate any internal hierarchy. They could speed across land (on horses), but could not make water move or do anything else supernatural. By the end of this inquiry, Lamana argues, Atahualpa had discerned that the Spanish were not gods but was deeply curious and worried about them. The massacre that followed shortly after his first meeting with Pizarro's representatives resulted not from Atahualpa's imagining the Spanish were divine, but from the dangerous situation created by both sides trying to size each other up.[46]

In sixteenth-century Mesoamerican painted manuscripts postdating the fall of Tenochtitlan, Spaniards are commonly shown seated in European style chairs or atop horses with beards, swords, and distinct types of clothing (including hats and shoes), as well as their own banners and armor.[47] In the *Lienzo de Quauhquechollan*, a painted depiction of the conquest of Guatemala created by Native allies from that altepetl around 1540, a single African – surely undercounting the number of Africans that would have accompanied the Spanish – is clearly demarcated with unique, rustic costume and barefoot, but with a long Spanish spear. The Maya are also portrayed as barefoot and rustic, a typical convention of barbarism justifying conquest in Mesoamerican pictorial writing. The Quauhquecholteca retain their own traditional warrior costumes of jaguar pelts and eagle feathers, but carry Spanish swords and are painted with the same pale skin tone as the Spanish, which Florine Asselbergs interprets as a visual assertion of their equivalence as conquistadors. The Spanish are shown with their conventional beards, hats, seats and horses, with one important exception: a single Spaniard traveling at the head of the departing troops dressed in full Quauhquecholteca warrior regalia.[48] Clothing here is not merely communicative but potentially transformative, and could work both ways. When Hernando Cortés executed the Mexica king Cuauhtemoc and his fellow ruler of Tlacopan during a journey through Yucatan in 1526, writes the Nahua historian Chimalpahin, he spared the life of a third lord and named him Cuauhtemoc's successor. The surviving lord was prepared for his return journey home with a gift that under the circumstances must have been fraught with meaning: 'their [i.e., the Spaniards' type of] clothing and a sword, a dagger, and a white horse.'[49]

As the colonial period progressed, Mesoamericans began to depict themselves in Spanish-style dress and with beards. This stylistic shift often marked the line between ancient and more recent history. In the 1691 *Tira de Santa Catarina Ixtepeji*, which traces a Zapotec elite lineage from the fourteenth through the seventeenth century, even the ancients have beards. A shift in costume occurs, however, with the Zapotec lord Coqui Lay who allied with the Spanish in the sixteenth century, shown brandishing a sword and in European-looking dress next to a Spanish conquistador on a horse. Coqui Lay's descendants are thereafter also dressed in European style. In these later paintings the claim of being 'we people here' from 'time immemorial' was important, but so was the change in rulership that came with Europeans and Christianity. Affiliation with the Spanish world – in this case, visually signaled through dress, swords and the claim of being Indian conquistadors – asserted both local authority and obedience to the Spanish Crown.[50] Conversely, Inca-descended lords who in everyday life likely pronounced their authority in part by wearing European dress processed in the festival of Corpus Christi in Cuzco in the late seventeenth century in richly ornamented Inca costumes, presenting themselves as living mediators between the ancient past and the colonial present.[51] A century and a half after contact with Europeans and Africans, these Native elites depicted and reimagined *themselves* according to distinctly colonial codes.

A more satirical tone is struck in the famous drawings of Guaman Poma de Ayala, the Quechua-speaking Andean who wrote the 1,189-page *Nueva corónica y buen gobierno* styled as a report and letter to the Spanish king. Like el Inca Garcilaso de la

Vega, Guaman Poma wrote his history of the Spanish invasion and conquest of Peru from a self-consciously Native perspective. In 398 illustrations that accompany the *Nueva corónica*, Spaniards and Africans are judged by the care or cruelty they show the Native population and their own good or bad habits, while those who have sex outside their 'pure' group and the products of these relationships, Mestizos and Mulatos, are ruthlessly criticized.[52] Like the *Florentine Codex*, the *Nueva corónica* offers a complex portrait of the Spanish. One idealized Spanish couple 'show charity, and rule with love the Indians of this kingdom' while another are 'great gluttons'. Priests are shown lovingly aiding Natives with their petitions, or fornicating with Indigenous women and beating their charges with sticks. Africans are depicted mostly sympathetically: as servants who must deliver punishment to Natives, who are also punished themselves, and who (like good Andeans) can be the most devout converts to Christianity. Again, dress marks identity. Africans, Spaniards, Mestizos and Mulatos dress mostly the same. Andeans wear their own distinctive garb, although some Andean elites are shown adopting elements of Spanish dress such as their hats.[53] For Guaman Poma, clothing signaled Native identity and served as a form of protection against sexual and cultural contamination: 'Spaniards, mestizos and mestizas and black women, mulatos, and mulatas, should not wear the clothes of Indians nor should Indians wear the clothes of Spaniards. All of this is a great offense to God.'[54] This is not so much imagining a faraway Other as creating social boundaries in a very crowded, chaotic social reality.

Indeed, a great deal of colonial Latin American history – as separate from Atlantic Worlds history – considers how Indigenous peoples fit European and African epistemologies into their own understandings of a world that had dramatically, irrevocably changed, often in very immediate ways. Some scholars focus on religious, medical or cosmological questions via language, art and ritual – categories, it should be pointed out, whose definitions cannot be assumed.[55] Some have tracked changes and continuities in Indigenous worldviews via philological analysis of secular historical or 'mundane' texts.[56] Some have sought out entirely different hermeneutics, for instance Carolyn Dean's reading of Inca stonework or Frank Salomon's historic-anthropological readings of the Andean khipu.[57] The question of power is inescapable, particularly when it comes to the Christian intellectual frameworks that underpinned Iberian colonialism. Mesoamerican painting could preserve and rework ancient histories, but only very carefully could it reference fundamentally Native understandings of sacrifice and renewal. Guaman Poma wrote in defense of Andeans, but using the tools of the colonizer and as a devoted Christian whose apparently sincere piety allowed him his voice. The very techniques of preserving and creating knowledge had been forcibly altered, and later generations of Indigenous intellectuals would be products of this hybridity. Under the weight of all this, the Atlantic Worlds category of 'imagining the Other' collapses.

CONCLUSION

Where does this exercise leave us? Of the three themes I have chosen to explore, one – imperial warfare – comes off as unhelpfully Eurocentric. Another – imagining the Other – seems both impossibly large given the profound impact of colonization on the Indigenous world (intellectually, materially, spiritually, artistically, linguistically, etc.), and dangerously colonial itself in its attempt to create some equivalency between experiences fundamentally marked by unequal power relations. The theme of transatlantic migration, however, challenges the 'we people here' of Indigenous American history in useful ways. It reminds us of the early and brief but important Native slave trade. It encourages us to look for Natives not only in transatlantic crossings but also up and down both the American coasts, for instance survivors of King Philip's War sent to the Caribbean, Nicaraguan slaves and Nahua warriors invading Peru, or Native sailors.[58] And it raises important questions about the cultural acceptance, rejection and assimilation of Indigenous people and Indigenous history in Europe versus the Americas, in comparison with the experience of other groups in the Atlantic World such as Jews, North Africans and Asians that do not quite fit into the European–African–Indigenous trichotomy.[59]

Perceptive readers will have noticed that throughout this essay I have tipped my hat towards the Indigenous history of the North Atlantic.[60] This comparative potential is perhaps the most important reason for Indigenous American history not to bypass the Atlantic World completely. Atlantic history's delight in spaces and situations 'shot through with a multiplicity of entangled actors and agendas'[61] may run counter to the agenda of much Indigenous history, which seeks to reclaim and prioritize Indigenous narratives for their own sake.[62] Some of the questions asked of the Atlantic World simply make no sense in the context of Indigenous history. But in its best manifestations – crossing national and linguistic boundaries, tracing overlapping epistemologies, emphasizing the global chains into which the individual, the familial, the local, and the regional were inserted during the early modern period – Atlantic history encourages us to see connections between the South and North that constitute an increasingly important part of Indigenous activism and scholarly research in the Americas. A great deal more could be gained, for instance, by comparing and supporting research on the relationships between the two largest populations facing east from the Americas in the early modern Atlantic: transplanted Africans and Natives.[63] Indigenous American history, for its part, has much to offer Atlantic World studies in its sophisticated analyses of power, loss, transculturation and survival. Neither field should be imagined completely without the other.

NOTES

1 Weaver 2011: 422.
2 Cohen 2008.
3 Lockhart 1992: 115–17.
4 Farriss 1984: 67–78; Matthew 2012a; Warren 2014.
5 Weaver 2014.
6 Lee 2011: 3–8.
7 Prescott and Lockhart 2001: 818.
8 Hassig 1994 and Lockhart 1993 were fundamental to this reorientation. See also Restall 2003; Asselbergs 2008 [2004]; Townsend 2006; Matthew and Oudijk 2007; Oudijk and Restall 2008; Altman 2010; Matthew 2012a; Levin Rojo 2014.
9 Oudijk and Restall 2007: 42–54.
10 Yupangui, ed. Julien 2006: viii–ix.
11 Oberem 1974; Salomon 1987.

12 Dean 1999; 185–99; Lamana 2008: 159–81.
13 Francis 2007; Thornton 2012: 175–81.
14 Whitehead 1990; Whitehead 1992; Gallup-Díaz 2001; Kars 2011.
15 Whitehead 1992.
16 Hämäläinen 2008: 323–25; Barr 2007.
17 Zavala Cepeda 2008.
18 Saunt 2006b.
19 Lamana 2008: 147–57
20 Bailyn 2005: 62–64; see also Blackhawk 2006.
21 Mira Caballos 2000: 46–48; Pagden 1982: 31; Weaver 2014: 38–50.
22 Van Deusen 2012; Metcalf 2005: 174; Meuwese 2012: 155.
23 Mira Caballos 2000: 107–13.
24 Ibid.: 82–84, 94–105.
25 Ibid.: 86–90.
26 Cline 1969: 70–90.
27 Metcalf 2005; Yannakakis 2008.
28 Loayza 1948: 7–94.
29 Ibid.: 92.
30 Townsend 2006: 188–204.
31 Mangan 2013: 277, 284–86, 291.
32 Chang-Rodríguez 2006: 15–38.
33 López-Baralt 2008.
34 One of Garcilaso's main sources was the *Historia occidentalis* of the Jesuit Blas Valera, who like Garcilaso was a Mestizo of Spanish-Inca origin and author of an extensive history of the Inca rooted in his Native heritage. Like Fr. Calixto, Valera would end his life exiled in Spain – although in his case, the same religious order that had adopted him was responsible for his denunciation and imprisonment.
35 Castañeda de la Paz 2013: 216–27.
36 Baber 2009: 36–37.
37 Muñoz Camargo and Acuña 2000.
38 De la Puente Luna 2012: 29n22.
39 De la Puente Luna 2012: esp. 26n19, 28, 30. Fear of subversion was also expressed towards Mestizos; see Burns 2007: 197–99.
40 On African diasporas, see O'Toole 2007; Sweet 2003. On European migrants to America, see Lockhart 1994; Altman 2000; Herrera 2003.
41 Chipman 2005.
42 For example Wey Gómez 2008; Cañizares Esguerra 2006; Bleichmar 2012.
43 Lockhart 1993: 31, 186–87.
44 Ibid.: 80–81.
45 Ibid.: 14–21; Restall 2003: 110–18; Townsend 2003; Gruzinski 1992: 41–53.
46 Lamana 2008: 31–53
47 Boone 2000: 47–48.
48 Asselbergs 2008.
49 Chimalpahin et al. 1997: 169. On the potential transformations induced by dress, see Carrasco 1999: 115–63; Olivier and Sule 2004: 144–45.
50 Boone 2000: 127; Florescano 2002; Cuadriello 2004; Matthew 2012b.
51 Dean 1999: 122–59.
52 Adorno 2000.
53 Det Konelige Bibliotek, The Guaman Poma Website 2006: images 220, 217, 235, 202, 276, 275, 200.
54 Ibid.: folio 553.

– CHAPTER 5: Facing East from the South –

55 Alberro 1988; Harris 2000; Sell and Burkhart et al. 2004–9; Durston 2007; Wake 2010; Hanks 2010; Ramos 2010; Tavárez 2011; Solari 2013.
56 Lockhart 1993; Schroeder 1997; Terraciano 2001; Wood 2003; Haskett 2005; Osowski 2010; Townsend 2010; Pizzigoni 2012.
57 Dean 2010; Salomon 2004.
58 Weaver 2014: 431, 437.
59 Compare to Vaughn 2006.
60 Beyond specific references, the section titles come from Den Ouden 2005; Deloria 2004; Shoemaker 2006.
61 Cañizares Esguerra and Breen 2013: 602
62 Weaver et al., 2006.
63 Saunt 2006a; Klopotek 2011; Sweet 2003; Restall 2005, 2009.

REFERENCES

Adorno, R., 2000. *Guaman Poma: Writing and resistance in colonial Peru.* University of Texas Press, Austin.

Alberro, S., 1988. *Inquisición y sociedad en México, 1571–1700.* Fondo de Cultura Económica, México.

Altman, I., 2000. *Transatlantic ties in the Spanish empire: Brihuega, Spain & Puebla, Mexico, 1560–1620.* Stanford University Press, Stanford, Calif.

——2010. *The war for Mexico's west: Indians and Spaniards in New Galicia, 1524–1550.* University of New Mexico Press, Albuquerque.

Asselbergs, F.G.L., 2008 [2004]. *Conquered conquistadors: the Lienzo de Quauhquechollan: a Nahua vision of the conquest of Guatemala.* University Press of Colorado, Boulder, Colo.

Baber, R. J. 2009. 'Categories, Self-Representation and the Construction of Indios,' *Journal of Spanish Cultural Studies* 10:1, 27–41.

Bailyn, B., 2005. *Atlantic history: concept and contours.* Harvard University Press, Cambridge, Mass.

Barr, J., 2007. *Peace came in the form of a woman: Indians and Spaniards in the Texas borderlands.* University of North Carolina Press, Chapel Hill.

Blackhawk, N. 2006. *Violence Over the Land: Indians and Empires in the Early American West.* Harvard University Press, Cambridge, MA.

Bleichmar, D., 2012. *Visible empire: botanical expeditions and visual culture in the Hispanic Enlightenment.* The University of Chicago Press, Chicago; London.

Boone, E.H., 2000. *Stories in red and black: pictorial histories of the Aztecs and Mixtecs.* University of Texas Press, Austin.

Burns, K., 2007. 'Unfixing Race,' in *Rereading the black legend: the discourses of religious and racial difference in the Renaissance empires*, eds. Margaret R. Greer, Walter D. Mignolo, and Maureen Quilligan, University of Chicago Press, 188–202.

Cañizares-Esguerra, J., 2006. *Nature, empire, and nation: explorations of the history of science in the Iberian world.* Stanford University Press, Stanford, Calif.

Cañizares-Esguerra, J., Breen, B., 2013. 'Hybrid Atlantics: future directions for the history of the Atlantic World,' *History Compass* 11:8, 597–609.

Carrasco, D., 1999. *City of sacrifice: the Aztec empire and the role of violence in civilization.* Beacon Press, Boston.

Castañeda de la Paz, M. 2013. *Conflictos y alianzas en tiempos de cambio: Azcapotzalco, Tlacopan, Tenochtitlan y Tlatelolco (siglos XII-XVI).* Instituto de Investigaciones Antropológicas, UNAM, México.

Chang-Rodríguez, R., 2006. *Franqueando fronteras: Garcilaso de la Vega y La Florida del Inca.* Pontificia Universidad Católica del Perú, Fondo Editorial, Lima.

Chimalpahin Cuauhtlehuanitzin, D.F. de S.A.M., Anderson, A.J.O., Schroeder, S., Ruwet, W., 1997. *Codex Chimalpahin*. University of Oklahoma Press, Norman, Okla.

Chipman, D.E., 2005. *Moctezuma's children: Aztec royalty under Spanish rule, 1520-1700*. University of Texas Press, Austin.

Cline, H.F., 1969. 'Hernando Cortés and the Aztec Indians in Spain.' *The Quarterly Journal of the Library of Congress* 26, 70–90.

Cohen, Paul 2008. 'Was there an Amerindian Atlantic? Reflections on the limits of a historiographical concept.' *History of European Ideas* 34, 388–410.

Cuadriello, J., 2004. *Las glorias de la república de Tlaxcala: o la conciencia como imagen sublime*. Instituto de Investigaciones Estéticas, UNAM : Museo Nacional de Arte, INBA, México.

Dean, C., 1999. *Inka bodies and the body of Christ: Corpus Christi in colonial Cuzco, Peru*. Duke University Press, Durham, N.C.

——2010. *A culture of stone: Inka perspectives on rock*. Duke University Press, Durham, NC.

De la Puente Luna, J.C. 2012. 'A costa de Su Majestad: indios y dilemas indianos en la corte de los Habsburgo,' *Allpanchis* 39 (72), 11–60.

Deloria, P.J., 2004. *Indians in unexpected places*. University Press of Kansas, Lawrence, Kan.

Den Ouden, A.E., 2005. *Beyond conquest Native peoples and the struggle for history in New England*. University of Nebraska Press, Lincoln.

Det Konelige Bibliotek, 2006. The Guaman Poma Website, http://www.kb.dk/permalink/2006/poma/info/en/frontpage.htm (accessed March 14, 2014).

Deusen, N.E. van, 2012. 'Seeing Indios in Sixteenth-Century Castile.' *The William and Mary Quarterly* 69, 205–234.

Durston, A., 2007. *Pastoral Quechua: the history of Christian translation in colonial Peru, 1550–1650*. University of Notre Dame Press, Notre Dame, Ind.

Farriss, N.M., 1984. *Maya society under colonial rule: the collective enterprise of survival*. Princeton University Press, Princeton, N.J.

Florescano, E. 2002. 'El canon memorioso forjado por los títulos primordiales,' *Colonial Latin American Review* 11, 183–230.

Francis, J.M., 2007. *Invading Colombia: Spanish accounts of the Gonzalo Jiménez de Quesada expedition of conquest*. Pennsylvania State University Press, University Park, Pa.

Gallup-Díaz, I., 2001. *The door of the seas and key to the universe: Indian politics and imperial rivalry in the Darién, 1640–1750*. Columbia University Press, New York.

Gruzinski, S., 1992. *Painting the conquest: the Mexican Indians and the European Renaissance*. Unesco : Flammarion, Paris, France.

Hämäläinen, P., 2008. *The Comanche empire*. Yale University Press, New Haven.

Hanks, W.F., 2010. *Converting words: Maya in the age of the cross*. University of California Press, Berkeley.

Harris, M., 2000. *Aztecs, Moors, and Christians festivals of reconquest in Mexico and Spain*. University of Texas Press, Austin, TX.

Haskett, R.S., 2005. *Visions of paradise: primordial titles and Mesoamerican history in Cuernavaca*. University of Oklahoma Press, Norman.

Hassig, R., 1994. *Mexico and the Spanish conquest*. Longman, London; New York.

Herrera, R.A., 2003. *Natives, Europeans, and Africans in sixteenth-century Santiago de Guatemala*. University of Texas Press, Austin.

Kars, Marjoleine 2011. '"Cleansing the Land": Dutch Amerindian Cooperation in the Suppression of the 1763 Slave Rebellion in Dutch Guiana' in *Empires and Indigenes: Intercultural Alliance, Imperial Expansion and Warfare in the Early Modern World*, ed. Wayne Lee, New York University Press, New York, 251–276.

Klopotek, B., 2011. *Recognition odysseys: indigeneity, race, and federal tribal recognition policy in three Louisiana Indian communities*. Duke University Press, Durham.

– CHAPTER 5: *Facing East from the South* –

Lamana, G., 2008. *Domination without dominance: Inca-Spanish encounters in early colonial Peru*. Duke University Press, Durham.

Lee, W.E., 2011. *Empires and indigenes: intercultural alliance, imperial expansion, and warfare in the early modern world*. New York University Press, New York.

Levin Rojo, D., 2014. *Return to Aztlan: Indians, Spaniards, and the invention of Nuevo Mexico*. University of Oklahoma Press, Norman.

Loayza, F.A., 1948. *Fray Calixto Túpak Inka, documentos originales y, en su mayoría, totalmente desconocidos, auténticos, de este apóstol indio, valiente defensor de su raza, desde el año de 1746 a 1760. Las doce dudas, códice del año de 1570, de autor anónimo*. D. Miranda, Lima.

Lockhart, J., 1992. *The Nahuas after the conquest: a social and cultural history of the Indians of central Mexico, sixteenth through eighteenth centuries*. Stanford University Press, Stanford, Calif.

——1993. *We people here: Nahuatl accounts of the conquest of Mexico*. University of California Press, Berkeley.

——1994 (1968). *Spanish Peru, 1532–1560: a social history*. University of Wisconsin Press, Madison, Wis.

López-Baralt, M. 2008. 'Tinku, concordia y ayni: Tradición oral andina y neoplatonismo en dos obras del Inca Garcilaso' in *Nuevas lecturas de La Florida del Inca*, eds. Carmen de Mora y Antonio Garrido Aranda, Madrid, Iberoamericana, 31–54.

Mangan, J.E., 2013. 'Moving Mestizos in Sixteenth-Century Peru: Spanish Fathers, Indigenous Mothers, and the Children In Between.' *The William and Mary Quarterly* 70, 273–294.

Matthew, L.E., 2012a. *Memories of conquest: becoming Mexicano in colonial Guatemala*. University of North Carolina Press, Chapel Hill.

——2012b. 'Lost and found: Three hundred year old manuscript found in Milwaukee,' http://marquettehistorians.wordpress.com/2012/04/03/lost-and-found-three-hundred-year-old-mexican-document-found-in-milwaukee/#more-164 (accessed March 14, 2014).

Matthew, L.E., Oudijk, M.R., 2007. *Indian conquistadors: indigenous allies in the conquest of Mesoamerica*. University of Oklahoma Press, Norman.

Metcalf, A.C., 2005. *Go-betweens and the colonization of Brazil, 1500–1600*. University of Texas Press, Austin.

Meuwese, M., 2012. *Brothers in arms, partners in trade: Dutch-indigenous alliances in the Atlantic world, 1595–1674*. Brill, Leiden; Boston.

Mira Caballos, E., 2000. *Indios y mestizos americanos en la España del siglo XVI*. Iberoamericana; Vervuert, Madrid; Frankfurt am Main.

Muñoz Camargo, D., Acuña, R., 2000. *Descripción de la ciudad y provincia de Tlaxcala*. El Colegio de San Luis; Gobierno del Estado de Tlaxcala, San Luis Potosí [Tlaxcala de Xicohténctal].

Oberem, U. 1974. 'Los cañaris y la conquista española de la sierra ecuatoriana, otro capítulo de las relaciones interétnicas en el siglo xvi.' *Journal de la Société des Américanistes* 63 (1), 263–274.

O'Toole, R.S., 2007. 'From the Rivers of Guinea to the Valleys of Peru: Becoming a Bran Diaspora Within Spanish Slavery.' *Social Text* 25, 19–36.

Olivier, G., Sule, T., 2004. *Tezcatlipoca: burlas y matamorfosis de un dios azteca*. Fondo de Cultura Económica, México.

Osowski, E.W., 2010. *Indigenous miracles: Nahua authority in colonial Mexico*. University of Arizona Press, Tucson, Ariz.

Oudijk, M.R., Restall, M. 2007. 'Mesoamerican Conquistadors in the Sixteenth Century,' in *Indian Conquistadors: Indigenous Allies in the Conquest of Mesoamerica*, eds. Laura Matthew and Michel Oudijk, University of Oklahoma Press, Norman, 28–64.

——2008. *La conquista indígena de Mesoamérica: el caso de Don Gonzalo Mazatzin Moctezuma*. Universidad de las Américas Puebla: Secretaría de Cultura del Estado de Puebla: Instituto Nacional de Antropología e Historia, Puebla; México, D.F.

Pagden, A., 1982. *The fall of natural man: the American Indian and the origins of comparative ethnology.* Cambridge University Press, Cambridge [Cambridgeshire]; New York.

Pizzigoni, C., 2012. *The life within: local indigenous society in Mexico's Toluca Valley, 1650–1800.* Stanford University Press, Stanford, California.

Prescott, W.H., Lockhart, J., 2001. *History of the conquest of Mexico.* Modern Library, New York.

Ramos, G., 2010. *Death and conversion in the Andes: Lima and Cuzco, 1532–1670.* University of Notre Dame Press, Notre Dame, Ind.

Restall, M., 2003. *Seven myths of the Spanish conquest.* Oxford University Press, New York.

——2005. *Beyond Black and Red: African-native Relations in Colonial Latin America.* UNM Press.

——2009. *The Black Middle: Africans, Mayas, and Spaniards in Colonial Yucatan.* Stanford University Press.

Salomon, F., 1987. 'Ancestors, Grave Robbers, and the Possible Antecedents of Cañari "Incaism."' In *Natives and Neighbors in South America: Anthropological Essays,* ed. Harald O. Skar and Frank Salomon, Museum of World Culture, Göteborg, Sweden, 207–232.

——2004. *The cord keepers: khipus and cultural life in a Peruvian village.* Duke University Press, Durham.

Saunt, C., 2006a. *Black, white, and Indian: race and the unmaking of an American family.* Oxford University Press, New York.

——2006b. '"Our Indians": European Empires and the History of the Native American South,' in *The Atlantic in Global History, 1500–2000,* eds. Jorge Cañizares-Esguerra and Erik R. Seeman. Prentice Hall, New York, 61–76.

Schroeder, S., et al., 1997. *Codex Chimalpahin,* 2 vols. University of Oklahoma Press, Norman OK.

Sell, B.D., Burkhart, L, 2004–2009. *Nahuatl theater,* 4 vols. University of Oklahoma Press, Norman.

Shoemaker, N., 2006. *A Strange Likeness: becoming red and white in eighteenth-century North America.* Oxford University Press, Oxford; New York.

Solari, A., 2013. *Maya ideologies of the sacred: the transfiguration of space in colonial Yucatan.* University of Texas Press, Austin.

Sweet, J.H., 2003. *Recreating Africa: culture, kinship, and religion in the African-Portuguese world, 1441–1770.* University of North Carolina Press, Chapel Hill.

Tavárez, D., 2011. *The Invisible War: Indigenous Devotions, Discipline, and Dissent in Colonial Mexico.* Stanford University Press, Stanford, CA.

Terraciano, K., 2001. *The Mixtecs of colonial Oaxaca: Ñudzahui history, sixteenth through eighteenth centuries.* Stanford University Press, Stanford, Calif.

Thornton, J.K., 2012. *A cultural history of the Atlantic world, 1250–1820.*

Townsend, C. 2003. 'Burying the White Gods: New Perspectives on the Conquest of Mexico,' in *American Historical Review* 103:3, 659–687.

——2006. *Malintzin's choices: an Indian woman in the conquest of Mexico.* University of New Mexico Press, Albuquerque.

——2010. *Here in this year: seventeenth-century Nahuatl annals of the Tlaxcala-Puebla Valley.* Stanford University Press, Stanford, Calif.

Vaughan, A.T., 2006. *Transatlantic encounters: American Indians in Britain, 1500–1776.* Cambridge University Press, Cambridge; New York.

Wake, E., 2010. *Framing the sacred: the Indian churches of early colonial Mexico.* University of Oklahoma Press, Norman.

Warren, S., 2014. *The worlds the Shawnees made: migration and violence in early America.* University of North Carolina Press, Chapel Hill, N.C.

Weaver, J. 2011. 'The Red Atlantic: Transoceanic Cultural Exchanges,' *The American Indian Quarterly,* 35 (3), 418–463.

—2014. *The Red Atlantic: American indigenes and the making of the modern world, 1000–1927*. The University of North Carolina Press, Chapel Hill.

Weaver, J., Womack, C.S., Warrior, R.A., 2006. *American Indian literary nationalism*. University of New Mexico Press, Albuquerque.

Wey Gómez, N., 2008. *The tropics of empire: why Columbus sailed south to the Indies*. MIT Press, Cambridge, Mass.

Whitehead, Neil L. 1990. 'Carib Ethnic Soldiering in Venezuela, the Guianas, and the Antilles, 1492–1820.' *Ethnohistory*, 37 (4), 357–385.

—1992. 'Tribes Make States and States Make Tribes: Warfare and the Creation of Colonial Tribes and States in Northeastern South America,' in *War in the tribal zone: expanding states and indigenous warfare*, eds. R. Brian Ferguson and Neil Whitehead. School of American Research Press; University of Washington Press, Sante Fe, N.M.; Seattle, Wash, 127–150.

Wood, S.G., 2003. *Transcending conquest: Nahua views of Spanish colonial Mexico*. University of Oklahoma Press, Norman [Okla.].

Yannakakis, Y., 2008. *The art of being in-between: native intermediaries, Indian identity, and local rule in colonial Oaxaca*. Duke University Press, Durham.

Yupangui, D. de C., Julien, C.J., 2006. *History of how the Spaniards arrived in Peru*. Hackett Pub. Comp., Indianapolis.

Zavala, J.M., 2008. *Los mapuches del siglo XVIII: dinámica interétnica y estrategias de resistencia*. Editorial Universidad Bolivariana, Santiago, Chile.

CHAPTER SIX

SOUTHERN AFRICA
AND THE ATLANTIC WORLD

—·◆·—

Gerald Groenewald

Why is southern Africa so rarely covered in volumes on the Atlantic World? Although, in the wake of the Second World War, some pioneer historians and advocates of a unified analysis of the four continents bordering the Atlantic considered southern Africa to be part of this 'community',[1] this was not borne out in the subsequent developments of Atlantic history which has been little concerned with the deep southern part of the ocean. Thus, a major new synthesis such as Thomas Benjamin's *The Atlantic World* contains no discussion of Africa south of Angola and hardly mentions the Cape of Good Hope.[2] This state of affairs is partly related to the fact that early practitioners of Atlantic history viewed the ocean as 'a basin around which a new civilization slowly formed'.[3] But this basin was not completely bounded or closed-off: the original purpose for crossing the Atlantic was to connect Europe with the East Indies, and the passage around the Cape of Good Hope in the south Atlantic continued to provide this throughout the period covered by this volume, as is increasingly being acknowledged.[4] But perhaps the main reason for this state of affairs in the historiography of the Atlantic is the result of the isolation of South African historians until the 1980s and their own inward-looking habits and practices.[5] For a long time historians of the colonial Cape tended to look to the hinterland and the interior of Africa, forgetting that the inhabitants of the Cape during this period were mostly ocean-oriented. This is what will be described in this chapter, which also affords one the opportunity to rethink the traditionally conceived notion of the Atlantic World as being bounded and closed-off. Serving as it did as a pivot between two oceans; the existence of a colonial society at the Cape of Good Hope made possible the development of a globalised, unified oceanic world by the nineteenth century.

The colonial history of South Africa traditionally gets divided between the Dutch and British 'periods'.[6] From the establishment of a refreshment station in Table Bay in 1652 until the conquest, in the context of the Napoleonic wars, of the Cape of Good Hope by Britain in 1795, the west and south coasts of southern Africa were under the control of the Dutch East India Company (VOC). From that year, except for a brief interregnum during 1803–6 when the Cape reverted to control by the Dutch Batavian Republic, southern Africa remained part of the British Empire until the creation of the Union of South Africa in 1910. For most of the twentieth century this historical 'division' was replicated in the historiography of the country with the VOC period considered the almost exclusive terrain of Afrikaans-speaking historians (who viewed themselves as the descendants of the European settlers who came to southern Africa during the VOC period). These historians reinterpreted the early modern history of South Africa to serve the Afrikaner nationalist paradigm prevalent for most of the twentieth century. In practical terms this meant a concentration on settler disputes with the VOC (demonstrating a desire for freedom and sovereignty from oppressive 'foreign' powers) – thus revealing an innate nationalism on the part of Afrikaner forebears – and on the advancing frontier of the colony which was driven by the needs of pastoralists farmers. The latter (called *trekboers*) were seen as the forerunners of the nineteenth-century *Voortrekkers* who, in Afrikaner mythology, opened up the hinterland (the southern African Highveld) for the Afrikaners,[7] thus spreading them all across what would later become 'South Africa'.[8] It is noticeable how these Afrikaner historians of the seventeenth and eighteenth centuries virtually ignored the history of the (very cosmopolitan) early modern Cape Town, as well as the larger place of the Cape in the world of the VOC and in the context of European expansion and global interaction. These were not historians who would have encouraged their students to adopt a broader perspective on the history of colonial South Africa.[9]

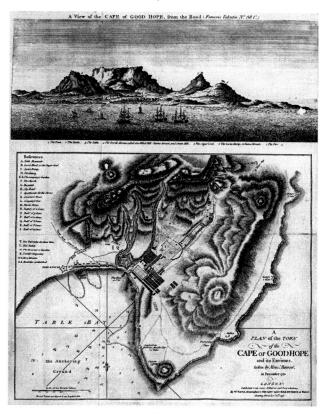

Figure 6.1 A view of the Cape of Good Hope and a plan of the town of the Cape of Good Hope and its environs, published 1795 (engraving) Private Collection/Bridgeman Images

This state of affairs changed radically during the late 1970s and 1980s when a group of mostly English-speaking younger scholars, influenced by the so-called revisionist or radical school of South African historiography, started to challenge perceived interpretations of southern Africa's colonial past and, particularly, to uncover new topics and subjects for research. For the first time South Africa's slave past was seriously studied, while hitherto ignored groups such as the Khoikhoi (the original inhabitants of the Cape) and freed slaves ('free blacks') received sustained attention. Important new interpretations of the colonial Cape's economy, its racial structure and the role of the frontier were also developed. In addition to a number of important monographs, the major achievement of this era was the edited volume, *The Shaping of South African Society*, which appeared in 1979 and in a much revised and expanded version in 1989, and which played a major role in providing an impetus for the study of colonial southern Africa.[10] Much of this work was heavily influenced – in topics, approaches and methodologies – by the new histories of colonial British North America appearing during this time. This was partly a consequence of the Anglophone background of these new practitioners,[11] but was primarily due to the parallels between colonial southern Africa and the United States: both were settler colonies[12] deeply marked (and scarred) by their experiences of slavery, the impact of which could still be felt in the twentieth century. Thus, not only were the new monographs on Cape slavery heavily influenced by North American examples,[13] but certain aspects such as the influence of the frontier and the rise of white supremacy were being actively compared.[14]

Although much of the impetus for this new work came from North American historiography, all of this new work remained firmly rooted in a land-based analysis with little or no cognisance of the Cape's broader oceanic contexts (excluding, of course, work on the slave trade). In addition, this work continued the old Afrikaner concentration on the immediate hinterland of Cape Town, virtually ignoring the centrality of the port city. With the advent of a democratic South Africa, it seems as if the previous obsession with the history of the Cape's slave and Khoikhoi populations began to work itself out. Alongside the New South Africa's desire to create a new society less concerned with issues of race, some of the pioneers of Cape historiography, along with a younger generation of scholars, started to investigate new topics of the Cape's colonial past. As was to be expected, much of this new work took its inspiration from the New Cultural History and concerned itself with issues relating to identity, individuality and personal relationships. However, a significant deviation from previous studies of the colonial era was a new interest in the history of Cape Town as an urban, cosmopolitan space in the context of a transoceanic world. Historians of the Dutch period finally started to consider the place of the Cape of Good Hope in the wider world of the VOC, while those of the British period considered the role and place of the Cape in the new transnational history of the British Empire. At last Cape historians began to break their isolation and to interact actively with the work of scholars outside of the Anglophone world.[15] Although this work has recently been criticised for going too far in its neglect of class and race, and for being too parochial and microhistorical in some instances, it has nevertheless paved the way to start thinking about the Cape in a more global context since the historiography of colonial southern Africa has now reached a complexity and depth of understanding which make fruitful considerations of broader contexts possible.[16]

* * *

Latter-day tourists to Cape Town are often sold the idea that what they are looking down upon at Cape Point – the southernmost tip of the Cape peninsula – is the 'meeting of two oceans'. This is of course technically a lie: Cape Town firmly falls within the Atlantic Ocean since the southernmost point of the African continent is at Cape Agulhas some 100 kilometres to the east.[17] It is here, as the local tourist board valiantly tries to convince visitors, that the two oceans actually meet rather unspectacularly. But in terms of human geography, and certainly historically, Cape Town can certainly claim to being at the crossroads of two oceanic worlds, of serving as a pivot which connects the Indian and the Atlantic oceans. Thus already by the eighteenth century the Cape of Good Hope had earned the nickname of 'the tavern of two seas'.[18] How did this come about?

'Atlantic history is the story of a world in motion,' Bernard Bailyn recently remarked.[19] Thus too the history of colonial southern Africa, which is unthinkable without ocean-crossing ships. Ships made the exploration of the Atlantic Ocean possible, and it was because of the inherent shortcomings of early modern ships in overcoming the tyranny of time and distance that the Cape of Good Hope became part of this world. From the start of the Portuguese discovery of a route to the East via the Cape of Good Hope in the late fifteenth century, southern Africa has served as a much-needed refreshment point for passing sailors. At first Table Bay was the obvious stopping place, but after the viceroy of the Portuguese East Indies, Francisco de Almeida, was killed there in 1510 during a skirmish with the indigenous Khoikhoi, the Portuguese avoided the Cape and preferred to have their stops-over further along the east coast of Africa.[20] The southern point of Africa only really became part of the Atlantic orbit when the Dutch and English started to challenge the Portuguese hegemony in the late sixteenth century. Since the establishment of the English East India Company (EIC) in 1600 its ships usually used Table Bay as a stop-over. The ships of the VOC, founded in 1602, had various roughly halfway calling places, especially the islands of St. Helena, Mauritius and Madagascar, but in 1616 the VOC determined its sailing course and insisted that its ships – except in emergencies – use Table Bay as its stop-over.[21] In 1619 the VOC and EIC formally agreed that both would use the Cape as a halfway station en route to the East.[22] Thus, from the 1620s onwards, Table Bay and its inhabitants firmly entered the transoceanic world created and exploited by the mercantile companies of the Atlantic. Hundreds of (mostly Dutch and English, but also French and Danish) ships, and thousands of the men who sailed them, thus called at the Cape during the first half of the seventeenth century.[23]

But this was not only a case of the North Atlantic world encountering a new 'New World'; it meant that the process of Africans interacting with Europeans which had been occurring further north along the African coast, repeated itself at the southern point of the continent, albeit in a different way, yet with equally deleterious effects. After de Almeida's fateful encounter with the pastoralist Khoikhoi, who had been practising transhumance in the south-western areas of southern Africa for upward of a thousand years by the time of European interaction,[24] an image developed of them as ferocious barbarians. This went hand-in-hand with the reigning perception of southern Africa in the Iberian imagination as the Cape of Storms where Adamastor (in the form of Table Mountain) stood guard over 'a forbidden portal – a crucial threshold between East and West' which the Cape represents.[25] It is for these reasons that Portuguese sailors preferred to bypass Table Bay. But, as Dutch and English sailors started to experience in the seventeenth century, the Khoikhoi were not at all unwilling to engage in small-scale trade with passing crews and the ready supply of meat created by this, coupled with the bountiful nature surrounding Table Bay (and the discovery of its relative meteorological calm during certain parts of the year), soon meant that it became widely known as the Cape of Good Hope.

Very early on the Cape became more than a mere 'halfway station': by the late 1610s, the EIC sent an annual ship to the South African west coast to hunt seals and whales, although this venture died after a few years.[26] During the same period, English ships also at various times off-loaded a few convicts and other unwanted persons at Table Bay or on Robben Island, some of whom were taken by other ships to the East.[27] During this period some individual Khoikhoi were also taken – some willingly, others not – to either Europe or the East Indies where they picked up the rudiments of Dutch and English. Those who returned could use their experience and expertise to act as mediators in the trade between passing Europeans and the various Khoikhoi groups.[28] Although what is described here concerns – by North Atlantic standards – relatively few people engaged in relatively unimportant economic activities, it does demonstrate how from even before more permanent European settlement in southern Africa, the region and its inhabitants partook of larger processes created by ships from the Atlantic plying the oceans around its coast.

Southern Africa became firmly part of the globalising world created by transoceanic merchant companies when the VOC formally founded a refreshment station for its ships in Table Bay. Its first commander, Jan van Riebeeck, landed with just over a hundred men (and a few women and children) in 1652 with the instructions to build a 'fort and garden' and to maintain friendly (and profitable) relations with the local Khoikhoi. Although van Riebeeck was by no means the 'founding father' Afrikaner mythologizing tried to make of him later (constantly applying, as he did, for promotion to the East Indies), his tenure at the Cape changed the fate of southern Africa's history. Not only did he manage – after some difficulty – to establish successfully a station and to prove its usefulness to the VOC and its ships and crews, but two of his decisions set into motion processes with far-reaching effects on the subsequent history of the region. First, in an attempt to improve the profitability of the station and ensure its long-term survival, the VOC allowed some of its employees to leave its service in 1657 and to settle as farmers on the understanding that they will sell their produce to the Company. These people were known as 'free burghers' – they were 'freed' from their original contracts with the VOC, although they remained subjects of the Company. Second was the decision, in 1658, to import slaves to southern Africa to serve both the VOC and the newly created group of free burghers. Slaves had to be imported since the VOC forbade van Riebeeck from enslaving the local Khoikhoi population for fear that it may lead to reprisals and a drop in the much-needed supply of livestock for passing ships.[29]

With these events of the 1650s the future development of a unique colonial society was set in motion. Like the contemporary societies of the Americas, the Cape of

Good Hope became a settler society predicated on imported slave labour. Unlike most of them, though, and in line with other VOC possessions in the East Indies, the Cape remained until 1795 firmly the possession of a merchant company which strictly controlled all aspects of life – but especially the economy – in its colony: as one high-ranking VOC official reminded the Cape's free burghers in the 1780s when some of them agitated for greater liberty: 'it is a truth which nobody can deny...that this whole establishment [the Cape of Good Hope] exists only because of, and for the sake of, the Company...'.[30] Already by the 1680s and 1690s, free burghers and their slaves had established extensive grain and wine farms in the arable regions of the south-western Cape (the immediate hinterland of Cape Town), and from the early 1700s onwards, their descendants gradually moved into the northern and eastern interior where they mostly engaged in pastoral farming.[31] By the end of Dutch rule, most of the non-desert western part of modern South Africa was settled by free burghers who were all connected – legally, economically, culturally and mentally – to the centre of the colony, Cape Town. As elsewhere in the Atlantic world, this expansion of Europeans had deleterious effects on the indigenous population: already by the second decade of the eighteenth century there were no more independent Khoikhoi remaining in the south-western arable districts of the colony – having succumbed to a combination of diseases and wars – while those who fled to or originally lived in the interior continually came into conflict with the pastoralist European settlers who competed with them for resources.[32]

* * *

Although the aforegoing may seem to have been a *sui generis* process, this was not the case: the developments on the frontiers of the Cape colony, hundreds of kilometres inland from the port city which was its centre, were influenced by much larger processes driven by the globalising north Atlantic world. Thus, by the end of VOC rule in 1795, there were some 17–18 000 European colonists in southern Africa (of which 2–3 000 were Company personnel) and about the same number of slaves (of which 500 belonged to the Company and the rest to the free burghers).[33] Most of these people, and the vast majority of their immediate ancestors, came to the Cape from elsewhere, brought here by ships whose routes were determined by trade patterns. Thus, throughout the existence of Cape Town as a VOC station, some forty to sixty Dutch ships annually called here on their way between north-western Europe and the eastern rim of the Indian Ocean basin. But this was by no means all: for the eighteenth century we know that the VOC figures only represent some 60 per cent of the total number of ships which called at the Cape: every year ships belonging to other nations – mostly the English and French, but also American and Scandinavian countries – would stop at the Cape, ranging from only a handful each year to more than a hundred by the end of the eighteenth century. Overall, the figures fluctuated somewhat due to changing war and trade imperatives, but one significant development was that from the 1770s onwards, and especially during the 1780s and 1790s, the number of 'foreign' ships calling at the Cape increased significantly and overtook that of VOC ships: for example, of the 622 ships which stayed over here between 1790 and 1793, only 233 were of Dutch origin.[34]

The aforegoing demonstrates how significant a node Cape Town was in a network of population movement between the North Atlantic and the Indian Ocean. We know that about 10 per cent of those people who embarked in the Dutch Republic disembarked in Cape Town – some simply because they needed to recuperate in the local hospital and took a later ship to the East – but mostly because they chose to stay at the Cape.[35] In this way, the vast bulk of Cape colonists during the VOC period came here as individuals in service of the VOC – only a very small percentage (such as the group of just over a hundred Huguenots from France in the late 1680s) were direct immigrants who arrived in larger groups. Most people who disembarked from the VOC's ships were soldiers in service of the VOC who – after working in the Cape Town garrison – were released from their Company contracts and became free burghers.[36] The bulk of these indirect immigrants who came to the Cape as VOC soldiers were German speakers from central Europe who, because of political and economic turmoil, first went to the Dutch Republic and thence tried their luck overseas.[37] In fact, about the same percentage of the 'progenitors' of the colonial Dutch in southern Africa who identified themselves as Afrikaners by the nineteenth century came from German as from Dutch-speaking lands:[38] the fact that during the early decades of the colony most of the free burghers were of Dutch origin, coupled with the fact that most of these German immigrants married the locally born daughters of earlier migrants, meant that the colony maintained its Dutch 'character', certainly in linguistic terms.[39] This was an ongoing process. Colonial southern Africa had always been a country of migrants and settlers maintained contact with their relatives elsewhere: we know that there existed a form of chain migration at the Cape whereby successful colonists here were followed in due course by family members from Europe.[40] In this way too, southern Africa formed part of a process of dislocation, migration and settlement starting in north-western Europe and continuing across the Atlantic to the 'new worlds' which bordered it; a process made possible by ocean-crossing ships.[41]

While the free burghers of early modern southern Africa shared the same European origins, background and immigrant experience as their fellow colonists in the Americas, the same cannot be said of the slaves who were brought to the colonial Cape. Here too slaves were forced migrants from elsewhere, but very few of them came from the Atlantic world: except for the first two consignments of slaves taken to the Cape in 1658, who derived from Dahomey and Angola,[42] the vast bulk of Cape slaves originated in the Indian Ocean world. This was the consequence of the fact that – despite its geographic position – the Cape formed part of a trading network based on the Indian Ocean: because it existed for the sake of the VOC, it followed that its slaves should also derive from VOC sources.[43] In this sense too the Cape is unusual since only a small percentage of slaves were obtained and imported specifically for the Cape, namely those who were imported on behalf of the local VOC administration from Madagascar.[44] The bulk of slaves arrived in small numbers aboard the trading ships of the VOC – not as part of large slave cargoes.[45] And they came from all over the Indian Ocean world: the 63,000 or so slaves imported to southern Africa between 1658 and the end of the legal slave trade in 1808 derived in roughly equal proportions from four geographical areas, namely Madagascar, India and Ceylon, the Indonesian archipelago and Mozambique. The sources of Cape slaves changed over time, and at different periods certain areas predominated: thus most Cape slaves in the seventeenth and early eighteenth centuries came from Madagascar and the Indian sub-continent, while Mozambique started to dominate slave imports to the Cape only in the final decades of the eighteenth century.[46] The latter development was partly due to the rise in importance as a source for slaves of the Swahili coast, Madagascar and the Mascarenes from the late eighteenth century onwards, and many American (especially Brazilian) slavers sold part of their cargoes in Cape Town on their way to the Atlantic.[47]

During the early modern period the Western hemisphere was, as Felipe Fernández-Armesto has argued, unified through the trade in and use of African slaves.[48] Southern Africa did not form part of this particular aspect of the Atlantic experience – or at least not in the same format. Not only did slaves arrive from a wide and diverse geographic area in the Indian Ocean region, the nature of Cape slavery also differed from the better-known plantation slavery which was so wide-spread in parts of the western Atlantic. Although, from the 1710s onwards, slaves at the Cape slightly outnumbered colonists, this numerical supremacy was never more than about 10 percent. In addition, except for Cape Town which had a sizeable slave population, slaves were distributed in small holdings (on average 5–10) on relatively isolated farms.[49] Coupled with the disparate cultural and linguistic background of Cape slaves and the fact that they came here in small numbers, this meant that no unified slave culture developed here akin to other slave societies, which partly explains why there were no large-scale slave uprisings in Dutch South Africa.[50] Slaves had to adapt to the culture of their owners and had to speak their language – although they certainly did contribute to the formation of Afrikaans.[51] Although miscegenation did occur and there existed a small 'free-black' community in Cape Town, the numbers were such that the development of a mestizo-type culture – as existed in Dutch Batavia for instance – was not possible.[52] Although newly discovered evidence shows that some slaves and free blacks managed to keep up links with other parts of the Indian Ocean world,[53] the extent of this is unlikely to be comparable to the network of links that colonists had with relatives in Europe. Thus, although colonial South Africa was a settler society based on Indian Ocean slave labour – and while this experience certainly left a deep impact on aspects of this society, such as race relations – it remained in many respects a remarkably 'Atlantic' society in which European culture and ideas dominated. This was certainly something which contemporary visitors to the Cape recognised for which reason it did not, in their view, compare favourably to the exoticism and splendour of the East Indies.[54]

* * *

From the start colonial southern Africa was linked to the Atlantic world of the north through a web of words, ideas, discourses and images made possible through the infrastructure created by the VOC: its ships and their routes. Stories of people who visited the Cape soon piqued the interest of the scholars of Europe keen to expand their knowledge of the new worlds which were opened up through trade and travel. Via a web of connections linking Europe with various people 'on the ground', knowledge of the Cape's flora, fauna and indigenous inhabitants entered the discussions and discourses of people in the northern Atlantic.[55] Thus, thanks to the networks created by the VOC, the philosopher Leibniz was able to include discussion of the Cape Khoi language in his disquisitions on the origins of language.[56] This inclusion of southern Africa in the world of knowledge and imagination created by the Atlantic ocean extended beyond correspondence – both official and private – and word-of-mouth. Since the start of the European encounter with southern Africa, visitors to the Cape capitalised on European interest in the local Khoikhoi (and, from the late eighteenth century, the Xhosa) and the natural wonders of Africa by publishing books and images of their experiences. Although much of this fed into certain tropes and discourses, and while much of this literature borrowed extensively from one another (especially images), over time knowledge about southern Africa started to accumulate in Europe which helped to create a certain image and expectation of Africa and the colonial experience in the European mind.[57] This was a dynamic process influenced both by new and expanding knowledge of the South African reality and of changes in European thinking about the world: thus by the late eighteenth century the original depiction and conception of the Khoikhoi as being subhuman and degenerate gave way to Rousseau's conception of them as being 'noble savages' hitherto untainted by European influences.[58]

Just as knowledge about the Cape spread northwards through the Atlantic via ships and people, so too did newly developing ideas and ways of thinking percolate down to the Cape. Thanks to the role of intermediaries such as ministers of religion who trained in Europe, the Cape elite were able to follow debates and controversies raging in the northern world, even though the public sphere at the Cape was small and overt, formal debate limited. Nonetheless, books and knowledge emanating from the European Enlightenments found their way here.[59] And knowledge of these new ways of thinking certainly impacted on the lives of ordinary people at the Cape: thus, a new generation of Cape clergy influenced by European and American pietism implemented radically different policies about female morality in their churches during the 1780s and 1790s.[60] The same period, what Palmer called the 'Age of Democratic Revolutions', also witnessed the free burghers at the Cape questioning the VOC's restrictive trade policies and demanding both greater political rights and more economic freedom.[61] These people too were influenced by reading texts emanating from elsewhere in the Atlantic, and listening to the talk of sailors and other visitors to Cape Town.[62] As has recently been demonstrated for other parts of the Atlantic, revolutionary ideas were distributed (and acted upon) by all groups of people who crossed this ocean, and new ideas spread as much through talk in taverns as they did through books and newspapers.[63] The Cape formed part of this network of radical ideas being spread by working-class people, including black sailors from America.[64] This information network extended to slaves in southern Africa by the late eighteenth century – individual (albeit isolated) cases of slaves resisting owners and insisting that they have rights reveal that some of the ideas which caused such turmoil in the northern Atlantic percolated down even to isolated farms in the Cape Town hinterland.[65] Recent work has revealed that, certainly by 1808, revolutionary talk and rumours could be used by Atlantic sailors to incite Cape slaves to the only large-scale (albeit unsuccessful) slave uprising in the history of South Africa.[66] In these ways, then, southern Africa formed part of the complex nexus of ideas, rumours and knowledge made possible by people and ships from different parts of the Atlantic criss-crossing the ocean.

* * *

The changes which started to affect the Cape during the last decades of the eighteenth century were in part made possible through its greater contact with other parts of the

– CHAPTER 6: *Southern Africa and the Atlantic World* –

Atlantic world, influenced by wider geopolitical and economic developments. Thus, in 1780 – in the context of the Fourth Anglo-Dutch war – a British fleet was sent to capture Cape Town so that it could aid in the further development of British interests in the Indian Ocean. In the event, the British were thwarted by the French, the allies of the Dutch, who were keen to keep the Cape out of British hands in order to protect their own interest in the Mascarene Islands. During the 1780s several French-speaking regiments were stationed in Cape Town to protect it. This had a huge impact on the economy and culture of the town, earning it in short time the nickname of 'Little Paris'.[67] The last decades of the eighteenth century also saw an increase in American shipping around the Cape as East Coast merchants increasingly started trading with the East Indies.[68] But it was the British, with growing involvement in the Indian Ocean, whose interest in the Cape – which became a real threat in the context of the Napoleonic wars because of the Dutch–French alliance – led to it being conquered from the Dutch in 1795. Except for a brief period when the Cape reverted to the Batavian Republic in 1803–6, the Cape remained firmly in the British sphere for the rest of the nineteenth century. This can be seen in the make-up of merchant shipping calling at Table Bay: in 1806, about 40 British ships anchored here, with about the same number of American ones and 20 ships from other European powers. By 1820, the 28 European ships were dwarfed by the number of British vessels which were almost twentyfold that of other powers.[69] This picture changed somewhat over the next few decades as other ports on the Cape south coast, notably Port Elizabeth, started trading with Cape Town, leading to an increase in locally based merchant ships, and American and European ships continued to call in Table Bay. But throughout the nineteenth century southern African waters remained firmly in the sphere of the British navy and merchant fleets.[70]

From the late eighteenth century and through the nineteenth, southern Africa played a major role in the process of the decline of the Atlantic World system and the rise of a more globalised world interconnected through commerce.[71] This is because of the strategic position of especially Cape Town in connecting the Atlantic Ocean and its system with that of the Indian, thus acting as a pivot from one world to the other during this crucial period of transition.[72] Under the VOC, the Cape's primary aim was to support the Dutch trading network. While Dutch South Africa's economy certainly was dynamic (albeit small), it was nonetheless crucially dependent on the VOC's shipping traffic.[73] This started to change radically under the British: the introduction of free trade and the greater availability of imported goods led to the rapid development of a merchant class consisting of both settled Dutch and newly arrived British colonists. The Cape benefitted much from the large-scale conflicts in which Britain was engaged: not only provisioning the fleet but also providing all kinds of goods and services for St. Helena in the Atlantic.[74] From the 1830s, when the Cape economy was injected with a great deal of capital from Britain as compensation for the abolishment of slavery, southern Africa increasingly became part of a global British economy.[75] Southern African merchants operated in both London and Cape Town while exports and imports from the various Cape ports increasingly integrated this part of the world with the north Atlantic, a process which accelerated sharply with the discovery of minerals in the interior during the 1870s.

The increased ship traffic to and from southern Africa did not only affect the economy: many of these ships also brought new migrants to the Cape. The British

109

take-over of the Cape resulted in large numbers of both administrators and soldiers being settled here, as well as more permanent settlers – not only new immigrants from Britain but also those who served in India and chose to settle at the Cape rather than return to Europe.[76] But the bulk of migrants to southern Africa in the first half of the nineteenth century came from Europe: not only were there the well-known mass migration of a few thousand poor people from the British isles to the eastern districts of the Cape Colony in the early 1820s,[77] but a steady stream of immigrants from the Dutch- and German-speaking parts of Europe continued to arrive throughout the nineteenth century, much as they did in the eighteenth.[78] In this way, colonial southern Africa remained a country of migrants who, as before, brought with them ideas and notions from elsewhere in the Atlantic. Thus, the pietist movement which swept throughout the north Atlantic in the last decades of the eighteenth century started to have a major impact on life in southern Africa from the early 1800s when missionaries inspired by their religious ideals arrived in the country and – for the first time – seriously started to labour among the remnants of the Khoikhoi and, somewhat later, among the Xhosa.[79] By the 1820s and 1830s, the presence of missionaries in southern Africa with strong links to influential interest groups in Britain, coupled with local discourses surrounding the freedom of press, free trade and the supremacy of the rule of law, led to the victory of the so-called humanitarian movement at the Cape.[80] In some ways the Cape experience became paradigmatic for the British Empire, as shown in how it drove the 1835 *Select Committee on Aborigines* instituted by the British parliament. But southern Africa was not just unified with the British world through shared ideas and ideals – during the same period it became firmly entrenched, thanks to the ships passing it from the Atlantic to India and Australia, in a transnational world which debated, rumoured and gossiped about ideas emanating from both the metropole and the colonies: both news and scandals – like people and commodities – could cross the oceans via the Cape.[81] Thus, although at first the Cape of Good Hope was but part of a route to the Indies, it still afforded the one portal from the Atlantic to the Indian Ocean, and hence to a global world – a development which was complete by the late nineteenth century when industrialising southern Africa formed part of a world united through capital and crime, news and migration.[82]

NOTES

1 Carlton Hayes and Charles Verlinden, quoted in Bernard Bailyn, *Atlantic History: Concepts and Contours* (Cambridge, Mass. & London, 2005), 13 and 19.

2 Thomas Benjamin, *The Atlantic World: Europeans, Africans, Indians and their Shared History, 1400–1900* (Cambridge, 2009), 34.

3 Godechot and Palmer in Bailyn, *Atlantic History*, 25.

4 Kerry Ward, '"Tavern of the Seas?": The Cape of Good Hope as an Oceanic Crossroads during the Seventeenth and Eighteenth Centuries', in J.H. Bentley, R. Bridenthal and K. Wigen (eds), *Seascapes: Maritime Histories, Littoral Cultures, and Transoceanic Exchanges* (Honolulu, 2007), 137–52.

5 Thus, with the exception of Gerrit Schutte, virtually no Dutch historian paid any attention to colonial South Africa from the 1960s to the 1990s, despite the growth of VOC scholarship in the Netherlands during this period.

6 One of the greatest desiderata for the historiography of colonial South Africa is an integrated study of the two periods. As this chapter illustrates, the period of the late

– CHAPTER 6: *Southern Africa and the Atlantic World* –

eighteenth to the early nineteenth centuries was crucial for establishing Cape Town's central role in the development of a cross-oceanic world; a view which gets lost when historians of the Dutch period stop abruptly in 1795 or, as often happens, when scholars of British South Africa ignore the earlier history of the colony.

7   In fact, as demonstrated by Norman Etherington, *The Great Treks: The Transformation of Southern Africa, 1815–1854* (Harlow & London, 2001) this was but one of several large dislocations and upheavals various groups in the interior of southern Africa experienced between the 1820s and 1840s, completely transforming the politics of the Highveld and bringing it firmly into the orbit of Western power centred on the South African coast.

8   Cf. the masterful trilogy of books P.J. van der Merwe published between 1937 and 1944 which – along with its author – had a stifling influence on VOC historiography in South Africa until the 1970s. See on the significance and influence of van der Merwe, Nigel Penn, 'Trekboers Revisited', *African Affairs* 95, 378 (1996), 126–30 and J.S. Bergh, 'P.J. (Piet) van der Merwe en D.J. (Dirk) Kotzé aan die Stuur by Stellenbosch, 1959–77: Goue Jare of Verspeelde Geleenthede?' *Historia* 53, 2 (2008), 208–62.

9   Cf. on Afrikaner nationalist historians and VOC historiography, Ken Smith, *The Changing Past: Trends in South African Historical Writing* (Johannesburg, 1988), chapter 3 and Nigel Worden, 'New Approaches to VOC History in South Africa', *South African Historical Journal* 59 (2007), 3–18.

10 Richard Elphick, 'Hermann Giliomee and *The Shaping of South African Society*: Memories of a Collaboration', *South African Historical Journal* 60, 4 (2008), 553–61.

11 Most of the influential scholars of this generation, such as Richard Elphick, Leonard Guelke, Robert Ross, Nigel Worden, Susan Newton-King and Robert Shell, were either raised in the UK or the USA, or else received their postgraduate training there.

12 In this sense South Africa deviates rather sharply from other Dutch colonies, except for New Netherland which passed from Dutch control too early to be usefully compared to the VOC Cape.

13 Cf. Greg Cuthbertson, 'Cape Slave Historiography and the Question of Intellectual Dependence', *South African Historical Journal* 27 (1992), 26–49.

14 Howard Lamar and Leonard Thompson (eds), *The Frontier in History: North America and Southern Africa Compared* (New Haven & London, 1981); G. Frederickson (ed.), *White Supremacy: A Comparative Study in American and South African History* (New York & Oxford, 1981).

15 For example, an international conference at the University of Cape Town in 2006 which brought together scholars of the VOC world from Asia, Africa, Europe and North America. This was followed up in 2008 with a conference on written culture in the colonial world which, for the first time ever, brought together historians of colonial Africa and Latin America; cf. Nigel Worden (ed.), *Contingent Lives: Social Identity and Material Culture in the VOC World* (Cape Town, 2007) and Adrien Delmas and Nigel Penn (eds), *Written Culture in a Colonial Context: Africa and the Americas, 1500–1900* (Cape Town and Leiden, 2011). For a consideration of the development and import of this new historiography, see Worden, 'New Approaches to VOC History' and Laura J. Mitchell and Gerald Groenewald, 'The Pre-Industrial Cape in the Twenty-First Century', *South African Historical Journal* 62, 3 (2010), 435–43.

16 Cf. Nicole Ulrich, 'Time, Space and the Political Economy of Merchant Colonialism in the Cape of Good Hope and VOC World' and the response by Nigel Worden, 'After Race and Class: Recent Trends in the Historiography of Early Colonial Cape Society', *South African Historical Journal* 62, 3 (2010), 571–88 and 589–602.

17 Cf. http://www.southafrica.info/about/geography/oceansmeet.htm (accessed 10 March 2012).

18 C.R. Boxer, *The Dutch Seaborne Empire, 1600–1800* (London and New York, 1965), 242.

19 Bailyn, *Atlantic History*, 61.

20 Nigel Worden, Elizabeth van Heyningen and Vivian Bickford-Smith, *Cape Town: The Making of a City* (Cape Town, 1998), 13–14.

21 Karel Schoeman, *Armosyn van die Kaap: Voorspel tot Vestiging, 1415–1651* (Cape Town, 1999), 181.

22 R. Raven-Hart, *Before Van Riebeeck: Callers at South Africa from 1488 to 1652* (Cape Town, 1967), 97.

23 At least 363 VOC ships called at the Cape between 1610–51, most of which stayed here on average for two to three weeks. No such complete figures have been published for other nations, but from those which have left literary records of their visits between 1610 and 1649, at least 62 were English with 23 from other powers; figures compiled from J.R. Bruijn, F.S. Gaastra and I. Schöffer, *Dutch Asiatic Shipping in the 17th and 18th Centuries*, 3 volumes (The Hague, 1979–87) and Raven-Hart, *Before Van Riebeeck*, 46–181.

24 Richard Elphick, *Khoikhoi and the Founding of White South Africa* (Johannesburg, 1985), chapters 1–3.

25 Nicolas Vergunst, *Hoerikwaggo: Images of Table Mountain* (Cape Town, 2000), 55; cf. Hedley Twidle, 'Prison and Garden: Cape Town, Natural History and the Literary Imagination' (Ph.D. thesis, University of York, 2010), chapter 1 on the figure of Adamastor in Camões and subsequent literary representations of the Cape. David Johnson, *Imagining the Cape Colony: History, Literature, and the South African Nation* (Edinburgh, 2012), chapter 1 discusses the various historiographical and literary treatments of the Khoikhoi's victory over de Almeida.

26 Raven-Hart, *Before Van Riebeeck*, 63.

27 Ibid., 67–84.

28 Cf. on the two most famous such individuals, Coree and Autshumao, Elphick, *Khoikhoi*, 76–86. Apparently Coree was kept in London for 'Six Months in Sir Thomas Smiths House then Governor of the East India Company' where 'he would daily lye on the ground, and cry out very often in broken English, *Coree home go...*', quoted from Edward Terry, 'A View of the Bay of Souldania near the Coast of Good Hope on the Coast of Africa', *Quarterly Bulletin of the South African Library* 1, 3 (1947), 75.

29 Earlier work on the 'founding moment' in South Africa's colonial history has now been replaced by the synthesis of Karel Schoeman, *Kolonie aan die Kaap: Jan van Riebeeck en die Vestiging van die Eerste Blankes, 1652–1662* (Pretoria, 2010).

30 Quoted from G.J. Schutte, *De Nederlandse Patriotten en de Koloniën: Een Onderzoek naar hun Denkbeelden en Optreden, 1770–1800* (Groningen, 1974), 66 (my translation).

31 Leonard Guelke, 'Freehold Farmers and Frontier Settlers, 1657–1780', in Richard Elphick and Hermann Giliomee (eds), *The Shaping of South African Society, 1652–1840*, 2nd ed. (Cape Town, 1989), 66–108.

32 Cf. from a large literature, Richard Elphick and V.C. Malherbe, 'The Khoisan to 1828', in Richard Elphick and Hermann Giliomee (eds), *The Shaping of South African Society, 1652–1840*, 2nd ed. (Cape Town, 1989), 3–65; Susan Newton-King, *Masters and Servants on the Cape Eastern Frontier, 1760–1803* (Cambridge, 1999) and Nigel Penn, *The Forgotten Frontier: Colonist and Khoisan on the Cape's Northern Frontier in the 18th Century* (Athens, OH and Cape Town, 2005).

33 P. van Duin and R. Ross, *The Economy of the Cape Colony in the Eighteenth Century* (Leiden, 1987), 112–15.

34 On shipping figures, its fluctuations and the causes thereof, see Bruijn, Gaastra and Schöffer, *Dutch Asiatic Shipping*, and Willem H. Boshoff and Johan Fourie, 'Explaining Ship Traffic Fluctuations at the Early Cape Settlement, 1652–1793', *South African Journal of Economic History* 23, 1–2 (2008), 1–27. Data for foreign ships come from Coenraad Beyers, *Die Kaapse Patriotte gedurende die Laaste Kwart van die Agtiende Eeu en die Voortlewing van hul Denkbeelde*, 2nd ed. (Pretoria, 1967), 333–35; see also, for a detailed

– CHAPTER 6: Southern Africa and the Atlantic World –

study of part of this period, Maurice Boucher, *The Cape of Good Hope and Foreign Contacts, 1735–1755* (Pretoria,1985).

35 Bruijn, Gaastra and Schöffer, *Dutch Asiatic Shipping*, vol. 3, 168. No similar figures exist for the homeward journeys from the East, nor for foreign ships (although it is unlikely that the contribution to the local population from privateers was significant since all people who wished to live at the Cape of Good Hope needed the permission of the VOC as the latter considered the colony its private possession).

36 J.E. Louwrens, 'Immigrasie aan die Kaap gedurende die Bewind van die Hollandse Oos-Indiese Kompanjie' (D.Phil. thesis, University of Stellenbosch, 1954) and R.C.-H. Shell, 'Immigration: The Forgotten Factor in Cape Colonial Frontier Expansion, 1658 to 1817', *Safundi: The Journal of South African and American Comparative Studies* 6, 2 (2005), online.

37 J.R. Bruijn, 'De Personeelsbehoefte van de VOC Overzee en aan Board, Bezien in Aziatisch en Nederlands Perspectief', *Bijdragen en Mededelingen betreffende de Geschiedenis der Nederlanden* 91 (1976), 218–48 and Roelof van Gelder, *Het Oost-Indisch Avontuur: Duitsers in Dienst van de VOC* (Nijmegen, 1997), chapters 1–2. On German–Dutch migration and experience, cf. Jan Lucassen, *Migrant Labour in Europe, 1600–1900* (London, 1987) and Erika Kuijpers, *Migrantenstad: Immigratie en Sociale Verhoudingen in 17e-eeuwse Amsterdam* (Hilversum, 2005).

38 34.8 per cent Dutch and 33.7 per cent German; cf. J.A. Heese, *Die Herkoms van die Afrikaner, 1657–1867* (Cape Town, 1972).

39 The large number of second-language speakers of Dutch certainly influenced the development of a unique version of Dutch, viz. proto-Afrikaans, during the eighteenth century; cf. e.g. Fritz Ponelis, *The Development of Afrikaans* (Frankfurt am Main, 1993), 17–21. The VOC also tried through most of its tenure to prevent the Cape's Germans from developing into a 'group apart' by inter alia refusing the establishment of a Lutheran church in Cape Town before 1780. Officially the colony maintained its Dutch character in spite of the large number of foreign elements in it.

40 This process has not yet been studied systematically for the colonial Cape, but see Gerald Groenewald, 'Entrepreneurs and the Making of a Free Burgher Society', in Nigel Worden (ed.), *Cape Town between East and West: Social Identities in a Dutch Colonial Town* (Johannesburg and Hilversum, 2012), 48–49 for some pertinent examples. Cf. on the workings of this process for German–Dutch migration, Kuijpers, *Migrantenstad*.

41 Cf. Bailyn, *Atlantic History*, 91–94 for brief remarks on this process for the better-known western parts of the Atlantic world. Likewise, the Cape formed part of a network of political patronage which crossed both the Atlantic and Indian Ocean worlds but with its origins firmly in the Netherlands where it was determined which high-ranking VOC officials would be stationed where, much as happened in Spanish and British America; ibid., 50–51 and, on the Cape, Robert Ross and Alicia Schrikker, 'The VOC Official Elite', in Worden (ed.), *Cape Town between East and West*, 26–44.

42 See on this first slave import to South Africa, Karel Schoeman, *Early Slavery at the Cape of Good Hope, 1652–1717* (Pretoria, 2007), 50–83.

43 Markus Vink, '"The World's Oldest Trade": Dutch Slavery and Slave Trade in the Indian Ocean in the Seventeenth Century', *Journal of World History* 14, 2 (2003), 131–77.

44 Between 1652 and 1795 we know of 33 VOC-sponsored voyages to Madagascar, and five to Mozambique and Zanzibar (in the late eighteenth century), with the aim of trading slaves; James C. Armstrong and Nigel A. Worden, 'The Slaves, 1652–1840', in R. Elphick and H. Giliomee (eds), *The Shaping of South African Society, 1652–1840*, 2nd edn. (Cape Town, 1989), 112; cf. Karel Schoeman, *Portrait of a Slave Society: The Cape of Good Hope, 1717–1795* (Pretoria, 2012), 119–70.

45 Many VOC personnel who repatriated from the East Indies sold their personal slaves (who accompanied them on the first leg of the journey) in Cape Town since it was

technically illegal to bring slaves to the Netherlands. In addition, small numbers of 'excess' slaves were sometimes sent from Batavia or Colombo; Armstrong and Worden, 'The Slaves', 116–17 and Schoeman, *Portrait*, 266–314.

46 R. C.-H. Shell, *Children of Bondage: A Social History of the Slave Society at the Cape of Good Hope, 1652–1838* (Johannesburg, 1994), chapter 2 and Nigel Worden, 'Indian Ocean Slavery and its Demise in the Cape Colony', in Gwyn Campbell (ed.), *Abolition and its Aftermath in Indian Ocean Africa and Asia* (London and New York, 2005), 30–38.

47 Worden, 'Indian Ocean Slavery', 37–38; cf. Richard B. Allen, 'The Mascarene Slave-Trade and Labour Migration in the Indian Ocean during the Eighteenth and Nineteenth Centuries', in Gwyn Campbell, *The Structures of Slavery in Indian Ocean Africa and Asia* (London, 2004), 33–50.

48 Felipe Fernández-Armesto, *The Americas: A Hemispheric History* (New York, 2003), 64–65.

49 Robert Ross, *Cape of Torments: Slavery and Resistance in South Africa* (London, 1983), 14–15 and Nigel Worden, *Slavery in Dutch South Africa* (Cambridge, 1985), 94–95.

50 Nigel Worden, 'Revolt in Cape Colony Slave Society', in Edward A. Alpers, Gwyn Campbell and Michael Salmon (eds), *Resisting Bondage in Indian Ocean Africa and Asia* (London, 2007), 10–23.

51 Slaves and the Khoikhoi were second-language speakers of Dutch. The fact that their numbers – and the rate at which it increased – were just right (not too many or too fast) meant that it was possible for a new Dutch-based language to develop during the seventeenth and eighteenth centuries at the Cape but not in other Dutch colonies such as New Netherland or Batavia where the balance of first- versus second-language speakers and the rate of change did not create favourable conditions for language genesis; cf. Gerald Groenewald, 'Waarom Afrikaans? Die Ontstaan van Afrikaans in die Konteks van die Nederlandse Koloniale Wêreld', forthcoming.

52 Cf. on Batavia, Pauline D. Milone, '*Indische* culture, and its relationship to urban life', *Comparative Studies in Society and History* 9, 4 (1967), 407–26; Jean Gelman Taylor, *The Social World of Batavia: European and Eurasian in Dutch Asia*, 2nd ed. (Madison and London, 2009) and, for the lack of creolisation at the Cape, Richard Elphick and Hermann Giliomee, 'The Origins and Entrenchment of European Dominance at the Cape, 1652–c. 1840' in Richard Elphick and Hermann Giliomee (eds), *The Shaping of South African Society, 1652–1840*, 2nd ed. (Cape Town: Maskew Miller Longman, 1989), 521–66; Ad Biewenga, *De Kaap de Goede Hoop: Een Nederlandse Vestigingskolonie, 1680–1730* (Amsterdam, 1999), 267–90.

53 Susan Newton-King, 'Family, Friendship and Survival among Freed Slaves', in Worden (ed.), *Cape Town between East and West*, 153–75.

54 Thus the Lammens sisters found in 1736 that, except for the omnipresence of slaves, 'the habits, attire and food here are all as in the mother country', while two decades earlier Maria van Riebeeck, the granddaughter of the founder of the Cape station and the wife of the governor-general of the Dutch East Indies, compared the Cape very unfavourably with the East; Gerald Groenewald, 'Friends Old and New: The Lammens Sisters at the Cape, 1736', *Quarterly Bulletin of the National Library of South Africa* 59, 4 (2005), 160 and 161 (quote).

55 Mary Gunn and L.E. Codd, *Botanical Exploration of Southern Africa* (Cape Town, 1981); L.C. Rookmaaker, *The Zoological Exploration of Southern Africa, 1650–1790* (Rotterdam, 1989) and Siegfried Huigen, Jan L. de Jong and Elmer Kolfin (eds), *The Dutch Trading Companies as Knowledge Networks* (Leiden, 2010). See below on the Khoikhoi.

56 Gerald Groenewald, 'To Leibniz, from Dorha: A Khoi Prayer in the Republic of Letters', *Itinerario* 28, 1 (2004), 29–48.

57 Siegfried Huigen, *De Weg naar Monomotapa: Nederlandstalige Representaties van Geografische, Historische en Sociale Werkelijkheden in Zuid-Afrika* (Amsterdam, 1996)

– CHAPTER 6: *Southern Africa and the Atlantic World* –

and *idem, Knowledge and Colonialism: Eighteenth-Century Travellers in South Africa* (Leiden and Boston, 2009).

58 Cf. Johnson, *Imagining the Cape Colony*, 37–56; Huigen, *Knowledge and Colonialism*, 132–35; Malvern van Wyk Smith, '"The Most Wretched of the Human Race": The Iconography of the Khoikhoin (Hottentots), 1500–1800', *History and Anthropology* 5, 3 (1992), 285–330; Linda E. Merians, *Envisioning the Worst: Representations of 'Hottentots' in Early Modern England* (London, 2001) and Francois-Xavier Fauvelle-Aymar, *L'Invention du Hottentot: Histoire du Regard Occidental sur les Khoikhoi, XV-XIX Siecle* (Paris, 2002).

59 Gerald Groenewald, 'On Not Spreading the Word: Ministers of Religion and Written Culture at the Cape of Good Hope in the 18th Century', in Adrien Delmas and Nigel Penn (eds), *Written Culture in a Colonial Context: Africa and the Americas, 1500–1900* (Cape Town and Leiden, 2011), 302–23.

60 Gerald Groenewald, '*Een Spoorloos Vrouwspersoon*: Unmarried Mothers, Moral Regulation and the Church at the Cape of Good Hope, circa 1652–1795', *Historia* 51, 2 (2008), 5–32.

61 The standard study remains Beyers, *Kaapse Patriotte*, although new and forthcoming work by Teun Baartman, e.g. 'Protest and Dutch Burger Identity', in Worden (ed.), *Cape Town between East and West*, 65–83, is bound to deepen our understanding of the so-called 'Patriot Movement'. For a study of the Cape movement in the context of the wider Dutch world, see Schutte, *Nederlandse Patriotten*, chapter 4.

62 Beyers, *Kaapse Patriotte*, 170–234.

63 Peter Linebaugh and Marcus Rediker, *The Many-Headed Hydra: The Hidden History of the Revolutionary Atlantic* (London and New York, 2000); Alan Gregor Cobley, 'That Turbulent Soil: Seafarers, the "Black Atlantic" and Afro-Caribbean Identity', in J.H. Bentley, R. Bridenthal and K. Wigen (eds), *Seascapes: Maritime Histories, Littoral Cultures and Transoceanic Exchanges* (Honolulu, 2007), 153–68.

64 Keletso E. Atkins, 'The "Black Atlantic Communication Network": African American Sailors and the Cape of Good Hope Connection', *Issue: A Journal of Opinion* 24, 2 (1996), 23–25.

65 Cf. examples in Nigel Worden and Gerald Groenewald, *Trials of Slavery: Selected Documents Concerning Slaves from the Criminal Records of the Council of Justice at the Cape of Good Hope, 1705–1794* (Cape Town, 2005), 606–8 and 612–19. This topic has not yet received the attention of Cape historians it deserves, but for important pointers see Nicole Ulrich, 'Counter Power and Colonial Rule in the Eighteenth-Century Cape of Good Hope: Belongings and Protest of the Labouring Poor' (Ph.D. thesis, University of the Witwatersrand, 2011), chapter 5.

66 Nigel Worden, '"Armed with Swords and Ostrich Feathers": Militarism and Cultural Revolution in the Cape Slave Uprising of 1808', in Jane Rendall, Richard Bessel and Nicholas Guyatt (eds), *War, Empire and Slavery, 1770–1830* (London, 2010), 121–38 and Nicole Ulrich, 'Abolition from Below: The 1808 Revolt in the Cape Colony', in Marcel van der Linden (ed.), *'Humanitarian Intervention' and Changing Labour Relations: Long-term Consequences of the British Act on the Abolition of the Slave Trade, 1807* (Leiden and Boston, 2011), 193–222.

67 Worden, van Heyningen and Bickford-Smith, *Cape Town*, 81–83.

68 Cf. James R. Fichter, *So Great a Profitt: How the East Indies Trade Transformed Anglo-American Capitalism* (Cambridge, Mass., 2010).

69 Cf. Worden, van Heyningen and Bickford-Smith, *Cape Town*, 164.

70 E.A.G. Clark, 'Port Sites and Perception: The Development of the Southern and Eastern Cape Coast in the Nineteenth Century', *South African Geographical Journal* 59, 2 (1977), 150–67 and idem, '"The Spirit of Private Adventure": British Merchants and the

Establishment of New Ports and Trades in the Cape of Good Hope, 1795–1840', in Stephen Fisher (ed.), *Innovation in Shipping and Trade* (Exeter, 1989), 111–30.

71 Cf. Benjamin, *Atlantic World*, 661: 'A fragmented world of more or less autonomous cultures, societies and states gave way to an increasingly connected, interdependent and uniform world.'

72 This suggestion builds on Kerry Ward's description of how the disintegration of the Dutch empire in South Africa helped in building up that of the British; *Network of Empires: Forced Migration in the Dutch East India Company* (Cambridge, 2009), 297–307.

73 The Cape of Good Hope was an unusual combination of both extractive and settler economies; cf. Willem H. Boshoff and Johan Fourie, 'The Significance of the Cape Trade Route to Economic Activity in the Cape Colony: A Medium-Term Business Cycle Analysis', *European Review of Economic History* 14, 3 (2010), 469–503.

74 See on the economy of the Cape during the transitional period from the Dutch to the British, Robert Ross, 'The Cape of Good Hope and the World Economy, 1652–1835', in Richard Elphick and Hermann Giliomee (eds), *The Shaping of South African Society, 1652–1840*, 2nd ed. (Cape Town, 1989), 243–80.

75 Cf. Lalou Meltzer, 'Emancipation, Commerce and the Role of John Fairbairn's *Advertiser*', in Nigel Worden and Clifton Crais (eds), *Breaking the Chains: Slavery and Its Legacy in the Nineteenth-Century Cape Colony* (Johannesburg, 1994), 169–99 and Wayne Dooling, *Slavery, Emancipation and Colonial Rule in South Africa* (Scottsville, 2007).

76 R.R. Langham-Carter, 'The "Indians" in Cape Town', *Quarterly Bulletin of the South African Library* 35, 4 (1981), 143–50.

77 Alan Lester, *Imperial Networks: Creating Identities in Nineteenth-Century South Africa and Britain* (London and New York, 2001).

78 In fact, more Dutch immigrated to the Cape in the three decades, 1808–37, than in the preceding three decades when the Cape was largely under Dutch control. But even this figure was dwarfed by the 30–40,000 Germans who moved to South Africa in the nineteenth century; C. Pama, *Die Groot Afrikaanse Familienaamboek* (Cape Town, 1983), 18.

79 Elizabeth Elbourne, *Blood Ground: Colonialism, Missions, and the Contest for Christianity in the Cape Colony and Britain, 1799–1853* (Montreal, 2002).

80 Timothy Keegan, *Colonial South Africa and the Origins of the Racial Order* (Cape Town & Johannesburg, 1996).

81 Cf. Kirsten McKenzie, *Scandal in the Colonies: Sydney and Cape Town, 1820–1850* (Melbourne, 2004) and Christopher Holdridge, 'Circulating the *African Journal*: The Colonial Press and Trans-Imperial Britishness in the Mid-Nineteenth Century Cape', *South African Historical Journal* 62, 3 (2010), 487–513.

82 For compelling case studies of these developments, focusing particularly on the link between capital and crime on the Highveld, see Charles van Onselen, *The Fox and the Flies: The Criminal Empire of the Whitechapel Murderer* (London, 2007) and *idem, Masked Raiders: Irish Banditry in Southern Africa, 1880–1899* (Cape Town, 2010).

CHAPTER SEVEN

EMIGRATION FROM THE HABSBURG MONARCHY AND SALZBURG TO THE NEW WORLD, 1700–1848

—·◆·—

William O'Reilly

AUSTRIA, AMERICA AND A TYPOLOGY OF MIGRATION

Migrations are nothing new in Austrian and Central European history. Political and religious motivated migration, the migration of elites, seasonal trade workers and agricultural labourers, or the travelling of tradesmen and students were common along the highways and bye-ways of Central Europe in the eighteenth century. The transportation revolution which accelerated the process of economic integration in the Holy Roman Empire in the eighteenth century also facilitated the expeditious movement of Austrians both within the country and without.[1] Yet Austria's position in the history of European migration in the pre-1848 moment is a particular, and peculiar, one. By the commencement of the nineteenth century, three distinct strands of migration were in evidence in the German-speaking parts of the Habsburg monarchy:

First, the political and religiously motivated forced *emigration* of Protestants to Prussia and America, as well as the Ländler who travelled, and were deported, respectively, during the reigns of Charles VI and Maria Theresia, from Karnten, Oberösterreich and Steiermark to the Banat and to Siebenbürgen.[2] Second, the more common European phenomenon of seasonal *migration*, inspired by local over-population, from the Alps and from the lands bordering the Carpathians to the agrarian regions of the Bavarian Schwabian Alpenvorland and to inner Hungary (*Schwabenziige* and *Sachsenganger*). And third, the *immigration* of political, artistic and crafts elites from abroad to the imperial capital Vienna. These immigrants included the soldier and army leader Prince Eugen von Savoyen, the composer Mozart from Salzburg, Beethoven from Bonn and Clemens Metternich from Koblenz, who count among the illustrious many who came to the hereditary lands (*Erblander*) during this time.[3]

Yet the history of emigration from Austria, and the Habsburg Monarchy more generally, is a curiously nineteenth-century phenomenon; curious, when compared with Austria's neighbours in western Europe. In an eighteenth century which saw fierce competition for colonists in many parts of the Holy Roman Empire, in France and in further parts of western Europe, few Habsburg subjects crossed the Atlantic in search of opportunity and a new life. This paper will explore this subject, and will suggest that it was the availability of sites of relocation much closer to the *Heimat*,

117

most notably in parts of Hungary, which both dissuaded many migrants from crossing the Atlantic and which spurred the Viennese administration in the eighteenth century to prohibit practically all subjects from legally departing the territory. Only with a relaxation in legislative prohibitions on freedom of movement and a renewed literary interest in America, from the end of the eighteenth century, did emigration to America become both a possibility and an ambition for many in the Austrian lands.

From 1453 until 1806, the Holy Roman Empire was governed, almost without interruption, predominantly from Vienna by a Habsburg emperor. Within the Holy Roman Empire there existed the Austrian Hereditary Lands and the lands of the Bohemian crown, typically governed by the selfsame individual as the emperor, but wearing a different crown, being *Oberhaupt* of the House of Austria, King of Bohemia and Hungary, and having a myriad titles for each and every territory governed. And lastly, there were the possessions and dominions of the House of Austria outside the borders of the Empire, comprising Hungary and, later, Galicia and Bukowina. In 1804, an 'Austrian' Empire proper was created and continued to exist until 1918. The Austrian Monarchy in the eighteenth century was a mildly centripetal agglutination of bewilderingly heterogeneous elements.[4] 'Austria' was much more than a 'composite' monarchy, for some of the territories of the House of Austria were part of the Holy Roman Empire, whereas other possessions were not. It is for this reason that the true nature and extent of 'Austrian' emigration to America in the period 1700–1848 is very difficult to assess, for at times 'Austrians' behaved as 'Germans' and are, as such, difficult to distinguish. While emigration to the Austrian lands was marginal in comparison with inner migration to Hungary, its very marginality makes it all the more interesting; why might an individual decide to emigrate from Styria to America, rather than take the much shorter route to Hungary much closer to hand? These points serve to highlight the more general shapeshifting nature of migrants' identities in the long eighteenth century, when regional identity sometimes gave way to a linguistic identity, sometimes to a religious or political badge of identity. A prime example is Salzburg, which lay outside Austria proper until 1815.

Salzburgers who left the city in the nineteenth century were not 'Austrians', but shared most aspects of quotidian life with their neighbours who were. In America in the eighteenth century, they were known as 'Salzburgers' and as 'Germans', but never as 'Austrians'. Use of 'Austria' in the period here considered can be anachronistic but it will be used for the remainder of this paper to refer to the German-speaking regions within the Austrian Habsburg lands between 1700–1848.[5]

Emigration from Austria in the eighteenth century followed, largely, an established movement from the east to the west, with the exception of Protestant migration from within Austria to the east of the Habsburg-governed territories. Migrations in the pre-industrial period, however, impacted only on a small percentage of the entire population. In the mercantilist economic and populationist politics of the eighteenth century, emigration was perceived as a direct challenge to the well-being of the state, by challenging the maintenance of a stable, and full, population. Overtaken by the popularity of the British American colonies, lands 'granted special blessings',[6] the Habsburg Monarchy had great difficulties in persuading willing migrants that the preferred direction in which to travel was east, and not west; to Hungary rather than to America.[7] Stories of the opportunities available to those willing to live and work in America became ever more common and popular in the eighteenth century as agents, many in the pay of Dutch shipping houses, tramped the highways and byways of Central Europe, earning *Kopfgeld* for every man or woman they recruited for the colonies. These recruiters, known colloquially as *Seelenverkaufer*, *Werber* or *Menschendiebe*, retailed stories of endless land, of opportunities unequalled anywhere other than America. America became the stuff of fairy-tales, where hunger never existed and people sailed on rivers of milk and honey. Belief in a better world, sometimes leaning very heavily towards a mythical 'Eldorado' was reinforced by the appearance of recruiters with their story-telling ability.[8] In the face of such competition with agents working for the settlement of the American colonies, it proved difficult to convince willing migrants of the merits of Hungary, known by many as the 'German graveyard'. The primary initiative for the Habsburg Monarchy's internal colonisation drive was a reaction to shortcomings in the political and administrative system controlling Habsburg governmental practice.[9] The greatest advocate of this change was Wenzel Anton Graf Kaunitz, who recognised the socio-political, economic, and political advantages in settling the Habsburg territories outside the hereditary lands with loyal subjects.[10] Kaunitz saw no other alternative but to revert to a dualist policy of prohibiting subjects from departing the Austrian lands, while often covertly directing those who were en route to travel to Hungary rather than America.[11] Yet eighteenth-century Austrian recruiting efforts to, at times, prohibit and, at other times, sanction emigration appeared outdated, ineffective and unattractive and remained closed to change and innovation.[12] The lure of the American colonies was proving too powerful to be challenged by neighbouring Austrian-administered territories as rival destinations.[13] Yet while emigration to America was illegal, families had at the very least access to information about conditions there. Hungary remained under-marketed and thus unattractive to those subjects who would be potential colonists. Bad communication and the lack of an information network seemed to be the greatest obstacles to a greater success in the imperial colonisation of Austrian territories. In general, the settlement of parts of Hungary with Austrian and German migrants was exceptionally badly organised and lacked both official scrutiny and interest, especially when compared with the activities of agents for North America and for other contemporary European absolutist states engaged in the attraction and settlement of migrants.[14] Agents working for Vienna failed to imbibe the methods employed by agents working for Pennsylvania or any of the American colonies and by the time new methods were attempted it was too late. Those settlers who became agents in the Hungarian Banat were quick to realise that opportunities there were just as advantageous as in America: they ascribed the name 'Europe's America' to the Banat in the hope of increasing the popularity of the destination.[15] Agents were quick to realise that much of the determination to move to America was associated with the name, and referring to the Banat as 'Europe's America' infused Hungary's reputation with positive attributes previously only associated with North America. But the administration in Vienna, which approved of this migration to the east, had not learned from the successes of recruiters for America in the 1740s and 1750s.

EMIGRATION FROM THE MONARCHY

This point goes some way in explaining why emigration from the Austrian lands was a relatively rare occurrence in the eighteenth century. While incentives certainly existed for many subjects of the Habsburg Monarchy to cross the Atlantic, emigration was limited to a few thousand people at most. Whereas by 1734, an estimated 10,000 families had moved through Austrian lands, with the approval of the Viennese administration, to settle lands in Hungary, perhaps as few as 1 percent of that number had crossed the Atlantic to America.[16] Knowledge of America was prevalent and common in the Monarchy, but emigration was curtailed for a variety of reasons.[17] By the eighteenth century, Europe and the Americas were linked economically, socially and culturally as never before, with America acquiring a reputation as the land of opportunity, advancement and adventure. Yet the Habsburg Monarchy was not, like many western European neighbours, a state with a tradition of overseas migration. While attempts were made to establish trading centres, most notably at Trieste, little came of these efforts, largely as a result of restrictions imposed during negotiations over the Pragmatic Sanction. Unlike its regal neighbours to the west, the Austrian Habsburgs did not possess colonies in the Atlantic, Indian or Pacific Oceans, nor was it likely they ever would. The House of Habsburg continued to share a lengthy border with an Ottoman Empire which in the early eighteenth century was entering a period of steady decline. Conscious that land regained in military successes from the Ottoman Empire would need to be absorbed into the Habsburg administrative system as speedily and efficiently as possible, civil and military administrators alike recognised the need to colonise these new territories with the greatest speed and by planting the most loyal subjects. Hungary, and particularly the Banat of Temesvar, was to be an experiment in colonial government of a type the Habsburg administration had not tried before. What began with the end of the siege of Vienna in 1683 would continue until the close of the eighteenth century; a unique process of expansion not limited to extra-European activities, but operated within the continent, too.[18] Colonisation and expansion within continental Europe were intrinsic parts of contemporary developments in the Atlantic world and the continental processes of reconquest and settlement were either modelled on, or directly imitated, practices in North America.[19] The Banat was to be an entrepot for merchants and ministers, soldiers and settlers, a new site for development and design. Just as in North America, these early years of conquest and colonisation in southern Hungary had economic and administrative success as the ultimate objective, and most hinged on the successful plantation of the country with colonists. This was a unique opportunity for a Habsburg Monarchy which desired and badly needed wealth; a near land-locked power with far-reaching ambitions for expansion and growth. For the first time, the Habsburg administration found itself in the role of coloniser: not in the *terra incognita* of the Americas, nor in the *res nullius* of the Pacific, but in the 'lost lands' of Europe.[20]

The Habsburg Monarchy thus became a colonial enterpriser in the more unusual position of colonisers within the European continent. The experiment of colonial government which led Sweden to colonise New Sweden along the Delaware took place in the Nordic north in the lands of the Sarni; Britain had its colonial experiment in Ireland before venturing to New England in North America. The Habsburg Empire had its experiment in the Banat of Temesvar in Hungary, before pushing later in the eighteenth century into Galicia in the north and thereafter consolidating her government of the northern Balkans in the nineteenth century. In a model which was advocated in England's colonies and in the Balkans alike, colonists were the worker

– CHAPTER 7: *Emigration to the New World* –

bees of colonial industry, and the hive could be transplanted to different landscapes.[21] The early eighteenth century ushered in choice for potential colonists, and competition for their labour was inevitable. Colonists, the worker bees who built eighteenth-century Empires, were presented with the one great directional choice: to go east or go west, to Hungary or to America. And the Monarchy needed to ensure that emigrants were dissuaded, or legally prohibited, from moving to America. The cameralist state duly responded in a slew of codes which limited the right of movement and prohibited the colonial American competition for colonists.

EMIGRATION, LAW AND THE EMPIRE

Significant changes in legislation governing emigration to the Americas and the Habsburg dominions occurred from the beginning of the eighteenth century. The century began with prohibitions on movement, even though the Aulic Chamber, the *Reichshofrat,* ruled in 1725 that 'it is against the nature of German freedom to remove the *ius emigrandi* from German subjects'.[22] Many German states attempted to dissuade emigration by introducing a departure tax, similar to a quit rent, which emigrants were required to pay. Without exception, all states in the Holy Roman Empire prohibited emigration at certain times during the nineteenth century. On 7 July 1769, Emperor Joseph II, in order to avoid the 'intolerable evil of depopulation', especially 'of young men', stated that the 'emigration of Imperial subjects to foreign lands will no longer be tolerated.[23] This imperial decree was implemented by many states, but the gap between the *de iure* position and the *de facto* reality was often wide, and laws may not have disseminated sufficiently to prohibit emigrants leaving the state. Over the course of the nineteenth century, successive bans on emigration seriously curtailed movement from Austria to North America at a time when over 100,000 migrants from elsewhere in the Empire were crossing the Atlantic.

From 1932, emigration from Austria required official sanction (*Emigrationskonsens*), without which emigration was illegal. This permission incorporated the resignation of, or release from, citizenship and subjectship on a variety of levels (*Ortsobrigkeit, Kreis amt, stadtischer Magistrat*). In the first half of the nineteenth century, just as in the course of the nineteenth century, the principal wish of the state remained the maintenance of a strong population, most easily attained through the strict control of departure from the state. Emigration from Austria and the lands of the Habsburg Monarchy to North America remained the final refuge rather than the first choice; the reserve of religious refugees and political patriots, denied a voice at home and seeking refuge in republican America.[24] Only with the basic law of 1967 (*Staatsgrundgesetz*) did the situation change in any significant way, when Austria-Hungary bestowed upon its citizens the right to make decisions concerning the crossing of state borders for reasons of emigration (*das Prinzip der Freiheit der Auswanderung*),[25] limited, however, by military service. While in reality, such possibilities were already in existence from the *Grundentlastung* of 1949, such a legislative change was highly significant and facilitated the mass emigration of many Austro-Hungarian subjects to the United States in the second half of the nineteenth century. No longer were emigrants from Austria and the lands of the Monarchy exceptional individuals or political refugees, but constituted the over 400,000 emigrants who sought a better life in the United States.[26]

121

THE GREAT EXCEPTION:
THE SALZBURG MIGRATION TO AMERICA

The sole exception to the micro-migration of individuals or singular families from the Monarchy to America was the migration of Protestants from Salzburg which took place in the 1730s. Protestants had lived in parts of Austria from the earliest stages of the Reformation.[27] The forcible expulsion of Protestants from parts of the Austrian lands, however, reached a new turn in the later seventeenth century, as with events in the east Tyrolian Defregger valley.[28] In the winter of 1684 Prince-Bishop (*Förstbischof*) Max Gandolph Graf von Kuenburg (1668–87) expelled the Evangelical farmers of the Defregger Valley, giving them fourteen days to leave and forcibly retaining these families' children behind.[29] Four years later, one of the most famous of all Austrian exiles (*Exulanten*) of the late seventeenth century, Josef Schaitberger (1658–1733), was expelled from the salt mining region of Dürrnberg bei Hallein. In the winter of 1685/86 he, and many others, were forced to emigrate, leaving their children behind to be raised as Catholic, and from his base in Nürnberg he attempted to raise the spirits, and raise to arms, his brother Protestants in Austria. Through his *Sendbrief* and his more famous song, 'Ich bin ein armer Exulant', he became a champion of crypto-Protestants throughout the Austrian lands.[30] Events escalated when, in 1728, the Price-Bishop Leopold Freiherr von Firmian (1727–44) called the Jesuit Order to Salzburg who attempted, through active preaching and campaigning, to convert the many Protestants of the Pongau to Catholicism. Appointing Hieronymus Cristani von Rall as his chancellor in 1731, Firmian initiated investigations into the state of Protestantism in his territory, vowing to preserve 'the old glory of the Catholic religion', despite one-fifth of the population being 'Acatholic'.[31] In seven legal petitions to the *Corpus Evangelicorum* of the Holy Roman Imperial Diet in Regensburg, over 19,000 Protestant farmers drew the attention of the Protestant lands in the Empire to events underway in Salzburg. The farmers were intent on protecting themselves and their Protestant culture, and gathered in Schwarzach on 5 August 1731, swearing by salt (*der Salzbund von Schwarzach*) to stand together against the incursion of Jesuitical Catholicism in their district. Prince-Bishop Firmian saw this as an act of rebellion, as the beginning of a Protestant Peasants Revolt in his territory, and called on Emperor Charles VI for military support. On 31 October 1731 Prince-Bishop Firmian, again in violation, certainly of the spirit, of the 1648 Osnabrück Peace treaty, declared that all adherents of the Augsburg Confession must depart the territory of Salzburg by April 1732; as this was a matter of expelling 'rebels' from the territory, the established practice of granting three years to sell property was denied the Salzburg Protestants. Instead, non-landowners had to leave within eight days, landowners had three months to sell up and leave. Firmian confidently reminded all who challenged his actions that his predecessor, Prince-Bishop Graf Paris Lodron, had not signed the Osnabrück Instrument of Peace.[32] Over 20,000 adherents of the Augsburg Confession departed the Prince-Bishopric in 1731 and early 1732. The majority – approximately 16,000 – travelled north to Prussia, where King Friedrich William I had invited the expelled Salzburgers to settle in East Prussia, under an Edict of 2 February 1732. The economic and military development of Prussia in the course of the eighteenth century owes a not-inconsiderable amount to the productivity, and the rich taxes paid, by

– CHAPTER 7: *Emigration to the New World* –

this successful colony of *Salzburg* Protestants.[33] Other Salzburgers settled on the Dutch–Flemish island of Cadsand; others in Holland, in Denmark, in the neighbouring German regions north-west of Salzburg; a small number in England and in other overseas European territories. A relatively small number, but significant in the history of Colonial America, settled in Georgia.

Largely as a result of the efforts of the pastor and Senior Samuel Urlsperger (1685–1772), who had held office at the German St. Mary's church in the Savoy, London, was a corresponding member of the 'Society for Promoting Christian Knowledge' (SPCK), and whose own ancestors had been exiled from Steiermark as Protestants during the Thirty Years War, Salzburgers found themselves on a path across the Atlantic. Urlsperger, from 1723 pastor at the St. Anna Church in Augsburg, used his contacts in London – especially his friendship with one of the chaplains of the German Court Chapel at St. James's, London, Friedrich Michael Ziegenhagen, who had also studied at Halle – to promote the idea of transplanting emigrating Salzburgers to the British North American colonies. When the *'Trustees for Establishing the Colony of Georgia in America'* received a royal charter from George II in 1732, the area between South Carolina in the north and Florida in the south was bestowed upon them for the founding of a colony. With the triumvirate aims of driving back Spain's aims on the east coast of America; to philanthropically serve the 'relief of poor subjects made poor by misfortune or want of employment'; and to create new markets for English products, they immediately thought of the fleeing Salzburgers as suitable colonists.[34] As time moved on, most of the future settlers of the Georgia colony would come to be called 'Salzburgers', irrespective of whence German-speaking Central Europe they came. On 15 December 1732 the Trustees decided to settle Salzburgers in Georgia and at the beginning of September 1732, some Salzburg Protestants gathered in Augsburg where, being provided for spiritually by Urslperger, they waited until 31 October 1733. On that date, 42 men and their families, 78 people in all, sailed on the Main and Rhine downstream to Rotterdam under the leadership of Baron Philipp Georg Friedrich von Reck (1710–98).[35] At Rotterdam, where they arrived on 27 November, two pastors joined the group – Johann Martin Bolzius (1703–65) and Israel Christian Gronau (1714–45) – who would accompany the emigrants on their voyage to Georgia and care for the group's pastoral needs. On 2 December 1733, the Salzburg migrants departed Rotterdam on the *Purysburg* for Dover and whence for North America. While at Dover, the cleric Henry Newman wrote to Philipp von Reck, wishing a speedy crossing and noting that 'our German Missionaries to East India commonly get the English Language in their Voyage thither, but I hope Your Voyage will not be long enough for that purpose'.[36] After 67 days out from England, the group reached the harbour of Charleston in South Carolina, where they spent five days recovering from the trans-Atlantic crossing. A further day sailing on the Savannah River brought them to Savannah on Tuesday, 12 March 1734, at around 2 p.m. A total of 143 days had passed from leaving Augsburg to arriving in Savannah. The colony would soon see the establishment of 'Ebenezer', the new home of the Salzburgers in America. On 28 December 1734, a second transport of 57 Salzburgers arrived under the leadership of Jean Vat aboard the *Prince of Wales*. This was an important contribution to the fledgling colony, as many of the new colonists were trades- and craftsmen. A third group arrived on 17 February 1736 under the leadership of Baron Philipp von Reck, although of the total 227, only a small number were

Salzburg emigrants. A fourth and final group would arrive on 2 December 1741, under the leader Johann Friedrich Vigera, accompanied by the 'surgeon' Johann Ledwig Mayer (Meyer). Each Salzburg family received 25 hectares of land, ground for a house and place for a fruit and vegetable garden. After five years construction and development, the settlement of Ebenezer was a functioning settlement.

Many colonial investors and proprietors began to realise the possibilities intrinsic to the supply of information to the Austrian lands concerning the New World. Pastor Johann Martin Bolzius maintained such a correspondence from Georgia with his Lutheran superior, the Reverend Samuel Urlsperger at Augsburg.[37] He noted that the Salzburg migrants did not venture along the much shorter voyage to Hungary for a number of reasons, including the obvious fear of religious persecution, although German Protestants did settle in Hungary during this time.[38] Rather, the Salzburgers were encouraged in their westward journey by news of America as a 'New Canaan'.[39] Being passively anti-Habsburg at the very least, these migrants were further discouraged from moving east by the prevalent and circulating malevolent reports of Hungary as the 'colonist's graveyard'. Bolzius cannot be accused of lavishing praise on life in the new colonies, nor did he encourage his contemporaries in Germany to uproot and undertake the voyage. 'Certain German news printed in Jena and Hanover about Carolina and Georgia', he wrote, 'contains much that I either do not find here at all, or the advantages of these provinces are much too exaggerated. It is a good, healthy, and well-situated land, but there are many difficulties in cultivating it. [...] He who makes a reasonable living in his Fatherland, and has freedom of conscience [...] does better if he remains where he is. But if [...] God provides willingness and opportunity for the journey to America, and he is not too old yet nor unfit for work, may he come in God's name; he will not rue it.'[40] Yet even Bolzius was open to manipulation. Little did he know that his letters were being edited with the deliberate intention of removing any disparaging and negative remarks about America, to promote Protestant movement to America.[41] The favourable reports given in the published version of the travelogue were, in part, due to the careful bowdlerising of his text by the Reverend Samuel Urlsperger. The unexpurgated versions show that Bolzius's fellow Salzburg passengers aboard vessel bound for North America had far more immediate concerns than contemplating the wonders of God, including lack of food, of clean water and of sanitation. Only when the original correspondence is compared with the printed version can the 'cleansing process' be fully appreciated. Samuel Urlsperger went so far as to edit out all references to sickness, infertile soil and the high level of mortality at Ebenezer, Georgia.[42] One Salzburg colonist, Matthias Braunberger, audaciously disparaged the settlement in Georgia, but luckily for Urlsperger the potentially calumnious letter fell into his hands and he censored it, concealing all adverse news concerning the settlement of Ebenezer from a potential readership in Austria and Germany.

While written correspondence from both America and Hungary to the Austrian lands varied greatly in style, it addressed similar themes of family issues; food, drink, land and religious practice.[43] Of course, not all letters were flattering to the new land, and many promoters found it necessary to alter correspondence to support claims of a better life overseas. Still others ascribed the name 'Europe's America' to Southern Hungary in the hope of increasing the popularity of the destination in the Empire.[44] Despite its distance and legal prohibition on travel to the country, America remained at the forefront of the 'Austrian' imagination, and this conceptualisation of America as a 'land of milk and honey' would intensify at the end of the eighteenth century.

THINKING ABOUT AMERICA: AUSTRIA LOOKS WEST

In the eighteenth century 'Austrians', like other peer Europeans, looked upon America as the home of children of nature, noble red-men and savages, who possessed all the virtues of the human race uncorrupted by the contaminating influences of civilisation and government. Thousands of Europeans knew America only through the letters that came from across the sea, and from the travel literature and emigrant guides that appeared in all the leading European languages.[45] The 'image' of America was comprised of a complex group of associations, phrases, ideas and attitudes in varying forms and combinations that evoked America in the readers' minds.[46] It was in the nineteenth century that the ordinary people of Europe looked to America as the land of their dreams; the nineteenth century was 'the American century' in that America stood as the ideal and goal of many of Europe's masses. It was for countless Europeans, just as for Austrians, 'the Century of the Common Man', the century of mass emigration to America.[47]

In general, from the end of the eighteenth century German-language publications looked to America with a curious, yet sympathetic, eye.[48] One can find in the German-language literature of the early nineteenth century two pictures of America. One, emphasising its rawness, hypocrisy, and materialism, and the curse of slavery; the other, representing the United States as a country where the refugees of Austria and Germany could find freedom from caste systems, from secret police, from bureaucracy and censorship, and from a standing army.[49] Significant publications from this period became the common currency in the exchange of opinions about America; frequently, these publications were first published in Vienna or were re-published for the Austrian market. It is no coincidence that the works of that Habsburg subject and explorer Ignaz Edler von Born (1742–91) would have an impact on his peers in Vienna in the last decades of the eighteenth century and would lead to the publication in Vienna of the first systematic geological description of America, written by Johann David Schopf.[50] These works informed a new audience of the possibilities, and potential, of America as a site of success and a resource for refuge. Such sentiments were not uncommon from the earliest years of the United States. Austrian interest in America awoke with a vengeance through the provocation of such authors as the enigmatic Karl Postl, a Kreuzherr from Moravia who had moved to Vienna and changed his name to Charles Sealsfield.[51] Sealsfield made five visits to America and his stories circulated widely in Austria and Hungary;[52] his writings had a decided influence on emigration from Austria in the early nineteenth century.[53] Another neglected, but equally important figure in understanding Austria's image of America and Austrian emigration to the United States in the nineteenth century is the Austrian poet Nikolas Lenau.[54] Lenau wrote parodies on Yankee Doodle, referred to the United States as the 'verschweinte' instead of the 'Vereinte Staaten' and helped to spread such misinformation about the United States among the population at home in Austria as the belief that birds do not sing and flowers do not smell in America.[55] Such negative opinions became more frequent as a growing body of clerics and academics challenged the reputation of America as a *deus ex machina* for life's woes and worries. One such voice was the Reverend Philip Schaff, who reported in 1854 that many respectable men of high culture, especially in Austria, spoke only with contempt of America, which they regarded as 'a grand bedlam, a rendezvous of European scamps and vagabonds.'[56] Debates about the advisability, or otherwise, of allowing information about America to circulate freely were contentious. It was even reported that the Emperor Franz-Joseph had refused permission for the establishment of chairs of American history at Prague and Vienna.[57]

CONCLUSION

While emigration from the Austrian Monarchy, and the Austrian lands in particular, was exceptional in the eighteenth century, it nonetheless established a pattern for the mass emigration to the United States in the nineteenth century. Had Habsburg administrators not been so preoccupied by mercantilist economic practices which stressed the need for a strong population – *ubi populus, ibi obulus* – then perhaps more immigrants would have departed the country to live across the Atlantic. But this is too simple; in reality, opportunities within the Empire in the eighteenth century far and away outweighed those overseas, at least for the majority of subjects. Only an elite of the population – skilled craftsmen, artists, clerics and nobles and political and literary activists – expressed any great desire to travel to the Americas, and they could, and did, without great difficulty. Others were denied the luxury of choice in this matter, as in the Salzburg migration. Religious refugees fled the Empire as they were forced to do so; their petitioning having failed, Salzburg Protestants had no other option but to emigrate. And a small number of highly motivated, part-Pietist, *part-Europamude*, refugees made their way to America. Austria and the Americas had been inextricably linked before the eighteenth century, but by the end of that century, Austria and the United States were forging a new relationship. If America became the first new nation, then its relationship with Austria and Austrians would ensure that neither could ever be an 'old nation' again.[58]

NOTES

1 David F. Good, Uneven Development in the Nineteenth Century: A Comparison of the Habsburg Empire and the United States, in: *The Journal of Economic History* 46 (1986), 137–51, here 145.

2 See Erich Buchinger, Die Geschichte der Kaminer Hutterischen Bruder in Siebenburgen und in der Walachei (1755–70), in: Russland und Amerika. Ein Beitrag zum Schicksal von Kaminer Transmigranten und zur Geschichte der heutigen Hutterischen Bruderhiife in den USA und Kanada, in: *Carinthia* I 172 (1982) 145–303; William O'Reilly, Agenten, Werbung und Reisemodalitaten. Die Auswanderung ins Temescher Banal im 18. Jahrhundert, in: Matthias Beer/Dittmar Dahlmann (Hg.), *Migration nach Ost-und Sudosteuropa vom 18. bis zum Beginn des 19. Jahrhunderts*. Ursachen-Formen-Verlauf-Ergebnis (= Schriftenreihe des Instituts für Donauschwabische Geschichte und Landeskunde, Bd. IV, 1999), 109–20.

3 Heinz Fassmann/Rainer Munz (Hg.), Einwanderungsland Osterreich? Historische Migrationsmuster, aktuelle Trends und politische Maßnahmen. Wien 1995, 131.

4 R.J.W. Evans, *The Making of the Habsburg Monarchy 1550–1700*. Oxford 1979, 446.

5 For a full and detailed consideration of these issues, see: Grete Klingenstein, Was bedeuten 'Osterreich' und 'österreichisch' im 18. Jahrhundert? Eine begriffsgeschichtliche Studie, in:

– CHAPTER 7: *Emigration to the New World* –

Richard G. Plaschka/Gerald Stourzh/Jan Paul Niederkorn (Hg.), *Was heisst Osterreich? Inhalt und Umfang des Osterreichbegriffs vom 10. Jahrhundert bis heute.* Wien 1995, 149–220.

6 Christopher Sauer writing in the *Pennsylvanische Berichte*, 1 December 1754.

7 See, *inter alia*, William O'Reilly, Migration, Recruitment and the Law: Europe Responds to the Atlantic World, in: Horst Pietschmann (Hg.), *Atlantic History. History of the Atlantic System 1580–1830* (= Proceedings of the Joachim Jungius Gesellschaft der Wissenschaften/ Universität Hamburg History of the Atlantic System Conference). Göttingen 2002.

8 Dirk Hoerder/Horst Rossler (Hg.), *Distant Magnets: Expectations and Realities in the Immigrant Experience.* New York 1993.

9 Konrad Schunemann, *Osterreichs Bevölkerungspolitik unter Maria Theresia.* Berlin 1835, 16.

10 Imre Takacs, Die wirtschaftlichen und sozialen Folgen der Wiederbesiedlung der ungarischen Tiefebene im 18. Jahrhundert, in: *Ungarische Jahrbücher* XIII (1933), 103.

11 Anton Tafferner, Ouellenbuch zur Donauschwabischen Geschichte Bd. Ill. München 1978, 244–46, no. 147–48; Konrad Schunemann, Die Einstellung der theresianischen Impopulation (1770–71), in: Jahrbuch des Wiener Ungarischen Instituts Bd. 1 (1931), 173 f., *Bevolkerungspolitik*, wie Anm. 9, 271, 303–16.

12 Schunemann, *Bevolkerungspolitik*, wie Anm. 9, 170.

13 William O'Reilly, Conceptualising America in Early Modern Central Europe, in: *Explorations in Early American Culture. Pennsylvania History* 65 (1998), 101–21.

14 See: Georg Reiser, Zur spat-theresianischen Ansiedlung im Banal. Gottlob, Triebswetter, Ostern, in: Neue Heimatblatter I (1935), 258 f; Friedrich Reschke, Genese und Wandlung der Kulturlandschaft des süd-ostlichen jugoslawischen Banats im Wechsel des historischen Geschehens. Dissertation Universitat Koln 1968, 571.

15 Roger Bartlett/Bruce Mitchell, State-Sponsored Immigration into Eastern Europe in the Eighteenth and Nineteenth Centuries, in: Roger Bartlett/Karen Schönwalder (Hg.), *The German Lands and Eastern Europe.* Basingstoke 1999, 91–114, here 105; Mark Haberlein, *Vom Oberrhein zum Susquehanna. Studien zur Auswanderung nach Pennsylvania im 18. Jahrhundert.* Stuttgart 1993, 89–92.

16 F. Milleker, Die erste organisierte deutsche Kolonisation des Banates unter Mercy 1722–26. Werschetz 1939, 8; M. Braess, Die Schwaben im Banal, in: Deutsche geogr. Blatter hg. v. d. geogr. Gesellschaft in Bremen, Bd. XXI, Heft 2 (1898), 70; K. Moller, *Wie die schwabischen Gemeinden entstanden sind*, 2 Bde. Temesvar 1923, here Bd. 1, 9; H. Zerzawy, Die Besiedlung des Banats mil Deutschen unter Karl VI. D.Phil. Dissertation Universitat Wien 1931, 30.

17 For a more detailed consideration of the recruitment of German-speaking migrants and colonists for North America and lands of the Austrian Monarchy in the eighteenth century, see: William O'Reilly, *To the East or to the West? Agents and the Recruitment of Migrants for British North America and Habsburg Hungary, 1717–80*, Dissertation University of Oxford 2002 (to be published by Cambridge University Press in 2015 as *Selling Souls. The international trade in German migrants, 1680–1780*).

18 Ronald Robinson, Non-European Foundations of European Imperialism: Sketch for a Theory of Collaboration, in: Roger Owen/R. Sutcliffe, *Studies in the Theory of Imperialism.* London 1972, 117–42. More recently, Richard Drayton, Nature's Government. Science, Imperial Britain, and the 'Improvement' of the World. New Haven/London 2000, esp. Preface, xi–xviii, highlights the importance of understanding the reverse processes of colonization at work in Europe in the 'Age of Expansion'.

19 Review of Nicholas Canny, Europeans on the Move. Studies on European Migration, 1500–1800. Oxford 1994, by Jeremy Black, in: *English Historical Review* CXll (1997), 201.

20 Anthony Pagden, *Lords of All the World. Ideologies of Empire in Spain, Britain and France c.1500–c.1800.* New Haven/London 1995, 76.

21 'Endorsed by both ancient wisdom and nature, the hive seemed to offer a perfect model for colonization. Just as bees swarmed from the overfull hive, English men and women should

leave England, groaning under its heavy burden of overpopulation, for the good of the commonwealth,' Karen Ordahl Kuppermann, The Beehive as a Model for Colonial Design, in: Dies. (Hg.), *America in European Consciousness 1493–1750.* Chapel Hill/London 1995, 272–92, here 273. Of course, the hive is also a familiar analogy in Central Europe and the Balkans: the seal of the constitution of the *Matica srpska,* published in 1864, shows a bee-hive, out of which bees are flying.

22 Robert Jutte, *Poverty and Deviance in Early Modern Europe.* Cambridge 1994, 203; U. Scheuner, *Die Aus wanderungsfreiheit in der Verfassungsgeschichte und im Verfassungsrecht Deutschlands.* Tübingen 1950, 210, n. 4, 'das es wider der teutschen Freiheit laufe, den Untertanen das *ius emigrandi* zu entziehen' [it ran contrary to Teutonic liberties to withdraw from the subjects the 'jus emigrandi' (i.e. the rights of religious emigration)]: G.H. van Berg, *Handbuch des Teutschen Policeyrechts.* Hannover 1799–1806, part II, 19 and 47. By the end of the century, the *Handbuch des deutschen Polizeirechts* (1799) suggested that the emigration of a 'surplus' in society was advantageous for the general population and the state.

23 Berg, *Handbuch,* wie Anm. 22, vol. 1, part VI, 1 18.

24 Traude Horvath/Gerda Neyer (Hg.), *Auswanderungen aus Osterreich. Von der Mitte des 19. Jahrhunderts bis zur Gegenwart.* Wien 1996, 14–1 5.

25 Erich Zollner, *Geschichte Österreichs van den Anfängen bis zur Gegenwart.* Wien 1970, 444.

26 Hans Chmelar, *Höhepunkte der Österreichischen Auswanderung.* Wien 1974, 20–21; Ders. (Hg.), *Nach Amerika. Burgenlandische Landesausstellung 1992.* Eisenstadt 1992, esp. 'Exportgut Mensch. Hohepunkt der Österreichischen Auswanderung bis 1914', 72–91.

27 A correspondence survives between the Hofgastein-resident Martin Lodinger and Martin Luther. See Gerhard Florey, *Geschichte der Salzburger Protestanten und ihrer Emigration 1731/32.* Wien/Koln/Graz 1977, 39–42.

28 Peter G. Trapper, Emigriert–missioniert–deportiert. Protestanten und Geheimprotestantismus in Osterreich und Salzburg zwischen Gegenreformation und Toleranz, in: *Rottenburger Jahrbuch für Kirchengeschichte* 13 (1994), 179–89.

29 Erich Buchinger, *Die 'Landler' in Siebenbürgen. Vorgeschichte, Durchtuhrung und Ergebnis einer Zwangsumsiedlung im 18. Jahrhundert.* München 1980, 35–40.

30 Gustav Reingrabner, *Jose ph Schaitberger, Bergmann und Exul Christi.* Wien 2000.

31 Florey, *Geschichte der Salzburger Protestanten,* wie Anm. 27, 79.

32 J.K. Mayer, Die Emigration Salzburger Protestanten von 1731/32, in: *Mitteilungen d. Gesellschaft f. Salzburger Landeskunde,* Bde. 69–71 (1929–31); C.F. Arnold, Die Austreibung der Salzburger Protestanten und ihre Aufnahme bei den Glaubensgenossen. o.O. 1900; Gerhard Florey, Bischofe, Kelzer, Emigranten. Salzburg 1967.

33 Martin Behaim-Schwarzenbach, Hohenzollnerische Colonisationen. *Ein Beitrag zu der Geschichte des preu Bischen Staates und der Colonisation des Östlichen Deutschlands.* Leipzig 1874.

34 W.K. Kavenagh (Hg.), *Foundations of Colonial Georgia. A Documentary History,* Vol. 3. New York 1973, 1822 f. Thomas J. Müller-Bahlke/Jürgen Grosch/ (Hg.), *Salzburg – Halle – Nordamerika.* Tübingen 1999, Llll-LXV.

35 George Fenwick Jones (Hg.), *Detailed Reports on the Salzburger Emigrants Who Settled in America. Edited by Samuel Urlsperger,* Vol. X, 1743. Athens, Georgia 1988, 131–68; Florey, *Geschichte der Salzburger Protestanten,* wie Anm. 27, 185.

36 George Fenwick Jones, *Henry Newman's Salzburger Letterbook.* Athens, Georgia 1966, 89.

37 [Samuel Urlsperger], Detailed Reports on the Salzburger Emigrants Who Settled in America, hg. v. George Fenwick Jones, Marie Hahn, vols. I-XVIII. Athens, Georgia, 1968–95. For the background to Salzburg emigration in 1733, see Mack Walker, *The Salzburg Transaction.* Ithaca, NY, 1993. Klaus G. Loewald/Beverly Starika and Paul S. Taylor (Hg.), Johann Martin Bolzius Answers a Questionnaire on Carolina and Georgia, in: *William and Mary Quarterly.* XIV (3rd series, 1957), 218–62.

– CHAPTER 7: *Emigration to the New World* –

38 Mack Walker, *The Salzburger Migration to Prussia*, 70, in: Hartmut Lehman/Hermann Wellenreuther/Renate Wilson (Hg.), *In Search of Peace and Prosperity: New German Settlements in Eighteenth-Century Europe and America*. University Park, Pennsylvania 2000.

39 Paul Raabe/Heike Liebau/Thomas Muller, Pietas Hallensis Universalis. Weltweite Beziehungen der Franckeschen Stiftungen im 18. Jahrhundert (= Katalog der Franckeschen Stiftungen, Bd. II). Halle 1995, esp. 85: 'Durch Vermittlung des Augsburger Theologen Samuel Urlsperger, der eng mit den halleschen Pietisten zusammenarbeitete, wurde eine Gruppe van Salzburgern in der kurz zuvor gegründeten Kolonie Georgia angesiedelt und van Halle aus mit Pastoren versorgt' [Through the mediation of the Augsburger theologian Sam Urlsperger, who worked closely with the Pietists of Halle, a group from Salzburg was settled in the recently founded Georgia colony and was supplied with pastors from Halle].

40 Rev. Samuel Urlsperger, *Der ausführlichen Nachrichten von der Koniglich-Gross-Brittannischen Colonie Saltzburgischer Emigranten in America*. Halle 1735–52, in 19 Teilen, 3 Bde., here Bd. 3, 951.

41 George Fenwick Jones, *The Salzburger Saga. Religious Exiles and Other Germans Along the Savannah*. Athens, Georgia 1984, 13.

42 Ebd., 18; Oers., German-Speaking Settlers in Georgia, 1733–41, in: *The Report. A Journal of the German American History* XXXVlll (1982), 35–51.

43 A.G. Roeber, *Palatines, Liberty and Property: German Lutherans in British Colonial America*. Baltimore 1993, 23.

44 Roger Bartlett/Bruce Mitchell, State-Sponsored Immigration into Eastern Europe in the Eighteenth and Nineteenth Centuries, in: Roger Bartlett/Karen Schonwalder (Hg.), *The German Lands and Eastern Europe*. Basingstoke 1999, 91–1 14, here 105; Hiiber/ein, Vern Oberrhein zum Susquehanna, wie Anm. 15, 89–92; Marianne S. Wokeck, *Trade in Strangers. The Beginnings of Mass Migration to North America*. University Park, Pennsylvania, 1999, 27–31 and 116.

45 Carl Wittke, The American Theme in Continental European Literatures, in: *The Mississippi Valley Historical Review* 28 (1941), 3–26, here 3. See also Stephan W. Gorisch, Information zwischen Werbung und Warnung. Die Rolle der Amerikaliteratur in der Auswanderung des 18. und 19. Jahrhunderts. Darmstadt/Marburg 1991, *passim.*

46 Merle Curti/Kendall Birr, The Immigrant and the American Image in Europe, 1860–1914, in: *The Mississippi Valley Historical Review* 37 (1950), 203–30, here 204.

47 47 ibid., 203.

48 Hildegard Meyer, *Nord-Amerika im Urteil des Deutschen Schrifttums bis zur Mitte des 19. Jahrhunderts*. Hamburg 1929; Heinrich Schneider, Lessing und Amerika, in: *Monatshefte für Deutschen Unterricht* 30 (1938), 424–32; Walter Wehe, Das Amerika-Erlebnis in der deutschen Literatur, in: Geist der Zeit Bd. 17 (Wien), 96–104; James T. Hatfield/Elfriede Hochbaum, The Influence of the American Revolution upon German Literature, in: *Americana Germanica* vol. 3 (1900), 338–65.

49 Meyer, *Nord-Amerika*, wie Anm. 48, 38f., 41, 60.

50 Johann David Schopf, *Beytrage* zur mineralogischen Kenntniss des ostlichen Theils von Nordamerica und seiner Geburge was first published in the review *Physikalische Arbeiten* in Wien 1785; it was later published by Joh. Jakob Palm in Erlangen in 1787. For Born, see: lgnatz Edler von Born, *Briefe Ober mineralogische Gegenstande, auf seine Reise durch das Temeswarer Bannat, Siebenbörger [...]* Frankfürt/Leipzig 1774; Ders., Catalogus bibliothecae bornianae publica auctione vendetur die 10 novembris 1791. Wien 1791.

51 For the reverse view, that of Austria from America, see: Karin M. Schmidlechner, Splitting Images. US-lmpressionen Oberösterreich, in: Ursula Prutsch/Manfred Lechner (Hg.), *Das ist Österreich. lnnensichten und Außensichten*. Wien 1997, 311–33.

52 William P. Dallmann, *The Spirit of America as Interpreted in the Works of Charles Sealsfield*. Washington University Studies. St. Louis 1935. Interpreted as a champion of theories of 'race'

– William O'Reilly –

and 'blood', Sealsfield was claimed by the Nazis as their own, in an article in the *Berliner Lokal-Anzeiger* (26 May 1939); see: Wittke, American Theme, wie Anm. 45, 10, n. 23.

53 B.A. Uhlendorf, *Charles Sealsfield, Ethnic Elements and National Problems in his Works*. Chicago 1922; A.B. Faust, Charles Sealsfield's Place in Literature, in: *Americana Germanica* vol. 1 (1897), 1–18; Otto Heller/Theodore H. Leon, *Charles Sealsfield, Bibliography of His Writings* (= Washington University Studies). St. Louis 1939; Eduard Castle, *Der grosse Unbekannte. Das Leben von Charles Sealsfield (Karl Postl)*. Wien/ München 1952.

54 Paul C. Weber, *America in Imaginative German Literature in the First Half of the Nineteenth Century*. New York 1926, 162 f.

55 Anton X. Schurz, Lenau's Leben. Stuttgart 1855, Bd. 1, 204.

56 Philip Schaff, *America. A Sketch of the Political, Social, and Religious Character of the United States*. New York 1855, vii.

57 *Appleton's Journal*, 9:494 (12 April 1873), after Merle Curti, The Reputation of America Overseas (1776–1860), in: *American Quarterly* 1/1 (1949), 58–82, here 62 and n. 16.

58 In contradistinction to the claims of Peter J. Katzenstein, The Last Old Nation: Austrian National Consciousness since 1945, in: *Comparative Politics* 9/2 (1977), 147–71, here 147.

CHAPTER EIGHT

SEAFARING COMMUNITIES,
1800–1850

——— ·◆· ———

Brian Rouleau

In 1849, no less an authority than Herman Melville reflected upon the sailor's instrumentality to the Atlantic world. Himself a seaman before moving on to write memorable maritime novels such as *Moby Dick* and *Billy Budd*, Melville could speak from experience as he sketched out what it meant to be a waterborne worker. Seafarers, in his estimation, were 'the true importers, and exporters of spices and silks; of fruits and wines and marbles; they carry missionaries, ambassadors, opera-singers, armies, merchants, tourists, [and] scholars to their destination;' they acted as 'a bridge of boats across the Atlantic' and were, fundamentally, the '*primum mobile* of all commerce.' If they suddenly disappeared, he reminded his readers, 'almost everything would stop here on earth.' Yet the centrality of seamen to the basic functioning of Atlantic exchange systems, Melville concluded, was easily overlooked. For, the author asked, 'what are sailors?' 'What in your heart do you think of the fellow staggering along the dock?' These were, ultimately, men 'deemed almost the refuse and offscourings of the earth.' Seafaring communities crucial to the daily lives of millions around the Atlantic, Melville complained, were hidden in plain sight.[1]

That paradox – of the central and yet largely overlooked role seafarers played within the broader nineteenth-century Atlantic world – remains the focus of this essay. We know a great deal about the circulation of goods, peoples, and knowledge which comprises Atlantic history, and yet, the sailors who moved those items, individuals, and ideas are often ignored or taken for granted. There are many possible explanations for our selective amnesia regarding the waterborne world, but the most significant factor is almost certainly the strange disciplinary divides which still insist on treating sailors as a distinct class of people worthy of separate inquiry. In the words of one early American maritime historian, 'the sailor lives in a little world of his own,' and 'is like the inhabitants of some undiscovered country.' As that attitude became consensus opinion, seafaring communities were often studied as discrete and bounded entities unto themselves, almost entirely cut off from the world which surrounded them. This insistence upon sailor isolation was ironic, though, given the influential role mariners played in weaving together the disparate threads of the Atlantic basin. Even a cursory glance at the early nineteenth-century maritime world belies claims about the sailor's relative isolation, and forces us to concede that seafaring communities have long been at the center of the Atlantic world.[2]

REVOLUTIONARY BEGINNINGS

One defining moment for transatlantic seafaring communities was the era of revolutionary upheaval initiated by the American war for independence. A top down history of that conflict has gentlemen assembled in Philadelphia to draft declarations and coordinate a united colonial response to the supposed tyranny of British policy. Examining events leading up to (and during) the formal break between Great Britain and thirteen North American colonies from the bottom up, however, situates sailors in the thick of anti-imperial protest. The American Revolution, in a very real sense, began on the waterfront. It was mariners, after all, who were deeply affected by interruptions in trade instigated by Parliament's attempts to more stringently police colonial commerce after the Seven Years' War. Many sailors made up the mob of irate Bostonians – a 'motley rabble of saucy boys, Negroes, mulattoes, Irish teagues and outlandish Jack Tars,' in John Adams' disapproving words – fired upon by British soldiers during the infamous 'massacre' of 1770. And seafarers more generally turned out en masse to protest the practice of impressment, wherein the Royal Navy, to replenish its ranks, seized subjects from port cities and forced them into service aboard ships of war.[3]

Impressment was itself a truly Atlantic practice, given the British navy's size, dominance, and omnipresence. But, if experience with the press gang united disparate seaside communities throughout the region, so did the politics and tactics of anti-impressment. Imperious naval officers seeking to forcibly recruit seamen often ran up against the determined resistance of mariners and local populations willing to lose neither friends and relatives nor the value of their labor. The press was a threat to personal liberty, but bad for business as well, given the commercial disruptions resulting from the extraction of men from merchant vessels. Prior to the American Revolution, therefore, several sizeable anti-impressment riots rocked both colonial seaports and British cities. And many sailors were in the vanguard of the independence movement exactly because it would – at least in theory – put an end to the experience of servitude aboard His Majesty's ships. Liberty, at times an abstract concept for the nation's founders, had more immediate meaning for people subject to involuntary work under arduous conditions. Seafaring communities throughout America therefore saw much to gain from political separation with Britain, and threw themselves into the effort.[4]

When Thomas Jefferson inserted impressment into the Declaration of Independence's list of grievances against George III, he merely ratified what was already popular sentiment along the waterfront. Indeed, anti-impressment was *the* source of politicization for plebian peoples (not simply sailors, but many other of the harbor's denizens as well) during the revolutionary era, and it is nearly impossible to overstress the pervasive climate of fear and resentment produced by the regularity of capture and forced labor. The arm of the imperial state, in other words, often fell most forcefully on seafaring communities. Sailors' violent resistance, meanwhile, pushed others less inclined to act closer to rebellion. Hence one patriot's assessment that the uprising against the crown had been precipitated by seamen, fishermen, and

– CHAPTER 8: Seafaring communities –

harbor workers: 'an army of furious men, whose actions are all animated by a spirit of vengeance and hatred against the English, who had destroyed their livelihood and the liberty of their country.'[5]

At times during the revolutionary struggle, allegiances could be fickle and survival often depended upon flexible loyalty – mariner John Blatchford's chronicle of the revolutionary Atlantic spoke of repeated capture and re-capture by British and American authorities on the high seas – but a high percentage of now self-consciously American seamen remained loyal to the patriot cause despite inducements offered by their British captors. By the end of the war many sailors proudly spoke of their centrality to the struggle for independence. Iconography and memorialization of the conflict in the United States, moreover, often valorized the contributions and heroic sacrifices of seamen. In a new democratic republic nominally devoted to the advancement of ordinary people, common sailors stood as potent symbols. Maritime issues, moreover, continued to percolate throughout public discussion of the new nation's place within the wider Atlantic world.[6]

'BRAVE REPUBLICANS OF THE OCEAN'

With independence secured by 1783, the new United States was now free to crawl out from under the restrictive legislation which had sought to confine colonial trade within the boundaries of the British empire. American ships began to fan out across the globe, reaching as far as China within a few short years of the Revolution's conclusion. But this new-found liberty to traffic with the world carried with it certain dangers. The most pressing of these was the absence of the Royal Navy's protection. Previously, ships departing North America could rely on military escort. The young republic's ships, on the other hand, were potential prey for both marauders and rival maritime states. Waters around North Africa proved especially troubling, given the prevalence of piratical powers. Those societies' ruling classes made their money extracting tribute from foreign governments in exchange for safe passage through the Mediterranean. Nations which could or would not pay, on the other hand, were considered fair game for plundering. Captured crews, meanwhile, were often brought ashore and sold into slavery unless ransomed.[7]

By 1784, an American vessel had been seized by a Moroccan raider, with Algerian, Tripolitan, and Tunisian pirates quick to follow suit, oftentimes with the encouragement of British officials eager to exact vengeance against their former dependents. The United States paid tribute and spent money to free hostages when it could, but these expenditures at times represented over one-sixth of the young nation's budget, and quickly overwhelmed the treasury. The number of captive sailors, meanwhile, continued to grow. Generally confined to port cities, enslaved seamen were set to work on chain gangs constructing roads and fortifications, while those with artisanal skills saw service as forcibly enlisted blacksmiths or carpenters. But the men were also objects of public fascination at home in the United States. Redeemed captives wrote narratives detailing their suffering, popular plays were performed describing the experience of Barbary captivity, and port-city subscriptions raised money to alleviate their suffering. Much of the Barbary literature, moreover, became a roundabout way of publicly discussing the contradictions posed by slavery within the United States itself. Abolitionists wondered how 'Turkish' slavery could horrify Americans, given the nation's own population of unfree laborers. In what would become a trend across the early nineteenth century, seafaring communities were enlisted to examine and discuss some of the larger problems plaguing American society. The maritime world often tested the definition and limits of national sovereignty, not to mention the very meaning of 'liberty' itself. Sailors heavily publicized their many miseries abroad, and drove a larger conversation about the implications of independence. Was the nation truly sovereign if it allowed its 'brave republicans of the ocean' (a term many American sailors used to refer to themselves) to remain suffering captives abroad? How could a country for which mariners had sacrificed abandon them?[8]

That question became all the more urgent as the British continued the practice of impressment. With Napoleon's rise to power and France's strengthening position on the European continent, Great Britain looked to its naval supremacy as a key bulwark. But, chronic manpower shortages prolonged the Royal Navy's dependence upon the abduction of seafarers. The United States, which pursued an official policy of neutrality in what was considered a European affair, nevertheless found itself repeatedly drawn into the conflict. This was largely the result of maritime actors. American merchants (and a federal government almost entirely dependent upon customs receipts for its basic solvency) expected to profit from the wars of the French Revolution by acting as a carrier for belligerent powers. Essential food and other commodities could be transshipped by U.S.-flagged vessels, allowing the republic to flourish even as monarchical Europe imploded. Of course, the exercise of neutral rights requires that states at war respect those rights, and this was something the British in particular were not inclined to do.

Britain's infamous 'Orders in Council' granted the country's naval personnel the right to board nominally neutral shipping, impress alleged subjects found aboard, and interdict any goods thought potentially beneficial to an enemy power's war effort. The British justified their behavior as that which was necessary to preserve liberty throughout the Atlantic basin, threatened as it supposedly was by Napoleonic tyranny. And moreover, they rejected American claims that mariners naturalized as U.S. citizens were immune from naval seizure. Rather, British authorities subscribed to the idea of indefeasible allegiance, which is to say, once a subject of the crown, always a subject. The figures remain imprecise, but it is believed that between 1803 and 1812, between six and eight thousand sailors were forcibly removed from American ships. Relations between the United States and Great Britain deteriorated all the more rapidly after the Royal Navy began to target even ships afloat in American territorial waters. The most notorious of these episodes saw HMS *Leopard* open fire on USS *Chesapeake* outside of Norfolk, Virginia. Three American sailors were killed outright, while another four were stolen out of the damaged ship. Public demonstrations of outrage spread throughout the country, with seafaring communities again at the center of a maelstrom. Seafarers led the charge in agitating for punitive measures, and once again, waterfront districts proved themselves among the most politically active and highly radicalized spaces within the Atlantic world.[9]

The rallying cry which ultimately resulted in an American declaration of war was 'Free Trade and Sailors' Rights.' Emblazoned on a banner flown by American naval war hero Captain David Porter, the slogan was intended as a defiant display meant to rally seamen and goad adversaries. Yet each half of that singular equation possessed a history prior to the 1812 conflict with Britain which made American citizens

– CHAPTER 8: *Seafaring communities* –

particularly receptive to it as a rationale for combat. 'Free trade' was an elastic term possessed of multiple meanings. But, at some basic level, it expressed hostility to the then-reigning paradigm of mercantilism, with its emphasis on protectionist policy meant to enrich individual empires and cripple rival states. American revolutionaries had imagined themselves rebelling against such antiquated policies and ushering in a new era of international relations rooted in the free and peaceful exchange of goods on seas open to the ships of all nations. 'Sailors' rights,' on the other hand, possessed a more plebeian meaning. It spoke to a long tradition of popular resistance to impressment. When combined, the concepts proved a potent justification for the War of 1812 with Great Britain, a war fought largely over what Americans saw as

Figure 8.1 John Archibald Woodside's painting, entitled: We Owe Allegiance to No Crown
© 2014 Photo National Portrait Gallery, Smithsonian/Art Resource/Scala, Florence

repeated violations of their sovereignty on the high seas. The fighting itself remained inconclusive and the 1814 treaty ending hostilities settled nothing; the belligerent powers merely agreed to resume the *status quo antebellum*. But, with the decisive defeat of Napoleon, the British war machine was rapidly disassembled, thus ending impressment and interdiction. Seafaring communities in the United States of course elected to see the war as one fought for their interests, and a conflict in which their contributions effectively allowed the republic to win a 'second independence' from an oppressive foe. America, many of its sailors insisted, would not become a mere client state to its former overlord. Popular iconography during the war often pictured American sailors, swaddled in the flag, proclaiming 'We Owe Allegiance to No Crown.' European powers, in other words, had no right to treat the nation's citizens – and particularly its sailors – as subjects. The War of 1812, while divisive at home, and often disastrous at the battlefront, seemed to have established that principle, if little else. And yet, for those who remained in power at the end of the era's many wars of revolution, the politicized waterfront looked dangerous.[10]

CONTAINING THE CONTAGION OF RADICALISM

In one sense, Atlantic seafaring communities settled down after 1815. The chaos of war and revolution had been contained by the forces of reaction, and an efflorescence of transoceanic trade was the result. But important changes were nevertheless afoot throughout the region. Counterrevolutionary forces had, in the space of a few decades, borne witness to the role of maritime workers in circulating seemingly 'dangerous' ideologies. In response, there was a concerted, state-driven effort to curtail what powerbrokers saw as the seafaring sector's worst tendencies. The revolutionary potential of plebeian radicalism along the waterfront had been useful during the struggle for American independence, and sailor grievances had helped mobilize vast constituencies in subsequent Atlantic conflicts designed to make watery highways safe for national commerce. But some people clearly worried that the insurrectionary potential of maritime workers could be put to far more unwholesome ends.

Hints of these efforts at stymieing the saltwater powder keg were apparent by the early eighteenth century at least. The British state took the lead in suppressing piracy throughout the Atlantic world, given the threat to mercantile interests such sea-robbers represented. The quest to contain piracy was ironic, to some extent, given that England itself had helped create the problem by issuing copious letters of marque authorizing the plunder of Spanish treasure ships. Privateers without enemy targets, it turns out, would begin to turn on their former masters, and the problem soon required a solution before ceaseless marauding and skyrocketing insurance rates made transatlantic commercial enterprise entirely unprofitable. But buccaneers were more than a military threat to the secure conduct of trade. Many pirates were notable for their democratic and egalitarian practices – the election of officers and sharing of wealth – within a maritime world where shipboard norms tended toward hierarchy and authoritarianism. Piracy should not, of course, be confused with utopian socialism. Their brutality often replicated the very state-sanctioned violence they claimed to rebel against, while many more pirates reinforced the Atlantic world's worst human rights violations by trafficking in slaves and plantation-based commodities. And yet, the existential threat pirates represented to the intertwined interests of mercantile capitalism and the nation-

– CHAPTER 8: *Seafaring communities* –

state was taken seriously. No expense was spared in exterminating seaborne raiders, whose often gruesome executions stood as very public warnings to any who might wish to imitate their crimes.[11]

The seagoing community showed itself disposed to other forms of labor radicalism as well. Perhaps not as drastic or dramatic as piracy, efforts at shipboard combination and organization still appeared dangerous enough to warrant violent response on the part of the maritime state. There is no better example of this than the spring 1797 mutinies aboard Royal Navy vessels anchored at Spithead and the Nore. The complaints centered on low wages and abuse by certain unpopular officers, and sailors organized a fleet-wide 'floating republic' of elected delegates to negotiate with officials and maintain discipline within their own ranks. Sailors couched their grievances in patriotic language, and promised to return to duty should an invading French force appear. The Admiralty settled the Spithead dispute peacefully, but when mutineers at the Nore began to blockade London and issue demands for the dissolution of Parliament and immediate peace, authorities took a harder line. The principal ringleaders were captured and executed, with many more sentenced to penal colonies or flogging. Though ultimately suppressed, episodes such as these are instructive for their involvement with the etymology of the term 'strike.' Mariners who crippled their ships by striking (or lowering) the sails made serious contributions to the origins of collective labor action.[12]

In the United States, the potentially subversive qualities of seafaring communities often revolved around the issue of race. Black sailors, in fact, were viewed by slaveholding interests as a potential conduit for abolitionist agitation. There was certainly precedent for believing as much. The Haitian Revolution was a particularly crucial flashpoint in the creation of African-American communication networks spreading news of slave insurrection throughout the West Indies and U.S. South. One historian, for example, has traced the life of Newport Bowers, an African-American mariner constantly on the move from Boston to Baltimore and St. Domingue, and at the latter location acting as an intermediary between ships and shore while assisting escaped slaves. More generally, black sailors and waterfront workers combined with Haitian refugees to circulate rumor and information regarding uprisings, often inspiring imitators elsewhere. Denmark Vesey, in Charleston, South Carolina was one such individual. His life as a free black laborer (and former Haitian slave) in a southern port city placed him in a prime position to act as intermediary between West Indian radicalism and American plantation laborers. During his 1822 trial for allegedly masterminding a slave insurrection, it came out that Vesey was in contact, through the aegis of mariners, with revolutionaries in Haiti. Hence the fears many slaveholders harbored regarding the insurrectionary potential of maritime communication networks. Black sailors, in a general sense, set dangerous examples of mobility and freedom for plantation slaves. But local black maritime workers – enslaved and free river pilots and watermen – were also notorious conduits for the spread of news and anti-slavery literature from harborside to outlying countryside, as well as agents of the underground railroad helping to sneak escaped slaves aboard ships bound north. The many complaints of slaveowners about African-American mariners are revealing; the *Wilmington Aurora*, for example, editorialized that black sailors 'are of course, all of them, from the very nature of their position, abolitionists, and have the best opportunity to inculcate the slaves with their notions of freedom and liberty.[13]

137

There were, in fact, long-standing patterns within black communities around the Atlantic of seeing seafaring as an opportunity to escape some of the worst injustices of landward life. As romantic nationalism intertwined with racism to harden prejudices ashore, life afloat presented some amelioration; the barbaric Middle Passage, in other words, was not the only way by which peoples of African descent experienced the ocean. By 1820, some estimates place the number of black sailors at something close to 20 percent of the Anglo-American maritime workforce. Most of these individuals served as cooks, stewards, and other lower-status positions aboard ship, though a smaller (but significant) number rose to places of influence and authority as officers and river pilots. As these men found, the ordered and hierarchical nature of shipboard society tended to downplay the significance of race. Vessels required cooperative endeavor on the part of their inhabitants, and black sailors often worked as equals alongside white shipmates, thus experiencing a degree of racial tolerance and harmony not often found on shore. Seafaring labor also provided geographic mobility, allowing black sailors to travel to places beyond their immediate horizon, sometimes experience better treatment elsewhere, and even participate in events thought momentous in the advancement of their particular race. The floating world was, of course, no paradise, and black sailors could be subjected to indignities and humiliations no different than what they were accustomed to within segregated societies at home. This was particularly true as the nineteenth century progressed and nonwhite seamen began to fill more and more of the shipping industry's most menial positions. But, on the whole, black mariners saw shipboard labor as a reliable source of wages, which in turn offered opportunities for advancement and upward social mobility uncommon for most other people of their color within the Atlantic world. Free black communities throughout the area were often anchored by their relatively prosperous seagoing members. Given those circumstances, it makes sense that Maryland slave Frederick Douglass could refer to sailing ships plying the Chesapeake Bay as 'freedom's swift-winged angels, that fly round the world.' 'I am confined in bands of iron,' he complained, but 'O that I were free! O, that that I were on one of your gallant decks, and under your protecting wing!' Tellingly, the famed abolitionist later escaped bondage dressed as a mariner and carrying a seaman's protection certificate provided by a free black sailor from the North.[14]

Such a state of affairs was of course, from the perspective of slaveholders, unacceptable. It was only further evidence of the seafaring community's fundamental subversiveness, and, just as authorities in England had moved against insurgent strikers, so would masters act to crush this menace to slavery. And so, in response to the threats posed by the polyglot maritime world, South Carolina in 1822 passed a Negro Seamen Act. That law was, in turn, swiftly replicated by other southern legislatures. Collectively, these regulations required the detention of all black sailors aboard ships in slaveholding ports. Nonwhite seamen were arrested, marched ashore, and imprisoned until their vessel's departure, with ship captains responsible for the posting of a bond meant to subsidize incarceration. Northern merchants complained of the immense inconvenience and expense such a policy presented, while Britain and France lodged formal diplomatic complaint about their free citizens of color being unlawfully detained by American authorities. But legal challenges to the laws were turned back. Southern jurists argued that the Negro Seamen Acts were no different than the laws which governed black life in the North. If Yankee states could prevent

African Americans from voting, segregate them in public accommodations, and prevent their intermarriage with white people, then what prevented slaveholders from enacting their own restrictions? More pressingly, the law's champions argued that just as the basic right of self-preservation granted states the authority to enact quarantines against sick people to avoid epidemics, so could that same impulse allow for the quarantine of people who might spread the 'contagion' of slave insurrection. For in southern ports, one of the Seamen's Acts' apologists argued, 'we think the presence of a free negro, fresh from the lectures of an Abolition Society equally dangerous' as any other traveler carrying some communicable tropical malady. The laws withstood efforts to overturn them, and represented further challenge to the relatively unrestricted border-crossing which had characterized an earlier Atlantic world. Class and race began to exercise far greater control over the lives of seafaring communities previously insulated, more or less, from those divisive ideologies.[15]

Thus currents of resistance and revolution which subverted the status quo circulated the Atlantic, but these were, at the same time, routes along which repression traveled. The variety of 'racial quarantine' practiced by southern U.S. states was one component of a broader transoceanic effort. These restrictions were crafted in response to exactly the sort of insurgent impulses the seafaring community helped transmit. In Great Britain, for example, Parliament passed the Merchant Shipping Act of 1823. It was a law designed to deal with the island's own 'racial contagion,' represented by so-called Lascar (or South Asian) seamen shipped to English ports aboard East India Company vessels. According to the bill's terms, Lascar sailors were, while in Britain, to be housed within their own segregated facilities. And, those who did not return home aboard their vessels could be arrested, charged with vagrancy, and imprisoned. Meanwhile, the British colony of Sierra Leone was conceptualized, at least in part, as a dumping ground for black seamen mustered out of the Royal Navy – but unwanted on the streets of London – during the massive demobilizations sweeping Europe after Napoleon's defeat. These laws were all rationalized as efforts to strengthen the national bloodline by expelling foreign-born and nonwhite 'impurities.' In Cuba too, local authorities, protective of slaveholding interests, and hoping to wall the island off from the revolutionary agency of seafarers, began to enforce their own Negro Seamen Act. Recognizing the seafaring community's insurgent capacity, burgeoning nation-states and anxious colonial leaders throughout the Atlantic world began to draw lines and enforce boundaries.[16]

REFORMING THE ATLANTIC WATERFRONT

In attempting to delimit and contain a 'dangerous' free-floating maritime class, states did not act alone. Seafaring communities also increasingly became the objects of interest for reform societies seeking to better, as they saw it, the sailor's condition. Mariners, many complained, led immoral and self-destructive lives, characterized by excessive drinking, sexual licentiousness, and brutal brawling. Taken as a whole, those vices were certainly problematic, but the larger problem again connected to the issue of 'contagion.' For the issue here was exactly that the sailor's dissolute lifestyle might infect and pervert communities throughout the Atlantic where seafarers regularly made landfall. Cleaning up the waterfront would help purify seaport cities, but would also prevent mariners from spreading the 'infection' of depravity as they circulated among locations throughout the Atlantic. Diplomats and missionaries stationed overseas painted a picture of mariners as, in the words of one evangelist, 'white-faced heathen.' Prone to sickening displays of viciousness, men of the sea needed to be restrained for the good of the entire project of social, economic, religious uplift that was the 'civilizing mission.' Descriptions of seafarers as 'rogues,' 'rascals,' and 'miscreants' peppered more official chatter within the Atlantic world's diplomatic channels, all used to express a growing sense that maritime rambunctiousness demanded containment before more catastrophic damage could be done. Transformation of the sailor's habits, pursued through a variety of methods, became a common answer to the problems presented by an aquatic class of supposedly questionable moral fiber.[17]

And so, during the nineteenth century, waterfront reformers – mostly evangelical Christians inspired by a series of transatlantic religious revivals known as the Second Great Awakening – founded organizations dedicated to the advancement of the sailor's material and spiritual conditions. These were the so-called Bethel Societies. Beginning first in Britain and quickly scattering throughout the Atlantic, ships, churches, and harborside meetinghouses raised the Bethel flag, calling sailors to worship, asking them to renounce their supposedly sinful ways. Meanwhile, associations such as the American Seamen's Friend Society and Port of London Society (later the British Sailors' Society) pressured ship owners and mercantile firms to donate money that would be used to distribute bibles, build churches, erect boarding houses and reading rooms, and establish banks for the benefit of common seamen. Commercial hubs where sailors swarmed became attractive targets for those seeking a solution to what middle-class activists increasingly referred to as the recklessness of the ocean's nautical ambassadors. While typically understood as one part (and a relatively insignificant one when compared to abolition or temperance) of the era's larger reform movements, we might better view these efforts as part of a consequential and coordinated international assault against the threat to the stability of the mercantile economic order posed by mariner misdeeds. Powerful interests aligned behind this crusade, and couched their proposed solution to a perceived crisis in Atlantic capitalism in the language of religious uplift. The steady, sober, spiritually sound habits of businessmen needed to become those of sailors as well.[18]

'Proper' authorities – mostly merchants and their allies in government – the argument went, would be secure in their profits once they had taught mariners the virtues of sobriety and self-respect. This was, of course, a self-interested claim. Drunken and degenerate crews endangered ships and their valuable cargoes, thereby driving up marine insurance rates and the costs of doing business more generally. A concerted effort to instruct seamen to 'behave,' to bring some semblance of discipline to transatlantic waterfront communities more generally, would ensure a more compliant workforce. The secure conduct of trade now depended upon toughening the temperament of the era's largest and most influential class of transnational intermediaries: sailors. With the many 'villainies [that] have been practised' by mariners on his mind, it was, as one U.S. diplomat argued, 'absolutely necessary to retrieve the character of Americans' at his outpost, and presumably, elsewhere. 'Character' – a concept central to reform movements of the long nineteenth century – became a word repeated in diplomatic correspondence, and spoken about as crucial to the commercial contacts which sustained the Atlantic world. Missionaries,

— CHAPTER 8: *Seafaring communities* —

meanwhile, saw in their efforts at sailor conversion a dual advantage: the preservation of valuable economic relations jeopardized by mariner radicalism and disruptiveness, as well as the creation of additional evangelists who would spread the Word as they traveled the world. Reformers divined in the omnipresence of American sailors at all the planet's parts a prophetic possibility. Mariners, 'confined to no place,' men of 'extensive influence,' if brought to Christ, could prove instrumental to 'the spread of truth in the world.' Sailors became itinerant evangelists in a double sense: of the nation, and, given proper exertions, the word of God. As one rapturous waterfront prophet enthused, 'let the seamen of our land be converted…and an influence is brought to bear upon the missionary enterprise which will give it a mighty impulse; the Gospel will have free course and be glorified throughout the world!'[19]

But nor were sailors the sole 'problem.' Harborside districts more generally were often the subject of middle-class suspicion, ire, reformism. The seafaring community consisted not only of sailors working at sea, but their wives, children, and families ashore, all of whom performed much of the labor which allowed Atlantic waterfronts to operate. Women were absolutely crucial actors here, and though life on the open ocean was an almost entirely male pursuit, the era's so-called 'gentler sex' performed a good deal of the rough work which allowed families with husbands, brothers, and sons at sea to scrape by. With men absent, waterfront households, marketplaces, and lives more generally were run overwhelmingly by female entrepreneurs. To make ends meet, women performed piecework spinning yarn and canvas for sails and flags, opened their homes to paid boarders, and operated taverns or brothels. They managed money, property, and made other financial arrangements, thus cultivating a dependency among seafarers upon their partners back home. These were individuals, in short, who did not comport with emerging ideals and standards regarding the 'proper' place of women within society. Bourgeois ideologues might have insisted that the women's sphere remain confined to the household and isolated from the tawdry and hypercompetitive commercial world, but for the waterfront's denizens, such separation of men's and women's roles made little practical sense. Part of the problem with seafaring labor from the reformers' point of view, then, was that it degraded women by forcing them into the sort of independent role in the world for which they were ill-equipped. It turned women into producers of wealth rather than passive, if prudent, consumers. Moreover, they contended, men were supposed to support their dependents; with charities and poor-relief for seafaring families straining city tax revenues, observers pointed to the deficient masculinity of mariners – who failed to provide for their families – as a source of urban disorder and moral decay. Port-city women, however, even if rarely empowered by the assumption of responsibilities otherwise coded 'male,' showed remarkable resourcefulness despite the rampant poverty and broader disapproval surrounding their lives. Many proved scornful of attacks against their character as women who propagated vice and impropriety.[20]

Seafarers themselves were also usually unenthusiastic about reformist agendas considered to be efforts at curtailing their freedom. To be sure, some sailors appreciated waterfront reformers, and took seriously their attempts to save souls and improve conditions afloat and ashore. Mariners, like many other peoples exposed to missionary work throughout the Atlantic world, used evangelism to their own ends, took advantage of what opportunities it presented, and discarded what they disagreed with. Indeed, many sailors were especially supportive of transatlantic campaigns against corporal punishment at sea; flogging afloat was eventually outlawed in the United States by 1850 and Great Britain by 1879. But, the overall thrust of the historical record suggests that many more men were actively hostile toward maritime improvement organizations. Customary understandings of liberty within the seafaring community placed emphasis upon the very drinking and 'vice' reformers sought to eradicate. The bonds of fraternity among shipmates could potentially be disrupted if the activists' vision triumphed. Most individuals appear to have looked upon the changes as, in the words of one seafarer, 'a new instrument of tyranny.' This was a particularly provocative assessment amongst American sailors, given their sense of themselves as crucial instruments in the republican revolution against oppression. Efforts to curtail their traditional liberties – not considered immoral, but rather, as necessary release after the close confinement of an ocean voyage – were to be met with skepticism if not outrage.[21]

ATLANTIC ANOMIE

But for seafaring communities on the defensive vis-à-vis their customary rights and privileges, the nineteenth century proved a befuddling age throughout the Atlantic. Norms related to the time-honored waterfront conception of liberty began to disintegrate at a rapid rate. This was an era characterized by swift technological and structural change, and maritime peoples at mid century would gaze upon a world transformed. It was difficult, circa 1850, to point to much that was definitively Atlantic about an increasingly globalized industry. The pace of change was different depending upon one's location within the Atlantic world. Large seaports such as London, Liverpool, and New York had begun to transform by the eighteenth century and earlier. Smaller seaports like Salem or Newport experienced definitive alterations over the course of the nineteenth century. But no matter the precise chronology, the results were largely similar: voyages were becoming more capital intensive, labor intensive, and difficult as time progressed.[22]

Seafaring at an earlier moment had, with some important exceptions, been characterized by the basic familiarity of ships' crews with one another and their officers. Men knew their shipmates within the larger context of the local community in which they all resided, and while on the open ocean, crews were governed by long-standing norms within that community. Individuals who went to sea, moreover, did so as a stage in their working lives. They were not, in other words, part of a permanent class of maritime workers, but rather, a collection of young men who had grown up near the sea, and took to the ocean because it was expected of them, and because seafaring was a natural way to make ends meet early in life before settling down ashore. The vast majority of Atlantic voyages were short, coastal excursions which connected places relatively close to one another, and most who labored afloat rarely had occasion to speak of their duties as something out of the ordinary. Today, we are accustomed to think of maritime work as something extraordinary, and sailors as relatively eccentric or exotic persons. But the construction of seafaring communities as fundamentally 'different' or 'distinct' from other places or types of labor was itself a process, a set of ideas with a history of their own.[23]

And that process accelerated rapidly during the nineteenth century, the result of both technological change and the increased volume of transatlantic trade. The burgeoning dimensions of commercial traffic was itself a product of concomitant industrial and market revolutions sweeping across the western hemisphere. Seafaring

– CHAPTER 8: *Seafaring communities* –

labor fed a massive machine comprised of captive African laborers extracting cotton, sugar, and other staples in the Americas, as well as the manufacturing facilities in Europe which processed those commodities. But, as more ships plied the Atlantic, carriers faced stiffer competition. Profit margins significantly narrowed, and premiums were placed on speed, as well as on turnaround in port. In this more rapidly paced economic environment, costs were cut wherever possible in order to preserve a particular shipping firm's competitive advantage. Those saving measures usually impacted common sailors most significantly. So while many basic elements of the seaman's duty – to hand, reef, knot, splice, and steer – remained familiar enough, the context in which they were performed had been transformed. Larger vessels, longer voyages, strange destinations, and different crew composition gave to life afloat in the nineteenth century a flavor quite unlike that of earlier eras.[24]

The faster-paced tempo of nineteenth-century seafaring life is best reflected in the rise of packet ships traversing the Atlantic. In 1817, several New York textile merchants proposed to redefine oceanic shipping by introducing regularly scheduled service between their homeport and Liverpool. The draw was supposed to be speed. Tramp shipping had long moved from port to port in a fairly haphazard way, picking up cargo and ballast at a captain's discretion. Packet service – named for the packets of mail innovators expected to deliver regularly between North America and Europe – promised instead to adhere to defined timetables. Their motive was to secure profit from postal service contracts, passengers, and freight. Their prices came at a premium, but with the promise of speed and dependability. Shifts in shipping technology, pushed by packet companies, made those promises possible. The box-like ships of the seventeenth and eighteenth century were replaced by narrower, sleeker designs capable of carrying more sail and cutting through the water at faster pace. These were the so-called Baltimore clippers, forebears of the famously majestic clipper ships of the 1840s and 1850s, and they sailed as the 'Black Ball Line,' named for the dark spheres painted on their canvas. A new era of rapid transit was inaugurated, further advanced by technological changes. The advent of steam power was gradually, if fitfully, brought to bear on oceanic commerce, which resulted in American entrepreneur Edward Collins and Englishman Samuel Cunard operating several Atlantic steamship lines. The Atlantic world itself was becoming more fast-paced, with an emphasis placed on reliability, timetables, and scheduling.[25]

Yet the thinning profit margins along which highly competitive carriers operated took a real toll on seafarers. Across the nineteenth century, shippers shaved labor costs by skimping on pay, while at the same time, hard-driving captains and 'bucko' mates imposed stricter disciplinary regimes in order to extract more labor from men driven to push vessels across the ocean far faster than ever before. In the aggregate, voyages between 1800–1850 became more arduous, crew sizes were reduced, and real wages shrank. All of this meant, for common sailors, harsher punishment, longer periods of time spent at sea, more labor for each individual while afloat, and all for diminishing compensation. A key element in this new maritime regime was the heterogeneous social composition of nineteenth-century crews. Previously, a ship's complement consisted of people who knew one another, moved in roughly comparable social circles, and only in rare instances, expected to spend their entire working lives at sea. Now, larger and larger numbers of vessels shipped crews composed of men who were strangers to one another, and whose officers were more responsive to

143

shipping firms than the needs of ordinary seamen. The pressures of the bottom line helped create a more distinct, perpetual, and self-perpetuating class of mariners.[26]

In a word, the nineteenth-century Atlantic seafaring community was experiencing rapid proletarianization. Maritime work was shifting from something one did temporarily to something connoting more permanent status. Upward social mobility within seafaring communities declined precipitously; generally, men became locked into position rather than climbing the ranks. Waterfront districts were increasingly populated by a permanent underclass of shipboard workers trapped in persistent cycles of poverty and debt-dependency. Rather than being dispersed throughout the population, specific urban arenas arose to cater to the needs of impoverished seafarers, while the mercantile elite and a better-paid officer class occupied the healthier, wealthier zones of ever more stratified Atlantic seaport cities. Hence one historian's assertion that the period from 1850 to 1950 was 'the great era of the proletarianized waterfront.' Seafaring was riven by the cleavages of class more than ever before, and shipmasters responded to the risks of employing perennially discontented and underpaid workers by running a tighter ship. And, as the scores of cases before courts sitting in admiralty testify, shipmasters and their officers were much quicker to reinforce their commands with physical abuse. Sailors showed their dissatisfaction by jumping ship; the swift rise in rates of desertion reflects these sweeping changes in seafaring labor.[27]

Voting with one's feet became a popular tactic within the Anglo-American maritime world. The United States and Great Britain still dominated shipping lanes in the Atlantic, but, by the 1850s, British and American citizens abandoned the ocean in large numbers. They turned inward, seeking opportunities in industry ashore, and were replaced by sailors from northern Europe, South Asia, and the Pacific Rim. But it was not only the maritime labor pool which was globalizing at this point in time. The Atlantic basin was becoming less a bounded commercial entity and more a jumping off point for the wider world. Or, that is to say, the commerce of the Atlantic world was integrating more thoroughly into a world system of exchange. These changes, of course, were not all-encompassing. Specialized, localized seafaring populations ended the 1850s looking much the same as they had during the 1800s. Coastal trade networks still flourished and interior waterways were expanded with the reshaping of rivers and the construction of canals. Fishermen still plied the North Atlantic's waters, whaleships continued to thread their way through familiar seas, and colliers still hauled their sooty loads across the North Sea. The sheer diversity of seafaring communities cannot be overstated. But nor can the broader trends shaping those communities be denied. As the volume of trade increased exponentially, waterborne work became more and more sweated. The composition of the labor force in turn shifted. Shipowners from the Atlantic world's principal maritime powers increasingly recruited foreign-born workers to man vessels and subjected those ships to more stringent discipline. Maritime labor, meanwhile, became a much less remunerative occupation. It was now low-status work performed by those individuals thought too 'intemperate,' 'restless,' or 'aimless' to succeed on shore.[28]

Indeed, seafaring was thought the destiny of a 'degraded' and altogether 'different' caste of men exactly because it increasingly looked retrograde within the burgeoning 'free-labor' (or 'freer labor,' at least) markets of industrial capitalism coming to dominate Atlantic seaport cities. Men who labored on ships, by the developing standards of the time, were subject to what was considered an unusual degree of regulation by public authorities. And, moreover, sailors were still harshly disciplined within their floating workplaces by masters given broad legal authority to maintain order and compel labor. Sailors, therefore, simply looked like something of a breed apart within the capitalist system's growing army of workers. For while a factory worker could, at least in theory, walk away from his job whenever he pleased, a seafarer could be legally obliged to continue serving. Deserting a textile mill was not a crime; deserting a ship, on the other hand, was considered an offense, and the seaman in question could be arrested, jailed, and forced back on board. This made seamen appear as anachronisms, as something closer to a slave or an indentured servant. Seaman Roland Gould thus explained the increasingly anomalous position of seafaring communities within the liberalizing order of the Atlantic world by asking his nineteenth-century readers an easily answerable question: 'What American would ever be content to rivet the chains of slavery upon himself?' The externally coercive and largely patriarchal command structure of seafaring communities were now things to be avoided; Gould's query implied as much. The rigidity of shipboard discipline marked seafaring as odd in a world coming to consensus about the importance of internalized self-discipline – rather than legal and physical coercion – in the maintenance of labor relationships. Fewer men, therefore, chose that watery way of life unless absolutely necessary.[29]

Sailors were no longer celebrated as the bulwark of republican liberty, or the proud keepers of the British empire's wooden walls. They were now alternately pitied and excoriated as a quasi-enslaved class of unfree laborers radically out of step with the modernizing transatlantic basin. In the United States, the free-ranging western settler became the 'stock' national hero, while in Great Britain, the pith-helmeted pioneers of empire attained greater renown than their floating forebears. America turned to the commercial world locked within its own vast territorial empire; its former mother country's interests simply grew to encompass more of the planet's peoples beyond the Atlantic. Meanwhile, those who remained at sea were increasingly thought of by people on shore as strangers, aliens, and exotic. Seafaring communities, which had started the nineteenth century as powerful symbols and important political icons, had become, as Melville complained, the perceived 'refuse and offscourings of the earth.' Beginning at the center of events, the noted novelist implied, mariners were, by the 1850s, now at the periphery; they had, by and large, been 'forgotten.' Crucial actors in helping craft the connective linkages that defined the Atlantic world, seafarers had become a transnational proletariat removed from much of the public's consciousness. They were less 'Atlantic' and more 'global.' Sailors had, in effect, been swallowed whole – reduced to poverty and condemned to anonymity – by the same forces they had helped unleash.

NOTES

1   Herman Melville, *Redburn* (New York: Harper & Brothers, 1849), 178–79.
2   Frank T. Bullen, *The Men of the Merchant Service* (New York: Stokes, 1900), 251–53.
3   Paul Gilje, *Liberty on the Waterfront: American Maritime Culture in the Age of Revolution* (Philadelphia: University of Pennsylvania Press, 2004), 97–129; Gary Nash, *Urban Crucible: Social Change, Political Consciousness, and the Origins of the American Revolution* (Cambridge, Mass.: Harvard University Press, 1979).
4   Denver Brunsman, *The Evil Necessity: British Naval Impressment in the Eighteenth-Century Atlantic World* (Charlottesville, VA: University of Virginia Press, 2013).

5   Jesse Lemisch, 'Jack Tar in the Streets: Merchant Seamen in the Politics of Revolutionary America,' *William and Mary Quarterly* 25, No. 3 (July, 1968), 371–407, and quoted 401; Jesse Lemisch, *Jack Tar Versus John Bull: The Role of New York's Seamen in Precipitating the Revolution* (New York: Routledge, 1997); Peter Linebaugh and Marcus Rediker, *The Many-Headed Hydra: Sailors, Slaves, Commoners, and the Hidden History of the Revolutionary Atlantic* (Boston: Beacon Press, 2000), 211–47.

6   Blatchford in Gilje, *Liberty on the Waterfront*, 97–98.

7   Kariann Yokota, *Unbecoming British: How Revolutionary America Became a Postcolonial Nation* (New York: Oxford University Press, 2011), 115–52; Robert J. Allison, *The Crescent Obscured: The United States and the Muslim World, 1776–1815* (New York: Oxford University Press, 1995).

8   Hester Blum, *The View from the Masthead: Maritime Imagination and Antebellum American Sea Narratives* (Chapel Hill: UNC Press, 2008), 46–70; Lawrence Peskin, *Captives and Countrymen: Barbary Slavery and the American Public, 1785–1816* (Baltimore: Johns Hopkins University Press, 2009); 'Brave republicans of the ocean' in Gilje, *Liberty on the Waterfront*, 130–62.

9   Gilje, *Liberty on the Waterfront*, 163–91.

10 Paul Gilje, *Free Trade and Sailors' Rights in the War of 1812* (Cambridge: Cambridge University Press, 2013); Troy Bickham, *The Weight of Vengeance: The United States, the British Empire, and the War of 1812* (New York: Oxford University Press, 2012), 20–48.

11 Marcus Rediker, *Villains of All Nations: Atlantic Pirates in the Golden Age* (Boston: Beacon Press, 2004); Kris E. Lane, *Pillaging the Empire: Piracy in the Americas, 1500–1750* (Armonk, N.Y.: M.E. Sharpe, 1998); Robert C. Ritchie, *Captain Kidd and the War Against the Pirates* (Cambridge, Mass.: Harvard University Press, 1986).

12 N.A.M. Rodger, *The Wooden World: An Anatomy of the Georgian Navy* (New York: W.W. Norton, 1996); James Dugan, *The Great Mutiny* (New York, 1965).

13 Julius Scott, 'Afro-American Sailors and the International Communication Network,' in Howell and Twomey, eds., *Jack Tar in History: Essays in the History of Maritime Life and Labour* (Fredericton, New Brunswick: Acadiensis Press, 1991), 37–52; W. Jeffrey Bolster, *Black Jacks: African American Seamen in the Age of Sail* (Cambridge, Mass.: Harvard University Press, 1997); David S. Cecelski, *The Waterman's Song: Slavery and Freedom in Maritime North Carolina* (Chapel Hill: UNC Press, 2001), quoted p. 28.

14 Bolster, *Black Jacks*; Cecelski, *Waterman's Song*; Paul Gilroy, *The Black Atlantic: Modernity and Double Consciousness* (Cambridge, Mass.: Harvard University Press, 1993). Frederick Douglass, *Narrative of the Life of Frederick Douglass* (London: H.G. Collins, 1851), 61.

15 Bolster, *Black Jacks*, 200–214 and Leon Fink, *Sweatshops at Sea: Merchant Seamen in the World's First Globalized Industry, from 1812 to the Present* (Chapel Hill: UNC Press, 2011), 50–55; Michael Schoeppner, 'Navigating the Dangerous Atlantic: Racial Quarantines, Black Sailors, and United States Constitutionalism,' (Ph.D. Diss., University of Florida, 2010), passim, and quoted, p. 69.

16 Isaac Land, 'Bread and Arsenic: Citizenship from the Bottom Up in Georgian London,' *Journal of Social History* 39, No. 1 (Fall 2005), 89–110 and Land, *War, Nationalism, and the British Sailor, 1750–1850* (New York: Palgrave Macmillan, 2009). On Cuba, see Schoeppner, 'Navigating the Dangerous Atlantic,' 188–213.

17 *Berkshire County Whig*, Vol. 1, Issue 42, Dec. 23, 1841. The best treatment of waterfront reform movements appears in Gilje, *Liberty on the Waterfront*, 195–227.

18 Gilje, *Liberty on the Waterfront*, 195–227. The more general spirit of reform is covered in Bruce Dorsey, *Reforming Men and Women: Gender in the Antebellum City* (Ithaca, NY: Cornell, 2002). Valerie Burton argues that reformers propagated the stereotype of the rowdy sailor as a foil to the sort of workers – soberly inclined, fastidious – they hoped to raise within Britain and the U.S. in '"Whoring, Drinking Sailors": Reflections on

– CHAPTER 8: *Seafaring communities* –

Masculinity from the Labour History of Nineteenth-Century British Shipping,' in Margaret Walsh, ed., *Working Out Gender: Perspectives from Labour History* (London: Ashgate, 1999), 84–101. Stereotypes about sailors, then, tell us next to nothing about maritime lives, but rather speak to the imperatives of capitalist development ashore.

19 RG 59, M101, Consular Despatches from Canton, China, Reel One, letter dated May 11, 1795; *The Sailor's Magazine and Naval Journal*, Vol. 5, No. 1 (Sept., 1832), 1–2 and New Bedford Port Society quoted in ibid., 15; 'Communications and Selections: The Shipmaster' in *Sailor's Magazine and Naval Journal* Vol. 8, No. 1 (Sept. 1835), 9; 'When Shall the World be Converted Unto God?' in *The Sailor's Magazine and Naval Journal* Vol. 7, No. 67 (March, 1834), 204–5; 'Who Prays for the Conversion of Seamen?' in *The Sailor's Magazine and Naval Journal* Vol. 7, No. 75 (Nov., 1834), 67. As Isaac Land argues in *War, Nationalism, and the British Sailor*, 77: 'Jack Tar ruled the waves, but until he could master himself, he would remain a suspect figure.' Broader importance of 'character' to nineteenth-century reformers is seen in James Salazar, *Bodies of Reform: The Rhetoric of Character in Gilded Age America* (New York: NYU Press, 2010).

20 The lives of women in port in Seth Rockman, *Scraping By: Wage Labor, Slavery, and Survival in Early Baltimore* (Baltimore: Johns Hopkins University Press, 2009); Ellen Hartigan-O'Connor, *The Ties That Buy: Women and Commerce in Revolutionary America* (Philadelphia: University of Pennsylvania Press, 2009); Elaine Forman Crane, *Ebb Tide in New England: Women, Seaports, and Social Change, 1630–1800* (Boston: Northeastern University Press, 1998); Lisa Norling, *Captain Ahab Had a Wife: New England Women and the Whalefishery, 1720–1870* (Chapel Hill: UNC Press, 2000).

21 Gilje, *Liberty on the Waterfront*, 195–227, quoted 221; Myra C. Glenn, *Campaigns Against Corporal Punishment: Prisoners, Sailors, Women, and Children in Antebellum America* (Albany: State University of New York Press, 1984); Margaret Creighton, *Rites and Passages: The Experience of American Whaling, 1830–1870* (Cambridge: Cambridge University Press, 1995).

22 Daniel Vickers, *Young Men and the Sea: Yankee Seafarers in the Age of Sail* (New Haven, Conn.: Yale University Press, 2005).

23 Vickers, *Young Men and the Sea*, 163–213.

24 Ibid.

25 Alex Roland, W. Jeffrey Bolster, and Alexander Keyssar, *The Way of the Ship: America's Maritime History Reenvisioned, 1600–2000* (Hoboken, NJ: John Wiley and Sons, 2008), 158–71.

26 Vickers, *Young Men and the Sea*, 163–213.

27 'Proletarianization' of deep-sea labor in Marcus Rediker, *Between the Devil and the Deep Blue Sea: Merchant Seamen, Pirates, and the Anglo-American Maritime World, 1700–1750* (Cambridge: Cambridge University Press, 1987); Linebaugh and Rediker, *Many-Headed Hydra*; Vickers, *Young Men and the Sea*, 248–51; John R. Gillis, *The Human Shore: Seacoasts in History* (Chicago: University of Chicago Press, 2012), 112–13, who refers to the period from 1850–1950 as the 'great era of the proletarianized waterfront.'

28 Emphasis on coastal and interior waterways in Roland, Bolster, and Keyssar, *Way of the Ship*. Fisheries are discussed in Christopher P. Magra, *The Fisherman's Cause: Atlantic Commerce and the Maritime Dimensions of the American Revolution* (Cambridge: Cambridge University Press, 2009) and W. Jeffrey Bolster, *The Mortal Sea: Fishing the Atlantic in the Age of Sail* (Cambridge, Mass.: Harvard University Press, 2012).

29 Vickers, *Young Men and the Sea*, 214–47; Roland Gould, *The Life of Gould, An Ex-Man-of-War's-Man; With Incidents on Sea and Shore, Including a Three-Year's Cruise on the Line of Battle Ship* Ohio, *on the Mediterranean Station, Under the Veteran Commodore Hall* (Claremont, N.H.: Claremont Manufacturing Company, 1867), 191.

PART III
CULTURAL ENCOUNTERS

CHAPTER NINE

COLOUR PREJUDICE
IN THE FRENCH ATLANTIC WORLD

——·◆·——

Mélanie Lamotte

From the beginning of French settlement in the Caribbean in the seventeenth century, physical and cultural differences significantly shaped social relationships. This was a time of significant interaction between the peoples of Europe, of Africa and of the New World. The mental impact of seeing foreign bodies and cultures could generate negative reactions. Naturally, some Europeans had already encountered black and Amerindian individuals before this period, and had conveyed varying images of them. There were old ideas inherited from classical writers such as Pliny the Elder, Herodotus, and the medieval writer Leo Africanus, who depicted Africans as either hospitable or monstrous and brutish.[1] From the fifteenth century, Spanish and Portuguese travellers encountered the inhabitants of the Lesser Antilles, whom they called 'Caribs', and they began bringing African slaves to the New World at the beginning of the sixteenth century. From an early date, there were numerous reports, including those of Christopher Columbus, depicting the people of the Americas either as hospitable or as fierce cannibals on the border of humanity.[2] It is difficult to assess the extent to which these writings influenced the French settlers, officials and missionaries who came to the Lesser Antilles in the seventeenth century, but they were probably read by a significant number of people since many were translated into French.

This article focuses on the development of colour prejudice in the early modern French Atlantic World and examines inter-ethnic encounters on the ground, in the context of French Guadeloupe – an island located in the Lesser Antilles. The period covered spreads from the beginning of French colonisation in Guadeloupe in 1635 to 1759, the first year of the English occupation of the island, which would last until 1763. Reactions to inter-ethnic encounters in the French Atlantic were extremely complex, fluctuating according to economic, demographic, social and political contexts. Thus this article presents specific incidents of colour prejudices and considers general conclusions that might be drawn from them. By the mid-eighteenth century, several French Caribbean islands, including Guadeloupe, had developed labour-intensive plantation regimes based on large enslaved workforces of black, mixed and Amerindian captives controlled by a small minority of French settlers. The need to maintain this socio-economic system contributed to the formation of a particularly segregated and prejudiced society.

In this essay, I frequently use the expression 'colour prejudice' instead of the word 'race'. Definitions of the word 'race' vary, but it frequently refers to the classification of humankind into groups supposedly having distinct hereditary physical and intellectual characteristics.[3] Some believe that the word 'race' should be avoided, because of its connections with the nineteenth-century theories positing the existence of inferior and superior races. Others argue that 'race' should be avoided because scientists have demonstrated that there is no biological basis to racial categories.[4] Today it is clear that 'race' is a cultural and social construction. It reflects a way people think about some aspects of human differences, generating discriminations and antagonisms visible in the sociocultural reality. Historians are now embracing 'constructivist' approaches, by examining how concepts of 'race' were built throughout history. This essay does not deny the fact that the concept of 'race' already existed in early modern Guadeloupe; in fact, it highlights some embryonic evidence of the presence of 'racial thinking', and when this is the case, the word 'race' is always used. In the seventeenth century, however, physical and intellectual differences were generally not perceived as being fixed biologically and hereditarily through several generations. They were, instead, often considered to be the products of environmental and cultural causes, such as territorial sun exposure or foreign customs. Thus, in 1667, French missionary Jean-Baptiste DuTertre, who had been in the Antilles between 1640 and 1657, argued that Africans only had flat noses and thick lips because their parents crushed their faces during their childhood. He explained that he once owned a slave raised in Dominica and Guadeloupe with 'the face as beautiful as those of French people because [the] Fathers had categorically forbidden his mother to flatten his nose'.[5] Intelligence too was frequently considered to have resulted from cultural factors and not from an innate capacity. For example, Father Mongin, who travelled to Martinique and St. Christopher, pointed out in 1682 that 'some blacks do not lack intelligence and are capable of all sorts of arts and sciences, if they are raised that way'.[6] Creole slaves, who were born and raised in the colonies, were often thought to be more intelligent than Africans for this reason.

In addition, factors such as divergences in religion, customs, social status and the simple perception of unfamiliar physical features not considered to be innate and hereditary, were more important than 'racial thinking' in shaping inter-ethnic relations in the seventeenth-century French Caribbean. Thus the concept of 'colour prejudice' – defined as the hostility, dislike and antagonism causing an unfavourable and a discriminatory treatment of people who have a different skin tone, physical appearance and cultural heritage – can do justice to this historical context. The category of 'ethnicity' is here used to refer to particular cultural heritages and physical features, 'racial' or not.

During the period covered by this essay, the word 'race' generally meant lineage or ancestry either in relation to animals or to noble families. The *Dictionary of the French Academy* (1694) defined the French word 'race' as the 'ancestry, lineage, origin' of animals and old noble families. By the seventeenth century, the French élite often believed that the assumed values and virtues of the old nobility (*Noblesse de Race*) were transmitted through blood and that consequently, commoners were unable to become equal to the old nobility, even when they bought titles of nobility. Marriages of members of the old nobility with commoners were increasingly perceived as *mésalliances* – unions with people of inferior birth and social status, which corrupted blood purity.[7] It has been argued that by the beginning of the eighteenth century, these metropolitan discourses had migrated to the French Atlantic World colonies and consequently, the French regarded inter-ethnic marriages as *mésalliances* threatening the purity of white blood.[8] This essay suggests that, by the beginning of the eighteenth century in Guadeloupe, such notions had emerged, at least among a few élite men.

Historiography focusing on the emergence of racial antagonisms in the French Atlantic World seems relatively underdeveloped in comparison to the considerable number of works on the construction of 'race' in the British Atlantic.[9] In the second half of the twentieth century, some historians had begun work on the history of cross-ethnic attitudes in early modern France, the French Antilles, as well as in the broader early French Atlantic World.[10] When a substantial number of analysts began to study the history of racial antagonisms in the early modern French empire, they often focused their attention on the eighteenth century.[11] Interestingly, today, the historiography of the French Caribbean also largely focuses its attention on the eighteenth century.[12] A few English-speaking scholars have recently begun to investigate the early French Caribbean, however.[13]

Similarly, over the last two decades, a substantial number of historians have become interested in early cross-ethnic attitudes in the French Atlantic World. A few historians have worked on the emergence of 'ethnic prejudices' in the seventeenth- and eighteenth-century French Caribbean.[14] Others have focused their attention on early modern France.[15] But in comparison, historians working on cross-ethnic attitudes in the early French settlements in North America remain more numerous.[16]

This essay carries these works further by examining the less studied early phase of development of colour prejudice in the French Caribbean. It relies on under-exploited sources including judicial records, censuses and parish registers, as well as the works of the missionaries who, from the first years of settlement, came to the Caribbean to serve the settlers and to evangelise the Caribs. As far more attention has been granted to the early modern history of Martinique and Saint-Domingue, this paper provides a much needed exploration of the early modern history of Guadeloupe.[17] It shows that blacks and Amerindian people contributed to the development of colour prejudice along with the Europeans, an idea that has rarely been examined in historiography. This essay also argues that negative attitudes became more entrenched in the first half of the eighteenth century, this being particularly visible in increasingly prejudicial legislation enacted by the French colonial planter élite and by the mother country across the Atlantic. Finally, it suggests that, in spite of these regulations, and in addition to existing antagonisms, there were significant instances of cross-ethnic fluidity in social relations and in the structure of the society in Guadeloupe during the entire period covered by this essay.

EMERGENCE OF COLOUR PREJUDICE

From the beginnings of European settlement in the 1630s to the turn of the seventeenth century, colour prejudice emerged in the French Caribbean, alongside positive attitudes. The first decades of this period have been called the 'Frontier-Era' because the plantation regime had not yet developed and black slaves were still a minority in the French Caribbean.[18] It is necessary to be cautious when considering early modern censuses. The 1698 census denounced, indeed, the 'lack of regularity and accuracy which characterise the work of militia officers when they make the censuses'.[19] But one of the first documents providing a demographical count of the Guadeloupian population suggests that, by 1671, African slaves and their descendants had reached demographic parity with the white population. In that year, 4,267 *'nègres'* ('negroes') were listed in the Guadeloupian census, amounting to 57.6 per cent of the population.[20] This was partly because the Guadeloupian sugar industry had begun to develop. The proportion of black inhabitants increased slightly until the end of the seventeenth century. In 1699, 6,185 slaves were recorded (64 per cent of the population).[21] The authorities feared slave insubordination. In a letter written in 1672, Governor Claude Francois Du Lion complained of black unruliness in Guadeloupe arguing that, 'the *nègres* understand that their number is increasing' and as a result 'they stand stronger and are less submissive'.[22] Only 47 *mulâtres* ('mulattoes', people of mixed heritage 0.6 per cent of the population) were listed in the 1671 census and 291 (2.78 per cent of the population) in 1696.[23] The free people of colour (*libres*), comprising blacks, *mulâtres* and Amerindians, represented a growing minority in Guadeloupe in 1697 (457 individuals, or 11.49 per cent of the free population).[24] Contemporary accounts of missionaries Raymond Breton and Jean-Baptiste DuTertre, active in the early French Antilles, suggest that the number of indigenous people inhabiting Guadeloupe during the first decades of colonisation was substantial. But between the 1640s and the 1660s, the number of Caribs diminished considerably, due to disease and exile. Following the Franco-Carib wars that lasted until 1660, Caribs signed a peace treaty requiring them to move to Grande-Terre, Dominica and St. Vincent. There were only a dozen *sauvages* ('savages', referring to the Amerindian population) recorded in the 1664 census.[25]

In the seventeenth-century French Caribbean, the different ethnic groups adopted both negative and positive attitudes toward each other. To Europeans not used to seeing blacks, black skin colour could appear shocking and repulsive. Missionaries, in particular, often said that people of African ancestry were ugly and blacks were often considered to have a bad smell. In 1667, DuTertre stated: 'One cannot verify the proverb which says that love is blind in a better way than by considering the dysfunctional love which conduces some of our French men to love their negresses despite the blackness of their faces, which makes them hideous, and their unbearable smell, which should, in my opinion, extinguish the ardour of their criminal fire'.[26] In addition, missionaries described the *nègres* they encountered as primitive, passive, and, in the words of missionary Pierre Pelleprat, who lived in the Antilles between 1651 and 1653, 'not very intelligent'.[27] They also often charged blacks with moral vices such as laziness, drunkenness and theft.[28]

Commentaries concerning people of African descent were not entirely negative, however. In the French Caribbean, settlers seem to have thought more highly of Angolan slaves than of other Africans. In 1659, missionary André Chevillard, who stayed in the French Caribbean from 1647, stated that while blacks from the Cap Vert were 'stupid' and 'rude', those from Angola and Guinea possessed 'subtle intelligences'.[29] Clerics also developed optimistic opinions concerning blacks, perhaps because people of African descent often became very good Christians. Although one must be cautious with the evidence because the clerics probably wanted to instruct the French in Christianity, early missionaries celebrated African converts as excellent Christians 'who very often serve as an example of piety to our French people'.[30]

– CHAPTER 9: *Colour prejudice in the French Atlantic World* –

French attitudes toward the indigenous populations of the Antilles varied as well. Comments regarding the Caribs' skin colouring, which was considered to be 'sallow', were usually neutral.[31] Early missionaries such as DuTertre, Pelleprat and De Rochefort described the Caribs as being physically well built.[32] Caribs were also ascribed virtues such as politeness, bravery and gentleness.[33] The first clerics sent to the *Iles du Vent* also tended to regard them as 'noble savages', uncorrupted by the vanities of the Old World.[34]

But descriptions of the indigenous population were not always positive. Early chroniclers such as Breton, Chevillard and Du Puis sometimes considered the Caribs to be barbarous.[35] Although the Caribs did not, apparently, eat human flesh very often, some missionaries liked to underscore their reputation for cannibalism.[36] The Caribs were also thought to lack intelligence. Breton, with faint praise, declared, 'They are not too stupid, considering the fact that they are savage people.'[37] The meaning of the term *sauvage*, often used among French settlers to designate the indigenous inhabitants of the Americas was negative in the seventeenth century. The 1694 *Dictionary of the French Academy* described *sauvages* as 'people who usually live in the woods, without religion, law, and fixed abode, more like animals than like humans'. Such negative ideas were perhaps due to French feelings of cultural superiority following the conquest.

In Guadeloupe, ethnic categories surfaced in literary discourses and administrative papers from the first years of settlement, reflecting a form of discrimination. Censuses from this period provide information concerning the state of mind of the administrators in charge of managing the making of local censuses – as well as of the state officials in charge of gathering the data. In the Guadeloupian census of 1664 and in the missionaries' writings of the same period, the categories *nègre*, *négresse* ('negress'), *nègre libre* ('free negro'), *sauvage* and *mulâtre* are noted.[38] From 1671, census-makers began to divide these groups more visibly, by creating tables and columns with headings and the category *serviteur blanc* (white servant) appeared.[39] This grouping was probably created in order to clearly distinguish the remaining white indentured servants from black and *mulâtre* domestic servants.

It is more difficult to attain information concerning early attitudes toward white settlers among non-Europeans. Some people of African descent considered whites to be depraved, miserable, rude, ignorant and incompetent. In 1698, Labat stated that 'the *nègres* always attribute to white people all the bad faults which make a person despicable and they commonly say that blacks only go bad by associating with whites and by following their example'.[40] In the same year, Labat also reported how, in the French Lesser Antilles, blacks particularly enjoyed observing white people to identify their defects and 'to mock them when they are together'.[41] Moreover, black slaves might have developed feelings of superiority over the *petits blancs* (poor whites). Labat related how, in 1698, one of his black slaves decided to give his savings to a white beggar, 'in order to have the pleasure of calling him poor white man'. He explained how this same slave told him that only white people could be poor because, unlike white people, blacks were too 'big-hearted' to leave someone in such a miserable state.[42] The same missionary also devoted a section of his book to rumours circulating from Africa to the Antilles through slave ships, according to which the French were fierce cannibals, bringing the Africans overseas with the sole intention of eating them. He explained that 'because of this slander, many slaves became desperate

155

during the Atlantic crossing, and they preferred throwing themselves overboard to going to a country where people would supposedly devour them'.[43]

The Caribs also expressed negative opinions concerning French people, especially about their physical features. While to Europeans, beards symbolised virility and power, the Caribs abhorred body hair. According to De Rochefort, 'the Carib think that it is a great deformity to have a beard'.[44] The indigenous population also commented negatively on European habits. In 1654, DuTertre wrote: 'they never stroll and they laugh a lot when they see us going from one place to another without any purpose. They think that is one of the stupidest things that we do.'[45] Non-European people's prejudiced attitudes toward the French may be interpreted as a form of resistance against white people's attempt to dominate them or, in the case of slaves, as a reaction to the masters' harsh treatments. Feelings of cultural superiority may have caused some of these negative attitudes too.

Antagonisms were apparently strong between Caribs and people of African descent. In 1694, Labat explained that one of the reasons why the settlers should avoid using Carib servants was the 'reciprocal dislike between them and the *nègres*' and that 'their pride make them believe that they are extremely superior to the *nègres*'.[46] This was partly due to the fact that blacks quickly became associated with slavery and the Caribs highly prized their freedom. These feelings were reciprocal. In 1667, DuTertre noted blacks' 'dislike for our Caribs'.[47] Labat also commented that 'the *nègres*, who are at least as proud as the Caribs, look at them with disdain, especially when they are not Christians, and they always call them "*sauvages*"'.[48] Thus, blacks apparently disliked the Caribs because they did not acculturate and, by referring to them as '*sauvages*', they helped to reinforce the common prejudice directed against the indigenous population.

In the 'Frontier-Era' of the early French Caribbean, Europeans were, in some instances, open to the possibility of mixing socially with black, *mulâtre* and indigenous people, although demographic constraints may have played a part in this phenomenon too. With regard to the non-Europeans, French settlers seem to have favoured concubinage over marriage, possibly due to social pressures. The scarcity of primary sources does not allow a precise assessment of the level of Guadeloupian inter-marriages for the period between 1635 and the 1660s. But evidence indicates that some trans-ethnic unions took place during this period. In 1669, Du Lion wrote, 'there are many more men and boys than girls in age of getting married, as a result some masters married their *négresses*'.[49] Among a few instances of intermarriages, this document mentions Manuel Vaze, a thirty-five-year-old 'free' *nègre* married to the presumably white 'Mary Blanche' and living with her in Capesterre.[50] In 1667, DuTertre also claimed to 'have seen some [*mulâtres*], who had married French women'.[51]

In addition, there were cases of white settlers forging friendships with people of colour. At the beginning of the eighteenth century, an Englishwoman living in Guadeloupe, whose name was recorded as Elizabeth Catinquiesme, approached a notary to free her *mulâtre* slave, André, 'for the friendship that she and her husband feel toward him'. The authorities suspected André to be the son of Elisabeth's husband, an Englishman named Richard Longly and of Elizabeth's *mulâtresse* slave, Jeanneton. When Elizabeth died, André lived with Richard Longly, according to the Guadeloupian authorities, 'as if he were his own child, and as a free man'. Then Longly entrusted André to Capuchin priests who taught him 'how to read and write'

– CHAPTER 9: *Colour prejudice in the French Atlantic World* –

and trained him as a carpenter. When André later decided to claim the freedom that had been given to him by his deceased mistress, the authorities refused perhaps partly because he had become 'a skilful carpenter of a considerable price'.[52]

In addition, white people and free people of African ancestry – not just domestic slaves – sometimes shared the same household. Although there is no way to determine whether genuine friendship or necessity brought these individuals together under the same roof, the 1664 census mentions a free *mulâtre* named Jean Bourdain and his daughter Marye Bourdain, who lived together in a *case* (a cabin) with a presumably white 'vagabond' named Jean Delabord, in St. Amand.[53] Moreover, in the second half of the seventeenth century, few white families had any qualms about raising their own children alongside those of their slaves. In 1667, DuTertre explained that 'there are few families on the Islands, who do not raise the little *nègres* together with the children of the house'.[54]

Fluid relations also existed between the indigenous community and the French. The case of Father Breton, who lived among the Guadeloupian Caribs between 1641 and 1653 and achieved a remarkable knowledge of the Carib language, is well known. Moreover, some settlers apparently married indigenous women. The unique early parish register of Capesterre shows instances of marriages between Frenchmen and indigenous women. For example, Charles des Champs and Susanes Belamée, a *sauvagesse* ('savage woman'), married each other before baptising their twin boys Charles and Jean, in August 1648.[55] In the second half of the seventeenth century, a substantial number of the few remaining Caribs were recorded as educated or living in French households. Thus, in 1671, Sieur Du Buisson and his wife Anne Jardin, residents of Grande-Terre, possessed eight 'male and female *sauvages* being educated by Mme Jardin'.[56] By associating with each other and living together, these individuals may have developed interethnic friendships.

Alongside these instances of cross-ethnic fluidity, there were significant antagonisms. By the 1660s, there were strong oppositions to intermarriages. The case of a Flemish settler named Jacob Michel, who was taken to the court of the Guadeloupian Sovereign Council in 1667, illustrates this point. Some of Michel's relatives wanted to exclude his free black wife Marie Läcotti from family inheritance by annulling their marriage. The court approved their request and declared Jacob and Marie's marriage null and void due in part to 'the shame cast on the family'.[57] Official opposition to intermarriages was also apparent in 1703, when the Council of Martinique refused to register the title of nobility of two Frenchmen because 'they had lived a contemptible life and married two *mulâtresses*'.[58] As blacks occupied an inferior position, several white officials and at least some settlers thought such marriages to be humiliating. The authorities also wanted to prevent free blacks from improving their socio-economic status in order to maintain the developing social hierarchy. By the end of the seventeenth century in Guadeloupe, social and governmental pressures had apparently deterred most French people from marrying people of colour. In 1695, Father Labat reported that on the *Iles du Vent* he had only met two white men who had married black women. One of these men was the Lieutenant of the Militia of Pointe-Noire in Guadeloupe, named Antoine Lietard, who married a 'very beautiful *négresse*' called Barbe in 1673 and they 'had handsome little *mulâtres*'. While Labat's comment seems rather favourable, the parish register of Pointe-Noire indicates that nobody came to their wedding 'for very grave reasons'.[59]

157

There was also antagonism between the Caribs and people of African ancestry. Although the well-known appearance of the 'black Caribs' in seventeenth-century St. Vincent attests that, in the Caribbean, there were alliances between black and indigenous people, in Guadeloupe, the Amerindians rarely united with blacks. Labat also observed that 'it is very rare to see a Carib willing to marry a *négresse* and a *négresse* would never decide to marry a Carib'.[60] Indeed, DuTertre reported that Caribs 'do not want to associate with the *nègres* at all, they never eat with them, and they build their *cases* separately because they all think that people would look at them as if they were slaves if they see them talking to the *nègres*'.[61]

Between 1635 and the 1660s, white people, the indigenous populations and the people of African descent formed a moderately flexible social hierarchy. During the first decades of settlement, the social order was not defined along a clear colour line, to a large extent because not all unfree people were black. Numerous *engagés* (indentured servants) worked in conditions that were very similar to those of slaves. DuTertre reported, regarding the *engagés,* that 'the settlers often force them to work with the slaves, and this afflicts these poor people more than all the excessive maltreatments that they have to endure'.[62] In August 1669, Du Lion even considered the indentured system to be 'a form of slavery'.[63] There were far fewer Amerindian slaves than indentured servants and indigenous people were often thought to be too indolent to be reduced to slavery.[64] As a result, the missionaries recommended that masters assign Caribs to less demanding tasks, such as fishing or hunting. Colour prejudice seems to have shaped the formation of a discriminatory social status for black slaves, because of all unfree people, they were given the most arduous tasks. In 1667, DuTertre even related how, when asked to perform hard work, indigenous slaves responded that 'these sorts of work are only good for the *nègres*'.[65]

By the end of the seventeenth century a social hierarchy more clearly defined along a colour line and yet slightly flexible had taken form. Although areas of sugar cane plantations expanded slowly, the number of indentured servants began to diminish rapidly by the 1660s: the 1698 census lists only two *engagés*.[66] At the end of the seventeenth century, the authorities had to reduce the period of engagement from three years to eighteen months because the number of volunteers was too small.[67] Word of bad treatment experienced by the *engagés* may have reached France. As a result, black labour became the predominant mode of production in the French Antilles. In the last decades of the seventeenth century, most African slaves newly arrived in the French Caribbean cultivated the land, positioned at the bottom of the social hierarchy. Craft industry offered esteemed positions to free and unfree people of colour. Labat stated: 'I have seen some of them, who were so proud to be masons and joiners that they were going to Church with their ruler and in their work overalls'.[68] Consequently, white fathers liked placing some of their *mulâtre* offspring in workshops for apprenticeships and although there were also black creole and African artisans, *mulâtres* frequently occupied this higher position, as was the case with the previously mentioned *mulâtre* André Richard, who became a 'skilful carpenter'. As white indentured servants gradually vanished from the French Antilles, people of colour began to take up the relatively distinguished status of servant, allowing them to be 'well fed and well dressed'.[69] Towards the end of the seventeenth century, household servants were often *mulâtres* or blacks. Thus, in 1671 in Trois Rivière, Leger Millard Champagne and his wife Marguerite owned a 'mulâtresse

– CHAPTER 9: *Colour prejudice in the French Atlantic World* –

servant'.[70] In the same year, in Vieux Fort, Mr. Jean Baptiste Delaseine had a black servant named Marie Mamachou, the 'spouse' of presumably white Jacques Valette, who was 'master of *case*, bourgeois and merchant'.[71] The fact that a few women of colour married Frenchmen of high social standing, like Jacques Valette and Marie Mamachou or Lieutenant Lietard and freed black Barbe (the latter couple in 1673 in Pointe-Noire), confirms the belief that the socio-economic hierarchy was not completely rigid. Since in seventeenth-century censuses free *mulâtres*, blacks and Caribs were recorded together without any distinction, it is not possible to examine the ethnic origins of the free people of colour. *Mulâtres* were, apparently, more likely to be manumitted than blacks, since they had a white parent. For this reason, skin colour may have acted as a factor of social mobility for individuals of fairer skin, while increasing discrimination against darker people.

Finally, during this same period, the French governmental élite issued a raft of discriminatory regulations. In the early modern period, the legislation related to colour prejudice resulted from centrifugal influences in Guadeloupe and the broader Caribbean, as well as from the metropolitan authorities. Guadeloupe came under the direct authority of the French Crown in 1674 and it felt the effects of Louis XIV's politics of centralisation through legal and administrative control. Each colony influenced royal decisions and laws through dispatches; thus the ministry of the Marine received colonial guidance, supervising the entire French empire through orders and legislation. The Governor General of the *Iles du Vent* received and carried out general orders and policies from the mother country into the French Antilles, but the Governor of Guadeloupe also influenced local judicial and administrative decisions. In October 1664, a royal order established a Sovereign Council of Guadeloupe 'to judge with sovereign power and in the last resort criminal and civil trials'. This judicial and legislative body also registered regulations and on some occasions, it issued *arrêts* (regulations). In the seventeenth century, the Governor of Guadeloupe normally headed the Sovereign Council with a few councillors who were nominated among the élite of Guadeloupe.[72] From 1668, Guadeloupe came under the administrative dependence of the Superior Council of Martinique, which began to register an important number of regulations for Guadeloupe.

In the late seventeenth century, the metropolitan authorities were apparently influenced by negative attitudes when they determined the legal status of *mulâtre* children in the Antilles. Before the 1670s, *mulâtres* were usually freed after reaching the age of twenty-four years. But when Guadeloupe was placed under the direct authority of the French Crown in 1674, royal authorities decided that '*mulâtres* whose mothers are slaves will remain enslaved for life', according to Roman law.[73] First Intendant of the Antilles Jean-Baptiste Patoulet argued in 1681 that the unique reason for ending the systematic manumission was the 'depraved inclinations of *mulâtres* and *mulâtresses*', who once freed were devoted to 'libertinism'.[74] Article IX of the 1685 Code Noir, an ordinance regulating slavery in the French Antilles, also stated that *mulâtre* children born of enslaved mothers were to remain enslaved and according to this same article, fathers refusing to marry the mothers of their *mulâtre* offspring had to pay a fine of 200 pounds of sugar.[75]

However, in Guadeloupe, the political élite seemed opposed to such unions. An *arrêt* issued in December 1667 by the Sovereign Council of Guadeloupe attempted to restrict intermarriages between whites and blacks by forbidding 'to all priests and

159

clergymen to perform any marriage ceremony between a white man and a black woman or a white woman and a black man without the agreement of the Governor or the Commandant of this island'.[76] In 1681, Governor General of the *Iles du Vent* Count of Blénac also obliged white fathers of *mulâtre* children to pay a fine of a hundred pounds of sugar to the Church.[77] By the end of the seventeenth century, the use of article IX seems to have mirrored a form of colour prejudice in Guadeloupe: when the *mulâtre* master Jean Boury fathered an illegitimate child with one of his black slaves, the Sovereign Council of Guadeloupe refused to apply the sentence provided by the article, arguing that Jean was not white.[78] Despite an exhaustive review, no other instances of application or non-application of these regulations were discovered in the judicial records. But these measures may have created discriminations by rendering black slaves 'forbidden' to white people.

THE INTENSIFICATION OF COLOUR PREJUDICE

Promoted by demographic, economic, social and political factors, colour prejudice intensified from the beginning of the eighteenth century to 1759. From the end of the seventeenth century to the 1710s, the slave population increased, significantly outnumbering whites. In 1710 Guadeloupe, 9,706 slaves were listed in the census (representing 65 percent of the population).[79] From the 1720s, largely owing to the vacant fertile lands of Grande-Terre, Guadeloupe grew into a flourishing centre of sugar production.[80] As a consequence, the number of slaves increased considerably. In 1731, 27,087 black captives were recorded in censuses, amounting to 75 percent of the population of the island and this proportional figure continued to increase until the 1750s, as a Guadeloupian census made in 1753 mentioned 40,525 black slaves, corresponding to 81 percent of the population.[81] White settlers became, consequently, a small minority attempting to control a large-scale enslaved labour force. During this period, the number of indentured servants remained relatively small: the 1707 census mentions only one *engagé*, although this figure rose to 142 in 1718.[82] The number of free people of colour in Guadeloupe remained relatively low until 1732, as only 580 *libres* were recorded in 1710 (11 percent of the free population) and this figure rose to 1,314 *libres* in 1732 (14 percent).[83] Between 1733 and 1759, censuses stopped quantifying free people of colour. Yet the number of manumissions taking place in the French Antilles seems to have increasingly preoccupied the authorities. In 1711, 1713, 1729 and 1736, ordinances prevented French people from freeing their slaves without the agreement of the local authorities.[84] From the 1720s to the 1740s, bad weather and the War of Austrian Succession (1742–48) generated food shortages and general misery.[85] As the servile group was the first to suffer, maroonnage and slave revolts multiplied.[86] All of these factors may have reinforced colour prejudice.

Indeed, from the 1690s to 1759 in Guadeloupe, negative attitudes toward people of African ancestry seem to have become more intense. By the 1720s, 'racial thinking' had emerged, as evidenced by the fact that at least a few élite men had begun to classify people into groups presumably having common hereditary traits transmitted through blood. The case of a white surgeon named Gilles Petit who was taken to the court of the Guadeloupian Sovereign Council by his brother-in-law Jacques Denis Huard in March 1727 is a case in point. Similar to the Michel case of 1667, Jacques

– CHAPTER 9: *Colour prejudice in the French Atlantic World* –

Denis sought to exclude Gilles' black wife Magdelon from the family inheritance by nullifying their marriage. This confirms the idea that some white settlers and politicians wanted to prevent blacks' economic ascendancy and thereby protect their own position at the top of the social hierarchy, though it is impossible to say how far this particular incident can be attributed to prejudice or mainly to greed. Magdelon and Gilles were married in Pointe Noire and then moved to Grand Cul-de-Sac where they had 'numerous male and female *mulâtre* children'. *Procureur Général* Monsieur Dorillac believed their marriage to be void partly due to 'the considerable inequality of their conditions'. He wanted to satisfy Jacques Denis's request, arguing that such *mésalliances* were 'scandalous', 'monstrous' and 'shameful'. He explained that 'on these islands, there are people of equal rank for all colours and for all species' and concluded that since 'there is no lack of men and women of equal blood' in Guadeloupe, such unions should be categorically prohibited. In his opinion, therefore, the people of colour had to marry within their own supposedly inferior racial and socio-economic groupings. Interestingly, Dorillac also questioned the integrity of the Dominican priest who had performed the marriage, pointing toward possible divergences of opinion concerning interracial marriages, between the priests and some of the political élite. There were probably some divergences of opinion among the political élite too: for we find that, in the end, seven Council members declared the marriage to be legally acceptable, against four members willing to invalidate the union. The final outcome of this trial is unknown.[87]

In addition, during the first half of the eighteenth century the classification of the different ethnic groups of Guadeloupe in administrative papers became more defined. While preserving the categories of 'nègre', 'négresse', 'mulâtre', 'mulâtresse' and 'sauvage', in 1729 the census-makers created the category, *blanc* ('white').[88] Thus the settlers could differentiate themselves more clearly from people of colour. Similar types of categorisations appeared in administrative papers in other early-modern French colonies, suggesting that a process of imperial administrative unification was perhaps taking place. The administrative papers of French Louisiana also contain numerous occurrences of the words 'nègre', 'négresse', 'sauvage', 'sauvagesse', 'mulâtre', 'mulâtresse' and 'blanc'.[89]

In the first half of the eighteenth century, social tensions intensified too. The available documentation shows that interracial marriages between whites and blacks were very rare during this time. For the period between 1700 and 1759, the well-preserved parish registers of Le Gozier in Guadeloupe mention only one union between a white individual and a person of colour: the French woman Marie Madelaine Delbourg married François Thaouira, a 'free *mulâtre*', in 1757, but this was probably because that they already had two illegitimate children, Charles and François.[90] However, the most striking aspect of accentuated colour prejudice was the considerable increase in the number of illegitimate mixed children. Illegitimate children were relatively rare in seventeenth-century censuses. Between the 1720s and the 1750s, in the single parish of Le Gozier, fifteen illegitimate mixed children were baptised. In April 1740, for example, the priest baptised a *mulâtre* named Charles 'born out of the libertinage of Marie Rose Girard free *négresse* and the Frenchman Guillaume Le Roux'.[91] Rejection of interracial unions was not restricted to Le Gozier, as more illegitimate children appear in all the Guadeloupian parish registers. For example, in 1703 in St. François, a priest baptised Magdeleine 'a little *mulâtresse*,

161

daughter of Marie Thomas unmarried free *négresse*, who says that Gabriel Leblond, assistant warrant officer, is the father'.[92] These circumstances suggest that consensual or forced cross-ethnic sexual encounters were numerous and the fact that some Frenchmen refused to recognise their *mulâtre* offspring suggests that social pressures were significant. Such situations were also probably related to the 1667 legislation aimed at preventing intermarriage.

It might be said that in the first half of the eighteenth century, the intensification of colour prejudice was most visible in the legislation issued by the governmental élite across the Atlantic. In 1758, the lawyers Monsieurs Nadau and Marin proposed a reform of the 1685 *Code Noir* for the French *Iles du Vent*, and decided that 'It is necessary to always maintain freed slaves in an inferior position, and to prevent them from associating with whites' on the basis that with 'article VI of the Edict of March 1724, his Majesty forbad the inhabitants of Louisiana to marry blacks'. It was eventually decided that, as already stated in the regulation of 1667, the *Gouverneur Général* and the *Intendant* should be allowed to forbid marriages between white individuals, and the people of colour.[93]

In addition, discriminatory measures against miscegenation and free individuals of colour became numerous. An ordinance issued in November 1704 prevented the administrators of the French *Iles du Vent* from providing titles of nobility to all Frenchmen who had married women of colour, thus precluding people of colour from becoming nobles.[94] A royal declaration of February 1726 prevented free people of colour from receiving donations from whites '*inter vivos*, because of death or for any other reason'. According to the authorities, this law merely aligned local legislation with the newest iteration of the *Code Noir*, issued for Louisiana in March 1724.[95] By the 1720s, discriminatory laws against free people of colour in the French Antilles had begun to threaten them with re-enslavement as punishment. Thus, a decree issued in June 1720 in Martinique prevented free people of colour of the French Antilles from wearing luxurious clothes, and forced them to dress with 'clothes of little value, without silk, gold-effect and lace, unless they are very inexpensive', under threat of loosing their freedom in the event of a second offence.[96] Six years later, a royal declaration imposed fines on free people of colour who harbored maroon slaves in their houses. Those unable to pay would be 'reduced to the condition of slave' also, claimed authorities, 'in accordance with the Edict of March 1724 which is used in our province of Louisiana'.[97] These regulations may be interpreted in light of the persistence of instances of cross-ethnic fluidity in the social life and the social structure of the society, which despite the consistently low proportion of free people of colour in Guadeloupe, threatened white people's position at the top of the social order in a time of economic crisis.

PERSISTENT INSTANCES OF CROSS-ETHNIC FLUIDITY

All evidence shows that, despite these regulations and alongside other negative attitudes, some instances of social fluidity occurred in Guadeloupe. In cabarets, inter-ethnic social relations may have tended to undermine the development of antagonisms. From the seventeenth century in the French Caribbean Islands, cabarets were places in which people smoked, ate, drank and gambled. According to several regulations issued between the end of the seventeenth century and the beginning of the eighteenth

– CHAPTER 9: *Colour prejudice in the French Atlantic World* –

century, the slaves of Basseterre and Saint-François frequented these cabarets 'day and night'.[98] A regulation issued in August 1711 explained that 'most freed slaves manage Cabarets, even in white people's houses who are despicable enough to support their indecent activities'.[99] An ordinance dated 1729 explained how white vagabonds often drank and gambled in cabarets with domestic servant slaves, free blacks and *mulâtres*. It prohibited 'the people running Cabarets, especially the free *mulâtres*, *nègres* and *négresses*, to offer an accommodation to [these vagabonds] under threat of paying a fine of two hundred pounds'.[100] Cabarets also offered accommodation to a substantial number of Europeans travellers and sailors.[101] The evidence suggests that fluid inter-ethnic relations may have also occurred in even more public settings. In a letter written in 1727, First Councillor to the Councils of the *Iles du Vent* Sr. Menier complained that 'the *mulâtresses* walk together with merchants' wives, either in churches or on the streets in public' and 'they assume the appearance of being placed under the too great protection of white people who are thrown with them in libertinage and filth'.[102] Indeed, some whites acted as protectors and defenders for blacks and this is especially true of some missionary priests. In the 1730s, the sermons of a Jesuit priest named Marcé generated heated discussions in Guadeloupe. During the Sunday service, he asked white masters to treat their slaves with humanity and declared that 'by revolting against their masters, the *nègres* would soon avenge God' for all the mistreatments that they were enduring. The witnesses reported how some '*nègres*' woke up their companions who had fallen asleep during the service to listen to this sermon, and how several black women began to laugh. The authorities protested that such types of discourses were extremely dangerous since there were, in Guadeloupe, 'more than thirty thousand slaves' always ready to revolt to 'shaken the yoke of slavery'.[103] A few white people might even have taken part in some of the slave rebellions that took place in early modern Guadeloupe. During the slave revolt of 1737, the slave Valentin Jacquot was arrested on a pirogue 'where there was a white man', both were allegedly on their way to the coast to 'tell *case* slaves to get ready for the revolt'.[104]

Finally, there is evidence of friendship ties between free mixed people and free blacks. *Mulâtres* sometimes chose blacks to be the godparents of their children. This was the case of Guillaume Galopin and Jeanne, both '*mulâtres*' from Capesterre, who chose Jean Dupont and Angelique Sabré 'free *nègres*' as godparents for their daughter Angélique in June 1702.[105] For the period between 1700 and 1759 in Le Gozier, 39 percent (seven cases) of the mentioned wedded free blacks had married non-black individuals and 82 percent (14 cases) of the mentioned wedded *mulâtres* had married another mixed individual.[106] This pattern cannot really be interpreted as evidence of antagonism because, as will be shown below, most free people of colour were *mulâtres*.

During the first half of the eighteenth century, the socio-economic hierarchy was, apparently, not completely defined along a colour line. In early eighteenth-century Guadeloupe, the vast majority of the free people of colour were mixed individuals, which confirms the idea that mixed people often occupied a higher status than blacks. There were 597 free *mulâtres* in 1718, amounting to 82 percent of the number of free people of colour, and this figure rose to 1,177 in 1732, corresponding to 90 percent of the free people of colour.[107]

However, in many instances, the colour lines of the social order blurred; this is especially true of interrelations in towns. The judicial and legal registers in this period express major concerns about a category of enslaved people of colour who were, according to the authorities, 'almost free' (*presque libres*).[108] In accordance with Article 28 of the 1685 *Code Noir*, slaves were not allowed to possess any property.[109] However, a significant number of slaves seem to have managed to work for their own interest, to earn money and sometimes to become wealthy. Most of these slaves lived in the towns of Guadeloupe, especially in Basseterre and Saint-François. According to a general order of 1749, these slaves 'rent their services for a day or a month, to work as sailors, porters, domestic servants as if they were independent' and their masters left them 'to their own devices provided that they pay regularly the price imposed on them for a day or a month'.[110] A regulation issued in August 1711 also protested that, in the broader French Caribbean, several masters offered to their slaves the possibility of buying their freedom, therefore driving them to commit thefts or to work independently.[111] The 1749 regulation described the 'almost free' people of colour as being able 'to undertake any trade and any profession, with the same liberty as white people'. They worked as independent bakers, peddlers and seemingly very often, as merchants. Some of them became wealthy enough to lease houses and shops from whites who, according to the authorities, had enough 'baseness of soul' to offer them places to rent. Many of these slaves also worked as tavern and cabaret managers and some were, apparently, involved in prostitution. In Guadeloupian towns, some maroon slaves were also able to sell their services. It allegedly became impossible to recognise slaves anymore, because the 'almost free' people of colour enjoyed 'immoderate luxury' with 'apparels very much above their rank, their bold and insolent attitudes, the jewels that they wear, their feasts and the balls and gambling parties that they organise in cabarets'.[112] Already in 1720, the authorities in Martinique and Guadeloupe had protested that 'the apparel of the *mulâtres* and free *nègres* or slaves is often above that of the free people to whom they are subjected'. It also described the people of colour as 'a nation marked by the seal of colour due to the sin of their first father, all born in the character of baseness and yet, subjected to a spirit of vanity'.[113] This statement suggested a hereditary state of inferiority perhaps in reference to the Curse of Ham – a religious myth that emerged in late medieval Europe according to which black people were the descendants of Canaan, who had been cursed by Noah in Genesis IX. Both dark skin and black slavery were sometimes thought to have resulted from this divine curse.[114] The first half of the eighteenth century saw a significant rise in new regulations aimed at suppressing the existence of the 'almost free' people of colour. The regulation of 1749 prohibited slaves from renting out their services without obtaining written permission from their masters.[115] Different regulations issued between 1711 and 1755 by the royal authorities in France, the Government General of the French Antilles in Martinique, as well as by the Superior Council of Guadeloupe prevented slaves from selling commodities.[116] The political authorities wanted to prevent thefts and prostitution, but also to keep the 'almost free' people of colour in a position of economic inferiority in order to preserve a sharp colour line and protect the institution of slavery.

In Guadeloupe some people of colour apparently became quite wealthy. This was the case of an 'almost free' slave named Jeanne Fary belonging to Sr. Houel. According to the 'Inventory of the properties of Jeanne Fary in favour of Sr Houel of October 6 1716', Sr. Houel had allowed Jeanne 'to enjoy the profit that she made by delivering the babies of the women of this country.' When she died, her freed nephew Jean

– CHAPTER 9: *Colour prejudice in the French Atlantic World* –

inherited her properties, which he possessed until 1716, when he died without having an heir. Jeanne's inheritance must have been quite significant, since Sr. Houel went so far as to write to the King in order to obtain all of Jean's properties. These included a farm and a 'residence' located on Sr. Houel's lands in Guadeloupe.[117] The evidence also reveals that some free people of colour were wealthy enough to become slave owners themselves. This was the case of a *mulâtresse* named Alegre. In 1720, the Superior Council of Martinique protested that she, as well as other slave owners in Basseterre and Saint-François, did not send their slaves to accomplish the Easter Duty.[118] On other rare occasions, people of colour acquired power and renown as well. This was the case of a French free *mulâtre* pirate named Louis Serville, who commanded the Spanish ship La Vierge du Bail and its French, Martinican, Spanish, English and Amerindian sailors and black slaves. In the 1720s, he became rich by stealing Spanish commodities and silver from the French and English ships that sailed in the Caribbean. He was a much-dreaded pirate because his crew comprised Amerindians able to make poisoned arrows. He also stole an English ship named La Marguerite and kidnapped its British crew. The Guadeloupian authorities eventually confiscated his ships and belongings and he was arrested, judged in Basseterre, and sent to the galleys.[119]

It can be seen, therefore, that the history of colour prejudice in the early modern French Atlantic World was extremely complex. In Guadeloupe, the political élite, missionaries, settlers, *petits blancs* (poor whites), whether in urban or rural areas, all adopted different attitudes toward non-Europeans. Even within these different groups, reactions could vary significantly from one individual to another. Like other French Caribbean islands such as Saint-Domingue or Martinique, Guadeloupe developed an intense plantation regime which gave birth to a particularly prejudiced and segregated society, but the nature of this prejudice was by no means universal. Additionally, while it would eventually benefit them the most, Europeans had no monopoly on colour prejudice. Black and Amerindian people adopted their own prejudicial attitudes toward each other and toward whites, but political, economic, social and technological supremacy gave Europeans the possibility of theorising colour prejudice and of applying it in the socio-economic reality in a much more virulent way than non-Europeans could ever do during this period. The discriminatory laws created by the French colonial planter authorities and metropolitan governmental élite across the Atlantic in the first half of the eighteenth century contributed to this phenomenon. But as demonstrated above, in Guadeloupe, the highly discriminatory attitudes of these colonial planters and state officials did not always prevent instances of inter-ethnic fluidity from existing alongside colour prejudice.

NOTES

I am grateful to the Centre des Archives d'Outre Mer, where I began research on early modern Guadeloupe. Thanks also to Saliha Belmessous, Philip Boucher, Myriam Cottias, John Garrigus, Sue Peabody and Cécile Vidal for their helpful suggestions and comments. I owe a special debt of gratitude to my advisors William O'Reilly, Pernille Roge, François-Joseph Ruggiu and to my friends Nathan Marvin, Benjamin Osborn and Mary White, who commented on several drafts of this article.

1 Bostock and Riley 1893: V, chp 1, *passim*; P. Du Ryer, 1645: III, IV *passim*; Africain 1556, *passim*, e.g. I, Livre 1.
2 Estorach and Lequenne 1979–91: *passim*, e.g. 'Lettre à Luis de Santangel' II, 45–55.

3 *Compact Oxford English Dictionary of Current English* 2005; *Collins English Dictionary* 2008.

4 Feldman, Lewontin and King 2003: V, 374.

5 DuTertre 1667: II (Traité VIII), 508.

6 Châtillon 1984: 130.

7 Devyver 1973; Jouanna 1977 and 1981.

8 Aubert 2004: 439–78.

9 For an outline of the numerous debates concerning the relationship between 'race' and colonial slavery among historians of Virginia, see Vaughan 1989: 311–54.

10 Andereggen, 1988; Cohen 1980; Debbasch 1967; Duchet 1971; Hall 1971.

11 E.g: Bonniol 1992; Hudson 1996; Smedley 1993; Rogers 2009.

12 Debien 1974; Dubois 2004; Garrigus 2010; Geggus 2002; Pluchon and Abénon 1982; Popkin 2007; Régent 2004.

13 Boucher 2008; Moitt 2001; Peabody 2005.

14 Aubert 2004; Boucher 1996; Dorlin 2006; Elisabeth 1974; Garraway 2005; Peabody 2004; Régent 2010.

15 Boulle 2007; Curran 2011; Palmer 2010; Peabody 1996.

16 Aubert 2004; Belmessous 2005; Hall 1992; Ingersoll 1999; Nash 1974; Spear 2009; Usner 1992; Vidal 2009.

17 Elisabeth 2003.

18 Boucher 2008: 3, 62–144 *passim.*

19 Centre des Archives d'Outre Mer (CAOM) G1 469.

20 CAOM G1 469 (Census for Basse-Terre, Grande-Terre and Les Saintes).

21 CAOM G1 469 (Basse-Terre, Grande-Terre and Les Saintes).

22 CAOM C7A2, f.87.

23 CAOM G1 469 (Basse-Terre, Grande-Terre and Les Saintes); CAOM G1 469 (Basse-Terre, Grande-Terre and Marie-Galante).

24 CAOM G1 469 (Basse-Terre, Grande-Terre and Les Saintes).

25 CAOM G1 469 (Basse-Terre).

26 DuTertre 1667: II (Traité VIII), 511.

27 DuTertre 1654: (Partie V), 474–75; Pelleprat 1655: 56.

28 DuTertre 1667: II (Traité VIII), 497; Labat 1724, II (Partie IV), 59.

29 Chevillard 1659, 193; DuTertre 1667: II (Traité VIII), 496.

30 DuTertre 1654: (Partie V), 475.

31 Breton 1647: I, 53; DuTertre 1654: (Partie V), 398.

32 Ibid.

33 Rochefort, 1658: 407; Du Puis 1652: 206; DuTertre 1667: II (Traité VII), 356, 377.

34 DuTertre 1667: (Traité VII), 357–58.

35 Breton 1647: I, 81; Chevillard 1659: 171; Du Puis 1653: 204.

36 PetitJean-Roget 1996: 65; Boucher 1992: 7; DuTertre: 1654, (Partie V), 450–51.

37 Breton 1647: I, p. 53.

38 CAOM G1 469.

39 CAOM G1 468.

40 Labat 1742: IV, 486.

41 Labat 1724: II (Partie IV) 58.

42 Labat 1742: IV, 484–85.

43 Labat, 1742: IV, 450–51.

44 Rochefort 1658: 385.

45 DuTertre 1654: (Partie V), 399.

46 Labat, 1722: II, 75.

47 DuTertre 1667: II (Traité VIII), 491.

– CHAPTER 9: *Colour prejudice in the French Atlantic World* –

48 Labat, 1722: II, 75.
49 CAOM C7A1 f58.
50 CAOM G1 469.
51 DuTertre 1667: II (Traité VIII), 513.
52 CAOM F3 225, 291–332.
53 CAOM G1 469.
54 DuTertre 1667: II (Traité VIII), 510.
55 CAOM 85MIOM182.
56 CAOM G1 468.
57 CAOM F3 133, 36.
58 CAOM F132, 639.
59 Labat 1724: II (Partie II), 35; CAOM 85MIOM276.
60 Labat 1724: I (Partie II), 26.
61 DuTertre 1667: II (Traité VIII), 491.
62 DuTertre 1667: II (Traité VII), 477, 488.
63 CAOM C7A1, f58.
64 DuTertre 1667: II (Traité VIII), 486, 488–89.
65 DuTertre 1667: II (Traité VIII), 493, 486.
66 CAOM G1 469.
67 CAOM B2 f.175v.
68 Labat 1724: I (Partie III), 328.
69 Labat 1724 I (Partie II),330.
70 CAOM G1 468.
71 CAOM G1 468.
72 CAOM F3 221, pp. 365–67 and F3 236 pp. 382–83.
73 Labat 1724: I (Partie II), 37.
74 CAOM F3 248, f.687.
75 *Receuil D'Edits* 1744: II, 85.
76 CAOM CAOM F3 133, f.36.
77 CAOM F3 248, f.687.
78 Debbasch 1967: 46.
79 CAOM G1 497 (Basse-Terre, Grande-Terre and Les Saintes).
80 CAOM F3 236, p. 775.
81 CAOM G1 497 (Basse-Terre); CAOM G1 497 (Guadeloupe and its dependent islands).
82 CAOM G1 497.
83 CAOM G1 497 (Basse-Terre, Grande-Terre and Les Saintes); CAOM G1 497 (Basse-Terre and dependent islands).
84 CAOM 6DPPC 1323; F3 222, p. 189; F3 236, pp. 680–81; F3 224, pp. 485–89; A 25, f.173–74; F3 224, pp. 485–86, 489; F3 236, pp. 681–83.
85 CAOM F133, p. 47; F3 223, pp. 145–47; F3 223, pp. 207–9; F3 225, pp. 433–36; F3 225, pp. 611–12; F3 225, p. 649; F3 226, pp. 413–17.
86 CAOM C7 A10, p. 19; F3 225, pp. 183–90, pp. 209–41.
87 CAOM F3 224 pp. 213–39; F3 224 pp. 241–44.
88 CAOM G1 497.
89 Vidal 2009.
90 CAOM 85MIOM197.
91 Ibid.
92 CAOM 85MIOM352.
93 CAOM F3 90, f.85–89.
94 Moreau de St. Méry 1784: I, 716.
95 CAOM F3 236, pp. 676–77.

96 CAOM F3 236, p. 701; CAOM 6DPPC 1323.
97 CAOM A25, f.59.
98 CAOM F3 226, p. 475.
99 CAOM F3 222, p. 189.
100 CAOM 6DPPC 1323.
101 CAOM F3 236, p. 342.
102 CAOM F3 224, pp. 359–61.
103 CAOM F3 224, pp. 791–96.
104 F2 225, pp. 209–41.
105 CAOM 85MIOM182.
106 CAOM 85MIOM197.
107 CAOM G1 497 (Basse-Terre) and CAOM G1 497 (Basse-Terre and dependent islands).
108 CAOM F3 226, p. 476.
109 *Receuil D'Edits*, 1744: II, 90.
110 CAOM F3 226, pp. 475–86.
111 CAOM F3 222, p. 189.
112 CAOM F3 226, pp. 475–86; F3 222, p.189.
113 CAOM 6DPPC 1323.
114 Braude 1997; Braude 2011.
115 CAOM F3 226, p. 485.
116 CAOM 6DPPC 1323; F2 222, p. 189; F2 226, p. 484; F3 227, pp. 1–3.
117 CAOM F3 222, pp. 451–52.
118 CAOM F3 222, pp. 643–45.
119 CAOM F3 224, pp. 429–35.

REFERENCES

Lucien Abénon, *La Guadeloupe de 1671 à 1759: Etude politique*, économique *et sociale* (2 vols., L'Harmattan, Paris, 1987).

Léon Africain, *Historiale Description de l'Afrique* (2 vols., Christophe Plantin, Anvers, 1556).

Guillaume Aubert, '"The Blood of France": Race and Purity of Blood in the French Atlantic world', *William and Mary Quarterly*, third series (2004), Vol. 61, No.3, pp. 439–78.

Amon Andereggen, 'The image of the African in the French collective psyche', *Peuples Noirs Peuples Africains* (1988), No. 59–62, pp. 129–40.

Saliha Belmessous, 'Assimilation and racialism in seventeenth and eighteenth century French colonial policy', in *The American Historical Review*, (2005), No. 110, 2, pp. 1–56.

Jean-Luc Bonniol, *La couleur comme maléfice: une illustration créole de la généalogie des 'Blancs' et des 'Noirs'* (Albin Michel, Paris, 1992).

John Bostock and Henry Riley eds. and trans., *The Natural History of Pliny* (6 vols., George Bell & Sons, London, 1893).

Philip Boucher, *Cannibal encounters: Europeans and Islands Caribs, 1492–1763* (Johns Hopkins University Press, Baltimore, 1992).

——'Race and Slavery in France and in the French Caribbean before 1700', paper given at the French Colonial History Conference in 1996.

——*France and the American tropics to 1700: tropics of discontent?* (Johns Hopkins University Press, Baltimore, 2008).

Pierre Boulle, *Race et esclavage dans la France de l'Ancien Régime* (Perrin, Paris, 2007).

Benjamin Braude, 'The Sons of Noah and the Construction of Ethnic and Geographical Identities in the Medieval and Early Modern Period', *The William and Mary Quarterly*, Third Series, (Jan, 1997), Vol. 54, No. 1, pp. 103–42.

— 'The Curse of Ham in the Early Modern Era: The Bible and the Justifications for Slavery.' *Catholic Historical Review* (July, 2011), Vol. 97, No. 3, pp. 587–88.

Raymond Breton, *Relation de L'isle de la Guadeloupe*, Reproduction of the editions of 1647, 1654 and 1656 by the Bibliothèque d'Histoire Antillaise (Société d'histoire de la Guadeloupe, Basse-Terre, Guadeloupe, 1973).

—*Relations de l'Ile de la Guadeloupe, 1647–1656* (2 vols., Publication of the Société d'Histoire de la Guadeloupe, Basse-Terre, 1978).

Marcel Châtillon, 'L'évangélisation des esclaves au XVIIe siècle. Lettres du R. P. Jean Mongin, 1676', *Bulletin de la Société d'Histoire de la Guadeloupe* (1984), No. 61–62, pp. 3–136.

André Chevillard, *Les desseins de son Eminence de Richelieu pour l'Amérique: reproduction de l'édition de 1659* (Basse-Terre, Société d'histoire de la Guadeloupe, 1973).

William Cohen, *The French encounter with Africans: white response to blacks, 1530–1880* (Indiana University Press, Bloomington, 1980).

Andrew Curran, *The Anatomy of Blackness: Science and Slavery in an Age of Enlightenment* (Johns Hopkins University Press, Baltimore, 2011).

Yvan Debbasch, *Couleur et liberté: le jeu du critère ethnique dans un ordre juridique esclavagiste Caraïbe: 1635–1833* (Dalloz, Paris, 1967).

Gabriel Debien, *Les esclaves aux antilles françaises XVIIe-XVIIIe siècles* (Société d'Histoire de la Guadeloupe, Basse-Terre, 1974).

André Devyver, *Le sang épuré: Les préjugés de race chez les gentihommes français de l'Ancien Régime 1560–1720* (Editions de l'Université de Bruxelles, Bruxelles, 1973).

Elsa Dorlin, *La matrice de la race. Généalogie sexuelle et coloniale de nation française* (La Découverte, Paris, 2006).

Laurent Dubois, *A colony of citizen: Revolution & Slave Emancipation in the Caribbean 1787–1804* (University of North Carolina Press, Chapel Hill, 2004).

Michèle Duchet, *Anthropologie et histoire au siècle des Lumières* (François Maspero, Paris, 1971).

Mathias Du Puis, *Relation de L'Etablissement d'une colonie Françoise dans la Gardeloupe Isle de L'Amerique et des Moeurs des Sauvages* (Marin Yvon, Caen, 1652).

—*Relation de l'establissement d'une colonie françoise dans la Gardeloupe (sic) isle de l'Amérique et des moeurs des sauvages Reproduction de l'édition de 1652* (Société d'histoire de la Guadeloupe, Basse-Terre, 1972).

Jean-Baptiste DuTertre, *Histoire générale des Isles de Saint-Christophe, de la Guadeloupe, de la Martinique et autres dans l'Amérique* (Jacques & Emmanuel Langlois, Paris, 1654).

—*Histoire Générale des Antilles habitées par les François* (4 vols., Thomas Iolly, Paris, 1667–71)

Léo Elisabeth, 'The French Antilles', in *Neither Slaves Nor Free: The Freedman of African Descent in The Slave Society of the New World*, David Cohen and Jack Greene eds. (Johns Hopkins University Press, Baltimore, 1974), pp. 134–71.

—*La société martiniquaise aux XVIIe et XVIIIe siècles 1664–1789* (Karthala, Paris, 2003).

Solelad Estorach and Michel Lequenne trad., *Christophe Colomb: La découverte de l'Amérique* (3 vols., La Découverte, Paris, 1979–91).

Marcus Feldman, Richard Lewontin and Mary-Claire King, 'Race: a genetic melting-pot', (2003), *Nature*, 424: 374.

Doris Garraway, *The Libertine Colony: Creolization in the Early French Caribbean* (Duke University Press, Durham, 2005).

John Garrigus, *Before Haiti: Race and Citizenship in French Saint-Domingue* (Palgrave Macmillan, New York, 2010).

David Geggus, *Haitian Revolutionary Studies* (Indiana University Press, Bloomington, 2002).

Gwendolyn Mildo Hall, *Social control in slave plantation societies: a comparison of St Domingue and Cuba* (Johns Hopkins University Press, Baltimore, 1971).

—*Africans in Colonial Louisiana* (Louisiana University Press, Baton Rouge, 1992).

Nicholas Hudson, 'From "nation" to "race": The origin of racial classification in eighteenth-century thought', *Eighteenth-Century Studies*, (1996), Vol. 29, No. 3, pp. 247–64.

Thomas Ingersoll, *Mammon and Manon in Early New Orleans: The First Slave Society in the Deep South, 1718–1819* (University of Tennessee Press, Knoxville, 1999).

Arlette Jouanna, *Ordre social: Mythes et hiérarchies dans la France du XVIe siècle* (Hachette, Paris, 1977).

——*L'idée de race en France au XVIe siècle et au début du XVIIe* (2 vols., Université Paul-Valéry, Montpellier, 1981).

Jean-Baptiste Labat, *Nouveau Voyage aux isles de l'Amérique* (2 vols., La Haye, 1724).

Jean-Baptiste Labat, *Nouveau Voyage aux isles de l'Amérique* (6 vols., Guillaume Cavelier, Paris, 1722).

——*Nouveau Voyage aux isles de l'Amérique* (6 vols., P. Husson, T. Johnson, P. Gosse, J. Van Duren, R. Alberts, & C. Le Vier , the Hague, 1724).

——*Nouveau Voyage aux isles de l'Amérique* (8 vols., Ch. J.B. Delespine, Paris, 1742).

Bernard Moitt, *Women and Slavery in the French Antilles, 1635–1848* (Indiana University Press, Bloomington, 2001).

Louis-Elie Moreau de St. Méry, *Loix et Constitutions des Colonies Françoises Sous le Vent* (6 Vols., Quillau, Paris, 1784–90).

Gary Nash, *Red, White, and Black: The people of Early America* (Englewood Cliffs, Prentice-Hall 1974).

Jennifer Palmer, 'What's in a Name? Mixed-Race Families and Resistance to Racial Marginalization in Eighteenth-Century La Rochelle,' *French Historical Studies* (Summer 2010), Vol 23, No. 3, pp. 357–85.

Sue Peabody, *'There are no slaves in France': the political culture of race and slavery in the Ancien Régime* (Oxford University Press, New York, 1996).

——'"A Nation Born to Slavery": Missionaries and Racial Discourse in Seventeenth-century French Antilles', *Journal of Social History*, (Fall 2004), Vol. 38, No. 1, pp. 113–26.

——'Négresse, Mulâtrese, Citoyenne: Gender and Emancipation in the French Caribbean, 1650–1848', in *Gender and Slave Emancipation in the Atlantic World*, Pamela Scully and Diana Paton eds. (Duke University Press, Durham, 2005).

Pierre Pelleprat, *Relation des missions des PP de la Compagnie de Jésus dans les isles et dans la Terre Ferme de l'Amérique Méridionale* (Sebastien and Gabriel Cramoisy, Paris, 1655).

Henry PetitJean-Roget, 'Les femmes caraïbes insulaires: lecture comparée des chroniques françaises du XVIIe et du XVIIIe sur les petites Antilles', *Bulletin de la société d'histoire de la Guadeloupe* (1996), No. 109, pp. 45–69.

Pierre Pluchon and Lucien Abénon, *Histoire des Antilles et de la Guyane* (Privat, Paris, 1982).

Jeremy Popkin, *Facing racial revolution: eyewitness accounts of the Haitian insurrection* (University of Chicago Press, Chicago, 2007).

Frédéric Régent, *Esclavage, métissage, liberté: la révolution française en Guadeloupe, 1789–1802* (Grasset & Fasquelle, Paris, 2004).

——, 'Unité ou variétés du genre humain dans le cadre de l'esclavage colonial français du XVIIe au XIXe siècle' (IHRF, Université Paris 1, workshop 'Fait colonial', 23 November 2010).

Charles de Rochefort, *Histoire Naturelle et Morale des Iles Antilles de l'Amérique* (Arnould Leers, Rotterdam, 1658).

Dominique Rogers, 'Raciser la société: un projet pour une société domingoise complexe', *Journal de la Société des Américanistes* (2009) Vol. 95-2, pp. 235–60.

Audrey Smedley, *Race in North America: origin and evolution of a worldview* (Westview Press, Boulder, 1993).

Jennifer Spear, *Race, Sex and Social order in Early New Orleans* (Johns Hopkins University Press, Baltimore, 2009).

– CHAPTER 9: *Colour prejudice in the French Atlantic World* –

Daniel Usner, *Indians, Settlers & Slaves in a Frontier Exchange Economy: The Lower Mississippi Valley Before 1783* (University of North Carolina Press, Chapel Hill, 1992).

Alden Vaughan, 'The Origins Debate: Slavery and Racism in Seventeenth-Century Virginia', *The Virginia Magazine of History and Biography*, (Jul., 1989), Vol. 97, No. 3, pp. 311–54.

Cécile Vidal, 'Francité et situation coloniale. Nation, empire et race en Louisiane française, 1699–1769', in *Annales, Histoire, Sciences Sociales*, 64 (2009), pp. 1019–50.

Les Histoires D'Herodote mises en François par P. Dv Ryer (3 vols., Antoine de Sommaville & Augustin Courbé, Paris, 1645).

Receuil D'Edits, Declarations et Arrests de Sa Majeste Concernant l'Adiminstration de la Justice & de la Police des Colonies Françaises de l'Amérique, & les Engagés (les Libraires Associez, Paris, 1744).

CHAPTER TEN

ATLANTIC SLAVERIES
Britons, Barbary, and the Atlantic World

———·◆·———

Catherine Styer

In the late 1580s, the Englishman Thomas Saunders was serving on board the *Jesus* voyaging to Tripoli in North Africa along with a multinational crew containing at least 23 of his countrymen. On leaving Barbary, the machinations of two Frenchmen brought the ship under suspicion and 'Turkish' pirates seized the crew and merchants and chained them up 'foure by foure.' The Turks despoiled the vessel, hanged the mate Andrew Dier, and made the rest of the company slaves 'perpetuall unto the Great Turke.' Saunders and his comrades had their heads shaved and were set half naked to row in the galleys and to quarry stones under the hot North African sun. He reported that two of the crew were forced to convert to Islam and were raped. The rest struggled with the violence of their overseers, the hardship of their labors, and the inadequacy of their food and clothing. They were redeemed one year later by the efforts of Sir Edward Osborne, but half of the company had already perished from disease and overwork. Saunders was among those fortunate enough to survive their enslavement and, on returning to England, published an account of his ordeal in 1587.[1]

One hundred years later Thomas Phelps also printed the story of his experiences as a slave in Barbary, this time in Morocco. Phelps was employed on board the *Success of London* sailing for Madeira, and was captured shortly after leaving the Irish coast. He was put to work quarrying and building, 'not Living…but Starving and Dying daily.' Attempts to ransom him failed and in desperation he fled from his captors on gouty legs and frantically rowed to a nearby English man of war. Phelps had his revenge, however: he piloted the English man of war to burn some of the Moroccan fleet before returning home and publishing his tale of enslavement and escape in 1685.[2]

Stories of Barbary slavery were still popular a century later. In the 1790s, for instance, James Wilson Stevens was one of several Americans eager to recount the horrors suffered by his countrymen enslaved in Algiers to readers at home. Stevens recorded how American slaves were 'subjected to a series of misery which humanity blushes to record,' weighed down with chains, and set to work at the marine and in public quarries before their ransom was finally paid.[3] Eighteenth-century Englishmen also remained interested in shocking tales from North Africa. Authors titillated British readers with fictive tales of slavery and escape, and ex-captives rehearsed the depredations they had suffered for a fascinated audience at home.

– CHAPTER 10: *Atlantic slaveries* –

Throughout the period associated with the British Atlantic world, Britons were enmeshed in two slave systems.[4] In their new colonies, Britons acted as traders and slave-owners, abducting and transporting men, women, and children from Africa and establishing a brutal system of racial slavery. At the same time, they were also involved in a slave system based in the Barbary States of North Africa. There, Britons' roles were more diverse. In the early 1600s, some Britons operated as Barbary pirates and slavers themselves. Later in the seventeenth century, Britons more frequently acted as redeemers and activists, protesting the enslavement of their fellow countrymen and working to have them released. Most Britons who found themselves in the Barbary States in this period, however, were there as slaves.

This second slave system in which early modern Britons were involved has received little attention from Atlantic historians. Barbary slavery is usually analyzed as a domestic, political problem of limited impact and duration. It enters the national narrative of seventeenth-century Britain only as a precursor to the Civil Wars and finds a place in the American story solely as a crisis point in the early years of the new republic's foreign policy.[5] Barbary slavery was, however, a more enduring and significant problem for Britons at home and in their Atlantic colonies than its current scholarly treatment suggests. American colonists and merchants fell victim to attack throughout the period and the most devastating years of British enslavement in North Africa were actually during the 1670s and 1680s. Barbary slavery was, furthermore, very much a problem of empire and the Atlantic world, spilling out beyond the concerns of domestic politics. As Britons established overseas colonies they became more inviting prey, and the trade routes between America, continental Europe, and Britain were haunted by Barbary slavery's ever-present threat.

The number of enslaved Britons taken to North Africa was, of course, dwarfed by the number of African people abducted to the Americas, but this second slave system was nonetheless an important component of the early modern British Atlantic world. There are, perhaps, two main ways to assess its impact on British life: the number of British slaves taken to North Africa and the visibility of the Barbary problem back home and in England's Atlantic colonies. The number of men taken is hard to calculate with great precision; the archival material available to study the enslavement of Britons in the early modern Barbary States is patchy, fragmented, and scarce. There are no North African ledgers of men taken or captives sold, and lists of abducted men compiled by English merchants, local authorities within Britain, and the London government are incomplete. Most of those enslaved were poor men, seized from small fishing boats off the English and Irish coasts or coming home from Newfoundland, whose disappearance often went unrecorded unless a petition from his family for aid happens to have survived. The archival records which are available, however, do indicate that many thousands of men were captured and offer some insight into the geographical and temporal patterns of Barbary enslavement.

As early as the sixteenth century, English, Irish, and Scottish shipping suffered regular attacks from the Barbary pirates. The *Jesus* was captured in 1587 with 23 men on board, the *Mary Marten* of London appears to have been seized in the 1590s with her crew, and the *Three Half Moons* was taken in the same decade and her crew enslaved at Alexandria, as was the *Toby of London* whose twelve-strong company were all detained in Morocco until redemptions could be arranged.[6] The capture of many small fishing vessels may well have gone unrecorded in this period, before any bureaucratic redemption process was established, if no one from their small crews lived to carry the news back to Britain. A more revealing approach when trying to assess the number of men taken in this early period, therefore, is to look at how the problem was perceived at home and what efforts were thought necessary to redeem men missing in North Africa. Such efforts were substantial and the frequency and geographical spread of collections to raise money to redeem abductees in the late sixteenth century indicates a fairly significant loss of men. The evidence of widespread, and sometimes annual, collections, suggest that as many as 1,000 Britons fell victim to these corsairs before 1600.

The pace of slaving quickened after 1600 and the numbers of men reported captured in letters from North African and British ports are startlingly large. It is possible that numbers were exaggerated in an effort to persuade the government in London to act. That different sources provide fairly similar estimates does lend the reports credibility however. In a missive to Lord Salisbury of July 1611, Sir Fernando Gorges reported that 2,000 English, Irish, and Scots men were enslaved in Barbary as a whole.[7] An anonymous report in the state papers estimates that 70 English ships were taken between 1609 and 1611, and 330 more between 1611 and 1616 by the Algerians alone.[8] If each ship had a crew, on average, of around fourteen men, that would indicate about 5,600 slaves captured from the British Isles and taken to Algiers.[9] In 1619 the Privy Council, having collected reports from merchants and sailors in London and the outports, believed 300 ships, and therefore around 4,200 men, had been captured by vessels from Algiers and Tunis in 'recent years.'[10] As Britons were being taken into Tripoli and Morocco as well – indeed there were around 260 British slaves in Salé alone in 1610 – it seems reasonable to estimate that at least 7,000 men were taken out of British ships and enslaved in North Africa in the years between 1600 and 1620.

Throughout the 1620s and 1630s similarly large numbers of Britons were enslaved by North African pirates. Richard Ford estimated that already by 1622 a further 500 men had been brought into Algiers, a number that is corroborated by the outports: the Mayor of Dartmouth, for instance, reported 130 men taken from just his region by Turks in the same period.[11] Men continued to be captured in the following years, with 1625 proving particularly disastrous. The Mayor of Plymouth informed the privy council that the 'Turks' had taken over 1,000 men in that one year alone and there are records of 37 named ships captured between 1624 and 1625 with possibly as many as 518 men on board, all of whom were killed or enslaved.[12] Although many attacks were recorded, reports of total figures – for instance that there were 3,000 Britons enslaved in Algiers and 1,500 in Salé in 1626 – suggest the capture of small ships often left no trace in the archives.[13] Between 1629 and 1638 attacks by the Barbary corsairs intensified yet further. At least 2,420 men, women, and children were enslaved from land raids and from the capture of more than 115 ships.[14] Again such large figures reported from sailors returning to British ports are corroborated by the 'men on the ground' in Barbary. In 1637, for instance, the consul James Frizell informed the king and council that 1,524 Britons had been sold in Algiers between 1630 and 1637 and that the Salé corsairs had sold over 800 in the same period.[15] Between 1639 and 1641 another 1,200 were enslaved by men operating out of Algiers and Salé. A petition to the king from 3,000 slaves in Algiers in 1640 reported that 957 new slaves had been brought in since May 18, 1639.[16] They attached a list of these men's names which, sadly, has been lost.

There were several factors involved in this upsurge in Barbary pirate attacks against British targets in the early seventeenth century. It resulted partly from a

Figure 10.1 Barbary Pirates
© Mary Evans Picture Library

change in the domestic politics of North Africa. After 1600, Constantinople's grip on the regencies of Libya, Tunisia, and Algeria, and influence over the Kingdom of Morocco, was loosening and oligarchies arose in each of these locations whose power was based on piracy. The British had also become more inviting prey. In the 1570s the English 're-entered' the Mediterranean in large numbers and in the following decades trade to the Levant flourished.[17] English ships were also venturing to the 'new world' in ever greater numbers, providing more targets for those pirates operating out of the Atlantic 'pirate republic' of Salé.

The situation continued to worsen at mid-century and the 'British were largely powerless in stopping the corsairs' during the British Civil Wars and the Protectorate.[18] In 1640 a fleet of 60 Algerian ships cruised the English Channel; in 1641 60 Cornishmen were seized from St Michael's Mount near Penzance; in 1645 another 240 were taken from the Cornish coast; and 'Salé rovers were still busy plundering the West Country, hauling off fresh captives by the score from the villages and fishing boats of Cornwall and Devon' into the 1650s.[19] After 1650, Tripoli also temporarily became a more important center of operations for the corsairs. Tripolitan vessels took the *Ursula Bonadventure* in 1654, an unidentified Scottish ship in 1656, and the Levant Company's *Resolution* in 1657.[20] Although it is once again difficult to calculate exact figures for this period, the evidence supports an estimate of at least 9,000 Britons captured between 1620 and 1660. Such a figure is possibly conservative, for David Delison Hebb has suggested that 8,000 English, Irish, and Scotsmen were taken to Barbary between 1616 and 1640, and in 1641 the English Parliament estimated that there were four or five thousand Englishmen enslaved in Algiers alone.[21]

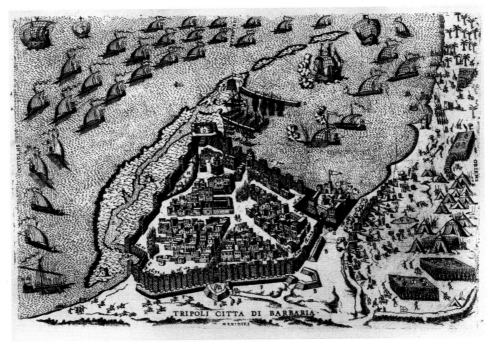

Figure 10.2 Tripoli – stronghold of Barbary Pirates
© Private Collection/Bridgeman Images

– CHAPTER 10: *Atlantic slaveries* –

The rate of attacks after the Restoration by pirates operating out of North African ports increased, culminating in an overwhelming number of seizures and enslavements between 1677 and 1682 when Britain and Algiers were openly at war. The archives contain reports of 182 named British ships captured between 1660 and 1682 with around 2,000 men on board. In addition there are 1,368 individually named captives in the sources for the same period – some of whom were likely serving on these ships, and some of whom were probably captured in unrecorded attacks. Contemporary reports again contain large numbers. William Hagget estimated that at least 2,000 Britons had been captured by Algerian and Moroccan pirates before 1669, and Thomas Baker, consul at Algiers, later recorded around 3,000 more enslaved during the official war time years.[22] An English newsletter estimated there were 2,500 Englishmen enslaved at Algiers by 1681.[23] It seems likely that at least another 7,000 Britons were captured between the Restoration and the peace of 1682 with Algiers. The following 20 years were occupied with redeeming surviving captives from Algiers – as late as 1695 there were still several hundred Britons there – and attacks on British shipping declined somewhat.[24] Morocco, however, was becoming increasingly hostile towards the close of the seventeenth century, and upwards of 500 Britons were enslaved there between 1680 and 1700.[25]

As late as the eighteenth century, when Britain was established as a dominant and slave-owning imperial power, hundreds of Britons were still being abducted to North Africa, with Morocco the most common destination. At least 470 Britons are recorded as being transported to Morocco in the first two decades of the new century, and during the 1730s 29 Britons were taken at Oran with the Spanish and over 130 more were captured at sea and enslaved.[26] More were abducted in the 1740s, and by 1759 there were over 350 British slaves in Morocco despite numerous efforts to free them.[27] Including the steady stream of men enslaved at Algiers, at least another 1,500 Britons were likely enslaved during the eighteenth century.

In total, as many as 26,000 men (and a few women) were abducted from English, Scottish, Irish, and colonial ships and shores between the late sixteenth and late eighteenth centuries and were set to work as slaves in North Africa. Such large numbers of missing men would surely have had an impact. Each of those enslaved men left behind parents and often a wife and family who quickly had to become knowledgeable about Barbary slavery. If 26,000 British men were captured, therefore, maybe three or four times that number were deeply affected by the loss of a husband, father or son.

Barbary slavery was also highly visible throughout England, and even those who had not lost friends and family members to the corsairs were aware of the problem. Early modern Britons published numerous pamphlets and books recounting skirmishes with Turks at sea and offering harrowing accounts of slavery in Algiers and Morocco, with some texts going through several editions. Thomas Troughton's *Barbarian Cruelty* was reprinted twice, for example, and Joseph Pitt's *A True and Faithful Account of the Religion and Manners of the Mahommetans* went through four editions. For those who could not read, there were plays about the Ottoman Empire and slavery, and spectacular water fights between Turks and Britons were staged in English towns. Huge crowds turned out to witness the occasional processions of British ex-slaves through the streets of London. These parades were theatrical and eye-catching, with emaciated men dressed in rags displaying the horrors of their enslavement for all to see.[28]

177

There were also frequent requests for charity to help Barbary slaves throughout England and Wales, and giving alms to the widows of captives, or to ex-slaves returned from North Africa, was commonplace. Churchwardens' accounts from English parishes show a steady stream of charity to ex-captives and local people seeking to free loved ones, especially after 1650. There were also several national collections and in the 1690s ministers were required to go 'from House to House to ask and receive from all Parishioners, as well Masters and Mistresses, and Servants, as Lodgers, Sojourners, or others in their Families, their Christian and Charitable Contributions, and to take the Names of all those which shall Contribute thereunto.'[29] Records from Somerset suggest the collection instructions were carried out carefully and everyone, from local landowners to servants, contributed. It would have been difficult in such circumstances for many in England or Wales to be left unaware of the Barbary slave problem.

Barbary attacks were also well known in Scotland and Ireland, both of which lost disproportionately large numbers of men to North African slavery. In Scotland there were frequent local and regional collections to redeem abductees, and the Barbary pirates were an ever-present threat to Irish ships and coastal villages. One of the most spectacular attacks by North African corsairs occurred in 1631 on the south coast of Ireland when 109 men, women, and children were snatched out of their beds to a lifetime of slavery.[30] Algerian and Moroccan ships were a common sight off the coast of Ireland, and many Irish ships travelling to England or the continent were captured and the men enslaved. In 1632 there were even rumors that the Turks planned to invade.[31] For two centuries Irish mariners, and their families on shore, lived in fear of attacks by Barbary pirates, and their depredations became the stuff of folklore, legend and public house names.[32]

Britons overseas in North America and the Caribbean were also acutely aware of the danger posed by North African slavers. The supply lines and trade routes between Atlantic colonial ports and Europe were constantly disrupted, especially by pirates operating out of Salé, and numerous ships and men were captured. Nine of the 24 ships appearing on an unpublished list of vessels 'taken and destroyed' by the Algerians in 1684, for instance, were travelling between Europe and North Africa – two coming from Newfoundland, two bound for New England, and five involved in trade with Virginia.[33] As Paul Baepler has noted, by the 1660s 'Massachusetts merchants regularly encountered Barbary privateers on their way to Europe' and a number of high profile colonists were seized: Jacob Leisler of New York; William Harris, one of the original founders of Rhode Island; and Seth Southel, the Governor of Carolina.[34] The danger of Barbary piracy was frequently publicized in North American ports as officials tried to alert seamen of the need to be cautious. In 1679, for example, the king ordered that notices be put up along the quays in Newfoundland that all shipping must return home in convoy or risk being captured and the crews enslaved in North Africa. In 1701 a circular letter was sent to the governors of England's American colonies notifying them of the recent peace agreement with Algiers and the workings of the new Barbary 'pass' system. Records from the Council of Virginia show the information was taken seriously and circulated to local officials.[35]

Like their fellow nationals in the British Isles, men and women in the colonies also learned of Barbary slavery as they watched collections being undertaken to redeem their relatives, friends, and neighbors. On August 17, 1678 a brief was granted to

– CHAPTER 10: *Atlantic slaveries* –

church officers in New York to collect money for redemptions, and later Governor Benjamin Fletcher gave permission for colonists to beg charity to rescue their relatives.[36] In 1693, 4,302 New Yorkers raised the generous sum of £400 to help Barbary slaves, an amount which compares favorably to the totals amassed in the larger English towns during the highly bureaucratic 1692 national collection. Of those who contributed to the New York collection, 13 percent were listed as 'negroes.'[37] Perhaps experiences of the early Atlantic trade in enslaved African people and its horrors encouraged black New Yorkers to sympathize with fellow colonists who they imagined were held in like conditions. There are also several records of collections held in Massachusetts: the 1698 minutes of the Council of Massachusetts show a collection was ordered in all congregations to raise money to redeem some New England men who had been taken captive, and in preceding years several briefs had been issued to raise money for specific slaves.[38] Some colonists even plotted, or at least invested in, revenge. Recent work by Mark Hanna has demonstrated the extent to which anti-Muslim and anti-Barbary pirate sentiments motivated the 'Red Sea Pirates' operating out of American ports in the 1690s. Ex-slaves such as Jacob Leisler were keen investors in such projects.[39]

The number of early modern Britons affected by Barbary slavery was significant and England's Atlantic colonies and trade routes were shadowed by potential pirate attack. Barbary slavery was highly visible in British culture, ex-slaves were a commonplace sight in many towns, and Britons across the Atlantic world were interested in the subject. When an ordinary Englishman of the period contemplated his country's embryonic empire, he may have thought about exploration and exotic goods, but he would also have been mindful of the costs paid in the enslavement of British sailors, merchants, and would-be settlers. Not only were early modern Britons interested in the fate of their countrymen abducted to North Africa, but they also seem to have understood capture by the Barbary pirates to be a form of slavery. Historians have generally been unwilling to share this assessment and, so far, have directed little scholarly attention to the lives of those who were captured. The experience of British slaves in Barbary varied greatly with time, place, and luck and there is much still to learn about their labor and treatment. The evidence surviving in British archives nevertheless allows a glimpse into these slaves' lives and indicates why abduction to Barbary looked like slavery to those captured and to those watching anxiously from home.

Britons seized by pirates operating out of North African ports in the decades before the Restoration endured a dismal existence. The majority were sold at Salé and Algiers, most to private owners and some to the state. While the range of their experiences and of the labor they were expected to carry out was wide, the majority were used on board corsair ships or in the Turkish fleet. Gunners, carpenters, sail makers, and pilots were much sought after and forced to ply their trade for their new owners. The rest of the able-bodied seamen likely endured a new life as a galley slave, a life from which relatively few returned. Many died at the oar of exhaustion, starvation, and violence, or on shore from the plague and other diseases that were a constant presence in the crowded, unsanitary 'bagnios' where galley slaves were kept during the winter months. Francis Knight, an English merchant who was himself enslaved in the galleys of Algiers between 1631 and 1638, wrote movingly of the experience of his fellow oarsmen in his 1640 account. Life in the galleys was so terrible, he recounted, that it caused the men 'to curse the day of their Nativities.' They were forced to drink salt water, were so exhausted they were in 'continual extasties' (ecstasies), had to endure heat so fierce the flesh was 'burned off their backs,' were made to sit continuously for days, were compelled to row so hard they sweated blood and broke their hearts, and were 'beaton to put on their clothes and beaten to take them off...beaten to eate, drinke, sleepe, and wash, and beaten for doing any of these.'[40]

The chance of any man captured before 1660 returning to Britain was very small. Robert C. Davis, in his study of Italian slaves in the North African Ottoman regencies, has concluded that for an Italian seized between 1530 and 1780 there was a 'less than 50/50 chance of returning home,' and this despite the strenuous efforts made by the relatively effective Catholic Orders of Redemption.[41] The redemption rate for Britons, especially in the early decades of the seventeenth century, appears to have been significantly lower than for Davis' Italian slaves. The English were notorious for the lackluster efforts of the state and the protestant church to redeem enslaved men. There was never enough money and those funds that were collected were often misapplied, and very few slaves in this period managed to help themselves. Most men captured between 1580 and 1660, therefore, probably lived out the remainder of their lives in North Africa. If a generous interpretation is given to every reference to redemptions in the British archives, the total recorded as redeemed during this 80-year period is 2,673. This is a small proportion, 15.7 percent, of the estimated 17,000 enslaved.

The experiences of British slaves in the second half of the seventeenth century varied even more widely. Most were enslaved at Algiers and Salé, with a few in Tripoli and Tunis. Generally they were owned privately, although some were public slaves employed on building works, especially in Morocco during and after the reign of Muley Ishmael (1673–1727). Galley slavery also remained a possible fate: as late as 1694, the English consul at Algiers was still providing relief to British galley slaves. Other slaves were set up by their owners in shops and taverns, forced to ply a trade, and made to hand over their profits to the men who had bought them.

Redemption rates after 1660 did improve slightly. The archives contain the names of 1,084 slaves liberated in the two decades following the Restoration and 567 redeemed between 1681 and 1701, making a total of 1,651. If approximately 7,500 British men, women, and children were enslaved in North Africa during these decades, around 22 percent subsequently made it home again. Most redemptions in this period were carried out either by fleets sent to North Africa, by consuls or negotiators in Barbary ports, or, most frequently, by merchants directed by the London government to re-purchase British slaves. Between 1660 and 1700, as in the earlier period, very few men escaped, managed to redeem themselves or were freed by their families. Redemption records for this period are fairly reliable as a bureaucratic system was in place allowing redeemers to re-claim money from the London government for the men and women they freed.

By the eighteenth century, redemption efforts by the London government were better organized and more slaves were eventually rescued, but slavery could still be relatively long and many British slaves died of exhaustion, starvation, violence, over-work, and disease while they waited for their liberty to be re-purchased. Of 388 Britons enslaved in Morocco between 1714 and 1719, for example, 290 were eventually freed, but 78 died and 20 converted to Islam despairing of rescue.[42] For men captured after 1700, slavery could still be extreme and arduous. Slave life in Morocco was so bad, Thomas Troughton wrote, and conditions so appalling, that he and his fellow slaves were forced to consider cannibalism in order to survive.[43] Most Britons who were enslaved in eighteenth-century Algiers, furthermore, were never re-claimed from their servitude at all.

The evidence suggests that the overwhelming majority of captured Britons, especially those taken in the seventeenth century, never returned home. Most died laboring in foreign lands of disease, starvation, and over-work. Most had their labor appropriated by coercion and violence, whether or not they rowed in the galleys or quarried stone. Most were permanently separated from their families and communities and joined a servile class defined by its members' cultural and religious identities. There were probably some British slaves who met with good treatment and charity in North Africa, and lived comfortable, even profitable, lives. But an examination of the few who did should not shift the historian's gaze from the many more who suffered in the galleys and quarries of their masters. Nor should it blind scholars to the fact that even those Britons who were well treated had usually been abducted from their friends and family, and were, in most cases, held in North Africa against their will.

In Atlantic world scholarship there has understandably been a great moral and intellectual imperative to distinguish white slavery in North Africa from black slavery in the Americas and the Caribbean. The two slave systems were not at all alike, and there has been an impulse among scholars to differentiate the two and to find another category than 'slavery' for those Britons and Americans abducted to Barbary. Historians have offered varying justifications for their reluctance to employ the word 'slavery' to describe the abduction and forced labor of Britons (and other Europeans and, later, Americans) captured by the Barbary pirates in the early modern period. For some scholars, the Atlantic slave trade in abducted African people has come to define the term, and all other forms of unfreedom require a different word. Others have denied that Barbary slavery was 'slavery' because of its socio-economic context, arguing it was not part of an economic system based on the commodification of labor, but rather some crusader relic in which a few Europeans were held captive as a show of status. A third group has argued that too few men were taken and that there was a short temporal limit to many Europeans' captivities with most being quickly repatriated. It was more like being a captive or a prisoner of war, they suggest, than being a slave.[44]

The archival evidence, however, undermines these arguments. It is clear, for example, that the enslavement of Christians was central to the seventeenth- and early eighteenth-century economies and militaries of Morocco and Algiers. Ellen G. Friedman has even demonstrated that the labor of captives and the money raised by their ransom was 'critical to the Algerian economy' until late into the eighteenth century.[45] Nor were slaves held by North Africans only for reasons of prestige. Davis has recently argued, 'in Mediterranean slavery, as in the Americas, human beings were commodities' bought and sold for profit and for their labor.[46] There existed in Algiers, moreover, just as in any other city with a lively slave market, men who speculated on the trade in men and for whom buying and selling people was a business like any other. In early modern North Africa, European men and women were a commodity traded in the market place for profit and put to hard labor under the threat of violence. An analysis of the available archival data for British slaves also suggests that enslavement in North Africa was usually life-long. The majority of enslaved Britons, especially in the seventeenth century, never returned home and did not opt to change religion, or were prevented from doing so by their owners. Most either died quickly from disease or worked as slave laborers for the remainder of their lives.

While acknowledging that the North African trade in enslaved Britons and the Atlantic European trade in enslaved Africans were very different phenomena, approaching the former by comparison with the latter is not especially helpful. We need to place British slavery in North Africa in its own time and context. Very few men living in the seventeenth century understood or evaluated this problem by comparison with the Atlantic trade in enslaved African people. As late as 1700, for many Britons, European abduction to Barbary was all they knew of slavery. To them, slavery was something European Christians endured under African Muslim masters. To them, slavery often had a white face. When they thought of empire and enslavement, they were as likely to imagine the dangers of Turkish galley slavery as the horrors of plantation slavery in their new American colonies.

Barbary slavery was an enduring, significant, and well-known problem in the British Atlantic world, and contemporaries most certainly considered it slavery. If historians are to excavate the ideas and cultural issues surrounding early-modern slaving practices, it may be more helpful to think in terms of Atlantic slaveries. These two slave systems, the Atlantic trade in enslaved Africans and Barbary slavery, had a parallel history in this period. Both, as they affected Britons, were products of imperial expansion and both underwent important changes in the late seventeenth century. Both also endured into the nineteenth century when changing attitudes to African slavery made tolerance of the last remaining slaves in Barbary impossible.

This re-assessment of Barbary slavery has important ramifications for Atlantic historians. It complicates the recent groundbreaking work by David Eltis on slavery in the Americas. Eltis has argued that by the early modern period it had become unthinkable to enslave certain categories of people – Europeans and Christians – but that it remained legitimate to enslave others for far longer. He sees the dividing line between these categories in racial terms. Barbary slavery, he suggests, although a significant problem, actually demonstrates how strongly Europeans felt it was illegitimate to enslave other Europeans. He maintains that Europeans went to great lengths to free their fellow countrymen who fell into the hands of the North Africans. Eltis, however, over-estimates the zeal of Europeans in this cause. Most enslaved Britons languished in slavery for years with the government unwilling to do much to help them. There were, furthermore, circumstances in which Britons were enslaved with the collusion of merchants and with the approval of their king and government. Britons knew their countrymen could be and often were enslaved. There was not, in practice or in their understanding of slavery, any clear racial line distinguishing those who could and could not be enslaved. It is important to recognize this complexity if historians are fully to understand the Atlantic discourse on slavery and freedom, and the development of more modern conceptions of racial slavery in the Americas.

Finally, this re-assessment of Barbary slavery also raises questions as to what it meant to be British in the seventeenth and eighteenth centuries. In precisely the period when Britain was emerging as a major imperial power and celebrating its subjects' special claim to freedom, thousands of Britons were languishing in North African slavery. A closer examination of those slaves – whose enslavement was protested and

– CHAPTER 10: *Atlantic slaveries* –

whose was not – may reveal much about British identity in the period. An expansive view of Atlantic slaveries, one which replaces Barbary slavery into the Atlantic narrative, offers new insights into the central Atlantic world questions of race, unfreedom, empire, identity, and belonging.

NOTES

1   Saunders 1587.
2   Phelps 1685.
3   Stevens 1797.
4   For brevity, 'Britons' is used in this essay to mean Englishmen, Irish, Scots, and English Atlantic world colonists.
5   For England see Matar 2005; Andrews 1991; Hebb 1994. For the United States see Allison 1995; Lambert 2005; Peskin 2009; Tucker 1963.
6   APC (1580–81): 90, 265; Saunders 1587; Webbe 1590; Hasleton 1595; Fox 1589.
7   Letter dated July 5, 1611, CSPD (1611–18): 55.
8   TNA SP 71/1, f. 96.
9   An average crew size of 14 for captured ships in this period seems to be a conservative estimate. An unpublished list in the state papers dated 1627 indicates the average size of the crews on the ships it details as taken was 14. TNA SP 71/1, f. 84. A similar list for ships taken between 1629–39 reveals the average crew size on each captured ship was 18. TNA SP 71/1, f. 163.
10   Letter from the Council to Lord Zouch dated February 7, 1619. CSPD (1619–23): 12.
11   Letter from Richard Ford to the king and council dated February 24, 1622. TNA SP 71/1, f.39; letter from the Mayor of Dartmouth to the king and council dated June 20, 1622. CSPD (1619–23): 409.
12   Letter to the Council dated August 12, 1625. CSPD (1625–26): 83.
13   Letter dated June 10, 1626. CSPD (1625–26): 343.
14   TNA SP 71/1, f.163; TNA SP 71/1, f.105; TNA SP 71/1, f.84; CSPD (1633–34): 357; The London Guildhall, MS 30045; CSPD (1635): 389, 398; CSPD (1635–36): 302; CSPD (1636–37): 4, 60, 140; CSPD (1637): 478; RPCS (1633–35) :142; RPCS (1635–37): 169, 387; RPCS (1638–43): 440; Calendar of State Papers: Ireland (1625–32): 617, 621; Calendar of State Papers: Colonial Series (1574–1660): 214.
15   Letter dated October 18, 1637. TNA SP 71/1, f.165; Calendar of State Papers, Colonial Series: America and West Indies (1675–76): doc 181.
16   CSPD (1640–41): 134.
17   Andrews 1984: 88, 97; Davis 1969: 78–98.
18   Davis 2009: 34.
19   Davis 2009: 34; Edmund Rossington to Viscount Conway, newsletter, July 4, 1640 in Playfair 1972: 54.
20   CSPD (1655–56): 313; CSPD (1657–58): 55.
21   Hebb 1994: 140, 269.
22   Letter dated May 25, 1669. CSPD (1668–69): 342; Letter dated January 24, 1702. TNA SP 71/4, f. 46.
23   CSPD (1680–81): 598.
24   Letter dated February 8, 1691. TNA SP 71/3, f. 103; Letter dated November 21, 1694. TNA SP 71/27.
25   'A List of the Subjects of their Majesty of great Brittain that are in Captivity att Maccaness and Elsewhere under the Emperor of Morocco.' Gloucestershire Record Office, D1833x2, Letter 45; TNA, CO 5/785: 175, 304; John Ellis, letter dated August 16, 1698. CSPD (1698): 374.

26 TNA SP 71/15, f.57, f.166; TNA SP 71/5: 453, 478, 485, 509, 515; TNA SP 71/6: 51–53, 104, 309, 405, 415; TNA SP 71/16, ff. 233, 256, 348; Norfolk Record Office, LC 27/3; Anon 1721; Windus 1725; de La Motte 1736.
27 TNA SP 71/8: 269; TNA SP 71/20, f. 237.
28 Munday 1610; Naile 1613; Taylor 1613. There were processions of redeemed slaves in 1637 and 1734.
29 Somerset Archives, DD\SAS\C/795/SE/93.
30 Calendar of State Papers: Ireland (1625–32): 621. Only three of those abducted from Baltimore were ever heard from again.
31 Calendar of State Papers: Ireland (1625–32): 640.
32 Barnby 1969: 101–29.
33 TNA SP 71/2.
34 Baepler 1995: 95–120.
35 Calendar of State Papers: Colonial Series (1701).
36 Fernow 1987: 31; O'Callaghan 1850: Vol III, 417.
37 Baepler 1995: 114–15.
38 Calendar of State Papers Colonial Series: America and West Indies (1697–98): 175.
39 Hanna 2006.
40 Knight 1640: 28–29.
41 Davis 2003: 173. No doubt the chance of being redeemed for an Italian slave in the first decades of the seventeenth century was considerably less.
42 Anon 1721; TNA SP 71/16, ff. 233, 247; TNA SP 71/5: 453, 478, 509, 515; TNA SP 71/6: 51–54.
43 Troughton 1751: 23.
44 Allison 1995; Baepler 1999; Colley 2004; Wheeler 2000.
45 Friedman 1980: 618.
46 Davis 2009: 15.

REFERENCES

Primary

Acts of the Privy Council of England, volume 12, 1580–81. John Roche Dasent (ed.), 1896, p. 90.

Anonymous. *A Description of the Nature of Slavery among the Moors and the Cruel Sufferings of those that fall into it.* London, 1721.

——*A Narrative of The Shipwreck of The British Brig, Surprise of Glasgow, John William Ross, Master, On the Coast of Barbary on the 28th December 1815 And Subsequent Captivity of the Passengers and Crew by the Arabs until Ransomed by the Worshipful Company of Ironmongers.* London, 1817

Cason, Edmund. *A Relation of the whole proceedings concerning the Redemption of the Captives in Ariger and Tunis.* London, 1646.

Fox, John. 'The Worthy Enterprise of John Fox, in Delivering 266 Christians out of the Captivity of the Turks' in *The Principall Navigations Voyages and Discoveries of the English Nation*, Richard Hakluyt. London, 1589.

Hasleton, Richard. *Strange and wonderfull things. Happened to Richard Hasleton.* London, 1595.

Knight, Francis. *A Relation of Seaven Yeares Slaverie under the Turkes of Argeire, suffered by an English Captive Merchant.* London, 1640.

de La Motte, Philémon. *Several Voyages to Barbary.* Translated by Joseph Morgan. London, 1736.

Munday, Anthony. *Londons love, to the Royal Prince Henrie.* London, 1610.

Naile, Robert. *A relation of the royall magnificent, and sumptuous entertainement, given to the High and Mighty Princesse, Queene Anne, at the renowned citie of Bristoll.* London, 1613.

– CHAPTER 10: Atlantic slaveries –

Phelps, Thomas. *A true account of the captivity of Thomas Phelps at Machaness in Barbary and of his strange escape in company of Edmund Baxter and others.* London, 1685.

Saunders, Thomas. *A true description and breefe discourse, of a most lamentable voyage, made latelie to Tripolie in Barbarie, in a ship named the Jesus.* London, 1587.

Stevens, James Wilson. *An Historical and Geographical Account of Algiers.* Philadelphia, 1797.

Taylor, John. *Heavens blessing, and earths joy.* London, 1613.

Troughton, Thomas. *Barbarian Cruelty.* London, 1751.

Webbe, Edward. *The rare and most wonderfull things which Edw. Webbe an Englishman borne, hath seene and passed in his troublesome travailes.* London, 1590.

Windus, John. *A Journey to Mequinez.* London, 1725.

Secondary

Allison, Robert J. *The Crescent Obscured: The United States and the Muslim World, 1776–1815.* Oxford: Oxford University Press, 1995.

Andrews, Kenneth R. *Trade, Plunder and Settlement: Maritime Enterprise and the Genesis of the British Empire, 1480–1630.* Cambridge: Cambridge University Press, 1984.

——*Ships, Money and Politics: Seafaring and Naval Enterprise in the Reign of Charles I.* Cambridge: Cambridge University Press, 1991.

Baepler, Paul. 'The Barbary Captivity Narrative in Early America,' *The Journal of Early American Literature*, 30.2 (1995), pp. 95–120.

——ed. *White Slaves, African Masters: An Anthology of American Barbary Captivity Narratives.* Chicago: University of Chicago Press, 1999.

Barnby, Henry. 'The Sack of Baltimore,' *Journal of the Cork Historical and Archeological Society*, 74 (1969), pp. 101–29.

Birchwood, Matthew. *Staging Islam in England: Drama and Culture, 1640–1685.* Cambridge: D.S. Brewer, 2007.

Burton, Jonathan. *Traffic and Turning: Islam and English Drama, 1579–1624.* Newark: University of Delaware Press, 2005.

Clissold, Stephen. *The Barbary Slaves.* New York: Barnes and Noble Books, 1992.

Clowes, William Laird. *The Royal Navy: A History from the Earliest Times to the Present.* 1903; repr., Annapolis: Naval Institute Press, 1996.

Colley, Linda. *Captives: Britain, Empire, and the World, 1600–1850.* New York: Random House, Inc., 2004.

Davis, Ralph. 'English Foreign Trade 1660–1700' in *The Growth of English Overseas Trade in the Seventeenth and Eighteenth Centuries*, ed. W. E. Minchinton. London: Methuen & Co., 1969, pp. 78–98.

Davis, Robert C. *Christian Slaves, Muslim Masters: White Slavery in the Mediterranean, the Barbary Coast, and Italy, 1500–1800.* New York: Palgrave Macmillan, 2003.

——*Holy War and Human Bondage: Tales of Christian-Muslim Slavery in the Early-Modern Mediterranean.* Santa Barbara: Praeger Press, 2009.

Eltis, David. *The Rise of African Slavery in the Americas.* Cambridge: Cambridge University Press, 2000.

Fernow, Berthold, compiler. *New York (Colony) Council: Calendar of Council Minutes 1668–1783.* New York: Harbor Hill Books, 1987.

Friedman, Ellen G. 'Christian Captives at "Hard Labor" in Algiers, 16th–18th Centuries,' *The International Journal of African Historical Studies* 13.4 (1980), pp. 616–32.

Hanna, Mark. *The Pirate Nest: The impact of piracy on Newport, Rhode Island and Charles Town, South Carolina.* Ph.D. Dissertation in History, Harvard University, 2006.

Hebb, David Delison. *Piracy and the English Government, 1616–1642.* Aldershot: Scolar Press, 1994.

Lambert, Frank. *The Barbary Wars: American Independence in the Atlantic World*. New York: Hill and Wang, 2005.

Matar, Nabil. *Britain and Barbary, 1589–1689*. Miami: University Press of Florida, 2005.

O'Callaghan, E. B. ed., *The Documentary History of the State of New York, arranged under the direction of the Hon Christopher Morgan, Secretary of State*. Albany: Weed, Parsons and Co., Public Printers, 1850. Vol III.

Peskin, Lawrence A. *Captives and Countrymen: Barbary Slavery and the American Public, 1785–1816*. Baltimore: John Hopkins University Press, 2009.

Playfair, Robert L. *The Scourge of Christendom: Annals of British Relations with Algiers prior to the French Conquest*. New York: Books for Libraries Press, 1972.

Tucker, Glen. *Dawn Like Thunder: The Barbary Wars and the Birth of the US Navy*. Indianapolis: Bobbs-Merrill, 1963.

Wheeler, Roxann. *The Complexion of Race: Categories of Difference in Eighteenth-Century British Culture*. Philadelphia: University of Pennsylvania Press, 2000.

Wolf, John B. *The Barbary Coast: Algiers under the Turks, 1500–1830*. London: W. W. Norton and Company, 1979.

CHAPTER ELEVEN

MOROCCO AND ATLANTIC HISTORY

—·◆·—

James A. O. C. Brown

In 1603, Aḥmad al-Manṣūr, sultan of Morocco from 1578 until that year, wrote to Elizabeth I of England (r. 1558–1603) outlining preparations for a joint Anglo-Moroccan attack on the Spanish possessions in the New World. His plan was a response to an initial English suggestion that such an attack would be more effective than a direct attack on Spain itself, which had been the subject of previous discussions with the Moroccans. Al-Manṣūr affirmed that he was willing to fund the expedition – something well within his capacity as the recent conqueror of the Songhay Empire in West Africa, which brought such wealth to the sultan that he is known to history as al-Dhahabī, 'the golden' – but he had requested a suitably well-armed English ship in which to transport the treasure.[1]

Al-Manṣūr further requested that more detailed thought be given to the long-term management of any successful conquests. He did not, he wrote, contemplate merely sacking Spanish territories and leaving. Rather he envisaged colonies perpetually attached to the English and Moroccan crowns, whose revenues would be divided between them. He also enquired whether or not Elizabeth intended to send English colonists, or whether she would agree that Moroccans would be better, as being more suited to the heat.[2]

In some ways, the recollection of this project brings to mind the counter-factual description by J.H. Elliot in his re-imagining of English history were Christopher Columbus to have taken service with Henry VII of England rather than Isabella and Ferdinand of Spain.[3] The involvement of a Muslim state in the conquest and colonisation of the New World would conceivably have had even more dramatic consequences for the course of world history. Yet perhaps it was only the deaths of Elizabeth and al-Manṣūr shortly after one another in the same year as the proposed project that prevented its realisation.

To most historians of the Atlantic world, the unfulfilled possibility of an Anglo-Moroccan attack on the Americas probably appears as little more than an unlikely, if intriguing, footnote to any serious account of the processes by which that world was formed. Historians of Morocco might respond that such a collaboration was not such a remote prospect as might easily be assumed. There were substantial and complex diplomatic exchanges between the two countries, particularly in the late

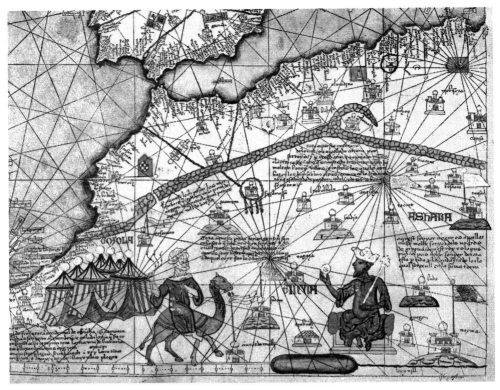

Figure 11.1 Catalan Map of Europe and North Africa
© British Museum, London, UK/Bridgeman

sixteenth century, when shared enmity of Spain motivated their alliance and when both countries were embarking upon imperial projects of expansion.[4]

Yet, leaving aside counter-factual exercises, any such dialogue between the historians of the Atlantic world on the one hand and Morocco on the other would expose some important and neglected questions for both groups.[5] For the former, it must be immediately evident that Morocco is a missing piece of the jigsaw puzzle. Despite a significant stretch of Atlantic coastline – currently longer, even excluding the disputed Western Sahara, than any African state north of Angola, for example – it is barely mentioned within discussions of Atlantic history, defined recently as 'the evolving history of the zone of interaction among the peoples of Western Europe, West Africa and the Americas'.[6] Although a semantic argument might be made that Morocco is included in that list, in terms of historiographical output it is clear that it is not. Of course, bare geographical statistics do not necessarily merit Morocco's inclusion in analyses of the field, but the case for its consideration in the debate, as we will see, rests on considerably more.

The problem might equally be posed from the reverse standpoint, however. Since at least the beginning of the Muslim period, Morocco has been fundamentally defined by its position on the Atlantic. It is *al-Maghrib al-Aqṣā*, literally 'the farthest West', where 'Uqba b. Nāfi', leader of the first Muslim army to reach the Atlantic, is said to

– CHAPTER 11: *Morocco and Atlantic history* –

have ridden into the sea and lamented that there were no more lands before him to conquer for Islam.[7] The ocean thus lay squarely before generations of Moroccans, simultaneously forbidding and inviting, as it did for the European peoples further north whose curiosity is often described as having fuelled the epochal voyages of exploration into it; like many other peoples around the Atlantic basin, Moroccans 'too feel the wind and watch the waves crash against the shore'.[8]

Yet despite the ocean's presence, Moroccan historiography has so far paid little attention to Atlantic history as a field. Interest in Atlantic perspectives may, as Games has noted, be uneven among specialists of different regions; among Moroccanists, it seems practically non-existent.[9] Partly, this is a result of the long-standing tendency in the field to emphasise the country's supposed withdrawal from and resistance to the great processes of modern globalisation of which the formation of the Atlantic world was a crucial part.[10] However, there have of course been important studies on various aspects of Morocco's relationship with the Atlantic, to which we can happily refer as the foundation of any attempt to develop a more explicitly Atlantic perspective.

This chapter, therefore, offers some preliminary outline answers to the question of the relationship between Morocco and the Atlantic world as it is now studied. It will argue first that Moroccan history has some important elements that need to be integrated into the study of the Atlantic system. Patricia Pearson has rightly argued that 'knowledge of the context in which the Atlantic World [sic] was formed and functioned – that is, the past of all the regions involved – is required for complete and accurate understanding of the region and period'.[11] It is clear that Morocco is among those regions in that it was significantly involved in the economic, cultural and technological processes that resulted in European expansion around and across the Atlantic, and equally clear that Moroccan history was heavily shaped by that involvement. The intensity of the relationship between Morocco and the Atlantic world did decline after around 1600, however, indicating the important truism of Moroccan history that the country faces many directions at once. Its relationship with the Atlantic system, while undoubtedly significant, was not definitive in the way that it was for some other regions in the ocean's basin.

Second, it will be argued that this relative ambiguity of Morocco's relationship to the Atlantic world is itself significant in the context of some important debates that are still shaping the relatively novel, if notably fertile, field of Atlantic history. In this sense, Morocco's absences from both the historical Atlantic world and the discourse of Atlantic history are perhaps just as significant as its presence. They not only point to the nature of the relationship between the Atlantic and other regional networks, but also further clarify some of the ambiguities and tensions within the project of Atlantic history as a framework within which different impulses simultaneously deconstruct and reinforce the West's role as the arbiter of historical change in the modern era. In presenting both of these arguments, I offer a conventional but sincere caveat that they are those of a Moroccanist venturing – historiographically if not literally – into the wide waters of the Atlantic for the first time, and as such are intended to begin a debate and not in any sense to conclude it definitively.

The first and perhaps most significant aspect of Morocco's role in the evolution of the Atlantic world is the country's position as a crucial site of what we might call its pre-history. There is obviously a strong argument for defining the origins of the Atlantic world by the watershed of 1492 and the subsequent processes of the

'Columbian exchange'.[12] Yet any attempt to account for and understand that defining event must surely include the technological, economic and cultural context in which it took place, and in that context Morocco's position was significant.

It is clear, for example, that long before the establishment of sustained connections between the eastern and western coasts of the Atlantic basin came centuries in which the foundations for that leap across the ocean were laid. As David Abulafia's recent study has argued, European voyages to the Canary Islands in the fourteenth century were an important precursor, not only geographically, but also intellectually for later discoveries further west.[13] These voyages – although not their results – repeated those made as long ago as the first century under the aegis of Juba II, king of the Roman client state of Mauretania (roughly equivalent to what is today northern Morocco and western Algeria), who sent voyages to the islands to expand the already flourishing trade in the region around the Strait of Gibraltar.[14]

The knowledge of these voyages seems to have been inherited by Muslim geographers and sailors, who also subscribed to the classical idea that the Atlantic (known among other titles as *al-baḥr al-muḥīṭ*, 'the encircling sea') surrounded the entire landmass of the earth. At least one state-sponsored attempt, recorded by the Sicilian geographer al-Idrīsī, was made by the Moroccan sultanate to repeat Juba's voyages, when the Almoravid sultan 'Alī b. Yūsuf b. Tāshfīn (r. 1106–43) unsuccessfully planned a fleet to conquer the islands. Al-Idrīsī and others also mention voyages made from the Iberian peninsula heading south and west into the Atlantic, and report islands opposite the coast of Safi in Morocco and elsewhere.[15]

It is tempting to speculate on how these sporadic contacts influenced the culture of the Islamic West (i.e. al-Andalus and the Maghrib), and whether or not they had any effect similar to the reshaping in Christian Europe of ideas about the nature of humanity, the role of revelation in human societies, the salvation of previously unknown peoples, and so on.[16] The reports of an island or islands to the west of the Atlantic coast of Morocco were fragmentary and fantastical – al-Idrisī counted among them the island 'of the two sorcerer brothers' (*al-akhawayn al-sāḥirayn*), for example – and therefore provided all the more scope for speculation.[17] It seems at least credible, for example, to consider some kind of relationship between knowledge of these strange, isolated islands and the influential philosophical allegory *Ḥayy ibn Yaqẓān* ('*Alive the Son of Aware*') by the Andalusi polymath Ibn Ṭufayl (d. 1185 CE). A scholar and a minister to the Almohad sultan Abū Ya'qūb Yūsuf (r. 1163–84), Ibn Ṭufayl used the story of the eponymous boy growing up alone on a isolated island to analyse the relationship between revelation and reason.[18] There were certainly at this time important links between the practical experiences of sailors and the development of scientific knowledge in the fields such as astronomy and cartography, but whether or not there was a similarly definite link with philosophy now seems impossible to determine.[19]

We return to more certain ground, however, by mentioning the development of maritime links along the Atlantic coasts of North Africa and the Iberian Peninsula during the medieval period, which gave that region of eastern Atlantic an important degree of unity before the first phases of the European 'age of discovery'. As Picard has shown in his detailed study of 'the Muslim Atlantic' during the medieval period, the western coasts of al-Andalus and Morocco were an important site of maritime trade and navigational development.[20] The routes of regular trade along this part of the Atlantic seaboard linked dozens of ports between the Tagus river to the north and

Wadi Sous in the south.[21] These routes were themselves linked through the Straits of Gibraltar to the commercial networks of the Mediterranean, as well as providing the launching pad for exploratory voyages further south.[22] This relative familiarity is reflected in the use of the term by some medieval Muslim geographers of *baḥr al-maghrib*, 'the Western sea', i.e. the Atlantic immediately around the coasts of the Iberian peninsula and Morocco. This suggests a distinct unity separate from the unknown ocean beyond, and linked rather to the Mediterranean through the Straits of Gibraltar, similar perhaps to the Portuguese term Mar Pequeña, and the later concept used by some historians of the 'Atlantic Mediterranean'.[23]

Thus, the nascent European maritime powers in the Atlantic of the thirteenth century were by no means emerging into a *marum incognitum*. Rather they were inserting themselves into a system of maritime trade and communication which already existed, albeit one which was rapidly changing in response to their arrival. Morocco's Atlantic coast became the training ground for European expansion, providing both cartographical knowledge and human experience. Once through the Straits of Gibraltar, ships coming from the Mediterranean were often forced south by the prevailing winds; their sailors became familiar with Moroccan ports, and began to consider for the first time the possibilities of sailing south around Africa or west to the Indies.[24] For the Genoese and Portuguese in particular, the coast of Morocco on either side of the straits was the site for the creation of important initial outposts, either through treaty agreements and the establishment of fondouks by the former or in the form of the militarised fortress–factories of the latter.[25]

The coast of Morocco was not, however, just a physical waypoint on the eventual routes established across the ocean, but was intimately connected to the motives for and the manner of their development. Strategies developed to address the economic problems fuelling European expansion found early expression in the emergent network linking the western Mediterranean with the Canary Islands and the Atlantic coasts of Morocco and the Iberian Peninsula, before the same pressures pushed the expansion beyond the eastern seaboard and across the ocean. Thus, the economic processes which did so much to shape the Atlantic world also heavily impacted on Morocco.

Among these strategies was first the attempt to gain direct access to the source of bullion, in order to overcome the adverse balance of trade dogging Europe's overseas commerce; in this case by trying either to participate in or bypass the existing networks of the trans-Saharan gold trade.[26] Second, Morocco became an important source of agricultural produce and raw materials – most notably sugar, but also grain, copper, iron and saltpetre – during the late fifteenth and sixteenth centuries. Sugar production had already reached Morocco by the ninth century, and was particularly well-established in the warm, well-watered Sous valley in the south of the country. It expanded rapidly, however, as a result of the growing trade with Europe, in which the Moroccans exchanged sugar particularly for weapons and also cloth. Thus, although the transfer of sugar from the Mediterranean into the Atlantic is generally associated with the cultivation of the crop on the Atlantic islands of Madeira and the Canaries and then in the New World, this shift was already underway through the growth of sugar production in Morocco and the Iberian peninsula, although these would themselves decline significantly after the sixteenth century under pressure of competition from Brazil and the Caribbean.[27]

Thus, as Cornell has argued, far from being 'out of the loop' of the processes of incorporation into the emerging system of the world economy, as is often asserted, Morocco was central to its early phases.[28] An indication of this was the intense competition among different European states to control the trade with Morocco. Portugal, for example, bitterly resented the growth of English trade there, which they considered reserved to themselves by papal decree. Elizabeth I ignored their threats to prohibit English trade with Portugal in retaliation, on the grounds that the trade with Morocco was more important to her subjects.[29] Besides the English, the merchants of Genoa, Venice, France and Flanders competed for trade, dodging the coastal patrols of the Portuguese intended to suppress the 'illegal' commerce of their rivals, and establishing their own links in the areas of northern Morocco controlled by the Wattasid dynasty (1472–1554) where Portuguese influence was limited.[30]

It was in this quest for resources along the Moroccan coast that Europeans developed many of the new tactics and technologies that underpinned later military–commercial expansion in the New World and elsewhere: a mixture of trade, slaving and privateering 'which were turned into the "voyages of discovery"'.[31] The Portuguese, most notably, developed alliances and tribute relationships in Morocco that anticipated similar strategies in their later empire building.[32] The country was also an important early source of slaves for the Portuguese, whose raids into the countryside around their enclaves ultimately contributed to the erosion of the stability of their position in the country. It is difficult to quantify the number of slaves taken from Morocco by the Portuguese, but it was certainly in the thousands annually during the early 1500s, when the exportation of slaves was sometimes the largest single source of revenue from their colonies there.[33] Although little information survives about individuals among this group, who were mainly transported to Spain and Portugal, an intriguing exception is 'Estebánico the Black', a tribesman from Azzemour who travelled to the New World as the servant of the Spanish explorer Alvaro Nuñez Cabeza de Vaca. He was subsequently among the first explorers of the American Southwest and whose memory was preserved in folk tales of the Pueblo Indians.[34] Thus Morocco was thus among the sources for 'the recruitment of a wide variety of peoples, their interaction, their conflicts, their partial absorption and their creation of new cultures' – a defining process of Atlantic history.[35]

The early Iberian slave trade, also including West Africans and Moriscos, anticipated and partly prepared the way for the much larger-scale plantation slavery of the New World.[36] Like other economic and military aspects of the growing European influence in Morocco, it was related to the cultural attitudes which defined European, especially Iberian, attitudes to their expansion in the Atlantic. The Reconquista and the subsequent processes of attempting to assimilate the conquered non-Christian population in Spain and Portugal were fundamental to the evolution of Iberian ideas about racial and religious purity that shaped the societies of Latin America.[37] Morocco was in many ways the site of an intermediate stage in this transmission, since the religious dimension of Europe's conquest of the New World was equally engrained into its commercial and military exploits in the Maghrib. From the papal bull of crusade granted before the conquest of Ceuta in 1415 onwards, it was at least in part religious motives – such as the prospect of victory over the Muslims, a route to the Holy Land through North Africa or the possibility of a grand alliance against Islam with the mythical Christian king of Africa, Prester John – which motivated this 'neo-Reconquista'.[38]

– CHAPTER 11: Morocco and Atlantic history –

This role as both the physical and conceptual waypoint for European expansion was not confined to that stemming from Iberia. Matar, for example, has highlighted the importance of the 'triangle' between England, North Africa and North America and its role alongside other, more well-known trading triangles around the Atlantic. It was no accident, for example, that Drake stopped in Morocco during his famous voyage to the Americas in 1577. Similarly, the idea of the 'Moor', to some extent conflated with the 'Turk', played a crucial role in the development of English understandings of the Native American population. There were even proposals, paralleling the debate in Iberia, for the English to colonise Morocco.[39]

Morocco was, therefore, significant as a crucible in which important elements of the Atlantic world were first forged. This was true both in economic terms and in the processes of cultural transformation, which, as Eltis has argued, are crucial to understanding them.[40] Hindsight should not obscure the fact that for the better part of a century after Columbus' first crossing of the Atlantic, the decisive weight of Iberian expansion hung in the balance between the Americas and North Africa, in other words between trans-Atlantic and eastern Atlantic/Mediterranean, between New World and Old. It was only with the Battle of al-Qaṣr al-Kabīr (also known as the Battle of the Three Kings) in 1578 that Portuguese ambitions in Morocco were finally curtailed, at the same time as bringing about, albeit indirectly, the unification of the Iberian peninsula under Philip II. As Hess has argued, Iberia did not shake off its centuries-long engagement with the societies of the Muslim Mediterranean and reorient itself toward the New World overnight in 1492; the following century or so was heavily shaped by external competition with the Ottoman Empire and internal attempts to assimilate Iberia's mixed religious heritage that did not reach their conclusion until the final expulsion of the Moriscos in 1614.[41]

If the Iberian footholds of the fifteenth and sixteenth centuries had become more significant – not an unrealistic prospect, given that, for example, the Portuguese and their Moroccan allies were raiding as far as the outskirts of Marrakesh in the 1510s[42] – it surely would have retrenched their interests in the Mediterranean and the Old World, perhaps decisively, and certainly giving the Atlantic world a very different character. Access to land, labour and precious metals much closer at hand would in themselves have been attractive, and the Iberian combination of material ambition and religious fervour would have found an outlet against the historic religious enemy, instead of the substitutes of the New World onto whom the crusading impulse was partly sublimated.

However, despite Morocco's place in the working out of some eventual trajectories of European expansion around the Atlantic basin, it should not be seen as only the site of the activity of outsiders. On the contrary, Morocco was profoundly affected by these events, and can certainly be counted among those societies whose 'transformations, experiences and events' may be, at least in part, explained by the processes created by the intersection of the four landmasses of Atlantic history.[43] The Iberian incursions in Morocco were not just a crucial phase of European expansion, and hence of Atlantic integration, but 'decisive in the formation of modern Morocco'.[44]

This process similarly had cultural, technological and economic aspects. Economically most significant was the rapid growth of sugar production aforementioned, which also ultimately encouraged the export to Europe of other Moroccan agricultural produce and, in the later sixteenth century, copper and

193

saltpetre. It has been argued, although not conclusively, that this provoked the utilisation of slave labour on a large scale for sugar production in southern Morocco, mirroring the 'strange connection between sugar and slavery' that developed in the New World. Whether or not this was the case, the increase in agricultural and mining production did encourage the growth of wage labour, as peasants left their own cultivation to work in those industries.[45]

In the political sphere, one very significant result of the Iberian incursions of the fifteenth and sixteenth centuries was the entrenchment of the practice and rhetoric of *jihād* (here, 'religious war') as a defining element of political legitimacy in Morocco. This became a fundamental aspect of the exercise of state power under both the Sa'di and 'Alawi dynasties well into the nineteenth century.[46] Paralleling this rhetorical development, efforts to resist Iberian incursions also prompted advances in military technology and tactics in Morocco, particularly the use of gunpowder weapons, and also the reorganisation and equipping of the Moroccan army.[47]

On the other hand, the presence of Christian enclaves also engendered other, more complex intersections with local socio-political structures. As we have already mentioned, the Portuguese had local allies in their military raids inland. In other regions Europeans found a niche within existing Moroccan social institutions, such as the Genoese merchants who traded at the weekly country markets around Fes.[48] Some of these co-operative relationships were formalised by agreements such as the treaty between Portugal and the Wattasid dynasty in 1471, which conceded both Asilah and Tangier to the Portuguese, while others developed in a more *de facto* fashion.[49]

By a similar paradox, the processes of resistance engendered by the military and commercial expansion of Portugal and Spain on Morocco's coasts actually contributed toward the country's greater engagement with wider Atlantic networks. Successive rulers during the sixteenth century encouraged trade with England, Holland and France in order to diversify their maritime trade and also to secure access to European military supplies.[50] This pushed Morocco toward an 'Atlantic policy' both diplomatically and economically, as it tried to outflank its expansionist Iberian neighbours to the north.[51] It was during this period, for example, that Anglo-Moroccan relations blossomed under Aḥmad al-Manṣūr and Elizabeth I. As Matar has pointed out, Morocco consequently had substantial involvement in 'European' diplomacy during the sixteenth century.[52] These simultaneous but divergent responses to the impact of European power and the nascent networks of European influence in the Atlantic point to the fundamental ambiguity of Morocco's overall relationship to the Atlantic world. Moroccan history during the period between the fifteenth to nineteenth centuries was to a significant degree defined in terms of the tension between those forces drawing the country and its society seaward and those directing them inland. Since at least the late tenth century, and particularly under the Almoravid and Almohad empires, the development of state structures in Morocco and in the Maghrib generally had been closely tied to the control of overland trade, particularly the trans-Saharan gold trade, and much less closely related to maritime affairs.[53] That is not to say that control of Morocco's ports and shipping was unimportant to the country's rulers – as we have already noted, both were important for military and economic reasons during the medieval period. However, generally speaking the inland entrepôts and the routes connecting them were the centres of gravity around which the state coalesced, from where it exercised more indirect power on the country's ports.[54] Then, as a result of the growth of European commercial influence and military threat, Moroccan society underwent a slow, spasmodic reorientation toward the sea, as maritime connections became increasingly integrated into the political and economic life of the country. This process tended toward the Atlantic more than the Mediterranean in part because, with their very first incursion in Morocco by the conquest of Ceuta, the Portuguese effectively shut off the country's historic outlet to the Mediterranean and its most important medieval port. The trend toward the sea was encouraged both by the gradual decline of the trans-Saharan trade and by Morocco's periodic instability, which facilitated the entrenchment of European influence and the growth of semi-autonomous local powers, especially but not exclusively in coastal regions, using the revenues of foreign trade and access to military supplies to resist central control.[55] In another manifestation of the simultaneous engagement with and confrontation of European expansion, the maritime orientation was also driven by the growth of Moroccan piracy and privateering in the seventeenth century. This reinforced local autonomy in the ports concerned, and disrupted European shipping on both sides of the Straits of Gibraltar to the extent that it provoked several campaigns to suppress it.[56]

These centrifugal forces in turn tended to provoke a reassertion of state power, a pattern exemplified in the growth of Portuguese power and the emergence of the Sa'di dynasty during the fifteenth and sixteenth centuries, with which we have been most concerned here, but which was repeated during the early establishment of 'Alawi rule in the late seventeenth century, and again in the renewal of the 'Alawi state under Sīdī Muḥammad b. 'Abd Allāh (r. 1757–90). In those cases, European influence was exercised mostly by the British, Spanish and, to some extent, the French. Sīdī Muḥammad sought both to benefit from but also control the growth of maritime commerce in order to prevent its negative impact on the power of the Moroccan state. In doing so, he refashioned the traditional symbiosis of state and commercial interests in Morocco in a way that institutionalised the shifting balance of trade from land to sea.[57] Similarly, he brought piracy under closer state control in order to use Morocco's capacity to disrupt commerce in order 'to force Western powers into closer dialogue and negotiation'.[58]

However, this gradual maritime reorientation should not be read simply as Morocco's inexorable integration into the Atlantic system. It is obvious but bears repetition in this context that Morocco lies in an overlapping zone between or at the meeting point of several important regions – Saharan, Mediterranean, and Maghribi as well as Atlantic – each with its own historic economic and cultural coherence. As David Abulafia has suggested, relatively empty spaces such as these, whether or not actual seas or oceans, 'have played an essential role in the transformation of societies across the world by bringing into contact with one another very diverse cultures'.[59] Morocco participated historically to a greater or lesser extent in each of these systems – something already implicit in the discussion above – so that its position was primarily defined by being between, or rather part of, all of them, rather than wholly in one or another. Thus the Atlantic dimension of the country's development was in constant dialogue with its other faces, even as the country's Atlantic orientation increased in importance.

It is necessary, therefore, to highlight the context of the country's relationship to the Atlantic world. After the early period of initial European expansion to around

1600 that most directly concerned Morocco, its links to that system continued to develop but became less intense. Partly this was because the focus of the expansion had definitively broadened beyond its first targets around the 'Atlantic Mediterranean', of which Morocco's Atlantic coast had been a crucial part. It was also because the Sa'di dynasty had successful restored state power and resisted Morocco's further colonisation and/or peripheralisation.

This reduced intensity manifested itself diplomatically, for example, in the relegation of Morocco to a position of lesser strategic importance for the European Atlantic powers. The addition of Tangier to England's early colonies in 1661 seemed significant to contemporaries, offering both control of the Straits of Gibraltar and an eastern Atlantic port to complement the acquisition of Jamaica a few years earlier; but it proved impossible to hold in the face of renewed Moroccan resistance, and was soon removed from England's developing Atlantic network.[60] The trade of Morocco continued to be the subject of rivalry between England, Spain and France in the eighteenth century, but not to the same degree as it had been during the initial period of European expansion.[61] It was only in the late nineteenth and early twentieth centuries that the competition of the 'Great Powers' in Morocco reached its second peak, in a different context of globalised colonialism.

The movement of people between Morocco and the rest of the Atlantic world similarly declined after the relatively high numbers of, on the one hand, Moroccan slaves being taken out and, on the other, European merchants venturing beyond the country's ports to its inland cities and trade routes. Some Moroccan Jews seem to have been among the early Jewish communities in the New World, as might be expected given the community's strong connections to the Marrano population expelled from Iberia and generally to Sephardic networks in Holland and elsewhere.[62] Occasionally, too, we also find Muslim Moroccans in the Americas – a half-Dutch, half-Moroccan privateer who settled in New Amsterdam, for example, or a merchant trading to Baltimore.[63] European merchants and consuls remained in Morocco, but were increasingly confined to its ports except for occasional diplomatic missions to see the sultan. The only Europeans and Americans in the country otherwise were generally captives taken by privateers and pirates or enslaved after being shipwrecked, a particular risk for any ship bound for West Africa because of the currents running toward the Moroccan coast to the east of the Canary Islands.[64]

So although we have seen that Moroccan history was certainly 'Atlantic' in the sense that it experienced the 'creation, destruction and re-creation of communities as a result of the movement, across and around the Atlantic basin, of people, commodities, cultural practices and ideas',[65] its position among several regional systems and the declining intensity of its engagement with the Atlantic world suggest that these processes of refashioning and exchange were also shaped by the waves washing on its other 'shores'.

Thus, for example, at the same time as beginning to import European military materials and techniques in the fifteenth and sixteenth centuries, the Moroccan sultanate also looked to the Ottomans for such expertise. Military reforms in the Ottoman Empire and Egypt similarly influenced Morocco in the eighteenth and nineteenth centuries.[66] While Aḥmad al-Manṣūr developed his 'Atlantic policy', he was also strongly committed to the extension of Moroccan influence across the Sahara.[67] Culturally and religiously, Morocco continued to look eastwards toward

– CHAPTER II: *Morocco and Atlantic history* –

the historic centres of the Muslim world, the most likely destinations for any Moroccan traveler well into the nineteenth century, whether pilgrim, merchant or scholar.[68] While Sīdī Muḥammad did promote Morocco's Atlantic trade and engage with the Atlantic powers diplomatically (most famously, perhaps, as the first sovereign to recognise the independent United States of America), he also looked to his relationship with the Ottoman Empire and promoted his role as defender of Muslims in the Mediterranean, particularly through the ransoming of Muslim slaves.[69] During his rule, Atlantic trade was boosted by the founding of Essaouira (Mogador) and a generation of merchants began to shift their investments toward maritime commerce and away from the traditional caravan trade. Yet despite this the caravan trade eastwards to Algiers and beyond, the trade axis linking the great emporium of Fes to the sea through Tetuan, and to some extent the trans-Saharan trade remained important for Moroccan trade well into the nineteenth century.[70]

The overlapping circuits of trade through Morocco are also recorded in the late-eighteenth-century travels of one merchant, 'Abd al-Salām Shabānī, who travelled from his home town of Tetuan to Timbuktu, residing there for several years travelling further south into Hausaland for several more years, from where he returned to Morocco. He set out again from Tetuan, this time eastwards to Egypt and then to the Hijaz, where he performed the Muslim pilgrimage of *ḥajj* while also continuing his trade. Upon returning from this trip, he engaged in the commerce between Tetuan and the British colony of Gibraltar, which encouraged him to extend his business further into Europe with a trip to Hamburg.[71]

Of course, this multi-faceted relationship to the outside world was not unique to Morocco among those societies engaged in the Atlantic system; but this characteristic – being both of the Atlantic world and not of it – was perhaps more strongly pronounced in Morocco than in many other regions. The societies of the New World were essentially products of the 'Columbian exchange'. For the European societies engaged in the Atlantic world, their involvement in it was almost as definitive, even if were to be argued that it was only so as the first stage of an ultimately global process. In sub-Saharan Africa, the impact of European arms and the population transfers of the Atlantic slave trade were certainly of clearer immediate significance than the slower, more hesitant spread of European influence in Morocco.[72] Uniquely among the non-European societies of the Atlantic basin, Morocco had a long history of interaction with Europe before the late fifteenth century (even if to some extent mediated through al-Andalus), which muted the transformative effect of the intensification of this interaction during the period of European expansion.

Herein lies the ambiguity of considering Morocco from an Atlantic perspective; while productive, it is in itself insufficient. While focusing on the coherence and unity of the ocean basin – natural enough in the field's early phases – Atlantic history has yet to clarify as fully the relationship of the Atlantic system to other regional or supra-regional systems. There is a lively and important debate about the place of the Atlantic as the axis or meeting point for the other circuits of trade and cultural exchange underpinning the processes of globalisation.[73] The example of Morocco tends most strongly to support the position of some in this debate that although the Atlantic system was in many ways coherent, it does not necessarily follow that it was self-contained or necessarily unitary at all levels. While the various parts of the Atlantic world obviously had a relationship with each other and together formed a

197

system that had a certain relationship with other regional systems, the different parts may also at other levels have had their own particular relationships with other regions. For example, the emergence of the Atlantic world from the Mediterranean has been an object of consideration for some time (albeit with some ellipses discussed here), but less attention has been paid to the question of how this relationship continued.[74] Although the results did not make themselves felt instantaneously of course, expansion into the Atlantic basin ultimately made the Mediterranean into a relative backwater for the new European powers, but for Morocco this shift was not so conclusive, putting it among those regions we might, using Colcanis' term, label 'conjuncto-Atlantic'.[75]

In this regard, Morocco is perhaps difficult to accommodate for Atlantic historians because it was part of the Old World, and continued to be so. Its conceptual relationship with the processes of European expansion has more in common with those societies and economic networks of Asia that were much more difficult for European expansion to uproot than those in the New World.[76] If, as Fernández-Armesto has argued, what defined Atlantic, as opposed to Mediterranean, colonisation by the European powers was the possibility of 'plantation' methods – bringing in slave or other populations to work land that was either empty or rapidly depopulated upon European arrival – Morocco could not fundamentally be incorporated into the new Atlantic world of Europe's creation.[77] It was able to adapt to and deflect the acceleration of European expansion, unhampered by some of the major factors that facilitated European conquest elsewhere: the shock of their arrival, technological disparity, vulnerability to new diseases. Once again, we can see Morocco is simultaneously of the Atlantic world, and yet not of it, at least as historians have largely constructed it.

This problem is a telling one in the context of the related critique of Atlantic history as imperial history or histories rehashed, 'a neo-colonial, politically correct attempt at re-writing European history with some "other bits" given deferential treatment'.[78] The consequent calls for greater recognition of the 'black Atlantic' are well known.[79] The implications of Morocco's complex ethnic and racial history in this context, the country's relationship to sub-Saharan Africa and the validity of analysing it in a specifically African framework are separate questions too complex to be addressed adequately here, but at the very least it can be said that the argument for including Morocco in the framework of Atlantic history is related to the overall process of addressing its residual imperial, Eurocentric biases, whether these are ultimately deemed justifiable or not.[80] It is unfortunate, after all, for any defence against the charge of Eurocentrism that in omitting Morocco almost completely from their analyses, Atlantic historians have ignored a region of the ocean basin in which European control was relatively weak for so long, despite, as outlined above, Morocco's role in the formation of the Atlantic system.

Overall, therefore, it seems that an analysis of Morocco within an Atlantic framework would be 'for better and worse'.[81] On the one hand, there is no doubt that 'the explanatory power and suggestive implications created by the vision of the Atlantic region as a coherent whole' have some important implications for understanding a country's relationship to and role within it.[82] Particularly during the early phase of European expansion, Morocco was an important site in many aspects of the processes of economic change and cultural encounter that came to define the

– CHAPTER 11: *Morocco and Atlantic history* –

Atlantic system. Likewise, the history of Morocco itself was strongly influenced by its experience of these processes.

However, at other levels the experience of Morocco points beyond a unitary Atlantic paradigm, supporting the trend toward relating that system to others in various ways. Atlantic history provides a way to understand a world that was created as the different parts of the oceanic basin were brought into contact for the first time, and whose development was subsequently defined to a large extent by the creation of those relationship; but from a Moroccan perspective neither the novelty of the system nor its unity can really be said to apply in the same way as to other regions. Although Morocco was deeply influenced by the development of the Atlantic world, that experience was shaped by the long history of contact between Islam and Christendom in the western Mediterranean and eastern Atlantic, as well as by the country's continuing relationship to other cultural and economic spheres. These factors ultimately helped drive European expansion further into the Atlantic, to a certain extent relegating Morocco to the margins of the oceanic system. They should not, however, push historians of the Atlantic similarly to bypass it. Although Morocco poses difficulties for the sustaining of the traditional, mainstream Atlantic paradigm, it equally offers material for the development of a richer, more subtle and more sustainable successor.

NOTES

1   On the Songhay Empire, its invasion by Morocco and the empire's subsequent decline, see S. M. Cissoko, 'The Songhay from the 12th to the 16th Century', in D. T. Niane (ed.), *Africa from the Twelfth to Sixteenth Century*, General History of Africa IV (London, Paris & Berkeley, CA, 1984), pp. 187–210; Michel Abitbol, 'The End of the Songhay Empire', in B. A. Ogot (ed.), *Africa from the Sixteenth to the Eighteenth Century*, General History of Africa V (London, Paris & Berkeley, CA, 1992), pp. 300–326.

2   Henry de Castries (ed.), *Les sources inédites de l'histoire du Maroc: première série – dynastie Saadienne: archives et bibliothèques d'Angleterre*, 3 vols. (Paris, 1918), Vol. 2, pp. 206–9. For an introduction to al-Manṣūr and his reign, see M. García-Areñal, *Ahmad al-Mansur: The Beginnings of Modern Morocco* (Oxford, 2009).

3   See J. H. Elliott, 'Atlantic History: A Circumnavigation', in David Armitage and Michael J. Braddick (eds.), *The British Atlantic World, 1500–1800* (Basingstoke & New York, 2002), pp. 233–49.

4   For an introduction to the Arab-Muslim conquest of North Africa, see M. Brett, 'The Arab Conquest and the Rise of Islam in North Africa', in J. D. Fage and R. Oliver (eds.), *Cambridge History of Africa* (Cambridge, 1978), Vol. 2, pp. 490–544.

5   On Anglo-Moroccan relations around this time, see in particular Nabil Matar, 'The Anglo-Spanish Conflict in Arabic Sources c.1588–96', in Mohammad Shaheen (ed.), *From Silence to Sound: Studies in Literature and Language. Festschrift for Hussam el-Khateeb / Min al-ṣamt ilā 'l-ṣawt* (Beirut, 2000), pp. 456–38 [sic]. For an interesting theoretical discussion of the early contacts and exchanges between Morocco and England by the same author, see Nabil Matar, 'The Question of Occidentalism in Early Modern Morocco', in Patricia Ingham and Michelle Warren (eds.), *Postcolonial Moves: Medieval through Modern* (New York, 2003), pp. 154–70. This shared enmity remained an important aspect of Anglo-Moroccan relations subsequently as well. See, for example, R. Lourido-Díaz, 'Relaciones politicas anglo-marroques en la segunda mitad del siglo XVIII. Bases militares espanolas en Tanger durante el bloquero de Gibraltar por Carlos III', *Hispania: Revista Española de*

Historia, 31 (1971), pp. 337–83. On Morocco's imperial ambitions during this period, see Mohamed Chérif, 'Les prétentions califales dans l'expédition d'Ahmed al Mansur au Soudan (1590)', in M. Balard and A. Ducellier (eds.), *Le partage du monde: échanges et colonisation dans la Méditerranée médiévale*, Série Byzantina Sorbonensia (Paris, 1998), pp. 375–84; Nabil Matar, 'The Maliki Imperialism of Ahmad al-Mansur: The Moroccan Invasion of Sudan, 1591', in Elizabeth Sauer and Balachandra Rajan (eds.), *Imperialisms: Historical and Literary Investigations, 1500–1900* (New York & Basingstoke, 2004), pp. 147–62; and most recently, Nabil Mouline, *Le califat imaginaire d'Ahmad al-Mansûr* (Paris, 2009).

6   The use of the terms 'Morocco' or 'Moroccan' to indicate or describe a political entity or geographical area before the modern period is problematic. It is used here with reference to the period before the establishment of the Sa'di dynasty in 1554 as a purely geographical term, meaning the approximate area that is now the modern state of Morocco, to distinguish it from the wider Maghrib. Used in reference to subsequent periods, these terms refer to the place and the dynasty that ruled it, in the awareness that this might strictly be considered anachronistic. Although this usage is somewhat arbitrary, it is adopted here with its shortcomings for the sake of convenience and brevity.

7   Bernard Bailyn, 'Introduction: Reflections on Some Major Themes', in Bernard Bailyn and Patricia L. Denault (eds.), *Soundings in Atlantic History: Latent Structures and Intellectual Currents, 1500–1830* (Cambridge, MA, 2009), pp. 1–43 at p. 1. See also Horst Pietschmann, 'Introduction: Atlantic History – History between European History and Global History', in Horst Pietschmann (ed.), *Atlantic History: History of the Atlantic System 1580–1830* (Göttingen, 2002), pp. 11–55 at p. 35, where Atlantic history is defined as 'a connecting element between European, North American, Caribbean, Latin American and West African history'. Morocco's total coastline is 1,835 km, very slightly more than Portugal's 1,793 km, although of course around one-quarter of the Moroccan coast lies inside the Straits of Gibraltar ('CIA World Factbook – Coastline' [https://www.cia.gov/library/publications/the-world-factbook/fields/2060.html – accessed 12 December 2009]).

8   Peter C. Mancall, 'Atlantic Colonies', *New England Quarterly* 75 (2002), pp. 477–87 at p. 477.

9   Alison Games, 'Atlantic History: Definitions, Challenges, and Opportunities', *American Historical Review* 111 (2006), pp. 741–57 at p. 750.

10   Julien, for example, described Moroccan history from the Sa'dis onwards as 'one of increasingly marked withdrawal...[By 1820] Morocco was taking virtually no part in the economic life of a world in which commercial exchanges were developing with increasing speed' (Charles-André Julien, *History of North Africa: From the Arab Conquest to 1830* [New York & Washington, 1970], pp. 269–70). Miège concluded similarly that in 1830 'Morocco remained isolated from the grand revolutions in Europe of politics, demography and technology, from that growth of men, ideas and money which...began the decisive shift in relations between Europe and the rest of the world' (J. L. Miège, 'Relations exterieures XVIe siécle – debut du XXe siécle', in *Maroc: les tresors de royaume, 15 avril – 18 juillet 1999* [Paris, 1999], pp. 217–23 at p. 222). For a critical review of this aspect of Moroccan historiography, see J.A.O.C. Brown, 'Anglo-Moroccan relations in late eighteenth and early nineteenth centuries, with particular reference to the role of Gibraltar', Ph.D. thesis, University of Cambridge, 2009, pp. 3–16.

11   Patricia Pearson, 'The World of the Atlantic before the "Atlantic World": Africa, Europe, and the Americas before 1450', in Toyin Falola and Kevin D. Roberts (eds.), *The Atlantic World, 1450–2000* (Bloomington, IN, 2008), pp. 3–26 at p. 3.

12   Games, 'Atlantic History', p. 747.

13   David Abulafia, *The Discovery of Mankind: Atlantic Encounters in the Age of Columbus* (New Haven & London, 2008), pp. 31–62.

– CHAPTER 11: *Morocco and Atlantic history* –

14 Pliny the Elder, *Natural History*, Book VI, 201–5. See Dunae W. Roller, *The World of Juba II and Kleopatra Selene: Royal Scholarship on Rome's African Frontier* (London & New York, 2003), pp. 196–97.

15 See Christophe Picard, *L'océan Atlantique musulman. De la conquête arabe à l'epoque almohade. Navigation et mise en valeur des côtes d'al-Andalus et du Maghreb occidental (Portugal-Espange-Maroc)* (Paris, 1997), pp. 34, 161 & 181; *Encyclopaedia of Islam*, 2nd ed. (Leiden. 1954–99) [hereafter *EI2*], 'Al-Baḥr al-Muḥīṭ', Vol. 1, p. 934; ibid., 'Al-Djazā'ir alKhālidāt', Vol. 2, p. 522.

16 See Abulafia, *Discovery of Mankind*.

17 See Halima Ferhat, 'Demons et merveilles: l'Atlantique dans l'imaginaire Marocain medieval', in Abdelmajid Kaddouri (ed.), *Le Maroc et l'Atlantique* (Rabat, 1992), pp. 31–49; Picard, *L'océan*, pp. 31–35. The Atlantic was also known as *al-baḥr al-muzlim* or *baḥr al-ẓulumāt*, 'the sea of shadows', an indication of its perceived mysterious character.

18 For an English translation, see *Ibn Tufayl's Hayy Ibn Yaqzan: A Philosophical Tale*, trans. Lenn Evan Goodman (Los Angeles, 2003) For some perspectives on the work's significance and later reception, see Lawrence I. Conrad (ed.), *The World of Ibn Ṭufayl: Interdisciplinary Perspectives on Ḥayy ibn Yaqẓān* (Leiden, 1996); G. A. Russell, 'The Impact of the *Philosophus autodidactus*: Pocockes, John Locke and the Society of Friends', in G.A. Russell (ed.), *The 'Arabick' Interest of the Natural Philosophers in Seventeenth-Century England* (Leiden, 1994), pp. 224–65.

19 Picard, *L'océan*, p. 36.

20 ibid. See also Christophe Picard, *La mer et les musulmans d'Occident au Moyen Age VIIIe-XIIIe siécle* (Paris, 1997).

21 See Picard, *L'océan*, p. 187ff.

22 On early Muslim voyages along the Atlantic coast, see J.F.P. Hopkins and N. Levtzion (eds.), *Corpus of early Arabic sources for West African history* (Cambridge, 1981), pp. 130–31, 190–91 & 272–73. On the link with the Mediterranean, see Olivia Remie Constable, *Trade and Traders in Muslim Spain: The commercial realignment of the Iberian peninsula, 900–1500* (Cambridge, 1994).

23 See *EI2*, 'Al-Baḥr al-Muḥīṭ', Vol. 1, p. 934; John K. Thornton, 'The Portuguese in Africa', in Francisco Bethencourt and Diogo Ramada Curto (eds.), *Portuguese Oceanic Expansion, 1400–1800* (Cambridge, 2007), pp. 138–60 at pp. 139–40; Felipe Fernández-Armesto, *Before Columbus: Exploration and Colonisation from the Mediterranean to the Atlantic 1229–1492* (London, 1987), p. 152; David Abulafia, 'Mediterraneans', in W. V. Harris (ed.), *Rethinking the Mediterranean* (Oxford, 2005), pp. 64–93 at pp. 80–82.

24 See Fernández-Armesto, *Before Columbus*, p. 153; David Abulafia, *A Mediterranean emporium: the Catalan kingdom of Majorca* (Cambridge, 1994), p. 208; Abulafia, *Discovery of Mankind*, p. 38.

25 See H. C. Krueger, 'Early Genoese Trade with Atlantic Morocco', *Medievalia et Humanistica* 3 (1945), pp. 3–15; Georges Jehel, 'Les relations entre Gênes et le Maghreb occidental au moyen age, aspects politiques et économiques', in Mohammed Hammam (ed), *L'occident musulman et l'occident chretien au moyen age* (Rabat, 1995), pp. 107–22; Malyn Newitt, *A History of Portuguese Overseas Expansion, 1400–1668* (London & New York, 2005), pp. 1–20.

26 Ibid., pp. 26, 90 & 140–48.

27 See Salmi-Bianchi, 'Anciennes sucreries'; Sidney W. Mintz, *Sweetness and Power: the Place of Sugar in Modern History* (New York, 1986), pp. 24–29; J.H. Galloway, 'The Mediterranean Sugar Industry', *Geographical Review* 67 (1977), pp. 177–94 at pp. 190–94; V.J. Cornell, 'Socioeconomic Dimensions of Reconquista and Jihad in Morocco: Portuguese Dukkala and the Sadid Sus, 1450–1557', *International Journal of Middle East Studies* 22 (1990), pp. 379–418 at pp. 402–3. On the role of sugar in the growth of trade between

Morocco and England in particular, see T.S. Willan, *Studies in Elizabethan Foreign Trade* (Manchester, 1959), *passim*.

28 Cornell, 'Socioeconomic Dimensions', pp. 379–80 & 407–9.

29 See P.G. Rogers, *A History of Anglo-Moroccan Relations to 1900* (London, n.d.), pp. 9–10.

30 Cornell, 'Socioeconomic Dimensions', pp. 395–96.

31 Newitt, *History*, p. 12.

32 A.J.R. Russell-Wood, 'Patterns of Settlement in the Portuguese Empire, 1400–1800', in Bethencourt and Curto (eds), *Portuguese Oceanic Expansion*, pp. 161–97 at p. 166.

33 Cornell, 'Socioeconomic dimensions', pp. 387 & 393–387 & 394.

34 See Robert Ricard, *Études sur l'histoire des Portugais au Maroc* (Coimbra, 1955), p. 156; Hsain Ilahiane, 'Estevan de Dorantes, the Moor or the slave? The other Moroccan explorer of New Spain', *Journal of North African Studies* 5 (2000), pp. 1–14.

35 Bernard Bailyn and Philip D. Morgan (eds.), *Strangers within the Realm: Cultural Margins of the First British Empire* (Chapel Hill, CA & London, 1991), p. 31.

36 See Ruth Pike, 'Slavery in Seville in the Time of Columbus', in H. B. Johnson Jr. (ed.), *From Reconquest to Empire: the Iberian Background to Latin American History* (New York, 1970), pp. 85–101.

37 See H.B. Johnson Jr., 'Introduction', in Johnson (ed.), *From Reconquest to Empire*, pp. 3–40; M. García-Arenal, 'Moriscos and Indians: A Comparative Approach', in G.J.H. van Gelder and Ed C.M. De Moor (eds.), *The Middle East and Europe: Encounters and Exchanges*, Orientations 1 (Amsterdam, 1992), pp. 39–55.

38 A.R. Disney, *A History of Portugal and the Portuguese Empire*, 2 vols. (Cambridge, 2009), Vol. 1, pp. 1–26.

39 De Castries (ed.), *Sources inédites*, Vol. 2, p. 222ff & Vol. 3, p. 129; Nabil Matar, *Turks, Moors, and Englishmen in the Age of Discovery* (New York, 1999), pp. 83–109. For an analysis of the ways in which the paradigms of English understandings of Native Americans and Muslims related to each other, see Nabil Matar, 'Britons, Muslims, and American Indians: gender and power', *Muslim World* 91 (2001), pp. 371–80.

40 David Eltis, 'Atlantic History in Global Perspective', *Itinerario: European Journal of Overseas History* 23 (1999), pp. 141–60 at pp. 143–44.

41 See Newitt, *History*, p. 19; Filipe Themudo Barata, 'Portugal and the Mediterranean: a Prelude to the Discovery of the "New World"', *Al-Masaq* 17 (2005), pp. 205–19; Andrew C. Hess, *The Forgotten Frontier: A History of the Sixteenth Century Ibero-African Frontier* (Chicago & London, 1978). On the expulsion of the Moriscos, see Már Jónsson, 'The expulsion of the Moriscos from Spain in 1609–14: the destruction of an Islamic periphery', *Journal of Global History* 2 (2007), pp. 195–212.

42 Cornell, 'Socioeconomic dimensions', p. 387.

43 Games, 'Atlantic History', p. 747.

44 Mohamed Ennaji, 'Le Maroc et l'Atlantique durant les temps modernes', in Kaddouri (ed.), *Le Maroc*, pp. 95–120 at p. 100. See also Ahmed Bouchareb, 'Les conséquences socio-culturelles de la conquête ibérique du littoral marocain', in Maria García-Arenal and María J. Viguera (eds.), *Relaciones de la Península Ibérica con el Magreb siglos XIII-XVI: Actas del coloquio, Madrid 17–18 diciembre 1987* (Madrid, 1988), pp. 487–537.

45 Mintz, *Sweetness*, p. 29. Berthier asserts that the need for slave labour for the production of sugar was one of the motivations for al-Manṣūr's conquests in the Sudan (see Paul Berthier, 'L'archéologie, source de l'histoire économique. Les plantations de canne à sucre et les fabriques de sucre dans l'ancien Maroc', *Hespéris-Tamuda* 7 (1966), pp. 33–40 at p. 40). On the use of wage labour and the absence of large-scale agricultural slavery, see Cornell, 'Socioeconomic dimensions', pp. 403–4.

46 See Amira K. Bennison, *Jihad and its Interpretations in Pre-colonial Morocco: State-society Relations during the French Conquest of Algeria* (London, 2002), pp. 15–33. It is true that

– CHAPTER 11: *Morocco and Atlantic history* –

jihād had long been established as an important element of political legitimacy in al-Andalus and the Maghrib under the Umayyads, the Almohads and the Almoravids. However, this tradition was reshaped and reinvigorated in the fifteenth and sixteenth centuries in response to the first direct Christian attacks on Morocco itself and in the unstable conditions of the Wattasid era, when central authority in the country seemed unable to resist such incursions. I am grateful to Dr. Bennison for her insights into this topic.

47 See Weston F. Cook, *The Hundred Years' War for Morocco: Gunpowder and the Military Revolution in the Early Modern Muslim World* (Boulder, CO, 1994); A. Dziubinski, 'L'armee et la flotte de guerre marocaines à l'époque des sultans de la dynastie saadienne', *Hespéris-Tamuda* 13 (1972), pp. 61–94.

48 See Ricard, *Études*, pp. 124–27.

49 See Mohamed Mezzine, 'Les rélations entre les places occupées et la localités de la région de Fès aux XVième et XVIième siècles, à partir de documents locaux inédits: les *Nawāzil*', in García-Areñal and Viguera (eds.), *Relaciones*, pp. 539–60.

50 See Jacques Caillé, 'Ambassadeurs et représentants officieux de la France au Maroc', *Hespéris* 38 (1951), pp. 355–65; Jacques Caillé, 'Ambassades et missions marocaines aux Pays-Bas à l'époque des sultans saadiens', *HespérisTamuda* 4 (1963), pp. 5–67; Jacques Caillé, 'Le commerce anglais avec le Maroc pendant la seconde moitié du XVIe siècle: importations et exportations', *Revue Africaine* 84 (1940), pp. 186–219; Willan, *Studies*, p. 92ff; Rogers, *AngloMoroccan relations*, pp. 7–20.

51 See Bernard Rosenberger, 'Les Sa'diens et l'Atlantique au XVIe siècle', in Mohamed Tahar Mansouri (ed.), *Le Maghreb et la mer à travers l'histoire* (Paris, 2000), pp. 201–22; Dahiru Yahya, *Morocco in the Sixteenth Century: Problems and Patterns in African Foreign Policy* (Harlow, 1981).

52 Matar, 'Anglo-Spanish conflict'. Later Moroccan rulers also understood and attempted to exploit the dynamics of religious rivalry in Europe, as in the case of Mawlay Ismā'īl's (r. 1672–1727) well-known letter to the exiled Catholic James II of England (see Henry de Castries, *Moulay Ismail et Jacques II: une apologie de l'Islam par un sultan du Maroc* [Paris, 1903], pp. 7–8).

53 See Yves Lacoste, 'General characteristics and fundamental structures of mediaeval North African society', *Economy and Society* 3 (1974), pp. 1–17; James L. Boone *et al.*, 'Archeological and Historical Approaches to Complex Societies: The Islamic States of Medieval Morocco', *American Anthropologist* 92 (1990), pp. 630–46; Ronald A. Messier, 'Sijilmâsa: l'intermédiaire entre la Méditerranée et l'ouest de l'Afrique', in Mohammed Hammam (ed.), *L'occident musulman et l'occident chretien au moyen age* (Rabat, 1995), pp. 181–96; James A. Miller, 'Trading through Islam: the Interconnections of Sijilmasa, Ghana and the Almoravid Movement', in J.A. Clancy-Smith (ed.), *North Africa, Islam and Mediterranean World: from the Almoravids to the Algerian War* (London & Portland, OR, 2001), pp. 29–58. On the importance of the Maghrib's position as an intermediary zone between West Africa and the Mediterranean, see Fernand Braudel, *The Mediterranean and the Mediterranean World in the Age of Philip II*, 2 vols. (London, 1972), Vol. 1, pp. 467–77. On trade across the Sahara generally, see D.T. Niane, 'Relationships and exchange among the different regions', in Niane (ed.), *Africa*, pp. 614–35.

54 Lacoste, 'General characteristics', pp. 3–4. On the political importance of maritime power in the medieval period, see Picard, *L'océan*, pp. 341–61 & 459–82. For the actual operation of this power and the relative autonomy of Maghribi ports, see J.D. Latham, 'The Rise of the 'Azafids in Ceuta', *Israel Oriental Studies* 2 (1972), pp. 263–87.

55 On the decline of the trans-Saharan trade with Morocco, see Michel Abitbol, 'Le Maroc et le commerce transsaharien du XVIIe siècle au début du XIXe siècle', *Revue de l'Occident Musulman et de la Méditerranée* 30 (1980), pp. 5–20. On the relationship between regional autonomy and European trade in Morocco, see J.A.O.C. Brown, 'AngloMoroccan

relations and the embassy of Aḥmad Qardanash, 1706–8', *Historical Journal* 51 (2008), pp. 599–620 at pp. 603–7.

56 See J. Bookin-Weiner, 'The "Sallee Rovers": Morocco and the Corsairs in the seventeenth century', in Reeva S. Simon (ed.), *The Middle East and North Africa: Essays in honour of J.C. Hurewitz* (New York, 1990), pp. 134–40; J. BookinWeiner, 'Corsairing in the economy and politics of North Africa', in George Joffé (ed.), *North Africa: Nation, State and Region* (London & New York, 1993), pp. 3–33.

57 For a more detailed analysis of this process, see Brown, 'Anglo-Moroccan relations in the late eighteenth and early nineteenth centuries', pp. 27–63. On Sīdī Muḥammad's foreign and trade policy generally, see Fatima Harrak, 'Foundations of Muhammad III's Foreign Policy', in Jerome Bookin-Weiner and Mohamed El Mansour (eds.), *The Atlantic Connection: 200 Years of Moroccan-American Relations 1786–1986* (Rabat, n.d.), pp. 31–48.

58 Linda Colley, *The Ordeal of Elizabeth Marsh: How a Remarkable Woman Crossed Seas and Empires to Become a Part of World History* (London & New York, 2008), p. 66.

59 See Abulafia, 'Mediterraneans', esp. pp. 75–76 & 91–93. Although he does not refer to the Maghrib specifically in this sense, others have interpreted the region in this spirit (see Brent D. Shaw, 'A Peculiar Island: Maghrib and the Mediterranean', *Mediterranean Historical Review* 18 [2003], pp. 93–125).

60 See Rafael Valladares Ramirez, 'Inglaterra, Tanger y el "estrecho compartido": los inicios del asentamiento ingles en el Mediterraneo occidental durante la guerra hispano-portuguesa (1641–61)', *Hispania: Revista Española de Historia* 51 (1991), pp. 982–93; José Ignacio Martínez Ruiz, 'De Tánger a Gibraltar: el estrecho en la praxis comercial e imperial Británica (1661–1776)', *Hispania: Revista Española de Historia* 65 (2005), pp. 1043–62; E. M.G. Routh, *Tangier: England's lost Atlantic outpost, 1661–1684* (London, 1912); Linda Colley, *Captives: Britain, Empire and the World, 1600–1850* (London, 2002), pp. 21–43.

61 See, for example, Lourido-Díaz, 'Relaciones politicas'; Brown, 'The embassy of Aḥmad Qardanash'. On the development and decline of a 'French Atlantic' during the first period of French colonialism see Silvia Marzagalli, 'The French Atlantic', *Itinerario: European Journal of Overseas History* 23 (1999), pp. 70–83.

62 'Morocco', *Encyclopaedia Judaica*, 16 vols. (Jerusalem, 1971), Vol. 12, pp. 326–47. Jewish immigration to the Spanish and Portuguese colonies before independence was of course limited because of the religious restrictions placed on them there (see, for example, Eva Alexandra Uchmany, *La vida entre judaísmo y el cristianismo en la Nueva España, 1580–1606* [Mexico City, 1992]). Greater toleration in the Dutch colonies particularly, and to a lesser extent those of Britain and France, resulted in the establishment of Jewish communities to which some Jews from Essaouira (Mogador) emigrated in the eighteenth century and which maintained links with Morocco through charitable donations (see André Chouraqui, *Histoire des Juifs en Afrique du Nord* [Paris, 1985], p. 357; I.S. Emmanuel and S.A. Emmanuel, *History of the Jews of the Netherlands Antilles*, 2 vols. [Cincinnati, 1970], Vol. 1, pp. 166–68; Mordehay Arbell, *The Jewish Nation of the Caribbean: the Spanish-Portuguese settlements in the Caribbean and the Guianas* [Jerusalem, 2002], p. 26). Jewish migration to South America also increased after independence, as testified by among other things visas issued from the Moroccan consulate at Gibraltar (see Victor Mirelman, 'Sephardim in Latin America after Independence', in Martin Cohen and Abraham Peck [eds.], *Sephardim in the Americas: Studies in Culture and History* [Tuscaloosa, AL & London, 1993], pp. 235–67 at pp. 240–49; Anita Novinsky, 'Sephardim in Brazil: the New Christians', in R. D. Barnett and W. M. Schwab [eds.], *The Sephardi Heritage: Essays on the History and Cultural Contribution of the Jews of Spain and Portugal – Vol. 2: The Western Sephardim* [Grendon, Northants, 1989], pp. 431–41 at pp. 440–41; Nadia Erzini, *'Hal yaslah li-taqansut* [Is He Suitable for Consulship?]: The Moroccan Consuls in Gibraltar during the Nineteenth Century',

– CHAPTER 11: *Morocco and Atlantic history* –

Journal of North African Studies 12 [2007], pp. 517–29 at pp. 524–25). On the Sephardic community in Holland and its links to Morocco, see for example Jonathan I. Israel, 'The Sephardim in the Netherlands', in Elie Kedourie (ed.), *Spain and the Jews: The Sephardi Experience, 1492 and After* (London, 1992), pp. 189–212; Mercedes García-Arenal and Gerard Albert Wiegers, *A Man of Three Worlds: Samuel Pallache, a Moroccan Jew in Catholic and Protestant Europe* (Baltimore, 2003).

63 Peter Lamborn Wilson, *Pirate Utopias: Moorish Corsairs & European Renegadoes* (Brooklyn, NY, 2003), pp. 205–12; National Archives, London, Foreign Office papers 52/14, ff. 121–28.

64 On the geographical factors contributing to shipwrecks on the Moroccan coast, see Suzanne Schwarz, *Slave Captain: the Career of James Irvine in the Liverpool Slave Trade*, 2nd ed. (Liverpool, 2008), pp. 40–43. On various aspects of the general phenomenon of European captives in North Africa, see for example Paul Baepler (ed.), *White Slaves, African Masters: An Anthology of American Barbary Captivity Narratives* (Chicago, 1999); E.G. Friedman, *Spanish Captives in North Africa in the Early Modern Age* (Madison, WI, 1983); Robert C. Davis, *Christian Slaves, Muslim Masters: White Slavery in the Mediterranean, the Barbary Coast, and Italy, 1500–1800* (Basingstoke, 2003); Daniel Vitkus (ed.), *Piracy, Slavery and Redemption: Barbary Captivity Narratives from Early Modern England* (New York, 2001).

65 Elliott, 'Atlantic History', p. 239.

66 See Cornell, 'Socioeconomic dimensions', pp. 399–400; Dziubinski, 'L'armee,' p. 93; Cook, *Hundred Years' War*, pp. 243–51; Abderrahman El Moudden, 'Looking Eastward: Some Moroccan Tentative Military Reforms with Turkish Assistance (18th–early 19th centuries)', *Maghreb Review* 19 (1994), pp. 237–45; Amira K. Bennison, 'The "New Order" and Islamic Order: The Introduction of the Niẓāmī Army in the Western Maghrib and its Legitimation, 1830–73', *International Journal of Middle East Studies* 36 (2004), pp. 591–612.

67 See note 4 above.

68 See Abderrahman El Moudden, 'The Ambivalance of Rihla: Community Integration and Self-Definition in Moroccan Travel Accounts, 1300–1800', in Dale F. Eickelman and James Piscatori (eds.), *Muslim Travelers: Pilgrimage, Migration and the Religious Imagination* (Berkley & Los Angeles, 1990), pp. 69–84.

69 See Abderrahmane El Moudden, 'Sharifs and Padishahs: Moroccan-Ottoman Relations from the 16th through the 18th Centuries', Ph.D. thesis, Princeton University, 1992; R. Lourido-Díaz, 'La obra redentora del sultan marroquí Sîdî Muhammad b. Abd Allàh entre los cautivos muslumanes en Europa (siglo XVII)', *Cuadernos de Historia del Islam* 11 (1984), pp. 139–84; R. Lourido-Díaz, 'El Sultan alawi Sidi Muhammad b. Abd Allāh (1757–90) y sus sueños de hegemonía sobre el Islam occidental', *Orientalia Hispanica* 1 (1974), pp. 472–89; Thomas Freller, '"The Shining of the Moon" – The Mediterranean Tour of Muhammad ibn 'Uthmān, Envoy of Morocco, in 1782', *Journal of Mediterranean Studies* 12 (2002), pp. 307–26. On the recognition of the United States, see J. Bookin-Weiner, 'The Origins of Moroccan American Relations', in Bookin-Weiner and El Mansour (eds.), *The Atlantic Connection*, pp. 19–31.

70 See Mohamed El Mansour, *Morocco in the Reign of Mawlay Sulayman* (Wisbech, 1990), pp. 11, 62–63 & 71; Brown, 'Anglo-Moroccan Relations in the late Eighteenth and Early Nineteenth Centuries', p. 140ff.

71 Shabānī's career was recorded in an interview at Dover in England, where he had ended up following his capture and the seizure of his goods by Russian privateers on his return voyage from Hamburg (see James Grey Jackson, *An Account of Timbuctoo and Housa Territories in the Interior of Africa by El Hage Abd Salam Shabeeny with Notes, Critical and Explanatory* [London, 1820]).

72 On the relationship between integration to the Atlantic and socio-economic change, see for example James F. Searing, *West African Slavery and Atlantic Commerce: The Senegal River valley, 1700–1850* (Cambridge, 1993).

73 For a review of works deconstructing a unitary Atlantic framework and Eurocentric conceptualisations of world trade during the early modern period, see for example Peter Colcanis, 'Atlantic World or Atlantic/World?', *William & Mary Quarterly* 63 (2006), pp. 725–42.

74 See Fernández-Armesto, *Before Columbus*.

75 Colcanis, 'Atlantic World', p. 739. He usefully adds this term to Armitage's threefold internal division of the Atlantic system into 'trans-Atlantic', 'circum-Atlantic' and 'cis-Atlantic' (see David Armitage, 'Three Concepts of Atlantic History', in Armitage and Braddick [eds], *The British Atlantic World*, pp. 11–27).

76 See Barata, 'Portugal and the Mediterranean'.

77 Fernández-Armesto, *Before Columbus*, pp. 170–71.

78 William O'Reilly, 'Genealogies of Atlantic history', *Atlantic Studies* 1 (2004), pp. 66–84 at p. 69.

79 See for example Paul Gilroy, *Black Atlantic: Modernity and Double Consciousness* (London, 1993); Alan Rice, *Radical Narratives of the Black Atlantic* (London & New York, 2003).

80 For a review of the debate among historians of the Maghrib about the region's conceptual and analytical relationships with its neighbours, see L. Carl Brown, 'Maghrib Historiography: the Unit of Analysis Problem', in Michel Le Gall and Kenneth Perkins (eds.), *The Maghrib in Question* (Austin, TX, 1997), pp. 4–16.

81 Colcanis, 'Atlantic World', p. 725.

82 Bailyn, 'Reflections', p. 2.

CHAPTER TWELVE

THE ATLANTIC
AND PACIFIC WORLDS

Paul D'Arcy

The vast majority of maritime historians focus on bodies of water defined by their continental margins, even though their particular interest might be thematic rather than regional connections and coherence. Four such ocean spaces attract the attention of most maritime historians: the Atlantic Ocean, the Mediterranean Sea, the Indian Ocean and the Pacific Ocean. The Pacific Ocean is the largest by far and the only one of these four not to have a substantial body of scholarship that conceptualizes it as a coherent, inter-linked space (see Figure 12.1).

This lack of coherence is largely the result of the sheer size of the Pacific. It covers an area greater than all of the land in the world combined. The Pacific is also larger than the Atlantic, Indian and Mediterranean combined: 165,721,000 kilometers squared as opposed to 158,048,000 kilometers squared.[1] A hemisphere cartographic projection taken from the centre of the Pacific is largely aquatic, and therefore blue and featureless in keeping with the terrestrial priorities of most mapping traditions. The Pacific is devoid of islands for thousands of miles in its northern and eastern sections, but also contains the vast majority of the world's islands within a roughly triangular wedge jutting out from its western margins to Rapanui (Easter Island) in the southeast Pacific.[2] While the former subdivisions have similar academic approaches to Atlantic maritime spaces, the latter 'sea of islands' as the late Tongan scholar Epeli Hau'ofa referred to it, has a quite distinct body of scholarship because of its cultures, history and seascapes.[3] After comparing the Atlantic and Pacific as oceanic environments, this chapter largely focuses on scholarship on the Pacific Islands, the most oceanic habitat of humankind, before suggesting approaches that might enhance key problems in contemporary Atlantic scholarship. The following observations favour the Pacific world over that of the Atlantic on the assumption that this collection's readership will be better versed in the latter than the former and will therefore benefit from exposure to another world and another body of scholarship.

The Pacific's sea of islands and the history of its coastal inhabitants are particularly relevant to Atlantic World historians seeking to conceptualize their field more in terms of histories *of the sea* than histories *across the sea*. Calls have mounted recently to balance essentially continental, Euro-centric outlooks emphasizing the flow of goods and people across the sea as measures of cultural and regional coherence with

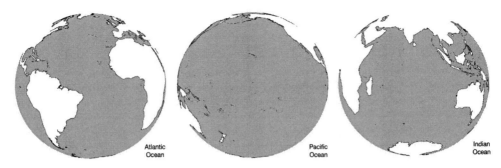

Figure 12.1 Map of the Atlantic, Pacific and Indian Oceans

more oceanic ones. The sea is not merely a passage for people between terrestrial stages of historical actions but also one of rich spaces of historical enactment, and cultural meaning and memory. As Karen Wigen noted in her introduction to a recent forum on oceans in history, 'No longer outside time, the sea is being given a history, even as the history of the world is being retold from the perspective of the sea.'[4]

Pacific Studies has much to offer those seeking to make the sea more prominent in history. Pacific Island maritime history is intimately linked to indigenous history, and has been enhanced by the survival of indigenous seafaring traditions and maritime cultural outlooks and priorities through the era of European and Japanese colonial rule. While Atlantic scholars are blessed with an abundance of written sources, Pacific scholars by necessity must employ more multidisciplinary approaches to take account of cultures whose history was recorded orally and who live in seas less travelled by those who recorded their observations in written form. Pacific Islands and the Pacific seas have however been intensively studied by anthropologists in particular since World War II and are today still more closely linked to local environments for their subsistence and well being than many in the Atlantic World who have grown less dependent on local seas because of their central place in the global economy their overseas' expansion helped create. These features combine to produce populated seas that are used intensively, culturally mapped in intimate detail and imbued with history.[5]

THE PACIFIC AND ATLANTIC AS OCEAN ENVIRONMENTS

The Pacific Islands are sometimes referred to collectively as Oceania. They are generally divided into three geographical areas: Melanesia, Micronesia and Polynesia. These terms were coined by the nineteenth century French explorer Dumont d'Urville, who deemed them to be racial and cultural classifications.[6] He also included Island Southeast Asia as a fourth area which he named Malaysia, although this four way grouping did not remain coherent within academia. Malaysia is today part of Southeast Asian studies while the other three are part of Pacific Island studies. With the exception of a number of Pacific archaeologists tracing Pacific migration routes back to their ultimate homelands, few scholars have linked the two regions as interacting entities. Recent studies by historians are challenging this divide as an *ex post facto* intellectual imposition.[7]

– CHAPTER 12: The Atlantic and Pacific Worlds –

D'urville's Polynesia consisted of all the islands east of a line running along the west coast of New Zealand to Fiji and up to the western end of the Hawai'ian chain. The only place where another race existed in close proximity was Melanesian Fiji, which lay a few days' sail northwest of Tonga. Micronesia consisted of all the islands from Palau, Yap and the Mariana Islands in the west across to Kiribati in the east. Its cultural borders were all clearly demarcated by large sea gaps, although d'Urville's Micronesia extended much further north than the current Micronesian political entities extend to incorporate islands closer to Japan. Melanesia stretched from Fiji to New Guinea and down to Australia. D'Urville's Malaysia incorporated much of Island Southeast Asia. Its only close Oceanic neighbours were the peoples of western New Guinea.

Two distinct bio-geographical zones are recognized within Oceania: Near Oceania and Remote Oceania.[8] These divisions map the progressive diminution of terrestrial and marine species' diversity eastward from their dispersal point into the Pacific as the gaps between islands increase.[9] Near Oceania is located in the Western Pacific, and encompasses most of the islands designated as Melanesia under the existing classification. This area demonstrates a great deal of environmental continuity with Island Southeast Asia in terms of its large 'continental' islands, and small gaps between islands. In contrast, Remote Oceania, broadly coinciding with Micronesia and Polynesia, is characterized by large gaps between smaller Oceanic islands and archipelagoes. It is also notable for its very limited land area relative to ocean area. Oceania was settled from the west which meant that its colonizers encountered a gradual transition from islands similar to their homelands in the western archipelagic margins of the Pacific to island environments that were increasingly more oceanic in nature as they moved east. It was an ideal transition zone to hone their already considerable seafaring skills as they sailed onwards in search of new island homes, spurred on by generations of successful discoveries of under-populated and increasingly unpopulated homes in the expanse of islands. Sailing predominantly into the wind was also beneficial for exploring new seas as the key issue was ensuring the ability to return home rapidly in case of adversity or failure to discover new lands before food supplies ran short.[10]

The boundary between Near and Remote Oceania lies east and south of the present day Solomon Islands.[11] It then passes east and north of the Bismarck archipelago, extending westward off the north coast of New Guinea before turning north to pass east of the Philippines. To the west of this line humans can usually travel between islands without losing sight of land because of the high mountains on these islands and the relatively narrow sea gaps between them. In contrast, Remote Oceania is made up of islands clustered into archipelagos that are now separated by at least 350 kilometres of ocean. Islands in this region tend to be smaller than in Near Oceania, and their flora and fauna more attenuated. This is because it was populated by an extremely limited Indo-Malayan biota that dispersed from the larger islands in Near Oceania. New Caledonia and Aotearoa/New Zealand[12] are exceptions. Both are continental in terms of size and diverse resource base, although New Caledonia is nevertheless relatively impoverished compared to islands of a similar size in Near Oceania. Otherwise, the only island landforms in this eastern sector are high volcanic islands, coral atolls and other kinds of coralline islands.

Short-term variation in atmospheric circulation patterns, temperature and rainfall are the most important environmental influences on Pacific Islanders. Regular voyaging between islands requires intimate knowledge of wind patterns which dictate inter-island travel as well as rainfall patterns to nourish island crops. In the more open eastern two-thirds there are zones crossing the ocean from east to west, each with a distinct pattern of surface winds. In the higher latitudes of both hemispheres, strong westerly winds blow for most of the year. Between these two belts are two zones of trade winds. In the Northern Hemisphere these blow from the northeast, while south of the equator they blow from the southeast. Their strength diminishes in the western third of the Pacific. The trade winds are not continuous, but generally blow for at least part of every month. They are most consistent between May and September. For the remainder of the year winds blow from both east and west. The equatorial area between these belts of trade winds is known as the doldrums, which generally experiences light, variable winds and total calm. However, it is also subject to occasional squalls, heavy showers and thunderstorms.[13]

The western Pacific is dominated by monsoon and typhoon weather patterns arising from the periodic heating and cooling of the Asian landmass. The monsoon winds blow from the northwest away from Asia in the Northern Hemisphere winter, and from the southeast towards Asia in the Northern Hemisphere summer. Typhoons or hurricanes occur in much of the western tropical Pacific. These spiral storms begin as areas of slowly circulating cloud that gather energy from the warm ocean waters that they pass over. They develop into giant mobile whirlwinds that can last for weeks. Their high winds and torrential rains carve a path of destruction, while the accompanying storm waves devastate coastal areas and low lying coral islands.

There is great variability within these seasonal climatic patterns. Typhoons can occur during any month of the year. Similarly, storms with gale force winds may occur during any month over much of the region.[14] Rainfall also varies widely. Generally areas near the equator experience high rainfall with limited seasonal variation. Further from the equator annual rainfall diminishes substantially, and is subject to marked seasonal variation.[15] In such variable conditions, the worst-case scenario rather than the overall average determines the viability of a community.

During *El Niño* conditions zones of convergence that cause heavy rainfall in this part of the Pacific move towards the equator. The usual areas of convergence such as the Carolines and Fiji then experience a decline in rainfall. Variation even occurs within the Caroline Islands. Islands that normally have high rainfall like Palau and Pohnpei may experience drought, while drier areas further east such as the Marshalls may experience high rainfall.[16]

A phenomenon known as the *El Niño* involves the periodic disruption of weather patterns and fisheries across the Pacific Ocean as well as into the Americas and Asia. This phenomenon is explained in terms of variations in the strength of the southeast trade winds. When strong, these winds were believed to allow upwelling by displacing surface water westward away from the coast. *El Niño* conditions resulted from a weakening of these winds. Much of the world's climate is determined by the exchange of heat and moisture between ocean and atmosphere. As the largest body of water, the Pacific has a crucial role. When pressure gradients lead to weaker than usual easterly winds in the eastern Pacific, this leads to a deepened warm surface layer off Peru that is far less productive than the upwelling mix that occurs otherwise.[17]

Rather than being abnormal, *El Niño* is merely the extreme warm surface phase of an eighteen to twenty-four month cycle that also exhibits an extreme, cool surface water phase known as *La Nina*. The occurrence of these cycles is irregular, although they seem to occur on average every three to seven years. Historical records also suggest that these cycles vary in intensity. In a *La Niña* phase the opposite conditions apply. These conditions may cause strong trade winds that push water westward, so that the sea level in the western Pacific is up to 2 feet higher than in the east.[18]

The movement of seawater influences life at sea, just as terrestrial flora is influenced by atmospheric circulation. Much of the daily and seasonal behaviour of near-shore marine biota is oriented around tidal patterns.[19] Seawater also circulates in ocean currents. Two vast loops, or gyres, dominate the Pacific. The one north of the equator flows clockwise, while the other flows anti-clockwise. The currents on the western side of these gyres increase in intensity as they flow away from the equator. Islands deflect these currents, particularly the southern, westward-moving flow. Between these two gyres is the Equatorial Countercurrent, which flows from the Carolines across to Panama. These tropical currents vary seasonally in strength, and even location. Seasonal wind shifts account for much of this variation. As well as these larger, general flows there are smaller, irregular currents that result from local eddies, islands and other barriers to flows on the ocean floor. Such currents may also exhibit seasonal variation because of changing winds and weather conditions.[20]

These currents have important consequences for life in the ocean. Surface currents affect human travel and subsistence. They either facilitate or hinder boat travel. Either way, their variability required that mariners acquire an intimate knowledge of local conditions. Plankton, the basis of all ocean food chains, is one such organism.[21] Deep ocean currents also affect the food chain by transporting decomposing organic matter that falls from surface waters enriched by the sun's penetration. Such currents transport this matter away from tropical seas towards the polar seas, where it rises to the surface and moves back towards the equator along surface currents. The result is that most tropical seas have much poorer offshore habitats than their temperate and polar equivalents. Tropical seas tend to consist of intense concentrations of marine biota surrounded by large tracts of relatively impoverished seas.

Oceanographers now generally accept that all marine ecosystems are in constant flux, and that they are open systems influenced by marine and climatic influences generated elsewhere. Such ecosystems are characterized by short-term perturbations and disruptions as well as more regular, seasonal patterns. People who live in such environments must view the world differently from those who inhabit more closed, stable environments. Short-term environmental perturbations and unpredictable changes from external elements fostered expectations of unheralded elements intruding from beyond the horizon, curiosity about where these elements came from, and flexible, opportunistic strategies to cope with this, at times, uncertain world. Once established, most Pacific Islander societies developed some form of magazine economy and inter-island marriage or trade links with other communities to insulate themselves against climatic variability in rainfall, *El Niño* cycles, and natural disasters such as typhoons.

A host of factors promote the rich fisheries so valued by sea peoples. Most marine species inhabit the benthic (ocean floor) or neritic (near shore) zones rather than the pelagic (open ocean) zone. Sunlight is a key factor. Approximately 90 per cent of the entire marine bio-mass is made up of phytoplankton, tiny plant plankton that combine sunlight, carbon dioxide and nutrients to produce organic matter in a manner similar to terrestrial plants. To enable photosynthesis they concentrate in the upper level of the sea where sunlight penetrates, which is down to 100 or 150 metres in clear conditions.

Phytoplankton forms the basis of the marine food chain.[22] Shallow seas concentrate marine life and organic fallout near the surface. Areas with a lot of turbidity or upwelling re-circulate decomposing organic matter back into the living ecosystem. Landmasses with high runoff periodically flush land nutrients into offshore waters.

The main ecosystems in the coastal waters of Remote Oceania are coral reefs, lagoons, and mangrove swamps. Some locations lack these buffers, allowing waves to break directly against the shoreline. The reef–lagoon complexes are among the most productive ecosystems on the planet. Only tropical rain forests rival reef–lagoon complexes in terms of productivity and diversity. The 150 kilometre long barrier reef surrounding Palau has nine species of sea grass, more than 300 species of corals, and approximately 2000 species of fish.[23] Most, but not all areas of high productivity are geographically fixed and in shallow near-shore locations. Tidally driven sea fronts on continental shelves, fronts along subtropical climatic transition zones, and areas of counter currents, gyres and eddies are also highly productive.[24] Other highly productive open ocean ecosystems are areas of shallow water shoals, or areas where upwelling enriches the upper layers with nutrients. Fijian fishermen refer to one as Thakau Lala, the 'Empty Reef'. It has no land, just a circular reef enclosing a shallow, sheltered body of water.[25] Bukatatanoa is the name given to a reef 11 miles east of the island of Lakeba that encloses a lagoon nearly 200 square miles in extent.[26] Similarly, the Marshallese were familiar with a huge, current-free area of ocean south of the atoll of Ailingalaplap. They call it Eon Woerr, literally 'over coral' in reference to its presumed shallow depth.[27] As will be discussed in the final section of this chapter, such offshore areas of plenty extended the cultural worlds, boundaries and tenure regimes of Pacific Islanders beyond sight of land.

Atlantic maritime spaces are shaped by many of the same broad processes at work in Pacific spaces, particularly those shaping the movement of oceanic waters and the concentration of marine biota. Rich fisheries were first found in near-shore shallow seas and continental shelves such as the North Sea and the Grand Banks off Newfoundland and later in sea mounts further out to sea.[28] Just as in the Pacific, the main surface currents are two large gyres separated by the eastward flowing Atlantic Equatorial Countercurrent. The North Atlantic gyre rotates clockwise, while the South Atlantic gyre flows counterclockwise, driven by northeast and southeast trade winds respectively. The trade winds and equatorial currents of the gyres facilitate voyaging westward across the shortest width of the open ocean Atlantic from the Cape Verde Islands to the West Indies, while the return passage continued along the gyres away from the equator until the currents began to change direction eastward in zones of westerly winds. The approximate 10,000 mile circuit averaged five months sailing and a further four months waiting for the right winds. Hurricanes began forming off the West African coast and moved westward towards Florida and the West Indies before moving north towards the Atlantic seaboard of North America.[29]

SEAS OF HISTORY AND SEAS OF ANTHROPOLOGY

Few have attempted to construct an image of the Pacific Ocean as a coherent entity in the way Fernand Braudel has for the Mediterranean, or K.N. Chauduri and David Pearson have for the Indian Ocean. To Braudel the whole Mediterranean 'shared a common destiny, a heavy one indeed, with identical problems and general trends if

– CHAPTER 12: *The Atlantic and Pacific Worlds* –

not identical consequences'.[30] For Chauduri, long distance trade, the monsoon climatic system, and broadly similar historical forces created a degree of cohesion amongst the four great civilizations that spanned the region. In the Irano-Arabic, Hindu, Indonesian and Chinese worlds 'the idea of a common geographical space defined by the exchange of ideas and material objects was quite strong, not only in the minds of merchants but also in those of political rulers and ordinary people'.[31]

No such coherence has ever been attributed to the vastly more expansive world/s encompassed by the Pacific Ocean. The few Pacific-wide histories that have been attempted focus on the region's integration into a wider global economy which is seen as beginning when Europeans began to move into the Pacific. The modern concept of a Pacific community is essentially based on the modern economic relationship between East Asia and North America. It is a relationship with little legacy of pre-existing cultural or historical ties, and one that has only been made possible by communications and transport revolutions in the last two centuries.[32]

Prior to this phase the Pacific is generally viewed as a prohibitive void rather than an avenue for movement. Pre-European Pacific peoples are usually considered to have conducted localized interactions only, with a resultant consciousness that was at best regional rather than pan-Pacific.[33] Such pan-Pacific passages were dominated by European vessels. European encounters with the South Pacific began in 1567 when Magellan sailed westward across Oceania from South America. Other Spanish voyages of discovery followed in his wake. A series of violent encounters and the decimation of colonies in Melanesia from malaria soon ended Spain's South Pacific engagement. Henceforth, the Spanish focused on Micronesia and the trans-Pacific galleon trade carrying goods between the colonial ports of Manila and Acapulco. Their route bypassed most inhabited islands in the Pacific, while former links between Guam and the Caroline Islands diminished with the violent establishment of Spanish rule in the Marianas and the subsequent loss of seafaring capacity within the island chain.[34] European contact with the Pacific became more sustained from the late 1760s onwards as voyages of exploration by a number of European nations gradually mapped Australasia and Oceania, most famously and comprehensively through the three expeditions of Captain James Cook from 1768 to 1779. Focusing on the flow of traffic between the Pacific's terrestrial margins removes indigenous voices and overlooks interactions with the sea that were part of daily life of most islanders and which we argue offer the greatest contrast to Atlantic approaches.

Despite its relatively late development, Pacific Island history has nevertheless produced a large body of published studies, and developed a distinct character. Most of its studies have been on inter-cultural relations between Pacific Islanders and Europeans over the last two and a half centuries.[35] Pacific historians have largely focused on the impact of Western products, peoples and ideas on Pacific Islanders, with much emphasis placed on presenting Pacific Islanders as rational, active agents in this process. The majority of Pacific Islanders' millennia of history was recorded and conveyed orally, which has meant that much Pacific history has become multidisciplinary to incorporate non-literate sources such as oral traditions, linguistic patterns and material remains. This has enhanced rather than diluted the nature of Pacific history.

Until quite recently even those studying Pacific Islanders tended to treat individual communities in relative isolation. Arbitrary colonial boundaries assisted by cutting the Pacific into administrative units of study that bore no resemblance to voyaging spheres.[36] Modern academic writings of even the most geographically wide-ranging field of study, the pre-European period of Oceanic history, portray external contacts as being of limited significance in the development of individual islands after their initial colonization by humans. Pre-European cultural development is usually depicted as driven by the interaction of internal processes. These include: adaptation of the founding culture to a new environment; population growth on a limited land area; environmental change, both natural and human-induced; and cultural emphasis on competition for status channelled into warfare, or the intensification of production for redistribution to forge social and political obligations. The possibility of new arrivals introducing cultural innovations is not dismissed, but it is almost always considered of secondary importance.[37]

Concern at this tendency to treat islands as closed cultural systems was expressed in the late 1970s when a series of well-argued articles called for an end to the pervasiveness of narrowly focussed studies. Kerry Howe called this approach 'monograph myopia', which he and others characterize as 'finding out more and more about less and less'.[38] These critics noted that there seemed to be no guiding direction or overall purpose beyond accumulating information and filling gaps. Oskar Spate observed that such historians 'may on occasion not see the Ocean for the Islands, may be content to be marooned on the tight but so soft confines of their little atolls of knowledge, regardless of the sweep of the currents which bring life to the isles'.[39]

Calls for academics to view the sea more as a means of communication than as an isolator have mounted. Now Island communities are increasingly portrayed as connected 'in a wider social world of moving items and ideas.'[40] Local traditions, the distribution of cultural traits, and observations by literate outsiders all attest to inter-island voyaging within most archipelagos. Voyaging between archipelagos was also apparent in the eighteenth and nineteenth centuries in at least three regions of Remote Oceania. Such external contacts probably waxed and waned, as did their impact. For example, Ian Campbell notes that archaeological, linguistic and traditional evidence all suggest that the period from c. AD 1100 to 1500 was an era of significant upheaval and inter-island movement through much of Oceania.[41]

Such a world created a wider sense of community and belonging. Perhaps the most articulate voice for this new vision has been the late Epeli Hau'ofa. In his 1994 article 'Our Sea of Islands', Hau'ofa asserts that:

> The world of our ancestors was a large sea full of places to explore, to make their homes in, to breed generations of seafarers like themselves. People raised in this environment were at home with the sea. They played in it as soon as they could walk steadily, they worked in it, they fought on it. They developed great skills for navigating their waters, and the spirit to traverse even the few large gaps that separated their island groups.
>
> Theirs was a large world in which peoples and cultures moved and mingled, unhindered by boundaries of the kind erected much later by imperial powers.[42]

To overcome this legacy, Hau'ofa believes that Pacific Islanders must now decolonize their minds, and recast their sense of identity by rediscovering the vision of their ancestors for whom the Pacific was a boundless sea of possibilities and opportunities.

Others have begun to argue for the need to incorporate the sea into our vision in ways that go beyond merely tracing the highways of sea travel between islands. Geoff Irwin notes that: 'Most prehistorians have concentrated on the evidence for intervals of *time* between islands but it could help our explanations to give more consideration to the intervening *space* – which is ocean – and the changing social and environmental circumstances of the islands and people in it.'[43] While Irwin suggests a way forward, he does not discuss the ocean environment in detail. His work also remains rooted in Western scientific discourse. The only discussion of Islanders' conceptions of the ocean relates to their navigational techniques.

The sea must also be seen as a cultural space in the worldview of the inhabitants of the islands. Hau'ofa makes this point in a sequel to 'Our Sea of Islands'. He notes 'for us in Oceania, the sea defines us, what we are and have always been. As the great Caribbean poet Derek Wolcott put it, the sea is history'.[44] Few studies examine the sea as both a physical and cultural space. Three works on Pacific seascapes are noteworthy in this regard: Bob Johannes' *Words of the Lagoon,* Michael D. Lieber's *More Than a Living* and Edvard Hviding's *Guardians of Marovo Lagoon*.[45] Johannes' book is essentially a study of fishing knowledge and practice, reflecting his background in marine biology. An anthropologist by training, Lieber traces the role of fishing activities in the social, political and ritual life of the inhabitants of Kapingamarangi Atoll. Hviding's work is the most comprehensive. Also trained in anthropology, he attempts to knit together the physical and cultural worlds that make up the territory of the people of the Marovo Lagoon in the Solomon Islands. To Hviding, 'the sea plays a crucial role in Marovo as a focus of cultural and social relations; it is the context for practice, interaction, and encounters, and is a cornerstone of Marovo identity, history, and material sustenance'.[46] He suggests that the inhabitants of the lagoon construct their perception of nature through their day-to-day use of that environment. It is not a cultural system that is merely transferred from the mind of the elders to the memory of the young. Such a system would be imposed upon the environment, but not influenced by it. There is no nature–culture dichotomy here. The Marovo peoples' view of nature emerges from engagements with the environment in multiple forms of knowledge and practice.[47] Hviding's work is also significant in demonstrating that some maritime environments can be endowed with as much cultural value and detail as terrestrial environments.

The general consensus is now that the first Pacific Islanders were skilled seafarers and explorers who evolved sophisticated navigational techniques involving waves, swells, stars and signs of land such as land-based seabirds to map the oceans as well as the lands they came across. Linguistic reconstructions of their proto-language suggest they came into the Pacific with canoes and food storage techniques capable of supporting long open sea voyages into the unknown which then evolved in situ over time.[48] Early European explorers such as Captain Cook marveled at the seafaring capabilities of Pacific Islanders and their canoes, many of which exceeded those of Cook in both carrying capacity and maneuverability. To traditional navigators, islands were not tiny specks in a vast sea but rather broad screens of signs such as shore-based seabirds fishing up to 50 miles out to sea and returning home at dusk, reflections of land and near-shore surfaces on the underside of clouds, and the pattern of waves bounced off or diverted around island barriers. These signs considerably expanded the navigator's target area and therefore made voyaging less haphazard.[49]

Few Island communities were restricted to one island. They often travelled by sea, and knew or suspected worlds beyond their usual voyaging range. Expectations of forces from beyond the horizon were deeply embedded in their worldviews long before the tall ships of Europeans sailed into view. Centuries of experience had taught them that new lands, new opportunities and new and old threats hovered just beyond the walls of heaven where sea met sky and which defined the boundaries of the world of usual experiences. Pacific Islander communities were highly localized in their affinities, expansive, even regional in their interactions, and subject to rapid and significant changes resulting from external influences.[50]

Studies since Hau'ofa's call for a re-examination of indigenous maritime history have detailed a variety of ways in which the oceanic environment shaped Islander societies, and Islanders shaped the sea. Most felt at home in the water. The waters of the Pacific were cultural seascapes rich in symbolic meaning; crowded with navigational markers, symbols of tenure, fishing and surfing sites, and reminders of gods and spirits in the form of maritime familiars and sites of their exploits. These seascapes altered as territories changed hands, navigational knowledge expanded and contracted, and storms and climate effected reef and shore configurations, and the distribution of species. To truly understand Pacific Islanders' relationship with the sea it is necessary to look at all maritime activities; swimming, diving, fishing, seafaring and navigation, boat building, religion and ritual, naval warfare and strategies for dealing with familiar outsiders and unexpected intrusions.[51]

The Atlantic is much less well endowed with seas of islands, and those it does contain lacked the indigenous seafaring traditions and marine economies of the Pacific. Felipe Fernández-Armesto and David Abulafia have both characterized the tropical eastern Atlantic archipelagos of the Madeira group, the Azores, the Canaries, the Cape Verde Islands and São Tome as an Atlantic Mediterranean because civilization was transplanted here by southern European cultures into islands that with the exception of the Canaries were uninhabited. Nautical technology and navigational limitations created an island world that traded within itself and back with Europe, but lacked the infrastructure to push further east despite the belief shared with Pacific Islanders that more islands surely lay ahead awaiting discovery and colonization.[52] The Caribbean was the other sea space within the Atlantic world that was a sea of islands with well-established indigenous cultures spread throughout its islands when Europeans first arrived. While the shores of the Caribbean's continental margins hosted elaborate civilizations with monumental stone architecture, elaborate ritual and sophisticated agriculture as occurred in a few Pacific archipelagos such as those of Hawai'i and Tonga,[53] most island cultures of the Caribbean left less grand legacies. Many of their coastal inhabitants shared with Pacific Islanders a heavy reliance on the sea for sustenance, while keeping a wary eye out for sea raids from marauding Carib peoples. By and large however, their maritime technology and sophistication did not match that of the Pacific.

Three themes and approaches stand out in Atlantic studies to an historian trained in Pacific ways of seeing. The first is that the sea is primarily viewed as either a neutral or hostile passage for people, ideas, germs and goods, but not as a habitat. Second, despite brilliant works of environmental history that have set the standard for Pacific specialists to follow such as Alfred Crosby's *The Columbian Exchange*, the focus of Atlantic studies is overwhelmingly cultural, especially the creation of hybrid creole cultures or colonial offshoots of founding European nations and their relations with their European founding nation – the English Atlantic, the Portuguese Atlantic and so on. Lastly, indigenous peoples are portrayed overwhelmingly as victims, especially of disease, or as silent and marginalized with the possible exception of post–slave trade West African history.

PACIFIC APPROACHES FOR ATLANTIC SPACES

Studies such as this volume continue a long tradition among Atlantic historians of periodically rethinking their approaches in highly creative ways. Today, perhaps more so than ever before, Atlantic World scholars appear more willing than ever to adopt new ways of reflecting upon and extending this now mature and increasingly crowded field of historical endeavour. In a recent review of Atlantic scholarship, Alison Games noted that the Atlantic as an ocean and the continents that bound it are modern creations that have been superimposed upon smaller worlds perceived by earlier generations – the Atlantic has been viewed as a number of seas for most of its history.[54] Increasingly trans-Atlantic and later global exchanges of peoples, goods and pathogens linked these worlds and gave them a common destiny and coherence formerly lacking. The price has perhaps been to lose sight of or marginalize local interactions with local environments, and particularly with the sea.

A re-exploration of these local maritime worlds will not necessarily unravel the intellectual coherence of the Atlantic World, but rather modify and enrich it by expanding zones of cultural interaction out to sea where cultural boundaries are more fluid and contested, and adding more of a human–environment interaction dimension to Atlantic studies. Were the first trans-Atlantic cultures essentially mono-cultural, homeland–colony relationships within distinct British, French, Spanish worlds spanning the Atlantic but not part of the Atlantic, or did they arise offshore as multicultural and multilingual exchanges between fisher-folk who were divided by national jurisdictions in which they were marginal but bonded by the dangers of the sea? Coming from the Pacific where European whaling and trading vessels were soon host to crews drawn from across the Pacific and Asia, I have always wondered why more is not made of incidents such as that noted by Michel Mollat du Jourdin in his *Europe and the Sea* that even when their nations were engaged in the Hundred Years' War during the fourteenth century, British and French fishers could still work together and interact peacefully.[55]

Five maritime themes common to the Pacific that might enhance Atlantic World historians' efforts to make the sea a more integral part of Atlantic history: the near to shore sea as a human habitat; the sea as a culturally differentiated space; the sea as a contested space, and sea as a zone of culture contact, and finally the sea as a decisive influence on human history rather than merely an environmental stage for history. All are present in Atlantic histories, but most are marginal in influence.

The sea was an integral and welcome part of coastal dwelling Pacific Islanders' daily lives. The sights, sounds and smells of the sea pervaded their lives, while the tastes of the sea were often on their lips. Marine species made up a significant part of the diet. Cook's expeditions recorded 150 types of fish known by Tahitians in the 1770s, at least forty-eight of which were identified as edible.[56] They felt at ease in the sea, and excelled at swimming and diving. The missionary William Ellis went so far as to describe Hawai'ians as 'almost a race of amphibious beings.' He detailed how

> Familiar with the sea at birth, they lose all dread of it, and seem nearly as much at home in the water as on dry land. There are few children who are not taken into the sea by their mothers the second or third day after birth, and many who can swim as soon as they can walk.[57]

Ellis's description is not isolated. Numerous observers were struck by how comfortable Islanders were in the water, and often described them in terms usually reserved for marine creatures. There are a number of accounts of Islanders surviving for long periods in the water, or swimming long distances in rough seas. When the Tahitian Tamaha took offence at the treatment meted out to him by the boatswain's mate on a United States' vessel sailing from the Marquesas Islands, he jumped overboard and swam off. He did so despite the fact that their last port of call was 20 miles distant, and 'it was blowing fresh with a considerable sea.' Tamaha made it back safely, claiming to have been in the water for one day and two nights.[58]

In contrast, many British seamen could not, and still cannot, swim. Contemporary British writer James Hamilton-Paterson found that most of the crew of a lifeboat in the British fishing community of Fraserburgh could not swim. Only recent generations had learnt to swim in the comfort of indoor swimming pools as part of their school education. Most displayed an almost fatalistic attitude to the sea, derived from an underlying assumption that once you fall into the sea's clutches you are finished.[59] This outlook may simply reflect the grim realities of the colder latitudes and waters of the north Atlantic, but it is also true that these feelings run deep in European sea cultures and have a long heritage. Cultural attitudes affect our ability at sea. Our bodies are insulated with subcutaneous fat like marine mammals, so that we are buoyant and streamlined. The more relaxed you are in the water the less chance you have of drowning. Something like 15 percent of all drownings are 'dry drownings', as people panic when they inhale their first water, sending their larynx into violent spasms that result in suffocation.[60]

The use of the sea as a place for leisure and social gatherings is a relatively recent phenomenon in European cultures. Until the nineteenth century many coastlines were almost deserted outside of ports. Watchtowers and lighthouses were perhaps the two main structures associated with European coasts, and both were responses to dangerous elements from the sea.[61] The Atlantic coasts of North America were only subject to hostile fleets periodically and correspondingly evolved different cultural landscapes along their shores.[62] Whether they embraced the sea more than their European cousins in swimming ability is unclear, but a history of trans-Atlantic variations in swimming and maritime leisure activities strikes one as an important way to embrace the sea as a factor in Atlantic cultural construction and identity.

Cultural attitudes not only affect our comfort in the sea but also how we map and otherwise percieve the sea. Hawai'ian sources are among the richest repository of sea lore in the Pacific and confirm Hviding's observations that Solomon Island cultural maps of the sea both affect and are affected by practical use of the sea. The seas surrounding the Hawai'ian islands were divided into regions on the basis of which aquatic aumakua (spirits) and gods held sway. The waters off O'ahu were protected from man-eating sharks by order of the shark gods Kanehunamoku and Kamohoali'i. Hawai'ians claimed that in 1834 a rogue shark was killed by guardian shark aumakua off Waikiki when it came seeking food.[63] A number of fishing grounds were marked

– CHAPTER 12: *The Atlantic and Pacific Worlds* –

out by 'Ai'ai, the son of the fishing god Ku'ula-kai. Various sites mark places of significance on 'Ai'ai's voyages of discovery. Thus a long thin outcrop of pahoehoe lava on the Hana coastline at Leho'ula is the backbone of the giant puhi (eel) slain by 'Ai'ai for raiding his father's fishponds. The puhi was called Koona, and had made its home in a nearby sea cave called Ka-puka-ulua (the hole of the crevalle). Prior to this it had lived in the sea just off Wailau on the windward coast of Moloka'i. However, it had moved to Hana after a battle with a large mano (shark) at Wailau. A large sea cave marked the spot where Koona had killed the mano by causing part of a sea cliff to collapse upon it.[64] While most fishing occurred near to shore, deeper offshore waters were also exploited regularly; by trolling, angling, netting near the surface, and long lining or more rarely by the use of traps. Traps might be set down to depths of seventy-five fathoms, while some Hawai'ian long lines used for benthic species could reach down 1200 feet. The result was knowledge of the seabed beyond the sight of the naked eye, and less anxiety about what dwelt below the surface.[65]

Ocean depths have always held a fascination and fear for Europeans. They were unknown and unknowable until well into the twentieth century. It was only in the last century that European science overturned a long-held belief that water increased in density as well as pressure with depth. Until then, it was believed that water density caused sunken ships and drowned sailors to drift suspended at middle depths according to their weight. Below this, was the azoic layer, forever dark, freezing and lifeless because of the inability of the sun's rays to penetrate it.[66] The Atlantic passage was feared with considerable trepidation by many seafarers and successful arrival at the destination was seen as an act of providence.[67] European cultures generally exhibit fear and hatred of sharks in equal measure in dramatic contrast to Pacific Islanders distinguishing between friendly and hostile sharks and adoption of individual sharks as guardian ancestral spirits. On the other hand, tales of close relationships between sea peoples and seals and dolphins are common to both the Pacific and Atlantic. Tales of silkies linking humans and seals along the west coasts of the British Isles resemble stories of humans mating with dolphins and porpoises common throughout Micronesia. Associated clans refrained from killing or eating them, and often had porpoise tattoo designs on their bodies.[68]

Many Pacific Islanders maintained tenure claims offshore. The most detailed studies deal with the Western Carolines, where the sea was crowded with fishing banks, reefs, and smaller, uninhabited atolls that were regularly exploited. Evidence collected around the turn of the twentieth century reveals that Puluwatese fished on Oraurau-feis (Manila Bank) southwest of Puluwat, Suat Reef (Enderby Bank) to the northwest, Asebar Reef in the east, and Maianjor to the southeast. All these fisheries were less than a day from Puluwat. Canoes would leave about midnight to arrive at the fishing grounds early the next day. After fishing for the remainder of the day, they departed in the evening, and arrived back at Puluwat the following day. Most of these fishing grounds lie between 20 miles and the 100 mile average overnight sailing range from Puluwat.[69]

Maritime rights needed to be constantly protected and asserted. Confrontations occurred along borders and within maritime territories, and ranged from low-level raiding of individual fish traps to attempts to permanently seize control of enemy fishing grounds. Polish ethnographer Jan Kubary noted that in Palau it was 'considered perfectly natural to rob the traps of the weaker neighboring villages, although the same offence practiced against kin or fellow villagers would not be accepted'.[70] When the trader Andrew Cheyne visited Yap in 1864 he found that the people of Tomil and Weeloey were at war after the Tomil people killed two Weeloey men over a fishing ground dispute.[71] On other occasions groups attempted to forcibly seize fisheries. The districts of Ko'olau and Kona on the Hawai'ian island of Moloka'i went to war over a disputed fishing ground. Kona emerged victorious in battle and held on to the fishery.[72]

Most cultural contacts at sea did not result in violence. Pacific Island historians have particularly focused on the dynamics of culture contact. Their approaches and focus has potential application to the Atlantic World, particularly at sea where historian David Chappell argues ships became liminal spaces that extended the usual coastal zone of contact out to sea. Broadly speaking, three approaches dominate. In the 1990s a hotly contested debate took place on the nature of western contact between Gananath Obeyesekere and Marshall Sahlins on why Hawai'ians killed Captain James Cook after initially treating him with great reverence. Sahlins advocated that culturally specific worldviews were key determinants of actions in situations of culture contact, and Obeyesekere argued for more pragmatic, universally understood influences behind actions. Historian Ian Campbell argues that a distinct culture of contact arose as both sides realized they faced unusual circumstances and resorted to more flexible behaviour themselves in an attempt to accommodate these circumstances.[73]

Much of this culture contact between Pacific Islanders and Europeans took place at sea as a number of individuals moved between cultures in the years following sustained European contact. From 1770 vessels themselves became zones of encounter, as Islanders took the opportunity to travel on Western vessels. What began as a trickle of invited guests in the late 1700s and early 1800s, became a flood as Islanders who eagerly sought employment on commercial vessels. Hawai'ians, Tahitians, and Māori were particularly prominent as crew because of their islands' popularity as ports of call. Most Islanders who travelled on these vessels spent their time within Oceania, with occasional visits to ports on the Pacific Rim such as Sydney and Valparaiso. Some sailed into the Indian and Atlantic Oceans.[74]

Melanesians joined this outpouring from the 1860s when vessels began recruiting them as labour for the emerging plantation economies of settler colonies such as Queensland, Fiji and New Caledonia.[75] Islanders travelled out of a sense of curiosity and adventure, or a desire to free themselves from constraints at home. Like earlier Polynesian crew members on Western vessels they hoped to enhance their status through the exotic tales and goods they returned with. The Melanesian labour trade involved tens of thousands of people and has generated significant interest among historians. Interpretations broadly divide between those seeing it as exploitation and deceit and those seeing it as a process in which Islanders had a great deal of choice and control.[76]

In most books and articles the environment is relegated to the general introduction that outlines environmental and cultural structures to set the stage for the human drama that then unfolds. A few works by archaeologists explore the potential of a more thorough integration of environmental considerations into historical narratives. In Tom Dye's study of Marquesan fishing, and Kirch's component of the Anahulu study, changes in resource use are related to particular historical eras, albeit in a largely generalized, systemic way.[77] While regular, seasonal events shaped the rhythm of human activity, shorter-term, less predictable elements of the environment such as typhoons also intruded into the actions and attitudes of Pacific Islanders. On occasion, such intrusions had dramatic and far-reaching implications for the communities that they affected. For example, a super typhoon in the late eighteenth century seems to have caused such devastation and deaths in the Caroline Islands that it shattered the power of two dynasties and required the resettlement of one island.[78] The most obvious point of comparison is the impact of typhoons in the Pacific and hurricanes in the Caribbean and Atlantic seaboard of North America. Pacific Island societies in Micronesia's Typhoon Alley extend their resource base through marriage-based kin links, magazine economies and maintaining sophisticated sailing technology to enable temporary or permanent relocation.

There is one final argument for making the sea more central to Atlantic and all ocean history. Criticisms of Atlantic historians for converting Atlantic crossings into mere passages of time across undifferentiated maritime spaces somewhat distort the reality of the time-space continuum at sea. The Tongan concepts of *Ta* and *Va* construct oceanic space, and particularly maritime space, and time as fluid and inter-related. Pacific Islander notions of space have long been recognized as distinct from Western ones, but the closer linking of both to the conception of time is an important refinement that moves us closer towards core issues of cultural identity.[79] It is also an important way of spanning the divide between cultural and environmental explanations in ocean history. Humans are far less able to shape the sea than the land, and so must adjust their rhythms and cultures to suit. Closer examination of the interaction of island and ocean space and time may therefore reveal key influences on Pacific Islander culture and identity, and perhaps to a lesser extent that of Atlantic coastal peoples as well? As scholars as diverse as Michael Adas and Greg Dening have argued, concepts of time lie at the heart of cultural identity and social, political and economic relationships.

NOTES

1 These figures are used here as relative measures rather than absolute measures. They are taken from A.G. Poynter (ed.), *The Grolier Atlas of Asia and the World*, London, George Philip & Son, 1985, 7, which lists the relative sizes of oceans and seas in descending order as: Pacific 165,721,000 sq km, Atlantic Ocean 81,660,000 sq km, Indian Ocean 73,422,000 sq km, Arctic Ocean, 14,351,000 sq km, and the Mediterranean Sea, 2,996,000 sq km. This calculation distinguishes some contiguous bodies of water to the Atlantic (Caribbean, 1,942,000 sq km, Gulf of Mexico, 1,813,000 sq km, and North Sea, 575,000 sq km) and Pacific (Bering Sea, 2,274,000 sq km, Sea of Okhotsk, 1,528,000 sq km, East China Sea, 1,248,000 sq km, and Sea of Japan, 1,049,000 sq km) as separate entities.

2 William L. Thomas Jr., 'The Pacific Basin: An Introduction', in A.P. Vayda (ed.), *Cultures of the Pacific: An Anthropological Reader*, Garden City, New York, The Natural History Press, 1963, 7–38, and Ben Finney, 'The Other One-Third of the Globe', *Journal of World History*, vol. 5(2), 1994, 273–97.

3 Epeli Hau'ofa, 'Our Sea of Islands', *The Contemporary Pacific*, vol. 6 (1), 1994, 148–61, and K.R. Howe, *Nature, Culture, and History: The 'Knowing of Oceania'*, Honolulu, University of Hawai'i Press, 2000.

4 Karen Wigen, 'Introduction', *Oceans of History Forum, The American Historical Review*, vol. 111(3), June 2006, 717–21 (http://www.historycooperative.org/journals/ahr/111.3/wigen.html, accessed 2 August 2014), para 1, and Alison Games, 'Atlantic History: Definitions, Challenges, and Opportunities', *The American Historical Review*, vol. 111(3),

June 2006, 741–57 (http://www.historycooperative.org/journals/ahr/111.3/games.htm, accessed 2 August 2014), paras 10, 17–19.

5 Paul D'Arcy (ed.), *Peoples of the Pacific: The History of Oceania to 1870*, Aldershot, Ashgate Publishing, 2008, xix–xlv.

6 See Geoff R. Clark (ed.), *Dumont d'Urville's Divisions of Oceania: Fundamental Precincts or Arbitrary Constructs?* special issue of *The Journal of Pacific History*, 38(2), 2003.

7 Some works span these regional dividing lines within academia. For works linking Southeast Asia and Oceania for example, see P. Swadling, *Plumes from Paradise: Trade Cycles in Outer Southeast Asia and Their Impact on New Guinea and Nearby Islands until 1920*, Boroko: Papua New Guinea National Museum in association with Robert Brown and Associates, 1996, and Peter Bellwood, James Fox & Darrell Tryon (eds.), *The Austronesians: Historical and Comparative Perspectives*, Canberra: Department of Anthropology, Research School of Pacific and Asian Studies, Australian National University, 1995. For recent revisionist history of Southeast Asian–Oceanic interaction see Matt K. Matsuda, *Pacific Worlds: A History of Seas, Peoples, and Cultures*, Cambridge: Cambridge University Press, 2012, and Paul D'Arcy, "Sea Worlds: Pacific and Southeast Asian history centered on the Philippines" in Rila Mukherjee (ed.), *Oceans Connect: New Directions in Maritime Studies*, Primus Books, Delhi, 2012, 20–35.

8 R.C. Green, 'Near and Remote Oceania: Disestablishing Melanesia in Culture History', in Andrew Pawley (ed.), *Man and a Half: Essays in Pacific Anthropology and Ethnobiology in Honour of Ralph Bulmer*, Auckland, Polynesian Society, 1991, 491–502, especially 493–95.

9 See E. Alison Kay, *Little Worlds of the Pacific: A Essay on Pacific Basin Biogeography*, Harold L. Lyon Arboretum Lecture no. 9, May 9, 1979, Lyon Arboretum, Honolulu, 1980, 25, 33.

10 Geoffrey Irwin, *The Prehistoric Exploration and Colonisation of the Pacific*, Cambridge, Cambridge University Press.

11 Excluding the Santa Cruz Group, 352 kilometres to the east of the main chain.

12 Aotearoa is the Polynesian word for modern day New Zealand and is used here to refer to that landmass before there was a significant European presence there in the 1840s.

13 For a good succinct summary, see Douglas L. Oliver, *Oceania: The Native Cultures of Australia and the Pacific Islands*, 2 vols., Honolulu, University of Hawai'i Press, 1989, vol. 1, 409–12.

14 On seasonal wind patterns and their variability see Oliver, *Oceania*, vol. 1, 14, and Ben R. Finney et al, 'Wait for the West Wind', *Journal of the Polynesian Society*, vol. 98(3), 1989, 261–302, especially 265–67, 272–73.

15 Oliver, *Oceania*, vol. 1, 15–17.

16 Christopher S. Lobban and Maria Schefter, *Tropical Pacific Island Environments*, Mangilao, Guam, University of Guam Press, 1997, 104–6.

17 This overview is based on Harold V. Thurman, *Essentials of Oceanography*, Columbus, Ohio, Charles E. Merrill Publishing Co., 1983, 261–62; David B. Enfield, 'Historical and Prehistorical Overview of El Nino/Southern Oscillation', in Henry F. Diaz & Vera Markgraf (eds.), *El Nino: Historical and Paleoclimatic Aspects of the Southern Oscillation*, Cambridge, Cambridge University Press, 1992, 95–117; Lobban & Schefter (1996) 103–7; and Tom Spencer, 'Changes in the Global Environment: Uncertain Prospects for the Pacific', in Ben Burt & Christian Clerk (eds.), *Environment and Development in the Pacific Islands*, National Centre for Development Studies, Australian National University, Canberra, 1997, 243–63, especially 253–54.

18 Good overviews of global weather patterns associated with the ENSO phenomenon are found in Enfield (1992) 100–102, and Matthias Tomczak & J. Stuart Godfrey, Regional Oceanography: An Introduction, Oxford, Pergamon, 1994, 364–67. A recreation of historical ENSO patterns using such data is attempted by William H. Quinn, 'A Study of

– CHAPTER 12: *The Atlantic and Pacific Worlds* –

Southern Oscillation-related Climatic Activity for A.D. 622–1990 incorporating Nile River Flood Data', in Henry F. Diaz & Vera Markgraf (eds.), *El Nino: Historical and Paleoclimatic Aspects of the Southern Oscillation*, Cambridge, Cambridge University Press, 1992, 119–49.

19 Good discussions of tidal patterns are found in Harold J. Wiens, *Atoll Environment and Ecology*, Yale University Press, New Haven, 1962, 207–15; William A. Anikouchine, & Richard W. Sternberg, *The World Ocean: An Introduction to Oceanography*, Prentice Hall, Englewood Cliffs, N.J., 1973, 133–38; and Thurman (1983) 152–56.

20 This discussion of Pacific currents is based on information drawn from Thurman (1983) 125–35; Anikouchine & Stenberg (1973) 96–117; Wiens (1962) 188–90; Tomczak & Godfrey (1994) 118–31; and Oliver (1989) vol.1, pp. 7–8.

21 For example, see Rudolf S. Scheltma, 'Long-distance Dispersal by Planktonic Larvae of Shoal-water Benthic Invertebrates among Central Pacific Islands', in Kay, E. Alison (ed.), *A Natural History of the Hawai'ian Islands: Selected Readings II*, University of Hawai'i Press, Honolulu, 1994, 171–86, especially 178–79.

22 On ocean food chains see Thurman (1983) 258–60; Anikouchine & Sternberg (1973) 235–39; and Taivo Laevastu, & Herbert A. Larkins, *Marine Fisheries Ecosystem: Its Quantitative Evaluation and Management*, Fishing News Books Ltd., Farnham, Surrey, 1981, 20–21.

23 On lagoon-reef ecosystem productivity see Sequoia Shannon & Joseph R. Morgan, 'Management of Insular Pacific Marine Ecosystems', in Elisabeth Mann Borgese, Norton Ginsburg & Joseph R. Morgan (eds.), *Ocean Yearbook 10*, University of Chicago Press, Chicago, 1993, 196–213, especially 199–200; Asahitaro Nishimura, 'Fishing in Indonesia from the Marine Ethnological Viewpoint with Respect to Wallace's Line', in Bela Gunda (ed.), *The Fishing Culture of the World: Studies in Ethnology, Culture and Folklore* (2 vols.), Budapest, Akademiai Kiado, 1984, vol.2, 677–703, 696–97.

24 For discussions on the optimal conditions for fisheries see G.D. Sharp, 'Fish Populations and Fisheries: Their Perturbations, Natural and Man-Induced', in H. Postma & J.J. Zijlstra (eds.), *Ecosystems of the World 27: Continental Shelves*, Amsterdam, Elsevier, 1988, 155–202, especially 172; Anikouchine & Sternberg (1973) 214ff.; Thurman (1983) 224, 264; David Sopher, *The Sea Nomads: A Study of the Maritime Boat People of Southeast Asia*, Singapore, National Museum of Singapore, 1977, 22–25, 31, 34; and T. Stell Newman, 'Man in the Prehistoric Hawai'ian Ecosystem', in E. Alison Kay (ed.), *A Natural History of the Hawai'ian Islands: Select Readings*, University of Hawai'i Press, Honolulu, 1972, 559–603, especially p. 577.

25 Lorimer Fison, *Tales from Old Fiji*, London, The De La More Press, 1907, 162–63.

26 R.A. Derrick, *A History of Fiji*, volume 1, Suva, Government Press, 1968 (reprint of 1950 revised edition), p. 37, note 1.

27 Max W. de Laubenfels, 'Ocean Currents in the Marshall Islands', *Geographical Review*, vol. 40(2), 1950, 254–59, especially 258.

28 Callum Roberts, *The Unnatural History of the Sea*, Island Press, Washington D.C., 2010, 17–44.

29 Ian K. Steele, *The English Atlantic 1675–1740: An Exploration of Communication and Community*, Oxford, Oxford University Press, 1986, 3–5; and Thurman (1983), 129–30.

30 Fernand Braudel, *The Mediterranean and the Mediterranean World in the Age of Philip II*, 2 vols., New York, Harper and Row, 1972–73; vol. I, 14; K.N. Chaudhuri, *Trade and Civilization in the Indian Ocean: An Economic History from the Rise of Islam to 1750*, Cambridge, Cambridge University Press, 1985; and Michael Pearson, *The Indian Ocean*, London, Routledge, 2003.

31 Chaudhuri (1985) 21.

32 See Arif Dirlik, 'The Asia-Pacific Idea: Reality and Representation in the Invention of a Regional Structure', *Journal of World History*, vol. 3(1), 1992, 55–79 for an overview of the concept.

– *Paul D'Arcy* –

33 Dirlik (1992) 64.

34 See O.H.K. Spate, *The Pacific since Magellan: Vol. 1: The Spanish Lake*, Canberra, Australian National University Press, 1979.

35 The terms Pacific Islander and Islander are used here interchangeably to refer to Pacific Islanders in general, while the terms European and Western are used interchangeably to refer to influences and people emanating from European and North American Caucasian societies.

36 Jocelyn Linnekin, 'Contending Approaches', in Donald Denoon (ed.), *The Cambridge History of the Pacific Islanders*, Cambridge, Cambridge University Press, 1997, 3–36, 6.

37 This scheme is most elegantly argued in P.V. Kirch, *The Evolution of the Polynesian Chiefdoms*, Cambridge, Cambridge University Press, 1984, 71–216. For a concise overview on the evolution of theory in Oceanic prehistory see P.V. Kirch, 'Prehistory' in Alan Howard & R. Borofsky (eds.), *Developments in Polynesian Ethnology*, Honolulu, University of Hawai'i Press, 1989, 13–46.

38 K.R. Howe, 'Pacific Islands History in the 1980s: New Directions or Monograph Myopia?', *Pacific Studies*, vol. 3(1), 1979, 81–90, 81.

39 O.H.K. Spate, 'The Pacific as an Artifact', in Niel Gunson (ed.), *The Changing Pacific: Essays in Honour of H.E. Maude*, Melbourne, Oxford University Press, 1978, 32–45, 34.

40 Irwin (1992) 204. For an early exploration of this concept, see P.V. Kirch, 'Exchange Systems and Inter-island Contact in the Transformation of an Island Society: the Tikopia Case', in P.V. Kirch (ed.), *Island Societies: Archaeological Approaches to Evolution and Transformation*, Cambridge, Cambridge University Press, 1986, 33–41.

41 I.C. Campbell, *A History of the Pacific Islands*, Christchurch, University of Canterbury Press, 1989, 36.

42 Epeli Hau'ofa (1994) 153–54.

43 Irwin (1992) 136.

44 Epeli Hau'ofa, 'The Ocean in Us', *The Contemporary Pacific*, vol. 10(2), 1998, 392–410, 405.

45 R.E. Johannes, *Words of the Lagoon: Fishing and Marin Lore in the Palau District of Micronesia*, Berkeley, University of California Press, 1981; Michael D. Lieber, *More Than a Living: Fishing and the Social Order on a Polynesian Atoll*, Boulder, Colorado, Westview Press, 1994; Edvard Hviding, *Guardians of Marovo Lagoon: Practice, Place, and Politics in Maritime Melanesia*, Honolulu, University of Hawai'i Press, 1996.

46 Hviding (1996) xiii.

47 Hviding (1996) 27, 369, 371.

48 See K.R. Howe (ed.), *Waka Moana: Voyages of the Ancestors: the Discovery and Settlement of the Pacific*, Honolulu, University of Hawai'i Press, 2007.

49 See Ben Finney and Sam Low, 'Navigation' in K.R. Howe (ed.), *Waka Moana: Voyages of the Ancestors: The Discovery and Settlement of the Pacific*, Honolulu, University of Hawai'i Press, 2007, 154–97.

50 Paul D'Arcy, *The People of the Sea: Environment, Identity, and History in Oceania*, Honolulu, University of Hawai'i Press, 2006.

51 D'Arcy (2006), and Howe (2007).

52 Felipe Fernández-Armesto, *Before Columbus: Exploration and Colonisation from the Mediterranean to the Atlantic, 1229–1492*, London, Macmillan, 1987, 152, and David Abulafia, 'Mediterraneans', in W.V. Harris (ed.), *Rethinking the Mediterranean*, Oxford, Oxford University Press, 2005, 64–93, 80–82.

53 See for example, Kirch (1984) 223–63.

54 Games (2006) paras 4–5.

55 Michel Mollat du Jourdin, *Europe and the Sea*, Oxford, Blackwell Publishers, 1993, 152. He does note that on other occasions fishers from different nations came to blows at sea – 147–52.

– CHAPTER 12: *The Atlantic and Pacific Worlds* –

56 Gordon R. Lewthwaite, 'Man and the Sea in Early Tahiti: Maritime Economy through European Eyes', *Pacific Viewpoint*, vol. 7(1), 1966, 28–53, 34, citing J.R. Forster, *Observations made during a Voyage round the World*, London, G. Robinson, 1778, 440–41.

57 William Ellis, *Polynesian Researches: Hawai'i*, Rutland, Vermont, Charles E. Tuttle Co., Publishers, 1969a (reprint of new edition, 1842), 369.

58 Captain David Porter, *Journal of a Cruise made to the Pacific Ocean*, 2 vols., Upper Saddle, New Jersey, The Gregg Press, 1970, 140, 180.

59 James Hamilton-Paterson, *Seven-Tenths: the Sea and Its Thresholds*, London, Vintage, 1993, 198–99.

60 Thomas Farber, *On Water*, Hopewell, New Jersey, The Ecco Press, 1994, 48–49.

61 Jourdin (1993) 41, 92, 195–96, 223, and Alain Corbin, *The Lure of the Sea: The Discovery of the Seaside 1750–1840*, London, Penguin, 1995.

62 John R. Stilgoe, *Alongshore*, New Haven, Yale University Press, 1994.

63 Dorothy Barrere (ed.), *Ka Po'eKahiko: The People of Old*, by Samuel Kamakau, Honolulu, Bernice P. Bishop Museum, 1964, 73–74.

64 On the legend of 'Ai'ai see Martha Beckwith, *Hawaiian Mythology*, Honolulu; University of Hawaii Press, 1970, 22–23.

65 See; Hommon (1975) 123. One fathom equals 6 feet.

66 Hamilton-Paterson (1992) 151, 154–56.

67 Steele (1986) 11–12.

68 See William H. Alkire, 'Porpoises and Taro', *Ethnology*, vol. 7(3), 1968, 280–89, and Katharine Luomala, 'Porpoises and Taro in Gilbert Islands' Myths and Customs', *Fabula*, vol.18(1), 1977, pp. 201–11.

69 H.P. Damm, P. Hambruch, and E. Sarfert, 'Inseln um Truck (Polowat, Hok, Satowal)', in G. Thilenius (ed.), *Ergebnisse der Südsee-Expedition 1908–1910*, vol. II, B, VI(1935), 1–288, Hamburg, Friederichsen, De Gruyter & Co., 1935, 50, 56.

70 J.S. Kubary, *Ethnograpische Beitrage zur Kenntnis de Karolinische – archipels*, Leiden, P.W.M. Trap, 1895, 148.

71 Andrew Cheyne, *Journal of a Voyage to the Islands of the Western Pacific in Brigantine 'Acis' A. Cheyne Commander*, 21 February 1864.

72 Abraham Fornander, *An Account of the Polynesian Race*, 2 vols., Rutland, Vermont, Charles E. Tuttle Co.,1969, 282.

73 See Gananath Obeyesekere, *The Apotheosis of Captain Cook: European Mythmaking in the Pacific*, Princeton, Princeton University Press, 1992, and Marshall Sahlins, *How 'Natives' Think: About Captain Cook, For Example*, Chicago, University of Chicago Press, 1995. See also I.C. Campbell, 'European-Polynesian Encounters: A Critique of the Pearson Thesis', *The Journal of Pacific History*, 29(2), 1994, 222–31.

74 See David A. Chappell, *Double Ghosts: Oceanic Voyagers on Euroamerican Ships*, Armonk, New York, M.E. Sharpe, 1997, especially 28–40, 158–63.

75 K.R. Howe, *Where the Waves Fall: A New South Sea Islands History from First Settlement to Colonial Rule*, Sydney, Allen and Unwin, 1984, 329–43.

76 See Doug Munro, 'Revisionism and its Enemies: Debating the Queensland Labour Trade', *The Journal of Pacific History*, vol. 30(2), 1995, 240–49. For the impact of returning labourers, see Peter Corris, *Passage, Port and Plantation: A History of Solomon Islands Labour Migration*, Melbourne, Melbourne University Press, 1973, 111–25.

77 Tom Dye, 'The Causes and Consequences of a Decline in the Prehistoric Marquesan Fishing Industry', in D.E. Yen & J.M.J. Mummery (eds.), *Pacific Production Systems: Approaches to Economic Prehistory*, Canberra, Occasional Papers in Prehistory no. 18, Department of Prehistory, RSPAS, Australian National University, Canberra, 1990, 70–84; and P.V. Kirch *The Archaeology of History. Anahulu: The Anthropology of History in the Kingdom of Hawai'i*, vol. 2., Chicago, University of Chicago Press, 1992.

78 D'Arcy (2006) 128–33.
79 On the centrality of senses of time to cultural identity, see Greg Dening's 'Reflection: On Civilizing' in his *Islands and Beaches. Discourse on a Silent Land: Marquesas 1774–1880*, Honolulu, University of Hawai'i Press, 1980, 263–67, especially 264, and Michael Adas, *Machines as the Measure of Men: Science, Technology, and Ideologies of Western Dominance*, Ithaca, Cornell University Press, 1989, 241ff.

CHAPTER THIRTEEN

AN ENSLAVED ENLIGHTENMENT
Rethinking the intellectual history
of the French Atlantic

————— •◆• —————

Laurent Dubois

In 1971, Michèle Duchet published *Anthropologie et histoire au siècle des lumières* (*Anthropology and History in the Century of the Enlightenment*), which provided a sweeping analysis of the French production of knowledge about Africa and the Americas during the eighteenth century. Her work remains one of the most careful and convincing analyses of the complex and contradictory tangle of Enlightenment intellectual currents that both celebrated the universality of the human race and put forth hierarchical and differentialist theories about different groups that are often of startling arrogance and racism.[1]

In a few early sections of her work, Duchet traced out how the Enlightenment critiques of colonial slavery in the Caribbean emerged in the second half of the eighteenth century in relation to the daily problem of colonial governance in the colonies themselves. Administrators in the slave colonies of the Caribbean during this period, she argued, were deeply concerned with the interrelated problems of marronage (the frequent escape of the enslaved from the plantations), high mortality and the violence of masters. They wrote extensively about these problems, creating analyses and documents that informed the writing of central texts of the period, particularly the Abbé Raynal's multi-volume history of European colonialism, *L'Histoire des Deux Indes*.[2] The criticism of slavery that expanded over the course of the eighteenth century, then, was not 'the progress of a humanism that created its own values and succeeded in imposing a conception of man'. In fact, the 'humanism' of the *philosophes* adjusted itself to economic, social and political realities, and proposed solutions that coincided with those advocated at the same time by administrators of different colonies and the clerks at the *Bureau des colonies*.[3]

Duchet placed the phenomenon of marronage at the centre of her analysis, noting the continuous preoccupation with maroons (fugitive slaves) in texts stretching over the entire eighteenth century. She called attention to 'the persistence of an anxiety' driven by 'the impossibility of ending a rebellion', arguing that the ongoing presence of maroons created 'a new situation'. Moreover, she insisted that the heroic slave rebels who appeared in a number of Enlightenment works, affirming 'the dignity of man' through the 'refusal of injustice', were directly based on 'real models' in the Caribbean such as Makandal and Cudjoe. The 'revolt' that 'found its voice' in

Enlightenment texts, then, had 'already taken form in the plantations of Surinam or Saint-Dominigue', in insurrections that reflected 'a collective attitude of refusal or revolt'. The resistance practised in the Caribbean, therefore, was part of the field of intellectual and political activity that comprised the Enlightenment. Even if, for the most part, they did not themselves participate in the production of writing about the basic questions regarding humanity, nature and rights that slavery raised, Duchet suggested, enslaved rebels were nevertheless key actors in this broader history.[4]

Since Duchet's work was published there has been a steadily growing interest among scholars regarding the ways in which Enlightenment thinkers dealt with questions of cultural difference, 'race' and slavery. This work has shown us the variety and complexity of writing on these themes, and highlighted many of the contradictions within the work of particular Enlightenment thinkers. However, this work in intellectual history has not taken up the theoretical and methodological challenge issued by Duchet: writing a history of the Enlightenment whose actors include not only the familiar literate intellectuals that historians and theorists have long studied, but others who did not for the most part articulate their political philosophy in writing – the slaves.

Writing an intellectual history of the enslaved might strike many scholars of the history of ideas as a quixotic enterprise. To do so, scholars obviously must confront major obstacles: the fragmentary nature of the relevant written record, a dependence on profoundly hostile observers for much of this record, and the necessity of reading backwards from political action to political philosophy. But these obstacles are not insurmountable. Historians working in Caribbean and African-American history have for some time been engaged in exploring the history of political thought within enslaved communities, providing us in the process with methods that can also be used to gain a fuller understanding of the Atlantic currents of thinking that produced the Enlightenment. Hillary Beckles, for instance, has insisted that we move beyond the idea that 'slaves existed in an atheoretical world which was devoid of ideas' and 'political concepts', and expand our understanding of the ways slaves 'made definite political analysis of the power structure they encountered' and resisted in ways that made them central protagonists in the demolition of slavery.[5]

In seeking to write an intellectual history of the enslaved, we should begin by acknowledging that in their dependence upon small numbers of literate members or allies for news, and in their focus on oral exchange of information and ideas, they were in fact like many other communities throughout Europe and the Americas during the same period. Even among elites, spoken transmission of ideas and news was an important part of the intellectual process. Although the ability to participate in textual production obviously enhanced these exchanges and expanded the distances and modes of transmission through which they could take place, there is no convincing reason to conserve a solid categorical distinction between the intellectual activities of free and enslaved individuals. We should begin from the assumption that there was an intellectual life within slave communities, and that this life involved movement between ideas and action, between the abstract and the particular, between past, present and future.

In this article I imagine how we might write a history of the Enlightenment – and particularly its development in the French Atlantic – that integrates the thought and action of a range of communities in France and the Caribbean. In doing so I build

– CHAPTER 13: *An enslaved Enlightenment* –

upon the work of scholars who have insisted on the diversity of Enlightenment thought's engagement with questions of race and slavery. Sankar Muthu, for instance, has recently emphasized that the term 'the "Enlightenment" groups together an extraordinarily diverse set of authors, texts, arguments, opinions, dispositions, assumptions, institutions and practices', and insists on the need to 'pluralize' our understanding of the political thought of this period, notably by acknowledging important strands of thought that issued powerful critiques of European imperialism. The 'pluralization' of the Enlightenment he proposes, however, focuses on what I see as only one particular field within it: that of written texts generated, distributed and debated within continental Europe. Here I argue, following Duchet, that scholars of the Enlightenment should consider taking another step in expanding their understanding of the diversity of the thought of this period. By developing a truly Atlantic approach to the history of the ideas during this period, I suggest, we can make connections not only between literate elites on both sides of the ocean but also between the diverse spheres of intellectual debate which took place in a world that was quite integrated by currents of trade in commodities, and in news and ideologies. The construction of a more integrated intellectual history of the Enlightenment can contribute to the broader rethinking under way in a variety of fields of the ways in which the set of discursive and intellectual habits wrongly identified as 'western' thought emerged through the process of imperial conquest and consolidation, and the responses it engendered.[6]

Because it produced both a stunningly successful slave revolution and, as a result, numerous documents and memoirs about the course of this revolution, Saint-Domingue's slave revolution provides a particularly useful site for examining the political culture within slave communities. This revolution, furthermore, ranks as perhaps the greatest political triumph of the Age of Revolution, and it might even be said that it best embodies the promises of Enlightenment universalism.[7]

In order to situate the political and intellectual contributions of this revolution, I begin with an examination of recent scholarship on Enlightenment approaches to the question of slavery and race. I then turn to a set of questions that are curiously absent from this scholarship. What were the enslaved talking about and reading in the late eighteenth century? How did they articulate their political visions and demands? Although it is unlikely that we will ever have more than an extremely partial answer to this question, there are enough traces to suggest that their access to intellectual and political debates was wider than might be assumed.

A number of the classic and nearly sacred thinkers of the French Enlightenment have been, during the past decades, on the receiving end of a blistering set of critiques on the part of scholars concerned with the seeming contradiction between their celebration of natural rights and their open justification for, or their lack of, direct criticism of the Atlantic slavery that was a bedrock of their societies. Leading the charge has been Louis Sala-Molins who, in two works published over a decade ago, took Montesquieu and Rousseau, as well as abolitionist thinkers like the Marquis de Condorcet and Dénis Diderot, to task for their racist views. More recently, Laurent Estève has expanded Sala-Molins's critical approach to Enlightenment treatments of slavery through a close analysis of Montaigne, Rousseau, Buffon and Diderot.[8]

The best French representative of a 'racist Enlightenment' is the Comte de Buffon who, in his *Histoire naturelle*, published between 1748 and 1778, laid out a hierarchical portrait of the human species that not only justified but actually rendered necessary the slavery of certain groups. A similar way of thinking informed the approach of the Baron de Montesquieu, one of the central theorists of natural rights. While in his *L'Esprit des Lois*, published in 1748, he argued that slavery was contrary to natural rights, in the rest of his work he suggested that different climates required different laws, and accepted the idea that slavery might be required in certain contexts. Indeed, he went so far as to argue that while 'peoples of the North' were in a 'coerced state' if they were not free, most people in warmer zones were in fact in a 'violent' state if they were *not* enslaved. He called the colonies of the Antilles 'admirable' and, in his *Pensées*, wrote that 'Negroes' were so 'naturally lazy' that those who were 'born free do nothing'. The broad principles of natural law laid out by Montesquieu were immediately and comfortably denied to a good portion of the human race.[9]

Jean-Jacques Rousseau represents a more ambiguous case: Estève and Sala-Molins lambaste him primarily for his 'silence' surrounding the actually existing slavery. As Sala-Molins complains, having established that the word 'slave' and the word 'rights' are contradictory, Rousseau nevertheless speaks not a word in criticism of the blatant violation of this principle in the French kingdom. Rousseau mentions the 'sadness and desperation' of a group of people forced onto ships and brought far from their homes by force: individuals from Iceland transported to Denmark. Rousseau must have known about the slave trade, about slavery in the Caribbean, about the *Code Noir* itself, yet he mentions none of them. The reality of the 'middle passage' is off the page, in the distance, and appears barely as a trace: Rousseau mentions that the 'Hottentots' at the Cape of Good Hope are able to see, with their naked eyes, ships on the sea that the Dutch can only see with the 'aid of glasses'. Estève wonders whether the ships they saw so clearly might be those carrying 'human cargo'; but Rousseau did not make this leap in his writing. Although Rousseau frequently and incisively critiqued concrete examples of inequality and tyranny in his society, he conspicuously avoided any attack on slavery as it actually existed. Although, to Sala-Molins, Rousseau's blindness to Atlantic slavery was inherited by the 'revolutionaries of 1789', who had read Rousseau 'very well', 'they were the ones who were the slaves, and it was up to them to break their own chains and get rid of their tyrants'. The problem of the enslaved in the Caribbean 'was not part of the instruction manual for the revolution'.[10]

The eighteenth century did have, as both Sala-Molins and Estève concede, prominent thinkers who directly attacked slavery, detailing and decrying the horrors of the middle passage and those inflicted by white masters in the Caribbean, particularly Dénis Diderot in his famous contributions to the Abbé Raynal's *Histoire des Deux Indes*. Sankar Muthu has forcefully argued, through an examination of Diderot's contributions to Raynal's work and his *Supplément au Voyage de Bougainville*, that he articulated a powerful critique of imperialism by presenting 'New World peoples as conscious, fully rational and cultural beings' and, more broadly, theorizing all humans as being '*constitutively* cultural beings'. Diderot, as Muthu notes, 'describes gleefully' the prospect of Europeans 'having their throats slashed open' by slaves. This is true both in his famous passage predicting the arrival of a 'Black Spartacus' and in a lesser-known dialogue between a master and a slave in which the latter tells the former not to 'complain if my tears open your chest to find your heart' or 'when you feel, in your cut-up intestines, the taste of death, which I

– CHAPTER 13: *An enslaved Enlightenment* –

have stirred in with your food'. Diderot also, Muthu argues, insisted that Europe was not superior to other cultures and had no right to impose its culture on other peoples.[11]

Estève, however, is less impressed by Diderot's contributions, and notes that, while Diderot took an important step in explicitly identifying slavery as a 'crime', his work also includes many ambiguities and a hierarchical vision of blacks that remains tied to the differentialist attitudes of other thinkers of the time. Sala-Molins, meanwhile, acknowledges the contributions of the Marquis de Condorcet in his 1781 anti-slavery work *Réflexions sur l'esclavage des nègres*, but ultimately criticizes Condorcet for presenting racist visions of slaves in his insistence on the need for an extremely slow and gradual process of emancipation. Estève's conclusion – which differs in important ways from that of Muthu – was that even the most progressive thinkers of the Enlightenment, such as Diderot, ultimately failed to 'think difference' outside of 'hierarchy'. He writes that from the Enlightenment we should retain the possibilities of universalism, but he also warns against letting the 'celebration of natural rights' allow us to 'make the corpses disappear from our closets'.[12]

Sala-Molins attacks a habit of convenient forgetting even more forcefully when he asks, referring to the debates about the holocaust: 'Who has ever asked the question: "How can one think after Saint-Domingue?" We think peacefully after Saint-Domingue.' There was, he insists, a crucial link between the celebrated Enlightenment and the brutality of slavery, and it is crucial for us to confront that. 'How should we read the Enlightenment? With the Code Noir in hand.' The work of Sala-Molins and Estève identifies, then, within Enlightenment discourse, a set of operations that are by now all too familiar to students of slavery and emancipation, and empire more broadly: universal claims were intertwined with justifications for exclusions based on the incapacity of certain 'others' to enjoy their natural rights. We must confront the Enlightenment, Estève and Sala-Molins suggest, not as a foundation for democracy and humanism but as a set of discourses saturated with racism and hierarchical thinking.[13]

This critique, however, does not fully answer the challenge posted by Duchet decades ago, for neither Sala-Molins nor Estève situate the complexities of Enlightenment thought about slavery and the colonies within the complexities of the social world that generated the knowledge they articulated. Despite the length of trans-Atlantic journeys, information about the colonies was constantly circulating through conversations among merchants, sailors, planters and all types of vagabonds who travelled between Europe, Africa and the Americas, through newspapers and travel accounts, novels and plays and, of course, administrative reports that made the ocean crossing. And though the vast majority of slaves lived and died in the colonies, slavery was not only a far-off problem: there were significant populations of slaves, as well as free people of African descent, in London and Paris as well as port towns like Bordeaux and Bristol. In both Britain and France, too, there were widely discussed court cases through which some slaves won their freedom from masters by arguing that enslavement was not legal within the boundaries of Europe. All of this meant that European intellectuals lived in a world into which the colonies were integrated on many levels. The multiple currents of Enlightenment thought were always already shaped by the realities of the Americas, and the explosion of political thought and activity that occurred after 1789 was rooted not only in France itself but in the larger Atlantic world. It is this reality – of a world integrated not only through the circulation of chained bodies and of the commodities slaves produced, but also through the

231

circulation of declamations, ideas and hopes generated by this onslaught of injustice – that I would argue we need to understand better.

Sala-Molins takes to task the idea that the Enlightenment set in motion the Haitian Revolution through a sarcastic reading of the 'fable' (included in, among other works, C. L. R. James's *The Black Jacobins*) that Toussaint Louverture was inspired by Raynal's work, particularly the passages calling for a 'Black Spartacus' to break the chains of the slaves. In order to be so inspired, Sala-Molins writes, Louverture would have had to read them while 'systematically skipping' the racist passages of the same text. But, asks Sala-Molins, how did the rebel of Saint-Domingue 'succeed in the subtle academic exercise that consists in deducing from a discourse that, occasionally, concerns him, what this discourse does not say or suggest, what it eliminates with complete serenity and clarity?' Having emphasized throughout his work that the Enlightenment worked either openly to justify or wilfully to overlook slavery in the Atlantic, Sala-Molins insists that it had no role in shaping revolution in the Caribbean: 'The black, always a slave and still always standing, truly invented his liberty'.[14]

Are these, in fact, the terms of the choice before us as historians? Is the only alternative to a reading that sees the Haitian Revolution as a derivative sideshow to the French Revolution, which Sala-Molins rightly derides, to ridicule the idea of Louverture reading Raynal, and to simplify the complexity of the Enlightenment to the point that it is impossible for those who wish to resist slavery to draw on it in some form? Can we not see the enslaved both as independent political and intellectual actors, inspired by their own experiences and hardly dependent on masters or European administrators for their agency or love of liberty, *and* – precisely because we see them as independent political and intellectual actors – as readers, listeners, thinkers, and generally participants in a broader Enlightenment debate? If we escape the prison of what Sala-Molins rightly calls a 'Franco-centric' approach that sees everything emanating from Paris, is our only choice to run headlong into another interpretive prison – a mirror image – in which there are two worlds, one a corrupt and endlessly hypocritical world of Europe and another a zone of spontaneous liberation in the Caribbean?

What if, instead, we seek to construct a picture of an integrated space of debate over rights, of universalism, over governance and empire? What if we populate this space with different actors, with different perspectives, and admit among the central actors in this story the enslaved, for whom the questions of rights were never only abstract? They, along with the widely recognized colonial free people of colour, were participating in a debate at once profoundly real and inherently theoretical. To understand the Atlantic as an integrated intellectual space is not to succumb to a reading that places Europe at the centre of all intellectual production. Indeed, this integration, I would argue, is the only way to destabilize the still-strong, at times seemingly unmovable, presumption that Europeans and European colonists were the exclusive agents of democratic theorizing. Instead, we might understand more about the complex and contradictory inheritances of the Enlightenment if we explore the possibility that it was crafted not only in Europe but also in the Caribbean. It may then begin to make a bit more sense that what many thinkers of the twentieth century wish to inherit from the Enlightenment – the principle that all human beings, of all colours and origins, are born with natural human rights that they have a right to defend, with force if necessary – is both promulgated and contradicted by the texts we think of as the foundations of modern political thought. Why this disjuncture? Because

– CHAPTER 13: An enslaved Enlightenment –

what we have inherited – particularly ideas of universal rights generally understood as the product of the European Enlightenment – were to a large extent generated by thinkers and actors located not in Europe but on the plantations of the Caribbean.

In addition to 'pluralizing' our idea of what constitutes the Enlightenment, then, we need to revise our sense of where it took place. Over the course of the eighteenth century, particularly during its final decades, there was indeed a space in which powerful theorizations of, and demands for, universal rights were articulated and put into practice, ultimately overthrowing long-standing and brutal forms of repression and tyranny and opening the way for new ways of conceiving of humankind. This space of theorization and debate, however, was an Atlantic one that included the classic texts and debates we understand as constituting the Enlightenment, to be sure, but which was also fundamentally shaped by the actions of individuals, both enslaved and free, who were subjected to the violent forms of racial exclusion that undergirded the imperial systems of the eighteenth century.

In *Colonialism and Science*, James McClellan III provides an analysis of the philosophical and legal activities of wealthy creoles in Saint-Domingue during the eighteenth century. McClellan details the intellectual pursuits of a number of men in Saint-Domingue who, organized around a scientific society called the *Cercle des Philadelphes*, sent the first balloon in the Americas into the sky, carried out horticultural experiments, and debated politics and governance. Some of them, most notably Moreau de Saint-Méry, made important contributions to debates about governance and slavery over the course of the eighteenth century.[15]

In a brilliant analysis of the legal culture of Saint-Domingue in the eighteenth century, Malech Ghachem suggests that the legal activities of free people of colour and the enslaved in the colonies had an influence on the evolution of administrative practice and even the law itself. As in other slave societies, the process of constant negotiation and, sometimes, open conflict between masters and slaves shaped debates over the governing of slavery. This can be seen particularly well in the controversies surrounding the royal reforms in slavery promulgated in 1784 and 1785, and the storm of controversy that ensued. As Ghachem shows, the debates about these reforms took place under the shadow of the threat that slave revolution might well break out. Planters argued that intervention on the part of the state would incite uprisings, while administrators riposted that unchecked violence on the part of masters was sure to lead to the same thing. The actions slaves took to testify and to challenge masters, notably in the famous LeJeune case, allowed them, though of course in very circumscribed ways, to participate in this broader debate.[16]

The enslaved, then, were understood to be potential political actors in late eighteenth-century Saint-Domingue. The danger that revolution might take place – and Ghachem has shown that commentators did in fact use the word 'revolution' – shaped public discourse not only among Enlightenment intellectuals in Paris but also among administrators and planters in the colonies. Although few commentators explored in detail the question of what the slaves were discussing and thinking, there was at least a sense of the possibility that they might emerge as a dangerous political force. Such fears accelerated – and became part of the violent debates over the rights of free people of colour and the question of slavery – after 1789.

The revolutionary context brought about an increased circulation of political tracts as well as rumours of both dreaded and hoped-for events. Many administrators

233

and planters quickly became preoccupied with the question of how information and ideas might influence the actions of slaves. In July 1789 several slave women arriving in French ports were detailed and sent back to the colonies, under the pretext that they might hear or learn things in France that could be dangerous in the colonies. Planter representatives from Saint-Domingue wrote back to the colony in August 1789 recommending that any writings in which the term 'liberty' appeared be seized, and that free people of colour arriving from Europe be intercepted. In September, moreover, the Club Massiac requested that merchants in port towns prevent those of African descent from embarking for the colonies, and received several assurances from captains that they would do so. Measures were taken in Saint-Domingue to control the flow of information: in April 1790 local officials in Le Cap directed the town's postal director 'to stop all arriving or departing letters that are addressed to mulattos or slaves and to deliver these letters to the municipality'. They were to keep this procedure a secret, presumably so that officials could use this surveillance to uncover evidence of sedition or conspiracy.[17]

After the uprising of 1791, such measures were redoubled: the Colonial Assembly of Saint-Domingue responded by passing a 'provisional decree, prohibiting the sale, impression, or distribution of any pieces relative to the politics and revolution of France'. The question of what political ideas had been circulating within slave communities, furthermore, became a focus of a great deal of polemic in writings and debates about the insurrection. Many writers claimed that the ideas of Enlightenment anti-slavery, as well as the various documents and ideologies that emerged through the French Revolution, had incited the uprising. The planter Félix Carteau famously wrote in a memoir that slaves learned of revolutionary ideals through pamphlets, engravings and conversations between slaves and sailors working together on the docks. Carteau claimed he had seen abolitionist texts 'among the hands of some Negroes'; and though few of them could read, 'all it took among the slaves of a plantation was one who could read to the others, as the plots were being formed, to give them proof of how much they were pitied in France, and how much people wanted them to free themselves of the terrible yoke of their pitiless masters'. The fact that most slaves could not read obviously did not mean that they could not hear, transmit and respond to ideas present in written texts circulating in the colony. Indeed, by writing that the abolitionist texts slaves read provided 'proof' to slaves of 'how much they were pitied in France', Carteau suggests that they had already heard information about European abolitionism through the spoken word. Carteau also emphasized the powerful role abolitionist images might play among the enslaved, blaming anti-slavery activists for having disseminated 'among the Negroes of the Colony many books that showed pity for their fate, and many similar engravings'. Slaves, he wrote, only had to open their eyes 'and listen to the interpretation of the subject, which was repeated from mouth to mouth', in order to understand that across the Atlantic there were those who would support them if they revolted.[18]

It is tempting, and reasonable, to dismiss writings blaming abolitionists for having stirred up revolution in the Caribbean as part of a broader set of reflexes of denial that made independent slave action unimaginable to most European writers. But in doing so we overlook an interesting admission that is made by these admittedly hostile observers: in blaming European abolitionists for slave action, they perhaps unwittingly portrayed the slaves as both interpreters of texts and political actors engaged in the

– CHAPTER 13: *An enslaved Enlightenment* –

pursuit of alliance and support. This is particularly clear in the writings of some who blamed not simply abolitionists but the culture of the Enlightenment as a whole for having set off the slave revolt. In order to make this argument, they implicitly had to accept that slaves had been influenced by, and responded to, the intellectual currents of eighteenth-century thought. Writers such as Carteau, and others, clearly understood that, even if the enslaved could not read, they could hear about and exchange news and ideas orally. Planters and administrators also clearly acknowledged through their writings and their actions that slaves were responding to the broader debates about slavery and governance that were taking place in the Atlantic world.[19]

Of course, the interpretations and trading of accusations on the part of planters, abolitionists and administrators about the causes of slave revolution – while they can suggest to us the contours of the debates within slave communities – can take us only so far into the mental world of the insurgents of Saint-Domingue. What other routes are there? Once the insurrection began, the insurgent leaders produced a number of documents that issued demands and sought to negotiate a variety of outcomes with the French administration. White prisoners, some of whom were used as secretaries, produced accounts of their time among insurgent camps that nevertheless provide us with important insights into the debates within these camps; and political symbols whose meaning we can seek to interpret were used by insurgents.[20]

One debate regarding the politics of insurrection in Saint-Domingue has revolved around the seeming contradiction between the use of royalist and republican symbols on the part of insurgents. In presenting themselves and articulating their demands, insurgents sometimes made reference to the discourses of republicanism, particularly the Declaration of the Rights of Man, but more often they made use of royalist symbols. Rather than signifying a fragmented or contradictory set of political ideologies, however, the cohabitation of these forms provides us with an entry into the particularities of the Caribbean political culture embodied in the slave revolution of 1791–93. Indeed, to analyse the political culture of the insurgents in terms of dichotomies defined according to the specific European political context of the time is to obscure the complex realities of the Caribbean political context. Both royalist and republican discourses were deployed, indeed subsumed, by insurgents in the articulation of their central goal: a reform and, eventually, an abolition of slavery. By laying claim both on the authority of the king and on the promises of republican rights emanating from the evolving metropolitan power structure, slave insurgents intervened in a long-standing conflict between colonial planters and the metropolitan administration, taking advantage of a new virulence in this conflict, and ultimately deepening it.[21]

The king served as a gathering point for demands for abolition because, in the context of colonial politics, he was seen as a counter-weight to the planters, primarily because of the important attempts at reforming slavery issued in 1784 and 1785. These royal actions incited widespread and vociferous opposition on the part of planters, and their angry conversations about them would have provided one way for the enslaved to learn about them. In these reforms, the king was presented quite forcefully as a friend and defender of the slaves. The articles on the reforms were all issued directly from the authority of 'His Majesty'. One article, for instance, declared strongly that in cases where managers of masters killed one of their slaves, the king 'wished them to be' pursued as 'murderers'. The reforms, furthermore, promised changes that would have had a great impact on the daily lives of slaves, particularly by securing for them both the right to cultivate their own garden plots and the right to receive food from their masters or managers. Had these reforms been followed, the amount of profit slaves could have gained from their own work would have increased.[22]

Evocations of the king were often combined quite comfortably with the use of republican symbols by insurgents, who often evoked both the king and the National Assembly as authorities whom they hoped would hear their demands. Georges Biassou, for instance, wrote in late 1791 of his willingness 'to serve his King, the nation and its representatives'. This was logical enough, since at the time both were centres of authority in Paris. But the combination of royalist and republican symbols continued into 1793, when one insurgent flew a tricolor flag decorated with *fleur-de-lys*. Over the course of 1793, however, as the conflict between republicanism and royalism became superimposed in a clearer way onto the conflict between pro-slavery masters and sympathetic republican administrators, many insurgents came to throw in their lot with the republic and embrace its symbols.[23]

As for the language of rights, and the broader Enlightenment context out of which it emerged, there are several reports that describe insurgents demanding their 'rights' when asked what they were pursuing. One group, when questioned shortly after the beginning of the insurrection, apparently stated that 'they wanted to enjoy the liberty they are entitled to by the Rights of Man'. There are other reflections of the circulation of Enlightenment ideas, too, notably in letters sent by Jean-François and Biassou to local administrators in late 1791 in which the term 'general will' was used in referring to the demands of the 'multitude' of African slaves who made up the majority in the insurgent camps. The term may, of course, have been the addition of the white secretary who seems to have written these letters. There is no way to rule this out, but it is worth at least allowing for the possibility that the insurgents themselves might have found this a useful concept in laying out what they wished written in the letters their secretaries penned for them.[24]

Acknowledging the place of a republican language of rights in insurgent discourse does not mean, as I have already suggested above, interpreting the revolution in Saint-Domingue as the result of the 'contagion' of republican ideas. Although this is an enticing intellectual habit – one that curiously ties together planter idealogues with some current interpretations of the revolution – the crucial point is not that ideas from Europe might have inspired insurgents in Saint-Domingue but that insurgents in Saint-Domingue made use of, and profoundly transformed, the very meaning of republicanism. Caribbean political culture was as much a part of the formation of what we consider republican political culture as it was an inheritor of it. Insurgents in the Caribbean, in effect, generated new strands of discourse that were, like all discourse, both embedded and in tension with the web from which they emerged. That many of the texts that Sala-Molins and others have rightly deconstructed for their racism and hypocrisy – the *Code Noir* and the writings of *philosophes* – were at times evoked and used by insurgents in pursuit of liberation in the Caribbean suggests not that this revolution was derivative but that it was a zone of engagement and debate with broader discourses. That the king could be invoked as a protector of slaves, because royal codes had been presented as such by the French administration and lambasted as interventionist by planters, shows not a lack of understanding on the part of the enslaved but a sense of the power and possibility of political symbolism. That the Enlightenment arguments for rights were taken up and the justifications for

– CHAPTER 13: *An enslaved Enlightenment* –

leaving Africans out of them were left behind shows precisely that insurgents in the Caribbean were not imprisoned by someone else's interpretation of them.

The centrality of Caribbean insurgents in shaping the ultimate meaning of Enlightenment discourses is particularly clear if we follow the chronology from 1791 to 1794, and acknowledge that the pinnacle of republicanism during the era of the French Revolution was the decree abolishing slavery and granting citizenship to all people, of all colours. The evolution of insurgent political ideologies in the years after 1791 was a varied and complex process, one that took a different course in each province of the colony and even in each group of insurgents. As Carolyn Fick has examined in detail, the demands made expanded from more reformist calls, including the abolition of the whip and the granting of three free days per week, to more radical demands for an end to slavery itself. Michel Rolph Trouillot has argued that the revolution 'thought itself out politically and philosophically as it was taking place' in a process where 'discourse always lagged behind practice'. It is certainly true that the revolutionary transformations opened up new spaces for the political imagination, created new contexts for free debate and the exchange of ideas, and infused many with a sense of exuberant possibility that may have been rare indeed in a world dominated by a seemingly unmovable institution of slavery. But I would add that pre-revolutionary political discourse among slaves may have been more complex than we might generally assume, sustained by the decades of conversations and debates tied to choices made on and off the plantations. As the enslaved had sought openings within the legal system, for example, they necessarily engaged a key strand of political discourse: legal reasoning.[25]

The central point about this political evolution, of course, is that it was sustained and accelerated by a powerful military force constituted by the insurgent armies. Because of this, the evolution of the tactics and ideological justifications presented by metropolitan commissioners like Sonthonax and Polverel must be seen primarily as the product of a response to, and negotiation with, the insurgent political force represented by men like Jean-François, Biassou and Louverture, but also Pierrot, Macaya, Sans-Souci and many others. Their ultimate choices were, of course, inflected by the agenda of the Spanish officers who supported these insurgents for a time, but even there the Spanish were clearly never in control of what they wishfully called their 'auxiliaries', as David Geggus has noted. In other words, having won territorial control over parts of Saint-Domingue through their military exploits, the insurgents were able to gain ideological control over the process that led to the dramatic abolition of slavery in 1793 in Saint-Domingue and in 1794 throughout the French empire.[26]

Perhaps the most difficult part of understanding this process, however, is the task of seeking to understand the role of political ideologies that drew on the home traditions of the African-born people who made up a majority in Saint-Domingue at the time of the revolution. Pioneering work in this regard has been done by John Thornton, who has argued provocatively that the Kongo can be seen as as much a fount of intellectual resources for the revolution as metropolitan France. At the same time, David Geggus has warned, the problem of avoiding 'the twin perils of exoticizing or occidentalizing the slaves' and imagining the 'attitudes and beliefs of those Africans and children of Africans of two centuries ago' is an 'intractable' one. Obviously, the first challenge is reconstructing as precisely as possible the varied and contested political strands that were shaping political life in West and Central Africa during the latter half of the eighteenth century. This, however, is not enough, since we must also come to understand how these political ideologies were transplanted and transformed as they confronted the very particular situation of plantation slavery as it existed in Saint-Domingue at the time. To put it another way, we must ask ourselves: would we recognize an 'African' political ideology if we saw one? Would it be possible to distinguish it from one rooted in 'European' traditions, or from the complex strands of Caribbean political thought emerging from within the plantation complex? Here a constant questioning of categories is in order, for to begin truly to grasp the intellectual history of the eighteenth-century Caribbean we must understand the layering of transformations and translations, rooted in Africa, Europe and the Americas, that produced it.[27]

What if, as we sought to understand the history of universalism in the Atlantic world, we could tell an integrated story that goes something like this: the discovery of the Americas generated a space for new ways of thinking about humanity and natural rights, and out of encounters between Native Americans, Africans and Europeans there emerged new ways of thinking about belonging, governance, subjecthood and, eventually, citizenship. These new ways of thinking may have been written down overwhelmingly by the educated elites in Europe and the colonies, yet they drew on the circulation of meanings and ideas in which those who were not literate participated; through their labour but also through their resistance – both in actions and in speech – enslaved peoples in the Atlantic world both generated problems of governance and began to propose new solutions by insisting on their own dignity and denying the justifications issued for their enslavement; as thinkers in Europe argued against slavery and for the primacy of natural rights, drawing on this broader context of which they were a part, they in turn influenced colonial administrators who witnessed the actions and sufferings of the enslaved, who saw and heard them, and who in turn produced new interpretations that emphasized the need for limits on the power of masters and for abuse; these reformist tendencies, though certainly limited in scope and ultimately aimed at preserving colonial production and societies in which people of African descent were viewed primarily as sources of labour, nevertheless opened up windows and possibilities for change; in and through these decades of debate in France there was a parallel set of debates in communities of the enslaved on both sides of the Atlantic, about tactics but also about ideas; together, these debates laid the foundations for the intellectual and political explosion that would take place during the 1790s in the Caribbean.

One could then, perhaps, go one step further and argue that this explosion generated what we view today as the true thinking of the Enlightenment – a concrete and radical universalism that overthrew profit for principle and defended human rights against the weapons of empire and the arguments of racial hierarchy. This advance, unsurprisingly, was met with hostility and with reaction; its victory was turned back in some ways; and it became saturated with many of the contradictions that infused the thinking of the Enlightenment itself. But precisely this process of reaction, the combination of planter nightmares and slave hopes, played out in crucial ways during the next decades to lead to other phases of liberation, followed by other phases of reaction, a cycle in which we still reside.

What if we took up the task of writing such a story – or one like it? Actually doing so, of course, is more difficult than simply envisioning it, but incorporating silence and subordinated voices into our broader narrative may enable us to tell a better history

– CHAPTER 13: *An enslaved Enlightenment* –

– one more grounded in the integrated political and intellectual reality of the Atlantic world – of the ideas and practices surrounding universalism and human rights.

NOTES

I wish to thank Christopher Schmidt-Nowara for inviting me to write on the topic of slavery and the Enlightenment, and both him and the editors of *Social History* for their helpful comments on the article. The ideas presented here have been profoundly shaped by the work of, discussions with, and comments by Julius Scott and Rebecca Scott. Earlier versions of this article were presented at the Colloquium of the Interdisciplinary Program in Anthropology and History at the University of Michigan in January 2005, at the conference 'L'expérience coloniale: Dynamiques des échanges dans les espaces Atlantiques à l'époque de l'esclavage' in Nantes in June 2005, and at the conference 'Atlantic History: Soundings' at Harvard University in August 2005. My thanks to the participants at all these events for their comments, particularly Ira Berlin, Chandra Bhimull, Douglas Chambers, David William Cohen, Myriam Cottias, Alejandro de la Fuente, Dena Goodman, Jean Hébrard, David Pedersen, Emma Rothschild and Stuart Schwartz.

1 Michèle Duchet, *Anthropologie et histoire au siècle des lumières* (Paris, 1971).
2 This work went through a large number of editions in the late eighteenth century in French, and parts were also published in English translation: Guillaume Thomas François Raynal, *A Philosophical and Political History of the Settlements and Trade of the Europeans in the East and West Indies*, trans. John Justamond (London, 1783).
3 Duchet, op. cit., 145.
4 Ibid., 139.
5 Hillary Beckles, 'Caribbean Anti-slavery: The Self-liberation Ethos of Enslaved Blacks', *Journal of Caribbean History*, XXII, 1 & 2 (1988), 1–19. Among the many contributions to the history of political thought in enslaved communities is C. L. R. James's *The Black Jacobins* (New York, 1963), to which this article owes an obvious debt, as well as Emilia Viotti da Costa, *Crowns of Glory, Tears of Blood: The Dememara Slave Rebellion of 1823* (Oxford, 1994); David Barry Gaspar, *Bondsmen and Rebels: A Study of Master–Slave Relations in Antigua* (Durham, 1993); and Steven Hahn, *A Nation Under Our Feet* (Cambridge, 2003). I have attempted to detail the intellectual and political currents in the revolutionary French Caribbean, particularly Guadeloupe, in *A Colony of Citizens: Revolution and Slave Emancipation in the French Caribbean, 1787–1804* (Chapel Hill, 2004).
6 Sankar Muthu, *Enlightenment Against Empire* (Princeton, 2003), 1–2 and Conclusion; see also Emmanuel Chukwudi Eze, *Race and the Enlightenment: A Reader* (Cambridge, 1997), 1–2. The foundation work on circuits of news in the Atlantic is Julius Scott, 'The Common Wind: Currents of Afro-American Communication in the Era of the Haitian Revolution' (Ph.D. dissertation, Duke University, 1986); see also Peter Linebaugh and Marcus Rediker, *The Many-Headed Hydra: The Hidden History of the Revolutionary Atlantic* (Boston, 2000).
7 The same is true, of course, of other contexts in which enslaved peoples played important military and political roles in struggles for liberation, such as the wars of independence in Latin America. On this see, for instance, Peter Blanchard, 'The Language of Liberation: Slave Voices in the Wars of Independence', *Hispanic American Historical Review*, LXXXII, 3 (2002), 499–523.
8 Louis Sala-Molins, *Le Code Noir; ou, la calvaire de Canaan* (Paris, 1987) and *Les Misères des Lumières: sous la raison, l'outrage* (Paris, 1992); Laurent Estève, *Montesquieu, Rousseau, Diderot: du genre humain au bois d'ébène* (Paris, 2002). The broadest treatment of how Enlightenment writers in France, including novelists and playwrights, dealt with

the question of slavery remains Edward Seeber, *Anti-Slavery Opinion in France during the Second Half of the Eighteenth Century* (Baltimore, 1937).

9 Estève, op. cit., 30–34, 153; on Buffon see also Duchet, op. cit., part II, chap. 1.

10 Sala-Molins, *Le Code Noir*, op. cit., 241, 249, 254; Estève, op. cit., 163–202, quote 178, n.455.

11 Muthu, op. cit., 66–67, 109, 299, n.26.

12 Estève, op. cit., 205, 210, 255–56; on Condorcet see Sala-Molins, *Les misères*, op. cit., chap. 1; I present an examination of Condorcet, and link up the contradictions in his thought to the 'Republican racism' of post-emancipation administrators in the revolutionary French Caribbean, in Dubois, op. cit., chap. 6.

13 Sala-Molins, *Les misères*, op. cit., 14, 17.

14 Ibid., 158–60.

15 James E. McClellan III, *Colonialism and Science: Saint Domingue in the Old Regime* (Baltimore, 1992).

16 Malech Walid Ghachem, 'Sovereignty and Slavery in the Age of Revolution: Haitian Variations on a Metropolitan Theme' (Ph.D. dissertation, Stanford University, 2001). On the influence of Enlightenment ideas on legal decisions in another context see Colin Maclachan, 'Slavery, Ideology and Institutional Change: The Impact of Enlightenment on Slavery in Late Eighteenth-century Maranhao', *Journal of Latin American Studies* XI, 1 (May 1979), 1–17.

17 Gabriel Debien, *Les colons de Saint-Domingue et la Révolution: Essai sur le Club Massiac* (Paris, 1951), 97, 158–59; Mitchell Bennett Garrett, *The French Colonial Question, 1789–91* (Ann Arbor, 1916), 23; Chaela Pastore, 'Merchant Voyages: Michel Marsaudon and the Exchange of Colonialism in Saint-Domingue, 1788–94' (Ph.D. dissertation, Berkeley, 2001), 59.

18 *Philadelphia General Advertiser*, 322 (11 October 1791); Félix Carteau, *Soirées Bermudiennes, ou entretiens sur les événements qui ont opéré la ruine de la partie française de l'isle Saint-Domingue* (Bordeaux, 1802), 75–76.

19 For two examples of writers who blamed the Enlightenment for the revolt, see the poem in *Moniteur général de la partie française de Saint-Domingue* I, 1 (15 November 1791), 1; and Antoine Dalmas, *Histoire de la Révolution de Saint-Domingue* (Paris, 1814), vol. I, 159.

20 For a good analysis of one important prisoner's narrative, that of Gros, see Jeremy Popkin, 'Facing Racial Revolution: Captivity Narratives and Identity in the Saint-Domingue Insurrection', *Eighteenth-Century Studies*, XXXVI, 4 (2003), 511–33.

21 On this, in the following paragraphs I draw on a more extended argument about insurgent ideology I have presented in '"Our Three Colors": The King, the Republic and the Political Culture of Slave Revolution in Saint-Domingue', *Historical Reflections/Réflexions Historiques*, XXIX, 1 (Spring 2003), 83–102; and *Avengers of the New World: The Story of the Haitian Revolution* (Cambridge, 2004), chaps 4 and 5.

22 A copy of the royal reforms is available within the 'Mémoire rélatif à l'ordonnance du 4 Décembre 1784 sur les gérens [sic] et la police des noirs', Beineke Rare Books Library, Documents Relating to the French Participation in the American Revolution, Gen MSS 308, Box 1, Series III, Folder 32. On the importance of these reforms for slaves, see Carolyn Fick, 'Emancipation in Haiti: From Plantation Labour to Peasant Proprietorship', *Slavery and Abolition*, XXI, 2 (August 2000), 11–40 and Ghachem, op. cit.

23 Biassou to Commissioners, 23 December 1791, AN DXXV 1, Folder 4, No. 20; Moniteur générale...de Saint-Domingue III, 104 (28 February 1793), 419.

24 See *Philadelphia General Advertiser*, 321, 322 and 349 for examples of the use of a language of rights by insurgents; Jean-François and Biassou to the Commissioners, Archives Nationales, DXXV 1, Folder 4, No. 6.

– CHAPTER 13: *An enslaved Enlightenment* –

25 Carolyn Fick, *The Making of Haiti: The Saint-Domingue Revolution from Below* (Knoxville, 1990), provides an excellent account of the evolution of insurgent tactics and demands; see also Michel Rolph Trouillot, *Silencing the Past: Power and the Production of History* (Boston, 1995), 89; a recent addition to our knowledge of this evolution is a paper by Yves Benot, 'La parole des esclaves insurgés de 1791–92: indépendance immédiate!' presented at 'La traite, l'esclavage colonial, la Révolution de Saint-Domingue et les droits de l'homme', UQAM, Montréal, 4–5 March 2004.

26 David Geggus, 'The Arming of Slaves during the Haitian Revolution', in P. Morgan and C. Brown (eds), *The Arming of Slaves in World History* (New Haven, 2006), 209–32. I emphasize and explore the important contributions of Caribbean insurgents to the broader discourse of universalism in *A Colony of Citizens*, op. cit.

27 David Geggus, *Haitian Revolutionary Studies* (Bloomington, 2002), 42; John Thornton, 'I Am the Subject of the King of Kongo: African Political Ideology and the Haitian Revolution', *Journal of World History*, IV (Fall 1993), 181–214.

PART IV
WARFARE AND GOVERNANCE

CHAPTER FOURTEEN

VIOLENCE IN THE ATLANTIC WORLD

—·◆·—

John Smolenski

Where did colonial Atlantic cultures come from? This question has animated many of the longest running scholarly debates about the history of the Americas. Historians of Anglo-America have written both of European 'seeds' shaping colonial cultures and of the transforming power of the frontier.[1] Scholars of Afro-Atlantic cultures have pondered the enduring strength of African 'survivals' in the face of the horror that was plantation slavery.[2] Latin Americanist anthropologists have examined how a Spanish 'culture of conquest' crystallized in a colonial order and how conquest ruptured the pre-colonial past and created a *mestizo* imaginary.[3] These debates have waxed and waned, with scholars in each respective field showing greater or lesser interest over time. Crucially, however, they have seldom talked to each other, confining their arguments to interlocutors within their own area of specialty. This tendency – entirely understandable, given the immense complexity of colonial Atlantic history and the dizzying amount of scholarly literature produced on the topic – has unfortunately made it difficult to see common themes across the whole. The big question – where did colonial Atlantic cultures come from? – has devolved into many smaller ones, to the detriment of scholars working in all subfields of colonial Atlantic history.

I propose here to explore the question through a thematic, rather than geographic, approach. Seeking origins in process rather than place, I contend in this essay that violence played a determinative, perhaps even *the* determinative, role in creating Atlantic cultures. It facilitated linkages among Europe, the Americas, and Africa. It shaped the development of local colonial cultures on these different continents. In other words, it helped make and remake Atlantic worlds and *the* Atlantic world over and over again from the fifteenth through the eighteenth centuries.

The argument here requires establishing some definitions. *Violence* here refers to the infliction of pain, whether physical or psychological, or coercion through the threat of violence, whether implicitly or explicitly stated. It includes war, juridically imposed forms of punishment, and forms of 'private' coercion, such as labor discipline or sexual assault.[4] *Culture* here is treated as both socially learned sets of practices, and the public meanings ascribed to these practices as they circulated through a given community or communities.[5] The usage of *Atlantic* draws from David Armitage's useful delineation of 'three concepts of Atlantic history': *circum*-Atlantic, to describe transnational history; *trans*-Atlantic, to describe international history; and *cis*-Atlantic, to describe local histories framed in a wider Atlantic context.[6] Though intended to be suggestive rather than comprehensive or conclusive, this essay aims to highlight the mutually constitutive relationship between culture and violence in generating trans-Atlantic ties and cis-Atlantic cultures (with a brief discussion of circum-Atlantic trends), in the hopes of outlining a common history of violence and culture in the colonial Atlantic world. Let me begin by looking at the cultural foundations of trans-Atlantic exploration and colonization.

* * *

Colonial discourses of conquest played a central role in the creation of trans-Atlantic connections in the early modern period. Indeed, one might say that they almost preceded Atlantic colonization itself. Ideologies of chivalry and crusade motivated Iberian explorers and conquerors in the Canaries, Azores, Madeira, and Cape Verde Islands in the fourteenth and fifteenth centuries.[7] Portuguese authors celebrated victories over Muslim opponents in northern Africa; the royal chronicler Gomes Eanes de Zuara wrote with pride about priests celebrating mass in the main mosque in Ceuta after that city had fallen in 1415 to Portuguese forces.[8] Though Portuguese explorers traveling along the west African coast did not attempt to conquer the kingdoms they encountered in the fifteenth century, they nonetheless sought to expand the Christian faith on their travels. They achieved their greatest success in 1491 when the Kongolese ruler Nzinga a Nkuwu accepted Christian baptism and adopted the name João I, honoring the Portuguese monarch.[9]

Meanwhile, the so-called '*Reconquista*' – that centuries-long Christian struggle to expel Muslim kingdoms from the Iberian peninsula – captured the imagination of Spanish soldiers and rulers. By the time Christopher Columbus arrived in the 'Indies' in 1492, he had already been conditioned to see this trans-Atlantic voyage in terms of this on-going Christian crusade. Indeed, as Stephen Greenblatt has noted, Columbus referred to his landfall in these new islands as a great victory. His choice of 'a phrase more appropriate in 1492 to the conquest of Granada than to landfall in the Caribbean' showed the impact of this crusading ideology on the Genoese navigator.[10] Both the Portuguese and the Spanish crowns saw their overseas endeavors as latter-day variations of the Roman empire, Renaissance heirs to this ancient tradition but empowered by a new, Christian Rome.[11]

Iberians were not the only ones possessed of this chivalric spirit.[12] English explorers also saw their overseas endeavors as crusades of their own sort. Sir Francis Drake's swashbuckling attacks on Spanish enemies furthered the nation's glory but also represented Protestant strikes against a spreading Catholic menace. Epic tales of Drake's endeavors inspired Englishmen for decades thereafter.[13] Richard Haklyut, England's greatest colonial promoter, believed that the crown should fund overseas exploration 'to plant Christian Religion,' 'to trafficke,' and 'to conquer.' In each case, English colonizers would have to contend with Spanish rivals as well as indigenous peoples.[14] As literary scholar Michael Warner has noted, these epics and promotional writings represented the first 'Anglo-American' literature, emerging in England before the first attempts to establish overseas settlements and predating the establishment of

– CHAPTER 14: *Violence in the Atlantic World* –

permanent American colonies by decades.[15] These fantasies of conquest acted as models of and models for North American colonization.[16]

Moreover, for Europeans of various stripes, stories of American colonization acted as tools of self-definition. Imperial powers justified their endeavors through comparison with other countries. For the Jesuit theologian José de Acosta, colonial expansion was part of a grand providential story in which God had intended the Spanish to use American gold and silver to fight 'infidel' Muslims and 'heretic' Protestants.[17] For the Dutch, denunciations of Spanish depredations against Native Americans closely mirrored cries of outrage against Hapsburg attempts to quash rebellion in the Netherlands; this 'black legend' of Spanish perfidy stood in sharp contrast to Dutch dealings with Indian peoples in the Americas.[18] The English, meanwhile, focused on two types of cruelty when writing about their imperial rivals: the cruelty Spanish conquistadors inflicted upon Native Americans and that which Dutch soldiers inflicted upon English colonizers. They became critics of victimization and victims themselves.[19] In all of these cases, though, these charges and counter charges affirmed the moral superiority of Spanish, Dutch, or English colonization, respectively; all that differed was the nationality of the one telling the tale. In a very real sense, condemnations of other European nations became stories they told themselves about themselves, authorizing continued American colonization.[20]

Of course, the opening of American colonization spurred the elaboration of other forms of colonial discourse as well: legal narratives of intrusion legitimating the dispossession of indigenous peoples and the assertion of sovereignty over them. Spanish jurists first pointed to a 1493 papal donation granting them the Americas, but developed more elaborate theories as the sixteenth century went on. Francisco de Vitora and Juan Ginés de Sepúlveda took pains to show that Native American societies failed to follow natural law, rendering them incapable of self-governance and fit to be governed by the Spanish crown. English promoters, meanwhile, rejected these claims, not least because they denied the authority of the pope to award lands to Catholic princes. Instead, they declared the Americas *terra nullius*, uninhabited land over which Europeans could extend their authority. Though this required a certain amount of intellectual gymnastics, including the assertion that since indigenous peoples seemingly lacked private land ownership, they therefore lacked sovereignty over American territory, it nonetheless provided at least a patina of authority.[21]

Upon settling in the Americas, European powers relied on a variety of different rituals to take possession of the land and peoples they encountered. All sought to convince indigenous rulers to cede power diplomatically, whether through voluntary surrender (as Hernán Cortés claimed the Mexica ruler Moctezuma had done), willing subordination to a European monarch (as when the Powhatan paramount chief Wahunsonacock 'allowed' Christopher Newport to crown him as a vassal of King James), or ceremonies that established colonizers as superior partners in a European–Indian alliance.[22] Spaniards read before any military attack a *Requerimiento* intended to give native peoples the opportunity to submit to authority of pope and crown or be conquered by force. English settlers built houses, planted gardens, and fenced in farms to mark 'empty' lands as their own. These rituals enacted the legal justifications for conquest and dispossession countless times from the sixteenth through the eighteenth centuries. They proclaimed the legitimacy of colonial settlement to one's compatriots, rival European powers, and native peoples.[23]

That colonizers developed somewhat dense explanations of the nature of conquest should not perhaps be surprising. Writing about the creation of the production of cultural authority, anthropologist Greg Urban argues that there is nothing inherent in any culture that allows it to claim superiority over any other. Culture, he writes, 'is inert. It contains no force that would cause it to spread, to perpetuate itself, in the face of resistance in the form of alternatives.' The motive force that would allow a claim to authority over other cultures or peoples, he continues, can only come from arguing *about* culture; this force is, in a word, metacultural.[24] In the Atlantic world, European narratives of identity and destiny – the stories they told themselves about themselves – helped create national imperial cultures. Narratives of legality acted as metacultural commentaries on these imperial stories, allowing particular European powers to claim theirs as the legitimate sovereignty. And the rituals of possession made these imperial narratives and metacultural justifications 'true,' even as violence frequently played a significant, if not always acknowledged, role in the rituals themselves.

And yet, the reality proved more complicated. Spanish jurists intended the *Requerimiento* to be a performative text, one whose utterance instantiated new social relationships.[25] Supposedly, its reading instantly transformed alien peoples – the indigenous inhabitants of the Americas – into either vassals or enemies. But as contemporary critics recognized, the linguistic gap that existed between Spaniards and Indians prevented the latter from even understanding the text, let alone complying with its requirements. Violence, under the guise of legality, was inevitable. Conquering Spaniards may have wanted to do things with words; they ended up saying things with wars.[26]

English claims to authority faced similar dilemmas. Colonizers did more than deny Indians' collective ownership of land as sovereign territory. They similarly denied native ownership of land as private property, suggesting that the 'wilderness' was *vacuum domicilium*, vacant land ripe for the taking. Such beliefs, however, reflected a fundamental misunderstanding of Indian conceptions of territorial sovereignty and land use. English colonizers – and their governments – persistently missed the ways in which Indian nations read the boundaries of their political communities on the landscape. They also failed to see how native farmers and hunters actually used supposedly 'empty' lands. The English believed their building, fencing, and planting to be assertions of mastery that made space, culture, and sovereignty isomorphic. But their supposedly transparent forms of taking possession of the land were anything but, leading to confusion and conflict during the first decades of colonization, especially as they used violence, implied or otherwise, to ensconce their values into law.[27]

Native Americans adapted to English ceremonies of possession in many regions of North America, adopting animal husbandry and European modes of agriculture. Wampanoag leader Metacom (known to Anglo-New Englanders as 'King Philip') became a 'keeper of swine,' domesticating animals for protein and profit. He even proved willing to use colonial courts to defend his interests against rival claimants. His fellow Wampanoags on the island of Martha's Vineyard, off the coast of Massachusetts, did likewise.[28] In some respects, this represented a triumph of colonial codes (using the word in both a cultural and legal sense), as English ways of living in the landscape took predominance. But it also helped sustain Indian communities in the face of English encroachment. What might have appeared as Indian acculturation was instead part of a process of transculturation in which indigenous peoples in New

– CHAPTER 14: *Violence in the Atlantic World* –

England integrated aspects of English life into their own society, but for native ends and to sustain native economic and political power.[29]

Indeed, Anglo-American colonizers in New England saw these changes in Indian communities as threat more than triumph. Settlers' responses revealed the seriousness of the challenge: having justified their claims to 'waste' lands on the grounds that Indians had done nothing to improve (and thus possess) them, some colonists threatened violence when faced with Indian fences marking the boundaries of Native lands.[30] Anglo-American courts frequently upheld the claims of English farmers while denying those of Indian ones, making the legal system a tool of colonization. Such problems contributed to the outbreak of one of the bloodiest wars in colonial Anglo-America, King Philip's War. This war, which spanned 1675 and 1676, came after decades of tension over land use, years in which indigenous peoples tried to incorporate some English values into their way of life. As one historian has noted, Metacom launched the war, in some respects, 'on behalf of cooperation,' upset about the passing of the rough harmony that had existed.[31] English colonizers, then, needed violence to make their narratives of conquest and the practices through which they enacted these narratives fit together. Violence helped them believe the stories they told themselves about themselves.[32]

Nowhere was the reciprocal relationship between violence and the formation of trans-Atlantic cultures more apparent than in wars between colonizers and natives. Violence in the colonial Americas, like violence everywhere, proved 'a vivid expression of culture values,' freighted with symbolic meaning. Conceptions of which forms of violence were appropriate (and when), and who could be fit objects of appropriate violence were culturally bounded. Conflicts between Spaniards and Mexica during the siege of Tenochtitlan, between Dutch and Indian nations in New Netherlands during Kieft's War, and England and Wampanoag and Narragansett Indians in King Philip's War in New England witnessed a similar phenomenon: revulsion at Indian styles of warfare – and the resultant belief that this kind of unrestrained violence placed natives outside the bounds of civilized society – encouraged European soldiers to resort to early modern variations of 'total war.'[33] Conceptions of violence thus helped reinforce cultural boundaries through the construction of what Michael Taussig has called 'the colonial mirror which reflects back onto the colonists the barbarity of their own social relations, but as imputed to the savage or evil figures they wish to colonize.'[34] Put another way, these colonial wars helped make true the narratives of conquest that played a role in driving overseas expansion.

These conflicts generated literary responses that attempted to explain, and contain, colonial violence. Cortés's 'Letters of Relation,' detailing his exploits to Emperor Charles V, declared that 'no race, however savage, has ever practiced such fierce and unnatural cruelty, as the natives of these parts.' First published in 1522, Cortés's writings inaugurated a new genre of Spanish chronicles celebrating American conquests.[35] Meanwhile, King Philip's War prompted much soul searching – quite literally – among Anglo-Americans in New England, leading them to question, then reaffirm, their covenant with God. In the end, they felt secure that their behavior during the war had been justified and that they had shown themselves superior to 'savage' Indians and the cruel Spanish of the 'Black Legend.'[36] Even where Europeans denounced the violence of colonial wars, they did so in terms that fit with the national narratives that justified imperial expansion, as when Dutch authors condemned

William Kieft, Governor of New Netherlands, for demonstrating a capacity for viciousness that matched that shown by the Spanish in their wars in the Low Country and the Americas.[37] These chronicles, polemics, histories, and denunciations all acted as metacultural glosses that helped trans-Atlantic colonial cultures take root in the Americas. In doing so, they enabled imperial expansion.

In this light, Urban's assertion that cultural authority emerges only through metacultural argument about culture leads to a disturbing conclusion. 'Violence,' he notes, 'is metacultural and, indeed, may be a fundamental manifestation of metaculture.'[38] Historically, culture and violence had a symbiotic relationship in the colonial Atlantic – perhaps even more so because the definitions and boundaries of cultural authority were so unclear as European powers tried to establish (and maintain) their rule. Colonial violence helped create a 'space of death' that was, in Taussig's words, 'one of the crucial spaces where Indian, African, and white gave birth to the New World.'[39]

* * *

These trans-Atlantic histories unfolded within a broader system of exchange, conquest, and context. The creation of an increasingly integrated Atlantic system accelerated the movement of peoples and goods within and among four continents, drawn from societies along the littoral. Local communities became enmeshed in translocal flows. Emerging networks of violence, some of which built on preexisting patterns, played a crucial role in this process. Understanding the reciprocal relationship between violence and culture in particular cis-Atlantic histories – local stories framed in an Atlantic context – requires an exploration of the relationship between violence and culture in particular circum-Atlantic histories.

The history of slavery in the colonial Atlantic provides the best example of these Atlantic changes. Slavery in western Africa predated the arrival of Europeans in the fifteenth century. Africans acquired slaves through warfare, judicial punishment, or self-sale (though the last was extremely rare). But if slavery was omnipresent, it was not the defining element of society. Kinship and lineage determined social structure; elders controlled the means of production and divisions of age and sex mattered more than the line between slave and free. Slaves worked in a wide variety of different occupations, rather than being confined to a single social stratum. Moreover, slavery existed as one system of dependency among others, albeit the most extreme form. Only slaves could be bought and sold, but others – including junior kin or individuals held in pawnshop – had their labor controlled by others.[40] The slave trade predated the arrival of Europeans as well. West Africa occupied one end of a trans-Saharan slave trade from the seventh century on. Muslim traders, prohibited from enslaving their coreligionists, purchased and shipped west African slaves as far east as the Indian Ocean. Nearly one million slaves went east in this trade between 1400 and 1600 – approximately as many as went west across the Atlantic during the fifteenth, sixteenth, and seventeenth centuries.[41]

The opening of an Atlantic world, however, wrought several changes. First, it changed *how* slaves were acquired. Military enslavement continued to be the most significant source of slaves as the trans-Atlantic trade developed. But where African rulers previously waged wars for political ends and took slaves as spoils of battle,

– CHAPTER 14: *Violence in the Atlantic World* –

they showed an increasing willingness after the mid-seventeenth century to fight for the primary purpose of gaining slaves. As the volume of the trade grew, so too did the cycles of warfare.[42] Second, it changed *who* was enslaved. Traditionally, African slave owners preferred adult women or children, each of whom might be incorporated into a lineage through marriage or adoption. Increasingly, however, African slavers targeted adult males as commodities, who commanded a higher price from trans-Atlantic merchants.[43] Third, it changed *where* slaves came from and where they went. African communities in the hinterlands increasingly found themselves vulnerable to warfare, kidnapping, and enslavement as the seventeenth century passed into the eighteenth. Moreover, the volume of the trans-Atlantic trade outstripped the trans-Saharan trade after 1700. In all of these cases, earlier patterns of slavery and the slave trade changed in response to growing demand for bound laborers on American plantations, particularly after the dramatic rise of sugar production after 1650.[44] Regional histories of violence changed as they became part of a larger circum-Atlantic history of violence. Moreover, these new patterns of enslavement and slave trading in turn helped fuel the growth of slave systems that would be so important throughout the colonial Americas, shaping countless local histories.

* * *

So what, then, of those countless locales that existed within these larger circum-Atlantic circuits? How can we make sense of their histories? I would argue that studying violence throughout the Atlantic offers a way to see histories of local cultures as parts of a larger picture. In other words, such an analysis presents a way to do cis-Atlantic history, smaller stories told with an eye to the much broader context. For violence played a role in creating local Atlantic communities, regimes of citizenship, and cultures of slavery. These communities grew, in part, out of colonial economies of violence – the range of permissible exchanges of violence that determined who could inflict pain upon whom and under what conditions.[45] These official and unofficial regulations, managed and reinforced through everyday life, lay at the heart of the imperial project.

As many scholars have noted, the Iberian Atlantic colonies were characterized by a high degree of intercultural mixture that lead to the growth of a *mestizo* or creole population. Indeed, some have celebrated the 'fusion' of Europeans and indigenous peoples off the coast of Africa and in the Americas. Echoing creole rejections (dating back to the colonial period) of continental claims that interracial sexual relations had led to biological and cultural degeneration, more modern authors have presented mixed populations as a source of vitality.[46] These communities, however, owed their existence to systemic sexual violence. The creole population of Cabo Verde, the first Atlantic colony which contained a permanent settler society, was comprised almost entirely of the children of male Portuguese slave owners and their female African slaves. Colonizers there quickly established administrative structures that institutionalized the slave regime, protecting not just the nascent African coastal slave trade but also owners' sexual exploitation of their female slaves, which both proved crucial to the rise of a plantation slave system.[47] On the western side of the Atlantic, sexual assault played a role in the Spanish conquest of the Americas from the start. Chroniclers wrote of Indian women's fondness for 'Christians' and their willingness to 'debauch and prostitute themselves,' even as Spanish soldiers seized women as spoils of war or accepted them as captive 'gifts' from native allies. (Indeed, the most famous such 'gift,' celebrated by Cortés as the famed Doña Marina, played a crucial part in the conquest of the Mexica empire.)[48] Sexual violence, in other words, had a central role in the origin of different colonial Atlantic cultures.

The symbiotic relationship between violence and culture lay at the center of emerging slave systems across the ocean as well. The growth of the trans-Atlantic slave trade and the rapid expansion of European colonies in the Americas relied upon a constant infusion of new, bound labor. New world plantations became sites of cultural creativity, even as work there was 'grinding [slaves] into sugar, coffee, and other crops for export' for slave owners' profit. As numerous scholars have noted, slave cultures in places such as in Cuba, Mexico, Minas Geras, and the Carolina low country (to name only a few examples) reflected different African elements, fused in a crucible of death and destruction.[49] Plantations also required the creation of new imperial regimes to accommodate an institution that had largely faded into disuse in most western European nations by the fifteenth century.[50] Colonizers developed cultures of slavery, dynamic mixtures of racial, legal, and labor practices that undergirded slavery as an institution. Power mediated these developments at every step.

The creation of full-blown cultures of slavery proved essential for the survival of those European colonies that relied upon the production of agricultural exports. The well-documented 'ordeal' of Virginia, England's first permanent Atlantic colony, epitomized this problem. Settlers navigated a delicate balance between tradition and novelty during the colony's first decades. If one 1649 traveler called the Chesapeake 'English grounde in America,' it was only tenuously so.[51] Though some scholars have claimed that colonizers tried earnestly to recreate older traditions across the Atlantic, their efforts in this respect seem, in retrospect, fitful at best.[52] Colonial law proved an early example of this trend. Seventeenth-century English vocally celebrated common law traditions that guaranteed their famed 'liberties.' Indeed, the law occupied a central place in Anglo-Americans' self-definition.[53] But Thomas Dale's imposition of the *Laws Divine, Moral, and Martiall* in 1609 foreshadowed future legal changes in the colony. Dale's *Laws* saved the colony, but also represented an abrogation of liberties Englishmen across the Atlantic never could have tolerated.

This trend accelerated after the colonizers established the House of Burgesses in 1619. Now with the power to craft their own laws, they soon showed that Virginia's legal distinctiveness resulted from conscious choice, rather than a dearth of legal knowledge among provincial judges.[54] When faced with the choice of following English examples or following their own path, Anglo-Americans chose a particularly American path. Planters initially tried to use the Statute of Artificers (1563), which regulated hireling labor in England, in America. After the 1630s, however, they abandoned English-origin statutes regarding labor entirely, instead creating a legal culture of labor that focused almost entirely on servitude. They made the conditions of servitude significantly more onerous, empowering masters to use harsher methods of corporal punishment against servants, gave servants fewer rights, and increased the number of offenses that could lead to a servant's time under indenture being extended. Towards the end of the century, they would also alter the law to make the market in servants' contracts run more smoothly and decided that their laws governing the emancipation of servants took precedent over English ones.[55]

– CHAPTER 14: *Violence in the Atlantic World* –

Moreover, by this time Anglo-Virginian colonizers had already spent decades crafting a regime of racial slavery that would play a dominant role in the colony's labor regime. The English had no true experience with slavery before the arrival of the first '20 and odd Negroes' that arrived as slaves in 1619. In the 1640s, however, legislators in Virginia began to draw racial distinctions that facilitated the institution's rise, passing a law that defined women of African descent as 'laborers,' while exempting Euro-American women from that category.[56] In 1662, the Assembly passed two laws that first created a culture of labor that clearly delineated slavery from other forms of labor and that allowed for slavery's indefinite perpetuation. One gave indentured servants protections, for the first time, from mistreatment at the hands of their masters; it outlawed the physical disfigurement of persistent runaway servants, prohibited immoderate correction of wayward servants, and confirmed servants' ability to complain of abuses in court.[57]

Meanwhile, another law declared that 'all children borne in this country shalbe held bond or free only according to the condition of the mother.'[58] This law represented a radical rejection of colonists' Anglo-American legal heritage. Previously, slaves had won freedom suits by proving that their father had been free; as judges in those cases admitted, English common law had always determined patrilineal descent more significant than matrilineal descent. In deciding that children's status should follow the condition of the mother, legislators had decided to abandon the common law to follow the civil law maxim that *partus sequitur ventrem* – the offspring follows the womb. In doing so, they adopted customs practiced elsewhere in the Americas, where Spanish, Portuguese, French, and Dutch slave-owners followed ancient Roman traditions.[59]

Nor did the legislature stop in 1662. In 1669, they enacted a law declaring that baptism did not lead to freedom, meaning that Christians could enslave other Christians – as long as the slaves were of African descent. And in 1691, they outlawed all interracial sexual relations, drawing lines between black and white as starkly as they could. Legislators had through these actions created a culture of slavery, one in which certain individuals were fit to labor for life and others were not; one in which some individuals had their legal personhood stripped away and others had theirs affirmed; one in which some individuals' bodies were subject to particular forms of corporal punishment and others were not; and one in which race defined the lines between the two groups. They developed, in other words, a particular economy of violence which underwrote the colonial economy. This culture underwrote the growth of Virginia's plantation economy, as the slave population grew from under 4 percent of the colony's total population in 1670, to 30 percent of the colony's total population in 1700, to over 40 percent of the colony's total population in 1720.[60]

Englishmen in Barbados had a similar experience. First settled by the English in 1627, colonizers on that island created a plantation system that deviated from English norms. Sugar production especially proved a problem, as it had a longer growing season and required new technologies and different forms of agricultural organization than any crop grown in England. Where Portuguese planters in Brazil had embraced African slavery fairly rapidly on their sugar plantations, their counterparts in Barbados continued to draw on the labor of bound Englishmen for some time after they began sugar cultivation. Bound labor on the island, however, became 'a new and different institution' based on 'the systematic application of legally sanctioned force and violence' – a sharp deviation from traditional practice across the Atlantic.[61]

253

Indentured servants lost customary rights and legal protections to which they had been entitled in England, while finding themselves subject to unprecedented forms of physical punishment. According to European visitors to the island, their condition resembled that of slaves more than of indentured servants in England.[62]

The creation of this culture of labor helped the development of a culture of slavery after mid-century. The number of slaves in Barbados nearly equaled the number of white bound laborers in 1655. By the 1670s, there were three slaves for every two white servants; a decade later, slaves outnumbered servants 2.3:1.[63] Moreover, Barbadian legislators moved more quickly to pass laws defining and protecting slavery, culminating in a comprehensive 1661 'Act for the Better Ordering and Governing of Negroes.' Declaring Africans to be 'of barbarous, wilde and savage nature' and thus 'wholly unqualified to be governed by the Laws, Customs, and Practices of our Nation,' the act detailed the ways in which masters and magistrates could work, discipline, and punish enslaved laborers. Though this act borrowed to some degree from English precedents regarding the regulation of servants and, tellingly, the declaration of martial law, it nonetheless represented a significant innovation in a land 'largely free of English oversight, tradition, and law.'[64]

That same year, the assembly passed an act for the regulation of servants that gave them, at least on paper, protection from some of the worst abuses of the plantation system – protection denied slaves. Just as their counterparts in Virginia would do a year later, Barbadian lawmakers established an institutional edifice to undergird the particularly brutal system of human exploitation they had developed. The existence of two separate acts revealed leading colonists' desire to create two different kinds of workers whose persons could be owned – and bodies could be regulated – in different ways. (Tellingly, they never adopted a law tracing slave status through the line of the mother, as Virginians did; this simply seems to have been customary.) They had created a culture of slavery within a true space of death. In 1700, Barbados had a black population of approximately 50,000; colonizers had imported over 212,000 enslaved Africans over the previous seventy-five years, this demographic disaster a testament to the world plantation owners had made.[65]

Other European colonial powers, too, created new Atlantic cultures of violence as they created new cultures of slavery. Slavery existed in Spain and Portugal before the opening of the Atlantic world, as did legal prescriptions and proscriptions regulating the treatment of slaves. The 'Reconquista' increased the slave population, though Iberian Christians were more likely to enserf defeated Muslims than enslave them during these wars.[66] Spain and Portugal (but especially the latter) embraced African slavery after the opening of an Atlantic trade in the 1440s, and African slaves comprised as much as 15 percent of the population in some Portuguese port cities. Nonetheless, African slaves worked largely in the same occupations as Muslim slaves – primarily as domestic servants – and in the same conditions.[67]

But with the opening of Atlantic colonies off the coast of Africa, these patterns changed. By mid-century, Portuguese settlers had established sugar works on Madeira, drawing on enslaved Africans for the lion's share of their workforce. Shortly thereafter, Castilian conquerors established sugar plantations almost immediately after conquering the Canaries, though the near total destruction of the native population through war and disease required them to seek an alternative source of labor: Africans. By the sixteenth-century, the Azore islands became large sugar producers; São Tomé boasted sixty sugar plantations in 1522, some of which had as many as 300 slaves. And by 1550, Portuguese planters had begun what would become the largest plantation complex in the Americas in the sugar cane fields in Brazil. The growth of plantation agriculture necessitated multiple transformations. Enslaved peoples in the colonial Atlantic worked in different occupations and in larger units than their predecessors had. It also involved an intensification not just in the labor demands made of slaves, but also in the types of punishments used to keep these slave economies going. If the laws governing slaves changed little during the rise of the Iberian plantation complex, the cultures of slavery that defined life in Madeira, the Canaries, São Tomé, and Brazil quickly deviated from any 'Old World' traditions.[68]

In the case of France, the law prohibited the practice of slavery on French soil. It quickly became apparent, however, that this proscription did not apply to the Americas.[69] French planters attempted to emulate other European colonizers, establishing sugar plantations on their Caribbean possessions. Initially, they tried to rely on *engagés* – indentured servants – as a permanent labor force in a growing plantation economy. Thousands of French laborers headed to the Caribbean between the 1620s and 1660s, working in desperate conditions that shocked visiting missionaries to the islands.[70]

Ultimately, however, this experiment in *engagé* labor failed and planters turned to imported Africans. By 1660, for example, slaves comprised more than half of Martinique's population; by 1684, they would be more than two-thirds of the population.[71] Colonizers in St. Domingue embraced slavery somewhat less slowly, but in 1713 more than 81 percent of the colony would be enslaved, working in the same brutal conditions as enslaved workers elsewhere on Atlantic sugar plantations. Meanwhile, royal officials promulgated the *Code Noir* in 1685, a collection of laws regulating slavery in the colonies. Not as harsh as English slave laws but without some of the more moderate provisions of Spanish slave laws, it defined slaves' status as property while allowing masters to punish their slaves, up to the point of torture, for infractions. In other words, it denied their humanity in ways far worse than the 'inhumane' environment the *engagés* faced.[72]

The creation of colonial cultures of slavery did more than simply regulate official and unofficial labor regimes. It also involved the creation of increasingly elaborate legal categories of race, as well as laws governing sexual relations across racial boundary lines. In Spanish America, legislators adapted laws regarding *limpieza de sangre* (purity of blood) passed in Europe for use in the colonies. Where these statutes had previously been used to track the Jewish and Muslim ancestry of *conversos* and *moriscos*, respectively, in Spain, they came to be used to track Indian and African ancestry among colonial residents of mixed ancestry.[73] In French colonies, meanwhile, the 1685 *Code Noir* established, among other things, the legal privileges of those born of interracial relationships. In this way, the management of race, gender, and sexuality played a role in maintaining colonial cultures of slavery just as interracial sexual violence played a role in creating those cultures.[74]

It can be easy enough to examine these histories discreetly, to write the stories of race and slavery in the English, French, Spanish, or Portuguese Atlantic separately. One could also, quite productively, write comparative histories of conquest colonization within and among these imperial powers. Looking at the relationship between culture and violence in communities within these empires, however, provides a way of seeing them in a particular combination, of showing how they existed as part of a larger whole. Though these local histories might, when viewed from a particular angle, look like discrete stories, each occupied a place within a kaleidoscope of Atlantic colonialism, one held together by the exercise of force and coercion in ways large and small.

* * *

Of course, this essay is, as noted at the outset, suggestive rather than conclusive. One could easily attempt to find the origins of Atlantic cultures elsewhere, perhaps with a different thematic focus or geographic outlook. One might also write different histories of violence in the Atlantic world, perhaps focusing on material rather than on cultural forces. The preceding discussion hardly forecloses the possibility of other narratives about this era and these places. But focusing on the intertwined history of violence and culture in the Atlantic has its own merits, as I hope I have shown.

Looking at the mutually constitutive relationship between violence and culture has three primary benefits. First, it provides an opportunity to engage with multiple levels of Atlantic history (drawing again on Armitage's three concepts of American history) simultaneously, analyzing trans-Atlantic histories while keeping cis-Atlantic variations on a theme in mind. Second, it suggests a way of making sense of historical entanglements and entangled histories, together. One of Atlantic history's virtues is the fact that it lets its practitioners move beyond nationalist assumptions, revealing the importance of connections that spanned old empires and the forces that criss-crossed the ocean. At the same time, some scholars have argued that its true value lies in the fact that it destabilizes nationalist narratives, allowing for more rigorous comparative work of those societies that emerged out of the colonial Atlantic world. Exploring the history of violence and culture gives scholars a means to address the history of trans-Atlantic ties that linked Europe, Africa, and the Americas, while also giving scholars a way of telling a larger trans-Atlantic history that spans multiple regions and historiographies.

Lastly, analyzing violence and culture together captures something crucial about life within the Atlantic in this era. Feeding off of each other – with particular cultural preconceptions legitimating and encouraging specific forms of violence, and practices of violence and domination spawning new cultures – they acted as a sort of perpetual motion machine of colonial domination. Atlantic cultures of violence determined who suffered, how they suffered, and who occupied positions of power in which they could inflict suffering. This was the world in which Europeans, Africans, and Americans lived and died. As such this particular way of telling the history of the Atlantic world has, I think, a resonance all its own.

NOTES

I would like to thank Michael Goode, Katie Harris, and Natalie Troxel for thorough, and very helpful, readings of this essay at the last minute.

1 Fischer, 1989; Hartz, 1964; Turner, 1975.
2 Frazier, 1978; Herskovits, 1941; Price, 2001.

– CHAPTER 14: *Violence in the Atlantic World* –

3 Foster, 1960; Gruzinski, 1993, 2002.
4 Plank, 2010; Smolenski, 2005.
5 Bourdieu, 1977; Geertz, 1973c; Greenblatt, 1988; Ortner, 1999; Sewell, 2005; Urban, 1991.
6 Armitage, 2002: 15.
7 Cañizares-Esguerra, 2006: 7.
8 Newitt, 2010: 25.
9 Thornton, 1998: 257, 2013: 57–60.
10 Elliott, 2006: 17; Greenblatt, 1991: 53.
11 Pagden, 1995: 11–62; Županov, 2010: 26–27.
12 Cañizares-Esguerra, 2006: 7.
13 Shields, 2007, 2009.
14 Mancall, 2007: 164; Oberg, 1999.
15 Warner, 2000: 55–56.
16 See Geertz, 1973b: 93.
17 Brading, 1991: 2, 22.
18 Schmidt, 2001.
19 Pestana, 2011; Shields, 2009.
20 Geertz, 1973a: 448.
21 Armitage, 2000: 96–98; Jennings, 1975: 82, 135; Pagden, 1990, 1998; Tomlins, 2010: 113–20.
22 Cortés and Elliott, 2001: xxvii–xxviii; Richter, 2011: 114.
23 On the Requirement and fences, see Seed, 1995: 16–40 and 69–99
24 Urban, 1993: 228.
25 On the cultural dynamics of this process, see Urban, 2001: 144.
26 Austin, 1975; Faudree, 2012.
27 On ideas of land ownership among Indians and Europeans, see Shoemaker, 2004: 16–20. On cultural space and sovereignty, see Greene, 1992; Smolenski, 2005.
28 Anderson, 1994; Richter, 2001: 98; Silverman, 2003; Smolenski, 2005: 1–3.
29 Robert Blair St. George defines transculturation as 'the action whereby a politically dominated culture appropriates some of the symbolic forms of a dominant or imperial culture in order to articulate its own continuing vision of autonomy' under colonialism: St. George, 2000: 26. See also Mazzotti, 2000; Mignolo, 2000: 14–16, 167–70.
30 Silverman, 2003: 528.
31 On Indians' difficulties in court and conflicts over land helping cause King Philip's War, see Anderson, 1994: 602. On Philip as a 'rebel for cooperation,' see Richter, 2001: 105.
32 Geertz, 1973a.
33 Clendinnen, 1993; Haefeli, 1999: 18; Lepore, 1998.
34 Taussig, 1984: 495.
35 Brading, 1991: 25–58; Clendinnen, 1993; Cortés, 2001: 262.
36 Lepore, 1998: xiv.
37 Schmidt, 2001: 276–80.
38 Urban, 1993: 228–29.
39 Taussig, 1984: 468.
40 Lovejoy, 2011: 11–15. Paul Lovejoy describes pawnship as a practice in which individuals could be 'held as security for a debt' whose value was based not on their productive capacity but on 'the expectation that their relatives would repay the debt and thereby release the pawn from bondage' (p. 13). See also Thornton, 1998: 98–125.
41 Lovejoy, 2011: 27; http://slavevoyages.org/tast/database/search.faces?yearFrom=1400& yearTo=1700 (accessed May 1, 2014).
42 Lovejoy, 2011: 83–87. On changes in war, see Heywood and Thornton, 2007: Chapter 3.
43 Eltis, 2000: 287; Lovejoy, 2011: 20.
44 Lovejoy, 2011: 19, 27.

45 See Smolenski, 2005: 14.
46 Green, 2012: 104; Martinez-Echazabal, 1998; Miller, 2004.
47 Green, 2012: 104–5.
48 Wood, 1998: quotation on 12. Karen Vieira Powers has raised a caution against a recent historiographic tendency to cast indigenous women as completely passive victims of *conquistador* violence, arguing this totalizing discourse discounts female agency. This point, while well-taken, nonetheless concedes the centrality of coerced sex in the space conquest (Powers, 2002).
49 Brown, 2008: 49. The literature on slave cultures in the Americas is vast. For some introduction to the literature, see the references cited in note 3, as well as Mintz and Price, 1992. For some of the more recent work that highlights the role of violence in the formation of slave societies, see Brown, 2008; Smallwood, 2007; Sweet, 2003; Trouillot, 2002.
50 Blackburn, 2010: 31–93; Eltis, 2000: Chapter 1.
51 Colonel [Henry] Nowood, *A Voyage to Virginia* (1649), cited in Horn, 1994: 138.
52 Handlin, 1957: 4.
53 Greene, 2002.
54 Billings, 1979: 242–44. James Horn argues that nonetheless the legal system in the Chesapeake would have been extremely familiar to settlers: Horn, 1994: 338.
55 Billings, 1991; Horn, 1994: 271; Morgan, 1975: 216–17; Pagan, 2003; Tomlins, 2010: 263–75.
56 Brown, 1996: 107–36.
57 Tomlins, 2010: 455–59f.
58 Tomlins, 2010: 455.
59 Billings, 1991: 57; Tomlins, 2010: 455–59. Jonathan Bush has pointed out that colonial slave law resembled Roman slave doctrines only through its embrace of matrilineal descent was was otherwise 'new' law: Bush, 1993: 425.
60 McCusker, 2006: 5:561, 653.
61 Beckles, 1989: 5.
62 Beckles, 1990: 511.
63 Beckles, 1990: 505.
64 Gaspar, 1999; Newman, 2013: 55, 192 (act quoted at 192); Nicholson, 1994.
65 Newman, 2013: 214.
66 Elliott, 2006: 107; Klein, 1986: 9.
67 Klein, 1986: 6, 14.
68 Blackburn, 2010: 107–12; De La Fuente, 2004; Fuente, 2008; Schwartz, 1985, 2004; Viera, 2004.
69 Peabody, 1994.
70 Blackburn, 2010: 281–82; Boucher, 2008: 144, 153; Moitt, 2001: 2–18; Pritchard, 2007: 94–95.
71 Garrigus, 2006: 25.
72 Garrigus, 2006: 39; Peabody, 2011: 603.
73 Martínez, 2008.
74 Aubert, 2004; Garrigus, 2006: Chapter 1.

REFERENCES

Anderson VD (1994) King Philip's Herds: Indians, Colonists, and the Problem of Livestock in Early New England. *William and Mary Quarterly*, Third Series, 51(4), 601–24.

Armitage D (2000) *The Ideological Origins of the British Empire.* New York: Cambridge University Press.

——(2002) Three Concepts of Atlantic History. In: Armitage D and Braddick MJ (eds), *The British Atlantic world, 1500–1800,* New York: Palgrave Macmillan, pp. 11–30.

– CHAPTER 14: *Violence in the Atlantic World* –

Aubert G (2004) The Blood of France: Race and Purity of Blood in the French Atlantic World. *William and Mary Quarterly*, Third Series, 61(3), 439–78.

Austin JL (1975) *How to do things with words*. 2nd edn. Oxford: Clarendon Press.

Beckles H (1989) *White servitude and Black slavery in Barbados, 1627–1715*. Knoxville: University of Tennessee Press.

Beckles HM (1990) A 'riotous and unruly lot': Irish Indentured Servants and Freemen in the English West Indies, 1644–1713. *William and Mary Quarterly*, Third Series, 47(4), 503–22.

Billings WM (1979) The Transfer of English Law to Virginia. In: Andrews KR, Canny NP, and Hair PEH (eds), *The Westward Enterprise: English Activities in Ireland, the Atlantic, and America, 1480–1650*, Detroit: Wayne State University Press, pp. 215–44.

——(1991) The Law of Servants and Slaves in Seventeenth-Century Virginia. *Virginia Magazine of History and Biography*, 99(1), 45–62.

Blackburn R (2010) *The making of New World slavery: from the Baroque to the Modern, 1492–1800*. 2nd. ed. New York: Verso.

Boucher PP (2008) *France and the American tropics to 1700: tropics of discontent?* Baltimore: Johns Hopkins University Press.

Bourdieu P (1977) *Outline of a theory of practice*. New York: Cambridge University Press.

Brading DA (1991) *The first America: the Spanish monarchy, Creole patriots, and the liberal state, 1492–1867*. New York: Cambridge University Press.

Brown KM (1996) *Good wives, nasty wenches, and anxious patriarchs: gender, race, and power in colonial Virginia*. Chapel Hill: University of North Carolina Press.

Brown V (2008) *The Reaper's Garden: Death and Power in the World of Atlantic Slavery*. Cambridge, Mass: Harvard University Press.

Bush JA (1993) Free to Enslave: The Foundations of Colonial American Slave Law. *Yale Journal of Law & the Humanities*, 5(2), 417–70.

Cañizares-Esguerra J (2006) *Puritan Conquistadors: Iberianizing the Atlantic, 1550–1700*. Stanford, California: Stanford University Press.

Clendinnen I (1993) 'Fierce and Unnatural Cruelty': Cortés and the Conquest of Mexico. In: Greenblatt S (ed.), *New World Encounters*, Berkeley: University of California Press, pp. 12–47.

Cortés H (2001) *Hernan Cortes: Letters from Mexico*. Rev. Pagden A (ed.), New Haven, CT: Yale University Press.

De La Fuente A (2004) Sugar and Slavery in Early Colonial Cuba. In: Schwartz SB (ed.), *Tropical Babylons: Sugar and the Making of the Atlantic World, 1450–1680*, Chapel Hill: University of North Carolina Press, pp. 158–200.

Elliott JH (2001) Cortés, Velázquex, and Charles V. In: Pagden A (ed.), *Hernan Cortes: Letters from Mexico*, New Haven, CT: Yale University Press, pp. xi–xxxviii.

——(2006) *Empires of the Atlantic World: Britain and Spain in America, 1492–1830*. New Haven: Yale University Press.

Eltis D (2000) *The rise of African slavery in the Americas*. New York: Cambridge University Press.

Faudree P (2012) How to Say Things with Wars: Performativity and Discursive Rupture in the Requerimiento of the Spanish Conquest. *Journal of Linguistic Anthropology*, 22(3), 182–200.

Fischer DH (1989) *Albion's Seed: Four British Folkways in America*. New York: Oxford University Press.

Foster GM (1960) *Culture and conquest: America's Spanish heritage*. New York: Wenner-Gren Foundation for Anthropological Research.

Frazier EF (1978) *Race and culture contacts in the modern world*. Westport, Conn: Greenwood Press.

Fuente A de la (2008) *Havana and the Atlantic in the Sixteenth Century*. Chapel Hill: University of North Carolina Press.

Garrigus JD (2006) *Before Haiti: Race and Citizenship in French Saint-Domingue*. The Americas in the early modern Atlantic world, New York: Palgrave Macmillan.

Gaspar DB (1999) With a Rod of Iron: Barbados Slave Laws as a Model for Jamaica, South Carolina, and Antigua, 1661–97. In: Hine DC and McLeod J (eds), *Crossing boundaries: comparative history of Black people in diaspora*, Bloomington: Indiana University Press, pp. 343–66.

Geertz C (1973a) Deep Play: Notes on a Balinese Cockfight. In: *The Interpretation of Cultures; Selected Essays*, New York: Basic Books, pp. 412–54.

——(1973b) Religion as a Cultural System. In: *The Interpretation of Cultures; Selected Essays*, New York: Basic Books, pp. 87–125.

——(1973c) Thick Description: Toward an Interpretive Theory of Culture. In: *The Interpretation of Cultures; Selected Essays*, New York: Basic Books, pp. 3–30.

Green T (2012) *The Rise of the Trans-Atlantic Slave Trade in Western Africa, 1300–1589*. New York: Cambridge University Press.

Greenblatt S (1988) The Circulation of Social Energy. In: *Shakespearean Negotiations: the Circulation of Social Energy in Renaissance England*, Berkeley: University of California Press, pp. 1–20.

——(1991) *Marvelous Possessions: the Wonder of the New World*. Chicago: University of Chicago Press.

Greene JP (1992) Mastery and the Definition of Cultural Space in Early America: A Perspective. In: *Imperatives, Behaviors, and Identities: Essays in Early American Cultural History*, Charlotsville: University Press of Virginia, pp. 1–12.

——(2002) 'By Their Laws Shall Ye Know Them': Law and Identity in Colonial British America. *Journal of Interdisciplinary History*, 33(2), 247–60.

Gruzinski S (1993) *The conquest of Mexico : the incorporation of Indian societies into the Western world, 16th-18th centuries*. Cambridge, MA: Blackwell Publishers.

——(2002) *The Mestizo Mind: The Intellectual Dynamics of Colonization and Globalization*. New York: Routledge.

Haefeli E (1999) Kieft's War and the Cultures of Violence in Colonial Americas. In: Bellesiles MA (ed.), *Lethal imagination: violence and brutality in American history*, New York: New York University Press, pp. 17–40.

Handlin O (1957) The Significance of the Seventeenth Century. In: Smith JM (ed.), *Seventeenth-Century America*, Chapel Hill: University of North Carolina Press, pp. 3–12.

Hartz LM (1964) *The Founding of New Societies: Studies in the History of the United States, Latin America, South Africa, Canada, and Australia*. New York, NY: Harcourt, Brace & World Inc.

Herskovits MJ (1941) *The Myth of the Negro Past*. New York, London: Harper & Brothers.

Heywood LM and Thornton JK (2007) *Central Africans, Atlantic Creoles, and the Foundation of the Americas, 1585–1660*. New York: Cambridge University Press.

Horn JPP (1994) *Adapting to a new world: English society in the seventeenth-century Chesapeake*. Chapel Hill: University of North Carolina Press.

Jennings F (1975) *The Invasion of America: Indians, Colonialism, and the Cant of Conquest*. Chapel Hill: University of North Carolina Press.

Klein HS (1986) *African slavery in Latin America and the Caribbean*. New York: Oxford University Press.

Lepore J (1998) *The Name of War: King Philip's War and the Origins of American Identity*. New York: Knopf.

Lovejoy PE (2011) *Transformations in slavery: a history of slavery in Africa*. 3rd ed. New York: Cambridge University Press.

Mancall PC (2007) *Hakluyt's Promise: An Elizabethan's Obsession for an English America*. New Haven, CT: Yale University Press.

Martínez ME (2008) *Genealogical Fictions: Limpieza De Sangre, Religion, and Gender in Colonial Mexico*. Stanford, Calif: Stanford University Press.

Martinez-Echazabal L (1998) Mestizaje and the Discourse of National/Cultural Identity in Latin America, 1845–1959. *Latin American Perspectives*, 25(3), 21–42.

Mazzotti JA (2000) Mestizo Dreams: Transculturation and Hetereogeneity in Inca Garcilaso de la Vega. In: St. George RB (ed.), *Possible Pasts: Becoming Colonial in Early America*, Ithaca, N.Y.: Cornell University Press, pp. 131–47.

McCusker JJ (2006) Colonial Statistics. In: Carter SB, Gartner SS, Haines MR, et al. (eds), *Historical Statistics of the United States Millennial Edition*, New York: Cambridge University Press, vol. 5, pp. 627–64.

Mignolo W (2000) *Local Histories/Global Designs: Coloniality, Subaltern Knowledges, and Border Thinking*. Princeton, N.J.: Princeton University Press.

Miller MG (2004) *Rise and fall of the cosmic race: the cult of mestizaje in Latin America*. Austin: University of Texas Press.

Mintz SW and Price R (1992) *The birth of African-American culture: an anthropological perspective*. Boston: Beacon Press.

Moitt B (2001) *Women and slavery in the French Antilles, 1635–1848*. Bloomington: Indiana University Press.

Morgan ES (1975) *American slavery, American freedom: the ordeal of colonial Virginia*. New York: W.W. Norton.

Newitt M (ed.) (2010) *The Portuguese in West Africa, 1415–1670: a documentary history*. New York: Cambridge University Press.

Newman SP (2013) *A new world of labor: the development of plantation slavery in the British Atlantic*. Philadelphia: University of Pennsylvania Press.

Nicholson BJ (1994) Legal Borrowing and the Origins of Slave Law in the British Colonies. *The American Journal of Legal History*, 38(1), 38–54.

Oberg ML (1999) *Dominion and civility: English imperialism and Native America, 1585–1685*. Ithaca, New York: Cornell University Press.

Ortner SB (1999) *The fate of 'culture': Geertz and beyond*. Representations books; 8, Berkeley: University of California Press.

Pagan JR (2003) *Anne Orthwood's bastard : sex and law in early Virginia*. New York: Oxford University Press.

Pagden A (1990) Dispossessing the Barbarian: Rights and Property in Spanish America. In: *Spanish Imperialism and the Political Imagination: Studies in European and Spanish-American Social and Political Theory, 1513–1830*, New Haven: Yale University Press, pp. 13–36.

——(1995) *Lords of All the World: Ideologies of Empire in Spain, Britain and France c. 1500–c. 1800*. New Haven, Conn.: Yale University Press.

——(1998) The Struggle for Legitimation and the Image of Empire in the Atlantic to c.1700. In: Canny NP (ed.), *The Oxford History of the British Empire: Volume I: The Origins of Empire British Overseas Enterprise to the Close of the Seventeenth Century*, 1: New York: Oxford University Press, pp. 34–54.

Peabody S (1994) Race, Slavery, and the Law in Early Modern France. *Historian*, 56(3), 501–10.

——(2011) Slavery, Freedom, and the Law in the Atlantic World, 1420–1807. In: Eltis D, Engerman SL, Eltis D, et al. (eds), *The Cambridge World History of Slavery*, Cambridge: Cambridge University Press, pp. 594–630.

Pestana CG (2011) Cruelty and Religious Justifications for Conquest in the Mid-Seventeenth Century English Atlantic. In: Gregerson L and Juster S (eds), *Empires of God: religious encounters in the early modern Atlantic*, Philadelphia: University of Pennsylvania Press, pp. 37–57.

Plank G (2010) Violence. In: Burnard T (ed.), *Oxford Bibliographies Online: Atlantic History*, New York: Oxford University Press.

Powers KV (2002) Conquering Discourses of 'Sexual Conquest': Of Women, Language, and Mestizaje. *Colonial Latin American Review*, 11(1), 7–32.

Price R (2001) The Miracle of Creolization: A Retrospective. *New West Indian Guide / Nieuwe West-Indische Gids*, 75(1), 35–64.

Pritchard J (2007) *In Search of Empire: The French in the Americas, 1670–1730.* 1st ed. New York: Cambridge University Press.

Richter DK (2001) *Facing East from Indian Country: a Native History of Early America.* Cambridge: Harvard University Press.

——(2011) *Before the Revolution: America's ancient pasts.* Cambridge, Mass: Belknap Press of Harvard University Press.

Schmidt B (2001) *Innocence abroad: the Dutch imagination and the New World, 1570–1670.* New York: Cambridge University Press.

Schwartz SB (1985) *Sugar plantations in the formation of Brazilian society: Bahia, 1550–1835.* New York: Cambridge University Press.

——(2004) A Commonwealth within Itself: The Early Brazilian Sugar Industry. In: Schwartz SB (ed.), *Tropical Babylons: Sugar and the Making of the Atlantic World, 1450–1680,* Chapel Hill: University of North Carolina Press, pp. 158–200.

Seed P (1995) *Ceremonies of Possession in Europe's Conquest of the New World, 1492–1640.* New York: Cambridge University Press.

Sewell WH (2005) The Concept(s) of Culture. In: *Logics of history: social theory and social transformation,* Chicago: University of Chicago Press, pp. 152–74.

Shields DS (2007) The Genius of Ancient Britain. In: Mancall PC (ed.), *The Atlantic World and Virginia, 1550–1624,* Chapel Hill: University of North Carolina Press, pp. 489–510.

——(2009) Sons of the Dragon; or, The English Hero Revived. In: Bauer R and Mazzotti JA (eds), *Creole Subjects in the Colonial Americas Empires, Texts, Identities.,* University of North Carolina Press, pp. 101–17.

Shoemaker N (2004) *A Strange Likeness: Becoming Red and White in Eighteenth-century North America.* New York: Oxford University Press.

Silverman DJ (2003) 'We Chuse to Be Bounded': Native American Animal Husbandry in Colonial New England. *William and Mary Quarterly,* Third Series, 60(3), 511–48.

Smallwood SE (2007) *Saltwater Slavery: A Middle Passage from Africa to American Diaspora.* Cambridge: Harvard University Press.

Smolenski J (2005) Introduction: The Ordering of Authority in the Colonial Americas. In: Smolenski J and Humphrey TJ (eds), *New World orders: violence, sanction, and authority in the colonial Americas,* Philadelphia: University of Pennsylvania Press, pp. 1–16.

St. George RB (2000) Introduction. In: St. George RB (ed.), *Possible Pasts: Becoming Colonial in Early America,* Ithaca, N.Y.: Cornell University Press, pp. 1–29.

Sweet JH (2003) *Recreating Africa: Culture, Kinship, and Religion in the African-Portuguese World, 1441–1770.* Chapel Hill: University of North Carolina Press.

Taussig M (1984) Culture of Terror – Space of Death. Roger Casement's Putumayo Report and the Explanation of Torture. *Comparative Studies in Society and History,* 26(3), 467–97.

Thornton JK (1998) *Africa and Africans in the making of the Atlantic world, 1400–1800.* New York: Cambridge University Press.

——(2013) Afro-Christian Syncretism in the Kingdom of Kongo. *Journal of African History,* 54(01), 53–77.

Tomlins CL (2010) *Freedom Bound: Law, Labor, and Civic Identity in Colonizing English America, 1580–1865.* New York: Cambridge University Press.

Trouillot M-R (2002) Culture on the Edges: Caribbean Creolization in Historical Context. In: Axel BK (ed.), *From the Margins: Historical Anthropology and Its Futures,* Durham, NC: Duke University Press, pp. 189–210.

Turner FJ (1975) The significance of the Frontier in American History. In: *The frontier in American history,* Huntington, N.Y.: R. E. Krieger Pub. Co., pp. 1–39.

– CHAPTER 14: *Violence in the Atlantic World* –

Urban G (1991) *A discourse-centered approach to culture : native South American myths and rituals*. Texas linguistics series, Austin: University of Texas Press.

——(1993) Culture's Public Face. *Public Culture*, 5(2), 213–22.

——(2001) *Metaculture: how culture moves through the world*. Public worlds; v. 8, Minneapolis, MN: University of Minnesota Press.

Viera A (2004) Sugar Islands: The Sugar Economy of Madeira and the Canaries, 1450–1650. In: Schwartz SB (ed.), *Tropical Babylons: Sugar and the Making of the Atlantic World, 1450–1680*, Chapel Hill: University of North Carolina Press, pp. 42–84.

Warner M (2000) What's Colonial About Colonial America? In: St. George RB (ed.), *Possible pasts: becoming colonial in early America*, Ithaca: Cornell Univ Press.

Wood S (1998) Sexual Violation in the Conquest of the Americas. In: Smith MD (ed.), *Sex and sexuality in early America*, New York: New York University Press, pp. 9–26.

Županov, Ines (2010) 'The Wheel of Torments': Mobility and Redemption in Portuguese Colonial India (Sixteenth century). In: Greenblatt S (ed.), *Cultural mobility: a manifesto*, New York: Cambridge University Press, pp. 24–74.

CHAPTER FIFTEEN

WAR AND WARFARE
IN THE ATLANTIC WORLD

——— ·◆· ———

Geoffrey Plank

Warfare shaped the Atlantic world between 1400 and 1815, but many of the dynamics that operated in that period had already revealed themselves in the medieval period with the Viking occupation of the Faero Islands, Iceland and southern Greenland, and the establishment of a small Norse outpost on the northern tip of Newfoundland. The Vikings acquired the ability to enter the North Atlantic only as a consequence of their military successes in Europe. Warfare secured them the necessary wealth and political power, and helped motivate the technological innovations that made crossing the ocean possible. The Norse built their first sailing ships around the year 700 and deployed them against Anglo-Saxon, Frankish and Irish enemies before sailing into the Atlantic. The resulting warfare spurred migration. The Icelandic sagas embellish the events they recall, but there is no reason to doubt the political dynamic they describe. A series of military confrontations, with rulers jockeying for position, establishing outposts on distant islands and carrying warriors and settlers with them, drove Viking colonization on Greenland and Newfoundland.

The fate of the Vikings' Newfoundland colony at the start of the eleventh century serves as an instructive tale on the vulnerability of European settlements in the Americas. The settlers did not encounter any indigenous people at first, but when they did they entered combat. According to one saga, the Vikings abducted two Native boys and sent them to Greenland in the hope that they would learn Norse, embrace Christianity and help pacify their kinsmen. That colonisation project came to nothing, and after a few years, sensing that they were surrounded in a hostile territory, the colonists gave up. A larger settlement with easier access to supplies from Greenland might have soldiered on, but under the circumstances the outpost seemed too risky and expensive to maintain.[1]

The Europeans who entered and travelled the Atlantic after 1400 in many respects resembled their ill-fated predecessors. The ships that carried the Portuguese into the ocean and down the coast of Africa in the fifteenth century were the product of a shipbuilding tradition in which designers had long sought to reconcile the requirements of commerce and war.[2] The Portuguese were able to finance their expeditions as a consequence of their military success against Muslim adversaries on the Iberian Peninsula, which secured them a measure of political stability, fiscal resources, and a charge from the Pope to extend their campaigns into Africa. Similarly, Spain's conquest of Granada provided an impetus for its ventures across the Atlantic, and the later colonizing efforts by other European powers were inspired in part by violent dynastic, commercial and sectarian rivalries. Like the Vikings in the eleventh century, Europe's colonists after 1492 frequently fought each other and their colonizing efforts led to warfare with and among indigenous peoples. New colonies were particularly vulnerable in the early years of settlement because of their dependence on ships for protection and trade.

In contrast to the Norse settlers on Greenland and Newfoundland, the Europeans who entered and crossed the Atlantic after 1400 eventually established permanent settlements and transatlantic communication links that persist to this day. Their success stemmed in no small part from their readiness to engage in endemic armed conflict. From the fifteenth century onward warfare in the Atlantic world was peculiarly destructive. In Africa and the Americas noncombatant populations were targeted and captive taking escalated as the belligerents sought to terrorize each other, assert their own dominion, and gain riches through the slave trade. Warfare transformed politics on every continent ringing the Atlantic and ultimately helped bind the ocean's peoples together. By the eighteenth century the Europeans and the Americans were experiencing periods of war in sync, as large-scale conflicts typically spread from one side of the ocean to the other. Transatlantic warfare sharply distinguished a period of global history, one that ended with the fall of Napoleon in 1815.

WAR AND COMMERCE AT SEA, 1400–1815

The vessels that first carried the Portuguese down the coast of Africa resembled those that had plied the coasts of Europe and the Mediterranean through the Middle Ages, but ship design began to change radically in the fifteenth century, partly under the influence of military considerations.[3] The Portuguese had placed guns on some of their ships as early as the fourteenth century, but the practice became much more widespread after the 1470s, when shipbuilders in Venice found a way to mount a cannon on the bow of a galley. Over the next century Scottish, English and Portuguese ship designers struggled to place heavy artillery on larger sailing ships. They succeeded by the 1580s, and cannons become essential to the military operations of ships. The heavy guns were used to bombard coastal targets, and when ships confronted each other on the water they maneuvered close together, typically fired a single volley, and prepared for boarding and combat on deck.[4]

Not all of the armed vessels that visited the shores of Africa and the Americas belonged to navies, as even merchant ships had the power to awe and intimidate. The shock of first seeing a European sailing ship became the stuff of legend among Native Americans and Africans alike.[5] As carriers of passengers and trade goods, large ships were the most persistent and efficacious technological advantage the Europeans held over the indigenous peoples of the Americas and sub-Saharan Africa. They were essential to the operations of the nascent transatlantic empires, and therefore they became targets as well as instruments of military force. On rare occasions Native American warriors seized sailing vessels and used them in attacks against colonial forces.[6] West Africa's rulers were in a better position to organize sustained, large-scale campaigns, and more regularly policed their harbors, on occasion taking to sea and attacking European ships.[7] Nonetheless, throughout the sixteenth, seventeenth and eighteenth centuries, except in the close vicinity of Africa, the vessels plying the

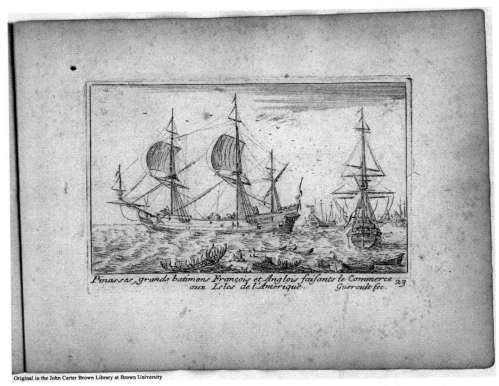

Figure 15.1 Pinasses, large French and English ships trading with the Americas.
Courtesy of the John Carter Brown Library at Brown University

open Atlantic belonged to the Europeans and their colonial descendents. Native American and African seamen may have served on ships, but from the perspective of the commanders naval warfare was an exclusively European or colonial concern.

On the ocean it was often difficult to distinguish commerce from warfare. English, Dutch and French pirates and privateers struck Portuguese ships off the coast of Africa and Spanish vessels in the Caribbean. Even the Portuguese fishing fleet off Newfoundland faced attack. The men who invested in these campaigns and manned the vessels did so for profit. By the 1580s a customary shares system was in place for compensating the men who worked on privateers. While hoping to make profits, private raiders also frequently served the interests of their sectarian and political leaders. In the late 1580s the English government issued licenses to an average of 100 privateering enterprises a year, as part of its ongoing struggle against Spain.[8] Particularly for the English, the violence reshaped the ships themselves. With access to relatively cheap iron cannons, English merchants routinely armed their vessels. This limited their ability to carry heavy, bulky produce, but it gave them an advantage during times of conflict, providing a measure of security and creating new economic opportunities.[9]

The prospect of raiding Spanish shipping lanes was a powerful early motive for colonization, helping to inspire the French Huguenot effort to settle in South Carolina, the English projects at Roanoke, Jamestown and Bermuda, and all of the early Dutch, French and English ventures into the Caribbean. The Spanish claimed all the islands

– CHAPTER 15: *War and warfare in the Atlantic World* –

of the Caribbean under the terms of two papal bulls issued in 1493 and the 1494 Treaty of Tordesillas between Spain and Portugal. Nonetheless, by the mid-sixteenth century it had become clear that neither Spain nor Portugal possessed a fleet large or powerful enough to keep French, English, or Dutch interlopers out of their claimed territorial waters. Neither country was willing to formally cede its authority on the seas, but at the same time the other powers, recognizing Spanish and Portuguese weakness, refused to stay out. Under these circumstances a new pragmatic understanding developed, that the Caribbean Sea and all the waters off of North and South America lay 'beyond the line,' meaning that Europe's diplomats agreed among themselves that no act of violence or depredation on the American side of the Atlantic would be construed as a cause for full-scale war.[10]

Spain invested enormous resources defending its most valuable cargo, the silver it extracted from the mines of Peru. Peruvian silver sailed through the Caribbean once a year escorted by a fleet of heavily armed ships.[11] Pirates and privateers dreamed of taking the treasure fleet, but never succeeded. The silver was captured only once, by the Dutch navy in 1628.[12] Private maritime raiders were more successful pursuing smaller prizes, and they found more riches to seize later in the seventeenth century and in the early decades of the eighteenth century after sugar cultivation and the slave trade transformed the Caribbean economy. Before the eighteenth century the competing European powers differed in the extent to which they invested in centralized navies or relied on privateers. From the sixteenth century forward Spain sought to strengthen its navy, possibly to the detriment of its merchant fleet. England's Queen Elizabeth, by contrast, privatized naval warfare on a grand scale, and even after the English navy gained greater support and fiscal resources in the second half of the seventeenth century, privateers remained an essential component of Britain's maritime strategy. By the middle decades of the eighteenth century the British, the French and the Spanish were all relying heavily on privateers, though Britain by that time possessed the most potent navy in the world.[13]

When they reached the shores of the Americas navies could wield enormous power. In most colonized regions in the seventeenth and eighteenth centuries the settlers remained dependent on overseas trade for the necessities of life, and therefore colonial combatants were almost always vulnerable to naval blockade. The colonists were not only economically but also politically subordinate to Europe, however, and therefore navies were often deployed away from America in order to answer the concerns of the home countries. Britain, for example, possessed the largest fleet in the world in the eighteenth century, but in wartime the British government usually kept most of its ships in European waters to ward off any possible attack from the continent.[14]

When deployed in colonial waters, large navies often played a decisive role in combat. The planters in the Caribbean were always conscious of their vulnerability to blockade.[15] In the seventeenth century the Dutch relied on naval superiority to seize Portuguese outposts in Angola and Brazil as well as along the coasts of the Indian Ocean.[16] Naval forces were decisive when the English conquered New Netherland from the Dutch in 1664 and when the Dutch retook the colony in 1673.[17] The British campaigns against the French in Acadia in 1690, 1704, 1707 and 1710 similarly demonstrated the importance of armed ships. The British were finally able to conquer and hold the colony (renamed Nova Scotia) only after the leaders of the 1710 expedition secured support from the Royal Navy.[18] Britain's campaigns against

267

French Canada followed the same pattern. Ambitious plans to attack the colony in 1709 and 1746 were abandoned because the Admiralty was unwilling to send its ships across the ocean. They took that risk in 1711, but the effort failed because the fleet foundered in a storm. Success came only in the period between 1758 and 1760, when the British navy arrived in full force and, coordinating its operations with the army, assumed a dominant position across the Gulf of St. Lawrence and the nearby North Atlantic. Britain maintained its blockade of the St. Lawrence River only intermittently, but when it did the French in Canada were starved.[19]

The American wars of independence exhibited a decline in the power of Europe's navies. The failure of the British blockade of Boston in 1774 and 1775 demonstrated one of two things: either that the American economy – in New England at least – had grown and diversified to such an extent that a naval embargo could no longer be relied upon to defeat a colonial adversary; or that a revolutionary movement could not be easily suppressed by a siege.[20] The French (and the British) would learn a similarly ambiguous lesson in Haiti in the 1790s, as would the Spanish early in the nineteenth century during the dissolution of their mainland American empire. Nonetheless, navies continued to play an important role in determining the balance of power. Whenever European troops were deployed in the Americas they relied heavily on naval support. Therefore their success in land battles often depended on their control of the shipping lanes. The United States declared independence from Britain in 1776 in part to give the revolutionary movement access to military aid from France and, more specifically, help from the French navy. The gambit paid off in 1781 when a French fleet took control of the waters off Yorktown and, operating in conjunction with George Washington's Continentals, surrounded Charles Cornwallis and his men, forcing them to surrender.[21] For the next two years, until the Treaty of Paris was signed in 1783, the erstwhile 'revolutionary' war was fought primarily in the Caribbean between the British, the French and the Spanish, with navies playing prominent roles.[22]

For the rest of the revolutionary era, through the Napoleonic period and for decades after that, the superior size and strength of the British navy affected the course of American politics. In Brazil, Buenos Aires, Chile and elsewhere in the crumbling Portuguese and Spanish Empires, Britain's naval interventions helped determine the outcome in colonial wars for independence.[23] The Royal Navy also defined the parameters of North America's War of 1812. During that conflict U.S. expansionists dreamed of defeating the British in Canada, but they knew they could not challenge Britain at sea. Though American privateers cruised the Caribbean during the war, no one in America contemplated seizing any British-ruled islands.[24]

COLONIZATION, SLAVERY, AND WARFARE ON LAND

Though they fought among themselves, from the fifteenth century forward the Europeans and their descendents dominated the Atlantic Ocean. The expansion of European power was more contested on land, and for centuries the relative strength of European and indigenous military forces along the coasts of Africa, on the islands of the Caribbean, and on the mainland of the Americas depended on an array of variables including spectacularly discriminatory disease environments and shifts in the pattern of trade. With the exception of the Azores, Madeira, and a few other

– CHAPTER 15: *War and warfare in the Atlantic World* –

uninhabited islands in the Atlantic, nearly everywhere the Europeans colonized in the early modern period they met armed resistance, and endemic warfare continued on the margins of most of their colonies and trading posts. Imperial soldiers, settlers and traveling merchants sought local allies, and consequently they often incorporated themselves into African and Native American diplomatic, military and commercial networks. The newcomers and the indigenous peoples struggled to understand each other, find common interests and exploit the opportunities that arose with the expansion of transatlantic commerce. Conflicts arose as a consequence of ongoing cultural misunderstandings and conflicting conceptions of justice and the appropriate use of force. Additionally, in many theatres of combat profits could be made by exploiting political instability. African, Native American and colonial leaders amassed riches, power and prestige in the context of war. Many indigenous and colonial communities felt vulnerable and believed that they had to engage in aggressive military action – or, at a minimum, issue dramatic threats – in order to survive. New ways of fighting developed, often involving a combination of hostage taking, torture, mutilation and other forms of exemplary punishment, or enslavement and the sale of captives.

The custom of taking captives in wartime and putting them to work as slaves had been common in many parts of Europe, Africa and the Americas before the fifteenth century.[25] Medieval Christian crusaders used war captives as slaves on sugar plantations they established on conquered Mediterranean islands.[26] In the sixteenth century Portuguese colonists adopted a similar practice on islands off the coast of Africa, forcing slaves they acquired through military action to work in their fields.[27] In the early days of colonization on Madeira, the Portuguese may have sent raiders to the Canary Islands to seize workers. It did not take long for them to realize, however, that they were better off purchasing workers in Africa. That continent's economy was already well organized for the delivery of slaves. In many societies along the African coast individuals were enslaved as a punishment for crime. The convicts joined other slaves who had been illicitly kidnapped, and those – a large portion of the enslaved population – who had been captured in war.[28] At least since the late 1750s when the antislavery campaigner Anthony Benezet began to protest against the Atlantic slave trade, activists and historians have been engaged in a debate over the slave trade's influence on warfare in Africa.[29] The transatlantic slave trade was not the only cause of Africa's wars, but there can be no doubt that the trade enriched and empowered the continent's wartime leaders, increased the cost of warfare and profoundly altered the consequences of military defeat.

The transatlantic economy that developed in the sixteenth century could not have been established or sustained without warfare and other forms of physical violence on a massive scale. Spain's first large-scale colonizing effort in the Americas, the conquest and settlement of Hispaniola, arguably set a pattern for much of what was to follow, though in its severity the episode may have been unique. In accordance with the *repartimiento* system introduced by Columbus in 1497, individual colonists demanded labor and tribute from indigenous islanders. Wielding this authority they broke up families and destroyed entire communities, sending men to work in gold mines and placing women and children to work on newly established farms. The local economy collapsed, resulting in famine and tens of thousands of deaths. Some of the islanders killed themselves, but more died of disease, and by 1520 their numbers may have dropped to as low as 500 from an initial population of about a quarter of

Figure 15.2 Slave traders in Gorés

– CHAPTER 15: War and warfare in the Atlantic World –

a million.[30] Throughout the Americas, indigenous populations were vulnerable to Eurasian and African pathogens. Epidemic diseases repeatedly wrecked Native communities and limited their ability to resist colonization. The Indians were susceptible not only because they were missing certain biological immunities, but also often because they suffered through food shortages, forced migrations, and other stresses that came as a direct consequence of war.[31]

Over the next two hundred years, on several of the Caribbean islands, colonization led to the total destruction of the indigenous population, a turn of events that encouraged the planters to turn to the transatlantic slave trade as a source for labor.[32] By contrast, Native populations seldom disappeared on the mainland of North or South America. Quite the contrary; at least until the eighteenth century in many regions the European colonists were outnumbered and needed assistance from Native allies if they were to conduct successful military campaigns. In 1519 Hernan Cortés succeeded against Moctezuma only with assistance from a large body of disaffected indigenous Mexicans. Many of his Native allies had grievances against the Aztec Empire, but others were simply trying to make the best of a difficult situation. All of them were impressed by the newcomer's military potential and they recognized the logistical advantage Cortés held over his opponents with his ability to send men and supplies quickly across long distances on horses and large ships.[33] Cortés was able to establish Spanish hegemony over the heartland of Mexico, but later in the colonial period on the margins of Spanish settlement, perhaps most dramatically in and around New Mexico, in times of crisis the colonists' survival could depend on the outcome of complex negotiations with a variety of powerful, disunited Native groups.[34]

While the Spanish frequently reached accommodations with Native leaders in order to secure and maintain power, their official policy toward the peoples of the Americas, especially in the sixteenth century, was uncompromising. Citing the Papal Bull of 1493, they insisted that they crossed the ocean with full legal authority and for the benefit of the Native Americans. The rituals that the Spanish army conducted to establish and dramatize the delegated power of the church and the crown encouraged colonial officials and missionaries alike to interpret resistance as rebellion and treat it as a crime.[35] On occasion the Spanish responded to perceived disobedience with severe punitive measures that blurred any distinction between labor discipline, criminal sanction, religious instruction, and full-scale war. Often church officials and military men asserted their authority most vehemently in outposts where they felt vulnerable, in the Yucatán, for example, or New Mexico.[36]

In Hispaniola, Mexico, Guatemala, and Peru, Spain's empire in the Americas was associated with the forcible expropriation of land and resources, the imposition of new social hierarchies, and coercive, exploitative labor relations.[37] From the perspective of many observers, violence seemed endemic to the entire colonial system, and the pattern of Spanish imperialism had lasting effects on the actions of subsequent colonizers. The Spanish subjugation of Hispaniola and Mexico, recounted graphically in the writings of the first bishop of Chiapas, Bartolomé de las Casas, convinced many imperial promoters in France, England, and Holland that the Native peoples of the Americas needed protectors and champions, that they were desperate for liberation from the Spanish, and that they would therefore welcome colonization by any other European power. Las Casas, of course, was Catholic, and he insisted that the crimes of the Spanish colonists violated the precepts of Catholic Christianity. Nonetheless after his work was translated and published in northern Europe, his accounts of Spanish atrocities were repeated by Protestant propagandists who increasingly came to view the Americas as a potential new zone of conflict in the ongoing wars of the Protestant Reformation. But even as Protestant colonial promoters claimed to espouse an alternative model of imperial expansion, at the same time in many respects they hoped to replicate the Spanish experience. The rhetoric the English used to support their early transatlantic colonial enterprises closely resembled Spanish imperial propaganda.[38] This was not merely the result of emulation. In their recent histories, England and Spain had much in common. Though they took opposite sides in the controversies dividing Christendom, England's Protestants and Spain's Catholics both adopted old arguments that had been used to support earlier crusading ventures. Spain and England were also similar in that both countries had long been engaged in struggles against allegedly benighted peoples on their own frontiers. The Spanish launched its transatlantic imperial enterprise immediately after defeating Muslim Granada, and many of the juridical and military practices they took to the Americas – including their way of distributing land, bound labor, and political authority to the officers of its conquering armies – drew on precedents from the period of the *reconquista*.[39] England's ongoing struggles in Ireland and along its border with Scotland similarly informed its behavior across the ocean.[40]

In the early 1560s, when French Protestants arrived in the Carolinas and built the first European fort on the Atlantic coast of mainland North America, the French quickly discovered how difficult it could be to establish durable, productive alliances with Native American groups. The Huguenots, unfamiliar with the norms of North American diplomacy, slighted those who had initially cooperated with them, tried to shift alliances, and ended up antagonizing almost everyone in their immediate vicinity, leaving them vulnerable to Spanish attack.[41] The early Virginia colonists made similar mistakes, and the two major conflicts that resulted, in 1622 and 1644, can accurately be described as simply pitting Native American warriors against armed colonists. The warfare that beset French Canada, New Netherland, and New England in the first half of the seventeenth century was more complex, as competing colonial groups and Native confederacies jockeyed for power and access to trade goods. Muskets became an important item of commerce, transforming Native American warfare and altering the balance of power among the tribes.[42]

Acquiring arms as a consequence of successive alliances with the Dutch and the English, the Iroquois League violently asserted itself and eventually became a dominant player in the fur trade by securing hunting grounds, demanding furs as tribute from others, and occupying trade routes across the St. Lawrence Valley and as far south as the Ohio. Long ago historians labeled the Iroquois League's seventeenth-century campaigns the 'Beaver Wars,' and the designation appropriately highlights the role of commerce in promoting bloodshed. The fighting became almost self-perpetuating. As Daniel K. Richter has shown, at the height of the wars the Iroquois League was struggling to maintain its own population. Families and villages sought to adopt outsiders to replace the men, women, and children they were losing, and their desire to acquire war captives became, in and of itself, a powerful motive for military raids.[43] Captive taking had been part of Native American warfare for centuries, but it escalated nearly everywhere in the context of colonization, and particularly in the early decades of the eighteenth century in the southeast, the

– CHAPTER 15: *War and warfare in the Atlantic World* –

practice was directly and simply tied to the operation of the Atlantic economy. Native groups sold their captives to the British and the French, and the British shipped many of them to the Caribbean where they worked and died as slaves.[44]

There is a consensus among historians that Native Americans military culture changed in the context of colonization, but scholars continue to debate whether the colonists' way of fighting 'Indian Wars' represented a sharp departure from the customs of their ancestors. John Grenier argues that a new 'way of war' emerged among the English in America, with distinctive features including 'the destruction of enemy noncombatants and their agricultural resources,' ranging, and 'scalp hunting.'[45] While it is certainly true that practices such as scalping were distinctly American, it is also important to remember that armies fighting in Europe engaged in other practices closely associated with American frontier warfare, in sixteenth- and seventeenth-century Ireland, for example, and in the Highlands of Scotland in 1746. When soldiers committed widespread rape, burned houses and fields across large areas, killed prisoners or displayed body parts along the sides of roads, early modern European commentators often described their conduct as 'lawless.' In most instances, however, those episodes resulted from an overlay of conflicting customs and laws.[46] When fighting men from differing military traditions faced each other, the antagonists on both sides were frequently shocked by the other's behavior and responded with a kind of unflattering mimicry, animated by a desire for revenge. This happened on occasion in Ireland and Scotland and repeatedly in the woods of North America when English colonists and Native American warriors fought.[47]

The incongruity of competing military traditions contributed to the ferocity of frontier warfare, but in Ireland, Britain, and North America another kind of cultural conflict had equally devastating consequences. Judicial officers and soldiers applied coercive force according to different rules, and problems arose when military forces were deployed against armed opponents in order to execute the sanctions of the criminal law. This happened, for example, in Ireland in 1569 and 1574, in New England in 1676, in Scotland in 1746, and in Nova Scotia in 1749. Government agents seeking to defend the sovereignty of the British crown suspended the protocols that normally governed European military conduct. Facing alleged rebels and traitors, commanding officers insisted that they had the authority – indeed the obligation – to expose prisoners taken on the field of battle to trial, punishment, and in some cases death. Adopting this stance made negotiation difficult, and it had the effect of prolonging and intensifying conflict.[48] Perhaps the ultimate manifestation of this dynamic in British North America came in 1763, when Colonel Jeffery Amherst, seeking to defend the uncontested sovereignty of George III, refused to honor the rituals of Native American diplomacy.[49] Amherst antagonized the most powerful Native leaders of the trans-Appalachian west, and when attacked he pursued a range of punitive measures that included one effort to infect Native peoples with small pox.[50] He may not have actually made anyone ill, but his actions are still worth examining. Amherst did not champion lawless behavior. It is likely that he believed that even his attempt to spread infectious disease enjoyed legal sanction. He was operating in a hostile environment, seeking to punish people he believed to be savages and rebels, but he could not rely on the orderly judicial machinery that in Europe might have been used to uphold the sovereign's monopoly on the use of violence.

273

A similar fusion of military and judicial functions affected the conduct of the Peruvian colonial authorities in 1780 and 1781 when they confronted the indigenous army of Tupac Amaru, and operated more commonly throughout the Western Hemisphere when slaveholders met large-scale resistance from those they intended to control as slaves.[51] The notorious brutality of Maroon warfare, with men, women and children targeted, homes and fields destroyed, prisoners decapitated or burned alive, and corpses placed for weeks or months on display, reflected the desperation of both runaways and planters. In the British Caribbean and elsewhere, slaveholders denigrated Maroons as traitors, murderers, and savages reverting to a vicious African culture. The British disdained negotiating with them, but on those few occasions when Maroon communities acquired enough strength to endure, most notably on Jamaica, the colonial authorities had little choice but to consider the limits of their own power and at least temporarily agree to terms. Colonial officials faced similar dilemmas on the periphery of Surinam and near many other slaveholding societies in the Caribbean and the American mainland. Even more clearly than in Africa, the maintenance of chattel slavery as a labor system sparked a relentless cycle of warfare on the margins of the American colonies.[52]

TRANSATLANTIC WAR

In 1654, in the closing months of the first Anglo-Dutch war, a ship captain and merchant from Massachusetts named Robert Sedgwick received a commission from Oliver Cromwell to attack the Dutch colony of New Netherland. He was given command of four ships and 200 English troops, and returned to America where he recruited 700 more colonial volunteers. By the time this force had been raised, however, news had arrived from Europe that England and Holland had concluded a peace. Sedgwick's intended siege of New Amsterdam was cancelled, but he was unwilling to disband his forces and therefore to make the best use of them he could, he sailed east and took control of the French colony of Acadia. England's treaty with Holland had effectively precluded a move against the Dutch colony, but from the New Englanders' perspective it was acceptable to attack the French even though England and France were not formally at war.[53]

The Sedgwick expedition illustrates a general pattern in the relationship between European diplomacy and colonial warfare in the seventeenth century. The governments of Europe frequently took an interest in the defense of their colonial possessions, and diplomatic and military events in Europe could, on occasion, determine American outcomes. This happened repeatedly during the contest over New Netherland. Often, however, wars between the colonists followed their own timetable. French and English settlers could fight each other even when Europe remained at peace.

The pattern was different in the eighteenth century, though arguably this was a difference of degree rather than kind. There were still major wars fought in North America, such as the French colonists' Fox Wars, for example, or the Massachusetts war against the Abenaki, that did not correspond directly to any European conflicts. Similarly there were European wars such as the mid-1730s War of the Polish Succession that did not trigger combat in the colonies. Overall, however, after 1689 most major wars in Europe resulted in fighting across the ocean, and conflict in the

Americas roiled European affairs. With the exception of the American Revolution, from 1689 until 1815, in every major conflict between France and Britain, French and British forces engaged each other on both sides of the Atlantic.

Transatlantic diplomacy and warfare profoundly affected politics in both America and Europe. Native American polities, already reconfigured in the aftermath of epidemic disease, dislocation and conflict in the seventeenth century, again were reordered, as power and wealth gravitated toward those groups who most successfully positioned themselves in an ever-more elaborate set of alliance networks incorporating rival colonial empires. The Iroquois, in particular, became sophisticated negotiators sensitive to European affairs.[54] Some scholars have questioned whether there ever was such a thing as an 'Amerindian Atlantic.'[55] The simple chronology of Native American history answers the question. From 1689 through 1713 and again from 1744 through 1763, imperial warfare devastated many Native communities. Conversely, in much of North America Native peoples prospered in the period from 1713 to 1744, when Britain and France maintained a fragile peace.[56]

Colonial warfare had an equally pervasive influence on the direction of politics in Europe. Almost as soon as it began in 1701, the War of the Spanish Succession became a contest between France and Britain over access to the trade of the Spanish Empire.[57] Britain gained important concessions in the treaty that ended that conflict, including a license to sell slaves to the Spanish in the Caribbean. The next major transatlantic war began in 1739 as a result of Britain's efforts to defend and expand its colonial trading privileges. The War of Jenkins' Ear initiated an expanding cycle of violence that eventually engulfed most of Europe as the War of the Austrian Succession.[58] The Seven Years War, the climactic global confrontation between the British and French empires, similarly started in the Americas. As the powers of Europe were drawn into increasingly prolonged and expensive conflicts to defend their colonial interests, the very structure of their governments changed. While Britain developed a robust and effective fiscal–military state, France struggled to finance its wartime adventures.[59] The cost of its intervention in the American Revolution contributed to the financial crisis that brought down the Bourbon monarchy.

The eighteenth century was the first age of transatlantic warfare, and that era gradually came to a close as a consequence of the political upheavals that began with the American Revolution and ended with the defeat of Napoleon. In order to win their independence from Britain, the Patriots in America allied themselves with France, but soon after the fighting ended many citizens of the new republic began to look askance at what George Washington called 'entangling alliances.' The divisive, pro-British policies of the Adams administration, culminating in America's 1798–1800 'Quasi-war' with France, reinforced a widespread apprehension that if the U.S. confronted any European power militarily, the resulting conflict would divide the country, undermine its autonomy and corrupt its republican principles. Presidents Thomas Jefferson and James Madison, in turn, struggled to maintain American neutrality. They experimented with trade embargos in an effort to discover a way to resolve international conflicts without resort to warfare.[60]

Meanwhile, during the first two decades of the nineteenth century, most of the Western Hemisphere witnessed war. Britain, France, Spain, and Portugal were drawn into a protracted series of conflicts that ultimately had the effect of weakening the ability of all four countries to control large parts of their transatlantic empires.[61]

Sailing became more dangerous as the belligerents targeted shipping in an effort to strangle their opponents economically. There were violent confrontations in the Caribbean including Napoleon's disastrous, unsuccessful effort to restore French sovereignty and slavery in Haiti. Independence movements broke apart the Spanish Empire on the mainland of North and South America, and the Portuguese monarchy, losing control of Portugal, established a new and separate polity in Brazil. All of these developments had the effect of distancing the Americas from Europe politically, facilitating the establishment of the nineteenth-century diplomatic order which drew a distinction between European and American affairs.

Of all the Europeans, the British retained the greatest power on both sides of the Atlantic, thanks to the strength of their navy. The British also held strategically important colonies on the mainland of North America and remained influential in Native American affairs. Many in the United States viewed Britain as a rival, and a series of controversies involving naval operations and the arms trade west of the Appalachians culminated in the Anglo-American conflict known in North America as the 'War of 1812.'[62] The U.S. and Britain fought for three years. Though no territory changed hands the war was hardly inconsequential, because it ended with a set of peace agreements that helped reshape the pattern of diplomacy and warfare across the Atlantic world.

The Napoleonic Wars ended in Europe with the Congress of Vienna and the creation of a new diplomatic order based on a balance of power between several European states. The new system discouraged international conflict and proved so resilient that nearly a century passed before the continent experienced another protracted large-scale war. The settlement that ended the War of 1812 in North America had different implications. The conflict had strengthened the standing of those within the United States who argued that the country should distance itself from European affairs. At the same time, Andrew Jackson's performance in the Battle of New Orleans, his subsequent campaigns against the Creeks, his invasion of Spanish Florida and his political triumph in 1828 empowered those who supported militant U.S. expansionism. Under the terms of the treaty ending the War of 1812 Britain had promised to desist from trade with Native Americans living within the borders of the United States. In effect Britain left the United States free to pursue its own wars south of the 49th parallel free from British interference.[63] In 1823 the Monroe Doctrine established an enduring policy framework in which the United States sought to bar any new European intrusion into North or South America. Partly as a consequence, for the rest of the century, wars would be conducted only on one side or the other of the Atlantic Ocean. The first age of transatlantic warfare was over.

NOTES

1 See W.W. Fitzhugh and E.I. Ward, eds, *Vikings: The North Atlantic Saga*, Washington: Smithsonian Institution Press, 2000.

2 F.M. Hocker and J.M. McManamon, 'Medieval Shipbuilding in the Mediterranean and Written Culture at Venice', *Mediterranean Historical Review* 21, 2006, 1–37.

3 R.C. Smith, *Vanguard of Empire: Ships of Exploration in the Age of Columbus*, Oxford: Oxford University Press, 1993, pp. 30–49; J.R.S. Phillips, *The Medieval Expansion of Europe*, Oxford: Oxford University Press, 1998, p. 230.

4 N.A.M. Rodger, 'Guns and Sails in the First Phase of English Colonization, 1500–1650', in N. Canny, ed., *The Origins of Empire: British Overseas Enterprise to the Close of the*

– CHAPTER 15: *War and warfare in the Atlantic World* –

Seventeenth Century, Oxford: Oxford University Press, 1998, pp. 79–98; Smith, *Vanguard of Empire*, pp. 148–70.

5 G. Fox, *The Journal of George Fox*, ed. N. Penney, 2 vols, Cambridge: Cambridge University Press, 1911, vol. 2, 251; E.E, Clark, *Indian Legends of Canada*, Toronto: McClelland and Stewart, 1960, p. 150; S.T. Rand, *Legends of the Micmacs*, New York, 1894, p. 225; G.H. Loskiel, *History of the Mission of the United Brethren Among the Indians in North America* trans. G.I. La Trobe, London: Brethren's Society for the Furtherance of the Gospel, 1794, p. 123; J.A.U. Gronniosaw, *A Narrative of the Life of James Albert Ukawsaw Gronniosaw* (Bath, n.d., 1780?), 11; O. Equiano, *The Interesting Narrative and Other Writings*, ed. V. Caretta, London: Penguin, 2003, p. 55; M. Rediker, *The Slave Ship: A Human History*, New York: Viking, 2007, p. 104.

6 See O.P. Dickason, 'La "Guerre navale" des micmacs contre les britaniques, 1713–63', in C.A. Martijn, ed., *Les Micmacs et la mer*, Montreal: Recherches amerindiennes au Québec, 1986, p. 244.

7 J. Thornton, *Africa and Africans in the Making of the Atlantic World, 1400–1800*, 2d ed., Cambridge: Cambridge University Press, 1998, pp. 37–38; J. Thornton, *Warfare in Atlantic Africa, 1500–1800*, London: UCL Press, 1999, p. 23.

8 K.R. Andrews, *Elizabethan Privateering: English Privateering during the Spanish War, 1585–1603*, Cambridge: Recherches amerindiennes au Québec, 1964, pp. 33, 39, 44.

9 Rodger, 'Guns and Sails', pp. 79–98, 86–87.

10 E.H. Gould, 'Zones of Law, Zones of Violence: The Legal Geography of the British Atlantic, c. 1772', *William and Mary Quarterly* 3d ser., 60, 2003, pp. 471–510, here pp. 479–81.

11 K.R. Andrews, *The Spanish Caribbean: Trade and Plunder, 1530–1630*, New Haven: Yale University Press, 1978, pp. 64–70.

12 C.R. Phillips, *Six Galleons for Spain: Imperial Defense in the Early Seventeenth Century*, Baltimore: Johns Hopkins University Press, 1986, pp. 4–5.

13 C.E. Swanson, *Predators and Prizes: American Privateering and Imperial Warfare, 1739–1748*, Columbia: University of South Carolina Press, 1991.

14 N.A.M. Rodger, 'Sea Power and Empire, 1688–1793', in P.J. Marshall, ed, *The Oxford History of the British Empire: The Eighteenth Century*, Oxford: Oxford University Press, 1998, pp. 169–83.

15 A.J. O'Shaughnessey, *An Empire Divided: The American Revolution and the British Caribbean*, Philadelphia: University of Pennsylvania Press, 2000, pp. 49–50.

16 A.J.R. Russell-Wood, *The Portuguese Empire, 1415–1808*, Baltimore: Johns Hopkins University Press, 1992, pp. 23–24.

17 R.C. Ritchie, *The Duke's Province: A Study of New York Politics and Society, 1664–1691*, Chapel Hill: University of North Carolina Press, 1977, pp. 20–24, 87–88.

18 G. Plank, *An Unsettled Conquest: The British Campaign Against the Peoples of Acadia*, Philadelphia: University of Pennsylvania Press, 2001, pp. 10–67.

19 See A.J.B. Johnston, *Endgame 1758: The Promise, the Glory, and the Despair of Louisbourg's Last Decade*, Lincoln: University of Nebraska Press, 2007; J.R. Dull, *The French Navy and the Seven Years' War*, Lincoln: University of Nebraska Press, 2005; see also generally F. Anderson, *Crucible of War: The Seven Years' War and the Fate of Empire in British North America, 1754–1766*, New York: Knopf, 2000.

20 R. Buel, *In Irons: Britain's Naval Supremacy and the American Revolutionary Economy*, New Haven: Yale University Press, 1998.

21 See generally R. Middlekauff, *The Glorious Cause: The American Revolution, 1763–1789*, New York: Oxford University Press, 1982; D. Higginbotham, *The War of American Independence: Military Attitudes, Policies and Practices*, Boston: Northeastern University Press, 1983.

22 W.M. James, *The British Navy in Adversity: A Study of the War of American Independence*, London: Longmans, Green, 1926, pp. 316–65.

23 See D.E. Worcester, *Sea Power and Chilean Independence*, Gainesville: University of Florida Press, 1962, and more generally G.S. Graham and R.A. Humphreys, *The Navy and South America, 1807–1823*, London: Navy Records Society, 1962.

24 T. Bickham, *The Weight of Vengeance: The United States, the British Empire, and the War of 1812*, Oxford: Oxford University Press, 2012, pp. 91–92, 152–54.

25 See in particular C. Snyder, *Slavery in Indian Country: The Changing Face of Captivity in Early America*, Cambridge: Harvard University Press, 2012.

26 W.M. Evans, 'From the Land of Canaan to the Land of Guinea: The Strange Odyssey of the "Sons of Ham"', *American Historical Review* 85, 1980, 34.

27 Thornton, *Africa and Africans*, p. 34.

28 Rediker, *The Slave Ship*, pp. 73–107.

29 A. Benezet, *Observations on the Inslaving, Importing and Purchasing of Negroes*, Germantown, Penn.: Christopher Sower, 1759, pp. 3–5.

30 K.R. Andrews, *The Spanish Caribbean: Trade and Plunder, 1530–1630*, New Haven: Yale University Press, 1978, pp. 4–11.

31 D.S. Jones, 'Virgin Soils Revisited', *William and Mary Quarterly* 3d ser. 60, 2003, 703–42.

32 On the fate of the Indians of the Lesser Antilles see K.F, Kiple and K.C. Ornelas, 'After the Encounter: Disease and Demographics in the Lesser Antilles', in R.L. Paquette and S.L. Engerman, eds, *The Lesser Antilles in the Age of European Expansion*, Gainesville: University Press of Florida, 1996, pp. 50–67; P.P. Boucher, *Cannibal Encounters: Europeans and Island Caribs, 1492–1763*, Baltimore: Johns Hopkins University Press, 1992.

33 C. Townsend, 'Burying the White Gods: New Perspectives on the Conquest of Mexico', *American Historical Review* 108, 2003, 659–87.

34 R. Gutierrez, *When Jesus Came, the Corn Mothers Went Away: Marriage, Sexuality, and Power in New Mexico, 1500–1846*, Palo Alto, Cal.: Stanford University Press, 1991; J.F. Brooks, *Captives and Cousins: Slavery, Kinship, and Community in the Southwest Borderlands*, Chapel Hill: University of North Carolina Press, 2002.

35 P. Seed, 'Taking Possession and Reading Texts', *William and Mary Quarterly* 3d se. 49, 1992, 202–7.

36 I. Clendinnen, 'Disciplining the Indians: Franciscan Ideology and Missionary Violence in Sixteenth-Century Yucatán', *Past and Present* 94, 1982, 27–48; Guteirrez, *When Jesus Came*, 44–45, 53–54.

37 For events in Guatemala and Peru, see W.G. Lovell, *Conquest and Survival in Colonial Guatemala: A Historical Geography of the Cuchumatan Highlands, 1500–1821*, Montreal: McGill-Queen's University Press, 1985; S.J. Stern, *Peru's Indian Peoples and the Challenge of Spanish Conquest: Humanga to 1640*, Madison: University of Wisconsin Press, 1982.

38 J.C. Esguerra, *Puritan Conquistadors: Iberianizing the Atlantic, 1500–1700*, Stanford, Cal.: Standford University Press, 2006.

39 M. Góngora, *Studies in the Colonial History of Spanish America*, trans. Richard Southern, Cambridge: Cambridge University Press, 1975, pp. 1–32; D.J. Weber, *The Spanish Frontier in North America*, New Haven: Yale University Press, 1992, pp. 23, 124–25; but see also L. Benton, *Law and Colonial Cultures: Legal Regimes in World History*, Cambridge: Cambridge University Press, 2002, pp. 33–45.

40 N.P. Canny, 'The Ideology of English Colonization: From Ireland to America', *William and Mary Quarterly* 3d ser. 30, 1973, 575–98.

41 D.B. Quinn, *North America from its Earliest Discovery to First Settlements*, New York: Harper and Row, 1975, pp. 240–61.

– CHAPTER 15: *War and warfare in the Atlantic World* –

42 For a vivid account of the transformative impact of muskets see F. Anderson and A. Cayton, *The Dominion of War: Empire and Liberty in North America*, New York: Penguin, 2005, 1–53.

43 D.K. Richter, 'War and Culture: The Iroquois Experience', *William and Mary Quarterly* 3d ser. 40, 1983, 528–59.

44 A. Gallay, *The Indian Slave Trade: The Rise of the English Empire in the American South*, New Haven: Yale University Press, 2002, pp. 299–301. For discussions of captive taking in other parts of North America, see E. Haefeli and K. Sweeny, *Captors and Captives: The 1704 French and Indian Raid on Deerfield*, Amherst: University of Massachusetts Press, 2003; B. Rushforth, '"A Little Flesh We Offer You": The Origins of Indian Slavery in New France', *William and Mary Quarterly* 3d ser. 60, 2003, 777–808; B. Rushworth, 'Slavery, The Fox Wars, and the Limits of Alliance', *William and Mary Quarterly* 3d ser. 63, 2006, 53–80; Brooks, *Captives and Cousins*.

45 J. Grenier, *The First Way of War: American War Making on the Frontier, 1607–1814*, Cambridge: Cambridge University Press, 2005, pp. 21, 43. For a starkly different assessment of early American warfare see G. Chet, *Conquering the American Wilderness: The Triumph of European Warfare in the Colonial Northeast*, Amherst: University of Massachusetts Press, 2003.

46 For a discussion of this dynamic in the British-colonial context see Gould, 'Zones of Law, Zones of Violence', pp. 474–75.

47 A.J. Hirsch, 'The Collision of Military Cultures in Seventeenth-Century New England', *Journal of American History* 74, 1988, 1187–1212.

48 Canny, 'Ideology of English Colonization', pp. 581–82; J.H. Pulsipher, *Subjects Unto the Same King: Indians, English and the Contest for Authority in Colonial New England*, Philadelphia: University of Pennsylvania Press, 2005, pp. 119–34; G. Plank, *Rebellion and Savagery: The Jacobite Rising of 1745 and the British Empire*, Philadelphia: University of Pennsylvania Press, 2006, pp. 29–52, 156–57.

49 R. White, *The Middle Ground: Indians, Empires, and Republics in the Great Lakes Region, 1650–1815*, Cambridge: Cambridge University Press, 1991, pp. 256–60.

50 E.A. Fenn, 'Biological Warfare in Eighteenth-century North America: Beyond Jeffery Amherst', *Journal of American History* 86, 2000, 1553–80.

51 A.F. Galindo, 'The Rebellion of Tupac Amaru', in D. Castro, ed., *Revolution and Revolutionaries: Guerilla Movements in Latin America*, Wilmington, Del.: Scholarly Resources, 1999, pp. 1–10.

52 A.O. Thompson, *Flying to Freedom: African Runaways and Maroons in the Americas*, Kingston, Jamaica: University of the West Indies Press, 2006, pp. 144–74, 265–94; M. Caton, *Testing the Chains: Resistance to Slavery in the British West Indies*, Ithaca, N.Y.: Cornell University Press, 1982; M.C. Campbell, *The Maroons of Jamaica, 1655–1796: A History of Resistance, Collaboration and Betrayal*, Granby, Mass.: Bergin and Garvey, 1988; W. Hoogbergen, *The Boni Maroon Wars in Suriname*, New York: Brill, 1990; Richard Price, ed., *Maroon Societies: Rebel Slave Communities in the Americas*, Baltimore: Johns Hopkins University Press, 1979; Benton, *Law and Colonial Cultures*, 59–66.

53 R. Gildrie, 'Segwick, Robert,' *Oxford Dictionary of National Biography*, Oxford: Oxford University Press, 2004, vol. 49, 653; J.G. Reid, *Acadia, Maine and New Scotland: Marginal Colonies in the Seventeenth Century: Marginal Colonies in the Seventeenth Century*, Toronto: University of Toronto Press, 1981, pp. 135–38.

54 J. Parmenter, 'After the Mourning Wars: The Iroquois as Allies in Colonial North American Campaigns, 1676–1760', *William and Mary Quarterly* 3d ser, 64, 2007, 39–82.

55 P. Cohen, 'Was there an Amerindian Atlantic? Reflections on the Limits of a Historiographical Concept', *History of European Ideas* 34, 2008, 388–410.

56 D.K. Richter, *Facing East from Indian Country: A Native History of Early America*, Cambridge: Harvard University Press, 2001, pp. 151–88.

57 S.J. Stein and B.H. Steiin, *Silver, Trade, and War: Spain and America in the Making of Early Modern Europe*, Baltimore: Johns Hopkins University Press, 2000, pp. 106–44.

58 R. Browning, *The War of the Austrian Succession*, New York: St. Martin's Press, 1993, pp. 21–23, 28–29.

59 J. Brewer, *The Sinews of Power: War, Money, and the English State, 1688–1783*, Cambridge: Harvard University Press, 1990; J. Pritchard, *Louis XIV's Navy, 1748–1762*, Montreal: McGill-Queen's University Press, 1987, pp. 184–205; S. Schama, *Citizens: A Chronicle of the French Revolution*, New York: Knopf, 1989, p. 65.

60 D. McCoy, *The Elusive Republic: Political Economy in Jeffersonian America*, Chapel Hill: University of North Carolina Press, 1980, pp. 209–35; J.C.A. Stagg, *Mr. Madison's War: Politics, Diplomacy, and Warfare in the Early American Republic, 1783–1830*, Princeton: Princeton University Press, 1983, pp. 22–25.

61 See J. Adelman, *Sovereignty and Revolution in the Iberian Atlantic*, Princeton: Princeton University Press, 2006, pp. 101–40.

62 J. Latimer, *1812: War with America*, Cambridge, Mass.: Belknap, 2007; D.R. Hickey, *The War of 1812: A Forgotten Conflict*, Urbana: University of Illinois Press, 1989.

63 For a fuller discussion of this transition see E. Gould, *Among the Powers of the Earth: The American Revolution and the Making of a New World Empire* Cambridge: Harvard University Press, 2012.

CHAPTER 16

POLITICAL THINKING, MILITARY POWER, AND ARMS BEARING IN THE BRITISH ATLANTIC WORLD

——·◆·——

Charles R. Drummond, IV

In *Federalist* 41, James Madison celebrated both British and American military institutions. Both countries, unlike the great powers of Western Europe, possessed military forces that would not lead to oppression. This was only possible, he explained, because they had been similarly blessed by geographic insulation from foreign entanglements by the English Channel and the Atlantic Ocean, respectively. They were thus able to do without large, regular army forces, which would have undoubtedly introduced military despotism and eroded civil liberties. Instead, they could largely rely upon citizen-based militias and the fleet.[1] Madison clearly discerned a large degree of consonance between British and American attitudes about military power, and this article argues that the 'British Atlantic world' proves a useful organizing principle for examining political thinking on military power in the British Isles and early America.[2] This article treats the period between *c.* 1640 and *c.* 1868, that is, from a little before the outbreak of the English Civil Wars to a little after the conclusion of the American Civil War. Such a large-scale study, albeit one primarily concerned with the American founding, might call to mind Lovejovian unit ideas that persisted and were transmitted, unaltered, across the Atlantic. This is not my contention. Indeed, while commonalities are emphasized, attention is also given to the transformation of ideas over time.[3]

MILITARY VOCABULARIES IN THE BRITISH ATLANTIC

This study represents an analysis of the language and vocabularies used to discuss military power in the early modern British Atlantic world. There is a recognition that such languages were neither stable nor monolithic, and reference is given to a wide spectrum of views about military power, running from broadly 'republican' to more 'courtly' paradigms. The study begins with a justification of the focus on the *British* Atlantic world. There follows an examination of the two poles of 'republican' and 'courtly' paradigms explaining their shared terminologies and divergent conclusions. Attention is then directed to the key categories and controversies related to military power in the British Atlantic world, including: the debate over the 'militia power,' which attempted to locate military power in the executive (king/president) in relation to the legislative (parliament/congress); the fundamental dichotomy of the 'militia'/'standing army'; the debate over the differential military powers of the center/periphery; resistance theory; and arms bearing, especially in relation to the Second Amendment. It is argued that the Second Amendment must be understood in light of early modern British Atlantic discussions on military power. It is further suggested that the Second Amendment should be read in light of a broader 'distributist approach,' which focuses on the *distribution* of military power within the early American polity.

In the later half of the seventeenth century, beginning with the English Civil Wars, Britons engaged in an extended discussion about the interaction between military power and politics. This discussion can best be described as a series of debates relating to political thinking about military power centered on three axes. First, Britons wondered who held ultimate sovereign military power: either king or parliament? Second, they wondered what form of military organisation was best, both in terms of geopolitical strength and domestic political ramifications: either the militia or a professional army? Finally, many worried how military power might be linked to the religious controversies of the day. Fears revolved around how military power could be used in order to impose Anglicanism, toleration for religious dissenters, or, perhaps most terrifyingly, Catholicism through the use of a 'popish army.' These questions were pressing, following as they did upon the heels of the 'military revolution,' and they cast a long shadow, shaping attitudes towards military power on both sides of the Atlantic until the middle of the nineteenth century.[4]

These early modern British Atlantic debates and controversies, of course, were not entirely without precedent. Concern about the political ramifications of military power had been a mainstay of political thinking stretching back to antiquity. Probing questions about the relationship between political and military power had also been raised in the Italian peninsula by civic humanists, including Bruni and Machiavelli, who warned of the dangers of *condottieri* and celebrated civic militias.[5] This legacy of reflection on military power was, of course, important to the development of British ideas. Nonetheless, one can bracket off a distinctly British style of reflection on these matters, informed by the area's peculiar institutional arrangements, memory of the Civil Wars, and politics.

By the same token, in America, political thinking about military power occurred within the context of a broader Atlantic world, in which different European powers, including the Spanish, Portuguese, French, and Dutch used military means to bolster imperial designs. One might expect North-South influence of the colonial powers on one another, especially in terms of their attitudes about military power, rather than a mere East-West transmission of British ideas across the Atlantic.[6] Nonetheless, this intra-colonial impact was not remarkably pronounced, and American discussions were more heavily inflected by British viewpoints and attitudes. Early Americans largely transferred British military institutions across the Atlantic and continued to think about military power in a way remarkably similar to their British cousins.

Of course, the presence of a shared language did not mean that political thinking about military power was without variation. Generally speaking, there was a spectrum of positions running from a 'republican' to a more 'courtly' paradigm of military power. Proponents of the former inveighed against professional armies kept up in peacetime (or 'standing armies' in the contemporary parlance), and argued for the importance of the militia. These views often occurred alongside preferences for parliamentary and/or local control over military power, as opposed to royal and/or centralized control.[7]

By focussing on the widespread distribution of military power, many advocates of the republican paradigm hoped to equip people with the means to rebel against a future despotic government. This republican paradigm came into being in the 1640s and 1650s, with much of it present in the writings of Sir Henry Vane and James Harrington, as well as in a more obscure anonymous pamphlet, *The peaceable militia* (1648).[8] It was further articulated by Whig opponents of the Stuarts in the Restoration period, and it persisted in the writings of authors such as Andrew Fletcher, John Toland and John Trenchard in the 1690s. It was then preserved into the eighteenth century by 'Country Party' writers, including Henry St John, first Viscount Bolingbroke, and the authors of *Cato's letters*.[9] In early America, the republican paradigm was widespread and dominated critiques of British military power in the 1760s and 1770s. Later in the century, Anti-Federalists, most notably Patrick Henry, were vocal advocates of these ideas in their attacks on the Constitution, and the republican paradigm continued to motivate American analyses of military power until around the period of the American Civil War.

The courtly paradigm, on the other hand, reversed almost all of these positions. It emphasized the power of the king over parliament, the importance of the standing army over the militia, the center over the localities, and it abhorred popular resistance against the regime. This constellation of ideas proved to be the natural position taken by kings and courtiers, who recognized the potential of monarchically controlled regular forces to bolster kingly and state power. The courtly paradigm can be seen in many of the remarks of Charles II and James II, and it is further reflected in the Earl of Orrery's *A treatise of the art of war* (1677) and Sir Bernardo Gascoigne's memoranda on military matters prepared in the mid-1680s for James II.[10] During the 'land forces controversy' (1697–1701) (sometimes called the 'standing army controversy') following the conclusion of the Nine Years' War, some elements of this paradigm were taken up by Lord Somers and the Whig Junto, who were helped in their propaganda efforts by a young Daniel Defoe.[11] The torch of the courtly paradigm was thereafter carried on by 'Court Whigs,' and it was eventually taken up, at least in some form, by the Federalists, perhaps most vociferously by Alexander Hamilton.[12]

POLARITIES OF POWER

The first major controversy over political thinking about military power in the early modern British Atlantic world revolved around the balance of military power between the executive and the legislative. This important question first surfaced during the 'Militia Ordinance controversy' (1641–1642) in the lead-up to the outbreak of the English Civil Wars. Amidst a fraught political scene, two contradictory commands issued forth from king and parliament on the raising of the trained bands. The issuing of *both* the king's Commissions of Array and the parliament's Militia Ordinance forced the English people to grapple with the thorny constitutional question of who held ultimate sovereignty over the military.[13] This difficult question persisted well after the 1640s and continued to inform discussions about military power for decades to come. After the Restoration of the Stuart monarchy, there was a general understanding that the king alone possessed the militia power – that is, ultimate sovereignty and command over the realm's military forces. This was then confirmed in acts of parliament in 1661 and 1662, in which the king's possession of *sole power* over the militia was proclaimed. Throughout the Restoration period, however, republican thinkers questioned the notion of the royal militia power, and argued that control over the military should be vested in parliament, or even directly in the people.

The dispute over the 'militia power' was remembered in colonial America, and it was recapitulated in similar debates about the division of federal military power between the executive and legislative branches.[14] Many shared Edmund Randolph's concern that the president represented the 'foetus of monarchy.'[15] Some were concerned that a future president might be a second Cromwell, a military dictator who would use the army for self-aggrandisement and the establishment of autocracy.[16] The transition from king to commander-in-chief, from prerogative to presidency, was complex and controversial, most notably due to the fact that post-Revolutionary America was emphatically a *republic*, which claimed to have sloughed off monarchy. In the Articles of Confederation, the legislature (namely, the Confederation Congress) was given the 'sole and exclusive right and power of determining on peace and war.'[17] Under the Constitution, the new Congress had the power to declare war, and was given substantial new powers over regulating the professional army, the militia and the navy, but the President was also declared Commander-in-Chief and was given wide powers over the military and foreign affairs.[18]

A tendency to mistrust monarchical (and presidential) power was pronounced in some circles, especially amongst Anti-Federalists, in early America.[19] The pseudonymous author Tamony, writing in Virginia, similarly attacked what he believed to be the overly vast powers granted to the president with respect to the military. In fact, 'Tamony' argued that the new president would possess even vaster powers over the military than the King of Great Britain. Although he admitted that the president would not have the 'magic name of King,' he attacked the 'great prerogatives' of the American executive, whom he believed would command a force 'unrestrained by law or limitation.'[20] 'Philadelphiensis,' a Pennsylvanian Anti-Federalist with some of the most overheated anti-monarchical rhetoric of the period, warned that the president would prove an '*Emperor*,' a militaristic king at the head of a standing army. He would prove a veritable Asiatic despot 'surrounding by thousands of blood-suckers, and cringing sycophants,' supported by 'Turkish Janissaries,' who were 'better acquainted with plundering their country than fighting for its protection.'[21]

Opposed to such criticisms were Federalists, especially Hamilton, who were less concerned about the dangers of executive absolutism.[22] The tendency on the part of Anti-Federalists to draw parallels between the president and the king of Great Britain was described by Hamilton as preposterous, and he carefully delineated the vast differences between these offices.[23] While the king of Great Britain was a hereditary monarch ruling with prerogative powers existing outside the warp and woof of ordinary law, the president was an elected official, holding a tenure of four years, who possessed clearly enumerated powers under Article II and was recallable through impeachment.[24]

– CHAPTER 16: *Political thinking and military power* –

Figure 16.1 The specter of the standing army in eighteenth-century America (*above*): This famous engraving of the Boston Massacre was prepared by Paul Revere and printed only three weeks after the incident. A famous piece of propaganda, the engraving portrays the British regular troops in a menacing manner. They stand arrayed in a straight column on the right, muskets raised, firing upon the citizens of Boston. Anti-standing army rhetoric was strong in colonial America, and this image can be seen as a visual representation of concerns about a British standing army of regulars. © De Agostini Picture Library/Getty Images

THE MILITIA *VS* THE STANDING ARMY

It is also worth pointing out that political thinking about military power in the early modern British Atlantic was overwhelmingly concerned with land forces and less interested in the navy, largely since it was less readily apparent how the fleet might interfere with domestic politics. When the navy was discussed in political terms, it was typically celebrated leading to the kind of easy elision of the fleet, Protestantism, and liberty immortalized in 'Rule, Britannia!' (1740).[25] Considering this neglect of sea forces, the fundamental principle running through early modern British Atlantic political thinking on military power was the drawing of a stark division between the 'militia,' a military force made up of civilian soldiers levied and armed based upon a property-based tax and the 'standing army,' a centralized, professional fighting force, which increasingly was maintained even after the conclusion of hostilities. This militia/standing army dichotomy was first formulated in the 1640s and 1650s under the pressures of the English Civil Wars, but was only fully articulated during the 'land forces controversy' (1697–1701) after the conclusion of the Nine Years' War as William III attempted to keep up a massive standing army of more than 30,000 soldiers in light of concerns about a recrudescence of Anglo-French hostilities. To supporters of the republican paradigm, the militia was a peculiarly privileged form of military organization – 'quasi-feudal' in origin and directly controlled by the gentry and nobility in the localities. It was seen to possess special liberty-preserving qualities distinctly lacking among regular forces.[26] The militia, moreover, was celebrated not only as a military force but also as a vehicle for societal reform and the cultivation of republican virtue. It was considered to be, at least theoretically, the people-at-arms (*populus armatus*). As such, it was utterly inconceivable that it could have any interests opposed to the general population.

The standing army, however, was a different beast altogether. Etymologically the army was *standing* because it was kept up even after the negotiation of peace – a taboo in an age that traditionally considered both armies (as well as parliaments) to be events rather than institutions. In addition, the term 'standing army' was often used in a loose way to refer to regular troops more generally, or, in fact, to refer to any military force deemed to have particular interests opposed to the common good. It is, perhaps, not surprising that the standing army was deemed one of the preeminent threats to freedom of the age, and contemporaries worried that a standing army might be used to crush representative institutions, destroy due process, and extirpate the Protestant religion. To the more courtly-inclined, however, the militia was a sorry affair, ineffective in the face of professional soldiers.[27] Far preferable were regular troops who had made fighting their trade, and who were able to devote all of their time to training and honing their expertise in the art of war.

A tendency to distinguish between standing armies and militias persisted throughout the eighteenth century, and it was eventually transmitted across the Atlantic.[28] While in England the peerage had exercised a significant degree of control over the militia, especially through service as Lords Lieutenant, the absence of hereditary aristocracy on American soil precluded the persistence of aristocratic dominance.[29] Despite this, early America inherited a great number of beliefs about the militia informed by the earlier British republican paradigm. The Maryland Constitution (1776) and the New Hampshire Constitution (1784) reflected a broadly shared belief that 'a well-regulated militia' was the 'proper' and 'natural' defence of a free state.[30] The militia, as well, continued to be a local organization, which was largely colony- and later state-based.

If the militia was clearly a *state-based organization* under the Articles of Confederation, the Constitution significantly complicated this distinction. Under the new Constitution, Congress was given vast powers over 'organizing, arming, and disciplining' militia forces. On top of this, the Congress was entrusted with the power of training the militia 'according to the discipline prescribed by Congress', and the even more significant power of 'calling forth the Militia' in order to 'execute the Laws of the Union, suppress Insurrections and repel Invasions'.[31] Reaction to greater federal control over the state militias was broadly negative among those who valued the local roots of the militia.

Another question that continued to dog political actors throughout the early modern period was the size and extent of the militia.[32] If the militia, according to republican theory, was meant to be, essentially, the people-at-arms, then it followed that all citizens needed to be mustered together in militia forces. Despite this, plans to include the totality of the citizenry (even if it was restricted to male property owners) were always more aspirational than achievable. Indeed, there were several proposals for the creation of 'select militias' of men, especially chosen for increased training and preparation, who would be better versed in military exercises than other, more nominal, members of the militia. This idea had a long history in England, especially in the institution of the 'trained bands,' a special subset of the militia forces, who underwent more vigorous training and drilling. Such ideas, however, were anathema to some Anti-Federalists, who remained attached to a vision of the militia that encompassed *all* of the citizenry.[33]

If the militia was typically celebrated in the early modern British Atlantic, the same could not be said of the standing army. In fact, one of the great mainstays of British Atlantic political discourse was the almost universal aversion to standing armies.[34] Potent historical memories, including Cromwell's Major-Generals scheme and the *dragonnades* of Louis XIV ensured that anti-standing army rhetoric remained a dominant chord in British discourse for centuries. Similar views were echoed in America, which itself had witnessed 'garrison government' under the British and had reacted with fits of apoplexy to the stationing of large British forces of regulars in Boston and elsewhere before the Revolutionary War.[35] One slight difference in the eighteenth century, however, was the waning of Catholicism as a theme in anti-army discourse. While in late seventeenth-century Britain much of the fear of the standing army centered on the 'popish army,' which would impose despotism and Catholicism on the peoples of the British Isles, after 1689 these themes increasingly receded into the background. Nonetheless, Americans followed their British cousins in an almost hereditary aversion to standing armies.[36] Indeed, as one Anti-Federal writer put the matter, the standing army was 'useless and dangerous,' an infection, which would encourage vice and dissolute behaviour and destroy civil liberties.[37] Meanwhile, the 'Maryland Farmer' advised his readers to engrave on the tender minds of their children the dictum that '*There is no form of government safe with a standing army, and there is none that is not safe without,*' a principle that he took to represent the 'first article' of his 'political creed.'[38]

Americans attacked the standing army of the British stationed in the colonies in the 1760s and 1770s, and critiques of standing armies formed an important trope in the *Declaration of Independence* (1776). Moreover, a large number of state constitutions included language opposed to standing armies.[39] The ratification controversy, however, represented the biggest single outburst against standing armies in early America. Anti-Federalist criticisms of the military clauses were heated and formed one of the movement's most pronounced lines of attacks on the proposed Constitution. Complaints invoking standing armies made by Anti-Federalists generally centered upon two clusters of related issues, namely excessive presidential and federal power over the military.

Anti-standing army discourse was integral to the Anti-Federalists' polemical efforts, and it highlighted both of these core complaints. The 'Son of Liberty' argued that a standing army was a threat to freedom and a support for tyrants.[40] Patrick Henry, at the Virginia ratifying convention, was deeply concerned about what he perceived to be the unlimited nature of Congress's power to raise armies. He imagined that Congress would keep up armies continually on foot, even in peacetime, and billet them on the people (a concern reflected in the later Third Amendment). According to Henry, such 'unlimited authority' would inevitably lead to despotism.[41] Luther Martin, similarly, argued that the Constitution gave Congress untrammelled authority to raise and support standing armies in peacetime, without any restrictions to their number. In this way, the Constitution provided for the introduction of the standing army, 'that *engine* of *arbitrary power*, which has so *often* and so *successfully* been used for the *subversion* of freedom.'[42]

CENTER, LOCALITIES AND ARMED RESISTANCE

Perhaps the most distinctive element of American thinking about military power was its intense focus on issues related to the center/localities, especially with respect to federalism.[43] This is not surprising, considering the fraught nature of state–national relationship in early America, as thirteen previously distinct colonies struggled to define their relation to one another. These federalism concerns, however, must be understood as being intimately linked with the 'militia'/'standing army' dichotomy discussed in the previous section. The regular forces were largely seen as falling within the ambit of the national government. This was, in fact, a natural conclusion given British practice and the importance of the Continental Congress's role in the erection of a national Continental Army.

In the British Isles, the regular forces were distinctly national organizations, existing in English, Scottish and Irish establishments. These forces bore a special relationship to royal power and were largely disconnected from the offices and structures of local government, including the commissions of the peace, the lieutenancy and the boroughs.[44] This was sharply contrasted with the organization of the militia, which was local and county-based, each force being presided over by a Lord Lieutenant (generally the most important peer of the region) appointed by the king. The Lord Lieutenant was assisted by a collection of Deputy Lieutenants drawn from the local gentry. The lieutenancy thus was held in great esteem throughout the period, as a source of patronage and as a mechanism for recognizing local elites.[45] Some ancient constitutionalist writers, in fact, even traced the main contours of the lieutenancy to pre-Norman practice, equating the Lord Lieutenant to the ancient Anglo-Saxon office of the *heretoch*.[46] In America, the arrangement of the militia was

– CHAPTER 16: *Political thinking and military power* –

similar, but was state-based rather than county-based. The chief executive of each state – variously called a 'governor' or 'president' – indeed acted in a manner akin to a Lord Lieutenant.

The U.S. Constitution transformed the general distribution of military competencies by giving significantly more control over military power to the national government, in the process radically altering the careful distribution of military power, to which Americans had become accustomed. The earlier Articles of Confederation had represented itself as an agreement of the states to enter into a 'firm league of friendship' with one another 'for their common defence.' However, there was little which made this aspiration a reality.[47] Financial charges incurred in the promotion of the common defense were to pass onto the states, but there was no mechanism available to the Confederation Congress to compel the discharge of these requisitions.[48] This haphazard situation was considered one of the main defects by those in attendance at the Philadelphia Convention.[49] As such, the Constitution made providing for the common defense one of its core *desiderata*, and in the process, it drastically shifted military initiative away from the states and towards the national government.[50]

The proposed breadth of federal control over military power caused some degree of concern at the Convention.[51] Elbridge Gerry was perhaps most outspoken in this respect, and he openly wondered whether this change would destroy the 'Sovereignty and Liberty of the States' and lead to the introduction of a regal system of government, overseen by an over-powerful president. Increased federal control over military power was, indeed, one of the chief complaints of Anti-Federalists against the proposed Constitution. Luther Martin considered the Constitution's exaggerated power over national regular forces and the militia as tending to the utter destruction of the state governments, and to the erection of an irresistible federal government that could never be overthrown by state military power.[52] The writer 'Philadelphiensis' attacked the regular army as the '*mighty basis*' of the new federal constitution, the cornerstone of its entire monstrous, despotic edifice.[53]

In the state ratifying conventions and among Anti-Federalist writers, there was special concern about the national government's ability to call forth the state militias to assist the federal government in time of emergency (i.e. the federal government's ability to 'federalize' state militias). Luther Martin complained that a limitation on this extensive power had been vainly urged at the convention.[54] On the other hand, there were fears that the federal government, far from being overly involved in the state militias, would neglect them by failing in its responsibilities to arm and organize the militias, thus paving the way, indirectly, for the dominance of regular forces.[55] Furthermore, among New York Anti-Federalists of an abolitionist bent, there was the added concern that militia forces would be dragged into southern states in order to quell slave revolts or for the further enslavement of peoples.[56] Supporters of ratification attempted to assuage Anti-Federalist fears, and Madison responded that it was extraordinarily unlikely that the federal government would entirely take the initiative with regard to military power from the states.[57]

Today, military power *qua* military power is generally conceptualized as exclusively falling within the purview of a government, possessing a Weberian monopoly on the use of coercive force (*Gewaltmonopol des Staates*). In the early modern British Atlantic, however, especially among more republican-inclined thinkers, military power was often viewed in a very different manner. Although the Weberian model was slowly coming into being, the experience of the English Civil Wars and the Glorious Revolution ensured there was a tradition within the early modern British Atlantic recognizing the potential for non-governmental exercise of military power especially through resistance against a despotic regime. This viewpoint, however, existed side-by-side more courtly visions, emphasizing the royal monopoly on the 'militia power' as well as broader norms prohibiting rebellion as treason. In fact, the conceptual apparatus for resistance against the state, at least as articulated in Locke's *Second treatise*, was conceived as a radical rejection of this notion of the royal 'militia power' by providing justification for violent and popular resistance against tyrants.[58]

This tradition of 'revolution principles' persisted well into the eighteenth and nineteenth centuries in the early modern British Atlantic world.[59] Even the celebrated English jurist William Blackstone, criticized by Jefferson for his 'honeyed Mansfieldism,' cited Article VII of the English Bill of Rights ('That the subjects which are Protestants may have arms for their defence suitable to their conditions and as allowed by law') in justification of an ultimate right of resistance possessed by the English people, linked to arms bearing. He saw this 'auxiliary right' as, essentially a 'natural right of resistance when the sanctions of society and laws are found insufficient' to protect the people's inalienable rights.[60]

America was heir to this republican tradition and, indeed, many of these concepts helped form the core of the founding generation's claims to a right to resistance against their British colonial overlords.[61] The great *locus classicus* on this point is undoubtedly the *Declaration of Independence* (1776), whose ringing words have been so endlessly quoted.[62] According to Jefferson, all men were 'endowed by their Creator with certain unalienable Rights' including the rights to 'Life, Liberty, and the pursuit of Happiness.' The failure of the British government under George III to secure these rights, accompanied by his regime's 'long train of abuses' of the peoples' rights, justified the violent, military overthrow of the current government.

However, it is important to realize that this set of concerns about resistance was intimately connected to concerns about executive power, standing armies, and the militia. Indeed, there was a tendency, first apparent in late seventeenth-century British republican writers to distinguish between government by 'law' or by 'the sword.'[63] The latter involved the use of coercive military force to impose policies upon an unwilling people, paradigmatically through standing armies, which would be instrumental not only in denying peoples liberties, but also in preventing any *future resistance* against the government. Coercive military government by the standing army, in essence, locked a people into a terrifying scenario from which it would be impossible to break free. Increased national control over the militia, as proposed by the U.S. Constitution, prompted strong fears that the military might be used to institute government by the sword, forcing the troops of the army and the militias to 'subdue their fellow citizens who dare to rise against the despotism of government.' Anti-Federalists warned that the proposed Constitution in its erection of a federal standing army and its enervation of the state-based militias would forever 'rivet the shackles of slavery on you and your unborn posterity.' The 'Maryland Farmer' argued that the envisioned national standing army was problematic precisely because, if erected, it would destroy 'all hopes of a revolution in favor of the rights of mankind.'[64]

However, if the standing army threatened the possibility of future resistance against despotism, the mechanism for implementing such resistance was somewhat more complicated. It had been typical within British discourse to speak of the collective *people's* right to resistance, but by the same token, there was also a tendency to see the *militia*, deemed to be the people-at-arms, as the natural organ of resistance. This elision of the people and the militia persisted in the American context. Unsurprisingly, in light of federalism concerns, the state-based militia were also sometimes conceptualized as an important locus for resistance to a future tyrannical national government. Luther Martin bemoaned the proposed Constitution's increased control over the state-based militias, and wondered whether they would now be fit 'to preserve their *existence* against a general government armed with powers *sufficient* to destroy them.'[65] Professor Akhil Amar clearly is right to note that many late eighteenth-century Americans imagined that the state militia acted 'in some sense *outside* of government, rather than as a professional and permanent government bureaucracy.'[66] In the event of an overly powerful federal government, the state militia would be used as the Pennsylvanian Anti-Federalist 'The Deliberator' suggested, to prevent the 'annihilation of the state governments.'[67] Perhaps the latest instantiation of this manner of thinking about resistance vis-à-vis the militia, is in fact the American Civil War, in which the state militias of the Confederacy were thought of in precisely such terms.[68]

ARMS BEARING AND THE SECOND AMENDMENT

Arms bearing, especially in analyses of the Second Amendment, is often abstracted from debates over military power. This is a major error. Indeed, early modern British Atlantic conceptions of arms bearing were largely *military* in nature. The major impetus behind preserving widespread, population-level arms bearing was driven by assumptions present in the republican paradigm of military power, as discussed above. Widespread arms bearing, indeed, was crucial primarily in facilitating the training and armament of men who might serve within the militia. An arms-bearing population, arrayed as the militia, in turn, was useful in that it obviated the need for large standing armies, which posed a threat to liberties. Further value was derived from an arms-bearing population's ability to serve as a potential locus for resistance in the event of the rise of a tyrannical government.

Arms bearing, therefore, was located directly within the matrix of concerns explored within this article. The ideological interconnections between the republican paradigm on military power and arms bearing can best be seen in two documents, separated in time from one another by over 140 years and by the Atlantic Ocean. The first is Thomas Erle's 'Papers of instructions for the Parliamentary meeting' prepared around the time of the Glorious Revolution.[69] The West Country gentleman Erle put pen to paper with his views for governmental reform in light of the disastrous reign of James II, and he argued that every householder with more than £10 per annum be armed with a musket to be used in case of invasion. He further argued the need for a reform of the militia laws, in order to revive the trained bands as a viable force. The benefit of these reforms would be the disappearance of the standing army, which would no longer be needed, and could be reduced to a small number of troops kept in the Cinque Ports and other coastal garrisons.

These themes and ideas are remarkably similar to those found in the American Joseph Story's influential *Commentaries on the Constitution* of 1833, which has been described as 'the most massive and most widely discussed treatise on constitutional law in pre-Civil War America.' Story's explanation of the meaning of the Second

Amendment, in particular, bears a number of parallels to Erle's 'Paper of instructions'.[70] Story, in fact, recognized that the core language of the Second Amendment could be traced back to the English Bill of Rights. However, in doing this, he did not claim that the amendment was unmoored from military concerns nor that the right to bear arms was individual and unconnected to the militia – a point foregrounded in the recent decisions by Heller and McDonald by the Supreme Court.[71] According to Story, the Second Amendment was intimately connected to the militia, which he described as 'the natural defence of a free country.' Moreover, he argued that the militia was crucial precisely because of its role in making unnecessary the need for a standing army, which could easily be used by 'ambitious and unprincipled rulers to subject the people' to tyranny. While locating the right to bear arms within this military context, he also focused on the importance of widespread arms bearing amongst the citizenry in connection to resistance. Widespread arms bearing was crucial, he argued, as a 'strong moral check against the usurpation and arbitrary power of rulers'.[72]

Story was not aberrant in his yoking of the Second Amendment to military concerns. In fact, the dominant manner of discussing arms bearing in early America followed this pattern. Although it is, of course, impossible in the space allotted to discuss at any great length, or with any degree of certainty what precisely the Second Amendment's original meaning might have been, nonetheless, this article suggests a greater need for a focus on the military context of the Second Amendment through what might be called a 'distributist approach' to the amendment centered on exploring how the Second Amendment reflected republican attitudes about the appropriate distribution of military power within a 'free state.' A broad commitment to arms bearing in eighteenth-century America was almost always connected to ideas about the distribution of military power. This, in fact, is eminently clear in the state constitutions of the period.[73] The Pennsylvania Constitution (1776) claimed that the people had a right to bear arms 'for the defence of themselves and the state.' The same provision went on to argue that standing armies in peacetime were 'dangerous to liberty' and that the military should be kept under strict subordination to the civil power.[74] The Massachusetts Constitution (1780) claimed that the people had a right to keep and bear arms 'for the common defence,' and mentioned that standing armies could not be kept up without the consent of the state legislature.[75] Although some of the language of these amendments suggests that arms bearing was tied to personal defense, issues of military power, especially in relation to bolstering the militia and curbing standing armies, were omnipresent.

The Second Amendment was similarly related to the issue of military power, as the debate over ratification and the passage of the Bill of Rights makes clear. The Constitution represented a radical expansion of national control over not only the regular forces but also the state militias. Anti-Federalists, in particular, were concerned about this development, and criticisms were brought at state ratifying conventions and by pamphleteers about a number of different issues, including: undue presidential power over the militia; the threat to the militia represented by increased national control, especially in the possible disarmament of the militias; the likely expansion of regular forces to create a 'standing army'; and the disturbing implications greater national control had in preventing necessary rebellion against an overly powerful federal government. It should be apparent that the Second Amendment was largely motivated by the genuinely *military* debates explored throughout this article, and it is only within the context of such debates that its original meaning can be understood.

In light of this, it is worthwhile to pause for a moment to look at one proposal from the Virginia ratifying convention, which helps contextualize how a number of ideas about military power were seen to relate to one another. The ratifying convention mentioned in the *same proposed amendment* to the Constitution a number of different points. First, that the people had the right to keep and bear arms. This sat alongside, however, language claiming that a well-regulated militia 'composed of the body of the people trained to arms' was the 'proper, natural, and safe defence of a free state.' In addition, the amendment included harsh verbiage condemning standing armies in time of peace as 'dangerous to liberty,' and it included a further clause supporting the constitutional principle that military power be under subordination to the civil power.[76] All these issues were of a piece and intimately connected to the right to bear arms.[77] The military context of arms bearing was eminently clear to the members of the Virginia ratifying convention, even if it may no longer be clear to historians.

The Bill of Rights was prompted by Anti-Federalist concerns, yet its provisions were drafted by defenders of the Constitution, who wished to preserve the Constitution's structural arrangements and integrity.[78] Understanding the Second Amendment's precise original meaning has proven difficult, a difficulty further exacerbated by the often-unhelpful vehemence of the historical debate over the past few decades, which has inevitably been tied to modern political and legal considerations.[79] Despite this, it seems apparent that a thorough understanding of political thinking about military power in the early modern British Atlantic is a necessary precondition for anyone wishing to appreciate the original meaning of the Second Amendment. The language of the amendment itself is spare, only twenty-seven words: 'A well regulated Militia, being necessary to the security of a free State, the right of the people to keep and bear Arms, shall not be infringed.' The amendment grants a right to bear arms to the 'people,' but which 'people'? The crucial debate amongst historians (and legal scholars) has hinged on who these *people* were precisely, i.e., the *scope* of the amendment). Was the right to bear arms intended to be restricted to militia service, or was it a general right of citizenship? Too little attention, however, has been given to the amendment's *purpose* in light of political thinking about military power in the broader British Atlantic world.

This article does not present a hegemonic 'model' of the Second Amendment, accompanied by grandiose claims of having finally ascertained the historical 'original meaning' of this difficult sentence, but this article does propose that a proper way to gain a fuller understanding of the Second Amendment's original meaning is through a 'distributionist approach' to the amendment.[80] The Second Amendment represents a somewhat cryptic and rather perfunctory nod in the direction of the republican paradigm, favoring a more widespread distribution of military power throughout the states and the localities. This view privileged representative institutions over the executive, the militia over the standing armies, the state government over the national government, and the people over governmental authority. Of course, it hinted towards this viewpoint without interrupting the actual institutional arrangements found in the Constitution. Nonetheless, its codification of the principle of the ideal of an armed populace, arrayed together as a militia, was thought important to contemporaries, who assumed that such an arrangement would serve as a bulwark against excessive power in the centralized organs of the national government. In addition, in the event of despotic disaster, widespread arms bearing would facilitate a Lockean 'Appeal to Heaven.' Appreciating this radically different vision of military power is difficult, particularly on the other side of the American Civil War, a conflict that did so much to tear asunder the earlier republican paradigm on military power. However, undertaking an imaginative engagement with the past is essential for historians and jurists who are interested in the Second Amendment, and it is only by unearthing the complex set of beliefs about military power held by early modern Britons and Americans that it is possible to construct a comprehensive and nuanced account of this controversial amendment's original meaning.

NOTES

1   *Federalist*: No. 41.
2   Inspiration for this approach comes from Bailyn 1967; Wood 1969 and Pocock 1975, but I embrace a history of political thinking rather than a history of political thought, in line with Rory Rapple 2002; Finnegan 2007 and Midgley 2008.
3   Lovejoy 1936. Instead my article follows an approach more similar to that of Armitage 2012.
4   On the military revolution see Parker 1996; Black 1991 and Downing 1992
5   Pocock 1975: chs. 5–8. On the reception of Machiavelli see Raab 1965; Pocock 1971 and Rahe, 2006.
6   See Cañigares-Esguerra 2003.
7   Worden 2002; Scott 2004 and Browning 1982.
8   Vane 1656; Harrington 1977; Anon. 1648.
9   Fletcher 1997; Robertson 1985; Toland 1698; Trenchard 1697 and 1698. See also Kramnick 1992 and McMahon 1990.
10 Boyle 1677; Gascoigne 1685.
11 Somers 1697; Defoe 1698a and 1698b.
12 Federici 2012.
13 Schwoerer 1971: 45–76.
14 Eliot 1836–45: III, 418.
15 Farrand 1911: I, 66.
16 Storing 1981: III, 55.
17 Articles of Confederation 1781: art. 9.
18 U.S. Constitution 1787: art. I, sect. 8; art. II, sect. 2.
19 *Federalist*, No. 3. Eliot 1836–45: I, 350–51.
20 Storing 1981: V, 146.
21 Storing 1981: III, 107, 129.
22 *Federalist*: Nos. 71–72.
23 *Federalist*: Nos. 66, 68.
24 *Federalist*: Nos. 69, 73.
25 Thomson 1763: II, 191.
26 Goring 1955: 17.
27 Storing 1981: III, 111.
28 Boynton 1967; Stater 1994; Western 1965; Cress 1979; Cornell 2006 and Breen 1972.
29 *Federalist*: Nos. 62–63.
30 Thorpe 1909: 1688, 2456.
31 U.S. Constitution 1787: art. I, sect. 8.
32 Eliot 1836–45: III, 428.
33 For discussion of the citizen militia conceptualized as the body of the people, see, for instance, Williams 2003: 46–49.

- CHAPTER 16: *Political thinking and military power* -

34 On standing armies see Schwoerer 1974; Reid 1981.
35 Webb 1979, 1966, 1977.
36 Storing 1981: III, 61–62.
37 Storing 1981: III, 76.
38 Storing 1981: V, 28.
39 E.g. Thorpe 1909: 1688.
40 Storing 1981: III, 59.
41 Eliot 1836–45: III, 410.
42 Farrand 1911: III, 207.
43 On federalism see LaCroix 2011.
44 Clode 1869; Hindle 2000.
45 See Stater 1994.
46 On the ancient constitution see Pocock 1957. For the idea of the 'heretoch', see Lambarde 1568: fos. 136r-v and Blount 1661: 157.
47 Articles of Confederation 1781: arts. II, III.
48 Articles of Confederation 1781: art. VIII.
49 Farrand 1911: I, 273; *Federalist*: No. 44.
50 U.S. Constitution 1787: art. I, sects. 8, 9.
51 For a discussion of federalism concerns in relation to the Second Amendment see Higginbotham 1998.
52 Farrand 1911: II, 635; III, 208–10, 259–60.
53 Storing 1981: III, 115.
54 Farrand 1911: III, 157.
55 Eliot 1836–45: II, 521; III, 418.
56 Storing 1981: VI, 35, 62.
57 *Federalist*, No. 45.
58 A reading of Locke's *Second Treatise* along these lines can be found in Drummond 2014: ch. 2. On Locke more generally see Ashcraft 1986; Goldie 1983: 61–85.
59 The term is taken from Kenyon 1977.
60 See Cottrol and Diamond 1995: 995–1026.
61 *Federalist*, No. 43.
62 On the intellectual context of the *Declaration of Independence*, see Armitage 2007. Many early state constitutions contained explicit criticisms of 'non-resistance', a doctrine attacked as 'slavish', e.g. Thorpe 1909: 3422
63 Storing 1981: V, 45.
64 Storing 1981: III, 153; V, 25, 42.
65 Farrand 1911: III, 208.
66 See Amar 2005.
67 Storing 1981: III, 177.
68 Amar, indeed, has argued that the Civil War represented a radical constitutional shift in how the armed forces were understood. The overwhelming importance of the regular forces of the national government in crushing the Confederacy ensured the primacy of the national army. Amar 2005: 380.
69 Although the MS suggests the document is from 1689, Professor Mark Goldie has persuasively argued that it was prepared in December 1688, see Goldie 1995; Erle 168[8].
70 Powell 1985: 1285.
71 Story 1833: III, 746–47.
72 Goldie 1995.
73 Adams 2001.
74 Thorpe 1909: 3083.
75 Thorpe 1909: 1892.

76 Farrand 1911: III, 157.

77 Eliot 1836–45: III, 659.

78 A point made in Finkelman 2000: 117–47.

79 A good introduction to the main contours of the exceedingly dense historiography on the Second Amendment can be found in Bogus 2000. See also Kates 1983; Cress 1984; Shalhope 1986; Lund 1987; Levinson 1989; Halbrook 1989; Cottrol and Diamond 1991; Uviller and Merkel 2003; Konig 2004; Cornell 2006; Churchill 2007; Halbrook 2008; Charles 2010 and 2011.

80 Legal rules need to be understood through recourse to background norms, which can be thought to ground them, so too originalist 'models' purporting to present a hegemonic account of amendments can be thought of as being backed by historical 'approaches' privileging certain themes and categories. My distributist approach would highlight the importance of the distribution of military power to the amendment's original meaning.

REFERENCES

Adams, William Paul. *The First American Constitutions: Republican Ideology and the Making of the State Constitutions in the Revolutionary Era*, trans. Rita Kimber and Robert Kimber (expanded ed., Lanham, MD, 2001).

Amar, Akhil Reed. *America's Constitution: A Biography* (New York, NY, 2005).

Anon., *The peaceable militia* (London, 1648).

Armitage, David. 'What's the Big Idea? Intellectual History and the *Longue Durée*,' *History of European Ideas* 38.4 (Dec., 2012), pp. 493–507.

——. *The Declaration of Independence: A Global History* (Cambridge, MA, 2007).

Ashcraft, Richard. *Revolutionary Politics: Locke's Two Treatises of Government* (Princeton, NJ, 1986).

B[lount], T[homas]. *Glossographia, or, A dictionary interpreting all such hard words of whatsoever language now used in our refined English tongue with etymologies, definitions and historical observations on the same: also the terms of divinity, law, physick, mathematicks and other arts and sciences explicated* (London, 1661).

Bailyn, Bernard *The Ideological Origins of the American Revolution* (Cambridge, MA, 1967).

Beckett, Ian F.W. *Britain's Part-Time Soldiers: The Amateur Military Tradition, 1558–1946* (Manchester, 1991).

Black, Jeremy. *A Military Revolution?: Military Change and European Society, 1550–1800* (London, 1991).

Bogus, Carl, ed. *The Second Amendment in Law and History* (New York, NY, 2000).

Boyle, Robert. *A treatise of the art of war dedicated to the Kings Most Excellent Majesty* (London, 1677).

Boynton, Lindsay. *The Elizabethan Militia, 1558–1638* (1967).

Breen, T.H. (1972). 'English Origins and New World Development: The Case of the Covenanted Militia in Seventeenth-Century Massachusetts' *Past & Present* 57.1 (1972), pp. 74–96.

Browning, Reed. *Political and Constitutional Ideas of the Court Whigs* (Baton Rouge, LA, 1982).

Cañigares-Esguerra, Jorge. 'Some Caveats About the "Atlantic" Paradigm,' *History Compass* 1 (2003), pp. 1–4.

Charles, Patrick. 'The 1792 National Militia Act, the Second Amendment, and Individual Militia Rights: A Legal and Historical Perspective,' *Georgetown Journal of Law & Public Policy* 9.2 (2011), pp. 323–92.

——. 'The Right of Self-Preservation and Resistance: A True Legal and Historical Understanding of the Anglo-American Right to Arms,' *Cardozo Law Review De Novo* 18 (2010), pp. 18–60.

– CHAPTER 16: *Political thinking and military power* –

Churchill, Robert. 'Gun Regulation, the Police Power, and the Right to Keep Arms in Early America: The Legal Context of the Second Amendment,' *Law & History Review* 25.1 (2007), pp. 139–75.

Clode, Charles. *The Militia Forces of the Crown, Their Administration and Government* (London, 1869).

Cornell, Saul. *A Well-Regulated Militia: The Founding Fathers and the Origins of Gun Control in America* (New York, NY, 2006).

Cottrol, Robert and Raymond Diamond. 'The Fifth Auxiliary Right: Review of Joyce Lee Malcolm's, *To Keep and Bear Arms: The Origins of an Anglo-American Right*' (Cambridge, MA, 1994), *Yale Law Journal* 104.4 (1995), pp. 995–1026.

——. 'The Second Amendment; Toward an Afro-Americanist Reconsideration,' *Georgetown Law Journal* 80 (1991), pp. 309–61.

Cress, Lawrence Delbert. 'An Armed Community: The Origin and Meaning of the Right to Bear Arms,' *Journal of American History* 71.1 (1984), pp. 22–42.

——. 'Radical Whiggery on the Role of the Military: Ideological Roots of the American Revolutionary Militia,' *Journal of the History of Ideas* 40 (1979), pp. 43–60.

Defoe, Daniel. *A brief reply to the History of standing armies in England with some account of the author* (London, 1698).

——. *An argument shewing, that a standing army, with consent of Parliament, is not inconsistent with a free government, &c* (London, 1698).

Downing, Brian. *The Military Revolution and Political Change: Origins of Democracy and Autocracy in Early Modern Europe* (1992).

Drummond, Charles. 'Political Thinking and Military Power in Later Stuart Britain, 1660–1701' (Ph.D. diss., Cambridge, expected 2014).

Eliot, Jonathan, ed., *The Debates in the Several State Conventions on the Adoption of the Federal Constitution* (Washington, D.C., 1836–45).

Erle, Thomas. 'Paper of instructions for the Parliam^ty. meeting after the revolution' (*c.* 168[8]) Churchill College, Cambridge Archive Centre Erle MS 4/4/5.

Farrand, Max, ed. *Records of the Federal Convention of 1787*, 3 vols. (New Haven, CT, 1911).

Federici, Michael. *The Political Philosophy of Alexander Hamilton* (Baltimore, MD, 2012).

Finkelman, Paul. '"A Well Regulated Miltia": The Second Amendment in Historical Perspective' in Carl Bogus, ed., *The Second Amendment in Law and History* (New York, NY, 2000).

Finnegan, Michael. 'The Impact of the Counter-Reformation on the Political Thinking of Irish Catholics, c.1540-c.1640' (unpub. Ph.D. diss., University of Cambridge, 2007).

Fisher, Louis. *Military Tribunals and Presidential Power: American Revolution to the War on Terrorism* (Lawrence, KA, 2005).

——. *Presidential War Power* (2nd ed., Lawrence, KA, 2004).

Fletcher, Andrew. *Political Works*, ed. John Robertson (Cambridge, 1997).

Gascoigne, Bernardo. 'Memoranda to James II' (*c.* 1685) British Library, Additional MSS 38,850.

Goldie, Mark. 'John Locke and Anglican Royalism,' *Political Studies* 31 (1983), pp. 61–85.

——. 'Thomas Erle's Instructions for the Revolution Parliament, December 1688'. *Parliamentary History* 14.3 (1995), pp. 337–47.

Goring, J.J. 'The Military Obligations of the English People, 1511–58' (unpub. Ph.D. diss., University of London, 1955).

Halbrook, Stephen. *A Right to Bear Arms: State and Federal Bill of Rights and Constitutional Guarantees* (Westport, CT, 1989).

——. *The Founders' Second Amendment: Origins of the Right to Bear Arms* (Chicago IL, 2008).

Harrington, James. *The Commonwealth of Oceana and A System of Politics*, ed. J.G.A. Pocock. (Cambridge, 1977).

Higginbotham, R. Don. 'The Federalized Militia Debate: A Neglected Aspect of Second Amendment Scholarship', *William and Mary Quarterly* 55 (1998).

Hindle, Steve. *The State and Social Change in Early Modern England, c. 1550–1640* (Basingstoke, 2000).

Kates, Don. 'Handgun Prohibition and the Original Meaning of the Second Amendment,' *Michigan Law Review* 82 (1983).

Kenyon, J.P. *Revolution Principles: The Politics of Party, 1689–1720* (Cambridge, 1977).

Koh, Harold. *The National Security Constitution: Sharing Power After the Iran-Contra Affair* (New Haven, CT, 1990).

Konig, David. 'The Second Amendment: A Missing Transatlantic Context for the Historical Meaning of the Right of the People to Keep and Bear Arms,' *Law & History Review* 22 (2004), pp. 119–60.

Kramnick, Isaac. *Bolingbroke and His Circle: The Politics of Nostalgia in the Age of Walpole* (Ithaca, NY, 1992).

LaCroix, Alison. *The Ideological Origins of American Federalism* (Cambridge, MA, 2011).

Lambarde, William, ed., *Archaionomia, siue de priscis anglorum legibus libri sermone Anglico, vetustate antiquissimo, aliquot abhinc seculis conscripti, atq[ue] nunc demum, magno iurisperitorum, & amantium antiquitatis omnium commodo, è tenebris in lucem vocati* (London, 1568).

Levinson, Sanford. 'The Embarrassing Second Amendment' *Yale Law Journal* 99 (1989), pp. 637–60.

Lovejoy, Arthur. *The Great Chain of Being: A Study of the History of an Idea* (Cambridge, MA, 1936).

Lund, Nelson. 'The Second Amendment, Political Liberty, and the Right to Self Preservation,' *Alabama Law Review* 39 (1987).

May, Thomas. *Arbitrary government display'd to the life, in the tyrannic usurpation of a junto of men called the Rump Parliament, and more especially in that of the tyrant and usurper, Oliver Cromwell. In which you have a clear view of the arbitrary, illegal, and unjust proceedings, of those persons under the notion of liberty. And a compendious history of those times, faithfully collected: with the characters and lives of several of those usurpers, and a brief account of the several persons that suffered death, and imprisonment under them for their loyalty to their king and country* (London, 1683).

McMahon, Marie. *The Radical Whigs, John Trenchard and Thomas Gordon: Libertarian Loyalists to the New House of Hanover* (Lanham, MD, 1990).

Midgley, Henry. 'The Political Thinking of the New Model Army 1647–54' (unpub. Ph.D. diss., University of Cambridge, 2008).

Parker, Geoffrey. *The Military Revolution, 1500–1800: Military Innovation and the Rise of the West* (2nd ed., Cambridge, 1996).

Pocock, J.G.A. *The Ancient Constitution and the Feudal Law: A Study of English Historical Thought in the Seventeenth Century* (Cambridge, 1957).

——. 'Machiavelli, Harrington and English Political Ideologies in the Eighteenth Century' in *Politic, Language, and Time: Essays on Political Thinking and History* (Chicago, IL, 1971), pp. 104–47.

——. *The Machiavellian Moment: Florentine Political Thought and the Atlantic Republican Tradition* (Princeton, NJ, 1975).

Powell, H. Jefferson. 'Joseph Story's Commentaries on the Constitution: A Belated Review,' *Yale Law Journal* 94.5 (Apr. 1985). pp. 1285–314.

Prakash, Saikrishnar and Michael Ramsey. 'The Executive Power over Foreign Affairs' *Yale Law Journal* 111 (2001), pp. 231–356.

Raab, Felix. *The English Face of Machiavelli: A Changing Interpretation, 1500–1700* (London, 1965).

Rahe, Paul. 'Machiavelli in the English Revolution' in Paul Rahe, ed., *Machiavelli's Liberal Republican Legacy* (Cambridge, 2006), pp. 9–35.

Rapple, Rory. 'The Political Thinking and Mentality of English Military Men in the Reign of Elizabeth I, 1558–88' (unpub. Ph.D. diss., University of Cambridge, 2002).

Reid, John Philip. *In Defiance of the Law: The Standing-Army Controversy, the Two Constitutions, and the Coming of the American Revolution* (Wilmington, NC, 1981).

Robertson, John. *The Scottish Enlightenment and the Militia Issue* (Edinburgh, 1985).

Schwoerer, Lois. "'The Fittest Subject for King's Quarrel'": An Essay on the Militia Controversy, 1641–42' *Journal of British Studies* 11.1 (Nov. 1971), pp. 45–76.

——. *"No Standing Armies!" The Antiarmy Ideology in Seventeenth-Century England* (Baltimore, MD, 1974).

Scott, Jonathan. *Commonwealth Principles: Republican Writings of the English Revolution* (Cambridge, 2004).

Shalhope, Robert. 'The Armed Citizen in the Early Republic' *Law and Contemporary Problems* 49 (1986), pp. 125–44.

Somers, John. *A letter balancing the necessity of keeping a land-force in time of peace: With the dangers that may follow on it* (London, 1697).

Stater, Victor. *Noble Government: The Stuart Lord Lieutenancy and the Transformation of English Politics* (Athens, GA, 1994).

Storing, Herbert J. ed. *The Complete Anti-Federalist* (Chicago, IL, 1981).

Story, Joseph. *Commentaries on the Constitution of the United States: With a Preliminary Review of the Constitutional History of the Colonies and States Before the Adoption of the Constitution* (3 vols., Boston, MA, 1833).

Thomson, James. *The Works of James Thomson*, 2 vols (London, 1763).

Thorpe, Francis, ed., *The Federal and State Constitutions, Colonial Charters, and the Organic Laws of the State, Territories, and Colonies; Now or heretofore Forming the United States of America.* (Washington, D.C., 1909).

Toland, John. *The Militia Reform'd and The Danger of Mercenary Parliaments* (London, 1698).

Trenchard, John. *A Short History of Standing Armies in England* (London, 1698).

——. *An Argument, shewing that a Standing Army is Inconsistent with a Free Government and Absolutely Destructive to the Constitution of the English Monarchy* (London, 1697).

Uviller, H. Richard and William Merkel. *The Militia and the Right to Arms, or, How the Second Amendment Fell Silent* (Chapel Hill, NC, 2003).

Vane, Sir Henry. *A healing question propounded and resolved upon occasion of the late publique and seasonable call to humiliation in order to love and union amongst the honest party, and with a desire to apply balsome to the wound, before it become incurable* (London, 1656).

Webb, Stephen Saunders. 'Army and Empire: English Garrison Government in Britain and America, 1569–1763' *William and Mary Quarterly*, 3rd ser. 34 (1977).

——. 'The Strange Career of Francis Nicholson' *William and Mary Quarterly*, 3rd ser. 23 (1966), pp. 513–48.

——. *The Governors-General: The English Army and the Definition of the Empire, 1569–1681* (Chapel Hill, NC, 1979).

Western, J.R. *English Militia in the Eighteenth Century: The Story of a Political Issue, 1660–1802* (London, 1965).

Williams, David C. *The Mythic Meanings of the Second Amendment: Taming Political Violence in a Constitutional Republic* (New Haven, CT, 2003).

Wood, Gordon. *The Creation of the American Republic, 1776–1787* (Chapel Hill, NC, 1969).

Worden, Blair. *Roundhead Reputations: The English Civil War and the Passions of Posterity* (London, 2002).

CHAPTER SEVENTEEN

ATLANTIC PERIPHERIES
Diplomacy, War, and Spanish–French Interactions in Hispaniola, 1660s–1690s

—·◆·—

Juan Ponce-Vázquez

In 1690, a French force of 900 men entered the northern Spanish region of Hispaniola and headed to the town of Santiago de los Caballeros, in the north of the island. When the Spanish lookout stationed at the edge of town informed the commander of Hispaniola's northern forces, Antonio Pichardo de Vinuesa, of the appearance of the advancing troops, he mustered the city's fighting force, called for reinforcements from nearby Spanish towns, and readied the defenses. Once they reached the outskirts of town, the French soldiers sent a message to the Spanish troops: no harm would befall the townfolk of Santiago as long as they swore loyalty to the king of France. If they refused, they would suffer a merciless attack. Pichardo gathered all the captains in a military council, who agreed to allow the enemy to enter the town and surround it, which would let the French wreak havoc and destroy a great number of houses. As part of the scheme, two captains volunteered to ambush the enemy.

The Spanish ambush was very successful, killing over eighty French soldiers. In the aftermath of the attack, it was rumored that as the Spanish forces attacked, some French soldiers had shouted 'Treason! Treason!' pointing to a possible pact between the invading force and some local residents. Another rumor stated that the attack was the result of debts incurred by Antonio Pichardo's nephew Pedro Morel de Santa Cruz and his business associates in their dealings with French merchants.

Pedro Morel, who had been absent from Santiago at the time of the attack, returned that same afternoon from Santo Domingo where he had been promoted to the military rank of *maestre de campo* by the governor in the capital.[1] According to the information received later in Santo Domingo, everyone expected that Morel would convince his uncle Pichardo to organize a force to pursue the French and attack them as they withdrew, 'thus eradicating the reputation he had accumulated during the period of peace in that city [Santiago] and this one [Santo Domingo] of a great merchant with the French.'[2] Instead, his first act was to gather all the captains to inform them of his new rank and reaffirm their obedience. Next, he chastised the men who participated in the ambush against the French troops and did everything he could to disparage their performance in the field. Morel also secured a letter signed by the *Cabildo* (Town Council) of Santiago requesting the relocation of the town of Santiago to another part of the island due to its proximity to French territory. The governor and members of the *Audiencia* of Santo Domingo in the capital interpreted this move as a scandalous and abhorrent capitulation of the territory to French settlers. The two captains responsible for the attacks against the French, however, refused to cede any land, claiming that 'they wanted to live there, they would, and they would defend their land to death.'[3]

The behavior of the military leaders of Santiago to the French attack, allowing the enemy to enter the town, and avoiding direct combat (with the exception of the two captains leading the ambushes) baffled Ignacio Pérez Caro, the governor of Santo Domingo. Pérez Caro proceeded to send the canon of the cathedral of Santo Domingo, a close friend of Pedro Morel, to convince the residents to rebuild their houses and resettle. It was also rumored that the canon received much of the merchandise that Morel and his allies bought from the French merchants and sold in Santo Domingo. Eventually, the governor himself traveled in person to Santiago to investigate the attack and its aftermath. Pedro Morel and the Cabildo of Santiago apologized for writing the letter asking for the town's relocation, and Antonio Pichardo was removed from his post and general of the Spanish forces in the north of the island for allowing the enemy troops to enter Santiago unopposed.[4]

Figure 17.1 Santo Domingo, 1671
© Universal Images Group Limited/Alamy

The actions of the local military leadership in Santiago and the events that surrounded the 1690 French attack of the city of Santiago raise numerous questions regarding the relationship between French and Spanish residents of Hispaniola during the last decades of the seventeenth century, the nature of such relations, and the role Spanish residents played in the implementation of Spanish imperial policy in Hispaniola during these years, both of which proved to be crucial for the future of the island in the last decades of the seventeenth century.

The actions of Pedro Morel and the captains who participated in the ambush against the French troops represent the two extremes in Spanish attitudes towards their French neighbors in Hispaniola throughout the last two decades of the seventeenth century. In this chapter, I argue that by the last decades of the 1600s, French and Spanish residents in Hispaniola had developed a deeply ambivalent and fluid relationship that ranged from open violence to collaboration. By the end of the century, however, Spanish residents on the island, organized in patronage networks of associates and dependents, came to rely on French merchants and settlers as the most secure sources of commerce, and as such, afforded them a level of economic prosperity Spanish traders operating in Santo Domingo could not provide. I also argue that the rise of intercolonial trade occurred alongside the growing efforts of the Spanish Crown to eliminate French settlements from Hispaniola. The participation of Spanish local residents in the war effort allowed them to manipulate the Spanish offensive and foil imperial designs of a unified Spanish colony of Hispaniola. Spanish residents of Hispaniola played a direct role in foiling Spanish imperial plans for the island, thus choosing the short-term benefits of accommodation to the neighboring French presence over a unified island under Spanish control that remained isolated from Atlantic markets.

I

The lands of western Hispaniola had been uninhabited since the Spanish population was forcibly removed in 1605 to prevent them from dealing with English, French, and Dutch merchants. By the 1630s, English and French adventurers had inhabited the western shores of the island. These men, popularly known as buccaneers due to their habit of cooking meat in an Arawak-style grill known as *boucan*, dedicated their time to hunting feral cattle and planting tobacco, which they would take to Tortuga for sale to European merchants. Situated off the northwestern tip of Hispaniola, the island of Tortuga became the most important non-Spanish settlement in the region from the 1630s to 1670s. As Tortuga increased in importance as an entrepôt, it also attracted the attention of the Spanish governors in Santo Domingo, who saw the presence of these foreigners both in Tortuga as well as in the western parts of Hispaniola as encroaching on Spanish territory. These so-called trespassers were killing feral cattle that, at least nominally, belonged to the long-time Spanish residents of Hispaniola. In two separate instances, 1635 and 1652, the governors of Santo Domingo organized expeditions to expel the foreigners from Tortuga. They were successful in both instances, but due to the inability to garrison Tortuga, or to populate the area with Spanish settlers, the French and English peoples who had been expelled from Tortuga soon returned.

– CHAPTER 17: *Atlantic peripheries* –

Figure 17.2 Buccaneer in the West Indies, 1686
© Private Collection/Bridgeman Images

By the late 1650s, Northern Europeans had become a permanent fixture on the island's depopulated regions. Writing in 1653, a governor of Santo Domingo informed the Council of the Indies in Spain that his troops had caught English, Irish, Dutch, and French prisoners during their patrols through western Hispaniola.[5] Earlier that same year, an *oidor* from the *Audiencia* of Santo Domingo reported that in the two years he had been on the island, fifty-seven foreigners, most of them

French, had been apprehended, sent to Santo Domingo, and shipped to Spain.[6] These prisoners only represented a small sample of those residing in the theoretically depopulated regions. By the middle of the seventeenth century, Hispaniola had become a contested borderland where Spanish authorities struggled to maintain control over their territorial claims while groups of Northern Europeans attempted to benefit from the uneven control Spain had over large swaths of the island. This is the implied message in a travel narrative published in London in 1655, in which its author claims that 'The Cattel of Europe, which have been transported thither, have thriven abundantly and multiplied into such incredible numbers, [...] especially in Hispaniola, and in many parts of the Continent beside, live wilde in herds upon the Mountains, and may be killed by any body that will take the pains to doe it.'[7] Such open invitations as this one to exploit the riches of the New World surely increased the appeal of places as dimly populated as Hispaniola at a time when Northern European monarchies were more interested than ever in expanding in the Caribbean in opposition to the expansionist tendencies of the Spanish monarchy. In 1655, those aspirations became apparent when the English attacked Santo Domingo. The English attack became a powerful reminder to colonial administrators of the imminent and recurring danger that Spanish Caribbean possessions faced during those years.[8]

It was precisely the 1655 English attack that forced Spanish forces stationed in Tortuga since its capture in 1652 to hurriedly return to Santo Domingo, thus allowing the French settlers to return. In the years that followed, the French colony of Tortuga flourished. Its population of 900 people in 1660 jumped to 6,500 individuals (2,012 of them black, and 200 colored) in 1681. A population estimate for that same year in the Spanish colony placed it at 6,312 individuals, including soldiers from the garrison, slaves, and free blacks.[9] Even though the Spanish estimates seem rather conservative, there is little doubt that the explosive growth of Tortuga represented a clear threat to the territorial integrity of the Spanish colony, particularly after 1670, when the settlement of Cap François, on the northern coast of Hispaniola, quickly became the most important port of the new French colony.

II

As the population of the French colony grew, the Spanish colony faced its own internal troubles. Starting in the 1660s, there were reports of repeated waves of epidemics ravaging the population of Santo Domingo. As early as 1659, Governor Juan de Balboa believed that the city was prone to the spread of leprosy due to the constant contact between sick residents and their relatives, as well as their disregard for the advice of the local doctor.[10] The repeated outbreaks of smallpox and measles that ravaged the population through the 1660s were much more serious, and affected both slave and free populations. In 1677, an already debilitated population faced a wave of dysentery that killed what seemed like a significant number of residents, although the testimony of witnesses do not offer data on the number of deaths. The only data available is that offered by the Archbishop, who documented the baptism of 638 children and the death of 780 individuals. Therefore, the city of Santo Domingo experienced negative growth during these years, which probably also impacted the city's business and trade. It is unclear whether the waves of disease also impacted the countryside and the island's other villages, although it seems possible that they were spared.[11]

In addition to attacking its human inhabitants, the diseases spreading through Santo Domingo also affected crops. Beginning in the 1630s and 1640s, cacao trees had been introduced in Hispaniola as an alternative to the previous crops such as ginger, whose profits were on the decline. Cacao was embraced by the elites and religious institutions as the only viable cash crop, and was produced extensively. By the late 1650s, Rodrigo Pimentel, the wealthiest man in the colony, had planted a total of 38,000 cacao trees on his various properties. His slaves harvested an average of 1,000 *cargas* of cacao annually, which earned him a reported 12,000 pesos.[12]

In the 1660s, cacao was well on the way to becoming the cash product that residents needed to turn the economy of the colony around from the economic decline that had affected the island since the 1570s. Between 1669–71, such optimistic prospects had vanished. That year, numerous letters from Santo Domingo reported that cacao trees were falling prey to a disease that prevented the trees from producing fruit and eventually killed them.[13] A look at the tithe collected by the Archdiocese of Santo Domingo during these years seems to indicate that trend. In 1666, the Archdiocese collected almost 13,000 pesos. Only three years later, it managed to collect only 4,000 pesos.[14] The ruin of the cacao trees due to 'blasts,' which contemporaries also experienced in Cuba and Jamaica, was felt by everyone in the colony, particularly those near the capital. The disappearance of the crop interrupted the incipient trade that the port of Santo Domingo had begun to experience due to the cacao bonanza. Most planters were reduced yet again to practice subsistence agriculture and cattle ranching.[15]

As if diseases affecting both humans and crops were not enough, natural disasters also challenged Hispaniola residents. In 1673, an earthquake hit the island, causing great destruction in the capital. Many private residences and religious buildings, some dating back to the early 1500s and shaken by years of torrential Caribbean rain and winds, could not withstand the tremors and collapsed. Writing almost twenty years later, in 1691, the governor of Santo Domingo reported that with the exception of the cathedral, most of the buildings around the main square still lay in ruins.[16] The owners, possibly pressed by economic hardship, seem to have been unable or unwilling to rebuild their houses. In 1680, a hurricane swept over the island, causing even more destruction.[17]

III

Despite those challenges faced by the population and economy of the colony, Spanish officials continued their efforts to thwart French advances. Beginning in 1647, the Crown authorized the formation of two companies of thirty men each to patrol the northern and southern coasts of the island and capture buccaneers and marauders living in the western parts of the island. The troops filled their ranks with professional Spanish soldiers, but the difficulty of maintaining an adequate number of soldiers in the Santo Domingo garrison led to compromises: professional soldiers were appointed to leadership positions, while local black and mulatto recruits represented the bulk of the troops when professional soldiers were not available. In 1653, one of the *oidores* of the *Audiencia* wrote to Spain announcing that he had sent over fifty-seven foreigners to Europe, including English, French, and Dutch, which seems to indicate that these troops were indeed an effective tool to at least keep in check the Europeans who inhabited the borderlands.[18]

For reasons that are unclear, the two companies were disbanded during the governorship of Juan de Balboa (1659–61). According to a witness, the governor thought that the troops were useless and claimed that, 'His Majesty did not pay blacks or mulattoes,' a statement that was clearly false but was used as an excuse to renege on payment of the salaries owed to those locals when the troops were disbanded, at a time of deep economic constraints by the local Treasury. It could have also been a way for the governor to pocket the money himself. The governor's statement also provides an example of the racialized disdain that many Spanish officials serving in Hispaniola showed for the increasingly colored population of the island. In this sense, Balboa's elimination of the two companies might have been due to the fact that most of the soldiers at this point were indeed local free black and mulatto residents.[19]

The absence of these two companies patrolling the borderlands allowed Europeans free movement through the island, which most Spanish residents did not mind, even benefited from, so long as this movement was peaceful. During governor Balboa's tenure, French people (very possibly, French indentured servants who escaped their patrons) were at times seen walking in and out Santo Domingo working as teamsters, which seems to indicate that the labor needs of local residents might have taken precedence over fears of invasion.[20] For inhabitants of borderland regions, and unlike Spanish colonial administrators, birthplace was not a cause of concern, as long as these individuals abided by the local codes of conduct.

Foreigners had resided in Santo Domingo and other towns on Hispaniola since the early days of the colony. The presence of Portuguese families and merchants in Santo Domingo dates to the origins of the city in the early 1500s. During the seventeenth century, foreigners of all origins had made Hispaniola their home. Some married into local society and stayed and were considered members of the community. In Hispaniola, as in many other places in Latin America, a person's belonging to the local community was not determined by birthplace, but by his ability to situate himself within the community and extract rights and fulfill duties to society.[21] Ricardo Ermenzon (Richard Emmerson?) was one of those men. He is described in the sources as a surgeon and *vecino*, that is, a permanent member of the community. In 1672, he was called by the governor to translate some English documents recently received from Jamaica. He managed to translate only part of them, arguing that the ink was too dark to read the handwriting and that 'he had not exercised [his tongue] in over twenty years.'[22] Not only was Ricardo's status as a *vecino* not questioned by the authorities, but by his own admission, he had been away from English territory (possibly in Hispaniola) for a good part of his adult life and become naturalized into Spanish society.

But not all foreigners crossed into Spanish territory to work or reside peacefully among the local residents. The disbandment of the two patrol companies emboldened other French colonists to initiate attacks on Spanish settlements. In 1660, thirty men guided by a Spanish mulatto attacked the settlers in the region of Guaba, taking them prisoner.[23] That same year, 300 Frenchmen from Tortuga sacked the town of Santiago, killing 150, and forcing its remaining inhabitants to seek refuge in the mountains. When an *oidor* of the *Audiencia* went to Santiago in the aftermath of the attack to investigate the state of its defenses, he found a few Frenchmen who had been residing in Santiago for a time. The fact that the oidor found them there indicates that they feared no reprisal from their neighbors for their countrymen's attack to the city, proving yet again that birthplace or nationality held little importance to the ways that local residents defined their neighbors.[24]

The 1660 attack on Santiago led Governor Balboa to create a permanent garrison containing at least fifty soldiers in the town.[25] In the following years, some of these soldiers established ties with the local population, married local women and formed their own families. Others, confronted with the pressures of living in a frontier town like Santiago, deserted their posts to live as ranchers and hunters in the countryside. The posts that they left open were filled by local Santiago residents, for whom working the land or tending cattle had become very challenging due to the constant threat of a French attack. Their salary as soldiers allowed them to continue earning a living at a time of increasing conflict. It also accelerated the creolization of the garrison and the connections between the soldiers and the local residents.[26]

During the 1670s, the clashes between Spanish and French settlers continued as the French expanded their control over the western part of the island. Such instability led to a reconstitution of the two companies who had previously patrolled the island. This time, however, the troops were formed from the start with local residents and led by professional soldiers. These troops were involved in the constant clashes between Spanish and French forces along the frontier. The two Spanish companies, however, were insufficient to stop French attacks on Spanish settlements. In 1673, French forces attacked the towns of Cotuy and La Vega, the latter only 70 miles away from the capital. The attackers burned part of the towns and killed residents and cattle. The town of Santiago, located farther north, was much more exposed to attacks. Many of its residents had land and cattle stretching all the way to what once was the town of Bayahá (today Port Dauphin, Haiti), but faced with the French attacks, they had to abandon it. Francisco Sánchez, *alcalde mayor* of the northern lands, viewed the growing French presence on the island with increasing worry, and warned the Council of the Indies in Spain that once the French took root in the land, it would be almost impossible to expel them. This in turn would create 'great inconvenience to this city [Santo Domingo] and to all the Indies, because this island is in the middle of their commerce, and every year the enemy captures many vessels, to great prejudice to Your vassals and Your Royal treasury.'[27]

Sánchez's attempts to alert the crown of the dire situation that Hispaniola residents were experiencing seemed to produce little results. The *Cabildo* (City Council) of Santo Domingo wrote in even starker terms, referring to the colony as 'the almost cadaverous...body of the unhappy Hispaniola.' Its members complained of the death of many slaves in the epidemics that ravaged the island and the lack of slave ships arriving in Santo Domingo. They also claimed that the few merchants that came to Santo Domingo sold their products 'without fear from God...at prices that provide them over 100% profit, and against human and divine laws.'[28]

In the second half of the 1670s, the Spanish residents of Hispaniola, and especially those located in the area surrounding Santo Domingo, found a new source of labor thanks to the proximity of their neighbors. As the French transitioned from a system that employed indentured servitude to one dependent on slavery, many African slaves started escaping their new masters and crossing the borderland region into Spanish territory. These slaves were captured by Spanish authorities and questioned to find out if they had been previously taken from other Spanish territories in the Caribbean.[29]

Once it was established that they had not, they were given in deposit to powerful local residents and Crown officials to work on their lands or households. According to Jerónimo Chacón, a new *oidor* who arrived in 1675, some members of the elites had pressured the governor to have the slaves sold at auction, but those who had the slaves in deposit resisted the sale.[30] Another member of the *Audiencia* pointed out an alternative option: setting the slaves free as a reward for escaping the French.[31] By 1675, the Crown had decided to keep the slaves in deposit with local residents, but the depositaries would have to pay a salary to the Treasury for the use of their labor.[32] As slaves continued arriving in the Spanish territory, the *Audiencia* of Santo Domingo sought a more permanent arrangement for the status of these slaves. In 1677, another twenty slaves arrived, and after a disputed trial among the elites and the Audiencia's attorney to decide the future of these runaway slaves, the Audiencia decided to declare all slaves escaped from French territory free, hoping that this would encourage other slaves to escape and would weaken the French colony. The governor also created a settlement on the outskirts of Santo Domingo for the former slaves called San Lorenzo de los Minas, in reference to Elmina Castle, on the African Gold Coast, and the port of origin of some of the new residents. The creation of towns of runaway slaves, which was later applied to other border regions such as St. Augustine in Florida, became a way to increase the population of border regions, as well as increase the supply of food to local markets, and improve the defenses of Spanish territories. These new settlers were also trained in the use of spears so they could participate in the defense of the colony if it ever became necessary to do so. By 1686, the initial settlement of fifty former slaves had already grown to 150 individuals, and it continued to grow as more slaves escaped French control.[33]

IV

Beginning in the 1680s, the diplomatic relationships between the Crowns of Spain and France changed in important ways. Formalized in the peace of Nijmegen in 1678, the end of the Franco–Dutch war, in which Spain sided with the latter, marked the beginning of a time of peace between the two kingdoms. The news of the peace agreement reached the Spanish officials in Santo Domingo in 1680, and the period of peace lasted until 1689. The governor of Santo Domingo decided to send an envoy to Tortuga to inform the governor there of the new peace between the two monarchies. The person chosen to carry out the mission was Juan Bautista Escoto, a cleric from Santiago. Escoto was very well received, and French officials informed him of the wealth, trading prowess, and strength of their military in case of a Spanish attack. He also observed that the island of Tortuga was a very busy port in which Spanish ships regularly stopped to trade, as well as ships from the Bay of Biscay, in northern Spain, Italy, and many other European ports. He also noted the frustration of French settlers towards the Spanish policy of welcoming French indentured servants and slaves into their lands, thus depriving the French of their labor force.[34]

The reaction of the French governor of Tortuga to the news of the peace was tepid at best. Even though he acknowledged the peace treaty, he observed that the document did not make any reference to Hispaniola. He promised to do everything in his power 'according to justice and reason,' and would keep French subjects from Spanish lands, but they would still make provisions in Hispaniola, in those lands they had acquired 'by right of conquest.' He also expressed his desire to come to an agreement on borders.[35] The French governor thus intended to keep his options as open as possible while extracting some concessions from the Spanish.

The mistrust between the governors was evident, both in their handling of the peace as well as in their interpretations of each other's moves. On January 1, 1681, once Escoto had returned to Santo Domingo, the French governor sent four men by land with a new letter to his Spanish counterpart. The men were intercepted in the north of the island and asked to return to French territory, due to fears that they might be encouraging trade between French and Spanish residents. Their letter was taken to the governor in Santo Domingo. The members of the *Audiencia* did not like the fact that the French governor had sent four men by land. Such an act was perceived as a discourtesy (as opposed to sending one single cleric, as the Spanish had done) and an attempt to survey Spanish lands and defenses. In his communication, the governor of Tortuga interpreted the letter of the peace rather liberally in the eyes of his counterpart. He tried to convince the Spanish that the exchange of prisoners contained in the peace agreement signaled that the Spanish had to return the French indentured servants and slaves that had escaped from French territory, while the governor of Santo Domingo argued that he could not return those that had come of their own will.[36] These exchanges between the imperial authorities of both colonies underscore the fragility of the Franco–Spanish peace in Hispaniola and the self-serving reading that each side made of the text. While the Spanish saw it as an opportunity to stop French advances, the French interpreted it as a way to legitimize their territorial gains and recover some of their lost labor.

From the north, others raised the alarm about the French. Jerónimo de Robles, *alcalde mayor* of Santiago, declared that the four French men sent by the governor of Tortuga had said in his presence that 'it is impossible their [French settlers'] removal from the island, and that we [the Spanish] should get the idea off our heads.' Jerónimo also claimed that the French had all the provisions they desired from Europe, and they had become bolder since the time of the peace, going into territories that they would have never dared to enter during times of war. His letter is signed by all the officers serving in the northern region of the island to add credibility to his statement.[37] The urgency that the letter conveys might also be motivated by his desire to highlight the risks of his job in order to receive his long delayed salary, but the threat of French encroachment, as perceived by some peninsular royal officials, is nonetheless evident.

Not all peninsular officials saw French encroachment as a threat. When Artillery General Andrés de Robles (1684–90) took office as governor of Santo Domingo, he was faced with the island's deep budgetary deficit, and so decided to once again eliminate the two companies in charge of patrolling the frontier, claiming that during peace times such troops were no longer necessary.[38] His actions earned him a scathing reply from the Council of the Indies: '…[R]egarding that island, treaties do not apply because, as I have informed you in numerous decrees, foreigners inhabiting those lands do it illegally, and they are merely tolerated.'[39] From this reaction, we can extract at least a couple of conclusions. First, it is curious that the attitude of the Crown here is very similar to that first reaction of the governor of Tortuga when he received the Spanish cleric with the news of the peace treaty. Both the Spanish Crown and the governor of Tortuga contested the validity of the treaty for Hispaniola (even though the governor of the French colony did try to use the treaty for his own advantage later, as we saw). Second, despite being inhabited by French settlers for decades, the Crown refused to acknowledge the French presence as legitimate, and still held out hope of a future reunification of the island under Spanish control. The position of the royal officials on the ground was based on the reality of the circumstances and the very real financial constraints of the island, while the Crown still held western Hispaniola as sovereign Spanish territory and expected its governor to behave accordingly.

Despite some continuing tension along the border areas over land and cattle during these years, the reality on the ground seems to have been quite different from the images that soldiers serving in Santiago painted or that Crown officials in Madrid imagined. During peace time, the French and Spanish attacks on each other's territory completely halted. At the same time that military actions ceased, commercial relations flourished. They had undoubtedly existed before, but during these years, the documentary evidence of these exchanges is much more abundant, which might indicate an increase of those exchanges.[40] It seems that the peace between France and Spain was interpreted by some French merchants as an opportunity to gain new customers. In a letter addressed 'to the Spanish gentlemen whose hands found this [letter] and to those from San Juan de Guaba,' the French merchant Carlos de Orange informed his prospective customers that 'observing that your very Christian king has made peace with ours, we joyfully look forward to meeting you, [...] you can come here as safely as if you were with your own brothers.' He insisted that the governor of Tortuga himself sanctioned these deals and that they would find everything they wished at a good price.[41] If it was true that the governor of Tortuga supported French merchants' attempts to expand their business into the Spanish colony, it might indicate that he embraced the peace as an opportunity to seek non-military avenues to benefit the French colony. There is evidence of at least one other letter like this one, but it is very difficult to ascertain how many of these letters circulated, how many people read them and participated in these exchanges.

The existing documentation seems to indicate that commercial interactions with French merchants became increasingly common during this period. Even among Spanish settlers at the border, where armed scuffles with French groups still occurred, trade was unavoidable. For example, talking about the Spanish residents of the settlement of Banica, within the border region, Governor Robles wrote that, 'even though they ordinarily trade with the enemies with great disorder and little faith, I have decided to leave them there because they maintain the enemies at a distance from their settlement.' These settlers, the governor added, were 'the worst vassals that Your Majesty has on this island.'[42] The fact that despite Robles' negative assessment of the settlers he was willing to leave them indicates the importance of these populations to deter French advances. The behavior of these settlers (both combative toward and collaborative with the French) provides a window into the ambiguous experience of living in a porous borderland, where enemies and trading partners were just roles that individuals and communities adopted according to necessity and opportunity.

By the end of the 1680s, commerce with the French had spread through the Spanish border regions of Hispaniola. Governor Robles was informed that even some of the most respectable residents of the town of Santiago were engaged in these deals, selling cattle, horses, and mules to the French, but it was impossible to find evidence because the Spanish residents protected each other. The governor only managed to arrest two mulatto brothers who lived in Santiago. Two members of the local militia accused them of selling 150 heads of cattle for 7 to 10 pesos each to the French in 1686, and another 120 in 1687. The two men who provided the information to the governor did it in secret, because 'it is true that [the informants] would have been speared if [Santiago residents] had known that they gave me the news.' As punishment, the two brothers were exiled for six years to the Araya fortress, which sits along what is today's Venezuelan coast.[43] The fact that these two brothers were of mixed race and quite successful in their deals with the French might have made them easy targets for their neighbors. The denunciation of the two mulatto brothers gave the authorities in Santo Domingo someone to blame, while it eliminated two market rivals. It is also relevant that the two individuals who reported the two brothers to the governor were both local militia captains, since there is ample evidence that members of both the *Cabildo* of Santiago and the local militia (whose leaders were often members of both bodies) were actively involved in the trade. Among those mentioned are Antonio Pichardo de Vinuesa and his nephew Pedro Morel de Santa Cruz, both active participants in the 1690 defense of the town of Santiago that opened this chapter. They were both members of the local elite, and both served as *alcaldes* of Santiago at different times. The Pichardo family had resided in northern Hispaniola for over a century.[44]

Pichardo made a career as a militia captain, and had led multiple expeditions against the French in the northwest beyond the Dajabón river and the Guaba valley. According to the Archbishop of Santo Domingo, Pichardo was 'the knife and scourge of the French on this island.'[45] His accomplishments on the military front did not, however, ensure that he was treated well by the governing forces on the capital. Salaries of soldiers in the northern frontier were often delayed for years, if ever paid at all. Pichardo was no exception. Writing in 1688, he complained that he had not received any salary in the previous three years, and since his appointment of *cabo general* (highest ranking military officer in the northern frontier), he had only received a small fraction of his salary.[46] Unable to exert enough political influence in Santo Domingo, the needs of soldiers in general, and especially those in the northern frontier, were regularly ignored in the capital. The military elites in Santiago constituted the first line of defense against a possible French invasion, but at the same time, deprived of their salaries almost permanently, they actively participated in trade deals with French settlers as their only means of survival. In the Hispaniola borderlands, militia solders embodied this duplicity despite its apparent incompatibility. They were both the defenders of the colony, and active trading partners with those who they were supposed to defeat and expel from the island.

During the peaceful years of the 1680s, as the northern residents of the island began dealing with their French neighbors, the circulation of French and Spanish peoples and cattle across the frontier could not have passed unnoticed to the militia or the soldiers patrolling the northern frontier. In most cases they were active participants in these deals. Governor Robles believed that French settlers were trading with the owners of every cattle ranch in the north. He tried to persuade local authorities to act, but these officials claimed they did not know anything about the deals. The governor took this attitude as an excuse not to act. He pointed out that the local justices and Pichardo were in on these deals, and questioned how local residents had gathered 200 heads to be sold to the French on a ranch belonging to Pichardo's brother without his knowledge and collaboration.[47]

V

The year 1689 brought to an end a period of relative peace between the residents of the Spanish colony of Hispaniola and the French settlers who inhabited the western shores of the island, as France and Spain renewed hostilities in Europe.[48] It is in this context that the French attack of Santiago in 1690 took place. If colonial officials in Santo Domingo already had doubts about the ability or even the willingness of the garrison and militia from Santiago to defend the north of the island from French encroachment, the events surrounding the 1690 French attack just confirmed their worst suspicions. As early as 1689, the viceroy of New Spain had started the preparations for a Spanish assault to eradicate all French settlements on the western part of the island. The offensive was planned as a dual attack: local militias and professional soldiers in the Spanish colony would strike by land, and the *Armada de Barlovento,* the Spanish Caribbean fleet, would attack by sea.

At the head of the royal bureaucracy at this time was Ignacio Pérez Caro, who had been appointed Governor of Santo Domingo in exchange for monetary compensation owed to him by the Crown. More than any of his predecessors, Pérez Caro's time in office became a business venture whose success depended on his good relations with the local elites. The fleet arrived in Santo Domingo in November 1690. Governor Pérez Caro called a meeting of the military captains of the island. Even though Pichardo was no longer commander of the northern forces, he attended as a captain, as did his nephew Morel. The newly appointed commanders of the troops in Santiago and the captains of the border patrolling forces, who according to some witnesses were 'subordinates' of Pichardo and Morel, were also in attendance. Despite Morel's carelessness in the defense of Santiago that year, the governor initially appointed him head of the land forces. The news pleased Morel's allies, but the great majority of captains did not hide their dissatisfaction with the governor's choice. The governor was thus forced to reconsider and finally settled on a professional soldier who was a popular choice among the Santo Domingo elites. Pedro Morel was then appointed his second in command, as a way to keep the elites from the north of the island content.[49]

In January 1691, the area of Cap François and its nearby settlements were surrounded by a Spanish force of 1,300 men who were supported from the sea by the fleet. They killed 200 men and captured significant quantities of coin, textiles, and other valuable products. Once the region was secure, the captains of the army gathered to discuss whether they should move forward and attack Port-de-Paix. Arguing that they lacked ammunition and food, despite having seized ample amounts of both in Cap François, many of the captains refused to continue the attack.[50] *Sargento mayor* José de Piña, in a letter to an *oidor* of the *Audiencia* of Santo Domingo, described how Pedro Morel, who many considered the real commander, took every possible measure to slow the attack and benefit from it. He gave quarter to prisoners in exchange for secret caches of money and jewels, and protected the property of some French landowners from pillaging. Morel accumulated a significant amount of loot, which he shared with his uncle Pichardo, other relatives, and his allies, while leaving everyone else without a reward.

Piña, who was the third in command of the expedition, believed that the overwhelming momentum that the Spanish force had experienced could have led to the expulsion of the French from Western Hispaniola had it not been for Morel's

– CHAPTER 17: *Atlantic peripheries* –

actions. The success of the mission was, in fact, impeded by the unwillingness of the local militia to continue the campaign, which preferred to concentrate its efforts in the pillaging and accumulation of the loot acquired in the sack of Cap François. Piña did not mince words when describing the actions of Morel, his relatives and allies. He depicted the local elites as committed 'to discredit[ing] our arms to cover their malice and cowardice.' After only two weeks in French territory, the Spanish force retreated, leaving the property and houses of many French settlers untouched. Any loot left over after Morel had taken his share was loaded into the fleet ships and taken to Veracruz, thus depriving the rest of the participating local militia of their reward for the campaign.[51]

In 1692, a second expedition was organized. This time, the governor gathered 1,700 men from the Spanish fleet, the garrison of Santo Domingo, and the local island militias. This last group was very reticent to join due to the treatment they had received from Pedro Morel in the 1691 expedition. Governor Pérez Caro had to resort to giving each man five pesos as an incentive to join the campaign. Many of them replied that they did not need the money to serve the king. They only needed an experienced commander who treated them well. As an added incentive, Pérez Caro gave them permission to take as much property from the French as they wanted as a reward for the participation, something that Morel had not allowed in 1691. Still reluctantly, the militia nonetheless gathered in Santo Domingo to prepare for the attack.[52]

Once the entire force was gathered in the capital, the governor announced that the commander of the expedition would be, once again, Pedro Morel, with some members of the *Cabildo* of Santo Domingo as second. This decision angered many soldiers of the fleet, who expected to be commanded by a professional soldier. It also disappointed many among the local militias, who saw themselves once again in the hands of a man they did not respect. Some members of the local militias left for their hometowns after the new commander was announced, but most stayed, and eventually set out with the army towards French territory.[53]

The army set up camp not far from the enemy in anticipation of the attack. The local militia units were grouped according to their villages of origin. In the camp, Morel rearranged the units, separating men from their neighbors and trusted friends. He also removed local militia captains from the command of each unit. Following Governor Pérez Caro's instructions, Morel took merchants of certain wealth but little military experience, who were unknown to the militia forces, and without any knowledge of the men and terrain in which they would be fighting, and appointed them captains. As if these changes were not enough to undermine the morale of the militia soldiers, Morel also prohibited members of the army from taking any property from the French settlers with the exception of used clothing. This order clearly contradicted the promises the governor made to the militia soldiers when they were recruited. The reorganization of the local militias, the substitution of local captains, and the prohibition against looting the enemies proved too much for the militias. That same evening, they left the camp en masse and returned to their homes. Morel attempted to continue without them, but deprived of the most experienced men and those with the best knowledge of the territory, he was forced to abort the campaign. A few days later, the expedition returned to Santo Domingo without facing the enemy. Once the Spanish forces returned to Santo Domingo, Perez Claro wrote to his superiors in Spain claiming that the militia had left the camp because they were afraid upon the news of the arrival of French reinforcements. Such claims exculpated Morel, and the governor himself, from any wrongdoing.[54]

In 1697, the treaty of Ryswick put an end to the War of the League of Augsburg and settled the future of Western Hispaniola. Spain acknowledged France's possession of the western part of the island, thus giving up on its aspirations to expel the French and unify the territory. As French settlers consolidated their position in the western lands of the island in the second half of the seventeenth century, the place of the island in the geopolitical struggle between the Spanish and French crowns was forever altered. The Spanish residents of the island had to protect their territory and property from French encroachment, but at the same time, their neighbors provided new opportunities for trade and, to a certain degree, prosperity in ways that had been impossible to them for nearly one hundred years, during which the Spanish crown never gave up its hopes of expelling the French from Western Hispaniola and placing the entire island once again under its control. Those aims, however, were dependent upon the collaboration of royal officials on the ground and local residents, which proved hard – at times impossible – to count on due to the divergent objectives of these three groups: Crown, royal officials, and local residents.

Even though the relationship between French settlers and Spanish residents was prone to constant violent clashes, both groups accommodated to their circumstances, particularly in times of peace between the Crowns. Trade flourished and peaceful interactions across the border increased. Runaway French indentured servants and slaves escaped to Spanish lands, and although their escape created diplomatic tensions between the governments of both colonies, their presence in the Spanish local economy, after years of disease and death, proved extremely positive. Spanish residents of Hispaniola learned to live with the risks associated with having French neighbors as they increasingly enjoyed the benefits of their presence in the western lands. These benefits were always uneven, with certain sectors of the local elite benefiting from it more than the rest of the population. In Santo Domingo, being part of a powerful network was a crucial aspect of leading a prosperous life in this borderland colony.

Eventually, however, the power and influence that these elites wielded locally played a crucial role in the ambitions of two Atlantic empires in the Caribbean stage. For France, the intervention of local Hispaniola residents allowed the colony to survive and go on to become its most valuable possession in the Americas during the eighteenth century. As for Spain, the effect of local interference in imperial plans thwarted the attempt to unify the island and to eliminate the center of operation of a powerful enemy in Caribbean waters. While Atlantic imperial projects strived to accomplish unambiguous triumphs, both Spanish and French residents of Hispaniola struggled to balance the directives of their respective royal imperatives without granting either a complete victory. It was precisely in this ambiguous balance that the local residents of a peripheral colony found the most profitable conditions for their survival.

NOTES

1 Governor Ignacio Pérez Caro to the Council of the Indies. August 6, 1690. Archivo General de Indias (henceforth AGI), Santo Domingo (SD). 65, Ramo (R). 6, Number (N). 215; Oidor Fernando de Araujo Rivera to the Council of the Indies. April 24, 1691. AGI, SD. 55, R. 20, N. 126.

- CHAPTER 17: *Atlantic peripheries* -

2 '...desvaneciendo por este medio el crédito que en tiempo de paces tenía de gran comerciante con dichos franceses así en aquella ciudad como en esta.' *Oidor* Fernando de Araujo Rivera to the Council of the Indies. April 24, 1691. AGI, SD. 55, R. 20, N. 126.

3 'que allí querían y habían de vivir y defender el lugar hasta morir.' Ibid.

4 Ibid.

5 Governor Andrés Pérez Franco to the Council of the Indies. April 23, 1653. AGI, SD. 57, R. 5, N. 70.

6 *Oidor* Francisco de Montemayor y Cuenca to the Council of the Indies. December 14, 1653. AGI, SD. 57, R. 5, N. 79.

7 Gent 1655: 138.

8 For a description of the 1655 English attack on Santo Domingo as well as the motivations behind it and its aftermath, see Carla G. Pestana, 'English Character and the Fiasco of the Western Design,' *Early American Studies* 3 (Spring 2005): 1–31.

9 French population data was extracted from Michel Camus (1985). Cited in Philip P. Boucher, *France and the American Trophics to 1700. Tropics of Discontent?*. Baltimore: Johns Hopkins University Press, 2008, pp. 238. The Spanish population data is extracted from a letter from Friar Domingo de Navarrete, Archbishop of Santo Domingo, to the Council of the Indies, April 30, 1681. AGI, SD. 93, R. 5, N. 241.

10 Balboa could not know that most people are immune to leprosy. Governor Juan Balboa Mogroviejo to the Council of the Indies. November 7, 1659. AGI, SD. 58, R. 6, N. 80.

11 The information regarding the measles and smallpox outbreaks are from February 3, 1669. AGI, SD. 76, R. 1. The report of the dysentery epidemic is contained in a letter of *oidor* Juan de Padilla to the Council of the Indies, August 24, 1677. AGI, 63, R. 3, N. 32, document 4. The demographic data comes from a letter by Archbishop Friar Domingo de Navarrete to the Council of the Indies, April 30, 1681. AGI, SD. 93, R. 5, N. 241. The Archbishop did not specify how many of the dead were Spanish and how many were people of color, either slave or free.

12 1 *carga* amounts approximately to 50 pounds. AGI, Escribanía de Cámara, 22A, fol. 323v

13 For testimonies of the death of the cacao trees, see for instance the letter by Governor Ignacio de Zayas Bazán to the Council of the Indies, May 29, 1671. AGI, SD. 76, R.1; or letter by resident Manuel González Pallano to the Council of the Indies, May 2, 1675. AGI, SD. 90, R. 2.

14 AGI, SD. 93 and 94. For a full table of the tithe of the Archdiocese of Santo Domingo in the 17th century, see Ponce-Vázquez 2011: 169.

15 To see the effects of the disease in the neighboring Jamaica, see Momsen and Richardson 2009: 482.

16 Governor Ignacio Pérez Caro to the Council of the Indies. July 27, 1691. AGI, SD. 91, R. 4.

17 Anonymous: 1680.

18 Information about the formation of the troops can be found in a letter by the treasury officials to the Council of the Indies, November 12, 1666. AGI, Escribanía, 12A; *Oidor* Francisco de Montemayor to the Council of the Indies. December 14, 1653. AGI, SD. 57, R. 5, N. 79

19 The witness was Francisco de Luna, a veteran soldier who had served for 37 years on the island and one of the officers of the companies that Balboa dismantled. He testified in Balboa's residency trial. AGI, Escribanía, 12A, bundle 1.

20 These men were likely indentured servants that escaped their French masters and found work for Spanish residents. Ibid.

21 See Herzog 2003.

22 'Había más de veinte años que [la lengua] no la ejercitaba.' Governor Ignacio Zayas Bazán to the Council of the Indies. January 27, 1672. AGI, SD. 62, R. 5, N. 31

23 *Oidor* Andrés Martínez de Amileta to Governor Juan de Balboa. April 21, 1660. AGI, Escribanía, 12B, bundle 8.

24 Ibid.

25 The number of soldiers in this garrison is unclear in the sources.

26 Lope de las Marinas y Nevares, *alcalde mayor* of Santiago, to Governor Juan Balboa. July 4, 1661. AGI, Escribanía, 12B, bundle 8, col. 65r.

27 '...se siguen grandes inconvenientes a esta plaza y a todas las Indias por estar esta isla en medio del trajín de ellas y que todos los años apresa el enemigo muchas embarcaciones del comercio, todo el daño y perjuicio de vuestro vasallos y disminución de vuestra Real Hacienda.' Francisco Sánchez Calderón to the Council of the Indies. Undated (but information within the letter seems to indicate it was written in 1674), AGI, SD. 90, R. 2.

28 'El cuerpo...casi cadáver de la Infeliz Española....Nos venden sin temor de Dios lo que le compraron a más de cien por ciento de ganancia y contra lo que prohiben las leyes divinas y humanas.' The *Cabildo* of Santo Domingo to the Council of the Indies. April 24, 1679, in Rodríguez Morel 2007: 373.

29 A good number of the slaves captured in pirate incursions of Spanish possessions around the Caribbean were sold in Western Hispaniola. This is the case of the slaves captured in the attack on Veracruz in 1684. In the cases in which Spanish authorities were able to establish Spanish ownership of a slave, they sent word to the slave's master. See for instance, Governor Andrés de Robles to the Council of the Indies November 24, 1684. AGI, SD. 64, R. 6, N. 156.

30 *Oidor* Jerónimo Chacón Albarca to the Council of the Indies. June 6, 1675. AGI, SD. 63, R. 2, N. 14, document 6.

31 *Fiscal* Juan Garcés de los Fayos to the Council of the Indies. January 22, 1675. AGI, SD 63, R. 1, N. 1

32 Royal Decree, June 15, 1675. AGI, SD. 63, R. 2, N. 15.

33 Interim Governor Juan de Padilla to the Council of the Indies. October 25, 1677. AGI, SD. 63, R. 3, N. 62; Governor Andrés de Padilla to the Council of the Indies. December 9, 1686. AGI, SD. 303. For more on the town of runaway slaves created in St. Augustine in the 1730s, see Landers, 1999.

34 Governor Francisco de Segura to the Council of the Indies. 1681. AGI, SD. 64, R. 3, N. 061.

35 '...todo lo que sea de justicia y razón...'; '...por derecho de conquista...' Letter of Jacques Nepveu de Pouançay, governor of Tortuga, to Governor Francisco de Segura [1681] translated into Spanish by Oidor Antonio Cemillán Campuzano. Ibid.

36 Ibid.

37 Jerónimo de Robles Cornejo, *alcalde mayor* of Santiago, to the Council of the Indies. June 28, 1681. AGI, SD. 294.

38 Governor Andrés de Robles to the Council of the Indies. April 24, 1687. AGI, SD. 65, R. 3, N. 44.

39 '...[R]especto de que por lo que mira a esa isla no se entienden los tratados de ellas porque los extranjeros que las habitan están mal introducidos y sin derecho alguno. Sólo es una tolerancia la permitida, como os tengo remitido en diferentes cédulas.' Royal Decree, January 29, 1690. AGI, Escribanía, 26C, R. 2, fol. 121r.

40 In fact, the excuse that the governor of Santo Domingo gave the governor of Tortuga about not allowing his four men to arrive in Santo Domingo was 'the issue of prohibited trade' ('por el tema de los comercios prohibidos'). Francisco de Segura, governor or Santo Domingo to Jacques Nepveu de Pouançay, governor of Tortuga. January 25, 1681. AGI, SD. 64, R. 3, N. 061.

41 'A los señores españoles que la hallaren o a cuyas manos viniese y a los de San Juan de Guaba'; '[V]iendo que vuestro rey cristianísimo ha establecido la paz con el nuestro de que nos hallamos gozosos y deseando encontrados [...] podéis venir aquí seguramente como con vuestros propios hermanos.' Carlos de Orange, February 24, 1681. AGI, SD. 92.

CHAPTER 17: *Atlantic peripheries*

42 'Aunque el trato y comercio con los enemigos es común y ordinario con ellos con gran desorden y poca fe todavía los he dejado estar allí porque detienen los enemigos más cerca de sus poblaciones.' Governor Andrés de Robles to the Council of the Indies. May 5, 1687. AGI, SD. 65, R. 3, N. 49; 'Los peores vasallos que Vuestra Majestad tiene en esta isla.' Governor Andrés de Robles to the Council of the Indies. July 20, 1687. AGI, SD. 65, R. 3, N. 66.

43 '[...] es cierto que los alancearían si supieran quién me había dado la noticia.' Governor Andrés de Robles to the Council of the Indies. November 17, 1688. AGI, SD. 65, R. 4, N. 98.

44 Pichardo's grandfather had been alcalde of the town of Puerto Plata in 1582. For a full list of merits and family tree of Antonio Pichardo de Vinuesa, see AGI, Indiferente General, 127, N. 5. Pedro Morel was the son of one of Pichardo's sisters.

45 'Ha sido años ha el cuchillo y azote del francés en esta isla.' Friar Domingo de Navarrete, Archbishop of Santo Domingo, to the Council of the Indies. April 4, 1679. AGI, SD. 93, R. 5, N. 230.

46 From 1669 to 1679 he only received seven pesos and a half per month of his salary. From 1679 to 1685, twelve pesos and a half. Antonio Pichardo de Vinuesa to the Council of the Indies. April 6, 1688. AGI, SD. 91, R. 3.

47 Governor Andrés de Robles to the Council of the Indies. April 13, 1688. AGI, SD. 65, R. 4, N. 120.

48 A Royal Decree sent to the governor of Santo Domingo in May 24, 1689, announced the start of the war with France. Governor Andrés de Robles acknowledged its receipt in September 15, 1689. Governor Robles to the Council of the Indies. AGI, SD. 65, R. 5, N. 187.

49 *Oidor* Fernando de Araujo Rivera to the Council of the Indies. April 24, 1691. AGI, SD. 65, R. 7, N. 229; Eagle, 2005: 93.

50 Ibid.

51 '...deslucir nuestras armas por encubrir su mal obrar y cobardía.' *Sargento mayor* of Santo Domingo José de Piña to Fernando Araujo Rivera, *oidor* of the Audiencia of Santo Domingo. January 25, 1691. Ibid.

52 Unsigned letter (possibly written by Fernando de Araujo Rivera, *oidor* of the *Audiencia* of Santo Domingo.) April 18, 1692. AGI, SD. 66, R. 1, N. 1.

53 Ibid.

54 Ibid.

REFERENCES

Anonymous. (1680) *Relación verdadera en que se da cuenta del horrible huracán que sobrevino a la isla y puerto de Santo Domingo de los Españoles el día 15 de agosto de 1680*. Madrid: Lucas Antonio de Bedmar, printer.

Boucher, Philip P. (2010) *France and the American Tropics to 1700: Tropics of Discontent?* Johns Hopkins University Press.

Camus, Michel (1985) *Correspondance de Bertrand Ogeron, gouverneur de l'île de la Tortue et coste de Saint-Domingue au XVIIe siècle*. Port-au-Prince, Haiti: Ateliers Fardin.

Eagle, M. (2005) The Audiencia of Santo Domingo in the Seventeenth Century. Ph. D. Tulane University.

Gent, N. N (1655) *America: or An exact description of the West-Indies more especially of those provinces which are under the dominion of the King of Spain*. Faithfully represented by N.N. Gent. London: printed by Ric. Hodgkinsonne for Edw. Dod.

Grivetti, L. E. and Shapiro, H.-Y. (2011) *Chocolate: History, Culture, and Heritage*. John Wiley & Sons.

Herzog, T. (2003) *Defining nations: immigrants and citizens in early modern Spain and Spanish America*. New Haven: Yale University Press.

Landers, J. (1999) *Black Society in Spanish Florida*. Urbana, IL: University of Illinois Press.

Momsen, Janet Henshall and Richardson, Pamela (2009) 'Caribbean and South America. Caribbean Cocoa: Planting and Production', in *Chocolate: History, Culture, and Heritage*, eds. Louis Evan Grivetti and Howard-Yana Shapiro. Hoboken, NJ: Wiley.

Pestana, C. G. (2005) 'English Character and the Fiasco of the Western Design', *Early American Studies: An Interdisciplinary Journal*, 3(1), pp. 1–31.

Ponce-Vázquez, Juan J. (2011) Social and Political Survival at the Edge of Empire: Spanish Local Elites in Hispaniola, 1580–1697. Ph.D. University of Pennsylvania.

Rodríguez Morel, Genaro (2007) *Cartas del cabildo de Santo Domingo en el siglo XVII*. Santo Domingo: Publicaciones del Archivo General de la Nación.

PART V
RELIGION

CHAPTER EIGHTEEN

CATHOLICISM

——•◆•——

E. L. Devlin

The Christians who established the foundations of the Catholic tradition in Africa and South America came from a society which defined itself, to a significant extent, through its common Catholic identity. Christendom was a Europe of the Catholic Church, and the extension of that faith and its institutional apparatus were bound together amidst the commercial and colonial imperatives which also informed the creation of the Atlantic world in the fifteenth and sixteenth centuries. Although a desire to establish more efficient trade routes to the east led to the arrival of Christian Europeans in both Africa and South America, from the moment of that arrival an evangelistic purpose of conversion emerged as central to their intentions in both continents. Although significant local and regional differences and distinctiveness existed throughout western Europe, a common Catholic identity was still potent at the beginnings of extra-European evangelical and entrepreneurial enterprises. In such a context Christopher Columbus can be described as a 'militant Catholic' even though Christian evangelism was not initially a central motivation behind his voyages.[1] The first Portuguese to arrive in West Africa in the fifteenth century introduced themselves first and foremost as Christians, and left a drawing of the cross to identify themselves to potential converts.[2] John Cabot landed in Newfoundland in 1497, sponsored by the English king Henry VII and claiming the territory in the name of the pope while armed with a crucifix. The most striking contrast underlying the spread of Catholicism throughout the Atlantic world can be found in the precise nature of the Catholicising process and, especially, the political context informing it. The conversion of the Amerindians was part of an outright territorial conquest, while the willing adhesion of some African leaders to Christianity played a significant role in establishing a more 'diplomatic' relationship between the European powers and the African elite; a distinction between an 'inclusive' version of Catholicism incorporated traditional beliefs into a Catholic framework, against an 'exclusive' one focused on confessional purity.[3] The later development of a French presence in North America operated as a kind of midpoint on this spectrum: neither a native-led movement nor part of a full-scale territorial conquest, the experiences of French missionaries had sustained and significant echoes with some of the counter-reformation responses to Catholic unorthodoxy within post-Reformation Europe itself.[4] In the British territories, the experiences of the Catholic minority were shaped by the ingrained nature of Protestant anti-Catholicism, and respite from persecution was found only in those few colonies which supported religious toleration.[5]

From the first arrivals of European Catholics, traditional African and Amerindian beliefs informed responses to the newcomers along established religious lines. In that sense, in the white heat of first contact, the story of the beginnings of Atlantic Catholicism was often understood to be a story of returns. In the Kongo, the kingdom's founder Lukeni lua Nimi (c. 1380–1420) was reinterpreted as a prefiguration of the Catholicising leadership of Afonso I (c. 1456–c. 1542), although sometimes the comparison was hostile.[6] The paleness of Christian skin marked them as liminal creatures, and the first Europeans in the Kongo in 1483 were regarded as 'water or earth spirits of the *mbumba* dimension'.[7] Christian historians of Aztec culture were keen to draw attention to identifications of Hernán Cortés, or even St Thomas, with the serpent-god Quetzalcoatl, who had been prophesised to return to Mexico. The initial welcome granted the Christians on those terms gave Cortés an important foothold in Aztec society, and was significant in facilitating its eventual destruction.[8] Similarly, the Christian response to the discovery of the New World replicated the importance of religious belief in dealing with the sudden appearance of unfamiliar peoples. Instead of elevating them to godhood, the Europeans – by and large – relegated them to the role of savage and slave. God was present in these events insofar as the discoveries, conquests and conversions were part of His unfolding of the divine narrative, a process of continuing revelation decanting the progressive story of mankind, even if the discovery of the New World raised difficult questions about what it was to be human, and what this might mean for global Catholic responsibilities.[9] Debates about the nature of humanity and the hierarchy of societies identified in the world were central to Catholic thinking about the peoples of the Americas from the early sixteenth century. The most famous of those public disputes, in 1550–51 between Juan Ginés de Sepúlveda and Bartolomé de Las Casas, explored the nature of Amerindian humanity.[10] In practical terms, these debates were about the inter-relations of Catholic evangelism and Iberian colonial interests, for they sought to decide whether natives had souls, and asked if they could be truly converted and achieve salvation. The intellectual disagreements these debates highlighted, and the tensions identified between the balance of religious or colonial imperatives in motivating Iberian activity in the New World, demonstrate that from the beginnings of Catholic involvement in the Americas, disagreements were incumbent between the church (or, at least, missionaries) and the crown. These issues would only become more prominent as time passed, especially in the evolving tensions between crown control of the Atlantic colonies, and the various ecclesiastical institutions which emerged in Africa and the Americas over the centuries. Rivalries developed between those structures themselves, and throughout the centuries Rome aspired to make those hierarchies subordinate to its oversight.[11]

INSTITUTIONS

Although the Portuguese had been actively pursuing Catholic evangelisation in the Kingdom of the Kongo since the 1480s, papal recognition of these efforts was formally made only in 1494. Through the Treaty of Tordesillas, the papacy awarded Saharan

Africa to the guiding leadership of the Portuguese crown, while at the same time the Castilian monarchy was given greater authority over the Americas.[12] In 1493, Pope Alexander VI had recognised the importance of 'the propagation of religion and the augmentation of holy worship and the exaltation of the Catholic faith and the salvation of souls' as central to the Iberian expansionist mission.[13] A few years later, in 1501, Alexander authorised the granting of tithes for the maintenance of churches and clergy in the New World, celebrating the 'exaltation of the Catholic faith and the subjugation of barbarous and infidel nations' with the promise of new churches being built.[14] Papal claims to dispense with continental territories in this way were, of course, borne from the Church's universalist claims to jurisdiction over all God's created landmasses and peoples, but the impact of such decrees was, in reality, already superseded by the spread of Catholic spirituality in both Africa and the Americas.

Catholicism already had a long history in Ethiopia, and continued to survive in parts of North Africa and Egypt despite the successes of Islam.[15] In the Kongo, the first baptisms were understood within the context of the *mbumba* cult, but gifts from the Portuguese king, as well as the discovery of a black stone cross, won supporters from the political elite to the new cult-religion.[16] As in Benin and elsewhere in Africa, the focus of missionary activity in the Kongo continued to be the conversion of monarchs.[17] When he converted to Catholicism, the Kongolese king Nzinga a Nkuwu adopted the name Joao I (after the Portuguese king) and, somewhat against his wishes, Christianity soon moved beyond being just the purview of the Kongolese elite.[18] It secured support through the broadest similarities between its beliefs and native religions; for instance, the notion of 'two worlds'. But Catholicism was separate and distinct from traditional practices too. The liturgy remained in Latin, and the focus of sacramental activity emphasised ritual and sensory engagement. Joao's successor, Afonso I, was concerned to establish a Christian Kongo as part of the 'larger religious, diplomatic, and symbolic system of the early modern Atlantic as a land belonging to the realm of Christendom'. The cathedral at Sao Salvador was built in 1549, and the city became a 'symbol of Kongolese Catholicism', famous for its bell, while the king was usually present at the cathedral's ritual activities. Kongolese Catholicism remained a religion of the state, and benefited from strong monarchical leadership in the sixteenth century, despite undulating tensions between the monarchy and ecclesiastical authority.[19]

At various times in its history, the Kongo's kings were hostile to the Jesuits and episcopal claims to jurisdiction. Through ambassadors sent to Rome, appeals were made to the popes for more direct influence over the church and its personnel, against the influences claimed by the Portuguese crown. At least in the short-term, such calls were often successful, but complicated dynamics between the Portuguese and Kongolese monarchies, as well as ecclesiastical authority, remained an issue.[20] Efforts by the pope and the Portuguese king to subordinate the Kongolese monarchy to the bishop of São Tomé in the 1530s failed, but in 1596 the creation of the diocese of Sao Salvador allowed the Portuguese crown to nominate its bishops.[21] The new diocese also gave more influence to the Kongo's own leadership and, despite resistance from the Iberian monarchs, the Kongolese kings secured more control over the patronage of dioceses in their territories and administrative jurisdiction over the tithe. Italian regular clergy became much more prominent in the Kongo from the mid-seventeenth century, undermining Iberian dominance of the African church, a development

323

encouraged by the monarchy.[22] Clerical activity was supported by the Franciscans and Augustinians in the first instance; from the 1550s the Jesuits and Dominicans, and from the 1580s the Carmelites.[23] However, the presence of missionary orders was relatively meagre until the arrival of the Capuchins in the 1620s, and a sustained bout of missionary activity would last – in decline – until the nineteenth century.[24] Through the Capuchin presence in Soyo, something like a direct link between the Kongolese monarchy and Rome was established.[25] Portuguese interest in the Kongo waned in the late seventeenth century, and its focus – along with the Jesuit mission – moved to Angola. Over the course of the early modern period, Catholic evangelism had moved throughout Africa. The Kingdom of Warri was effectively converted in the late sixteenth century by Augustinians based in São Tomé and the rulers of Sierra Leone were converted by Jesuits in the early seventeenth century.[26] But a few decades later, official interest in such activities declined, and African Catholicism was sustained by the smaller remnants of earlier missions, especially through the efforts of native catechists who maintained Catholic beliefs and ritual practices when the imperial and commercial imperatives of the European empires directed the attention of the central authorities elsewhere.[27]

Catholic evangelisation was an important part of Spain's civilising mission in the Americas, and a significant motivation for the conquistadores.[28] Although the counter-reformation effort had not yet taken hold in continental Europe, the Spanish and Portuguese experience of the reconquest of the Iberian Peninsula in the late fifteenth century ensured that the loyal subjects of the crown were sensitive to the importance of evangelisation to the spread of Spanish civilisation, and were able to employ ready-made institutions and other mechanisms to consolidate the faith.[29] The Inquisition, and its associated bureaucracy, was introduced into the Americas in 1520.[30] Its presence, alongside the harsh deployment of native labour in the earliest years of Spanish colonial activity, was essential to the emergence of the anti-Spanish 'black legend', which interpreted Spain's Catholic empire as a brutal and repressive society, and contributed to the centrality of anti-Catholicism as an important characteristic of Protestant settlements in the New World.[31] The Spanish Inquisition was an institution not established in Rome by the central ecclesiastical authorities of the church, but created under the auspices of the Spanish crown to deal with racial and religious purity in the Iberian Peninsula. Its translation into New Spain highlighted the centrality of a Catholicising agenda to crown interests in Mexico, but also drew attention to the problem of authority, leadership and power in the Catholic Atlantic world. Even Cortés was strongly motivated by his desire to secure souls for the church – and consequently, subjects for the crown too. Writing to the king in October 1524, he commented 'Each time I have written to Your Sacred Majesty I have told Your Highness of the readiness displayed by some of the natives of these parts to be converted to Our Holy Catholic Faith and to become Christians'; Cortés goes on to explain that the quantity and quality of Catholic missionaries sent to Spain had been inadequate.[32] His letter is a reminder of some of the problems posed by the power structures of the Catholic Church, the role of the monarchy in its territories, and the relative independence of many of the religious orders in establishing their own missionary spaces in an environment influenced by so many competing agendas.

At the beginning of Spanish activity in the Americas, the crown played the central role in church administration. Under a Papal Bull of 1508, all ecclesiastical benefices

– CHAPTER 18: *Catholicism* –

lay within the king's jurisdiction. The archbishop of Seville held the primary authority over American clergy until independent dioceses began to be established in the 1540s, with the crown nominating bishops. By 1564 there were twenty-two dioceses and five archdioceses.[33] Within those structures a variety of clerical and missionary activities took place. The establishment of *reducciones*, closed Catholic settlements led by missionaries, offered protection to Catholic converts while ensuring clerical authority and religious orthodoxy were preserved.[34] Out of the *reducciones* emerged new generations of native-born Catholic missionaries who evangelised among their own peoples, although the acceptability of this practice from the European perspective changed over time.[35] While the conversionary efforts of various religious orders achieved significant successes, rivalries between them were common, often deeply political and ultimately disruptive. The arrival of new orders in the Americas or Africa antagonised those who had established earlier foundations. The Jesuit mission in the Kongo in 1548–55 failed because of tensions between the orders, the secular European priests and the indigenous clergy.[36] In the early seventeenth century, against the background of Portuguese conflict with Spain, Spanish Jesuits argued that their Portuguese counterparts were offering inadequate Catholic education in Africa.[37] At the same time, on the island of São Tomé, serious economic decline encouraged the question of Catholic orthodoxy to become prominent. Descendants of Jews who had long since been Catholic were now labelled 'New Christians', and the language of the Catholic reconquest of Iberia surfaced more than a century after the expulsion of the Moors.[38] The people of São Tomé were seen by Iberian overlords and the institutional church as potential Jews or subject to Moorish influence, demonstrating that, despite the profoundly Catholic history of the island's population – complicated marginally with the assimilation of African religious practices from the resident slave population – racial mixing could still surface as a problematic factor for contemporaries interpreting the purity and orthodoxy of Catholic populations in an imperial context.

Atlantic Catholicism emphasised participation in ritual activity alongside a basic catechistical knowledge. As in continental Europe, lay Catholics were expected to pursue an active and committed life of prayer and sacramental enthusiasm, and in most communities, missionaries and clerics led these pursuits. However, the relative paucity of available priests also meant that the full rigours of Catholic sacramental life could not always be enforced. Significantly, the sacraments of ordination and confirmation required a presiding bishop, and not every Catholic jurisdiction had one to hand.[39] Processes of 'translation' were also in play throughout the Catholicising effort in the Kongo. Missionaries used salt in baptisms as a possible defence against witches, reflecting how 'Kongolese ideas of evil were incorporated into Christianity'.[40] The sacramental life of the missions created a bureaucratic record which now survives as a vital source for exploring the numbers and nature of Catholic conversions. The creation of baptism records is one example of how missionaries in Africa echoed the responsibilities of the Tridentine parish priest in Europe, establishing a paper trail between the central ecclesiastical authorities and the missions, which included Catholic slaves in the Americas too.[41]

Supporting the formal sacramental practices of the church, missionaries and crown officials encouraged the creation of confraternities across the Atlantic world. As in Europe, these bodies were a corporation with some kind of shared spiritual interest, often dedicated to a specific saint or to the Virgin. They were at the vanguard of

325

syncretic Catholicism, which merged traditional religious practices with Catholic ritual, and native belief with Catholic teachings. The confraternities were also a means through which lay Catholics could be granted a leadership role within their communities, even if clerical oversight ensured orthodoxy. Race and ethnicity could become a key aspect of confraternal identity and used to further incorporate native Africans and Amerindians into the church's institutions. The first confraternity for black Catholics in Spain was founded in Cadiz in 1593.[42] Lay confraternities were especially important in the Kongo and Angola, and crown and ecclesiastical authorities encouraged Africans to establish and lead their own congregations. This was 'a means of social control' for the authorities, but it also reflected two of the most significant characteristics of Atlantic Catholicism: a desire to shape church practice to the pre-existing norms of African society, while also being influenced by shifts in continental European Catholicism (in this case renewed enthusiasm for lay confraternities in the Tridentine Church).[43] In Africa, while Capuchin missionaries assisted the spread of confraternities, the organic evolution of these social orders is apparent in myriad examples from across the Atlantic world. The Confraternity of Our Lady of the Rosary in Luanda comprised slaves and free black Catholics and was founded in 1658, requesting formal recognition from Rome within a few years. It took almost two hundred years for the confraternity of the same name in Lisbon – with its membership of African descendants – to be recognised, even though the confraternity had been extremely successful in the sixteenth century.[44] In 1682 Lourenço da Silva, an Afro-Brazilian anti-slavery campaigner at the court of Madrid, became procurator of the Confraternity of Our Lady Star of the Negroes, with a focus on turning the confraternity into a global one. There were regional differences in the spread of confraternities for black Catholics; until the eighteenth century they were less prominent in Brazil than in Portugal, but by that time most Brazilian towns had several black confraternities.[45] In the middle of the eighteenth century, twenty-four black Catholics founded a confraternity in Madrid, almost two hundred years after the first had been established in Spain.[46] Confraternities continued to be created and supported by crown and church authorities into the eighteenth century, often adapting to new ideas about racial or ethnic identities.

The ecclesiastical leadership based in Rome, concerned with the question of discipline and orthodoxy in Europe, was equally determined to maintain a watchful eye on developments in the Iberian presence in South America and Africa. The consolidation of clerical and episcopal discipline in the Tridentine Church was a keynote of a more intense commitment to evangelism and the maintenance of Catholic orthodoxy in the extra-European world. As in continental Europe, the bishops in Africa and the Americas achieved a new social standing and more conspicuous leadership role, and could find themselves openly and explicitly challenging crown policies in their dioceses. They could also challenge the local power structures too; through the 1610s tensions increased between the resident bishop of Sao Salvador Manuel Baptista Soares and King Alvaro III.[47] Sometimes, the complicated power structures between Catholic monarchies and ecclesiastical authorities benefited the consolidation of both church and monarchical power over native elites. In 1622 the inauguration of a Roman congregation with oversight over overseas missions, *Propaganda Fide*, transformed the church's administration of Catholic communities in the Atlantic world, and challenged the established power of monarchy and colonial governments. The *Collegium urbanum* was created to train missionaries, and catechisms in various languages were printed in Rome and transported throughout the Atlantic world by its agents. Such texts were also developed by missionaries working in Africa and the Americas.[48] As early as the 1550s the first translations of the catechism into Kikongo by the Jesuit Diogo Gomes were printed in Lisbon.[49] These developments ensured the Tridentine church was not just confined to rejuvenating the Catholic tradition in Europe, but also directed its response to Protestantism within a broader global mission of evangelisation and the defence of Catholic orthodoxy.

The experiences of Catholics in North America were more directly connected to confessional tensions incumbent between Catholics and Protestants and new attitudes towards empire-building and colonial rivalries in the aftermath of the Reformations. The inability or disinterest on the part of the sixteenth-century French crown to embroil itself in the Atlantic world stemmed primarily from the weaknesses of the monarchy during the period when other powers consolidated their extra-European activities. Until the seventeenth century, French interest in the New World had been limited to the profit-making enterprises of colonial companies who established a loose network of French settlements in North America, accompanied – at the fur traders' insistence – by Catholic missionaries.[50] New France's Catholic identity had been central since the 1630s, when Cardinal Richelieu prohibited Protestants from living in the colony.[51] In 1658, François de Laval became the first vicar apostolic, a papal appointee, but also a leading member of the Sovereign Council, and eventually the king's close ally.[52] As part of the process of re-consolidating the power of the crown within France itself, Louis XIV successfully deprived the companies of their independence and subordinated the church and its missionaries to crown authority in the early 1660s. In New France, Louis claimed the right to nominate ecclesiastical appointments, and the church became profoundly dependent on the crown for its financial security. After 1663, the king nominated bishops, and 40 percent of church funds came from the crown. The local *intendant* and the Sovereign Council oversaw the administration of the colonial church.[53] This translation of French Gallican privileges into North America is another potent indication of the different assumptions Catholic monarchs made about their position vis-à-vis the papacy, and the broader institutional apparatus of the Church. In 1674, the apostolic vicariate was turned into the diocese of Quebec, and in 1819 it became an archdiocese.

The evolution of these jurisdictional forms highlights the longer-term success of Catholic consolidation in Quebec. Its episcopal structures remained intact even after the territory was lost to the Protestant British in 1760.[54] In the newly formed United States, debates continued in the eighteenth and nineteenth century about the administration of the church, especially its finances and evangelical purpose. Before independence, the various missionary orders had fallen under the jurisdiction of the vicars apostolic in England, but now Catholic bishops based in America argued about the dynamics between church and state.[55] In the 1820s, John England, bishop of Charleston, South Carolina, opposed the use of state finances by the church, while the archbishop of Baltimore, James Whitfield, supported federal financing of Christian – including Catholic – evangelism among Native Americans. In the commonplace anti-Catholicism which remained potent in the United States, Catholics were assumed to oppose the separation of church and state, and religious liberty. In 1832, Pope Gregory XVI issued a papal bull condemning precisely those concepts, as well as freedom of the press. But five years later, in 1837, the American bishops formally pronounced their support for liberty of conscience.[56] The nationalities of the bishops alone – French, English, Irish – demonstrate the complexity of the church's evolving presence in the Americas. Bishop England was central to establishing the first Provincial Council of Baltimore, which alongside diocesan synods, would prove a relatively effective way for the American church to govern its disparate components, and engage with problems of sacramental orthodoxy, church structure and administration, as well as the need for evangelisation among African Americans, former slaves and western Indians.

THRESHOLDS

The emergence of a more disciplined and centralised global church in the mid-sixteenth century generated problems of contemporary interpretation and assessment for global Catholic evangelism. Since the late fifteenth century a popular and enforced syncretic Catholicism had emerged throughout the Atlantic world, and responses to this required contemporaries to address the problematic question of defining Catholic orthodoxy in the Atlantic context and, particularly, deciding how far native religious and social practices could be allowed to coalesce with Catholic beliefs and teachings. Throughout the history of the global church in the sixteenth and seventeenth centuries, this question of 'the merging of religions' would become even more contentious and embittered, as the disciplining of Tridentine renewal, geopolitical conflicts, and rivalries between the missionary orders emerged. These debates were not absent before the Reformation either, but the history of Catholic syncretism in the Atlantic world highlights that 'religion responded both to its internal dynamic and to the new dynamic created by culture contact and physical transfer'.[57] Although Catholic missionaries and evangelists often led these processes, they sometimes emerged organically from engagement with native interpretations too. This equilibrium – the creation of new forms of Christianity which allowed Africans and Amerindians to embrace the faith while at the same time preserving a connection to traditional beliefs and customs – ultimately gave an extraordinary strength, potency and longevity to Atlantic Catholicism, and insulated it from many of the most debilitating debates within European Catholicism in the modern period.

The origins of syncretic Catholicism in Africa and the New World can be seen in the complicated attitudes Europeans held towards native peoples and societies. Although they were usually understood as barbaric and uncivilised, native religious practices fascinated missionaries, and are often prominent in the detailed descriptions assembled by Europeans throughout the early modern period.[58] They were not quite denigrated but, rather, understood as a manifestation of the devil's active work in these territories. They were sinful, but not pagan or heretical.[59] Other African 'characteristics' were appreciated as pseudo-Christian: the Kongolese willingness to share was 'truly Apostolic' and resonated with concepts of Catholic charity.[60] The Europeans' appreciation of some similarities between Catholicism and native religions only served to underscore the diabolic manipulation of Christian practice apparent in native understandings. Aspects of Amerindian beliefs – notably serpent-deities – made the devil's real presence even more conspicuous.[61] In other cases, stories from the classical and biblical traditions were interpreted to indicate a kind of mythological universalism; the fables of Nipinoukje and Pipinoukhe in North America were read as a version of Castor and Pollux.[62] Syncretic Catholicism emerged from a sense that

– CHAPTER 18: *Catholicism* –

many aspects of native ritual and religious tradition could legitimately be incorporated into Catholic practice. Indeed, one of the most significant features of the Iberian crowns' interest in the New World, and their method of colonialism, itself hinged on a biological syncretism being established between subject peoples. Miscegenation between Europeans and Amerindians was actively encouraged, and within a few generations the Spanish colonies were dominated by a native, mixed-race, Catholic community. The *mestizo* became another category in the Iberian fascination with race and religion long-since prominent even before the discovery of the New World. African Catholicism had a very profound reaction on the nascent American church too, for the arrival of Africans – often as slaves – transported syncretic Catholic practices to another continent, where they often flourished and joined with American Catholicism in an even more complicated interplay of plural Catholicisms.[63]

Although Europeans had successfully established Catholicism in the Kongo in the late fifteenth century, its position was still insecure in the early decades of the next century. Joao I's support for the faith became more circumspect later in his reign, and it was not until his son became king in 1509 as Afonso I (Mvemba a Nzinga) that the conversion of the kingdom was consolidated. This full-scale Catholicisation was heralded by Afonso's witnessing the appearance of a cross in the sky or, in other versions, a vision of St James.[64] As in his father's reign, its native elite led the Kongo's embrace of the faith. Afonso used 'a range of regalia, narratives and ritual apparatus' to consolidate his authority, and following his conversion he 'imposed Christianity as the kingdom's state religion and integrated it into the symbolic and historical fabric of the realm'.[65] Afonso regarded the Portuguese king as his equal, a 'brother', and the Kongolese kings were usually recognised as monarchs in their own right by the church.[66] In Afonso's reign, the *Mani Vunda*, the religious leader who balanced the crown's political influence among the nobles, was given a 'Christian religious role', while the nobles as a group were willing to embrace Catholic sacramental life, adopt Portuguese names, and celebrate the main feasts of the church and its saints. Kongolese terms from traditional religious practices were used in a Catholic context; for instance, 'nganga', the word for priest, was now used to describe Catholic clergy.[67] Nevertheless, non-Christian *nganga* were assimilated into a Christian diabolist framework, and it was assumed that the Devil was working through them.[68] The regalia and politico-religious arguments for Afonso's policies demonstrated a 'cross-cultural manipulation of symbols and narratives' allowing him to establish his position as a Catholic monarch who respected his heritage – even if he destroyed African artworks to impress the Portuguese as part of his assault on traditional religious idols.[69] Despite Afonso's longer-term success at establishing Catholicism's centrality to the Kongo's religious identity, there remained considerable resistance from adherents of traditional African religious practises. The evolution of a syncretic Catholicism was partially the result of this organic negotiation between political and religious authorities within the Kongo, and the broader influences of traditional religious belief and practice, which allowed some Catholics in Africa to be accused of witchcraft.[70] The tropes of African witchcraft and Christian ideas could even come to share the same linguistic forms.[71] Later, in the reign of kings Garcia and Antonio, concessions were made to an 'indigenous religious revival' threatening Catholicism's established standing. Nevertheless, with the help of missionaries, Kongolese Catholics would survive the collapse of central government in the 1660s and sustain 'an African variant of Christianity' for decades.[72]

One of the most potent examples of syncretism in the Kongo can be observed in the emergence of the cross as a symbol of the connections between syncretic spirituality and materiality in the early modern Kongo. Brass crucifixes created in Africa became the most prominent symbol of the success of Catholicism, and they 'brought together local ideas of death and regeneration…and Christian beliefs in the passing and resurrection of Christ'.[73] The cross came to be the strongest symbol of an African Catholicism fusing European figurative sculpture – the image of Christ – with traditional Kongolese images and ideas, for instance the 'Four Moments of the Sun'. This was an emblem symbolic of life's journey and the passing of the day from morning to night, and the 'Four Moments' motif was often represented in the form of the human body.[74] A 'cross' was apparent in the placement of the figure's limbs which was twice echoed in the materiality of the Catholic crucifix – first, in Christ's own body, and second, in the cross itself. The popularity of the cross in African Catholicism highlights how brass-workers in the Kongo brought 'their own cultural assumptions' to bear in their creation of a distinctive Catholic material culture, and could themselves be as sophisticated and sympathetic to the potentials of religious fusion as Catholic missionaries. In sixteenth-century Benin, sculptural artefacts from the period of Christian interaction highlight 'the indigenous African cosmologies into which the early Portuguese travellers entered, and through which these strangers were reconfigured', and so African sculptors were granted interpretative agency. By this time, carved African objects were being used in Catholic ritual and achieved a sacred purpose in the new religion.[75] In the same way, traditional native ritual was adapted. As late as 1740, the Capuchin Bernardino d'Asti described how dancers of the *sangamentos* wore regalia dating back to Afonso's reign to perform a series of 'martial dances' after Mass on major Catholic feast days. These *sangamentos* had moved from being about agricultural cycles and hope for prosperity, to a commemoration of particular holy days – 'an altered symbolic realm'.[76] They are emblematic of the 'cross-cultural manipulation of symbols and narratives' defining Catholic material culture in the Kongo during, and after, Afonso's reign.[77]

Similar trajectories occurred in South America, fuelled both by the specific conversionary purposes of Europeans, and by the response of Amerindians to Catholicism in their own right. In South America, the position of the mixed-race *mestizo* was important to the cultural syncretism which defined the nature of Catholic society and ritual. Confraternities focused on several significant saints encouraged a hybrid baroque art to merge Catholic and native Amerindian styles and subjects.[78] The appearance of the Virgin Mary to the Indian Juan Diego in 1531 confirmed to Iberian Catholics, and the global Catholic Church as a whole, that European engagement with the Atlantic world was pre-ordained as part of the divine narrative and a core aspect of the ongoing process of Christian revelation. The Americas became a truly, if contested, Catholic space, and images of the Virgin of Guadalupe were often flanked by smaller depictions of various miraculous occurrences, received and welcomed equally by both Europeans and non-Europeans alike. Even into the modern period, the Virgin remained a potent symbol of Catholic universalism, and its transcendent righteousness in the sacred and secular worlds.[79] In one such image from 1774, she forms the centrepiece flanked by depictions of saints in the ether, with their miraculous interventions occurring in the temporal world. Below the Virgin are two figures representing the embodiment of continuing ideals for the Catholic Atlantic world: at the base of her right foot is the contemporary pope, Benedict XIV, and at her left, a native Amerindian princess and symbol of conquered – or assimilated – Spanish Mexico.

Figure 18.1 Virgin of Guadalupe
© Denver Art Museum

This female figure is also a reminder of how adeptly Catholic missionaries used gendered images and ideas to win converts, and the spread of Catholicism was followed by an increasing celebration of female spirituality in the Americas.[80] From the beginning, Europeans in Africa had been associated with the liminal and the feminine, and the church's emphasis on female saints and holy figures only heightened this connection.[81] The most obvious manifestation of female prowess in the Atlantic Catholic world was the emergence of female convents and the prominence of nuns in the spiritual lives of Catholic communities. These women were usually of Spanish descent, but often born in Iberian America, and could be controversial.[82] Juana Inés de la Cruz (1651–95), a Hieronymite nun born near Mexico City, became one of the leading poets of her age, and was condemned by her Archbishop for supporting female education.[83] St Anne was assimilated into pre-existing interpretative models, while Catherine Twkakwitha and Rosa da Lima represented a potent female American Catholicism. The profundity of female spiritual writings from New Spain demonstrates the intensity of female religiosity.[84] Outside the cloisters, it also led to an increased emphasis on females in traditional Amerindian history, religion and myth. An ancestor portrait from Peru in the early 1800s depicts a woman identified as the first Catholic convert in the Andes. The male head she holds by its hair, dripping his blood onto her white dress, is her prize decapitation, the result of an attempt to force her to break her (Christian) vow of chastity. The imagery emphasises her essentially 'native' identity and is intended to do so; her violent resistance imitates the conquest of Cuzco by the first Incan queen, Mama Occllo, who beheaded her rival, as well as the biblical story of Judith's decapitation of Holofernes. It is a perfect example of how the tropes of Amerindian and Christian history were being assimilated and synchronised throughout the early modern period. Even at the beginning of the nineteenth century, it was still important and relevant to identify and celebrate these legacies. For American Catholics, they were not a mark of impurity or imperfection, but rather of genuine Catholic enthusiasm and recognition of the vitality of Catholic Amerindian society.

Despite the successes implied in the spread of syncretic Catholicism, it also created significant problems for the reputation of Catholics who could not always control how they were interpreted within the context of native traditions. In 1528 the followers of one of Cortés's rivals, Panfilo de Narvaez, were shipwrecked off the coast of Texas. There were four survivors, including a Moorish slave and a Spaniard, Cabeza de Vaca, who would later write an account of his experiences. Enslaved by Karankawa Indians, they 'reluctantly became magical healers at the Indians' insistence'. The Indians assumed that, since the Europeans had brought with them a variety of illnesses, then they could also cure them. The Europeans sought to cure using Catholic ritual, 'by making the sign of the cross over them and blowing on them and reciting a Pater Noster and an Ave Maria; and then we prayed as best we could to God our Lord to give them help and inspire them to give us good treatment.'[85] In this instance, the Europeans fell back on Catholic ritual as a means of alleviating their persecution by the Indians, but this approach could lead to an accidental syncretism, and assimilated Catholic practice within a dominating native interpretative framework. It was not uncommon in North America for Catholic prayer and ritual to be interpreted within pre-existing shamanic tropes, and for the impact of the European presence in the New World to be considered in this way. When people did die because of diseases brought by Europeans, or indeed through other natural causes, missionaries were often accused

Figure 18.2 Inca Princess
© Denver Art Museum

of shamanism, and of poisoning the natives. The missionaries themselves were interpreted as diabolic agents.[86] The use of sugar as a means of winning over native children to baptism and in catechising classes was one way in which Catholics found themselves accused of attacking natives, poisoning their children and complicit in the destruction of native societies.[87] The perceived loss of traditional talismanic powers following Christian conversion could lead to despair. In 1639, native Amerindians asked 'what is the use of believing?' as missionaries were actively confronting

333

'sorcerers' and their diabolic compacts.[88] Many Amerindians did not want to go to Heaven, for their relatives would not be there, and many were disturbed to find that embracing Christian culture meant more than simply building some churches.[89] As Catholicism became established in the French territories, new converts developed illustrated catechisms and new techniques for self-mortification more suited to their own society – an instance of organic syncretism at work.[90] They enthusiastically pursued the sacramental life, rising early in the morning for Mass and instruction, while their society was also blighted by the introduction of French brandy and the rise of new 'vices' centring on alcohol.[91] The complexity of the Amerindian response to Catholic evangelism, at different times and different places, was marked by one sustained similarity. Most Catholic converts who were won over were children or the dying; if the latter survived, the legitimacy of their 'conversion' could be problematic, while the focus on children encouraged a missionary focus on long-term education as a means of securing orthodoxy, catechistical knowledge and true belief.

In New France, the establishment of missionary activity was heavily indebted to the support of wealthy French Catholics, and in the first instance was inspired by the example offered by the Spanish in South America.[92] Over the course of several decades, French missionaries sought to evangelise by learning native languages, and attempting to synchronise established beliefs within Catholic thought and practice. Although conflict between the French and native peoples was almost constant, Catholics were encouraged to engage with Iroquois culture. But in contrast to the syncretic missionary activity of Catholics in New Spain, the *coureurs des bois* acted more as a buffer between the French settlements and the American natives, rather than a Catholicising presence. It was a new generation of counter-reformation missionaries which had most success in making evangelising inroads into the North American territories, as missionary orders like the Recollets emerged to create a particularly distinct association between Catholicism and France. The Jesuits were, perhaps, the most important of the missionary orders, and their annual reports back to Europe, with their 'unparalleled richness of...ethnographic detail' reflect the broader Catholic interest in native cultures, and an emphasis on understanding it.[93] They engaged with almost every native nation in north eastern America, and made clear distinctions between them. Although the French were closely allied to the Algonquins, the Jesuits regarded the Iroquin nations as superior because they more closely resembled European society.[94] Catholic missionaries were assisted in their efforts by the assumption that they were agents of the French crown and trading companies, and the Iroquis, at least, were very interested in developing trading connections with Europe.[95] As in other parts of the Atlantic world, aspects of native beliefs were assumed to reflect the nascent understanding of the Christian God. The Jesuit Jean de Brebeuf, in 1636, believed the 'poor Indians' really acknowledged the Christian God in their prayers 'though blindly, for they imagine in the heavens an *oki*...a demon of power which rules the seasons of the year, which holds in check the winds and the waves of the sea'. Because of these similarities, it would be 'easy' to 'lead these peoples to a knowledge of their Creator'.[96] However, the various North American nations proved more difficult to immerse within the faith in the absence of a territorial conquest. Amerindian attitudes to Catholicism in North America were not always hostile, but it was nearly always predicated on a kind of cultural relativism, and an openness to a concept of 'multiple and relative supernatural truths', in which

Catholic and native beliefs co-existed side-by-side.[97] Catholic evangelicals were stymied by this unwillingness to commit absolutely to a Catholic worldview, even a syncretic one.

TENSIONS

The primacy of syncretism might suggest the emergence of Catholicism in Africa and the Americas was chiefly and happily a process of assimilation, encouraged by Catholic missionaries, pursued by natives with enthusiasm, and ultimately a core aspect of global Catholic triumphalism after the Reformation. That is true, to a point, but neglects the use and threat of violence as one means by which Catholicisation was achieved. King Afonso was reputed to have buried his mother alive for refusing to abandon native icons, and this story was reported well into the modern period as a sign of the intensity of his faith.[98] The vibrancy of Catholicism in the Atlantic world gave sustenance to counter-reformation missionaries who moved further afield, to Asia and the Philippines in the seventeenth and eighteenth centuries, as well as those who moved deeper into Africa and the Americas during the modern period. But suspicions about these syncretic processes had been present since the fifteenth century, and continued to be prominent, and not just among Catholic missionaries and visitors nervous that they had failed to stamp out traditional beliefs.[99] Europeans, Africans and Amerindians were all equally concerned – in different ways – with the question of preservation, authenticity and truth in their beliefs and the rituals used to inscribe them in their cultures. Conflicts within and between these groups could be deeply political, challenging assumptions about the nature of power and its ownership. Hostility to Catholic syncretism became a cornerstone of Atlantic anti-Catholicism, and Protestant evangelism was dubious about the quality of syncretic Christianity, preferring to destroy native religions outright, rather than assimilate them.[100] Some of the most radical challenges to Roman Catholicism in the Atlantic world came not just from Protestant opponents but from within the syncretic Catholic tradition too.

From the perspective of Catholic Europeans observing, or participating, in the emergence of syncretic Catholic practices in the Kongo, the key challenge to orthodoxy was to be found in the legacy of so-called 'festishes', material artefacts worshipped in traditional religion and used in various social rituals. It was not always easy to identify the boundaries between objects totally assimilated into the new Catholic culture, and those understood purely within the contexts of earlier native traditions. The use of fetishes were not just limited to religious practices, but also had a broader social role as medicinal and healing objects. Catholics confronting them in the Kongo found themselves in a similar position to their peers working to remove practices in Europe which had simply been part of local folklore and social custom, but which in the post-Reformation period were being re-designated as witchcraft or heresy.[101] In October 1621, Bishop Pedro da Cuhna Lobo at São Tomé witnessed what he believed to be a procession of Jews carrying a golden calf past the cathedral. His interpretation was informed by increasing hysteria about the purity of Catholic practice in São Tomé at this time, and was most probably a Catholic procession mixed with traditional African rites. The 'golden calf' was some kind of fetish which had survived in the island's Catholic culture. The problems of liminality, fetish survivalism and the porosity of religious orthodoxy in the Catholic world remained potent.

Even so obvious an orthodox symbol as the cross – and the use of crucifixes in Catholic ritual – was not unchallenged. In the early eighteenth century, a female mystic named Dona Beatriz, sometimes called Kimpa Vita, experienced a series of visions in which she saw the Holy Family as members of Kongolese society, and emerged from this experience with her body inhabited by St Anthony.[102] The Antonian movement she led developed in the context of a Kongo destabilised by economic failure and civil conflict. The much-weakened Catholic monarchy was upbraided for abandoning Sao Salvador, and Beatriz claimed that Christ had been born in the city. In 1705, she occupied the ruined cathedral and gathered thousands of Catholic zealots – chiefly peasants – around her. The conflict which followed between King Pedro, supported by the Capuchins and other missionaries in Africa, and the Antonians, supported by rival Kongolese aristocrats, hinged on the meanings of Catholic materiality and sacramentalism; its symbolic and social functions. Beatriz destroyed many *nkisi* (African objects with spiritual powers), declared the cross to be a fetish, and burned it. In this dispute, there was a real 'danger of repudiating the entire sacramental teaching which the Kongo had accepted for two hundred years as the structural core of its public religion'.[103] The cross became one of the recurring motifs for the defenders of royal authority and Catholic sacramentalism, and King Pedro embraced it as his personal symbol, ensuring 'the struggle lay between the cross upon the one hand and the "Salve Antoniana" symbolised by the crown which St Anthony and her male followers always wore, upon the other'.[104] Beatriz was captured and burned for heresy in July 1706 and crucially, the decision to execute her was made by the *Mani Vunda*, a powerful statement of the legacies of pre-Christian Kongolese power structures, ameliorating Beatriz's attempts to further 'Africanise' the Catholic Church in the Kongo. Pedro retook Sao Salvador in February 1709, the king reputedly armed only with a cross. The defeat of Antonianism's anti-sacramentalism consolidated the cornerstone of syncretic Kongolese Catholicism as it had emerged since the fifteenth century. But Beatriz had offered a potent challenge, and consolidated a material tradition which continued into the eighteenth and nineteenth centuries. Images of Christ, the Virgin and other significant Catholics figures would increasingly be depicted as Kongolese, while sculptures of St Anthony – although invoked by the Capuchins in the war against Beatriz – continued to hold associations with her millenarian movement.[105] One metal sculpture of the saint, 'Toni Malau', offers an image of a kind of reconciliation: in his right hand he holds a cross, and in his left, stands the Christ-child, contemplating a goldfinch, a portent of the crucifixion.

If the Antonian movement represented a challenge within the African church, the broader legacies of the split within European Christianity were felt in other parts of the world. The establishment of British colonies in North America highlighted some of the tensions emerging between Catholics and Protestants in the New World, within the context of strong anti-Catholic sentiment in the British Isles. The establishment of Maryland by Lord Baltimore in the 1630s was a direct riposte to the Protestant-minded sensibilities of other British colonies. Rejecting Virginia's oaths of supremacy and allegiance, the Catholic Baltimore secured a charter for a colony allowing Catholics to participate in civic life and freely pursue their religious beliefs.[106] But Maryland was not a Catholic colony, and Catholics were a minority, even if they held significant influence and were often quite wealthy. Throughout the seventeenth century the number of Protestant settlers increased significantly. Many of them subscribed to normative English attitudes about Catholicism: it was intolerant, associated with European absolutist government, and a threat to the commercial and imperial aspirations of Protestant Britain. Baltimore seemed to recognise that the success of his experiment relied on the Catholic population remaining quiet and, in contrast to the very public sacramental life of Catholics elsewhere in the Americas, called for Catholic ritual to be practiced in private.[107] Although Maryland witnessed a rise in the numbers of Catholic schools, and most of the public religious buildings in seventeenth-century Maryland were Catholic churches, they were austere when compared to their European counterparts.[108] There was little ornate religious art or stained glass on public display, and chapels were often based in private houses.[109]

Despite this private lifestyle, the Catholic minority still antagonised their Protestant neighbours. The most prominent religious order was again the Jesuits, who had some success in finding Catholic converts, and extended their activity throughout British America.[110] After thirty years of focusing on Indian natives, they turned their attention towards the Protestant English instead.[111] As they became more established, the Jesuits asserted their own independence against Baltimore's assumptions of a private Catholicism subscribing to a central secular loyalty, in tensions which echoed those between crown and cleric elsewhere in the Atlantic world.[112] Despite Baltimore's hostility to a strong Catholic evangelism, the colony suffered three rebellions against Catholic proprietorship in the seventeenth century, all connected to broader political and religious crises back in mainland Britain: during the British civil wars in 1645–46, the Interregnum in 1652–58 and finally in 1689 in the aftermath of the Glorious Revolution.[113] The latter consolidated the introduction of anti-Catholic legislation during the eighteenth century and this defined Colonial American perspectives, and then those of the early United States, towards Catholics, even if many later supported the American Revolution and its enthusiasm for private religiosity.[114] Attitudes towards Catholics marked a kind of syncretic assimilation of post-Reformation European fears about the religion in the American context: 'in Maryland, an anti-Catholic ideology was in place which built upon the English anti-Catholic tradition, fused the fears and concerns of many mainstream Protestant Maryland planters, and located the sources of those fears in the proprietor and his Catholic governors.'[115] It was sustained in part by continuing Catholic immigration, especially from Ireland and through slaves from Africa. Conflict with Spain and France in the 1750s led to an intensification of anti-Catholic sentiment, and a return to the old tropes of conflating tyrannical government with popery.[116] Irish Catholics were seen as sympathetic to Spain, and in the 1630s and 1640s had led revolts in Barbados. In June 1689 they were encouraged by the Jacobite governor general to destroy the English plantation of St Kitt's.[117] Fears of Catholics were grounded in contemporary reality, while at the same time embracing an earlier discourse identifying the pope as Antichrist and interpreting the Catholic Church within a millenarian framework. Fears of Catholics, slaves, and Catholic slaves all existed within a similar paradigm, interpreted as a significant threat to Protestant security. The arrival of Catholic slaves from Africa, as well as the conversion of slaves to Catholicism while living within British territories, was an attack not just on British interests, but more intimately, on Protestant households too.[118] Slaves were expected to observe the sacramental calendar of the church, and participated in the same services as free Catholics. The ecclesiastical hierarchy resisted attempts to exempt slaves from their religious responsibilities until tensions over the collection of the tobacco crop on saints' days became too sustained in the late eighteenth century, and some Jesuits granted dispensations.[119] Of course, many of the slaves were owned by Jesuits, Recollets or other missionary orders, emphasising that the Catholic Church was not fundamentally opposed to slavery, even if it was sensitive to abuses within the institution.[120]

The exportation of slaves from Africa to the Americas connected Catholic communities across the Atlantic. Many slaves were themselves Catholic, and found themselves part of a broader Catholic society if they were transported to Iberian or French America, or part of a different Christian tradition if in British or Dutch territories. From the early sixteenth century, King Afonso had objected to the capture and trading of Kongolese subjects on religious grounds, arguing that the abduction of his subjects was an affront to his position as a Catholic king and his sacred role in the Catholic world. Similarly, Catholic missionaries in the Americas were actively involved in attempts to prohibit the exploitation of native peoples as labourers or slaves. The most powerful advocates were those whose condemnation was built 'not merely on abstract principles, but on their personal knowledge of the evils arising from the actual operation of the slave trade'.[121] Pope Paul III issued a bull on the issue and in 1534 Charles V ordered that natives should not be compelled to work in the mines.[122] One hundred and fifty years later, Lourenço da Silva – who claimed descent from the Kolgolese royal family – campaigned for Roman intervention against perpetual slavery, especially for Catholics who 'with holy baptism [God] had directed towards the enjoyment of eternal glory'. Pope Innocent XI referred these complaints to Propaganda Fide, and both pope and congregation viewed slavery as 'a disgraceful offence against Catholic liberty' with practical consequences for evangelisation: 'the progress of the missionaries in spreading the holy faith remains impeded' by slavery.[123] Rome turned to crown authorities to ensure that abuses were stamped out, and Capuchin missionaries won the support of the Holy Office to condemn perpetual slavery. However, this did not amount to a full condemnation of 'just enslavement', as articulated by Aristotle and the Roman legal tradition. In the end, the efforts by the Holy Office to defeat perpetual slavery were ignored, although Catholic opponents of slavery throughout the eighteenth and early nineteenth centuries referred to its conclusions. The reason for this defeat was the result of the complex nature of government in the Atlantic world: 'the Holy Office could define questions of ethics, but the enforcement of its decisions depended on clerics and laity whose immediate ecclesiastical and ultimately political loyalties lay elsewhere'.[124] Slavery was another long-running cause of tensions between the religious, economic and colonial motivations behind European empire-building, and the complicated interplay of authority between papal and ecclesiastical hierarchies, colonial administrations, and European monarchical interests.

CONCLUSION

The story of Catholicism in the Atlantic world might be reduced to one of burgeoning empires using Catholicism as a label for justifying commercial and territorial exploitation, securing land and power in the name of the Lord, but the experience of Catholicism – and of all kinds of Catholics – was so varied in the spiritualities, cultures and social practices which emerged that such a simplistic approach cannot be sustained. Instead, the evolution of different forms of Catholic thought and practice throughout the Atlantic world demonstrate the vitality and flexibility of the nascent global church from the late medieval period and into the modern. That adaptability also generated significant problems, concerns and challenges for the Church's leadership and Catholics' broader associations with the societies in which they lived. Because 'the church was not only the church of the poor and the oppressed...it was also the church of the privileged and of the conquistadores', Atlantic Catholicism generates many questions about the nature of Catholic orthodoxy over four centuries and three continents.[125]

Although there were broad similarities in the ways Catholicism evolved in Africa and the Americas, particularly in the development of syncretic approaches merging Catholic materiality and ritual with traditional social practises, there were significant differences too. The extent to which South American populations embraced Catholicism needs to be quantified by the reality that the Iberian presence reflected a territorial conquest as well as a spiritual one. If that quality was not entirely absent in some parts of the African experience, it was at least mitigated by the more willing embrace of its political leadership throughout much of Western and Central Africa to tolerate or actively encourage, the spread of Catholicism in their territories. Catholic Africa was strongly connected to the emerging trading systems joining continental Europe to the Americas, partially as a result of emergent slaving networks, and the strong Christian traditions which had existed in that continent since the fifteenth century contributed to Catholic evangelism in the post-Reformation period. In North America, a strident contrast emerged between the experiences of Catholics living in French Canada and those within British settlements. Even in the most religiously tolerant British settlements, Catholics remained a minority and anti-Catholicism had a potent impact on these communities and in the later United States.[126] The residue of traditional anti-Catholicism, a stronger sense of 'orthodoxy' within the modern Catholic Church in Europe, and a shared disdain of syncretic approaches from both Catholics and Protestants in the Enlightened world had a significant impact on how non-European Catholicism was appreciated – or not – in the modern period. In the nineteenth century, the particularities of Kongolese Catholicism especially, were perceived to undermine the integrity of the universal (European) Catholic tradition, and many of the most successful and potent practices in the African Catholic experience were dismissed as 'fetishes', when in fact, they had been introduced and adapted to precisely counter native practice and the survival of various traditions.[127]

This raises the question of how the success of Catholicism in the Atlantic world might be assessed. Certainly, contemporary missionaries believed that God was on their side in this struggle, and that they had made enormous progress in winning converts to the new faith. The key was education, and it is not surprising that Catholics in the Atlantic world focused on the catechism and the building of schools; harnessing local elites and winning rulers to the cause, while at the same time concentrating their focus – often controversially – on children. One Jesuit in New France bemoaned native abhorrence of corporal punishment; 'How much trouble this will give us in carrying out our plans of teaching the young!' he exclaimed.[128] But missionaries were always nervous that conversions were based on misunderstandings, ambition or fear. It was not unknown for deathbed converts to abandon their new faith the moment they returned to life, and the targeting of the dying also brought Catholics into disrepute among natives. And, of course, Catholic evangelism was nearly always invested with the broader colonial ambitions of the imperial powers. Nevertheless, accounts of confrontations between Indian converts visiting Dutch settlements adjacent to New France greatly satisfied their Jesuit observers: 'When they return from the land of the Dutch, they relate to us with much pleasure their success in the disputes they have had with the Dutch on points of religion, to the shame and confusion of those heretics'. Atlantic Catholicism not only saved natives from diabolic influence and barbarism, but put them in the frontline of European confessional disputes as well. But although the legacies of Reformation and counter-reformation were strongly felt in the Atlantic territories where Catholics sought to sway souls, Atlantic Catholicism was never just a proxy for European concerns. Instead, it offered a profound opportunity for the expansion of the faithful, and posed complicated challenges for an institution whose claims for universalism now extended far beyond the borders of an erstwhile Christendom, into a world in which new forms of Catholic thought and practice became a central part of a global religion. The responsibility was keenly felt, and converts and missionaries alike understood their purpose as a cross to be continually borne as much as it was a triumph to be celebrated.[129]

NOTES

1 Taylor 2001: 33.
2 Elbl 1992: 169.
3 Thornton 1984: 152–53.
4 Eccles 1987: 27–28.
5 Taylor 2001: 214.
6 Hilton 1985: 45.
7 Hilton 1985: 50.
8 Carrasco 2008.
9 Elliott 2007: 184.
10 Huxley 1980.
11 Wright 2005: 26–27.
12 Elliott 2007: 68; Hastings 1995: 72.
13 Symcox 2001: 39.
14 Symcox 2001: 58.
15 Hastings 1995: 3–45, 62–67.
16 Fromont 2011b: 111–12.
17 Hastings 1995: 77–89.
18 Hastings 1995: 73.
19 Hastings 1995: 81; Thornton 2001: 96, 102.
20 Thornton 1984: 162–64.
21 Hastings 1995: 87; Thornton 1984: 163.
22 Thornton 1984: 164.
23 Hastings 1995: 85.
24 Hastings 1995: 94–102.
25 Thornton 1984: 161–62; Gray 1983.
26 Thornton 1988: 264.
27 Thornton 1988: 273.
28 Headley 2000: 1119–55.
29 Elliott 2007: 67.

– CHAPTER 18: *Catholicism* –

30 Boxer 1978: 84–93.
31 Taylor 2001: 33.
32 Cortes 2001: 332.
33 McAllister 1984: 194–95.
34 Greer 2000: 6.
35 Boxer 1978: 2–11, 14–22.
36 Thornton 1984: 149.
37 Thornton 1988: 269.
38 Garfield 1990.
39 Pyne 2008: 45.
40 Thornton 2003: 279–80.
41 Thornton 1977: 509–10; Pyne 2008: 34.
42 Gray 1987: 56.
43 Gray 1987: 54.
44 Gray 1987: 55.
45 Gray 1987: 54.
46 Gray 1987: 56.
47 Hastings 1995: 89–90.
48 Thornton 1984: 155–56; Hastings 1995: 82.
49 Hastings 1995: 82.
50 Eccles 1987: 27; Trigger 1965.
51 Elliott 2007: 213.
52 Eccles 1987: 30.
53 Eccles 1987: 29, 34.
54 Clark 1993: 273.
55 Pyne 2008: 31.
56 Carey, 338–43.
57 Thornton 1998a: 235.
58 Thornton 1979a; Thornton 1979b; Thornton 1987: 409.
59 Thornton 1984: 151, 156.
60 Thornton 2003: 283; Greer 2000: 48.
61 Greer 2000: 50.
62 Greer 2000: 30.
63 Thornton 1988: 262, 270.
64 Fromont 2011a: 57; Hilton 1981: 192n.8
65 Fromont 2011a: 53.
66 Thornton 1981: 183.
67 Thornton 1984: 156.
68 Thornton 1984: 158.
69 Fromont 2011a: 57.
70 Thornton 1998a: 256.
71 Thornton 2003: 278–79.
72 Thornton 1984: 165–66; Thornton 1988: 262.
73 Fromont 2011a: 53.
74 Thompson 1981.
75 Fromont 2011a: 57.
76 Fromont 2011a: 53.
77 Blier 1993: 376.
78 Davidson 2007.
79 Brading 2003.
80 Thornton 2006: 441–42.

81 Blier 1993: 380, 386; Gray 1999.
82 Soeiro 1974; Black 2003; Deslandres 2003; Greer 2003; Myers 2003; Taylor in Greer and Bilinkoff 2003; Brading 2003; Gray 1999; Kiddy 2000; Pearsall in Armitage and Braddick 2002; Thornton 2006.
83 Thomas 2012; Prendergast 2007.
84 Ibsen 1999.
85 Taylor 2001: 69.
86 Taylor 2001: 110; Tuer 1993: 86–92.
87 Greer 2000: 88.
88 Greer 2000: 75.
89 Greer 2000: 81.
90 Greer 2000: 151.
91 Greer 2000: 140.
92 Taylor 2001: 107.
93 Greer 2000: 1.
94 Greer 2000: 7.
95 Greer 2000: 12.
96 Greer 2000: 47.
97 Taylor 2001: 109.
98 Thornton 2001: 100–101.
99 Thornton 1988: 266–67.
100 Pestana in Armitage and Braddick 2002: 79.
101 Thornton 1988: 277.
102 Thornton 1998b.
103 Hastings 1998: 153.
104 Hastings 1998: 153–54.
105 Hastings 1998: 152–53.
106 Krugler 1979: 55.
107 Krugler 1979: 55, 75.
108 Bosworth 1975: 546; Fogarty 1986: 583.
109 Pyne 2008: 22.
110 Pyne 2008: 18, 23.
111 Krugler 1979: 62; Pyne 2008: 19.
112 Krugler 1979: 66–73.
113 Pestana in Armitage and Braddick 2002: 83; Stanwood 2010; Stanwood 2007; Stanwood 2011.
114 Fogarty 1986: 574, 584; Farrelly 2011.
115 Graham 1993: 216.
116 Bosworth 1975: 540.
117 Brown in Armitage and Braddick 2002: 224.
118 Bosworth 1975: 546.
119 Pyne 2008: 31, 33–34.
120 Eccles in Armitage and Braddick 2002: 174.
121 Gray 1987: 52.
122 Gray 1987: 57.
123 Gray 1987: 60.
124 Gray 1987: 66.
125 Gray 1987: 67.
126 Krugler 1979: 59.
127 Thornton 1984: 166.
128 Greer 2000: 36.
129 Greer 2000: 153.

REFERENCES

Abé, Takao, *The Jesuit mission to New France: a new interpretation in the light of the earlier Jesuit experience in Japan* (Brill, 2011).

Black, Charlene Villasenor, ' St Anne imagery and maternal archetypes in Spain and Mexico' in Allan Greer and Jodi Bilinkoff (eds.), *Colonial saints: discovering the holy in the Americas, 1500–1800* (Routledge, 2003), 3–30.

Blier, Suzanne Preston, 'Imaging otherness in ivory: African portrayals of the Portuguese ca. 1492', *Art Bulletin*, 75.3 (1993), 375–96.

Bosworth, Timothy W., '*Anti-Catholicism* as a political tool in mid-eighteenth century Maryland', *Catholic historical review* 61.4 (1975), 539–63.

Boxer, C.R., *The church militant and Iberian expansion, 1440–1770* (John Hopkins University Press, 1978).

Brading, D.A., *Mexican phoenix: Our Lady of Guadalupe: image and tradition across five centuries* (Cambridge University Press, 2003).

Brown, Christopher L., 'The politics of slavery' in David Armitage and Michael J. Braddick (eds.), *The British Atlantic world, 1500–1800* (Palgrave Macmillan, 2002).

Carey, Patrick W., 'American Catholics and the First Amendment: 1776–1840' *Pennsylvania magazine of history and biography* 113.3 (1989), 323–46.

Carrasco, David, 'Spaniards as gods: the return of Quetzalcoatl' in Bernal Diaz del Castillo, *The history of the conquest of New Spain*, David Carrasco (ed.) (UNM Press, 2008).

Casares, Aurelia Martin and Christine Delaigue, 'The evangelization of freed and slave black Africans in Renaissance Spain: baptism, marriage, and ethnic brotherhoods', *History of religions*, 52.3 (2013), 214–35.

Clark, J.C.D., *The language of liberty, 1660–1832: political discourse and social dynamics in the Anglo-American world* (Cambridge University Press, 1993).

Cortes, Hernan, *Letters from Mexico*, Anthony Pagden (ed. and trans.) (Yale University Press, 2001).

Dantas, Mariana L.R., 'Humble slaves and royal vassals: free Africans and their descendants in eighteenth-century Minas Gerais, Brazil' in Andrew B. Fisher and Matthew D. O'Hara (eds.), *Imperial subjects: race and identity in colonial Latin America* (Duke University Press, 2009).

Davidson, Peter, *The universal baroque* (Manchester University Press, 2007).

Deslandres, Dominique, 'In the shadow of the cloister: representations of female holiness in New France' in Allan Greer and Jodi Bilinkoff (eds.), *Colonial saints: discovering the holy in the Americas, 1500–1800* (Routledge, 2003), 129–52.

Eastman, Scott, *Preaching Spanish nationalism across the Hispanic Atlantic, 1759–1823* (Louisiana, 2012).

Eccles, W.J., *Essays on New France* (Oxford, 1987).

Elbl, Ivana, 'Cross-cultural trade and diplomacy: Portuguese relations with West Africa, 1441–1521', *Journal of world history*, 3.2 (1992).

Elliott, J.H., *Empires of the Atlantic world: Britain and Spain in America, 1492–1830* (Yale University Press, 2007).

Farrelly, Maura Jane, *Papist patriots: the making of an American Catholic identity* (Oxford University Press, 2011).

Fisher, Linford D. and Lucas Mason-Brown, 'By "Treachery and Seduction": Indian baptism and conversion in the Roger Williams Code', *William and Mary Quarterly*, 71.2 (2014), 175–202.

Fisher, Andrew B. and Matthew D. O'Hara (eds.), *Imperial subjects: race and identity in colonial Latin America* (Duke University Press, 2009).

Fogarty, Gerald P., 'Property and religious liberty in Colonial Maryland Catholic thought', *Catholic historical review* 72.4 (1986), 573–600.

Fromont, Cécile, 'Dance, image, myth, and conversion in the Kingdom of Kongo, 1500–1800', *African arts* 44.4 (2011a), 52–63.

——, 'Under the sign of the cross in the kingdom of Kongo: religious conversion and visual correlation in early modern Central Africa', *Res* 59/60 (2011b), 109–23.

Garfield, Robert, 'Public Christians, secret Jews: religion and political conflict on Sao Tome Island in the sixteenth and seventeenth centuries', *The sixteenth century journal*, 21.4 (1990), 645–54.

Graham, Michael, 'Popish Plots: Protestant fears in early colonial Maryland, 1676–89', *Catholic historical review* 79.2 (1993), 197–216.

Gray, Richard, 'A Kongo princess, the Kongo ambassadors and the papacy', *Journal of religion in Africa*, 29 (1999), 140–54.

——, 'The papacy and the Atlantic slave trade: Lourenço da Silva, the Capuchins and the decisions of the Holy Office', *Past and present* 115 (1987), 52–68.

——, '"Come vero Prencipe Catolico": the Capuchins and the rulers of Soyo in the late seventeenth century', *Africa*, 53.3 (1983), 39–54.

Graziano, Frank, *Cultures of devotion: folk saints of Spanish America* (Oxford University Press, 2006).

Greer, Allen, 'Iroquois virgin: the story of Catherine Tekawitha in New France and New Spain' in Allan Greer and Jodi Bilinkoff (eds.), *Colonial saints: discovering the holy in the Americas, 1500–1800* (Routledge, 2003), 235–50.

Greer, Allen (ed.), *The Jesuit relations: natives and missionaries in seventeenth-century North America* (Bedford/St Martin's, 2000).

Hastings, Adrian, 'The Christianity of Pedro IV of the Kongo, "The Pacific" (1695–1718)' *Journal of religion in Africa*, 28.2 (1998), 145–59.

——, *The church in Africa, 1450–1950* (Oxford University Press, 1995).

Headley, John M., 'Geography and empire in the late Renaissance: Botero's assignment, western universalism, and the civilizing process', *Renaissance quarterly*, 53.4 (2000), 1119–55.

Hilton, Anne, *The kingdom of Kongo* (Oxford University Press, 1985).

——, 'The Jaga reconsidered', *The journal of African history*, 22.2 (1981), 191–202.

Huxley, G. L. 'Aristotle, Las Casas and the American Indians', *Proceedings of the Royal Irish Academy*, 80C (1980), 57–68.

Ibsen, Kristine, *Women's spiritual autobiography on Colonial Spanish America* (Florida, 1999).

Karras, Allan L. and John Robert McNeill (eds.), *Atlantic American societies: from Columbus through abolition, 1492–1888* (Routledge, 1992).

Kennedy, J.H., *Jesuit and savage in New France* (Yale University Press, 1950).

Kiddy, Elizabeth E., 'Congados, Calunga, Candombe: Our Lady of the Rosary in Minas Gerais, Brazil' *Luso-Brazilian review*, 37.1 (2000), 47–61.

Krugler, John D., 'Lord Baltimore, Roman Catholics and toleration: religious policy in Maryland during the early Catholic years, 1634–49', *Catholic Historical Review* 65.1 (1979), 49–75.

Law, Robin, 'Religion, trade and politics on the "slave coast": Roman Catholic missions in Allada and Whydah in the seventeenth century' *Journal of Religion in Africa*, 21.1 (1991), 42–77.

Matthew, Laura E., *Memories of conquest: becoming Mexicano in colonial Guatemala* (University of North Carolina Press, 2012).

Maxwell, David James and Ingrid Lawrie (eds.), *Christianity and the African imagination: essays in honour of Adrian Hastings* (Brill, 2002).

McAllister, Lyle N., *Spain and Portugal in the New World, 1492–1700* (Minnesota Press, 1984).

Mulvey, Patricia A., 'Slave confraternities in Brazil: their role in colonial society', *The Americas*, 39.1 (1982), 39–68.

Murphy, Thomas, *Jesuit slaveholding in Maryland, 1717–1838* (New York and London, 2001).

Myers, Kathleen Ann, '"Redeemer of America": Rosa da Lima (1586–1617), the dynamics of identity, and canonization' in Allan Greer and Jodi Bilinkoff (eds.), *Colonial saints: discovering the holy in the Americas, 1500–1800* (Routledge, 2003), 251–76.

Osokowski, Edward W., *Indigenous miracles: Nahua authority in colonial Mexico* (University of Arizona Press, 2010).

Pearsall, Sarah M. S., 'Gender' in David Armitage and Michael J. Braddick (eds.), *The British Atlantic world, 1500–1800* (Palgrave Macmillan, 2002).

Pestana, Carla Gardina, 'Religion' in David Armitage and Michael J. Braddick (eds.), *The British Atlantic world, 1500–1800* (Palgrave Macmillan, 2002), 69–92.

Prendergast, Ryan, 'Constructing an icon: the self-referentiality and framing of Sor Juana Inés de la Cruz', *Journal for early modern cultural studies*, 7.2 (2007), 28–56.

Prieto, Andrés I., *Missionary scientists: Jesuit science in Spanish South America, 1570–1810* (Vanderbilt University Press, 2011).

Pyne, Tricia T., 'Ritual and practice in the Maryland Catholic community, 1634–1776', *U.S. Catholic Historian* 26.2 (2008), 17–46.

Randall, Catharine (ed.), *Black robes and buckskins: a selection from the Jesuit relations* (Fordham University Press, 2011).

Rushforth, Brett, *Bonds of alliance: indigenous and Atlantic slaveries in New France* (University of North Carolina Press, 2012).

Soeiro, Susan A., 'The social and economic role of the convent: women and nuns in Colonial Bahia, 1677–1800' *Hispanic American historical review*, 54.2 (1974), 209–32.

Stanwood, Owen, *The Empire reformed: English America in the age of the Glorious Revolution* (University of Pennsylvania Press, 2011).

——, 'Catholics, Protestants, and the clash of civilisations in early America' in Chris Beneke and Christopher S. Greanda (eds.), *The first prejudice: religious tolerance and intolerance in early America* (University of Pennsylvania Press, 2010).

——, 'The Protestant moment: antipopery, the Revolution of 1688–89, and the making of an Anglo-American empire', *Journal of British studies*, 46 (2007), 481–508.

Sweet, James H., 'Defying social death: the multiple configurations of African slave family in the Atlantic World', *William and Mary Quarterly*, 70.2, (2013), 251–72.

Symcox, Geoffrey (ed.), *Italian reports on America, 1492–1522: letters, despatches and papal bulls*, Giovanna Rabitti (textual ed.) and Peter D. Diehl (trans.) (Turnhout: Brepols, 2001).

Tavrez, David Eduardo, *The invisible war: indigenous devotions, discipline and dissent in colonial Mexico* (Stanford University Press, 2011).

Taylor, Alan, *American colonies: the settling of North America* (Penguin, 2001).

Taylor, William B., 'Mexico's Virgin of Guadalupe in the seventeenth century: hagiography and beyond' in Allan Greer and Jodi Bilinkoff (eds.), *Colonial saints: discovering the holy in the Americas, 1500–1800* (Routledge, 2003), 277–97.

Tevarez, David, 'Legally Indian: inquisitorial readings of indigenous identities in New Spain' in Andrew B. Fisher and Matthew D. O'Hara (eds.), *Imperial subjects: race and identity in Colonial Latin America* (Duke University Press, 2009).

Thomas, George Antony, *The politics and poetics of Sor Juana Inés de La Cruz: women and gender in the early modern world* (Ashgate, 2012).

Thompson, Robert Farris and Joseph Cornet, *The four moments of the sun: Kongo art in two worlds* (National Gallery of Art, 1981).

Thornton, John K., 'Elite women in the Kingdom of Kongo: historical perspectives on women's political power', *Journal of African history*, 47.3 (2006), 437–60.

Thornton, John, 'Cannibals, witches, and slave traders in the Atlantic world', *William and Mary quarterly*, 60.2 (2003), 273–94.

——, 'The origins and early history of the Kingdom of Kongo, c. 1350–1550', *International journal of African historical studies*, 34.1 (2001), 89–120.

——, *Africa and Africans in the making of the Atlantic world, 1400–1800* second edition (Cambridge University Press, 1998a).

Thornton, John K., *The Kongolese Saint Anthony: Dona Beatriz Kimpa Vita and the Antonian movement* (Cambridge University Press, 1998b).

Thornton, John, 'The African experience of the "20. and Odd Negroes" arriving in Virginia in 1619', *William and Mary quarterly* 55. 3 (1998c), 421–34.

Thornton, John K., 'On the trail of Voodoo: African Christianity in Africa and the Americas', *The Americas*, 44. 3 (1988), 261–78.

——, 'The correspondence of the Kongo kings, 1614–35: problems of internal written evidence on a central African kingdom', *Paideuma*, 33, (1987), 407–21.

Thornton, John, 'The development of an African Catholic Church in the Kingdom of Kongo, 1491–1750', *Journal of African history*, 25.2 (1984), 147–67.

——, 'Early Kongo-Portuguese relations: a new interpretation', *History in Africa* 8 (1981), 183–204.

——, 'The slave trade in eighteenth century Angola: effects on demographic structures', *Canadian Journal of African Studies/Revue Canadienne des Études Africaines* 14.3 (1980), 417–27.

Thornton, John K., 'A note on the Archives of the Propaganda Fide and Capuchin Archives', *History in Africa* 6, (1979a), 341–44.

——, 'New light on Cavazzi's seventeenth-century description of Kongo', *History in Africa* 6, (1979b), 253–64.

Thornton, John, 'Demography and history in the Kingdom of Kongo, 1550–1750', *The journal of African history*, 18.4 (1977), 507–30.

Thornton, John K., and Linda M. Heywood, *Central Africans, Atlantic Creoles, and the making of the Foundation of the Americas, 1585–1660* (Cambridge University Press, 2007).

Trigger, Bruce G., 'The Jesuits and the fur trade', *Ethnohistory* 12.1 (1965), 30–53.

Tuer, Dot, 'Old bones and beautiful words: the spiritual contestation between Shaman and Jesuit in the Guarani missions' in Allan Greer and Jodi Bilinkoff (eds.), *Colonial saints: discovering the holy in the Americas, 1500–1800* (Routledge, 2003), 77–98.

Vainfas, Ronaldo, 'St Anthony in Portuguese America: saint of the Restoration' in Allan Greer and Jodi Bilinkoff (eds.), *Colonial saints: discovering the holy in the Americas, 1500–1800* (Routledge, 2003), 99–111.

Verhoeven, Timothy, *Transatlantic anti-Catholicism: France and the United States in the nineteenth century* (Palgrave, 2010).

Watts, Edward, *In this remote country: French colonial culture in the Anglo-American imagination, 1780–1860* (University of North Carolina Press, 2006).

Williams, Margaret Todaro, 'Integralism and the Brazilian Catholic Church', *Hispanic American historical review*, 54.3 (1974), 431–52.

Wright, A.D., *The counter-reformation: Catholic Europe and the non-Christian world* (second edition, Ashgate, 2005).

CHAPTER NINETEEN

PROTESTANTISM
IN THE ATLANTIC WORLD

———·◆·———

Travis Glasson

Protestantism was born in Europe, but it came of age in the Atlantic world. For much of the sixteenth century, it was uncertain whether either reformed Christianity or the Atlantic colonization schemes of the northern European states that most readily embraced Protestantism would endure. By the seventeenth century, though, it is possible to discern an interconnected, vibrant Protestant Atlantic world that provided the setting for many important developments in religious and cultural history. This Protestant Atlantic was but one segment of the Atlantic world as a whole, overlapping with other subdivisions of that wider zone of interaction and exchange: the multinational commercial Atlantic, the Atlantic empires of European powers, the black Atlantic, and those parts of the Atlantic world where Catholicism, Islam, Judaism, west African religions, or an array of American indigenous religions predominated. Differentiating part of the Atlantic world as the Protestant Atlantic risks obscuring the myriad connections between it and other 'Atlantics' as well as places and people elsewhere in the world. However, focusing on the Protestant Atlantic as an expansive but integrated space allows its particular features to be seen in relief. Here, three of those features will be stressed: the way the Atlantic functioned as a zone of religious contact and competition; the central role that the circulation of people, texts, and practices played in this space; and how these patterns of contact and circulation fostered a creativity that produced new and significant forms of religiosity.[1]

* * *

From the outset of Iberian expansionism, European voyages of exploration and colonization blended political, commercial, and religious goals. Similarly intertwined motivations affected how elites and common people in early modern Europe responded to the new theology and practices introduced by Protestant reformers, and these patterns were repeated as Protestant people moved out into the Atlantic. The foundational documents for most Atlantic colonies included clauses that promoted religion in the new world even as their backers dreamed of rich earthly rewards. Many of the earliest Protestant ministers to visit the Americas and west Africa were chaplains employed by

European explorers, navies and trading companies. The growth of commerce and European strategic control initially spread Protestantism around the Atlantic.

By the seventeenth century, the dividing lines between Catholics and Protestants in Europe and between European empires in the Americas had hardened considerably. Warfare between European powers, which often though not always included a confessional dimension in the seventeenth century, was a near constant phenomenon. Internal disputes within European states over the domestic fate and course of the Reformation spilled into their Atlantic holdings. Such conflicts, including the Thirty Years War in central Europe, the Dutch Republic's long fight for independence from Spain, disputes over the place of Protestantism in France, and the oscillating fortunes of the Reformation within the seventeenth-century English church, made the Atlantic a site where disputes between Catholics and Protestants were played out.

This often bloody rivalry between European Catholics and Reformers circumscribed the Protestant Atlantic. Europe's most powerful Protestant states, England (and after 1707, Britain) and the Dutch Republic, and, to a lesser extent, other Protestant polities like Sweden and Denmark, controlled the places in the Atlantic where Protestantism would predominate. For much of the seventeenth century, the relatively narrow band of North American and Caribbean territories controlled by these powers had a precarious existence, threatened by the Catholic powers of France, Portugal, and Spain. This sense of a looming Catholic danger in the western Atlantic mirrored Protestant concerns in Europe about the possibility of reformed territories there – Britain, the Netherlands, Protestant lands in Germany – being conquered and returned to Catholicism by force. By the eighteenth century, the long-term future of the Protestant Atlantic colonies looked more secure, but continuing warfare between European powers and the mingling of confessional with national animosities, as in the case of the eighteenth-century rivalry between Britain and France, helped ensure that hostility to Catholicism remained one of the common currencies of the Protestant Atlantic world.

It has rightly been observed that differences between Catholics and Protestants can be overemphasized, and that Protestants in the Atlantic world inherited an array of common Christian worldviews that pre-dated the Reformation.[2] Nonetheless, parts of the Atlantic world became vigorously contested territory between Catholics and Protestants. Ireland, home to a predominantly Catholic population and a succession of Protestant colonization schemes, was an early site of such conflict.[3] The Caribbean colony of Providence Island was central to early Puritan hopes; it was attacked and destroyed by the Spanish in 1641.[4] The English took Jamaica from the Spanish in 1655, and many other islands changed hands, often repeatedly. Competition in Atlantic borderlands also underlined differences. French Catholic and Dutch/British Protestant missionaries vied for converts and allies among the Iroquois.[5] The sense of Protestant common identification and shared opposition to Catholicism was strengthened by the events of 1688, the 'Anglo-Dutch moment' that brought the Dutch William of Orange to the English throne and marked England's rejection of the possibility of a return to Catholicism. To be sure, in some places Protestants and Catholics found ways to live together and not all or even most conflicts in the Atlantic world were motivated primarily by religion. Nevertheless, the ubiquity of conflict in the Atlantic meant that the subjects of

– CHAPTER 19: Protestantism in the Atlantic World –

Protestant European empires often fought against foes that were conceptualized as both national and theological enemies.

* * *

To look at this process another way, confessional conflict also helped transform Protestantism from a European movement into a much wider phenomenon. This occurred partly because the Atlantic world served as a place of refuge for European Protestants during the seventeenth and eighteenth centuries. This process began in Europe, with Britain, Switzerland, and the Netherlands becoming home in the sixteenth century to Protestant migrants from elsewhere in Europe. Beginning with the journey of separatist English Protestants to the Netherlands and then to the Plymouth Colony in the 1620s and the subsequent, larger 'Great Migration' of some 20,000 Puritans to Massachusetts Bay in the 1630s, the movement of Protestants to the Americas created dense webs of connections stretching across the Atlantic.[6]

These New Englanders shared a view with many subsequent groups of Protestant émigrés that trans-oceanic migration would afford them the space to live in societies that conformed with their religious beliefs. Crucially for the development of the Protestant Atlantic world, while the British and the Dutch controlled most of the territories to which Protestant people emigrated, the migrants themselves represented a broad cross-section of European Protestantism. French Protestants, for example, made up a large share of the population of New Netherland and contributed to the British Protestant plantations established in Ireland in the seventeenth century. The emigration of Huguenots into the Atlantic ballooned after 1685, when the Revocation of the Edict of Nantes subjected them to new persecution at home.[7] Economic opportunities further jumbled populations; Dutch speakers, for example, were prominent among the early generations of planters in the Danish West Indies. German-speaking Protestants began crossing the Atlantic from the 1680s, punctuated by episodes of mass migration such as those by the 'poor Palatines' in the 1700s and the 'Salzburgers' in the 1730s. Total German migration may have reached 75,000 by about 1760. The period between 1701 and 1780 saw approximately 60,000 Scottish Lowlanders and 70,000 Ulster Protestants, most of whom were Presbyterians, migrate to Britain's colonies.[8] Most Protestant migrants did not move primarily for religious reasons, nor did they all travel west. Large numbers of Huguenots, for example, migrated to Prussia. However, against the backdrop of Europe's Catholic/ Protestant divisions, these trans-Atlantic migrations reinforced senses of interconnection grounded in a shared faith that many had suffered in order to retain.

These population movements also helped make the Atlantic world a zone of contact and competition between different forms of Protestantism. In the seventeenth century, emigrant groups often attempted to establish societies where their own views on theological principles, structures of church governance, and patterns of worship could be put into effect. Among Britain's early colonies, both 'Puritans' and adherents to the episcopal Church of England gave their churches legal protection and financial support in New England, Virginia, and in the Caribbean. The Dutch established the Calvinist Dutch Reformed Church in their continental and Caribbean colonies, making it 'the central institution in shaping and maintaining Dutch identity in the New World.'[9] Similarly, the Danes established the Lutheran Danish National Church in the Virgin Islands. While 'toleration' of 'dissent' was widespread in the Protestant

349

Atlantic and a few colonies enshrined the principle of religious freedom in their foundational laws, the more standard approach in the seventeenth and early eighteenth century was to legally establish a church and thereby stamp it with the support and approval of the forces of authority.[10]

However, these state-allied churches very rarely had the institutional resources or the strong metropolitan backing that would have been required to enforce genuine Protestant uniformity. Before the eighteenth century, most colonial societies outside of New England lacked the numbers of church buildings and university-trained ministers that would have been necessary to replicate European patterns of institutional Protestant religious life. The eighteenth century saw a dramatic effort to build and staff new churches, a process that in Britain's thirteen North American colonies Jon Butler has characterized as part of the sacralization of the American landscape.[11] However, this process occurred only after patterns of toleration and religious and ethnic diversity had been established. The Atlantic colonies therefore put Protestants of different affiliations in much closer proximity with each other than they tended to live in most European places or than the founding generations of many communities had hoped. This fostered the rich mixture of beliefs and practices that became a defining feature of Protestant life in the Atlantic world.

This cacophony of Protestant voices led to concerns among some that, despite initial hopes, colonies in the Americas were dangerously unregulated, ungodly societies. These fears emerged quite early in New England, as Puritan leaders struggled with the challenges posed by Quakers and dissidents like Anne Hutchinson and Roger Williams.[12] These concerns were also central for the resurgent Church of England that emerged from the tumultuous second half of the seventeenth century. While several early colonies had seen the establishment of the Church of England along lines similar to English practice, little else was done to expand and staff the church abroad on a scale commensurate with the growth of the English empire. With the development after 1688 of a more stable Church of England committed to an episcopal ecclesiology and hopeful about the prospects for close cooperation between the established church and a now reliably Protestant state, Anglicanism became a powerful force around the Atlantic. Under the leadership of Thomas Bray, two new organizations, the Society for Promoting Christian Knowledge (SPCK) and the Society for the Propagation of the Gospel in Foreign Parts (SPG), were founded to strengthen the Church of England at home and abroad. Many early supporters of these organizations shared a belief that 'dissenters' and outright irreligion were dangerously dominant in Britain's Atlantic colonies.[13]

This reinvigorated Anglicanism produced political activity: New York, Maryland, North Carolina, South Carolina, and Georgia all enacted full or partial Anglican establishments between 1690 and 1758. While the bulk of the work of the SPG and the SPCK was directed at providing colonial Anglicans with ministers, churches, and literature, these groups' periodic efforts to use their political influence in London or the colonies brought them into conflict with other Protestants. Anglican drives to secure legal establishments for the Church of England were often bitterly opposed by other Protestants. SPG challenges to the monopoly position of Puritanism in New England led to wars of words between ministers on both sides. Above all, repeated but ultimately unsuccessful Anglican attempts to create colonial bishops activated deep fears among other Protestants.[14]

The diversity and interconnectedness of Protestantism around the Atlantic also produced conflicts within denominations. From the 1730s, Congregationalist,

– CHAPTER 19: *Protestantism in the Atlantic World* –

Presbyterian, and Anglican ministers all faced challenges from within their own traditions by proponents of new and unsettling forms of emotion-laden religious revivalism. These religious revivals, collectively labeled as the Great Awakening, crossed the sea, with historians uncovering evidence of interrelated sets of revivals in the Americas, Britain, Ireland, and the Netherlands.[15] Revivals often produced bitter controversies between opponents and proponents of new, 'enthusiastic' forms of religiosity that revealed deep disagreements about what it meant to be a Protestant. This revivalism appealed to broad swathes of the Atlantic's Protestant population, but it also challenged ministerial and political authority by transcending established gender, racial, and class divisions.[16]

Conflicts within Protestantism were real but should not be overstated. Lay people were on the whole much less concerned about the intricacies of disputes between different denominations than ministers were.[17] In many regions, the difficult conditions and sparse populations typical of rural and frontier life minimized the influence of ministers and formal worship practices in favor of simple, accessible types of familial or communal worship. Just as importantly, clerical and political supporters of established churches had only limited abilities to insist on and enforce uniformity. Even 'Puritan' New England was home to many views and voices on how to live a godly life.[18] For colonial representatives of churches, like the Church of England, that looked to Europe for authority and support, communications across the Atlantic were regular but often slow. It could take years of back and forth communication to resolve disputes over many issues including finances, building new churches, and ministerial misconduct.

Even for leaders of groups like Congregationalists, Quakers, and Presbyterians that erected independent structures of denominational authority in the colonies, the possibilities for settler mobility in the Atlantic world meant that non-conformers of all sorts could move relatively easily beyond the pale of their control. Two of the British colonies where religious authority was most zealously established, Massachusetts and Virginia, were soon bordered by colonies, Rhode Island and Maryland, that became known as bastions of religious liberty. These obstacles to control meant that in most Atlantic colonies, the balance of power and influence within congregations was tilted more toward the laity and local elites and away from ministers and metropolitan elites than was the norm in Europe. As individuals or in communities, Atlantic Protestants had considerable freedom to choose how to live and worship. Collectively, their choices produced a rich and varied religious landscape.

* * *

The differences between denominations, or indeed between Protestants and Catholics, appear especially small when considered alongside a third type of contact and conflict that shaped the Protestant Atlantic world: reformed Christianity's encounter with the varied non-Christian faiths of Native Americans and Africans. The missionary impulse played a mixed and often minor role in initiating imperial expansion by Protestant powers.[19] Nevertheless, as Protestant people moved across the Atlantic contact with non-Christian populations became inescapable and many Protestants shared with European Catholics the perception that Native American and black African populations should be categorized as 'heathens' and converted. They differed at times, however, on how that should be accomplished and what 'conversion' actually entailed.[20]

351

Protestant conversion efforts lacked the deep institutional and financial resources that underpinned early Catholic efforts to convert Native Americans in the Atlantic territories controlled by Spain, Portugal, and France. This is not to say that Protestant individuals and communities were uninterested in evangelization. The documents establishing the Virginia Company in 1606 emphasized that the Christianization of Native Americans would be to 'the glorrie of hys divyne maiestie.'[21] The first seal for Massachusetts Bay famously featured an Indian and the wishful slogan 'Come Over and Help Us,' and Puritans capitalized on the sympathy of Cromwell's Parliament to found the New England Company (1649), a missionary organization dedicated to spreading 'the Gospel of Christ unto and amongst the heathen natives in or near New England and parts adjacent in America.' Lowland Scottish Presbyterians founded the Scottish Society for Promoting Christian Knowledge (1709), which promoted the conversion of Scotland's Highland population and Native Americans as twin branches of a program to further the Reformation around the Atlantic.[22] The need to produce ministers and Anglo-Indian intermediaries for this conversion work was a major impetus behind the founding of some of British America's earliest colleges, including both Harvard (founded in 1636) and William and Mary (1693). This link long persisted, reappearing in George Berkeley's failed attempt to create a college in Bermuda in the 1720s and the trans-Atlantic effort to found Dartmouth College (1769), originally chartered 'for the education and instruction of Youth of the Indian Tribes in this Land...and also of English Youth and any others.'

Among some settlers and early promoters of colonization, the existence of Native Americans – a population confusingly not mentioned in the Bible – was explained by identifying them with one of the 'lost tribes' of Israel. This raised millenarian hopes that the conversion of Native Americans would herald the second coming of Christ. These hopes, and the wider Puritan interest in the conversion of Native Americans, reached their apogee in the work of John Eliot, who undertook a systematic effort to remake Indian society as more godly and more 'civilized,' that is more like the society settlers were working to create in their New England. Eliot's plan effected the resettlement of indigenous people into what became fourteen new towns of 'Praying Indians,' where the essential skills of literacy could be taught and patterns of right living could be inculcated. Eliot's dreams for a Christianized Indian population, never entirely popular with his fellow settlers, were engulfed by the violence of King Philip's War, which hardened notions that there were insurmountable differences between Europeans and Native Americans and destroyed the idea that New England could be a place they might amicably share.[23]

More generally, the experiences of seventeenth-century New England's Protestant 'Praying Indians' raise questions of how 'success' should be defined and what part assessing 'success' should play in histories of missionary activity. While many generations of historians have taken the failure of most Protestant missionary efforts to produce conversions of Native Americans en masse as evidence of either lack of zeal or the product of some inherent and essentially unchanging feature of indigenous cultures, these approaches now seem rather arid. In part this is because defining what did and what did not count as 'conversion' was problematic for many Protestants and often intertwined with notions of civility. Reception of Catholic sacraments and participation in communal worship did not amount to genuine conversion for most Protestant commentators, and they were often critical of Catholic missions on these grounds. It seems likely that efforts to count 'converts' based on the reports of European missionaries underestimate the possibilities for creative adaptation and partial adoption of Protestantism by Native Americans. The story of colonial New England Indians' interactions with Christianity, for example, has been effectively characterized as 'a tale of ebb and flow, engagement and disengagement, affiliation and deaffiliation, which varied by individual and community.'[24] This applies particularly to the eighteenth century, when the native peoples of eastern North America had been in contact with Protestantism for a century.

Variety, therefore, was a theme. Many Native Americans long rejected Protestantism because they remained more attached to other religious beliefs and practices. While disease and expanding settler populations put Native American communities under tremendous pressure, the power of colonists to coerce indigenous peoples into patterns of behavior remained limited. This is especially the case because, as Daniel Richter has noted, the vast interior of North America remained 'Indian Country' throughout the colonial period.[25] Like other residents of the Atlantic world, eastern North American Indians could and did avail themselves of opportunities to move, sometimes in defense of their religious and cultural traditions. It is also clear that in some cases individuals and groups used Protestantism to meet their own spiritual and communal needs. A segment of the Mohawks adopted Anglicanism in the eighteenth century as part of a political, military, and religious alliance with Britain that endured even through their resettlement in Ontario after the American Revolution. Characterizing these Indian choices as 'failures' or 'successes' for Protestant missions obscures the more complex dynamics at play in these interactions.

The history of Protestantism's encounter with African peoples and west African religions unfolded differently. While Protestant settlers and intellectuals tended to conceptualize Native Americans as an array of autonomous peoples to whom missionaries needed to be sent, African 'heathenism' arose as an area of concern for Protestants because of its presence within their own households, where enslaved black people were becoming a growing presence. The trans-Atlantic slave trade, slavery, and the effort to spread Protestantism among Africans and their descendants were therefore entangled early on, and this had a number of effects. While Catholicism had a much older presence, there was not a sustained, large-scale Protestant missionary outreach to free African populations in Africa before the nineteenth century. In North American colonies and in the Caribbean, early efforts to convert African-born people and their descendants were neither particularly systematic nor the purview of dedicated Protestant missionaries or organizations like the New England Company. For example, in the Anglophone Atlantic there were not seventeenth-century or early eighteenth-century texts, analogous to those produced by John Eliot or the SPG-sponsored translation of the Book of Common Prayer into Mohawk (1715), designed to further the conversion of speakers of African languages. Instead, the conversion of enslaved people was long left to those masters who might be interested in exercising their patriarchal authority to promote the conversion of their 'servants' and to ministers who viewed their primary responsibility as tending to their settler congregations. In some places in the seventeenth century, such as New Holland and early Virginia, this led to the incorporation of relatively small, though too easily forgotten, numbers of enslaved people into Atlantic congregations.

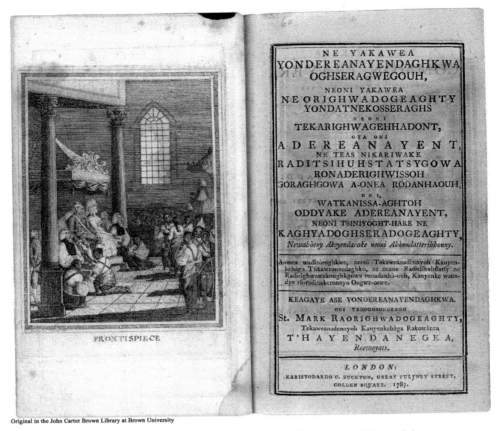

Figure 19.1 Frontispiece and title page of the 1787 edition of the
Mohawk Book of Common Prayer
Courtesy of the John Carter Brown Library at Brown University

More commonly, ministers reported that their white congregations were deeply hostile to efforts to convert their slaves. Initially, this opposition may have been attributable to the fact that the non-Christian status of many west Africans formed part of the legal and religious justifications that Europeans produced to legitimize their enslavement. Early British colonial laws tended to differentiate permanently enslaved people from other types of unfree laborers by reference to their 'heathenism,' which raised the theoretical possibility that Christian baptism might provide the basis for an enslaved person to claim temporal freedom. In response, settler-controlled colonial legislatures passed acts designed to make explicit that conversion had no bearing on the legal position of enslaved people. Colonial ministers, particularly Anglicans, tended to support and even promote these efforts to eliminate potential conflicts between Protestantism and Atlantic slavery. They did so based on a widely shared understanding that the Bible sanctioned slavery and in the hope that such measures would lessen masters' resistance to conversion efforts. Other aspects of missionary activity also activated settler fears. The centrality of reading the Bible and other texts to many forms of Protestantism seemed to some to entail teaching enslaved potential converts to read. Some masters and ministers did so, but most saw equipping enslaved people with literacy as a dangerous step that magnified the possibilities for resistance and rebellion.

Protestantism's place within black populations around the Atlantic world first changed as the numbers of enslaved people in Atlantic colonies exploded in the late seventeenth and eighteenth centuries. Paradoxically, while white Atlantic Protestantism was shaped by the freedom of movement enjoyed by European settlers, black Atlantic Protestantism was molded by forced migration and Africans' and African-Americans' experiences of enslavement. First, this led to some individuals in the colonies looking to call wider attention to the 'plight' of so many unconverted enslaved people in the Atlantic world. The Quaker founder George Fox criticized the physical cruelty of masters and their neglect of enslaved peoples' spiritual welfare, calls echoed by the Anglican minister Morgan Godwyn. This rising awareness of the black population of the Atlantic as a field for mission affected the SPG as it began its missionary program, leading the Society's leadership in England and the Bishop of London to promote this branch of their work among their European benefactors, and to appoint a small number of specialized catechists with particular responsibility for converting enslaved people.[26]

Through approximately 1730, members of the Church of England were the most active advocates for the conversion of black populations in the Protestant Atlantic world. Because the Church of England and other state-allied churches regularly signaled their support for the existing colonial order, including slavery, their messages may have held limited appeal for enslaved people. The SPG, for example, worked to develop Codrington College on Barbados as a place for training future missionaries, whose duties would include converting enslaved people. In a plan that blended mastership with mission, the college was to be supported by profits from an attached sugar plantation worked by enslaved people, whom the SPG hoped to convert as a model of Christian paternal slave owning for other masters.[27] The principle that black Christianization and Atlantic slavery could complement each other was also echoed in west Africa and Europe. The first black man ordained as a minister of the Dutch Reformed Church, Jacobus Capitein (c. 1717–47), was a west African who was trained and employed as a chaplain by the slave-trading Dutch West India Company. The missionary efforts of the Church of England and other national churches produced some converts – certainly numbering in the thousands in total around the Atlantic by 1730 – but these conversions occurred in ones and twos rather than in large groups or whole communities.

This situation changed more dramatically in the mid-eighteenth century. By then, the enslaved population in mainland North America had become more 'creolized,' mitigating some of the language and cultural barriers that had limited earlier conversion efforts. The religious environment there also had been altered by the growth of denominational diversity and the onset of the Great Awakening, with religious revivalism beginning to appeal to African-American people in significant numbers. These developments set the stage for the growth of Protestant Christianity, largely Baptist and Methodist, among free and enslaved black people in North America. In several Caribbean islands too, the revivalist-minded Moravians established missions to communities of enslaved people in the mid-eighteenth century.

Figure 19.2 Engraved portrait of the Afro-Dutch minister Jacobus Capitein
© The Trustees of the British Museum

– CHAPTER 19: *Protestantism in the Atlantic World* –

Revivalist preachers offered hope for salvation to any person who experienced conversion, and this message of equality could reach across divides of race and enslavement. While every Protestant church in the Atlantic world made accommodations with slavery, groups like the Baptists, Moravians, and Methodists that grew through revivalism were less closely identified with colonial slave traders and owners. The predominance of lay leadership and popular preaching within these movements meant that black people themselves, rather than just white ministers, acted as agents of evangelization to black communities.[28] The comparative malleability of these forms of Protestantism, in which patterns of worship and points of theology were less rigidly articulated than in state churches, also meant that African-American people could shape practices and principles to make them meaningful in their own lives and incorporate African views on spirituality. By the last quarter of the eighteenth century, these developments led to black Protestantism becoming a new and powerful source of connection and community around the Atlantic world.[29]

* * *

Movement was central to the development of the Protestant Atlantic world. However, it was not just one-time or one-way movement that helped define this space. Instead, the Protestant Atlantic featured the continual circulation of people, texts, and practices. These patterns of circulation spread European developments through the colonies, forged connections between colonies, and allowed colonial innovations to cross back to Europe. Mobility characterized the lives of many of the key figures in the history of Atlantic Protestantism. Despite the dangers of maritime travel and the hardships endured by those who journeyed over colonial roads and rivers and into undeveloped backcountries, many individuals completed astounding circuits to promote their faith. In 1671, the founder of Quakerism George Fox decided to travel to Britain's Atlantic colonies, both to visit with emigrant Quakers and to keep his young, fractious religious movement unified. Fox's travels took him to Barbados, Jamaica, Maryland, New York, Rhode Island, and North Carolina. Fox's travels in the colonies not only promoted Quakerism, the circum-Atlantic journey he undertook in the early 1670s also shaped the Friends' distinctive beliefs and commitments. Fox experienced Atlantic slavery first hand in Barbados, and his writings from there on it marked the starting point of debates within the Society about the legitimacy and godliness of slavery, discussions that would ultimately put Quakers at the forefront of Atlantic abolitionism.

George Fox developed his ministry through circum-Atlantic motion; George Whitefield's career was founded on it. As a young man, Whitefield was a member of the 'Holy Club' that John Wesley founded while a student at Oxford in the 1730s. After his ordination as an Anglican minister, Whitefield decided to join the Wesley brothers as a missionary in America. From this first voyage there in 1738 until his death in 1770, Whitefield was to cross the Atlantic thirteen times and visit most British North American colonies, where his preaching spread revivalism and Calvinistic Methodism. He also made fourteen separate journeys from England to Scotland, and visited places as far-flung as Bermuda, Gibraltar, Ireland, and the Netherlands. Like the revival movement itself, Whitefield ignored denominational distinctions and sought to bring his message to anyone who would hear him. Whitefield's itinerant preaching helped him become 'the most famous person in America' in the mid-eighteenth century and he was lionized by his backers and attacked by his opponents in both the colonial and British press.[30]

Fox and Whitefield were celebrated figures in their own days. A third example of the way that circulation marked the Protestant Atlantic world is provided by a less exalted but no less remarkable person, the Moravian woman Rebecca Protten. As Jon Sensbach has uncovered, Rebecca was probably born of mixed European and African parentage on the British island of Antigua. As a young girl, she was kidnapped by slave traders and sold to a Dutch-speaking planter living on the Danish island of St. Thomas. There, she learned how to speak, read, and write Dutch and was exposed to Christianity through the Dutch Reformed Church. Despite the confession of the household in which she lived, a Catholic priest baptized the young woman as Rebecca. Her life changed again when, now a freed woman, she joined a Moravian church recently founded on the island. Moravianism radically challenged both Euro-American race and gender roles, which Rebecca capitalized on to fashion a 'self-appointed role as Christian apostle' and a teacher to enslaved people on the island.

In the early 1740s, Protten traveled with other Moravians on a trans-Atlantic voyage that ended at the Moravian settlement of Herrnhaag, Germany. There, in 1746, Rebecca married Christian Protten, a man of mixed-race parentage who had been born at a Danish slave trading station in west Africa. The couple and their daughter, Anna Maria, lived in German Moravian communities for a decade, where Rebecca rose to become a deaconess. In 1765, she joined her husband as a missionary to west Africa's Gold Coast, where they planned to build a 'Negro village for the Lord' and where Rebecca would serve as a schoolmistress. The Prottens were not welcomed by many in this slave-trading outpost, but Rebecca continued to work in west Africa until her death in 1781 at the age of sixty-two. Her life, shaped by her faith and lived in the Caribbean, Europe, and west Africa, documents the mobility and connectedness that marked the Protestant Atlantic.[31]

Protestant travelers like Fox, Whitefield, and the Prottens brought their messages to many, but even more people were affected by the texts that religious networks sent around the Atlantic in the seventeenth and eighteenth centuries. Publishers in both Europe and the colonies found a ready market for religious literature of all sorts. Books were valuable commodities in Atlantic colonies and religious texts of various kinds – bibles, sermons, works of theology, and tracts on practical morality, reports of revivals – made up much of the reading material that circulated in them.[32] As one reflection on life in eighteenth-century Connecticut reported, 'The Bible and Dr. Watt's Psalms and Hymns were indispensable in every family, and ours was not without them. There were also, on the "book shelf", a volume or two of Sermons [...] and very few other books and pamphlets, chiefly of a religious character.'[33] The view that good religious literature was essential and too scarce in many colonial households motivated European-based groups like the SPCK and the SPG to ship thousands of copies of religious texts to North America and the Caribbean in the eighteenth century. Protestants of all varieties used the printed word to bridge distances of time and space, promote shared principles, and create senses of circum-Atlantic community.

Similarly, religious practices moved through the Atlantic world. The practices of religious revivalism are the best documented example of this phenomenon, with congregations in the colonies and Europe learning of how religious revivals were

– CHAPTER 19: *Protestantism in the Atlantic World* –

conducted in other places and replicating those patterns in their own communities. In another vein, Susan Juster has documented the culture of prophecy as a trans-denominational, trans-racial, and trans-gender phenomenon in the late eighteenth-century and early nineteenth-century Anglo-Atlantic world.[34] To this can also be added the practice of congregational singing, which was promoted by Moravians and Methodists, spread by revivalism, and adopted and modified by black, white, and Native American Protestants of multiple denominations around the Atlantic to promote faith and fellowship.[35]

* * *

The circulation of religious practices highlights another noteworthy characteristic of the Protestant Atlantic: the way the patterns of contact, competition, and circulation present in this space produced a tremendous outpouring of religious creativity in the seventeenth and eighteenth centuries. The twin trunks of European Lutheranism and Calvinism branched in many directions when planted in the early modern Atlantic world. A number of groups – Quakers, Methodists, Moravians, and the panoply of black Protestantism in all its varied denominational forms – were born in this place and time. The founding generations of these faiths lived in the Protestant Atlantic and much of what marked these types of Protestantism as new and distinct emerged from the ways that Atlantic cultures and institutions functioned.

Perhaps the strongest example of this is the rise of Methodism in the mid-eighteenth century, a Protestant church whose foundation can be plausibly traced not just to the Atlantic world but to a specific trans-Atlantic crossing. When the devout young brothers John and Charles Wesley sailed to Georgia in 1735 as Anglican missionaries, they met a group of Moravians on their ship. These Moravian travelers left a deep impression on John Wesley when they responded to a life-threatening storm at sea by calmly praying together. The Wesleys' nearly two years in Georgia were difficult. The brothers struggled to make much headway among Georgia's settlers and the experience left John Wesley depressed and uncertain when he returned to England. He sought solace in the fellowship that he had witnessed on his voyage out to Georgia, worshipping with a Moravian community in London and then traveling to Herrnhut in Germany to visit the movement's home. After a period of intense self-examination under the guidance of the Moravian Peter Böhler, Wesley in 1738 felt his 'heart strangely warmed' at the meeting of a small religious society in London, the conversion experience that underpinned his future evangelizing.[36]

Wesley soon broke his formal connection with the Moravians, but he combined many of their techniques for promoting community and affective religiosity with the traditions of the Church of England in developing Methodism. In the coming years, Wesley, along with George Whitefield and a growing number of other preachers, would spread Methodism's calls for personal conversion and the adoption of Methodist practices throughout Britain and the Atlantic world. While it grew from within Anglicanism, and it was to suffer its own internal divisions, Methodism attracted adherents from many sources. Lay preachers became essential to the spread of Methodism and through them Methodism's approaches to worship and living a Christian life – outdoor preaching, 'classes' for seekers and 'bands' for the converted, the communal meals and services known as love feasts, the singing of hymns, and

359

others – became part of the spiritual landscape of Europe and Atlantic colonies. As befitting a movement that drew on multiple sources, Methodism long functioned for some as an additional set of practices and connections that existed alongside membership in the Church of England and for others as the defining affiliation of their religious lives.[37]

Methodism's vibrancy and effort to appeal to people who had been marginalized within Atlantic culture helped make the movement a powerful one within black communities.[38] Black adherents to Methodism were prominent in places like Virginia and Maryland from the 1760s and by the late eighteenth century there was a circum-Atlantic network of black Methodists, including people and places like Phillis Wheatley in Boston, Anne and Elizabeth Hart in Antigua, Olaudah Equiano in London, and Boston King in Nova Scotia and later Sierra Leone. This religious network also became a platform that some of its members would use to launch criticisms of Atlantic slavery. Equiano's autobiography, for example, blends an account of his own spiritual journey with an attack on the horrors and injustices of the slave trade.[39] John Wesley himself was converted to the cause of antislavery and issued the tract 'Thoughts on Slavery' in 1774, lending his weight to the developing movement.

Not all white Methodists in the late eighteenth century welcomed the growing presence of black people within their congregations. When some black Methodists in Philadelphia grew tired of discrimination at the hands of their co-religionists they responded creatively as other Atlantic Protestants had often done when they disagreed with the forces of institutional authority. They elected, in 1787, to leave their congregation and establish one of their own, a movement that would develop into the African Methodist Episcopal Church in the nineteenth century. As the history of early Methodism illustrates, the religious inventiveness that the Atlantic fostered did not flow in only one direction from Europe to the colonies. Instead the various currents within Atlantic Protestantism crossed and mingled with each other and with faith traditions outside those of the European Reformation.

* * *

The Protestant Atlantic world described here was most integrated in the seventeenth and eighteenth centuries. The connections and circulations that characterized the Protestant Atlantic certainly did not disappear all at once or at the same rate in all places after this period, but by the mid-nineteenth century, a number of new developments reoriented the ways that many Protestants thought about their communities and the ways that Atlantic churches were functioning. In the most heavily settled colonies in mainland North America, separation from Britain and the creation of the independent United States gradually eroded institutional ties between churches in the former colonies and Europe. This was most dramatic in the case of the Church of England, which was disestablished in the new states and which was reborn as the independent Protestant Episcopal Church. The dislocations and reevaluations caused by the American Revolution also affected the Church of England in other colonies in Canada and the Caribbean that remained part of the British Empire because it spurred the creation of a new class of colonial bishops. American Methodists undertook similar measures to create a distinct ecclesiastical structure in the period immediately following the Revolution. These changes put these churches on a more secure and effective local footing, but this independence limited the importance of continuing connections to Europe and the rest of the Atlantic.

At the same time, the rise of new religious movements signaled wider reorientations within North American societies away from the Atlantic coast and towards the north American interior and different sources of identity. The paradigmatic religious example of this reorientation is the development of Mormonism in the 1830s, a faith whose origins and sacred texts were rooted not in Europe or the Atlantic but in the westward-facing young republic of the United States. When early Mormons, like other religious minorities before them, faced persecution they looked to find new spaces to live and worship as they chose. But, unlike the Huguenots or Salzburgers of a previous era, early Mormons sought space for their beliefs not by using the Atlantic as a highway to their own New Jerusalem, but by moving steadily westward to Illinois and then to the dry lands of the American southwest.

Changes on the eastern side of the Atlantic similarly decreased the centrality of this space to various groups of Protestants. In Britain, a vigorous missionary evangelicalism emerged in the early nineteenth century, but it was oriented towards new and expanding sites of empire in the African interior and Asia rather than towards the Atlantic world. Missionary interest in the Caribbean and North America continued, but this was now one relatively small aspect of a much larger program. In this way the Atlantic Protestantism of the seventeenth and eighteenth centuries was subsumed within the global Protestantism that developed in the nineteenth and twentieth centuries. In the last two hundred years Protestantism has grown into a worldwide movement, with congregations not only in Europe and the Americas, but also millions of adherents in Asia, Africa, and Latin America. The diversity that characterizes this contemporary global Protestantism is largely a legacy of reformed Christianity's development in the early modern Atlantic world.

NOTES

The author thanks Rebecca Goetz for her insightful comments on this essay.

1   C. Pestana, *Protestant Empire: Religion and the Making of the British Atlantic World*, Philadelphia: University of Pennsylvania Press, 2009; and and C. Pestana, 'Religion,' in D. Armitage and M. Braddick (eds.), *The British Atlantic World, 1500–1800*, New York: Palgrave Macmillan, 2009, pp. 69–92 treat the British Atlantic. Important surveys of religion in early America include P. Bonomi, *Under the Cope of Heaven: Religion, Society, and Politics in Colonial America*, New York: Oxford University Press, Updated Edition, 2003; and J. Butler, *Awash in a Sea of Faith: Christianizing the American People*, Cambridge: Harvard University Press, 1990.

2   J. Canizares-Esguerra, *Puritan Conquistadors: Iberianizing the Atlantic, 1550–1700*, Stanford: Stanford University Press, 2006, pp. 3–31.

3   J. Ohlmeyer, 'A Laboratory for Empire: Early Modern Ireland and English Imperialism,' in K. Kenny (ed.), *Ireland and the British Empire*, Oxford: Oxford University Press, 2006, pp. 26–60.

4   K. Kupperman, *Providence Island, 1630–1641: The Other Puritan Colony*, Cambridge: Cambridge University Press, 1993.

5   D. Richter, *The Ordeal of the Longhouse: The Peoples of the Iroquois League in the Era of European Colonization*, Chapel Hill: University of North Carolina Press, 1992; J. Axtell, *The Invasion Within: The Contest of Cultures in Colonial North America*, New York: Oxford University Press, 1985, pp. 71–178.

6 A. Games, *Migration and the Origins of the English Atlantic World*, Cambridge, MA: Harvard University Press, 1999.

7 B. Van Ruymbeke and R. Sparks (eds.), *Memory and Identity: The Huguenots in France and the Atlantic Diaspora*, Columbia: University of South Carolina Press, 2003; J. Butler, *The Huguenots in America: A Refugee People in a New World Society*, Cambridge, MA: Harvard University Press, 1983.

8 B. Bailyn, *Voyagers to the West: A Passage in the Peopling of America on the Eve of the Revolution*, New York: Vintage Books, 1988, p. 25; J. Horn, 'British Diaspora: Emigration from Britain, 1680–1815,' in P. J. Marshall (ed.), *The Oxford History of the British Empire. Volume II. The Eighteenth Century*, Oxford: Oxford University Press, 1998, p. 31.

9 D. Voorhees, 'Tying the Loose Ends Together,' in J. Goodfriend (ed.), *Revisiting New Netherland: Perspectives on Early Dutch America*, Leiden: Brill, 2005, p. 316.

10 Bonomi, *Under the Cope of Heaven*, pp. 15–33; Butler, *Awash in a Sea of Faith*, pp. 98–128.

11 Butler, *Awash in a Sea of Faith*, p. 98.

12 C. Pestana, *Quakers and Baptists in Colonial Massachusetts*, Cambridge: Cambridge University Press, 1991.

13 R. Strong, *Anglicanism and the British Empire, c. 1700–1850*, Oxford: Oxford University Press, 2007, pp. 40–117.

14 J. Bell, *The Imperial Origins of the King's Church in Early America, 1607–1783*, Houndmills: Palgrave Macmillan, 2004, pp. 166–85; C. Bridenbaugh, *Mitre and Sceptre: Transatlantic Faiths, Ideas, Personalities, and Politics, 1689–1775*, New York: Oxford University Press, 1962; J. Clark, *The Language of Liberty, 1660–1832: Political Discourse and Social Dynamics in the Anglo-American World*, Cambridge: Cambridge University Press, 1994.

15 S. O'Brien, 'A Transatlantic Community of Saints: The Great Awakening and the First Evangelical Network, 1735–55,' *American Historical Review*, 91, 1986, pp. 811–32; L. Schmidt, *Holy Fairs: Scottish Communions and American Revivals in the Early Modern Period*, Princeton: Princeton University Press, 1990; F. van Lieburg, 'Interpreting the Dutch Great Awakening (1749–1755),' *Church History*, 77, 2008, pp. 318–36.

16 T. Kidd, *The Great Awakening: The Roots of Evangelical Christianity in Colonial America*, New Haven: Yale University Press, 2007; P. Bonomi, *Under the Cope of Heaven*, 131–60; R. Isaac, *The Transformation of Virginia, 1740–1790*, Chapel Hill: University of North Carolina Press, 1982.

17 C. Pestana, 'Between Religious Marketplace and Spiritual Wasteland: Religion in the British Atlantic World,' *History Compass*, 2, 2004, pp. 3–5.

18 D. Hall, 'Narrating Puritanism,' in H. Stout and D. Hart (eds.), *New Directions in American Religious History*, New York: Oxford University Press, 1997, pp. 51–83.

19 D. Armitage, *The Ideological Origins of the British Empire*, Cambridge: Cambridge University Press, 2000, pp. 61–69; B. Schmidt, *Innocence Abroad: The Dutch Imagination and the New World, 1570–1670*, Cambridge: Cambridge University Press, 2001, pp. 176–84.

20 J. Elliott, *Empires of the Atlantic World: Britain and Spain in America, 1492–1830*, New Haven: Yale University Press, 2006, pp. 66–78; J. Axtell, *The Invasion Within: The Contest of Cultures in Colonial North America*, Oxford: Oxford University Press, 1985.

21 R. Goetz, *The Baptism of Early Virginia: How Christianity Created Race*, Baltimore: Johns Hopkins University Press, 2012, p. 35.

22 M. Szasz, *Scottish Highlanders and Native Americans: Indigenous Education in the Eighteenth-Century Atlantic World*, Norman: University of Oklahoma Press, 2007.

23 R. Cogley, *John Eliot's Mission to the Indians before King Philip's War*, Cambridge, MA: Harvard University Press, 1999.

24 L. Fisher, *The Indian Great Awakening: Religion and the Shaping of Native Cultures in Early America*, New York: Oxford University Press, 2012, p. 8.

– CHAPTER 19: *Protestantism in the Atlantic World* –

25 D. Richter, *Facing East from Indian Country: A Native History of Early America*, Cambridge, MA: Harvard University Press, 2001.

26 T. Glasson, *Mastering Christianity: Missionary Anglicanism and Slavery in the Atlantic World*, New York: Oxford University Press, 2012.

27 J. Bennett, *Bondsmen and Bishops: Slavery and Apprenticeship on the Codrington Plantations of Barbados, 1710–1838*, Berkeley: University of California Press, 1958.

28 On the importance of non-white missionaries to the spread of Protestantism more generally, see E. Andrews, *Native Apostles: Black and Indian Missionaries in the British Atlantic World*, Cambridge, MA: Harvard University Press, 2013.

29 S. Frey and B. Wood, *Come Shouting to Zion: African-American Protestantism in the American South and British Caribbean to 1830*, Chapel Hill: University of North Carolina Press, 1998; A. Raboteau, *Slave Religion: The 'Invisible Institution' in the Antebellum South*, Oxford: Oxford University Press, 1978; M. Sobel, *Trabelin' On: The Slave Journey to an Afro-Baptist Faith*, Westport: Greenwood Press, 1979; J. Thornton, *Africa and Africans in the Making of the Atlantic World, 1400–1800*, 2nd ed., Cambridge: Cambridge University Press, 1998, pp. 235–71.

30 H. Stout, *The Divine Dramatist: George Whitefield and the Rise of Modern Evangelicalism*, Grand Rapids: William B. Eerdmans Publishing, 1991; F. Lambert, *'Pedlar in Divinity:' George Whitefield and the Transatlantic Revivals, 1737–1770*, Princeton: Princeton University Press, 1994; and and B. Schlenther, 'Whitefield, George (1714–1770)', *Oxford Dictionary of National Biography*, Oxford University Press, 2004 ([http://www.oxforddnb.com/view/article/29281, accessed August 7, 2014).

31 J. Sensbach, *Rebecca's Revival: Creating Black Christianity in the Atlantic World*, Cambridge, MA: Harvard University Press, 2006; A. Fogleman, *Jesus is Female: Moravians and the Challenge of Radical Religion in Early America*, Philadelphia: University of Pennsylvania Press, 2007, pp. 34–104.

32 D. Hall, 'Introduction,' in H. Amory and D. Hall (eds.), *The History of the Book in America, Vol. I, The Colonial Book in the Atlantic World*, Cambridge: Cambridge University Press, 2000, pp. 1–13.

33 D. Hall, *Cultures of Print: Essays in the History of the Book*, Amherst: University of Massachusetts Press, 1996, p. 37.

34 S. Juster, *Doomsayers: Anglo-American Prophecy in the Age of Revolution*, Philadelphia: University of Pennsylvania Press, 2003.

35 D. Hempton, *Methodism: Empire of the Spirit*, New Haven: Yale University Press, 2005, pp. 68–74; D. Stowe, *How Sweet the Sound: Music in the Spiritual Lives of Americans*, Cambridge, MA: Harvard University Press, 2004, pp. 16–63; M. Sirini, 'Hymnody as History: Early Evangelical Hymns and the Recovery of American Popular Religion,' *Church History*, 71, 2002, pp. 273–306; and W. Pitts, *Old Ship of Zion: The Afro-Baptist Ritual in the African Diaspora*, Oxford: Oxford University Press, 1993, pp. 11–51.

36 H. Rack, *Reasonable Enthusiast: John Wesley and the Rise of Methodism*, 3rd ed., London: Epworth Press, 2002, pp. 107–45.

37 Hempton, *Methodism*, pp. 13–85.

38 Frey and Wood, *Come Shouting to Zion*, pp. 80–148; Hempton, *Methodism*, pp. 24–25, 105–8, 132–35.

39 V. Carretta (ed.), *Unchained Voices: An Anthology of Black Authors in the English-Speaking World of the Eighteenth Century*, Lexington: University Press of Kentucky, 2003, pp. 7–14.

CHAPTER TWENTY

THE FREEST COUNTRY
Jews of the British Atlantic World,
ca. 1600–1800

———·◆·———

Natalie A. Zacek

In a letter to his friend, the Cambridge don Charles Mason, the Reverend William Smith, a Church of England minister on the island of Nevis, described a recreational outing which took place 'in the Month of July, 1719', at which time 'Mr Moses Pinheiro a Jew and myself, went to angle in Black Rock Pond', a body of water 'situate[d] a quarter of a mile or better Northwards from Charles Town our Metropolis or Capital, and about thirty yards distant from the Sea'.[1] Smith lived in Nevis from 1719 to 1724, serving as rector of the parish of St. John's Fig Tree, outside Charlestown, before returning to England to take up the well-endowed living of St. Mary's, Bedford.[2] As the island's principal clergyman, he possessed considerable social capital, and his letters are filled with references to the elite men and women which whom he socialised. That he chose to befriend a Jew, and to give this relationship a prominent mention in correspondence with a friend in the metropole, implies that it was possible for Jews to form bonds of acceptance and friendship with Gentiles, even churchmen. But that Smith felt it necessary to identify Pinheiro exclusively in terms of his religion suggests that their friendship was complicated by the latter's status as a member of a religious minority within colonial British America.

Jews were a numerically small but economically significant presence in the British Atlantic world from the middle of the seventeenth century to the end of the eighteenth, a period which saw the birth and rapid development of the sugar industry in the Caribbean, and the formation of transatlantic mercantile communities in the port towns and cities therein and on the North American mainland. The economic and social development of both regions was greatly influenced by the diaspora of Jewish settlers from Brazil in the mid-seventeenth century. In 1654, Portuguese forces seized control of the Dutch colony of Recife, the centre of northern Brazil's burgeoning sugar industry. With the possibility of religious persecution looming, Jewish colonists looked to settle elsewhere in the Atlantic world. The Spanish and Portuguese colonies, with their active Inquisitorial institutions, clearly offered no haven to Jewish refugees, and Louis XIV's increasing hostility towards non-Catholics both at home and overseas forestalled resettlement within the French empire.[3] For those Jewish settlers who preferred not to return to the Netherlands, the only places which seemed to offer refuge were the English and Dutch settlements in the Americas, particularly those in which the Recifean Jews' experience of the cultivation and commerce of sugar were likely to be an asset. By 1680, the earliest census of Barbados listed 54 Jewish households, consisting of 184 individuals, in the capital and principal entrepot of Bridgetown, with at least another hundred resident in the island's second town, Speightstown; by 1750 the four to five hundred Jewish residents comprised about 3 per cent of the island's total population.[4] Estimates suggest that Jews, who settled first in Port Royal and, after that city's destruction by an earthquake in 1692, in the capital city of Spanish Town, constituted 10 per cent of Jamaica's white population by the eighteenth century; in 1724 the Reverend Robert Robertson estimated that the white population of Nevis, which with Antigua, Montserrat and St. Kitts made up the federated Leeward Islands colony, consisted of 'about seventy householders with their families, being in all (children included) some three hundred whites of which one-fourth are Jews'.[5] Smaller Jewish communities emerged in the port towns of British North America, particulary Newport, New York, Philadelphia, Charleston and Savannah, where 'they comprised an almost infinitesimal proportion...of the population. At the time of the first national census of the United States, approximately 1500 of the nation's three million inhabitants were Jews, and the largest Jewish American communities, New York and Charleston, consisted of only a couple of hundred people.'[6]

Seventeenth-century English attitudes towards Jews, though considerably more accommodating than those of Europe's Catholic powers, were not particularly welcoming. For Britons, metropolitan and colonial alike, religious tolerance failed to generate a willing acceptance of alien groups such as Jews and Gypsies, with whom the former were frequently linked in the popular imagination, due to their alleged shared 'criminality, itinerancy, commerce, cohesion, and threatening and deviant sexuality'.[7] Many Englishmen might have found farfetched William Hughes of Gray's Inn's 1656 assertion, echoing centuries of the notorious practice of the blood libel, that Jews 'make it their annual practice to crucifie children', but they might have deemed more convincing the warning of the MP Thomas Papillon (1623–1702) that Jews, though not necessarily a threat to national security, were so culturally and socially alien that it would be impossible to assimilate them into the English body politic.[8] After their expulsion by Edward I's decree in 1290, Jews were virtually absent from England until Oliver Cromwell authorised their readmission in 1655. A seventeenth-century Englishman was more likely to have met a Muslim, or 'Moor', than to have had a personal encounter with a Jew, and in this instance unfamiliarity bred, if not contempt, then at least suspicion.[9] In his posthumously published *Second Part of the Institutes of the Lawes of England* (1642), the influential jurist Edward Coke described Jews as 'wicked and wretched men' who used 'cruell' means to enrich themselves and 'shewed no mercie' in their dealings with English Christians. Although Coke, who died in 1634, had probably never encountered a Jew – those few who lived in England before 1655 presented themselves publicly as Spanish or Italian Catholics, and practiced their faith in secrecy – he was convinced that Jewish character was eternal and immutable, and that it was not necessary to be personally acquainted with Jews in order to understand their nature.[10]

Following their readmission, English distaste for Jews is evident from a number of anonymous broadsides of the early eighteenth century, which, following the Act of Union, attempted to defame the Scots by comparing them to Jews. A 1721 verse

365

which satirised the 'Caledonian Clans' opened by inquiring of the reader, 'Was you ne'er, in a Cabbin/Confin'd like a religious *Rabbin?*' and went on to compare the Jewish clergyman to 'a Monkey ('Tis all by Way of Simile)/Imprison'd in a Cage'.[11] Still cruder in its satire was an earlier screed against the Scots, which claimed that they were 'down-right Egyptians by the[ir] Lice', but that their allegedly penny-pinching, double-dealing nature branded them simultaneously as 'right Jews in their Hearts'.[12] In the popular imagination, Jews and Scots, though represented by the very different physical stereotypes of the swarthy, hunched Semite and the freckled, gangly Caledonian, both served as representatives of the undesirable qualities of miserliness, greed, and untrustworthiness, particularly within the context of commerce and finance. Seventeenth- and eighteenth-century Scots and Jews tended to be both educated and unlanded, attributes which encouraged their participation in the fields of trade and speculation as the sorts of 'sophisters, economists, and calculators' whom Edmund Burke would deplore towards the end of the eighteenth century as bringing about the end of 'the age of chivalry'.[13] Of course Scots were, in the eyes of most Englishmen, less foreign and more assimilable than Jews; both groups might have suffered frequent ridicule, but only the latter had their civil and political rights abridged by both law and custom. Popular distaste towards Jews was a constant in eighteenth-century England, and although this hostility might remain dormant for years, it could easily flare up at moments of social or political stress. In the summer of 1753, Parliament passed the Jewish Naturalization Bill, which gave foreign-born Jews the right to own land and ships, and to engage in commerce with Britain's colonies 'without receiving the Sacrament of the Lord's Supper', only to be surprised by a tremendous popular furore in response. Pamphlets and sermons poured forth depicting Jews as 'money grubbing, dishonest, cunning interlopers…blasphemous, clannish, and traitorous', and Jewish men were attacked in the streets of London by those convinced of the existence of a Jewish conspiracy against British authority, property and masculinity, including the mandatory circumcision of all male Britons.[14] Fearing for public order, Parliament quickly repealed the Bill.

Despite these powerful undercurrents of anti-Semitism, England was, after the Cromwellian era, 'probably the freest European country a Jew could find', and its colonies, particularly those which lacked the resources, and in many instances the desire, to establish a strong Church of England presence therein appeared as potential havens to the dispossessed Jews of Recife.[15] Nonetheless, the assemblies of several of the English colonies imposed substantial disabilities upon their Jewish inhabitants. In 1661, only a few years after the onset of the Brazilian Jewish diaspora, a delegation of the merchants of Barbados, at that time the wealthiest colony in English America, petitioned the Lords of Trade and Plantations to bar Jews from participation in island commerce, pleading that 'the Jews are a people so subtle in matters of trade…that in a short time they will not only ingross trade among themselves, but will be able to divert the benefit thereof to other places…', presumably by deploying their supposedly innate craftiness and trickery in order to construct tightly knit networks of their co-religionists throughout the Americas.[16] Barbados was by the late seventeenth century already becoming physically and commercially over-crowded, and would grow ever more so over the next century, encouraging a climate of hostility against Jewish settlers; in 1739 the long-established Jewish community at Speightstown was dispersed after a mob attacked local Jews and destroyed their synagogue, due to a rumour that a band of Jewish men had assaulted a Christian.[17] Although the majority of Jewish migrants to the English colonies had paid the substantial fees to acquire Letters Patent of Denization, which granted them the status of English subjects, and thus the right to engage in transatlantic trade without violating the provisions of the Navigation Acts, they were subject to still stricter controls in Jamaica, where they were obligated to pay heavy additional taxes as well as being excluded from holding public office and serving in the militia, both major institutions of political influence and masculine prestige within island society.[18] In addition to accepting these disabilities, the Jews of Jamaica also felt it necessary to propitiate the local authorities from time to time by presenting them with what Christian islanders termed 'Jew pies', pastry crusts filled with coins, which they hoped would yield them improved treatment, or at least prevent their situation from worsening.[19] In Barbados, they were further burdened by being barred from testifying in court against any Gentile whom they felt had mistreated them, and they were similarly unable to defend themselves against accusations from their non-Jewish neighbours.[20]

Attitudes and practices such as these encouraged Jewish settlers in the larger English islands, such as the Abudiente, Senior, and Levy Rezio families of Barbados, to try their luck in the Leeward Islands colony.[21] But these smaller communities were not initially more welcoming to Jews; in 1694, the Antiguan House of Assembly approved a bill which attempted to relegate Jewish islanders to a second-class legal and economic status by forbidding them to engage in trade with slave peddlers and, more threateningly, by licensing local magistrates to try Jews suspected of criminal activities by using 'any such evidence as the said Justices shall judge sufficient in their own judgments and consciences'.[22] Even in Nevis, which by the early eighteenth century boasted the highest percentage of Jews in its white population among the English colonies in island and mainland alike, Jews were the subject of punitive legislation as 'evil-minded Persons, intending nothing but their own private Gain, and the Ruin of the Poor', who were known to 'ingross and buy whole Cargoes of Provisions at a cheap Rate, and to retale them again at excessive Prices, thereby forestalling the Market'. They were also accused of profaning the Christian Sabbath by 'trading with Negroes...on the Lord's Day', participating in the semi-illegal markets which slaves conducted on Sundays.[23] These misdeeds appeared to threaten the island planters' control both of their bondspeople and of local commerce, and as such generated considerable anxiety regarding their Jewish neighbours.

Burdened as they were by these legal proscriptions and popular prejudices, Jews nonetheless flourished in the English West Indian colonies. The Recifean exiles and their descendants constructed and participated in an extensive network of contacts which connected them with their co-religionists elsewhere in the Caribbean, in the Dutch colony of Surinam, and in the Netherlands, as well as in British North America, particularly New York and Newport. Their extensive experience in the business of sugar cultivation and their familiarity with the languages and commercial practices of the Spanish and Portuguese colonies allowed them to function as conduits of information, finance, and commerce across the imperial boundaries of the Atlantic world.[24] In addition to these valued skills and networks, Jews also possessed the advantage of their whiteness; as the ratio of black slaves and free people of colour rose steadily in relation to the number of white settlers, Jews' very complexion became a badge of their comparative trustworthiness to their fellow islanders. By 1740, the passage of the Plantation Act by Parliament exempted Jews in the colonies (though not those in the metropole) from the need to take the Oaths of Supremacy and Allegiane, acknowledging the sovereign as the supreme head of the Church of England, and provided for the naturalisation of foreigners who had lived in Britain's American colonies for seven years. These concessions allowed both English- and foreign-born Jews to attain a greater degree of inclusion within colonial society, though to a certain extent they simultaneously reified their position as social outsiders.[25]

Because they stood outside the world of local political life in colonial British America, and were almost exclusively endogamous in relation both to marital choice and to social life more generally, it is through the wills left by Jews of the seventeenth- and eighteenth-century British Atlantic world that it is most possible to understand the extent to which these men and women were connected both to their Christian neighbours and to fellow members of the diasporic Jewish community of the Americas. The will of Haim Abinum de Lima, for example, depicts this Nevisian Jew as enmeshed in a network of personal and commercial relationships with Jews and non-Jews alike, one which crossed both colonial and imperial boundaries. De Lima was open in his profession of Judaism, as is indicated by his stated wish 'to be buried after the rites of the people called Jews,' by his philanthropic activity in connection with the Mikve Israel synagogue in the Dutch colony of Curaçao, and by his bequests of a 'Little Sepher for Sr Eustacia Rodes for the Kaal, [and] the great Sepher for my cousin David the son of Ab[raha]m Piza, senior'.[26] But his status as an observant Jew did not forestall the development of close contacts, and even friendship, with Christian islanders. None of the three men who served as witnesses to his will – William Liburd, John Burke senior and Adam Brodie – were Jews. This situation might be considered axiomatic; in many instances, island law barred Jews, like other non-jurors, from acting as witnesses to any kind of legal transaction. But Liburd, Burke and Brodie were men of considerable property and prestige in Nevis, and their apparent willingness not merely to witness de Lima's will, but also to accept the responsibility of carrying out its provisions and bequests indicates an instance of a significant degree of Anglo-Jewish amity. Such a responsibility was not a trivial one, particularly in cases such as that of de Lima, who chose to distribute his property among a large number of heirs in St. Kitts, Barbados and Curaçao, and whose estate was therefore complicated and time-consuming to administer.[27]

Considerably more elevated than Haim Abinum de Lima in both the economic and social realms was the Pinheiro family, with whose son Moses the Reverend William Smith had socialised. The family's progenitor, the prosperous merchant and rum distiller Isaac Pinheiro, was born in Spain and became a freeman of New York in 1695, but maintained Charlestown, Nevis, as the headquarters of his rapidly expanding mercantile network.[28] He died in 1710 in the course of a visit to New York, to which he may have travelled in order to carry out his responsibilities as commercial agent to Abraham Bueno de Mezqueta, another Jewish resident of Nevis and a member of a family whose business interests extended throughout colonial British America.[29] Perhaps sensing the approach of death and doubting that he would survive the long voyage back to Nevis, Isaac drew up a new will in New York, the provisions of which reveal the extent of both his wealth and his affective relationships. Isaac's wife Esther was his principal legatee, inheriting 'all the Houses and Land...in Charles Towne', but his resources were sufficient to allow him to make sizable

– CHAPTER 20: *Jews of the British Atlantic* –

bequests to his five adult children, and to leave annuities to his father Abraham and sister Rachel in Amsterdam and to his sister Sarah Mendes Goma in Curaçao.[30] To serve as 'Trustees and Overseers of this my Will', Isaac selected two Nevisians. One was Solomon Israel, a prosperous merchant and a leading figure in the Jewish community; the other was Captain Samuel Clarke, a prominent planter and the commander of the island's militia.[31] The relationship between Pinheiro and Clarke appears to have been an intimate one; not only did the former refer to the latter as 'my Loving Friend', but he also bequeathed to him the sum of 'Tenn pounds currant Money of this Island...to buy...a Mourning Sute', the practice of wearing mourning clothes being reserved at this time to the family and intimate friends of the decedent.[32] No less eminent a person than New York governor Rip Van Dam, whom Esther Pinheiro named as 'my friend', served as one of two 'special attornies' who assisted the widow in her role as executor of the will.[33]

After Isaac's death, Esther assumed his place at the head of his commercial network, maintaining and expanding the family's business interests, primarily through the acquisition of a small fleet of merchant vessels which travelled between New York, New England, Britain and the West Indies, with an occasional stop at Madeira to take on casks of the sweet wine so popular among West Indian planters.[34] Between 1716 and 1718, Esther herself made a series of voyages to the ports of New York and Boston in her 20 ton sloop, the *Neptune*, exchanging cargoes of sugar, molasses, and other island commodities for New England timber and provisions and imported European manufactured goods.[35] By 1720, Esther was the owner of the *Samuel*, a 25 ton sloop with a crew of five, which made several voyages each year between Boston and Nevis from 1720 to 1722. The *Samuel* ceased to appear in Nevis's Naval Office records after 1722, implying that it had been lost at sea or had been sold to someone off the island, but by the beginning of 1724 it had been replaced in the Pinheiro fleet by the brigantine *Esther*, a 60 ton vessel which the eponymous Mrs. Pinheiro owned in partnership with Jonathan Dowse of Charlestown, Massachusetts, where the ship had been built the previous winter. Initially, the *Esther* appears to have replaced the defunct *Samuel* on the Boston-Nevis route, but by 1728, when the merchant Ebenezer Hough, another Bostonian, had replaced Dowse as the ship's co-owner, it began to make far more ambitious transatlantic voyages between Nevis and the ports of London and Cork. Around this time Esther acquired yet another ship, the *Abigail*, a small brig of 35 tons, which plied the route between Nevis, London and Madeira.[36] As a participant in both local and transatlantic commerce, Esther's influence stretched beyond the spheres of both her family and Nevis's Jewish community. Her entrepreneurial activities assured her a prominent place in the mercantile community in which she lived, and further allowed her to integrate her family into Nevisian society and, beyond, into the economic life of New England shipping and commerce.

The small worlds which Jews constructed for themselves in the port towns of the British Atlantic, on the North American mainland as well as in the West Indies, were largely parallel to, rather than intertwined with, those of their Gentile neighbours. Most Jews lived, by choice or by necessity, in closed communities. They were almost entirely endogamous, marrying other members of their communities or looking to Jewish enclaves throughout the British and Dutch colonies for spouses. Endogamy was desirable from the perspective of religious adherence and cultural persistence,

369

but it prevented Jewish settlers from reaping the numerous benefits which could be gained through intermarriage, such as the possibility of acquiring land, money, and political influence through participation in the kinship networks of the 'great tangled cousinry' which allowed white elites throughout colonial British America to gain and retain hegemony.[37] It is noteworthy than the Nevisian Solomon Israel, one of very few colonial British American Jews to sit upon a jury, and therefore to claim the legal and political rights of an Englishman, had married a Christian woman, an action which encouraged 'his disassociation from the faith...and his ability to move within the upper social, political, and economic classes' of the wider community.[38] By contrast, Moses Pinheiro might have gone fishing with an Anglican clergyman, but when he came to take a wife, he chose a Barbadian Jewish woman named Lunah.[39]

Of course, endogamy did not prevent Jews from attaining wealth. It did, however, ensure that Jews would remain outside the formal and informal spheres, those of office-holding and kinship, which presented those who settled in the Anglo-American colonies with their most promising opportunities to rise in influence and esteem within local white society. Even the wealthiest Jew could not sit on the Governor's Council or in the Assembly, or even serve as a juror, a justice of the peace, or a member of the militia, despite the fact that adult white males were so few in number in many of these communities that it was difficult to fill these offices. In times of war, Jews were encouraged to 'assist and defend [their communities] with the utmost of their Power, Strength, and Ability', but in less fraught moments the sole civic responsibility entrusted to them was 'to behave themselves fairly and honestly amongst us'.[40]

The cosmopolitan nature of Jewish identity in the Atlantic world allowed Jews to develop networks of kinship which stretched over thousands of miles and which benefited its participants in their search for marital and commercial opportunities, and allowed the small number of synagogues in the eighteenth-century Americas to flourish in financial and cultural terms and to function as nodes of support and cultural survival for Jewish enclaves.[41] But Judaism marked a boundary more definite than that of even the most radical and alarming deviations within Protestantism, as is shown by the trajectory of Quaker and Huguenot settlement and social integration in colonial British America. Huguenots and Quakers could, and often did, distance themselves from their suspect heritage through intermarriage with Anglicans and at least outward observance of Church of England practices. Jews, in contrast, neither desired nor were encouraged to marry outside their faith, and the stamp of otherness marked even those who were less than entirely committed to their religion. Alternative Protestant identities were permeable to processes of Anglicisation and Anglicanisation in a way which could not be true of Jews. Jacob Marcus, the pioneering historian of Judaism in the Americas, claimed that 'the typical colonial Jew was true to his heritage because he was not pressed to be untrue to it', but nor was he in any way encouraged to connect himself (or herself) to a more general sense of Englishness.[42]

The apparently rapid disappearance of many of the Jewish communities of colonial British America is reflective of the tenuous nature of the relationship between the Jewish population and the wider local community. As the sugar trade began to decline in the final decades of the eighteenth century, and as a series of hurricanes devastated the eastern Caribbean, Jewish islanders, at least some of whom had family connections in the region which stretched back over a century, quickly abandoned the West Indian colonies in favour of the Anglo-American settlements on the mainland, or relocated to the Dutch colony of Curacao, the most vital Jewish outpost of the Atlantic world.[43]

These migrations were accelerated by the aftermath of the American Revolution, which cut the commercial bonds which had developed for more than a century between Jews in the English West Indies and those on the North American mainland.[44] As Jonathan Sarna has noted, all of the organised Jewish communities of colonial North America, which he enumerates as New York, Philadelphia, Newport, Savannah and Charleston, developed in port cities and catered to the needs of transatlantic merchants.[45] In comparison with the Jews of the Caribbean, who were almost exclusively of Sephardic heritage and tradition, many of those on the mainland were Ashkenazim from central or eastern Europe, most notably in Philadelphia, home to the Polish Jewish financier Haym Solomon and the German immigrant merchants Nathan and Isaac Levy. Although these Ashkenazi Jews often intermarried with local Sephardim, who were widely perceived as having higher social status within the Jewish community, they were also more prone than their West Indian compatriots to join with their Gentile neighbours in commercial ventures, social life, and even marriage.[46] The trajectory of the Franks family of Philadelphia illuminates the extent to which 'Jews of sufficient gentility...were accepted as members of an anglicized Philadelphia elite, to which Quakers, Anglicans, and Presbyterians all belonged'. While the family's progenitor, Jacob Franks, had been the *parnas*, or president, of the Shearith Israel synagogue in New York, and he and his wife Abigail Levy raised their nine children as observant Jews, his son David married Margaret Evans, the daughter of a leading Philadelphia Quaker family. David and Margaret's children were raised as Christians, and reached the heights of Philadelphia society. Abigail married Andrew Hamilton, who served as attorney general and as acting governor of Pennsylvania, and Rebecca, a notable local belle, was selected as one of the 'Queens of Beauty' at the Meschianza, a grand ball in full British aristocratic style which was held in 1778, which British army officers gave for their Loyalist friends before the forces left the city.[47]

While the high degree of assimilation experienced by elite Jews in Philadelphia was not representative of the wider experience of Jews in eighteenth-century North America, the small size of their communities, even in comparison with those of the Caribbean, encouraged a dilution of identity through intermarriage between Ashkenazim and Sephardim, and also between Jews and Christians. When, following the Revolution, it became increasingly difficult for mainland and island Jews to trade and communicate with one another, as they had done for nearly a century and a half, 'the Atlantic world that colonial North American port Jews had known ended...and Jews ceased to identify themselves...as "members of the nation"'.[48] Under these strains, American Jewish communities began to fragment in the final years of the eighteenth century, losing their sense of themselves as 'port Jews' and becoming simply another minority group within an ever larger and more diverse United States. So insignificant and unthreatening were these Jewish communities that anti-Semitic rhetoric and activity, always a threat in colonial North America up to the Revolution, relinquished its influence in the political and social sphere, and would not revive until the latter half of the nineteenth century, when large numbers of Jews, mostly impoverished and almost exclusively Ashkenazi, began to immigrate to the United States.

As a final point, it may be useful to speculate about the apparent assimilability of Quakers and Huguenots, which offers an interesting contrast to the continued distinctiveness of Jews in colonial British American society. All three groups encountered significant opposition and even persecution in seventeenth-century England, wracked as it was by every kind of disorder, and in its empire, yet all succeeded in creating niches for themselves in colonial society by the early decades of the eighteenth century. Jews, however, remained within self-contained enclaves centred upon a handful of port towns. They participated in imperial commerce and, to a certain extent, in neighbourly rituals of sociability, but, unlike the Quakers and Huguenots, they appear, other than amongst the Philadelphian elite, very rarely to have intermarried with Anglican settlers, nor did they gain a role in the political or military establishments which were a principal source of local prestige and patronage.

Huguenots and Quakers were on some levels far more assimilable than Jews into the mainstream of Anglo-Atlantic society, but this assimilability was at least in part the result of their apparent willingness to become part of the larger society, a tendency which few Jews seem to have shared. Societal inclusion resulted from the combination of the *ability* of a group or an individual to accommodate itself to certain norms and its *willingness* to do so. In other words, inclusion in a community was the result, not of a completely autonomous decision on the part of one side or the other, but of a negotiation between the two. The Jews of the English colonies might under certain circumstances be *integrated* into the wider community, but they would very rarely be *assimilated* within it. The persistence of anti-Jewish sentiment among seventeenth- and eighteenth-century Englishmen dovetailed with the communal and self-enclosed tendency of Jewish settlers to create a subtle yet distinct sense of cultural distance which both groups were willing to enforce through law and custom alike. In the end, most of these Jewish colonists were prototypical sojourners within the early modern Atlantic world, moving between islands and mainland and across imperial boundaries, and leading lives characterised by fluidity and mobility. Perhaps only those who were laid to rest in the Jewish cemeteries which remain their most notable material legacy can be described as permanent residents of most of their communities within the British Atlantic world.

NOTES

Some of this material has been previously published in Natalie A. Zacek, *Settler Society in the English Leeward Islands, 1670–1776* (Cambridge, 2010), chapter 3, and in Zacek, '"A People So Subtle": Sephardic Jewish Pioneers of the English West Indies', in Caroline Williams, ed., *Bridging the Early Modern Atlantic World* (Aldershot, 2009), pp. 97–112.

1   William Smith, *A Natural History of Nevis, and the rest of the English Leeward Charibee Islands in America* (Cambridge, 1745), p.10.
2   Elsa V. Goveia, *A Study on the Historiography of the British West Indies* (Mexico City, 1956), p. 34.
3   In Article One of the *Code Noir* of 1685, Louis XIV instructed French colonial officials 'to expel from our islands all the Jews who have settled there; to them, as declared enemies of Christianity, we command to leave within three months from the publication of this edict, on pain of loss of liberty and property' (reprinted in F. R. Augier and S. C. Gordon, *Sources of West Indian History* [London, 1962], p. 92).

– CHAPTER 20: *Jews of the British Atlantic* –

4 Mordechai Arbell, *The Jewish Nation of the Caribbean* (Jerusalem, 2002), p. 199.

5 Thomas G. August, 'An Historical Profile of the Jewish Community of Jamaica', *Jewish Social Studies* 49 (1987), pp. 303–26, here p. 304; Robertson, quoted in Arbell, *Jewish Nation*, p. 221.

6 William Pencak, 'Jews and Anti-Semitism in Early Pennsylvania', *Pennsylvania Magazine of History and Biography* 126 (2002), pp. 365–408, here pp. 366, 367.

7 Dana Rabin, 'Seeing Jews and Gypsies in 1753', *Cultural and Social History* 7 (2010), pp. 35–58, here p. 37.

8 Frank Felsenstein, *Anti-Semitic Stereotypes: A Paradigm of Otherness in English Popular Culture, 1660–1830* (Baltimore, 1995), p. 40; Daniel Statt, *Foreigners and Englishmen: The Controversy over Immigration and Population, 1660–1760* (Newark, Del., 1995), p. 82.

9 Nabil Matar, *Turks, Moors, and Englishmen in the Age of Discovery* (New York, 1999), pp. 3–4.

10 Holly Snyder, '"Usury, to the English Mind": The Image of the Jewish Merchant in the British Atlantic World', paper presented to the Ninth Annual Conference of the Omohundro Institute of Early American History and Culture, New Orleans, Louisiana, June 2003, pp. 1–2.

11 'To ******** *******, Esq.,' in Samuel Keimer, ed., *Caribbeana* (Millwood, N.Y., 1978), vol. 2, pp. 54–55; italics in original.

12 *Caledonia; or, The Pedlar turn'd Merchant: A Tragi-Comedy, as it was Acted by His Majesty's Subjects of Scotland, in the King of Spain's Province of Darien* (London, 1700), p. 9. In early modern English parlance, 'Egyptians' denoted gypsies.

13 Burke, *Reflections on the Revolution in France* (London, 1790), p. 113.

14 Dana Rabin, 'The Jew Bill of 1753: Masculinity, Virility, and the Nation', *Eighteenth-Century Studies* 39 (2006), pp. 157–71, here 157, 158; Rabin, 'Seeing Jews and Gypsies', pp. 36, 40.

15 David Brion Davis, *Slavery and Human Progress* (New York, 1984), p. 100. For a useful survey of recent scholarship, see Isaac Land, 'Jewishness and Britishness in the Eighteenth Century', *History Compass* 3 (2005), pp. 1–12.

16 Report of the Council for Foreign Plantations to the King [Charles II], 24 July 1661, in W. Noel Sainsbury (ed.), *Calendar of State Papers: Colonial Series: America and West Indies, 1661–1668* (London, 1880), p. 49. As Nuala Zahedieh has observed, 'the skill with which Jewish merchants managed to comply with English [trade] regulations, and their success at commerce, combined to cause resentment' on the part of non-Jewish English colonists. See Zahedieh, 'The Capture of the *Blue Dove*, 1664: Policy, Profits, and Protection in Early English Jamaica,' in Roderick A. MacDonald (ed.), *West Indies Accounts* (Barbados, 1996), p. 45.

17 Arbell, *Jewish Nation*, pp. 203, 207.

18 Frank Wesley Pitman, *The Development of the British West Indies* (New Haven, 1917), p. 27. See also Samuel J. Hurwitz and Edith Hurwitz, 'The New World Sets an Example for the Old: The Jews of Jamaica and Political Rights, 1661–1831', *American Jewish Historical Quarterly*, 55 (1965), pp. 37–56. Sacramental requirements prevented Jews in England and its colonies from voting for or holding office, receiving a naval commission, being called to the bar, or taking a degree at a university, placing them on the same footing as all other non-Anglicans at this time (Rabin, 'Seeing Jews and Gypsies,' p. 40).

19 Jacob R. Marcus, *The Colonial American Jew* (Detroit, 1970), vol. 1, p. 108.

20 Arbell, *Jewish Nation*, 204.

21 Arbell, *Jewish Nation*, pp. 214, 215.

22 Quoted in Mindie Lazarus-Black, *Legitimate Acts and Illegal Encounters: Law and Society in Antigua and Barbuda* (Washington, D.C., 1994), p. 25.

23 *Acts of Assembly Passed in the Island of Nevis, from 1664, to 1739, inclusive* (London, 1740), pp. 11, 12. As Karen Fog Olwig has noted, Jews in Charlestown, Nevis, 'were alleged to deal with slaves who sold them stolen goods and thus to practice unfair trade.

Similar accusations were made against Jews throughout the West Indies and seem to have been occasioned by the fact that they controlled a large part of the trade on several islands.' See Olwig, *Global Culture, Island Identity: Continuity and Change in the Afro-Caribbean Community of Nevis* (Chur, Switzerland, 1993), p. 63.

24 Angus Calder, *Revolutionary Empire* (New York, 1981), p. 317.

25 Holly Snyder, 'Rules, Rights, and Redemption: The Negotiation of Jewish Status in British Atlantic Port Towns,' *Jewish History* 20 (2006), pp. 147–70, here p. 153.

26 Will and codicil of Haim Abinum de Lima, 27 June 1765 and 2 December 1765, 'Abstracts of Nevis Wills in the P[rivy]. C[ouncil]. C[ollections],' in Oliver, *Caribbeana*, vol. 2, pp. 158–59. The term 'Sepher' or 'Sefer' refers to any of a number of Jewish sacred books, most commonly the Torah.

27 Will of de Lima, *Caribbeana*, vol. 2, p. 159.

28 Marcus, *Colonial American Jew*, vol. 1, p. 99.

29 'Jews of Nevis', unattributed typescript, Nevis Historical and Conservation Society, Charlestown, Nevis, p. 3. De Mezqueta appears in 1692 as 'Mr Abraham Buino Demesquieta', one of nine Barbadian Jews possessed of 'houses and plantations on the island'; see Frank Cundall, et al., 'Documents Relating to the History of the Jews of Jamaica and Barbados in the Time of William III', *Publications of the American Jewish Historical Society* 23 (1915), pp. 25–30, here p. 29.

30 Will of Isaac Pinheiro, in Leo Hershkowitz, *Wills of Early New York Jews, 1704–1799* (New York, 1967), pp. 21–24; Stern, *American Jewish Families*, p. 250.

31 Ibid., p. 24. Solomon Israel also served as a witness to the wills of the vintner George Richardson and the merchant Azariah Pinney, founder of the 'West-India Fortune' analysed by Richard Pares; he is notable for being perhaps the only Jew in the English West Indian colonies to have been permitted to serve as a juror, a responsibility restricted by law and custom to members of the Church of England.

32 Marcus, *Colonial American Jew*, p. 99.

33 Friedman, 'Wills', p. 158.

34 See David Hancock, 'Commerce and Conversation in the Eighteenth-Century Atlantic: The Invention of Madeira Wine', *Journal of Interdisciplinary History* 29 (1998), pp. 197–220.

35 C.O. 187/1 and 187/2, Naval Office Returns, Nevis, 1720–29, National Archives of the United Kingdom, Kew.

36 C.O. 187/1 and 187/2.

37 The phrase is that of Bernard Bailyn in 'Politics and Social Structure in Virginia', in James M. Smith, ed., *Seventeenth-Century America* (Chapel Hill, 1959), p. 111.

38 Michelle M. Terrell, *The Jewish Community of Early Colonial Nevis* (Gainesville, Fla., 2005), p. 147.

39 Malcolm H. Stern, *First American Jewish Families: 600 Genealogies, 1654–1977* (Cincinnati, 1978), p. 250.

40 'An Act to repeal a certain Act against the Jews', *The Laws of the Leeward Islands*, in *Acts of Assembly Passed in the Island of St. Christopher; From the Year 1711, to 1769* (St. Christopher, 1769), p. 11.

41 Seventeenth- and eighteenth-century synagogues appeared in the English colonies in Barbados (Bridgetown and Speightstown), Jamaica (Port Royal, Spanish Town, and Kingston), Nevis (Charlestown), New York (New York City), Georgia (Savannah), Pennsylvania (Philadelphia), Rhode Island (Newport), South Carolina (Charleston), and Virginia (Richmond).

42 Marcus, 'The American Colonial Jew: A Study in Acculturation', The B. G. Rudolph Lecture in Judaic Studies, Syracuse University, 1968, p. 19.

43 Arbell, *Jewish Nation*, p. 221.

- CHAPTER 20: *Jews of the British Atlantic* -

44 See Richard Pares, *Yankees and Creoles: The Trade between North America and the West Indies before the American Revolution* (London, 1956).

45 Sarna, 'Port Jews in the Atlantic: Further Thoughts', *Jewish History* 20 (2006), pp. 213–19, here 214.

46 Sarna, 'Port Jews,' p. 215; Pencak, 'Jews and Anti-Semitism', pp. 368, 369, 374.

47 Pencak, 'Jews and Anti-Semitism', p. 371; Leo Hershkowitz, 'Rebecca Franks, 1760–1823', *Jewish Women's Archive* (http://jwa.org/encyclopedia/article/franks-rebecca), consulted 16 February 2014.

48 Sarna, 'Port Jews', pp. 216, 217.

CHAPTER TWENTY-ONE

ISLAM AND THE ATLANTIC

——·◆·——

Denise A. Spellberg

The phrase 'Islam and the Atlantic' invokes more than the category of religion, for Islam as a political and cultural presence has had a real but also imagined presence in what we implicitly define as a Europeanized, Christian Atlantic world since its inception. Muslims lived in this Atlantic but, ironically, their practice of the faith was often obscured in favor of discourses about notional Muslims who, whether depicted as eternal enemies or as future citizens, provided a foil to emerging definitions of European religious persecution and tolerance, particularly in the Anglo-Atlantic.

A history of Islam in the Atlantic world in all its imperial incarnations has yet to be written. What follows is a thematic, anecdotal introduction to the permutations of Islam – and the presence of Muslims, largely focused on the British and Spanish imperial spheres, with some attention to the Dutch and Portuguese realms. But let us commence with a very different possible beginning for Islam in the Atlantic...

Europeans may receive credit for the maritime 'discovery' and colonization of the Atlantic world, but some historians now assert that Muslims crossed this ocean first. The most serious of these claims, however, are hardly definitive, nor have they enjoyed widespread acceptance or even acknowledgment by Atlantic historians. The earliest of these reports within the Islamic sphere dates from the tenth century, when the historian al-Mas'udi (d. 956), who never ventured west of Egypt, stated in his chronicle that beyond the navigable ocean, Muslims accepted that there was yet another ocean, described as 'unnavigable due to its darkness' (Sezgin, 2011: 130). This, of course, was the Atlantic. There even exist reports that Sultan Muhammad Abu Bakr, the ruler of Mali, not only dispatched a fleet from his West African kingdom, with the directive that they reach 'the other side of the ocean,' but that after a first unsuccessful attempt, the Muslim ruler joined a second naval expedition, which 'never returned.' The year was 1312 (Sezgin 2011: 132).

The claims that Muslims discovered a 'New World' by crossing the Atlantic have not met with much academic acceptance, and those who have attempted to teach these events as fact have met with ridicule and significant resistance, particularly in the U.S. (Bennetta 2003). However, historically, we are on more solid ground when appreciating that the Atlantic world's discovery by Christian Europeans succeeded, in part, because of their reliance on earlier Islamic scientific breakthroughs. Beyond

376

the astrolabe and nautical compass, Muslim navigators excelled in determining longitudinal precision as early as the eleventh century, a skill which Columbus inherited directly (Sezgin 2011: 149). For example, he would have known from Islamic calculations that 'one equatorial degree equals 56 and 2/3 miles' (Sezgin 2011: 154). There is also evidence that Muslim pilots were used by the Portuguese explorer Vasco da Gama to explore the West coast of Africa (Sezgin 2011: 151). Among the crew who sailed with Columbus, including the part owner of the *Pinta* and *Nina*, there were reputedly Spaniards of Muslim descent (Dirks 2006: 62–64). The presence of these *moriscos*, former Muslims forcibly Christianized, has been accepted by serious historians (Gomez 2005: ix).

Yet whether these individuals still practiced Islam in their transatlantic trek has not been verified and, indeed, is unlikely, at least, officially. The reason? By 1501, practicing Muslims and Jews were banned from crossing the Spanish Atlantic (Gomez 2005: 14). By 1508, the 'children and grandchildren of the converts of Jews and Muslims' were also forbidden passage across the Atlantic by order of King Ferdinand, an assertion which would be repeatedly reaffirmed by Spanish authorities (Cook 2008: 37). The intent of this policy was to keep the 'corrupting' influence of Islam and Judaism away from Native Americans, destined for conversion to the 'true' Catholic faith. Despite these prohibitions, Karoline P. Cook has discovered roughly 100 individuals who were accused of practicing Islam in the Spanish New World, most often the charges are recorded in Inquisition records (Cook 2008: 5).

There is more conclusive evidence that European forays into North Africa resulted in the enslavement of Muslims who then, against their will, traversed the Atlantic. One such notable, documented case is that of a Moroccan from Azemmour, whose hometown on the eastern Atlantic littoral had fallen to the Portuguese in 1513. Enslaved as the result of Portuguese conquest, this Muslim served his Spanish owner and became known as Estevanico de Dorantes. He crossed the Atlantic during a Spanish expedition to Florida in 1527, which was driven aground near Tampa, due to a hurricane. Thus began Estevanico's trek, along with the remaining survivors, to Mexico via Texas. The Moroccan not only survived privation and a second enslavement by Native Americans in Texas, he later joined a Spanish expedition of exploration in search of the fabled Seven Cities of Gold, which led him overland through New Mexico and Arizona. Estevanico was killed by Native Americans in New Mexico in 1539 (GhaneaBassiri 2010: 11–12). He and other members of his party are credited with the earliest Spanish exploration of Texas – and the Southwest, which remains the first documented account of a probable Muslim explorer taking active part in the European quest to expand the borders of their New World. His Spanish contemporaries referred to Estevanico as black and Arabic-speaking, but Christian, possibly because of the prohibition against Muslims in the Spanish New World (GhaneaBassiri 2010: 10, n. 6; Gomez 2005: 5). This transatlantic tale reminds us that the Atlantic coast of West Africa included a considerable Islamic presence and point of contact with Europeans. It was also not uncommon for European traders, captured by North African corsairs, to convert to Islam, be ransomed and expand their commercial reach into the Caribbean, which Kristen Block has documented for Spanish, French, and English merchants (Block 2012: 57, 68, 159).

Whether former Muslims sailed with Columbus or not, it is certain that these European voyages of discovery had been initiated to find alternative routes around the

Islamic-controlled Mediterranean and Red Sea, then the only maritime access to coveted commodity markets in the Indian Ocean and China. In sailing west, across the Atlantic, Europeans really intended to go east, avoiding the powerful presence in Egypt of the Mamluks (1250–1517) and, later, the Ottomans (1517–1923). The European discovery of the Atlantic was thus propelled by avoidance of Islamic political and commercial dominance in the Mediterranean. The two bodies of water cannot be separated when writing a history of Islam in the Atlantic (GhaneaBassiri 2010: 10). A case for this 'triangle' (England, the Muslim Mediterranean, and America) has been advanced by Nabil Matar for the English since the sixteenth century (Matar 1999: 83–84).

Once Europeans navigated successfully across the Atlantic, they brought with them foodstuffs for cultivation that had been discovered in the eastern Islamic world under the patronage of the Abbasid dynasty (r. 750–1258) in Baghdad. These new crops were then diffused westward to Islamic North Africa, Spain, and Sicily. Muslims not only spread these new crops of sugar cane, rice, cotton, and citrus; they hybridized them in areas that would fall under Christian control in the Iberian peninsula by 1492 (Watson 1983: 15–51). Muslim agricultural breakthroughs were accompanied by Islamic technological advances in irrigation in places like Valencia, Spain. These were replicated by Franciscan monks around their San Antonio, Texas, missions in the seventeenth century (Glick 1972). Most of these Muslim-pioneered crops required not just advanced irrigation techniques, but the importation of African slave labor to both South and North America.

Among these West African slaves were many practicing Muslims. Estimates of this population are not precise and vary geographically, but at highest count the expert Sylviane Diouf has proposed, for all of the Americas and the Caribbean, that 15 to 20 percent of African slaves were Muslim, while another historian suggests the lower figure of 10 percent (Diouf 1998: 48). Many Muslims from West Africa, particularly from Senegambia and Sierra Leone, often possessed agricultural expertise in rice cultivation. White, British colonists preferred these mostly Muslim slaves for their plantations in the southern states of North America, particularly South Carolina, Georgia, and Louisiana (Carney 2001; Diouf 1998:47). The demand for slaves to tend crops first developed in the Islamic world, especially sugar cane, rice, and cotton, ironically, propelled the transport of the greatest number of Muslims throughout the Atlantic world. The very appellations in Spanish and English for key Islamic crops reflect Arabic origins: *al-sukkar*, for *zucar* in Spanish or sugar in English; and *al-ruz*, for *arroz* in Spanish or rice in English. And these are just a few of the terms for New World crops with similar linguistic antecedents.

European Christian voyages of discovery were propelled by reactions against Islamic maritime dominance, on the one hand, while, on the other, they succeeded because of Muslim breakthroughs in navigational technology. Although Europeans refused to credit these Islamic precedents as ingredients in their successful Atlantic ventures, they also brought with them knowledge about Islam as a religious and political system, which they transplanted in their New Worlds. Indeed, learned historians such as Nabil Matar, have argued that the English template for understanding Native Americans had been shaped by earlier, violent encounters with Muslims in the North African and the Ottoman sphere: 'As they [the English] began their conquest of the Americas they transported their anti-Muslim ideology of religious war across the Atlantic and applied it to the American Indians' (Matar 1999: 130).

This doctrine of a holy war against Muslims, transplanted to the New World's indigenous inhabitants, also existed in Spanish lands. There, Santiago, the patron saint of the Christian Reconquista against Islamic political control in Iberia, received the honorific *Matamoros*, or Muslim Slayer, a title which morphed in his New World incarnation into *Mataindios*, the Slayer of Native Americans. When Santiago's birthday is recalled annually on July 26th throughout the Catholic Mediterranean and Spanish America, it is customary to celebrate still with mock conflicts between *Moros* (Muslims) and *Cristianos* (Christians). At the end of these public performances, Santiago Matamoros appears on a white horse, holding a thunderbolt, ready to exterminate the Muslim threat, a holiday annually celebrated in Chimayo, New Mexico, by actors on horseback (Harris 2000: 18–19, 183, 206–8). The original conflict in New Mexico, however, was not between the Spanish and enemy Muslims, but between the Spanish and Native Americans at the Battle of Acoma, where the Pueblo were defeated in 1598 (Spellberg 2004: 152).

This is but one example of the enduring antipathy to an Islamic enemy from Europe reincarnated on the other side of the Atlantic. The phrase *moros y cristianos* persists less dramatically in Cuba and Brazil as a dish combining black beans (the Muslims) and white rice (the Christians). As we shall see, the imputation of blackness to Muslims was part of their definition on both sides of the Atlantic. Sometimes the comestible combination is referred to simply as *arroz moro*, or Muslim rice, a reference that did *not* honor the special agricultural skills of Islamic slaves cultivating that crop.

The transposition of Islam as the religion of a more powerful political enemy also existed in the English Atlantic world. Nabil Matar argues that Britons, who could not assert dominance over the Ottomans or against North African corsairs in the Mediterranean by the end of the sixteenth century, 'began to demonize, polarize, and alterize' Muslims (Matar 1999: 12). For some English explorers, such as Captain John Smith, this was not difficult to do. He had begun his life of adventure battling the Ottomans in Hungary, where he was captured and became the slave of a Muslim woman (Marr 2006: 2). After escaping, he created a coat of arms emblazoned with the heads of three Turks, whom he had slain. When his ventures of exploration and conquest became transatlantic, Smith named a coastal area of northern Massachusetts after the Muslim woman who had once owned him but had treated him kindly and then named three coastal islands after those infamous three Turks from his earlier crusading life (Marr 2006: 2). Just as a Muslim woman had once come to his rescue, but is seldom remembered, Smith would become more famous for his encounter with the Native American woman, Pocahontas. But, he opined in 1616 that his countrymen 'were more interested in the Mediterranean than in America' (Matar 1999: 58). Thus, individual not just collective British experiences with Islam 'prefigured' interactions with Native Americans as the barbaric enemy Other (Marr 2006: 2–3).

The very terms used by Europeans to define Muslims reflected the fusion of hostility and misunderstanding which also crossed the Atlantic (Spellberg 2013: 25–26). The two most common pre-modern terms in English for Muslims were 'Turk' and 'Mahometan.' The former, because of the Ottoman military threat, became synonymous with all Muslims, regardless of ethnicity. By the sixteenth century, the word was hardly neutral: it signified someone 'cruel' and 'tyrannical,' a barbarian (Spellberg 2006: 489–91) Even after the Ottoman military threat subsided following the second, unsuccessful siege of Vienna in 1683, the rulers of the Ottoman North

African regencies of Tripoli, Tunis, and Algiers, were still correctly recognized by Europeans as rulers of Turkish extraction.

The word 'Mahometan,' in English usage since the sixteenth century, indicated one who (incorrectly) worshipped Muhammad, rather than, God, the more accurate description of a Muslim's beliefs (Oxford English Dictionary 1970: 6:38). Orthographical variations of this term abounded in English, while both the French and English also employed the more accurate form of 'Mussulman' or 'Mussulmen,' which was closer to the Arabic collective noun: *muslimun*. The latter European variation is still employed by the French today (Dakhlia and Vincent 2011). The English and, eventually, Americans also employed the word 'Moor,' which originally meant an inhabitant of North Africa as defined by the Roman province Mauretania, the home of the 'Maurus.' In Spanish, the equivalent became *moro*, which, like Moor, implied that the individual in question possessed dark or black skin. Hence, the term 'blackamoor' in English, the variation in Portuguese is *blackmoor* (Gomez 2005: 7; Spellberg 2013: 26).

According to Maria Elena Martínez, the evolution of an Islamic religious identity into a racial one reached its final destination in seventeenth-century Spanish America, where the word *morisco*, which originally meant a Muslim convert to Christianity, would be transformed in Mexican *casta* paintings into a reflection of racial hierarchies in the Spanish New World (Martínez 2008: 165). Thus, the Mexican Inquisition reviewed the case of Beatriz de Padilla, described in 1658 as 'an unmarried *morisca*, daughter of a Spaniard and a free *mulatta*' (Martínez 2008: 165). (The Spaniard father was understood as white, while the mother's designation as *mulatta* meant a female descendant from a white Spanish male and a black woman.) Thus, the original implication of the term *moro*, with its heritage of Islamic belief and insinuation of blackness, morphed into part of a *raza*, or race. This racial identity finally prevailed over any retention of Islam as a religious marker for the inhabitants of Mexico through the eighteenth century.

What Europeans knew about Islam on both sides of the Atlantic was the product of a Christian print culture that demonized Muslims and their beliefs. Christians, whether Catholic or Protestant, envisioned the Antichrist as an incarnation of Muhammad or the Ottoman sultan. Martin Luther (1483–1586) asserted that 'the Antichrist is at the same time the pope and the Turk, meaning the Ottoman sultan' (Forrell 1945: 264). German woodcuts dramatically reproduced these images for the illiterate (Scribner 1994: 182–83). In linking this Islamic Antichrist to his commentaries on the book of Daniel, Luther merely reconstituted and redirected an earlier Catholic theological stance, which defined the Prophet as the Antichrist's harbinger (Daniel 1966: 184–85).

Like Luther, the Protestant reformer John Calvin (1509–64) believed that the Prophet Muhammad and the pope represented the two-horned Antichrist (Slomp 1995: 134). In the sixteenth century, Catholic theologians responded to these Protestant polemics with charges of their own that excoriated Luther as no better than the Turks:

> The Turk tears down churches and destroys monasteries – so does Luther, the Turks turn convents into horse stables and make canon out of church bells – so does Luther. The Turk abuses and treats lasciviously all female persons, both secular and spiritual. Luther is just as bad for he entices monks and nuns out of their monasteries into false marriages.
>
> (Miller 1994: 146)

– CHAPTER 21: *Islam and the Atlantic* –

For one Christian, no matter what denomination, to defame a fellow believer in terms of Islam would continue as a standard libel, beginning in the sixteenth century, a slur which still persists in the Atlantic world (Spellberg 2013: 20–22).

The Englishman John Foxe (1516–87) detailed the horrible suffering of Protestant martyrs at the hands of the Ottoman Turks, with illustrations, a tract which flourished on both sides of the British Atlantic. In this text, Protestants perceived Catholics and Muslims as cruel religious enemies, with twin missions of conquest and conversion, a logical extension of their theological depiction as the Antichrist (Spellberg 2013: 17–18). In 1697, the Anglican cleric Humphrey Prideaux's anti-Islamic polemic, *The True Nature of Imposture Fully Display'd in the Life of Mahomet* became the equivalent of an Anglo-Atlantic best seller, with multiple editions in England and editions printed in Philadelphia (1758), Connecticut (1784), and Vermont (1798) (Allison 2000: 14). Great Awakening preachers such as Jonathan Edwards (1703–58) interpreted the book of Revelation to include the destruction of Islam (Marr 2006: 89). These virulently anti-Islamic Christian polemics represented the most dominant vision of Islam, not as a religion but as a heresy invented by a violent, fanatical prophet, a view that had changed little since the eighth century (Spellberg 2006: 488–89).

Yet among these predominantly anti-Islamic treatises, versions of the Qur'an also crossed the Atlantic into Dutch and British North America. To focus on just four that survived the trip reveals the variety of their provenances and reception. One of these, perhaps the earliest in North America, belonged to a man named Anthony Jansen van Salee, also known as Anthony 'the Turk' (GhaneaBassiri 2010: 9). Presumably, his surname indicates his origin from the Moroccan Atlantic citadel of Salé, a notorious port for Muslim corsairs. As Kambiz GhaneaBassiri recounts: 'Anthony immigrated to New Amsterdam sometime around 1630 as a colonist for the Dutch West India Company' (GhaneaBassiri 2010: 9). His father was, most likely, a Dutch privateer, who had fought the Spanish in the Mediterranean, but was captured by Muslim raiders from North Africa and converted to Islam, reaching the status of admiral under the ruler or Morocco. Anthony's mother was believed to be Moroccan. When he died in 1676, he left in his will to his New York City descendants his copy of the Qur'an (GhaneaBassiri 2010: 9). In what language was this Qur'an? We do not know. But its preservation and passage to his descendants by this man of Islamic heritage suggests the importance it retained for its owner.

Although 'the Turk's' Qur'an was probably the earliest copy to reach North America, there were others which followed close behind. Cotton Mather (d. 1728), a scion of Puritan Massachusetts Bay, made several un-ironic allusions to the Qur'an in *The Christian Philosopher* (1721), a treatise which asserts 'the harmony between science and religion' (Mather 1994: lxix). The section which refers to the Qur'an begins rather unflatteringly: 'To render us more sensible thereof [of modern philosophy], we will propose a few points of the Mahometan Philosophy, or Secrets reveal'd unto Mahomet, which none of his Followers, who cover so much of the Earth at this Day, may dare to question' (Mather 1994: 110). Mather, as Christian Scientist, then goes on to paraphrase Qur'anic references to natural phenomenon such as the stars in the heavens (Mather 1994: 111, 346–47; Qur'an 37: 6–10); earthquakes (Mather 1994: 111, 347; Qur'an: 214:33), and thunder/thunderbolts (Mather 1994: 111, 347; Qur'an 18:40). Mather probably owned the first English translation of the Qur'an, done in 1649 by Alexander Ross, based on an earlier

French version (Matar 1998: 79). There was an initial uproar in London over this translation, which many feared would encourage good Christians to embrace Islam. For a time, the publisher was thrown in prison (Matar 1998: 76–82). Ross ultimately defended his work, asserting that staunch Christians would not be inveigled away from their faith. The history of European translations of the Qur'an continued to be inextricably linked to Christian polemic (Elmarsafy 2009: 1–2). Thus, owning a Qur'an did not necessarily contribute to a Christian's accurate understanding of Islam.

Yet the Christian philosopher Mather referenced not only the Qur'an, but also a quite different translation of a work of medieval Islamic philosophy by Ibn Tufayl (d. 1185). This work, originally titled *Hayy ibn Yaqzan* in Arabic, Mather cited from either a Latin version, translated in 1671 as *Philosophus Autodidactus*, or a later seventeenth-century English translation of the tale, which came to be known as *The Self-Taught Philosopher*. Mather praised the Muslim philosopher, who, 'more than five hundred years ago,' had demonstrated that 'without any Teacher, but Reason in a serious View of Nature, led to the Acknowledgment of a Glorious GOD' (Mather 1994:11–12). Mather praised Ibn Tufayl for already demonstrating in his allegory what the native of Massachusetts also attempted to prove in his Christian philosophy: that by simply 'using his Rational Faculties,' one would inevitably come to understand not only natural science, but also accept the existence of God. Mather exclaimed: '*God has thus far taught* a Mahometan!' which Mather intended, in turn, as a lesson for fellow Protestant Christians (Mather 1994: 12). In the midst of a plethora of predominantly biased, negative information about Islam, Cotton Mather demonstrated that other avenues of Islamic learning also could influence devout Christians across the Atlantic.

Mather was not alone in being influenced by this Islamic philosophical tract. It is probable that John Locke derived his view of the mind as a *tabula rasa* from it, for the son of Edward Pococke, his favorite professor and first chair of Arabic at Oxford, had translated the treatise in 1671, the year in which John Locke began his *Essay on Human Understanding*. Historians speculate about the impact of this Islamic philosophical tract on Locke's work (Russell 1994: 236–53). But Locke was not alone in this regard. Englishmen as different as the Society of Friends' leader George Keith and Daniel Defoe were influenced by Ibn Tufayl's work, with many suggesting that the prototype for *Robinson Crusoe* had been derived from the Islamic allegory (Russell 1994: 236–53).

The Qur'an bought by Thomas Jefferson in 1765, eleven years before writing the Declaration of Independence, was the first translation made directly from Arabic to English. The task was undertaken in 1734 by the Anglican lawyer George Sale. He learned his Arabic in London from two Syrian Christians. At the time Jefferson bought the Qur'an, he was a student of law in Williamsburg, Virginia (Spellberg 2013: 81–82).

Although this version of the Qur'an was financed by an Anglican missionary society, Sale's Qur'an, as it came to be known, was by far the most accurate translation then available. Jefferson would have been struck by Sale's depiction of the Prophet Muhammad as 'the lawgiver of the Arabians' (Sale 1984: A2). Most Europeans had long denied the Qur'an as a book of revelation, defaming the Prophet as an 'impostor' and religious fanatic. However, Sale, in his 200-page

– CHAPTER 21: *Islam and the Atlantic* –

'Preliminary Discourse' demonstrated, for the time, a more even-handed approach to the faith of Islam. Although he defamed the Prophet as the author of a 'false religion,' he nevertheless praised his virtues, which included 'piety, veracity, justice, liberality, clemency, humility, and abstinence' (Sale 1984: 178). Sale also denied that Islam had been spread by the sword, a common Christian claim since the eighth century, and refused to condemn the Prophet's polygamy, a standard defamation, asserted in contrast to the celibate Jesus. Instead, Sale emphasized that the Hebrew prophets had taken more than one wife (Sale 1984: 178). For his condemnation of the anti-Islamic polemic of his countryman Humphrey Prideaux, the historian Edward Gibbon would dub Sale posthumously in 1788 as 'half a Mussulman' (Spellberg 2013: 271).

There is no direct evidence about what Jefferson learned from his Qur'an or its lengthy 'Preliminary Discourse,' in which Sale outlined Islamic history, ritual, and law. But he would not be the only American president to own the Muslim sacred text. In 1806, former president John Adams bought the first edition of the Qur'an printed in the U.S. at Springfield, Massachusetts (Qur'an 1806). This was not Sale's translation, but the American printing of the first English version of 1649, a text translated from a French original. Arabic Qur'ans have been identified among Muslim slaves in Georgia, Trinidad, Brazil, and Jamaica (Diouf 1998: 113).

Despite access to the Qur'an, it is clear that during Jefferson's lifetime he absorbed and expressed quite negative views of the faith, based on European precedents. For example, in 1776, he advanced the argument that Muslims only wanted to know what was in their Qur'an, and nothing more, a view he adopted directly from the French *philosophe* Voltaire (Spellberg 2013: 103). This assertion he raised in debate in the Virginia House of Delegates, arguing that Islam, like Catholicism, repressed 'free enquiry' (Spellberg 2013: 103).

However, in the very same year, a few months after writing the Declaration, Jefferson recorded in his notes this pivotal precedent from his intellectual hero, the English philosopher John Locke's *Letter on Toleration* (1689): '[He] sais: "neither Pagan nor Mahometan nor Jew ought to be excluded from the civil rights of the Commonwealth because of his religion"' (Jefferson 1950, 1: 548; Spellberg 2006: 490). Jefferson would reaffirm this same assertion in his autobiography in 1821, five years before his death. Despite prosecuting as president an undeclared war against the North African kingdom of Tripoli, the Founder insisted that his most important legislation, A Bill for Establishing Religious Freedom, made law in 1786, included protections for Muslim civil rights. He asserted that the Bill 'meant to comprehend within the mantle of its protection, the Jew and the Gentile, the Christian and Mahometan, the Hindoo, and the Infidel of every denomination' (Jefferson 1998: 46; Spellberg 2006: 490). Presumably, Jefferson's principled forecast for the inclusion of future Muslims as American citizens construed them as white – and free.

It is clear that Jefferson never connected the Muslims in his theory of political equality with the actual practice of Islam in America, where practitioners of the faith may well have labored on his own plantations. Although this cannot be proved for Jefferson, based on slave nomenclature, we know that George Washington owned at least two Muslim slaves. We find on his 1774 list of taxable 'items' the names of two Muslim slaves: 'Fatimer' and 'Little Fatimer,' two women indubitably named after the Prophet's daughter, Fatima (d. 632) (Thompson 2010: 2:392–93).

383

As the historian Michael Gomez has stated, 'Muslims arrived in North America by the thousands, if not tens of thousands' (Gomez 2005: 166). This means that this religious minority outnumbered Jews in the eighteenth century, and possibly, Catholics awash in a Protestant majority. Neither Washington nor Jefferson ever attested to witnessing the practice of Islam on their plantations. Reasons for this may vary, but certainly include the fact that Muslims were a minority among slaves, and may well have practiced their faith singly – and in secret.

Jefferson's inclusive view of future Muslim citizens co-existed with his predominantly, but not exclusively, negative view of Islam as a faith (Spellberg 2013: 236–39). In this seemingly contradictory position, he was not alone, for Roger Williams, often designated as the earliest champion of religious liberty in North America, professed similar views. Although Jefferson adopted the idea of Muslims as future citizens with civil rights from Locke, not Williams, the founder of the Providence Colony in Rhode Island also condemned Islam, even while he defended the liberty of conscience of its adherents. Echoing standard Protestant defamations of both the Prophet and the head of the Roman Catholic Church, Williams forecast that 'the Pope and Mahomet' would soon be in the 'Ashes' of hell (Williams 1963: 5: Dedication 3). Muslims, in his estimation, had no chance of salvation.

But the heretical belief that Muslims, indeed all believers, would be saved regardless of their faith – did exist among some Catholics throughout the Atlantic world, as Stuart Schwartz has demonstrated for both the Portuguese and Spanish empires (Schwartz 2008). In cases brought before the Inquisition, this belief would be condemned as the heresy of Origen of Alexandria (d. 254). It was not unknown for even Old Christians, those without the 'taint' of previous Jewish or Muslim ancestry, to swear, as the peasant Juana Perez did before the Spanish Inquisition in 1488 that 'the good Jew would be saved and the good Moor, in his law, and why else had God made them?' (Schwartz 2008: 22). But, it also should be remembered, that Roger Williams described his own brother in Providence as one who 'runs strongly to Origins's [sic] notion of universal mercy at last, against an eternal sentence' (Williams 1963: 5: xxxii, n. 1). While such beliefs are not quantifiable, they existed among both Protestants and Catholics in the Spanish and British Atlantic spheres amidst virulent anti-Islamic sentiment.

Also coexisting with Williams' dire salvific forecasts, we see the earliest expression of his embrace of universal religious toleration that included Muslims in his *The Bloudy Tenent of Persecution, for Cause of Conscience*, published in 1644.

More than ten times, Williams defended the right of Muslims to worship freely, without coercion or violence perpetrated upon them by Christian ruling authorities (Spellberg 2013: 58). In one such passage, he invoked their future as neighbors whose beliefs should not be the subject of state control.

> And I ask, whether or no such as may hold forth other *Worships* or *Religions* (*Jews, Turkes,* or *Antichristians*) may not be peaceable and quiet *Subjects*, loving and helpfull *neighbours*, faire and just *dealers*, true and loyall to the *civill government*? It is clear they may from all *Reason* and *Experience* in many flourishing *Cities* and *Kingdoms* of the World and so offend not against the *civill State* and *Peace*; nor incurre the punishment of the *civill sword*...
>
> (Williams 1963: 3: 142)

– CHAPTER 21: *Islam and the Atlantic* –

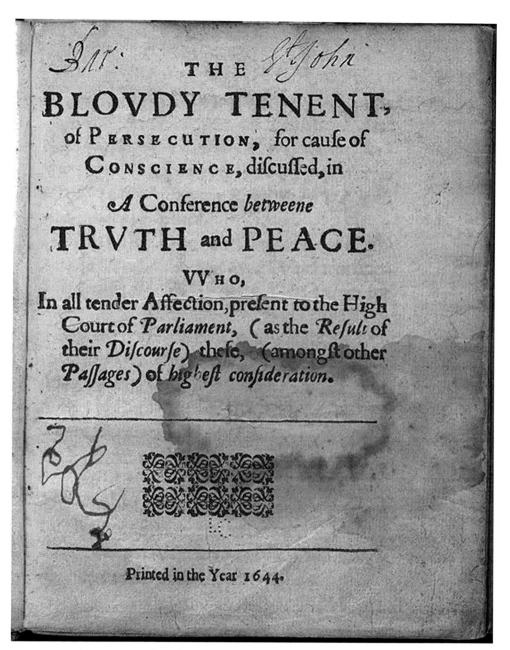

Figure 21.1   The title page of Roger Williams' 'Bloudy Tenent' 1644
Courtesy Library of Congress

As a working template for an ideal government, Williams as President of Providence Plantations, adopted a truly Atlantic metaphor – a ship of state – in 1655, one in which 'It hath fallen out sometimes, that both papists and protestants, Jews and Turks, may be embarked upon one ship; upon which supposal I affirm, that all the liberty of conscience, that I ever pleaded for, turns upon these two hinges – that none of the papists, protestants, Jews or Turks, be forced to come to the ship's prayers or worship..., if they practice any' (Williams 1963: 6: 278–79). In this vessel, he made room, once again for Muslims – and Jews – and even Catholics, at a time when all three were despised on both sides of the Atlantic by English Protestant majorities. Historians who have remarked upon the inclusion of Jews in this vision often have argued that by adding Muslims to this list of believers, Williams was actually further marginalizing Jews from the normative Christian viewpoint (Cohen 1992: 17). But this was not his intention, for Williams sought to extend the religious toleration of the government to *all* believers. By including Muslims in his purview, he was making a case for a universal, if still theoretical, category of religious inclusion in the Atlantic world, one that would be echoed indirectly by both Locke and Jefferson.

Although Williams claims to have met and conversed with real Muslims in his homeland (Williams 1988: 2:664), there is no evidence that any actual Muslims applied to become members of his colony, despite a recent rather dubious declaration in *Jews and Muslims in British Colonial America: A Genealogical History*, which states as an unverified assertion: 'The presence of Jews and Muslims among its [Rhode Island's] settlers, and Freemasons, is to be expected' (Hirschman and Yates 2012: 187). While there is certainly evidence of a Sephardic Jewish population in Newport, there is absolutely no proof of an active Muslim presence in Williams' colony of Rhode Island.

Yet, even in Dutch Long Island, settlers forecast and defended the ideal of Muslim religious liberty from government control in 1657, presumably, without the presence of real practitioners of Islam. (This was two years after Williams' vision of his multi-religious ship of state.) We find this idea endorsed in a document that would come to be known as the Flushing Remonstrance. The thirty-one signatories invoked the Golden Rule 'desireing to doe unto all men as wee desire all men shoulde doe unto us,' and included 'Jews, Turkes and Egyptians' in their plea for the colonial government of Long Island to stay out of religious matters – for all believers (Dreisbach and Hall 2009: 108–9).

While Williams forecast that Muslims might one day be passengers on his ideal ship of state, he never envisioned the very different transatlantic voyage described by a real Muslim named Ibrahima Abd al-Rahman, a West African slave from Guinea, bound for servitude in North America in 1788. (The Arabic *Ibrahim*, for Abraham, as pronounced by native speakers of African languages, ended in a vowel.) As part of an autobiography he dictated, Ibrahima wrote:

> They sold me directly, with fifty others to an English ship. They took me to the island of Dominica. After that I was taken to New Orleans. Then they took me to Natchez, and Colonel F[oster] bought me. I have lived with Colonel F. 40 years. Thirty years I labored hard. The last ten years I have been indulged a good deal.
>
> (Austin 1997: 81)

– CHAPTER 21: *Islam and the Atlantic* –

Through a series of extraordinary coincidences, Ibrahima was granted his freedom, with the proviso by his owner that he only exercise it once he returned to Africa. Pleading on Ibrahima's behalf, a local newspaper editor wrote the senator from Mississippi, identifying the slave as Moroccan, with a plea that he be allowed to return to his homeland (Alford 2007: 98). This mistake reflected the enduring but false American assumption that all Muslims must be from North rather than West Africa, even in 1826. Ibrahima played up this distinction, insisting that he was a 'Moor,' and not a 'negro' (Gomez 2005: 181–82). Included in the letter sent to the senator was a missive written by Ibrahima in Arabic, which was supposed to be a letter to the ruler of Morocco, but, in reality, was a passage of the Qur'an. The U.S. government attempted to use Ibrahima's Islamic identity to curry favor with the ruler of Morocco, and the sultan volunteered to pay for the slave's passage to his putative homeland. However, when Ibrahima actually met the president, he admitted that he would rather go to Liberia, which was closer to his actual home (Alford 2007: 120).

By 1828, Ibrahima would be described as 'the most famous African in America,' because before returning across the Atlantic to Africa, he went on a tour of northeastern cities, speaking and often demonstrating his Arabic literacy. When asked to write the Lord's Prayer in Arabic, he instead wrote the *Fatiha*, the Qur'an's opening chapter, a subterfuge never identified by his audiences (Austin 1997: 66).

Ibrahima pretended to embrace Christianity to merit the sponsorship of the American Colonization Society, dedicated to sending free blacks back to Africa to do business and spread Christianity. In multiple appearances, he attempted to raise money to free all of his children and grandchildren, but he failed, and Ibrahima despaired: 'I desire to go back to my country again; but when I think of my children, it hurts my feelings. If I go to my own country, I cannot feel happy, if my children are left' (Austin 1997: 81). Although his American supporters were convinced of his Christianity, when Ibrahima spied the shores of Africa in 1829, he began to pray publicly as a Muslim, a faith he had never renounced. He died a few months after his return, never finding his way back to his original homeland. His story has been told by Terry Alford, in his biography, *Prince Among Slaves* and, most recently, on television by the Public Broadcasting Corporation, as narrated by Mos Def, in 2008.

The Arabic literacy of Ibrahima changed his life, providing him with the singular opportunity to return from America across the Atlantic to Africa. More than seventy-five other cases of Arabic literacy have been documented throughout the Atlantic world exclusively among men (Austin 1997). However, in West Africa, some estimate that up to 20 percent of Muslim girls would have attended Qur'an schools, the equivalent of primary instruction, and, along with boys would have learned some Arabic (Diouf 1998: 7). Evidence of female Muslim slave literacy does not exist, but that does not mean that all Muslim women who crossed the Atlantic were illiterate. Fewer literate girls and women were enslaved and transported, and fewer of those who survived the Middle Passage would have known Arabic, resulting in this dearth of written evidence. However, while such literacy might signal the particular intelligence of individual Muslim male slaves, it often became part of a tactic for asserting their 'superiority' over non-Muslim slaves. Michael Gomez has explained this tendency as the result of some Muslims identifying in their past African lives as slaveholders themselves, who often traced their ancestry to early Arab conquerors

387

Figure 21.2 Ibrahima Abd al-Rahman, also known as 'Prince'.
Caption in Arabic in his own hand reads: 'His name is Abd al-Rahman.'
Courtesy Library of Congress

(Gomez 2005: 178–79). In Africa, too, Muslims would have elevated their practice of Islam over other, enemy tribes of non-Muslims. This pronounced self-definition of Muslim slave superiority was further enhanced by education and literacy in Arabic, which, in turn, allowed slave masters to singularize those who professed Islam among the Africans they owned.

While Muslim demonstrations of Arabic literacy often resulted in elevated status and better treatment, the ability to read and/or write was often viewed as suspect by white owners, and could be dangerous, because in the U.S. teaching any slave to write was illegal (Diouf 1998: 106–8; Lepore 2002: 125–28). But, when Muslims arrived from Africa with Arabic literacy, there was little colonial officials throughout the Atlantic world could do. There is no question that literacy linked Muslim identity to slave agency.

The Inquisition in Spanish colonies actively prosecuted those thought to be writing Islamic amulets for protection. And Spanish colonial authorities repeatedly blamed Muslim slaves and former slaves as troublemakers for precipitating uprisings among Native Americans in Hispaniola (1522–32), Mexico (1523), Cuba (1529), Panama (1550–82), Venezuela (1550), Peru (1560), Ecuador (1599), Guatemala (1627), Chile (1647), and Martinique (1650) (Diouf 1998: 147).

By the time of the Haitian slave revolt in 1791, there was a clear connection between the written Arabic word and the uprising, according to both Michael Gomez and Sylviane Diouf (Gomez 2005: 86–87; Diouf 1998: 128–34). On this sugar-producing island, Tamerlan, a forty-four year old slave named after the Turkic world conqueror Tamerlane (d. 1405), 'had written over twenty lines,' of Arabic. When questioned by a French authority, he identified the writing as 'a prayer' (Gomez 2005: 86–87). Two months later, the Haitian Revolution began. French authorities insisted that the leaders were Muslim – and that they were communicating in Arabic. Michael Gomez believes it more likely that these short texts were, in fact, amulets, verses of the Qur'an preserved on paper, designed to be worn, usually in leather wrappings, concealed on one's person as protection (Gomez 2005: 87–90; Diouf 1998: 128–31).

Arabic amulets served a similar function in the slave revolt in Bahia, Brazil in 1835, where sugar was also the main export (Reis 1993: 15). There remains some irony in the economic centrality of this crop, pioneered and diffused by Muslims to Europe, then transferred to imperial colonies throughout the Atlantic, which then required a steady stream of West African, often Muslim slaves, for production. The sugar economy spun a connective Islamic web from the introduction of this crop to Europe, through to the Atlantic presence of Muslim slaves, who would foment revolts against those who used their labor to produce this commodity.

The classic treatment of the Bahia slave revolt is by João José Reis, who notes that while Muslims may have led the revolt, they were not in the religious majority (Reis 1993: 97). However, Reis emphasizes that this uprising was not equivalent to *jihad*, or any exceptional Islamic quest for dominion in the New World (Reis 1993: 128). While leaders of the revolt were often designated as *Malês*, from *mu'allim*, for religious teacher, they also rallied non-Muslims to join them. Islamic leaders united Africans, all of whom were black and unfree. That these scraps of paper bore writing, even in Arabic, proved a powerful part of the attraction for non-Muslims who had known only oral culture (Diouf 1998: 129).

One of the reasons non-Muslims joined the Bahia revolt may be explained by their belief in the power of Islamic amulets. Almost always these papers included the *bismillah* in Arabic: 'In the name of Allah, the compassionate, the merciful' (Reis 1993: 100–101). But this ubiquitous phrase in Muslim life might then also include either verses from the Qur'an about protection from the 'infidel,' or other, more magical repetitions of shapes and letters. For example, one talisman invoked the names of the angels Gabriel and Michael, the former believed by Muslims to have conveyed God's word in Arabic to the Prophet (Reis 1993: 100). The power of these amulets lay not just in their religious statements, but was also the product of the *baraka*, or blessing, imbued by the special spiritual power of the men who produced them. All of them were apotropaic in design, but some warded off mundane threats from humans and spirits. Others were intended to ward off death, most directly in the revolts. In contradiction to this hope, some of these amulets were recovered from the bodies of slaves who died in the Brazilian uprising, a testament to the finite limits of their power (Reis 1993: 99–100).

'With a documented presence of five hundred years,' writes Sylviane Diouf, 'Islam was, after Catholicism, the second monotheist religion introduced into post-Columbian America' (Diouf 1998: 179). If one counts Judaism, it was, perhaps, the third. Yet Diouf is right to point out that unlike other religions brought by Europeans, 'not one community currently practices Islam as passed on by preceding African generations' (Diouf 1998: 179). While a few survivals of Muslim practice were recorded along the coast of Georgia in the 1930s by the WPA, only tantalizing glimpses of possible survivals in other African religions, as well as material culture and music echo today (Gomez 2005: 155–56). They are the subject of continuing study. Islam, as a living monotheism, would not return to the Caribbean, South America, and the United States until the last quarter of the nineteenth century, when new Muslim immigrants from the Middle East appeared.

While the remnants of Islam as a religion introduced into the Atlantic world with a real West African Muslim slave population in the pre-modern era have withered, what remains robust is the struggle to define the place of the faith as an intellectual and religious construct with resonant implications for contemporary Muslims. Images of Muslims as the eternal enemy Other thrive, sharing much in common with pre-modern Atlantic antecedents. Such negative precedents continue to conflict with those unique voices who once challenged the predominance of these stereotypes, and, in a variety of radical assertions, insisted upon the premise of tolerance, inclusion, and civic equality for all believers, including the adherents of Islam. The outcome of this embattled Atlantic past remains to be resolved – on both sides of the ocean.

REFERENCES

Terry Alford, *Prince Among Slaves* (New York: Oxford University Press, 1977, rptd 2007).
Robert J. Allison, *The Crescent Obscured: The United States and the Muslim World, 1776–1815* (Chicago: Chicago University Press, 2000).
Allan D. Austin, *African Muslims in Antebellum America: Transatlantic Stories and Spiritual Struggles* (New York: Routledge, 1997).
William J. Bennetta, '*Arab World Studies Notebook* lobs Muslim propaganda at teachers.' The Textbook League, October 2003. http://www.textbookleague.org/spwich.htm (accessed April 30, 2014).
Kristen Block, *Ordinary Lives in the Caribbean: Religion Colonial Competition, and the Politics of Profit* (Athens: Univgersity of Georgia Press, 2012).
Judith Ann Carney, *Black Rice: The African Origins of Rice Cultivation in the Americas* (Cambridge, MA: Harvard University Press, 2001).
Naomi Cohen, *Jews in Christian America: The Pursuit of Religious Equality* (New York: Oxford University Press, 1992).

– CHAPTER 21: *Islam and the Atlantic* –

Karoline P. Cook, 'Forbidden Crossings: Morisco Emigration to Spanish America, 1492–1650,' (PhD diss., Princeton University, 2008).

Jocelyne Dakhlia and Bernard Vincent, eds., *Les musulmans dans l'histoire de l'Europe* (Paris: Albin Michel, 2011).

Norman Daniel, *Islam and the West: The Making of an Image* (Edinburgh: Edinburgh University Press, 1966).

Sylviane Diouf, *Servants of Allah: African Muslims Enslaved in the Americas* (New York: New York University Press, 1998).

Jerald F. Dirks, *Muslims in American History: A Forgotten Legacy* (Beltsville, MD: Amana Publications, 2006).

Daniel L. Dreisbach and Mark David Hall, eds., 'The Flushing Remonstrance,' in *The Sacred Rights of Conscience: Selected Readings on Religious Liberty and Church-State Relations in the American Founding* (Indianapolis, IN: Liberty Fund, 2009).

Ziad Elmarsafy, *The Enlightenment Qur'an: The Politics of Translation and the Construction of Islam* (Oxford: Oneworld Press, 2009).

George W. Forrell, 'Luther and the War against the Turks,' *Church History* 14:4 (1945): 256–71.

Kambiz GhaneaBassiri, *A History of Islam in America* (New York: Cambridge University Press, 2010).

Thomas S. Glick, *The Old World Background of the Irrigation System of San Antonio, Texas* (El Paso, TX: University of El Paso Press, 1972).

Michael A. Gomez, *Black Crescent: The Experience of African Muslims in the Americas* (New York: Cambridge University Press, 2005).

Max Harris, *Aztecs, Moors, and Christians: Festivals of Reconquest in Mexico and Spain* (Austin, TX: University of Texas Press, 2000).

Elizabeth Hirschman and Donald Yates, *Jews and Muslims in British Colonial America, A Genealogical History* (Jefferson, NC: McFarland, 2012).

Thomas Jefferson, 'Autobiography,' in *The Life and Selected Writings of Thomas Jefferson*, eds. Adrienne Koch and William Peden (New York: The Modern Library, 1998), 7–104.

——, *The Papers of Thomas Jefferson*, ed. Julian P. Boyd et al. 40 vols. (Princeton: Princeton University Press, 1950).

Jill Lepore, *A Is for American: Letters and Other Characters in the Newly United States* (New York: Alfred A. Knopf, 2002).

Timothy Marr, *The Cultural Roots of American Islamicism* (New York: Cambridge University Press, 2006).

'Mahometan,' in *The Oxford English Dictionary*, 13 vols (Oxford: Clarendon Press, 1970), 6:38.

María Elena Martínez, *Genealogical Fictions: Limpieza de Sangre, Religion, and Gender in Colonial Mexico* (Stanford, CA: Stanford University Press, 2008).

Nabil Matar, *Islam in Britain, 1558–1685* (New York: Cambridge University Press, 1998).

——, *Turks, Moors & Englishmen in the Age of Discovery* (New York: Columbia University Press, 1999).

Cotton Mather, *The Christian Philosopher*, ed. Winton U. Solberg (Urbana and Chicago: University of Illinois Press, 1994).

Gregory H. Miller, 'Holy War, Holy Terror: Views of Islam in German Pamphlet Literature,' (PhD diss., University of Michigan, 1994).

Oxford English Dictionary. 13 vols. (Oxford: Clarendon Press, 1970).

The Qur'an: Commonly Called the Alcoran of Mahomet (Springfield, MA: Henry Brewer for Isaiah Thomas, 1806). John Adams Library, Boston Public Library, Boston, Massachusetts.

João José Reis, *Slave Rebellion in Brazil: The Muslim Uprising of 1835 in Bahia*, Arthur Brakel, trans. (Baltimore, MD: Johns Hopkins University Press, 1993).

G.A. Russell, 'The Impact of the *Philosphus Autodidactus*: Pocockes, John Locke and the Society of Friends,' *The 'Arabick' Interest of the Natural Philosophers in Seventeenth-Century England*, ed. G.A. Russell (Leiden: E.J. Brill, 1994): 236–53.

George Sale, trans. *The Koran* (1734) (New York: Garland Press, 1984).

Stuart B. Schwartz, *All Can Be Saved: Religious Tolerance and Salvation in the Iberian Atlantic* (New Haven, CT: Yale University Press, 2008).

R.W. Scribner, *For the Sake of the Simple Folk: Popular Propaganda for the German Reformation* (Oxford: Clarendon Press, 1994).

Fuat Sezgin, *Mathematical Geography and Cartography in Islam and Their Continuation in the Occident*. Vol. 4. English version of Vol. XIII of *Geschichte Des Arabischen Schriftums*. Translated by Renata Sarma and S.R. Sarma. Revised by Guy Moore and Geoff Sammon (Frankfurt am Main: Institute for the History of Arabic-Islamic Science at the Johann Wolfgang Goethe University, 2011).

Jan Slomp, 'Calvin and the Turks,' in *Christian-Muslim Encounters*, ed. Yvonne Y. Haddad and Wadi Haddad (Gainesville, FL: University of Florida Press, 1995), 126–142.

Denise A. Spellberg, 'Inventing Matamoras: Gender and the Forgotten Islamic Past in the United States of America,' *Frontiers: A Journal of Women Studies* 25:1(2004): 148–64.

——, 'Could a Muslim be President? An Eighteenth-Century Constitutional Debate', *Eighteenth-Century Studies*, 39:4(2006): 485–506.

——, *Thomas Jefferson's Qur'an: Islam and the Founders* (New York: Alfred A. Knopf, 2013).

Mary V. Thompson, 'Mount Vernon,' *Encyclopedia of Muslim-American History*, ed. Edward E. Curtis IV, 2 vols. (New York: Facts on File, 2010), 2: 392–93.

Andrew M. Watson, *Agricultural Innovation in the Early Islamic World: The Diffusion of Crops and Farming Techniques, 700–1000* (Cambridge: Cambridge University Press, 1983).

Roger Williams, *The Bloody Tenent of Persecution*, ed. Samuel L, Calwell, vol. 3 in The Complete Writings of Roger Williams, 7 vols. (New York: Russell and Russell, 1963).

——, *The Correspondence of Roger Williams*, ed. Glen LaFantasie, 2 vols. (Providence, RI: Brown University Press/University Press of New England, 1988).

——, *George Fox Digg'd out of His Burrowes*, ed. J. Lewis Diman, vol. 5 in The Complete Writings of Roger Williams, 7 vols. (New York: Russell and Russell, 1963).

——, *The Letters of Roger Williams*, ed. John Russell Bartlett, vol. 6 in The Complete Writings of Roger Williams, 7 vols. (New York: Russell and Russell, 1963).

CHAPTER TWENTY-TWO

AMERICAN IDENTITY AND ENGLISH CATHOLICISM IN THE ATLANTIC WORLD

——·◆·——

Maura Jane Farrelly

The American Revolution was more than just a physical conflict or the ultimate articulation of an Enlightenment, 'contractarian' approach to government.[1] When they broke away from the parent country and declared their full and absolute independence from Great Britain, England's colonists in North America took a step that had profoundly cultural and psychological implications, as well.

The colonists had always thought of themselves as 'English,' after all.[2] Even the ones who came to Pennsylvania from Saxony or New York from Sweden understood in the eighteenth century that what they were living in was an 'English' colony. Indeed, one of the many paradoxes of the American Revolution was that when they rebelled against England, the Patriots claimed to be doing so in the name of the 'rights of Englishmen.' England's government, they believed, had once been the world's most ardent protector of human beings' natural rights to property, political representation, personal security, and the rule of law. The English system had become corrupt, however – sullied by the power-mongering of dishonest MPs who had grown greedy and 'corpulent' as a consequence of the wealth brought into England by the mercantilist, colonial system.[3] To protect themselves from the gangrenous qualities of this unfortunate corruption, the colonists believed they needed to separate themselves from the disease's source – to 'chop off their right arms,' so to speak, and forge a new identity for themselves without the assistance of that appendage that had been such a vital part of who they were.

To protect their rights as Englishmen, in other words, the residents of England's colonies had to proclaim that they were not 'English' anymore. The success of the independence movement, then, raised the unavoidable question of who these former colonists were, now that they were no longer English. More to the point, it challenged the first two or three generations of Americans to forge a cultural path for their grandchildren and great-grandchildren to follow in a brand-new country that had no common language or religion, and where many of the traditional ties of national heritage had been thrown off voluntarily.

Historians have typically taught that the creation of a distinct and recognizably 'American' national identity took place between 1815 and 1860. It was during these decades that the United States expanded its reach to the Pacific Ocean; the steam

393

engine, 'Waltham System,' and a growing network of canals, railroads, and telegraph lines launched the so-called Market Revolution; race-based slavery was challenged and ultimately outlawed; and Calvinist Orthodoxy, with its high-minded intellectualism, limited atonement, and staunchly individualistic approach to salvation was replaced by a gentler, more 'democratic' variety of evangelicalism that was still pretty judgmental and individualistic, but nevertheless offered the promise of salvation to everyone, not just the elect – and also did not require a Harvard degree, as barely literate itinerate preachers like the Methodist Peter Cartwright made clear.[4]

I am not looking to challenge this narrative in any way. I think it is useful – but more than that, I also think it is quite accurate.

I do want to suggest, however, that there were pockets of people who became 'American' long before the Erie Canal was built in 1824, if by 'American' we mean an identity that is committed to more than just democratic individualism and free-market capitalism. If we add to that mix a commitment to republicanism, church–state separation, and religious pluralism – and if we remember that to become 'American' one had to see oneself as 'non-English' first – then I think one of the first populations of Americans may actually have been the Catholic population in eighteenth-century Maryland, making colonial Maryland very important to scholars' understanding of how New World experiences shaped – and even changed – Old World identities.

Now, anyone who is familiar with the Catholic mindset or the Church's history will realize that the claim I am making is a somewhat bizarre one. The Catholic Church, after all, did not actually embrace the principle of church–state separation until 1965, when the Second Vatican Council drafted its statement on religious freedom, *Dignitatis Humanae*. The Catholic Church, of course, is hardly democratic in its sensibilities. True freedom has never been the purview of the individual for a Catholic, the way it is for most Americans; true freedom for a Catholic is found within the community – and with the assistance – of the Church. On top of this, the rhetoric leading up to the American Revolution, which was really the ultimate articulation of the principles that would define American identity, was vehemently anti-Catholic. George III's decision to allow the free practice of Catholicism in Quebec was *the key* development that convinced the colonists that the King, as opposed to simply Parliament, could no longer be relied upon to protect their liberties. As one veteran from New Hampshire recalled in 1821, the common cry of the Patriots was, 'No King, No Popery.'[5]

'American' identity, scholars such as John McGreevy and Jay Dolan have acknowledged, is not – and never has been – a natural fit for Catholics. There is an inherent tension between the individualistic foundation of America's cultural identity and the communal and hierarchical orientation of Catholicism's understanding of society, authority, morality, and salvation. It would be wrong to say that the American and Catholic traditions are entirely incompatible with one another; nevertheless, it is true that Catholicism is, in the words of Dolan, 'rooted in traditions very different from those of American culture' – and that before the Church reforms of the 1960s, the differences between the two traditions could be quite sharp.[6]

Yet, the Catholics living in British colonial America at the time of the Revolution understood the individualistic, rights-oriented language of America's Founders and embraced the notion of republican government and church–state separation that animated the first generation of Americans. Outside Canada, most of Britain's colonial Catholics lived in Maryland, a colony that had been founded in 1634 by an English Catholic nobleman. They supported the independence movement in numbers that were proportionately greater than those of their Protestant neighbors, as evidenced by their donations to the Continental Army and their service in that army, as well as their membership in local committees of safety and the militia units from Maryland that patrolled the Chesapeake Bay and saw action in New Jersey and Long Island.[7]

Protestants in Maryland, who were the majority, were quite reluctant initially to participate in the boycotts and non-importation agreements leading up to the Revolution, prompting John Adams to recall many years later that 'neither the State of Maryland, nor [any] of their Delegates were very early in their conviction of the necessity of independence.'[8] Unlike the other colonies, Maryland had £25,000 sterling in the Bank of England, which allowed it to get around a prohibition on the issuing of paper money that was a part of the widely hated Currency Act of 1764. In 1766, Maryland's assembly issued more than £40,000 in paper bills, an action that no other colony could take and a freedom that tended to make the imperative of independence less economically obvious to merchants in Maryland.[9]

But not everyone in Maryland looked at independence primarily in economic terms. John Adams might be forgiven for not noticing that the colony's sluggish response to the question of independence was peppered with a healthy dash of Catholic ardency. The only Catholic man present at the meeting of the First Continental Congress in 1774 was Charles Carroll of Carrollton, and he was there in an advisory capacity only; as an advisor, Carroll tended to express his opinions solely within the confines of Maryland's delegation. Nevertheless, Charles Carroll revealed his staunch support for the independence movement a year and a half after the Continental Congress met for the first time, when he and his cousin, John – a priest who had been born in Maryland and trained by the Society of Jesus in Europe – traveled to Quebec on the Congress's behalf in a failed effort to get Canada's Catholic majority to sign onto the independence movement.[10]

Why Maryland's Catholics were so willing to embrace independence from England when their Protestant neighbors were not – and when the individualistic tenets that the independence movement rested upon were far more compatible with a Protestant theological outlook than they were with a Catholic one – is a story that reveals much about both the role of cultural context in the creation of Catholic identity and the role of religious experience in the creation of American identity. As such, the story of Maryland's Catholics in the decades leading up to the American Revolution has much to teach scholars who are seeking to understand the parameters of cultural exchange in the Atlantic World.

Until Quebec became a part of the British Empire in 1763 as a consequence of France's loss to England in the Seven Years War, Maryland was home to the largest concentration of Catholics in British colonial America. St. Mary's County, on the southern tip of the western shore of the Chesapeake, was the initial area settled when the first colonists arrived in Cecilius Calvert's colony in 1634, and for the entire colonial period, then, St. Mary's was the county that had the largest number of Catholics living within it.

395

Figure 22.1   Virginia, Maryland, Chesapeake Bay
©Antiquarian Images/Mary Evans

– CHAPTER 22: *American identity and English Catholicism* –

Not only that, but the Catholics who lived in St. Mary's and neighboring Charles Counties tended to be quite wealthy – a consequence of the fact that they and their ancestors had come to Maryland from England, where the recusancy fines that began to be levied during the reign of King James I all but guaranteed that only the wealthy (or those who had wealthy benefactors) could afford to remain Catholic. In 1675, for example, 40 percent of Maryland's Catholics owned estates that were worth more than £100, whereas just 25 percent of the freemen overall could make that claim. More than 80 years later, in 1758, ten of the 20 largest landowners in Maryland were Catholic, at a time when just 13 percent of the colony's population identified with the Church of Rome.[11]

In spite of the fact that they had a lot to lose – precisely because they were so wealthy – 79 percent of the Catholic men who married in St. Mary's County between 1767 and 1784 swore their allegiance to the free state of Maryland, donated money and supplies to the American war effort, and served in the Continental Army or the St. Mary's County Militia. Fifty-eight percent of the men who belonged to the Jesuits' congregation at St. Inigoes Manor in 1768 did the same, and a genealogical analysis of the lives of more than 2,000 men from St. Mary's County who aided the independence movement reveals that slightly more than half of them were probably Catholic at a time when the Catholic population of St. Mary's County was just 25 to 32 percent.[12]

In contrast, it is estimated that just 30 to 40 percent of Maryland's population overall actively supported the war effort. The willingness of Maryland's merchants to participate in the boycotts and non-importation agreements leading up to the war seems to have been tied largely to the health of the colony's economy, which was good in the 1760s, but not-so-good after 1772, thanks to a glut in the international tobacco market. Another relevant factor in Maryland's ultimate support for independence was – perhaps ironically – the dependence that the merchant community had on the Port of Philadelphia. In the eighteenth century, Baltimore Harbor could not handle ships that had a draft of more than 8 feet, and many of Maryland's merchants, therefore, relied on Philadelphia, where the ideological commitment to the boycotts was much stronger.[13]

But why were Maryland's Catholics so committed to the independence movement, when the movement itself was animated by anti-Catholic rhetoric, and its ideology rested upon an understanding of natural rights as outside the social order that was anathema to the Church until the twentieth century? Catholic leaders in Europe, such as Arthur O'Leary, a Franciscan priest from Ireland, condemned the movement as a 'sedition' that would most assuredly lead to the revolutionaries' damnation, in spite of the fact that England's government had been no friend to the Catholic Church.[14]

That Catholics *did* support the American Revolution was for many years an assumed, but entirely unproven proposition. Early Catholic historians such as Martin Griffin and Peter Guilday looked at muster rolls from the revolutionary period and considered every Irish name they found there to be evidence of Catholic support. In doing so, these scholars ignored the reality that a sizeable number of the Irish living in colonial America, especially in the slaveholding South, were Protestants from Ulster, rather than Catholics from Munster, Leinster, and Connaught. They also failed to appreciate that the Catholic community in colonial Maryland was English for the most part, rather than Irish.[15]

Undoubtedly, part of the reason Catholic historians from the early twentieth century assumed that their colonial co-religionists had been ardent Patriots was that the converse – namely, that they had been Loyalists – was unflattering and certainly not the message that Catholic scholars needed to be sending to their Protestant countrymen in an age when fears of 'rum, Romanism, and rebellion' were still running high.[16]

But one other reason these early historians assumed that Catholics had been Patriots may have been that the first two generations of lay Catholics who followed the Revolutionary War were known – by contemporary priests and non-Catholic observers alike – to have had some rather strongly democratic sensibilities. These sensibilities manifested themselves most frequently in the phenomenon of 'lay trusteeism,' a system whereby boards of elected laymen would weigh in on a host of non-theological matters affecting the Church, ranging from whether or not and how a new roof might be placed on a chapel, to the selection of priests and the payment of their salaries.[17]

John Carroll, the first bishop of the United States, was generally supportive of the laity's democratic pretensions – though his reactions to their efforts to treat their priests as elected servants did, occasionally, smack of the Old World training he had received from the Jesuits in French Flanders. In 1785, Carroll accused the members of New York City's first Catholic parish of 'acting nearly in the same manor as the Congregational Presbyterians of your neighboring New England states' when they expressed a desire to choose their priest and control the new parish's budget. Nevertheless, the native of Prince George's County, Maryland, did assure the laymen in New York that he would extend a 'proper regard' to them 'in the mode of the presentation and election [of pastors].'[18]

Carroll's willingness to work with the laity in this way was an impulse that some of his contemporaries – and certainly many of the bishops who came over from Europe to assume their positions in the early decades of the nineteenth century, as the Church's infrastructure in the new United States grew – did not share. Some clergy, such as the French-born Stephen Badin of Kentucky, decried the 'extravagant pretentions of Republicanism' that they found among the laypeople they were working with in the 1790s. Bishop Louis William Dubourg of New Orleans, who was born in the Caribbean but was sent to live with his grandparents in France at the age of two, lamented in 1816 that 'the principles of freedom and independence' had been 'imbibed by all the pores in these United States,' including the Catholic pores. In 1829, Bishop James Whitfield, who was born in England and succeeded John Carroll as the Bishop of Baltimore after Carroll's death in 1815, convened the First Provincial Council of Baltimore to address the 'problem' of lay trusteeism in the American Church. At this gathering, the nation's bishops, nearly all of whom were foreign-born, designed a plan that they hoped would weaken the power of lay trustees by requiring that all church properties be deeded to an appropriate bishop. 'It would be a great good to religion,' the clergy in attendance noted, 'if this simple plan were universally adopted and the system of church trustees entirely abolished.'[19]

But in spite of the clerical opposition that the laity faced, America's Catholics were still exhibiting 'pretensions of Republicanism' three years after the First Provincial Council of Baltimore met. These pretensions were 'extravagant' enough to attract the attention of the English journalist, Harriet Martineau, during her tour of the United States. Although Martineau believed it was 'the Pope's wish to keep the Catholics of America a colonial church,' she observed that the Catholic population in America was 'democratic in its politics and made up of the more independent-minded occupations.' She noted with delight that 'the Catholic religion is modified by the spirit of the time in America; and its professors are not a set of men who can be priest-ridden to any fatal extent.'[20]

Martineau's idea that the Catholic faith had been 'modified by the spirit of the time' is how scholars who study the pre-immigrant Church have generally explained lay trusteeism and the existence of a strongly democratic element in the American Catholic community during the first few decades that followed the Revolutionary War. The country's first Catholics, historian James O'Toole has written, were 'influenced by broader American notions of authority.' They were 'accustomed to the republican idea that ordinary people such as themselves were the source of power in civil society,' and they assumed, then, that that meant they were the source of at least some power within the Catholic Church, as well.[21]

Undoubtedly, early American Catholics *were* influenced by the broader American notions of authority that characterized their time. This explanation for the Catholic republicanism found in the early national period certainly has many merits. But the fact that Catholics in colonial Maryland were more likely than their Protestant neighbors to support the independence movement – again, in spite of the anti-Catholic rhetoric that animated that movement – does suggest that something more than just broad American notions of authority may have been at work in the making of an 'American' Catholic identity. Indeed, there may have been something about their specific experiences *as English Catholics in eighteenth-century Maryland* that influenced the members of America's first Catholic community and encouraged them to support the Patriots' cause and embrace the implications that cause had for their national identity.

The Catholic community in the lower thirteen colonies at the time of the Revolution was small. A census conducted at the behest of London's Bishop Richard Challoner found that there were 16,000 Catholics living in Maryland in 1763, another 8,000 in Pennsylvania, and approximately 1,500 in New York. No other English colony had a measurable Catholic population. The Catholics in New York were not served by any priests, and the census-takers concluded that the New Yorkers' sense of themselves as 'Catholic' was minimal, at best. The border between Maryland and Pennsylvania was highly contested until 1776, when the surveyors Charles Mason and Jeremiah Dixon finally settled an 84-year-old boundary dispute between the Calvert and Penn families. It is possible, therefore, that some of the Catholics whom Challoner's census-takers placed in Pennsylvania were actually living in Maryland. Regardless of which colony they actually lived in, though, all of the Catholics in Maryland and Pennsylvania were served by the Maryland Province of the Society of Jesus, which never had more than 21 priests working in British North America – and frequently had fewer than a dozen.[22]

On the surface, the ratio of one priest for every 1,191 Catholics in colonial America may seem like a good one, considering that in 2009, the Archdiocese of Boston had just 749 priests serving a community that was 1.8 million strong (a ratio of 1:2,403). Colonial Maryland, however, did not have a regular postal service or even a network of paved roads, let alone the 310 primary and secondary schools, six colleges, 40 Councils of the Knights of Columbus, three newspapers, and one public access television station that the Archdiocese of Boston has at its disposal to sustain Catholics in modern-day Massachusetts. In colonial Maryland, many lay Catholics were fortunate if they were able to interact with a priest as frequently as once a month – and some had to reconcile themselves to making their confessions and receiving Communion just one time a year.[23]

In such an environment, it would have been very easy to simply abandon one's religious identity – and a few people did. Being Catholic in Maryland was not like being Catholic in Spain or France, where the cultural and legal landscape was dominated by the Church. In colonial Maryland, one could not just 'go with the flow' and be Catholic. A man or woman had to actively assume responsibility for his or her religious identity.

People assumed this responsibility when they named their sons after Catholic saints, even though a name like 'Ignatius' or 'Francis Xavier' essentially guaranteed that a boy would never have a political career in Maryland. They asserted their Catholic identity when they arranged to have their slaves baptized and then married by a priest, even though slave marriage, which was sacramental for Catholics, was illegal in the colony. Catholics in Maryland maintained their religious identity by forming lay sodalities, which did not become popular in Continental Europe until the Vatican started promoting them in the early nineteenth century as a response to the secularism and anti-clericism of the French Revolution. In these sodalities, lay Catholics agreed to pray about the Sacrament of the Eucharist at certain times throughout the week – often during months when the Eucharist was completely unavailable to them because weather conditions prevented one of Maryland's few priests from visiting them.[24]

In Maryland, one had to *choose* to be and remain a Catholic. That decision – made every single day by individual Catholics, on their own, without the constant presence and support of a clerical advisor – facilitated the development of a new Catholic identity that was unlike anything found in Europe and comfortable with the democratic language of the independence movement. The 'ownership' that colonial Catholics assumed over their religious identity did not, in and of itself, turn them into Patriots. It was, however, one of the factors that helped to prepare them to accept the new national identity that was held out to them in the 1770s.[25]

Of course, Catholics in early-modern England had had to assume a substantial degree of responsibility for their religious identity, as well – secreting clergy away in 'priest holes' and accepting the onerous obligation of recusancy fines. Certainly Catholic identity became a choice in eighteenth-century England, just as it did in colonial Maryland, and this choice did have implications for the meaning and nature of Catholic identity in England at the dawn of the nineteenth century. The Cisalpine Movement of the 1780s and 1790s revealed a liberal mindset among some of England's Catholics that stressed the importance of individual autonomy within the community of the Church, the limited scope of the Pope's jurisdiction in England, and the need for membership within a particular religious organization to be completely voluntary.[26]

Many of the same forces that compelled Catholics in British colonial America to take responsibility for their faith also compelled some Catholics in England – whence Maryland's Catholics came – to construct a new and personal understanding of what it meant to be Catholic. Whereas those forces empowered the English to challenge their church to become more compatible with English identity, in America, the forces prepared Catholics to accept an entirely new national identity, one that came wrapped in the rhetoric of anti-Catholicism, but which offered Maryland's Catholics their best

– CHAPTER 22: *American identity and English Catholicism* –

hope for a return to the more tolerant times their ancestors had enjoyed at the time of Maryland's founding by a Catholic proprietor.

Those more tolerant times – or specifically, the 'memory' that Maryland's Catholics constructed of those tolerant times in the decades that followed their demise – hold the key to understanding how and why British colonial Catholics became something different from their co-religionists in both England and Continental Europe. To become 'Americans,' after all, Catholics in British North America had to do more than simply find a way of reconciling their faith with the democratic and individualistic principles upon which American identity would rest. They also had to view themselves as something other than 'English' before they could choose to break away from the parent country.

Maryland had been founded in 1634 by Cecilius Calvert, an English Catholic convert who owned a barony in Ireland known as 'Baltimore.' For the first 55 years of Maryland's existence, Catholicism had been tolerated there, in spite of the colony's ties to England. Lord Baltimore's charter gave him the authority to do whatever he deemed was necessary to keep the peace among Maryland's religiously mixed residents, and in 1649, after a particularly nasty rebellion that had been launched by Calvinists who resented being under the rule of a Catholic proprietor, Cecilius Calvert used his authority to push an act of religious toleration through the colony's assembly. It applied to all Christians and was the first act of religious toleration in the English-speaking world – passed a half-century before John Locke published his now-famous 'Letter Concerning Toleration.'

Calvert's 'Act Concerning Religion' was designed to keep religious bigotry at bay so that Maryland's residents could learn how to live and work with one another and start turning a profit in the colony for themselves and their proprietor. The law did more than simply prevent the government from establishing a church or penalizing people for worshipping within a particular Christian tradition – practices that were standard in England, where Catholic priests were guilty of treason simply by virtue of their vocation and the recusancy fines levied against religious dissenters were high enough to bankrupt some of them. Calvert's act also placed an obligation upon the citizens of Maryland themselves; it required them to be mannerly when it came to the subject of religion. Residents were barred from using 'reproachfull words' about one another's religious beliefs, and anyone who used an epithet such as 'Roundhead,' 'Puritan,' 'Antinomian,' or 'Jesuited Priest' was to be fined or flogged under the provisions of the act.[27]

The years that followed the passage of the Act Concerning Religion were far from consistently peaceful. Many Protestant settlers continued to chafe under the leadership of a Catholic proprietor and governor, and their displeasure with Calvert and his co-religionists occasionally expressed itself in ways that became quite violent. Battles were fought; fines were levied; floggings were ordered. Yet, for the most part, religious toleration did characterize life in Maryland throughout Cecilius Calvert's tenure as proprietor. That toleration continued into the first two decades of his son's proprietorship, as well. So long as Maryland's residents swore that they would 'be not unfaithfull to the Lord Proprietary, or molest or conspire against the civill Government,' Cecilius Calvert showed himself willing to extend a degree of religious toleration to them that occasionally went beyond even the limits of the law – as a Jewish doctor named Jacob Lumbrozo discovered in 1658, when his loyalty to Lord Baltimore resulted in his being pardoned of the charge of blasphemy, in spite of the fact that the Act Concerning Religion actually called for the execution of anyone who denied the divinity of Jesus.[28]

401

Figure 22.2 Cecil Calvert, first Lord Baltimore
© Mary Evans Picture Library

– CHAPTER 22: *American identity and English Catholicism* –

Lord Baltimore's religious toleration, however, was destined to be short-lived. In 1689, angry Protestants in Maryland, emboldened by the Glorious Revolution back home in England, once again rose up against their Catholic proprietor, who was, by this point, Cecilius Calvert's son, Charles. The fighting lasted for nearly three years. In 1692, then, the Lords of Trade, operating under England's newly crowned King William III – who had, himself, achieved his position by challenging the authority of an English Catholic ruler – revoked Charles Calvert's charter and appointed a royal governor who quickly disenfranchised Catholics and began the process of establishing the Church of England in Maryland. That goal was finally achieved in 1702.[29]

The Calvert family eventually got the charter back, but only after Charles Calvert's son and grandson had converted to Anglicanism. For nearly 90 years, then – from the Glorious Revolution in 1689 until the American Revolution in 1776 – Maryland's Catholics were subjected to a host of laws, drafted and passed by their Protestant neighbors, which restricted their civil, military, educational, economic, religious, and even parental rights and behavior.

The legislative onslaught was not continuous, however. It came in fits and starts. Maryland's Protestants tended to enact anti-Catholic legislation during times when they were feeling most insecure about their 'English' identity. Historian Jack Greene has noted that the eighteenth century was a time of high anxiety for many British colonists when it came to the topic of their national identity. By 1720, after all, the North Atlantic seaboard was populated with people who thought of themselves as 'Englishmen' and relished the rights and liberties that came with that identity, but had not been born in England – had not even been born to people who had been born in England – and would probably never visit the island. Throughout the 1720s, 1730s, and 1740s, therefore, these colonists clung desperately to their English identity, filling their houses with British furnishings and sipping their tea from British china, 'so that they might,' Greene tells us, 'with more credibility think of themselves and their societies – and be thought of by the people in Britain itself – as demonstrably English.'[30]

In Maryland, the anxieties about English identity were particularly high at times – at least among Protestants – because of the colony's Catholic history and its concentration of Catholic families. The Glorious Revolution, after all, had firmly established that to be 'English' was to be 'Protestant.' The first charge that Parliament levied against the Catholic King James II when they ousted him and replaced him with his Dutch Calvinist son-in-law, William of Orange, was that he 'did endeavor to subvert and extirpate the Protestant religion' in England. Noting that it was 'inconsistent with the safety and welfare of this Protestant kingdom to be governed by a popish prince,' the Declaration of Right barred Catholics from inheriting the throne and prevented any monarch or heir apparent from marrying a Catholic. To this day, a Catholic is still not allowed to become the king or queen of England. In 2011, however, the leaders of the sixteen nations that were technically ruled by England's sovereign did agree to allow their future monarchs to marry members of the Roman Catholic faith.[31]

Maryland's identity as a proper, 'English' colony was suspect in a way that the identities of the other colonies were not because of its Catholic origins. Protestants in the colony were keen, therefore, to shore up Maryland's connection to England by limiting the size and activity of the colony's Catholic population. Anti-Catholicism, like tea and china, was a way for Maryland's eighteenth-century Protestants to think of themselves and their society as 'demonstrably English.'

403

Their anxieties, however, were not perpetually high; one of the more bizarre layers to the story of anti-Catholicism in colonial Maryland is the reality that Catholics and Protestants were married to one another, descended from one another, and involved in business partnerships with one another. They lived near one another and sometimes even attended one another's worship services whenever the Anglican or Catholic priests who represented their own religious traditions were unavailable. Fourteen percent of the marriages that Frs. Joseph Mosley and John Bolton performed for Catholics in Queen Anne's and Cecil Counties in 1768 involved Anglican and Calvinist partners. In 1734, the Reverend Samuel Smith of All Hallow's Parish in Anne Arundel County admitted to his friend, Arthur Holt, that sometimes when he was too sick to hold Anglican services, his congregants would visit the homes of their Catholic neighbors and attend Mass there.[32]

It was whenever they perceived an overt threat to Maryland's status as an 'English' colony that political leaders proposed and implemented legislation that taxed Catholic lands or restricted Catholic gun ownership or denied Catholic widows and widowers the right to rear their own children.[33] Those overt threats came after the failed Jacobite rebellions of 1715 and 1745, when dozens of prisoner-servants arrived in the colony, denying the legitimacy of the Glorious Revolution and proclaiming their loyalty to the son and grandson of King James II. The threats came again in 1756, when *Le Grand Dérangement* brought more than 900 Acadian exiles to Maryland as part of the English government's plan to disperse the French-speaking Catholic population of Nova Scotia. Those Canadian Catholics had been rendered suspect by the French and Indian War (1754–63), a conflict that took place just across Maryland's borders in southwestern Pennsylvania; this war, too, heightened Protestant anxieties about Maryland's status as an English colony.

The Catholics in Lord Baltimore's colony did not share the anxieties of their Protestant neighbors, of course. While there was still much about English identity that they wished to claim for themselves – the right to be represented in the legislative deliberations that governed their lives, for starters – Maryland's Catholics understood after the revocation of Charles Calvert's charter and the establishment of the Church of England in Maryland that English identity alone was not going to be enough to provide them with the rights they sought. The fact that their colony was tied to England, after all, was the reason the religious toleration their ancestors had been allowed to enjoy in the seventeenth century had disappeared. Those ancestors, Charles Carroll of Annapolis wrote in 1754, had 'transported themselves into this Province, then a Wilderness, and in the Hands of a barbarous People,' precisely because they understood that 'by such a Sacrifice they should procure to themselves and their Descendants all the religious and Civil Rights they were deprived of in his Majesty's Dominions in Europe.'[34]

If Maryland had not been an English colony, the Glorious Revolution might not have reverberated there to the extent that it did. This was how Catholics understood the situation. Protestants in Maryland believed that to protect their natural rights, they needed to strengthen their ties to England; Catholics, however, knew that the colony's ties to England were precisely the reason their natural rights were being denied.

Throughout the eighteenth century, Maryland's Catholics constructed a collective 'memory' for themselves of a time in their colony's past when their seventeenth-century ancestors had enjoyed the benefits of full-citizenship. The

– CHAPTER 22: *American identity and English Catholicism* –

memory emphasized Maryland's autonomy vis-à-vis England. It was a bit selective, however. It tended to avoid the rampant religious nepotism that characterized Charles Calvert's leadership of the colony after 1675, and it also downplayed the violent episodes of religious bigotry that did take place in the colony even during the years when the Act Concerning Religion was the law of the land. The memory was not meant to be an actual history of religious life in Maryland, however. In the short-term, Catholics used it to prevent the extension of England's anti-Catholic laws to the landscape in Maryland; in the long-term, they used the memory to sustain themselves as a religious community during a period in their colony's history when being Catholic had become decidedly inconvenient. The memory preserved Catholic identity, in spite of the inconveniences that came with it, by linking that identity to liberty and tradition and, in so doing, ennobling it. In emphasizing Maryland's autonomy, the memory also prepared Catholics in the colony to jump at the chance to be independent from England when the opportunity finally presented itself.

The earliest surviving articulation of this memory dates back to 1718, in a protest that was written by an English Jesuit serving in Maryland named Peter Atwood. The protest was entitled 'Liberty and Property, or The Beauty of Maryland Displayed,' and the circumstances surrounding Atwood's authorship of the essay are a little convoluted. The priest wrote the essay to protest an effort on the part of Maryland's assemblymen to repeal a piece of anti-Catholic legislation that the colony's lawmakers had previously passed and implemented. Atwood was certainly not pleased to be living under the law that the assemblymen were looking to throw out; he insisted, however, that the lawmakers' intentions in repealing the law were far more dangerous than the law itself, because those intentions violated the autonomy of Maryland's 'constitution.'

The situation was as follows: In 1704, shortly after the Church of England was established in Maryland, the colony's locally elected assemblymen ordered the sheriff of St. Mary's County to put a padlock on the door of the Catholic chapel there, and they passed, then, an 'Act to Prevent the Growth of Popery in this Province.' The law was similar, but not identical to a law that had been passed by Parliament in England two years earlier. Its primary mechanism for curbing the growth of popery was a tax that was placed on all Catholic servants brought into the colony from Ireland.

Following the Jacobite rebellion of 1715, however, Maryland was one of several British colonies that were forced to accept as servants those supporters of the deposed King James II who had been taken prisoner during the rebellion. A large number of these prisoner-servants were Catholic, prompting the colonial assembly to take a serious look at the Catholic population in Maryland and conclude that the 'growth of popery' had not, in fact, been curbed.

Noting that 'professed Papists still multiply and increase in number' in spite of the law, the Lower House of the assembly proposed that the local law from 1704 be thrown out, so that the colony could defer to that 'one Act of Parliament made in... the Reign of His late Majesty, King William the Third, whereby there is good Provision made to prevent the Growth of Popery, as well as in this Province, as throughout all his Majesty's Dominions.'[35] Protestants, the Lower House concluded, need not resign themselves to being overrun by propagating papists; they simply needed to stop trying to solve the problem on their own. If Maryland's lawmakers repealed their indigenous Act to Prevent the Growth of Popery and deferred to the one passed in 1700 by Parliament in England instead, the problem of punishing popery in Maryland would become the purview of the English courts. Anyone caught violating the well-codified recusancy laws of the parent country would be subject to deportation, and the colony's Catholic population would consequently be curbed.

The proposal was a flagrant violation of Maryland's separate constitution, according to Peter Atwood. The priest was naturally concerned about the anti-Catholic goals of the legislative maneuver; knowing that he could not rely upon the religious sympathies of Maryland's assemblymen, however, he chose to emphasize the autonomy that Maryland's lawmakers would be giving up if they implemented their plan. 'That the Penal Laws of England extend not hither was for 70 years and more the opinion of all in Maryland,' Atwood reminded the assemblymen, drawing their attention to the distinctive nature of the principles and practices that animated society in colonial Maryland. Criminal laws in the colony had always been drafted by Maryland's assembly, not by Parliament. Any attempt, therefore, to extend anything to the colony other than those English laws 'deemed an Englishman's birthright' was 'highly prejudicial to, if not destructive of our constitution.'

The word 'constitution' cropped up time and again in Atwood's essay. 'Altho our Government is framed...according to the model of that of England,' the priest insisted, Maryland had its own assembly, and the separate and unique nature of the constitution that guided that assembly had made it such that religious toleration was 'far from...inconsistent' with the colony's identity. Respect for the collective Catholic right to worship freely may not have been a characteristic of life in England, but in Maryland, it was a 'fundamental part of our constitution,' according to Atwood. Indeed, 'Liberty of Conscience' was the 'reason behind the peopling of this province' and the 'perpetual and inherent birthright of each Marylandian.'[36]

It is noteworthy that Atwood spoke of both 'an Englishman's birthright' and the 'birthright of each Marylandian.' The distinction was essential to his argument in 1718, and it was one that would ultimately have revolutionary ramifications when Protestant leaders in New England and Virginia articulated it in a different context 60 years later. Even as they insisted that they were good Englishmen, deserving of English rights, Maryland's Catholics did not – and could not – make their argument without appealing to a related, but different birthright: the one that they had as residents of a colony that, unlike England itself, had been founded with their best interests in mind.

To be sure, Peter Atwood was no revolutionary. He and the lay Catholics who utilized his argument – his 'memory' – in the years that followed were not bold enough during the Penal Period to insist that they were not English subjects. They did not have the freedom in the first half of the eighteenth century to make such an argument; many people in North America and England, after all, were arguing that Catholics could not be trusted to be good Englishmen by virtue of their enslavement to the Pope in Rome. There was much about what it meant to be an Englishman that Maryland's Catholics wanted to see applied to themselves. They were not interested, therefore, in throwing off the mantle of English identity entirely.

But the fact is that long before Protestant colonists recognized that they had evolved into something different from their supposed countrymen in England,

– CHAPTER 22: *American identity and English Catholicism* –

Catholic colonists understood that to be English in Maryland meant something different from what it meant to be English in England. When, in the wake of the Stamp Act of 1765, colonial leaders in Anglican Virginia, Congregationalist Massachusetts, and Quaker Pennsylvania started to insist that their rights as Englishmen were being violated by an English government that refused to recognize the separate nature of their colonies' constitutions, Catholics in Maryland heard an argument that was quite familiar to them.

The Lower House of the Assembly approved the proposal to repeal Maryland's indigenous law and defer to the recusancy laws of England, but the Upper House blocked the measure. Squabbling between the two houses, however, rather than Peter Atwood's eloquence, seems to have been the reason that the repeal failed. Atwood was called to appear before the assembly following the publication of his essay, but for unknown reasons he never actually appeared, and there is no further discussion in the assembly's minutes of his ideas. The Lower House would try at least two other times in the next 40 years to repeal Maryland's anti-Catholic laws and defer to the laws of England, however, and several private individuals brought lawsuits against Catholics, charging those Catholics with having violated the laws not of Maryland, but of England.[37]

Atwood's beliefs about the separate nature of colonial constitutions had not yet found a mainstream audience in Maryland. His words, however, do seem to have had an impact on the Catholic community to which he belonged. Catholics in Maryland echoed his sentiments throughout the rest of the eighteenth century – primarily during their efforts to protect their property from taxes and inheritance restrictions that applied to Catholics in England but had not yet been written into the local laws of Maryland.

During one dispute, a court in England issued a ruling that – in hindsight – was extremely significant, though it failed to attract much attention in the colonies at the time. In 1724, the Catholic heirs of Robert Brooke used Atwood's understanding of Maryland's constitution to defend their inheritance against the challenges of Robert's brother, Thomas. Thomas was an Anglican convert, and Robert had been a Catholic priest. Thomas had not challenged his brother's share of their father's estate when the property had been left to them in 1689, but following Robert's death in 1723, Thomas insisted that his brother could not pass the property on to anyone in his will, since the property had never rightfully been his.

Thomas challenged his brother's claim to their father's estate on the grounds that England's Act for Further Preventing the Growth of Popery had made it illegal for Catholic clergy to inherit land. The Maryland native John Darnall – who had been reared a Catholic, but converted to Anglicanism so he could practice law – represented Robert Brooke's heirs. He argued that British statutes did no apply to Maryland. The colony, after all, had it own 'act against Popery,' and that act, Darnall pointed out, did not prohibit the clergy from inheriting anything.

After five years, a British court finally determined that Fr. Robert Brooke's claim to the estate was, in fact, legitimate because he had inherited 'lands in the Plantations,' as Britain's colonies were called, 'where our Act against Popery…does not extend.'[38] It was a seemingly unremarkable decision in 1729. In three-and-a-half decades, however, the idea that the laws passed by Parliament in England did not 'extend' to 'lands in the Plantations' would become an animating argument in the Stamp Act

Riots, the non-importation agreements, the Boston Tea Party, and, ultimately, the war for American independence.

* * *

As it turned out, the gamble that Catholics waged paid off. The state constitution that Maryland's leaders adopted in 1776 following their declaration of independence from England mirrored the historical constitution that Catholics insisted had animated the colony's political and cultural life at the time of its founding. Gone were all of the restrictions on Catholic voting and office-holding that had governed Maryland for nearly 90 years. Consequently, the Maryland *Gazette*, which had used the terms 'Popery' and 'arbitrary power' interchangeably in 1774, was able to congratulate a Catholic convert, Thomas Sim Lee, on his election in 1781 as the second governor of the free state of Maryland.[39]

In the 1770s, Maryland's Catholics were among the colonists most prepared to accept the cultural and psychological implications of independence from England. The independence movement's emphasis on personal freedom and its insistence on the separate nature of the colonies' constitutions resonated with a population that had been self-consciously defining itself for generations – and had also experienced, first-hand, the negative consequences of being tied politically to England. Maryland's Catholics were not like their co-religionists in England or in Continental Europe. The story of Catholicism's survival in seventeenth- and eighteenth-century Maryland, therefore, reveals much about how the constellation of trade, settlement, violence, technology, conversion, epidemiology, and law that scholars now call the 'Atlantic World' was able to create religious, cultural, and ultimately national identities that were unheard of in the Old World.

NOTES

1   For more on the rise of contractarianism in seventeenth-century English political thought – and its ultimate manifestation, then, in the American independence movement of the 1770s – see Michael Zuckert's *Natural Rights and the New Republicanism* (Princeton, NJ, 1994).

2   Jack Greene, *Pursuits of Happiness: The Social Development of Early Modern British Colonies and the Formation of American Culture* (Chapel Hill, NC, 1988), 70, 175.

3   Bernard Bailyn, *The Origins of American Politics* (New York, 1967), 11. See also Pauline Maier, *From Resistance to Revolution: Colonial Radicals and the Development of American Opposition to Britain, 1765–1776* (New York, 1972); and Edward Countryman, *The American Revolution* (New York, 1985).

4   For a recent example of this narrative, see David Walker Howe, *What Hath God Wrought: The Transformation of America, 1815–1848* (New York, 2007).

5   Daniel Barber, *The History of My Own Times* (Washington, DC, 1827), 17.

6   Jay Dolan, *In Search of American Catholicism: A History of Religion and Culture in Tension* (New York, 2002), 7. See also John T. McGreevy, *Catholicism and American Freedom* (New York, 2003).

7   Maura Jane Farrelly, *Papist Patriots: The Making of an American Catholic Identity* (New York, 2012), 242.

8   John Adams to Tomas Jefferson, September 24th, 1821, in *Adams-Jefferson Letters: The Complete Correspondence between Thomas Jefferson and Abigail and John Adams*, ed. Lester J. Cappon (Chapel Hill, 1988), 577.

– CHAPTER 22: *American identity and English Catholicism* –

9 Jack P. Greene and Richard M. Jellison, 'The Currencty Act of 1764 in Imperial-Colonial Relations, 1764–76,' *William and Mary Quarterly* 18 (1961): 493–94; Katherine L. Beherns, *Paper Money in Maryland* (Baltimore, 1923), 51–52.

10 Charles Carroll, *Journal of Charles Carroll of Carrollton during his Visit to Canada in 1776*, ed. Brantz Mayer (Baltimore, 1876).

11 Francis Edgar Sparks, *Causes of the Maryland Revolution of 1689* (Baltimore, 1896), 50; Michael Graham, 'Meetinghouse and Chapel: Religion and Community in Seventeenth Century Maryland,' in *Colonial Chesapeake Society*, ed. Lois Green Carr, Philip D. Morgan, and Jean B. Russo (Chapel Hill, NC, 1988), 268–69; William Hand Brown et al., eds., *Archives of Maryland* (Baltimore, 1883–), :315; Ronald Hoffman, *Princes of Ireland, Planters of Maryland: A Carroll Saga, 1500–1782* (Chapel Hill, NC, 2000), 267. For more on the gentrification of English Catholicism in the seventeenth century, see Christopher Haigh, 'From Monopoly to Minority: Catholicism in Early Modern England,' *Transactions of the Royal Historical Society* 31 (1981): 129–47.

12 The religious affiliations of most of the Patriots from Maryland are unknown. With the help of Henry C. Peden, however, I have identified 2,035 men from St. Mary's County who aided the independence movement, and at least 51 percent of them were either Catholic – as evidenced by the fact that they were married, baptized, or buried in the Church, left money or property to the Church, or had their children baptized in the Church – or the sons, fathers, and brothers of Catholics – as evidenced by the names and property that they shared with known Catholics, their residential proximity to known Catholics, and their involvement in the probate proceedings of known Catholics. We do not know what percentage of the St. Mary's County population, overall, was Catholic in the 1770s. We can, however, make logical estimates. Governor Horatio Sharpe believed that around 7 percent of Maryland's entire population was Catholic in 1758, but the only surviving county-by-county census of the Catholic population before the Revolution was done in 1708. At that time, 32 percent of the households in St. Mary's County were Catholic, and around 9 percent of the colony's entire white population was Catholic. The overall Catholic population in Maryland, in other words, was 23 percent smaller in 1758, when Governor Sharpe wrote about it, than it had been 50 years earlier, when Catholic households made up 32 percent of the population in St. Mary's County. A 23 percent reduction in the Catholic population of St. Mary's County would put the population at 25 percent – which is why I estimate that the population in the 1770s was between 25 and 32 percent. See 'Marriages, St. Francis Xavier and St. Inigoes Churches,' 'Baptisms, St. Francis Xavier and St. Inigoes Congregations,' 'Maryland Catholic Subscribers to Boston Relief, 1760,' 'Catholics Listed in Manorial Rent Rolls, St. Mary's County,' 'Census, St. Inigoes, St. Mary's County, 1768,' and 'Presumed Catholic Births Recorded at St. Andrew's Episcopal Church,' in Timothy J. O'Rourke, comp., *Catholic Families of Southern Maryland* (Baltimore, 1985), 1–39, 43–70; Henry C. Peden, *Revolutionary Patriots of Calvert and St. Mary's Counties, Maryland, 1775–1784* (Westminster, Md., 2006); Gaius M. Brumbaugh, *Maryland Records: Colonial, Revolutionary, County and Church, from Original Sources* (Baltimore, 1928), 2: xi, 63–78, 314–411; Lois Green Carr and David William Jordan, *Maryland's Revolution of Government, 1689–92* (Ithaca, 1974), 33n.

13 Robert M. Calhoon, 'Loyalism and Neutrality,' in Jack P. Greene and J. R. Pole, eds., *A Companion to the American Revolution* (Malden, Mass., 2000), 235; *Archives of Maryland*, 9: 315, 25: 258–59; M. Christopher Newton, *Maryland Loyalists in the American Revolution* (Centreville, Md., 1996); Ronald Hoffman, *A Spirit of Dissension: Economics, Politics, and the Revolution in Maryland* (Baltimore, 1973), 80–82, 98–100; David Curtis Skaggs, 'Maryland's Impulse toward Social Revolution, 1750–76,' *Journal of American History* 54 (1968): 771–86.

14 Zachary R. Calo has pointed out that there is a lively scholarly debate about the origins of 'rights language' in Catholic social thought. Some scholars, such as Jacques Mariatain, John Finnis, and – of course – John Courtney Murray, have rightly pointed to the existence of 'natural rights' in the 'natural law' tradition of Thomas Aquinas. The natural law tradition, however, was premised on the notion of *duties*, and all rights were presented as being a consequence of the duties that men and women had within the social order; rights were not conceived by Aquinas as being inherent to the individual, in other words. Some scholars have noted that Pope Leo XIII did, occasionally, use the word 'right' in the modern, individualistic sense – particularly in *Rerum Novarum*, which was released in 1891. But most agree that it was not until after Vatican II that the Church embraced modern 'rights language.' See Calo, 'Catholic Social Thought, Political Liberalism, and the Idea of Human Rights,' *Journal of Christian Legal Thought* 1 (2011): 1–13, here 8; Jean Porter, 'From Natural Rights to Human Rights: Or, Why Rights Talk Matters,' *Journal of Law and Religion* 14 (1999–2000): 77–90; Brian Tierney, 'Religious Rights: A Historical Perspective,' in *Religious Human Rights in Global Perspective: Religious Perspectives*, ed. John Witte, Jr. and Johan D. van der Vyver (The Hague, 1996), 17–45; J. Bryan Hehir, 'Religious Activism for Human Rights: A Christian Case Study,' in ibid., 97–119. For Fr. Arthur O'Leary's understanding of the Revolution, see his *Address to the Common People of the Roman Catholic Religion* (1779), ed. Michael Bernard Buckley (Dublin, 1868), 103–5.

15 See Martin Griffin, *Catholics and the American Revolution*, 3 vols. (Ridley Park, PA, 1907–11), 2: 185, 217; Peter Guilday, *The Life and Times of John Carroll* (New York, 1922), 86; David T. Gleeson, *The Irish in the South, 1815–1877* (Chapel Hill, NC, 2001), 13; Farrelly, *Papist Patriots*, 20, 148.

16 The phrase 'rum, Romanism, and rebellion' was used by the Presbyterian minister Samuel Burchard to describe the foundation of the Democratic party in the presidential election of 1884. See Mark Wahlgren Summers, *Rum, Romanism, and Rebellion: The Making of a President, 1884* (Chapel Hill, NC, 2000).

17 For more on lay trusteeism, see *Patrick Carey, People, Priests and Prelates: Ecclesiastical Democracy and the Tensions of Trusteeism* (Notre Dame, IN, 1987).

18 'John Carroll's Letter on Lay Trusteeism in New York City,' (1786) in Mark Massa and Catherine Osborne, eds., *American Catholic History: A Documentary Reader* (New York, 2008), 32.

19 Dolan, *In Search of an American Catholicism*, 40–43.

20 Harriet Martineau, *Society in America* (New York, 1837), 2: 323.

21 James O'Toole, *The Faithful: A History of Catholicism in America* (Cambridge, MA, 2008), 59.

22 *Account of the Condition of the Catholic Religion in the English Colonies of America* (1763), rpt. *Catholic Historical Review* 6 (1920–21), 517–24; Robert Emmett Curran, *American Jesuit Spirituality: The Maryland Tradition* (New York, 1987), 10, 13; Jason K. Duncan, *Citizens or Papists? The Politics of Anti-Catholicism in New York, 1685–1821* (New York, 2005), 22–23; 'Regulations for the Maryland Mission, 1759, by Father Corbie, English Provincial,' Maryland Province Archives (MPA), Special Collections, Georgetown University, Box 2, Folder 9; Box 18, Folder 6.

23 Robert O'Grady, ed. *The Boston Catholic Directory, 2009* (Braintree, MA, 2009), 235; MPA, Box 18, Folder 6; 'Official report from the Superior, Father G. Hunter, to the Provincial, Father Dennett, July 23rd, 1765,' in *History of the Society of Jesus in North America, Colonial and Federal, Documents*, ed. Thomas Hughes (New York, 1907), 1: 337; Tricia T. Pyne, 'Ritual and Practice in the Maryland Catholic Community, 1634–1776,' *U.S. Catholic Historian* 26 (2008): 14–46, here 24.

24 Farrelly, *Papist Patriots*, 152–87. For more on the nineteenth-century development of sodalities and other forms of devotionalism in Europe, see Mary Heimann, *Catholic*

Devotion in Victorian England (New York, 195); Derek Holms, *The Triumph of the Holy See: A Short History of the Papacy in the Nineteenth Century* (Shepherdstown, WV, 1978); Ann Taves, 'Context and Meaning: Roman Catholic Devotion to the Blessed Sacrament in Mid-Nineteenth-Century America,' *Church History* 54 (1985): 482–95; McGreevy, *Catholicism and American Freedom*, 27–29.

25 Patricia Bonomi was one of the first scholars to talk about how religious experience helped to 'prepare' the colonists to accept the ideology of the Revolution. She focuses on evangelical Protestants, though, and does not consider Catholics at all. See her *Under the Cope of Heaven: Religion, Society, and Politics in Colonial America* (New York, 1986), 10, 132.

26 Eamon Duffy, 'Ecclesiastical Democracy Detected, II (1787–96),' *Recusant History* 10 (1969–170), 317–27; Joseph Chinnici, *The English Catholic Enlightenment: John Lingard and the Cisalpine Movement, 1780–1850* (Sheperdstown, WV, 1980), 93–97.

27 Farrelly, *Papist Patriots*, 99; 'An Act for the better discovering and repressing of Popish Recusants,' Jac. I, c. 3,4, in *Statues of the Realm*, ed. T.E. Tomlins et al. (London, 1810–28), 4: 1071–73; 'An Act Concerning Religion,' April 21, 1649, *Archives of Maryland*, ed. William Hand Brown et al. (Baltimore, 1883–present), 1: 244–47. The recusancy fines levied during the reign of King James I gave Parliament the right to seize two-thirds of a recusant's estate if the MPs determined that the fines levied previously were not arduous enough to force the recusant to start attending the Church of England.

28 Jacob Lumbrozo had immigrated to Maryland from Portugal in 1656. He was charged with blasphemy two years later, after he admitted in public that he believed Christ's miracles had been works of 'magic' and that the Resurrection was a rumor that had been started when Jesus' disciples removed his body from the tomb. The Act Concerning Religion did not apply to anyone who denied 'our Saviour Jesus Christ to bee the sonne of God.' Jacob Lumbrozo, however, had sworn his loyalty to Cecilius Calvert not long before making his public statements about Jesus. Maryland's governor, therefore – claiming to be acting on behalf of the proprietor – pardoned Lumbrozo ten days after his arrest. The Portuguese Jew went on, then, to receive his papers of denization, which allowed him to acquire property and vote. He ended up having a very lucrative career in Maryland as one of the colony's few doctors. See ibid., 41: 203, 258–59, 591, and 3: 488; J. H. Hollander, 'Some Unpublished Material Relating to Dr. Jacob Lumbrozo,' *Publications of the American Jewish Historical Society* 1(1893): 25–40.

29 Lois Green Carr and David William Jordan, *Maryland's Revolution of Government, 1689–1692* (Ithaca, NY, 1974), 161.

30 Greene, *Pursuits of Happiness*, 70, 175.

31 'English Bill of Rights, 1689,' *The Avalon Project: Documents in Law, History and Diplomacy*, Lillian Goldman Law Library, Yale University, August 31, 2009, http://avalon.law.yale.edu/17th{_}century/england.asp (accessed 2008); 'Ban on British monarch marrying a Catholic to be lifted,' Catholic Herald, October 31, 2011. For more on the link between 'Protestant' and 'English' identity that was established by the Glorious Revolution, see Owen Stanwood, 'The Protestant moment: Antipopery, the Revolution of 1688–89, and the Making of an Anglo-American Empire,' *Journal of British Studies* 46 (2007): 481–508; Colin Haydon, '"I love my King and my Country, but a Roman catholic I hate": Anti-Catholicism, Xenophobia, and National Identity in Eighteenth-Century England,' in *Protestantism and National Identity: Britain and Ireland, c. 1650–c.1850*, ed. Tony Claydon and Ian McBride (New York, 1998), 33–52; Jeremy Black, 'Confessional State or Elect Nation? Religion and Identity in Eighteenth-Century England,' ibid., 53–74; Linda Colley, 'Britishness and Otherness, an Argument,' *Journal of British Studies* 31 (1992): 309–29; and J. C. D. Clark, *The Language of Liberty: Political Discourse and Social Dynamics in the Anglo-American World* (New York, 1994), 237–57.

32　Marriage Register for St. Joseph's Parish, Cordova, Talbot County, and St. Francis Xavier, Bohemia, Cecil County, Maryland State Archives (MSA), SC4649; Arthur Holt to Samuel Smith, May 21, 1734, in *The Fulham Papers in the Lambeth Palace Library, American Colonial Section*, ed. William Wilson Manross (Oxford, UK, 1965), 3: 76–77.

33　'An Act for Laying an Additional Duty...on all Irish Servants, being Papists,' *Archives of Maryland*, 33: 109, 'Papists and Dissenters,' ibid., 25: 582–582; 'An Act for the Better Administration of Justice in Testamentary Affairs,' ibid., 30: 334.

34　'Charles Carroll Protests Against the Assembly's Act,' rpt. in *The American Catholic Historical Records*, ed. Martin I. J. Griffin (Philadelphia, 1908), 261–64.

35　*Archives of Maryland*, 33: 288–89; 'William III, 1998–99: An Act for the Further Preventing the Growth of Popery' (11 and 12 William III, c. 4), in *Statutes of the Realm, 1695–1701*, ed. John Raithby (London, 1820), 7: 586–87.

36　Peter Atwood, 'Liberty and Property, or the Beauty of Maryland Displayed,' rpt., *United States Catholic Historical Magazine* 3 (1889–90): 237–63, here 248, 249, 252, 242.

37　Beatriz Bentacourt Hardy, 'Papists in a Protestant Age' (Ph.D. dissertation, University of Maryland, 1993), 265; *Maryland Gazette*, November 13, 1755; Thomas Hughes, *History of the Society of Jesus in North America, Colonial and Federal, from the First Colonization till 1645, Text* (New York, 1908), 2: 533.

38　*History of the Society of Jesus in North America, Colonial and Federal, from the First Colonization till 1645, Documents*, ed. Thomas Hughes (New York, 1907), 1: 225.

39　*Maryland Gazette*, September 8th, 1774, and April 21st, 1781.

CHAPTER TWENTY-THREE

NAVIGATING THE JEWISH ATLANTIC
The state of the field and opportunities for new research

—·◆·—

Holly Snyder

Adam Sutcliffe opened a 2009 essay on early modern Jewish historiography with the rhetorical question, 'Are we all Atlanticists now?'[1] One could certainly wonder whether this tongue-in-cheek query – a parody of the declarative way David Armitage opened a 2002 essay on historiographical frameworks for *The British Atlantic World* – was intended to poke a metaphorical sharp stick at the reader. For any assessment of work in the field to date reveals that Jewish historians[2] of the present moment, with a few rare exceptions, are hardly Atlanticists at all. A thorough reading of Sutcliffe's piece finds him, in a pattern that has become all too typical among Jewish historians, sloughing off the potential contribution of a broad Atlantic paradigm for Jewish history in favor of a constrained Sephardic model of the early modern Atlantic. Indeed, Sutcliffe points to several 'dangers' that he believes the Atlantic paradigm may pose for Jewish historiography: that historians may simply replace old-fashioned nation-based Jewish historical writing with an equally limited binary division between the Atlantic and the non-Atlantic regions ('the West' and 'the Rest,' as he terms it), that historians will use an Atlanticist approach as a method of avoiding discussion of unsettling issues within particular national historiographies, and that the lack of a global context will only perpertuate a kind of peculiar orientalism within Atlantic Jewish historiography that juxtaposes romanticized notions of medieval Spain against a decisively Ashkenazi version of modernity.[3] While these cautions are well-advised, it seems to me that they spring from a deeper unease, and constitute perhaps a self-reflexive defense of Jewish historiography as it is presently practiced, against the suspicion that an Atlantic Jewish paradigm might undermine the very premises on which more traditional forms of Jewish history writing have relied for several generations now. The essay thus proves less provocative than Sutcliffe's opening would lead the reader to suspect; Sutcliffe has instead crafted a historiographical apologetic for the sloth with which practitioners of Jewish history have approached the Atlantic paradigm.

Why have Jewish historians largely ignored the potential for re-examining Jewish history through the Atlantic lens – an approach to historical analysis that an outside observer might think they would find of keen interest for their work, given the 'vitally important role' of Iberian Jews, Conversos, and crypto-Jews in Atlantic networks, as readily documented by Sutcliffe and other Jewish historians? In part, this has been a product of the particular methodologies of Jewish history, but a larger truth is that it is the end result of the effective ghettoization of Jewish history as a field. Although not entirely by intent, historians working in national historiographies writ large, as David S. Katz pointed out in 1991, have traditionally viewed Jews as just a small and exotic minority of their respective national populations, and decided that Jewish aspects of various topics were of marginal relevance, at best, to the national story. Thus, these aspects have been routinely ignored. Jewish historians, by contrast, have chosen, instead, to examine the meaning of these same aspects but only within a narrow context that is nominally and specifically Jewish, thus ignoring their significance for a nationalist approach.[4] The few historians who do engage topics with an eye toward both their Jewish and national aspects tend to emphasize their importance to the Jewish community of a particular place or in a particular time (thus inflating them out of scale to their importance within the national, international, and temporal contexts), or to portray them in an excessively patriotic light. Either way, the results invite dismissal as either anecdotal or antiquarian, or perhaps both. It would be fair to say that the larger framework for historiography of the Jewish experience in the Atlantic world has thus far suffered the ignominy of being seen as neither fish nor fowl by the very historiographical trajectories that might be thought principally responsible for enlarging and sustaining such a paradigm.

The lack of engagement by Jewish historians with the broader Atlantic paradigm thus far underscores a number of ongoing tendencies within Jewish historiography itself that have come to frame the field as a whole. As early as 1999, David Sorkin declared, 'it is by now belabouring the obvious to lament the "ashkenazification" of modern Jewish history,' noting that the then-extant understanding of early modern Jewish history 'tends to marginalize the sephardim.'[5] It is telling that though the field has grown substantially beyond the intensive study of Ashkenaz[6] alone in the past decade and a half, the geographical center of Jewish historical study for the early modern period has remained grounded in Central Europe ever since the field was first established in the early nineteenth century. And if the keen interest among academics in Atlantic history is, as Sutcliffe suggests, the byproduct of faltering relations between the United States and Europe in the wake of the toppling of the Berlin Wall, Jewish historians are just as imprisoned by the internal politics of the modern Jewish world. Jewish historians, themselves predominantly of Ashkenazi background, have long been in denial about the diversity of the Jewish diaspora. It took, for example, the 1977 electoral victory by the ethnically diverse Likud block under Menachem Begin – the first government of Israel not controlled by the Ashkenazi-dominated Labor Party – to bring serious attention by scholars to the significant subfields of Sephardic and Mizrachi Studies; scholarly interest in the Beta Yisrael (Ethiopian Jewry) lagged until Operations Moses and Solomon transferred tens of thousands of Ethiopian Jews to Israel between 1984 and 1991. There are many Jewish sub-cultures around the world that remain understudied, including those of the Magreb, Turkey, Subsaharan Africa, and all of Asia, from Iraq to India and Uzbekistan to China. Even now, scholarship on Sephardi, Mizrachi, and other non-Ashkenazi Jewish diasporas operates at the margins of the field, and early modernists in these areas find only modest support for their work, particularly outside of the limited arenas of the early modern religious, political, and economic development of Western Europe and the Mediterranean.[7]

– CHAPTER 23: *Navigating the Jewish Atlantic* –

Adam Sutcliffe is certainly not alone in his effort to circle the wagons around the ingrained traditions of Jewish historiography. A defensive tone threads through a number of works by the few Jewish historians who aim to address the larger field of historical study in a serious way, as they are pressed to grapple with public and defamatory distortions of historical realities disseminated by unscrupulous parties who invoke purported Jewish conspiracies of various sorts.[8] In recent decades, driven in part by such public attacks on Jews and Jewish history from various quarters and in part by a longstanding historiographical tradition that emphasized study of the Jewish community in its own right, Jewish historians of the early modern period have by and large turned their scholarly focus substantially inward, toward intensive study of the Jewish experience intended principally for a Jewish audience. Somewhat stymied by the tortuous difficulties of parsing out the Jewish role in race relations in the Americas and Africa before 1800, particularly in light of contemporary sensitivities surrounding public discussions of slavery and reparations, they have by and large left racial issues to Jewish historians of later periods, where Jews may more easily be presented as heroic – such as in Jewish participation in the twentieth-century push for civil rights in the United States – or, at least, as having had empathy for the oppressed.[9] Indeed, in the latter half of the twentieth century, Jewish historians in general limited their efforts to topics attaching lower levels of public controversy – that is to say, topics less likely to bring the opprobrium of a broader public down on the heads of the Jewish community – and in the process came to define Jewish history in narrow, insular ways that tend to maintain a central focus on Christian-dominated Europe to the exclusion of the rest of the Jewish diaspora, and even of the modern State of Israel. 'Here,' as Jonathan Schorsch has noted, 'Jewish history is more Eurocentric than the Europeans.'[10] And the study of Jews in the early modern Atlantic theatre has, until quite recently, been the case which proved this general rule. Jewish historians, as a body, simply have not yet taken seriously the potential for understanding early modern migration to the New World as a transformational event in the history of the Jewish diaspora, reflecting in degree if not in kind the neglect nationalist historians have shown for the varied roles that Jews and other minority actors played in shaping early modern nationalist and imperial trajectories in the Atlantic sphere after Columbus.

Of course, general historians are equally to blame for neglecting Jewish aspects of a wide variety of topics, as well as for dismissing the ways in which attitudes toward Jews shaped both Christian theology and the worldview of individual Christians, especially in their early encounters with the New World. Historians of the early modern Atlantic have, on the whole, ignored the prospects for examining Jewishness as a social category beyond the boundaries of Europe, just as if, in leaving the continent, Europeans had left all of their attitudes and assumptions about Jews behind them as being of no use to their settlement in the Americas. The records tell us a different story: many early accounts of European settlers and travellers in the New World, including that of William Penn, recount how native peoples of North America resembled European Jews. Moreover, the anti-Jewish bigotry displayed by Peter Stuyvesant in 1654 could hardly have originated with his experience of the Indians on Manhattan island.[11] As these samples attest, there are unrecorded trails in the historiographical forest that, having been passed by, still present possible pathways for exploration, allowing ample opportunity for those interested in

415

pursuing research on Jews in the Atlantic theatre after 1500. This essay provides an overview of existing research pertinent to the field and outlines opportunities for expansion, drawing attention to some of the many lacunae open for future pursuit.

WORK WITHIN NATIONAL HISTORIOGRAPHIES

The trend toward the creation of national historiographies, spawned at the juncture of the professionalization of historical study and the rise of nationalism in the nineteenth century, clearly shaped the establishment of a number of historiographical traditions – including that of Jewish history. The scientific study of Jewish history (originally called Wissenschaft des Judentums) was, in fact, first promoted about 1819 by Leopold Zunz and others through the Verein für Cultur und Wissenschaft der Juden (Society for Jewish Culture and History) in Berlin at the precise moment when German nationalism began its rise, culminating in the unification of the separate German states as a single nation state under Bismarck in 1871.[12] Jewish history as a field was therefore embedded from the moment of its conception in a nationalist agenda – though from the standpoint of Zunz and later proponents, right up to the creation of the State of Israel in 1948, this meant inculcating the vision of Jews in diaspora as an independent but landless, semi-nomadic transnational ethnic entity rather than a nation state fixed in space with geographical boundaries. The powerful impetus for nationalist historiographies since then has tended to shape Jewish historians, both professional and amateur, as proponents of the Jewish experience within a single nationalist frame – a paradoxical development belied, as it is or at least ought to be, by the transnational realities of the Jewish diaspora.

As the sense of periodization evolved within the field of Jewish history, the civil emancipation[13] of the Jews took on the mantle of a historical dividing line between the 'early modern' and 'modern' eras. For many Jewish historians, it is thus civil emancipation which forms the singular watershed moment within respective nationalist historiographies, precisely because it encapsulates a key tension of the modern diasporic experience: that is to say, at what point do diaspora Jews lose their distinctive status as a segregated minority group and become eligible for full subjecthood or citizenship in the nation? Indeed, Adam Sutcliffe's argument takes its bearings from recent work by Jewish historians (himself among them) that focuses new attention on the long process of European civil emancipation for Jews, which took place, roughly, between the French Revolution and the early twentieth century. Given that periodization, it should come as no surprise that the most interesting of these works have come from historians of the Jews of France and from those pursuing the broad impact of the Enlightenment on shifting attitudes toward Jews.[14]

But while this new work provides much needed attention to a significant lapse in the prior historiography on European Jewry, it has had the effect of subsuming the critical developments of the early modern era under the presentist trope of the Jewish entré into 'modernity' by means of acculturation and civil emancipation in Europe. Further, and in addition to misrepresenting the Jewish experience of the early modern era, it may not be the logical place to situate the development of 'modern' history for Jews living beyond Europe. Using civil emancipation as the organizing principle for a model of Jewish 'modernity' elides many critical issues for Jewish communities in places beyond the reach of Europeans – Bukhara (in present day Uzbekistan) is only one such example[15] – while emphasizing the underlying bias in the field for a Eurocentric narrative of Jewish history as a whole that remains grounded in Germany. Overall, it asserts a curious and pronounced disconnect with the Jewish experience writ large, especially for earlier times and non-European geographies. Yet despite its limitations, civil emancipation as an explanation for Jewish modernity has not, as of this writing, been seriously challenged, amended, or revisited by Jewish historians. In fact, David S. Katz is one of the very few Jewish historians working within a nationalist tradition who has argued for the efficacy of examining Jewish history from a more wholistic perspective.[16] Even a cursory examination of the nationalist historiographies of Western Europe reveals important questions about the general atmosphere for political, religious, and economic activity – questions with substantive impact both for Jewish communities and individual Jews, while monarchical absolutism gradually gave way to the imperial nation state, and the age of the court Jew (dated, by Jonathan Israel, at roughly 1650 to 1713 or, to put it into the broad framework of European history, from the end of the Thirty Years War to the end of the War of the Spanish Succession) gave way to the age of mercantilism. As Jonathan Israel persuasively argues, the transformation of the Jewish condition from enforced marginality into 'the mainstream of European life' can only be understood within the wider context of the political and social fracturing of Christian Europe wrought by the Reformation.[17] This is not to say that the nationalist framework has nothing to contribute. As David Katz points out, there is still value in examining Jewish interactions with given national subcultures, rather than simply trying to tie varied subcultures to a 'common' Jewish experience which, in many ways, they simply do not fit. A comparative synthesis of the Jewish experience in the early modern era would be empowered by a series of such national studies of respective Jewish communities.

As a whole, historians of American Jewry have been no better than their Europeanist counterparts, paying lip service to the Atlantic paradigm while failing to incorporate its broader methodology into their work, and in particular ignoring the call for comparative studies. In fact, there is a concerted dissonance between early modern European Jewish history and early American Jewish history that is unparalleled in the early modern Jewish historiography of other geographic regions. The neglect of transatlantic and other transnational connections has much to do with the way in which American Jewish history arose as a sub-field and its status within Jewish history, as well as with its curious approach to periodization, which until quite recently has trivialized anything that took place prior to 1850 (or, for that matter, anything that involved Sephardim). Originally created by a group of professional and amateur historians in America interested in studying Jews in America, its first practitioners in the 1890s pursued an agenda that sought to use every conceivable means to document Jewish advances in American life and to prove Jews had been good Americans from the moment of first settlement. From this overtly patriotic beginning, the field remained largely engaged in historical writing for a popular audience and thus did not gain sufficient strength as a discipline to win a place in academia until American universities began to hire faculty (both American- and European-born) with doctorates from German universities whose training emphasized the Wissenschaft approach.[18] As result, the writing of American Jewish history moved directly from a consistently patriotic to a patently Eurocentric model by the time it was being taught at American colleges and universities after World War II. Rooted in the distinctively European perspective that was part and parcel of the great Wissenschaft historiographical tradition, arising from Ashkenazi Jewish academics trained in German universities who focused their studies on German Jewry, the Jewish history of the United States was presented as having little, if any, significance prior to the first wave of German Jewish migration in the late 1840s.[19] In fact, there is a common underlying presumption among American Jewish historians, perhaps coming out of the American patriotism of the original founders of the sub-field as well as out of inattention to the seventeenth and eighteenth centuries from the later generation of both professional American and American Jewish historians, that civil emancipation was simply handed to American Jews by right-thinking founders, without discussion, debate, or effort by American Jews themselves – and this despite the evidence of documents from the early national period that have been extensively anthologized.[20] Until recently, little effort had been made by historians, whether Americanist, Atlanticist, or Jewish, to analyze the world inherited by these emigrants of the 1840s, let alone the peregrinations of earlier generations of Jews to Canada, Latin America, the Caribbean, or Africa. Indeed, Jewish historians have almost entirely ceded the latter two geographies to anthropologists.

This need not be the case. Work on the larger frame of Atlantic legal geographies, notably by Eliga Gould,[21] has begun to identify areas where Jewish historians could, were they so inclined, make a distinctive contribution. What strikingly emerges from the present over-reliance on the nationalist agenda, sadly, is the utter absence of any comprehensive discussion of Jewish civil emancipation during the Age of Revolutions. The potential for a long transnational dialogue about Jewish citizenship rights in the commonwealth and the republic has utterly missed, and been missed by, Jewish historians of the United States, Canada, Latin America, and the Caribbean; it is a story that remains, in large part, to be told.[22]

TOWARD TRANS-NATIONAL HISTORIOGRAPHIES

While, as a discipline, Jewish history potentially has important transnational perspectives to offer, it has been difficult to encourage Jewish historians to break away from the Eurocentric nationalist mindset when it comes to the writing of Jewish history. Indeed, Pierre Birnbaum and Ira Katznelson, in their *Paths to Emancipation: Jews, States and Citizenship* (1995) – the seminal volume on this topic – note that the available literature on Jewish civil emancipation in the late 1980s 'treated the incorporation of Jews into western modernity either as unitary experience in spite of considerable differences...or as *sui generis* in single-country studies.'[23] Although there has been much attention to the process of emancipation, beginning with the appearance of the Birnbaum and Katznelson volume, this work continues to center itself in Central and Western Europe, including examples from elsewhere, principally from the Mediterranean and Eastern Europe, only as counter-narratives. Comparative work on Jewish emancipation that crosses the great Atlantic divide, as noted above, is still wholly lacking; little effort has been made to examine how the guarantees of the U. S. Constitution (1787), specifically that for Freedom of Religion under the Bill of Rights, might have affected Jewish expectations for emancipation in other British colonies (Canada, Jamaica, and Barbados all had significant Jewish populations at the time) or Europe; nor has there been much serious consideration given to how the

American break with Britain effected, for good or for ill, rights talk by Jews in other places. Coordinated attempts to generate comparative study of Jewish societies and subcultures thus far appear to have resulted in little more than the occasional conference volume or edited compilation of articles in or from selected journals. Most of these efforts necessarily suffer – to greater or lesser degrees – from an uneven approach to their content. Even while they attempt to break the mold, the essays in these volumes betray Eurocentric standards of analysis and theoretical underpinnings; for example, of the 25 to 30 papers presented at the 1997 conference 'The Jews and the Expansion of Europe to the West, 1450–1800' at the John Carter Brown Library, only two dealt in any respect with North America, while more than half of those on Latin America focused on the Inquisition; another case in point is the 2002 volume *Port Jews: Jewish Communities in Cosmopolitan Maritime Trading Centers, 1550–1950*, which includes only a single article covering the Atlantic out of 13 pieces by 11 scholars included in the compilation. At that rate, conceptualization of a 'Jewish Atlantic' is little more than tokenism. The published volume from the first Lavy Seminar at Hopkins includes 10 essays, only one each from the Americanist and Africanist perspectives – a somewhat better balance than the JCB and *Port Jews* volumes, though the Europeanist perspective still predominates, comprising 80 percent of the content (author's disclosure: the single Americanist essay in the latter volume is mine).[24]

If early modern Jewish historians have not gone so far as to embrace the Atlantic history model, that has certainly not prevented them from devising an alternative model of their own to represent the development of early modern Jewry. This new model, developed over the course of the past decade by Lois Dubin and David Sorkin, both specialists on Jews in Enlightenment Europe, purports to address the character of 'acculturated Jewish merchants in port cities' for the express purpose of understanding their path toward integration into the broader Gentile society. Dubin coined the term 'Port Jew' in her work on Hapsburg Trieste, and the model has been known by that name ever since.[25] It was, however, Sorkin who created the theoretical underpinnings for the model, as a distinctive 'social type' consisting of 'merchant Jews of sephardi or...Italian extraction who settled in the port cities of the Mediterranean, the Atlantic seaboard and the New World' during the seventeenth, eighteenth, and nineteenth centuries. However, once the model began to assume popularity among other Jewish historians, as witnessed by the Southampton 2001 conference on this topic that resulted in the Cesarani volume, Sorkin attempted to limit the model by subsequently adding a second category, 'Jews in port cities,' as a catch-all applied without ethnic, geographical, or chronological specificity. He now stated that Port Jews should be distinguished from other early modern Jews by five traits: migration, the valuation of commerce, formation of community through voluntary association, re-education in normative Judaism, and a Jewish identity better characterized by ethnicity and rationalism than by religious belief. Sorkin's revisions ignored much historical evidence, including some documenting the activities of a number of Ashkenazi merchants of port cities in both the old and new worlds who fit Sorkin's Port Jew social type in every respect *except* their ethnicity – much as a number of early Sephardim were every bit the Court Jews of their respective times and places. And in proscribing particular categories of experience to define the Port Jew social type, Sorkin denied a range of Jewish experiences that were unique to and over time became characteristic of the Jewish experience in the New World, such as plantation ownership, as well as other non-mercantilist professions generally available to early modern Jews, like the practice of medicine.

In his attempt to bifurcate the Port Jew model, it would seem that Sorkin created a distinction without a difference, for the new category 'Jews in port cities' was only intended to allow the Port Jew concept to maintain its ethnic purity as a specifically Sephardic social type. In practice, this conception would render analysis of Jewish communal life endlessly confusing, as Sorkin's splitting of the categories would have classified Sephardi merchants of maritime communities as 'port jews' while their Ashkenazi and Mizrachi counterparts, along with religious functionaries who served communal purposes and non-merchant Sephardi professionals and laborers who lived alongside them would have been merely 'Jews in port cities.' Sorkin's motivation in his argument for the purity of the Port Jew model appears to have been, at least in part, to re-direct Jewish historians toward the Sephardi experience, as a counterpoint to the earlier dominance of court Jews as the principal subjects of Jewish historical writing. The latter model, arising as it did out of German Jewish history, was thus tagged among historians as ethnically Ashkenazi, although examination of the evidence indicates this was not exclusively true, suggesting that the rise of court Jews had much more to do with the process of the patronage/clientage system of court politics than with ethnic stereotyping.[26] Still, however noble his motivations, Sorkin's revisions have struck other Jewish historians as odd and ill-founded. In part, this is because 'Sephardi' as an early modern ethnic grouping is methodologically fraught, as evidenced in some detail through work on particular Jewish communities, notably Ken Stow's work on early modern Jewish Rome and Daniel Swetschinski's work on Jewish Amsterdam.[27] But a more significant, if little heeded, critique was offered by C. S. Monaco, whose study of the elite Sephardi merchant Moses E. Levy revealed a lived experience quite at odds with the theoretical underpinnings of Sorkin's model.[28] Even Lois Dubin was among the detractors to Sorkin's proposed revision to the model: in a 2004 piece, Dubin critiqued Sorkin's proposed categories and attempted to redefine the characteristics of Port Jews in ways that made them less driven by internal notions of identity and allegiance, to rather better reflect the ongoing discourse between Port Jews and their surrounding communities. Dubin suggested features that, in my experience, more appropriately describe Port Jews and their communities: a geographical focus in dynamic maritime centers driven by commerce, the perception within the broader society that Jews had commercial prowess and were therefore useful members, encouragement to merchants of all types to settle for the purpose of developing commerce, a favorable legal status for Jews (though not necessarily equivalent to full equality), a self-consciousness among Jews of the importance of building relationships with both Jews and non-Jews for the furtherance of commerce. Dubin, with direct experience interpreting the evidence of Jewish mercantile activity and its impact on Jewish individuals and communal life for Trieste, here lays out an agenda of themes ripe for expansion and comparative study throughout the Jewish world. Though she curiously neglects to mention the Americas or Africa, even while targeting Asia as a potential focus for study, the expansive nature of her vision is broadly applicable to the study of the Jewish Atlantic as well as to other portions of the diaspora. Prospective Jewish Atlanticists would be wise to review this essay and take up at least a few of the challenges Dubin profers.[29]

SAILING ON TO THE JEWISH ATLANTIC

Dubin's modelling brings us back to the topic of the historical work that actually touches on the Jewish Atlantic world. To date, very few studies have actually approached Jewish history, in any degree, from an Atlanticist perspective.[30] As one might imagine, with so few full-length studies available in the field, coverage of many important topics is still wholly lacking. Dutch West Indies trade and society, for example, have been well-documented for the Jews of New Holland, Curacao, Surinam, and New Amsterdam, while Jewish involvement in the French overseas colonies has received peculiarly scattered and inconsistent attention. In addition, Atlantic studies that discuss the role of the Jews divide fairly evenly among those which closely examine the Jewish experience and those which include Jews as part of a general historical portrait.

The pattern of publication suggests that if there is a central flaw to the methodological basis on which historians of all varieties have pursued the history of Jews in the early modern era it is that they have largely left the New World and its discovery out of the picture. In fact, it seems the neglect of this topic stems from a general lack of familiarity among Atlantic historians with recent work on Renaissance and early modern Jewish scientific thinking fostered over the past few decades by David Ruderman, Noah Efron, and André Neher, among others. Failing to find Jews written into the record of New World explorations, they have assumed that if Jews had any role in the systems that led to discovery of the New World it was at best a minor one; yet, as Patricia Seed notes, there has been a wholesale erasure from the historical record of the Jewish and Converso identity of many modern scientists and mathematicians working in Portugal in the fifteenth century.[31] That Jewish scientists discussed and interpreted the findings of Columbus, and attempted to map them (as did David Gans in Prague) or brought scientific skill with them to help settle the New World (as did metallurgist Joachim Gans) is similarly little heeded by Atlantic historians.[32] Then, too, American Jewish historians have perpetuated the misimpression that Jewish emigrants who settled in the New World remained more strongly tied to Europe than to their new home in the Western hemisphere. Jacob Rader Marcus, a leading figure in American Jewish history during the latter half of the twentieth century, as Jonathan Schorsch points out, claimed that 'the typical American Jew' turned his back to the frontier and looked to the east, to Europe, as the locus of 'the culture he knew and cherished.'[33] This broad claim distorts the realities of colonial settlement significantly by excluding the experience of Iberian Jews and Conversos, many of whom had experienced torture at the hands of the Inquisition prior to reaching American shores. The attitude of the latter was more succinctly captured by the sixteenth-century Converso apologist Samuel Usque, who wrote,

> O Europe, my hell on earth, what shall I say of you since you have won most of your triumphs at the expense of my limbs?[34]

In short, while Jews were just as 'European' as any other New World settler who originated from the northeastern shores of the Atlantic, they do not appear to have been more closely tied to Europe than non-Jewish settlers. To apply such a general characterization to the likes of, say, Asser Levy van Swellem, who spent many years in

New Netherlands, eking out a living in trade between New Amsterdam and Beverwijk through the Hudson valley, at times the only Jew in the colony, flies in the face of the evidence. Had Levy so desired, he could easily have gone back to Europe like his compatriots from the *St. Catherine* and lived a European life. But despite numerous trials, he chose to stay in the wilds of America. That alone says something about the engagement of individual Jews with the American wilderness.[35] The Gratz brothers, Barnard and Michael, who formed a partnership with George Croghan to further the development of the Pennsylvania backcountry in the mid-eighteenth century, and Luis de Carvajal (called 'el mozo,' so as to distinguish him from an uncle of the same name), crypto-Jewish martyr of the backcountry in New Spain in the sixteenth century, who persisted in his Jewish beliefs despite several rounds of imprisonment and torture at the hands of the Mexican Inquisition, provide yet other examples of American Jews who run counter to Marcus' claim.[36] For these Jews, the American wilderness promised the opportunity of refuge foreclosed to them in Europe.

Asser Levy, the Gratz brothers, Luis de Carvajal, and their respective colonial cohorts suggest that if we are to comprehend the varied experiences of early modern Jews in the Americas, a new approach is required – one that examines closely the evidence of geographical and social as well as religious identity. To do this requires tackling some fairly thorny issues; still, there are a number of important themes that deserve more attention from a transatlantic perspective than they have yet received. These include (though are by no means limited to) Jewish social networks, detailed study of Jewish mercantile activity, and Jewish participation in transatlantic labor systems, with a particular focus on slavery and the slave trade.

Early modern Jewish social networks present a theme that at present is poorly grasped, as historians have attempted to focus instead on religious identity. The religious self-definition of early modern Iberian Conversos is a Gordion knot that fascinates scholars while resisting easy analysis. In large part, its complexity owes much to the nature of the extant sources. But documents created by the Inquisition can hardly be said to be without bias. David Graizbord has offered some important cautions for approaching this material, and in particular about making too literal a reading of the Inquisitorial record; anyone aware of our contemporary public debate over the validity of confessions extracted through the use of torture will have a keen sense of the pitfalls Graizbord has described.[37] This problematique perhaps explains why the great bulk of historiography available on Jews in Latin America focuses almost solely on the issue of Converso religious identity.[38] But while tackling this task may be critical to understanding the survival of post-conversion Jewish identity in the Iberian Atlantic world, the corpus of scholarly attention devoted to it has also inhibited our comprehension of how professing Jews, crypto-Jews, and Conversos were linked together by blood, by marriage and by commerce, and how identity was shaped both by limitations imposed within areas where the presence of the Inquisition kept incipient Jews from ever having the safety to freely express their opinions without fear of retribution and links to areas where such freedoms could be taken as granted.

Within the last decade, new scholarship has demonstrated promise in suggesting other ways of approaching the question: Brazilian scholar Bruno Feitler, for example, describes a complex picture of Jewish life in Northeast Brazil, with individuals at some points publicly espousing Judaism and at others declaring themselves good Catholics.[39] Feitler's study reveals a plasticity to Jewish identity, as Conversos publicly bent their professed religious ideology to suit their immediate needs for individual and familial survival and upward mobility. It is a view that is reflected in the sources not only from Catholic territory but also in reports delivered to the Inquisition even from Protestant strongholds on the opposite side of the Atlantic – London, Amsterdam, Antwerp, Hamburg – where Jews were free to be openly Jewish without fear of reprisal. Until these works appeared, historians of all types routinely missed these nuances because their own present-minded notions of religion dictated that one could not be both Christian and Jewish (or, for that matter, Christian and Muslim) at the same time. Our current historiographical conventions hold that religious identity in the early modern period was fixed – whether given at birth or chosen in adulthood, individuals abode with it for life. But perhaps it was never so, and the convention on which we have relied for several generations now was unthinkingly created by historians for the sheer convenience of having populations which fit the categories that historians wanted to analyze. How difficult to imagine, then, that our historical subjects would defy us and act dynamically, choosing for themselves what religious identity seemed best to them at the time rather than waiting quietly in a box to be counted.

Indeed, it was not until the early nineteenth century, with the birth of the Reform movement, that Jews had the option to choose between normalized forms of Jewish ritual practice. Until that moment, those who disagreed with synagogue elders had nowhere else in Judaism to go. In the absence of a viable alternative, choosing to be 'Christian' for a while must have seemed, to some, more attractive than having no place at all to express one's faith.[40] But, of course, this going back and forth between religious identities poses new challenges for the historian. In the face of such choices by individuals, and even whole families, how can we judge religious commitment? Further, how can we hope to derive a meaningful measurement for apostasy?

It is here that we might turn for help to sub-fields of Jewish scholarship previously little used by historians of either the Jewish or general varieties: Jewish sociology, promoted and developed since the 1950s principally by the late Marshall Sklare (among others) and now in its maturity; and Jewish ethnology, the study of comparative Jewish cultures, a field that continues to evolve. Sklare, in particular, saw the importance of an understanding of history toward the development of sound sociological theory; in fact, he opened the 1958 compilation *The Jews: Social Patterns of an American Group* with the question of not 'whether' but 'how much' history a sociologist ought to know. Early modern historians might quibble with Sklare's decision to use, as his principle historical foil, an article by Bernard Weinryb that sets its opening with the great wave of Jewish immigration to the United States in the 1880s. However, it remains for historians to bring Jewish sociology into the early modern era by historicizing the work of Jewish sociologists – not vice versa.[41] Jewish ethnology is yet an emerging area, just beginning to take on a life of its own, as a 2009 conference at Brown University attests. Indeed, even ethnological studies of singular Jewish communities have already made useful contributions to the historical understanding of Atlantic Jewry.[42] With its focus on the culture, characteristics, and folkways of various groups, Jewish ethnology has the potential for important contributions to the writing of Jewish history, and in particular for the kind of comparative work that Atlantic history, as a discipline, proposes to foster.[43] One important example that suggests the potential efficacy this approach might have for

Atlantic Jewish history is the question of where and why Jewish slaveholders made concerted efforts to educate as Jews the mulatto offspring of their liasons with enslaved or free women of color, and these offspring (both male and female) then transmitted Judaism to their own children, giving rise to a population of Jews of color, as happened both in Surinam and, across the Atlantic, in Guiné.[44] Jewish slaveholders in other places, we know, behaved quite differently. In Jamaica, while Jewish men maintained relationships with free and enslaved women of color, they made little effort to acknowledge their paternity of the children resulting from these unions and none at all to transmit Judaism to their children or other slaves.[45] Here, a comparative study that examines this juxtaposition in some detail might illuminate aspects of early modern Jewish culture that are now poorly understood. Stephen Sharot has laid out a useful methodology for pursuing historical comparative studies of just this type, using religious separatism and religious syncretism as the poles on a sliding scale of Jewish cultural variation.[46]

Taking an Atlantic approach to Jewish history not only allows historians to expand the range of comprehending the Jewish diaspora beyond the boundaries of Europe; it also has potential for bridging chronological boundaries, allowing Jewish historians to push the Atlantic model beyond the rigid periodization and geographical boundaries that some of its chief advocates (notably Bernard Bailyn and David Armitage) have attempted to impose. Recent work by Arthur Kiron and Adam Mendelsohn, for example, focuses attention on Jewish literary and cultural networks that spanned the Atlantic in the mid-to-late nineteenth century, laying the groundwork for further development of a distinctively transoceanic Anglophone Jewish culture in the period when Jewish emigration from Europe to the Americas began in earnest.[47] There is perhaps no better example of the potential contributions of an Atlantic model for understanding Jewish history and culture than that of the Yiddish theatre, which, by the 1890s had begun its travels back from the Americas to Russia and Eastern Europe, coming to a pinnacle with the popularity of Yiddish film on both sides of the Atlantic in the years between the two world wars. Though long ignored by European-trained Jewish historians because of its genesis in the United States, the circuitous travels of American Yiddish theatre and film, including international stars such as Molly Picon and Boris Tomashevsky, gave a vibrancy to transnational Jewish culture that it has not recaptured since. Indeed, Yiddish theatre brought Jewish cultural traditions full circle, reaching generations of migrants and their now creolized children, making them not simply transatlantic voyagers but circumatlantic cosmopolitans.[48] Seen in this light, the study of Jewish history from an Atlantic perspective has great potential for enlarging the reach of Jewish historiography to all four of the Atlantic continents, bringing Africa, North America, and Latin America into focus along with Europe and allowing Jewish historiography to take the lead in reshaping the way in which historians understand history in general. And, indeed, it is from literary historians that the first tentative steps toward putting forward a transatlantic analysis of early modern Jewish culture have recently come.[49]

As to Jewish mercantilism, Derek Penslar points out that until the 1970s, Jewish historians focused their attention on politics and religion but paid little heed to Jewish economics. Jonathan Israel's magisterial *European Jewry in an Age of Mercantilism*, first published in 1985 and now in its third edition, was a groundbreaking study of the pathways created for Jewish communal life by European political economy in the

– CHAPTER 23: *Navigating the Jewish Atlantic* –

early modern period; Penslar himself has contributed greatly to our understanding of the economic thought of Jews themselves. Nevertheless, Penslar's focus has been on the modernization of Jewish economic culture, and in particular the key transition from marginal traders and vagrants to petit-bourgeois tradesmen and professionals between the eighteenth and nineteenth centuries, while Israel's has been on the larger picture of European politics and intellectual culture (that of the Netherlands in particular). That certainly leaves much more to be done on the internal political economy of Jewish communities and individuals in the early modern period, particularly for the period prior to the end of the Thirty Years War (1648), when Penslar begins his study.[50] Many of the best works on Jewish merchants do not cover transatlantic trade (a case in point is Francesca Trivellato's *Familiarity of Strangers*,[51] a study of Jewish merchants in Livorno and their trading networks in Europe and Asia); those few that do tackle Jewish Atlantic mercantilism often amount to less than their claims. An early example of the latter is that of Gedalia Yogev's *Diamonds and Coral* (1978), whose initial chapter titles seem promising but whose survey of Atlantic commerce is disappointingly brief and cursory. Still, Yogev's study could be excused for being a product of its time, as Yogev was particularly interested in the trade with Asia and there was then little research available on which to build an understanding of Jewish transatlantic commerce. Stephen Alexander Fortune's 1984 attempt to analyze the role of Jewish merchants in British West Indian commerce between 1650 and 1750 proved woefully inadequate with much less excuse, given the stated focus of the work and Fortune's contact with primary documents.[52] Sarah Abrevaya Stein's recent work on Jews in the feather trade provides an intriguing analysis of transatlantic trading patterns from Africa to Europe and the Americas but, alas, focuses on the twentieth century.[53] What *is* an early modernist to do?

While much work is in process on networks of those involved in trade, little attention has been paid to the particular role of Jewish commerce within and between wider imperial frameworks. Cathy Matson's work on New York merchants, while inclusive, speaks in such broad and general terms that it is impossible to see where and how the trading patterns of Jewish merchants may be distinguished from those of the English and Dutch merchants who dominated the city's mercantile elite.[54] Wim Klooster's ongoing work admirably captures Dutch West Indies trade out of Curacao, integrating the island's Jewish population into the picture, yet does not discuss how they did what they did.[55] Again, application of the framework recently laid out by Eliga Gould may be of some help in this regard. The involvement (or lack) of Jewish merchants in trading contraband, their interactions with illicit actors (pirates, slaves, maroon communities, and Indians), the relative success or failure of their legitimate trading activities, and the manner in which they were forced to manage competition from merchants operating with the backing of full imperial subjecthood are areas that merit further exploration but have not yet received adequate attention. Further, there is much to be done with exploring the nature of the trading activities embarked upon by early modern Jews and the strategies they used in pursuit of trade. How did their activities complement or supplement what other groups of merchants were doing? What different skill sets and connections did they bring to the table, and how did these help or hinder their prosecution of trade in a variety of early modern commodities, from foodstuffs to manufactured goods? Just how instrumental – or not – were Jewish merchants in the transatlantic slave trade?

425

Perhaps the most important area that Jewish historians have not yet addressed in a serious way is that of labor systems, and in particular Jewish participation in the institution of slavery. Here, again, is a topic worthy of serious examination and discussion within Jewish history, yet few works have managed to overcome a defensive posture in order to take a hard and critical look at the evidence of Jewish slave ownership. Certainly, it is difficult for Jewish historians conscious of the great pain suffered by the victims of slavery to avoid looking for some way of differentiating Jews from other classes of slaveholders and slavetraders, or to deter the effort to explain away Jewish participation in the system. But the undisputed fact is that Jews did participate in the transatlantic slave system and, like other groups of European Americans, benefitted from its unapologetic appropriation of the labor of Africans, creolized Blacks and Indians, not only as slaveowners and traders but as members of a somewhat privileged caste. It is time for Jewish historians to own that truth and confront this difficult and disturbing past. We will not have a credible handle on the world these Jews inhabited, their place within it, or their understanding of Judaism itself until we come to terms with the historical evidence that documents these simple facts, and learn to discuss them dispassionately and with great candor.[56] The ongoing work of Jonathan Schorsch has made a substantial contribution toward untangling some of these threads, in particular through close contrast of Jewish religious texts on slavery with the ritual behavior of individual early modern Jews and Jewish communities toward the African slaves in their midst. And recent work by Peter Mark and Jose da Silva Horta makes an enormously important contribution by documenting Jewish culture and communal life in West Africa, and shows great promise for enlarging our understanding of the complex relations between Jewish merchants, Africa, and Africans. However, there is ample room for more scholarship and new voices. As Schorsch pointed out, the relationship of Jewish slaveowners to their slaves in the Anglophone Caribbean is a tale yet to be explored.[57] It appears, for example, from my own cursory study of Jewish relations with slaves in Jamaica,[58] that Jewish slaveowners acted no differently than white Christians when it came to teaching their slaves about their faith; but little work has been done to elicit the history of the descendants of extra-legal relationships of Jamaican Jewish men with women of color. This begs the question of how we can hope to understand the extent of racial attitudes among early modern Jews, and the range of ways they chose to act toward people of color. What were the conditions in Jamaica that might explain why Jews in Jamaica have behaved so differently toward their children of color than their counterparts in Surinam?[59] How do we explain the seemingly widespread impetus of the Jews of the Joden Savanne and Guiné to teach Judaism to their children of color, while Jews elsewhere did not?

There are also ways in which historians ought to consider Jews as part of the larger framework of racial distinction in the early modern Atlantic world. Winthrop Jordan set the tone for our present discussion back in 1968 by suggesting that American racism began at the moment the English encountered Africans in West Africa.[60] But in his discussion, Jordan removed the very concept of race from its historical contexts, presuming that it sprang *de novo* from contact with Africa; he thus explored neither the earlier conceptions of 'blackness' in English culture or the religious and nationalistic contexts from which they sprang. As James Shapiro has since noted, the perceived 'blackness' of Africans has its antecedents in the specifically

English and more broadly Christian application of 'blackness' to Jews and other groups in sixteenth- and seventeenth-century Europe.[61] With the advantage of 40 years of hindsight and much new historiography on race, it would be worth revisiting Jordan's assumptions. Going back to the early modern religious understanding of the racial attributes of the sons of Noah, outlined so well by Benjamin Braude,[62] may help us give new life to a close examination of the role religion may have played in the transition of racial ideologies from Europe to the New World, and how European attitudes were then complicated by encounters with Africans and native peoples of the Americas. Was it only the 'shock of the new' that drove Englishmen to treat Africans as less than human, or is there a broader ideological genealogy to the way 'blackness' could be used to create the kind of dehumanization of a class of people that allowed for the psychological justification of their enslavement?

CONCLUSION

If Jewish historians are overly Eurocentric, Atlantic historians have certainly been unthinkingly Christocentric. Each side might argue that it is only following the obsessions of its subjects, but it may be worthwhile to ask whether both have taken their tired historiographical premises for granted. Was early modern Judaism really so limited to European geography, or has the modern historiographical focus on Jewish Europe blinded Jewish historians to the varied ways in which New World experiences began to reshape both Jews and Judaism?[63] Should we take early modern Christians only at their word, or do their motivations and actions bear a closer scrutiny than they have yet received? Might the general focus on Christians and their endeavors blind Atlanticists to some of the subtle elements of social reality in the Atlantic world – and in particular, to the Jewish aspects of their context – causing them to write histories that distort external realities of intergroup relations as they unthinkingly reflect a Christian inner reality? That is, taking the Christian perspective on that world for granted, do they fail to ask pertinent questions about the limitations of a text-based Christian worldview and how it may have reinforced the individual initiative to rationalize disregard for the humanity of Indians and Africans, in ways that Christians simply could not do with respect to Jews precisely because Jews were imbedded in Christian texts while Indians and Africans were not? By failing to explore the various roles of Jews and others in that Christian cosmology, have Atlantic historians been missing a gigantic piece of the puzzle for understanding racial distinctions in the New World context?

In an essay entitled 'A Domesday Book for the Periphery,' Bernard Bailyn imagined early North America as a place in which 'primitivism and civilization' were counterposed, each dominant in its own time and space, and equally responsible for defining the character of America and Americans. The essay closes with the poignant image of Thomas Jefferson, 'slave owner and *philosophe*,' gazing 'from Queen Anne rooms of spare elegance onto a wild, uncultivated land.' We must remain cognizant that the world of which Bailyn writes did not belong exclusively to Christians of European origin. It was peopled with a variety of cultural and linguistic forms, Indian and African as well as Euro-caucasian, Jewish, and Muslim as well as Protestant and Catholic, Spanish, Portuguese and French, as well as Dutch and British. This world of savagery and culture in equal measure, Bailyn wrote, was one that we historians 'can only grope' at; we are like Tantalus, he suggests, and understanding is always just out of our grasp. Adam Sutcliffe suggests another metaphor for the Jewish Atlantic: a 'fascinatingly alien' people, from a world profoundly unlike our own.[64]

Both of these images are, I think, self-limiting in ways that are not conducive to good historical writing.[65] The early modern Jewish Atlantic is a world whose knowledge has, over many generations, been carelessly misplaced. It is an attic full of ancient books we have not yet read, some of them in languages we have not yet mastered. The successful pursuit of Atlantic Jewish history will, then, require that we begin the process of reclaiming that lost information, browsing the shelves and opening dusty texts to unpack unfamiliar themes and restore them to the context of their making. We must rethink our assumptions of the shape of both the Jewish world and the Atlantic world. Jewish historians must allow the Americas and Africa into the story in a larger way, examine more closely the conversation between Jewish Europe and Jewish America, and listen to what the early modern Americas and Africa can contribute to our understanding of the Jewish diaspora. Atlantic historians also must expand their field of vision, taking in what is peripheral along with what is central, and must think more wholistically about the link between others here (Jews, Irish, Muslims) and others there (Indians, Africans), not as individuated groups but in terms of broader patterns of social inclusion and marginalization. The evidence is there, just waiting for us to discover it.

NOTES

1 Sutcliffe 2009.
2 For purposes of clarity, 'Jewish historians' and 'Jewish Atlanticists' are used throughout this essay to refer to practitioners in the field of Jewish history, not to historians who happen to be Jewish.
3 Sutcliffe 2009: 18–21, 23–24, 29–30.
4 Katz 1991.
5 Sorkin 1999: 87.
6 That is, German and East European Jewry.
7 In November 2008, for example, the Hebrew Union College-Jewish Institute of Religion sponsored a three-day conference entitled, 'Integrating Sephardi & Mizrachi Studies: Research and Practice' with the stated goal of 'reviewing the current state of sephardic studies within the academy' because 'in the last few decades the study of sephardi and mizrachi culture has increased significantly but Judaic studies as a field has not integrated a wider perspective on the diversity of Jewish experiences in the modern period.' The conference was held in Los Angeles, currently home to a sizeable community of Jewish immigrants from Iran.
8 One such attack, directly pertinent to the study of Atlantic history, has come through the much decried pseudo-scholarship of the Nation of Islam's Historical Research Department. See, e.g., Faber 1998, a work Faber researched and wrote as a direct response to claims that Jews had been largely responsible for the transatlantic slave trade, published by the Nation of Islam as *The Secret Relationship Between Blacks and Jews* in 1991. Though two eminent historians of the transatlantic slave trade have also refuted the claims, in a general way, with quantitative analyses, Faber's work attempted to recreate the historical context for the Anglo-American slave trade and put Jewish involvement into appropriate perspective. Faber's work has been the rare piece of dispassionate scholarship contributed to a body of literature otherwise dominated by scholarly polemics, including: Friedman

– CHAPTER 23: *Navigating the Jewish Atlantic* –

1998; Brackman 1994; and Caplan 1993. On the limitations of Faber's work, see Schorsch 2000: 130, note 51. Outside of this limited area, as Schorsch notes, work by Jewish historians on racial questions takes on an 'overwhelmingly apologetic' tone. Ibid.: 102.

9   In no way do I mean to imply here that American Jewish historians have neglected to address troublesome aspects of Black–Jewish relations in the twentieth century; anyone familiar with the historiography for this period will know of the plethora of recent work that tackles this important but problematic subject. My comments here refer only to the apparent lack of interest by Jewish historians of the early modern period in addressing such issues. On this point, see also Schorsch 2000: pp. 102–3. As to works on the twentieth century which portray Jews in a positive light vis-à-vis the struggle for civil rights for African Americans, see, for example, Schultz 2001; Mohl 2004; Diner 1977.

10   Schorsch 2000: 104.

11   Daiutolo 1983, citing an account by William Penn. In a tract originally published in 1607 that remained popular in Spain, being reprinted in 1625 and 1729, Fray Gregorio Garcia made similar observations about the resemblance to Jews of Indians living in the vast territory controlled by Spain. See, also, Popkin 1993; Williams 1998; and, especially, Parfitt 2012: 67–69.

12   Sutcliffe, in a footnote, points to Jacob Katz (1904–98) as 'most influentially associated' with what he calls the 'Germanocentric paradigm.' Sutcliffe 2009: 223, note 3. While Katz was certainly among the most influential Jewish historians of the late twentieth century, scholarship in Wissenschaft des Judentums preceded his birth by nearly a century. For a useful discussion of Katz's predecessors in the field, see Liberles 1995: 94–124.

13   Throughout this essay, the term 'civil emancipation' is used to refer to the removal of political disabilities, and 'emancipation' will refer only to extinguishing the bonds of chattel slavery.

14   See, e.g., Malino 1978; Schechter 2003; Sutcliffe, 2003. See, also, Israel 2006. A few works on emancipation in other nations, notably the Netherlands, also fit into this frame. See, e.g., Michman 1995.

15   Kaganovich 2003; Thompstone 1995; Poujol 1986.

16   Katz 1991: 61–62, 74.

17   Israel 1985: 258–59.

18   See, for example, the extended discussion of Columbia's search for a Jewish historian, as recounted in Liberles 1995: 1–93; Schorsch 2000: 123, note 18; and Robinson 1994.

19   See, e.g., Ira Katnelson's synthesis, entitled 'Between Separation and Disappearance: Jews on the Margins of American Liberalism,' in Birnbaum and Katnelson 1995: 157–205. Sources cited by Katznelson focus on post-1848 German immigration and ignore the state by state struggle for Jewish civil emancipation and political participation that took place between 1776 and 1875. As Adam Mendelsohn notes, American Jewish historians 'have eschewed a transnational approach' to the historiography, thus leaving unaddressed many topics of significance for the development of American Jewry. Mendelsohn 2007: 179.

20   See, e.g., Sarna and Dalin 1997; Sarna, Kraut and Joseph 1985; Schappes 1950 (also reprinted in 1952 and 1971); Marcus 1959.

21   See, especially, Gould 2007A (presented at the Library of Congress conference *Seascapes, Littoral Cultures, and Trans-Oceanic Exchanges* in February 2003 and since published in the conference volume *Seascapes*) and Gould 2007B.

22   For American Jewish history, see Chyet 1958; for Canadian Jewish history, see Godfrey and Godfrey 1995. Both works constitute general surveys of legal statutes within these respective nations but provide little in the way of an interpretative framework for understanding the differences found at the state, provincial or regional levels; neither draws connections to similar laws in other colonies or nations. For a beginning in this direction, see Snyder 2000, Snyder 2006A and Snyder 2006B.

23 Birnbaum and Katnelson 1995: ix–x.

24 One popular volume, Todd M. Endelman's *Comparing Jewish Societies* comprises selected articles drawn from the journal *Comparative Studies in Society and History*; conference volumes that have appeared since that date include: Bernardini and Fiering 2001, consisting of papers from the June 1997 conference by the same name convened at the John Carter Brown Library in Providence, Rhode Island; Cesarani 2002, comprising papers delivered at a 2001 conference sponsored by the AHRB Parkes Centre at the University of Southampton and originally published as a special issue of *Jewish History and Culture*; a special issue of *Jewish History* in May 2006, comprising essays presented as a panel at the 35th Annual Conference of the Association for Jewish Studies in December 2003; and Kagan and Morgan 2009, drawn largely from papers delivered at the first Lavy Seminar at Johns Hopkins University in March 2005. On the uneven content of these volumes, see, for example, my reviews of the Bernardini and Fiering volume in *New West Indian Guide*, Vol. 78, No. 3&4 (2004), pp. 7–8, and *The European Legacy: Toward New Paradigms*, Vol. 9, No. 1 (2004), pp. 128–30, and of the Cesarani volume in *International Journal of Maritime History*, Vol. XVII, no. 1 (June 2005), pp. 315–16. An exception is the new volume edited by Jane S. Gerber of the City University of New York, which arose out of the first academic conference ever held on the topic of Caribbean Jewry; the conference took place in Kingston (Jamaica) in January of 2010 and was jointly sponsored by CUNY and the United Congregation of Israelites in Jamaica.

25 Sorkin, David, 'Enlightenment and Emancipation: German Jewry's Formative Age in Comparative Perspective,' in Endelman 1997: pp. 104–5; Sorkin 1999: 87–97 (see, especially p. 88, note 7); Dubin 1999; Dubin, Lois, 'Researching Port Jews and Port Jewries: Trieste and Beyond,' in Cesarani 2002: 47–58; Sorkin, David, 'Port Jews and the Three Regions of Emancipation,' in Cesarani 2002: 31–46.

26 On Court Jews, the seminal work is that of Selma Stern, first printed in Germany as *Der Hofjude im Zeitalter des Absolutismus: ein Beitrag zur europäischen Geschichte im 17. und 18. Jahrhundert*, and republished in English translation by the Jewish Publication Society in 1950; see, also, the essays in Mann and Cohen 1996. On court culture, the seminal work is Elias 1983.

27 Stow 2001: 23–29; Swetschinski 2000, p. xii. Both Stow and Swetschinski point to the problematique of using the term 'Sephardi' as a catch-all term for non-Ashkenazi Jews of the early modern period; Stow, for example, indicates that the Jewish community of Rome was well established prior to the mid-fifteenth century, a generation before the expulsion from Spain; indigenous Roman Jews therefore cannot be said to be 'Sephardim,' as they had no historical or genealogical connection to Iberia. In fact, Stow points to Shlomo Ibn Verga's account of Sephardi refugees from Spain being turned away by Rome's Jewish inhabitants in 1492, requiring the intercession of the pope in order to enter the city, Stow 1992: 286–87. Further, Swetschinski observes that during the seventeenth century Portuguese Jews of Amsterdam never used the term Sephardi when referring to themselves.

28 Monaco cites Levy's 1819 observations of the backward nature of the Jewish community of Curacao to highlight the model's false presumption of enlightened cosmopolitanism. Monaco 2009: 138, 143–49; Monaco 2005.

29 Dubin 2004: 14–17.

30 These have included, over the course of the past two decades or so, a half dozen monographs and perhaps the same number of doctoral dissertations that have not yet found their way into monograph form, along with a fair number of shorter article-length publications. Among the former are: Klooster 1998; Feitler 2003; Schorsch 2004; Zacek 2010; Rupert 2012. The latter include work by Noah Gelfand (NYU, 2008) on Jews of the Dutch Atlantic world and my own dissertation, a comparative study of Jewish identity and social place in the British Atlantic world (Brandeis, 2000), along with the important

– CHAPTER 23: *Navigating the Jewish Atlantic* –

study by Catana Tully Cayetano (SUNY Albany, 1989) on Jewish involvement in early New World sugar production.

31 Seed, Patricia, 'Jewish Scientists and the Origin of Modern Navigation,' in Bernardini and Fiering 2001: 82–83.

32 Neher 1986: 102–68; Grassl 1998. See, also, Ruderman 1995.

33 Schorsch 2000: 104, *citing* Marcus 1970: 1, xxviii.

34 Efron, Noah, 'Knowledge of Newly Discovered Lands Among Jewish Communities of Europe (from 1492 to the Thirty Years War),' in Bernardini and Fiering 2001: 54. The quotation comes from Usque's *Consolation for the Tribulations of Israel,* which was translated from the original Portuguese by Martin A. Cohen and published by the Jewish Publication Society of America in 1964.

35 On Asser Levy, see Snyder, Holly, 'English Markets, Jewish Merchants, and Atlantic Endeavors: Jews and the Making of British Transatlantic Commercial Culture,' in Kagan and Morgan 2009: 57–63.

36 On the Gratz brothers, see Byars 1916. On Carvajal, see Hordes 2005; Cohen 1973; Toro 1944. Carvajal's writings have also been the subject of several literary studies, including: Dollinger 2002.

37 See Graizbord 2008: 32–65.

38 In the Bernardini and Fiering volume, for example, all of the seven essays on the Ibero-Atlantic world deal in some fashion or other with Converso religiosity, and of these five address directly their confrontations with the Inquisition.

39 Feitler 2003; Feitler, Bruno, 'Jews and New Christians in Dutch Brazil, 1630–54,' in Kagan and Morgan 2009: 123–51. It seems the trends that Feitler documents may have become something of a cultural tradition: a later example from nations under Protestant control is the case of Abraham Gabay Crasto, a descendant of Portuguese Conversos who lived both as a Jew (while in his native Surinam) and as a Christian (while sojourning in New York) between 1810 and 1850; see Bennett 1994. Feitler's findings certainly call into question Bennett's surmise that the case of Gabay Crasto was 'unique.'

40 Excommunication was occasionally used by early modern Jewish communities as a means of keeping restive congregants in line, the case of Baruch Spinoza in Amsterdam being perhaps the most prominent. See, e.g., Kaplan 1984: 153–55; Kaplan provides an Appendix showing more than 30 instances of excommunication between 1622 and 1683. See, also, Nadler 2001; Wesselius 1990; Yovel 1977. The practice of *Herem* was widespread in the Jewish world; at least one case took place in New York's Shearith Israel Congregation during the eighteenth century. See Snyder 2001: 17; original documents for this case are transcribed in Godfrey and Godfrey 1991: 401–6.

41 See Sklare 1958: 3–39; also, Sklare 1971.

42 The only serious full-length academic study of the Jewish community in Jamaica published to date, for example, was that of anthropologist Carol Holzberg (1984). Holzberg's study suggests some important ways in which the Jews of Jamaica have historically interacted with other components of Jamaican society. Holzberg's ethnographic study stepped in where historians had previously failed: in the mid-1960s, Samuel and Edith Hurwitz went to Jamaica for a year intending to write a history of the community; however, the book that resulted from their efforts was, instead, a general history of the island. See Hurwitz and Hurwitz 1965; Hurwitz and Hurwitz 1971.

43 The conference was entitled 'Cultured Jews: The Art and Science of Jewish Ethnography.'

44 Cohen 1991: pp. 157–62; Ben-Ur, Aviva, 'A Matriarchal Matter: Slavery, Conversion, and Upward Mobility in Suriname's Jewish Community' in Kagan and Morgan 2009: 152–69; Mark, Peter and Jose da Silva Horta, 'Catholics, Jews and Muslims in Early Seventeenth Century Guiné,' in Kagan and Morgan 2009: 170–94.

45 Snyder 2007: 155–59.

46 Sharot, Stephen, 'Religious Syncretism and Religious Distinctiveness: A Comparative Analysis of Pre-Modern Jewish Communities,' in Endelman 1997: 23–60.

47 Kiron 2006; Mendelsohn 2007; Mendelsohn 2008. Mendelsohn's study further stretches the paradigm by including Australia (along with Britain, Canada, the United States and South Africa), thus making it trans-Pacific as well as transatlantic.

48 See Warnke 2004; Hoberman 1991. On the application of the terms 'transatlantic' (crossing the ocean), and 'circumatlantic' (travelling around the ocean) to historical study, see Armitage 2002.

49 Leibman 2012; Hoberman 2011.

50 *See* Penslar 1997; Penslar 2001.

51 Trivellato 2009.

52 Fortune 1984; for a detailed discussion of its problems, see also the review by James Walvin in *William & Mary Quarterly*, 3rd Series, Vol. 42, no. 3 (July 1985), pp. 413–15.

53 Stein 2008.

54 Matson 1998.

55 Klooster 1998.

56 For a model of how this might be done, see Hancock 1995.

57 Mark, Peter and Jose da Silva Horta, 'Catholics, Jews and Muslims in Early Seventeenth Century Guiné,' in Kagan and Morgan 2009: 170–94; Schorsch 2000: 130.

58 See Snyder 2007: 151–61. For further study of this body of records, see also Mirvis, Stan, 'Sexuality and Sentiment: Concubinage and the Sephardi Family in Late Eighteenth-Century Jamaica' in Gerber 2014: 223–40.

59 On Surinam, see Cohen 1991; Ben-Ur, Aviva, 'The Cultural Heritage of Eurafrican Sephardi Jews in Suriname' in Gerber 2014: 169–94. Ben-Ur is currently at work on a book project documenting Jewish identity among Jews of color in Suriname between 1660 and 1863.

60 Jordan 1968: 4–7.

61 Shapiro 1996: 162, 170–73, 197; see also, Felsenstein 1996: 248, 316 n. 9.

62 Braude 1997.

63 See, e.g., Sarna 2004: xiv, xviii, 137–44. Far from embracing the declensionist model, Sarna emphasizes the dynamic nature of American Judaism, from the colonial period to the present, finding multiple examples of reinvention and revitalization alongside examples of assimilation across time.

64 Bailyn 1987: 111–31; Sutcliffe 2009: 30.

65 A case in point is the traditional historiographical neglect on the topic of Muslims in early America, recently redressed by Denise Spellberg's book on Jefferson and his Qur'an (2013). Here, Spellberg moves our perspective beyond its traditional Eurocentric limits by exposing how knowledge and study of Islam by Jefferson and others of his generation helped to shape founding notions of religious pluralism for the United States.

REFERENCES

Armitage, David, 'Three Concepts of Atlantic History' in Armitage, David and Michael J. Braddock (eds.), *The British Atlantic World, 1500–1800* (Basingstoke, UK: Palgrave Macmillan, 2002), pp. 11–30.

Bailyn, Bernard, *The Peopling of British North America: An Introduction* (New York: Alfred A. Knopf, 1987).

Bennett, Ralph G., 'The Case of the Part-Time Jew: A Unique Incident in Nineteenth-Century America,' *American Jewish Archives*, Vol. 46, no. 1 (1994), pp. 38–61.

Bernardini, Paolo and Norman Fiering (eds.), *The Jews and the Expansion of Europe to the West, 1450–1800* (New York: Berghahn Books, 2001).

– CHAPTER 23: *Navigating the Jewish Atlantic* –

Birnbaum, Pierre and Ira Katnelson (eds.), *Paths of Emancipation: Jews, States and Citizenship* (Princeton, New Jersey: Princeton University Press, 1995).

Brackman, Harold, *Ministry of Lies: The Truth Behind the Nation of Islam's 'The Secret Relationship Between Blacks and Jews'* ([New York]: Four Walls Eight Windows, 1994).

Braude, Benajamin, 'The Sons of Noah and the Construction of Ethnic and Geographical Identities in the Medieval and Early Modern Periods,' *William & Mary Quarterly*, 3rd Series, Vol. 54, no. 1 (January 1997), pp. 103–42.

Byars, William Vincent, *B. and M. Gratz: Merchants in Philadelphia, 1754–1798; Papers of Interest to Their Posterity and the Posterity of Their Associates* (Jefferson City, Missouri: The Hugh Stephens Printing Co., 1916).

Caplan, Marc, *Jew-Hatred as History: An Analysis of the Nation of Islam's 'The Secret Relationship Between Blacks and Jews'* (New York: Anti-Defamation League of B'nai B'rith, 1993).

Cayetano, Catana Tully. *Outcasts of Jewish Descent and the Early Develoment of the Sugar Industry in the New World* (State University of New York at Albany diss. 1989).

Cesarani, David (ed.), *Port Jews: Jewish Communities in Cosmopolitan Maritime Trading Centres, 1550–1950* (London: Frank Cass, 2002).

Chyet, Stanley F., 'The Political Rights of the Jews in the United States: 1776–1840,' *American Jewish Archives*, Vol. 10, no. 1 (1958), pp. 14–75.

Cohen, Martin A., *The Martyr: The Story of a Secret Jew and the Mexican Inquisition in the Sixteenth Century* (Philadelphia: Jewish Publication Society of America, 1973).

Cohen, Robert, *Jews in Another Environment: Surinam in the Second Half of the Eighteenth Century* (Leiden: E. J. Brill, 1991).

Daiutolo, Robert, Jr., 'The Early Quaker Perception of the Indian,' *Quaker History*, Vol. 72, no. 2 (1983), 103–19.

Diner, Hasia, *In the Almost Promised Land: American Jews and Blacks, 1915–1935* (Westport, Connecticut: Greenwood Press, 1977).

Dollinger, Karen R., *In the Shadow of the Mexican Inquisition: Theological Discourse in the Writings of Luis de Carvajal and in Sor Juana's 'Crisis de un Sermon'* (Ohio State Univ. doc. diss., 2002).

Dubin, Lois, *The Port Jews of Habsburg Trieste: Absolutist Politics and Enlightenment Culture* (Stanford, California: Stanford University Press, 1999).

——, '"Wings on their feet...and wings on their head": Reflections on the Study of Port Jews,' *Jewish Culture and History*, Vol. 7, no. 1–2 (2004), pp. 14–17.

Elias, Norbert, *The Court Society* (Oxford, England: B. Blackwell, 1983).

Endelman, Todd M., *Comparing Jewish Societies* (University of Michigan Press, 1997).

Faber, Eli, *Jews, Slaves, and the Slave Trade: Setting the Record Straight* (New York: NYU Press, 1998)

Feitler, Bruno, *Inquisition, Juifs et Nouveaux-Chrétiens au Brésil: le Nordeste XVIIe et XVIIIe Siécles* (Leuven: Leuven University Press, 2003).

Felsenstein, Frank, *Anti-Semitic Stereotypes: A Paradigm of Otherness in English Popular Culture, 1650–1830* (Baltimore: Johns Hopkins University Press, 1996).

Fortune, Stephen Alexander, *Merchants and Jews: The Struggle for British West Indian Commerce, 1650–1750* (Gainesville: University of Florida Press, 1984).

Friedman, Saul, *Jews and the American Slave Trade* (New Brunswick, New Jersey: Transaction Books, 1998).

Garcia, Gregorio, *Origen de los Indios de el Nueuo Mundo, e Indias Occidentales* (Valencia: Pedro Patricio Mey, 1607).

Gelfand, Noah. *A People Within and Without: International Jewish Commerce and Community in the Seventeenth and Eighteenth Centuries* [sic] *Dutch Atlantic World* (New York University Diss. 2008).

Gerber, Jane S. *Jews in the Caribbean* (Oxford: Littman Library, 2014).

433

Graizbord, David, 'Religion and Ethnicity Among "Men of the Nation": Toward a Realistic Interpretation,' *Jewish Social Studies: History, Culture, Society*, n. s. Vol. 15, no. 1 (Fall 2008), pp. 32–65.

Godfrey, Sheldon and Judith Godfrey, 'The King vs. Moses Gomez et al: Opening the Prosecutor's File, Over 200 Years Later,' *American Jewish History*, Vol. 80 (Spring 1991), pp. 401–6.

Godfrey, Sheldon J. and Judith C. Godfrey, *Search Out the Land: The Jews and the Growth of Equality in British Colonial America, 1740–1867* (Montreal: McGill-Queens University Press, 1995).

Gould, Elija H., 'Lines of Plunder or Crucible of Modernity? Toward a Legal History of the English-Speaking Atlantic, 1660–1825,' in Jerry H. Bentley, Renate Bridenthal, and Kären Wigen (eds.) *Seascapes: Maritime Histories, Littoral Cultures, and Transoceanic Exchanges* (Manoa: University of Hawaii Press, 2007), pp. 105–20.

Gould, Eliga H., 'AHR Forum: Entangled Histories, Entangled Worlds: The English-Speaking Atlantic as a Spanish Periphery,' *The American Historical Review*, Vol. 112, no. 3 (June 2007), pp. 764–86.

Grassl, Gary C., 'Joachim Gans of Prague: The First Jew in English America,' *American Jewish History*, Vol. 86, no. 2 (1998), pp. 195–217.

Hancock, David H., *Citizens of the World: London Merchants and the Integration of the British Atlantic Community, 1735–1785* (Cambridge: Cambridge University Press, 1995).

Hoberman, J., *Bridge of Light: Yiddish Film Between Two Worlds* (New York: Museum of Modern Art and Shocken Books, 1991).

Hoberman, Michael, *New Israel/New England: Jews and Puritans in Early America* (Amherst: University of Massachusetts Press, 2011).

Holzberg, Carol, *Minorities and Power in a Black Society: The Jewish Community of Jamaica* (Lanham, Maryland: North South Publishing Co., 1984).

Hordes, Stanley M., *To the End of the Earth: A History of the Crypto-Jews of New Mexico* (New York: Columbia University Press, 2005).

Hurwitz, Samuel J., and Edith Hurwitz, 'The New World Sets an Example for the Old: The Jews of Jamaica and Political Rights, 1661–1831,' *American Jewish Historical Quarterly*, Vol. 55, no. 1 (1965), pp. 37–56.

Hurwitz, Samuel J. and Edith F. Hurwitz, *Jamaica: A Historical Portrait* (New York: Praeger, 1971).

Israel, Jonathan I., *Enlightenment Contested: Philosophy, Modernity, and the Emancipation of Man, 1670–1752* (Oxford: Oxford University Press, 2006).

——, *European Jewry in an Age of Mercantilism* (Oxford: Oxford University Press, 1985)

Jordan, Winthrop, *White Over Black: American Attitudes Toward the Negro, 1550–1812* (New York: W. W. Norton, 1968, 1977).

Kagan, Richard L. and Philip D. Morgan (eds), *Atlantic Diasporas: Jews, Conversos, and Crypto-Jews in the Age of Mercantilism, 1500–1800* (Johns Hopkins University Press, 2009).

Kaganovich, Albert, 'Rossiia "Absorbiruet" Svoikh Evreev: Imperrskaia Kolonizatsiia, Evreiskaia Politika i Bukharskie Evrei,' *Ab Imperio*, no. 4 (2003), pp. 301–28.

Kaplan, Yosef, 'The Social Functions of the *Herem* in the Portuguese Jewish Community of Amsterdam in the Seventeenth Century,' in Jozeph Michman (ed.), *Dutch Jewish History: Proceedings of the Symposium on the History of the Jews in the Netherlands, November 28 – December 3, 1982* (Jerusalem: Institute for Research on Dutch Jewry, 1984), pp. 153–55.

Katz, David S., 'The Marginalization of Early Modern Anglo-Jewish History,' *Immigrants & Minorities*, Vol. 10, no. 1–2 (1991), pp. 60–77.

Kiron, Arthur, 'An Atlantic Jewish Republic of Letters?,' *Jewish History*, Vol. 20, no. 2 (May 2006), pp. 171–211.

Klooster, Wim, *Illicit Riches: Dutch Trade in the Caribbean, 1648–1795* (Leiden: KITLV Press, 1998).

Leibman, Laura Arnold, *Messianism, Secrecy and Mysticism: A New Interpretation of Early American Jewish Life* (Portland, Oregon: Vallentine Mitchell, 2012).

Liberles, Robert, *Salo Wittmayer Baron: Architect of Jewish History* (New York: NYU Press, 1995).

Malino, Frances, *The Sephardic Jews of Bordeaux: Assimilation and Emancipation in Revolutionary and Napoleonic France* (Tuscaloosa: University of Alabama Press, 1978).

Mann, Vivian B. and Robert I. Cohen (eds.), *From Court Jews to the Rothschilds: Art, Patronage, and Power: 1600–1800* (Munich: Prestel, 1996).

Marcus, Jacob Rader, *American Jewry – Documents – Eighteenth Century: Primarily Hitherto Unpublished Manuscripts* (Cincinnati: Hebrew Union College, 1959).

——, *The Colonial American Jew* (Detroit: Wayne State University Press, 1970).

Matson, Cathy, *Merchants and Empire: Trading in Colonial New York* (Baltimore: Johns Hopkins University Press, 1998).

Mendelsohn, Adam, 'Tongue Ties: The Emergence of the Anglophone Jewish Diaspora in the Mid-Nineteenth Century,' *American Jewish History*, Vol. 93, no. 2 (2007), pp. 177–209, here p. 179.

——, *Tongue Ties: Religion, Culture and Commerce in the Making of the Anglophone Jewish Diaspora, 1840–1870* (Waltham, Massachusetts: Brandeis Univ. doc. diss., 2008).

Michman, Jozeph, *The History of Dutch Jewry During the Emancipation Period, 1787–1815: Gothic Turrets on a Corinthian Building* (Amsterdam: Amsterdam University Press, 1995).

Mohl, Raymond A., *South of the South: Jewish Activists and the Civil Rights Movement in Miami, 1945–1960* (Gainsville: University of Florida Press, 2004).

Monaco, C. S., 'Port Jews or a People of the Diaspora? A Critique of the Port Jew Concept,' *Jewish Social Studies: History, Culture, Society*, n.s. Vol. 15, no. 2 (Winter 2009), pp. 137–66.

——, *Moses Levy of Florida: Jewish Utopian and Antebellum Reformer* (Baton Rouge: Louisiana State University Press, 2005).

Nadler, Steven, 'The Excommunication of Spinoza: Trouble and Toleration in the "Dutch Jerusalem",' *Shofar: An Interdisciplinary Journal of Jewish Studies*, Vol. 19, no. 4 (2001), pp. 40–52.

Neher, André, *Jewish Thought and the Scientific Revolution of the Sixteenth Century: David Gans (1541–1613) and His Times* (Oxford: Oxford University Press, for the Littman Library, 1986).

Parfitt, Tudor, *Black Jews in Africa and the Americas* (Cambridge, Massachusetts: Harvard University Press, 2012).

Penslar, Derek J., 'The Origins of Jewish Political Economy,' *Jewish Social Studies*, new series Vol. 3, no. 3 (1997), pp. 26–60.

——, *Shylock's Children: Economics and Jewish Identity in Modern Europe* (Berkeley: University of California Press, 2001).

Popkin, Richard H., 'The Rise and Fall of the Jewish Indian Theory,' in Shalom Goldman (ed.), *Hebrew and the Bible in America: The First Two Centuries* (Hanover, New Hampshire: Brandeis University Press, 1993), pp. 70–90.

Poujol, Catherine, 'Les Juifs de Buhara: Ou la Permanence d'une Communaute,' *Cahiers du Monde Russe et Sovietique*, Vol. 27, no. 1 (1986), pp. 111–23.

Robinson, Ira, 'The Invention of American Jewish History,' *American Jewish History*, Vol. 91, no. 3–4 (Spring-Summer 1994), pp. 307–20.

Ruderman, David, *Jewish Thought and Scientific Discovery in Early Modern Europe* (New Haven: Yale University Press, 1995).

Rupert, Linda M. *Creolization and Contraband : Curaçao in the Early Modern Atlantic World* (Athens: University of Georgia Press, 2012).

Sarna, Jonathan D., *American Judaism: A History* (New Haven: Yale University Press, 2004).

Sarna, Jonathan D. and David G. Dalin, *Religion and State in the American Jewish Experience* (South Bend, Indiana: Notre Dame University Press, 1997).

Sarna, Jonathan D., Benny Kraut and Samuel K. Joseph, *Jews and the Founding of the Republic* (New York: Marcus Wiener Publishers, 1985).

Schappes, Morris U., *A Documentary History of the Jews in the United States, 1654–1875* (New York: Citadel Press, 1950), also reprinted in 1952 and 1971.

Schechter, Ronald, *Obstinate Hebrews: Representations of Jews in France, 1715–1815* (Berkeley: University of California Press, 2003).

Schorsch, Jonathan, 'American Jewish Historians, Colonial Jews and Blacks, and the Limits of *Wissenschaft*: A Critical Review,' *Jewish Social Studies*, Vol. 6, no. 2 (2000), pp. 102–32.

——, *Jews and Blacks in the Early Modern World* (Cambridge: Cambridge University Press, 2004).

Schultz, Debra L., *Going South: Jewish Women in the Civil Rights Movement* (New York: NYU Press, 2001).

Shapiro, James, *Shakespeare and the Jews* (New York: Columbia University Press, 1996).

Sklare, Marshall (ed.), *The Jews: Social Patterns of an American Group* (Glencoe, Illinois: Free Press, 1958).

Sklare, Marshall, *America's Jews* (New York: Random House, 1971).

Snyder, Holly, *A Sense of Place: Jews, Identity and Social Status in Colonial British America, 1654–1831* (Brandeis Univ. diss., 2000).

——, 'Customs of an Unruly Race: The Political Context of Jamaican Jewry,' in Barringer, Timothy, Gillian Forrester and Barbaro Martinez-Ruiz (eds.), *Art and Emancipation in Jamaica: Isaac Mendes Belisario and His Worlds* (New Haven: Yale University Press, 2007).

——, 'Declarations of Inter-Dependence: The Trans-Colonial Trajectory of Jewish Rights and Liberties in the Anglo-Atlantic Empire, 1740–1830,' 12th Annual Conference of the Omohundro Institute of Early American History and Culture (Quebec City, June 9, 2006).

——, 'Queens of the Household: The Jewish Women of British America,' in Nadell, Pamela S. and Jonathan D. Sarna (eds.), *Women and American Judaism: Historical Perspectives* (Hanover, New Hampshire: Brandeis University Press, 2001), pp. 15–45.

——, 'Rules, Rights and Redemption: The negotiation of Jewish status in British Atlantic port towns, 1740–1831,' *Jewish History*, Vol. 20, no. 2 (May 2006), pp. 147–70.

Sorkin, David, 'The Port Jew: Notes Toward a Social Type,' *Journal of Jewish Studies*, Vol. 1, no. 1 (Spring 1999), pp. 87–98, here p. 87

Spellberg, Denise, *Thomas Jefferson's Qur'an: Islam and the Founders* (New York: Alfred A. Knopf, 2013).

Stein, Sarah Abrevaya, *Plumes: Ostrich Feathers, Jews, and a Lost World of Global Commerce* (New Haven: Yale University Press, 2008).

Stern, Selma, *The Court Jew: A Contribution to the History of the Period of Absolutism in Central Europe* (Philadelphia: Jewish Publication Society of America, 1950).

Stow, Kenneth R., 'Ethnic Rivalry or Melting Pot: The "Edot" in the Roman Ghetto,' *Judaism*, Vol. 41, no. 3 (Summer 1992), pp. 286–97.

——, *Theatre of Acculturation: The Roman Ghetto in the Sixteenth Century* (Seattle: University of Washington Press, 2001).

Sutcliffe, Adam, 'Jewish History in an Age of Atlanticism,' in Richard L. Kagan and Philip D. Morgan (eds.), *Atlantic Diasporas: Jews, Conversos, and Crypto-Jews in the Age of Mercantilism, 1500–1800* (Baltimore: Johns Hopkins University Press, 2009), pp. 18–30.

——, *Judaism and Enlightenment* (Cambridge: Cambridge University Press, 2003).

Swetschinski, Daniel, *Reluctant Cosmopolitans: The Portuguese Jews of Seventeenth-Century Amsterdam* (London: Littman Library of Jewish Civilization, 2000).

Thompstone, Stuart, 'Central Asia's Jewish Minority and its Contribution to Tsarist Russia's Economic Development,' *Renaissance & Modern Studies*, Vol. 38 (1995), pp. 60–79.

Toro, Alfonso, *La familía Carvajal: Estudio Histórico Sobre los Judíos y la Inquisición de la Nueva España en el Siglo XVI* (Mexico City: Editorial Patria S.A., 1944).

– CHAPTER 23: *Navigating the Jewish Atlantic* –

Trivellato, Francesca, *The Familiarity of Strangers: The Sephardic Diaspora, Livorno, and Cross-Cultural Trade in the Early Modern Period* (New Haven: Yale University Press, 2009).

Usque, Samuel, *Consolation for the Tribulations of Israel* [Martin A. Cohen, trans.] (Philadelphia: Jewish Publication Society of America, 1964).

Warnke, Nina, 'Going East: The Impact of American Yiddish Plays and Players on the Yiddish Stage in Czarist Russia, 1890–1914,' *American Jewish History*, Vol. 92, no. 1 (2004), pp. 1–29.

Wesselius, J. W., 'Spinoza's Excommunication and Related Matters,' *Studia Rosenthaliana*, Vol. 24, no. 1 (1990), pp. 43–63.

Williams, James H., '"Abominable Religion" and Dutch (In)tolerance: The Jews and Petrus Stuyvesant,' *De Halve Maen*, Vol. 71, no. 4 (Winter 1998), pp. 85–87.

Yovel, Yirmiyahu. 'Why Spinoza was Excommunicated,' *Commentary*, Vol. 64, no. 5 (1977): 46–52.

Zacek, Natalie A. *Settler Society in the English Leeward Islands, 1670–1776* (Cambridge University Press, 2010).

PART VI
CREDIT, FINANCE, AND MONEY

CHAPTER TWENTY-FOUR

BRITISH JOINT-STOCK COMPANIES AND ATLANTIC TRADING

Matthew David Mitchell

Our sovereign lord and lady the king and queen's majesties, considering how much the improvement of trade concerns the wealth and welfare of the kingdom, and that nothing has been found more effectual for the improving and enlarging thereof than the erecting and encouraging of companies whereby the same may be carried on by undertakings to the remotest parts, which it is not possible for single persons to undergo...

(Records of the Parliaments of Scotland: 2013)

The preceding passage from the 1693 'Act for Encouraging of Forraigne Trade' succinctly sets out the reasons why an early modern state – in this case, Scotland – would choose to charter a joint-stock trading company. What the Scottish legislators wanted, and wanted quickly, was a homegrown Atlantic trading system that could rival England's already-established oceanic commerce. The 'Company of Scotland tradeing to Affrica and the Indies', as it was dubbed in a further piece of establishing legislation in 1695, seemed to offer just such a shortcut to commercial empire due to three special capabilities of joint-stock companies.

First, joint-stocks offered the opportunity to invest and profit to people from across the social spectrum, not only those expert in the mysteries of overseas trading. Fully 34 per cent of the Company of Scotland's initial capital subscription of 153,448 Scottish pounds came from Scotland's lairds, a share outweighing that of Scotland's merchants. Second, the great risks of oceanic trade in the early modern technological environment were spread among this multitude of investors rather than being borne by 'single persons', whether acting individually or in small partnerships. Third, a state by granting broad liberties to a joint-stock company could allow it to carry on its own diplomatic and military policy in the lands where it traded – an advantage thought to be particularly useful in the 'remotest parts' of the world where European state power could not extend and where the power of indigenous polities was thought to be too crude to provide proper security. None of these capabilities worked to the advantage of the Company of Scotland, which sank much of its capital – a sum amounting to one-sixth of the realm's circulating coinage – into a Central American colony that soon proved a dead loss. The consequences of this

441

Figure 24.1   The several journals of the Court of Directors of the Company of Scotland Trading to Africa and the Indies
Reproduced by kind permission of The Royal Bank of Scotland © 2014

– CHAPTER 24: *British joint-stock companies* –

disaster proved fatal for the Scottish Parliament, which in 1707 assented to its own dissolution and the creation of a United Kingdom ruled from Westminster as the price for Scottish access to the pre-existing English Atlantic system (Watt 2007: 28, 57, 82–83, 207–16, 251–54).

In the course of this system's development the English state had experimented with several chartered companies of its own, though none of them failed so dramatically as the short-lived Company of Scotland and none matched the success that the British East India Company achieved in Asian trade. Even so, the late seventeenth and early eighteenth centuries formed the classic period of English/British joint-stock commercialism in the Atlantic Basin. The Hudson's Bay Company (HBC) had been established in 1670 and its core business of purchasing beaver pelts from the inhabitants of the American far north for the supply of Europe's hatting industry would enjoy its greatest success following the conclusion in 1713 of the War of the Spanish Succession. The South Sea Company (SSC) would receive its charter in 1711 and though the expectations of its Parliamentary supporters that it would serve as a bedrock of government finance soon collapsed along with the great speculative bubble of 1720, the company would carry out its commercial role as Britain's official purveyor of enslaved African labourers to Spanish America for an additional two decades.

Figure 24.2 The South-Sea House in Bishops-gate Street, published according to Act of Parliament, for Stowe's Survey, 1754
Bleichroeder Print Collection, Kress Collection. Baker Library, Harvard Business School (olvwork 368953)

On the other hand, in 1707 a third great joint-stock trading firm, the Royal African Company (RAC), faced a political fight for its survival that it would soon lose. Like South Sea and Hudson's Bay Companies, the Royal African Company also enjoyed a charter that granted it a monopoly over a branch of British Atlantic trade, in this case the supply of African commodities to Britain itself and enslaved labourers to its American colonies. From the RAC's foundation in 1672 it faced illicit competition from 'separate traders', but by the 1690s these had organized themselves into a highly effective political lobby aimed at convincing Parliament and British public opinion that the RAC monopoly not only infringed the liberty of the individual subject, but actually held back the efficient development of British commerce as a whole.

The separate traders' wide-ranging critique questioned most of the fundamental premises for the very existence of joint-stock companies. Were they really the best way of raising the capital necessary for long-range trading while spreading the inherent risk? Did it really serve the interests of Crown or of country to grant such sweeping liberties to a specially chosen group of its subjects? Could the RAC really supply enslaved labourers to the colonies in greater numbers and at lower prices than the separate traders could if given the opportunity? Did the company really do the best possible job of exporting British manufactures and thus providing employment? In short, was the RAC – and by extension, other joint-stock companies – using the capabilities of the joint-stock form to conduct overseas commerce as efficiently as possible, or was it simply hiding behind the protection of its monopoly privilege to engage in inefficient yet profitable 'rent-seeking' behaviour?

THE FIRST ENGLISH JOINT-STOCKS, 1555–1660

Long before the establishment of the Royal African Company and its contemporaries, similar questions were being asked of the very first of England's joint-stock companies, the Muscovy or Russia Company. Chartered in 1555, the Muscovy Company made only a meagre contribution to the wealth of the realm, but it set the pattern for the Atlantic trading concerns of the seventeenth century and beyond in at least two important ways. First, from its beginning the company faced clandestine competition from fellow English subjects. In 1566 Parliament responded to company appeals for relief from these violations of its charter by passing an act calling for the seizure of Russia-bound non-company vessels and their cargoes. As would happen in virtually every subsequent case in which a joint-stock company sought to assert an exclusive privilege, the bolder 'interlopers' simply flouted this law, which was enforced only weakly. A related second problem confronting the Muscovy Company was the opportunistic behaviour of its own members and employees, some of whom participated in illicit trade on their own accounts (Willan 1948: 316–20).

As a rule the sixteenth-century English forays into Atlantic commerce lacked key elements common to the Muscovy Company and the later joint-stock companies. Beginning in 1553 a group of London merchants pooled their resources for the fitting out of a series of trading expeditions to the coast of West Africa, bringing back gold, spice, and ivory. Rather than the permanent joint-stock that characterized the Muscovy Company, the partners in these African ventures reclaimed their original capital plus a share of the profits after each individual voyage and then had the

– CHAPTER 24: *British joint-stock companies* –

option to reinvest in the next voyage. The operation also lacked a royal charter, let alone a monopoly privilege, although Queen Elizabeth herself invested in the voyages of 1561, 1563 and 1564. After this the slave-trading expeditions of the Plymouth-based John Hawkins eclipsed the activities of the London partners. Hawkins organized the financing of his commercial activities in Africa along similar lines as the Londoners had, as would the anti-Spanish privateers and Northwest Passage seekers that followed him such as Martin Frobisher, Thomas Cavendish and Francis Drake (Rabb 1967: 61–63; Scott 1912: 3–9). In 1588 while these men were occupied with harrying the Spanish Armada, eight merchants from London and Exeter took the next organizational step, receiving a royal charter that granted them a ten-year exclusive privilege to trade in Africa under the name of the Senegal Adventurers (Scott 1912: 10–11).

The first three decades of the seventeenth century saw a great surge of interest in the establishment of English joint-stock companies, though the goal of most of these was Atlantic colonization rather than commerce. Gentlemen investors, as opposed to merchants, were conspicuous by their numbers in many of these colonial projects, accounting for 560 of the 1,684 members in the Virginia Company, 26 out of 122 in the Massachusetts Bay Company, and 78 out of 105 in Sir Walter Ralegh's various South American ventures. By contrast, investors in the commercially focused East India Company were almost entirely merchants. This suggests that in comparison with the profit-minded merchants, gentlemen's investments may have been motivated more by the desire to expand England's territory, wealth and glory rather than their personal fortunes (Rabb 1967: 28–42).

Yet one Atlantic trading company, the Gynney and Bynney Company, counted thirty landed gentlemen among its thirty-eight identifiable members. This firm's 1618 charter from James I acknowledged the intention to 'run a uniform course in the setting up and prosecuting a trade of merchandise' to Africa, symbolized by its establishment and maintenance of the first English trading fort on the African coast. This company proved a rather spectacular financial failure: the first ship dispatched was lost at sea and the first three voyages together resulted in the loss of £5,600 out of its initial capital of about £7,000. It also proved as incompetent in restraining interlopers as it was inefficient in conducting its own trade. While the company apparently attempted to seize and condemn interloping vessels where it could, the interlopers successfully lobbied the Parliament of 1624 to declare the Gynney and Binney charter a grievance on the grounds that it raised the price English textile makers had to pay for African dyestuffs. After these reverses the company stopped fitting out voyages, instead licensing others to carry on the trade, including several of its own members (Porter 1968: 59; Rabb 1967: 30; Scott 1912: 11–15).

Despite the 1628 purchase of a controlling interest by one of its most prominent member-licensees, Nicholas Crispe, the Gynney and Binney Company succumbed to bankruptcy in 1631. Crispe, however, saw great commercial potential in West Africa and immediately reorganized the company under a new charter from Charles I with a 31-year monopoly clause. The new Company of Merchants Trading to Guinea (otherwise known as 'Nicholas Crispe and Company') took as its mainstay the trade in dyestuffs from Sierra Leone, but also attempted inroads into the trade of the Gold Coast. Crispe's company built at least four trading factories in this new region of interest, thus staking a claim alongside the more established Portuguese traders and the Dutch West India Company, the United Provinces' own Atlantic joint-stock trading firm. Though Crispe faced competition from these quarters as well as from the continuing challenge of English interlopers, he would later claim that his company imported half a million pounds worth of African gold from 1636 to 1644 (Porter 1968: 61–65).

The politics of the Civil War undid Crispe's success. Knighted in 1640, this staunch Royalist lost control of the Company of Merchants Trading to Guinea after Parliament froze his assets in 1644. The company's subsequent managers proved better at Interregnum politics than at trading with Africa. Interlopers including Samuel Vassall, a major figure in the growing transport of enslaved Africans to Barbados, continued to complain about the company monopoly, prompting a governmental inquiry into its affairs in 1651. This inquiry found that the company had lost some £100,000 during its existence, yet recommended the extension of its charter through 1664 on the grounds that the perils of trading with Africa made a joint-stock company necessary. Vassall later ceased his criticisms of the company and indeed bought a stake in it himself, but by 1657 the company no longer found its string of African forts profitable, leasing them to the East India Company as waystations (Porter 1968: 66–72; Smith 2006: 23).

THE HIGH PERIOD OF THE AFRICAN COMPANIES, 1660–1712

The Restoration of Charles II in 1660 brought about a new era of joint-stock enterprise as senior members of the House of Stuart took an interest in the possibilities of Atlantic commerce. Charles's brother James, Duke of York and their cousin Prince Rupert led the list of subscribers who in 1660 and 1663 obtained charters naming them the Company of Royal Adventurers Trading into Africa (CRA). The 1663 charter stipulated that the company should have the '"whole, entire and only trade for the buying and selling bartering and exchanging of for or with any Negroes, slaves, goods, wares and merchandises whatsoever to be vented or found at or within any of the Cities" on the west coast of Africa' (Donnan 1930: 169n; Zook 1919b: 148).

The appearance of 'Negroes' and 'slaves' at the head of the list reflected a major change in the emerging political economy of the English Atlantic. Colonists in Virginia and Maryland had long since identified tobacco as the cash crop best adapted to their climate, while Barbados and Jamaica proved ideal for sugar monoculture. By 1663 planters in all of these locations were abandoning their earlier experiments with white indentured servitude, turning instead to enslaved Africans as their main source of labour (Menard 2007: 310–12, 318). The killing labour regime and hostile disease environment of the plantations ensured that planters in the American colonies would face a constant need for newly imported slaves to replace the dead (Tadman 2000: 1536–37). The Company of Royal Adventurers obliged the planters by delivering nearly 16,000 enslaved Africans to America from 1662 to 1672, although the company's assertion of its exclusive rights to the trade did not prevent English interlopers from delivering an additional 7,000 slaves over the same period (Voyages).

The Royal Adventurers' most dangerous rivals were not their unchartered fellow English subjects, but the West India Company (WIC), the Dutch Republic's entry

– CHAPTER 24: *British joint-stock companies* –

into Atlantic joint-stock commerce. Since its foundation in 1621, the WIC had conquered the entire string of Portuguese fortresses along the West African coast, including the main Gold Coast castle of Elmina. Dutch dominance of the Gold Coast was by no means complete, for upstart West India Companies from Sweden, Denmark, and Brandenburg each maintained at least one tenuous settlement there, but when the Portuguese sought to re-enter the trade in 1689 the Dutch were able to force their ships to purchase passes at Elmina (Postma 1990: 14–18, 75–77).

Starting in 1664 the Company of Royal Adventurers mounted its own military challenge to Dutch control of the Gold Coast. The conquest by Sir Robert Holmes of several WIC ships and factories provoked a response in kind by a Dutch fleet under Michiel de Ruyter. In 1665, these mutual depredations between the two companies pushed England and the Dutch Republic themselves into open war, the second between the two states since 1650 (Zook 1919a: 177–82; 1919b: 153–56). The CRA's interests suffered badly in the war it fomented; the company sent eighty-nine ships to Africa to purchase slaves from 1662 to 1666, but only seven from 1667 through 1672 (Voyages). Rendered incapable of further trading, the CRA during the late 1660s resorted to the time-honoured expedient of selling licences to those who could, including several of its own shareholders. One group of licensees – perhaps seeing little possibility of loosening the Dutch grip on the Gold Coast trade – set up a separate uncharted joint-stock under the name of the Gambia Adventurers, paying the CRA £1,000 annually for the exclusive privilege of trading to the Senegambia region under the CRA charter (Zook 1919b: 156–58).

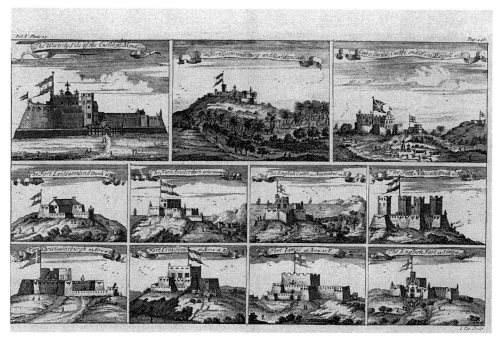

Figure 24.3 Views of forts and castles along the Gold Coast, West Africa, about 1700
© National Maritime Museum, Greenwich, London

This period of disarray ended in September 1672 with the establishment of the Royal African Company, the last in the series of joint-stocks chartered by the English crown to conduct the realm's trade with Africa. Like its predecessor the CRA, the RAC enjoyed substantial gentry and aristocratic involvement with ten out of twenty-four charter members ranking as esquires at least; on the other hand, the new company received about three-fourths of its initial capitalization of £110,100 from merchants (Donnan 1930: 179–80; Davies 1960: 64–66). Because the CRA's experience seemed to indicate that 'the powers and privileges in our said Letters Patents granted were not sufficient for those purposes for which they were designed', the Royal African Company received a much wider set of liberties than those possessed by its predecessor, including 'full power to make and declare peace and war with any of the heathen nations' within the charter's geographical limits. Second, the RAC would have the right of search and seizure and the assistance of customs officers and the Royal Navy (whose Lord Admiral, James Duke of York, was also the RAC's ceremonial Governor) in order to enforce the prohibition of interlopers from the 5,000 miles of coastline from Morocco down to the Cape of Good Hope. Finally, the charter provided that any interlopers captured on the African coast would be heard in a prerogative court administered by the RAC itself with authority to condemn ships and confiscate cargoes (Donnan 1930: 179, 188–91).

These powers went some way towards interdicting interlopers, especially on the coast of Africa (Carlos and Kruse 1996: 305; Davies 1960: 115–16), but the challenge of monopoly enforcement was much greater in the Americas. Here the sugar and tobacco planters who were the main purchasers of enslaved labourers also dominated colonial politics, and they wanted the largest possible labour supply at the lowest possible cost, giving them the incentive to connive in smuggling. Between 1679 and 1682 the RAC's Caribbean agents reported the arrival of thirty-two interloping vessels, but were able to seize only four of them. Colonial governors, anxious to curry favour with local elites, often refused to support the RAC's efforts to seize interlopers, and even when such seizures were successful, they stood little chance of being upheld in colonial courts (Davies 1960: 113–20; Zahedieh 2010a: 116–17). As a result, the RAC's powers to restrain competition were of limited use. The available documents of slave trading voyages show that from 1674, when the Royal African Company sent out its first slave ship, through 1688, British vessels embarked an approximate total of 141,807 enslaved human beings in African ports; seven out of every ten were embarked by RAC ships and the other three out of ten on interloping vessels (Voyages).

The Revolution of 1688 ended the reign of James II, the RAC's great Stuart patron who had succeeded his brother Charles only three years before, and simultaneously brought into disrepute the expansive view of the royal prerogative upon which the RAC's charter rested. In the following year the court of King's Bench, under its newly appointed Lord Chief Justice Sir John Holt, reversed an admiralty court's pro-company verdict in the 1684 case of *Nightingale v. Bridges*, finding in favour of the owners of an interloping vessel seized by a Royal Navy frigate on monopoly-enforcement duty. The RAC largely curtailed its coercive efforts against interlopers after this decision, which established common-law jurisdiction over cases involving its monopoly privileges and rendered the company's own prerogative court ineffective (Stump 1974: 29–32).

– CHAPTER 24: *British joint-stock companies* –

Much as happened simultaneously in the Indian Ocean trade, which split between partisans of the Old and New East India Companies, the battle between interlopers and the RAC over the state of the African trade now entered the halls of Parliament. A voluminous pamphlet literature on both sides of the question extended the dispute into the court of public opinion; indeed, 'the debate surrounding the African trade generated as much literature as, if not more than, any other economic controversy during this period' (Keirn 1995: 437). Sharing the mercantilist preoccupation with the realm's balance of trade, the mostly anonymous pamphleteers on both sides sought to convince readers that their preferred commercial system would maximize both the African demand for English goods and the African supply of enslaved labourers to the English plantations (Mitchell 2013b: 442–46). In 1697 the 'separate trade' lobby, representing the interests of interlopers along with the many colonial planters who believed themselves underserved by the Royal African Company, won a somewhat hollow victory in the form of an Act that confirmed their right to participate in the African trade, but required them to pay the RAC a duty of 10 per cent for the upkeep of its forts, on the grounds that all English traders in West Africa benefited from the protection of the forts (Zahedieh 2010a: 52).

Continued Anglo-Dutch hostilities in Africa lent credence to the perceived need for the forts, though the tactics on both sides had become less direct than they were in the 1660s. During the 1670s and 1680s the Royal African Company and the Dutch West India Company engaged in an increasingly expensive contest to offer the most lavish bribes to the African rulers and merchants who controlled trade on various parts of the coast in hopes of securing exclusive trading rights. The stakes increased during the 1690s when the RAC and WIC took sides in an eight-year succession battle in the kingdom of Komenda on the western Gold Coast, with each company encouraging its preferred claimant to attack the trading posts of the rival company. Though at the time England and the Dutch Republic shared a ruler in William of Orange and a common French enemy, officers in the African service of both the RAC and WIC considered their commercial rivalry as something separate from the policy of their sovereigns (Law 2007).

The spectre of Dutch competition loomed large in the economic thinking of Charles Davenant, the prolific pamphleteer engaged by the Royal African Company to write a plea for the renewal of its monopoly that ran to three volumes and 136 total pages. The Dutch, according to Davenant,

> have laid it down for a Maxim, that in all Foreign Trades where the Trade must be maintain'd by Force and Forts on the Land, and where they cannot conveniently keep up an Amity and Correspondence by Ambassadors alone, there seems to be an absolute Necessity of carrying on such Trades, by Joint-Stocks.
>
> (Davenant 1709: 28)

Davenant's lengthy treatise appeared in 1709 amid a welter of new pro- and anti-RAC publications as the so-called Ten-Percent Act approached its scheduled expiration in 1712. This time all the ink spilled on both sides of the question resulted in no new legislation at all, but with the burdensome ten-percent duty expired and the Royal African Company having gained no Parliamentary sanction of their privileges, the separate traders could claim complete political victory over the monopolists (Pettigrew 2013: 43–44).

449

Following this de facto opening of the slave trade, and contrary to the dire prophecies of Davenant and other pro-RAC pamphleteers, Britain actually expanded its overall share of the trade even as the company's share dwindled in the face of unrestrained competition from the private traders. From 1672 to 1712, Royal African Company ships delivered 133,551 enslaved persons to the Americas, an annual average of 3,257. By contrast, during the first decade of duty-free trade from 1713 to 1722, the separate traders delivered a collective annual average of 12,705 Africans for sale to colonial planters (Voyages). Savvy and well-capitalized traders like London's Humphry Morice, who would fit out at least seventy-three slaving voyages between 1709 and 1732, had effectively eroded what competitive advantages the RAC had possessed (Rawley 2003; Voyages). In the process, each year they condemned roughly four times as many human beings to involuntary transportation across the Atlantic and forced labour in the Americas as the Royal African Company had done during each year of its monopoly.

HUDSON'S BAY, SOUTH SEA, AND ROYAL AFRICAN COMPANIES AFTER 1713

If the political events of 1712 marked a precipitous decline in the fortunes of the Royal African Company, those of 1713 portended a brighter future for Britain's two other Atlantic trading companies of the day: the Hudson's Bay Company and the South Sea Company. The South Sea Company (SSC) received its charter from Queen Anne in 1711, the brainchild of the Tory circle around Lord High Treasurer Sir Robert Harley. The new firm was to serve in part as a holding company for over £9 million worth of the National Debt – a connection with state finances that in 1720 would lead to the inflation and bursting of the South Sea Bubble, by far the best-known event in the company's history (for which see the essay in this volume by Helen Julia Paul). From the beginning, however, Harley had pictured a commercial foundation for the SSC's financial functions, promising potential investors that the projected company would enjoy a monopoly on the previously clandestine trade between the British Caribbean islands and the Spanish Main. In 1711 with the War of the Spanish Succession in progress, this was a speculative proposition at best, but the peace negotiations in Utrecht resulted in a contract (the *asiento*) for the British crown to supply 4,800 slaves annually to Spain's empire for a period of thirty years, which Queen Anne immediately awarded to the South Sea Company (Wennerlind 2011: 197–203, 218–19).

Initially the South Sea Company conducted its branch of the trade in enslaved human beings in much the same way that the Royal African Company had approached the supply of slaves to the British plantations: chartering vessels and freighting them with cargo to be exchanged in Africa for slaves to be transported to Jamaica, where the slaves would be 'refreshed' on shore before the final transit to the markets in such Spanish Caribbean ports as Cartagena, Panama, Veracruz, or Havana. Later on the company sought ways to externalize some of the risks of this itinerary. One way of doing this was to allow the Royal African Company to exchange cargoes from Europe for slaves and then sell them to the South Sea Company, which would handle the Middle Passage. Another method involved the SSC's agent at Kingston in Jamaica purchasing Africans from private traders and transferring them to SSC vessels for the

– CHAPTER 24: *British joint-stock companies* –

run to the Spanish Main. From about 1729 the SSC concentrated on this short-haul slaving business along with its transatlantic supply of slaves to Buenos Aires and its privilege of sending one ship a year laden with European consumer imports to one of Spanish America's trade fairs (Palmer 1981: 9–12, 15–16).

The South Sea Company faced significant barriers in making this trade profitable, many of them similar to those the Royal African Company had faced. British interlopers and even the SSC's own opportunistic captains bit into company profits, while the planters of Jamaica attempted several times to impose duties on the landing and re-export of slaves, hoping to prevent Spanish slave purchasers from monopolizing the most productive enslaved agriculturalists. Even in peacetime South Sea captains and land-based agents quarrelled constantly with Spanish officials over the terms of the *asiento*. During wartime the trade ground to a halt, as it did during the war of 1718–20, while the outbreak in 1739 of the War of Jenkins' Ear (or to the Spaniards, the *Guerra del Asiento*) ended the SSC's trading operations more or less permanently, though it remained in existence as a manager of government securities well into the nineteenth century (Palmer 1981: 65–66, 83–94). Yet in contrast to the Royal African Company, the South Sea Company's profitability during its years of supplying slaves to Spanish America seems on the incomplete evidence available to have been 'far from unprofitable' and even 'better than good' (Palmer 1981: 155).

The end of war with France in 1713 also signalled improved prospects for the Hudson's Bay Company. Established in 1670, the Hudson's Bay Company (HBC) was the first Atlantic trading firm to extend the joint-stock model of commerce beyond Africa. Though joint-stock companies had initially set up several English colonies in America, individual merchants mainly took on the business of supplying them with European consumer goods and carrying away their agricultural products (Zahedieh 2010a: 80–81). Compared with trade to Barbados or Massachusetts-Bay, the fur trade of 'Rupert's Land' seemed better adapted for a joint-stock, since it involved 'an area without a structured government or governor and without permanent European settlers'. Within twenty years of its charter, the new company constructed four trading factories on the west coast of Hudson Bay. Until 1713, however, the factories existed under constant threat of French military action and the HBC's trade remained relatively small (Carlos and Lewis 2010: 3–5, 40–43).

With British authority over the Canadian Shield region recognized in the Treaty of Utrecht – and with populations of fur-bearing animals waning in Russia and around the North American Great Lakes – the company found that it controlled a large portion of the supply of pelts to the European hat industry. Nor did France attempt the conquest of the region in any of the five Anglo-French wars of the next hundred years; as a result, the Hudson's Bay Company enjoyed lower security costs than the Royal African Company, whose installations had always faced a greater threat from seagoing Europeans than from African attackers (Carlos and Lewis 2010: 5, 12, 43). If forts therefore represented a lesser liability to the HBC than to the RAC, their warehousing function also served as a greater asset. Pelts could be purchased and stored for months in expectation of the HBC's annual ship, but humans could not be kept for nearly so long in the heat and squalor of the RAC's slave dungeons.

French *coureurs de bois* operating from Quebec and Montreal did compete with the Hudson's Bay Company to purchase pelts from Native American hunters, often forcing the British factors to offer the hunters a significantly greater amount of

451

European-made consumer manufactures in exchange for each pelt than the company's official price standard indicated. Yet compared to the Royal African Company, whose factors also bartered for African commodities and enslaved persons according to an official list of prices, the directors of the Hudson's Bay Company could give their factors much more latitude to vary from the standard while still trading profitably (Carlos and Lewis 2010: 53–67). The hunters also did well out of this exchange, acquiring imported household goods and luxuries along with producer goods such as firearms that allowed them to harvest the products of the subarctic environment more efficiently. The resulting standard of living for Native Americans around Hudson's Bay arguably equalled that of labourers in England (Carlos and Lewis 2010: 78–95, 179–83).

In 1749 the Hudson's Bay Company faced a political test when representations from the projectors of a rival company prompted a Parliamentary inquiry into whether the revocation of the HBC monopoly might increase the supply of furs. The HBC's counterargument echoed that of the Royal African Company during its own political troubles by (erroneously) invoking the barbarity of their trading counterparts and (more credibly) the bogey of potentially violent competition from a rival European state, in this case France instead of the Dutch Republic. Unlike the RAC, the HBC prevailed; the investigating commission recommended to Parliament that the company retain its monopoly (Carlos and Lewis 2010: 134–39; Wagner 2012: 9). Even so, the halcyon days could not last forever for the Hudson's Bay Company. In the wake of the British conquest of Quebec during the Seven Years' War, a new British firm, the Montreal-based North West Company, rivalled the HBC's control for control of a trade in beaver pelts that was already declining due to overhunting (Carlos and Lewis 2010: 184–88).

As for the Royal African Company, it experienced a brief but extraordinary revival after James Brydges, first Duke of Chandos, led a coterie of mostly aristocratic investors in a successful bid to purchase the company during the Bubble year of 1720 (Shea 2011, 18–19). Though he assured his fellow shareholders that his short-term plans involved the recapture of the slave trade to British America, Chandos privately believed the company unable to compete with the separate traders in the post-1712 political environment (Mitchell 2013a: 546, 555n, 558–60).

Instead, over the next three years Chandos led a secret RAC 'bye committee' in organizing a series of expeditions aimed at locating and securing previously unknown sources of gold, spices and drugs within Africa itself. In time Chandos expected that imports to Europe of such newly discovered commodities would become the Royal African Company's main line of business, generating sufficient profits to allow the company to purchase and transport slaves at a loss until the separate traders were priced out and had to leave the trade. For the moment the company used Chandos's infusion of new capital to fund the largest trading volume in its history: over £100,000 of European goods and Asian re-exports sent to Africa in the single year of 1723. Fierce competition from other Europeans seeking to buy African commodities and enslaved persons meant that this massive investment of working capital produced only massive losses, starving the company of cash and stretching its credit to breaking point. Thus did Chandos's long-term project fail and by 1726 he and his friends had cut themselves loose from RAC affairs (Mitchell 2013a: 554–60, 567–73).

In 1731 the company sent out its last slaving voyage, thereafter focusing on the management of the trading posts for which purpose it received an annual Parliamentary

CHAPTER 24: *British joint-stock companies*

subsidy of £10,000. The revocation of this subsidy in 1746, and Parliament's decision in 1750 to give the management of the forts over to a newly organized consortium of traders to Africa, led to the RAC's final dissolution in 1752 (Davies 1960: 345; Hancock 1997: 175, 182–85). The evolution of the British Atlantic system had left the RAC behind.

CONCLUSIONS

Being chartered by the British state, joint-stock trading companies existed in the first instance as instruments of that state's policy. Once in existence they tended to operate quite independently of that policy, yet they maintained an interest in keeping the state convinced of their usefulness for its objectives. When a company failed in using politics to protect its chartered privileges, it then had to fall back upon the commercial expertise of its personnel to stave off its challengers and extend its existence. In large part this meant selecting cargoes in England that would prove in-demand and exchangeable for enslaved Africans, Canadian beaver pelts, or Peruvian silver several months and thousands of miles away. This was a daunting challenge for any prospective early modern transoceanic trader, but the HBC, RAC and SSC all seem to have used the wide range of their operations to achieve at least a temporary advantage in acquiring and handling market information. Yet when the political barriers that protected a company's markets from domestic competition did collapse, as happened to the Royal African Company beginning in the 1690s, it was only a matter of time before a significant number of separate traders gained sufficient experience and capital to erode the joint-stock's economies of scale while avoiding its diseconomies. Of course, even when a company did enjoy a market mostly protected from British rivals, competitors from elsewhere in Europe could make life difficult for its traders. The results of warmaking and diplomacy, both among European states and among the companies they chartered, therefore bore heavily on the differing fortunes of the companies.

The South Sea and Hudson's Bay Companies both enjoyed effectively protected markets thanks to the Treaty of Utrecht in 1713, lasting for the SSC until the renewal of war with Spain in 1739 and for the HBC until after the conquest of Quebec in the war of 1754–63. Aside from the relative handful of French–Canadian fur traders, continental Europeans largely conceded British control of each company's respective market. As for the African trade, the open violence in the 1660s between the Company of Royal Adventurers Trading into Africa and the Dutch West India Company proved disastrous for both, and the continued attempts of the WIC and the CRA's successor, the Royal African Company, to thwart each other left the door to African riches open for other Europeans. The English and Dutch states blundered by devolving diplomatic and military powers onto chartered companies, inadvertently blocking the way to a mutually profitable accommodation in the African trade. The Royal African Company also did less well than its two contemporaries in navigating the politics of the British Empire itself, proving unable to see off Parliamentary challenges to its monopoly privileges in the 1690s through 1710s as the Hudson's Bay Company did in 1749.

Though the literature on the British Atlantic joint-stock companies does allow for such insights, it is limited by the fact that most existing works consider individual companies in isolation rather than juxtaposing multiple companies. Comparative studies along four distinct dimensions will greatly expand our understanding of the

453

significance of joint-stocks. First, while this essay has attempted some broad comparisons among the three big British Atlantic joint-stocks, more detailed studies will surely produce additional evidence for the reasons underlying their divergent trajectories. Second, comparisons between these three companies and Atlantic joint-stocks from elsewhere in Europe may prove useful, particularly for understanding the joint-stocks as quasi-autonomous diplomatic and military actors on an international stage. The British East India Company offers a third potential counterpoint; recent work by Philip J. Stern has extended our understanding of its approach to the projection of political and military power, while James R. Fichter has demonstrated the means by which even this highly successful joint-stock trader eventually succumbed to commercial challenge by small-scale American merchants in the early nineteenth century. To most fully explain the phenomenon of joint-stock companies within the development of capitalism, however, the most essential comparison is with competing traders operating under different organizational forms. For instance, study of the methods by which the separate slave traders not only overcame the RAC's advantages, but also expanded the trade in enslaved labourers far beyond what the larger firm had ever managed, will suggest much about the difference that joint-stock companies made to the wider Atlantic economy.

The Hudson's Bay, Royal African, and South Sea Companies do seem to have achieved at least indifferent commercial success as they developed their respective branches of Britain's emerging Atlantic trading system. This success could last only as long as the keepers of the British state believed the companies' monopoly privileges to be justified. Yet the remarkable – and horrific – expansion in the volume of the slave trade once the Royal African Company lost its own privileged position suggests that perhaps the joint-stocks never were justified as an efficient means of conducting transoceanic commerce in the early modern Atlantic environment.

REFERENCES

Behrendt, Stephen D. (2001) 'Markets, Transaction Cycles, and Profits: Merchant Decision Making in the British Slave Trade', *William and Mary Quarterly*, 58, 1: 171–204.

Carlos, Ann M. (1994) 'Bonding and the Agency Problem: Evidence from the Royal African Company, 1672–91', *Explorations in Economic History*, 31, 3: 313–35.

Carlos, Ann M. and Jamie Brown Kruse (1996) 'The Decline of the Royal African Company: Fringe Firms and the Role of the Charter', *Economic History Review*, 49, 2: 291–313.

Carlos, Ann M. and Santhi Hejeebu (2007) 'Specific Information and the English Chartered Companies, 1650–1750' in Leos Müller and Jari Ojala, eds., *Information Flows: New Approaches in the Historical Study of Business Information*, Helsinki: Studia Historica.

Carlos, Ann M. and Frank D. Lewis (2010) *Commerce by a Frozen Sea: Native Americans and the European Fur Trade*, Philadelphia: University of Pennsylvania Press.

Carlos, Ann M. and Stephen Nicholas (1988) '"Giants of an Earlier Capitalism": The Chartered Trading Companies as Modern Multinationals', *Business History Review*, 62, 3: 398–419.

Davenant, Charles (1709) *Reflections upon the Constitution and Management of the Trade to Africa*, Vol. 1, London: Printed for John Morphew.

Davies, K. G. (1960) *The Royal African Company*, 2nd edn., London: Longmans.

Donnan, Elizabeth (ed.) (1930) *Documents Illustrative of the History of the Slave Trade to America*, Vol. 1, Washington, DC: Carnegie Institution of Washington.

Eltis, David (2000) *The Rise of African Slavery in the Americas*, Cambridge: Cambridge University Press.

– CHAPTER 24: *British joint-stock companies* –

Fichter, James R. (2010) *So Great a Profit: How the East Indies Trade Transformed Anglo-American Capitalism*, Cambridge, Mass.: Harvard University Press.

Hancock, David (1997) *Citizens of the World: London Merchants and the Integration of the British Atlantic Community, 1735–1785*, Cambridge: Cambridge University Press.

Jones, S. R. H. and Simon P. Ville (1996) 'Efficient Transactors or Rent-Seeking Monopolists? The Rationale for Early Chartered Trading Companies', *Journal of Economic History*, 56, 4: 898–915.

Keirn, Tim (1995) 'Monopoly, economic thought, and the Royal African Company' in John Brewer and Susan Staves, eds., *Early Modern Conceptions of Property*, London: Routledge.

Law, Robin (2007) 'The Komenda Wars, 1694–1700: A Revised Narrative', *History in Africa*, 34: 133–68.

Menard, Russell R. (2007) 'Plantation Empire: How Sugar and Tobacco Planters Built Their Industries and Raised an Empire', *Agricultural History*, 81, 3: 309–32.

Mitchell, Matthew David (2013a) 'Legitimate commerce in the eighteenth century: the Royal African Company under the Duke of Chandos, 1720–26', *Enterprise and Society*, 14, 3: 544–78.

——(2013b) 'Three English Cloth Towns and the Royal African Company', *Journal of the Historical Society*, 13, 4: 421–47.

Palmer, Colin (1981) *Human Cargoes: The British Slave Trade to Spanish America, 1700–1739*, Urbana: University of Illinois Press.

Pettigrew, William A. (2013) *Freedom's Debt: The Royal African Company and the Politics of the Atlantic Slave Trade, 1672–1752*, Chapel Hill: University of North Carolina Press.

Pincus, Steven C.A. (2008) 'A Revolution in Political Economy?' in Maximillian E. Novak, ed., *The Age of Projects*, Toronto: University of Toronto Press.

Porter, R. (1968) 'The Crispe Family and the African Trade in the Seventeenth Century', *Journal of African History*, 9, 1: 57–77.

Postma, Johannes Menne (1990) *The Dutch in the Atlantic Slave Trade, 1600–1815*, Cambridge: Cambridge University Press.

Rabb, T. K. (1967) *Enterprise and Empire: Merchant and Gentry Investment in the Expansion of England, 1575–1630*, Cambridge, Mass.: Harvard University Press.

Rawley, James (2003) 'Humphry Morice: Foremost London Slave Merchant of His Time', *London: Metropolis of the Slave Trade*, Columbia: University of Missouri Press.

'The Records of the Parliaments of Scotland to 1707' (2013), K.M. Brown et al., eds., St Andrews, http://www.rps.ac.uk/trans/1693/4/107 (accessed 14 November 2013).

Scott, W. R. (1912) *The Constitution and Finance of English, Scottish and Irish Joint-Stock Companies to 1720*, Vol. 2, Cambridge: Cambridge University Press.

Shea, Gary S. (2011). '(Re)financing the Slave Trade with the Royal African Company in the Boom Markets of 1720', Centre for Dynamic Macroeconomic Analysis Working Paper Series 201114.

Smith, S. D. (2006) *Slavery, Family, and Gentry Capitalism in the British Atlantic: The World of the Lascelles, 1648–1834*, Cambridge: Cambridge University Press.

Stern, Philip J. (2011) *The Company-State: Corporate Sovereignty and the Early Modern Foundations of the British Empire in India*, Oxford: Oxford University Press.

Stump, W. Darrell (1974) 'An Economic Consequence of 1688', *Albion: A Quarterly Journal Concerned with British Studies*, 6, 1: 26–35.

Tadman, Michael (2000) 'The Demographic Cost of Sugar: Debates on Slave Societies and Natural Increase in the Americas', *American Historical Review*, 105, 5 (Dec. 2000), pp. 1534–75.

Voyages: The Trans-Atlantic Slave Trade Database, www.slavevoyages.org (accessed 15 November 2013).

Wagner, Michael (2012) 'Managing To Compete: The Hudson's Bay, Levant, and Russia Companies, 1714–63', *Business and Economic History On-Line: Papers Presented at the Business History Conference Annual Meeting*, 10, http://www.thebhc.org/publications/BEHonline/2012/wagner.pdf (accessed 9 November 2013).

Watt, Douglas (2007) *The Price of Scotland: Darien, Union, and the Wealth of Nations*, Edinburgh: Luath Press Ltd.

Wennerlind, Carl (2011) *Casualties of Credit: The English Financial Revolution, 1620–1720*, Cambridge, Mass.: Harvard University Press.

Willan, T. S. (1948) 'Trade between England and Russia in the Second Half of the Sixteenth Century', *English Historical Review*, 63, 248: 307–21.

Zahedieh, Nuala (2010a) *The Capital and the Colonies: London and the Atlantic economy, 1660–1700*, Cambridge: Cambridge University Press.

Zahedieh, Nuala (2010b) 'Regulation, rent-seeking, and the Glorious Revolution in the English Atlantic economy', *Economic History Review*, 63, 4: 865–90.

Zook, George Frederick (1919a) 'On the West Coast of Africa', *Journal of Negro History*, 4, 2: 163–205.

Zook, George Frederick (1919b) 'The Royal Adventurers in England', *Journal of Negro History*, 4, 2: 143–62.

CHAPTER TWENTY-FIVE

SPECULATING ON THE ATLANTIC WORLD

————•◆•————

Helen Paul

The Mississippi and South Sea Bubbles of 1720 are two of the most famous financial bubbles in history, and amongst the earliest. Each owes its name to a great joint-stock trading company. John Law had restructured the French economy to conform to his 'System' or 'Système'. He combined a number of companies into one leviathan. It is known to posterity as the Mississippi Company and was involved in a number of Atlantic trading ventures.

The South Sea Company was founded in London in 1711 (Carswell, 2001: 45). It was to assist the state by restructuring part of the National Debt. It offered its shares in exchange for the debt obligations held by government creditors. For this, it was paid a fee by the British state. It was granted the monopoly right to trade slaves to Spanish America (the *Asiento*). It could also trade in goods, both with and without official sanction from Spain. Share prices in Paris and London rose to unsustainable heights during 1720, partly (but not solely) due to the activities of over-optimistic investors entering the market. The Paris market experienced a bubble first. As it was bursting, another bubble was inflating in London. The South Sea Company's shares rocketed in price and dragged the rest of the London stock market along as well. This chapter discusses how Atlantic Worlds intersected with the European financial system, with particular reference to the South Sea Company. These linkages have received less attention than lurid tales of gambling manias and frauds.

The standard explanation for the South Sea Bubble is that the company directors were engaged in some sort of fraud and the rest of the country went gambling mad. The contemporary pamphlets, songs, plays and prints which satirise the South Sea Bubble have been a fertile source for historians. However, they tell us very little about why investors chose to put their money into shares and into the South Sea Company in particular (Paul, 2011a: 88–101). Lord Macaulay (1986: 490), writing in the nineteenth century, used the word 'mania'. Mackay (1841) included the South Sea and Mississippi bubbles in his book *Extraordinary Popular Delusions and the Madness of Crowds*. The title says it all. (Logan (2003) describes how popular *Popular Delusions* was in the Victorian era.) Carswell (1960) wrote one of the classic texts on the South Sea Bubble. He thought that '"speculative fever" [...] is hardly a sufficient explanation' (Carswell, 2001: 12). He did believe that the company's trading prospects were negligible and

457

Figure 25.1 Trade label of the South Sea Company
© Lebrecht Music and Arts Photo Library/Alamy

of no interest to the company in any case. It had, he claimed, no 'real assets or even prospects' (Carswell, 2001: 241). Galbraith (1994: 47) got the terms of the *Asiento* wrong and claimed that only one ship a year was allowed to sail (Paul, 2011a: 56–57). Referring to the market conditions for both London and Paris, Galbraith (1994: 43) wrote, 'Insanity born of optimism and self-serving illusion was the tale of two cities'.

CHAPTER 25: *Speculating on the Atlantic World*

Figure 25.2 The Bubblers Bubbl'd or The Devil Take the Hindmost, 1720
© The Print Collector/Alamy

Some of the South Sea directors were unscrupulous and bribed prominent people (Carswell, 2001: 181–93). They provided loans to their shareholders which may have helped inflate prices for other shares temporarily. However, it is not necessary to posit that the entire financial market went gambling mad. Garber (1990) proposed that the South Sea and Mississippi bubbles were both rational bubbles. Only a minority of investors would have to be over-optimistic to start a price rise. If others rationally predicted that the price would continue to rise, they could buy in in order to sell out. Greenwood and Nagel (2009: 239) from their analysis of recent trading data, found that inexperienced investors are more 'prone to the optimism that fuels the bubble'. Inexperienced investors may well have come into the Paris and London stock markets, and this might have helped to inflate a bubble. However, they were also alongside experienced investors. There is no evidence that these people, as a class, went 'gambling mad'. Nor is it necessary for them to be viewed with suspicion for simply following a sensible trading strategy. Financial historians such as Hoppit (2002), Neal (1993) and Paul (2011a) reject stories of mysterious speculative manias. Such tales are not an accurate reflection of a more complicated history. The topic is plagued by what Hoppit (2002) has cogently termed 'the myths of the South Sea Bubble'. The matter is not helped by the fact that scholars like Carswell downplayed the role of the company's trading arm. This chapter will discuss the trading side of the company and also contemporary views of the Atlantic trading system.

The Atlantic trade routes linked Europe, Africa and the Americas and ensured a flow of goods, people and ideas around the Atlantic system. The dreadful trade in human beings underpinned the plantation economies of the Caribbean and boosted the labour force in the European colonies in continental America. Spain was unable to maintain her own transatlantic supply of slaves, due largely to the extra resources needed for the African side of the trade.

African kingdoms had a great deal of power, relative to their European trading associates. African traders brought slaves to the coast from the hinterland. Europeans were only really able to settle at the coast, often on land rented from African kings. For example, in the town of Ouidah (or Whydah), the local ruler had sited three different European trading forts cheek by jowl (Law, 2004: 17–19). Ouidah itself had no harbour and slave ships were forced to anchor offshore and to load goods by canoe. The Europeans were forced to compete with each other at a place convenient to the local Africans. It was not convenient for the Europeans, which shows where the real power lay. African traders required a mix of goods, which could change over time and by location. Thus Europeans needed access to a large range of products as the exact selection required was so variable. European companies had representatives who could then liaise with local traders and kings to determine their requirements. The companies also had trading forts to guard their unsold stock, house slaves and act as a base (Daaku, 1970: 38–39).

The requisite maritime expertise and naval support was also essential. Long sea voyages required particular technologies and skills, but also huge capital investments. The Spanish empire already claimed much of the state's resources, including bureaucratic costs and military support (Paul, 2011a: 40). Spain would have found her resources stretched further if she entered the competitive world at the African coast. The task was deputised to other nations, via the *Asiento*. (The Dutch had held the *Asiento* at one point, for example [Wright, 1924].) Eventually, the Spanish granted the *Asiento* to the British. The main British slave trading company was the Royal African Company (RAC). It had strong ties to the Royal Navy and supported the South Sea Company's trading activities (Paul, 2008). The RAC had its problems, but it had a network of forts along the coast and great experience in the trade.

The Atlantic World has been conceptualised as a series of overlapping 'worlds': the English Atlantic or the French Atlantic to name but two. It is important to note that the Baltic trading system interlocked with the Atlantic World. A particular type of ship was needed to cross the Atlantic, especially if it was fitted out to carry slaves. The ships needed to be large and sturdy enough to weather an Atlantic crossing. They had to be made of good quality materials to withstand the punishment inflicted by Atlantic gales.

– CHAPTER 25: *Speculating on the Atlantic World* –

Certain Baltic materials had few substitutes. Large ships required large masts, and such items were more readily sourced from the Baltic trade than from anywhere else (Paul, 2008). The best quality iron for anchors came from Sweden: known in Britain as Orgrund (Öregrund) iron after the port it was shipped from. Of course, Britain had its own ironmongers and manufacturers but their ironware was intended for different purposes, such as nail-making. The Royal Navy insisted on Orgrund iron for its anchors (Evans et al., 2002). Unsurprisingly, there was a great deal of overlap in the fortunes of the Baltic and Atlantic trading systems. There was also an overlap of personnel. Men who worked as Baltic merchants turned up in the Atlantic trading companies such as the Royal African Company and the South Sea Company. Carswell's (2001: 244–55) directory of South Sea men includes several. For example, William Astell was a director of the South Sea but also dealt in Baltic stores such as timber (Carswell, 2001: 245).

It is notable that the Baltic region had been disrupted by the Great Northern War (1700–21) between Sweden and an alliance of its neighbours led by Russia. The war may have officially ended in 1721 but the writing was on the wall when Charles XII of Sweden died in 1718. As Charles was the main belligerent, it was obvious that the war was coming to a close (Frost, 2000: 290–300). Its ability to dislocate trading patterns would be over. Not only did the ending of the Great Northern War reduce risks for international merchants, but it also freed up supplies needed to equip Atlantic shipping.

The War of the Spanish Succession (1702–13) had a much more direct effect on the Atlantic trade. The same peace dividend for both wars meant that risks were reduced and resources were freed up for private investment. For those merchants and financiers involved in both the Baltic and Atlantic trades, the ending of two main wars was a boon. Even those who were only involved in the Atlantic trade would have understood the value of Baltic supplies to shipbuilding. Another effect of the ending of the War of the Spanish Succession was that the *Asiento* was part of the peace negotiations. The Treaty of Utrecht (1713) conferred the *Asiento* upon Queen Anne, who transferred it to the South Sea Company.

The ending of two major wars may explain why there were excess resources to invest. In addition, the South Sea Bubble was partly inflated by funds coming from Paris when John Law's System unravelled. Neal (1993: 70–71) noted that funds moved from Paris to London and then to Amsterdam and Hamburg. Law's System requires some discussion as it too relates to the Atlantic trading system. John Law's programme of reforms for France was more radical than anything which occurred in England. The new Regent of France inherited all the economic problems of the regime of Louis XIV (died 1715). The Sun King's expenditures had been onerous. He had contracted war debts like other European sovereigns, but he had also built Versailles at great expense. Earlier in the reign the controller general of finances, Colbert, had undertaken financial reforms (McCollim, 2012: 1–13). At the very end of Louis's life, the king appointed another reformer. This was the cautious Desmaretz (or Desmarets). Desmaretz wished to reform the economy in a gradual way. He was the nephew of the great Colbert, and had been his principal assistant. According to McCollim (2012: 8), Desmaretz was only appointed at the 'nadir of the reign'. Previously, he had been excluded from power and viewed with suspicion by Louis. Desmaretz also made powerful enemies and they ensured his downfall after his master died in 1715. Amongst Desmaretz's key reforms was the *dixième*: a tax on income. Property owners were required to declare their income.

461

This tax [the *dixième*] violated one of the principles of French society at the time because it disregarded the social status of the property owner [...] In effect, the new law disregarded the privileges that Louis XIV's government had worked so hard to preserve or create in fashioning an ordered society.

(McCollim, 2012: 1)

John Law was more palatable to the French élite because he appeared to be able to harness reform to the existing social structure. His financial innovations, such as a paper currency, were far more radical than those of Desmaretz. They were also implemented at great speed. Law was appointed by the French Regent in 1715. Velde (2007) gives a good overview of Law's 'System'. Briefly, its main components were 'an operation in public finance, the other [the creation of] paper money' (Velde: 2007: 276). The paper money experiment was the first of its kind in Europe to create an official paper currency as legal tender. Paper instruments, such as records of government debts, did already circulate as a type of *money*. Money is anything, which is a medium of exchange, a unit of account and a store of value. However, Law's paper money was intended to be the dominant type of official currency. He even attempted to force its acceptance instead of commodity money (coins made from precious metals).

The Atlantic side of the System involved Law's battles with public finance. In 1717, Law created a large joint stock company which was to develop territory in Louisiana. Early modern Louisiana covered an area equivalent to 40 per cent of the modern United States. The land was unsettled by Europeans and the intention was to settle and develop it. The company took over the tobacco monopoly (Velde 2007: 277) and, eventually, it gobbled up most of the overseas trading ventures which held a royal charter. Murphy (1997) provides the definitive account of Law's life and career and he describes the System in great detail. Law's company had several names, but is known to posterity as the Mississippi Company. It included the trading companies, the Company of the East Indies (*Compagnie des Indes*) and the China Company (*Compagnie de la Chine*). Then the African Company (*Companie d'Afrique*) was added (Murphy: 1997, 188). Law embarked upon a complicated string of financial manoeuvres in order to finance all these mergers. Within his leviathan company were the components of much of France's Atlantic trade. Tobacco, African trade and American colonial development were all now under one heading. Investors in the Mississippi Company were not exclusively speculating on the French Atlantic World. They were still involved with the political project. The French elite believed that Law could use the riches of foreign trade to avoid the sort of social changes proposed by Desmaretz.

Law's potential success forced the British to restructure their National Debt too. Otherwise, the British could lose the next war. The British government had contracted a number of debts on unfavourable terms. It had tried to convert these debts to a more acceptable form, and reduce its bureaucratic costs. A number of debt conversions had already occurred successfully. The South Sea Company was to offer its shares in exchange for government annuities. Some of these annuities were called 'irredeemables' as the government had no right to convert them without the holder's permission. The government could not take advantage of lower interest rates and more favourable terms (Neal, 1993: 12–13). The South Sea Company did manage to convince annuity holders to convert, which was beneficial for the state. The South Sea company had been formed partly to deal with navy debt. Payments to Royal Navy contractors had fallen heavily into arrears. The situation was becoming desperate by the end of the War of the Spanish Succession. The South Sea Company was founded and shares given to naval contractors in lieu of cash payments. By this method, the great ironmaster Sir Ambrose Crowley gained enough shares to head the company (Flinn, 1960). From the first, the South Sea Company was a creature of the state. Viewing it solely as a private concern is a mistake. It was part of what Brewer (1989) termed 'the fiscal–military state'.

Brewer (1989) introduced the idea of a fiscal–military state which combined the activities of war and trade. Successful warfare brought trading privileges and colonies, but commercial tensions could lead to further warfare. Paul (2008) argued that a large joint-stock company was not merely a private entity. It performed services for the state and expected help in return. The Royal African Company was keeping a British presence in West Africa without which independent traders would not thrive. The other European nations would take over British forts and perhaps take over the whole coastal trade. The slave trade was important, not merely because of the slaves themselves, but also because of the industries associated with the trade. All sorts of manufactured goods were exported along the Atlantic slave routes and important imports were shipped back to Britain. The sugar and tobacco industries were part and parcel of the slave trade. It is not surprising that the entire trading issue was a politically important one. There were numerous Parliamentary enquiries held (Brown, 2007).

Like the RAC, the South Sea Company's future was bound up with the future of the state itself. Both companies worked closely with the Royal Navy to ensure that the merchant shipping had convoy protection. This was a major consideration. When the Royal Navy suspended convoy protection temporarily during the War of the Spanish Succession, the Royal African Company halted its shipments (Paul, 2011b: 213–16). Such close connections within the fiscal–military, or perhaps fiscal–naval state, were important. However, they are not usually highlighted in the secondary literature of the Bubble or in the contemporary propaganda. Perhaps the assistance was so obvious that it went without saying. As such, it has become less obvious to later commentators.

Investment in the South Sea has often been presented in black or white terms. On the one hand, there are the naïve investors who have been duped, gone gambling mad or both. On the other are the fraudsters and stock jobbers. Modern financial models often follow Black's (1985) categorisation of noise traders (those who do not trade on information) and informed traders. This may seem very similar to the black and white view of the Bubble, but it is not. Financial models are known to be abstractions from reality, whilst proponents of gambling mania arguments seem to believe that they reflect the truth. Rational or careful investment in the South Sea is overlooked, even though financial historians have found evidence of reasonable trading strategies. Altorfer-Ong (2007) uncovered the South Sea investments made by the cautious burghers of the Canton of Berne in Switzerland. Temin and Voth (2004) looked at the activities of Hoare's Bank and concluded that it advised its clients well.

Such insights are outweighed by the volume of works about gambling manias and frauds. Some of these do not present much in the way of evidence to back up their claims, or get details wrong. An early proponent of the genre was Archibald Hutcheson MP who was involved in the government inquiry into the crash: the Secret

Committee. This was probably the highlight of Hutcheson's career and he was loath to let anyone forget it. A large number of truly tedious pamphlets by Hutcheson are preserved in the archives. His oeuvre included little in the way of economic argument, but he provided figures and calculations purporting to show that the South Sea scheme was doomed to fail. Dale (2004: viii) praised Hutcheson as 'the unsung hero of the South Sea Bubble'. Paul (2012) argued that Hutcheson had originally predicted that the South Sea Company would be too successful. His calculations into the scheme's workings were flawed and hard to follow. It is unlikely that potential investors gleaned much from him, before the Bubble reached its height. His insight was that the Bubble would burst, but that was presumably obvious by the time he reached that conclusion. It is important to realise that contemporaries did not necessarily rely upon works which happen to have found a home in an archive.

Literary critics, amongst others, have studied the propaganda surrounding the scheme. For example, Downie (1979) has studied government propagandists including Defoe and Swift. Markley (1994) discussed Defoe's claims about the riches of the 'South Seas'. De Goede (2000) analysed how Defoe conceptualised credit as a female figure called 'Lady Credit'. Although such studies are illuminating, they cannot tell us how readers used such propaganda. It is unlikely that investors simply swallowed propaganda whole. Potential investors would also be able to obtain information and advice from professional brokers or from within their social circle. The professional advice of Hoare's Bank has already been mentioned. Laurence (2006) showed that Lady Betty Hastings and her sisters relied upon correspondents in London to give them information about the market. Coffee houses were also an important site of both share trading and of information about the market. A map of Exchange Alley shows a number of coffeehouses including the famous Garraway's (Dale, 2004: 32). Today, the only sign of it is a blue plaque affixed to the wall. In its time, Garraway's and its rivals would provide coffee, a location to meet and newspapers. Some publications, such as John Castaing's *Course of the Exchange*, printed the share prices of the major companies. An investor would need both information and the means to use it correctly. Either the investors or their advisor needed the skills set to trade in the market. Murphy (2009: 193) showed that a small subset of traders had developed skills in derivatives trading. She also discussed the information networks and financial press of the period (Murphy, 2009: 89–136).

There were rational reasons to invest in the South Sea scheme. Some would not have been captured in the propaganda of the day, and have received less attention as a result. One of the most obvious is that investors would have found it easier to diversify their portfolio if they could buy shares. If an individual had most of their capital tied up in their estate, house or business then joint-stock company shares were an important alternative. Shares could be bought for comparatively small amounts of money, especially if they were paid for by instalments. The South Sea Company offered subscription shares (Paul, 2011a: 84–87). Shea (2007) argued that investors could treat these shares as a put option: they had the option, but not the obligation to buy. Whether or not they did so, the returns from overseas trading companies were unlikely to be closely correlated to the returns from a landed estate. The shares themselves had diversification built into them. A South Sea share combined different types of potential return which had different probabilities of success. The government fee to the company was low risk and low return. The company's slave trade had a higher risk but was more lucrative, as was its trade in smuggled goods. And, if Spain's empire started to fray at the edges, then the company might have an advantage in taking over a former Spanish colony. This was a long shot, but if it paid off it would have generated a very high return indeed. There was also an element of portfolio diversification within the one share, which was another feature. A risk-averse purchaser might be attracted by the government payments. Thomas Guy clearly wanted a steady income for his proposed hospital. He purchased South Seas shares before the bubble started to inflate (Cameron, 1954). Others might also purchase a share because of one of the more risky streams of income attached to it.

A third reason, at least for government creditors, was a liquidity premium. Some of the more extreme accounts of the Bubble present investors throwing away solid government securities for worthless paper (for example, Chancellor, 2000: 93). Annuity holders were scattered and could not easily form a coherent pressure group, whilst a single company had more bargaining power. This was important when the government was in arrears. By the time of the South Sea conversions, Neal (1993: 91) showed that the targeted annuities were trading at a deep discount. In addition, annuities which were illiquid carried a risk. Joint-stock shares were assignable (i.e. could be easily transferred to another person) but annuities were not (Neal, 1993: 92–93). Neal (1993: 93–94) showed that there were liquidity premia for the previous successful conversions.

In addition, people who could not carry on a business themselves could invest in trade as rentiers. Women could buy and sell shares. If they were inclined to avoid Exchange Alley itself, they could act via a broker. Some ladies even conducted their business in the shops near to the Alley, where their brokers came to meet them. This is important, as married women lost their legal identity and became 'feme covert' (sic): i.e. their legal identity was covered by that of their husband. Their property, with a few exceptions, was owned by their husband. Women, like Lady Mary Wortley Montague, were able to trade in shares without their husbands being any the wiser (Paul, 2011a: 66–68).

Much has been made of the suspension of the South Sea Company's trading privileges in 1718. The Spanish temporarily halted the trade in this year, due to a dispute over territory between it and its opponents (Paul, 2011a: 27). The company was part of the wider fiscal–military (fiscal–naval) state. Therefore, it benefited from government support but was vulnerable to the vagaries of international politics. Whenever diplomatic relations between Spain and Britain broke down, the company was punished. This occurred in 1718 and again in 1726. The trade was stopped and some of the company's assets seized. Carswell (2001: 64) wrote, 'with its trade at a full stop for all to see, the Company became, from sheer necessity, a naked finance corporation'. Dale (2004: 49–50) argued that the stock market had never valued the South Sea's trade much in any case. Hence the share price was not greatly affected by the news. The lull in trade would have had a great effect if investors thought it was permanent.

Forward-looking investors did not simply consider a company's activities today. They also consider its future prospects. If South Sea investors believed that the company would ultimately prevail and recommence its trade, then they would still be interested in the company's shares. The strength of the Royal Navy had not diminished and Spain did not have a strong fleet to rival it. The Spanish fleet had been destroyed at the Battle of Cape Passaro in 1718 (Paul, 2011a: 27). Therefore, it was not clear

465

how Spain proposed to avoid the terms of the Treaty of Utrecht for any length of time. The history of the East India Company (EIC) is littered with similar setbacks. However, in the popular imagination the EIC has a Whig history of success and the South Sea has no trading history to speak of. These simplifications have come about over time. In some cases, the companies become mere ciphers in a wider Whig historical narrative: the EIC and the expansion of the British Empire, and the South Sea and financial folly.

It is a useful thought experiment to ask what a reasonably well-informed person knew about the South Sea trade. South America was the source of much of the bullion which flowed into Europe. Some of it then flowed out again to pay for goods from India, China and 'the East'. The Chinese in particular had no need for European manufactures. Chinese porcelain and silk were sought after in Europe. To trade with China, there was no option but to secure supplies of bullion. Spain controlled its colonies but restricted their ability to produce their own manufactures. In theory, the colonies purchased goods from Spain but they were also willing to purchase contraband imports. The slave trade was a way to bring in contraband as the Spanish seemed unable to maintain slave supplies themselves. When the British gained their *Asiento* contract, the Spanish had just seen the last of the Hapsburg monarchs of Spain. Under Hapsburg rule, the country had maintained a vast empire which looked as if it would collapse under its own weight. Scholars such as Kamen (1978) and Grafe and Irigoin (2012) have questioned whether or not Spain's economic health was indeed parlous. In any case, the new Bourbon monarchy did institute reforms and the Spanish held on to their empire. If there was a small, even very small, chance that the South Sea would be able to capitalise on Spain's weakness then this should be part of the investment decision. If the South Sea emulated the later success of the East India Company and staked out a colony, then the rewards could be enormous. Any stake, no matter how small, in the company would provide a huge return. If Georgians were prepared to venture a small amount of money on South Sea subscription shares they might stand a chance of a windfall. Such a decision may be gambling (or speculation), but it was gambling with small stakes, which investors could afford to lose. It was not gambling mania. It would be similar to buying a lottery ticket which promised a small chance of winning a large prize.

The notion of an Atlantic world allows scholars to consider the trading routes as they were imagined by traders themselves. The ocean itself becomes the common factor and its history replaces a piecemeal collection of national histories. Scholars decided to use the concept of particular Atlantic worlds, for example a British Atlantic world co-existing with a Spanish one. There may be several Atlantic worlds superimposed upon one Atlantic Ocean. However, whichever world we consider it did not function apart from other trading systems, such as the Baltic and the East Indian and Chinese trades. The trade goods required by African slave traders included items brought into Europe from the East. Chinese porcelain was found at Savi – the capital of the West African Kingdom of Hueda. Savi was abandoned in 1727 (Kelly, 1997). African preferences for certain high quality imports, such as porcelain, could not easily be substituted from within the Atlantic system. Similarly, the shipwrights who constructed the great transatlantic ships preferred high quality Baltic stores. Therefore, the Atlantic World had an overlap with the Baltic and 'Eastern' ones. Even someone who had never left England might have a mental map of the interlocking trading mechanisms, like the moving parts of a watch. This effect is not captured in the propaganda, even of writers such as Defoe. Defoe was an author, not an international merchant. Therefore, a narrow focus on the works of propagandists ignores the mental maps which merchants themselves would have developed. Defoe was not primarily writing for them, but for those who were not so well informed.

By comparison with the spectacular failures, the details of more successful investment strategies have largely been hidden from view. There are three main reasons for this state of affairs. First, some investors may have chosen to downplay their good fortune to avoid envy or confiscation. Second, the records detailing the investments may have been lost over time. Third, if the records exist they may not be in a suitable format for widespread consumption. One of the more immediately tangible effects of the Bubble is that a bookseller called Thomas Guy was able to sell his shares for far more than he paid for them (Cameron, 1954). Guy had originally bought South Sea shares as a long-term investment for his proposed charitable projects. The famous Guy's hospital in London was the result. Had Guy chosen to do something else with his money, his successful strategy may not have come to light. The records of men like Guy may not survive in a usable form, if at all. There is a clear selection bias in the types of materials which are kept and the type of people to whom they belong.

Famous authors, or those who could afford the vanity press, had a greater chance of being read in later years than the unknown merchants who made up the City of London. Even the records which do survive are not always clear. Isaac Newton's jottings about investments in the South Sea do not show conclusively how he fared in the Bubble (Hall and Tilling, 1977: 96–97). This is despite the popular tale that he suffered badly. He is credited with the (presumably apocryphal) remark that he 'could not calculate the madness of the people'. This witticism is far more entertaining than the reality of his account books, which are understandably somewhat dry. Yet it is in account books and ledgers that evidence of successful trades is found. The sources may not be easy for the layman, or even the professional historian, to access or to interpret. They are certainly not as racy as the jottings of Defoe or the prints of Hogarth. However, a number of authors have used account books to show how certain investors did fare well and without being part of a sinister plot. Even the entertaining tale of Lord Londonderry and John Law's high stakes bet regarding future share prices has only recently been told. Neal (2012) took several decades to bring together enough (initially uncatalogued) archival material to write his book. He described how two major financiers entered into an important financial contract with each other, just as the situation in Paris was becoming critical.

Historical financial crises are often treated differently to other recurrent crises, such as wars. Wars are treated as separate historical episodes with their own causes and effects. The context is foregrounded in any discussion. Financial crises are often grouped together into one or more basic types. Until very recently, their similarities, rather than their differences, receive the most attention. Abstract economic models of financial bubbles can help us to understand them, but obviously render them ahistorical. Even the twin bubbles of the Mississippi and South Sea were different events though linked. Both appeared after the War of the Spanish Succession, and towards the end of the Great Northern War. There were investors who were caught up in both. Neal (1993) has cogently argued that there was financial contagion between the Paris and London markets. However, this does not mean that either bubble can be explained by a simple discussion of fraud and gambling. Nor does it mean that the London and Paris bubbles had exactly the same features. The Mississippi bubble was tied to Law's system, whilst the British financial system was not radically overhauled.

This chapter considered how the Baltic and Atlantic trading systems interacted, and how they both benefitted from the ending of wars. Investors may have conceptualised the Atlantic system due to their personal knowledge, or from personal connections with brokers and merchants. The surviving propaganda does not necessarily capture the Atlantic world of the successful merchant. Nor are the quotidian considerations of liquidity, portfolio diversification or women's legal rights mentioned in the popular histories of the Bubble. Yet all these various details might be brought together as part of an investment decision. The competition between France and England may have also played a part. Those with spare funds could invest in companies engaged in the Atlantic trade, but which were also part of their own state's financial architecture. The states themselves were putting their trust in the strategic importance of the Atlantic World.

REFERENCES

ALTORFER-ONG, S., 2007. State investment in eighteenth-century Berne. *History of European Ideas*, 33, 4: 440–62.

BLACK, F., 1985. Noise. *Journal of Finance*. 41, 3: 529–43.

BREWER, J., 1989. *The Sinews of Power: War, Money and the English State 1688–1783*. New York: Alfred A. Knopf.

BROWN, C.L., 2007. The British Government and the Slave Trade: Early Parliamentary Enquiries, 1713–83. In: Farrell, S., Unwin, M. & Walvin, J. (eds), *The British Slave Trade: Abolition, Parliament and the People*. Edinburgh: Edinburgh University Press, 27–41.

CAMERON, H.C., 1954. *Mr Guy's Hospital, 1726–1948*. London: Longmans.

CANNY, N. and MORGAN, P., 2011. *The Oxford Handbook of the Atlantic World*. Oxford: Oxford University Press.

CARSWELL, J., 1960. *The South Sea Bubble*. London: Cresset.

——, 2001. *The South Sea Bubble*, revised ed. Thrupp: Sutton.

CHANCELLOR, E., 2000. *Devil take the Hindmost: A history of financial speculation*. Reprint ed. New York: Plume.

DAAKU, K.Y., 1970. *Trade and Politics on the Gold Coast, 1600–1720: A study of the African Reaction to European Trade*. Oxford: Oxford University Press.

DALE, R., 2004. *The first crash: lessons from the South Sea Bubble*. Princeton NJ: Princeton University Press.

DE GOEDE, M., 2000. Mastering 'Lady Credit': Discourses of Financial Crisis in Historical Perspective, *International Feminist Journal of Politics*, 2, 1: 58–61.

DICKSON, P.G.M., 1967. *The Financial Revolution in England: A Study in the Development of Public Credit, 1688–1756*. London: Macmillan.

DOWNIE, J.A., 1979. *Robert Harley and the press: propaganda and public opinion in the age of Swift and Defoe*. Cambridge: Cambridge University Press.

EVANS, C., JACKSON, O. and RYDÉN, G., 2002. Baltic Iron and the British Iron Industry in the Eighteenth Century, *Economic History Review*, 55, 4: 642–65.

FLINN, M.W., 1960. Sir Ambrose Crowley and the South Sea Scheme of 1711. *Journal of Economic History*, 20, 1: 51–66.

– CHAPTER 25: *Speculating on the Atlantic World* –

FROST, R.I., 2000. *The Northern Wars: War, State and Society in Northeastern Europe, 1558–1721*. London: Longman.

GALBRAITH, J.K., 1994. *A Short History of Financial Euphoria*. New York: Penguin.

GARBER, P.M., 1990. Famous First Bubbles. *Journal of Economic Perspectives*, 4, 2: 35–54.

GRAFE, R. and IRIGOIN, A., 2012. A Stakeholder Empire: the political economy of Spanish imperial rule in America, *Economic History Review*, 65, 2: 609–51.

GREENWOOD, R. and NAGEL, S., 2009. Inexperienced investors and bubbles. *Journal of Financial Economics*. 93: 239–58.

HALL, A.R. and TILLING, L., 1977. *The Correspondence of Isaac Newton*. Cambridge: Cambridge University Press.

HARRIS, R., 1994. The Bubble Act: Its Passage and Its Effects on Business Organization. *Journal of Economic History*, 54, 3: 610–27.

HARRISON, P., 2001. Rational Equity Valuation at the Time of the South Sea Bubble. *History of Political Economy*, 33, 2: 269–81.

HOPPIT, J., 2002. The Myths of the South Sea Bubble. *Transactions of the Royal Historical Society*, 12: 141–65.

KAMEN, H., 1978. The Decline of Spain: A Historical Myth. *Past & Present*, 81, Nov.: 24–50.

KELLY, K.G., 1997. The Archaeology of African-European Interaction: Investigating the Social Roles of Trade, Traders, and the Use of Space in the Seventeenth- and Eighteenth-Century Hueda Kingdom, Republic of Benin. *World Archaeology*, 28, 3: 351–69.

LAURENCE, E.A., 2006. Lady Betty Hastings, Her Half-Sisters, and the South Sea Bubble: family fortunes and strategies. *Women's History Review*, 15, 4: 533–40.

LAW, R., 2004. *Ouidah: The Social History of a West African Slaving 'Port', 1727–1892*. Athens OH: Ohio University Press.

LOGAN, P.M., 2003. The Popularity of Popular Delusions: Charles Mackay and Victorian Popular Culture. *Cultural Critique*. 54, Spring: 213–41.

MACAULAY, T.B., 1986. *The History of England*. Edited and abridged with an introduction by H. Trevor-Roper. Reprint ed. London: Penguin Classics.

MACKAY, C., 1841. *Extraordinary Popular Delusions and the Madness of Crowds*. London: Richard Bentley.

MARKLEY, R., 1994. 'So Inexhaustible a Treasure of Gold': Defoe, Capitalism, and the Romance of the South Seas. *Eighteenth-Century Life*, 18, 3: 148–67.

McCOLLIM, G.B., 2012. *Louis XIV's Assault on Privilege: Nicolas Desmaretz and the Tax on Wealth*. Rochester NY: University of Rochester Press.

MURPHY, A.E., 1997. *John Law: economic theorist and policy-maker*. Oxford: Clarendon Press.

MURPHY, A.L., 2009. *The Origins of English Financial Markets: Investment and Speculation before the South Sea Bubble*. Cambridge Studies in Economic History. Cambridge: Cambridge University Press.

NEAL, L., 1993. *The Rise of Financial Capitalism: International Capital Markets in the Age of Reason*, paperback edn. Studies in Monetary and Financial History. Cambridge: Cambridge University Press.

——, 2012. *'I Am Not Master Of Events': The Speculations of John Law and Lord Londonderry in the Mississippi and South Sea Bubbles*. New Haven and London: Yale University Press.

PAUL, H.J., 2008. Joint-Stock Companies as the Sinews of War: The South Sea and Royal African Companies. In: Torres, R. ed. *War, State and Development: Military Fiscal States in the Eighteenth Century*. Navarre: Universidad de Navarra, 277–94.

——, 2011a. *The South Sea Bubble: an economic history of its origins and consequences*. Routledge Explorations in Economic History. London: Routledge.

——, 2011b. 'The maintenance of British slaving forts in Africa: the activities of joint-stock companies and the Royal Navy'. In: Torres, R. and Conway, S. eds. *The Spending of the*

States: military expenditure during the long eighteenth century: patterns, organisation, and consequences. Saarbrücken: VDM Verlag, 213–36.

——, 2012. Archibald Hutcheson's reputation as an economic thinker: his pamphlets, the National Debt, and the South Sea Bubble. *Essays in Economic and Business History*, 30, 93–104.

SCOTT, W.R., 1911. *The Constitution of English, Scottish and Irish Joint-Stock Companies to 1720*, vol. 3. Cambridge: Cambridge University Press.

SHEA, G.S., 2007. Understanding Financial Derivatives during the South Sea Bubble: the Case of the South Sea Subscription Shares. *Oxford Economic Papers*, 59, i73–i107.

TEMIN, P. and VOTH, H-J., 2004. Riding the South Sea Bubble. *American Economic Review*, 94, 5, 1654–68.

VELDE. F.R., 2007. John Law's System. *American Economic Review*, 97, 2, 276–79.

WRIGHT, I.A., 1924. The Coyman's Asiento (1685–89). *Bijdragen voor Vaderlandsche Geschiedenis en Oudheidkunde*, 23–62.

CHAPTER TWENTY-SIX

PAPER MONEY, 1450–1850

———·◆·———

Dror Goldberg

INTRODUCTION

When piles of looted gold and silver began to be shipped from America to Spain in the sixteenth century, nothing seemed more certain than the continued use of precious metals as money in Europe. It must have seemed unlikely that the Atlantic World would become the epicentre of the antithesis of precious metal, namely paper money. Paper money could be merely a technical device of saving on transportation of precious metal coins, but the way paper money developed in the early modern Atlantic made it much more than that.

Commercial banks issued paper money in return for deposited coin and promised its redemption on demand but actually lent the deposited coin to others, and sometimes lent paper money without any coin being deposited. Banks thus took the control of the quantity of money from governments and miners. Their paper money fueled the commercial growth of the West and greased the wheels of the Industrial Revolution. Commercial paper money made economic miracles where it operated with the least regulation – eighteenth-century Scotland and nineteenth-century United States – but it opened the door to recurrent financial crises. The evil twin of the banknote – unbacked, inconvertible, government-issued paper money – became the ultimate tool of war finance. A doomsday device, it wrecked economies and governments after giving them victories on the battlefield. Paper money was one of the most important forces of the period and helped make the North Atlantic the seat of some of the greatest powers of the modern era. This chapter traces the evolution of paper money from humble beginnings to the centre of political and commercial debates as the modern era began, an era which paper money helped to launch.

WHAT IS PAPER MONEY?

There is often confusion about what constitutes 'paper money' in the early modern era, since there were numerous types of paper financial instruments and the boundaries between them were not clear, sometimes on purpose. Contemporary confusion has been exacerbated by home bias of patriotic historians who have a

471

'we were the first' agenda, and by appearances and terminologies that mislead modern scholars.

This chapter takes a narrow definition of paper money. Paper money is a type of currency: It is a *general* medium of exchange, circulating in the economy, regularly and casually used to buy goods and services in retail markets. Today currency can be defined as something that one can find in most cash registers. For a paper to function as currency it must have several properties. First, it must be legally easily transferable, on the spot, and payable to bearer. If transfer requires a visit to the issuer's office, this is not currency. Second, the denomination must be conveniently 'round.' A paper of £37.29 is not money because cognitive limitations of sellers (and today the structure of cash registers) make it too cumbersome to accept. Third, the denomination must be in the correct proportion to the prices of most goods and services. A paper note of £10,000 is not money because you cannot go shopping with it.

Paper money needs to be distinguished from two other paper financial instruments. Paper money was often a promise of precious metal coin, or an IOU. There are other types of IOUs which can be loosely called bonds, and which are not paper money. Their denominations are too large and often not round, and even when they pass from hand to hand, these hands are not of buyers and sellers in retail markets but hands of investors and speculators. This difference has consequences, especially when the issuer is a government. A government that issues too many bonds loses the trust of investors, and they stop buying its bonds. A government that issues too much paper money can get away with it for much longer. People still accept its money, because money has a grip on everyone's daily activities that makes it nearly impossible to avoid. Money, therefore, is much more powerful than bonds. Whereas government bonds are supposed to be repaid by future taxes, paper money inflation is a tax in itself, being paid implicitly through the increase of prices between the moment one accepts a bill and the moment one buys with it. Putting formalities aside, economists simply refer to an 'inflation tax,' which is just another type of tax.

Many bonds in the early modern era were called banknotes or looked like modern paper money, and are easily mistaken today for paper money. Due to the very different economic implications of bonds and money, this suggests a cautious approach. The burden of proof is on historians and numismatists who claim that something was 'paper money.' Evidence can come from facts about actual circulation, the ratio between the denomination and prices and wages, deliberations inside the government before issue, text of authorizing laws, and text on the notes. Often such evidence is not provided in the sources available to me, and then I use the more neutral term 'banknote' or 'note'.

Another paper financial instrument, which is distinguished here from paper money, is the bill of exchange, which includes the cheque as a special case. It involved a request to a third party to pay, and it usually had large, non-round denominations. Bills of exchange often passed among merchants and financiers, but not in retail markets. Governments could not easily finance wars by issuing them in unlimited quantities, nor could employers pay wages with them.

Being a currency with no intrinsic value, paper money also has to be distinguished from debased precious metal coin and token coin. Countless kings abused the trust given in their coins by replacing some of the precious metal in their coin with base metal. More coins were produced with the precious metal that thus became available,

– CHAPTER 26: *Paper money* –

resulting in extra war resources but also high inflation. In extreme cases, the coins were entirely made of base metal and were mere tokens. This is similar to printing paper money for war, but the scale is different. Paper can be produced in much larger quantities, much faster, and much cheaper than coin, without mining even one ounce of precious metal, and therefore it easily broke the records of coin inflation. Another difference has to do with fractional reserve banking. A bank could issue paper money to a depositor of coin while lending the deposited coin to a third party. This action, which increased the amount of money according to the needs of commerce and industry, could not be replicated by debasing coin.

MEDIEVAL BACKGROUND

By the end of the Middle Ages there were semi-mythological reports throughout Europe about the recent or ancient monetary use of small, presumably stamped pieces of leather, which were sometimes convertible into precious metal coin.[1] This was essentially a non-metallic token coin, which was perhaps somewhat close to paper because parchment was a standard material for writing. Marco Polo told Europeans about proper paper money in China, where every seller had to accept the paper money under penalty of death.[2]

Polo's Venice and other northern Italian city-states pioneered banking. Banks provided safe-keeping of coin and lending services. A depositor was given a receipt with his name that could be used only by him in redeeming the deposit at any time. Since it was not transferable, the receipt was not money. The cheque was also invented there. The more important form of paper was the banks' books, where transfers between accounts were made. This was money on paper, but not paper money.

Bonds of various types were common throughout Europe, often issued by governments to finance wars.[3] Initially they were not transferable, and even when transfer was allowed it usually required a visit to the issuer's office. Government bonds were issued to financiers and suppliers and had large denominations. In England they were usually not even paper but long notched sticks called tallies. All these instruments were not money. Any person could in principle pay for purchases with an IOU, if only both sides could read, and that was common practice among the merchants of northwest Europe.

Southern European merchants used the bill of exchange. The bill originally aimed at avoiding the cost and risk of sending coin over long distances to pay for imports. It can best be explained as a generalised form of a cheque. For example, London merchant L imported wine from Bruges merchant B and exported wool at the same value to Bruges merchant BB. Instead of sending gold back and forth (to B and from BB) he sent his creditor B an order addressed to his debtor BB, in which BB was asked to pay B. The only coin payment was thus made within Bruges.[4]

In general, there were four parties to a bill of exchange – one merchant and one banker in each port. London importer L paid coin to a London banker LL and got a bill of exchange asking Bruges banker BB to pay Bruges exporter B. This bill was sent by L to B. The inter-bank debt of LL to BB would be offset by future bills going in the other direction. Sometimes BB and LL were branches of the same banking house, such as the Medici.[5] Usually no coin travelled even within ports, but credits were transferred in the banks' books.[6] In the Middle Ages the bill could not be legally

473

transferred to others before reaching its final destination, and therefore it was clearly not money. But there was an important lesson: Coin could be completely and voluntarily set aside if paperwork was working properly and enforced by law.

EXPERIMENTS AND VARIANTS
IN THE EUROPEAN ATLANTIC: 1450–1700

The middle of the fifteenth century was associated with two events which were critical for the development of paper money in Europe. First, after centuries of abusing paper money to finance wars, the last Chinese paper money lost its value and China reverted to uncoined silver.[7] China then absorbed huge quantities of silver through trade with Europe, and even more so after the American looting began. Europeans needed silver to pay the international mercenaries which were their main fighting force, and the silver flows to China led to a perceived shortage of silver in Europe. This set Europe's course towards mercantilism first (each country trying to accumulate as much metal as possible) and paper money later. The second important event was that Gutenberg made the printing of paper money feasible.

Paper money evolved along two routes. One route was state money, used to finance war, and backed by promises or threats (as in China). Another route was commercial money, backed by promises of metal, land, or goods, and often improving on Italian practices such as banks, cheques, and bills of exchange. The two routes inspired each other and sometimes crossed paths.

Ironically, paper money first appeared in the early modern Atlantic in Spain.[8] During the reconquest of Granada, sometime in the period 1483–85, the commander of the town Alhama de Granada ran out of coin to pay wages to soldiers. He gave them papers on which he wrote denominations, promised to redeem the paper in coin later on, and forced the townspeople to accept these notes. In 1574, the Dutch city of Leyden did something similar with stamped paper coins when besieged by Spain. Nearby Middleburg stamped leather. Redemption in metal after the sieges was promised, and acceptance of this money in trade was probably not optional.

Both experiments were successful but not followed up in peacetime. Possible reasons include: Conservatism, fear of over-issue by either the legal authority or counterfeiters, and pessimism regarding the government's ability to supervise markets effectively in peacetime.

During the sixteenth century, as Antwerp replaced Bruges as the Atlantic financial centre, bills of exchange and IOUs started circulating but only among merchants.[9] Some were payable to bearer with the simplest informal transferability. Others were endorsed by signatures on their backs, and all those signing were jointly liable for payment with the initial debtor. Instruments of the latter type moved further away from being paper money, which for anyone other than the issuer is something that one pays and forgets about.

The war that brought paper money to Leyden also devastated Antwerp and led to an exodus of financiers and merchants to Amsterdam. The coinage situation there was complicated since hundreds of types of different coins arrived from many nearby mints.[10] The situation was initially handled by *kassiers* ('cashiers') who accepted deposits and provided cheques. They may have invented the banknote – a transferable printed receipt. No evidence has been brought to suggest that their paper instruments

– CHAPTER 26: *Paper money* –

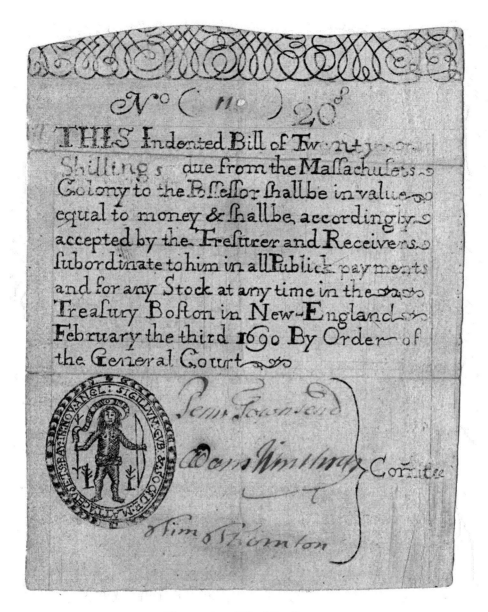

Figure 26.1 Bill of Credit, 1691
Image from the Massachusetts Historical Society. Not to be reproduced without permission.

were used among ordinary people. The receipts were probably in large, non-round denominations, and only used by merchants.

In 1609 Amsterdam replaced the *kassiers* with an imitation of Venice's exchange bank. The *Wisselbank* ('exchange bank', a.k.a. Bank of Amsterdam) entered the intrinsic value of each deposited coin in the depositor's account and did not issue paper money. Local law obliged merchants to settle large bill of exchange debts in the banks' books. Other Dutch cities imitated Amsterdam, which in 1621 allowed the *kassiers* to resume activity by working for the *Wisselbank*.

In England scriveners operated with deposits and loans on a small scale, while the Royal Mint was a safe for merchants' deposits.[11] In 1640 Charles I confiscated the deposits to pay for war. He soon kept one-third as a forced loan and returned the rest. This was the end of the Mint as a safe place and goldsmiths emerged as an alternative. They issued named receipts at first, and quickly imitated the *kassiers'* banknotes ('pay to bearer') and cheques ('pay to order').[12] Although often celebrated as 'paper money', these instruments were not fit for retail transactions. Their most common denomination was £100 and none was under £5.[13] For comparison, a simple laborer earned £12–15 *a year* and a carpenter £25.[14]

After the Civil Wars of the 1640s, Parliament was in debt to soldiers so it confiscated lands of its opponents. Every soldier was given a debenture which acknowledged the debt. The debentures could be used in purchasing confiscated land and were freely traded. Combined with the Italian pawn shop known as Lombard, it was probably this experiment which led to the idea of land banks, appearing in pamphlets in the 1650s.[15] It was essentially a money-printing pawn shop of mortgages.[16] A land owner who needed liquidity would deposit a land title and get a loan in convenient banknotes – printed by the pawn shop itself. While banknotes could not be redeemable in land directly, at least land would limit the amount of notes printed, and foreclosed land could be sold for coin which would then be available for note redemption. These banknotes, unlike other paper instruments, would be designed in their denominations and transferability to function as money. Their circulation would not be incidental as was the case with goldsmiths' receipts, cheques, and bonds.

The next few decades saw interesting experiments. Attempts to launch land banks in England failed. In 1661, near the Atlantic World, Stockholm's exchange bank experimented with proper paper money to substitute heavy copper coins (weighing up to 20 kg). Overissue led to loss of confidence by banknote holders and the government ended the experiment in 1664.[17] In 1667 the English government made its first mass issue of tradable paper bonds. These Exchequer orders were sometimes directly used by the government in purchases of war supplies, but they were not money. They were named, could be transferred only at the Exchequer, most had very large denominations, and most were immediately sold to goldsmith-bankers who held them until maturity. A 1672 royal bankruptcy ended the experiment.

The Glorious Revolution of 1688 led to a generation of expensive wars with France. The Bank of England was born in 1694 as a private institution. Its purpose, like that of Venice's latest public bank, was merely to recruit lenders from the public to help war finance.[18] Its effect on the money supply was incidental and initially negligible. Depositors could get various paper instruments with round denominations and bearer or order clauses, which were redeemable on demand. Historians often refer to these as 'paper money', especially those which were revealingly called 'running-cash notes.' However, after briefly experimenting with various types of notes of £5 and less, from 1697 the minimal denomination was £20. It is revealing that earlier proposals to imitate the *Wisselbank* in England had £20 as the threshold above which payments would have to be settled in the bank's books.[19] The Bank of England was a merchants' bank. In 1695 the Scottish Parliament chartered the Bank of Scotland, where the first notes had a minimal denomination of £5.[20]

– CHAPTER 26: *Paper money* –

Parliament also authorised land banks which failed to get off the ground, and reminted all coin in 1696. The resulting brief shortage of coin was partially answered by Exchequer bills. Unlike the 1660s Exchequer orders, they had round denominations as low as £5, were payable to bearer, transferred by simple endorsement, and receivable for taxes. But they were still government bonds, with denominations too large for retail transactions, paying interest, and given only for coin lent to the Exchequer rather than at the Mint.

The war of the 1690s also resulted in a brief monetary experiment in Norway.[21] Jorgen Thor Mohlen, a leading merchant and courtier, incurred losses to privateers and got permission in 1695 to print temporary notes with which to continue his business. It seems that these notes were paper money, as they were legal tender (meaning that creditors had to accept them) and convertible into coin with delay. The government revoked the notes the following year because the public had no faith in the notes and demanded immediate redemption. Perhaps the 1660s Swedish experiment gave inspiration for both issuer and the public.

Outside of Scandinavia the traditional use of paper as bonds and bills of exchange may have been too strong for experiments in small denominations. The population catered for in 1690s England was lenders to the government, which were typically nobles, financiers and merchants, rather than ordinary people. However, the same motive of war finance had just led to a different financial revolution in America, one that derived its power in the exact opposite way – by bringing paper instruments to ordinary people.

AMERICAN WARS, 1600–1700

The Spanish bonanza of precious metal indirectly caused American paper money. It motivated others to settle America, but instead of finding metal the colonists found themselves starved of coin even more than in Europe. They became expert monetary improvisers, and when wars magnified the problem, they found limited political freedom to solve it with paper money.

Virginia started as a gold-digging enterprise, but soon turned into a tobacco plantation. There was not enough coin around, and several culprits have been mentioned.[22] First, England prohibited exportation of its coin because it thought it had too little. Second, the balance of trade tended to keep coin in England. Any coin that the colonists obtained was shipped to England to buy the manufactures that were not available in America, leaving no coin for domestic circulation. Third, export of bullion or foreign coin from England was permitted, and early Virginia had the right to establish a mint, but it was too poor and chaotic to pull it off.[23]

Under such circumstances, it was natural to use the most common agricultural produce as money, as was the case in the financially backward areas of Europe. Dried tobacco leaves became official money, but they were very inconvenient. Tobacco-denominated private IOUs became common and in 1633 Virginia passed a law to establish exchange banks, to clear on paper all these IOUs.[24] The law was probably modeled on Dutch banks, but was not implemented, probably because the poor colony could not procure the physical infrastructure of storehouses and the boats needed to reach them. The use of IOUs as currency was later hampered when it was enacted that creditors holding IOUs could pass them on only with the issuers'

477

knowledge. Such difficult transferability probably emanated from excessive litigation or counterfeiting and eliminated the IOUs' monetary potential.

New England seemed to have suffered most from coin shortage.[25] Its growing, market-oriented, diversified economy had more paid laborers, more opportunities for internal trade, and no obvious single type of commodity money. It was not allowed to have a mint. Its balance of trade was worse because it had nothing like tobacco to export to England, while the high material demands of its middle-class families meant large imports from England.[26] To solve the problem, Massachusetts immediately enforced in law the transferring of IOUs, long before England did, thus enabling IOUs of important people to have limited circulation. Grain, bullets, fur, and Natives' seashells also became legal money. Opening of a mint had to await the abolishment of royalty in England in 1649.

In the meanwhile, the Dutch West India Company occupied Pernambuco in northeast Brazil. Dutch rule lasted from 1630 to 1654, and was accompanied by constant fighting with Portugal.[27] The local money was sugar. Governor Johan Maurits of Nassau was a scientifically minded noble who brought dozens of scholars and two financiers. Probably waiting for coin shipments from home, he issued emergency paper money to soldiers in 1640 and 1643 and forced its acceptance.[28] He was probably inspired by the Leyden episode, which was well known to every Dutch person and especially to Maurits whose family was prominent in that episode. This seems to have been the first paper money in America.

In 1669 the English colony of Antigua established two public tobacco banks which issued paper money for deposited tobacco.[29] The incidence of such a bold experiment in a tiny colony was perhaps related to the fact that the leading colonist was one Samuel Winthrop.[30] Just a few years earlier, his brother John Jr. – Governor of Connecticut and America's only scientist – presented a bank plan to the Royal Society of London (of which he was a member).[31] The details are unknown, except that it was not to be based on coin, and probably based on land or goods. In 1675 the Antigua banks closed due to fraudulent excessive issue of paper.

In the early 1680s England eliminated both the charter and the mint of Massachusetts. In 1685 the land bank idea came to Massachusetts with an English financier named John Blackwell.[32] He had been Cromwell's paymaster, prominent in the debenture market of the 1640s, and partner in a London land bank scheme which was attempted in 1683. It was this plan which he brought to Massachusetts. Getting the colony's elite on board, his plan won preliminary approval by the government in 1686. An English-appointed dictator of the short-lived Dominion of New England invalidated all the land titles in 1688, and so the land-based bank was immediately aborted.

Paper money came to French Quebec in 1685.[33] Soldiers were not paid due to delays in shipment of gold from France. The local government improvised money from playing cards, promising to redeem the notes in gold upon arrival. The promise was fulfilled, and the temporary measure was repeated intermittently in the following years, in spite of objections from the home government.

In 1689 Massachusetts regained its independence during the American phase of the Glorious Revolution. Involved in the Nine Years' War (known in America as King William's War), in 1690 it tried to occupy Quebec and ended up with a huge debt to troops and suppliers. Tax collections in grain were slow and the soldiers demanded pay. The government might have issued token coin or land-backed notes,

– CHAPTER 26: *Paper money* –

but there was no word from England regarding permission to reopen the mint or revalidation of land titles.[34] As a provisional government seeking restoration of its charter, it could not take the risk of alienating England.

Following common practice, Massachusetts issued debentures to the soldiers, but also made the debentures eligible for tax payments. Then, with partial inspiration from Canada, it allowed the debentures' conversion into bearer 'bills' with small, round denominations. The bills were not named, did not need endorsement for transfer, were acceptable in tax payments, and were theoretically redeemable at the empty treasury. They were not called 'money', and were not forced on anyone other than the treasury, so as not to look as if the colony once again violated the Crown's monopoly over money. The bills circulated at par after a rough start. Soon they came to be called 'bills of credit.' Once Massachusetts got a new charter in 1692, it was confident enough to upgrade the bills to the level of proper money: They could discharge any private debt. In later terminology, the bills became 'legal tender' for all debts and taxes. The bills received in tax payments were reissued by the Treasury over and over, and solved the coin shortage. The absence of precious metal coin at the treasury, and the lack of hope of a British shipment of coin, proved to be irrelevant for the bills' circulation.

It was the first time in Western civilization that paper money backed only by its ability to discharge debts and taxes (just like today's paper money[35]) circulated on a regular basis. Unlike the hybrid bills and notes soon to be issued in England and Scotland, the Massachusetts bills (like the Quebec and Brazil bills) were intentionally made for retail market transactions and were proper paper money. Their lowest denomination was 2 shillings, 50 times less than the lowest English and Scottish paper denomination (a pound had 20 shillings). Bringing paper instruments to the people was not an end in itself but a tool of war finance. Massachusetts could pay its soldiers with inconvertible, unbacked paper money because its soldiers were its own people, paying taxes there, and buying from local taxpaying sellers. England could not do something similar because it had to pay foreign mercenaries on the continent, and they wanted metal.

DIFFUSION AND INFLATION: 1700–75

There were no more major inventions of paper money after 1700. It was known that paper money could be used to finance war and fuel commerce, and could be backed by metal, land, goods, punishment, or its acceptance for debts and taxes. The following decades witnessed diffusion of paper money throughout the Atlantic World. In some places, paper money was adopted in imitation of foreign colonies and nations. In other places, local tradable bonds received more monetary features, such as lower denominations, and became paper money. Some places discovered paper money inflation.

In England paper money was still not materialised. Transferability of promissory notes still relied more on custom than on law, and only in 1704 Parliament made transferability enforceable in law.[36] The first £10 notes were issued in 1759. Smaller banks also stayed with large denominations. Exchequer bills, which originated in the 1696 recoinage, continued.

In 1704 the Bank of Scotland started issuing £1 notes, which would become the most common currency of Scotland for the rest of the century.[37] After the 1707 Union with England, Scotland experienced benign neglect. This led to relatively unregulated banking, which sometimes bordered on anarchy, but revolutionised a backward agrarian economy. The Royal Bank of Scotland was chartered in 1727 and attacked the older bank by presenting a large amount of notes for redemption. For protection, both banks used an 'option clause,' allowing them to postpone redemptions for half a year with interest. More banks were opened later and even small businesses issued small-denomination notes. In 1765 Parliament prohibited notes of less than £1 and the option clause. In Dublin, by the 1750s private banknotes of goldsmiths and others were common among merchants, and this practice later spread to the rest of Ireland.[38]

Louis XIV's wars exhausted the French treasury and economy. In 1701 a recoinage began. *Billets de monnaie* were issued as IOUs to those who handed their coin.[39] The government itself was confused about whether these were bonds or money. It tried to force their use in some transactions, but gave them large denominations and refused to accept them in some of its own transactions. By 1711 they were traded at heavy discounts and were converted into more ordinary bonds.

A Scottish financier, John Law, concocted a complicated scheme of handling the French government debt.[40] His fast evolving scheme (1715–20) remains a puzzle to this day. It included bonds which were more like stocks, stocks that were more like stock options, and paper money too.[41] The paper money was briefly imposed on all large transactions. When the scheme collapsed the paper money became worthless, and nobody in France wanted to hear about paper money and banks for decades to come. Outside the European Atlantic, paper money had already resumed in Sweden and diffused to Denmark. When Law's trauma was somewhat forgotten, it diffused to Austria and Russia as well.

Back in America, the long wars of Louis XIV made the military paper moneys of Massachusetts and Quebec permanent, unlike all previous military paper moneys in the West. The wars also led to diffusion to other colonies: French Acadia (today Nova Scotia) imitated Quebec's cards,[42] while South Carolina (1703), New Hampshire, Connecticut, New York, New Jersey (1709), Rhode Island (1710), and North Carolina (1712) imitated Massachusetts' legal tender.[43] After the wars these colonies kept their paper moneys. The discipline of the legislatures weakened and they were tempted to issue too much money.[44] The taxes legislated to absorb the bills were postponed more and more into the future. The quantity thus increased and the result was inflation. In Quebec, inflation led the French government to end card money in 1719, but it was revived in 1729.[45]

The land bank idea returned in a public form. In 1706 it was created in Barbados and soon shut down by England.[46] It was luckier on the continent, adopted in South Carolina (1712), Massachusetts (1714), Rhode Island (1715), and New Hampshire (1717).[47] It got another boost when suggested as a solution to the recession of the early 1720s (caused by the crash of John Law's 'system' and related British and Dutch bubbles). The land bank spread to Pennsylvania and Delaware (1723), New Jersey (1724), North Carolina (1729), Maryland and Connecticut (1733), and New York (1737). Some of Maryland's bills were freely distributed to taxpayers, and were all redeemable in sterling bills of exchange in the distant future. Antigua's public tobacco notes were revived in Virginia in 1717, vetoed by England, and resumed in 1730. In the 1730s Boston merchants circulated silver-backed notes, but other attempts of private banking in New England were shot down by either local

– CHAPTER 26: *Paper money* –

government or Parliament.[48] Colonial merchants circulated bills of exchange among themselves before sending them to London for payment.[49]

By 1740 Parliament started debating the New England inflation that was eroding the debts owed to British merchants.[50] As the War of the Austrian Succession spread to America (King George's War), the colonies printed more money than ever before. Massachusetts increased its money supply seven times from 1744 to 1748, and prices doubled. In 1749, with Parliament's gun pointed at its head, Massachusetts redeemed all its notes for coin that was owed to it by Britain for war expenses. Rhode Island, the worst paper inflationist, planned to continue printing, and led to Parliament's Currency Act of 1751. It forbade all New England colonies from issuing anything other than temporary bills, and from forcing these bills on private creditors. Meanwhile, tobacco notes diffused to Maryland (1747) and North Carolina (1754). The French and Indian War, which soon spread to Europe as the Seven Years' War, brought the last colonies on board the paper money train (land bank in Georgia and legal tender in Virginia). The end of war saw the elimination of card money in occupied Quebec,[51] and the 1764 Currency Act that restricted all the colonies' paper money.[52] The Act had a significant role in provoking the American Revolution.

In the Southern Atlantic metal still ruled, with a few exceptions. The British colony of Saint Helena, between Brazil and Africa, seems to have had paper money of 2.5 shillings in 1722.[53] The Dutch colony Surinam started issuing card money in 1761, initially only in large denominations and backed by bills of exchange. Later the denominations declined and the money was issued against mortgages.[54] Regarding Brazil there are claims that 'bonds of some trading companies circulated as money since the 1750s...for local transactions,' and that 'certificates' issued by the Inspector General of Diamonds since 1771 were money.[55] These claims should be treated with caution.

REVOLUTIONS: 1775–1820

British colonial paper money not only paved the way to the American Revolution. It also financed much of it.[56] The Continental Congress and colonies printed money from 1775, sometimes imposing criminal penalties on those refusing their currencies. Since the Continental Congress had no authority to tax, its money (called 'continental') lacked the anchor which states' paper moneys did have. Congress' empty promise to pay coin after the war lost value and by 1780 the continental became worthless. It was a massively successful inflation tax that gave Americans their independence.

After Independence, states kept issuing their own paper moneys to get out of the postwar recession, and some chartered private note-issuing banks.[57] Again Rhode Island abused the system, creating inflation on purpose to erode farmers' debts. The 1787 Constitution therefore prohibited state-issued legal tender paper money. Nothing was said about federal paper money, so according to standard legal interpretation there was no prohibition. It seems that there was a reluctance to block the possibility of using once more at war this most powerful financial weapon. The United States founded a mint and returned to metal. A partially public bank, the Bank of the United States, was chartered by Congress in 1791. Dozens of private banks followed, chartered by the states and issuing paper money because the states could not.

In 1811 Congress did not renew the charter of the Bank of the United States. During the War of 1812 all banks outside New England suspended convertibility in 1814 and their notes lost up to 30 per cent of their value. The U.S. Treasury, which issued war

481

bonds since 1812, printed its own paper money in 1815.[58] Congress chartered a second Bank of the United States in 1816, and convertibility was resumed in 1817. In the same war, the British forces in Canada issued convertible paper money, called Army Bills.[59]

Britain's European enemies helped the United States gain independence but paid a price. Spain's debt led it to issue the hybrid *vales reales* from 1780.[60] These were large-denomination bonds which were legal tender for large payments and had potential circulation mostly among merchants and financiers. The smallest denomination was equal to a carpenter's annual salary. Probably inspired by Venetian and English precedents, *Banco de San Carlos* was founded to help market these bonds.[61]

The American War led France to bankruptcy and all hell broke loose. France had chartered the private *Caisse d'Escompte* already in 1776, and modelled after the Bank of England it issued convertible banknotes.[62] Royal efforts to use the bank to prevent state bankruptcy led to bank runs and suspension of convertibility. More such notes were issued to close the 1789 government deficit. In that year the *assignat* bond was introduced to finance the tax-less regime.[63] The bonds could be used to buy confiscated church land. Soon the *assignat*'s interest rate was gone and its denominations plummeted until it became inconvertible paper money in 1792. This was partly done to replace the *Caisse*'s notes which were private and legal tender only in Paris.

Figure 26.2 Assignat (banknote) for 50 sols dated revolutionary year II (1793) of French Republic
© The Art Archive/Alamy

– CHAPTER 26: *Paper money* –

War led to massive printing of *assignats* as the almost only source of government revenue, and with it came the inevitable inflation. Harsh penalties for those refusing the *assignat* or accepting it at a discount did not help, nor did its imposition on occupied territories. In 1795 the *assignat* was worthless. A similar currency, the *mandat*, briefly circulated in 1796.

Although superficially similar to convertibility, the church land option could not help maintain the *assignat*'s value because the promise was not for a specific piece of land, or a piece of land of a certain pre-determined size. The promise was for purchase at market values. And when printing brought inflation, land prices rose too, leaving nothing to anchor the value of paper. Since nobody had to buy church land, this mechanism was also much weaker than the acceptance of paper in tax payments.

Napoleon restored monetary prudence by establishing the silver franc and restricting the new Bank of France that issued only old fashioned banknotes of large denominations for merchants and financiers.[64] The recent trauma was accompanied by fears that ordinary people would initiate bank runs in their ignorance, and that small denomination notes would drive silver out.

France's enemies also used bonds and paper money to maintain the war effort. In Spain, the *vales* declined in denomination (not enough for retail) and comprised much of the budget in some years.[65] By 1800 they lost most of their value. *Banco de San Carlos* briefly issued convertible notes in 1803.[66]

Portugal issued endorsable bonds in 1796.[67] In 1797 the denominations were lowered to enable the bonds to be used as money and they were forced on all transactions. The paper was accepted at heavy discounts, especially when France invaded. It circulated only in the large cities, as people elsewhere did not consider it to be real money. By 1813, prices more than doubled.

Even England succumbed to the pressure. In 1797, fears of a French invasion led to panic in London and depositors stormed the Bank of England.[68] The government ordered to suspend redemption of the Bank's notes and of the notes of the Bank of Ireland (established 1783). At the beginning of the suspension many merchants declared that they would continue to accept the Bank's notes in trade. Hoarding, war needs, and changes in the exchange rate between gold and silver led to a shortage of coin. In response, lower denominations appeared in the notes of the Bank of England (£1), and of other banks in England, Scotland, and Ireland.[69] Now banknotes in England finally reached ordinary retail transactions. The Bank of England wanted to resume convertibility already in 1797 and again in 1803 but the government refused in order to keep this potential source of revenue. There was some money printing and inflation, but nothing comparable to the American and French experiences.[70] During the suspension the notes were formally legal tender for taxes but not for private debts.[71] Until 1811 they were still universally accepted for private debts in practice, but then paper depreciated against gold. Traumatised by the *assignats*, Parliament refused to formally make the notes full legal tender, but did it in practice in 1812 with technical legal tricks.

The revolutions in Europe also affected Latin America. Wartime deficits increased Spanish taxation of the colonies, and then Spain was occupied by France. These events provoked American revolutions in 1810. In the disintegrating viceroyalty of New Granada, paper money was quickly issued in Venezuela and Colombia.[72] Argentina financed the war with bonds which 'took on, at times, the characteristics of quasi-

483

money and circulated, although by all accounts in a very limited fashion.'[73] The same goes for bonds of the *Caja Nacional de Fondos de Sud America*, which converted the variety of Argentine bonds into uniform *billetes*. In Brazil, bills of foundry houses backed by the Treasury are claimed to have functioned as money from 1803.[74]

Outside the main area of wars and revolutions, paper money quietly diffused to all corners of the Atlantic World. In 1790 the British Canadian province of the Island of Saint John (today Prince Edward Island) started issuing legal tender paper money with denominations as low as half a pound.[75] The usual colonial coin shortage led to the issue of paper money in Dutch South Africa, first by the government (1782) and later by a land bank (1793).[76] The British occupation chartered another note-issuing bank in 1809. In all cases there were over-issue and high inflation. Inflated Danish paper money diffused to the Atlantic Danish possessions of Iceland (1778)[77] and Norway (1791).[78] According to numismatists, emergency issues also spread to the Danish possessions of Faroe Islands, Greenland, and the Danish West Indies (today United States Virgin Islands), as well as to Haiti, French Guiana, and Puerto Rico.[79] These claims should be treated with caution.

THE DUST SETTLES: 1821–50

By the time the revolutions in Europe and America were over, the secret was out. Wars could be financed with paper money. Marco Polo was right. There is no need to mine gold or debase gold coins. All you need is paper, and some functioning branches of government to support it by either carrot or stick. Theories of money, inflation and war finance would never be the same. In the age of the greatest political revolutions, this in itself was a revolution.[80]

Most governments in the Atlantic World therefore strengthened their control on paper money, by nationalizing existing banks, establishing new national banks, or printing from the treasury. Nobody wanted inflation unless necessary, so nations in peace returned to metal, but with banknotes that were only partially covered by metal in the banks' vaults (fractional reserve banking). The decline in banknotes' denominations generally became permanent. They would henceforth belong to the common people as well as to financiers and merchants, because that proved to be useful for both war and commerce. The *assignat*-traumatised France, Belgium, and the Netherlands experienced significant delay in this trend.[81]

Leading by example was the Bank of England, still nominally private.[82] In 1821 it returned to gold. In 1833 its notes formally became legal tender for private debts (as long as they were convertible into gold). In 1844 it became the monopolist paper issuer in England and its Issue Department was separated from its Banking Department. Free entry into the paper-issuing business was closed in Scotland at the same time.[83] The same trends could be seen in Spain, Portugal, and Brazil.[84] Mexico, the world's leading producer of silver, rejected paper money.[85]

High inflation continued to be associated with wars, directly or indirectly. Argentina was continuously at war and paid for it with paper money.[86] Soon after independence, the Republic of Texas relied on paper money before joining the United States.[87] Long after independence, Haiti sent its gold to France as indemnity. Paper money replaced gold in domestic circulation, and this soon led the government to print its deficits away.[88]

– CHAPTER 26: *Paper money* –

In the United States, however, government control over paper money weakened.[89] The state-chartered banking system kept growing, and by 1825 there was twice as much capital invested in U.S. banks than in all the banks of England and Wales, even though the U.S. population was smaller. A bank charter, with the associated privilege of issuing paper money, became 'a democratic right,' while elsewhere it was a privilege restricted to few. As in Scotland, paper money allowed the leveraging of a limited supply of gold coins to develop an expanding economy with easy credit to anyone who could convince bankers to lend him money, and in principle anyone could become a banker. Congress again did not renew the charter of the Bank of the United States and it expired in 1836. The British possessions of Canada and South Africa also had private banks issuing the local paper money.[90]

CONCLUSION

There seem to be three effects of the Atlantic World on the development of paper money from curiosity and myth in 1450 to greatness in 1850. First, the countries of the European Atlantic dominated long-distance trade. The financial centres that facilitated this trade moved along the Eastern Atlantic shore once a century, from Bruges to Antwerp to Amsterdam and to London. The bills of exchange and promissory notes of that trade helped promote the idea that in various ways paper could replace metal on a voluntary, regular basis. Second, the contested great riches of maritime trade and colonialism increased warfare between the nations of the European Atlantic. This contributed to the progress of military paper money, which led the way in reaching ordinary people rather than merchants and financiers. Third, the American Atlantic outside the Iberian colonies found no metal, and had temporary political freedom to print paper instead.

The interaction between both sides of the Atlantic contributed to the progress of paper money. Wars that started on one side diffused to the other side. Ideas flowed back and forth and imitation was mutual. Before the American Revolution, Americans hated the Bank of England while the British despised the colonists' inconvertible paper money. After the American Revolution, however, the charter of the Bank of the United States was inspired by the Bank of England,[91] and Britain found wartime inspiration in the inconvertible paper money that the colonists perfected during the American Revolution.

Another recurring theme in the story is that a particularly bad experience with paper inflation traumatised a country and it reverted to precious metal as the anchor of its monetary system, until memory faded and the witnesses died, or until the next major war broke. Prime examples are France after John law and after the 1790s, the United States after Independence, and Great Britain after the Napoleonic Wars.

This story ends in 1850, just before the gold discoveries in California and Australia would change global money and lead the world to a Gold Standard, and just before the paper money in the United States would be nationalised in the Civil War.

NOTES

1 Einzig 1966: 216–17, 226, 236–37, 250–51, 259, 286; Sargent and Velde 2002, 219.
2 Polo 1871: I, 378–80.
3 van der Wee 1977.

485

4 Adapted from de Roover 1948: 58–59.
5 Adapted from Neal 1990: 5–8.
6 de Roover 1948: 57.
7 von Glahn, 1996.
8 These stories and similar ones are told in Sargent and Velde 2002, 219–22.
9 de Roover 1948: 54, 70–71 (fn. 37–38); van der Wee 1977: 324–29.
10 Spufford 1995.
11 Richards 1929 is the source of English facts in this section unless mentioned otherwise. However, his interpretation of various instruments as 'paper money' is disputed here.
12 Recent comprehensive work on the goldsmith-bankers and the *Wisselbank* can be found in various articles by Stephen Quinn (occasionally with co-authors).
13 Quinn 1997: 420. The smallest check reported by Richards is for almost £10 (p. 51).
14 Muldrew 1998: 81–83.
15 Goldberg forthcoming.
16 Horsefield 1960 reviews the theoretical literature on money and banking in England before 1710.
17 Jensen 1896: 393–95.
18 van der Wee 1977: 313.
19 Davis 1901: II, 6, 26.
20 Checkland 1975 is the standard reference for Scottish banking.
21 Norges Bank 2014.
22 Nettels 1934.
23 Goldberg forthcoming.
24 Goldberg forthcoming.
25 Sylla 1982: 23–25.
26 Goldberg forthcoming.
27 Boxer 1973.
28 Abreu and Lago 2001: 333, fn. 16.
29 McCusker 1976: 95.
30 Goldberg forthcoming.
31 Davis 1901: II, 63–67.
32 Goldberg 2011.
33 Shortt 1925: xlix–lv.
34 This episode is analysed in detail in Goldberg 2009.
35 McCusker 1976: 97.
36 Richards 1929: 48–49, 42–43.
37 Cameron 1967: Chapter 3.
38 Fetter 1955: 10–11.
39 Murphy 1997: 115–20.
40 Murphy 1997.
41 This interpretation is from Velde 2009.
42 Shortt 1925: lv.
43 Brock 1975: Chapters II–III. A recent survey is Sylla 2001.
44 Nettels 1934: 267–75.
45 Shortt 1925: lxi–lxxi.
46 Nettels 1934: 269–71.
47 Brock 1975: Chapters I–III.
48 Davis 1901: II, Chapters VI–XII.
49 McCusker 1976, 100–103.
50 Davis 1901: I; Brock 1975.
51 Shortt 1925: lxxxv–lxxxvii.

- CHAPTER 26: *Paper money* -

52 Ernst 1973; Brock 1975: Chapter IX.
53 Cuhaj 2008: 1045.
54 de Vries 2001: 135–36.
55 Macedo et al. 2001: 202, fn. 31; Abreu and Lago 2001: 336; Cuhaj 2008: 141.
56 Harlow 1929.
57 Sylla 2001.
58 Hurst 1973: 136.
59 Bordo and Redish 2001: 273–74.
60 Hamilton 1947: 79–82.
61 Tortella and Comín 2001: 160.
62 White 2001: 84; Bordo and White 1994: 252.
63 Aftalion 1990.
64 Cameron 1967: Chapter 4.
65 Hamilton 1947: 83.
66 Tortella and Comín 2001: 169–70.
67 Macedo et al. 2001: 210–12.
68 Fetter 1950.
69 Richards 1929: 43; Fetter 1955: 17–18.
70 Bordo and White 1994: 255–59.
71 Fetter 1950.
72 McFarlane 2014: 93, 104.
73 Cortés-Conde and McCandless 2001: 386–87; Millington 1992: 16–17.
74 Abreu and Lago 2001: 336.
75 Powell 2005: 15.
76 South African Reserve Bank 2014; Goosen et al. 1999: 16-7.
77 Central Bank of Iceland 2002: 7, 11–14; Jensen 1896: 375–76.
78 Norges Bank 2014.
79 Cuhaj 2008: 477, 623, 430, 644, 520, 999–1000, respectively.
80 See also McCusker 1976: 94.
81 Cameron 1967: Chapters 4–5; De Nederlandsche Bank 2014: 3.
82 Clapham 1944: II, Chapters 2–3.
83 Cameron 1967: Chapter 3.
84 Tortella and Comín 2001: 170, 161; Macedo et al. 2001: 212-17; Abreu and Lago 2001: 363–67; respectively.
85 Marichal and Carmagnani 2001: 302.
86 Cortés-Conde and McCandless 2001: 388–93, 402.
87 Miller 1949.
88 Logan 1961: 437; Lacerte 1981: 507, 510; Cuhaj 2008: 644–46.
89 Sylla 2001: 248.
90 Bordo and Redish 2001: 274–76; Goosen et al. 1999: 17–18; respectively.
91 Sylla 2001: 245–46, 258.

REFERENCES

Abreu, Marcelo de Paiva, and Luiz A. Correa do Lago. 2001. Property Rights and the Fiscal and Financial Systems in Brazil. In Bordo and Cortés-Conde.

Aftalion, Florin. 1990. *The French Revolution: An Economic Interpretation*. Trans. Martin Thom. Cambridge: Cambridge University Press.

Bordo, Michael D., and Roberto Cortés-Conde, eds. 2001. *Transferring Wealth and Power from the Old to the New World: Monetary and Fiscal Institutions in the 17th through the 19th Centuries*. Cambridge: Cambridge University Press.

Bordo, Michael D., and Angela Redish. 2001. The Legacy of French and English Fiscal and Monetary Institutions for Canada. In Bordo and Cortés-Conde.

Bordo, Michael D., and Eugene N. White. 1994. British and French Finance during the Napoleonic Wars. In Michael D. Bordo and Forrest Capie, eds., *Monetary Regimes in Transition*. Cambridge: Cambridge University Press.

Boxer, C. R. 1973. *The Dutch in Brazil, 1624–1654*. Oxford: Clarendon Press.

Brock, Leslie V. 1975. *The Currency of the American Colonies, 1700–1764*. New York: Arno Press.

Cameron, Rondo. 1967. *Banking in the Early Stages of Industrialization: A Study in Comparative Economic History*. New York: Oxford University Press.

Central Bank of Iceland. 2002. *The Currency of Iceland: Issues and Features of Icelandic Notes and Coins*. Reykjavik: Central Bank of Iceland.

Checkland, S. G. 1975. *Scottish Banking: A History, 1695–1973*. Glasgow: Collins.

Clapham, John Harold. 1944. *The Bank of England: A History*. 2 vols. Cambridge: Cambridge University Press.

Cortés-Conde, Roberto, and George T. McCandless. 2001. Argentina: From Colony to Nation: Fiscal and Monetary Experience of the Eighteenth and Nineteenth Centuries. In Bordo and Cortés-Conde.

Cuhaj, George S., ed. 2008. *Standard Catalog of World Paper Money: General Issues, 1368–1960*. 12th edition. Iola: Krause Publications.

Davis, Andrew McFarland. 1901. *Currency and Banking in the Province of the Massachusetts Bay*. 2 vols. New York: Macmillan.

De Nederlandsche Bank. 2014. History of DNB. Available at http://www.dnb.nl/en/about-dnb/organisation/history/. Accessed 1 April 2014.

Einzig, Paul. 1966. *Primitive Money: In its Ethnological, Historical and Economic Aspects*. 2nd edition. Oxford: Pergamon Press.

Ernst, Joseph Albert. 1973. *Money and Politics in America, 1755–1775: A Study in the Currency Act of 1764 and the Political Economy of Revolution*. Chapel Hill: University of North Carolina Press.

Fetter, Frank Whitson. 1950. Legal Tender during the English and Irish Bank Restrictions. *Journal of Political Economy* 58: 241–53.

——, ed. 1955. *The Irish Pound, 1797–1826: A reprint of the Report of the Committee of 1804 of the British House of Commons on the Condition of the Irish Currency*. Abingdon: Routledge.

Glahn, Richard von. 1996. *Fountain of Fortune: Money and Monetary Policy in China, 1000–1700*. Berkeley: University of California Press.

Goldberg, Dror. 2009. The Massachusetts Paper Money of 1690. *Journal of Economic History* 69: 1092–1106.

——. 2011. Why Was America's First Bank Aborted? *Journal of Economic History* 71: 211–22.

——. Forthcoming. *How Americans Invented Modern Money, 1607–1692*. Chicago: University of Chicago Press.

Goosen W., A. Pampallis, A. van der Merwe, and L. Mdluli. 1999. *Banking in the New Millennium*. Kenwyn: Juta & Co.

Hamilton, Earl J. 1947. *War and Prices in Spain, 1651–1800*. Cambridge: Harvard University Press.

Harlow, Ralph Volney. 1929. Aspects of Revolutionary Finance, 1775–1783. *American Historical Review* 35: 46–68.

Horsefield, J. Keith. 1960. *British Monetary Experiments, 1650–1710*. Cambridge: Harvard University Press.

Hurst, James W. 1973. *A Legal History of Money in the United States, 1774–1970*. Lincoln: University of Nebraska Press.

Jensen, Adolph. 1896. A History of Banking in the Scandinavian Nations. Trams. William Price. In *A History of Banking in all the Leading Nations*. New York: The Journal of Commerce and Commercial Bulletin.

Lacerte, Robert K. 1981. Xenophobia and Economic Decline: The Haitian Case, 1820–1843. *The Americas* 37: 499–515.

Logan, Rayford W. 1961. The U.S. 'Colonial Experiment' in Haiti. *The World Today* 17: 435–46.

Macedo, Jorge Braga de, Alvaro Ferreira da Silva, and Rita Martins de Sousa. 2001. War, Taxes, and Gold: The Inheritance of the Real. In Bordo and Cortés-Conde.

Marichal, Carlos, and Marcello Carmagnani. 2001. Mexico: From Colonial Fiscal Regime to Liberal Order, 1750–1912. In Bordo and Cortés-Conde.

McCusker, John. Colonial Paper Money. 1976. In Eric P. Newman and Richard G. Doty, eds., *Studies on Money in Early America*. New York: The American Numismatic Society.

McFarlane, Anthony. 2014. *War and Independence in Spanish America*. New York: Routledge.

Miller, E. T. 1949. The Money of the Republic of Texas. *The Southwestern Historical Quarterly* 52: 294–300.

Millington, Thomas. 1992. *Debt Politics After Independence: The Funding Conflict in Bolivia*. Gainesville: University of Florida Press.

Muldrew, Craig. 1998. *The Economy of Obligation: The Culture of Credit and Social Relations in Early Modern England*. Houndmills: Macmillan Press.

Murphy, Antoin E. 1997. *John Law: Economic Theorist and Policy-Maker*. Oxford: Clarendon Press.

Neal, Larry. 1990. *The Rise of Financial Capitalism: International Capital Markets in the Age of Reason*. Cambridge: Cambridge University Press.

Nettels, Curtis P. 1934. *The Money Supply of the American Colonies before 1720*. Madison: University of Wisconsin Press.

Norges Bank. 2014. Norges Bank's History. Available at http://www.norges-bank.no/en/about/history/norges-banks-history. Accessed 1 April 2014.

Polo, Marco. 1871. *The Book of Ser Marco Polo, the Venetian, Concerning the Kingdoms and Marvels of the East*. 2 vols. Trans. Henry Yule. London: John Murray.

Powell, James. 2005. *A History of the Canadian Dollar*. Ottawa: Bank of Canada.

Quinn, Stephen. 1997. Goldsmith-Banking: Mutual Acceptance and Interbanker Clearing in Restoration England. *Explorations in Economic History* 34: 411–32.

Roover, Raymond de. 1948. *Money, Banking and Credit in Mediaeval Bruges*. Cambridge: Mediaeval Academy of America.

Richards, R. D. 1929. *The Early History of Banking in England*. London: P. S. King & Son.

Sargent, Thomas J., and François R. Velde. 2002. *The Big Problem of Small Change*. Princeton: Princeton University Press.

Shortt, Adam, ed. 1925. *Documents relating to Canadian Money, Exchange and Finance during the French Period*. Ottawa: Canadian Archives.

South African Reserve Bank. 2014. History of South African Banknotes 1782 to 1902. Available at https://www.resbank.co.za/BanknotesandCoin/SouthAfricanCurrency/BankNotes/Pages/HistoryofSouthAfricanbanknotes1782To1920.aspx. Accessed 1 April 2014.

Spufford, Peter. 1995. Access to Credit and Capital in the Commercial Centres of Europe. In Karel Davids and Jan Lucassen, eds., *A Miracle Mirrored: The Dutch Republic in European Perspective*. Cambridge: Cambridge University Press.

Sylla, Richard. 1982. Monetary Innovation in America. *Journal of Economic History* 42: 21–30.

——. 2001. The United States: Financial Innovation and Adaptation. In Bordo and Cortés-Conde.

Tortella, Gabriel, and Francisco Comín. 2001. Fiscal and Monetary Institutions in Spain (1600–1900). In Bordo and Cortés-Conde.

Velde, François R. 2009. Was John Law's System a Bubble? The Mississippi Bubble Revisited. In Jeremy Atack and Larry Neal, eds., *The Origins and Development of Financial Markets and Institutions: From the Seventeenth Century to the Present*. Cambridge: Cambridge University Press.

Vries, Jan de. 2001. The Netherlands in the New World: The Legacy of European Fiscal, Monetary, and Trading Institutions for New World Development from the Seventeenth to the Nineteenth Centuries. In Bordo and Cortés-Conde.

Wee, Herman van der. 1977. Monetary, Credit and Banking Systems. In E. E. Rich and C. H. Wilson, eds. *The Cambridge Economic History of Europe, volume V: The Economic Organization of Early Modern Europe*. Cambridge: Cambridge University Press.

White, Eugene N. 2001. France and the Failure to Modernize Macroeconomic Institutions. In Bordo and Cortés-Conde.

CHAPTER TWENTY-SEVEN

THE CREDIT CRISIS OF 1772-73
IN THE ATLANTIC WORLD

———·◆·———

Paul Kosmetatos

INTRODUCTION

On 9 June 1772, Alexander Fordyce, the Scottish leading partner of the London bank of Neale, James, Fordyce, and Down, absconded to the Continent after being caught wrong-footed in his speculations in East India stock.[1] Fordyce's flight and eventual surrender the following September was the first act of a multifaceted financial crisis which raged for about a year.[2] The initial distress in the London market peaked on 22 June with a series of bank runs, when 'a universal bankruptcy was expected, and the stoppage of every banker looked for'.[3] The simultaneous impact in Scotland was even more spectacular, when the ambitious and experimental Ayr Bank (Douglas, Heron &Co.) was also forced to stop payment on 24 June with over £1.2 million in liabilities.[4]

A second phase of the crisis centred on Amsterdam in the winter of 1772–73, with the collapse of the bank of Clifford & Sons among others.[5] Ripples were felt across Europe and in the North American colonies, and the crisis closed its circle in London when Sir George Colebrooke, Chairman of the East India Company and a notorious speculator in his own accord, became its last prominent victim in March 1773.[6]

The on-going financial troubles of the East India Company are the connecting thread between the two phases of the crisis. Ever since the award of the *diwani* of Bengal to it in 1765 had raised expectations of a dividend windfall, its shares had become an object of intense speculation and had already followed a recognisable bubble trajectory in 1766–69. The credit crisis in June 1772 forced the Company to lower its dividend from the very high levels it had reached in previous years, particularly when the Bank of England discontinued the rolling short-term loans the Company had come to depend on as working capital ahead of its annual sale in England. The Company's finances were finally tidied over by the government and the Bank of England as part of the Regulating Acts of 1773, albeit at the price of some loss of independence, but the blow to its stock price in late 1772 helped break the Amsterdam speculators and the banks which had financed them.[7]

Although neither Horace Walpole's fears that 'one rascally and extravagant banker [had] brought Britannia, Queen of the Indies, to the precipice of bankruptcy',[8] nor James Boswell's prediction that '1772 [would] ever be remembered as a year of

491

confusion, dismay, and distress' proved accurate in the end,[9] the episode possesses several aspects that merit continued attention. Adam Smith's references to the Ayr Bank affair in Book II of the *Wealth of Nations* have attracted most of what modern academic interest persists,[10] but the affair as a whole is notable for being one of the first endogenous financial crises caused by growth itself, rather than war or government policy.[11] Its rapidity and geographical extent moreover can easily give the impression of causal relationships existing between its various episodes, and promote talk of financial contagion. Contemporaries were indeed quick to do just that, describing Fordyce's failure as the spark that 'set fire to the mine',[12] and marvelling at the speed with which news of it was brought to Edinburgh by 'a gentleman who came down in 43 hours'.[13] In the same passage quoted above, Boswell described the shock in Scotland as just that: 'like a company connected by an electrical wire, the people in every corner of the country have almost instantaneously received the same shock'. This conviction that the 1772–73 crisis displayed contagion characteristics is echoed in the limited modern literature on the affair. The actions of the Bank of England to limit the spread and severity of the shock are likewise proposed to constitute an early instance of a Lender of Last Resort (LOLR) in action, some thirty years before the classical formulation of the concept in Henry Thornton's *Inquiry on the Paper Credit of Great Britain*.[14] Charles Kindleberger considered 1772 as a typical example of financial contagion at work, and an almost canonical one on the desireability of a LOLR.[15] Fernand Braudel even suggested that the crisis' British origins signify that 'Amsterdam was no longer the [financial] centre or epicentre of Europe [and that] this had already shifted to London'.[16]

While an all-encompassing account of the 1772–73 crisis has yet to be written, some of its individual episodes have been described in detail. The North American side of the story is one, thanks in large part to the work of J. M. Price, T. M. Devine, and R. B. Sheridan.[17] All three have identified the financial connections associated with the colonial trades, tobacco foremost among them, as the likeliest route of transmission of the crisis from Europe to America. They have moreover drawn attention to the fact that the crisis occurred at a particularly interesting juncture in the relations between Britain and its American colonies, falling as it did between the breakdown of the colonial non-importation agreements in 1770 and the breakout of hostilities in 1775. The literature is universally (and commendably) careful not to make too much of the crisis as a direct 'cause' of the American Revolution, despite its close proximity in time. Circumstantial connections do remain, most notably the East India Company tea destroyed in December 1773, which had found its way to Boston Harbor through the provisions of the Regulating Acts that accompanied the government's rescue loan of £1,400,000. The most that can be safely said however, is that the crisis may have 'helped focus the discontent of the colonists...and thus helped to make [them] more responsive to anti-British propaganda',[18] though even this cautious a conjecture has been doubted in the literature.[19]

A more interesting question is to establish whether the crisis was indeed transmitted from Britain to America in the contagious manner claimed both by its contemporaries and by later literature. Quite apart from providing a satisfyingly causal narrative for the crisis, its propagation by genuine financial contagion would support the existence of systemic risk in the financial system of the 1770s. 'Contagion' can be a nebulous concept, and the literature is unfortunately all too ready to use words like 'spread' in

– CHAPTER 27: *The credit crisis of 1772–73* –

describing the sequence of the crisis episodes, and thus tacitly assume a causal relationship between them.[20] Causality however is easier to state than to prove in this as in so many other historical arguments. The mere coincidence of economic difficulties across different financial centres or economic sectors does not necessarily imply that contagion is at work. Going beyond this simple causal requirement, contagion in its purest sense arises from a narrow (or *idiosyncratic*) shock that is limited to a small set of institutions. Such a shock can include the outright failure of a small number of 'systemically important' market players (like Fordyce's bank or the Ayr Bank in 1772), but could just be the release of adverse news on them, or merely the heightening of suspicions on their financial health. Any further failures that occur afterwards must concern players who were completely insulated from this original shock.[21] Therefore such events as the breakout (or end) of war, bad (or bumper) harvests, and new (or repealed) legislation with broad effect such as regulations or tariffs, can be causes of a broad systemic crisis but generally *not* of contagion.

Contagion should moreover not be confused with the effects of economic recession, even if they have directly arisen from a financial shock, as these are usually too slow and open to other external impulses over the lifetime of the crisis. Therefore, contagion mechanisms are not only causal and sequential but also comparatively rapid.

THE AMERICAN COLONIAL TRADES AND THEIR FINANCIAL CONNECTIONS WITH BRITAIN

Contemporaries attributed the market break to what Adam Smith later termed 'overtrading',[22] a term which encompassed both asset speculation during a period of rapid economic growth, as well as imprudent monetary expansion. Later opinion is broadly in agreement, sometimes using the contentious word 'bubble' to describe the period preceding 1772.[23] According to this traditional narrative, the buyoancy of the British economy following the victorious end to the Seven Years War and Clive's advances in India very soon turned to excessively ambitious projects, conspicuous consumption, monetary fallacy such as the overuse of redrawn 'fictitious' bills of exchange, and speculation filled with 'roguery' and 'stupidity'.[24] This volatile mixture is supposed to have needed only a spark to 'set off the mine', as Sir William Forbes put it in his famous comment.

Scotland features prominently in this narrative. Following the final defeat of Jacobitism, the Scottish economy had entered an expansionary phase which accelerated in the late 1760s and peaked just before 1772. The growth of the Scottish share of the tobacco trade with North America after 1750 was especially noteworthy, growing from a fifth of the British total in 1744 to over half in 1769.[25] Almost all of this activity was centred on the Clyde and destined for re-export to England and, increasingly, the Continent, particularly after Scottish firms won the lucrative monopoly contract with the French Farmers-General.[26] The adoption of the non-importation agreements by the Americans had a predictably negative effect on imports after 1765, but after most of the Townshend duties were repealed in 1770 tobacco imports once again grew rapidly, reaching an all-time high of 47 million lbs in 1771.

This Scottish dominance of the tobacco trade was founded on the cost advantage Scots enjoyed over their English competitors. Part of this was due to the lower costs of locally produced manufactured goods that were supplied to the colonists. Henry

493

Hamilton estimated that £100 of Glasgow goods purchased £230 of tobacco in Virginia, although this margin may have incorporated the advantageous exchange between sterling and the Virginia currency.[27] Equally important were the advantages inherent in the Scottish system of tobacco purchasing in America.

The tobacco trade with Britain followed two distinct business models.[28] The older system, usually adopted by London traders and involving the produce of large plantations, was the plantation or consignment system. This involved the planter arranging for a British trader to assume the costs and risks of storing and marketing his entire crop in Europe (though not those associated with shipping and insuring it) in exchange for a commission. The merchant in turn arranged for the purchases of manufactured and consumer goods required by the planter and shipped them by return vessel. Any deficit (as was usually the case) between the price of the crop and that of the European goods was financed by the British merchant and secured on the planter's personal bond. The newer commercial, or store-based, system, which became increasingly prevalent among Glasgow traders after 1750, involved dispatching factors to America as 'supercargoes', or recruited them among the Scottish emigrants in the colonies. They in turn set up stores in the colonies which purchased tobacco directly and sold European goods to the planters on credit. Title to the crop passed to the factor on purchase, and all freight and insurance costs for transportation to Europe were assumed by the store. As in the case of the consignment system, any deficit incurred by the planter was financed by the British store owner

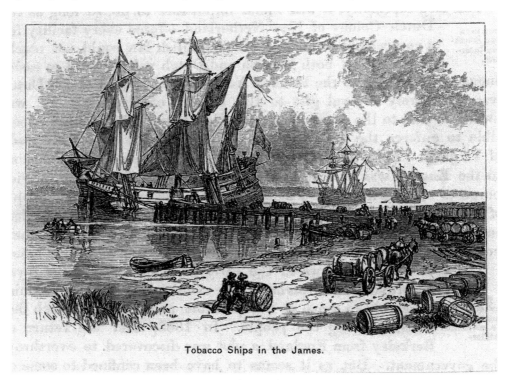

Figure 27.1 Tobacco ships in America
© Mary Evans Picture Library

– CHAPTER 27: *The credit crisis of 1772–73* –

and secured on land mortgages. Planters, both under the consignment and commercial systems of trade, generally ran credit balances with their British counterparts for at least 12 months, although store credit generally consisted of numerous small-sized debts compared to the larger balances run in the consignment trade.

The commercial system became increasingly popular as it proved better suited to the needs of smaller farmers and planters; by 1775 over three-quarters of Virginia tobacco were traded under it.[29] The reason for this was once again cost: Scottish ships achieved much quicker turn-around times due to the presence of their affiliated factors on the spot, who could arrange for the shipment of the produce of the smaller planters they traded with in more flexible manner than for the case of large consignments. Shipping to Glasgow rather than London also enjoyed the advantage of a round-trip that was shorter by four to six weeks, and which followed a route that was mostly immune to hostile action in case of war, unlike the Channel route typically used by English importers. Since freight charges could range from a third to a half of the prime cost of tobacco, the savings achieved by Glasgow merchants were substantial and allowed them to be much more competitive in the prices they offered to planters.[30]

The Clyde tobacco boom, and to a lesser extent the growth of other colonial trades such as sugar, rum, and cotton, gave some impetus to those Scottish industries which supplied the manufactured goods demanded by the colonies.[31] Banking services also saw increased demand, since tobacco importation through the store system was a particularly capital intensive business.[32] It is estimated that an initial investment of four times the cost of each hogshead of tobacco was necessary for the store system to function, not only because of the capital expenditure required in setting up the network of overseas stores, but also due to the planters running chronic deficits with their European counterparties. A contemporary estimate put it that £55,000 in goods and credit needed to be invested for an annual import rate of 2,200 hogsheads, at the time selling for £6 each.[33] These large capital requirements may have been partly behind the consolidation of the industry to a few large firms, which fell from 91 in 1728–31 to only 38 in 1773.[34] Some of these firms, like John Glassford & Co., or the Buchanan and Cunninghame groups of interconnected partnerships, were large concerns with tens of established stores in America and turnovers in the hundreds of thousands of pounds.[35]

Perhaps paradoxically given the comparative backwardness of its economy, Scotland's banks seem to have enjoyed a competitive advantage over the English in supplying capital for the colonial trades, and longer-term capital at that.[36] English private banks were still restricted to a maximum of six partners under the provisions of the 1708 Bank of England monopoly, which perforce constrained their assets even at the usual leverage for this period of 10–12.[37] Scottish banks by contrast functioned under a legal regime that allowed unincorporated partnerships of many persons, and enjoyed the advantage of operating as a separate legal personality (though not with limited liability).[38] The Royal Bank of Scotland and the Glasgow-based Ship, Arms, and Thistle banks had all supported the colonial trades at an early stage,[39] and the new Ayr Bank with its large resources and support of prominent landowners, merchants, and professionals throughout the Lowlands joined them in 1769. The Ayr Bank has been strongly (but not always justly) criticised by posterity for incompetent and venal management, and for fanning the flames of a huge credit bubble.[40] Its rapid credit growth supposedly consisted of 'taking up the bad loans of

495

the other banks'[41] and funding 'every kind of social pretention',[42] while its excessive paper money issuance was maintained by precarious short-term money market loans in London. Part of this credit was directed towards the purchase of sugar plantations in the Ceded Islands in the Caribbean, recently won from the French in the Seven Years War, particularly in Grenada where William Alexander & Sons, a major Edinburgh tobacco and banking concern, and the Home family from Berwickshire acquired plantations.[43] Both were to feature prominently in the aftermath of the 1772 crisis, albeit in different capacities: George Home of Branxton became the factor and manager overseeing (and, happily for posterity, meticulously recording) the unwinding of the Ayr Bank after 1773, while the surviving partners of Alexanders and their two large estates in Grenada were involved in long and bitter litigation with the Bank of England that took decades to resolve.[44]

When the non-importation agreements broke down in 1770, the tobacco trade intensified to compensate for the time it had been restricted, aided no doubt by the boom conditions in Britain. Sources agreed than an 'amazingly great' volume of goods was shipped from the mother country in 1771, and realised that the balance of trade, always in deficit from the point of view of planters, was turning even more against them.[45] Official estimates (which do not necessarily correspond to commercial values) put this deficit at £2.6 million in 1771 and almost £1.5 million at the time of the crisis in 1772. Total American debts outstanding just before the Revolution are estimated between £2–6 million. R. B. Sheridan estimates a possible figure of as high as £4–5 million for the peak of the boom, assuming a natural retrenchment of credit following the crisis in 1772.[46]

All tobacco merchants, whether Scots or English (or indeed, American), consignment- or store-based, and whatever their sources of capital, depended on the City of London for effecting their fund transfers. The bill of exchange drawn on London or Amsterdam bankers (and, increasingly, on aggressive Scottish newcomers like the Ayr Bank) was the long-established cornerstone of international trade in this period, allowing the fast and safe transfer of funds without the risk and expense of transporting specie, even had specie been abundantly available – which was far from the case.[47] Tobacco factors either drew or purchased existing London or Scottish bills, using either cash or – far more frequently – local paper money, and remitted those to their British parent companies. The inherent transferability of bills, by means of serial endorsements, made them convenient and somewhat mitigated their cost. This was invariably high: the structural deficits of the tobacco trade for the Americans, together with the scarcity of specie and the fact that American paper money issues in all their great variety, and (all too often) their inflationary disrepute, were not readily accepted by British merchants, drove demand for London bills ever higher – typically between 25–33 per cent in premium.[48] Going beyond cost, the bills system also introduced an extra dimension of credit risk to the transaction between exporter and importer, should any doubt befall the security of the London or Scottish banker who had 'accepted' (i.e. guaranteed) the bill.

Much has been made of the practice of drawing 'fictitious' bills during the 1770–72 boom, ever since Smith's analysis of the Ayr Bank failure in the *Wealth of Nations*. These were fiat financial instruments that did not correspond to real underlying commercial transactions, and which were often redrawn just before maturity so that the short-term loan (bills typically ran for 50–70 days) could be extended for a longer

– CHAPTER 27: *The credit crisis of 1772–73* –

duration.[49] Fictitious bills were certainly used heavily in Europe, particularly in effecting so-called 'accommodation loans', a form of interbank loan that made use of a bill drawn and accepted by established bankers in the major money markets like London or Amsterdam. This was not an innovation particular to this period, but long-established practice in the absence of a modern interbank market, nor was 1772 the first time such loans had been associated with a serious financial crisis.[50] Sources are nonetheless almost uniform in asserting that the practice had exceeded previous experience in 1772, particularly when Scottish bills were concerned. The bills employed in the tobacco and other colonial trades were very much 'real' however, supported by a voluminous trade in real commodities. Indeed, the very fact that the booming colonial trade created so many *genuine* bills which could be also used as a monetary instrument may have even fed the financial boom, by providing increased quantities of the very instrument that was its signature.

Although the preceding discussion has focused on the bilateral trade between colonies and mother country, not all commerce was conducted in this fashion, just as not all pre-1772 American debts were owed to British counterparties. Indeed, the case has been made that internal American debts outnumbered those owed to Britons.[51] Colonist merchants were already making their presence felt, trading directly either with the West Indies or with southern European countries, and participating in the tobacco and other colonial trades in their own account. Such 'cargo traders' were often based in the 'semi-open and commercially active...northern provinces',[52] which were not as tightly integrated with Britain as the southern colonies with their staple crop based economy operating under the restrictive colonial regime established by the Trade and Navigation Acts. They were however as dependent on the London money markets for their operations, since bills of exchange were the standard instrument through which their cash flows could be affected. This exposed them to the availability of short-term credit there, binding them to the British financial nexus as strongly as the southern planters with their large capital needs and chronic trading deficits with Britain.

THE IMPACT OF THE 1772–73 CRISIS ON TRANSATLANTIC FINANCE

Contemporary press reports and correspondence described an emotional outburst in the market and society at large when the crisis broke out. 'Public calamity', 'tragedy', 'catastrophe fatal to thousands', 'horror and confusion', are some of the statements found in only one London newspaper report.[53] David Hume talked of 'universal Loss of Credit and endless Suspicions' in Edinburgh,[54] while the *Scots Magazine* reported the 'whole city [of London] in uproar, and many of the first families in tears'. The same correspondent warned of suicides arising from this sense of desperation, and lurid tales indeed abounded in the press for a time, describing merchants cutting their own throats, shooting or hanging themselves, not to mention the by now proverbial jumping out of a 'window in agony of mind arising from the failure of the Bankers'.[55] Such reports were not entirely fantasy either: the younger Robert Bogle of the London Scottish tobacco house Bogle & Scott *did* jump out of the proverbial window 'in a phrenzy' when his firm stopped payment – although he survived.[56] Those involved in the colonial trade on both sides of the Atlantic quickly joined this chorus of alarm.

Even if he was by then somewhat calmer, the aforementioned Bogle repeated a few months later the exaggerated claim that 'the South Sea affair was a trifle to what has now happened' that was also appearing in the press.[57] George Norton of the large John Norton & Sons tobacco concern was typical in stating that 'were [he] to recount the many Catastroph'es that have happen'd & the many families reduced to want & Beggary [he] should fill a volume of Incidents'.[58] Joshua Johnson of the London and Maryland tobacco trading firm of Wallace, Davidson & Johnson estimated the situation in almost the identical phrasing as Hume: 'the breaking of Fordyce & Co. bankers has stagnated business; every man seems afraid of each other'.[59]

Such reactions are all too often described as 'panic' in the literature, sometimes even 'spreading panic', implying contagion of some sort.[60] It can also be argued, however, that the reactions of at least some market participants were in fact all too rational in view of the sudden change in market circumstances. The revelation of previously unavailable information can lead market participants to reassess their risk accordingly, even to the point of resorting to capital flight, forced asset liquidations, or the denial of new credit.[61] This 'informational contagion' presumes an imperfect information regime where 'the costs of acquiring and processing [market] information make a correct assessment of fundamentals difficult and a certain degree of ignorance rational',[62] a not altogether unreasonable assumption for the eighteenth-century British financial network. The 'wake-up call'[63] that can set off the contagion sequence in motion may be the outright failure of a market player who is considered systemically important (like Fordyce or the Ayr Bank), an increase in the rate at which bills are dishonoured or protested, or merely the suspicion that the behaviour of the financial establishment has altered drastically. In June 1772, it was not just that Fordyce was rumoured to have been deeply committed in the bills trade and in Alley speculations, but that his failure was attributed by many to ongoing – though unsubstantiated – rumours that the Bank of England was refusing to discount bills drawn by Scots and Amsterdam Jews.[64] The very fact that the Scot Fordyce had absconded could have been seen as proof of such a policy change, even if – as is more than probable – this never took place in reality.[65] The rate at which bills were protested certainly rose during the crisis to perhaps as high as 25 per cent,[66] and complaints about the Bank of England's discount policy continued both in Britain and on the Continent.[67] Any new knowledge that existing bills were being dishonoured by their drawers, or that new bills were being returned protested from their acceptors, or that the ultimate discounting power in the country was choosing to refuse them, could thus very rationally lead market participants to restrict their bills acceptances, or to call in what outstanding loans they could. Eight months after the breakout of the crisis, and after the January wave of stoppages in Holland had dealt a new blow to the bills of exchange network, Joshua Johnson described himself 'trembling with fear' lest more houses stop

> for, if they do, we most surely must have many more of our bills returned [i.e. protested] than is at present, and the quantity already is so great that I know not what to do about it. The Bank continues not to discount and they have by that means distressed the whole mercantile body and, unless they relapse soon, I fear the whole nation will become a bankrupt.[68]

Suspicion could encompass whole classes of market participants, assigning to them guilt by mere association. No other category in 1772 was suspected or publically

– CHAPTER 27: The credit crisis of 1772–73 –

excoriated more than the Scots, who had already been the subject of a virulent campaign in the Wilkite press for some years. As Walpole put it,

> As [Fordyce] is a Scotchman, and as the Scots have given provocation even to the Bank of England, by circulating vast quantities of their own banks' notes, all the clamour against that country is revived, and the war is carried very far, at least in the newspapers.[69]

Resentment at this 'deluge of Scotch paper for English gold' went beyond letters in the press or satirical prints.[70] The concurrent failures of other Scottish bankers in London like Fordyce, Grant & Co. and Charles Ferguson & Co. led to general consternation about the quality of Scottish bills, particularly as 'the foundation of them [was] very little understood, though of late much the topic of conversation'.[71] The stoppage of the Ayr Bank made such fears even more acute, although the bank eventually managed to fend off bankruptcy and satisfy drafts on it through the (ultimately ill-advised) issuance of £450,000 in life annuities.[72] John Norton specifically warned that he was 'credibly inform'd that Virginia Bills drawn payable in Scotland are now discharged by drafts on the Heron & Douglas Bank which lately stopt, for which reason those who purchase Bills ought to be carefull of whom'.[73] Johnson similarly cautioned his American correspondents to take particular care in purchasing any bills of exchange that might be tainted from any Scottish connections:

> It is hardly doubted that all your Scotch factors will be knocked up. I recommended to you caution in the last [letter] respecting the purchase of Scotch bills, but now let me beg of you not to have anything to do with them at any rate, for I assure you I am very doubtful of the ones I have by me will [be protested]; indeed no one will do anything with them; they are all so frighted, and I assure you that it is not only my opinion but everyone's else that there will be a total bankruptcy with the Scotch in most countries.[74]

There are indications that some transatlantic traders curtailed their trading activities in the face of the crisis. The large W. Cunninghame & Co. Scottish concern explicitly declared on 19 August the company's 'fixed resolution to adopt a new plan in carrying on their business more frugally…as they are morally certain that there will be but few goods imported into the colony [of Virginia] next year'. They accordingly warned their factors that they should expect 'very scanty supplies next year' and urged them to clear their inventories of goods. They furthermore instructed them to 'have more dependance on receiving payment of [their] debts', and restricted the leverage of their stores by limiting their ability of drawing bills on the parent company without first remitting a fraction of the face value of the bill in cash.[75] This restriction varied according to store location: from a leverage factor of 4 to 5 for their Rappahannock and Potomac stores, to 3–4 for the ones at Cabin Point and Petersburg, to only 2 or at most 3 for those at Shockoe and Rocky Ridge.[76] In general, the Cunninghame firm showed much hard-headedness in responding to the crisis, despite paying lip-service to the usual hyperbole about 'amazement, terror, astonishment, and suspicion [being] visible in every countenance'. In the same letter quoted above, they showed no little *schadenfreude* in stating that though

499

the shock must have been terrible, it will show who has and who has not a foundation and will make everyone be much more on their guard in what manner they trade beyond their bottom.

One of the Cunninghame representatives in America echoed this frustration at what he viewed as the excesses of the boom and the incursions of independent traders, by declaring himself

happy if this shock to credit has an effect to the advantage of the trade of this colony. If fewer goods are imported, fewer will trade on their own account and the advance of course may be increased.[77]

Such informational and behavioural effects aside, contagion can also be transmitted through strictly financial connections.[78] The most obvious way this can occur is through dishonoured debts, leading to cascading defaults as more debts are dishonoured in turn.[79] It is not very likely that such a direct route was a major factor in 1772, despite the large American debts due to British merchants. As mentioned above, most of those arose from the trading deficits of planters, and there had always been the option of discharging them by supplying staple commodities like tobacco instead of cash. Credit exposures arising from bills of exchange were a more serious matter, however. Bills were short-dated, generally running from 50 to 70 days and never longer than three months, and the bill holder in fact had a claim upon multiple counterparties, thus obscuring the credit risk picture. Not only was the original drawer and acceptor of the bill liable for its face value, but so were also any endorsers who might have signed on the bill in its path to the ultimate creditor's hands. This multiplicity of claim entitlement could rapidly transmit financial distress, as merchants were unsure whether they would be called upon for repayment of bills they had drawn, accepted, or endorsed to counterparties. Johnson's letters to his American factors frequently listed firms or persons who might be under a cloud of suspicion, or were already having their drafts protested in London, along with warnings against purchasing any bills that might be tainted by association, since

almost every merchant notes the bills drawn on them, so that it requires you use the utmost caution on your parts that you have good endorsers to those bills you purchase.[80]

Bills on London, Edinburgh, or Amsterdam were also held as liquid assets due to the chronic dearth of cash on both sides of the Atlantic. These were either sold on, discounted for cash, or remitted in payment of other debts, including other bills. The stoppage of any of the signatories on a bill could very easily drive its value downward, leaving the current holder with a sharply devalued (or worthless) asset.

Such distress did not necessarily lead to bankruptcy, at least not immediately. The numbers of British bankruptcy commisions instituted in 1772 *did* rise appreciably, in fact reaching the highest level since 1706 and would only be surpassed again in the war year of 1778.[81] The size of the proven debts for the major failures of 1772 was likewise very substantial.[82] In general however, comparatively few participants in the trade went immediately bankrupt in a way that would cause the cascading defaults

– CHAPTER 27: *The credit crisis of 1772–73* –

that would be evidence of financial contagion. Among tobacco traders only the London Scottish house of Bogle & Scott and their correspondents Simpson, Baird, & Co. went bankrupt during the June crisis, and there were no notable bankruptcies among the big warehousemen who supplied the transatlantic trade with goods.[83] The only equivalent in America was the stoppage of an unnamed Carolina house mentioned by Joshua Johnson, though whether it actually went bankrupt or not is not specified.[84] A second wave of failures coincided with the January 1773 Amsterdam crisis and continued all through the year. This time several big tobacco houses stopped, including some of the prominent Buchanan interlocking partnerships.[85] Others resisted longer before finally succumbing: William Alexander & Sons, who were connected with such central players of the crisis like the London private bank of Glyn & Hallifax as well as the Ayr Bank, received two large rescue loans from the Bank of England for a total of £220,000, and were the beneficiary of a further favourable – and contentious – loan from the Ayr Bank for £10,000 in 1774, as well as of another £5,000 in loan guarantees by no less a figure than Benjamin Franklin. Even so, they could not avoid eventual bankruptcy and long litigation over the family's estates in Grenada, before their last surviving partner eventually absconded, first to France, and finally the newly independent United States.[86]

Most debt cases took years to resolve, and in extreme cases like that of the Ayr Bank, decades. During that time other factors came into play, topmost of all of course being the rapidly deteriorating political situation culminating in the Revolution. R. B. Sheridan has tried to extract some information specific to the financial crisis from the Loyalist Claims Commission documents, while a write-down of £15,000 in the 1786 Ayr Bank balance sheet was attributed to Hamilton & Co. and Simon Brown, all of whose assets were in America.[87] In all cases however, it is difficult to distinguish which effects were due to the financial crisis and which to the political situation. In any event, bankruptcy was only the final resort for creditors. More often than not, debtors would open their books and try to come to some accommodation with creditors, either continuing operations in the meantime, or agreeing to an orderly wind-up. In some cases credit was extended over the crisis period until liquidity was reestablished, and in others debtors and creditors agreed to a composition, that is the payment of a fraction of the debts. Johnson's letterbook goes into some detail about this process, both concerning his company and also the arrangements of other troubled merchants. The timing of such a proposal was particularly crucial in view of the shaky confidence prevailing in the markets. Johnson described this dilemma in responding to such a proposal by his associates:

> You certainly don't recall the injury it has done many houses in raising a suspicion of their goodness or you would not have advised it...If we are to preserve the reputation of the house, I must by no means [call my creditors together to demonstrate our security is good]; that I was subject to be arrested and might be threw in gaol from the present exceeding ill temper amongst the tradesmen.[88]

Tobacco merchants trading under the store system were much more susceptible to mechanical contagion compared to those still operating under the old consignment one, since they depended on bills for effecting their remittances to their British creditors. Independent American 'cargo traders' operating outside both systems were

501

even more vulnerable, since they could neither benefit from long-term store credit, nor supply tobacco in part payment of their debts. Any disruption to the bills of exchange network could be instant and fatal for them, as would any retrenchment on the part of their London correspondents on whose short-term credit their solvency depended. By contrast, the greatest hardship those operating under the consignment system might encounter was a straightforward scarcity of capital. This might prevent them from purchasing more land and slaves to expand production, but would not pose an immediate threat to their solvency.

On the other hand, large planters were much more worth pursuing in court by their creditors, unlike stores who were typically owed numerous and individual small debts. For instance, the £63,000 owed to John Norton & Sons in 1773 arose from 398 distinct debts.[89] Table 27.1 shows the distribution of debts due to two stores in Port Royal and Fredericksburg by the failed Bogle & Scott firm. Close to half of the almost £9,000 owed arose from four comparatively large debts over £500, the largest of which was for a little over £1,700. These debts would have been worth pursuing. Another 14 debtors owed between £100 and £500 a total of about a third of the outstanding store debt. The remaining 15 per cent arose from 41 small debts whose originators would very likely have been safe from being pursued in court, and who could always move to the interior of the vast country if hard pressed. Indeed, one reason for the comparatively conciliatory attitude on the part of creditors was that the collection of debts in America posed major challenges. There had never been enough cash in the colony in the first place, and the disruption in the bills market removed the most ready alternative for making remittances to Britain. Payments in kind were still possible of course; the sugar from the Grenada plantations of William Alexander & Sons was explicitly used to service their large Bank of England rescue loans, and later became a major bone of contention in the laborious litigation involving them.[90] Tobacco could be used in the same way, although the glut caused by the bumper harvest reduced its usefulness in that respect.

Between the recovery of debts that would have been normally carried forward by the stores before the crisis, remittances in support of drawn bills of exchange, and the repatriation of specie to Britain by merchants who needed to support their credit there, there was a sudden drain of cash out of the colonies. One contemporary put the total amount of cash shipped out of the country at £100,000 for the nine months

Table 27.1 Debt distribution of Port Royal and Fredericksburg stores of Robert and Robert Bogle and William Scott, 22 June 1772

	Number of debts	Total owed (£)
Below £20	15	195
£20 - £50	16	468
£50 - £100	10	716
£100 - £500	14	3,453
£500 - £1,000	2	1,209
over £1,000	2	2,952
	59	8,994

Source: RBS SPS/12

preceding June 1773.[91] The discount in the rate of exchange between sterling and local currency rose from 20 to 30 per cent between October 1771 and May 1773, both due to this cash drain and the bidding up of the increasingly scarce good bills of exchange. Nevertheless, the colonial economy had been accustomed to specie shortages, as indeed was the British one as well. It is far more likely that the disruption in the bills of exchange market affected business more seriously than the removal of £100,000 of specie.

EFFECTS ON OVERALL TRANSATLANTIC BUSINESS AND THE QUESTION OF CONTAGION

It is not easy to establish whether the transmission of the British credit crisis to North America caused appreciable negative effects on overall business.There are no reports that the underlying demand for colonial commodities fell in Europe. Tobacco prices remained comparatively low throughout the crisis years of 1772–73, but that was more a result of five straight bumper crops starting in 1770.[92] At first glance, trade figures for England and Scotland as shown in Tables 27.2 and 27.3 do seem to indicate that transatlantic trade contracted due to the crisis. Volumes of imported tobacco fell more significantly for English importers than for Scottish ones (a fall of 11.5 per cent and 4.3 per cent year-on-year respectively). This apparent resilience of the Glasgow traders, despite the involvement of prominent Scots bankers in the crash, has been attributed to the fact that a large part of their re-exports were directed to French customers who paid in cash, unlike those Hamburg or Amsterdam customers of the English who instead relied on the bills market. Scottish exports to France had risen by almost 69 per cent by volume of merchandise, from 12 million lbs in 1771 to over 20 million lbs in 1772, and remained over 21 million lbs the following year.[93] Even the much smaller English tobacco exports to France jumped from 1771 to 1772, and although they retreated somewhat in 1773, remained at much higher levels than previously. There also remains the possibility, that the apparent drop in overall imports in the crisis year is either an artifact of the way the annual figures were collated, or of the clearing of inventories after the record imports of 1771. In fact, English tobacco imports more than cancelled this apparent drop with a rise of 12.4 per cent in the following year, while Scottish imports remained largely stable at their new slightly lower levels. Over the whole 1772–73 period therefore, overall tobacco imports remained broadly stable though somewhat below the 1771 all-time peak, while British exports to France stayed at record levels. Similarly, English sugar imports from the West Indies (Scottish sugar imports were dwarfed by comparison and are not as relevant) show a small year-on-year drop of 2.4 per cent for 1773, but then resume their strong upward trend they were on since 1765. Data for arrivals of British flagged slaving ships to the Caribbean underline this picture (Table 27.4), showing a very small drop for 1772 before recovering strongly in 1773. In all cases, what impact the financial crisis may have had on the volume of colonial trade is dwarfed by that of the war that was to break out only three years later. Tobacco imports completely collapsed to virtually zero then, never to recover again for the case of the Glasgow merchants, while the sugar and slave trades were also disrupted, particularly after the French capture of Grenada in 1779.

503

Table 27.2

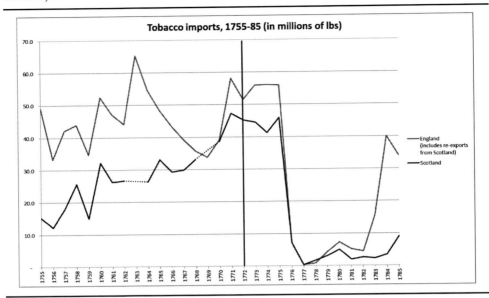

Sources: (1) English data: Elizabeth Boody Schumpeter, *English Overseas Trade Statistics 1697-1808* (Oxford, 1960), Tables XVI and XVII
(2) Scottish data: Henry Hamilton, *An Economic History of Scotland in the Eighteenth Century* (Oxford, 1963), Appendix IX

Table 27.3

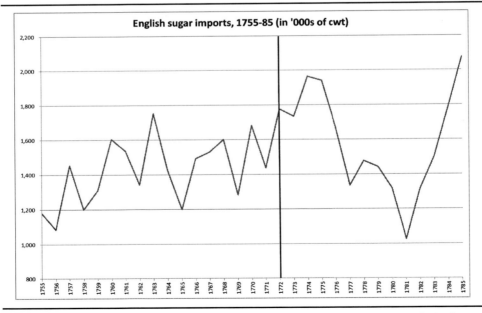

Source: Elizabeth Boody Schumpeter, *English Overseas Trade Statistics 1697-1808* (Oxford, 1960), Tables XVI and XVII

Table 27.4

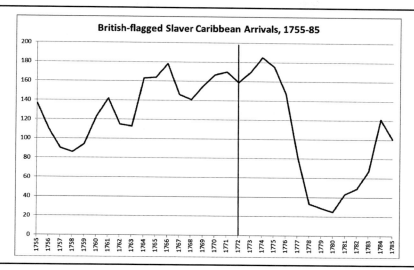

Source: *Voyages: The Trans-Atlantic Slave Trade Database*. http://www.slavevoyages.org (accessed March 28, 2014).

There is stronger evidence from wholesale commodity prices for Charleston, that have the further advantage of a finer data set than the annual totals of the import data.[94] These show an unequivocal peak just before the crash month of June 1772, following an almost steady rise since 1770. After the crash, prices fell by almost 30 per cent, and despite some volatility never regained the same peaks throughout the last three years of peace.

It is nonetheless difficult to depend on such aggregate figures as an explicit indicator of the effects of the financial crisis, and certainly not as evidence of contagion according to the specific definition. Contagious relationships between the American colonies and the distressed European money markets are certainly plausible, but the surviving evidence is sparse. Capital repatriation to Britain on the part of distressed traders is an appealing hypothesis, but there is at present little archival evidence to corroborate it. It is far more likely that the disruption in the bills market transmitted financial distress more decisively than the removal of even £100,000 in specie. Furthermore, there are other possible explanations for the difficulties faced by tobacco traders after 1772. The great surge in imports on both sides of the Atlantic that followed the normalisation of trade in 1770 may have been followed by a correction to more sustainable levels as built-up inventories were cleared. Moreover, the tobacco glut in Europe depressed prices by itself, thus worsening the chronic deficits of planters, and made it difficult for British importers to keep extending ever higher credit by supplying the same quantities of goods as in the peak year of 1771. In general terms too, 1772 paled in comparison with the economic dislocation that was to follow as political friction between mother country and colonists worsened into rebellion, and eventually into European war.

That said, we should not altogether dismiss the effects of the crisis on the transatlantic trading network, even if we remain sceptical of contemporary hyperbole which builds it up to an unprecedented disaster. The level of financial integration and sophistication of the international financial network in 1772 was such as to make the contagious transmission of the crisis both plausible and serious. Contemporaries certainly thought as much, stressing that 'such [were] the connexions of trade that the English could not feel complacent about the distress of Scottish bankers',[95] and that 'the failure of a great house in another country is very little different to a failure in our own'.[96] No other contemporary reaction underlined such fears better than the speed and decisiveness with which the Bank of England intervened to interpose the 'shelter of the Castle of Public Credit' to protect the financial system from the storm,[97] even if the first theoretical expression of the concept of the Lender of Last Resort still lay three decades in the future.

NOTES

1   *London Evening Post*, June 9–11, 1772.
2   *Bingley's London Journal*, September 5–12, 1772.
3   *Scots Magazine*, XXXIV (1772), p. 311.
4   Henry Hamilton, 'The Failure of the Ayr Bank, 1772', *Economic History Review* 8 (1956), 405–17.
5   Charles Wilson, *Anglo-Dutch Commerce and Finance in the Eighteenth Century* (Cambridge, 1941), 169–88.
6   Lucy S. Sutherland, 'Sir George Colebrooke's World Corner in Alum, 1771–73', *Economic History: A Supplement to the Economic Journal III* (1934), 237–58.
7   Lucy S. Sutherland, *The East India Company in Eighteenth Century Politics* (Oxford, 1952), 222–29.
8   Horace Walpole, *The letters of Horace Walpole: earl of Orford, Volume 5* (P. Cunningham, ed.) (London, 1891), 395–96.
9   James Boswell, *Reflections on the Late Alarming Bankruptcies in Scotland* (Edinburgh, 1773), 1.
10 Adam Smith, *An Inquiry into the Nature and Causes of the Wealth of Nations* (Oxford, 1976) (hereafter: *WoN*), II.ii.73–77. S. G. Checkland, 'Adam Smith and the Bankers', in A. S. Skinner and T. Wilson, eds., *Essays on Adam Smith* (Oxford, 1975), Hugh Rockoff, 'Parallel Journeys: Adam Smith and Milton Friedman on the Regulation of Banking', *Journal of Cultural Economy*, 4, 3 (2011), 255–83.
11 Julian Hoppit, 'Financial Crises in 18th Century England', *Economic History Review* 39, 1 (1986), 39–58. Jacob M. Price, *France and the Chesapeake; a history of the French tobacco monopoly, 1674–1791* (Ann Arbor, 1973), 639.
12 Sir William Forbes, *Memoirs of a Banking-House* (London and Edinburgh, 1860), 39–44, *Scots Magazine* (hereafter *SM*) XXXIV, 304–18.
13 *London Evening Post*, 18–20 June 1772.
14 Henry Thornton, *An Enquiry into the Nature and Effects of the Paper Credit of Great Britain* (London, 1802).
15 Charles P. Kindleberger, *Manias, Panics, and Crashes: A History of Financial Crises* (New York, 2000), 162.
16 Fernand Braudel, *Civilization and Capitalism 15th–18th Century, Vol. 3* (Berkeley, 1992), 268–69.
17 Jacob M. Price, 'The Rise of Glasgow in the Chesapeake Tobacco Trade, 1707–55', *William and Mary Quarterly*, 3rd ser., 11 (1954) 179–99, *Capital and Credit in British Overseas Trade: The View from the Chesapeake, 1700–1776* (Boston [Mass.], 1980). T. M. Devine, 'Glasgow Merchants and the Collapse of the Tobacco Trade, 1775–83', *Scottish Historical*

- CHAPTER 27: *The credit crisis of 1772–73* -

Review, 52, 153 (1973), 50–74, 'Sources of Capital for the Glasgow Tobacco Trade, c. 1740–80', *Business History*, 16, 2 (1974), 123–29. Richard B. Sheridan, 'The British Credit Crisis of 1772 and the American Colonies', *Journal of Economic History*, 20 (1960), 161–86.

18 Sheridan, 'The British Credit Crisis of 1772', p. 186.

19 Emory G. Evans, 'Planter Indebtedness and the Coming of the Revolution in Virginia', *William and Mary Quarterly*, 3rd ser., 19 (1962), 511–33.

20 For instance Sheridan, 'The British Credit Crisis of 1772', p. 172 (on two occasions), Kindleberger, *Manias, Panics, and Crashes*, p. 124.

21 This definition is adapted from Olivier De Bandt and Philipp Hartmann, 'Systemic risk in banking: a survey', in Charles Goodhard and Gerhard Illing (eds.), *Financial Crises, Contagion, and the Lender of Last Resort* (Oxford, 2002), 249–97. This review article is in general a good starting point for approaching the vast literature on this subject.

22 Smith, *WoN*, II.ii.57.

23 For instance Sheridan, 'The British Credit Crisis of 1772', p. 172, Price, *Capital and Credit*, p. 131, Julian Hoppit, *Risk and Failure in English Business 1700–1800* (Cambridge, 1987), p. 99.

24 Hoppit, *Risk and Failure*, p. 134.

25 Henry Hamilton, *An Economic History of Scotland in the Eighteenth Century* (Oxford, 1963), 255–56.

26 Price, *France and the Chesapeake*, pp. 608–9.

27 Hamilton, *Economic History*, p. 259.

28 Sheridan, 'The British Credit Crisis of 1772', pp. 168–71, J. H. Soltow, 'Scottish traders in Virginia, 1750–1775', *Economic History Review*, 12, 1 (1959), 83–98.

29 Sheridan, 'The British Credit Crisis of 1772', p. 169.

30 Hamilton, *Economic History*, p. 259. Price, 'Rise of Glasgow', 187–90.

31 T. M. Devine, 'The Colonial Trades and Industrial Investment in Scotland, c. 1700–1815', *Economic History Review*, 29, 1 (1976). 1–13. Hamilton, *Economic History*, p. 262.

32 Price, *Capital and Credit*, p. 124.

33 Devine, *Sources of Capital*, pp. 116–17.

34 Hamilton, *Economic History*, p. 266.

35 Soltow, 'Scottish traders in Virginia, 1750–1775', p. 85, Hamilton, *Economic History*, p. 266.

36 Devine, *Sources of Capital*, p. 116.

37 Examples include Barclays (Barlcays Group Archives [BGA] 364/1–40 &78–84), the Bristol Old Bank, and its London correspondent, Prescott Grote (Royal Bank of Scotland Archives (RBS) MCB/1/1 and PRE/263).

38 R. H. Campbell, 'The Law and the Joint-stock Company in Scotland', in P. L. Payne, ed., *Studies in Scottish Business History*, 136 (1967), 137–5. Charles W. Munn, *The Scottish Provincial Banking Companies, 1747–1864* (Edinburgh, 1981), 5–6.

39 Price, *France and the Chesapeake*, 607–8, *Capital and Credit*, 63–95.

40 Smith, *WoN*, II.ii.73–77. Committee of Inquiry appointed by the Proprietors, *The Precipitation and Fall of Mess. Douglas, Heron, and Company, Late Bankers in Air with the Causes of their Distress and Ruin, Investigated and Considered* (Edinburgh, 1778).

41 Kindleberger, *Manias*, p. 44.

42 Wilson, *Anglo-Dutch Finance*, p. 171.

43 National Archives of Scotland (NAS), Home-Robertson papers, GD267/1–4.

44 NAS, Court of Session papers, William Alexander vs Creditors of William Alexander: Sequestration; Proceedings in England, CS181/6942.

45 Quoted in Sheridan, 'The British Credit Crisis of 1772', p. 173.

46 Sheridan, 'The British Credit Crisis of 1772', p. 166, Devine, *Sources of Capital*, p. 117. Lawrence H. Gipson, 'Virginia Planter Debts before the American Revolution', *Virginia Magazine of History and Biography*, 69, 3 (1961), 259–77.

47 T. S. Ashton, *An Economic History of England: The 18th Century* (London, 1955), p. 186, Neal, pp. 5–9.

48 Roger W. Weiss, 'The Issue of Paper Money in the American Colonies, 1720–74', *Journal of Economic History*, 30, 1 (1970), 770–84.

49 For Smith on the Law of Reflux and the Real Bills Doctrine see David Glasner, 'The Real Bills Doctrine in the Light of the Law of Reflux', Lloyd W. Mints, *A History of Banking Theory in Great Britain and the United States* (Chicago, 1945), 9–30, Morris Perlman, 'Adam Smith and the Paternity of the Real Bills Doctrine', *History of Political Economy*, 21 (1989), 77–90.

50 Isabel Schnabel and Hyun Song Shin, 'Liquidity and Contagion: The Crisis of 1763', *Journal of the European Economic Association* 2, 6 (2004), 929–68. Stephen Quinn and William Roberds, 'Responding to a Shadow Banking Crisis: The Lessons of 1763', *Federal Reserve Board of Atlanta Working Paper Series*, 2012–18 (2012).

51 A. C. Land, 'Economic Behavior in a Planting Society', *Journal of Southern History*, 33 (1967), 479.

52 Sheridan, 'The British Credit Crisis of 1772', p. 168. Price, *Capital and Credit*, pp. 127–29.

53 *Middlesex Journal*, July 2–4, 1772.

54 David Hume to Adam Smith, 27 June 1772, *The Correspondence of Adam Smith* (Oxford, 1977), p. 162.

55 *Morning Chronicle*, June 24, 1772, *Bingley's London Journal*, July 4–11, 1772, *London Chronicle*, November 17–19, 1772, *General Evening Post*, July 2–4, 1772, Sheridan, 'The British Credit Crisis of 1772', p. 176.

56 RBS GM/1357, Robert Oliphant to William Putney, 22 June 1772. Robert Bogle Jr. to George Bogle, London, November November 19, 1772, quoted in Price, *France and the Chesapeake*, p. 640. Frances Norton Mason (ed.), *John Norton & Sons, Merchants of London and Virginia* (hereafter: Norton letterbook), p. 254 George F. Norton to John Hately Norton, July 8, 1772.

57 Bogle letter quoted in Price, *France and the Chesapeake*, op. cit.

58 Norton letterbook, op. cit.

59 Jacob M. Price (ed.), *Joshua Johnson's Letterbook, 1771–1774* (hereafter: Johnson letterbook) (London, 1979), 41d, 22 June 1772, p. 40.

60 For instance, Hoppit, 'Financial Crises', p. 54, Sheridan, 'The British Credit Crisis of 1772', p. 172, Price, *France and the Chesapeake*, p. 639 and *Capital and Credit*, p. 131.

61 Mervyn King and Sushil Wadhwani, 'Transmission of Volatility between Stock Markets', *Review of Financial Studies*, 3 (1990), pp. 5–33, Matt Pritsker, 'The Channels for Financial Contagion', pp. 67–97 in S. Claessens and K. Forbes (eds.), *International Financial Contagion* (Boston, 2001).

62 Thomas Moser, 'What is International Financial Contagion?', *International Finance*, 6, 2 (2003), 157–78.

63 Morris Goldstein, *The Asian Crisis: Causes, Cures, and Systemic Implications* (Washington, 1998), 18.

64 *Middlesex Journal*, 3–6 September 1772, *Bingley's Journal*, 6–13 June 1772, *General Evening Post*, 20–23 June 1772, NAS GD44/43/70/7, James Balfour to James Ross, 21 July 1772.

65 The only documented change in Bank official policy is a 13 May 1773 resolution to increase the discount rate on foreign bills to 5 per cent, starting on 24 June that year, that is a year after the crisis broke out (BOE, Extracts from court minutes relating to discounts, G29/1, fo. 6).

66 Price, *Capital and Credit*, p. 132.

67 For instance Anonymous, *Réflexions sur les dernieres banqueroutes en Anglettere & Hollande, et conduite du Ministere Anglois à ce sujet* (pamphlet claiming to be printed in London, 1773). Bogle letter quoted in Price, *France & Chesapeake*, op. cit. NAS GD267/22/7/57, George Home to Patrick Home, 29 June 1772.

– CHAPTER 27: *The credit crisis of 1772–73* –

68 Johnson letterbook, 61, 5 February 1773, p. 59.
69 Horace Walpole, *The Letters of Horace Walpole: Earl of Oxford, Volume 5* (P. Cunningham, ed.) (London, 1891), 395–96.
70 F. G. Stephens and M. D. George, *Catalogue of Political and Personal Satires in the Department of Prints and Drawings in the British Museum* (London, 1870), 'A view of the Deluge of Scotch Paper Currency for English Gold', anonymous satirical print, 1 August 1772 (BM Satires 4961).
71 *Scots Magazine, XXXIV,* 313.
72 Lloyds Group (Bank of Scotland) Archives, NAS945 20/30/3.
73 Norton letterbook, John Norton to john Hately Norton, 6 August 1772, p. 266.
74 Johnson letterbook, 42, 1 July 1772, pp. 40–41.
75 T. M. Devine (ed.), *A Scottish firm in Virginia, 1767–1777, W. Cunninghame and Co.* (hereafter: Cunninghame letterbook), to J. Neilson, 19 August 1772, p. 58.
76 Cunninghame letterbook, as above.
77 Cunninghame letterbook, to Messrs W. Cunninghame & Co. per the *Nelly,* Capt. Brown, 22 August 1772, p. 88.
78 Franklin Allen and Douglas Gale, 'Financial Contagion', *Journal of Political Economy,* 108, 1 (2000), 1–33.
79 Philippe Jorion, and Gaiyan Zhang, 'Credit Contagion from Counterparty Risk', *Journal of Finance,* 64, 5 (2009), 2053–87, David Marshall, 'Understanding the Asian crisis: Systemic risk as coordination failure', Federal Reserve Bank of Chicago, *Economic Perspectives,* 22 (1988), 13–27.
80 Johnson letterbook, 47a, 20 August 1772, p.45 and 52a, 7 October 1772, p. 49.
81 Hoppit, *Risk and Failure,* Appendix I, 182–83.
82 Paul Kosmetatos, 'The Winding-Up of the Ayr Bank, 1772-1827', *Financial History Review,* 21, 2 (2014), 165–190.
83 Price, *Capital and Credit,* p. 135.
84 Johnson letterbook, 41e, 22 June 1772, p. 40.
85 Sheridan, 'The British Credit Crisis of 1772', p. 177.
86 Price, *France and the Chesapeake,* p. 693–700.
87 NAS GD224/178/8.
88 Johnson letterbook, 83a, 28 June 1773, p. 80, and 86, 30 June 1773, p. 83.
89 Norton letterbook, p. 293.
90 NAS CS181/6942, William Alexander & Sons, sequestration proceedings in England, NAS CS222/278, sequestration proceedings in Scotland.
91 Sheridan, 'The British Credit Crisis of 1772', pp. 175, 178.
92 Price, *Capital and Credit,* p. 130.
93 Price, *France and the Chesapeake,* pp. 641–43.
94 George Rogers Taylor, 'Wholesale commodity prices at Charleston, South Carolina, 1732–91', *Journal of Economic and Business History IV* (1932), 366–77, quoted in Sheridan, 'The British Credit Crisis of 1772', pp. 174–75. Note also Sheridan, 'The British Credit Crisis of 1772', p. 174n, for further price index references.
95 *Bingley's Journal,* 20–27 June 1772.
96 *General Evening Post,* 2–5 January 1773
97 'Ship News Extraordinary', *Morning Chronicle,* 29 June 1772.

PART VII
COMMERCE, CONSUMPTION, AND MERCANTILE NETWORKS

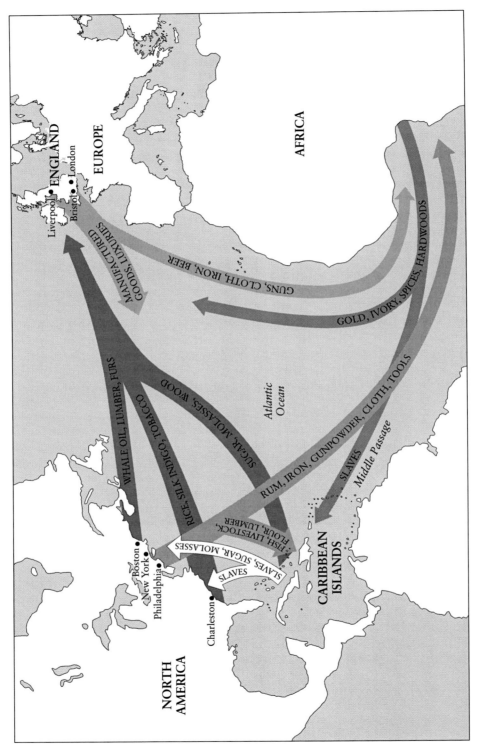

Trade routes in the Atlantic linking Europe, Africa and North and South America

CHAPTER TWENTY-EIGHT

REASSESSING THE ATLANTIC CONTRIBUTION TO BRITISH MARINE INSURANCE

A. B. Leonard

New world discoveries from 1492 increased the known land endowment per European capita six-fold. This enormous introduction of one of three factors of production into Europeans' early modern mercantilist economies could be exploited only after the addition of the other two, labour and capital. Historians have only recently begun to explore one important source of the latter in the context of Atlantic World development, the provision of capital through marine insurance. There as elsewhere, marine insurance provided individual merchants with crucial contingent capital, allowing them to trade with less resources than the perils of a specific voyage prudently demanded. It permitted the maximum investment of cash and credit into cargoes and vessels. As Captain John Butler wrote to a correspondent in Amsterdam in 1735, 'I could make no Ensurance here, and I beg of you that you would get insured for me two thousand pounds, for it is too great a Risque for me to run with my little fortune, without insurance'.[1]

Butler couldn't afford his planned venture without the backstop of an insurance policy, since he feared ruin if his vessel or trade goods were lost. However, he could limit his downside with insurance. If the ship had sunk, whether due to the rage of the seas or the actions of pirates or enemies, the underwriters would have paid him £2,000 towards the loss – presuming, of course, that his correspondent secured cover. Under the well-established structure of a marine insurance contract, the buyer receives the promise of an injection of capital from the underwriters (usually fellow merchants, but sometimes others with capital to risk) if an insured loss actually occurs. In exchange, the insured merchant pays an advanced fee, called a premium, calculated as a percentage of the maximum possible payout.[2]

This system of mercantile risk-sharing stretches back much further into the history of finance than the Atlantic discoveries of the early modern era. Underwriting – the practice of merchants sharing the risks of their endeavours amongst themselves through premium insurance – has been a catalyst of international trade since Italian adventurers developed the financial instrument in the later middle ages, during their commercial revolution. The structure of the marine insurance contracts was developed and standardised fairly rapidly, and has changed very little since, such that one historian has argued that the earliest Italian 'policies did not differ very much even at

513

the end of the fourteenth century from either those of the subsequent centuries or... from those of the present day'.[3]

Long before merchants began to insure the perils of Atlantic World ventures, they used their risk-sharing system to provide contingent capital for more local trade. The insurance structures developed in medieval Italy were adopted and routinely practised in major ports there at least as early as the first decades of the fourteenth century. Lombard émigrés brought the practice to London within a century. In 1426 Alexander Ferrantyn, a Florentine merchant resident in the city, insured his vessel the *Seint Anne of London*, and its cargo of French wine, for £250 with 17 other resident Italian merchants. The policy states that the agreement was governed by the customary practice of Florence. The example is not isolated. The ledgers of the merchant bank Filippo Borromei & Co. record insurance transactions in London from at least 1438, covering the bankers' cloth trade with the mainland. Other entries show that the bank was also sometimes an underwriter, illustrating the mutual nature of insurance practice.[4]

These examples show not only that insurance was practised in London in the fifteenth century, but also that its development was already advanced. Likewise, the basic structure of the market, with merchants insuring one another (making them 'merchant-insurers'), and sometimes deploying the capital of other wealthy men as underwriters, was copied from Italy, and was well established. Dispute resolution processes were already in place, and the contractual form, or policy, was already widely known and adopted. Trade statistics for the period are scant, but it is known, for example, that merchants in England imported an annual average of 7 million tonnes of dry wine in the first half of the fifteenth century, and exported 27.5 million cloths. This number increased to over 90 million in 1500 to 1561. This is the sort of commerce that was being insured in London during the period when marine insurance emerged there.[5]

As England's international insurance market evolved and matured, the trade risks which underwriters assumed was most often unconnected to the Atlantic World economy. In 1539 the Bristol merchant John Smythe insured a shipment of iron he was importing from San Sebastian in Spain. The policy, which covered only part of the value of the iron, cost about £1.6.0. Further evidence from Smythe's ledger shows that he insured often, although not always, on cargoes ranging from wine to wood. The Italian merchant Bartholomew Corsini, trading from London in the 1580s, routinely insured his ships and trade goods, which comprised primarily exports of English cloth and primary products, and imports of various Mediterranean goods. While such extant evidence is scant, court records show that the practice of insurance was widespread in London in the sixteenth century. Cases recorded then include more than a dozen heard in the High Court of Admiralty, nearly a score heard by the Privy Council, and a handful each in the courts of Chancery and King's Bench. *Mayne & Poyn* v. *De Gozi*, the earliest known case to have reached the formal courts, was heard in 1538.[6]

The sixteenth-century London insurance market was already ordered and increasingly institutionalised. Roughly 30 brokers and 16 notaries operated in London in the sector during the 1570s. The former group facilitated introductions and interactions between buyers and sellers of insurance, and managed financial relationships. The latter drew up policies, kept registers of their details, and managed client monies. Merchants and their insurers also sometimes dealt directly, without the intermediation of third parties. The activities of all were governed by a set of customs and principles based upon an inheritance from Italian merchants, such as those

CHAPTER 28: *Atlantic contribution to British marine insurance*

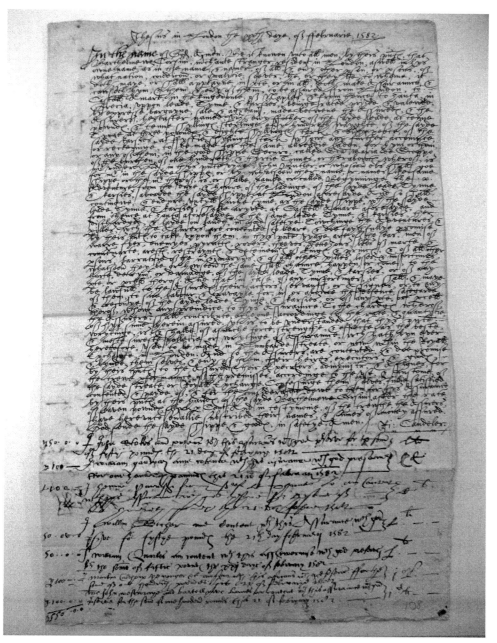

Figure 28.1 A 1583 policy drawn up at the Office of Assurances in London for Bartholomew Corsini
Guildhall Library

governing the Ferrantyn contract, and the modifications of merchant-insurers in Antwerp and Amsterdam. These insurance customs were an important component of the *lex mercatoria*, or law merchant. Most disputes were resolved internally according to these law merchant principles. When, in 1575/6, a number of frauds were perpetrated against underwriters, a royal patent was granted to the merchant Richard Candeler to operate the Office of Assurances, which possessed an exclusive right to draw up and register marine insurance policies in London (although it did not grant a monopoly over underwriting itself).[7]

Contemporary recognition of the importance to trade of marine insurance was widespread. The English marine insurance act of 1601 stated that, when they are insured, 'all Merchants, sp[ec]iallie the younger sorte, are allured to venture more willinglie and more freelie'. However, the causal relationship between the growth of trade and the rise of insurance is circular. Insurance indeed encouraged merchants to trade, but the increased demand for insurance which arrived with burgeoning English seaborne commerce helped to spur the expansion of the insurance market. This pushed down the cost of cover, which in turn boosted the take-up of marine insurance. As the market expanded in the later sixteenth century, inevitably driving up the number of disputes which could not be resolved to the satisfaction of all parties through non-binding arbitration, the need for a more formal system of dispute resolution was recognised. The Privy Council responded with a series of initiatives, and parliament established a Court of Assurance under the 1601 Act to settle cases arising in London.[8]

The purchase of insurance became ever more common in the seventeenth century. The journal of Baltic trader Charles Marescoe records that between June 1664 and April 1668 he purchased 108 policies from 31 underwriters who provided total cover of £39,715. His successor, Jacob David, purchased 36 policies worth £30,770 between 1673 and 1677, from 77 discrete underwriters (although some of Marescoe-David's trade went intentionally uninsured, or only partially covered). Many more examples could be cited which show that in the seventeenth century marine insurance was commonplace, widespread, and often – if not always – purchased by merchants when venturing aboard. A final example shows that London's marine insurance market was also becoming an international one. Writing in 1657, Samuel Lamb, a London trader, stated that English merchants usually shipped their wares in Dutch vessels, 'which ships were usually insured in London; and it is the Hollanders custom to this day, that when they send any single ship southward for their own accounts, oftentimes to insure them in England'. Lamb also states that heavily armed English merchant vessels were typically uninsured, but such vessels were not the norm.[9]

Readers are forgiven for wondering, at this point, why this chapter appears in a book about the Atlantic World. The reason is this: amongst the very limited recent published work in English about marine insurance, some has declared strongly that it was Atlantic World trade that led to the development and growth of the British marine insurance market. For example, Christopher Ebert has recently argued that 'Atlantic shipping was the great spur' in the development of marine insurance, from the time of the discoveries to 1630. He states that 'colonial trade tended to lead to accelerated state involvement in the activities of the merchants involved, and consequently spawned an evolving institutional framework...one [aspect] of which... was the development of maritime premium insurance practices situated partly in a state-supported institutional context mainly during the years 1550 to 1630'. Ebert's conclusions followed marine-insurance market analysis by Joseph Inikori, who presented calculations in his 2002 book *Africans and the industrial revolution in England* which purport to show, for the 1790s, that 'the [marine insurance] premiums for the slave trade and the West Indies trade together...is 63 percent of the whole [marine] insurance market in Great Britain'. When US risks insured in London are included, his total rises to 'very much above 70 per cent of the entire market'.[10]

While there can be no doubt that the marine insurance market received a great boost and much income from Atlantic trade, the drivers of its development were much broader than these simple Atlanticist arguments claim. As shown above, and in much more detail elsewhere, the practices and institutions of marine insurance were developed and established long before Atlantic World trade became significant. The balance of this chapter will attempt to deflate the recent assertion that Atlantic World trade was the main driver of the development of marine insurance.

Ebert's assertion specifies *colonial* trade as the catalyst to institutional developments in the marine insurance market, rather than the conventional seaborne trade between European ports, which was increasing significantly in the period 1550 to 1630. Ebert goes on to specify further that the 'spread of state-supported premium insurance practices [occurred] in order to facilitate Atlantic trade'. However, the balance of extant documents does not support this thesis. Evidence such as the extant London policies underwritten in the period shows that development of institutional structures supporting marine insurance responded primarily to disputes over policies which, in the vast majority, related to non-colonial trade to Europe and the Mediterranean. Six of eight relevant disputes heard and recorded in England's High Court of the Admiralty between 1547 and 1565 involved European trade; another was over a voyage to India. Nor was it specifically the trade of this period which 'spawned an evolving institutional framework'. As has been shown above, by 1550 the outline framework of marine insurance markets, including state involvement in them, had been evolving for many centuries in southern Europe. State involvement matured in England in the years culminating in the marine insurance act of 1601, but not due to the perils or pressures of Atlantic World trade. Of 17 relevant cases heard before the English Privy Council between 1573 and 1590/1, the ports of call are recorded for only three voyages. All were between ports in England and France or Spain. Arguably it was these cases, along with a petition from leading merchants about their desire for a state solution to the rising incidence of fraud against underwriters, which prompted the Privy Council into a flurry of marine insurance institution-building activity. The Councillors' three-pronged effort in the 1570s formalised the framework for the resolution of marine-insurance-related disputes in London under elected Commissioners of Assurance, established Candeler's monopoly Office of Assurances, and attempted to codify the customary law merchant which for at least a century had governed marine insurance in London and elsewhere. In 1601 the statutory Court of Assurances was established under parliamentary legislation drafted and presented by Francis Bacon.[11]

Ebert claims that 'Insurance was especially associated with "rich trades", that is, trade in overseas commodities.' Conventionally, the rich trades are those in high-value goods ranging from silks to spices, which comprise only a subset of 'overseas trade'. It has often been argued that higher-value trade goods were more likely to be insured, but much evidence shows that during the sixteenth century bulky, low-valued commodities were often covered. Above we saw the Bristol merchant John Smythe regularly insuring his shipments of iron in 1539. By the 1570s, even fishing vessels and their cargoes were also regularly insured. A tract about the Newfoundland fishery published in 1580 reports that 'A shippe of Excester is gone to the Warde house, to fishe for Codd and Lyng; the venture for the Shippe, Salte, and Victualls is three hundredth pounde; for eightene pownd [i.e., six per cent] all is assured.' Many more examples could be cited, showing incontrovertibly that marine insurance was not limited to luxury items.[12]

Ebert shows that some changes in insurance institutions occurred concurrently with the rise of Atlantic trade, but provides no evidence of a causal link. The absolute growth of trade in the period Ebert examines, including the entry into local marine insurance markets of many individuals who were unfamiliar with market practice, and, much earlier, the need of merchants to develop more efficient, more effective instruments which separated capital provision from risk transfer, were the key drivers of change in marine insurance markets. Atlantic trade was, at best, another factor among many.

Inikori's analysis is much better considered, and therefore deserves much more attention. His explanation of the strong link between marine insurance, trade, and trade finance is essentially correct: insurance spreads the risk of 'floating considerable property by sea' while 'mobilising funds for investment'. His description of early forms of marine risk transfer as 'little more than a loan' is also fundamentally correct. A group of financial instruments with origins dating back at least to the era of imperial Rome, and which together may be described as sea loans, connected the advance of trade capital to risk transfer through the forgiveness of the loans in case of actual loss. Inikori cites *bottomry*, a form of loan in which capital is advanced against the ship itself as security (strictly speaking for the repair or provisioning of a vessel in a foreign port, but commonly for trade finance). Bottomry and other early varieties of ocean-going trade finance, such as the *cambium nauticum*, had the distinctive characteristic of the discharge of the debt without repayment in case of loss of insured property. However, their medieval function was threefold. They advanced capital for trade, removed some of the risk of losses at sea, and third, they avoided usury laws through their risk transfer structure, with interest disguised as a risk premium (a ploy which the medieval Church accepted). Early risk transfer mechanisms for ocean-going trade thus combined borrowing and risk transfer.[13]

These forms of risk transfer were very early drivers of the development of marine insurance, in part because they were expensive. When bills of exchange became popular, and when merchants became sedentary, sea loans became less useful. Premium insurance emerged in medieval Italy to satisfy only the risk transfer element, disconnected from the advance of capital. The wording of marine insurance contracts was fixed in England, based on much older Mediterranean precedents, by Candeler in the 1570s, when England had only just begun to flirt with Atlantic trade. The policy wording remained almost completely unchanged until the 1980s. Bottomry was used well into the nineteenth century, but it had lingered long after the modern insurance contract was developed. Premium insurance was dominant in Atlantic World trade, and it did indeed mobilise funds for investment, but only contingent funds, to be paid only in cases of actual insured loss. It also helped to loosen

– CHAPTER 28: Atlantic contribution to British marine insurance –

commercial credit. For example, when colonial merchants consigned goods to metropolitan merchants, they would often draw bills against their consignees before the goods arrived, and insure the goods to reduce the likelihood that the bills would be dishonoured because the cargo failed to arrive. However, these systems and practices were not a product of the Atlantic World. They had been developed in Italy by the fourteenth century, and were widespread long before Atlantic trade gained great importance.[14]

Inikori offers a multi-stranded argument to support his contention that the 'Atlantic slave economy' was responsible for the development of marine insurance. He argues that demand for marine insurance was limited before the arrival of the Atlantic trade, which he asserts was more perilous than other trades, and therefore spurred insurance-buying. He dismisses the trade to India and the east as generally uninsured. Finally, as stated above, he calculates that an enormous share of Britain's total marine insurance business was related to the Atlantic trade.

Inikori first argues that limited demand for marine insurance slowed its development in England prior to the second half of the seventeenth century, but that the growth of English trade and its reorientation away from Europe to 'regions where the much greater risks compelled a more regular procurement of insurance cover' – the Americas – prompted its development. These arguments echo relatively common misconceptions about the under-development of marine insurance in England prior to about 1720. These include, for example, misrepresentation of the observation of Frederick Martin, the author of *The History of Lloyd's and of Marine Insurance in Great Britain*. Writing in 1876, Martin declared that 'up to the commencement of the great war [for supremacy of the seas from 1775] the insurance of ships, and of property sent by sea, had not been held to be *absolutely necessary*, and there were numbers of merchants who deemed it no more requisite to insure the vessels and cargoes they owned against loss than to insure their houses'. Inikori cites the second part of Martin's statement, but in context it is a far cry from his later assertion that 'the average merchant in England did not regularly insure his property at sea'. Nor is it in any way akin to characterising the marine insurance market as under-developed. Wright and Fayle, in their 1928 *History of Lloyd's*, found 'nothing to show that [the] system had proved inadequate to the requirements of commerce' even in the Elizabethan era.[15]

Prior to 1717 nearly all marine insurance underwriting in London was carried out by individual merchant-insurers, or sometimes by merchant partnerships. In essence, private traders comprised the insurance market. However, when joint-stock companies began to emerge in great numbers in the late seventeenth century, many merchants believed such a company would better serve the needs of insurance buyers. Leaving aside the protracted debates which surrounded the formation of joint-stock insurers, it needs only to be said that in 1720 the *Bubble Act* (which, ironically, was intended primarily to prevent the formation of new joint-stock companies) permitted 'two several and distinct corporations' to underwrite marine insurance under royal charter. All other corporations, societies and partnerships were prohibited from the business. The companies formed were the London Assurance and the Royal Exchange Assurance. However, individual underwriters were permitted to carry on trading.[16]

A 1958 article about the London Assurance Company by Arthur John cites an 1810 estimate of the potential maximum insured value of 'English foreign trade in 1720 at £20.3 millions, of which some £2.3 millions were underwritten by the two companies', and asserts that this 'merely confirms...what has long been known – namely, that a large part of coastal and foreign-bound shipping proceeded without cover'. Inikori draws heavily on this article to support his arguments, and repeats these same quotes. In a footnote, he states that 'As John suggests, the private underwriters could not have done much more business than the two corporations in the early years of the century.' As will be shown below, the two companies shared about 10 per cent of the total market at that time, while individual underwriters had the rest. John makes no suggestion that private underwriters could not handle demand for insurance, stating instead that the private underwriters, who numbered over 150 in London at this time, were 'better able, and thus more willing, to accept risks of all kinds'.[17]

Much evidence shows that private underwriters were able to meet the demand that existed. In 1719 Attorney General Nicholas Lechmere reported petitioners' claims that 'the Pretence of Difficulties in gaining Insurance is altogether Groundless'. More concretely, the merchant-insurer John Barnard stated in an affidavit that 'no sums which *English* or Foreign merchants have Occasion to Insure, are too large for the [private] Insurers to take at Reasonable Prices'. The broker John Bourne stated that 'it is very easy to procure Insurances for the largest Sums that are wanting to be Insured'. While the last two men were petitioning against the formation of a chartered joint-stock insurer which argued that, among other benefits, it would be able to assume larger risks, others in their camp later stated that 'no Proof has been made' by the proponents of incorporation that 'Trade had suffered from the Want of Ability in the [private] Insurers'.[18]

In any case, the supply-side argument does not support the contention that low demand slowed England's insurance-market development. Here, two qualifying observations may be made. First, it is obvious that as trade volumes rise, the amount of insurance purchased will also rise. The eighteenth century saw significant growth in trade volumes (see Table 28.1). Second, while there can be no doubt that a large share of trade went uninsured, there is much evidence that the opposite was true for a large share. While insufficient records survive to estimate market penetration with any worthwhile confidence, other evidence supports the assertion that marine insurance was a significant and much-used sector well before the English Atlantic trade was of importance.

Table 28.1: English (British) imports, exports, and re-exports, 1622–1824, official values, £ million[19]

	Imports	Exports	Re-exports
1598–1600*	n/a	0.22	n/a
1622	2.32	2.62	n/a
1663/69	4.4	4.1	n/a
1700	5.84	3.73	2.08
1725	7.10	5.67	2.81
1750	7.77	9.47	3.23
1775	13.55	9.72	5.48
1800	30.57	24.30	18.85
1824	37.5	48.7	10.2

– CHAPTER 28: *Atlantic contribution to British marine insurance* –

Consider, for example, the efforts of the Elizabethan Privy Council to create a formal framework for its operation, and the parliamentary creation of the Court of Assurance. These institutional development steps would have been taken only in response to a genuine demand for dispute resolution mechanisms in an important market. Given that the commonplace mechanism of adjudication in London's marine insurance market was arbitration, and that relatively few contracts would have led to a formal dispute (if this were not true, and it had been usual for insurance contracts to lead to disputes, surely no insurance market at all would have existed), then a need for state-backed dispute resolution mechanisms must indicate that the use of marine insurance was relatively widespread.

Inikori concedes that 'the practice of marine insurance was well-established in London in the sixteenth century', but he argues that it was not 'specialised'. Instead, it was 'undertaken as a sideline by merchants whose main activity was something else'. This observation is correct, but is a red herring. Many of London's leading underwriters, including the famous John Julius Angerstein, widely regarded as the father of modern Lloyd's, remained active in multiple branches of trade and commerce, including raising state loans with Alexander Baring, even after the Napoleonic Wars, when London was firmly established as the world's leading insurance centre. In 2013, private individuals whose main commercial activity was something other than underwriting provided more than £2.7 billion of capital to Lloyd's, widely recognised as the most specialised insurance market in the world.[20]

These facts together should not lead to the conclusion that the 'slow development of marine insurance as a specialized business in England was due to the limited size of the market for marine insurance arising from the absolute volume of England's seaborne commerce as well as the attitude of merchants to insurance'. While there can be no doubt that the growth of England's trade led to increasing demand for marine insurance, this alone did not determine the size of the London marine insurance market, as Lamb's testimony highlights. Further, while the 'attitude towards insurance' may have dictated that not all cargoes should be insured at all times for all voyages, it is not clear whether this was because full cover was not wanted for some reason, or that it was not purchased because it was not available. It may have been because, as seems most likely, complete coverage was uneconomic at the prices offered by London's insurers in the earlier part of a period which saw a long decline in insurance pricing. Nor is the prevalence of the attitude in any way certain, since many merchants did opt to insure. The West Indies merchant William Freeman, for example, explained that 'it's my general custom to insure when adventures are anything considerable, whether at peace or war. When the danger is least, premium is low, and so I look upon it as a safe way.'[21]

Although insurance was clearly well established in the seventeenth century and widespread in the sixteenth, Inikori claims that 'it is generally known that in the eighteenth century the average merchant in England did not regularly insure his property at sea'. Although this may be said of the seventeenth century despite the evidence of insurance activity cited above (and it may even be true), no such consensus has formed about the eighteenth. John states, citing an 1810 tract addressed to the then-chairman of Lloyd's, that in combination the two chartered companies underwrote policies with an annual insured value of about £2.3 million in their first year, 1720. Evidence delivered before a related parliamentary committee in 1810

521

heard that the chartered companies had about 10 per cent of the insurance market in their first year, suggesting a total sum insured of roughly £23 million. In 1720 the total international trade of England and Wales was, according to modern estimates, £13 million. The anonymous 1810 writer calculated the total value of insurable ships and cargoes entering and leaving England at £20.3 million (of which English foreign trade was £14 million). Thus, the total value of ships and goods insured in England in 1720 was greater than the total value of English trade goods and ships that year. Even if coastal trade, foreign insurance buying in London, and a significant understatement of the companies' market share are ignored, it must remain difficult to argue that the majority of England's early eighteenth-century ocean-going commerce was uninsured.[22]

What of the second of Inikori's arguments, that the risks faced by Atlantic traders, and especially slaving vessels, were greater than for other vessels, which prompted them to buy more insurance than the average merchant adventurer? Inikori states that 'the risks involved in trans-Atlantic trade in the eighteenth century were infinitely greater than those in the trade with nearby Europe [and] more so in wartime'. Hyperbole notwithstanding, this assertion deserves careful examination. Inikori states that 'war was by far the greatest hazard faced by the [European slave] traders... particularly so, because struggle over control of overseas trade was a major factor in these wars'. The contemporary comments quoted in his 1996 article *Measuring the hazards of the Atlantic slave trade*, in which he presents a detailed analysis of the causes of the loss of 1,053 slaving vessels in the period 1689–1807, indeed show that contemporaries believed the trade to be risky. However, the evidence he cites does not state whether slaving was made 'uncertain and precarious' by peculiar market risks, such as the variability of pricing, or by unusual transportation risks.[23]

According to Inikori's analysis of the causes of slave-vessel losses in the period 1689–1807, wartime capture was by far the leading peril, resulting in 679 losses, including 248 vessels taken during the French Revolutionary and Napoleonic wars. Yet the risk of capture was not intrinsically greater for slavers than for other vessels. During wartime, privateers operated often or sometimes in the approaches to most of the world's major ports, from India to the Spanish Main. The English Channel, given its proximity to major French privateering ports such as St Malo, was particularly vulnerable. All enemy vessels were fair game. No evidence has come to light that slave vessels were particularly favoured targets, and, in contrast, it is easy to speculate that the added challenges of assuming control of a vessel packed with human cargo – not easily sold without a long and perilous voyage – suggest the opposite. It seems likely that the capture of a slave vessel by privateers would lead to slave insurrection, making such vessels particularly unattractive targets. Further, vessels departing from major ports other than London, including Bristol, Glasgow and Liverpool, frequently took a 'Northabouts' route which avoided the privateer-infested Sound and Channel, despite it taking longer.[24]

An important aspect of capture is the ability to ransom vessels, and indeed to insure the cost of ransom. This, however, is not a product of the slave trade, nor was war necessarily the driver. In 1682 the Philadelphia merchant James Claypoole insured John Spread on his return voyage from New England 'personally against capture by the Turks at 2 percent by good men'. From the 1580s formal English policies always included, as named insured perils, 'Men of War...Enemies...Letters

– CHAPTER 28: *Atlantic contribution to British marine insurance* –

of Marque and Counter-Marque, Suprisals, and Takings at Sea'. Ships' masters were obliged to ransom their vessels if this was in the interests of the vessels' owners, and insurers were 'obliged to declare immediately that they will contribute towards the payment of the ransom'. If a ransomed ship was lost or taken again on the same voyage, insurers were twice liable. Capture-and-ransom became institutionalised, and was far more convenient than seizure for both captor and captured. It was perhaps less so for insurers. The cost of a ransom was less than that of a total loss of vessel and cargo, but the chance of a recapture negating the loss was eliminated, and efforts at evasion and resistance by crews were probably reduced.[25]

Recapture was another commonplace. For example, Williams recounts that the *Bud*, Captain Robert Tyrer, was captured in 1798 by a privateer while sailing for Guinea, but was retaken (with her captor) by navy vessels a week later. Thus capture did not mark the end of *Bud's* slave-trading career; the ship, under the same captain, completed triangular voyages in 1799 and 1801. Similarly Thomas and William Barton's slaver *Agreeable* was captured the same year in the West Indies, and drawn into service as a French cruiser, but was retaken by the *Concorde* and the *Amphitrite*, and completed seven more slave voyages. Clearly vessels lost in wartime were sometimes quickly returned to service. Finally, if the threat of wartime losses due to the capture of slave vessels were a significant driver of development of the insurance market due to an exceptional level of risk faced by slave ships, one would expect them to form a significant part of the total number of ships captured or captured and ransomed. However, the 679 losses of slavers during the 118 years between 1689–1807 attributed to capture by Inikori pales in comparison to 2,600 prizes and 1,100 ransoms against British vessels in just five years between the passage of the *Cruisers and Convoys Act* in March 1708 and the conclusion of the Treaty of Utrecht in April 1713.[26]

Loss due to wreck is non-discriminatory. Inikori states that 17.7% of the lost vessels he enumerated suffered their fate due to 'slave insurrection, conflict with local Africans, or wrecks on the African coast'. Unfortunately in neither article nor book has he offered more numerical detail, so it is impossible to know if, for example, losses due to the seas were more frequent in this location than the average casualty rate for all merchant vessels. A table including descriptive excerpts from *Lloyd's List* appears in the article, but as Inikori points out, in very many cases it is impossible to determine the specific cause of each loss from the brief descriptions reported. Several vessels are listed as 'blown up', a relatively frequent fate for armed merchantmen carrying powder and shot.[27]

Some of the vessels Inikori included as reported 'lost' appear not to have been lost at all. The *King David*, according to the *Lloyd's List* report quoted by Inikori, suffered a slave insurrection on its voyage from Old Calabar to St Kitts. The captain and all but four of the crew were killed. The survivors 'carried the ship into Guadeloupe'. While the cargo was lost to its owners, the vessel appears to have been saved. The same can be said of the *Lamb*, much of whose crew was dead or disabled, perhaps as a result of an insurrection in which 14 slaves were killed. Despite the hardships, Captain Anyon 'got fresh hands, and sail'd...for S. Carolina'. The *Mercer* was seized by slaves in 1789, but 'afterwards retaken by the *African King*'. All three vessels are included in Inikori's table of 188 'vessels lost due to insurrection of slaves, conflict with coastal Africans, and wrecks off the coast', but these three vessels, at least, were not lost.[28]

523

Slave insurrection is a peril which carriers of non-human cargoes clearly did not face, but comprises only a small proportion of the insurrection and African loss grouping. However, 'conflict with coastal Africans' is not. Instead, the examples cited in Inikori's enumeration appear to be incidents of the ancient peril of piracy, which is probably less likely to menace slave vessels than those without human cargo, for the same reasons that privateers steered clear of slavers. While Inikori muses that the motivation of local venturers who seized slaving vessels may have been solidarity with captives, the accounts he presents seem to present banditry, rather than rescue, as the principal driving interest of free Africans who boarded slavers. In 1785, the *Good-Intent* was 'plundered by the Natives at Gabon' then set on fire. The following year the *James* was 'totally lost', and 'his first boat plundered of 12 slaves'. Finally, Inikori acknowledges the gaps in the record which make impossible the calculation of accurate loss ratios – the measure of insurers' premium income versus claims against that income – but then goes on to compound the problem. 'Although there are indications of double counting in the reporting of losses, it may be reasonable to add about 200 vessels to the figure to make up for missing reports', he states, but does not justify his estimate. Equally, it may be reasonable to subtract 100, given the double-count and the inclusion in the totals of vessels which apparently were not lost.[29]

The assertion that 'the trans-Atlantic slave trade had the greatest amount of risk among all international trades of the period' is not supported by the analysis of the causes of losses in *Lloyd's List*. Inikori's claim that 'unlike merchants in some other trades, who could afford to be more relaxed in matters of insurance, the slave traders were compelled by the unusual level of risk involved in their business to secure insurance cover regularly to help spread the risk' is not supported by the evidence, and no comparative examples from 'other trades' are offered. Inikori goes on to cite examples of vessels which did not purchase insurance, or which intentionally underinsured their cargoes, including correspondence between merchants and captains which instructs them to be extra careful, since the enemy will be nearby and the cargo is uninsured or underinsured. 'Extraordinarily high premium rates' may have encouraged 'larger firms' to retain risk, Inikori suggests. If so, this means that wartime risks faced especially by Atlantic slavers were not a driver of the insurance market. More likely, however, is that some slavers chose to retain risk because they did not desire contingent capital at the price offered. If their own resources were sufficient to ensure that losses would not sink the firm, and their volume and frequency of trade was sufficient to ensure that they suffered only the mean statistical level of loss, the purchase of insurance was rendered merely a cash-swapping exercise with insurers. Still others may simply have possessed a larger-than-average risk appetite.[30]

Having argued that marine insurance demand was weak in England, and that Atlantic traders bought more cover because their trade was more risky, Inikori goes on to assess 'the contribution of the Atlantic slave economy to the expansion of the market for marine insurance that was central to the emergence of England as the centre of marine insurance in the world'. He does this by making assumptions about market size. First, he estimates the total size of the marine insurance market by extrapolating from the marine insurance premium income of a single market player – the London Assurance Company. He 'derived' his estimates of this premium income not from hard numbers, but through extrapolation from a line-graph in John's article. 'If it is accepted that the trend in growth of [the company's] premium income from

– CHAPTER 28: Atlantic contribution to British marine insurance –

1720 to 1820...represents roughly the general trend in the growth of the market as a whole, then a tolerably reliable estimate of the volume of business in the period 1720–1807 can be made'. For the critical period of his investigation, 1793 to 1807, Inikori uses this trend to arrive at a total average annual marine insurance market premium of £4 million. The average is based on a 'backwards projection' from a starting point of a £10.95 million in total premium income in 1809, a figure drawn from a contemporary declaration of Lloyd's chairman John Julius Angerstein (Inikori also mentions, in a footnote, an estimate of £10.3 million for 1811). In 1809 the benchmark London Assurance's premium income was 'roughly three times its average annual premium income from about 1793–1807'. Inikori then leaps to the conclusion that the entire insurance market grew threefold in the same years.[31]

He does not suggest the change to the London Assurance's premium income might be a result of a change in corporate underwriting policy, rather than a sudden tripling of the overall market size, but figures for marine premium levels at the London Assurance's parallel company, the Royal Exchange Assurance, strongly suggest this explanation. Supple found that the latter company's marine income, which averaged £23,000 per year in 1771–75, reached £275,000 in 1796–1800. From this example, it seems that a tenfold increase in premium income occurred at the Royal a decade before the trebling of premium at the London. Something other than overall market size must have been at play, then. There can be no doubt that the French wars which ended the long eighteenth century spurred significantly increased spending on marine insurance, but much of the change reflected in premium income totals was the result of price increases, rather than greater demand. As underwriters ventured their capital to insure risks when the predictable perils of peacetime were multiplied by much less-predictable actions of war, they raised their prices to ensure that the uncertainty was covered (although Gibb argues that the experience of the War of American Independence left Lloyd's underwriters able to 'frame their policy on the calculable risks of privateers'). This historian of Lloyd's also describes these war years as a time of great profitability for underwriters. In short, 1809, a year of blockade and vigorous belligerent naval activity, is an extremely poor index year on which to base market size estimates which span a century.[32]

It is not possible to accept the correlation between one company's premium growth and overall market size. According to Supple, the London Assurance and the Royal Exchange Assurance 'approached the expanding demand for [marine] insurance with such caution as to retain only a very small proportion', approximately 4 per cent between them. This is underlined by the lack of growth in the marine insurance premiums of the London Assurance in the years 1720–93, a period when the nation's international trade more than trebled, and when, according to Inikori, London became 'the centre of marine insurance in the world'. The trend in the company's marine insurance premium growth cannot be used to extrapolate growth rates or premium income figures for the marine insurance market as a whole.[33]

This error is in part attributable to another misinterpretation by Inikori of John, who wrote that 'the years 1730–39 and 1763–76 were clearly associated with a fall in marine insurance activity, which there is reason to believe was not confined to the London Assurance'. Inikori repeated this sentence in a footnote, adding: 'Arthur John thought the premium income trend of the London Assurance Company reflects the general trend of the market', although John suggested a correlation only in terms

525

of these periods of lower uptake. Inikori failed to cite John's claim that, unlike the private underwriters, 'the companies...tended to become more conservative in their business as the century wore on'. For example, of £656,000 in insurance cover underwritten on the frigate *Diana* and its cargo for an 1807 voyage from Vera Cruz to England, only £25,000 was written by the companies, just 4 per cent of the total (precisely the market share Supple estimated for the companies at this time). This misinterpretation of John undermines the basis of Inikori's argument about the drivers of the growth of marine insurance by beginning from incorrect assumptions about market size and development.[34]

Having presented arguments about the high levels of risk faced by slaving vessels, Inikori goes on to estimate the total amount of premiums spent by British slave traders to insure their triangular voyages, calculating the spend on cover for cargoes to Africa, slaves to the Americas, and ships for the entire voyage. His total for the period 1750 to 1897 is £11.72 million, of which £7.831 million was spent after 1790. The calculations he has made to determine these figures are, however, extremely opaque. Working backwards, two problems become clear. First, Inikori has assumed that all cargoes and vessels were always insured to their full value. As his own evidence states, this was particularly unlikely. Second, he has chosen to use insurance prices which are at the top end, or sometimes seemingly above, those which he has garnered from a small set of primary and secondary sources. Few of the periods for which a rate is given match the periods for which cargo and vessel values and slave numbers are tabulated in *Africans and the industrial revolution* or his 1992 article *The Volume of the British Slave Trade 1655–1807*. However, it is clear that assumptions made have maximised end results. The statement 'everything considered, it is likely that the figures in the table [Insurance Premiums in the British Slave Trade] understate the amount of premiums generated by the British slave trade in the period' therefore seems to be, at best, overly optimistic.

A similar set of calculations follows, presenting Inikori's estimates of the total cost of insuring goods shipped between Britain, the West Indies, and the United States. Inikori rightly states that commission trade was usually insured, although based on a single opinion, he assumes that only half the American exports to Britain were covered. He mentions the fact that following its independence US merchants purchased less of their insurance cover in London, which is indeed true: when independence freed the 13 colonies from the restrictions on corporate insurance formations introduced in the *Bubble Act* of 1720, American merchants, who had practised underwriting as individuals for many decades, quickly formed their own insurers. The business of insuring American trade in London declined quickly and dramatically. Inikori makes an adjustment to his estimate of premiums spent in London to insure US Atlantic trade as a result.[35]

Inikori next combines his estimates of annual average premiums for the slave trade and the West Indies trade in the 1790s, to reach a total premium figure of £2,522,000. He declares: 'this is 63 percent of the whole marine insurance market in Great Britain, put at about £4 million'. He notes that the addition of US risks insured in London raises the total 'above 70 percent of the entire market'. Unfortunately, as shown above, Inikori's estimate of a £4 million market is woefully inadequate, based on a regrettable backwards calculation which, at the very least, ignores a fall in the companies' market share from 10 per cent in the 1720s to 4 per cent in the 1800s,

– CHAPTER 28: *Atlantic contribution to British marine insurance* –

which suggests a total market size 150 percent larger, or £10 million. Such a figure seems also to be intuitively correct, since it is almost inconceivable that total market premium would have risen from £1.8 million to only £4 million in a period which experienced the multiplication of international trade, the increasing use of insurance, and the elevation of London to the position of world leader in marine insurance. Thus, Inikori's conclusion that 'the estimates presented can reasonably support...that premiums on British trans-Atlantic commerce (including the slave trade), the re-export trade in slave-produced American products, and on the trans-Atlantic commerce of other European powers constituted the bulk of the marine insurance market in England in the eighteenth century' is, again, overly optimistic. The error in the market-share multiplier alone suggests 25 per cent is a more likely figure.[36]

Another misinterpretation – one which allows Inikori to dismiss all eastern trade from being insured – makes the gross overestimate appear more plausible. 'The East India Company that dominated the other major long distance trade of the period carried its own risks', Inikori declares. While this is technically true, at least for the most part, a great deal of eastern trade was insured – that of the agency houses, of the private 'privilege' trade of EIC servants, the vessels owned by private merchants but leased to the Company, and even the private 'country' trade along the Indian coasts and between India and China. The Indiaman *Scaleby Castle*, for example, was insured in 1799 for £148,100. Insurers at Lloyd's also underwrote the 'country trade' along the India coasts, and between India and China. The 1807 risk book of the Lloyd's underwriters Clagett & Pratt comprises a record of the insurance they sold during the year. It shows, for example, that the London agency Bruce & Co. bought cover in February for goods shipped from Canton to Bombay on the vessel *Anna*, six weeks later for goods on the return voyage, and shortly after for the next Bombay run. Each entry in an underwriter's risk book reflects only one of many 'lines', or proportional shares, underwritten on specific risks. Edward Allfrey's 1809 underwriting records show that on 2 January he accepted lines worth £2,000 in total on three policies covering cargo belonging to Bruce & Co while in transit from Calcutta to London. The same day the underwriter John Janson insured £1,500 worth of Bruce & Co's cargoes for the same voyage. Janson wrote lines on Bruce & Co policies on 13 occasions during the year; on three of these risks, Allfrey also participated. This trade was sufficiently robust, and large enough to support the emergence of an new insurance-company sector in the Indian Presidencies and in Canton by the turn of the century.[37]

In conclusion, it seems that it was not trade in the Atlantic World which spurred the development of marine insurance institutions, nor was it the unique perils of Atlantic trade which encouraged merchants to take up insurance when otherwise they had typically chosen to go uninsured. The institutions and principles of marine insurance were well established long before the Atlantic trade gathered any great volume or velocity. The same can be said of London marine insurance institutions and Atlantic trade. The use of marine insurance was widespread in England in the sixteenth century, and a practical, efficient, and stable market existed to support demand. Institutional developments occurred, but were implemented primarily to avert costly disputes and fraud against underwriters, rather than to deal with unique Atlantic challenges, including those arising from the transport of slaves. The increased volume of British trade in the eighteenth century was certainly a driver of growth in insurance uptake, just as heightened wartime threats encouraged more insurance buying. However, these threats were not peculiar to Atlantic World trading. Recent arguments to the contrary appear to put the Atlanticist horse before the evidential cart.

NOTES

1   For the relative size of the new land endowment, see Webb, Walter Prescott: *The Great Frontier*, London: Secker & Warburg, 1953, p. 17. Butler quote cited in Inikori, Joseph: *Africans and the industrial revolution in England: a study in international trade and economic development*, Cambridge: University Press, 2002, p. 343.

2   In practice, Butler would probably not have received the entire £2,000, because an 'abatement', akin to a modern deductible, would probably have applied. For non-merchant underwriters in Italy, see Leone, Alfonso: 'Maritime insurance as a source for the history of international credit in the Middle Ages', *Journal of European Economic History*, 12 (1983), p. 367.

3   For a comprehensive exploration of the Mediterranean origins and early spread of marine insurance, see Leonard, A.B. (ed.): *Marine insurance: international development and evolution*, Palgrave History of Finance Series, Basingstoke: Routledge, forthcoming 2015. For the Italian commercial revolution, see Spufford, Peter: *Power and profit: the merchant in medieval Europe*, London: Thames & Hudson, 2002; Stefani, Giuseppi: *Insurance in Venice from the origins to the end of the Serenissima*, vol. I, Amoruso, A.D. (trans.), Trieste: Assicurazioni Generali, 1958, p. 61.

4   Bensa, Enrico: *Il contratto di assicurazione nel medio evo*, 1884, translated to French, Valéry, Jules, as *Histoire du contrat d'assurance au moyen age*, Paris: Anciemme Librairie Thorin et Fis, 1897, p. 20; Thomas, A.H. (ed.): *Calendar of plea & memoranda rolls of the City of London preserved among the archives of the Corporation of London at the Guildhall*, AD 1413–1437, Cambridge: Cambridge University Press, 1943, pp. 208–10; machine-readable data drawn from the Borromei ledgers is available at www. queenmaryhistoricalresearch.org/roundhouse/default.aspx (accessed 15 June 2014).

5   For the early development of marine insurance practice and law-merchant customs, see Leonard, *Marine Insurance*; for the nomenclature 'merchant-insurers' see, for example, the 1693 parliamentary 'Bill to enable divers merchants-insurers…', 9 December 1693, *Journal of the House of Commons*, 11 (1693–97), p. 26; Sacks, D. H.: *The widening gate: Bristol and the Atlantic economy, 1450–1700*, Berkley: University of California Press, 1991, pp. 22–23, 26.

6   Vanes, Jean (ed.): *The ledger of John Smythe, 1538–1550*, London: HMSO, 1974, p. 85; Guildhall Library, CLC/B/062/MS22281, CLC/B/062/MS22282, the Corsini papers, policies issued to Bartholomew Corsini; Ibbetson, D.: 'Law and custom: Insurance in sixteenth-century England', *Journal of Legal History*, Vol. 29, No. 3 (2008), p. 293.

7   BL Lansdowne MS 113/9, 'Some Merchants, Notaries, and Brokers petition Sir James Hawes, Lord Mayor of London, against Rich. Candley's grant for registering policies of assurance' (undated, 1574). For the development of insurance institutions in England, see Leonard, A.B.: *The origins and development of London marine insurance, 1547–1824*, unpublished Ph.D. thesis, Faculty of History, University of Cambridge, 2013. For the Law Merchant and codification in English marine insurance, see Rossi, Guido: 'The Book of Orders of Assurances: a civil law code in 16th century London', *Maastricht Journal*, Vol. 19, No. 2, (2012), pp. 240–61.

8   *43 Eliz. c. 12, 1601*, An Act Conc'nge matters of Assurances amongst Marchantes.

9   Roseveare, Henry (ed.): *Markets and merchants of the late seventeenth century: the Marescoe-David letters, 1668–80*, Oxford: University Press, 1987, pp. 582–884; Lamb, Samuel: 'Seasonal observations humbly offered to his Highness the Lord Protector' (1657), reprinted in *A collection of scarce and valuable tracts, sec. ed., vol. VI*, Scott, Walter (ed.), London: printed for T. Cadell and others, 1811, pp. 448.

– CHAPTER 28: *Atlantic contribution to British marine insurance* –

10 Ebert, Christopher: 'Early modern Atlantic trade and the development of maritime insurance to 1630', *Past & Present*, No. 213 (2011), pp. 89–90; Inikori, *Africans*, p. 356.

11 Ebert, *Atlantic trade and the development*, p. 100; TNA HCA 24/29 f. 45, policy underwritten for Anthony de Salizar, 05 Aug. 1555; Marsden, R.G.: *Select pleas in the Court of the Admiralty*, vols. I & II, London: Selden Society, 1897; Dasent, John R.: *Acts of the Privy Council of England, New Series*, Vols. VII–XX, London: H.M.SO., 1893–1900. On the Privy Council's insurance projects, see Leonard, A.B.: 'Contingent commitment: the development of English marine insurance in the context of New Institutional Economics, 1577–1720', in Coffman, D., Leonard, A., and Neal, L.: *Questioning 'credible commitment': re-thinking the Glorious Revolution and the rise of financial capitalism*, Cambridge: Cambridge University Press, 2013, pp. 48–75.

12 Ebert, *Atlantic trade and the development*, p. 102; Hitchcock, Robert: *A pollitique Platt for the development of the fisheries*, London: 1580, cited in Tawney, R.H. and Power, E. (eds), *Tudor economic documents*, three volumes, London: Longmans, Green & Co., 1924, III, p. 253.

13 Inikori, *Africans*, p. 338; de Roover, Florence Edler: 'Early examples of marine insurance', *Journal of Economic History*, Vol. 5, No. 2 (1945).

14 For the continuity of the insurance contract, see Leonard, *Origins and development*. On insurance gurantees for bills of exchange, see Price, Jacob: 'Transaction costs: A note on merchant credit and the organisation of private trade', in Tracy, James (ed.): *The political economy of merchant empires*, Cambridge: Cambridge University Press, 1991, pp. 289.

15 Emphasis added. Martin, Frederick: *History of Lloyd's and of marine insurance in Great Britain*, London: Macmillan & Co., 1876, p. 161; Inikori, *Africans*, pp. 339, 342; Wright, C. and Fayle, C.E.: *A history of Lloyd's*. London: Macmillan & Co., 1928, p. 35.

16 *6 Geo. 1. c. 18, 1720*, An Act for better securing certain Powers and Privileges, intended to be granted by His Majesty by Two Charters, for Assurance of Ships and Merchandize at Sea, and for lending Money upon Bottomry; and for restraining several extravagant and unwarrantable Practices therein mentioned (the *Bubble Act*).

17 John, A.H.: 'The London Assurance Company and the Marine Insurance Market of the Eighteenth Century', *Economica*, New Series, Vol. 25, No. 98 (May, 1958), pp. 128, 133; Inikori, *Africans*, p. 340 n; *The special report from the committee appointed to inquire into, and examine the several subscriptions for fisheries, insurances, annuities for lives, and all other projects carried on by subscription...*, London: House of Commons, printed by Tonson, J., Goodwin, T., Lintot, B., and Taylor, W., 1720, p. 45.

18 All quotations from Special Report 1720, pp. 44, 55.

19 For 1598–1600, Fisher, F.J.: 'London's export trade in the early seventeenth century', *Economic History Review*, Vol. 3, No. 2 (1950), p. 153; for 1622, Ormrod, *Commercial empires*, p. 56; for 1663/69, Davis, *English foreign trade*, p. 154; for 1700–1824, Mitchell, B.R.: *Abstract of British historical statistics*, Cambridge: Cambridge University Press, 1962, pp. 279–82. * London only.

20 *Eliz. Cap.* 12; arbitration clauses were included in marine insurance policies in England at least as early as 1555. TNA HCA 24/29 f. 45; Inikori, *Africans*, p. 339; Association of Lloyd's Members, *Lloyd's Market Results and Prospects 2013*, London: ALM, 2013, p. 6.

21 Inikori, *Africans*, pp. 339–40. For insurance price declines, see Leonard, A. B.: 'The pricing revolution in marine insurance', working paper presented to the Economic History Association, Sept. 2012, http://eh.net/eha/system/files/Leonard.pdf (accessed 15 June 2014); William Freeman to John Bramley, 16 July 1680, in Hancock, David (ed.): *The letters of William Freeman, London Merchant, 1678–1685*, London: London Record Society, 2002, p. 162.

22 Inikori, *Africans*, p. 342; John, *The London Assurance*, p. 127; Mitchell, *Historical statistics*, p. 448; A subscriber to Lloyd's: *A letter to Jasper Vaux*, London: Printed for J. M. Richardson,

1810, pp. 23, 47; *Report from the Select Committee on Marine Insurance, Sess. 1810*, London: House of Commons, 1824, committee report, p. 3, testimony of J.J. Angerstein, p. 68.

23 Inikori, J.E.: 'Measuring the hazards of the Atlantic slave trade', *Revue Française d'Histoire d'Outre-mer* 83, No. 312, (1996), p. 54.

24 Inikori, *Africans*, p. 253–54; MS Rawl Lett 66 fol 17, Letterbook of Joseph Cruttenden.

25 For a discussion of capture and ransom, see Leonard, A.B.: 'Underwriting Marine Warfare: Insurance and Conflict in the Eighteenth Century', *International Journal of Maritime History*, Vol. 25, No. 2, Dec 2013, pp. 173–86; the perils named were explicitly covered in all London policies which I have examined and which were issued between the seventeenth and nineteenth centuries, unless specifically excluded; Claypoole is cited in Zahedieh, Nuala: *The capital and the colonies: London and the Atlantic economy 1660–1700*, Cambridge: Cambridge University Press, 2010, p. 85 *n*; Weskett, John: *A complete digest of the theory, laws, and practice of insurance*, London: Printed by Frys, Couchman, & Collier, 1781, pp. 440–41; Wright and Fayle, *History of Lloyd's*, p. 154.

26 Williams, *Liverpool privateers*, p. 366–67; *TransAtlantic slave trade database*, www. slavevoyages.org (accessed June 15, 2014); Bromley, J.S.: 'The French privateering war, 1702–13', in Bell, H.E. & Ollard, R.L. (eds): *Historical essays 1600–1750 presented to David Ogg*. London: Adam & Charles Black, 1963, p. 229.

27 Inikori, *Africans*, p. 253.

28 Inikori, *Measuring the hazards*, p. 64, 71.

29 Inikori, *Measuring the hazards*, p. 70.

30 Inikori, *Africans*, pp. 342, 344.

31 Inikori, *Africans*, pp. 342, 342, n. 86.

32 Supple, Barry: *The Royal Exchange Assurance: A history of British insurance 1720–1970*. Cambridge: University Press, 1970, p. 191; Gibb, D.E.W.: *Lloyd's of London: a study in individualism*, London: Macmillan & Co., 1957, p. 49.

33 Supple, *Royal Exchange*, p. 53, 188; Mitchell, *British historical statistics*, pp. 448–50.

34 John, *The London*, pp. 131, 133; Inikori, *Africans*, p. 342; 'Report from the select committee on marine insurance, 18 April 1810', British Parliamentary Papers, 226 (1810), reprinted 11 May 1824, p. 58.

35 For a discussion of US underwriting before and after independence, see Leonard, A.B: 'From local to transatlantic: insuring trade in the Caribbean', in Leonard, A.B. and Pretel, D.: *The Caribbean and the Atlantic World economy: circuits of trade, money and knowledge, 1650–1914*, Cambridge Imperial and Post-Colonial Studies Series, Basingstoke: Palgrave Macmillan, forthcoming 2015; Inikori, *Africans*, p. 353–54.

36 Inikori, *Africans*, pp. 356–57.

37 Inikori, *Africans*, pp. 357; Testimony of Angerstein, 'Report from the select committee', p. 58; Clagett & Pratt, Risk book 1807, Lloyd's of London Archive (LLA); Edward Allfrey, Risk book 1809, LLA; Risk book of John Janson, 1809, British Library ADD MSS 346730; Leonard, A.B.: 'Underwriting British trade to India And China, 1780–1835', *Historical Journal*, Vol. 54, No. 4, Dec. 2012, pp. 983–1006.

CHAPTER TWENTY-NINE

THE ECONOMIC WORLD OF THE EARLY DUTCH AND ENGLISH ATLANTIC

——·◆·——

Edmond Smith

INTRODUCTION

In 1584, Richard Hakluyt, a well-known proponent of English overseas expansion, wrote a treatise extolling the benefits of English expansion in North America. In 'A Discourse on Western Planting', he highlighted the benefits of English activities in the north Atlantic through three arguments: the benefits of trade, the potential land available, and the importance of expansion in order to 'greately annoye' the 'proud and hatefulle Spaniardes' (Hakluyt and Deane, 1877: 55). Each of these points reveals how the English perceived the world beyond Europe and Peter Mancall considers the text to represent 'a comprehensive rationale for expansion' (2007: 155). While the development of expansion did not follow Hakluyt's plans, the plans do represent how the English understood the world. England was on the periphery of the Spanish and Portuguese Empires that dominated the Atlantic by the end of the seventeenth century, and English activities were often attempts to engage or compete with this existing, complex system.

The Dutch also engaged in activities in the Atlantic from an originally peripheral position, with activities in Brazil and the Caribbean as much a part of an overseas strategy to damage the Spanish–Portuguese Empire as a plan to trade in the East Indies. From the Dutch perspective, the two Iberian empires had no claim to monopoly privileges in the Atlantic or Asia (De Vries, 1997: 383). The success of the Dutch state was dependent on revolt against the Spanish empire in Europe, and the rapid development of overseas activities on a global level was very much a response to their need to damage the Hapsburg throne. As in the English example, Dutch activity overseas was also seen as beneficial 'for damaging the enemy and for security of the fatherland' (Oldenbarnevelt quoted in Boxer, 1979: 1). Consequently, the earliest history of Dutch overseas activity simultaneously sees expansion in the north Atlantic – particularly through fishing – and the development of long-distance trade throughout the Atlantic coast of Europe (Israel, 1990: 20–25). Raiding and trading in the Atlantic was an important third facet to Dutch expansion, but in many respects came second to the perspective of the state, leaving early Dutch activities in the hands of individuals already connected to the Atlantic economy (Da Silva, 2011: 7–32).

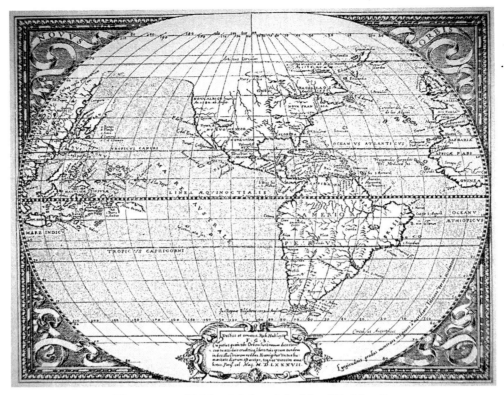

Figure 29.1 Hakluyt's Map of the New World 1587
© Private Collection/Peter Newark American Pictures/Bridgeman Images

Historians have written a significant volume of work on the development of the British, and to a much lesser extent the Dutch, Empire in the Atlantic world. The Dutch Atlantic has received the least attention of the two; indeed, Pieter Emmer and Wim Klooster (1998: 1) asked 'why has the history of Dutch expansion in the Atlantic been neglected?', and questioned whether the success of the Dutch in Asia has been detrimental to historians' interest in their activity elsewhere. Alongside Emmer, Klooster questioned whether the conception of a Dutch Atlantic is useful at all (Emmer and Klooster, 1999: 48–69). Recently, Gert Oostindie and Jessica Roitman (2012: 129–30) have noted a slow reversal of this trend, themselves arguing for a new typology for examining the Dutch Atlantic during this period. Lacking a formal colonial empire in the Atlantic for much of the early modern period (a contrast to successes in the East Indies), the Dutch in the Atlantic have instead been examined through the role played by individuals and intermediaries rather than a singular focus on the Dutch West India Company (WIC). Oostindie and Roitman (2012: 149–51) ask how the Dutch were able to dominate a substantial share of Atlantic trade without a colonial power and in a region dominated by competing imperial superpowers (first Spain and Portugal, then Britain and France)?

On the other hand, the British are often placed centre stage in Atlantic history, the dominant group in a theoretical paradigm intended to explore interconnectivity and the entanglement of imperial activity. For example, over the past 15 years this trend is clear in three key collections: Nicolas Canny's *The Origins of Empire* (1998); Elizabeth Mancke and Carole Shamms's *The Creation of the British Atlantic World* (2005); and Nicolas Canny and Philip Morgan's *The Oxford Handbook of the Atlantic World* (2011). However, the role of the English and Dutch in the earliest decades of their Atlantic activity should place them far from the centre of the Atlantic World. Instead, they should be seen as peripheral actors, engaging within (or in opposition to) the existing Spanish and Portuguese Empires, also taking on the role of supplicant in many of their interactions with indigenous groups in Africa and America. As Eliga Gould (2007: 764–86) has convincingly demonstrated, the English Atlantic world was very much a periphery of the Spanish Atlantic – part of an entangled Atlantic world.

During the early modern period, while the particular nature of relationships between each 'national' group might change, and competition shift, the Atlantic world remained an arena where participating states and individuals could profit themselves at the expense of the others. The early history of Dutch and English activity in the Atlantic world must therefore seek to understand the interaction, engagement and competition that defined relationships within the Ocean basin.

Critics of Atlantic history have argued that interconnectivity between the Atlantic and global activities of each country demonstrate the limitations of Atlantic history, suggesting instead that the idea of 'cosmopolitans' or 'global lives' would be a more all-encompassing approach. Numerous historians have argued these points over the past decade, notably Peter Coclanis' pieces 'Atlantic world or Atlantic/world?' (2006) and 'Beyond Atlantic history' (2009); Alison Games' article 'Beyond the Atlantic: English globetrotters and transoceanic connections' (2006); and Philip Stern's contribution 'British Asia and the British Atlantic: comparisons and connections' (2006). However, in spite of these objections, this Atlantic perspective has become particularly dominant within the historiography of overseas expansion and the British Empire. In some respects, the history of Dutch activities has had the reverse problem, with studies focusing far more on the development of the Dutch Empire in Asia, at the expense of a global perspective that includes Atlantic activities. In a recent review, Holly Rine (2011: 24–29) stressed the importance of 'putting the Dutch Republic back in New Netherland' and highlighted the significance of Jaap Jacob's work in bringing Dutch North American activities back into the limelight.

For both the Dutch and the English, participating in the Atlantic world was part of broader, global strategies and interests that drew much from continental aspirations and objectives. From the late sixteenth century onwards, English and Dutch actors entered the Atlantic world from their northern periphery, integrating and interacting with existing structures and adding a further level of entanglement. Much of this activity went hand-in-hand with other trade and colonisation, both in Europe and globally, and the influence of this broader picture was substantial in the Atlantic. In this chapter, Kenneth Andrews' (1984) three areas of overseas activity – trade, plunder and settlement – are each given a section, but space has also been made to include two important foundations for Atlantic activity: fishing and exploration. Throughout all of this analysis, commonalities and contrasts between the English and Dutch experiences are sought. Together, the English and Dutch entered an Atlantic world already dominated by existing Iberian empires, beginning a process of integration and usurpation that would continue to entangle the region over the proceeding centuries.

FISHING

For both the Dutch and the English, the Atlantic was not a region unknown when the Spanish and Portuguese were exploring the distant shores of Africa and America in the fifteenth century. However, earlier activities were restrained by practicality and many of them (beyond the occasional voyage of exploration) were limited to taking advantage of the original Atlantic commodity; the sea itself. Fishing was, throughout the early modern period, an essential industry for the British and the Dutch, with fish a staple of diets in both, and the Atlantic provided access to this resource in abundance.

During the early modern period, herring and cod were sought after by the fishing communities active in the Atlantic, with other goods like whale also attractive. Herring was a staple food source in much of Europe, partly due to the limitation on eating meat on certain days but also due to the relative ease of storing herring for long periods. Whale was also an important product, primarily because of the growing demand for large quantities of oil. Cod was a further important fishing product of the Atlantic, and in some respects, the first good to connect the English and Dutch Atlantic experience with the New World, as these fish were sought after in regions close to the Atlantic seaboard of North America, particularly in the region that would become known as Cape Cod. Transported back to Europe, each of these three commodities played important roles in their domestic economies, in turn connecting with the Atlantic coast of Europe through re-export of the fish and the purchase of essential fishing goods, such as salt.

In the Dutch case, superiority in herring fishing was a key ingredient for their commercial success (Israel, 1990: 23). In part, this was closely linked to interaction with the Atlantic coast of Europe, with salt brought from Spain vital for the success of the industry. Furthermore, shipbuilding developed rapidly to take advantage of their geographic situation, with efficient specialist vessels (herring *busses*) designed specifically for activity in the Atlantic. These were large boats with crews of 15 or 18 men, and were designed to weather ocean storms and provide room on board for the evisceration, salting and packing of the herring. Ownership of these ships was shared throughout the Dutch community, with investment available in shipping concerns from the sixteenth century. This spread the risk of these activities and laid the ground for the development of a larger community of investors willing to engage in overseas activities (Israel, 1990: 23). Even by the 1560s (before the Dutch revolt), the north Netherlands fishing industry operated over 500 herring *busses* and employed up to 7000 men (Israel, 1990: 24). Later, the importance of the industry and its dependence on access to salt meant it became a potential target for attack, with Spanish ministers believing that withdrawing access to Iberian salt would seriously hinder the Dutch economy (Israel, 1990: 22).

In the Atlantic world, English and Dutch fishing was seen, by friends and enemies alike, as foundations for the national economies of each. Such was the importance of English fishing, and the perceived strength obtained by the Dutch by their investment in this resource, that one merchant, Robert Kayll, wrote in 1615 that the East India trade should be abandoned in favour of further investment in this area (Kayll, 1615)! For the Dutch, the essential role of their herring industry to the economy continued into the seventeenth century. Attacks on the herring *busses* in the North Sea became regular aspects of war, with Spanish forces executing extensive attacks from as early as 1625 and the English attempting the same following the outbreak of war with the Dutch in 1652 (Unger, 1980: 279). David Ormrod (2003: 107) has highlighted how tensions over Atlantic fishing grounds were among the major sources of tension between the English, Dutch and other European states, and their role in the Atlantic world is important. The fishing industry was a central part of the English and Dutch Atlantic experience, and through re-export and competition with other European states formed part of the entangled Atlantic experience that spread across the ocean. Furthermore, it enabled both participants the opportunity to develop expertise and innovate in a manner that made further Atlantic participation achievable and attractive.

EXPLORATION

Beyond fishing, the English experience of the Atlantic world extended quite logically into voyages of exploration – even though many of these sought to establish links with Asia rather than lands bordering the Atlantic itself. In part, these were intended to enable the raiding and trading activities that are detailed later in this chapter, but they were also a separate aspect of English overseas expansion. As early as the fifteenth century the English had attempted to explore further into the Atlantic, with the voyages of Cabot an example of England's advanced approach to overseas activity from a period just as early as the Spanish. However, following Cabot there was a long period before further voyages were attempted, with these being a response to the Spanish and Portuguese monopoly over the southern trade routes. Instead, the English sought to explore alternative routes to reach Asia, with the Crown, the gentry and the merchant community funding a number of voyages to seek a north-east or north-west passage throughout the sixteenth century and into the seventeenth. Finding new sea routes would enable the English to circumvent the Iberian empires.

At the same time, the Dutch were participating to a much greater extent in Portuguese and Spanish expansion, in part due to the close relationship between the Iberian empires and the Low Countries before and after the Dutch revolt. With greater participation in these imperial activities, the Dutch were able to draw on considerable experience operating within the Atlantic, and wider, world. Merchants from Antwerp, and then the Northern provinces, could depend on existing commercial networks and therefore operate to a greater extent within the Iberian Atlantic, limiting the requirements of more extensive exploration. Also, following the Dutch revolt, using force to operate within these areas was not only possible but also an important motivator for Dutch participation in the Atlantic world – again making a northern passage unnecessary. As such, rather than seeing a concerted effort from the Dutch regarding exploration in the Atlantic, the later sixteenth century witnessed collaboration and information-gathering efforts on a huge scale. Interaction with the Iberian empires through relationships in Europe was thus a key facilitator for later Dutch activity in the Atlantic world. However, as war with Spain made the voyage to the East Indies increasingly troublesome following the establishment of the Dutch East India Company and subsequent increase in value of returning voyages, alternative routes were sought. In 1609, the Dutch East India Company engaged the English navigator Henry Hudson to explore for a northern passage, with English exploratory expertise now sought after. This Dutch expedition, led by an Englishman, enabled the Dutch to lay claim to a large region in North America where the Dutch colony of New Netherland would later be established.

While unable to find northern route to Asia, the English were successful in other respects. Large fisheries off the North American coast were discovered, trade with Muscovy was established, English cartography and navigation advanced, and English seamen obtained many new skills necessary for long ocean voyages. In the end, the requirement for voyages of exploration lessened. The English obtained the navigational knowledge for the sea route to Asia through Drake's circumnavigation and the capture of Portuguese charts, and war with Spain made imperial boundaries seem a lot less important. Furthermore, English translations of Spanish texts began to appear, although many of these were accounts of the Spanish conquest of America rather than practical information (Elliott, 2007: 6–7). Also, as mentioned, the Dutch had greater access to navigational information and some of this filtered through to England. Around the turn of the seventeenth century, there was significant exchange between these two peripheral nations as they both sought to enter the Iberian Atlantic. Throughout these many voyages of exploration, it is important to remember that the desired destination was the East Indies. Even though they did assist the development of English overseas activity in the Atlantic they were part of broader English attempts to develop a global presence overseas.

PLUNDER

Dutch and English exploration in the Atlantic world met with three, sometimes overlapping, results: raiding, trading, and/or colonisation. Each of these were experienced by the English and the Dutch during the late sixteenth and early seventeenth century. In the case of raiding, or privateering, in the Atlantic world, the primary incentive was often the need to break into the Spanish and Portuguese Empires and enter the lucrative markets of the Atlantic world.

English raiding in the Atlantic and further afield is a prominent aspect of the country's overseas activities during the final decades of the sixteenth century. Often a consequence of damaged relationships with Spain – at least when endorsed by the crown – English raiding in the Atlantic was a source of substantial profits and pride for participants. Of these, Drake's voyages are the most notable, resulting in the circumnavigation of the globe. These voyages covered substantial areas and raided possessions across the Spanish Atlantic, including the prized silver fleets (Appleby, 1998: 61–62). After 1585, war between England and Spain enabled the English to embrace a more aggressive naval stance towards Spain, an approach to the conflict necessitated by the relative weakness of the English crown. By allowing private interests to prosecute the war through privateering, not only did the Crown save money but private interests found an avenue for investment that would provide many with the experience and funds to trade and colonise following the end of the conflict (Andrews, 1984: 223–55). Many participants in this early privateering played a further role in supporting later English expansion – in particular, much of the silver obtained was used to invest in the English East India Company (EIC) after 1600.

After the turn of the century English raiding in the Atlantic declined, but it was still an intermittent threat to shipping, particularly in times of war with Spain – and later the United Provinces and France. To support the growing trade within the Atlantic world, whole fleets were also deployed against the Spanish in the Caribbean; attempts to reach peace diplomatically continued simultaneously. In one example,

Christopher Newport led a combined Anglo-French force against Spanish raiders from Cuba (Andrews, 1984: 285). Interestingly, English, French, and Dutch co-operation regarding the contraband trade in the Atlantic was a regular feature in this period. Many individuals crossed between these three groups to trade successfully. Throughout the first half of the seventeenth century, war in Europe created situations where northern European raiders could take advantage of Spanish weakness in the Atlantic. Sometimes this was through attacks on Spanish shipping, but more common was contraband trade with friendly ports and people throughout the Atlantic. To trade successfully, the English found it necessary to enter relationships in the Caribbean that were unnecessary in other regions, such as north American areas where no pre-existing European empires existed, again highlighting the entangled qualities of trading in the expanding world of seventeenth century commerce.

Following the start of the Dutch revolt, raiding Spanish fleets in the Atlantic was an important part of Dutch overseas policy. These raids had numerous benefits for the emerging state, damaging the Spanish enemy and providing a means of accessing the South American silver that would become an important foundation for their overseas trading activities. The prevalence of privateering within Dutch maritime activities was such that it enabled a dedicated privateering industry to develop during this period (Lunsford, 2005: 9–11). These predatory opportunities were taken up with particular gusto within Zeeland, where peace with Spain was greeted with little enthusiasm in 1609 (Price, 1994: 223). Like the English, Dutch raiding in the Atlantic was intermittent after the end of the war with Spain, but became an attractive proposition once more after war was renewed in 1621 and the Dutch West India Company (WIC) was founded. The founding of this Company had been based in some part due to the belief that raiding in the Spanish Atlantic would be hugely profitable. However, these profits were not always realised, with significant WIC losses before 1628, when they were successful in capturing the Spanish silver fleet. WIC raiding continued with limited success until 1646 (Emmer, 1998: 70–73). It was eventually replaced by attempts to conquer Spanish and Portuguese possessions in America and Africa, which enabled the emergence of dominant Dutch trading within a small region of the Atlantic.

TRADE

Raiding, which had made up such an important part of the early English and Dutch experience of the Atlantic, was rapidly substituted and overtaken by trade. In some cases this was undertaken beyond the reaches of the Iberian empires, but it also took place within these regions, often against the wishes of the colonial authorities. Supporting numerous trading circuits and providing access to a wide range of commodities, the Atlantic world provided an exceptional opportunity for merchants of both countries to make considerable profits. Intermediaries and transnational relationships were vital for trading success, and the interconnections within the Atlantic world are readily apparent.

Dutch trading in the Atlantic was a continuous presence throughout the early modern period, with war and peace offering different challenges for merchants rather than curtailing activity altogether. An important part of this trade was the Dutch salt trade to Venezuela, which replaced the Dutch salt trade with Spain and Portugal in the sixteenth century and enabled the continued success of the United Provinces' fishing industry. From 1601, over a hundred Dutch ships were visiting Venezuela each year, stopped only briefly by Spanish attempts to impose their authority with a navy. The success of the trade continued throughout the war with Spain, remaining both useful and profitable. Like other trading within the Atlantic world, the Venezuela trade is one example where working across the boundaries of jurisdictions was a requirement for the trades' success. To do so, the Dutch maintained positive relationships with numerous intermediaries across the Atlantic.

These relationships are primarily apparent in the brokering of trades across colonial boundaries. Cátia Antunes (2008) has demonstrated the entangled relationship between the Dutch trading world and the Hispanic empires further, highlighting how these connections played an important role in connecting merchants both within and across colonial boundaries. Particularly important for the Dutch were the relationships sustained within the Atlantic Jewish community, which enabled Dutch participation in the slave trade within and without the sphere of the Iberian monopoly (Da Silva, 2011: 7–32). Through their commercial relationships, and the ability of Dutch merchants to act across the Atlantic world, the ubiquity of Dutch shipping in the Atlantic is easily explained. With Amsterdam inheriting Antwerp's role in the distribution of Brazilian goods in Europe, and the city's ability to harness the developing tobacco trade in a similar manner, the Dutch obtained an important position within the Atlantic trading economy (Klooster, 2011: 171–73). Furthermore, when peace was finalised in 1609 between the Dutch and Spain, the obstacles that had limited Dutch activity were removed, enabling the consolidation of activities in America and complete Dutch domination of the north–south trade along Europe's Atlantic coast. This included the flow of Baltic grain and naval stores to Spain, and the return flow of American silver to the United Provinces (Israel, 1997: 37).

Partly in response to Dutch success, English merchants too returned to trading after 1602. With numerous ventures to South America the English trade started well. In these voyages, we continue to see the connectedness of English overseas trading endeavours. Where Atlantic raiding had provided access to silver for investment in the EIC, its members then used their new experience and income to invest once more into the Atlantic world. Trade continued successfully for the next two decades, with small settlements established along the coast of Brazil to engage with Portuguese plantations throughout the colony. However, conflict with Spain in 1621 and Portuguese attacks in 1623 and 1625 against the English and Dutch positions forced the expulsion of many traders. As a result, the English strategy reverted to raiding, with the Guiana Company founded in 1626 specifically to prosecute the conflict – albeit with no success. With the establishment of colonies in the Caribbean in the 1620s, alternatives were offered to these trading groups, who shifted their investment into these new colonial ventures.

Further north, English and Dutch trading in the Atlantic was less likely to form around pre-existing communities of Europeans and instead stemmed from engagement with the local communities. Although less profitable than the Caribbean and Brazilian trade, goods from the northern areas (such as furs) were highly sought after. With numerous expeditions launched to tap into the internal trade of North America, the

– CHAPTER 29: *The early Dutch and English Atlantic* –

English were able to access these products consistently. This trade was one of the incentives for founding English settlements in the north, similar to that attempted at Roanoke in the sixteenth century, but from the beginnings of the Virginia Company in 1607 the traders who founded the Company had broader aims: the cultivation of commodities that could be traded in the Atlantic world.

New products emerged from this expansion in trade. Tobacco in particular drew attention, both negative, such as King James' pamphlet *A Counter-Blaste to Tobacco*, and positive, such as the rapid increase in imports, which reached £60,000 by 1610 (Andrews, 1984: 295). Tobacco became a highly sought after commodity, first by English merchants and later by plantation owners seeking cash crops for the English market. Indeed, tobacco became a product typical of the Atlantic – of little use for sustaining settlements, but profitable when exported to Europe. Here, as in many other ways, colonial and trading activities in the Atlantic world were symbiotic.

The slave trade was also an area where both the Dutch and the English were active participants. While the Dutch only became major players following their acquisition of territory in Brazil in the 1630s, Dutch ships had participated in the trade from as early as 1596 (Emmer, 1998: 33). For the English on the other hand, the slave trade had been an important part of their Atlantic activities since Hawkins' voyages in the 1560s, with Hawkins willing to use force as a means of obtaining slaves in Africa in order to initiate peaceful trade with Spanish America. It was, however, a failure, and the English turned from slave trading for the next few decades (Appleby, 1998: 61). In the seventeenth century both the English and Dutch started to participate in the slave trade to a greater extent, by establishing outposts on the African coast and through direct trading with African rulers or Portuguese intermediaries along the coasts. Many of these slaves were transported to the Iberian colonies of South America, but others were sold in the developing Dutch and English colonies.

In addition to their competition with the Iberian empires, trade increasingly became a source of rivalry between the Dutch and English. As David Ormrod (2003) has made clear, English attempts to expand their trading activities, partly in the Atlantic but also in the Mediterranean, Baltic, and East Indies, were seen as a direct threat to Dutch trade. Beyond the North Sea, the Anglo-Dutch relationship became increasingly strained. In the East Indies, this conflict came close to open war on numerous occasions in the early seventeenth century, and was a source of ill feeling within merchant groups that made it difficult for closer relationships between the two states to develop effectively, even after the renewal of conflict between Spain and the United Provinces. From the English perspective, Dutch attempts at monopoly in the East Indies, and their treatment of English merchants, were part of attempts to create a universal monarchy and trading domination that would exclude the English (Pincus, 1992: 22).

The Dutch and English experiences of Atlantic trade were, therefore, experiences where their merchants were regularly crossing boundaries and actively engaging in activities within the boundaries of the Spanish and Portuguese imperial domains. Furthermore, through the re-export of Atlantic commodities throughout Europe this trade created interconnections on numerous levels and played an important part in integrating the Atlantic economy. With the role of intermediaries clear, the entanglement of the various trading circuits and their participants is apparent. To understand the Atlantic world of England and the Dutch it is essential to integrate them into the existing Atlantic world created by the Iberian empires.

539

SETTLEMENT

Building on many of the successes in the trading and raiding arenas that the Atlantic offered, both the English and the Dutch sought to increase their influence in the Atlantic world through colonisation. In both cases, the extent of this colonisation during the first decades of the seventeenth century was minimal, with only limited territorial gains made in North America, much of the Caribbean remaining in Spanish hands, and Dutch rule in Brazil weak and short-lived. On the African coast, forts were established, offering access to the trades described earlier in this chapter but not becoming major colonies in terms of population or territory. On the other hand, what the early colonies lacked in size they made up for in their importance to English and Dutch trading circuits. The colonies all enabled access to important commodities. As such, they were integral parts of the Atlantic economies experienced by both the Dutch and the English in early seventeenth century. Through colonial designs, these northern European states and their subjects become increasingly engaged in cultural and economic exchange with non-European peoples, interaction that significantly changed their perceptions of the world and the shape of their respective Empires.

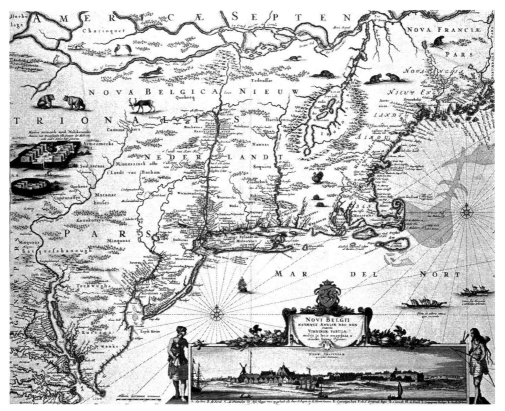

Figure 29.2   New Belgium, plate from 'Atlas Contractus', c. 1671
© Private Collection/Bridgeman Images

– CHAPTER 29: The early Dutch and English Atlantic –

Simultaneous to the raiding in the Atlantic, the late seventeenth century also saw numerous attempts to launch colonies across the Atlantic world. Some of these were merely theoretical and part of a strategy that was particularly apparent in the Hakluyt treatise mentioned previously. However, other plans came closer to fruition. Sir Walter Raleigh made extensive plans for the colonisation of Guiana for example, and the abortive but repeated attempts to colonise Roanoke also demonstrate the scope of English colonising plans during this period (Appleby, 1998: 62–65).

Although early colonisation efforts in Roanoke and the colonisation of Ireland had given many individuals the skills and desire to participate in further expansion, it was a significant step to turn this interest into investment and support for a North American colony. In 1606, merchant and gentry investment created the Virginia Company. A joint stock company with many of the same members as the EIC and, indeed, some of the same leaders, the Virginia Company sought to establish a significant and profitable colony on the Atlantic coast. Initial plans for the colony had focused on hoped-for access to mineral or other wealth that had been found by Spain to the south. The application for a grant for the colony made it clear that the colony would be 'planted' in North America in land considered unoccupied by the English – a significant difference to the conquest that characterised Spanish expansion (Elliott, 2007: 9). Little information was available regarding what was expected by the settlers and the lack of success of many ventures attests to the risks involved.

On their arrival, the English colonists found local groups who were already familiar with Europeans, and it was through intermediaries again that the English were able to enter existing trading circuits and gain access to the goods essential for survival (Games, 2006: 746). Over the next 15 years, the interaction between the two communities grew, with indigenous workers assisting the English in return for European goods and the development of consistent diplomatic efforts between the two groups, including what could be called a Wahunsonacock embassy to London in 1616. In spite of the early difficulties, the Virginia Company continued to see commercial opportunities and the Jamestown settlement soon became the centre of a plantation economy built around the desire to produce commodities for export to England. It took years for the community in Virginia to establish this agriculture effectively and the death toll was considerable, but experimentation in the end prevailed and the cultivation of tobacco was successful. However, in the end the Virginia Company failed. In 1622, the local leader Opechancanough attacked the colony, killing one-third of the colonists and making the future of the Virginia Company untenable. The Crown took over and continued to operate the colony as the first Crown colony in the Atlantic world, and the colony continued to develop (Games, 2011: 117–46).

However, the most successful attempts at colonisation in the early seventeenth century were not in North America but in the islands of the Caribbean. Following a series of failures to establish outposts in Guiana, English colonists started to consider the validity of island colonies. Between 1624 and 1632, these were established on St Christopher, Barbados, Nevis, Montserrat and Antigua. These colonies were more successful than those of other European states in attracting migrant labour from Europe, and each rapidly developed plantation economies built on the export of tobacco and cotton (Mc.D Beckles, 1998: 218–22). Roper (2009), for example, considers tobacco cultivation to be the most important aspect of early American history and the reason for support from commercial interests. These colonies added a further level on entanglement within the Atlantic. Christian Koot (2011) has recently demonstrated how English and Dutch participants depended on each other for support, and Dutch merchants played an important role in the success of English Caribbean colonies. As these plantation economies developed, the need for labour became increasingly important for their continued success, and as a result English merchants increasingly turned towards African slave trade. Through this trade, in addition to continued migration from England, Scotland and Ireland, the colonies grew rapidly. Their success in producing tobacco did cause a market glut in the 1630s and 1640s, but they continued to attract support and became integral aspects of England's overseas activity in the coming centuries, both providing Atlantic commodities for the English market and granting access to the commercial circuit of the developing Caribbean.

As suggested by the excerpt from Hakluyt in the introduction, colonisation in the Atlantic world had dual aims of economic and political gain. As Oostindie and Paasman (1998) have suggested, 'Dutch colonialism had started in the geopolitical context of the struggle against Spain' and this obvious rationale for overseas expansion is clear. In the Atlantic world this is particularly clear, with attempts to seize territory a consequence of the renewal of war with Spain in 1621. With the ending of the truce, it was no longer possible for the Dutch to continue their trade with Spanish-controlled South America, the Caribbean, or Africa in such large numbers. The establishment of the Dutch WIC sought to alleviate the impact of this curtailing of Dutch activities, but for the first decade the Company met with little success, relying on trade with Guinea and raiding in the Atlantic to stay solvent following defeat and expulsion from Brazil, Puerto Rico and Elmina (Guinea). It was only after 1634 that the situation improved, with military expansion in Brazil enabling the Dutch to seize considerable sugar-producing areas and begin the export of numerous commodities from Brazil back to Europe. The seizure of Elmina in Guinea from the Portuguese in 1637 bridged the Atlantic for the Dutch, giving them control, for the first time, of land and markets in all three continents shaping the Atlantic world. In turn, these colonies also invigorated the Dutch slave trade, with 23,163 Africans transported to the Dutch Brazilian territories between 1636 and 1645 (Israel, 1990: 162–63). For the Dutch as much as the English, forced migration was the main source of labour in the Atlantic colonies.

The governance of the English and Dutch colonies was a combination of military rule and planter oligarchy during the earliest period of expansion. In Africa, the forts along the coast were trading facilities, but also (usually) armed and operated as military outposts. In the case of the WIC this was particularly noticeable in the early period, as conflict with the Portuguese and Spanish and huge military expenses necessitated strict control on the part of the WIC government. Over time however, this strict military administration shifted, with colonists becoming increasingly important as part of local administrations – even going so far as to create a shared parliament of Dutch and Portuguese members in Dutch Brazil (Emmer, 1998: 81–82). In contrast, the English colonies had a much greater range of administrative styles. This was partly a consequence of the divided structure of English expansion, with different colonies falling under the administration of different trading and colonial bodies rather than a centralised company. As the seventeenth century continued, and migration to the North American coast increased, this divide in forms of administration and social structure increased – particularly in areas where religion was an important aspect of the colonising drive.

CONCLUSION

As the Dutch and English began to participate in the Atlantic world to a greater extent during the end of the sixteenth century and the beginning of the seventeenth they did so from a clearly peripheral position. Although their fishing activities and the English exploration for northern passages fell beyond the limits of Iberian activity, even these were dependent on interaction with the Iberian empires. For fishing, access to Portuguese and then Venezuelan salt was essential for Dutch prosperity, and interaction throughout the Atlantic developed because of this northern Atlantic aspect of English and Dutch Atlantic activity. Exploration was only necessary due to the Iberian monopoly over the southern routes and the inability of the English to access the navigational knowledge and experience of their Spanish and Portuguese competitors. The Dutch learned much from their access to the Iberian empire before the revolt, and the ongoing relationships between the Dutch merchant community and intermediaries throughout the Atlantic world remained a useful means of operating within the Iberian-dominated Atlantic.

The incentives for entering the Atlantic world for each group were also dominated by their interaction with Spain. Damaging the Spanish enemy was a key component for the English and Dutch states who could use private interests in raiding and trade to undermine the Spanish war effort at little or no cost to themselves. Furthermore, the colonial expansion of both the English and the Dutch sought to create possibilities for damaging the Iberian position. For the Dutch, their colonies were directly taken from the Portuguese in Brazil and on the African coast, and these were operated through predominantly military administration in their early stages. In the English case, the colonies in the Caribbean were taken in response to Spanish attempts to curtail their trading activities, and the islands were chosen in part for their potential as plantations for tobacco and cotton, but also for their potential role in providing accessible locations to launch raids against the Spanish. In the Caribbean and Brazil, the English and Dutch activities were, for much of this period, directly in opposition to the Spanish authorities in Madrid, trading in contraband or through networks of intermediaries that enabled trading activities within the boundaries of the Iberian Atlantic.

These relationships, and the permeable boundaries of the Iberian Atlantic, reveal another important facet of English and Dutch interaction with the Atlantic economy. To succeed, they were reliant on the support and co-operation of numerous groups, with transnational interaction common. In the Dutch case, communities that had spread between the northern and southern Netherlands survived the revolt against Spain and were particularly useful for Dutch traders in the Atlantic. Lisbon and Amsterdam for example were strongly connected by a Jewish community that facilitated contact between merchants from both cities and developed links throughout the Atlantic world. The entanglement of the Atlantic world is clear through the study of relationships such as these, as is the need for such relationships from the perspective of the peripheral players in the Atlantic economy.

The Atlantic world continues to represent a useful means of exploring the relationship between English and Dutch overseas agents and the Iberian empires that dominated the region. In this early period, the entanglement of different organisations and individuals is particularly striking and the economic development of the Dutch and English Atlantic was dependent on interaction and cooperation just as much as anti-Iberian aggression. However, overseas expansion by the English and Dutch was not limited to the Atlantic. It is important to remember that while the Atlantic world can reveal the entanglement of numerous empires we should not overlook the entangled and interconnected nature of both English and Dutch expansion elsewhere in the seventeenth century.

REFERENCES

Andrews, K. 1984, *Trade, Plunder and Settlement: maritime enterprise and the genesis of the British Empire, 1480–1630*, Cambridge University Press, Cambridge.

Antunes, C. 2008, 'Portuguese Jews in Amsterdam: an insight on entrepreneurial behaviour in the Dutch Republic', in Jarvis, A. and Lee, R. (ed.), *Trade, Migration and Urban Networks in Port Cities, c. 1640–1940*, International Maritime Economic History Association, St. John's, Newfoundland.

Appleby, J. 1998, 'War, politics and colonisation' in Canny, N. (ed.), *The Origins of Empire: British overseas enterprise to the close of the seventeenth century*, Oxford University Press, Oxford.

Blakemore, R. 2014, 'Thinking outside the gundeck: maritime history, the royal navy and the outbreak of the British Civil War, 1625–21', *Historical Research*, vol. 87, no. 236, pp. 1–24.

Boxer, C. 1979, *Jan Compagnie in War and Peace, 1602–1799: a short history of the Dutch East India Company*, Heinamann Asia, Hong Kong.

Canny, N. & Morgan, P. (eds.) 2011, *The Oxford Handbook of the Atlantic World, 1450–1850*, Oxford University Press, Oxford.

Canny, N. (ed.) 1998, *The Origins of Empire: British overseas enterprise to the close of the seventeenth century*, Oxford University Press, Oxford.

Coclanis, P. A. 2006, 'Atlantic world or Atlantic/world?' *William and Mary Quarterly*, vol. 63, no. 4, pp. 725–42.

—— 2009, 'Beyond Atlantic history', in Greene, J. D. & Morgan, P. D. (eds.), *Atlantic history: a critical reappraisal*, Oxford University Press, Oxford.

Da Silva, F. R. 2011, 'Crossing Empires: Portuguese, Sephardic, and Dutch Business Networks in the Atlantic Slave Trade, 1580–1674', *The Americas*, vol. 68, no. 1, pp. 7–32.

De Vries, J. 1997, *The First Modern Economy: Success, failure, and perseverance of the Dutch economy, 1500–1800*, Cambridge University Press, Cambridge.

Elliott, J. H. 2007, *Empires of the Atlantic World: Britain and Spain in America, 1492–1830*, Yale University Press, New Haven.

Emmer, P. 1998, *The Dutch in the Atlantic Economy, 1580–1880*, Ashgate, Farnham.

Emmer, P. & Klooster, W. 1999, 'The Dutch Atlantic, 1600–1800: expansion without Empire', *Itinerario*, vol. 28, no. 2, pp. 48–69.

Games, A 2006, 'Beyond the Atlantic: English globetrotters and transoceanic connections', *William and Mary Quarterly*, vol. 63, no. 4, pp. 675–92.

—— 2011, *Web of Empire: English cosmopolitans in an age of expansion, 1560–1660*, Oxford University Press, Oxford.

Gould, E. 2007, 'Entangled Histories, Entangled Worlds: the English-speaking Atlantic as a Spanish periphery', *The American Historical Review*, vol. 112, no. 3, pp. 764–86.

Hakluyt, R. & Deane C. (ed.) 1877, *A particular discourse concerning the great necessitie and manifold comodyties that are likely to growe in this Realme of England by the Western discoveries lately attempted*, Maine Historical Society, Cambridge [Mass].

– CHAPTER 29: *The early Dutch and English Atlantic* –

Israel, J 1990, *Dutch Primacy in World Trade, 1585–1740*, Oxford University Press, Oxford.

—— 1997, *Conflicts of Empires: Spain, the Low Countries and the Struggle for World Supremacy, 1585–1713*, Continuum, London.

Kayll, R. 1615, *The Trades Increase*, Nicholas Oakes, London.

Klooster, W. 2011, 'The Northern European Atlantic World' in Canny, N. & Morgan, P., *The Atlantic World, c.1450–c.1850*, Oxford University Press, Oxford.

Koot, C. J. 2011, *Empire at the Periphery: British colonists, Anglo-Dutch trade, and the development of the British Atlantic, 1621–1713*, New York University Press, New York.

Lunsford, V. 2005, *Piracy and Privateering in the Golden Age Netherlands*, Palgrave Macmillan, New York.

Mancall, P. 2007, *Hakluyt's Promise: an Elizabethan obsession for an English America*, Yale University Press, New Haven.

Mancke, E. & Shamms, C. (eds.) 2005, *The Creation of the British Atlantic World*, Johns Hopkins University Press, Baltimore.

Mc.D Beckles, H. 1998, 'The "Hub of Empire": the Caribbean and Britain in the Seventeenth Century', in Canny, N. (ed.), *The Origins of Empire: British overseas enterprise to the close of the seventeenth century*, Oxford University Press, Oxford.

Oostindie, G. L. & Paasman, B. 1998, 'Dutch attitudes towards colonial empires, indigenous cultures, and slaves', *Eighteenth Century Studies*, vol. 31, no. 3, pp. 349–55.

Oostindie, G. L. & Roitman, J. V. 2012, 'Repositioning the Dutch in the Atlantic, 1680–1800', *Itinerario*, vol. 36, no. 2, pp. 129–60.

Ormrod, D. 2003, *The Rise of Commercial Empires: England and the Netherlands in the Age of Mercantalism, 1650–1770*. Cambridge University Press, Cambridge.

Pincus, S. 1992, 'Popery, Trade and Universal Monarchy: the ideological context of the outbreak of the second Anglo-Dutch war', *English Historical Review*, vol. 107, no. 422, pp. 1–29.

Price, J. L. 1994, *Holland and the Dutch Republic in the Seventeenth Century: the politics of particularism*, Clarendon Press, Oxford.

Quinn, D & Quinn, A (eds.) 1993, *Discourse on Western Planting*, Hakluyt Society, London.

Rine, Holly 2011, 'Putting the Dutch Republic back in New Netherland', *Reviews in American History*, vol. 39, no. 1, pp. 24–29.

Roper, L. H. 2009, *The English Empire in America, 1602–1658: Beyond Jamestown*, Pickering and Chatto, London.

Stern, P. J. 2006, 'British Asia and the British Atlantic: comparisons and connections', *William and Mary Quarterly*, vol. 63, no. 4, pp. 693–712.

Unger, R. 1980, 'Dutch Herring, Technology and International Trade in the Seventeenth Century', *The Journal of Economic History*, vol. 40, no. 1, pp. 253–79.

CHAPTER THIRTY

THE CULTURAL HISTORY OF COMMERCE IN THE ATLANTIC WORLD[1]

———•◆•———

Jonathan Eacott

In 1789 the Connecticut merchant Elijah Boardman commissioned a particularly Atlantic portrait of himself. Merchant portraits were not specific to the Atlantic World; Eurasian merchants also sat for portraits to advertise their social and financial credit. Nevertheless, Boardman's upright posture, elegant clothing and tidy work spaces projected to Americans and Europeans a holistic sense of the individual as confident, stable and respectable that would not have been as obvious to their Asian counterparts.[2] The many books lined up prominently under Boardman's desk showcased Boardman's Atlantic, and particularly British Atlantic, definition of his character, as well as the lack of separation between one's self and one's business that characterized pre-corporate commercial life. Although some of the books may have been printed and bound in America, Britons on the other side of the ocean had written them, and only one was a business manual. The *London Magazine* underscored Boardman's knowledge of the politics and fashions of the Atlantic's leading metropolis, while Francis Moore's *Travels* and William Guthrie's *New System of Modern Geography* suggested knowledge of the greater world with which he traded. William Shakespeare's collected works, Samuel Johnson's *Dictionary*, and Benjamin Martin's *Philosophical Grammar* vouched for Boardman's participation in polite cultured society. John Milton's *Paradise Lost* suggested Boardman's caution for both the temptations of the devil's avaricious sidekick, Mammon, and the commercial monopolies Milton derided. Similarly, the bolts of cloth visible through the open door behind Boardman attested to the desirability of goods imported from Britain and Boardman's taste and skill as a merchant. One slightly unrolled bolt near the centre of the painting revealed a prominent British customs stamp suggesting that Boardman obtained his wares through legal and respectable channels, and more figuratively that they bore the stamp of approval of London fashion. Such prominent books and fabrics imported from Britain may seem out of place in a United States which had only recently fought for its independence from the British empire. Indeed, Boardman himself served as a patriot in the American Revolution, and some commentators see his portrait as evidence of a new national character.[3] The posture, clothing, books, and cloth in Boardman's portrait, however, tell a story not so much of American independence, but of both Boardman's and America's place in an Atlantic, and increasingly prominently British Atlantic culture of commerce.

546

– CHAPTER 30: *The cultural history of commerce* –

Atlantic commerce was 'a whole way of life' for merchants such as Boardman, and in many ways it increasingly shaped and was shaped by the lives of all sorts of people from Western Europe to the coast of Africa, the Caribbean and the Americas.[4] Commercial culture happened in the Atlantic World's portraits, such as Boardman's, and literature, such as Milton's, and in its shops, coffee houses, counting offices, manufactories, sugarcane fields, government halls and religious centres. This chapter follows the trading currents of the Atlantic as the ocean bubbled new practices, ideas, institutions and goods up into all of facets of life to help create a new network of commercial culture. It begins with a narrative that locates European activity in the Atlantic within larger processes of European imperial expansion that spanned the globe. Some of the cloth in Boardman's portrait, for instance, most likely came from Britain's possessions two oceans away in India. From Columbus' stumbling upon the West Indies on his way to seek such goods from Asia, to the support of state apparatuses, to the everyday activities of individuals, global commerce paid for global empires, and these empires, in turn created opportunities for commerce. This narrative also suggests that the commercial culture of the Atlantic World stimulated and was in turn stimulated by new trading practices, habits, tools and institutions; religious, scientific and political thinking; and mass forced and free migrations that provided new commodities and consumer markets. The three sections following the opening narrative, 'Practice and Profit', 'Faith, Morals and Markets', and 'Migration Based Production and Consumption' consider these themes in turn.

ATLANTIC COMMERCE IN A GLOBAL CONTEXT

When the *Lydia* sailed from London to Boston in 1770 it made an Atlantic voyage. Its cargo came from several European countries and included four trunks of books, six cases of stationary, numerous cases of glass and several sheets of lead. The *Lydia*, however, also brought several chests of tea and porcelain from China, hundreds of yards of cotton fabric from India, and a box filled with dozens of pounds of various East Indian spices.[5] Such voyages with complicated and cosmopolitan cargoes repeated tens of thousands of times between the fifteenth century and the middle of the nineteenth. During this period merchants integrated the Atlantic into the valuable and pre-existing coasting trades of Europe, the North Sea and the Mediterranean, as well as circuits of trade extending to Asia and, eventually, the Pacific Islands. Regardless of their locations, these trades grew largely out of the same imperial desires: profit and power. With their 'fluid centers' to borrow a phrase from the historian Victor Lieberman, recent histories of these various circuits of trade have done invaluable work in exposing the scale of exchange in many parts of the early modern world and the porousness of supposedly heavily regulated imperial trading systems.[6] Yet such histories often give the impression of bounded oceans analogous to the nationally bounded narratives that they have done so much to decentre. This is not to argue that the whole globe is the only reasonable geographic framework for the analysis of historical commerce. That merchants who traded with Europe, Western Africa and the Americas might also have traded with the Middle East, the Asian Subcontinent and beyond, does not necessarily suggest that an Atlantic commercial sub-culture was a fiction. These global activities do demand, however, that historians think rigorously about what differentiated the Atlantic commercial

547

culture and why that differentiation matters. The *Lydia's* voyage was Atlantic, but it was also a connection to the oceans beyond.

Fifteenth- and sixteenth-century Portuguese merchants both benefiting from and backing Portuguese and Spanish conquests set in motion many of the trades and network trading mechanisms which would characterize the culture of Atlantic commerce for centuries. Beginning in the early fifteenth century the Portuguese Crown led the development of European seaborne exploration along the West and East African coasts and across the Indian Ocean.[7] Portuguese merchants, particularly Jews and New Christians, embedded themselves, often violently, as small commercial colonies in African, Asian and South American ports previously unknown to Europeans. They emulated the networks of family members and friends that Genoese and Venetian traders already used in the Ottoman Empire and elsewhere in the Mediterranean. Network associates depended on personal letters, bills of exchange and lengthy terms of credit to facilitate trade. Portuguese trade bolstered government finances through duties, monopoly profits, and the development of a well-capitalized merchant elite that served as the primary lender to the Portuguese Crown, and from 1580 to 1640, the union Crown with Spain.[8] Networked Portuguese merchants increasingly dominated global trade through licit and illicit means, while the numerically and militarily stronger Spanish, with the assistance of Genoese merchants, focussed more on conquering foreign peoples, developing Caribbean and South American slave plantations, and extracting precious metals. The Spanish Crown dispatched regular fleets to and from Seville and Havana, Cartagena and San Juan. In Havana a heterogeneous population built vibrant trading, provisioning, and ship-building sectors for and through the regular *Carrera de Indias* fleets.[9] The Dutch in Antwerp too found a profitable role in the Iberian system, dispersing Atlantic imports throughout Northern Europe. Still, the Dutch desired greater access to the Atlantic, and during the Eighty Years War (1568–1648), they fought the Iberians not only for political independence but for control of the valuable spice, slave and sugar trades. The Dutch targeted Portuguese trading settlements which provided easier and in many ways more profitable targets than the Spanish territories in Mexico and Peru.[10]

Unable to participate easily in the closed Iberian system and more limited in resources than the Dutch, merchants in other Northern European ports such as Middelburg, La Rochelle and especially, London, focussed on consorting with their state governments to fund and fit out private vessels to capture valuable Iberian cargoes. Typically, these privateers needed little in the way of expensive armaments and relied on close-quarters combat and an overwhelming superiority of fighting men to take control of enemy vessels – sinking a merchant ship with heavy broadsides brought no profit. Many captains oscillated between privateering and pirating, the latter of which freed them from paying the Admiralty and the Queen their shares of the loot. A veneer of patriotism covered attacks on the Spanish and Portuguese. To take wealth from the Catholic Iberians both weakened the principal enemy of the Protestant English and Dutch, and strengthened the capital positions of the Northern powers. The merchants won doubly too: not only did they earn a share of the booty but in taking the booty they drove countless Iberian merchants into bankruptcy and out of competition in the regular trades. Privateers and pirates operated globally, but their Atlantic activities poaching valuable African, and South and Central American cargos held particular importance.[11] The resulting enhanced capital position of many

– CHAPTER 30: The cultural history of commerce –

English merchants encouraged a new round of investing in expansive business pursuits which would more clearly set the Atlantic and Indian Ocean trades off from each other.

The English and Dutch fused the pre-existing forms of state-sponsored monopoly trade and the joint stock company, fostering hopes of profits for investors and revenue for the state through the export of the valuable commodities expected to be found in Asia, Africa, and the Americas. The Portuguese Crown had already utilized monopolies to generate revenue in the fifteenth and sixteenth centuries, such as those granted to Prince Henry and the *Casa da India*. The Spanish Crown, too, attempted to enforce multiple royal monopolies. The English and Dutch, however, used the capital pooling and risk spreading nature of joint stock companies to offset political and capital weaknesses. The companies shared the same legal and ideological underpinnings, and within each country often the same investors from both the middling and upper sorts. English and Dutch companies such as the Turkey, later Levant Company (1581) and East India Companies (1600 and 1602) were initially focussed on trade, not settlement. English Atlantic companies, in contrast, focussed more on settlement to drive trade, and included the Virginia Company (1606), which established colonies in Virginia and Bermuda; the Massachusetts Bay Company (1629); and, the Providence Island Company (1629), which began settlements on Providence Island off the Mosquito Coast and Tortuga off San Domingo. Meanwhile, the Dutch West India Company (1621) ramped up privateering against the Iberians, and obtained a monopoly over the Dutch portion of the African slave trade and Dutch colonization in the West Indies and the Americas. With Portuguese shipping beset by English and Dutch privateers, King John IV adapted for defence the strategy which the English and Dutch had used offensively to muscle in on the Iberian trades, chartering the Brazil Company and granting it two naval squadrons for protection (1649).[12] After the English Restoration, the Royal African Company (1660) gained a legal monopoly over the English slave trade, and the Hudson's Bay Company (1670) challenged the French monopoly in the North American fur trade, extending often damaging European goods and relationships of commercial exchange to multiple indigenous peoples. Some also hoped to expand settlement aggressively in the Indian Ocean along Atlantic models. Whether in the Indian or Atlantic Ocean, trading profit was always the intended bottom line. Profit had such importance that early settlers, such as those at Jamestown in Virginia, often emphasized the procurement and production of exports at the expense of their own survival.[13] The English, Dutch, French (1664) and Swedish (1731) East India Companies proved enduring in conception if not in execution or profitability, while Northern European intra-oceanic trade in both the Atlantic and Indian Oceans quickly came to follow the earlier Portuguese New Christian model of private merchant networks. The advantages of joint stock companies in raising capital, spreading risk, and projecting power were thought to compensate for the greater distances and more powerful indigenous regimes that Europeans encountered in trade with Asia. In the accessible Atlantic trades, looser networks of private Northern European merchants displaced the joint stock companies over the seventeenth and eighteenth centuries. The Virginia Company had already lost control of Jamestown in 1624 and by 1792 the Hudson's Bay Company was the only remaining major British or Dutch chartered joint stock company focussed on the Atlantic.[14]

549

As the chartered companies collapsed trade expanded much more dramatically to the Americas and Africa than to Asia, to the benefit of private merchant networks and, if properly harnessed, their states. Intra-imperial trade was common and could be supported by governments when it seemed to be in the state's interests – it could even be vital to colonial development, as for English colonies trading with the Dutch.[15] Despite Dutch commercial success, however, the growth in Atlantic trade was increasingly driven by the English and, for a time, the French colonial presences in the Caribbean and North America. British shipping tonnage in the second half of the seventeenth century tripled through success in expanding colonial populations and conquering Dutch colonies, as well as the assumption of the *asiento de negros* to service the insatiable Spanish demand for slaves, creation of a slave and tobacco economy in the Chesapeake, evolution of the Navigation Acts, and formation of the Board of Trade.[16] Tonnage rose rapidly again from the middle of the eighteenth century, reaching 153,000 tons burden per year in the early 1770s. Meanwhile, English shipping to the East Indies increased from approximately 8,000 tons burden per year in 1663 to 29,000 tons, a similar rate of growth but a much smaller addition of tonnage.[17]

Debate raged over whether trade, like politics, was a zero sum game, but many agreed that economic growth should be aided by the state.[18] Imperial governments in Europe established a range of regulations to better harness expanding trades for metropolitan gain, most famously the mid-seventeenth-century English Navigation Acts. These acts required English ships with a crew at least three-fourths English to be used in all coastal and colonial trade, as well as trade from Asia, Africa and America. Additionally, certain 'enumerated' goods could only be shipped from the colonies to England, except when deemed helpful in furthering the national interest. Enforcement was erratic and difficult, but direct trade between English colonists and Holland declined sharply, while English Atlantic merchants and vessels came to dominate the trade between Britain and America and the West Indies, if not the trade between the colonies of England and the colonies of other European powers. By encouraging the use of English vessels and sailors, the Navigation Acts expanded shipping and naval power. Using a range of protections and taxes the state generated sizeable new revenues, enhanced its credit position, directed economic growth and gained tens of thousands of experienced seamen available to be impressed into the British navy in times of need. French kings passed similar laws, culminating in attempts by Louis XV which largely failed despite the grizzly penalty of 'banishment to the galleys'. Smuggling was a constant difficulty in the Atlantic World, and such acts were most successful when they reflected both metropolitan and colonial interests in protected markets.[19]

The expansion of European markets through the mass settler colonization of the Americas most dramatically marked seventeenth- and eighteenth-century Atlantic commerce as different from that in the other world oceans. By the late eighteenth century perhaps a few hundred thousand European migrants had ventured to the Indian Ocean. Europeans had also transported hundreds of thousands of individuals from Africa and Madagascar and unknown numbers of other peoples throughout the Indian Ocean as part of a much longer and larger Afroeurasian slave trade. In the Americas, Europeans attempted to turn indigenous labour and slaving practices to their benefit. After contact with Europeans, however, disease devastated indigenous

– CHAPTER 30: *The cultural history of commerce* –

communities in the Americas unlike in Asia. Large migrant populations became essential to colonization in the Atlantic. Approximately 1 million European migrants had already travelled to the Americas between 1492 and 1700, and millions more arrived before 1850. Europeans brought over 10 million people to the Americas as slaves from Africa, with the vast majority going to the West Indies, Brazil and Spanish America.[20] The enormous slave populations in the Atlantic produced new commodities in remarkable quantities for European markets, but were not major consumers of European goods. Utilizing slave production and large and rapidly growing colonial consumer markets, British power continued to expand during the eighteenth century. British merchants came to dominate most Atlantic trades, including lumber, fish, tobacco and eventually sugar to Europe, cloth to Africa, and cloth, slaves, guns, wine and pots to the Americas. While many of the mechanisms of trade and commodities traded were little different from those of the Portuguese two centuries earlier, the scale of trade and Britain's place within it had changed dramatically.[21]

Atlantic commercial culture was both part of, and distinct from, global imperial pursuits. Merchant networks, privateering, joint stock companies, imperial legal frameworks, and trade as warfare were not confined to the Atlantic World. The European struggle for profit and power was a global struggle. Nevertheless, the prominence of merchant networks over joint stock companies for direct trade to Europe; shifts in intellectual, moral and religious conceptions of trade and luxury; the settlement of Europeans, particularly in North America; and the forced migration of Africans as slaves, particularly to South America and the West Indies, all built on one another to set Atlantic commercial culture off from European trade with Asia. North America and the western coast of Africa became massive new markets for European goods, much more important than the markets offered by enslaved Africans or the populations of Asia. These expanding consumer markets made the Atlantic World an important subculture of global commerce, and the British increasingly dominant within that subculture.

PRACTICE AND PROFIT

Between the 1500s and the 1850s, Atlantic merchants transformed natural harbours into entrepot port towns to spread their networks of family, finance and trade. For Atlantic merchants, negotiation was not an abstract concept. Merchants constantly negotiated to enhance their social and financial credit, settle methods and rates of payment, buy and sell merchandise, and procure shipping. The sort of line often posited as modern today between business and personal affairs barely existed, if it existed at all. Trade depended on kinship ties and the establishment of personal credit – the lifeblood of the system. Establishing credit involved particular sets of performances and material displays that differed little in purpose across the time and space of the Atlantic World. The general practices of shipping, too, changed little before the middle of the nineteenth century. The most dramatic changes occurred, instead, in retailing, where many new institutions and advertising tactics served and encouraged consumer demand.

Merchants centralized Atlantic commercial functions in leading European cities such as Seville, Amsterdam and London; colonial economic functions in local port towns; and daily activities in their counting house residences. Characteristic of the major European entrepots that would follow it, Seville's population tripled in size during the sixteenth century. A host of Genoese, Portuguese and other European merchants established enclaves in the city. In the mid-seventeenth century, Amsterdam displaced Seville as the leading centre of trade and finance in the Atlantic World by utilizing a relatively open trading system and offering the most secure bank, the most capricious stock exchange, and the most developed insurance market. Amsterdam was also a hub of commercial information; published price lists, for instance, circulated from 1585.[22] In the eighteenth century, London, the Western Europe's largest metropolis and seat of commerce and government for an empire, quickly becoming the world's most powerful, usurped Amsterdam. As much as one-quarter of London's nearly 1 million inhabitants depended on commerce. And, according to one estimate, one in six male Britons in the eighteenth century lived in the city at some stage of their lives. Several thousand merchants from Britain, Europe and the Americas met daily on the Royal Exchange's quadrangle to swap letters, bills of exchange, stocks, goods, political petitions and gossip. The Exchange and its vicinity offered highly developed capital and commodity markets, several major insurers, and a range of banking services. Additionally, a slew of increasingly sophisticated printed circulars, such as *Lloyd's List* begun in 1692, distributed the details of ship movements, exchange rates, bullion prices and commercial news gathered from far-flung networks of correspondents.[23] Great London merchants had fortunes surpassing a half million pounds, several times the wealth of their colonial associates.[24]

Yet merchants in the colonial ports of all of the European powers played a critical dual role by simultaneously de-centralizing Atlantic trade and centralizing local trade. Generally, merchants did not prefer to pass all their goods through one primary imperial port. Instead, depending on the Atlantic currents and seasons, imperial legal restrictions, and one's willingness to trade evasively, merchants shipped goods as directly as possible from the regional port nearest the site of production to the port where the goods were most in demand. As in the leading ports of Europe, colonial port towns offered an enterprising merchant connections to government officials, financiers and consumers, as well as a critical mass of other merchants to associate or compete with. Many merchants acted both on their own account and as commission merchants or agents for other merchants, with the commission trade rising and falling in particular trades and ports at different times. Merchants congregated at coffee houses where they discussed trade, posted notices, sought out ship captains, and increasingly in the eighteenth century, read the local financial papers. While a quality port provided the foundation for urban growth, a city's success depended on the quantity of raw materials it could draw in and its access to markets in its rural hinterland.[25]

Individual merchants often centralized their work and family life in the same building, reflecting the extent to which trading made up a complete lifestyle. Clerks' offices generally occupied the first floor with the merchant's living accommodations above. Marriages often occurred between strategically associated merchant families, solidifying social, economic and political connections. Wives primarily looked after domestic responsibilities and managed household servants. Nevertheless, they often gained considerable knowledge of the family enterprise from their proximity to the book-keeping and business conversations of their husbands. Throughout the Atlantic World women could and did directly manage commercial concerns, often when their husbands were ill, abroad or deceased. Additionally, countless women often managed

– CHAPTER 30: *The cultural history of commerce* –

retail operations on accounts independent from their husbands.[26] Merchants frequently apprenticed sons, nephews, grandchildren or the children of friends in their counting offices to learn reading, writing and accounting. Eventually, merchants dispatched some of these young men as supercargos to gain additional experience to become partners, agents in distant ports, or independent merchants.[27] The broad characteristics of these relationships changed little until the middle of the nineteenth century when new commercial organizations and the increasingly common separation of a merchant's workplace from the home dovetailed with larger societal changes in the doctrine of separate spheres, at least in ideology, if not clearly in fact.[28]

A merchant's household needed to look wealthy and reputable, not just for reasons of personal vanity or social status, but because financial credit largely depended on the appearance of social credit and limited risk. The appearance of frivolous or tasteless spending had a negative effect on one's credit, and thus displays of wealth were ideally also displays of responsibility and virtue. While conspicuous consumption and virtue may appear to be mutually exclusive, a social code laying out proper behaviour and spending was negotiated throughout the Atlantic World.[29] By spending on tasteful and virtuous items one's credit was enhanced not impugned. Expensive musical instruments, books and curiosities most displayed the virtuous characteristics of a family of polite learning. A wealthy merchant also displayed virtue in his family's taste for stylish architecture, gardens, furniture, dress, carriages and civic improvements. Not only did one look reputable by showcasing good taste, knowing the fashionable market signified likely success in buying and selling goods to satisfy consumers. Spending needed to be complemented by a steady demeanor and carefully phrased letters and conversations, performances for associates and customers alike.[30] Such appearances, along with the recommendations of others, underpinned social credit, which, in turn, underpinned a merchant's financial credit and business opportunities. Much like merchants, labourers, artisans and others increasingly needed to establish, project and evaluate social credit to obtain and give financial credit for the goods and services that they desired. The widespread policy of imprisoning merchants and consumers who failed to meet their obligations reflected the lack of distinction between an individual and his or her financial credit.[31]

From the Portuguese, to the Dutch, to the British, merchants were caught in an awkward social and economic position dependent on paper and fraught with risk. Merchants enjoyed more wealth than the mass of the population, but typically less than the aristocracy. The value of land, the mainstay of aristocratic wealth in Europe, and of planter wealth in the Americas, increased slowly and more or less constantly. Merchant wealth, in contrast, was tied up primarily in commercial papers and merchandise which could change instantly from being assets to liabilities at any time.[32] A severely limited supply of gold and silver coins in many colonies made commercial paper particularly crucial from trans-Atlantic trade to the smallest transactions between shopkeepers and consumers. Merchants used bills of exchange, based on personal credit, as their primary tools for commercial transactions. A bill of exchange involved often four parties. The merchant paying for the goods (the payer) purchased a bill of exchange from a nearby second individual (the drawer) who was owed money by a third individual (the drawee) living near the seller of the goods (the payee). The payer sent the bill of exchange to the payee, who presented it to the drawee for payment at a specified time. The transaction paralleled the use of a cheque if one

553

imagines the payer's bank as the drawer and the payee's bank as the drawee. Without an international banking system, negotiating bills of exchange required both good credit and a network of trusted associates.[33] As one merchant firm wrote, 'there can be no connection in trade where there is not confidence.'[34] Bills of exchange, even backed by family or trusted friends, added a substantial level of risk as a party might go bankrupt or otherwise be unwilling or unable to pay his or her liabilities. Defaulted payments put other creditor merchants at risk. One merchant bankruptcy within a long chain of credit could bring down several merchants at once.[35]

Few merchants enjoyed stable wealth and none enjoyed the benefits of modern limited liability to protect their families from business failures. One study has shown that the majority of British trading families suffered a major financial collapse during the period, and these findings could likely be replicated throughout the Atlantic World.[36] To maintain, let alone increase their incomes, merchants needed to be constantly buying and selling goods within the constraints of their credit and the availability of shipping. Profits depended on good advice, instincts, timely market news from one's network, and chance. Although, as Ian Steele has explained, the Atlantic was in many ways more a highway than a barrier, communication was inconsistent, often incomplete, and regularly out of date.[37] Goods could thus be poorly chosen, bought too dearly, or sold too cheaply in a suddenly glutted market, in addition to the risks of loss at sea through shipwreck, privateers or pirates. The only protection came from the widespread expansion of often costly and unreliable insurance. French rates, for instance, rose as high as 40 per cent when the country was at war. Even such high rates did not guarantee protection; insurers frequently went bankrupt, and during the Seven Years' War those still in business stopped issuing policies.[38]

The willingness to face such risks might appear surprising; merchants, however, lived in a world in which planning for the long term was imprecise at best and pointless at worst. Multiple commissions, chains of bills of exchange, and transaction cycles lasting several months or years confused not only profits and losses but assessments of risk. In a world where sickness and death came quickly and often, the potential for handsome short-term gains trumped long-term fears of over-extension. Finally, a widespread belief that kin and friends should help a distressed associate and his family diffused risk. Failure, after all, could happen to anyone, at any time, and be caused by the collapse or death of a party far along a chain of bills. Allowing the total collapse of an associate's business, moreover, could drag down one's own.[39]

Once a merchant had negotiated bills and purchased goods, shipping had its own subculture involving shipowners, ship husbands, captains, supercargoes and ship and dock hands. Many merchants doubled as shipowners, but instead of owning ships outright they often owned shares in one or more vessels through what the Dutch called *rederij*. In both the Atlantic and Indian Ocean trades individuals ranging from butchers to aristocrats also purchased shares. The owner with the most shares served as the ship's husband and took added responsibility for managing the vessel as a business concern. Husbands advertised available freight tonnage in coffee houses, newspapers, and through word of mouth for one or more intended destinations. A merchant might accompany the goods or hire a supercargo for the voyage to oversee the unloading and sale of the cargo at the destination and to purchase and load new merchandise. The captain or ship master was responsible for the safety of the ship

– CHAPTER 30: *The cultural history of commerce* –

and command of the crew, although on slaving voyages captains often managed the sale of the slaves as well. Additionally, captains often managed side deals on their own accounts. On board, the captain, supercargo, and well-to-do passengers kept private cabins, but frequently dined and socialized together. They expected, and typically received, respect and deference from the crew.[40] Ship hands saw the world, but lived a risky life with low pay, poor rations, cramped space, and the threats of corporal punishment, illness and shipwreck. Life at sea and their own lively subculture made them immediately recognizable on land. The historian Charles Boxer has suggested that seventeenth-century Dutch efficiency in trade was due, in particular, to the severe exploitation of Dutch seamen.[41]

Many aspects of Atlantic commercial culture changed little throughout the period, but the rapid expansion of trade occurred alongside radical changes in retailing. The rise of the ready-made goods trade as well as an increasing separation between places of production and places of retail transformed how merchants and consumers interacted. Independent shop retailers and peddlers appeared in increasing numbers in cities and towns in the Netherlands, Britain and France, and in the European colonies across the Atlantic as early as the sixteenth century. By the middle of the eighteenth century retail shops were omnipresent, and large wholesalers had emerged to manage and distribute a growing range of products newly available in standardized cuts, sizes and qualities. Shopkeepers arranged such products in impressive interiors and window displays designed to stimulate consumer desire.[42] In the middle and late eighteenth century, print advertising became essential as a means of informing customers at each point in the retail chain of the lines of products available. North American colonial newspapers, in particular, carried a staggering quantity of advertisements with increasingly sophisticated presentations. Merchants emphasized the recent arrival and metropolitan origin of their produce, and promised the best prices, most fashionable selection, and longest credit. Imported goods had special importance in colonial societies that boasted few high-end artisan producers.[43] Looking to take better advantage of such markets by avoiding merchant middlemen, British manufacturers in the middle of the eighteenth century began dispatching their own agents to sell products directly to colonial shopkeepers. Agents and competing merchants circulated sample books and fabric swatches from which wholesalers and retailers throughout the Atlantic World could order specific goods and patterns.[44] When combined, these many changes in retail practice helped to remake consumption habits, urban landscapes and popular fashions.

European, African and American merchants developed a distribution network spread between various entrepots and across the Atlantic Ocean. This enduring and diffused system depended on credit and personal connections. Merchants used major and minor port cities to centralize market functions, economic decision making and commercial services, while they used their network connections to decentralize trade flows. Negotiations occurred through letters and personal conversations at all stages of a transaction. Trade depended, more than anything, on the negotiation of social and financial credit, which themselves were tightly intermingled. Merchants, therefore, worked diligently to establish and maintain not only their good reputations, but the networks of associates necessary to protect them if their reputations became sullied, often due to the failure of merchants far distant on the credit chain. This largely material-based performance of one's values and identities would come to characterize Atlantic consumer culture. Indeed, the most remarkable changes to commercial practices during the period came in retailing the consumer goods that the ever expanding networks of merchants moved throughout the Atlantic World.

FAITH, MORALS AND MARKETS

Increased trade and consumption did not go unquestioned. People disagreed sharply over the morality of profits, markets and new consumer goods, debates which ultimately played into the economic success of the Netherlands and, especially, Britain. On the one hand, the ideal qualities of a merchant: stability, honesty, frankness, charity, frugality and humility, varied little amongst the European powers, and closely followed the ideal qualities set forth for all individuals in the Catholic and Protestant faiths. On the other hand, successful merchants also needed to be highly competitive, guarded in the information that they shared, aggressive negotiators, frequent creditors and debtors and projectors of wealth.[45] As trade and consumer culture expanded, tensions between these two sets of qualities spilled over from merchant life to the life of a growing cross section of individuals. Religious, intellectual and political leaders became increasingly concerned with the moral and financial realities of burgeoning market economies. To use the terms of the historian Henry Clark, the 'gap' between the 'moral infrastructure' and daily commercial life caused considerable anxiety amongst thinkers and leaders in Atlantic communities throughout the period; how they bridged the gap, however, varied considerably.[46]

In the mid-seventeenth century the Jewish and New Christian Portuguese merchant network buoying up the Portuguese and Spanish states drained through the gap between ideals and realities forced wider by the Iberian Inquisition. Iberian merchants had been lobbying Spanish leaders for freer trade, the end of royal regulation over the timing of shipping, and the option to form joint stock companies to compete with Dutch and English merchants. Many in the church and court, however, feared merchant influence over public policy. They suspected merchants of working against the Catholic Church and the crown by syphoning off wealth through credit, usury and exchange unmoored from physical production. Thousands of persecuted, wealthy and well-connected merchants flowed out of the gap into the relative tolerance of protestant Northern Europe at precisely the moment that France, the Netherlands and England began to exert themselves as major players in Atlantic commerce.[47] Ultimately, neither France nor the Netherlands made the most attractive harbours for merchants fleeing persecution. The former with potential advantages in population size, productive capacity and state strength, lacked beneficial commercial policies; the latter with beneficial commercial policies lacked a powerful state.

French prejudice against commerce was less clearly an issue of religion than of monarchical conceit. Instead of depending upon the fortunes and financial expertise of merchants, the French court maintained both revenue and obedience by selling offices and charges to the nobility.[48] Arguments that self-interest and the interests of the public good were mutually exclusive dominated French political economy. French leaders widely denounced merchants and financiers as greedy, vain and profane. Those who believed in the competing theories of the *moralistes* and who hoped to emulate the commercial successes of the Netherlands and Britain struggled to gain influence over French policy. As France became an increasingly commercial society, rapidly expanding its Atlantic trade from the mid-seventeenth to the mid-eighteenth century, the gap between public ideals and economic reality continued to grow.[49]

In the Netherlands, in contrast, little such gap existed. Dutch thinkers, artists and governments celebrated the commercial basis and success of the republic.[50] Many Europeans in the sixteenth century described the Dutch as a most frugal people, but with economic growth in the seventeenth century came new attitudes towards consumption. Calvinist and humanist critics of heightened levels of consumer spending lashed out with sermons, rituals and engravings: increased spending was a sign of decreased virtue, which could lead only to public rot and decline. Yet few seemed to heed such distressing prognoses.[51] Writers of panegyrics, painters and engravers celebrated the activity, wealth and size of Dutch ports, and eagerly depicted the great range of commodities that poured into them. In Jurriaen van Streek's *Still Life with Moor and Porcelain Vessels* (c. 1670) the objects of commerce, including oranges, oysters, glassware, silver, porcelain and fabrics literally spill off of the table. A slave smiles submissively suggesting the basis of Dutch West Indian power and inviting the viewer to share. The partially consumed abundance bathed in a warm glow appears more cheerful than ominous. Such still lifes, popular as the Dutch rose to economic prominence in the seventeenth century, and different from the predominantly religious painting of Portugal, celebrated wealth, consumption and imperial power typically with little overt sense of criticism.[52]

Simultaneously, other Dutch etchers, painters and architects emphasized the importance and glory of seaborne commerce. Artists created a new genre of imagery fusing highly realistic and accurate depictions of ships with dramatic settings. Reinier Nooms' etchings of commercial and military ships were extraordinarily popular, attesting to the public's interest in celebrating Dutch command of the seas. Similarly, Hendrick Vroom's *View of the River Ij Near Amsterdam* (c. 1630) depicts countless vessels crowding out the panorama of the city behind, and emphasizing the source of Amsterdam's wealth.[53] Prominent wind-blown flags leave little doubt of a powerful sense of pride in Dutch commercial achievements. In his other works, Vroom's interchangeable use of bright blowing flags, warm golden lighting, great puffy clouds and tumultuous storms to depict heroic commercial and military struggles on the sea set the pattern for dozens of painters who followed. Dutch architecture, too, celebrated the dual economic and political importance of trade. Amsterdam's new town hall finished in 1655 and located in immediate proximity to the city's commercial weigh-house, provided a striking manifestation of the centrality of trade to the public's identity. Yet while the republic sought to enable commerce and spread a vision of reduced international trade barriers and vigorous consumption, it lacked the financial, regulatory and military strength of the French state, and ultimately more importantly, the English.[54]

Merchants increasingly found the most supportive landing across the English Channel where popular beliefs, economic philosophy and a powerful state combined. Already, by the end of the sixteenth century, few in England seriously doubted the value of market-based trade, or the importance of a strong state in regulating and enforcing the honest behaviour of both buyers and sellers. A fundamental humanist faith in contracts and market negotiations encouraged a sense of moral equality amongst individuals, a dramatic shift from a pre-modern, pan-European culture that had emphasized social inequalities. Indeed, the term 'interest' suggested not usury but a positive co-dependence whereby one person literally took a vested interest in the success of another. Popular portrayals of the landed upper classes as unproductive and outside the relationship of moral equals implicit in market society existed across Europe, but the English Revolution permanently embedded these beliefs into England's ruling ideology. The protectionists and anti-Orangist revolutionaries who gave rise to the Navigation Acts validated commerce as a national goal as well as merchants and mariners as national heroes. Upon the restoration of the monarchy, Charles II, the self-proclaimed 'King of Trade', entered London under triumphal arches depicting commercial and naval scenes that left little doubt of the centrality of merchant commerce to the English state. Similarly, the importance of commerce to the public good figured in much of Restoration theatre.[55] By 1720 belief in the market economy had become so firmly entrenched that the dramatic collapse of the South Sea Bubble, which brought down thousands of investors and battered the British economy, did not lead to a tear down of the commercial system.

The Bubble and other collapses did, however, foreground the risks of trade, the potential fictionality of wealth, and the importance of Christian teachings against the vices of mammon, covetousness and luxury. With market-based commerce established as both an individual and public good, questions about the Godliness of its corollary, consumption, received considerable attention. Some preachers attempted to reconcile these concerns, and such men as Locke, Milton, Defoe and Addison emphasized frugality to attempt to balance the risks and benefits inherent in a market-based economy. Defoe, for example, argued that luxuries stimulated economic growth and relieved the poverty of artisans, corrupting only those few consumers who overspent. Meanwhile, building on the English faith in the market and belief in the ordained morality of economic exchange, such thinkers as Thomas Mun, Jacob Vanderlint and Edward Misselden drafted a new economic science that encouraged greater consumption to generate economic growth. Such ideas caused little stir when published in economic tracts, but when the Dutch-born Bernard Mandeville claimed that heady spending and not Calvinist frugality drove Dutch economic success in his early eighteenth century, *The Fable of the Bees or, Private Vices, Public Benefits*, intended for widespread public distribution, he was attacked as an immoral advocate of vice and debilitating foreignness.[56]

During the eighteenth century, however, the discordance between support for market trade on the one hand and the denunciation of luxury on the other harmonized as the terms of what Maxine Berg has called 'the luxury debates' shifted across Europe and throughout the Atlantic World. Concerns over debilitating vice continued but were increasingly displaced by the growth of interest in taste, comfort and aesthetics.[57] Many Protestant Evangelical millenarians and supporters of the Newtonian Enlightenment who believed in a non-interventionist God increasingly also stressed that the market-based system dependent on consumption for its expansion mirrored the natural universal system of life.[58] In a sermon to the merchants of Bristol, for instance, the Reverend Alexander Catcott posited a line of godly commercial activity extending from the Biblical city of Tyre to the Britain of his present, quickly brushing aside Isaiah's contention that Tyre was ripe for God's judgement.[59] Additionally, the imagery of increasing British commerce and maritime power infused British painting, as in the Netherlands a century before. Heroic and patriotic scenes of naval engagements, such as Dominic Serres' *The Second Battle of*

– CHAPTER 30: The cultural history of commerce –

Finisterrer, 4 October 1747, and serene views of commercial ports, such as Samuel Atkins' *A View of the Pool Below London Bridge* (1790), increased dramatically over the eighteenth century. Collectively these patriotic works represented the interdependent duality of British seaborne power: force and commerce.

During the French Revolution, engravings, such as Isaac Cruikshank's *French Happiness/English Misery* (1793) patriotically celebrated the generous levels of consumption in Britain made possible by commerce and a strong state. Cruikshank ironically labelled emaciated Frenchmen fighting anarchically for a frog's leg as happy, in comparison to a party of jovial, fat Englishmen living under the banner of constitutional rule and supplied with great roasts, beer, white linen, and even an imported bird in a cage, as miserable. Living in plenty was not immoral nor simply fun, it was a sign of Britain's greatness. The increasing popularity of Adam Smith's *An Inquiry into the Nature and Causes of the Wealth of Nations* that packaged a range of economic and moral arguments for the mutually beneficial relationship amongst trade, public wealth, self-interest and consumption, further underscored the entrenchment of this new attitude towards consumer society.

The benefits of the market, however, still needed to be justly distributed, a point that became increasingly important in late-eighteenth-century attacks on the British East India Company and the slave trade. Both concerns grew out of the ideology of a moral political economy valued in Britain and in revolutionary America. British Americans came to see the East India Company monopoly over tea imports as a type of slavery, and as unjustly rewarding a company acting on non-free principles, both in its trade monopoly and its non-democratic government over India. During the non-importation movements the Boston Tea Party colonists made a moral political point about the freedom of the market. Britons at home likewise increasingly agitated against the East India Company monopoly and in favour of freer trade; with one alderman noting, for instance, that 'so soon as monopoly ceased to be necessary, it ceased to be just'.[60] Similarly, for most of the previous three centuries, the questions of morality implicit in the slave trade, although voiced, did not gain traction. With the alignment of Protestant theories of God-given liberty and market principles as part of the moral foundation of society, came growing acceptance that individuals must have legal free choice in their economic affairs and that both buyer and seller benefited from a market value for goods and labour.[61] The end of both the East India Company monopoly and the slave trade within less than a decade marked the maturing development of belief in the morality of market culture throughout the British Atlantic and indeed beyond.

The concordance of relative religious tolerance, popular faith in the social and economic importance of the market, trust in Newtonian science, belief in a Protestant natural order, and acceptance of the morality of consumption provided an environment conducive to the growth of British Atlantic commerce. Similar ideas existed in the Netherlands, but in Britain the gap between moral ideals and economic growth had been bridged with the aid of, and to the aid of, a powerful central state. The celebration of trade as patriotic and of a new market-oriented morality appeared in painting, architecture, theatre and literature in the Netherlands and Britain. Market morality was contested, but a major shift occurred in both countries as consumption went from being seen as corrupting, to potentially generative of liberty and justice. This new morality lent power to calls for the banning of British imports

559

into the Thirteen Colonies before the American Revolution, and the ending of the East India Company monopoly and the slave trade. Britons could purchase free labour sugar and Wedgwood porcelain branded in favour of abolitionism to make political points. Consumer choice and market justice had become particularly Atlantic moral obligations to be enforced by the state.

MIGRATION BASED PRODUCTION AND CONSUMPTION

State and religious leaders could support, displace, or destroy Atlantic merchants, but they struggled to control consumption. Sumptuary laws, increasingly common throughout much of Europe before the seventeenth century as a reaction against rising levels of consumption, disappeared, first in Britain and later in Continental Europe, as they dropped out of step with a spreading popular belief in the morality of market culture and consumerism.[62] By yoking a relatively tolerant and powerful state to the pursuit of self-interest, large colonial markets, and the widespread development of diversified and decentralized colonial trade, Britain developed a new model of Atlantic commercial culture particularly in contrast to the core urban centres, large bureaucracies, bilateral trade and transfer of precious metals favoured by Spanish rulers.[63] Although Europe had been the dominant locus of British trade for centuries, the eighteenth-century growth of British North America firmly established the potential of distant colonies as sites not only of production but of valuable and intense consumption. The value of these rapidly growing consumer markets transformed the importance of the Americas and of Atlantic commerce. While some differences existed in consumption tastes from colony to colony and nation to nation, differences in rates of consumption primarily depended upon economic opportunity and the availability of goods. Knowing how to spend became essential to the construction of self not only for the European middling ranks but for people ranging from African slaves to Native Americans to colonial farmers. Atlantic merchants and colonial producers encouraged and fuelled these markets, while, in a reciprocal action, the ever growing demand for new goods stimulated further trade.

Massive increases in Atlantic slave plantation agriculture during the long eighteenth century helped to transform early-modern consumer culture by expanding its reach downwards on the social spectrum and outwards around the Atlantic.[64] Under brutal and tragic conditions slaves produced goods that had previously been considered luxuries, such as tobacco, sugar, chocolate, coffee and mahogany in such quantities that they could become relatively widespread consumer items through a trans-cultural, trans-imperial and trans-Atlantic process of adaptation and adoption.[65] During the eighteenth century, European imports of tobacco, for example, increased from 50 million to 125 million pounds, while coffee imports increased from 2 million to 120 million pounds. Sugar, desired to sweeten coffee, chocolate and tea, grew in popularity most remarkably in Britain, with consumption rising to over 20 pounds per person per year. Euro-American consumer culture depended, not only on Atlantic production, but on products such as tea, porcelains and fabrics imported from China and India. These goods were combined into often elaborate social contexts, such as the porcelain tea service or the tobacco snuff box or pipe. Demand thus begot demand.[66] As the historian David Hancock describes, producers, merchants and

– CHAPTER 30: *The cultural history of commerce* –

consumers engaged in a shared cultural conversation to introduce and refine new goods and fashions.[67] These goods, moreover, increasingly 'mediated the relations between individuals and the social worlds they inhabited'.[68]

The growth of market-based consumer culture occurred first in the Dutch Republic, but most remarkably in British North America, where it gained a critical economic importance.[69] London served as the British empire's leading node of political power, commercial exchange, and manufacturing capacity; it was not, however, the only node, nor did the benefits of empire flow primarily one way.[70] The British American colonies enjoyed rapid economic development and rising real wealth levels while other colonies fell into economic decline. Entrepreneurial merchants, tradesmen, planters and industrialists took their wealth and ideas throughout the British empire with faith in the protection of the British navy and the assumed tolerance of British rulers. The widespread growth of small private farms on land secured often violently and unscrupulously from Native Americans offered a source of economic stability to the lower sorts, who in turn offered important markets for West Indian commodities and manufactured goods from Europe and Asia.[71] Although they may have found themselves geographically in the margins, many white migrants eventually gained economic agency in the colonies.[72] Colonists purchased a wide and growing range of imported consumer goods including cloth, shoes, furniture, soap, cooking utensils and dishware. One study of the Chesapeake suggests that over half of all expenditures were on such imported goods.[73] During the eighteenth century, and continuing after the American Revolution, the North American share of British exports grew from 5.7 to over 25 per cent, challenging continental Europe as Britain's main trading partner.[74] While British manufacturers and merchants clearly benefited in supplying them, these vibrant colonial communities belie simple conceptions of Britain as a wealthy core with a marginalized and dependent empire.

The advantages in colonial market size, freedom from religious persecution, and effective government increasingly enjoyed by British merchants and consumers appears clearly when contrasted against the situation of their French competitors. In 1700, non-slave settlers in British North America already outnumbered those in New France perhaps more than ten to one. This relative imbalance occurred for a variety of reasons, including a widespread French antipathy to emigration, and royal prohibitions banning Jews and Protestant Huguenots, in many ways the most eager migrants, from settling in New France. Several hundred thousand Huguenots left France to settle in the Netherlands, Britain and the British North American colonies, creating and expanding networks of French kin and associates but also further bolstering Dutch and British trading connections and capital. Despite dramatic growth in French sugar imports from the West Indies in the first half of the eighteenth century, an emphasis on slave plantation agriculture produced weaker colonial consumer markets. European settler colonists in North America tended to consume more. Major participants in the fur and sugar trades, French merchants operated under the constraints of small colonial markets, disruptive prejudices, and often unfavourable political policies. [75]

Consumer culture varied based on local conditions not only from one side of the Atlantic to the other, but from empire to empire, and colony to colony within empires. Individuals readily adapted fashions and the meaning of goods to their local environments, ideas and practices.[76] That Africans frequently assigned much higher value than Europeans to manufactured 'baubles', was not a sign of weaknesses, but an indication of the specificity of their local demand structure. Indeed, the terms of the slave trade increasingly favoured and profited those African leaders who played an active part in shaping and controlling it.[77] The French in New France, moreover, lived differently from the Spanish in New Spain and the English in New England, who lived differently from the Dutch in New Netherland, and indeed, from the English in Jamaica.[78] The importance of the intersection of imperial heritage and local conditions in the colonies has been explained by several historians.[79] David Hume's discounting of the effects of climate and geography, and his observation that 'the same set of manners will follow a nation, and adhere to them over the whole globe' captured an imperial ideal that played out differently on the ground.[80]

Nevertheless, in the context of commercial culture such differences should not be overstated. Commerce, trade and centralized production of everything from West Indian sugar to Irish linen, Dutch tulips and British cutlery caused a convergence in the material life of Atlantic consumers, if not for those enslaved. The products available and popular amongst Europeans throughout the Atlantic World, as well as general consumer attitudes, did not differ dramatically. The Dutch in New Amsterdam adapted when conquered by the English, as did the French inhabitants of Grenada after the Seven Years' War. The latter sent a memorial to the British government pledging 'to serve their new country with their persons, their talents, and their Fortunes', requesting only the right to remain Catholic.[81] Such offers were in part about self-preservation, but in offering their fortunes they likely expected to gain from better access to British trading networks and consumer goods.[82] Atlantic merchants eagerly traded with each other across imperial boundaries by legal or illegal means, and eighteenth-century consumers surveyed newspapers overflowing with advertisements boasting of the finest new importations from rival empires.

The origins of the goods were certainly global; nevertheless, the large settler colonies and European- and American-owned slave plantations made this new consumer culture far more prevalent in the Atlantic. By the middle of the eighteenth century thinkers and policy makers in other Atlantic powers saw the British culture of imperial commerce and state support as so successful that they tried to literally and figuratively translate it to their own economic and imperial situations.[83] In early-nineteenth-century Latin America, British merchants replicated in part their own success in North America by importing vast quantities of new mass-produced goods, further spreading the Atlantic consumer economy. By the middle of the century, Britain provided half of all of Brazil's imports. Slowly, India and to a lesser extent China became sizeable consumer markets for European goods. London's merchant bankers meanwhile, such as the Barings and Rothschilds, supported the development of industry and railways throughout the Atlantic and beyond, replicating new patterns and enhancing interconnections.[84] The middle of the nineteenth century marked a new phase characterized by a short-lived but relatively open British commercial framework, and more importantly, dramatic advances in steamship and rail transportation, telegraph communication, industrialization and urbanization across Europe and America.[85] From 1400 to 1850, merchants, consumers, producers and imperial states had transformed the Atlantic from a world of strikingly different cultures into a co-dependent market with a bewildering selection of broadly standardized goods critical for the projection of one's self.

CONCLUSION

All of the major Atlantic powers, including the early United States, traded and warred actively around the globe; the Atlantic was not, as Peter Coclanis has rightly pointed out, completely a world apart.[86] Many polities in Asia had systems of exchange and regional trading networks before seaborne European incursions in the sixteenth century. Due to the strength of their own manufacturing systems and cultures, people in these non-Atlantic networks had little interest in buying Atlantic goods, but they had plenty that people in the Atlantic world wanted. While thus tied to the Middle East, Asia, and Indonesia, people around the Atlantic participated in a shared set of habits and practices of trade, commercial thought and migration-based production and consumption patterns that made up a specific sub-culture.

North and South America, for reasons of disease and technological inequality, provided in European imaginations, if not always in fact, welcoming terrain for mass settlement. Notwithstanding their frequent positions as outcasts, radicals and slaves, Atlantic migrants brought with them many of the ideological and cultural norms of the lands which they left. For European migrants, in particular, this meant extending, adapting and at times re-inventing the cultural patterns of commerce common in Europe. European merchants trading to the Caribbean and North and South America typically found not only eager markets for new world products in Europe, but growing markets for old world products in the Americas and Africa. Yet the Atlantic World was bifurcated in theory if not always in practice by the competing claims of rival peoples and European empires with their own trade policies. European empires, with few exceptions, attempted to constrain trade between empires. Economic warfare went hand-in-glove with military warfare. Also with few exceptions, regulations were difficult to enforce and only partially successful. The similarities, indeed, the interoperability, legally or not, amongst the commercial cultures of all the Atlantic powers from Africa to the USA are too often lost by nationally based histories and by historical questions that emphasize change and difference. While different motivations for expansion, modes of possession, and intellectual currents should not be overlooked, fundamentally, all of the Atlantic powers depended directly on a broadly similar commercial culture for their success and failure.

Before the middle of the nineteenth century the leading imperial powers changed, but the practices of networked private merchants established by the Portuguese in the sixteenth century proved remarkably enduring. A failure to reconcile the commerce conducted by such merchants and the consumption that it supported with moral and political thought in Portugal, Spain and France created dangerous fissures. In the British Atlantic these gaps were bridged with a new market-based morality in an environment boasting a strong central state and support for an expensive navy capable of defending and expanding commerce. As the nineteenth century progressed, Britain expanded its influence in South America, and replicated its North American settlement patterns in Australia and New Zealand, encouraging, often violently, a global commercial culture of private trade. New theories of political economy, business and labour forms, and technologies started a new phase in the middle of the nineteenth century. The Atlantic commercial culture that from the earliest days of Portuguese exploration had transformed and been transformed by the wider world of which it was a part, fell away, taking with it merchants like Boardman and the tortures of slave plantations alike. As

America, Germany, Russia and Japan industrialized, Britain's economic leadership role too fell away. The legacy of the commercial culture of the Early Modern Atlantic, however, has been enduring, not least where fortunes are made and lost in stock markets, shopping malls displace Native American burial grounds and communist ideologies, and the wounds of a commoditized humanity continue to hurt.

Figure 30.1   Ralph Earl, *Elijah Boardman*, 1789
© 2014. Image copyright the Metropolitan Museum of Art/Art Resource/Scala, Florence

NOTES

1 The author thanks the members of the Mellon Workshop on the Global Nineteenth Century at the University of California, Riverside who read and commented most helpfully upon an early draft of this chapter.
2 For earlier colonial American examples of merchant portraits see, Roger B. Stein, *Seascape and the American Imagination*, New York: Clarkson N. Potter, 1975, pp. 10–15. Asian merchants posed in substantially different clothing and did not necessarily see a standing posture as one of authority and confidence. European merchants in Asia also often posed

– CHAPTER 30: *The cultural history of commerce* –

with elements of Asian clothing and decor to signify their position outside of the Atlantic. Hermione de Almeida and George H. Gilpin, *Indian Renaissance: British Romantic Art and the Prospect of India*, Burlington, VT: Ashgate, 2007, p. 72. For an example of a Dutch merchant posing under an Asian umbrella and pointing to his European vessels see, Julie Berger Hochstrasser, *Still Life and Trade in the Dutch Golden Age*, New Haven: Yale University Press, 2007, pp. 116. For an example of a painting of a British merchant with hookahs and other Asian objects see, *Charles D'Oyly*, 1820s, WD 4403, f.40, Asia, Pacific, and Africa Collections, British Library.

3 David Jaffee, 'Changing Modes of Furnishing' in Dena Goodman and Kathryn Norberg (eds), *Furnishing the Eighteenth Century: What Furniture Can Tell Us About the European and American Past*, New York: Routledge, 2006, pp. 82–83; Christopher John Murra, *Encyclopedia of the Romantic Era, 1760–1850*, New York: Taylor & Francis, 2004, p. 895; Eileen Rebeiro, 'Elijah Boardman, 1789', in Elizabeth Mankin Kornhauser *et al.*, *Ralph Earl: The Face of the Young Republic*, New Haven: Yale University Press, 1991, pp. 155–56. Several studies explore the relationship between the Early Republic and Britain's lasting influence. See for examples, Kariann Akemi Yokota, *Unbecoming British: How Revolutionary America Became a Postcolonial Nation*, London: Oxford University Press, 2011; Elisa Tamarkin, *Anglophilia: Deference, Devotion, and Antebellum America*, Chicago: Chicago University Press, 2008.

4 Raymond Williams, *Culture and Society, 1780–1950*, London: Chatto and Windus, pp. xviii, 232–42.

5 John Mein, *A State of Importations From Great-Britain into the Port of Boston*, Boston, 1770, p. 26–27.

6 Victor Lieberman, 'Transcending East-West Dichotomies: State and Culture Formation in Six Ostensibly Disparate Areas', in Victor Lieberman (ed.), *Beyond Binary Histories: Re-Imagining Eurasia to c. 1830*, Ann Arbor: The University of Michigan Press, 1999, 28. For examples of ocean and sea histories, see: Arne Bang-Andersen, Basil Greenhill, Egil Harald Grude (eds), *The North Sea: A Highway of Economic and Cultural Exchange, Character-History*, Stavanger: Norwegian University Press, 1985; Paul Butel, *The Atlantic*, Ian Hamilton Grant (trans.) New York: Routledge, 1999; Satish Chandra (ed.), *The Indian Ocean: Explorations in History, Commerce and Politics*, New Delhi: Sage Publications, 1987; K. N. Chaudhuri, *Trade and Civilisation in the Indian Ocean: An Economic History from the Rise of Islam to 1750*, New York: Cambridge University Press, 1985; Ashin Das Gupta, *India and the Indian Ocean World: Trade and Politics*, New York: Oxford University Press, 2004; Devleena Ghosh and Stephen Muecke, *Cultures of Trade: Indian Ocean Exchanges*, Newcastle: Cambridge Scholars Publishing, 2007; Om Prakash, *Bullion for Goods: European and Indian Merchants in the Indian Ocean Trade, 1500–1800*, New Delhi: Manohar, 2004.

7 For the classic overview see, Charles Boxer, *The Portuguese Seaborne Empire, 1415–1825*, New York: Knopf, 1969, pp. 1–83.

8 M. D. D. Newitt, *A History of Portuguese Overseas Expansion, 1400–1668*, New York: Routledge, 2005, pp. 147–48, 167–69, 180–81; Gunnar Dahl, *Trade, Trust, and Networks: Commercial Culture in Late Medieval Italy*, Lund, Sweden: Nordic Academic Press, 1998; Daniel Goffman, *The Ottoman Empire and Early Modern Europe*, New York: Cambridge University Press, 2002, pp. 169–88. On the role of the Genoese in the Atlantic see, Ruth Pike, *Enterprise and Adventure: The Genoese in Seville and the Opening of the New World*, Ithaca: Cornell University Press, 1966. J. H. Elliott, *Empires of the Atlantic World: Britain and Spain in America, 1492–1830*, New Haven: Yale University Press, 2006, p. 18; Daviken Studnicki-Gizbert, *A Nation Upon the Ocean Sea: Portugal's Atlantic Diaspora and the Crisis of the Spanish Empire, 1492–1640*, New York: Oxford University Press, 2007, pp. 65, 93, 105–30. The Portuguese did use slaves to create products to fuel their trade and

565

also pursued precious metals. The point remains, however, that their focus was dominating global trade in the sixteenth century. Boxer, *Portuguese Seaborne Empire*, pp. 150–57, 308, 318–26. Charles Verlinden, *The Beginnings of Modern Colonization: Eleven Essays with an Introduction*, Yvonne Freccero (trans.) Ithaca: Cornell University Press, 1970, pp. 79–157.

9 Butel, *The Atlantic*, pp. 69–74; Alejandro de la Fuente, César García del Pino, and Bernardo Iglesias Delgado, *Havana and the Atlantic in the Sixteenth Century*, Chapel Hill: University of North Carolina Press, 2008, pp. 51, 64, 120, 127–30, 223–27.

10 Butel, *The Atlantic*, pp. 73, 89–91; Boxer, *Portuguese Seaborne Empire*, pp. 109–15.

11 Kenneth R. Andrews, *Trade, Plunder, and Settlement: Maritime Enterprise and the Genesis of the British Empire, 1480-1630*, New York: Cambridge University Press, 1984, pp. 246–51. On Dutch and French privateers see, Butel, *The Atlantic*, pp. 100–101, 116–17, 130. Philip J. Stern, 'British Asia and British Atlantic: Comparisons and Connections', *William and Mary Quarterly*, 3rd ser., October 2006, vol. 63, no. 4, 694–710.

12 Boxer, *Portuguese Seaborne Empire*, pp. 60–62, 181–85, 222–24, 320–21; Charles Boxer, *The Dutch Seaborne Empire: 1600–1800*, New York: Knopf, 1965, pp. 43–53; Charles Wilson, *England's Apprenticeship, 1603–1763*, 2nd ed., New York: Longman, 1984, pp. 172–76. Kenneth Andrews, *Trade, Plunder and Settlement: Maritime Enterprise and the Genesis of the British Empire, 1480-1630*, New York: Cambridge University Press, 1985, pp. 316, 320–52, 360–61; Stern, 'British Asia and British Atlantic', pp. 694–707. Henk den Heijr, 'The Dutch West India Company, 1621–1791', in Johannes Postma and Victor Enthoven (eds), *Riches from Atlantic Commerce: Dutch Transatlantic Trade and Shipping, 1585–1817*, Boston: Brill, 2003, pp. 77–103.

13 Harold A. Innis, *The Fur Trade in Canada*, 1930, Reprint, Toronto: University of Toronto Press, 2001, pp. 47–48. On the need for export profits in New England see, Dwight B. Heath (ed.), *Mourt's Relation: A Journal of the Pilgrims at Plymouth*, Bedford: Applewood Books, 1963, pp. 16, 21, 33, 40. Additionally, both the Pilgrims and Puritans adopted corporate models to govern the distribution of land seized from native Americans into new towns for profit. John Frederick Martin, *Profits in the Wilderness: Entrepreneurship and the Founding of New England Towns in the Seventeenth Century*, Chapel Hill: Published by the Institute of Early American History and Culture, by the University of North Carolina Press, 1991, pp. 7–37, 79–86.

14 Henk den Heijr, 'Dutch West India Company', in Postma and Enthoven (eds), *Riches from Atlantic Commerce*, pp. 93–103; Victor Enthoven, 'An Assessment of Dutch Transatlantic Commerce, 1585–1817', in Postma and Enthoven (eds), *Riches from Atlantic Commerce*, pp. 387–417. The Marquis of Pombal chartered several new Portuguese monopoly companies to trade to South America in the 1760s. Briefly important, these companies accounted for little of the Atlantic World's overall trade and folded within a few decades; Boxer, *Portuguese Seaborne Empire*, pp. 181–84, 192–93, 227. The Hudson's Bay Company did face competition, particularly from the Northwest Company from 1779 to 1821, when the two companies merged to restore a monopoly position.

15 Christian J. Koot, *Empire at the Periphery: British Colonists, Anglo-Dutch Trade, and the Development of the British Atlantic, 1621–1713*, New York: New York University, 2011, esp. pp. 3–7, 13, 218–27.

16 Richard Sheridan, *Sugar and Slavery, An Economic History of the British West Indies, 1623–1775*, Baltimore: Johns Hopkins University Press, 1974, pp. 97, 397–98; Donna Merwick, *Possessing Albany, 1630-1710: The Dutch and English Experiences*, New York: Cambridge University Press, 2003, pp. 188–285; Edmund S. Morgan, *American Slavery, American Freedom: The Ordeal of Colonial Virginia*, New York: Norton, 1975, pp. 295–315; Lawrence A. Harper, *The English Navigation Laws: A Seventeenth Century Experiment in Social Engineering*, New York: Columbia University Press, 1939, pp. 239, 253; Ian K. Steele, *Politics of Colonial Policy: The Board of Trade in Colonial Administration, 1696–1720*,

– CHAPTER 30: *The cultural history of commerce* –

Oxford: Clarendon, 1968, pp. 10–41; Charles M. Andrews, *The Colonial Period of American History*, New Haven: Yale University Press, 1947, p. 4:64.

17 Ralph Davis, *The Rise of the English Shipping Industry in the Seventeenth and Eighteenth Centuries*, London: Macmillan, 1962, pp. 17, 395–406. On the Dutch see, Johannes Postma and Victor Enthoven 'Introduction', in Postma and Enthoven (eds), *Riches from Atlantic Commerce*, pp. 1–12; Boxer, *Dutch Seaborne Empire*, p. 280.

18 New attention is being paid to these debates. For more see the contributions to, 'Forum: Rethinking Mercantilism,' *William and Mary Quarterly*, 3rd ser., January 2012, vol. 69, no. 1, 3–70.

19 Harper, *English Navigation Laws*, pp. 387–414; Davis, *English Shipping*, p. 393; William Ashworth, *Customs and Excise: Trade, Production, and Consumption in England, 1640–1845*, London: Oxford University, 2003, pp. 5–205; John Brewer, *The Sinews of Power: War, Money and the English State, 1688–1783*, London: Unwin Hyman, 1989; Koot, *Empire at the Periphery*, p. 185; James Pritchard, *In Search of Empire: The French in the Americas, 1670–1730*, New York: Cambridge University Press, 2004, pp. 192–93.

20 Woodrow Borah, 'The Mixing of Populations', and Magnus Mörner, 'Spanish Migration to the New World Prior to 1800', in Fredi Chiappelli (ed), *First Images of America*, 2 vols, Berkeley: University of California Press, 1976, pp. 2:707–22 and 737–82. On native American enslavement see for examples, Brett Rushforth, *Bonds of Alliance: Indigenous and Atlantic Slaveries in New France*, Chapel Hill: Published for the Institute of Early American History and Culture, by the University of North Carolina Press, 2012; Alan Gallay, *The Indian Slave Trade: The Rise of the English Empire in the American South, 1670–1717*, New Haven: Yale University Press, 2002; William L. Sherman, *Forced Native Labor in Sixteenth-Century Central America*, Lincoln: University of Nebraska, 1979; Stuart B. Schwartz, 'Indian Labor and New World Plantations: European Demands and Indian Responses in Northeastern Brazil', *American Historical Review*, February 1978, vol. 83, no. 1, 43–79. Estimates of African enslavement numbers vary; see, Paul E. Lovejoy, 'The Volume of the Atlantic Slave Trade: A Synthesis', *Journal of African History*, 1982, vol. 23, no. 4, 494–500; Paul E. Lovejoy, *Transformations in Slavery: A History of Slavery in Africa*, 2nd ed, Cambridge: Cambridge University Press, 2000, p. 19. For a brief overview of the Afroeurasian slave trade see, Pier M. Larson, 'African Diasporas and the Atlantic', in Jorge Cañizares-Esguerra and Erik R. Seeman (eds), *The Atlantic in Global History, 1500–2000*, Upper Saddle River, NJ: Pearson, 2007, pp. 134–35. For European Indian Ocean forced migration and enslavement of Africans and others see, Richard B. Allen, 'Satisfying the "Want for Labouring People": European Slave Trading in the Indian Ocean, 1500–1850', *Journal of World History*, 2010, vol. 21, no. 1, 59–68.

21 P. K. O'Brien and S. L. Engermen, 'Exports and the Growth of the British Economy from the Glorious Revolution to the Peace of Amiens', in Barbara L. Solow (ed) *Slavery and the Rise of the Atlantic System*, New York: Cambridge University Press, 1994, pp. 180–99.

22 Youssef Cassis, *Capitals of Capital: A History of International Financial Centres, 1780–2005*, Jacqueline Collier (trans.), New York: Cambridge University Press, 2006, pp. 9–24; Simon Schama, *The Embarrassment of Riches: An Interpretation of Dutch Culture in the Golden Age*, New York: Knopf, 1987, pp. 345–50; Boxer, *Dutch Seaborne Empire*, pp. 19–20.

23 Marcus Rediker, *Between the Devil and the Deep Blue Sea: Merchant Seamen, Pirates, and the Anglo-American Maritime World, 1700–1750*, New York: Cambridge University Press, 1987, p. 21; Davis, *English Shipping*, pp. 34–36, 390; Wilson, *England's Apprenticeship*, p. 176; Neil McKendrick, 'The Consumer Revolution in Eighteenth-Century England', in Neil McKendrick, John Brewer, and J. H. Plumb (eds), *The Birth of a Consumer Society*, Bloomington: Indiana University Press, 1982, p. 21; Natasha Glaisyer, *The Culture of Commerce in England, 1660–1720*, London: Boydell, 2006, pp. 27–36; John J. McCusker and C. Gravesteijn, *The Beginnings of Commercial and Financial Journalism*, Amsterdam:

Rodopi, 1991, pp. 292–326; Larry Neal, 'The Rise of a Financial Press: London and Amsterdam, 1681–1810', *Business History*, April 1988, vol. 30, no. 2, 165–75.

24 David Hancock, *Citizens of the World: London Merchants and the Integration of the British Atlantic Community, 1735-1785*, New York: Cambridge University Press, 1995, p. 385; Thomas M. Doerflinger, *A Vigorous Spirit of Enterprise: Merchants and Economic Development in Revolutionary Philadelphia*, Chapel Hill: Published for the Institute of Early American History and Culture, by the University of North Carolina Press, 1986, p. 128; Phyllis Hunter, *Purchasing Identity in the Atlantic World: Massachusetts Merchants, 1670-1780*, Ithaca: Cornell University Press, 2001, p. 131.

25 Ian K. Steele, *The English Atlantic, 1675–1740: An Exploration of Communication and Community*, New York: Oxford University Press, 1986, pp. 1–93; Hancock, *Citizens of the World*, pp. 86–89; Doerflinger, *Vigorous Spirit*, pp. 41–47; Hunter, *Purchasing Identity*, p. 87; Jacob Price, 'Economic Function and the Growth of American Port Towns in the Eighteenth Century', *Perspectives in American History*, 1974, vol. 8, 130–70. Historians have debated the shifting importance of commissions; see, R. C. Nash, 'The Organization of Trade and Finance in the British Atlantic Economy, 1600–1830', in Peter Coclanis (ed), *The Atlantic Economy During the Seventeenth and Eighteenth Centuries: Organization, Operation, Practice, and Personnel*, Columbia: University of South Carolina Press, 2005, pp. 95–133.

26 Margaret R. Hunt, *The Middling Sort: Commerce, Gender, and the Family in England, 1680–1780*, Berkeley: University of California, 1996, pp. 125–46; Julie Hardwick, *Family Business: Litigation and the Political Economies of Daily Life in Early Modern France*, New York: Oxford University Press, 2009, pp. 128–33.

27 Hancock, *Citizens of the World*, pp. 89–101; Boxer, *Dutch Seaborne Empire*, pp. 282–83; Jacob M. Price, 'Directions for the Conduct of a Merchant's Counting House, 1766', *Business History*, July 1986, vol. 28, no. 3, 134–37. Studnicki-Gizbert, *Nation Upon the Ocean Sea*, p. 81; John F. Bosher, 'Success and Failure in Trade to New France', *French Historical Studies*, 1988, vol. 15, no. 3, 455–56.

28 Leonore Davidoff and Catherine Hall, *Family Fortunes: Men and Women of the English Middle Class, 1780–1850*, Chicago: University of Chicago Press, 1987, pp. 149–270, 357–60.

29 Craig Muldrew, *Economy of Obligation: The Culture of Credit and Social Relations in Early Modern England*, New York: St. Martin's, 1998, pp. 4, 148–49, 311; Bosher, 'Trade to New France', pp. 452–55. For examples of merchant advice guides see, Daniel Defoe, *The Complete English Tradesman*, London: Charles Rivington, 1727; Benjamin Franklin, 'Advice to a Young Tradesman', in *Works of the Late Doctor Benjamin Franklin, Consisting of His Life Written by Himself; Together with Essays, Humorous, Moral, and Literary, Chiefly in the Manner of the Spectator*, London: G. Dilly, 1796, pp. 39–42; Jacques Savary, *Le parfait negociant ou Instruction generale pour ce qui regarde le commerce de toute sorte de marchandises, tant de France que des pays estrangers*, Paris: Chez L. Billaine, 1675.

30 Studnicki-Gizbert, *Nation Upon the Ocean Sea*, pp. 65, 85–87; Hancock, *Citizens of the World*, pp. 258–376; Peter France, 'The Commerce of Self', *Comparative Criticism*, vol. 12, Cambridge: Cambridge University Press, 1990, pp. 39–56; in colonial ports, such as Charleston such ideals were grafted onto local conditions and planter societies; Emma Hart, *Building Charleston: Town and Society in the Eighteenth-Century British Atlantic World*, London: University of Virginia, 2010, pp. 125, 132–41, 156–76.

31 Margot C. Finn, *The Character of Credit: Personal Debt in English Culture, 1740–1914*, New York: Cambridge University Press, 2003, pp. 3, 17–18; Hardwick, *Family Business*, pp. 136–60, 169–78.

32 Hancock, *Citizens of the World*, pp. 292–95.

33 Elliott, *Empires of the Atlantic*, pp. 94–95; John J. McCusker, *Money and Exchange in Europe and America, 1600–1771. A Handbook*, Chapel Hill: Published for the Institute

– CHAPTER 30: *The cultural history of commerce* –

of Early American History and Culture, by the University of North Carolina Press, 1978, pp. 18–23, 116–30, 234–35.

34 Hayes and Polock to Harford and Powell, 17 May 1769, Box 2, Henry Marchant Papers, Mss 552, Rhode Island Historical Society.

35 Defoe, *Complete English Tradesman*, pp. 1:Supplement, 3–4; Bosher, 'Trade to New France', p. 451.

36 Hardwick, *Family Business*, pp. 133–35; Hunt, *Middling Sort*, pp. 23–34.

37 Steele, *English Atlantic*.

38 Cassis, *Capitals of Capital*, pp. 17–18; Davis, *English Shipping*, pp. 318–19; Bosher, 'Trade to New France', pp. 447–49.

39 Hunt, *Middling Sort*, pp. 34, 164–66; Peter Razzell and Christine Spence, 'The Hazards of Wealth: Adult Mortality in Pre-Twentieth-Century England', *Social History of Medicine*, 2006, vol. 19, no. 3, 381–405; Muldrew, *Economy of Obligation*, p. 61.

40 Boxer, *Dutch Seaborne Empire*, pp. 6, 19; Pike, *Enterprise and Adventure*, pp. 76–77; Davis, *English Shipping*, pp. 81–102; Holden Furber, *John Company at Work*, Cambridge: Harvard University Press, 1951, p. 275; GD1/453/1, National Archives of Scotland cited in Huw Bowen, *Business of Empire: The East India Company and Imperial Britain, 1756–1833*, Cambridge: Cambridge University Press, 2006, p. 284; Lucy Sutherland, *A London Merchant, 1695–1774*, London: Frank Cass, 1962, pp. 119–22. Studnicki-Gizbert, *Nation upon the Ocean Sea*, pp. 59–61.

41 Rediker, *Between the Devil*, pp. 10–13; Studnicki-Gizbert, *Nation upon the Ocean Sea*, p. 61; Boxer, *Dutch Seaborne Empire*, pp. 67–68.

42 Hoh-Cheung Mui and Lorna Mui, *Shops and Shopkeeping in Eighteenth-Century England*, Montreal: McGill-Queen's University Press, 1989; A. J. and R. H. Tawney, 'An Occupational Census of the Seventeenth Century', *Economic History Review*, 1934–35, vol. 5, no. 1, 30–39; Georgio Riello, *A Foot in the Past: Consumers, Producers and Footwear in the Long Eighteenth Century*, New York: Oxford University Press, 2006, pp. 95–98, 110; John Stobart, Andrew Hann, and Victoria Morgan, *Spaces of Consumption: Leisure and Shopping in the English Town, c. 1680–1830*, New York: Routledge, 2007; Claire Walsh, 'Shop Design and the Display of Goods in Eighteenth-Century London', *Journal of Design History*, 1995, vol. 8, no. 3, 157–76.

43 Colin Jones and Rebecca Spang, 'Sans-culottes, *sans café, sans tabac*: Shifting Realms of Necessity and Luxury in Eighteenth-Century France', in Maxine Berg and Helen Clifford (eds), *Consumers and Luxury: Consumer Culture in Europe, 1650–1850*, Manchester: Manchester University Press, 1999, p. 49; Timothy Breen, *The Marketplace of Revolution: How Consumer Politics Shaped American Independence*, New York: Oxford University Press, 2004, pp. 118–47.

44 Michael Edwards, *The Growth of the British Cotton Trade 1780–1815*, Manchester: Manchester University Press, 1967, pp. 147–80. German merchants tied to German producers in the pre-factory period performed a similar role to British manufacturers' agents; see, Klaus Weber, 'The Atlantic Coast of German Trade: German Rural Industry and Trade in the Atlantic (1680–1840)', *Itinerario*, 2002, vol. 26, no. 2, 108–13.

45 Glaisyer, *The Culture of Commerce*, pp. 18, 86–95.

46 Henry C. Clark, *Compass of Society: Commerce and Absolutism in Old-Regime France*, New York: Lexington Books, 2007, pp. 4, 8.

47 Studnicki-Gizbert, *Nation Upon the Ocean Sea*, pp. 119–31, 157–78.

48 Laure Chantrel, 'Les Notions de richesse et de travail dans in la pensée économique français da la seconde moitié du XVIe et au début du XVIIe siècle', *Journal of Medieval and Renaissance Studies*, Winter, 1995, vol. 25, no. 1, 129–245.

49 Clark, *Compass of Society*, pp. 4, 8.

50 Blair Hoxby, *Mammon's Music: Literature and Economics in the Age of Milton*, New Haven: Yale University Press, 2002, pp. 106, 191.

51 Schama, *Embarrassment of Riches*, pp. 295–99, 326–40.

52 Hochstrasser, *Still Life and Trade*, pp. 144–45, 264–75; Luís de Moura Sobral, 'The Expansion of the Arts: Transfers, Contaminations, Innovations,' in Fransisco Bethencourt and Diogo Ramada Curto (eds), *Portuguese Oceanic Expansion, 1400–1800*, New York: Cambridge University Press, 2007, pp. 390–459.

53 For examples of Reinier Nooms' work see, George S. Keyes (ed.), *Mirror of Empire: Dutch Marine Art of the Seventeenth Century*, New York: The Minneapolis Institute of Arts in Association with Cambridge University Press, 1990, pp. 301–12, 413; Hendrick Vroom's *View of the River Ij Near Amsterdam* reproduced in Jeroen Giltaij and Jan Kelch, *Praise of Ships and the Sea: The Dutch Marine Painters of the 17th Century*, Rotterdam: Museum Boijmans Van Beuningen; Berlin: Staatliche Museen zu Berlin, 1996, p. 93.

54 David Ormrod, *The Rise of Commercial Empires: England and the Netherlands in the Age of Mercantilism, 1650–1770*, New York: Cambridge University Press, 2003, pp. 9–27, 64, 337–50.

55 Muldrew, *Economy of Obligation*, pp. 134–47, 319–20; Hoxby, *Mammon's Music*, pp. 92–105; Steven Pincus, *Protestantism and Patriotism: Ideologies and the Making of English Foreign Policy, 1650–1668*, New York: Cambridge University Press, 1996, 24–79, 172–84; Richard Kroll, *Restoration Drama and 'The Circle of Commerce': Tragicomedy, Politics, and Trade in the Seventeenth Century*, New York: Cambridge University Press, 2007, pp. 1–8, 59–61, 234.

56 Glaisyer, *Culture of Commerce*, p. 86; Liz Bellamy, *Commerce, Morality, and the Eighteenth-Century Novel*, New York: Cambridge University Press, 1998, pp. 2–3, 13–21; J. G. A Pocock, *The Machiavellian Moment: Florentine Political Thought and the Atlantic Republican Tradition*, Princeton: Princeton University Press, 1975, pp. 462–505; Hoxby, *Mammon's Music*, pp. 20, 233–35; Sandra Sherman, *Finance and Fictionality in the Early Eighteenth Century: Accounting for Defoe*, New York: Cambridge University Press, 1996, pp. 3–4, 26–40; Thomas Keith Meier, *Defoe and the Defense of Commerce*, Victoria, Canada: University of Victoria, 1987, pp. 84–88; Schama, *Embarrassment of Riches*, p. 297.

57 Maxine Berg, 'From Imitation to Invention: Creating Commodities in Eighteenth-Century Britain', *Economic History Review*, 2002, vol. 55, no. 1, 2–3; Maxine Berg, 'In Pursuit of Luxury: Global History and British Consumer Goods in the Eighteenth Century', *Past & Present*, February 2004, no. 182, 94–95. On the endurance of concerns about luxury and their new manifestations, see James Raven, *Judging New Wealth: Popular Publishing and Responses to Commerce in England, 1750–1800*, Oxford: Clarendon, 1992, pp. 157–200.

58 Meier, *Defoe and the Defense of Commerce*, pp. 31, 40–42; Boyd Hilton, *The Age of Atonement: The Influence of Evangelicalism on Social and Economic Thought, 1795–1865*, Oxford: Clarendon, 1988, pp. viii, 13–15, 50, 126–33, 209–10; Margaret C. Jacob, *Scientific Culture and the Making of the Industrial West*, New York: Oxford University Press, 1997, pp. 73–80; Margaret C. Jacob, *The Radical Enlightenment: Pantheists, Freemasons and Republicans*, Boston: Allen & Unwin, 1981, pp. 81–88. It is important to note that what many political economists saw as limited government intervention was in fact substantial government intervention, but of a different kind than in sixteenth-century Spain or the twentieth-century Soviet Union; Karl Polanyi, *The Great Transformation*, New York: Rinehart, 1944, p. 139.

59 A. S. Catcott, *The Antiquity and Honourableness of the Practice of Merchandize. A Sermon Preached Before the Worshipful Society of Merchants of the City of Bristol, in the Parish Church of St. Stephen, November the 10th, 1744* (Bristol, 1744).

60 Breen, *Marketplace of Revolution*, pp. 151–85. Jonathan Eacott, 'Trading Language: British Merchants and Political Economy Between 1793–1815', MA Thesis, Queen's University, Kingston, 2001, pp. 55–76; Alderman Wray, quoted in *East India Trade. Report of the Proceedings of the Meeting at Kingston-Upon-Hull, 6th April, 1812, on the Subject of Laying Open the Trade to the East Indies*, Hull: J. Perkins, 1812, p. 7.

– CHAPTER 30: *The cultural history of commerce* –

61 Christopher Leslie Brown, *Moral Capital: Foundations of British Abolitionism*, Chapel Hill: Published for the Omohundro Institute of Early American History and Culture, by the University of North Carolina Press, 2006, pp. 27, 37–116, 158–59, 233–37, 326–27; G. R. Searle, *Morality and the Market in Victorian Britain*, Oxford: Clarendon, 1998, pp. 48–64.

62 Doerflinger, *Vigorous Spirit*, p. 60; James B. Collins, 'State Building in Early Modern Europe: The Case of France', in Lieberman (ed.), *Beyond Binary Histories*, p. 187. Chandra Mukerji, *From Graven Images: Patterns of Modern Materialism*, New York: Columbia University Press, 1983, p. 182. For an example of religiously enforced sumptuary laws functioning outside the state, albeit briefly, see Paul E. Johnson and Sean Wilentz, *The Kingdom of Matthias*, New York: Oxford University Press, 1995, pp. 31–33.

63 Guadalipe Jiménez Codinach, 'An Atlantic Silver Entrepôt: Vera Cruz and the House of Gordon Murphy' in Franklin W. Knight and Peggy K. Liss (eds), *Atlantic Port Cities: Economy, Culture, and Society in the Atlantic World, 1650–1850*, Knoxville: University of Tennessee Press, 1991, pp. 149–50; Lance R. Grahn, 'Cartagena and its Hinterland in the Eighteenth Century', in Knight and Liss (eds), *Atlantic Port Cities*, pp. 168–88; Jacob M. Price, 'Summation: The American Panorama of Atlantic Port Cities', in Knight and Liss (eds), *Atlantic Port Cities*, p. 267.

64 Mukerji, *From Graven Images*; Schama, *Embarrassment of Riches*, pp. 304, 314–18; Carole Shammas, *The Pre-Industrial Consumer in England and America*, Oxford: Clarendon, 1990; Lorna Weatherill, *Consumer Behaviour and Material Culture in Britain, 1660-1760*, New York: Routledge, 1988; Cissie Fairchilds, 'The Production and Marketing of Populuxe Goods in Eighteenth-Century Paris', in Roy Porter and John Brewer (eds), *Consumption and the World of Goods*, New York: Routledge, 1992.

65 On slavery in the cutting of mahogany see, Jennifer Anderson, *Mahogany: The Costs of Luxury in Early America*, London: Harvard University Press, 2012, pp. 156–83.

66 Jordan Goodman, 'Excitantia: Or, How Enlightenment Europe took to Soft Drugs', in Jordan Goodman (ed), *Consuming Habits: Drugs in History and Anthropology*, London: Routledge, 1995, pp. 126–33; Butel, *The Atlantic*, pp. 133–38; Marcy Norton, *Sacred Gifts, Profane Pleasures: A History of Tobacco and Chocolate in the Atlantic World*, Ithaca: Cornell University Press, 2008, pp. 141–200.

67 David Hancock, 'Commerce and Conversation in the Eighteenth-century Atlantic: The Invention of Madeira Wine', *Journal of Interdisciplinary History*, Autumn, 1998, vol. 29, no. 2, 197; see also, David Hancock, *Oceans of Wine: Madeira and the Emergence of American Trade and Taste*, London: Yale University Press, 2009, pp. 144–71.

68 Cary Carson, 'The Consumer Revolution in Colonial British America: Why Demand?' in Cary Carson, Ronald Hoffman, and Peter J. Albert (eds), *Of Consuming Interests*, Charlottesville: Published for the United States Capitol Historical Society by the University Press of Virginia, 1994, p. 487.

69 On the Dutch as first see Schama, *Embarrassment of Riches*, 323.

70 Luiz Felipe de Alencastro, 'The Apprenticeship of Colonisation' in Solow (ed), *Slavery*, p. 151.

71 Carson, 'Consumer Revolution' in Carson, Hoffman, and Albert (eds), *Consuming Interests*, pp. 502, 513; Shammas, *Pre-Industrial Consumer*, p. 44.

72 The many white migrants who entered America as indentured servants had little initial choice and power in the colonies. After their period of service was finished, these migrants typically had opportunities for advancement. Virginia Anderson, *New England's Generation*, Cambridge: Cambridge University Press, 1993, pp. 104–9; Marianne Wokeck, *Trade in Strangers: The Beginnings of Mass Migration to North America*, University Park: Pennsylvania State University Press, 1999, p. 192; Bernard Bailyn, *The Peopling of British North America*, New York: Alfred A. Knopf, 1986, pp. 60–64.

73 Timothy Breen, '"Baubles of Britain": The American and Consumer Revolutions of the Eighteenth Century', *Past & Present*, 1988, vol. 119, no. 1, 82–83; Shammas, *Pre-Industrial*

Consumer, p. 62; Lois Carr, Russell Menard, and Lorena Walsh, *Robert Cole's World: Agriculture and Society in Early Maryland*, Chapel Hill: Published for the Institute of Early American History and Culture, by the University of North Carolina Press, 1991, p. 85.

74 Jacob M. Price, 'What did the Merchants Do? Reflections on British Overseas Trade, 1660–1790', *Journal of Economic History*, 1989, vol. 49, no. 2, 274.

75 Pritchard, *In Search of Empire*, pp. 189–229; Butel, *The Atlantic*, p. 132; Marc Engel, *Divergent Paths: How Culture and Institutions Have Shaped North American Growth*, New York: Oxford University Press, 1996, pp. 71–72; François Crouzet, 'Angleterre et France au XVIIIe siècle, essai d'analyse comparée de leurs croissances économique', *Annales ESC*, March-April 1966, pp. 261–66; Richard Drayton, 'The Globalisation of France: Provincial Cities and French Expansion c. 1500–1800', *History of European Ideas*, 2008, vol. 34, no. 4, 427–28. John F. Bosher, 'Huguenot Merchants and the Protestant International in the Seventeenth Century', *William and Mary Quarterly*, 3rd ser., January 1995, vol. 52, no. 1, 77–102; R. C. Nash, 'The Huguenot Diaspora and the Development of the Atlantic Economy: Huguenots and the Growth of the South Carolina Economy, 1680–1775', in Olaf Uwe Janzen (ed) *Merchant Organization and Maritime Trade in the North Atlantic, 1660–1815*, St. John's, Newfoundland: Research in Maritime History, 1998, pp. 75–105; Price, 'What did the Merchants Do?', pp. 270–71.

76 Breen, '"Baubles of Britain"', p. 82.

77 David Eltis, 'Precolonial Western Africa and the Atlantic Economy', in Solow (ed.), *Slavery*, pp. 102–18; David Eltis, *The Rise of African Slavery in the Americas*, Cambridge: Cambridge University Press, 2000, pp. 131–70.

78 For a most concise and wide ranging, if too neatly compartmentalized overview of the translation of national European ideals to the Americas see, Patricia Seed, *Ceremonies of Possession in Europe's Conquest of the New World, 1492–1640*, New York: Cambridge University Press, 1995. The classic work on the similarities and differences amongst British colonies is, Jack P. Greene, *Pursuits of Happiness: The Social Development of Early Modern British Colonies and the Formation of American Culture*, Chapel Hill: University of North Carolina Press, 1988. On the English and Dutch in New Netherland see, Merwick, *Possessing Albany*. For the English compared to the Spanish see, Elliott, *Empires of the Atlantic*.

79 For a brief overview see, Elliott, *Empires of the Atlantic*, pp. xiv–xvii.

80 David Hume, *Essays, Moral, Political, and Literary*, 1742, pt I, essay XXI, par. 10–19. On a later British imperialist desire to replicate national European hierarchies see, David Cannadine, *Ornamentalism: How the British Saw Their Empire*, New York: Oxford University Press, 2001, p. xix.

81 'Memorial of the French Inhabitants of the Island of Grenada', Shelburne Papers, vol. 74, Clements Library, University of Michigan, Ann Arbor.

82 On the difficulties of commerce in the French empire and the benefits of trade with the British and Dutch see, Pritchard, *In Search of Empire*, pp. 201–29.

83 Sophus A. Reinert, *Translating Empire: Emulation and the Origins of Political Economy*, London: Harvard University, 2011, esp. pp. 13–16, 51–69, 136–42.

84 François Crouzet, 'Angleterre-Brésil, 1697–1850: Un siècle et demi d'échanges commerciaux', *Histoire, économie et société*, 1990, vol. 9, no. 2, 304–10. On British informal imperialism in Latin America see, Mathew Brown (ed.), *Informal Empire in Latin America: Culture, Commerce and Capital*, Oxford: Blackwell, 2008. On merchant bankers see, Stanley Chapman, *The Rise of Merchant Banking*, Abingdon: Routledge, 1984.

85 Kevin H. O'Rourke and Jeffrey G. Williamson, *Globalization and History: The Evolution of a Nineteenth-Century Atlantic Economy*, Cambridge, Mass.: MIT Press, 1999, pp. 29–55, 120, 286–87.

86 Peter A. Coclanis, 'Atlantic World or Atlantic/World?' *William and Mary Quarterly*, 3rd ser., October 2006, vol. 63, no. 4, 725–42.

CHAPTER THIRTY-ONE

'TO CATCH THE PUBLIC TASTE'
Interpreting American consumers in the era of Atlantic free trade, 1783–1854

———•◆•———

Joanna Cohen

In June 1853, George Wallis and several colleagues arrived in New York City, to conduct research on the state of American manufactures for the British government.[1] Their plan was to visit the New York Crystal Palace Exhibition, a vast display of American national industry. Intended to rival the great exhibition that had taken place in London only two years earlier, the New York Crystal Palace trumpeted America's industrial skill and proclaimed their free trade commitments to a watching world.[2] Unfortunately, this ambitious exhibition did not get off to a good start. Arriving in Gotham in good time for the grand opening, Wallis and his fellow travelers discovered the exhibition had been delayed by a month.[3] Undaunted, they chose to embark on a tour of the United States, hoping to see first hand the state of American manufacturing.[4]

Wallis approached this trip from an unusual perspective. As the headmaster of the National School of Design in Birmingham, his interest was not in the mechanical innovations or patented inventions that Americans had showcased in the London exhibition of 1851. Instead, Wallis wanted to see what he could of American taste and style. Travelling throughout New England and the mid-Atlantic, Wallis pored over cottons, woolens, worsteds, silks, lace, printed fabrics, tapestries and carpets as well as a variety of cutlery, edge tools, hardware, precious metalwork and ceramics, decorative furniture and even clothing. In short, he examined the full gamut of consumer goods that Americans made at midcentury.[5]

Within this context, Wallis was especially interested in the transatlantic relationships between British manufacturers and the American market. 'English manufacturers,' he mused, 'have it especially in their power to either assist in the formation of a purer taste in the American people, or by neglecting their growing judgment, to oppose, and retard but not crush it. By assisting its development they are likely to secure to themselves, or at least, share very largely in a market for a long time almost entirely their own, but which is gradually being occupied by their Transatlantic competitors.'[6] As one of the breed of emerging professional tastemakers in Britain, it was unsurprising that Wallis should have been interested in the development of American taste. But what was surprising was his belief that British manufacturers had a capacity to influence American taste through their productions and in doing so capture a foreign market. Such a supposition suggested that despite

573

nearly seventy years of American independence, men like Wallis still hoped to achieve a very specific cultural dominance in the United States that would work to serve Britain's political economy.[7]

Wallis's faith in the power of taste to influence the nature of transatlantic trade appeared confident. But in fact his comment revealed the questions that many Britons shared about how commerce would work in a world that was slowly embracing the tenets of free trade.[8] While exhibitions such as those in London and New York promised cooperation and commitment to the international project of free trade, these same exhibitions were competitive arenas, where the challenges of contending for international markets was abundantly clear. Embedded in Wallis's call for manufacturers to shape the taste of the American people was a concern that as markets became less protected and more integrated, a nation's ability to capture the taste of foreign consumers would become a far harder proposition.

Such concerns were well established by the 1850s. Even before these vivid expositions had been staged, some British manufacturers recognized that the only solution to this particular challenge of free trade would be to tailor their production in order 'to catch the public taste.'[9] Yet the project of catering to the consumer was not one that came easily to the tastemakers of Victorian Britain. The standards of taste had long been considered markers of civility and morality in England and the principles of design helped to constitute national pride and commercial prowess. Thus when men like Wallis suggested dictating the standards of taste to foreign consumers he was not just responding to concerns that England might lose its competitive edge, he was also trying to combat fears that bowing to foreign consumer demand could fundamentally alter the identity of a nation. This was the cultural conundrum of free trade philosophy.

Scholars have long recognized that implementing the tenets of free trade posed a problem for Victorian Britons and have explored the ways in which British politicians, diplomats and reformers worked to promote national interest while implementing the new framework of laissez-faire policy.[10] Free trade has also captured the attention of intellectual historians, who have done important work in tracing out the intricacies of theoretical debate that blossomed out of liberal doctrine in the eighteenth and nineteenth century.[11] But fewer historians have looked at the ways in which a different group comprising artists, designers, manufacturers and civil servants like Wallis grappled with the problems that free trade and foreign consumer taste posed for British politicians and manufacturers.[12] These men were confronted with the opposing demands of cosmopolitan commerce and patriotic production, and found no way to satisfy the claims of both. Looking beyond the familiar grounds of trade negotiations on the one hand and the intellectual debates over doctrine on the other, this essay illuminates how anxieties over national aesthetics complicated the implementation of free trade in the nineteenth century, shedding new light on the way in which the men and women of the Atlantic World understood the changing nature of capitalist markets.

Eighteenth- and nineteenth-century commentaries on the nature of consumer goods often characterized commodities as weapons in a war for commercial advantage. One anonymous American woman argued in 1786 that a vain female desire for consumer goods 'enfeebled [her] country with more speedy destruction than it was in the power of foreign arms to accomplish.'[13] Indeed, the idea gained traction over the course of the nineteenth century. Marx and Engels dubbed cheap commodities 'the artillery'

– CHAPTER 31: *American consumers in an era of Atlantic free trade* –

with which the free trade bourgeoisie battered down all commercial protections.[14] But such characterizations obscure the multilateral power of consumer goods. Goods were far more than weapons in the hands of the producers. British commodities, sold in America, were vehicles of taste and makers of identity, which carried cultural influence both ways and not always in a manner that the British found reassuring.[15] Catering to the tastes of Americans, manufacturers confronted the ways in which free trade opened up their own nation to the influences and preferences of foreign demands, subtly testing articulations of British national identity as well as the very idea of what national borders could in fact contain and protect.[16]

LONDON AND ABROAD: METROPOLITAN TASTE IN THE LATE EIGHTEENTH CENTURY

Long before George Wallis would puzzle over the preferences of Americans, Britons around the empire attempted to understand the slippery concept of taste. By the close of the eighteenth century, debates over the meaning and definition of the term dominated the realm of public and private discussion in Britain and America.[17] It was, as Edmund Burke suggested, a word 'like all other figurative terms...not extremely accurate...liable to uncertainty and confusion'.[18] In purely philosophical terms, understandings of taste had been subtly rethought over the space of several decades. Thinkers from Lord Shaftesbury and David Hume to Immanuel Kant, slowly introduced the idea that beauty and taste, far from being fixed measures, might be learned, subjective and even variable, cultivated best through the pursuit of politeness.[19] Theorists such as William Hogarth and Adam Smith added a different dimension to this debate. In *The Theory of Moral Sentiments* Smith acknowledged the effect that the mutable standards of fashion and custom might have on taste while Hogarth, writing in 1735 attempted to make a case for an aesthetics that was based on sensation and pleasure, rather than moral judgement.[20] Such arguments located the formation of taste in realms that were changeable and personal. It allowed for a diversity of taste that was new. Despite their many differences, by the end of the eighteenth century, these thinkers had de-stabilized aesthetic certainties and come to define the judgement of taste as a subjective and sensuous response to the material world.

Despite the shifting intellectual grounds upon which the idea of taste now stood, late eighteenth-century elite society remained convinced that good taste, when correctly identified, reflected a virtuous use of wealth. Those who possessed taste also possessed an ability to steer clear of the perils of excessive consumption.[21] Poor taste, most often identified through a person's indulgence in luxury goods, was a clear indication that an individual had succumbed to immoral, sensuous consumer habits. This elite conviction was reflected broadly across a cultural landscape of jeremiads, sermons, novels and satires. Yet the sheer proliferation of these cultural forms, most often summed up as the 'luxury debates' indicated that as commercial society grew, luxury itself had become an indeterminate category, both in conceptual and material terms.[22] Manifested in the seemingly endless production of novelties, baubles and trinkets that could adorn both bodies and homes, luxury consumer goods included calicoes and silks, porcelain and silverware, ribbons, shawls, teapots and sugar tongs.[23] Faced with this bewildering array of goods, eighteenth-century theorists and thinkers used the discourse of taste to give polite society a set of principles on how to

575

reconcile the aesthetic and moral realm with the baser demands of the commercial world.[24] Thus, taste was simultaneously an acknowledged reflection of morality and subjective expression of judgement, a tension that was reflected in the many anxious musings on the subject.

These tensions were heightened further still by the nationalist inflection embedded in the discussion of taste and design from the mid eighteenth century onwards. The rise of nationalist sentiment was not a solely British concern; indeed the interest in national culture and patriotic productions in Britain was matched by an equally pressing preoccupation with the same in France.[25] The competition over whose culture was the more superior only served to clarify differences and sharpen expressions of nationalistic pride. In Britain, concerns that elite Francoplihia was corrupting national tastes, manners and morals, manifested in a number of ways, including the active promotion of British manufactures and design to combat the French infiltration of British society. The Anti-Gallician Association, founded in 1754 by a collection of tradesmen, connected the cultivation of British design with increased national commercial strength. Similarly, the Society of Arts worked hard to promote technical innovations in British manufacturing, offering premiums for innovative product design and technological improvement.[26] This was in many ways a culture war, with both taste and technology acting as weapons in a battle to claim national supremacy. By the end of the eighteenth century, tradesmen and artisans argued that the production of tasteful goods could and should reflect national pride and commercial prowess.

The nationalist dimensions of these debates raised a series of questions over taste in Britain's Atlantic World empire. Between the Act of Union and the Seven Years War, trade between Britain and its colonial outposts expanded in astounding ways, with 95 per cent of the increase in Britain's commodity exports being sold to 'captive and colonial markets'.[27] This energetic exportation of 'British baubles' was not just the basis of a commercial ascendancy for Britain. It was also the foundation of a powerful new expression of British identity in the colonies, especially in North America, connecting consumers from Boston to Charleston back to London, through a shared taste for everything from textiles to teapots.[28] Many colonial followers of fashion looked to London for their standards of style and through this aesthetic expression, reinforced their own connection to a national identity they were proud to claim. But these same consumers of Britain's Atlantic World empire also posed a challenge to the elite tastemakers of London. British North Americans may have followed London fashions but they did not slavishly copy them. Through articulations of their different preferences and their distinctive demands, these colonial consumers subtly tested the idea that national taste emanated only from the metropole.[29]

The differing standards of taste in the colonies was no secret in late eighteenth-century England. Indeed, for some, this difference was old news. Merchants who shipped British manufactures and East India goods to the West Indies and North America had long been aware that colonial taste was somewhat different from that of the London beau monde or even England's provincial gentry. American consumers looked to buy textiles in colours that were less bright and patterns less elaborate. New York merchants worried that London fashions were too showy for American tastes and bought instead, differently figured fabrics that they hoped would suit their consumer's needs.[30] Moreover, North American consumers were subject to different

– CHAPTER 31: *American consumers in an era of Atlantic free trade* –

trade regulations that permitted the expression of different tastes. The colonial craze for calico textiles for example was specific to America; the vastly fashionable Indian cotton was banned in England after 1721, a result of pressure from silk and linen weavers.[31] In the practical world of commerce then, colonial taste had long been seen as separate from that of its metropolitan counterpart, a distinct but not necessarily inferior sector of the Atlantic World economy. The tastes of these colonial consumers did not at first cause as much concern amongst London social critics. Prohibited by colonial law from setting up their own manufacturing establishments and hemmed in by mercantilist restrictions on all sides, the preferences of these consumers could be easily managed and seemed unlikely to truly disrupt the production of goods or the manufacturing of standards of taste.[32]

Such metropolitan complacency did not last. Responding to the changing moral and political imperatives of the latter half of the eighteenth century, British social critics began to question the power of colonial taste in the empire. They turned first to the West Indies, where fortunes were made quickly and extravagance was rife. Metropolitan audiences partly attributed such extravagance to sheer distance from polite society. Planters (even those who did not reside permanently in the Caribbean) could not immerse themselves in the English culture of politeness. Thus they were not conditioned to temper greedy acquisition with tasteful and moral restraint. As a result metropolitan audiences judged that the planter class lacked the taste that was exhibited by the British-based gentry.[33] A caricature of a Jamaican plantation owner, published in London in November 1807 by William Holland demonstrated the dynamic with brutal directness.[34] The print showed a couple of 'West India Fashionables' dressed in absurdly large hats, drawn along by a procession of black slaves against a bleak and windy Caribbean backdrop. The exaggeration of the planter's fashion, so tasteless and out of place, sent a clear message about the failure of West Indian society to cultivate appropriate standards of taste, despite their wealth and pretensions.

But this particular print also illuminated a number of other problems that underlay the issue of taste in West Indian society. Although eighteenth-century philosophers had begun to frame taste as an attribute to be acquired, there were still limits on who could claim to possess that quality. In 1757, David Hume had elaborated on one of those limits, arguing that slaves were subjects utterly devoid of taste. Having deemed taste an acquirable property, philosophers like Hume, naturally considered what institutions, associations and values might also predispose an individual to fail in their acquisition of taste. Perhaps living among slaves was one such condition? Outnumbered by these ostensibly tasteless beings, as the print so clearly depicted, the image raised a question: did proximity to slaves preclude the acquisition of taste, or was it dependence on slavery as an institution that corrupted slave owners' taste?[35] These musings, along with the slow rise of abolitionist sentiment condemning the existence of sugar plantations and New World slavery, resulted in an underlying question as to whether or not the immorality of slavery would permit its proponents to exhibit good taste. Here was a case where commercial wealth could not be refined by the principles of good taste, since the society itself was founded on immoral precepts. Yet it could hardly be denied that the fortunes made in the Caribbean gave the planter class a great deal of wealth and power in metropolitan Britain. As Tobias Smollett had put it in 1771, 'planters, negro drivers, and hucksters from our American plantations...discharge their affluence without taste or conduct'.[36] Politically and culturally, this group of consumers, white Creoles and nabobs, had the capacity to shape consumer demand within British society.[37]

Metropolitan cultural critics also treated North American consumers with ambivalence. Merchants and manufacturers were keenly aware that the American market represented a crucial outlet for their goods.[38] Indeed, between 1710 and 1770 British exports to North America increased 8.6 times their initial level, mirroring a similar increase in American population levels.[39] Thus the defiant consumer politics of the Revolution created alarm in Britain, even as American efforts to exhibit good taste received satirical treatment from London's fashion commentators and cognoscenti. Mary Darly's print of *Miss Carolina Sullivan, one of the obstinate daughters of America*, published in 1776, followed a common visual joke of the day, a laugh at the overweight, oversized wigs worn in polite society.[40] Yet if the purchasers of Darly's print could laugh at the American failure to wear a tasteful wig and thus feel more secure in their own choice of accessories and moral superiority, the decoration of the wig would have certainly been more unsettling. Adorning the headdress was a series of canons, while perched precariously on the side of the wig was a line of military tents, standards flying. Most ominous, a small figure hanging from a gallows dangled at the front. The imagined wig signaled that American politics were refashioning American taste. For those Britons who had read or heard Benjamin Franklin's threat to parliament, that continued taxation would induce Americans to change their consumer habits as a means of protest, the boycotts of the Revolution must have seemed alarming in the extreme.[41] The new world, with its corrupt plantations and rebellious politics, seemed to create an entirely new order of consumer tastes to contend with by the end of the eighteenth century.

AMERICAN TASTE IN A POST-REVOLUTIONARY WORLD

If *Miss Carolina Sullivan's* wig forced British merchants and manufacturers to wonder whether the War of Independence had created a new kind of consumer, the same question of American taste only became more acute in the wake of the Revolution. The end of the conflict meant the end of America's colonial status and its place within the larger mercantilist political economy that had governed its trade for over a century. The abrupt transition forced British politicians, merchants and manufacturers to confront an uncomfortable possibility. Would American customers still have a preference for British goods, now associated with a former imperial enemy, or had the Revolution transformed the taste of the new nation? Even during the war, Patriots had asserted their revolutionary allegiance by rejecting British style and favoring Gallic fashions. As the war ended, Americans sought to establish new trade relationships with France.[42] By 1783 however British merchants were relieved to discover that business was resuming along its old lines, as they found themselves able to dump hundreds of thousands of pounds worth of their imports and manufactures onto the quays and docks of American cities.[43] In the short term, trade seemed to resume without a hitch, though not without debate.

Yet the mood back in Britain was far from sanguine and there was little consensus on how best to re-establish the long-term commercial relationship that Britain had with America. The question of how to retain access to the American market was

– CHAPTER 31: *American consumers in an era of Atlantic free trade* –

one that took precedence. This was in part a practical question, but it was one that was also partly influenced by the emerging doctrines of Adam Smith. In 1776, Smith's publication of *The Wealth of Nations* had made it clear that if Britain was to embark on the task of instituting free trade then producers would have to pay increased attention to their market. 'Consumption,' Smith wrote, 'is the sole end and purpose of all production; and the interest of the producer ought to be attended to, only so far as it may be necessary for promoting that of the consumer.'[44] Such an observation intensified British concerns about the American market. If consumer desire was, as Smith said, what powered the surging tides of commerce, then commanding that desire, both at home and abroad, became an issue of pressing national importance.

While Prime Minister Lord Shelburne could see the virtue of Adam Smith's doctrine of free trade, he was not instinctively inclined to institute laissez-faire policy towards America. This was in large part due to his persistent refusal to even countenance the idea of American independence, even as the war drew to a close. In 1782, Shelburne had worked hard to institute a policy that would negate the consequences of independence and it was out of this impulse that he proposed to maintain America's commercial privileges with Britain, thus hoping to perpetuate a commercial fiction that the newly United States had not in fact left the empire.[45] Shelburne, along with Pitt the Younger who took over the prime ministerial post in 1783, could see the virtue of negotiating a peace treaty that did not place barriers between Britain and its former colony and hoped to establish a new reciprocity between the former enemies.[46]

Yet despite a rising interest in the spirit of laissez-faire liberalism that was circulating slowly through Westminster, the more powerful voice in the immediate wake of the war was that of John Baker Holroyd, Lord Sheffield. In April 1783, he had published a pamphlet that had condemned the efforts of Pitt's government to establish free trade with America and urged the government to re-enshrine the principles of mercantilism. *Observations on the Commerce of the American States with Europe and the West Indies* was a sneering indictment of Englishmen's eager desires to resume trading as if nothing had happened. In his opening salvo, Sheffield pointed out that, '[b]y asserting their independence, the Americans have at once renounced the privileges, as well as the duties, of British subjects – they are become foreign states.'[47] Sheffield argued they should not be allowed to trade as they once had. American merchants had forfeited the right to the markets of the West Indies and the privileges of trading within the protective embrace of the British Empire.

Sheffield dismissed the anxious claims that Americans would turn their back on British goods as a result of this stance and was especially dismissive of concerns that Americans would look instead to France for their fashions. In discussing American reliance on British wool for example, he noted that during the Revolutionary War, France had granted Congress a sum of money to help pay for the clothing of the American troops. Much to the dismay of their Gallic allies however, John Laurens, acting as the US army's agent, had bought English cloth and sent it back to America to garb the Continental Army. Sheffield related this anecdote with an unbecoming glee, emphasizing that Laurens had told the French (who had accused him of being ungrateful if not downright disloyal) that his responsibility had been to find the best he could for his troops. Nor had this been an isolated incident. Sheffield was quick to point out that despite being at war with Britain, Americans had continued to import British manufactures whenever they could, until the French had threatened to withdraw their support from the US entirely.[48]

The decision to invoke their commercial victory over the French was surely deliberate on Sheffield's part. France had been Britain's long-time rival, and hatred of this Catholic nation was at the heart of British identity in the eighteenth century.[49] Yet at the same time this was the nation whose tastes had penetrated deep into the British beau monde's own understanding of fashionable standards, providing Britons with examples of both elegance and effeminacy. The debate over whether Britain or France could lay claim to superior taste remained unresolved by the end of the Revolution, but Sheffield hoped to allay British concerns about national pride and economic superiority by pointing to American consumer preferences. If Americans chose British woolens even as they waged a war against their manufacturers, then Sheffield thought that imposing the small penalty of being excluded from Britain's protective imperial umbrella would certainly not deter Americans from seeking out British goods. Sheffield's efforts carried the day despite Pitt's effort to liberalize trade. Americans remained subject to the restrictions of the Navigation Acts, their trade with the West Indies limited, although the Privy Council did introduce orders that attempted to encourage direct trade between America and metropolitan Britain.[50]

Sheffield's arguments were based partly on the idea that American consumers would respond to the quality of the goods alone in making their choices about what to buy and from whom.[51] It was an argument that reflected the eighteenth-century supposition that it was the proficiency of design and the quality of craftsmanship that yielded goods in the best taste.[52] Yet such an argument did not convince all observers and Britain's reluctance to negotiate a commercial treaty with the US in the wake of the war left others concerned. Richard Champion, the former deputy paymaster general of the army and a lobbyist working for the West India interest, warned '[a] great stress is laid upon the necessity which the Americans will be under to purchase English goods, from their not being able to procure them in any other country upon such cheap and advantageous terms.' But, he continued, '[it] is, however, a hazardous attempt to drive them to this necessity. Mankind are formed of materials which have a great aptitude to resist, when force is employed.'[53] Rather than forcing Americans down the path of increased self-sufficiency, Champion advocated for the 'radical cure' of free trade.

By opening up commerce to the natural competition between nations, he argued, Britain's manufacturing prowess and the tendencies of American taste would do the work of securing the future of transatlantic commerce. 'The Americans...are already relapsing into their former luxury and enjoyments,' he wrote. '[T]he orders for goods which have lately been transmitted, are filled with as many superfluities as necessaries. This is not a wise conduct in the infancy of a new Republick; the establishment of which ought to be founded in examples of frugality, not of luxurious enjoyments. But if their own Governments have not this consideration, and they offer a Trade which must in some measure produce a state of Dependence upon Europe, it will not be a wise conduct in us to neglect so advantageous a prospect.'[54]

Champion's analysis illuminates the dilemmas that accompanied the slow embrace of free trade policy in Britain. How could the politicians at Westminster be sure that

– CHAPTER 31: American consumers in an era of Atlantic free trade –

the supposed principles of laissez-faire economics, still poorly understood, would operate? Certainly Champion was quick to point out that cheap goods above all would act as an inducement to American consumers. But besides that, Champion realized that his argument for Britain's commercial future was based on two hopeful suppositions: first that the American government would not attempt to legislate into existence a republican political economy, one that would limit the influx of luxury British goods into the new nation, and second, that Americans themselves would not embrace the more austere qualities of republican civic virtue and would instead continue to maintain a taste for British superfluities. Both suppositions would prove to be of enduring concern and interest.

Despite the initial indications that Americans continued to hanker after British-made goods and the imports they shipped in from the East Indies, some of the republic's new citizens were quick to warn Westminster politicians and the British public more broadly not to rely on American preferences for British goods for too long. William Bingham, an influential Philadelphia merchant, living in London in 1784, replied to Sheffield's pamphlet thus:

> There may at present be some partiality in the States, for British manufactures; – yet this predilection arises from cradle prejudices and has greatly decreased during the war; – and it would be unwise in Great Britain to place any reliance on a continuation of it: – for the manufactures of other countries, if equally good, and afforded cheaper, will, by a continued competition, be eventually preferred; especially as there will be a constant succession of emigrants from different parts of Europe, who have no decided preference in favour of the fashion or quality of British manufactures, and who, by mixing with the mass of the people, will gradually effect a change in their taste.[55]

Bingham's warning emphasized one of the crucial conundrums facing British politicians, merchants and manufacturers as they contemplated the future: the question of how American consumer taste would develop as the new nation severed its political, economic and above all cultural ties with their former imperial mistress. What would an influx of new people combined with a separate government and a new range of economic imperatives do to the nature of American taste? There were few immediate answers to these questions. As the nineteenth century opened, politicians, like the philosophers and fashion cognoscenti before them, grappled with the nature of taste and its formation. No longer an objective category of judgement, now slipping beyond the reach of the metropolitan influence in new ways and imbued with enhanced commercial power through the political economy of Adam Smith, the nature of American taste and the scope of the American market posed a set of problems previously unknown to British politicians.

These were not issues that were resolved immediately in the wake of the War of Independence. In fact, the complexities of establishing new trade relations between Britain and America continued to provoke disputes well into the nineteenth century. Between 1783 and 1815, the governance of trade between Britain, the United States and France, caused both domestic and international tensions as first the infamous Jay Treaty, then the French Revolution, the Quasi War, the Napoleonic Wars and finally the War of 1812 itself, forced politicians on both sides of the Atlantic to confront the limitations of their commercial power in a changing Atlantic World.[56] With governments on both sides of the Atlantic threatening their rivals' commercial privileges and curtailing trade, using measures ranging from tariffs to embargoes, the Smithian vision of a laissez-faire global economy seemed far beyond reach. Indeed, by 1815, Europe was, as one scholar has claimed, 'an ocean of protectionism' with only a few small liberal islands exhibiting a different approach.[57]

More worrying for British merchants and manufacturers were the increased tendencies of Americans to erect the barriers of protection around their infant industries. One of the first acts of Congress had been to establish a revenue-raising tariff and between 1806 and 1815, first Jefferson and then Madison oversaw the passage of various trade restrictions, including an embargo, in an effort to punish European depredations on American commercial neutrality.[58] Although these were rescinded in 1815, the fortress mindset did not disappear. In the wake of the War of 1812, an increasingly vocal group of mid-Atlantic manufacturers were becoming more organized in their quest for protectionist tariffs. This quest culminated in 1824, when Congress passed a tariff explicitly designed to protect American woolens, establishing what political economist Henry Carey would call 'the American System'.[59] Yet as some historians have argued, the end of the Napoleonic Wars did usher in a new openness to shifting the basis of international trade relations towards freer trade, especially among the European powers.[60] Indeed, before free trade policy became a commercial reality, various British merchants, authors and ultimately politicians engaged indirectly with one of the key questions that free trade would pose: what determined the taste of the consumers who would drive the engines of productive economy: both at home and abroad.

KEEPING TRACK OF AMERICAN TASTE

Some British manufacturers were quick to assume that the political independence of America would naturally produce a taste for new designs. Most prominent among these examples was the canny potter Josiah Wedgewood. Wedgewood had extensive experience in producing for the American market. But in the wake of independence, he capitalized on this knowledge, producing goods that he thought would reflect the new patriotic sentiments of his customers. His designs for jugs, plates, toby jars and other items included images of patriotic emblems, portraits of George Washington and Benjamin Franklin, the eagle insignia and encouraging mottoes for American consumers to reflect on as they supped their tea or drank their punch.[61] Less well-known ceramic producers also cashed in on this design trend. One factory near Liverpool produced a design in the 1810s with a list of all the states, their date of joining the Union and their population inscribed on one side, while on the other, the female figure of Liberty was seated, holding aloft a plaque inscribed 'Agriculture, Commerce, Prosperity.'[62] It is difficult to judge whether such products were popular, but their manufacture points to the fact that British potters were labouring under the assumption that the Revolution had altered the tastes of the American market. Reflecting the idea that each nation possessed a unique set of tastes, British manufacturers attempted to cater to those demands.

Such an assumption helps to account for the persistent fascination that British visitors to the United States had for American manners and tastes in the early decades

– CHAPTER 31: *American consumers in an era of Atlantic free trade* –

of the nineteenth century. Henry Bradshaw Fearon for example, who travelled to the United States in 1818 to make a report for a group of prospective emigrants, paid particular attention to the habits of American consumers. He explored both the source of their goods and fashions as well as the nature of the people's taste. Among his first impressions of the country was the general inferiority of good taste despite a general expression of personal pride. '[The labouring class] were not better clothed than men in a similar condition in England,' he observed 'but they were more erect in their posture, less care-worn in their countenances...intermixed with these were several of the mercantile and genteeler classes. Large straw hats prevailed; trowsers were universal. The general costume of these persons was inferior to men in the same rank of life in England.'[63] Venturing further into the city of New York, Fearon commented not only on the lack of well-dressed white ladies but also on the 'number of blacks, [who] are finely dressed, the females very ludicrously so, showing a partiality to white muslin dresses, artificial flowers and pink shoes.'[64] Fearon's comments suggest that he was attempting to discern how nationhood had changed the tastes of American consumers. America's working class empowered through new habits of democracy exhibited their own sartorial preferences. American freedpeople, whose tastes Fearon thought worth it to mention, even if he did so with derision, demonstrated how even tastes deemed unworthy of consideration were nonetheless a part of this newly forming market. Politics and a racial order that were highly unfamiliar were imagined as having an impact on America's national tastes, rendering them both coarse and ridiculous.[65]

More sympathetic to the Americans, was the author Frances Wright, who travelled through America at the same time as Fearon did, from 1818 through to 1820. Wright was far more sympathetic towards the Americans, but she was also keenly aware of the difficulties Americans were facing in cultivating a national style and taste in dress. Like Fearon she was quick to see a connection between the new political order and its effect on taste. Discussing the unmarried youth of America she noted, 'their dress is elegant, sometimes too showy and costly than befits a republic', and she noted that from New York to the backcountry, American women were purchasing 'the flaunting silks of France and Indies'.[66] The liberal Wright believed that Americans' efforts to sustain their republic would be better served through 'the positive resistance to so becoming a dereliction of principle and good taste' and encouraged Americans to hold fast to their 'practice of clothing every member of their family in articles of domestic manufacture'.[67] But English readers of Wright's tale might have taken away another point from her observations. Throughout the eighteenth century and on into the nineteenth century, textiles from France and the East Indies had competed with English silk woven on the looms of Spitalfields workers.[68] Reading that Americans were developing such tastes, these workers may have worried about how they could adapt and compete with these powerful commercial rivals. Wright's comments about French silks might also have rung alarm bells for British merchants, hoping to supply the American market with the goods they had to offer. Through publications like Wright's and Fearon's then, Britons were left to wonder how American taste would develop as the republic matured and what effect that would have on English commerce, production and design. As the advocates for free trade policy in Britain became more insistent that they be heard, the debate over taste took on a new, more overtly political dimension.

583

– Joanna Cohen –

TASTE AND FREE TRADE:
THE SELECT COMMITTEE OF 1835

Historians have long been clear that the intellectual centre of the transition to free trade policy was in Britain, where a group of radical free traders, including Sir Henry Parnell, Richard Cobden and William Bright advocated for the establishment of free trade and in particular for the repeal of the Corn Laws.[69] By the 1830s, 'economic liberalism burst forth as a crusading passion', that brought with it new debates over how Britain could maintain its commercial prowess in a world of global competition.[70] It was against this backdrop that taste became the focus of intense interest among British politicians. But it was not the taste of their foreign markets that initially prompted concern; instead it was the dynamics of the domestic market that attracted attention. As the government began to dismantle the protections of an earlier era, politicians, merchants and manufacturers began to consider what would promote the purchase of British productions above all the other goods to be had on the open market. Concerned with production and supply, the focus of public debate quickly became the tastefulness of the goods themselves and by extension the aesthetic training of the British artisan.

In the summer of 1835, the radical MP for Liverpool William Ewart convened a Parliamentary Committee to hear evidence on the state of 'Art and Manufactures' in Britain.[71] Among the committee members were Sir Robert Peel, Henry Lytton Bulwer and Henry Warburton, all of who would be vocal supporters of free trade over the course of their careers. Warburton in particular had been schooled in politics by James Mill, was friends with David Ricardo and had joined the Political Economy Club at its founding in 1821.[72] Over the course of several months, between July and September, the committee would hear twenty-eight witnesses testify on the best way to 'extend among the People, especially the Manufacturing Classes, a knowledge and taste for Art'.[73]

The immediate presumption of both the committee members and the witnesses was that Britain's artisans required a level of government-sponsored art education that was unheard of in Britain but worryingly already a familiar part of both French, Belgian and German industrial education.[74] One witness, James Morrison, the head of a large commercial house in London and a twenty-year veteran of the dry goods trade lamented, 'I have felt so much the want of such institutions, especially since the discussions on the subject of free trade and the admission of foreign manufactures'.[75] The deliberate cultivation of tasteful production was key to the proponents of free trade. If the French or Germans could outdo British artisans in the precepts of design then the logic of free trade would mean that these competitors would outstrip British producers.[76] Charles Robert Cockerell, an associate of the Royal Academy, was even more damning in his demand for better industrial training. Echoing an older rhetoric that linked good taste to morality rather than commercial advantage alone, Cockerell thundered: 'I have deplored the indifference shown by Government on a subject which materially concerns the honour and character of England as respects arts and which is of paramount commercial and national importance in a manufacturing country, where the cultivation of taste only is wanting to give us superiority over the world.'[77]

However, the committee struggled with the question of whose taste ought to be cultivated. The initial aim of the committee had been to establish a model for a National School of Design, thus training producers to create better patterns for

– CHAPTER 31: *American consumers in an era of Atlantic free trade* –

textiles as well as more seductive designs for goods ranging from iron stove fronts to ormulu ornaments. The supporters of this project saw its benefits in clear commercial terms. Cockerell in particular was clear that 'the ignorance of the true principals of design' meant that there was a 'constant waste of capital in the capricious and random endeavour to catch the public taste'.[78] But Cockerell's rhetoric suggested a shift that was taking place when it came to thinking about taste. Alongside the training of artisans, this associate of the Royal Academy was arguing that the public as a collective whole had tastes that required attention. In fact, repeatedly the testimony of the witnesses suggested that training the artisan was not enough. If the British economy was to prosper, then the public taste would also require an education.

This education was not intended to teach the consumer to identify and purchase only British made goods. Rather, the liberal bent of the committee meant that witnesses and committee members alike were keen to prove that free trade had had the overall effect of improving the public taste to the benefit of the national economy. John Jobson Smith, the owner of a Sheffield Iron Foundry was quick to point out that opening of commercial intercourse with France had meant that 'French ornaments and French style [had] become introduced in [Britain] and [had] become ingrafted into [British] style'. Smith argued that this process of incorporating French style into British production had had the overall effect of improving 'national taste' as the committee termed it, an improvement that had led to consumers wanting a greater number of more expensive items. 'We cannot produce articles too expensive for the public taste of the present day,'[79] Smith pointed out with pleasure. Free trade, Smith was glad to confirm, had the potential to be good for business.

Nonetheless, the logical extension of this argument was that cultivating even better taste would be even better for business and here the committee was afraid that Britain was lagging behind the continent. All the evidence pointed to the fact that European governments were training their population in the principles of design, something that led directly to a people possessed of better standards of taste.[80] The debate over what kind of training to offer the British population certainly took up a large portion of the committee's attention. But in principle it seemed clear that the public taste could be educated through an exposure to classical art housed in galleries and museums, as well as exhibited through urban design and public architecture. A few also advocated for the introduction of drawing as a skill, but here consensus faltered. Witnesses seemed not to be advocating for the creation of formal schools of public taste, rather the more informal approach of a general environment of tastefulness.

Opinion also diverged as to who among the public should receive this education. Interestingly the committee did not specifically discuss consumer tastes as they related to gender. In referring to the 'public' this committee at least was oddly silent on the question of whether it was male or female preferences or both that would drive their decision to institute a more thorough programme of educating public taste.[81] However, when it came to the question of class, the discussion became slightly more overt. While some witnesses agreed with the committee that 'not merely the lower and middling classes, but a great portion of the upper classes have not had their taste proportionately cultivated' others were more sympathetic and argued that the English upper classes at least, had excellent taste.[82]

Ultimately however, the committee seemed to focus more on the education of the lower and middling classes, since the committee identified this group as having the greatest capacity for changing the dynamics of the British manufacturing economy. Yet a note of unease lingered throughout these months of testimony. While most witnesses seemed confident that the public taste could be trained, there was a disquieting undercurrent of comment that suggested that in fact it was the producer's task to simply understand and then cater to the public's taste. 'The dealer's study is not so much to improve the taste of the public, as to discover what goods will sell most readily and produce them to the largest profit' argued one C. Smith in front of the committee. He continued with brutal clarity: 'the taste of the public must infallibly operate upon the seller.'[83] Had the debate over taste been simply an argument about economic advantage this might not have been unsettling. But it was clear that these men also believed a public preference for tasteful goods to be a positive reflection of national character. Thus, the idea that the public taste and especially the lower classes' preferences ought to dictate the mode of production was one that did not come easily to an elite who planned to act as the architects of a newly powerful British political economy.

FOREIGN TASTE AND FREE TRADE?

The ultimate recommendation of the Select Committee was that the government should establish a School of Design in London to train teachers in the applied arts. The Committee authorized a grant of £10,000 for the purpose and gave operational control of the School over to the Board of Trade.[84] Their actions were not especially innovative. In fact, they were merely following the example laid out for them by the French, the Germans and even the Americans who had all established schools or institutes prior to this point, that educated producers in the art of tasteful production. In fact it had been the awareness of these initiatives that had been the starting point for the committee hearings. But of course, such initiatives were unable to help manufacturers who hoped to produce for foreign markets and consumers. They could not hope to train a foreign public to demonstrate better taste. Thus they monitored the American market, trying to ascertain what shaped American demands and desires.[85]

Before 1833, when American tariffs had risen to their highest levels, the tastes of American consumers had been almost a moot point. Instead, British manufacturers simply had to contend with the problem that the US Congress was continuing to obstruct British merchants in their efforts to do business with American retailers.[86] But in 1833, Senator Henry Clay brokered a legislative compromise in Congress that began the gradual reduction of American tariffs. The move away from tariffs seemed to present British manufacturers with an opportunity, but they worried it would be squandered by the Conservative government's adherence to the Corn Laws. By the late 1830s, free trade manufacturers argued that one of the Corn Laws' most devastating effects was that they legitimated American retaliatory efforts to shut out British goods from the American marketplace. 'It is impossible to multiply too greatly the proofs of the injury which the corn laws [sic] are inflicting upon our manufactures by cherishing foreign competition' reported *The Sheffield Independent* in 1839.[87] The proof that free traders sought seemed to arrive in 1842, when the Whig Congress reinstituted a prohibitive tariff to deal with the United States' growing public debt. For four years, a rising chorus of voices championed the end of protectionist tariffs on both sides of the Atlantic. Finally in 1846, Peel's ministry brought the Corn Laws

– CHAPTER 31: *American consumers in an era of Atlantic free trade* –

to an end and this was followed in short order by the passage of the Walker Tariff in the US, a tariff that lowered duties on a broad range of imports. Such reductions were only the beginning. In 1849, Britain abolished the Navigation Acts and up until 1861, the spirit of free trade seemed to envelop the two nations in unprecedented ways and a new interest in American consumer demand took shape in both America and Britain.[88]

Whether they supported free trade or not, by mid-century many Americans connected the widespread demand for finished consumer goods with a direct expression of a democratic political order. Addressing the crowds gathered at an exhibition of American-made manufactures staged by the Franklin Institute in Philadelphia in 1847, Joseph Chandler proclaimed: '[t]hose...who in this country are...transfusing into the lower classes...the *wants* of refinement are ministering to the diffusion and maintenance of true republicanism.'[89] A universal desire for refined consumer goods, accompanied by open access to them within the marketplace, argued Chandler, leveled out society. Moreover, Chandler implied that an equality of good taste in consumer goods was a core component of a democratic republic. Indeed, by the mid nineteenth century, many observers believed that consumption habits in America showcased a crucial aspect of democratic society. As Chandler's colleague at the Franklin Institute, William Kelley argued, America could be imagined as 'millions of luxurious citizens' all waiting to buy the goods that to him expressed the 'life of the nation'.[90]

This idealized democratic marketplace was not admired in Britain. At the Great Exhibition of 1851, the British press mercilessly mocked the American exhibit for its want of refinement and lack of exhibits.[91] Scathingly referred to as the 'prairie ground', London observers were quick to point to the tasteless and uninteresting character of American productions. This included condemnation for such practical items such as ice-making machines, corn-husk mattresses, fireproofed safes, india-rubber shoes and McCormick's Virginia Reaper.[92] All of these objects generated a lot of interest, but could hardly be described as the height of elegance. At a moment when the British believed good taste to be an expression of society's moral standards such a shocking lack of refinement intensified British scrutiny of American society.[93]

In attempting to explain this lack of taste, British commentators turned to an examination of the US' political economy. 'The absence in the United States of those vast accumulations of wealth which favour the expenditure of large sums on articles of mere luxury, and the general distribution of the means of procuring the more substantial conveniences of life, impart to the productions of American industry a character distinct from that of many other countries,' explained the authors of the *Official Description and Illustrated Catalogue* for the Great Exhibition. Pointing out that very few American productions were created solely as 'an object of *virtu*' the authors of the catalogue noted instead that, 'both the manual and mechanical labour are applied with direct reference to increasing the number or the quantity of articles suited to the wants of the whole people'.[94] The *London Observer* echoed such sentiments, claiming that the American industrial system was 'democratic in its tendencies' and that American manufacturers 'produce for the masses...and look for their reward to the public demand alone'.[95] Yet, these demands appeared to be the antithesis of good taste. The American exhibit thus challenged the idea that commercial progress produced a more civilized society. But the exhibit also raised a new set of questions. In the context of an international exhibition dedicated to spreading free trade, the American exhibit posed a problem: with freer trade came the freer flow of goods, demands and desires. Yet these productions and preferences had an acknowledged and potentially detrimental effect on the social and political fabric of society. The question was: could British manufacturers cash in on supplying the American market but resist the urge to lower their own standards of production and corrupt the quality of British taste in the process?

By the time of the New York Exhibition of 1853, the idea that the virtues of American democracy could be seen in the widespread diffusion of luxury goods was well established in American minds. The journalist Horace Greeley, describing the great lesson to be learned from the Exhibition, argued that American 'progress, in these modern times, then consists in this, that we have democratized the means and appliances of a higher life; ...we have brought...the masses of the people up to the aristocratic standard of taste and enjoyment and so diffusing the influence of splendor and grace over all minds.'[96] But British observers such as George Wallis were not convinced. Certainly Wallis, like other British observers before him, had found there was an elite taste for elegant goods in the US. Indeed, concerns that Americans preferred the productions of France, when it came to purchasing refined luxury goods continued to circulate in Britain.[97] But it was the goods intended for a mass market that caused greater anxiety. Instead of seeing refinement for the masses, Wallis found American manufacturing to be slapdash and hurried, meaning that American-made goods 'lack[ed] the perfect finish and completeness of appearance' which characterized European goods of a similar type.[98] Cottons were made plainly and cheaply, designed to use up the 'short waste of other branches of the woolen manufacture'.[99] These satinets, as they were called, replaced the imported fustians and velveteens that made up the clothes of the working classes in Britain. Wallis believed that they lacked durability and reflected a less than admirable desire for 'short-lived' articles that were made for appearance and not for long use.[100] American taste was 'tawdry and unimaginative' but as British tastemakers acknowledged, British manufacturers had to respond.[101]

The question of how to manage these tastes back in England worried tastemakers and manufacturers. Those invested in national design education urged the government to invest more heavily in training British manufacturers in the standards of good taste so that they might more effectively compete for 'the market of the world'. Especially those with a more conservative outlook clung to the idea that taste had 'laws, rules and principles' that 'were sanctioned by the reverence of all ages and of all countries'. But such assertions had lost ground by the middle of the nineteenth century.[102] Instead, British observers fretted that catering for the tastes of the American market was having a negative impact on the high standards of British manufacturing.

The prime example of this phenomenon was the British production of shoddy. Shoddy was the term given to textiles made from the scraps and rags that were collected and re-spun into yarn and then woven into fabric that might be bulked up by the addition of a little extra fresh wool. The centre of British shoddy manufacture were the small towns of Yorkshire, in particular Dewsbury, which had transformed from 'a village to a town of some thirty thousand inhabitants' as a result of this 'extraordinary transformation of old garments into new'.[103] In Dewsbury, men and women passed rags collected from all over Europe through iron toothed cylinders, stripping them of any cotton filaments until they disintegrated into short scraps of

– CHAPTER 31: *American consumers in an era of Atlantic free trade* –

yarn. Then amidst the lint-filled air, known as 'devil's dust' they would begin the process of cleaning and spinning these small strings of wool back into textile.[104] The result was a fabric that looked fine at first glance but that soon wore out once it was put into use. Horace Greeley reported having seen men pick handfuls of wool scraps off of their shoulders, as their shoddy coats wore down to the lining.[105]

Americans were well aware that shoddy constituted a large portion of the textiles that British merchants imported to the US.[106] Although they too recognized that shoddy was not especially durable, many did not seem to mind and indeed set about trying to imitate the production of such textiles. Indeed, the satinets that Wallis commented on were in all likelihood an effort to imitate shoddy. But British commentators were far less sanguine about the effects of shoddy on both the British economy and its reputation for adhering to high standards of taste and quality. Commenting on the escalation of the shoddy trade, a writer for *The Spectator* noted:

> There used to be a time when to say of any manufactured commodity that it was 'English' implied ipso facto that it was sterling – sound to the heart – made to stand wear and tear, and defying scrutiny to prove any falsity in its pedigree. That time has passed; and we may well say that the decline of English repute in that respect has reached an alarming point, when even the manufacture of woollen cloth, so long identified with our national name, has ceased to be sterling.[107]

Selling shoddy to the 'Yankee' customer might be easy to sustain for the time being, but this particular author was concerned that losing sight of British standards in an effort to cater to the not-so-discerning tastes of the Americans would ultimately undermine the entirety of British trade.

The concern voiced by *The Spectator* was of course in part about maintaining market share. But there was something else that was disturbing about shoddy. It seemed to be the ultimate expression of free trade production. Here was a product that was a cosmopolitan co-mingling of raw materials, made not out of any tradition of artisanal craft but was instead a manufactured commodity arising out of an international consumer demand. Although he did not condemn shoddy outright, it was Horace Greeley who captured this essence of shoddy. In the warehouses of Yorkshire, where the merchants of the rag trade collected their haul, Greeley reckoned a visitor would find 'the cast-off garments of Great Britain and the Continent of Europe...the tattered remains of the clothes, some of which have been worn by royalty in the various Courts of Europe, as well as by peers and peasants. The rich broadcloth of the English nobles here commingles with the livery of their servants and the worsted blouses of French republicans...American under-shirts, pantaloons, and all other worsted or woollen goods...reduced to one common level and known by the one common appellation of "rags".'[108] Shoddy seemed to embody the tawdry democratic tastes of its consumers, challenging the ideas that commerce should reflect progress, refinement and the quality of the nation in its entirety.

The concerns over shoddy revealed the deep anxieties that some Britons nurtured when it came to implementing free trade. Although the Great Exhibition itself seemed to promise Victorian Britons that the progress of commerce would secure the international community's journey towards a more civilized world, some British manufacturers and merchants were less sure of this progress.[109] Instead they saw the

589

de-stabilizing potential of responding to the diverse, democratic and potentially degraded tastes of a global market of consumers. Such recognition elevated the importance of the consumer in broad discussions about the operations of a national and international market. It put the dictums of Adam Smith to the test and revealed that free trade's promise challenged deeply held assumptions about quality, value and taste in Victorian society. What Britons learned from the Americans' consumer tastes was that market integration came with a cultural price tag attached. It was a price they were apparently willing to pay.

NOTES

The author would like to thank Erik Mathisen and Zara Anishanslin for their thoughtful and thorough reading of this essay as well as the challenging and fruitful questions they continued to ask. She would also like to thank D'Maris Coffman for the opportunity to become involved in the collection and her immense and generous patience throughout.

1 'English Commissioners at New York' *Farmer's Cabinet* (Amherst, NH) 16 June, 1853.
2 William R. Wallace, 'An Ode for the Inauguration of the American Crystal Palace' *New York Times*, 14 July, 1853. See also Charles Hirschfeld, 'America on Exhibition: The New York Crystal Palace' *American Quarterly* 9 (Summer 1957), 101.
3 'The Directors' *The Barre Patriot* (Massachusetts) June 3, 1853.
4 George Wallis and Joseph Whitworth, *The American System of Manufactures. The Report of the Committee on the Machinery of the United States in 1855 and the Special Reports of George Wallis and Joseph Whitworth* ed. and introd., Nathan Rosenberg (Edinburgh: Edinburgh University Press, 1969), 21–22.
5 This list reflects the items that Wallis had been commissioned to judge by the British government. See Wallis and Whitworth, *The American System of Manufactures*, 22.
6 Wallis quoted in 'Belfast Government School of Art – Annual Conversazione and Distribution of Scholarships' *The Belfast News-Letter* Issue 12012, April 7, 1854.
7 Michael Snodin, 'Victorian Britain, 1837–1901: Who Led Taste?' in Michael Snodin and John Styles, ed., *Design and the Decorative Arts, Britain 1500–1900* (London: V&A Publications, 2001), 369.
8 There is debate over the rate at which free trade was being embraced although most agree that the significant shift towards implementing free trade took place in 1846 with the repeal of the Corn Laws. See C.P. Kindleberger, 'The Rise of Free Trade in Western Europe, 1820–75' *The Journal of Economic History* 35 (March, 1975), 28–36; John Vincent Nye, 'The Myth of Free Trade Britain and Fortress France: Tariffs and Trade in the Nineteenth Century' *The Journal of Economic History* 51 (March, 1991), 23–46; Douglas A. Irwin, 'Free Trade and Protection in Nineteenth-Century Britain and France Revisted: A Comment on Nye' *The Journal of Economic History* 53 (March 1993), 146–52.
9 Arts and Manufactures Committee, *Report from Select Committee on Arts and Manufactures* (HC, 1835, 598–375), 102.
10 The classic account remains Karl Polanyi, *The Great Transformation: The Political and Economic Origins of Our Time* 2nd edition (Boston: Beacon, 2001). A great deal of the literature especially from the 1970s and 1980s focused on the theory of hegemonic stability, looking specifically at Britain as the free trade hegemon and British politicians and philosophers as the architects of free trade. For a review of this scholarship and of its limitations see Patrick K. O'Brien and Geoffey Allen Pigman, 'Free Trade, British Hegemony and the International Economic Order in the Nineteenth Century' *Review of International Studies* 18 (April 1992), 89–91 and Arthur A. Stein, 'The Hegemon's

Dilemma: Great Britain, the United States and the International Economic order' *International Organization* 38:2 (Spring 1984), 355, n.1. See also C.P Kindleberger, 'The Rise of Free Trade in the West'; James Ashley Morrison, 'Before Hegemony: Adam Smith, American Independence, and the Origins of the First Era of Globalization' *International Organization* 66 (Summer 2012), 395–428. Some recent articles to look beyond the hegemonic stability theory and examine a wider array of pressure groups and parties include Simon Morgan, 'The Anti-Corn Law League and British Anti-slavery in Transatlantic Perspective, 1838–46' *The Historical Journal* 52 (2009),: 87–109; Richard Huzzey, 'Free Trade, Free Labour and Slave Sugar in Victorian Britain' *The Historical Journal* 53 (June 2010), 359–79 and Anthony Howe, 'John Bull and Brother Jonathan: Cobden, America and the Liberal Mind' in Ella Dzelzainis and Ruth Livesey, ed., *The American Experiment and the Idea of Democracy in British Culture, 1776–1914* (Farnham: Ashgate, 2013), 107–20.

11 See especially Douglas A. Irwin, *Against the Tide: An Intellectual History of Free Trade* (Princeton, N.J.: Princeton University Press, 1996); *Free Trade and Protectionism in America, 1822–1890* vol. 1, ed. Lars Magnusson (London and New York: Routledge, 2000).

12 Some exceptions are Wolfram Kaiser, 'Cultural Transfer of Free Trade at the World Exhibitions, 1851–62' *Journal of Modern History* 77 (September 2005), 563–90; Lara Kriegel, 'Culture and the Copy: Calico, Capitalism and Design Copyright in Early Victorian Britain' *Journal of British Studies* 43 (April 2004), 233–65.

13 'Mr. Wheeler, Your attention is Requested to the enclosed Piece from a Female Correspondent' *The United States Chronicle, Political, Commercial and Historical* (Providence RI) 11 May, 1786.

14 Karl Marx and Frederich Engels with an introduction by A. J. P. Taylor, *The Communist Manifesto* 1888 (London: Penguin, 1985), 84.

15 The literature on consumer goods as markers of identity and makers of taste is expansive. See John Brewer and Roy Porter, eds., *Consumption and the World of Goods* (New York: Routledge, 1993); Cary Carson, Ronald Hoffman, and Peter J. Albert, eds. *Of Consuming Interests: The Style of Life in the Eighteenth Century* (Charlottesville, Va.: University Press of Virginia, 1994); T.H. Breen, *The Marketplace of Revolution: How Consumer Politics Shaped American Independence* (New York: Oxford University Press, 2004), Kate Haulman, *The Politics of Fashion in Eighteenth Century America* (Chapel Hill: University of North Carolina Press, 2010); Michael Zakim, *Ready-Made Democracy: A History of Men's Dress in the American Republic, 1760–1860* (Chicago: University of Chicago Press, 2003); John Styles and Amanda Vickery, eds., *Gender, Taste and Material Culture in Britain and North America 1700–1830* (New Haven: Yale University Press, 2006).

16 The relationship between material culture, taste and national identity is brilliantly explored in Leora Auslander, *Cultural Revolutions: Everyday Life and Politics in Britain, North America and France* (Berkeley: University of California Press, 2009). Auslander focuses on domestic productions and does not consider the ways in which foreign tastes or demands impacted this relationship.

17 Styles and Vickery, *Gender, Taste and Material Culture*, 14.

18 Edmund Burke, *A Philosophical Enquiry into the Origin of the Sublime and Beautiful* (London: J. Dodsley, 1759), 4 cited in Amanda Vickery, '"Neat and Not Too Showey": Words and Wallpaper in Regency England' in Styles and Vickery, *Gender, Taste and Material Culture*, 201.

19 Dabney Townsend, 'From Shaftesbury to Kant: The Development of the Concept of Aesthetic Experience' *Journal of the History of Ideas* 48 (April–June, 1987), 287–305.

20 Adam Smith, *The Theory of Moral Sentiments* ed. Knud Haakonssen (Cambridge, 2002), 227–29. On Hogarth see Maxine Berg, 'From Imitation to Invention: Creating Commodities in Eighteenth-Century Britain' *The Economic History Review* 55 (Feb 2002), 13.

21 On the luxury debates see *Luxury in the Eighteenth Century. Debates, Desires and Delectable Goods*, ed., Maxine Berg and Elizabeth Eger (New York: Palgrave, 2003); Michael Kwass, 'Ordering the World of Goods: Consumer Revolution and the Classification of Objects in Eighteenth Century France' *Representations*, 82 (Spring, 2003), 87–116; John Sekora, *Luxury: The Concept in Western Thought from Eden to Smollett* (Baltimore: Johns Hopkins University Press, 1977).

22 Maxine Berg and Elizabeth Eger, 'The Rise and Fall of the Luxury Debates' in *Luxury in the Eighteenth Century*, 1–14.

23 Maxine Berg, 'In Pursuit of Luxury: Global History and British Consumer Goods in the Eighteenth Century' *Past and Present* 182 (February 2004), 91–96; T.H. Breen, '"The Baubles of Britain": The American and Consumer Revolutions of the Eighteenth Century' *Past and Present* 119 (May 1988), 73–104. The classic account of the 'consumer revolution' is Neil McKendrick, John Brewer and J.H. Plumb, *The Birth of Consumer Society: The Commercialization of Eighteenth-Century England* (Bloomington, Ind.: Indiana University Press, 1982).

24 Simon Gikandi, *Slavery and the Culture of Taste* (Princeton, N.J.: Princeton University Press, 2011), 17.

25 Auslander, *Cultural Revolutions*, 7.

26 Linda Colley, *Britons: Forging the Nation 1707–1837* (New Haven: Yale University Press, 2009), 90–91; Berg, 'From Imitation to Invention,' 17–18. For another aspect of this debate over design, regarding Spitalfield silk weavers' competition with French weavers see Zara Anishanslin, *Embedded Empire: Hidden Histories of Labor, Landscape and Luxury in the British Atlantic World* (New Haven, forthcoming), chapter 1.

27 Colley, *Britons*, 69.

28 Breen, *The Marketplace of Revolution*, 76–200.

29 Haulman, *The Politics of Fashion*, 34–35.

30 Ibid., 18–20, 45.

31 Ibid., 32–33.

32 On the centrality of imports (legal and illegal) for British North Americans see Carole Shammas, 'How Self-Sufficient was Early America?' *Journal of Interdisciplinary History* 13 (Autumn 1982), 263–68; On the Navigation Acts see Linzy A. Brekke '"To Make a Figure": Clothing and the Politics of Male Identity in Eighteenth-Century America' in *Gender, Taste and Material Culture*, 235; on sumptuary laws in the colonies see Linzy A. Brekke '"The Scourge of Fashion": Political Economy and the Politics of Consumption in the Early Republic' *Early American Studies* (Spring 2005), 114.

33 Gikandi, *Slavery and the Culture of Taste*, 115,119.

34 [Print] J[ames] S[ayer], 'On a Visit – Taking a Ride – West India Fashionables' (London, William Holland, 1807).

35 Gikandi, *Slavery and the Culture of Taste*, 102.

36 Tobias Smollett, *The Expedition of Humphrey Clinker* (1771; London, 1884), 37.

37 Gikandi, *Slavery and the Culture of Taste*, 125.

38 Breen, *The Marketplace of Revolution*, xx

39 C. Knick Harley, 'British Industrialization before 1841: Evidence of Slower Growth During the Industrial Revolution' *Journal of Economic History* 42 (June 1982), 280.

40 'Miss Carolina Sullivan, one of the obstinate daughters of America,' printed by Mary Darly, London, September 1, 1776. Caricature and Cartoon File, PR 010 #1776–3, negative number 39754. Collection of The New-York Historical Society. Reproduced in Haulman, *The Politics of Fashion*, 159.

41 'Examination before the Committee of the Whole of the House of Commons,' Feb. 13, 1766 *The Papers of Benjamin Franklin* 3: 124 (http://franklinpapers.org) and Breen, *The Marketplace of Revolution*, 195–200.

– CHAPTER 31: *American consumers in an era of Atlantic free trade* –

42 On the wearing of French fashions see Haulman, *The Politics of Fashion*, 175–80. The controversy over the British Meschianza ball held in Philadelphia in May 1778 also illuminates this tension over British fashions. See Haulman, *The Politics of Fashion*, 172–73 and Susan Klepp, 'Rough Music on Independence Day: Philadelphia' in Matthew Dennis, Simon P. Newman and William Pencaks, eds., *Riot and Revelry in Early America* (University Park, Pa.: University of Pittsburgh Press, 2002). On trade see Merril D. Peterson, 'Thomas Jefferson and Commercial Policy, 1783–93' *William and Mary Quarterly,* Third Series, 22:4 (October 1965), 595–600.

43 See for example: 'Advertisement' *South Carolina Weekly Advertiser*, 12 March 1783, 'Albany June 16' *Pennsylvania Packet*, 3 July 1783, 'Advertisement' *Pennsylvania Packet,* 17 April 1783, 'Advertisement' *Pennsylvania Packet*, 8 July 1783, 'New-York, July 17 Advertisement' *Salem Gazette*, 7 August 1783, 'London May 29' *Pennsylvania Packet*, 16 August 1783. For an overview see Thomas Doerflinger, *A Vigorous Spirit of Enterprise: Merchants and Economic Development in Revolutionary Philadelphia* (Chapel Hill: University of North Carolina Press for the Institute of Early American History and Culture, 1986), 263; Peter J. Marshall *Remaking the British Atlantic: The United States and the British Empire after American Independence* (Oxford: Oxford University Press, 2012), 264.

44 Adam Smith, *The Wealth of Nations*, ed. Edwin Cannon, introduction Robert Reich (New York: Modern Library, 2000), 715.

45 John E. Crowley, *The Privileges of Independence. Neomercantilism and the American Revolution* (Baltimore: Johns Hopkins University Press, 1993), 70.

46 Ibid., 72. See also James Ashley Morrison, "Before Hegemony," 25.

47 John Baker Holroyd, Earl of Sheffield, *Observations on the Commerce of the American States with Europe and the West Indies* (London: J. Debrett, 1784), 2. See also George Chalmers, *Opinions on Interesting Subjects of Public Law and Commercial Policy Arising from American Independence* (London: J. Debrett, 1784).

48 Sheffield, *Observations on the Commerce of the American States*, 10–11.

49 Colley, *Britons*, 19–25.

50 Eliga H. Gould, *Among the Powers of the Earth: The American Revolution and Making of a New World Empire* (Cambridge Mass and London: Harvard University Press, 2012), 119.

51 Sheffield also assumed that the price of goods would play a significant role as well as the fact that Americans relied on the British for generous lines of credit. See Sheffield, *Observations on the Commerce of the American States*, 5.

52 Berg, 'From Imitation to Invention,' 18.

53 Richard Champion, *Considerations on the Present Situation of Great Britain and the United States of America, with a view to their further commercial connexions,* 2nd edition (London: John Stockdale, 1784), 58.

54 Ibid., 263–64.

55 William Bingham, *A Letter from an American, Now Resident In London, to a Member of Parliament on the Subject of Restraining Proclamation and containing Strictures on Lord Sheffield's Pamphlet on the Commerce of the American States* (London: J. Stockdale, 1784), 45.

56 See Gould, *Among the Powers of the Earth*, 136; Marshall, *Remaking the British Atlantic,* Donald R. Hickey, 'American Trade Restrictions during the War of 1812' *The Journal of American History* 68:3 (December 1981), 517–38.

57 Paul Bairoch quoted in Nye, 'The Myth of Free-Trade Britain and Fortress France', 24. See also C.P Kindleberger, 'The Rise of Free Trade', 27.

58 Act of July 4, 1789, c.2, *Stat.* 1. For the period 1807 to 1815 see Joanna Cohen, *Luxurious Citizens: Consumption and Civic Belonging in Nineteenth Century America* (Philadelphia: University of Pennsylvania Press, forthcoming) chapter 2. See also Hickey, 'American Trade Restrictions'.

593

59 Daniel Peart, 'Looking Beyond Parties and Elections: The Making of United States Tariff Policy during the Early 1820s' *Journal of the Early Republic* 33:1 (Spring 2013), 94, 107. See also Jonathan J. Pincus, *Pressure Groups and Politics in Antebellum Tariffs* (New York: Columbia University Press, 1977).

60 Kindleberger, 'The Rise of Free Trade', 27.

61 Regina Blasszczyk, *Imagining Consumers: Design and Innovation from Wedgewood to Corning* (Baltimore: Johns Hopkins University Press, 2000), 52–88.

62 Unknown maker, Jug, made Liverpool, England, ca. 1795, 414:1095–1885, Victoria and Albert Museum, London, UK. See also James and Ralph Clews, Jug, made in Cobridge, England, ca. 1825, C.38–1974, Victoria and Albert Museum, London, UK.

63 Henry Bradshaw Fearon, *Sketches of America, a narrative of a Journey of Five Thousand Miles* 2nd edition (London: Longman, Hurst, Rees, Orme and Brown, 1818), 6.

64 Ibid., 9.

65 It was not only Britons who thought free black people lacked taste. Americans were quick to mock and dismiss the tastes of free black people also, attitudes which in fact helped to reinforce British conceptions. See Nancy Reynolds Davidson, 'E.W. Clay: American Political Caricaturist of the Jacksonian Era', PhD. diss.,The University of Michigan, 1980.

66 Frances Wright, *Views of Society and Manners in America*, ed. Paul R Baker (Cambridge, Mass: The Belknap Press of Harvard University Press, 1963), 33.

67 Ibid., 201.

68 Anishanslin, *Embedded Empire*, chapter 1.

69 Kindleberger, 'The Rise of Free Trade', 28–30; Irwin, 'Free Trade and Protection in Nineteenth-Century Britain and France Revisited', 146.

70 Polanyi, *The Great Transformation*, 143.

71 29 Parl. Deb. (3rd ser.) (1835) 553–55.

72 Stephen Farrell, 'Warburton, Henry, (1754–1858)', *The History of Parliament: The House of Commons, 1820–1832* ed. D.R Fisher (Cambridge: Cambridge University Press, 2009) http://www.historyofparliamentonline.org/volume/1820-32 (accessed March 23, 2014).

73 *Report from Select Committee on Arts and Manufactures* (1835), 2.

74 Paul A.C. Sproll, 'Matters of Taste and Matters of Commerce: British Government Intervention in Art Education in 1835', *Studies in Art Education* 35:4 (1994), 107–8; Edward Bird, 'Art and Design in the Nineteenth Century – Dilemma and Conflict' in *Proceedings of the Conference of the European Academy of Design* 3: 1995.

75 *Report from Select Committee on Arts and Manufactures* (1835), 15.

76 Paul Young, *Globalization and the Great Exhibition: The Victorian New World Order* (London: Palgrave Macmillan, 2009), 23.

77 *Report from Select Committee on Arts and Manufactures* (1835), 102.

78 Ibid., 102.

79 Ibid., 11–12.

80 Ibid., 2–6; 22, 27, 88.

81 This is surprising since Victorians believed women to be especially susceptible to the beguiling nature of consumer goods. See Margot Finn, 'Working-Class Women and the Contest for Consumer Control in Victorian County Courts' *Past and Present* 161 (Nov., 1998), 135, 141. See also Lori Anne Loeb, *Consuming Angels: Advertising and Victorian Women* (New York: Oxford University Press, 1994).

82 *Report from Select Committee on Arts and Manufactures* (1835), 19, 39.

83 Ibid., 46.

84 Bird, 'Art and Design in the Nineteenth Century – Dilemma and Conflict', although ultimately the Select Committee were pre-empted and the government allocated £1600 for the foundation of a national School of Design in 1835. See Sproll, 'Matters of Taste and Commerce', 109.

- CHAPTER 31: *American consumers in an era of Atlantic free trade* -

85 'American Complaints of British Monopoly', *The Sheffield and Rotherham Independent,* 20 November, 1841, 1139.

86 This was despite British efforts to lessen the effects of the Corn Laws by introducing a sliding scale for manufactured goods in 1828. See Simon Morgan, 'America, Protectionism and Democracy in British Free Trade Debates, 1815–61' in *The American Experiment and the Idea of Democracy in British Culture, 1776–1914* ed. Ella Dzelzainis and Ruth Livesey (Farnham, Surrey: Ashgate, 2013), 94.

87 Foreign Intelligence, *The Sheffield Independent* April 13, 1839, 3.

88 American support for free trade came largely from southern pro-slavery intellectuals. See Michael O' Brien *Conjectures of Order: Intellectual Life and the American South, 1810–1860* II (Chapel Hill and London: University of North Carolina Press, 2004), 817, 891; Brian Schoen, *The Fragile Fabric of Union: Cotton, Federal Politics and the Global Origins of the Civil War* (Baltimore: Johns Hopkins University Press, 2009), 100–145; Walter Johnson, *River of Dark Dreams: Slavery and Empire in the Cotton Kingdom* (Cambridge, MA: Harvard University Press, 2013), 282–83. For an overview of American tariff policy see the classic F.W Taussig, *The Tariff History of the United States* (1892 reprint: New York and London: Knickerbocker Press, 1923). On British free trade see Morgan, 'America, Protectionism and Democracy in British Free Trade Debates', and Anthony Howe, 'John Bull and Brother Jonathan: Cobden, America and the Liberal Mind' in *The American Experiment and the Idea of Democracy in British Culture, 1776–1914* ed. Ella Dzelzainis and Ruth Livesey (Farnham, Surrey: Ashgate, 2013), 107–19.

89 Joseph R. Chandler, *Address Delivered at the Close of the Seventeenth Exhibition of American Manufactures Held by the Franklin Institute of the State of Pennsylvania for the Promotion of the Mechanic Arts, October 1847* (Philadelphia: Franklin Institute, 1847), 10.

90 William Kelley quoted in The Franklin Institute, *Report of the Twenty-Second Exhibition of American Manufactures, Held in the City of Philadelphia* (Philadelphia: R.W. Barnard, 1852), 14.

91 Society for Promoting Christian Knowledge, *The Industry of Nations, as Exemplified in the Great Exhibition of 1851* I (London: Society for Promoting Christian Knowledge, 1852), 101–2.

92 *Great Exhibition of the Works of Industry of All Nations, Official and Illustrated Catalogue by Authority of the Royal Commission* III (London: Spicer Brothers, 1851), 1431–62. On the prairie-ground reference see Wallis and Whitworth, *The American System of Manufactures, 7.*

93 John Styles, 'Victorian Britain, 1837–1901, Introduction' in *Design and the Decorative Arts, 336.*

94 *Official Catalogue and Illustrated Description* III, 1431 (cited in Wallis and Whitworth, n.2 p. 7).

95 Charles T. Rodgers, *American Superiority at the World's Fair* (Philadelphia: J.J. Hawkins, 1852), 127. Rodgers quoted the *Observer* with pride.

96 Horace Greeley, ed., *Art and Industry: As Represented in the Exhibition at the Crystal Palace, New York – 1853–4* (New York: Redfield, 1853), 58.

97 'America and Canada' (London), *Daily News,* May 23, 1849.

98 Wallis and Whitworth, *The American System of Manufactures, 204.*

99 C.R. Goodrich and B. Silliman, ed. *Science and Mechanism: Illustrated by Examples in the New York Exhibition, 1853–4* (New York: G.P. Putnam and Company, 1854), 161.

100 Wallis and Whitworth, *The American System of Manufactures, 304.*

101 'American Industry' *The Morning Chronicle* (London) March 30, 1854.

102 'Belfast – Government School of Art' *The Belfast News-Letter* April 7, 1854.

103 Greeley, *Art and Industry* 212.

104 The concerns over quality were accompanied by a worry for the work force used to produce shoddy. This was part of a wider debate over the problem of wage labour and its relationship to free trade. For the broader Anglo-American context see Marcus Cunliffe, *Chattel Slavery and Wage Slavery: The Anglo-American Context, 1830–1860* (Athens GA: University of Georgia Press, 1979).

105 Greeley, *Art and Industry* 211.

106 C.R. Goodrich and B. Silliman, ed. *Science and Mechanism*, 160.

107 'Caveat Venditor', *The Spectator* June 18, 1853, 18.

108 Greeley, *Art and Industry*, 208.

109 Young, *Globalization and the Great Exhibition*, 22–24.

PART VIII
THE CIRCULATION OF IDEAS

CHAPTER THIRTY-TWO

'EXCITED ALMOST TO MADNESS'[1]
Slave rebellions and resistance
in the Atlantic World

——•◆•——

Jeffrey A. Fortin

'About twelve or one clock in the night' of 6 April 1712, Governor Robert Hunter reported a 'bloody conspiracy of some of the slaves' aiming 'to destroy as many of the inhabitants' of New York City 'as they could.'[2] Meeting at an orchard in the middle of town and armed with knives, hatchets, swords, and guns, 'about three and twenty' enslaved Africans – and Native Americans, according to some unverified reports – 'resolved to revenge themselves.'[3] One slave torched his master's shed while the others gathered around. The 'noise of the fire spreading through the town' drew a quick response from the white inhabitants of the bustling seaport; immediately upon 'the approach of several' whites intent on controlling the flames, 'the slaves fired and killed them.'[4] Within minutes, nine white 'Christians' lay dead, with another six injured.[5]

Reports of the mayhem quickly reached Governor Hunter, who summoned the militia to capture the rebellious slaves. With the slaves retreating into the woods, a search of the town on the following day revealed that six of the conspirators 'first laid violent hands on themselves' by committing suicide.[6] Twenty-seven other slaves were captured and condemned to death. Twenty-one of those caught were 'burnt, [the] other hanged, one broke on the wheel' – the latter a particularly tortuous death whereby the bones were slowly, systematically broken and crushed so as to cause excruciating pain over a series of hours.[7] 'The most exemplary punishment inflicted that could possibly be thought of,' Governor Hunter earnestly reported, involved 'one' of the condemned who was 'hung alive in chains in the town' for all to see.[8] He died slowly of dehydration and exposure, with birds likely picking the man's bones clean of flesh after a few days' passing.

Within one year, the Common Council for the City of New York passed several new acts for the regulation and punishment of slaves. These new, stricter black codes focused mainly on controlling nighttime activities of slaves, making it illegal to travel without a 'Lanthorn and a Lighted Candle' or for slaves to inhabit certain parts of the city after sunset.[9] Most importantly, the rebellion hardened the practice of slavery in this city with a high concentration of slaves – approximately 20 percent of the total population in bondage.[10] The city's Common Council argued for better regulation of slaves to halt future revolts and to increase the number of 'White Servants' imported into the city.[11] Restrictions on manumission would also limit the number of free blacks in the city, supposedly making it more difficult for persons of African descent to gather and conspire against whites. Additionally, slaves could no longer claim a right to freedom through conversion to Christianity, a key highlight in this separate code of laws developed specifically for application to the slave population.

The reality of slavery in New York City was different from common modern perceptions of slavery, yet entirely familiar to citizens of the early-modern Atlantic World. New York City's slave population represented the vast diversity of the Trans-Atlantic Slave Trade: most had been born in the West Indies, Angola, the Congo, the Gold Coast of West Africa, and even along Africa's eastern Coast and Madagascar.[12] Urban slaves possessed a level of mobility uncommon for a plantation slave because often their duties were dependent on traveling to different establishments within town. New York City, in particular, was a mixture of ethnicities and races, some free and some enslaved, complicating the social and economic exchanges between individuals within the community. Tavern walls witnessed enslaved and free Africans, creoles, Native Americans and a milieu of Europeans drinking side-by-side and chattering about the latest news brought by ships from around the Atlantic, leading to an enslaved population intimate with the political and social fabric of the city. Undoubtedly on that Sunday night in mid-spring, the two dozen or so slaves involved in the uprising chose the Sabbath – a day of rest for colonial Americans – knowing the city's white residents' guard would be down. The slaves clearly played on growing anxieties in the city fueled by recent murders committed by slaves on Long Island and an increasing concern among whites about a newly opened school to educate and Christianize slaves and Indians.

Rebellions like the one in New York in 1712 occurred often throughout the Atlantic world between 1450 and 1850. Slave revolts took on a variety of meanings, but they represent one of the more extreme acts of resistance to enslavement. Rebellions large and small committed the participating slave to death: either caught and executed, or committing suicide before being captured, rebellious Africans rarely escaped with their lives or freedom.[13] As the slaves in the 1712 rebellion found out, insurrection could be an excruciating way to protest their bondage – a dramatic act of the desperate, or a valiant expression of agency. Death, according to many West African beliefs, provided an escape from slavery where individuals could be reborn in the company of their ancestors.[14]

Although rebellion is the most obvious and often discussed form of resistance to slavery, persons of African descent responded to their enslavement in a variety of ways. As Philip Morgan argues, 'In work and in play, in public and private, violently and quietly, slaves struggled against their masters,' making the act of resistance an evolving, continuous negotiation of power between master and slave, slave and master.[15] Slaves resisted their captivity by running away, through work stoppages/ slowdowns, playing on whites' anxieties, committing suicide and creating a new African–Atlantic culture, among other methods.[16] Each of these forms of resistance shared a common thread: enslaved Africans and Native Americans not only reacted to their oppressors, but often they influenced these relationships. For nearly 400 years of enslavement in the Atlantic world – Brazil was the final Atlantic nation to abolish slavery in 1888 – enslaved peoples developed numerous ways in which to combat their status and express agency over their situations.

– CHAPTER 32: Slave rebellions and resistance –

Resistance need not mean certain death for enslaved Africans or Native Americans in the Atlantic world. Nor was resistance to slavery an act of the powerless. Although in the past scholars have characterized slaves as passive and submissive, unwilling to fight their captors, contemporary scholarship offers a corrective, mostly identifying the variety of ways slaves challenged the master/slave relationship.[17] Enslaved peoples faced a world in which unimaginable despair and loss of hope would seem to rule; yet, because of individual resiliency and group cooperation acts of resistance became the critical conduit through which to shape their world. From everyday acts to grand insurrections – even revolutions – slaves acted out their humanity by confronting their dire situation directly.[18] Surprisingly successful in their resistance, slaves negotiated and renegotiated power relationships with their captors. Sometimes this meant gaining their freedom, sometimes this meant death, but it always meant a disruption in that individual's life of bondage – a powerful motivation even if escaping from the grind of slavery for only a few hours.

Difficult challenges await scholars attempting to understand resistance and rebellion in the Atlantic world. Beyond the multiple languages and broad geographic locations of archives that contain documents relative to slavery and the Trans-Atlantic Slave Trade, the most basic, and somewhat unavoidable problem in current scholarship is the lack of records left by the slaves themselves. Largely illiterate and purposefully kept from socio-political environments – such as courts, legislative bodies, churches, etc. – that often produced copious amounts of records, slaves' intentions and plans to resist slavery are difficult to trace. In short, slaves planning an insurrection or choosing to run away rarely recorded their objectives for fear of being uncovered. The written accounts of enslavement that do exist were produced by exceptional people in unique circumstances, such as Olaudah Equiano, Mary Prince, Frederick Douglass, and others that remain extremely valuable to historians but tell us little about the common slave's method of resistance.[19] Importantly, the only way to arrive at a true sense of resistance and rebellion in the Atlantic World is to consider a vast array of documents, whether slave narratives or records produced by the enslavers themselves.

By no means comprehensive, we will explore the nature of resistance and rebellion in much the same fashion enslaved peoples did. Until recently, studies of slave resistance often centered on mainland North America, suggesting that Africans resisted bondage immediately upon arrival from the Middle Passage. By exploring slave resistance and rebellion in an Atlantic context, it becomes clear that resistance started with the point of capture in Africa. From there, we will follow slaves along the routes they took to their final destination, whether on a plantation or as urban bonded labor, highlighting along the voyage moments of resistance, rebellion and the resulting negotiated power relationships that emerged. Frequently the smallest act of defiance warranted a change in the captive African's conditions; other times it took a massive, violent insurrection to shape the enslaved environment. At all times resistance endeavored to challenge that bleakest of human conditions: the absence of freedom.

* * *

In 1448, a Portuguese slave trader, Alvaro Fernandez, recounted his second voyage to West Africa to buy some slaves. Along with providing insight into the existing practice of slavery on the continent, where 'some Moors' sell 'those Negroes whom

601

– Jeffrey A. Fortin –

they have kidnapped' to Christian merchants, the narrative details early raiding missions by Europeans along the coast of Africa.[20] Inadvertently, the account also reveals the nature of resistance by potential captives. Well before Columbus' voyages to America Europeans were engaged in small-scale slavery aimed primarily at providing domestic servants as opposed to large plantation labor forces that would blossom in the seventeenth and eighteenth centuries. The hunt for these servants regularly brought Europeans to Africa. Historian Ira Berlin identifies the Africans involved in these early exchanges with Europeans as 'Atlantic creoles' because 'they became part of three worlds' – Africa, the Americas and Europe – 'in the Atlantic littoral.'[21] Not always enslaved, Atlantic creoles were often educated and highly culturally literate, able to move from one socio-cultural setting to another with ease.

Fernandez was not interested in acquiring potential Atlantic creoles. His mission was to capture slaves. Returning to 'the land of the Negroes,' Fernandez immediately encountered Africans' resistance to being enslaved by these ugly, hairy white men.[22] Once in Guinea, Fernandez 'journeyed along the sea coast' and 'in a few days…came upon a village, and its inhabitants issued forth like men who showed they had a will to defend their houses.'[23] After a futile attempt to engage the men of the village, Fernandez's men retreated, waiting for the opportune moment to launch a raid. The next day they 'espied some of the wives of those Guineas' collecting shellfish some distance from the village.[24] Descending upon them, Frenandez's men marveled at the 'strength of the woman,' whom, targeted for capture by the raiders, resisted with fortitude. 'For not one of the three men who came upon her,' Fernandez exclaimed, 'would have great labor attempting to get her to the boat.'[25] The people of this anonymous village along the coast of Guinea, including the mother whose two children were also taken into captivity, demonstrated the most basic form of resistance to slavery: fighting the initial capture.

Even when the seemingly weakest members of villages – children – were targeted they found ways to resist being kidnapped. Olaudah Equiano, a former slave who authored the widely selling *The Interesting Narrative of Olaudah Equiano, or Gustavus Vassa, the African,* recalled an incident when a slave raider entered his village after all the adults left to work in the fields for the day. Perhaps under the impression of easy pickings, a 'rogue' entered Equiano's neighbor's yard one day ready to 'carry off as many as they could seize.'[26] Alarmed by Equiano's calls, the 'stoutest' of the children surrounded the man, 'entangl[ing] him with cords, so that he could not escape till some of the grown people came and secured him.'[27] Equiano's detailed narrative illuminates how well versed even the youngest Africans were in the trickery of the slave traders – to the extent that they were able to fend off their captors.[28]

The process of enslavement began in Africa, as raiding parties led by African slave traders captured their bounties in the interior of the continent. Two-thirds male and primarily young, those Africans unable to fight off slave raiders were immediately confined or bound in some type of device to ensure compliance throughout the often long march to the coast where captives would be counted, classified, and readied for sale to the slavers laying in anchor in the bay. Wooden yokes, iron necklaces, and chains introduced stunned men, women, and children to the horrors of slavery.[29] These coffles – a line of people joined by mechanical devices such as a forked log – marched grimly over terra firma, with those unable to keep the pace hacked to death.

– CHAPTER 32: Slave rebellions and resistance –

For some, facing the unknown or experiencing the violence of the moment of capture inspired resistance. At any opportunity captives ran away. Occasionally, successful runaways formed de facto maroon communities perhaps made possible by the fact that most slaves were farmers or from agricultural backgrounds, providing a source of bonding in their mutual experiences. Many captives cried out, attempting to draw attention to themselves and their captors, willing outside aid to interrupt the long march. However, as Equiano reported in his *Narrative,* these cries were met with a stopper placed in the mouth, forcing them to march to the factories in silence. By the time the gag was released, captives were often so 'overpowered by fatigue' and hunger that resistance proved difficult.[30] Sleep, 'our only relief...allayed our misfortune for a short time,' providing only the slightest respite from the descent into bondage.[31]

At the factory, where slaves were counted, inspected, and classified, resistance continued. Initially, slaves were housed in weak enclosures, often able to escape by digging beneath the walls through the loose sand. These 'booths,' as one account refers to them, were constructed directly on the beach.[32] Sometimes 'compass'd round with a mud-wall, about six foot high,' these factories were lightly defended at first and often muddy, disease-ridden environments.[33] High death rates for both Africans and Europeans stationed at the factories made them less than desirable ports of call on the slavers' voyage. But, as the trade increased these structures grew in size and effectiveness, buildings were expanded to include full foundations and mortared walls, making it more challenging for slaves to escape and marking the factories' emergence as fully defended forts dotting the landscape of the Gold Coast of West Africa.[34] Inside, the forts were divided by gender, with men on one side and women on the other to maintain order and ease accessibility for buyers. Deep inside the bowels of these forts, Africans awaited sale, and their first sunlight in days, weeks, or months, before loading into one of the large canoes for transport to the slave ship anchored in the coastal waters.

Once on the water, new opportunities for resistance and rebellion revealed themselves to those Africans seeking escape. In what might seem like the confining gunwales of a canoe or thickly lumbered walls of a 700-tonne ship, Africans rose against their enslavement with might and intensity. Captains of the slave trade understood the most difficult portion of their voyage to be the run westward across the Atlantic. With the average crossing between six weeks and six months, 'the tediousness caus[ed] a great mortality among them.'[35] Facing such conditions, slave ship captains took several precautions against potential insurrections, including division of the sexes, highly regulated feedings of the cargo, heavy shackles, and cramped dimly lit quarters intended to further break the spirits of the Africans.[36] The most important precaution, according to experienced seamen, was avoidance of 'taking in too many...from want of knowing how to manage them aboard' with just enough care taken to ensure safe passage across the Atlantic and arrival in port in the West Indies with as many surviving cargo as possible.[37]

Sailing under the banner of England's joint-stock Royal African Company, a firm with nearly 40 percent of its trade composed of enslaved Africans, Captain Thomas Phillips kept a detailed journal that vividly described the process of enslavement from the moment after capture to their arrival in the West Indies.[38] Importantly, Phillips' journal reveals the degree to which Africans were willing to avoid enslavement and the new opportunities for resistance shipboard. As Phillips' *Hannibal* lay anchored off the coast of Guinea, the captain and his crew loaded some seven hundred newly purchased slaves onto heavy-duty oceangoing canoes for transport to the slaver. 'The men were all put in irons,' he reported, 'two and two shackled together, to prevent their mutiny, or swimming ashore.' For many newly enslaved Africans these attempts to prevent escape mattered little. 'The negroes are so wilful and loth to leave their own country,' affirmed Phillips, 'that they often leap'd out of the canoes, boats and ship, and kept under water till they were drowned…to avoid being taken up and saved by our boats.'[39] Intended to deter, the iron shackles only caused Africans to change their strategy of resistance. 'They [had] a more dreadful apprehension of Barbadoes than we can have of hell, though in reality' Phillips convinced himself, 'they live much better there than in their own country.'[40] Suicide offered a way out of Africans' earthly purgatory.

Despite witnessing seemingly common suicidal behavior, Captain Phillips remained detached from, and somewhat aggravated by his captives. 'We have likewise seen divers numbers of them eaten by sharks,' he stated, concerned by these sharks that 'kept about the ships in this place, and I have been told will keep about' the *Hannibal* until reaching port in Barbadoes, 'for the dead negroes that are thrown overboard in the passage' will provide a steady diet.[41] The grim reality of death, the ever-present moans as the weight of enslavement seemed to crush Africans, in the eyes of their captors, did little to raise emotion in Phillips' words. Apparently cool to the plight of his commodities, Phillips expressed little regret at losing some of his cargo to the sharks.

Perhaps the ultimate form of resistance, suicide illustrates the differences in European and African cultural beliefs as well as how attuned to their cargoes slave ship captains could be. Phillips himself understood the meaning behind the act for Africans, lamenting the loss of about '12 negroes who drowned themselves, and others starv'd themselves to death.' Phillips explained to his imagined audience that "tis their belief that when they [committed suicide] they return home to their own country and friends,' to which he mused, 'home is home, etc.' To prevent these suicides, other captains dismembered a few of the 'most unruly' offenders because 'they believe if they lose [a] member, they cannot return home again.' Professing to be stunned by such deeds, Phillips refused to practice this degree of 'barbarity and cruelty.'[42] Slave ship captains understood their captives to a degree that might seem unfathomable, yet it was essential to their success: they accepted resistance by Africans in limited amounts before acting to suppress it.

Later in the eighteenth century, Olaudah Equiano's explicit details about life shipboard during the arduous journey from freedom in Africa to slavery in the Americas depicted suicide as a mode of resistance infused with African spiritual beliefs. Under a pervasive stench of death, bodily fluids and rotting food, Equiano recalled expecting to 'share the fate of my companions…the inhabitants of the deep' who had jumped ship, releasing themselves from the torturous journey, becoming 'much more happy than myself.'[43] Confronting the unknown yet understanding his new status as enslaved, Equiano 'envied them the freedom they enjoyed' in the depths of the Atlantic.[44] Equiano's own despair became so intense that he attempted to go without food but was forced by the ship's crew to accept their rations. Combating the horrid conditions onboard a slaver became a struggle of life and death, crew versus cargo, and a battle of the individual's will.

Beyond Equiano's desire to live, whether enslaved or not, his *Narrative* captures the veracity with which petrified Africans took the situation into their own hands. On a day with smooth sailing and moderate wind, 'two of my wearied countrymen,

– CHAPTER 32: *Slave rebellions and resistance* –

who were chained together...preferring death to such a life of misery, somehow made through the nettings, and jumped into the sea.'[45] Far from surprised, Equiano recalled 'another quite dejected fellow...follow their example,' plunging himself into the ocean, rather than face a life in shackles.[46] Many Africans resisted their captors with a finality that was twofold. Suicide not only cost the traders financially but it made the slaver's crew anxious over the prospect of mass suicide or revolt shipboard, striking fear into the minds of those very men whose survival depended on coercion and violence aimed at their captive cargoes.[47]

A continual tension existed between slave ship crews and their enslaved cargo. Africans resisted their fate through suicide and crews did what they could to limit losses. A fine line governed these actions: how many suicides or beatings would it take before an entire cargo mutinied? This continual negotiation between the two groups illustrates how resistance did not always need to occur in large groups or dramatic episodes. Sometimes resistance took the form of individuals fasting; at other times resistance was the enhancement of an omnipresent fear of what could happen shipboard. Regardless, as experience mounted, European slave ship captains began to avoid carrying a cargo of too many Africans from the same ethnic background to avoid conspiracies and collaboration against themselves.

As the slaver prepared for its Trans-Atlantic crossing crews tended to the cargo, securing the holds to circumvent shipboard insurrection. For an imprudent crew, revolt could happen immediately after securing their cargo. A Dutch factor, William Bosman, recalled the 'carelessness of a master' who laid the ship's anchor in the hold of the male slaves.[48] Using the heavy anchor 'in a short time they broke all their fetters in pieces,' emerging on the deck where 'before all was appeased about twenty of them were killed.'[49] Despite this particular revolt's failure, Bosman heard of several more successful insurrections in the harbor. 'They resolve and agree together...to run away from the ship' by killing the Europeans, 'set the vessel a-shore; by which means they design to free themselves.'[50] Acutely aware of the desperation and fear amongst the captured Africans, slave ship crews needed to be alert and take care not to misplace items that could facilitate an uprising. Africans often took advantage of the first – and virtually every – opportunity they had to resist enslavement, whether through shipboard rebellions or some other means.

There exist numerous accounts of insurrections aboard slavers making the dreary, often monotonous Trans-Atlantic crossing. Alexander Falconbridge, a ship's surgeon who recorded a narrative of the events he witnessed on countless voyages involving the slave trade, offered perhaps the most powerful description of life onboard a slaver. He explained that 'few of the Negroes can so far brook the loss of their liberty and the hardships they endure, they are ever on the watch to take advantage of the least negligence in their oppressors.'[51] Reflecting further, 'insurrections are frequently the consequence...seldom' are these acts 'expressed without much bloodshed.'[52] Even when outright rebellion failed, 'they are likewise always ready to seize every opportunity for committing some acts of desperation to free themselves from their miserable state and notwithstanding the restraints which are laid, they often succeed.'[53] Writing in the Age of Revolution, Falconbridge cast his narrative in stark contrast to the recent American Revolution and burgeoning French Revolution. Few crewmembers onboard slavers commented on Africans' liberty, yet all understood that their captive cargoes were desperate to avoid the Middle Passage.

605

Most often ships' crews were able to beat down an insurrection, whether through brute force or, upon hearing rumors of a planned revolt, by punishing its presumed leaders. Countless times, however, revolts occurred with dire consequences. French trader John Barbot described one brutal episode on the vessel, *Don Carlos*. In a 'premeditated' attack, 'seeing all the ship's company, at best but weak and many quite sick,' several slaves had 'broken off the shackles from several of their companions' feet.'[54] Armed with all 'things they could lay their hands on' to 'use for their enterprise,' they 'fell in crouds and parcels on our men.'[55] Surprised by the rebellion, several crewmembers were quickly overrun. The armed men stabbed the 'stoutest of us all, who receiv'd fourteen or fifteen wounds' that killed him. Next, they sliced through the nerves of the boatswain's legs, rendering him immobile and highly susceptible to gangrene. Then, the mutineers cut the 'cook's throat to the pipe' and wounded three others, throwing overboard one of the wounded.[56] In a spectacular display of force the Africans overturned the hierarchy of the ship.

As chaos ensued, the crew gathered their weapons, 'firing on the revolted slaves, of whom we kill'd some, and wounded many: which terrify'd the rest' who returned between decks in defeat.[57] When it appeared the revolt would be quashed, the 'most mutinous...leapt over board, and drown'd themselves in the ocean with much resolution, shewing no manner of concern for life.'[58] Having lost twenty-eight slaves in the madness, with four or five crew members killed, Barbot's men identified the main conspirators and had each physically capable white man aboard severely whip the ringleaders. Spending two brief paragraphs in his lengthy journal describing the revolt suggests how ordinary the events were that day. In the moment when the slaves rose up against their captors, the captain and his crew acted swiftly to put down the insurrection; yet, the journal seems to describe a series of events altogether expected, almost routine in the way they unfolded. Despite their commonplace, shipboard resistance usually failed to release the Africans onboard from their captivity, resulting in the safe passage on average of roughly two-thirds of the captives who began the voyage.[59]

For those Africans who did not successfully resist bondage through suicide, successful shipboard insurrection, or by running away when slave traders attempted to kidnap them in Africa, another opportunity to affect their future awaited at the completion of the Middle Passage. Approximately 37 percent of slave voyages ended in the West Indies, while 58 percent culminated in South America, with the remainder scattered in mainland North America (just 4 percent) and Africa (1 percent).[60] In these far-flung locations slaves were redistributed through auction houses and markets. Sales could take the form of an auction, a parade through the port's streets, or even a 'scramble,' which involved a mass of buyers in a chaotic scrum, pulling and tugging at the arms of slaves they saw fit to purchase for a pre-arranged price. The slave-broker may appear to have held the power, yet Africans invented numerous ways to influence to whom they were sold, if not entirely break free from bondage. Whether in a scramble sale in Jamaica or an auction house in New Orleans, the market provided unique opportunities for the daring.

The market environment could be chaotic, where stunned Africans were examined, picked, and prodded, with potential buyers even tasting their sweat to determine the health of the slave. To the same degree Africans often resisted their kidnappers on the eastern side of the Atlantic, once in port on the western side they employed the most basic act of resistance: the attempt to flee their captors. The confusion of a scramble-style sale provided the opportune moment for 'the poor astonished negroes' who

– CHAPTER 32: *Slave rebellions and resistance* –

(Châtiment des quatre piquets, dans les colonies, par M. Marcel Verdier.)

Figure 32.1 Slavery/West Indies
Mary Evans Picture Library

'were so much terrified by these proceedings, that several of them…climbed over the walls of the courtyard, and ran wild about the town.'[61] Although eventually captured, the slaves briefly experienced freedom from the primeval scramble, where buyers tied together handkerchiefs or ropes to corral as many bodies as possible.

Evidence abounds for the myriad ways that slaves influenced their sale. As historian Walter Johnson argues, 'slaveholders were forced to consider their slaves a party to their own sale' because the slave held a unique position of power where even subtle acts could influence the price or sale of the individual.[62] Because sale meant another journey into the unknown for the slave – raising questions, to begin with, about what kind of treatment they may receive from their new owners – these human commodities resisted their own sale in numerous ways. Reports of individuals maiming themselves to make them less desirable in the marketplace – what good is a field worker with a missing hand? – demonstrate the lengths to which individuals would resort to remain with the same owner. Other slaves tried to make themselves more desirable to certain buyers with a reputation for treating their property in a more humane manner. Regardless of the method, slaves on the auction block understood that moment as ripe with opportunity to shape their own futures. Inside the domestic trade within antebellum America slaves could resist their sale through increasingly dramatic measures, even threatening suicide. In this manner, the individual targeted for sale could alter the stakes, renegotiating with his or her master where he or she was willing to be sold, if at all.[63]

In contrast to most other moments in the process of enslavement, life on a plantation in the Atlantic world offered Africans a plethora of opportunities for resistance to their bondage. It was on the plantation that slaves experienced stability: relatively sturdy housing, fairly consistent ownership, the ability to carve a semi-private space, and the prospect of negotiating power relationships with the overseer, owner, and other slaves. The wide-open landscape mocked Africans in bondage – the cleared land awaiting cultivation must have made freedom appear just beyond the horizon, or off in the rugged mountains that surrounded tillable lands. For many, the harsh labor and violence of plantation life provoked rebellion, resistance, and daily efforts to define the terms of their enslavement with the specter of life outside of bondage looming in the distance.

Perhaps the essential road to resistance for a plantation slave, however, resembled one of the most basic forms of resistance to slavery back in Africa. Running away from one's enslavement proved time and again to be a popular method through which the individual could gain – at least – temporary freedom. Runaway slave advertisements from the eighteenth century reveal that this act of resistance was commonplace.[64] A survey of newspapers throughout the American colonies contains numerous advertisements offering payment for the return of their slaves with reward amounts varying depending on a slave's value to the owner, which often depended on whether or not the slave was a skilled laborer.[65]

Runaway slaves patterns suggest this form of resistance was often aimed at temporary relief of strenuous work. In the Carolina Lowcountry, for example, reports of runaway slaves peaked in June when continuous work in the rice fields began, marking the most tedious and difficult two months on the plantation. Plantation overseers found a simple way to combat this seasonal upsurge in runaways, claiming

Figure 32.2   Black slaves working on a plantation and sugar factory
Iberfoto/Mary Evans Picture Library

that slaves were 'kept to their work by mere dint of Encouragement of a Beef and some Rum, added to lenient treatment by the Overseer.'[66] By running away in summer months, slaves reduced the amount of workers in the fields, which allowed weeds to overtake the rice and reduce the crop yield. Planters and Overseers knew that fewer workers meant less profit, making accommodating slaves' demands necessary, to some degree, in order to produce marketable rice. By simply providing extra food or some rum to appease their slaves, overseers knew this would ensure enough workers in the field to cultivate the rice successfully.

Despite the regular return of slaves to plantations, runaways were periodically successful in escaping bondage. Maroon communities composed of runaway slaves and their descendants sprang up in plantation-based slave societies throughout the Atlantic world, from the mainland American colonies to the French Caribbean island of Martinique to Portuguese Brazil.[67] Along the Savannah River in the Carolina Lowcountry stable, well-built maroon communities seemed to taunt white South Carolinians who found it necessary to mount military expeditions against the runaway communities.[68] Further south, maroon communities thrived in the West Indies. On the British sugar island of Jamaica, in particular, maroon-founded communities survived Spanish rule as well as the British take-over in the late seventeenth and early eighteenth centuries. Divided into numerous towns such as Spanish Town, Accompong, and Trelawney Town, maroons lived in tension with whites, as well as other free and enslaved blacks and mulattos on the island.

Periodically whites hired maroons to hunt down other runway slaves, prizing their knowledge of Cockpit Country, so-called for its rugged landscape that provided numerous spaces for hiding out. Despite momentary collaboration, maroons throughout the island caused havoc and cost planters money in stolen goods by raiding plantations for food, women, and alcohol. Noted scholar Orlando Patterson argues that 'Few slave societies present a more impressive record of slave revolts than Jamaica,' where maroon communities continuously put pressure on the island's slave system.[69] The First Maroon War, which occurred shortly after the English takeover from the Spanish and concluded with a treaty in 1739/40, yielded to decades of seemingly continuous plantation raids and land conflicts that eventually resulted in the Second Maroon War in 1796. The short war resulted in the deportation of an entire maroon community – the Trelawney Town Maroons – identified as the lone group responsible for the conflict.[70] Nevertheless, maroons in Jamaica rarely were returned to slavery, making them perhaps the most successful runaways in the Atlantic littoral in part because they fashioned an existence outside of slavery, working for whites when necessary and maintaining focus on guarding their own self-interest.

For Native Americans, fleeing their captors proved to be their greatest defense against widespread enslavement. In writing of colonial Louisiana – the very real melting pot of the Atlantic where Africans, Spaniards, Frenchmen, Englishmen, and Native Americans intermingled – historian Daniel Usner asserts that a 'more serious threat to the designs of colonial planners was the general recalcitrance of Indian slaves and their potential for collaboration' with African slaves. 'Given their knowledge of the terrain and familiarity with local tribes,' Native American runaways 'held the key to unlocking mass rebellion.'[71] Indian slaves fell out of favor once large numbers of Africans were imported into European colonies throughout the Atlantic in part because of the destabilizing threat they posed to the plantation system but also because they resisted bondage adeptly by running away. Knowing the lay of the land and able to use kinship networks unavailable to newly arrived Africans facilitated Indians' escape from slavery. Indeed, some Native Americans were hired to capture runaway African slaves because of their abilities to navigate the complex, always shifting social and environmental landscapes of the Americas.[72] For Native Americans, running away contributed significantly to the decline in Europeans using Indians for labor.

Life on the plantation provided many other opportunities for resistance. Slaves often faked illness or slowed work in order to combat harsh demands from an overseer or planter. These labor disputes were effective ways that slaves could renegotiate the type and length of task assigned to them, providing a level of input and influence over their work assignments.[73] With enough experience, overseers and slave masters understood that 'Should any owner increase the work beyond what is customary, he subjects himself to the...discontent amongst his slaves as to make them of but little use to him.'[74] Despite being held in bondage Africans could shape their daily lives through work, whether that meant gaining concessions in the form of extra food or alcohol, or by convincing the overseer to lower production expectations.

Many enslaved Africans resisted harsh conditions on plantations by steeling away enough money to buy freedom. Mary Prince, a slave in the West Indies during the late eighteenth and early nineteenth centuries, recalled, 'I had saved about 100 dollars, and hoped, with a little help, to purchase my freedom.'[75] Prince utilized those times 'When my master and mistress went from home, as they sometimes did...and made the most of it' by taking on odd jobs for extra pay.[76] Prince even occasionally bought and resold hogs to acquire 'a little cash' to buy her freedom.[77] Although not as widespread as running away or implementing work stoppages, purchasing one's own freedom proved to be an act of resistance of the highest order because slaves worked within the very financial systems that ensured their bondage in order to gain their freedom. In some parts of the Atlantic, self-purchasing was guaranteed by law. Once a slave initiated the legal mechanisms to purchase their freedom, a master or owner could do little to block the slave's manumission.[78]

Resistance to enslavement was as varied as the ethnicities of Africans held in bondage and it frequently occurred in the courts. In 1705, on the French sugar island of Martinique, Babet Binture sued for her freedom, testing the French colonial courts. 'Claiming to have been born of a free father and a free mother' but with no records available to support her claims, the case was 'dismissed...declar[ing] her a slave' and 'to punish her temerity to start inappropriate and groundless proceedings.'[79] Three years later, Jean Doussin, a public official, petitioned the court to change Binture's status because it had been determined that her sister was free since birth. Although the court agreed, declaring 'Babet, Negress, and all her children free and emancipated' their freedom was once again taken in 1713 after recently appointed Governor Phelypeaux argued successfully that they endangered public welfare, as well as placed the Binture's former owner, a widow, in a state of destitution.[80]

Clearly more troubling to the man was the 'ruin of the La Pallu family' – Binture's former owners – 'one of the better and the most numerous of this land,' to whom 'this judgement has caused extreme disorders.'[81] With dishonor brought to the family, Binture and two other free women 'currently play as nightclub proprietors, madams, whores, fences of stolen property and runaway slaves.'[82] Upset over the state of affairs in Martinique, Governor Phelypeaux was convinced that society as a whole suffered greatly with these freed women doing 'everything that is prohibited by the *Code Noir,*' the French laws aimed at controlling the empire's African population.[83] He seemed to wonder how degraded the island would become if Binture were allowed to remain free.

If courts refused to support the pleas for emancipation, Africans throughout the Atlantic tested other legal bodies to see if they would heed the calls for their enslaved brethren. In 1773, as revolutionary fervor grew in the American colonies, free blacks sought inclusion by petitioning provincial legislative bodies in the 'divine spirit of *freedom* [that] seems to fire every human breast on this continent.'[84] On 'behalf of our fellow slaves in this province,' Boston's petitioners joined together in resisting the institution that could easily reclaim these four freedmen and return them to enslavement.[85] Continuing the tradition of Martinique's Babet Binture, free and enslaved Africans alike challenged the very legal systems that upheld slavery for two centuries of Atlantic expansion to abolish the institution in the name of liberty for all. Such petitions often fell short of their intended goal. Yet, these petitions provided the foundation for future events that would see persons of African descent rise in frustration to raze the structures of plantation slavery on one Caribbean island, and infuse fear and anxiety throughout the entire Atlantic slave system. Beginning in 1791, a new, independent, free black nation would rise in the midst of some of the harshest, most brutal slave societies known to history.

* * *

In the spring of 1685, *Le Code Noir,* or the Black Code, a decree authored by King Louis XIV codified the nature of slavery in the French Atlantic World. Beyond casting all Jews out of French Atlantic holdings, and making Roman Catholicism the more or less official religion of the state, *Le Code Noir* laid out clear and sometimes brutal ground rules for slaves and their masters. Article XVI of *Le Code Noir* struck at slave owners' greatest fear: rebellion. To counter the most violent and, for whites in the Atlantic, dangerous form of resistance to enslavement, the article declared that 'slaves who belong to different masters' are forbidden 'from gathering, either during the day or at night, under the pretext of a wedding or other excuse,' risking 'corporal punishment that shall not be less than the whip and the fleur de lys, and for frequent recidivists and in other aggravating circumstances, they may be punished with death.'[86] *Le Code Noir* largely governed slaves' status and treatment in the French Atlantic, especially on the Caribbean islands of Martinique and Saint Domingue.

Just over one century later, on 29 August 1793, the French Commissioner Léger Félicité Sonthonax, issued a decree for the northern parts of the French colony of Saint Domingue. Building on *The Declaration of the Rights of Man and of the Citizen,* issued four years prior and proving to be the catalyst for the French Revolution, Sonthonax's decree extended to slaves and *gens de couleur* freedom and the full rights of citizenship.[87] A year later, the French National Convention issued a much more broad, sweeping repeal, declaring that 'the slavery of Negroes in all the colonies is abolished,' and 'that all men, without the distinction with regard to color...will enjoy all the rights ensured by the constitution.'[88] In short succession – just four years between the beginning of the French Revolution and the abolition decree in Saint Domingue – an uprising of slaves on the small but influential French

611

sugar island of Saint Domingue sparked what would become the most significant episode of slave resistance in the Atlantic World: the Haitian Revolution. Inspired by the French Revolution, African slaves, men of color – *gens de couleur* – and whites engaged in a long battle over the emancipation of the island's slaves. Although not always a rebellion defined in stark racial lines, slavery and bondage were at the heart of the conflict.

On an island nation where slaves numbered at least 200,000 and nearly two-thirds of the population had been born in Africa by the late eighteenth century, Saint Domingue was ripe for revolution.[89] The multi-layered existence of slavery in Saint Domingue provided unique circumstances that yielded the Atlantic's first independent free black nation. A growing mixed-race class of slaves, descended from their white masters and relieved of work on the plantation but not officially free, combined with a substantial population of free people of color who themselves owned plantations and slaves to make for a combustible atmosphere. *The Declaration of the Rights of Man* ignited the powder keg of Saint Domingue when slaves in the north burned approximately one thousand plantations, demanding the same freedoms of the *gens de couleur,* and driving slave owners to America to escape death at the hands of their former captives.

Despite the rhetoric of the French Revolution, the French Army responded to quash this freedom struggle but was quickly defeated by armies of ex-slaves. In a weakened state and virtually defenseless, Saint Domingue officials began to turn to the rebellious slaves for help: rather than lose the wealthiest colony in the world, limited emancipation was offered to slaves in exchange for their common defense against British and Spanish invaders. Full emancipation soon followed as whites, *gens de couleur* and ex-slaves fought off other European powers in 1794. For the next ten years Toussaint L'Overture ruled the nation embroiled in racial and class conflict. As the revolution cooled in France and Napolean seized power, he sent General Leclerc to Haiti to regain control and re-instill slavery – the sugar island proved too wealthy and tempting to ignore. Leclerc quickly arrested and exiled L'Overture, but failed to win the support of his *gens de couleur* allies who in turn united with the now free slaves to rebel against Napoleon's army, defeating the French with finality.[90]

Christened 'Haiti,' the new nation stood as a beacon to slaves and free blacks around the Atlantic World. Over the past century, scholars have often been fixated on the Haitian Revolution's sometimes brutal events, where 'massacres' were commonplace, representing a pervasive anxiety about the threat of black insurrections in the Atlantic World. Yet, the revolution significantly impacted slavery throughout the Atlantic, providing a unique example of resistance for Africans held in bondage. With a great deal of growing pains, Haiti emerged as a rare successful rebellion against slavery and in so doing it became the zenith of slave resistance, proving that escaping a life in bondage was possible.

What began with fighting off slave traders in Africa, continued on the forced march to slave factories along the coast, resuming once again with desperate struggles shipboard during the Middle Passage, acquiring new significance in the New World slave markets, and finally blossoming on the plantations driving the Atlantic economy. Less than a century after the failed insurrection in New York City in 1712, Haiti transformed the Atlantic World and beyond, becoming 'a crucial moment in the

CHAPTER 32: *Slave rebellions and resistance*

history of democracy, one that laid the foundation for the continuing struggles for human rights everywhere.'[91] Whether enslaved peoples resisted their bondage through revolt, suicide, work stoppages, or running away, their horrifying circumstances demanded defiance. In small and fantastic acts of insubordination, slaves were able to shape their own worlds by resisting their captors, overseers, and owners. It is a reflection of enslaved peoples' humanity and perseverance that they were able to rise against the racist institution and capitalistic system that enforced chattel bondage. For the vast majority of enslaved peoples the only true freedom achieved came upon their deaths, yet resistance enabled slaves to carve a slice of liberty if only for the briefest moment.

NOTES

1 *The Cincinnati Daily Gazette,* 29 January 1856 as reprinted in *Major Problems in African American History, Volume I: From Slavery to Freedom, 1619–1877,* eds. Thomas C. Holt and Elsa Barkley Brown. New York: Houghton Mifflin Company, 2000. p. 248.

2 'Letter from Governor Robert Hunter, June 23, 1712' in *Documents Relative to the Colonial History of the State of New York,* ed. E.B. Callaghan. Vol. V. pp. 341–42.

3 Ibid.

4 Ibid.

5 Ibid.

6 Ibid.

7 Ibid.

8 Ibid.

9 Minutes of the Common Council of the City of New York, 28 February 1713, Vol. III, p. 28.

10 Thelma Wills Foote, *Black and White Manhattan: The History of Racial Formation in Colonial New York City.* New York: Oxford University Press, 2004. p. 138.

11 Ibid. p. 132.

12 Thelma Willis Foote, *Black and White Manhattan: The History of Racial Formation in Colonial New York City.* New York: Oxford University Press, 2004. p. 133.

13 The Haitian Revolution, from 1791–1804, being the one major exception.

14 Walter C. Rucker, *The River Flows On: Black Resistance, Culture, and Identity Formation in Early America.* Baton Rouge: Louisiana State University Press, 2006. p. 86.

15 Philip D. Morgan, *Slave Counterpoint: Black Culture in the Eighteenth-Century Chesapeake and Lowcountry.* Chapel Hill: The University of North Carolina Press, 1998. p. xxii.

16 The formation of new cultures and retention of traditional African cultures and identities is viewed by many scholars as a distinct form of resistance to enslavement. For more on this complex discussion, see Philip Morgan, *Slave Counterpoint;* Michael A. Gomez, *Exchanging Our Country Marks: The Transformation of African Identities in the Colonial and Antebellum South.* Chapel Hill: The University of North Carolina Press, 1998; and John Savage, 'Black Magic and White Terror: Slave Poisoning and Colonial Society in Early Nineteenth Century Martinique,' in *Journal of Social History,* Vol. 40, No. 3 (Spring 2007), 635–62.

17 For example, Stanley Elkins introduced what later became known as the Sambo Thesis, concluding that the institution of slavery proved so overwhelming that Africans had little choice but accept their condition and become child-like dependents to their masters. See: *Slavery: A Problem in American Institutional and Intellectual Life.* Chicago: University of Chicago Press, 1959.

18 For varied treatments on slave rebellion and resistance in past several decades, see: Eugene Genovese, *From Rebellion to Revolution: Afro-American Slave Rebellions in the Making*

of the Modern World. Baton Rouge: Louisiana State University Press, 1979; Anne C. Bailey, *African Voices of the Atlantic Slave Trade: Beyond the Silence and the Shame.* Boston: Beacon Press, 2005; and for a somewhat comprehensive reference source, see *Encyclopedia of Slave Resistance and Rebellion*, ed. Junius Rodriguez. Westport, CT: Greenwood Publishing Group, 2007.

19 For examples of documents produced by enslaved or formerly enslaved Africans, see: *Phillis Wheatley, Complete Writings*, ed. Vincent Carretta. New York: Penguin Classics, 2001; and *The Classic Slave Narratives*, ed. Henry Louis Gates, Jr. New York: New Amsterdam Library, 1987. For an interesting perspective of reading between the lines of colonial documents to uncover slaves' voices, see Natalie Zacek, 'Reading the Rebels: Currents of Slave Resistance in the Eighteenth-Century British West Indies,' in *History in Focus*, 12 (2007) http://www.history.ac.uk/ihr/Focus/Slavery/articles/zacek.html (accessed 13 August 2014).

20 'Of how Alvaro Fernandez returned again to the land of the Negroes' in *Documents Illustrative of the History of the Slave Trade to America*, ed. Elizabeth Donnan. New York: Octagon Books, 1969. p. 39.

21 Berlin, p. 17.

22 'Of how Alvaro Fernandez returned again to the land of the Negroes,' p. 39. Africans were so startled by Europeans' appearances that some checked their bodies for gills. For more on Africans' perceptions of Europeans, see also David Northrup, *Africa's Discovery of Europe, 1450–1850*. New York: Oxford University Press, 2009.

23 'Of how Alvaro Fernandez returned again to the land of the Negroes,' p. 39.

24 Ibid. p. 40.

25 Ibid. p. 40.

26 Equiano (Gates). p. 25.

27 Ibid.

28 It should be noted that some scholars have raised questions about Equiano's claim to having been born in Africa. Vincent Carretta has uncovered records that show Equiano could have been born in South Carolina. Although this would seem to cast doubt on Equiano's description of his capture in Africa, Carretta suggests Equiano could have accurately reconstructed such events based on other Africans' experiences in, as well as widely known contemporary accounts of the slave trade. See Vincent Carretta, *Equiano, the African: Biography of a Self-Made Man*. New York: Penguin Books, 2005. pp. 15–18.

29 For a more detailed description, see Marcus Rediker, *Slave Ship: A Human History*. Boston: Beacon Press, 2008. p. 100.

30 Equiano, *Narrative*, pp. 25–26.

31 Ibid. p. 26.

32 'A Description of the Coasts of North and South Guinea...' by John Barbot, reprinted in *Documents Illustrative of the Slave Trade*, p. 293.

33 Thomas Phillips, 'A Journal of a Voyage Made in the *Hannibal* (1693–94) from England to Cape Monseradoe, in Africa,' in *Documents Illustrative of the History of the Slave Trade to America*, ed. Elizabeth Donnan. New York: Octagon Books, 1969. p. 399.

34 For more on the factories, see Stephanie E. Smallwood, *Saltwater Slavery: A Middle Passage from Africa to American Diaspora*. Cambridge: Harvard University Press, 2007. pp. 37–41.

35 'An Abstract of a Voyage to Congo River or the Zair, and to Cabinde, in the Year 1700,' in *Documents Illustrative of the History of the Slave Trade to America*, ed. Elizabeth Donnan. New York: Octagon Books, 1969. p. 460.

36 For more in-depth discussions of conditions on board slave ships, see: Emma Christopher, *Slave Ships and Their Captive Cargoes, 1730–1807*, New York: Cambridge University Press, 2006; Rediker, *Slave Ship;* and Smallwood, *Saltwater Slavery.*

– CHAPTER 32: *Slave rebellions and resistance* –

37 'An Abstract of a Voyage to Congo River or the Zair, and to Cabinde, in the Year 1700,' in *Documents Illustrative of the History of the Slave Trade to America*, p. 460.

38 Ann M. Carlos and Jamie Brown Kruse, 'The Decline of the Royal African Company: Fringe Firms and the Role of the Charter,' in *Economic History Review*, Vol. XLIX, No. 2 (1996), p. 292.

39 Thomas Phillips, 'A Journal of a Voyage Made in the *Hannibal* (1693–94) from England to Cape Monseradoe, in Africa,' in *Documents Illustrative of the History of the Slave Trade to America*, ed. Elizabeth Donnan. New York: Octagon Books, 1969. pp. 400–403.

40 Ibid. p. 402.

41 Ibid.

42 ibid.

43 Olaudah Equiano, *The Interesting Narrative of the Life of Olaudah Equiano, or Gustavus Vassa, the African*, in *The Classic Slave Narratives*, ed. Henry Louis Gates, Jr., New York: A Mentor Book, 1987. p. 35.

44 Ibid. p. 36.

45 Ibid.

46 Ibid.

47 For more on the tenuous relations between ships' crews and enslaved Africans, see Emma Christopher, *Slave Ship Sailors and their Captive Cargoes, 1730–1807*. New York: Cambridge University Press, 2005.

48 'A New and Accurate Description of the Coast of Guniea, Divided Into Gold, Slave, and the Ivory Coasts,' William Bosman, in *Documents Illustrative of the History of the Slave Trade to America*, ed. Elizabeth Donnan. New York: Octagon Books, 1969. p. 443.

49 Ibid.

50 Ibid.

51 Alexander Falconbridge, *An Account of the Slave Trade on the Coast of Africa*. London: J. Phillips, 1788. p. 30.

52 Ibid.

53 Ibid.

54 'An Abstract of a Voyage to Congo River or the Zair, and to Cabinde, in the Year 1700,' in *Documents Illustrative of the History of the Slave Trade to America*, ed. Elizabeth Donnan. New York: Octagon Books, 1969. p. 457.

55 Ibid.

56 Ibid. The man thrown overboard was able to catch on to a piece of the rigging, eventually pulling himself to safety.

57 Ibid.

58 Ibid.

59 Some ships could arrive in the West Indies with loss of 'only' 5–7 percent their cargo, but most had substantially higher rates of mortality reaching over 50 percent in some cases. See Herbert S. Klein and Stanley L. Engerman, 'Long-term Trends in African Mortality in the Transatlantic Slave Trade,' in *Routes to Slavery: Direction, Ethnicity and Mortality in the Transatlantic Slave Trade*, eds. David Eltis and David Richardson. London: Routledge, 1997. pp. 36–48.

60 http://slavevoyages.org/tast/assessment/estimates.faces (accessed 24 March 2009).

61 *An Account of the Slave Trade...*, Falconbridge, p. 34.

62 Walter Johnson, *Soul By Soul: Life Inside the Antebellum Slave Market*. Cambridge: Harvard University Press, 1999. p. 30.

63 Ibid. See specifically Chapter Two, 'The Chattel Principle,' pp. 30–44.

64 For an interesting and expansive collection of eighteenth-century runaway slaves see the University of Virginia's digitized collection at http://etext.virginia.edu/subjects/runaways (accessed 13 August 2014).

65 Lathan Algerna Whindey, 'A Profile of Runaway Slaves in Virginia and South Carolina from 1730–87,' in *Hammer in Their Hands: A Documentary History of Technology and the African-American Experience*, ed. Carroll Pursell. Cambrigde: MIT Press, 2005. pp. 9–15. See also, John Hope Franklin and Loren Schweninger, *Runaway Slaves: Rebels on the Plantation*. New York: Oxford University Press, 2000.

66 Josiah Smith to George Austin, 22 July 1773 – 22 July 1774, as reprinted in Morgan, *Slave Counterpoint*, p. 151.

67 For further reading on various maroon communities, see Wim S.M. Hoogbergen. *The Boni Maroon Wars in Suriname*. New York: Brill Academic Publishers, 1990; and *Maroon Societies: Rebel Slave Communities in the Americas*, ed. Richard Price. Baltimore: The Johns Hopkins University Press, 1996.

68 Morgan, *Slave Counterpoint*, pp. 450–51.

69 Orlando Patterson, 'Slavery and Slave Revolts: A Sociohistorical Analysis of the First Maroon War, 1665–1740,' in *Maroon Societies: Rebel Slave Communities in the Americas*, ed. Richard Price. Baltimore: The Johns Hopkins University Press, 1996. p. 246.

70 Jeffrey A. Fortin, '"Blackened beyond Our Native Hue": Removal, Identity and the Trelawney Maroons on the Margins of the Atlantic World, 1796–1800,' in *Freedom on the Margins: A Special Issue of Citizenship Studies*. Vol. 10, No. 1 (February 2006), pp. 5–34.

71 Daniel H. Usner, *Indians, Settlers, and Slaves in a Frontier Exchange Economy: The Lower Mississippi Valley before 1783*. Chapel Hill: The University of North Carolina Press, 1992. p. 58.

72 For more, see: Allan Gallay, *The Indian Slave Trade: The Rise of the English Empire in the American South, 1670–1717*. New Haven: Yale University Press, 2002. pp. 94–95.

73 Morgan, *Slave Counterpoint*, p. 184.

74 Ibid.

75 'The History of Mary Prince, A West Indian Slave,' in *The Classic Slave Narratives*, ed. Henry Louis Gates, Jr., p. 205.

76 Ibid.

77 ibid.

78 Berlin, *Many Thousands Gone*, pp. 212–13.

79 'A Tavern Keeper Sues for Her Freedom in Martinique,' in *Slavery, Freedom, and the Law in the Atlantic World: A Brief History with Documents*, eds. Sue Peabody and Keila Grinberg. Boston: Bedford/St Martin's, 2007. p. 37.

80 Ibid. p. 39.

81 Ibid. pp. 40–41.

82 Ibid. p. 41.

83 Ibid.

84 'Petition of Peter Bestes, Sambo Freeman, Felix Holbrook, and Chester Joie, Boston, April 20, 1773,' in *A Documentary History of the Negro People in the United States. Volume I: From Colonial Times through the Civil War*. ed., Herbert Aptheker. New York: The Citadel Press, 1968. pp. 7–8.

85 Ibid. For more see Thomas J. Davis, 'Emancipation Rhetoric, Natural Rights, and Revolutionary New England: A Note on Four Black Petitions in Massachusetts, 1773–77,' in *The New England Quarterly*, Vol. 62, No. 2 (Jun 1989), pp. 248–63.

86 As translated in *Slave Revolution in the Caribbean, 1789–1804: A Brief History with Documents*, eds. Laurent Dubois, John D. Garrigus. New York: Macmillan, 2006. p. 52.

87 As reprinted in *Slavery, Freedom and the Law in the Atlantic World*, p. 61.

88 Ibid. p. 62.

89 Population estimates based on Christopher L. Miller, *The French Atlantic Triangle: Literature and Culture of the Slave Trade*. Durham, NC: Duke University Press, 2008.

– CHAPTER 32: *Slave rebellions and resistance* –

p. 30. Other statistics suggest a slave population of 450,000 with only half of those persons born in Africa, see *Slavery, Freedom and the Law in the Atlantic World*, p. 8.

90 For more on the complex revolution in Saint Domingue, see: Laurent Dubois, *Avengers of the New World: The Story of the Haitian Revolution*. Cambridge: Harvard University Press, 2005; C.L.R. James, *The Black Jacobins: Toussaint L'Overture and the San Domingo Revolution*. New York: Vintage, 1989.

91 Dubois, *Avengers of a New World*, p. 7.

CHAPTER THIRTY-THREE

ECONOMIC THOUGHT AND STATE PRACTICE IN THE ATLANTIC WORLD
The 'Phénomène Savary' in context

——·◆·——

D'Maris Coffman

If the Cultural Turn of the last quarter of the twentieth century contributed to a slow marginalization of economic history and the history of economic thought, the financial crisis of 2007–8 and the Great Recession that followed arrested and eventually reversed that process. In the last few years, scholars have begun to re-visit many of the canonical works of political economy, beginning with Adam Smith's *Wealth of Nations*. Much of their enthusiasm lies in the prospect of interrogating the intellectual origins of the neoliberal emphasis on free markets and free trade. As a consequence of the renewed interest in putatively heterodox economic ideas, authors, classically dismissed as 'mercantilist' by mainstream economics, have received considerable attention, which in turn has mirrored an outpouring of empirical work on how early modern empires were actually governed. Smith's arguments about the central role of the Atlantic economy in catalyzing economic development in Britain, a narrative which inspired generations of scholars including Karl Marx himself, remain more widely accepted than his specific critiques of mercantilism (Zahedieh, 2010, pp. 1–3; Stern and Wennerlind, 2013, pp. 3–4).

At the same time and without denying the enduring significance of influential accounts of the role of ideology and confession in shaping the different political cultures of the respective European imperial powers, historians have begun to emphasize the convergence, rather than divergence, of state practice, especially in key areas like commercial regulation, taxation, and the policing of economic crimes (Pagden, 1995; Hont, 2005; Coffman et al., 2013; Reinert and Røge, 2013). In the process, scholars have come to appreciate the importance of neglected literary genres – including merchant manuals and published public accounts – and of the translation of economic treatises from one European language to another in spreading both commercial and fiscal practices (Reinert, 2011; Reinert and Røge, 2013; Soll, 2014). Recent revisionist scholarship has thus coalesced around three related preoccupations: exploring the possibility that these newly re-discovered non-canonical genres and texts might yield important insights into mercantile practice, understanding better what 'state' power meant in practice in the imperial frame, and finally questioning the presumption found in Montesquieu that promoting trade and commerce produced peace rather than war. The power of these new approaches can be illustrated through

– CHAPTER 33: *Economic thought and state practice* –

examination of the publication history of Jacques Savary's *Le parfait négociant* in France, which cannot be properly understood without reference to the Atlantic context and with it the intense rivalry between the French and English in realizing their overseas imperial projects. As the history text of successive editions of Savary's manual reveals, contemporaries themselves were often unsure how far international trade was a zero-sum game or an opportunity for all to prosper.

When Savary published *Le parfait négociant, ou Instruction générale pour ce qui regarde le commerce des marchandises de France et des pays* étrangers ('The Perfect Merchant, or the General Instruction regarding mercantile commerce of France and foreign nations') in 1675, he dedicated his efforts to Jean-Baptise Colbert. [Illustration 33.1]. From a merchant who prospered under Colbert's commercial policies, such a choice is unsurprising. Yet Savary's connection was more immediate than that of a remote admirer. Over the course of his public career, he served Nicolas Fouquet, Seguier, and Colbert. Savary came from a cadet branch of a minor noble family, was educated in the law, and made a fortune as a wholesale merchant. After increasing his position and wealth by strategic marriage and by tax farming, he became a commercial advisor to the crown. Under Colbert, Savary was appointed to the Council on Reform (of the commercial code) and played enough of a leading part that the president of the commission unveiled the new 'Code Savary' in his name. If the biographical information offered in an eighteenth-century edition of *Le Parfait Négociant* can be believed, the commission further honored him by asking him to prepare what they had learned for general publication in a manual, which might serve as a guide to noble families whose younger sons wanted to enter the mercantile trade, as was the practice in England.[1] Jacob Soll (2009, pp. 86–90) develops this theme in his treatment of the didactic intentions of the text for disciplining the French to Colbert's vision for world dominance through trade.

Albert Hirschman, one of the earliest modern historians to take *Le Parfait Négociant* seriously, noticed immediately that Savary was the first in this period to make the claim, later echoed by Montesquieu, that '[Divine providence] has dispersed its gifts so that men would trade together so that the mutual need which they have to help one another would establish ties of friendship among them. This continuous exchange of all comforts of life constitutes commerce and this commerce makes for all the gentleness of life' (Hirschman, 1977, pp. 59–60). Hirschman saw this shift in attitude towards commerce as a fundamental one in the development of the ideology of capitalism. Unfortunately, historians of early modern Europe have largely ignored both Hirschman's suggestion of the work's importance and the figure of Jacques Savary.

Despite thirty-one printings in three languages (French, German, and Dutch) in less than a century (1675–1777) and a thirty-second and thirty-third in 1800, *Le Parfait Négociant* has not attracted much scholarly attention in either French or English.[2] Jochen Hoock, one of the editors of the authoritative compendium of merchant handbooks and treatises, *Ars Mercatoria*, contributed an essay to *Innovations et Renouveaux Techniques de l'Antiquité à nos Jours*, a volume compiling conference papers from the tenth-anniversary meeting of the *Colloque International de Mulhouse* in 1987. With the exception of this excellent, if difficult to obtain, discussion of *Le Parfait Négociant* as a publishing phenomenon, the only full-length treatment in the secondary literature is a single article by Henri Hauser in *Revue d'Historie* Économique *et Sociale* in 1925 and a recent discussion by Trivellato which points to Savary as the

619

Figure 33.1 Frontispiece of 'Le Parfait Negociant' by Jacques Savary, Paris, 1665 (engraving)
Bibliotheque Nationale, Paris, France/Archives Charmet/Bridgeman Images

– CHAPTER 33: *Economic thought and state practice* –

source of the myth of the Jewish invention of bills of exchange (Hoock, 1989; Hauser, 1925; Trivellato, 2012). Otherwise, there are occasional references in the literatures on merchant mentalities, early modern accounting, and material culture (Rabuzzi, 1995–96; Bonno, 1948; Hirschman, 1977). Although Bonno's footnote proved erroneous, he too used a quotation from Savary to suggest that the French knew that the English nobility saw nothing wrong with participating in trade. Bonno begins his section on English commercial activity by citing Savary: 'en Angleterre le commerce est trouvé tellement honnête que la noblesse de la plus haute dignité fait le commerce de laine et de bétail' ('in England trade is found so honourable that the highest nobility engage in the trade of wool and cattle') (Bonno, 1948, p. 50).

Yet beyond a brief mention in the *Catholic Encyclopedia* of 1912, based almost entirely on the preface to the 1721 edition, no biographical treatment of the author exists (Goyau, 1912). The scholarly attention paid to *Le dictionnaire universel du commerce* by Savary's son, Savary des Bruslons, is not much greater: one article from the 1920s, one chapter in a recent monograph, and only the occasional reference otherwise (Vignols, 1929; Perrot, 1992). This is all the more surprising because the Goldsmiths'-Kress Library contains seventeen editions of *Le Parfait Négociant* (Rogers, 1986; Nicholes and Reeves, 1966). The editions chosen for this discussion – 1675 (Paris), 1676 (Geneva), 1679 (Paris), 1697 (Lyon), 1701 (Paris, Lyon), 1721 (Paris), and 1777 – were selected for their bibliographical interest and the relevance of the publication dates to their political contexts. Of additional interest, the 1676 edition is bilinear (French and High German) and the 1721 edition included, as part of the preface, the aforementioned 'La Vie de Monsieur Savary.' Of these, all but the 1777 edition, the last revised edition issued, were available on microfilm.

In their brief mention of *Le Parfait Négociant* in their companion volume to *Ars Mercatoria*, Jeannin and Hoock put it somewhere 'between a handbook and a treatise (zwischen Handbuch und Traktat)' (Jeannin and Hoock, 1991, pp. 168–69). For them, Savary's role as Colbert's advisor in framing commercial policy was the singular and most interesting aspect of the work. They argued that the cultural and literary significance of the text, particularly over the course of its hundred-year publication run, was not a product of its technical quality (Jeannin and Hoock, 1991, p. 169), which they regarded as inferior. Hoock (1989, p. 123) had developed this analysis at length in his earlier contributed essay, concluding that what he calls the

> 'Phénomène Savary'...exprime bien plutôt de façon emblématique les ruptures sociales, intellectuelles, techniques et technologiques qui ont lieu à l'extrême fin du XVIIe siècle. *Le Parfait Négociant* y participe par son discourse légitimant et l'action pédagogique qu'il représente.[3]

Hoock's analysis understands genre at the level of 'conjuncture' and sees a structural process by which elite commercial activity is made legitimate not only in France but also in the British Isles and in Italy. He sees *Le Parfait Négociant* of a piece with Lewis Roberts' *The merchants mappe of commerce* (1638) and Gio-Domenico's *Il negociante* (1638). All three make their information about good trading practice accessible to the reading public at large, but are targeted at the nobility in particular (Hoock, 1989, p. 119). In Hoock's view, Savary's sons both 'prolonged and modified' the enterprise; for him, the *Le dictionnaire universel du commerce* appropriated the genre of the alphabetical dictionary to formulate a complete and simple commercial vocabulary, available in one small and inexpensive volume, thereby making the information accessible to an even wider reading public, including those in the French overseas empire (Hoock, 1989, pp. 119–20). Without saying so explicitly, Hoock appeared to be taking his 'Phénomène Savary' as a kind of exemplar of Norbert Elias' *Civilizing Process* by which elite values were established in courtly circles and disseminated outward to commercial society by successive generations.

Hoock's argument is convincing in a general sense, but the text itself embodies the ambiguities contained within the popularization of Colbert's project. Some chapters, especially those containing information on trading in the Americas and Africa, were assiduously updated by the editors in successive editions, while others were left virtually untouched despite containing anachronistic and even outdated discussions. An examination of a single chapter over seven editions illustrates this tension, while also opening a window into the depth of English and French commercial rivalries. A three-page advertisement for the 1721 edition tells the reader that Savary's son, Jacques Savary des Bruslons, faithfully contributed additions to the chapter entitled 'Du Commerce d'Hollande & de Flandre' for the 1713 edition. This updated discussion offered information on the banks of Rotterdam and Amsterdam. The advertisement also mentioned even newer revisions, which the editor credited in marginal notations to their respective authors.[4] These additions, made to the second chapter of the second volume, were judged by the editor to be significant enough to convince potential buyers to purchase the new edition. Unlike the editorial attention paid to the treatment of Holland, the following chapter entitled 'Du Commerce d'Angleterre, d'Ireland, & d'Ecosse' was never updated. With the exception of orthographical changes and printers' conventions, the text of the 1777 edition is the same as the 1675 one. Over the hundred-year publication history, there were no additions, amendments, or marginal notations to the chapter on trading with the English. A close examination of this third chapter suggests something of the persistent intensity of the commercial rivalry between France and England as it played out in this text.

Consisting of a little over 2500 words, the chapter offers a litany of complaints, couched as warnings, about the bad treatment that French merchants can expect at the hands of the English. Apart from a single mention of Irish customs, there is no discussion of either Ireland or Scotland. Savary follows the first two paragraphs, which detail the items traded by the French and the English, with eighteen specific charges against English trading practices. The majority of the complaints turn on the extraordinary duties on French imports and exports (purportedly double those on native merchants and triple in the case of Irish cloth), prohibitions on the import of French cloth, tin and gold (lace, coins, silk or wire), the granting of monopolies to London merchants for the sale of merchandise to French traders, and the exclusion of French merchants from any form of retail or direct wholesale trade, including trade from the French overseas empire (Savary, 1777, p. 458–59).

The author finds equally odious the requirement that French merchants post bail bonds to guarantee good behavior, the mandate that they use British labor to load their ships, and the English practice of levying export duties on French re-export trade (Savary, 1777, p. 459). According to Savary, French wine merchants suffer especially bad treatment. They must first offer their wares to the purveyor of the king's household, who takes the best wines at any price he sees fit. The remainder they must market to the

– CHAPTER 33: *Economic thought and state practice* –

London firm holding the monopoly; because they cannot sell directly to tavern owners, they have to accept the prices offered (Savary, 1777, p. 459). French merchants are also forbidden to transport anything for a third party that might be carried on English ships and cannot easily be naturalized in England. Worse still, according to Savary, if they die intestate, their goods are forfeit to the English king; and, when parliament votes extraordinary supply it raises the funds by taxing resident French aliens double those of natives and other foreigners (Savary, 1777, pp. 459–60). Savary insists that the only way to do business in England is through a London agent with connections to a merchant house, but warns that, much like their government, individual English trading companies deal in bad faith. As evidence of this charge, he produces an example of a short vignette, a kind of picaresque of a fraud that an English agent perpetrated on his French employer, involving fraudulent invoices, forged bills of lading, and third-party endorsements (Savary, 1777, pp. 460–61; Mander, 2010, p. 73, n. 23).

Reconstructing the immediate contexts for most of Savary's charges was not difficult. The author warns his readers of 'la haine implacable qu'ils ont pour notre Nation' or 'the implacable hatred which they have for our nation' (Savary, 1777, p. 458). Stuart historians have long acknowledged the shift in English public opinion in the 1670s from an anti-Dutch to anti-French posture. The unpopularity of the Anglo-Dutch wars, fears of Louis XIV's ambitions towards universal monarchy, and increasing concern about the Duke of York's Catholicism all played a role (Pincus, 1995). So too did the public's perception, shared by members of parliament, of the 'unfavourable balance' of trade with France. As Margaret Priestley noted in her treatment of this dispute, there was a striking symmetry to the complaints on the English and French sides, as they alleged virtually identical practices (Priestley, 1951). In 1674, a year before the publication of *Le Parfait Négociant*, fourteen prominent London cloth merchants, led by Sir Patience Ward, estimated for the 'Lords Commissioners for the Treaty for Commerce with France' that trade imbalance with the French at £965,128 (Ward, 1674; Priestley, 1951, p. 39). In a footnote, the petitioners insisted their figures were understated because they excluded important imports, including 'toys for women and children, fans, jessamin-gloves, laces, point-laces, rich embroidered garments, and rich embroidered beds, and other vestments, which are an incredible value' (Ward, 1674). As Priestley argued in her investigation of the realities of Anglo-French trade, these figures were substantially over-stated, as too were their complaints about the consequences of Colbert's protective tariffs for the English woolen export market (Priestley, 1951, pp. 42, 48). Yet Priestley also acknowledged the significance of the million pound figure, exaggerated or not, in shaping both public opinion and economic policy (Priestley, 1951, p. 52).

Savary's complaints refer to specific aspects of the English parliament's mercantilist policies and the inherent conflicts between those protectionist objectives and the Crown's interest in maximizing the customs revenue. In 1663, three years after the Restoration, the government had reckoned French trade as the most important branch of foreign trade. According to C.D. Chandaman, a formidable historian of the English public revenue, the French import trade represented a sixth of the total London merchant trade, and the customs revenue from French imports more than twelve times that of exports (Chandaman, 1975, p. 15). The alliance between London merchants who wanted to protect domestic manufactures and the so-called 'Country Party' opposition in Parliament translated into a push, in the 1670s, for protectionist

623

legislation. Between 1673 and 1677, no fewer than four bills to prohibit French imports entirely were introduced to Commons (Chandaman, 1975, p. 18). Savary's complaints echo the details of Parliament's mercantilist policies: the singling out of French goods for selective imposition (levied as 'extraordinary revenue' in 1670) and the doubling of duties on French cloth in the same year (Chandaman, 1975, p. 17). The Wine Act of 1670, renewed at three-year intervals, increased the duties on French wine merchants. Although the additional duties payable by foreign merchants exporting English goods had been abolished in 1673, the eighteenth-month assessment passed in that year offered bounties to merchants exporting grain to the continent. By 1675, it would have been very difficult indeed for a French merchant to do business in London without an English agent.

Not surprisingly, English authors of the period produced similar attacks on French trading practices. The anonymous 'English Gentleman abroad' complained in 1679 in a 'letter to his Friend in England,' entitled 'Popery and Tyranny: or the Present State of France' of the following abuses:

> 5. Endeavouring to make his subjects sole merchants of all trades, as well imported as exported, and not only by the priviledges already mentioned upon their Commodities and Ships, but also by putting all manner of Discouragements upon all Foreign Factories and Merchants by Difficulty in their Dispatches, delayes in point of Justice, subjecting them to Foreign Duties and Seizures, not suffering them to be Factors to the French or any other Nation but their own, and in case of Death to have their Estates seized as *Aliens*, and the Countenance and conceiving the *French* have as to all Duty when employ'd in the Service of Foreigners.
>
> (Anonymous, 1679, p. 13)

The author also complained about French monopolies, rebating of customs duties to domestic shippers, the practice of 'giving their shipping preference of employment... obliging all [the king's officers] to fraught French ships at such a rate before any strangers, as also fifty *sols* per ton imposed on foreign vessels.'[5] Much like the anonymous author of *Monsieur Colbert's Ghost*, this author believed the foreign and imperial policy and mercantilist interests of France to be aligned (Anonymous, 1684).

Although the context for Savary's complaints about English trading practices can be easily demonstrated, the source for his anecdotal evidence for the perfidy of London agents, related at the end of the chapter, has proven elusive. The author concludes by reiterating his reasons for recounting this fraud: 'J'ai rapporté cet exemple pour faire voir la mauvaise foi des Anglois, & qu'il faut prendre de bonnes précautions pour négocier avec eux' (Savary, 1777, p. 461).[6] By contrast, Savary had, in the preceding chapter, conducted his discussion on Holland with a tone of neutrality. He concludes by reminding the reader of the even-handed treatment he should expect in there: 'En Hollande on paye les droits pour les marchandise qui entrent & qui sortent des leurs Etats, selon les fortes de marchandises, & suivant qu'ils font mentionnés dans le Tarif, qui vont environ à cinq pour cent' (Savary, 1777, p. 451).[7] His treatments of Flanders and Italy, also matter-of-fact, contained none of the vitriolic reserved for trading practices in the British Isles. In short, Savary's treatment of trading practices in the British Isles reads more like the polemical literature of the late 1670s than it does as a 'handbook' or pedagogical 'treatise.'

– CHAPTER 33: *Economic thought and state practice* –

Savary's description of the trading practices in the British Isles can only be read profitably within the context of the Anglo-French trade conflicts of the 1670s, which had intensified as the English tried to settle Hudson Bay. Even more surprising than the actual charges against English trading practices was the inclusion of this section in subsequent editions of the work, even after British sovereignty over the Hudson Bay was recognized in the Commercial Treaty of Utrecht in 1713. Unlike the chapter on trading with the English, the chapter on Holland, it was revised periodically to reflect changes in the trading climate. The 1721 edition included a 'nouvelle augmentation' introduced in the 1713 edition on 'Banques d'Amsterdam & de Rotterdam,' following the financial crises of 1719 and 1720 in Paris, Amsterdam, and London. The new edition gives the history of the banks from the early seventeenth century and describes how the cities act as guarantors and cashiers (Savary, 1777, pp. 451–52). Yet the 1697 and 1701 printings, much less the subsequent ones, make no reference of the founding of the Bank of England, despite the fact that other French writers commonly regarded the Bank of Amsterdam as its inspiration. Marginal references by the printer explain the expansion of the sub-section on Flanders in four installments: in 1701, 1713, 1715 and 1721 (Savary, 1777, pp. 454–57; Savary, 1721, v. 2, pp. 117–20). The most significant of these revisions (1713, 1715) appear to be in response to the commercial treaty of Utrecht. Jacques Savary des Bruslons, as the former inspector-general of the Customs House in Paris, would have had the expertise to re-write the section on the British Isles and even the incentive to grapple with the growing reputation of the English customs and excise service for aggressively policing smuggling (see Figure 33.3).

The omission becomes more striking because, on the English side, parliamentary opposition to ratification of the Utrecht treaty in 1713 rested in no small part on the recycling of statistics from the 'Scheme of Trade' in 1674 (Priestley, 1951, p. 40). Perhaps for the editors of *Le Parfait Négociant,* the disingenuous English were at it again. In any case, after the death of the elder brother, Louis-Philémon Savary, in 1727, the revisions ceased. William Reddy's explanation in *The Social Life of Things: Commodities in a Cultural Perspective* for the retention of dated material on the cloth trade in subsequent editions and knock-offs of Savary des Bruslons's *Dictionnaire Universel* hardly applies here (Reddy, 1986, pp. 264–70). According to Reddy, the exquisite attention to detail reinforced Colbert's maxim that 'quality was the key to prosperity' and 'reminded one that evaluating cloth in the eighteenth century required the skills of the connoisseur rather than those of a technician' (Reddy, 1986, p. 266). By contrast, no eighteenth-century Frenchman had to look as far as the third chapter of the second volume of *Le Parfait Négociant* for a reminder that Englishmen wished ill upon their continental commercial rivals.

Most of Savary's manual, however, was far more prosaic than the chapter on trading with the English. Beyond the material aimed at educating merchants on how to keep accounts, it contained a wealth of commercial intelligence. As other scholars have noted, it contained excellent advice on trading with Spain, including the importance of following the cargoes of ships arriving at Portobelo (Lamikiz, 2014). As Donald Harreld's recent treatment of the text within the context of a wider study of how business information was transmitted in early modern Europe suggests, Savary's work was part of a larger genre of French texts instructing French merchants in trading practices in Europe, Asia, and the Americas (Harreld, 2007). Most texts were specialized in their remit, concentrating on specific geographical areas or on particular trades, whereas Savary's sons opted for a more comprehensive treatment.

Figure 33.2 George Grenville looks to the North American colonial trade to balance the budget after the Seven Years War
Courtesy of the John Carter Brown Library at Brown University

In contrast to the willingness of Savary's sons to allow the entries on England to stand, their 'nouvelle augmentation' on French trading companies and the opportunities attendant to them revealed a remarkable sophistication both in their presentation of trading practices and in their historical account of relevant legislation (Savary, 1777, pp. 587–94). They offer an account of the origins of the Company of Senegal, the increasing importance of African slavery to its trading activities, and the relationship between the African activities of the *Compagnie française des Indes occidentales* and its expeditions in Quebec. The nuanced discussion of the War of Spanish Succession, which also attempts to estimate the effects of the asientos, stands in sharp contrast to the polemical treatment of English commercial legislation in the chapter discussed above (Savary, 1777, pp. 590–91). Ironically, whereas the Hudson Bay controversy was part of the context for the tension between France and England in the 1670s, it receives scant mention in the new material, which instead focuses on the creation and fortunes of the Mississippi Company, first established in 1684 (Savary, 1777, pp. 591–92). The Savary brothers give an account of the creation of the Company of the West in 1717, in which they firmly recognize the importance of

– CHAPTER 33: *Economic thought and state practice* –

mounting pressure on royal finances, while nevertheless minimizing John Law's role. Though this new material was incorporated in the 1721 edition, the discussion of the Mississippi Company ends in September 1719 with the issuance of fifty million new shares. Likewise the following chapter, which offers specific notes on trading practices in Martinique, the Antilles, Grenada, French Guinea, Guadeloupe, Saint-Domingue, and Canada, is evenhanded in its treatment. Particular care is taken to map the relationships between the imports to and exports from the regions of France, including Brittany, Normandy, La Rochelle, and Bourdeaux, and the corresponding activities in the imperial frame. The Canadian material received was immediately rewritten after the Commercial Treaty of Utrecht in 1713 (Savary, 1777, pp. 600–603).

In these new augmentations, colonial warfare is presented as a matter-of-fact handmaiden to commerce, without the moralizing that accompanied the earlier discussion of trading with the English. The chief impression given by the text, however, is the recognition on the part of the Savary brothers of the limitations of state power, both with respect to the African slave trade and to the governance of the Louisiana territories. At the same time, sympathetic treatments of the interests of the Dutch Republic, Spanish Empire, Scandinavian monarchies, Russian Empire, and Italian states repeatedly emphasize the gap between official policy and the practice on the ground. More is the pity that the British overseas trading empire never received the same treatment in subsequent revisions of the work, especially as the 1777 edition would have offered an opportunity to reflect on the outcome of the Seven Years War in 1763 and the financial consequences of the war for the British Atlantic system (see Figure 33.2).

Another interpretation of the violence of Jacques Savary's assessment of the English trading practices (and perhaps the willingness of successor editors to retain it) is suggested by Joan DeJean's article on Molière's *Le Festin de Pierre*, in which she positions censorship as part of the 'work of forgetting.' In her view, Molière's play hit too close to home:

> The official mission of French culture was to promote this vision of the civilizing effects of all things French. In this vision Molière's story of a society in which the boundary between market values and aristocratic values had been eroded had no place. The possibility that France might be becoming, like its models in the overseas trade, a nation of shopkeepers, more interested in the price of things than in proper social stratification – or in sexual conquest – was quite clearly unthinkable.
>
> (DeJean, 2002, p. 80)

Like Hoock, DeJean sees the civilizing process, except in reverse. In her view, the elite interests, embodied by state censors, were uncomfortable with the commercialization of society (this process of 'becoming English'), which Colbert simultaneously orchestrated as Comptroller-General of French finances and whitewashed as patron of the arts, including Molière. DeJean mentions Savary in passing, as the author of a manual whose purpose was to teach the nobility how to identify mercantile aptitude and cultivate it in their children (2002, p. 58). What she neglected to mention is that Savary did so at the behest of Colbert, who wanted to encourage both continental and overseas trade. Savary's participation in Colbert's political and economic project explains why Savary and his work have been all but forgotten by modern scholars, as the subsequent triumphs of the physiocrats in France and the political economists in

Figure 33.3 Modern Rendering of a seventeenth-century exciseman
leading an attack on smugglers[8]
Private Collection/© Look and Learn/Bridgeman Images

England marginalized both French and English mercantilist discourses. Taken together, Hoock and DeJean do provide complementary explanations of the paradox of the 'Phénomène Savary,' i.e. its publishing success and its subsequent consignment to obscurity. Modern scholars should benefit from its rediscovery, not least because Savary was participating in a process that was not a French but rather European and ultimately Atlantic phenomenon, as European nations emulated and imitated each other as they pursued their 'jealousies of trade' (Hont, 2005).

NOTES

For the helpful feedback and sympathetic hearing she received, the author is grateful to the audience of her paper entitled, 'Echoes of the Picaresque in Jacques Savary's *Le Parfait Négociant*,' which she presented at 'Early Modern Exchanges,' Launch Conference, 15–17 September 2011,

– CHAPTER 33: Economic thought and state practice –

UCL, London. As a result of this panel and a follow-up conference at Newnham College in July 2012 entitled 'Anglo-French Perspectives on The Literature of Commerce and the Commerce of Literature in the Long 18th Century,' Jenny Mander and D'Maris Coffman are undertaking the first English translation of *Le parfait négociant*.

1 Jacques Savary, *Le parfait négociant, ou Instruction générale pour ce qui regarde le commerce des marchandises de France et des pays étrangers* (Paris, 1721). This introduction, entitled 'La vie De Monsieur Savary' was written by his son, Louis-Philémon Savary.
2 For a comprehensive listing of the printings, see Pierre Jeannin and Jochen Hoock (1991, pp. 488–97).
3 English translation: 'the "Phenomenon Savary" expresses very nicely in an emblematic way the social, intellectual, technical and technological ruptures at the very end of the seventeenth century. *Le Parfait Négocians* participates in it by its legitimating discourse and the pedagogical action that it represents.'
4 *Advertissement, sur la huitiéme Edition du Parfait Negociant* (1721), pp. 2–3.
5 'Fraught' appears to be a variant early modern spelling for 'freight.'
6 English translation: 'I reported this example to show bad faith of the English & that it is necessary to take good precautions in order to trade with them.'
7 This text was preserved from the earlier editions, and directly precedes the addition about the banks of Amsterdam and Rotterdam. 'In Holland we simply pay ad-valorem duties upon entry and exit, and they are mentioned in their book of tariffs and are about five percent.'
8 Ironically although this is an early twentieth century work, it captures beautifully the belief that eighteenth-century commentators had about the ferocity with which the English prosecuted smuggling.

REFERENCES
Primary sources

Anonymous. *Popery and Tyranny: Or the Present State of France, in relation to its Government, Trade, Manners of People, and Nature of the Countrey. As it was sent in a Letter from an English Gentleman abroad, to his Friend in England.* (London, 1679).
——. *Monsieur Colbert's ghost, or, France without bounds being a particular account by what ways it has attain'd to that supream grandure, and relating the secret intreagues of the French Kings ministers at the courts of most of the princes and states of Europe, with remarkes there upon: also some reflections on the interest of those princes.* (Cologne, 1679; London, 1684).
Savary, Jacques. *Le parfait négociant, ou Instruction générale pour ce qui regarde le commerce des marchandises de France et des pays étrangers* (Paris, 1675).
——. *Le parfait négociant, ou Instruction générale pour ce qui regarde le commerce des marchandises de France et des pays étrangers / Der volkommene Kaufmann* (Genève, 1676).
——. *Le parfait négociant, ou Instruction générale pour ce qui regarde le commerce des marchandises de France et des pays étrangers* (Paris, 1679). 2nd edition.
——. *Le parfait négociant, ou Instruction générale pour ce qui regarde le commerce des marchandises de France et des pays étrangers* (Lyon, 1697). 5th edition.
——. *Le parfait négociant, ou Instruction générale pour ce qui regarde le commerce des marchandises de France et des pays étrangers* (Paris, 1701). 5th edition, re-print.
——. *Le parfait négociant, ou Instruction générale pour ce qui regarde le commerce des marchandises de France et des pays étrangers* (Paris, 1721). 8th edition.
——. *Le parfait négociant, ou Instruction générale pour ce qui regarde le commerce des marchandises de France et des pays étrangers* (Paris, 1777). 17th edition.
Ward, Sir Patience, et al. *A scheme of the trade, as it is at present carried on between England and France* (London: 29 November 1674).

Secondary literature

Appadurai, Arjun (ed.). *The Social Life of Things: Commodities in Cultural Perspective* (Cambridge: Cambridge University Press, 1986).

Bamford, Paul Walden. 'French Shipping in Northern European Trade, 1660–1789.' *The Journal of Modern History*, Vol. 26, No. 3. (Sep., 1954), pp. 207–19.

Bermingham, Ann and John Brewer (ed.). *The Consumption of Culture, 1600–1800: Image, Object, Text* (New York: Routledge, 1995).

Bonno, Gabriel. 'La Culture et la Civilisation Britanniques Devant L'Opinion Francaise de la Paix D'Utrecht aux Lettres Philosophiques (1713–34).' *Transactions of the American Philosophical Society*, New Ser., Vol. 38, No. 1 (1948), pp. 1–184.

Brewer, John and Roy Porter (ed.). *Consumption and the World of Goods* (London: Routledge, 1993).

Chandaman, C. D. The English Public Revenue 1660–1688 (Oxford: Clarendon Press, 1975).

Coffman, D'Maris; Leonard, Adrian and Neal, Larry (eds). *Questioning Credible Commitment: New Perspectives on the Rise of Financial Capitalism.* (Cambridge: Cambridge University Press, 2013).

Cole, Arthur H. *The Historical Development of Economic and Business Literature* (Rensselaer: Hamilton Printing Company, 1957).

Cole, Charles W. *Colbert and a Century of French Mercantilism.* 2 vols. (Hamden: Archon Books, 1964).

Crouzet, François (ed). *Le Négoce International XIIIe-XXe siècle* (Paris: Economica, 1989).

DeJean, Joan. 'The Work of Forgetting: Commerce, Sexuality, Censorship, and Molière's *Le Festin de Pierre*,' *Critical Inquiry*, Vol. 29, No. 1, Fall 2002, pp. 53–80.

Dewald, Jonathan. *Aristocratic Experience and the Origins of Modern Culture.* (Berkeley: University of California Press, 1993).

Eisenstein, Elizabeth. *The Printing Press as an Agent of Change: Communications and Cultural Transformations in Early Modern Europe.* 2 vols. (New York: Cambridge University Press, 1979).

Gauci, Perry. *The Politics of Trade: The Overseas Merchant in State and Society 1660–1720* (Oxford: Oxford University Press, 2001).

Goyau, Georges. 'Savary' in *The Catholic Encyclopedia, Volume XIII*, 1912.

Harreld, Donald J. 'An Education in Commerce: Transmitting Business Information in Early Modern Europe' in *Information Flows: New Approaches in the Historical Study of Business Information,* edited by Jari Ojala and Leos Müller (Helsinki: Suomalaisen Kirjallisuuden Seura, 2007).

Hauser, Henri. 'Le "Parfait Negociant" de Jacques Savary,' *Revue d'Historie Économique et Sociale*, Vol. 13 (1925), pp. 1–28.

Hirschman, Albert O. *The passions and the interests: political arguments for capitalism before its triumph* (Princeton: Princeton University Press, 1977).

Hont, Istvan. *Jealousy of Trade: International Competition and the Nation-State* (Cambridge, Mass.: Harvard University Press, 2005).

Hoock, Jochen. 'Le phénomene Savary et l'innovation en matière commerciale en France aux xviie et xviiie siècles,' in *Innovations et Renouveaux Techniques de l'Antiquité à nos Jours: Actes du Colloque International de Mulhouse.* ed. J.-P. Kintz (Strasbourg: Assoc. interuniversitaire de l'Est, 1989).

Howard, Stanley E. 'Public Rules for Private Accounting in France, 1673 and 1807,' *The Accounting Review*, Vol. 7, No. 2 (Jun., 1932), pp. 91–102.

Jeannin, Pierre and Jochen Hoock. *Ars Mercatoria: Handbücher und Traktate für den Gebrauch des Kaufmanns 1470–1820; Eine analytische Bibliographie*, Vol. II: 1600–1700, Vol III: Analysen: 1470–1700 (with Wolfgang Kaiser) (Paderborn: Schoningh, 1991).

– CHAPTER 33: *Economic thought and state practice* –

Kintz, Jean-Pierre (ed.). *Innovations et Renouveaux Techniques de l'Antiquité à nos Jours: Actes du Colloque International de Mulhouse 1987* (Strasbourg: Assoc. interuniversitaire de l'Est, 1989).

Lamikiz, Xabier. 'The Transatlantic Flow of Price Information in the Spanish Colonial Trade, 1680–1820' in *Merchants and Profit in the Age of Commerce, 1680–1830*, edited by Pierre Gervais, Yannick Lemarchand and Dominique Margairaz (London: Pickerring & Chatto, 2014).

Langford, Paul. 1989. *A Polite and Commercial People: England 1727–1783* (Oxford: Oxford University Press).

Mander, Jenny. 'Picaros, Pirates and Colonial History,' in *The Philological Quarterly*, Vol. 89, No. 1 (Winter 2010), pp. 55–74.

McVeagh, John. *Tradefull Merchants: The Portrait of the Capitalist in Literature* (London: Routledge & Kegan Paul, 1981).

Meuvret, Jean. *Études d'histoire économique, recueil d'articles* (Paris: A. Colin, 1971).

Mitchell, Brian R. ed. *British Historical Statistics* (Cambridge: Cambridge University Press, 1988).

Murris, Roelof. *Le Hollande et les Hollandais au XVIIe et au XVIIIe siècles, vus par les Francais* (Paris: E. Champion, 1925).

Nicholes, Eleanor L. and Dorothea D. Reeves. 'The Kress Library of Business and Economics and Some of Its Treasures.' *The Business History Review*, Vol. 40, No. 2 (Summer, 1966), pp. 237–49.

O'Brien, Patrick K. 1988. 'The Political Economy of British Taxation, 1660–1815,' *Economic History Review*, 2nd ser., 4Vol. 1, No. 1: 1–32.

Pagden, Anthony. *Lords of All the World: Ideologies of Empire in Spain, Britain and France, c.1500-c.1800* (New Haven: Yale University Press, 1995).

Parker, R. H. 'A Note on Savary's "Le Parfait Negociant",' *Journal of Accounting Research*, Vol. 4, No. 2 (Autumn, 1966), pp. 260–61.

Perrot, Jean-Claude. *Une histoire intellectuelle de l'économie politique: XVIIe-XVIIIe siècle* (Paris: Editions de l'Ecole des hautes études en sciences sociales, 1992).

Pincus, Steven C.A. 'From Butterboxes to Wooden Shoes: The Shift in English Popular Settlement from anti-Dutch to anti-French in the 1670s' *Historical Journal*, Vol. 38, No. 2 (1995), pp. 333–61.

Priestley, Margaret. 'Anglo-French Trade and the "Unfavourable Balance" Controversy, 1660–85,' *The Economic History Review*, New Series, Vol. 4, No. 1 (1951), pp. 37–52.

Rabuzzi, Daniel A. 'Eighteenth-Century Commercial Mentalities as Reflected and Projected in Business Handbooks,' *Eighteenth-Century Studies*, Vol. 29, No. 2 (1995–96), pp. 169–89.

Reddy, William M. 'The structure of a cultural crisis: thinking about cloth in France before and after the Revolution' in Appadurai, Arjun (ed.). *The Social Life of Things: Commodities in Cultural Perspective* (Cambridge: Cambridge University Press, 1986), pp. 261–84.

Redlich, Fritz. 'An Eighteenth-Century Business Encyclopedia as a Carrier of Ideas.' *Harvard Library Bulletin*, Vol. 19, No. 1 (1971), pp. 73–98.

Reinert, Sophus A. 2011. *Translating Empire: Emulation and the Origins of Political Economy*, Cambridge, Mass.: Harvard University Press, 2011.

Reinert, Sophus A. and Pernille Røge (eds). *The Political Economy of Empire in the Early Modern World* (Basingstoke: Palgrave Macmillan, 2013).

Rogers, Ruth R. 'The Kress Library of Business and Economics,' *The Business History Review*, Vol. 60, No. 2 (Summer, 1986), pp. 281–88.

Roseveare, Henry. *Markets and Merchants of the late Seventeenth century: the Marescoe-David Letters, 1668–1680* (Oxford: Oxford University Press, 1991).

Savary, Jacques. *Le parfait négociant, ou Instruction générale pour ce qui regarde le commerce des marchandises de France et des pays étrangers* (Paris, 1721).

Schaeper, Thomas J. *The French Council of Commerce 1700–1715: A Study of Mercantilism after Colbert* (Columbus: Ohio University Press, 1983).

Soll, Jacob. *The Reckoning: Financial Accountability and the Rise and Fall of Nations.* (New York: Basic Books, 2014).

——. *The Information Master: Jean-Baptiste Colbert's secret intelligence system* (Ann Arbor: University of Michigan Press, 2009).

Sonnino, Paul (ed.). *The Reign of Louis XIV: Essays in Celebration of Andrew Lossky* (Atlantic Highlands: Humanities Press International, 1990).

Stern, Philip J. and Carl Wennerlind (eds). *Mercantilism Reimagined: Political Economy in Early Modern Britain and its Empire* (Oxford: Oxford University Press, 2013).

Trivellato, Franesca. 'Credit, Honor, and the Early Modern French Legend of the Jewish Invention of Bills of Exchange' in *The Journal of Modern History*, Vol. 84, No. 2 (June 2012), pp. 289–334.

Turner, Raymond. 'The Excise Scheme of 1733'. *The English Historical Review*, Vol. 42, No. 165 (1927.), pp. 34–57.

Usher, Abbott Payson. 'Colbert and Governmental Control of Industry in Seventeenth Century France' *The Review of Economics and Statistics*, Vol. 16, No. 11 (Nov., 1934), pp. 237–40.

Vignols, Leon. 'Le dictionnaire universel du commerce de Savary des Bruslons; L'opinion des négociants nantais en 1738, etc.,' *Annales de Bretagne*, Vol. 38, No. 4 (1929), pp. 742–51.

Zahedieh, Nuala. *The Capital and the Colonies: London and the Atlantic Economy, 1660–1700* (Cambridge: Cambridge University Press, 2010).

CHAPTER THIRTY-FOUR

THE CLASSICAL ATLANTIC WORLD

——·◆·——

N. P. Cole

On the shore where the colony of Virginia had its first beginnings stands a monument to the tenacity and achievements of those early British settlers. Yet the pagan obelisk and Roman wreaths with which their seventeenth-century society is symbolized and celebrated reflect not their own understanding and representations of their community, but a vocabulary associated with the wider American achievement, and in particular the politics and political theory that in the late eighteenth century produced the modern American republic. Across the continent of America and around the Atlantic world, a similar classical vocabulary symbolizes legitimacy, civilization, learning and achievement. In the federal and state capitals of the United States, neo-classical buildings house the various branches of government, a connection between the ancient and modern world for which Thomas Jefferson, through his deliberate choice of the temple at Nîmes as the model for the post-Independence Virginian Capitol building, is in part responsible. Familiarity has perhaps dulled modern observers to some of the original impact of such buildings, but their original and striking impression can be glimpsed in the art of the late eighteenth and early nineteenth centuries. A watercolour by Benjamin Henry Latrobe, 'View of the City of Richmond From the Bank of the James River' painted in 1798 and now in the possession of the Maryland Historical Society, shows the newly constructed, unmistakably classical, capitol building rising above the modestly constructed houses of contemporary Richmond. Latrobe would go on to work on many important public buildings in America, not least of which is the national Capitol Building in Washington D.C., and he was important in promoting a style of Greek Revival architecture that has proved enduring and influential.

The connections between the ancient and the Atlantic world began long before the age of republican government. The first English translations of Ovid made in North America were by George Sandys, who lived in Virginia between 1621 and 1631, serving as the treasurer of the Virginia Company and as a member of the council. Elements of his translation and commentary were informed by his knowledge of and beliefs about the New World, though his beliefs were the product of reading rather than experience. In the 1940s, Richard Beale Davis wondered whether or not a work begun in England, continued during the voyage, completed in America and first published on return to England deserved to be called 'genuine American literature'. If this work sits uncomfortably in such a narrow category, however, it sits much more easily in a category of Atlantic literature. The translation is far from infused with constant reference to the New World – it was, after all, a translation of Ovid's text – but all the same, the books composed in America do contain references to the New World. As Davis noted, his commentaries on Ovid show a familiarity with works on the West Indies, Mexico and Florida.[1] More recently, James Elison has emphasized that both the 1626 edition of his translation, and the 1632 commentaries that Sandys published on Ovid, explicitly referred to the fact that they were a product of his time in America, contrasting the 'muses' of the classical text with the wars, tumults and 'rudenesse' of Virginia. He had not only brought civilization to the shores of Virginia, but he was making a claim to have produced its first work of learning and scholarship.

Since the very discovery of America, the classical past provided Europeans with one of the frameworks through which they understood and with which they described the nature of the American continent and their own role on it. Classical texts travelled to America with its earliest settlers, while in Europe writers struggled to reconcile classical views of the world with the discovery of a new continent and its peoples. Seeking to characterize the significance of this classical lens through which those living on both sides of the Atlantic viewed their relationship to the American continent, to the past and to each other, is a difficult task. Accurately capturing the view of many Europeans and their descendants over the centuries that this volume covers, Thomas Jefferson expressed the view that the classics formed the foundation of most and an ornament to all branches of human knowledge.[2] Events in history, scientific discovery, observations on newly discovered lands and peoples could all be discussed with classical allusion, citation and parallel, and in that sense, to chart in full the reach of the classics into the modern, Atlantic world, would be to write the history of western thought itself. One project begun in the 1980s did promise to survey the reception of the classics throughout the Atlantic World, though the ill health of one of its editors meant that only the first of six planned volumes in the series *The Classical Tradition and the Americas* ever appeared.[3] The scheme that project outlined, however, would have covered most areas of human endeavour in the Atlantic world in some form, and would have been a worthy monument as much to the place of the classics in western thought before the twentieth century as it would have been to the importance of the classics in the Atlantic world itself. It was, however, part of a longer and more controversial tradition of research.

In the mid-twentieth century, historians of both the United States and the rest of the continent bemoaned the fact that little work had been done on the significance of the modern understanding of the classical past for the shaping of American history.[4] Their works appeared at the same time that European scholars were beginning to make similar points about the contribution of the classical tradition to European thought.[5] Given the dependence of America on European classical scholarship and editions of classical texts, it is perhaps surprising that scholarship in this area, especially as it pertains to North America, has not been more consciously written within the framework provided by Atlantic History. By definition, American readers of classical texts were engaged in the exchange of goods and ideas across the Atlantic world. James Madison took advantage of Thomas Jefferson's appointment in Paris during

– CHAPTER 34: *The classical Atlantic World* –

the 1780s to ask him to acquire books on a broad range of topics, ancient as well as modern. Madison had made his specific request for classical works in a list of instructions sent to Jefferson in April. He wished Jefferson to find 'such of the Greek and Roman authorities where they can be got very cheap, as are worth having, and are not on the common list of school classics'. Beyond the ancient authors themselves, he was also interested in translations of their works, and he repeated a long-standing request for 'treatises on antient or modern foederal republics'.[6] As it turned out, it was Madison's request for classical texts that caused Jefferson the greatest difficulty. 'The Greek and Roman authors,' he explained, 'are dearer here than I believe anywhere else in the world. No body here reads them, wherefore they are not reprinted.'[7]

Historians of the United States have, for the most part, however, sought to identify the texts and histories that may have conditioned American thinking, often failing to integrate the classical influences on the revolutionary generation with other traditions of thought, and failing to emphasize properly the Atlantic context of American interest in the ancient world. One of the challenges for historians of this classicism is that similar classical motifs and imagery were present throughout the Atlantic world, and deployed by both imperial powers and young republics. Common to all Atlantic interest in the ancient world was a sense that the ancients represented ideals of civilization and knowledge and classical imagery could thereby confer a sense of legitimacy and connection to a greater civilization. In that sense, the ancient world provided a common language for certain ideas throughout the Atlantic world. Yet it is equally true that the same architecture in a European, imperial capital could make a very different statement when perched on the Atlantic's western shore.

It is not, perhaps, a coincidence that articles making the case that classical influences on America were worthy of greater study appeared in the late 1930s, when democracy in Europe seemed on the verge of extinction and Americans debated whether or not it was worth saving at all. They represented a challenge to the prevailing sentiment at the time that the American republican achievement and its intellectual basis was essentially a product of circumstance and the genius of one particular generation of Americans. 'Though students of American government in the last three decades of the eighteenth century,' wrote one scholar, 'were familiar with the political forms and experiences of these older so-called republics, they agreed that they found in them practically no helpful contribution to the American experiment.' Innovation in American government, it was argued, was the product of necessity, circumstance and the experience of colonial government.[8]

The early works drawing attention to the importance of the classical tradition in America need to be read in this context. These studies were initially written partly as a reaction against a general sense of American exceptionalism, in the context of growing interest in charting the contributions of previous traditions to the emergence and evolution of American republicanism.[9] Though the Revolution was increasingly understood as the product of European thought, one other significant result was a series of studies that specifically examined the contribution of the classics to American thinking before and after the Revolution.[10] All argued that the contribution of the classics had been significant, and aimed to counter the 'natural assumption' that American thought had been formed by English and French liberals, Deists and *philosophes*.[11] Other studies have since focused on the thought not of America generally but of particular thinkers.[12] Focussing on the contribution to American

635

political thought, Gilbert Chinard noted the importance of a theory of balanced government, derived ultimately from the ancient world, and the prominence of the use of ancient history in debate about the shape and function of the Senate, especially in Madison's thought.[13] He commented on the close connection between the American theory of the separation of powers and the ancient theory of balanced government. 'It is clear that in the opinion of several delegates [to the Constitutional Convention],' he wrote, 'the executive represented the monarchical power, the senate the aristocratical, and the house the popular power.'[14] Like all of these early studies that focused merely on the classical connections in American thought, he was rightly cautious about his conclusion, writing only that 'it is necessary to realise that the most modern form of government is not unconnected with the political thought and the political experience of ancient times'.[15]

The most extensive claim for the classical contribution to American thought was made by Richard Gunmere in an essay on the American Constitution that claimed unambiguously that ideas absorbed from classical reading had had a crucial role in helping to forge the shape of the Constitution of the United States, and had perhaps helped to shape the crisis that led to the Revolution itself.[16] Like many similar works, Gummere was clear that his intent was only to study the influence of the classics, and not to consider the contribution of other traditions. Indeed, in some of the detail of his commentary Gummere shied away from asserting the direct and decisive influence of the classics. In this caution, he followed broader trends of the time. Writing later, but reflecting on similar methodological problems, Trevor Coulborn, who examined the influence of Whig History on the thought of the Revolution, noted that he sought to avoid 'the contention that a colonist adopted a particular political opinion because he had read a particular book'.[17]

Gummere's essay provoked a gentle but firm corrective from Meyer Reinhold, who highlighted unease in early America at the presence of classics in education.[18] He drew attention to those voices in early America that disliked and were even suspicious of the emphasis on classical culture, and highlighted the complex attitudes towards the classical texts even of men, such as Jefferson, genuinely interested in them. Subsequent work examined this early dispute about education in more detail.[19]

More recently there has been a renewed effort to revive the idea that classical modes of thought were foundational to American ideas on government. Carl Richard has analyzed the American engagement with the ancient world by identifying classical models and anti-models in American thought, while David Bederman has explicitly outlined the 'classical foundations' of the American Constitution.[20] Both have stressed parallels between ancient and American institutions and American knowledge of the ancient world. Shalev's studies have charted in detail engagement with the ancient world and classical allusion in American political writing at the end of the eighteenth century.[21] Yet the difficulty of evaluating the significance of this influence alongside other sources of political thought remains a problem more often identified than confronted. Gummere acknowledged even while asserting classical thought as an organizing principle underlying American institutions that this did not always seem apparent to American republicans themselves. 'Colonials credited Bolingbroke with the doctrine of checks and balances, and Montesquieu with the separation of powers,' he noted, while at the same time arguing forcefully that both doctrines were to be found in Polybius' description of Rome.[22] Historians focused on the contribution of

– CHAPTER 34: *The classical Atlantic World* –

ancient thought have often consciously left this tension unresolved, but this option was not open to one particular group of historians who wrote explicitly about causation and the history of ideas.

From the late 1960s onwards, many historians sought to chart not merely the influences on the development of American thought but more ambitiously the ideology that in itself provided the primary explanation for the Revolution and subsequently the form of American government.[23] One of these movements, championed in particular by Gordon Wood, spoke explicitly about an era of 'classical politics', beginning before the Revolution and ending with the 1787 Constitution.

The 'classical republicanism' school earned their label from their assertion that the Americans were fluent in a language of virtue, a language that derived its vocabulary from classical – and especially Roman – texts. This language expressed and explained not a classical but a seventeenth- and eighteenth-century political philosophy that required the subordination of individual interests to those of the polity and the public good. They did not assert a distinctively American reception of the classics, indeed quite the reverse was either the explicit argument or the most natural inference from their comments. Rather the philosophy they identified echoed Machiavelli's suggestion that virtue was the sustaining spirit of a republic. The Americans they described, therefore, were 'classically republican' in the sense of a commitment to individual and collective virtue that seemed to echo Roman exhortations. They had inherited from the English a tradition of republicanism whose ideas had their roots in the ancient world,[24] and were committed to a system of politics that was alien to and would give way to the individualistic liberalism of the nineteenth century and beyond. As they explained it, the 'end of classical politics' was the creation of a system of government that no longer looked to English antecedents, 'the mixed constitution and the proportioned social hierarchy on which it rested,' to provide a source of stability. The transformation of politics at the end of the eighteenth century was a 'shattering' not of the influence of classical ideas but of ('classical') whig conceptions of politics, above all its sense of virtue.[25]

As far as explaining American interest in the classical heritage is concerned, the name usually applied to this school of historians can be misleading.[26] Searching for the source of the organizing ideas behind American politics, these historians drew an important distinction as far as the classics were concerned. Seeking to describe the most important sources of ideas for American thinking in the eighteenth century, and locating in particular the importance of Whig ideas, their methodology necessitated shifting emphasis away from the classical heritage itself. While they might provide language that was consonant with a developing American ideology, they did not themselves shape it. As Bernard Bailyn famously explained it:

> The classics of the ancient world are everywhere in the literature of the revolution, but they are everywhere illustrative, not determinative, of thought. They contributed a vivid vocabulary but not the logic and grammar of thought, a universally respected personification but not the source of political and social beliefs. They heightened the colonists' sensitivity to ideas and attitudes otherwise derived.[27]

The apparent interest of Americans in the ancient world was, Bailyn argued, deceptive. It was the product of habits formed at school and elites' intellectual fashion rather than deliberate choice. These historians viewed classical authors as significant primarily for the fact that they stood at the head of long traditions that ultimately gave rise to the American modes of thought.[28]

The third approach of historians has developed this idea of political culture even further and been more explicitly comparative. Here again, the conclusions can be negative as well as positive, and whereas Arendt saw strong comparisons between some American attitudes and Roman ones, Paul Rahe's survey of ancient and modern thought emphasized the gulf that separated the society and politics of the ancient world from those of modern states.[29] Modern political philosophers, he wrote, far from being in sympathy with the political philosophy of the ancient world, made the break between the two worlds stronger by 'systematically subordinating public to private concerns'.[30] How to protect the right to enjoy private property had become one of the defining questions of modern political philosophy from Harrington onwards, a question that had not been fundamental to ancient considerations of politics. Furthermore, the eighteenth-century mind, Rahe believed, was well aware of the break that had been made with the ancient tradition, and he quoted Edmund Burke on the point:

> It happened...that the great contests for freedom in this country were from the earliest times chiefly upon the question of taxing. Most of the contests in the ancient commonwealth turned primarily on the right of election of magistrates, or on the balance among the several orders of the state. The question of money was not with them so immediate. But in England it was otherwise.[31]

Rahe suggested that the very notion of the public good itself, devotion to which was the primary ingredient of virtue as identified by historians of classical republican America, was not a fundamental part of modern political philosophy. The emphasis seemingly placed upon it in the eighteenth century was, in Rahe's view, deceptive. Praise might be lavished upon the notion of the common good, but, 'they consistently defined that common good as the defence of their own lives, liberty and property'. He regarded as a universal political assumption of the period the observation that, 'no man when he enters into society does it from a view to promote the good of others, but he does it for his own good'. Even those Americans with the highest regard for the classical world – he cited Mercy Otis Warren as his example – praised the classical notion of virtue but nevertheless always subordinated the rights of the community to the rights of the individual.[32] Coupled with the notion that the modern world had seen, and continued to see, technological and material progress that further distanced it from the ancient,[33] he argued, it was important to stress not the similarities but the 'chasm separating the Americans from the ancient Greeks'.[34]

There has, then, been considerable and sustained interest in debating the contribution of the classics to the period of the revolution and early republic in the United States. Some works have extended these themes into the nineteenth century, though the claims of these works have typically been more modest, charting the classical dimension to enduring debates over religion, slavery and education rather than making the strong claims of the works focused on the eighteenth century.[35] One important work in recent years has taken up the challenge to examine the reception of the classics in Spanish America in more depth and has been notable for its claim

– CHAPTER 34: *The classical Atlantic World* –

that reception of the classics in the New World could influence the understanding of the classics in Europe too.[36] In doing so, it is one of the few monographs that really does attempt to write an Atlantic history of an aspect of classical reception.

Beyond the competing claims about the contribution of the classics to the creation of the American republic that have captured the interest of historians of the United States, the reception of the classics has interested historians of America because of the remarkable nature of the reception that transplanted wholesale an important element of European culture to the American continent, and caused classical texts to be read within a wholly new and unfamiliar context. As Wolfgang Haase captured it, Americans remained constantly in contact with European traditions of interpretation, and yet the constant 'confrontation with the fundamentally foreign' allowed 'over time, what were at least the elements of specifically American traditions'.[37] Local receptions of the classics in the Atlantic world all have their own unique elements, as individuals applied their classical learning to their own peculiar situations. If awareness of the ancient world infused European thinking throughout the Atlantic world and across centuries, merely charting the presence of classical reading, allusion and citation in the New World is unlikely to reveal much of value. Certain themes, however, stand out as being especially worthy of particular study, elements of which are common to the reception of the ancient world in different parts of the Atlantic world.

The first of these, important for its endurance and ubiquity, was the contribution that the classics made to the way in which Europeans, colonists and their descendants have understood the relationship between America and Europe. As Anthony Grafton suggested in his study of the intellectual shifts that accompanied the discovery of the Americas, from the moment of discovery those who had understood the world on the basis of classical and medieval authorities faced the difficult task of reassessing the classical and medieval authorities that had been proved fallible.[38] This was no easy process, and Grafton suggests that the result of this dramatic undermining of ancient authorities was, over the course of a hundred and fifty years, a growing emphasis on empirical knowledge. The authority of classical authors was far from destroyed, however, and continued to inform the way that people living on both sides of the Atlantic described their sense of the gulf that separated European and American life. In Europe, ideas of a civilized Europe contrasted with a wild and untamed America persisted, and frequently found expression in classical vocabulary. In 1775, the *London Magazine* published a frontispiece urging the reconciliation of Britain and her North American colonies. In it, America is depicted personified as a native American woman, dressed in a caricature of native costume. England, on the other hand, is depicted as a woman in fine, classical dress, almost indistinguishable from the Goddess Peace who stands between them, urging them to reconcile and return to commerce. It is not the only benefit of peace, however. As the verse underneath the image makes clear, it is the duty of 'England, unrivaled in the liberal arts' to continue spreading the learning of civilization 'to remotest parts'.

Yet for their part, Americans challenged this view of the relationship between Europe and America both before and after Independence. Jefferson's generation had inherited a curriculum and a mode of discourse that strongly privileged knowledge of the classics and discussion of antiquity. If knowledge of the classics was widely held to be the mark of the educated man, then a population widely schooled in the classics was the mark of a civilized and virtuous society. For this reason, some revelled in the

639

idea that Americans might be better guardians of the classical than the European nations. 'The learning of Greek and Latin, I am told,' Jefferson wrote in his *Notes on the State of Virginia*, 'is going into disuse in Europe. I know not what their manners and occupations may call for: but it would be very ill-judged in us to follow their example in this instance.'[39]

The suggestion that despite being separated by an ocean from Europe's ancient universities Americans were nevertheless well versed in the classical tradition both reflected and contributed to a growing sense of national confidence. In the years before the Revolution, Americans were eager to suggest that American knowledge of the classics was diffused more widely than in Europe, and some were even prepared to go further and suggest decay in European universities. The men who settled America, John Adams wrote in a 1765 essay, 'both the clergy and the laity' had been led by men familiar with 'the historians, orators, poets and philosophers of Greece and Rome', and some of their libraries still existed, 'consisting chiefly of volumes in which the wisdom of the most enlightened ages and nations is deposited', but which, he could not resist adding, their descendants, though educated in European universities, had difficulty in reading.[40] The famous *Letters from a Farmer in Pennsylvania*, written by John Dickinson and published anonymously in 1767 to spur opposition to the British, made a similar point in a more subtle way. Using the opportunity afforded by anonymity, Dickinson adopted the literary persona of a modestly successful farmer, whose hard work and property won him the leisure to read in his library and talk to 'two or three gentlemen of abilities and learning'. Through them and his private reading, this fictitious farmer acquired knowledge of history and law.[41] Each of these letters ended with a short Latin epigram.[42] These have several rhetorical purposes, but one of them is to suggest that even a self-taught, Pennsylvanian farmer might be familiar enough with the classics to be able to support his argument in such a way. If such learning was possible in the farms of Pennsylvania, perhaps American society was more cultured and virtuous than European.

A similar sentiment produced Jefferson's famous, if joking, comment to the author of *Letters from an American Farmer* that 'ours are the only farmers that can read Homer'. He had been indignant when he read in a French journal that the British had recently patented a type of wheel-making, held in London to be a great rediscovery of an ancient method, but which he knew to be similar to a method commonly known in New Jersey. Jefferson's consternation was increased all the more because 'Dr. Franklin, in one of his trips to London, mentioned this practice to the man now in London, who has the patent for making those wheels'. Seeing that a magazine article praised the British for rediscovering a method mentioned in Homer, Jefferson took offence on behalf of his countrymen. His sense of indignation was heightened all the more because the American method was in fact much closer to the one described in the Iliad than the method that the London workshop had adopted. He wished, therefore, to 'reclaim the honor of our farmers' – though, in seriousness, for their inventiveness rather than their classical learning.[43] Nevertheless, his jest also captures the classical tone of American politics and society after the Revolution. It captures, too, the desire of the American patriot to subvert European prejudices. During most of the eighteenth century, until the end of the War of Independence, British cartoonists depicted the colonists in North America as a boorish, even savage, people living on the very edge of civilization. It delighted Americans to suggest that America not only equalled Europe in learning,

– CHAPTER 34: *The classical Atlantic World* –

civilization and virtue, but surpassed her in important ways. American writers were able, thereby, to subvert the claims of cultural superiority made by those living in Europe, paradoxically relying upon the same language of classicism and in spite of the fact that there were scant examples of a genuine, American contribution to classical scholarship.

This, too, is the primary message presented by the many neo-classical public and private buildings erected after American Independence. Commenting on his design for the Virginia Capitol, Jefferson does not emphasize a moral or republican message, but an aesthetic one:

> I send by this conveiance designs for the Capitol. They are simple & sublime, more cannot be said, they are not the brat of a whimsical conception never before brought to light, but copied from the most precious, the most perfect model of antient architecture remaining on earth; one which has received the approbation of near 2000 years, and which is sufficiently remarkable to have been visited by all travellers.[44]

Writing to secure Madison's help in advancing his proposals for the Virginian capitol, Jefferson expressed concern for the reputation of his country and explained his choice of model for the building:

> It is very simple, but it is noble beyond expression, and would have done honour to our country as presenting to travellers a morsel of taste in our infancy promising much for our maturer age…But how is a taste in this beautiful art to be formed in our countrymen, unless we avail ourselves of every occasion when public buildings are to be erected, of presenting to them models for their study and imitation?…You see I am an enthusiast on the subject of the arts. But it is an enthusiasm of which I am not ashamed, as it's object is to improve the taste of my countrymen, to increase their reputation, to reconcile to them the respect of the world and procure them it's praise.[45]

Second, ancient authors provided a way for Europeans to explain and justify their treatment of other Atlantic peoples. The crimes of slavery and the destruction of native cultures were neither the products of nor sustained by classical reading, but ancient authors, and most especially Aristotle, did provide a language by which those who perpetrated them justified their actions. As Richard has shown, both sides of the debates over slavery and emancipation in nineteenth-century America debated the question in classical terms.[46] Nor was such an impulse confined to the English-speaking world. The Spanish had debated their treatment of the native peoples of America in similar, Aristotelian terms.[47] In 1748, Montesquieu's *The Spirit of the Laws* devoted Book XV to attacking European justifications of slavery, including a detailed attack on the grounds for slavery established by ancient authorities. To the shame of his American readers, who cited him liberally as an authority on other matters, the chapters on slavery seem to have made no impact on them at all.

At least in the structure of the one extended argument that he himself presented on the question of slavery, Jefferson also relied heavily on Aristotle. Although in general terms historians have noted the parallel between Aristotle's ideas on slavery and the views Jefferson expressed in *Notes on the State of Virginia*, and Richard hinted at a more direct link,[48] the full extent to which Jefferson structured his own text around Aristotle's discussion has not been fully examined. Of course, irrespective of anything he read in Aristotle, racism and a reception of certain contemporary 'scientific' notions on the origins of species are explanation enough for Jefferson's thinking.[49]

Yet although it is true to say that Aristotle stood simply at the head of a long tradition of pro-slavery thinking,[50] it is also possible to show that feeling pressure to defend slavery (and, in part, his own hypocracy) against European critics, Jefferson engages closely with Aristotle's discussion of slavery. Not only does the structure of the argument show a striking similarity with the structure of Aristotle's own discussion of the issue in *Politics I*, but also the scales of probability are tipped further towards the suggestion that Jefferson drew on Aristotle by an interesting remark he makes about the native Americans in Query VI of the *Notes*, where the topic under discussion was the native plants and wildlife. He thought that the native American male subjugated the female to 'unjust' hard labour, and that the roles of the male and female in that society were not sufficiently separated. This is a curious echo of the comment by Aristotle that among barbarian peoples insufficient distinction is made between the female and the slave (in 1252b), and suggests that Jefferson, at least in this work, chose to follow Aristotle's tripartite division: the citizen, the barbarian (who might be civilized, in Jefferson's view), and the natural slave (who could never be a citizen).

Two particular rhetorical choices by Jefferson have obscured his reliance on Aristotle. The first was his presentation of his findings on slavery as the result of his own private observations. This was not an unusual ploy of writers on disputed territory in the eighteenth century. To cite authorities for his view on slavery would have been to invite criticism of those writers, and would have weakened his case. The second rhetorical device is more interesting: Jefferson held the practice of ancient slavery as a counter-example to the American institution. He was making the rhetorical claim that the American example was more justly administered than the ancient example, and in fact selected the 'correct' people for slavery. His aim was to damn ancient slavery by contrast and thereby blunt attacks on the Virginian institution. Again, it would have weakened his case to have attacked the example of slavery in the ancient world as unjust at the same time as making any explicit relationship between his arguments and those of an ancient philosopher.

Jefferson drew his contrasts with ancient slavery in two ways. The less important was to find examples of the treatment of slaves in the ancient world that he could condemn as especially cruel. He contrasted, for example, Cato's selling of slaves 'and everything else that had become useless', or the 'common practice [of exposing to the elements and leaving to die]…diseased slaves whose case had become tedious' with his claim that the Virginians would not tolerate such action. He disapproves too of the ancient principle that slaves could give evidence in legal cases – under torture. He prefers instead the principle that they should not be able to give evidence at all.[51] These examples are meant to ease the conscience of the Virginian slave-owner, just as his rejection of environmentalist arguments he hopes will be bolstered by the observation that:

> …among the Romans, their slaves were often their rarest artists. They excelled too in science, insomuch as to be usually employed as tutors to their master's children. Epictetus, Diogenes, Phaedon, Terence, Phaedrus, were slaves. But they

– CHAPTER 34: *The classical Atlantic World* –

were of the race of whites. It is not their [the American slaves'] condition then, but nature, which has produced the distinction.

Third, Americans shared with Europe a tradition of political writing in which engagement with ancient authors was judged as a mark of serious scholarship. Montesquieu, one of the most cited thinkers in Revolutionary and post-Independence America,[52] commented frequently on Roman and Greek history in his *Spirit of the Laws*. Reflecting on this in the middle of his work, he wrote that 'One can never leave the Romans; thus it is that even today in their capital one leaves the new places to go in search of the ruins; thus it is that the eye that has rested on flower-strewn meadows likes to look at rocks and mountains.'[53] Before writing his more famous work, in fact, he had written *Considerations on the Greatness of the Romans and their Decline*, and in this followed many other writers who had explicitly combined an interest in political theory and contemporary politics with classical scholarship and observations on Roman and Greek history. Popular authors more famous for other works include Thomas Hobbes, whose translation of Thucydides had not shied away from comment on contemporary politics, and Robert Filmer, who had written an essay *Observations upon Aristotle's Politicks*; and Niccolò Machiavelli, who had presented his work on republics as *Discourses on the First Ten Books of Livy*. As Machiavelli wrote in the preface to that work, comparing ancient to modern events not only enabled better understanding of them both, but the reader to draw practical lessons from history.[54]

This motif is seen in overtly political works as well as theoretical ones. The translation of a fragment of Polybius – specifically his thoughts on the Roman constitution – could provide an opportunity to call for annual Parliaments, for example.[55] This tendency could be taken to an extreme: Johnathan Swift's *A Discourse of the Contests and Dissentions Between the Nobles and the Commons in Athens and Rome* (1701) is not, as it might first appear, primarily a history of the well-known turmoils of Greek and Roman politics at all, but, through the emphasis it gives to particular events, a cleverly worked commentary on contemporary British partisan struggles. The parallels are, however, mostly left for the reader to draw rather than being made explicit. Read out of its historical context the complexity of this subtext is, as one of its editors has noted, unintelligible to the modern reader without exhaustive notes explaining the allusions to contemporary affairs.[56]

At the end of the eighteenth century, revolutionaries and republican philosophers on both sides of the Atlantic discussed the example of ancient republics and democracies at length, and chose classical symbols to represent their experiments in government. All the same, no institutions in the new United States were created by directly following classical models, even if James Madison did prepare carefully for the 1787 Constitutional Convention by reading Greek and Roman History and preparing his *Notes on Ancient and Modern Confederacies*. The closest that America ever came to establishing any institution with a simple, obvious, classical precedent was during the Revolutionary War itself, when to Jefferson's disgust, his fellow Virginians considered creating a dictator on the Roman model to deal with the British invasion. 'What clause in our constitution,' asked an exasperated Jefferson in *Notes on the State of Virginia*, 'has substituted that of Rome, by way of residuary provision, for all cases not otherwise provided for?'[57] The idea of a dictator, with absolute power over life, property and law was, as Jefferson accurately observed, a proposal

643

with no precedent in English law and practice, and had instead been borrowed from the example of ancient Rome. In the event, however, the measure failed by narrow margins both times it was proposed.

In post-Revolutionary America the upper chambers of the various legislatures were frequently discussed as if they were recreations of ancient institutions, even if in their form and function they are more naturally explained as new versions of colonial-era councils. Certainly, the twenty-six-member Federal Senate created by the 1787 Constitution bears little close comparison with the four- to six-hundred-member debating chamber of the Ancient Roman state from which it took its name. However, lacking a theory of representation that coherently justified bicameral systems and still somewhat beholden to the notion that lower chambers should be understood as a direct substitute for direct democracy, Madison and other Federalists discussed the role and nature of the Federal Senate as if it was indeed a recreation of ancient Rome's. Urging the people of New York to adopt the Constitution, Madison wrote of the Senate's role:

> I shall not scruple to add that such an institution [a senate] may sometimes be necessary as a defence to the people against their own temporary errors and delusions...there are particular moments in public affairs when the people, stimulated by some irregular passion, or some illicit advantage, or misled by the representations of interested men, may call for measures which they themselves will afterwards be the most ready to lament and condemn.[58]

The Senate was to be able to provide the interference 'of some temperate and respectable body of citizens,' until 'reason justice and truth can regain their authority over the public mind'. In case anyone missed the point, he added that all of the ancient republics worthy of emulation had appointed a senate to control the passions of democratic government. He acknowledged that the appointment of senator for life on the Roman model would be 'repugnant to the genius of America', but nevertheless left his readers with a strong hint that the appointment of senators for six-year terms by state legislatures (that is, the appointment of a body beyond direct popular control), should be welcomed as emulating at least certain aspects of the Roman Senate:

> I am not unaware of the circumstances which distinguish the American from other popular governments, as well ancient and modern; and which render extreme circumspection necessary in reasoning from one case to the other. But after allowing due weight to this consideration it may still be maintained that there are many points of similitude which render these examples not unworthy of our attention. Many of the defects, as we have seen, which can only be supplied by a senatorial institution, are common to a numerous assembly frequently elected by the people, and to the people themselves.[59]

A classically inspired distrust of democracy even in an America committed to republican government remained common, though not universal, in American political writing well into the nineteenth century. Modern discussions of the Constitution would no doubt emphasize its Federal nature, rather than attempting to explain its institutions in quasi-classical terms, and a sensitivity to the fact that

– CHAPTER 34: *The classical Atlantic World* –

Madison's generation continued to reply on what were in a republican context increasingly awkward, classical models of government to describe their political institutions, reveals the gulf that separates them from modern thought about politics, democracy, representation and society. Perhaps the greatest legacy of all of this has been to inject into American political discourse a fear of institutional failure that contributes greatly to what Richard Hofstadter called the 'paranoid style' in American politics.[60] The founding texts of the American nation, including the much-read *Federalist Papers*, are infused with warnings that if America's political institutions fail to contain the dangers, the American experiment in republicanism will suffer the same disastrous fate that met ancient states.

On the western shore of the Atlantic, then, classical learning arrived with the first settlers, providing both a bridge back to European thought, reminding European settlers of their European roots while also providing them with the opportunity to justify their actions on a new continent and with a way to distinguish themselves from the Europe they had left behind. The classical corpus provided obvious motifs upon which those championing the achievements of the New World could draw. To be sure, the classics never had any monopoly on the Atlantic imagination. Pierre Eugene Du Simitière, an engraver who was involved in the creation of several seals for use in the early American Republic, proposed using coats of arms along more traditional European lines. The first committee charged with the creation of a national seal rejected both John Adams's proposal of a classical design and suggestions by Benjamin Franklin and Jefferson for a design based on Exodus. Instead they recommended a complex design based on Du Simitière's idea of a national coat of arms. It would have celebrated in six quarters the various nations that had peopled America, supported by the goddesses of liberty and justice. This design was not ultimately adopted, and the motto '*e pluribus unum*' and the eye of Providence were the only aspects of that committee's proposals that would be incorporated into the Seal eventually adopted by the United States.[61] Instead, the Great Seal of the United States, at least on its reverse, uses two lines from Virgil's Aeneid to make two claims that, while using a European source, separates America from Europe: first, that the American Republic is the will of Providence, and second that its creation marks a new epoch of time, one that is as significant a break with the past and as great in its importance as the founding of the city of Rome had been for the history Europe. Yet despite this attempt to divide the world into East and West hemispheres using a language of classicism, the most lasting legacy has been one of unity. Neoclassical public and private buildings ring the Atlantic world, monuments to shared tastes and an enduring deference to ancient aesthetics, and made possible by the wealth created by Atlantic trade.

NOTES

1 Richard Beale Davis, 'America in George Sandy's "Ovid"', *The William and Mary Quarterly*, Third Series, 4, number 3 (1947): 300–303.

2 Jefferson John Brazer, 24 August 1819.

3 Wolfgang Haase and Meyer Reinhold, editors, *The Classical Tradition and the Americas: European Images of the Americas and the Classical Tradition* (Berlin and Boston: Walter de Gruyter, 1993), VIII.

4 Charles F. Mullet, 'Classical Influences on the American Revolution', *Classical Journal* 35 (1935): 92–104; Tom B. Jones, 'The Classics in Colonial Hispanic America', *Transactions*

and *Proceedings of the American Philological Association* 70 (1939): 37–45, Gilbert Chinard, 'Polybius and the American Constitution', *Journal of the History of Ideas* 1, number 1 (1940): 38–58.

5 Harold Talbot Parker, *The Cult of Antiquity and the French Revolutionaries* (Chicago, Ill.: The University of Chicago press, 1937).

6 James Madison to Thomas Jefferson, 27 April 1785.

7 Jefferson to Madison, 1 September, 1785

8 George M. Dutcher, 'The Rise of Republican Government in the United States', *Political Science Quarterly* 55, number 2 (1940): 199, 201. For a history of American exceptionalism see Jack P. Greene, *The Intellectual Construction of America: Exceptionalism and Identity from 1492 to 1800* (Chapel Hill: University of North Carolina Press, 1993). The classical tradition was not alone in being cited by those challenging American exceptionalism before the 1950s. Other works included: Carl L. Becker, *The Declaration of Independence: A Study in the History of Political Ideas* (New York: Harcourt, Brace and Company, 1922); *America and French Culture, 1750–1848*; Merle Curti, 'The Great Mr. Locke: America's Philospher, 1783–1861', in *The Huntington Library Billetin*, no. 11 (1937), pp. 108–151.

9 Louis B. Wright, 'The Purposeful Reading of Our Colonial Ancestors', *ELH* 4, number 2 (1937): 85–111.

10 Mullet, 'Classical Influences on the American Revolution'; Chinard; George P. Schmidt, 'The Classics and Democracy', *Journal of Higher Education* 13, number 8 (1942): 414–19; Henry C. Montgomery, 'Thomas Jefferson as a Philologist (II)', *American Journal of Philology* 65, number 4 (1944): 367–71; Harvey Wish, 'Aristotle, Plato, and the Mason-Dixon Line', *Journal of the History of Ideas* 10, number 2 (1949): 254–66; Douglass Adair, 'A Note on Certain of Hamilton's Pseudonyms', *William and Mary Quarterly* 12, number 2 (1955): 282–97.

11 Chinard, 38.

12 Dorothy M. Robathan, 'John Adams and the Classics', *New England Quarterly* 19, number 1 (1946): 91–98; Douglass Adair, 'A Note on Certain of Hamilton's Pseudonyms', Author unclear in Journal. Editor assumed. *William and Mary Quarterly* 12, number 2 (1955): 282–97; Leo M. Kaiser, 'John Quincy Adams and His Translation of Juvenal 13', *Proceedings of the American Philosophical Society* 114, number 4 (1970): 272–93; James M. Farrell and John Adams, 'John Adams's Autobiography: The Ciceronian Paradigm and the Quest for Fame', *New England Quarterly* 62, number 4 (1989): 505–28; James M. Farrell, '"Syren Tully" and the Young John Adams', *The Classical Journal* 87, number 4 (1992): 373–90; Carl J. Richard, 'A Dialogue with the Ancients: Thomas Jefferson and Classical Philosophy and History', *Journal of the Early Republic* 9, number 4 (1989): 431–55; Lyon Rathbun, 'The Ciceronian Rhetoric of John Quincy Adams', *Rhetorica* 18, number 2 (2000): 175–215.

13 Chinard, 56.

14 Ibidem, 51.

15 Ibidem, 57.

16 Richard M. Gummere, 'The Classical Ancestry of the United States Constitution', *American Quarterly* 14, number 1 (1962): 3–18.

17 H. Trevor Colbourn, *The Lamp of Experience: Whig History and the Intellectual Origins of the American Revolution* (Indianapolis, IN: Liberty Fund, 1998), xviii.

18 Meyer Reinhold, 'Opponents of Classical Learning in America during the Revolutionary Period', *Proceedings of the American Philosophical Society* 112, number 4 (1968): 221–34.

19 Shevaun E. Watson, 'Complicating the Classics: Neoclassical Rhetorics in Two Early American Schoolbooks', *Rhetoric Society Quarterly* 31, number 4 (2001): 49; Caroline Winterer, *The Culture of Classicism: Ancient Greece and Rome in American Intellectual Life 1780–1910* (Baltimore, MD: John Hopkins University Press, 2002), 11–43,45–49.

– CHAPTER 34: *The classical Atlantic World* –

20 Carl J. Richard, *The Founders and the Classics: Greece, Rome, and the American Enlightenment* (Cambridge, MA: Harvard University Press, 1994); Carl J. Richard, 'The Classical Roots of the U.S. Congress: Mixed Government Theory', in *Inventing Congress: Origins and Establishment of the First Federal Congress*, edited by Kenneth R. Bowling and Donald R. Kennon (Athens, Ohio: Published for the United States Capitol Historical Society by Ohio University Press, 1999); David J. Bederman, *The Classical Foundations of the American Constitution: Prevailing Wisdom* (Cambridge; New York: Cambridge University Press, 2008).

21 Eran Shalev, 'Ancient Masks, American Fathers: Classical Pseudonyms during the American Revolution and Early Republic', *Journal of the Early Republic* 23, number 2 (2003): 151–72; Eran Shalev, *Rome Reborn on Western Shores: Historical Imagination and the Creation of the American Republic*, Jeffersonian America (Charlottesville: University of Virginia Press, 2009).

22 Richard M. Gummere, 'The Classical Ancestry of the United States Constitution', *American Quarterly* 14, number 1 (1962): 7–8.

23 Louis Hartz, *The Liberal Tradition in America* (Harcourt Brace, 1991); Robert E. Shalhope, 'Toward a Republican Synthesis: The Emergence of an Understanding of Republicanism in American Historiography', *William and Mary Quarterly* 29, number 1 (1972): 49–80; Robert E. Shalhope, 'Republicanism and Early American Historiography', *William and Mary Quarterly* 39, number 2 (1982): 334–56; Isaac Kramnick, 'Republican Revisionism Revisited', *The American Historical Review* 87, number 3 (1982): 629–64; Richard K. Matthews, 'Liberalism, Civic Humanism, and the American Political Tradition: Understanding Genesis', *Journal of Politics* 49, number 4 (1987): 1127–157; Daniel T. Rodgers, 'Republicanism: The Career of a Concept', *Journal of American History* 79 (1992): 11–38; Richard P. Gildrie, 'The Republican Synthesis Revisited: Essays in Honor of George Athan Billias (Review)', *Journal of Southern History* 61, number 3 (1995): 584–85; Steve Pincus, 'Neither Machiavellian Moment nor Progressive Individualism: Commercial Society and the Defenders of the English Commonwealth', *American Historical Review* 103, number 3 (1998): 705–36. Bailyn, interestingly, was gently critical of the extension of his approach past the Revolution, though his later attempts to nuance his position have not been widely noted. Bernard Bailyn, *The Ideological Origins of the American Revolution*, Second, First published 1967 (Cambridge, MA: Harvard University Press, 1992), v–vi; Jack N. Rakove, 'Gordon S. Wood, the "Republican Synthesis," and the Path Not Taken', *William and Mary Quarterly* 44, number 3 (1987): 621.

24 J.G.A. Pocock, *The Machiavellian Moment: Florentine Political Thought and the Atlantic Republican Tradition* (Princeton: Princeton University Press, 1975).

25 Gordon S. Wood, *The Creation of the American Republic 1776–1787* (Chapel Hill, NC: University of North Carolina Press, 1998), 606ff.

26 For an insightful analysis of the history of this label, see Gildrie, 'The Republican Synthesis Revisited', 102–6.

27 Bernard Bailyn, *The Ideological Origins of the American Revolution*, Second, First published 1967 (Cambridge, MA: Harvard University Press, 1992), 22–26; cf. Mullet, 'Classical Influences on the American Revolution', 93ff.

28 Douglass Adair, *The Intellectual Origins of Jeffersonian Democracy* (Lanham, MD: Lexington Books, 2000). For the influence of this thesis, see the introduction to that edition. For a 'Roman' and 'Greek' tradition in political thought see Eric Nelson, *The Greek Tradition in Republican Thought* (Cambridge: Cambridge University Press, 2004), 8ff.

29 Hannah Arendt, *On Revolution* (London; New York: Penguin Books, 1970), 180–214; Paul A. Rahe, 'Primacy of Politics in Classical Greece', *American Historical Review* 89, number 2 (1984): 206, 267.

647

30 Paul A. Rahe, *New Modes and Orders in Early Modern Political Thought*, volume 2, Republics Ancient and Modern (Chapel Hill, NC: University of North Carolina Press, 1994), 214.

31 Burke, *Speech on Moving Resolutions for Conciliation with the Colonies*, 22nd March 1775, quoted at ibidem, 214.

32 Ibidem, 121.

33 Ibidem, 108–10.

34 Paul A. Rahe, *Inventions of Prudence: Constituting the American Regime*, volume 3, Republics Ancient and Modern (Chapel Hill, NC: University of North Carolina Press, 1994), 191, 45–46.

35 Winterer, *The Culture of Classicism*; Caroline Winterer, *The Mirror of Antiquity: American Women and the Classical Tradition, 1750–1900* (Ithaca: Cornell University Press, 2007); Carl J. Richard, *The Golden Age of the Classics in America: Greece Rome and the Antebellum United States* (Cambridge, MA: Harvard Univeristy Press, 2009).

36 Sabine MacCormack, *On the Wings of Time: Rome, the Incas, Spain, and Peru* (Princeton, N.J.: Princeton University Press, 2007).

37 Wolfgang Haase and Meyer Reinhold, *Classical Tradition and the Americas: European Images of the Americas and the Classical Tradition*, volume 1 (Berlin: Walter de Gruyter, 1994), XI.

38 Anthony Grafton, *New Worlds, Ancient Texts: The Power of Tradition and the Shock of Discovery* (Cambridge, MA: Harvard University Press, 1992).

39 Thomas Jefferson, *Notes on the State of Virginia*, edited by William Peden (Chapel Hill, NC: University of North Carolina Press, 1954), 147.

40 John Adams, 'A Dissertation on the Canon and Feudal Law', in *The Revolutionary Writings of John Adams*, edited by C. Bradley Thompson (Indianapolis, IN: Liberty Fund, 2000), 24.

41 John Dickinson, 'Letters from a Farmer in Pennsylvania', in *Empire and Nation*, edited by Forrest McDonald (Indianapolis, IN: Liberty Fund, 1999), 3.

42 For analysis of which, see Richard M. Gummere, 'John Dickinson: Classical Penman of the Revolution', *The Classical Journal* 52, number 2 (1956): 84.

43 Jefferson to St. John de Cr'evecoeur, 15th January 1787.

44 Thomas Jefferson to James Currie, 28 January 1786.

45 Jefferson to James Madison, 20th September 1785.

46 Richard, *The Golden Age of the Classics in America: Greece Rome and the Antebellum United States*, 181–203.

47 Lewis Hanke, *Aristotle and the American Indians: A Study in Race Prejudice in the Modern World* (London: Hollis & Carter, 1959), 44–61.

48 Carl J. Richard, 'A Dialogue with the Ancients: Thomas Jefferson and Classical Philosophy and History', *Journal of the Early Republic* 9, number 4 (1989): 451.

49 Eric Foner, 'The Meaning of Freedom in the Age of Emancipation', *Journal of American History* 81, number 2 (1994): 443.

50 *The Problem of Slavery in Western Culture*, 18, *The Problem of Slavery in the Age of the Revolution*, 42.

51 Thomas Jefferson, *Notes on the State of Virginia*, edited by William Peden (Chapel Hill, NC: University of North Carolina Press, 1954), 141–42.

52 Donald S. Lutz, 'The Relative Influence of European Writers on Late Eighteenth-Century American Political Thought', *The American Political Science Review* 78, number 1 (1984): 193–95.

53 Charles Montesquieu, *The Spirit of the Laws*, edited by Anne M. Cohler, Basia C. Miller and Harold S. Stone (Cambridge: Cambridge University Press, 1989), 172.

54 Niccolo Machiavelli, *Discourses on Livy*, translated by Harvy C. Mansfield and Nathan Tarcov (Chicago and London: University of Chicago Press, 1996), 6.

– CHAPTER 34: *The classical Atlantic World* –

55 Edward Spelmen, *A Fragment out of the Sixth Book of Polybius, Containing a Dissertation upon Government in General, particularly applied to that of the Romans...To which is prefixed a Preface, wherein the System of Polybius is applied to the Government of England* (London: J. Bettenham, 1743).

56 Jonathan Swift, *A Discourse of the Contests and Dissentions Between the Nobles and the Commons in Athens and Rome*, edited by Frank H. Ellis (Oxford: Oxford Clarendon Press, 1967), vi.

57 Jefferson, *Notes on the State of Virginia*, 129.

58 James Madison, Alexander Hamilton and John Jay, *The Federalist Papers*, edited by Isaac Kramnick (London: Penguin, 1987), 371.

59 Ibidem, 372.

60 Richard Hofstadter, 'The Paranoid Style in American Politics', *Harper's Magazine* (1964).

61 Thomas Jefferson, *The Papers of Thomas Jefferson*, edited by Julian P. Boyd, volume 1 (Princeton: Princeton University Press, 1950), 494–97.

CHAPTER THIRTY-FIVE

THE ATLANTIC ENLIGHTENMENT

——·◆·——

William Max Nelson

Although the term 'Atlantic Enlightenment' is not yet widely used, it should be. The term – and more importantly, the category that it refers to – adds something useful to the study of the Enlightenment as well as the study of the Atlantic world. There is some risk, of course, in stretching the concept of Enlightenment too far or diluting it by adding yet another particular or peripheral Enlightenment to the constellation of Enlightenments that have emerged from the historiography in the last few decades; these Enlightenments range from the large and somewhat concentrated (French, Scottish, English, American, German, Protestant, Jewish, Radical, Vitalist, etc.) to the more modestly sized or dispersed (Socinian, Arminian, Swiss, Neapolitan, Utrechtean, etc.).[1] But the risk seems worth taking for several reasons. First, there are signs that there *was* a distinctly Atlantic Enlightenment composed of individuals whose intellectual development and contributions were deeply grounded in the mobility and fluidity, the interconnection and reciprocity, the circulation and contestation that characterized the early modern Atlantic world. The Atlantic contexts of colonialism and slavery profoundly affected the development of most aspects of Atlantic Enlightenment thought – whether political, economic, social, or scientific – and helped account for many of the differences between ideas emerging from the Atlantic and some European sites of the Enlightenment. Second, a better understanding of this Atlantic Enlightenment will give additional depth to one of the fundamental assertions of the historiography of the Atlantic world – that there was a highly integrated and meaningful circulation and connection in the early modern Atlantic world. Of the three pillars of the Atlantic world historiography – the circulation of people, commodities, and ideas – the history of ideas seems to be the least developed in terms of having a unified narrative. While there are excellent works about the circulation and development of ideas in the early modern Atlantic world (particularly in relationship to politics and science), there is still much to be determined about the nature and characteristics of the intellectual context of this circulation and development.[2] Finally, I would suggest that we can identify and analyze multiple Enlightenments, while still recognizing a single unified Enlightenment, and in fact, bringing the Atlantic world further into the historiography of the Enlightenment gives us a new angle from which to address persistent and important questions about *the* Enlightenment (which in the

650

– CHAPTER 35: *The Atlantic Enlightenment* –

work of most specialists of the Enlightenment is still generally located on the dry land of Europe, despite a historiography of an American Enlightenment).[3]

Although the Atlantic narrative of the Enlightenment is still in its early stages, the appearance of the first book to claim the title *The Atlantic Enlightenment* (2008) adds to the sense that the time for the study of the Atlantic Enlightenment has arrived.[4] The book seems to capture both the promise and the difficulty in writing the history of the Atlantic Enlightenment – for as the editors acknowledge in the introduction, the volume really focuses on 'a *North* Atlantic Enlightenment primarily protestant in denomination, and anglophone in orientation,' with 'its axis unashamedly tilted toward Scotland.'[5] While significant questions remain about the proper parameters and perspectives of this inchoate subject, I wish to suggest some of the ways that an Atlantic frame for the study of the Enlightenment can enrich existing approaches and point the way towards others. Even to pose the question of whether the Atlantic Enlightenment existed, begins to open up new avenues of research and new candidates for re-evaluation.

After identifying some of the representative figures and features of this Atlantic Enlightenment, I will suggest five topics or themes in the development of Enlightenment ideas that are particularly well suited to inquiries within an Atlantic framework. These are subjects that will probably reveal a greater Atlantic distinctiveness when investigated more closely: the new discourses of social and political inclusion and exclusion (primarily those discourses utilizing notions of natural rights and racial exclusion); the emergence of biopolitical ideas and practices; the contributions of the enslaved and free people of African descent; the development of liberal political economic theory; and the development of radical political ideas (e.g. radical egalitarianism, arguments for greater liberties, and justifications for national independence, revolution, and democratic institutions, etc.). Of these five topics, I will focus on the first two, since they appear to be the most promising avenues of research due to their high degree of Atlantic distinctiveness, their expansiveness (involving numerous people, places, and branches of knowledge), the depth and breadth of their historical impact, and their ability to yield a new perspective on persistent questions about the Enlightenment.

The year 1776 might function as a useful date to mark the beginning of the Atlantic Enlightenment. While the year was obviously important in America and the British Empire, it also had a profound effect across the Atlantic world, in European centers of the Enlightenment as well as European colonies. It was a time when American figures of the Enlightenment gained a new assertiveness and the *philosophes* in continental Europe became newly interested in America and the Atlantic world more generally. The year, for example, was a crucial turning point for the French *philosophe* Denis Diderot as he was both inspired by the American Revolution and discouraged by the blow that enlightened reform suffered in France when the *philosophe-administrator* Turgot was dismissed from his important ministerial position.[6] Diderot greatly admired the Declaration of Independence, and as he wrote his contributions to the radicalized 1780 edition of the influential *Histoire des deux Indes* (written by multiple contributors but published under the name of abbé Raynal), he created what was probably the most widely read eighteenth-century account of the American Revolution.[7] This account of the Revolution and the defense of the people's right to resist tyranny (drawing on the arguments made by another Atlantic Enlightenment author, Thomas Paine), joined a text that was already one of the most significant and widely read critiques of European colonization and slavery. The widespread popularity and impact of the *Histoire des deux Indes* captures some of the ferment and vitality of the nascent Atlantic Enlightenment. In its desire to rethink politics and commerce – particularly as they manifest in colonialism and slavery – as well as its broad view of the entire Atlantic world (and indeed the other Indies), *Histoire des deux Indes* stands as one of the monuments of the Atlantic Enlightenment.[8]

Diderot's Atlantic turn captures two of the most important characteristics of the Atlantic Enlightenment – that it emerged from the back-and-forth transmission and translation of ideas between Europe and the rest of the Atlantic world, and that the hybrid and dialectical ideas and disputes of the Atlantic Enlightenment came about in the era rightly characterized as the Age of Revolution. This revolutionary age was a newly self-aware era when those involved in politics, philosophy, and science gained a new sense of their ability to separate themselves from old ways of being and thinking (seen most radically in the desire of some French revolutionaries to construct a completely new future).[9] This type of self-aware assertion (and the link between intellectual and political revolutions) was captured by Thomas Paine in 1782 as he responded to the portrayal of the American Revolution in the *Histoire des deux Indes*: 'Our style and manner of thinking have undergone a revolution more extraordinary than the political revolution of the country. We see with other eyes; we hear with other ears; and think with other thoughts, than those we formerly used.'[10] While Paine's claims demonstrate the revolutionary self-awareness and sense of novelty that many of the figures of the Atlantic Enlightenment shared, the completeness of the break from the past should not be overstated. While there was often a desire to leave behind tradition and older ways of thinking, it was precisely the tension between old and new that defined so much of the Atlantic Enlightenment. It was the dialectic between influence and independence that formed the intellectual and political contours of the Atlantic Enlightenment as citizens of the Atlantic world self-consciously drew upon the European tradition while asserting the value (economic and epistemological) of their local particularities. It was not just a question of identity formation or the assertion of political or cultural autonomy; it was the search for a way to think through, as well as beyond, the forms inherited from the European tradition.

A strange ambivalence often resulted from this attempt to simultaneously be within *and* without the boundaries of European thought. This ambivalent dialectic can be seen in grand events like the American Revolution – where, for instance, revolutionaries drew on the European natural law tradition to fashion a new articulation of natural rights that helped justify their endeavor.[11] But it can also be seen in the dramatically more modest (yet symbolically important) events like when Benjamin Smith Barton, the American naturalist and eventual president of the American Philosophical Society, created the new hybrid name *Didelphis woapink* for a variety of opossum found in North America.[12] Retaining the bi-nomial structure of the Swedish naturalist Linnaeus and the Latin family name, *Didelphis*, Barton replaced the Latin term *marsupialis* with the Native American term *woapink* that supposedly described the animal's white face.

As figures of the Atlantic Enlightenment like Barton drew on the language and concepts of Europe to create their own hybrid knowledge and intellectual dispositions, the Atlantic Enlightenment came of age in the last quarter of the eighteenth century

– CHAPTER 35: *The Atlantic Enlightenment* –

and persisted into the first decades of the nineteenth century, when it slowly and unevenly transformed into something else. It had its moments of crystallization and realization in some of the democratic Atlantic revolutions and independence movements, although there was never a simple or direct relationship between Enlightenment theory and revolutionary practice. The existence of Enlightenment figures who were characteristically Atlantic and who embodied the Enlightenment's theoretical and practical concerns varied considerably over time and place. For much of its existence, the Atlantic Enlightenment was most present in North America and the French Caribbean colonies, with Philadelphia and Cap François (the capitals of the new United States and the French colony of Saint-Domingue respectively) coming closest to being its centers. In these places, there were many signs of the types of books, newspapers, learned societies, libraries, correspondence networks, colleges, and masonic lodges that functioned as the infrastructure of the Enlightenment.[13]

Some of the important and characteristic figures of the Atlantic Enlightenment were Benjamin Franklin, Thomas Jefferson, Benjamin Rush, James Madison, Thomas Paine, Joseph Priestley, Joel Barlow, Richard Price, William Bartram, Benjamin Smith Barton, Mark Catesby, John Witherspoon, Samuel Stanhope Smith, Bryan Edwards, Olaudah Equiano, J. Hector St. John Crèvecoeur, the marquis de Lafayette, Médéric-Louis-Élie Moreau de Saint-Méry, Pierre-Paul-François-Joachim-Henri Le Mercier de la Rivière, Michel-René Hilliard d'Auberteuil, Gabriel de Bory, Julien Raimond, abbé Raynal, Denis Diderot, Anne-Robert-Jacques Turgot, Marie-Jean-Antoine-Nicolas Caritat, marquis de Condorcet, Pierre-Samuel Dupont de Nemours, Jacques-Pierre Brissot de Warville, abbé Henri-Baptiste Grégoire, Constantin-Françoise Chasseboeuf, comte de Volney, José Antonio Alzate y Ramírez, Francisco José de Caldas, Hipólito Unanue, and Hipólito José da Costa. There were also men like John Locke, Hans Sloane, and Louis-Armand de Lom d'Arce, baron de Lahontan whose works helped lay some of the intellectual foundations of the Atlantic Enlightenment. Locke's *An Essay Concerning Human Understanding* was one of the foundational works of Enlightenment philosophy of mind and human perfectibility, he was directly involved in colonial administration (including a role in the authorship of the *Fundamental Constitutions of Carolina*), and his powerful arguments from the *Two Treatises of Government* were used to justify English colonization as well as American revolution.[14] Hans Sloane, a physician, founder of the British Museum, and president of the Royal Society in London, resided in the Caribbean for two years, brought back a number of material objects (many of which were put on public display in London), and wrote a prominent book about the Caribbean that provided a model of an encyclopedic natural history of the region.[15] Lahontan had been an army officer in New France and his popular written works played an important role in fostering European interest in native Americans, developing the notion of the 'noble savage,' and inspiring later critiques of European colonization.[16] There were also a number of figures of Enlightenment that resided in, or travelled through, the Atlantic world, but lived largely before the formation of the distinctively Atlantic Enlightenment. Scientist, statesmen, author, and printer Benjamin Franklin was the most important of these early figures, but the scientific activities of Cadwallader Colden and John Bartram, as well as the French scientific expedition led by Charles-Marie de La Condamine through Spanish America were important early steps in the development of the Atlantic Enlightenment.[17] They helped demonstrate the intellectual and

653

practical potential of the Atlantic world – a place that could produce great scientists and practical knowledge of great utility and commercial value.

There were a number of figures of Enlightenment spread throughout Spanish America. Although the concentration of these figures and the depth and breadth of supporting institutions seems to have been less than some of the colonies and states of North America or in Saint-Domingue, clerical Creole authors articulated a 'patriotic epistemology' in the mid-eighteenth century that established a critical tradition of engaging with figures of the European Enlightenment. Based on pointed critiques of historical and natural historical accounts of the New World, a number of authors questioned the epistemological assumptions, system building, and sweeping judgments of European authors, particularly in relation to the claims that the environment of the New World caused degeneration (as Buffon, Robertson, de Pauw, Kalm, and Raynal famously claimed).[18] Building on this tradition of critical epistemology that asserted the importance of local knowledge and first hand observation, a new generation of Enlightenment figures emerged in Spanish America in the 1780s and 1790s. Enabled by the Bourbon Reforms, people like author and publisher José Antonio Alzate y Ramírez took advantage of the Spanish government's policies minimizing the influence of the Church and supporting learned institutions and publications. Publishing two short-lived periodicals before founding and almost single-handedly writing and compiling the periodical *Gacetas de literatura de México* from 1788 to 1795, Alzate was a secular priest and a persistent critic of European accounts of the people, plants, and history of the Americas. In his periodicals, Alzate publicized news from the Republic of Letters and the learned academies of Europe while remaining an outspoken critic of what he saw as the de-contextualizing and homogenizing tendencies of Enlightenment systems of thought and the natural historical practices such as Linnaean taxonomy.[19] Alzate was surrounded in New Spain (Mexico) by a group of Creole authors who also attempted to merge native history and scientific traditions with European knowledge and scientific practices. This was also true of other figures of the Atlantic Enlightenment in Spanish America such as the distinguished naturalist, astronomer, and engineer Francisco José de Caldas in the vice royalty of New Granada (Columbia) and the physician, naturalist, and journalist Hipólito Unanue in the vice royalty of Peru.[20]

The lusophone presence in the Atlantic Enlightenment was rather limited until the so-called 'generation of the 1790s' emerged in the wake of Pombal's reforms in Portugal (which included the significant curriculum reform of the University of Coimbra). A number of small learned academies were established in Brazil in the eighteenth century, but none of them lasted for long – most of them dissolving or being disbanded within a year or two of their founding – and by the late eighteenth century Brazil still lacked a printing press or a university (Coimbra was in fact the only university in the Portuguese empire).[21] Many of the members of the reformist generation of the 1790s were born in Brazil, educated at Coimbra, and then became involved in correspondence networks and scientific expeditions that reached across the Atlantic world. Some of these figures who came of age in the 1790s were José Bonifacio de Andrada e Silva, Tomáso Antônio Gonzaga, Francisco Josée de Lacerda e Almeida, and José Joaquim de Cunha de Azerdo Coutinho, Hipólito José da Costa, Alexadre Rodrigues Ferreira, Manuel Galvão da Silva, Joaquim José de Silva, João da Silva Feijó.[22] Through their travels across and around the Atlantic, they made contact

– CHAPTER 35: *The Atlantic Enlightenment* –

with leading European and American figures of Enlightenment and they made their own contributions to the development of natural history, jurisprudence, and political philosophy. Hipólito José da Costa, for example, was a cosmopolitan editor and publisher of colonial origin, Portuguese education, and an Atlantic itinerary (for a time living in Philadelphia and journeying throughout North America and the Caribbean collecting natural historical samples) who eventually settled in London, where he printed his politically dissident monthly publication *Correio Braziliense*.[23]

Although the Atlantic Enlightenment was distributed throughout the Atlantic world, there were also sites of convergence when a number of important figures of the Enlightenment found themselves residing in the same place at the same time, such as the mid-1790s in Philadelphia. Already the center of the Enlightenment in America (and the home of the Library Company of Philadelphia and the American Philosophical Society), Philadelphia received an influx of people fleeing from the revolutionary tumult in France and Saint-Domingue (including Constantin-François Volney, Charles-Maurice de Talleyrand, and Médéric-Louis-Élie Moreau de Saint-Méry), as well as British sympathizers of the French Revolution (including the Scottish botanist Alexander Wilson and the Unitarian radical Thomas Cooper). Volney, Talleyrand, Moreau, Wilson, and Cooper all became members of the American Philosophical Society and contributed to the intellectual and political ferment that received additional animation from the immigration of the illustrious English chemist, Unitarian, and ardent republican, Joseph Priestley.[24]

While there are many figures who composed the Atlantic Enlightenment, I want to focus on four figures – Thomas Jefferson, Médéric-Louis-Élie Moreau de Saint-Méry, Michel-René Hilliard d'Auberteuil, and Thomas Thistlewood – who represent important characteristics of the intellectual and political developments. Thomas Jefferson is an exemplary figure for his Atlantic itinerary, with time spent in American and European centers of Enlightenment, but also because of the wide range of subjects that he wrote about (best represented by the diversity of topics in *Notes on the State of Virginia*); his personal acquaintance with and correspondence with many of the other figures of the Enlightenment; his authorship of the influential works that demonstrated some of the ideas that were central to the Atlantic Enlightenment (the Declaration of Independence containing one of the most important articulations of natural rights and *Notes on the State of Virginia* containing one of the most important articulations of a creole natural history and the importance of local and particular knowledge); his membership in (and presidency of) the American Philosophical Society; his collecting one of the most significant personal libraries in North America (which became the foundation for the collection of the Library of Congress); and his establishment of what became the University of Virginia.[25]

While Thomas Jefferson – the statesman, lawyer, political philosopher, architect, and naturalist – is a well-known figure with an enormous amount written about him, a similar breadth of learning and experience can be found in a more obscure figure whose life and works nonetheless embody so many characteristics of the Atlantic Enlightenment. Much in the way that Jefferson's *Notes on the State of Virginia* exemplified the combination of broad encyclopedic interest and a focus on local and particular knowledge, as well as practical political economic concerns and larger philosophical problems, Médéric-Louis-Élie Moreau de Saint-Méry's monumental *Description topographique, physique, civile, politique et historique de la partie*

655

française de l'isle Saint-Domingue (1796) was a similarly typical beacon of the Atlantic Enlightenment.[26] Beginning in the 1780s, as part of a large government project to reform French colonial law, Moreau began researching and editing a different encyclopedic work: the six-volume work, *Loix et contitutions des colonies françoises de l'Amérique sous le Vent*, which collected the laws and decrees relating to the French colonies in the Caribbean with the intention of codifying colonial law and providing a new resource for colonial administrators to use in making informed decisions.[27] During this research, with its unprecedented access to the ministerial archives, Moreau began to gather information for his monumental *Description*, which he originally envisioned as an enlightened encyclopedia covering all aspects of life in the Caribbean. Although he did not fulfill this grand vision, his *Description* remains one of the best sources for historical information about Saint-Domingue and it was one of the most wide-ranging books to be published during the Enlightenment.

As the full title of the *Description* indicated, it covered the history of the geographical, political, economic, and social structures of the French side of the island of Hispaniola, but it also touched upon elements of everyday life and culture. In places, the *Description* reads like an ethnographic study, with descriptions of linguistic creolization, the fashion tastes of free women of color in Cap François, the religious practices of the '*danse vaudoux*,' and the sexual predilections of the white men of Saint-Domingue. But the *Description*'s most original and troubling intellectual contribution to the Atlantic Enlightenment was the treatment of fractional racial difference. Moreau created an elaborate attempt to identify, name, and classify all of the combinations of descent between people of African and European origin. When he divided the range between complete whiteness and blackness into 128 genealogical parts, Moreau's racial calculus went far beyond the era's other discussions of racial classification. In fact, Moreau took his calculations even further and posited the hypothetical existence of someone who was 1 part black and 8,191 parts white.[28]

Born at mid-century in Martinique, Moreau travelled to Paris as a young adult, where he trained in law and gained a job in the Parlement of Paris during the turbulent years of 'the Maupeou revolution' when the Parlement and the crown struggled for legitimacy and power.[29] Upon returning to the Carribean, he settled in Saint-Domingue and began working as a lawyer and soon became a judge in the colonial judiciary. Through the 1780s, Moreau travelled back and forth between Saint-Domingue and Paris, researching and writing *Loix* and *Description*. In 1789, as the revolution began to take shape, Moreau found himself in France. He became a politic activist for both the colonial interests of the planters and the interests of the metropolitan members of the Third Estate.

After his political career was crippled by rumors that he wanted to end slavery, Moreau remained in France until he was forced to flee the Terror. Settling in Philadelphia, he was involved in proliferating Enlightenment ideas through print as an author, printer, and book-seller. He set up a printing press and bookstore that published his own work on Saint-Domingue, as well as books and pamphlets on Spanish Santo-Domingo, improving the breed of horses in the United States, Joseph Priestley's reflections on the chemical theory of phlogiston, a European perspective on American prisons, and an encyclopedic presentation of the arts and sciences for young people. He printed many of these works in both French and English, and throughout his life, he remained engaged with scholarly works from parts of the

– CHAPTER 35: *The Atlantic Enlightenment* –

Atlantic world quite distant from his own place of residence – as can be seen in his translation of a Spanish naturalist's observation on the quadrupeds of Paraguay.[30] Throughout his travels in the Atlantic world, Moreau participated in Masonic activities in Saint-Domingue, Paris, and Philadelphia, becoming a member of the illustrious Loge des Neuf Sœurs in Paris, which was packed with Enlightenment luminaries such as Franklin and Voltaire, and becoming president of the Loge's educational subsidiary the Musée de Paris. He was also a member of important learned societies including the American Philosophical Society and Saint-Domingue's Cercle des Philadelphes, which he helped gain royal letters patent, turning it into the Société Royale des Science et des Arts du Cap François.

Moreau was not simply a Frenchman or a Caribbean creole, a royal administrator or a French revolutionary, a cosmopolitan by choice or an émigré by necessity, a partisan of liberty or a theorist of racial difference – he was all of these things. He was 'a citizen of the Atlantic' and – while he has not been ignored by historians – there is still much to be learned about his life and the ways that his itinerant Atlantic existence played a role in his intellectual development and his lasting contributions to the Atlantic Enlightenment.[31] I suspect that as we know more about figures like Moreau, the contours of the Atlantic Enlightenment will become significantly clearer.

Michel-René Hilliard d'Auberteuil is an example of a more obscure – but still significant – figure of the Atlantic Enlightenment. He was a legally minded reformists who drew heavily on Montesquieu's legal and political ideas in his development of a creole jurisprudence, opposed the metropolitan *ancien régime* hierarchy and its enshrined special privileges, attacked mercantilism while articulating liberal economic arguments that were consistent with the new Enlightenment political economy, ardently supported the American Revolution, and implicitly built upon the new Enlightenment approaches to natural history and race.[32] His two-volume *Considérations sur l'état présent de la colonie française de Saint-Domingue* (1776– 77) remains one of the best historical sources for information on eighteenth-century Saint-Domingue.[33] It was one of the most vituperative critiques of colonial governance (rivaled in the francophone world only by the 1780 edition of the *Histoire des deux Indes*) and a strong articulation of the importance of local knowledge and empirical observation in the creation of law and the process of governing.[34]

Hilliard's *Considérations* also included a proposal for the racial engineering of Saint-Domingue that was one of the most surprising and extreme visions of biopolitics in the eighteenth century; in fact, it was one of the first plans ever to propose the racial engineering of a real population actually existing in the world.[35] Hilliard's plan drew on metropolitan developments in legal and biological theory in an attempt to address the social, political, and military circumstances of Saint-Domingue. The plan, proposed in the 1770s, was neither a metropolitan or colonial plan, it was an Atlantic hybrid, much as Hilliard was. His life exhibited the movement across great distances and between different cultures that was so typical of many of the most notable intellectual figures of the early modern Atlantic world. He was born in France and moved to Saint-Domingue as an adolescent, was exiled from the colony for his radical writing, spent time in New York during the American Revolution, returned to the Caribbean to take up the position of royal prosecutor in Grenada (from which he was quickly removed and exiled from the island), moved to Paris to earn his living as a writer (although he was jailed for his increasingly radical critiques of the monarchy and colonial policy), only to once more move to the Caribbean where he died in mysterious circumstances just as the French and Haitian Revolutions were getting underway (it was rumored that a group of planters had him murdered).[36]

In addition to a two-volume synoptic work on Saint-Domingue, Hilliard published a wide variety of works including histories of the American Revolution, an account of British financial policy, anti-mercantilist polemics, a novel set in America during the Revolutionary War, and a variety of pamphlets on morality. While in Paris, he was also a member, like Moreau, of one of the French Enlightenment's most exclusive and exemplary fraternal organizations, the masonic Loge des Neuf Sœurs. The lodge functioned much like a learned academy, fostering the egalitarian and cosmopolitan ideals that were associated with the more progressive masonic lodges of the era.[37]

While Hilliard had a less illustrious career than Jefferson or Moreau, there were even more peripheral figures in the Atlantic Enlightenment who often lived further from urban centers and the types of learned societies, libraries, book-sellers, and periodicals that would have allowed for a substantive engagement with the Enlightenment. These figures often did not make a significant direct contribution to the Enlightenment – or maybe even a modest one such as a short notice in the publication of a learned society – but many of them nonetheless put concerted effort into staying abreast of the philosophical and scientific developments of the day. Furthermore, they may have played an important role in the proliferation of Enlightenment dispositions and practices that contributed to the circumstances enabling some of the direct contributions to the Enlightenment for which we have textual or material evidence.

Thomas Thistlewood, for instance, was a stunningly violent, sadistic, and tyrannical plantation overseer and slave owner, who nonetheless aspired to make himself into a learned figure of the Republic of Letters. After moving to Jamaica from England in 1750, he acquired and built a number of scientific instruments such as telescopes, microscopes, and hydrometers. He amassed a library of approximately one thousand volumes while pursuing his practical interests in botany, horticulture, and meteorology.[38] Thistlewood also participated in a small informal network of provincial Jamaicans with whom he often traded and borrowed books. His commonplace book – where he transcribed interesting and instructive passages from his reading material – records a surprising number and variety of Enlightenment works. Most surprisingly – for a provincial plantation overseer and modest landowner in what would have appeared to be an intellectual backwater of the Atlantic world – many of the books were written by well-known Enlightenment authors including French *philosophes* such as Montesquieu, Rousseau, Voltaire, and the novelist and chronicler Louis-Sébastien Mercier.[39]

Thistlewood's engagement with these authors raises questions not only of the penetration of Enlightenment ideas into some of the most seemingly un-enlightened parts of the Atlantic world, they also raise question about the role of Enlightenment ideas in the re-assessment of even the most fundamental foundations of the Atlantic world, such as the institution of slavery. In addition to transcribing critiques of slavery from the books of Rousseau and Montesquieu into his commonplace book, Thistlewood copied the now famous passage from Mercier's futurist novel where he imagined a Paris in the distant future that included a statue celebrating 'the Avenger of the New World' who destroyed the tyranny of slavery through bloody violence.[40]

– CHAPTER 35: *The Atlantic Enlightenment* –

Historians today often invoke this passage as a sign of a rare and eerie prescience, and it has been used many times as an epigraph, title, or illustrative quotation.[41] Along with Diderot's invocation of a black Spartacus rising up to end slavery, Mercier's vision haunts the historiography of the Atlantic world and the Haitian Revolution, and it appears that it may have also haunted even one of the most sadistic and peripheral of slave owners in the eighteenth-century Atlantic world.

By way of conclusion, I would like to suggest five lines of inquiry that could contribute to the development of a historiography of the Atlantic Enlightenment. The first two of these topics build on the fact that all four of the men I have just discussed were all deeply involved in the world of slavery (with Jefferson, Moreau, and Hilliard giving great consideration to its political, economic, moral, and scientific dimensions). We still have much to discover about how the Enlightenment created such powerful discourses of inclusion based on ideas of toleration, equality, cosmopolitanism, and natural rights, while simultaneously creating powerful and lasting discourses of exclusion based on the perception (and creation) of differences such as race.[42] How this paradoxical situation emerged is still a central question (maybe *the* question) of the Enlightenment.[43] The Atlantic seems like the most promising frame to arrive at a compelling analysis of the simultaneous development of new ideas of inclusion and exclusion during the eighteenth century because the most powerful discourse of inclusion (self-evident natural rights) and one of the primary discourses of exclusion (racial differentiation) have distinctively Atlantic genealogies.

Recently, scholars have brought greater attention to the transatlantic nature of the development of ideas of human rights as well as the fact that 'perhaps more than any other set of ideas, race was Atlantic.'[44] Over the past ten to fifteen years, intellectual historians of the eighteenth-century Atlantic world have demonstrated how instrumental the eighteenth century was in the creation of the idea of race and how much the Atlantic was the crucible within which this idea was formed.[45] Yet, it is still unclear how some of the most prominent advocates of notions of equality, natural rights, and common humanity also held profoundly inegalitarian ideas in relation to race. The co-mingling of universalism and racism in a single person poses one of the most difficult problems for Enlightenment historiography and embodies one of the most seemingly contradictory legacies of Enlightenment ideas. This is particularly true because this strange admixture is found in some of the most noteworthy of Enlightenment figures, such as Voltaire, Kant, Hume, Buffon, and Jefferson, to name just a few.

Related to the development of these discourses – and another promising line of historical inquiry that I will suggest for future research on the Atlantic Enlightenment – is the manner in which the colonies in the Atlantic world functioned as 'laboratories of modernity' where biopolitical projects were developed and sometimes implemented. While Michel Foucault identified the eighteenth century as the era of the emergence of biopolitics, he did not mention the ways that colonial history in the Atlantic world – with the intertwined questions arising from the interaction of settler populations, slave populations, and native populations – was a major site of development of modern biopolitics. In fact, he largely ignored the issues of race and colonialism.[46] This oversight has been corrected for the literature on the development of biopolitics in the nineteenth century, but there has not yet been an adequate recognition of the role of the colonies during the eighteenth century or of the role of Enlightenment thought. It was precisely because of the colonization of places like Saint-Domingue (a society where roughly 90 percent of the population was enslaved in the late eighteenth century), that free residents of the colony, administrators in the colony and the metropole, as well as people connected to the colonial project through economic, scientific, and military activities, were forced to consider new questions about knowing, controlling, and transforming populations. Although they have received little attention from historians of Europe, some of the most extreme ideas of biopolitics were directly related to concerns with the relationship between the populations in the colonies and the population in the metropole. These plans go far beyond the demographic concerns or the development of techniques for monitoring populations that Foucault first drew attention to in his writing on the development of biopolitics.

Many of the most comprehensive, interventionist, and extreme biopolitical ideas and practices that attempted to know, regulate, and transform populations were developed in the context of the colonial slave societies of the Atlantic world. Elsewhere, I have attempted to situate a little known, yet highly troubling and complex product of the Atlantic Enlightenment: the first plans proposing the racial engineering of a real population actually existing in the world.[47] In addition to these proposals for racial engineering, the Atlantic world saw the creation of a great variety of biopolitical projects: the creation of numerous laws and ordinances to encourage or discourage marriage between whites and blacks; projects of political arithmetic like that of Benjamin Franklin; the creation of expeditions of royal midwives to Saint-Domingue to increase settler populations; the many attempts to increase the reproduction of slaves through improved health and birthing practices; calls for the creation of systems of identification, surveillance, and census for free people of color on Saint-Domingue; the introduction of the *Police des noirs* regulations in France in the 1770s; the purchasing of the legal status of whiteness from Spanish royal administrators through the process of *gracias al sacar*; Victor Hugues' racial census on Guadalupe in the 1790s; and a variety of proposals for the forced relocation or assimilation of emancipated slaves.[48]

The paradigm of the Atlantic Enlightenment also affords the opportunity to better include a number of figures of the early Black Atlantic diaspora in the history of the Enlightenment and to discover ways that enslaved peoples contributed to the development of Enlightenment knowledge and practices. It may enable scholars to find new connections between seemingly disparate phenomena and to create a broader picture of the contribution of slaves and free people of African descent.[49] These developments include: the writing of narratives of slavery and freedom by early authors of the Black Atlantic such as Ignatius Sancho, Philis Wheatley, Olaudah Equiano, and Quobona Ottobah Cugoano; the employment of rights discourse by the slave insurgents in the late-eighteenth-century Caribbean; the political radicalization of some sailors of African descent; the establishment in the mid-1780s of the masonic African Lodge No. 459 in Boston by Prince Hall, a black leather worker and veteran of the American Revolutionary War; the contribution of African slaves to Enlightenment practices such as smallpox inoculation; and the contributions of slaves to the development of valuable and useful botanical knowledge.[50]

Another promising area of inquiry into the character and impact of the Atlantic Enlightenment is the development of political economy. As scholars are beginning to demonstrate, the Atlantic economy played a much more important role in the development of liberal political economy than previously realized. The study of

– CHAPTER 35: *The Atlantic Enlightenment* –

political economy holds out the promise of better integrating European intellectuals into the Atlantic Enlightenment, as many of the most prominent figures in the development of political economy in the European Enlightenment – such as Adam Smith, the Physiocrats, Turgot, and Condorcet – were people with a significant interest in Atlantic trade, imperial conflict, and the peoples of the Atlantic world.[51] Some of these figures had direct and sustained involvement with the Atlantic world, such as Pierre-Paul Mercier de la Rivière who was an intendant of Martinique before becoming one of the most famous Physiocrats and a consulting expert to the French ministry in charge of the colonies. But more surprising and promising is the depth of Atlantic connections and interest that have recently been suggested for David Hume, someone who never left Europe and is 'at first sight a distinctively unAtlantic figure,' yet whose Atlantic entanglements (commercial, political, personal, aspirational, and imaginative) seem to have played a significant and unrecognized role in the formation of his influential political and economic ideas.[52] Through the study of political economy, there is also much to discover about the role of political economic theory in undermining metropolitan authority (particularly through anti-mercantilist critique) and its complicated role in the Bourbon reforms in the Spanish empire.

The last and largest topic – the development of radical ideas and revolutionary politics – is one of the topics that has received the most extensive treatment in the historiography of the Atlantic world. In fact, it was a focus from the beginning in the work of scholars like Robert Palmer and Jacques Godechot.[53] But several recent works demonstrate that there is much to learn about the broadly Atlantic character of radical ideas and their relationship to the great democratic revolutions and independence movements of the late eighteenth century and the early nineteenth century. Some of the most promising new literature illuminates the development of transatlantic revolutionary cosmopolitans, the role of the ideas of the Radical Enlightenment, the relationship between the Atlantic Revolutions, the broad Atlantic impact of the Haitian Revolution, the role of the Atlantic world in the French Revolution, and the role of the Declaration of Independence in providing a model for asserting national autonomy.[54]

There was a deep intellectual reciprocity between the European figures of Enlightenment and the Atlantic world that is still only beginning to be discovered. While the historiography of the early modern Atlantic world has taken off and established itself as a major field of study in the last several decades, the story of the Atlantic Enlightenment as a singular and coherent movement – or at least a useful framework to study this intellectual reciprocity – remains largely to be told.

NOTES

1 For the most significant arguments for multiple Enlightenments, see J. G. A. Pocock, *Barbarism and Religion*, 4 vols. (New York, 1999–2008); Dorinda Outram, *The Enlightenment* (New York, 1995); and Roy Porter and Mikulás Teich, ed., *The Enlightenment in National Context* (New York, 1981).

2 See Susan Manning and Francis D. Cogliano, eds., *The Atlantic Enlightenment* (Burlington, 2008); Bernard Bailyn and Patricia L. Denault, eds., *Soundings in Atlantic History: Latent Structures and Intellectual Currents, 1500–1830* (Cambridge, Mass., 2009); and Manuela Albertone and Antonino De Francesco, *Rethinking the Atlantic World: Europe and America in the Age of Democratic Revolutions* (New York, 2009). On the Sciences in the

Atlantic world, see James Delbourgo, *A Most Amazing Scene of Wonders: Electricity and Enlightenment in Early America* (Cambridge, Mass., 2006); Jorge Cañizares-Esguerra, *How to Write the History of the New World: Histories, Epistemologies, and Identities in the Eighteenth-Century Atlantic World* (Stanford, 2001); Neil Safier, *Measuring the New World: Enlightenment Science and South America* (Chicago, 2008); Londa Schiebinger and Claudia Swan, eds., *Colonial Botany: Science, Commerce and Politics in the Early Modern World* (Philadelphia, 2005); James Delbourgo and Nicolas Dew, eds., *Science and Empire in the Atlantic World* (New York, 2008); Susan Scott Parrish, *American Curiosity: Cultures of Natural History in the Colonial British Atlantic World* (Chapel Hill, 2006).

3   On the American Enlightenment, see Henry F. May, *The Enlightenment in America* (Oxford, 1976); Donald F. Meyer, *The Democratic Enlightenment* (New York, 1976); Robert A. Ferguson, *The American Enlightenment, 1750–1820* (Cambridge, Mass., 1997); and Nina Reid-Maroney, *Philadelphia's Enlightenment, 1740–1800* (Westport, Conn., 2001).

4   Manning and Cogliano, *The Atlantic Enlightenment*.

5   Manning and Cogliano, *The Atlantic Enlightenment*, 9–10.

6   Anthony Strugnell, *Diderot's Politics: A Study of the Evolution of Diderot's Political Thought After the* Encyclopédie (The Hague, 1973), 205–17.

7   *Histoire des deux Indes* is the commonly used title for *Histoire philosophique et politique des établissements et du commerce des Européens dans les deux Indes* which was published by abbé Guillaume-Thomas-François Raynal in 1772 (with 1770 printed on the title page), expanded in a co-authored revised edition of 1780, before being pirated and reissued in innumerable editions in various languages. For Diderot's contributions to the 1780 edition, see Michèle Duchet, *Diderot et l'Histoire des deux Indes, ou l'écriture fragmentaire* (Paris, 1978).

8   On the reception and importance of the *Histoire des deux Indes*, see Sankar Muthu, *Enlightenment Against Empire* (Princeton, 2003), 72–121; Hans-Jürgen Lüsebrink and Manfred Tietz, eds., *Lectures de Raynal: L'Histoire des deux Indes en Europe et en Amérique au XVIIIe siècle* (Oxford, 1991); and Hans-Jürgen Lüsebrink and Anthony Strugnell, eds., *L'Histoire des deux Indes: Reécriture et polygraphie* (Oxford, 1995).

9   On the French Revolution and the future see, Lynn Hunt, 'The World We Have Gained: The Future of the French Revolution' *The American Historical Review* 108, no. 1 (February 2003): 1–19.

10 Thomas Paine, 'Letter Addressed to the Abbé Raynal' (1782), in Philip S. Foner, ed., *Complete Writings of Thomas Paine* (New York, 1945), 2:243.

11 See Jack N. Rakove, ed., *Declaring Rights: A Brief History with Documents* (Boston, 1998); Pauline Maier, *American Scripture: Making the Declaration of Independence* (New York, 1997); and Michael P. Zuckert, *The Natural Rights Republic* (South Bend, 1997).

12 Parrish, *American Curiosity*, 134–35.

13 On correspondence networks between naturalists in the Atlantic world, see E. C. Spary, *Utopia's Garden: French Natural History from Old Regime to Revolution* (Chicago, 2000), 49–98; and Parrish, *American Curiosity*, 103–35. On politics and American, Dutch, and French correspondence networks, see Nathan Perl-Rosenthal, 'Corresponding Republics: Letter Writing and Patriot Organizing in the Atlantic Revolutions, circa 1760–92' (Ph.D. dissertation, Columbia University, 2011). On the history of printing, reading, newspapers, and books, see Hugh Amory and David D. Hall, eds., *The Colonial Book in the Atlantic World* (Cambridge, 2000); and David S. Shields and Caroline Sloat, et al., *Liberty! Égalité! ¡Independencia!: Print Culture, Enlightenment, and Revolutions in the Americas, 1776–1838* (Worcester, Mass., 2007). On the history of the theater, see Heather S. Nathans, *Early American Theatre from Revolution to Thomas Jefferson: Into the Hands of the People* (Cambridge, 2003) and Jenna M. Gibbs, *Performing the Temple of*

– CHAPTER 35: *The Atlantic Enlightenment* –

Liberty: Slavery, Theater, and Popular Culture in London and Philadelphia, 1760–1850 (Baltimore, 2014). On Freemasonry, see Margaret Jacob, *Living the Enlightenment: Freemasonry and Politics in Eighteenth-Century Europe* (Oxford, 1991); Stephen C. Bullock, *Revolutionary Brotherhood: Freemasonry and the Transformation of the American Social Order, 1730–1840* (Chapel Hill, 1996); and James E. McClellan III, *Colonialism and Science: Saint Domingue in the Old Regime* (Baltimore, 1992), 183–205.

14 On the colonial uses of Locke and Locke's colonial involvement, see James Tully, *An Approach to Political Philosophy: John Locke in Contexts* (Cambridge, 1993); Barbara Arneil, *John Locke and America: The Defense of English Colonialism* (Oxford, 1996); and David Armitage, 'John Locke, Carolina, and the "Two Treatises of Government",' *Political Theory* 32, no. 5 (October 2004): 602–27; On the American uses of Locke, see Bernard Bailyn, *The Ideological Origins of the American Revolution* (Cambridge, Mass., 1967); and May, *Enlightenment in America*.

15 Arthur MacGregor, ed., *Sir Hans Sloane: Collector, Scientist, Antiquary, Founding Father of the British Museum* (London, 1994).

16 Anthony Pagden, *European Encounters with the New World: From Renaissance to Romanticism* (New Haven, 1993), 117–40; Muthu, *Enlightenment Against Empire*, 11–71.

17 Gordon S. Wood, *The Americanization of Benjamin Franklin* (New York, 2004); Joyce Chaplin, *The First Scientific American: Benjamin Franklin and the Pursuit of Genius* (New York, 2006); Alfred R. Hoermann, *Cadwallader Colden: A Figure of the American Enlightenment* (Westport, Conn., 2002); Nancy E. Hoffmann and John C. Van Horne, eds., *America's Curious Botanist: A Tercentennial Reappraisal of John Bartram (1699–1777)* (Philadelphia, 2004). On the La Condamine expedition, see Safier, *Measuring the New World*. On science in the early modern Atlantic see, Delbourgo and Dew, *Science and Empire*.

18 Antonello Gerbi, *The Dispute of the New World: The History of a Polemic, 1750–1900*, trans. Jeremy Moyle (Pittsburgh, 1973); Cañizares-Esguerra, *How to Write the History of the New World*.

19 Fiona Clark, '"Read All About It": Science, Translation, Adaptation, and Confrontation in the *Gazeta de Literatura de México*, 1788–95,' in Daniela Bleichmar et al., eds., *Science in the Spanish and Portuguese Empires, 1500–1800* (Stanford, 2009); Cañizares-Esguerra, *How to Write the History of the New World*, 281–307; Antonio Lafuente, 'Enlightenment in an Imperial Context: Local Science in the Late-Eighteenth-Century Hispanic World,' *Osiris*, 2nd series, 15 (2000): 155–73.

20 Antonio Lafuente, 'Enlightenment in an Imperial Context'; and Jorge Cañizares-Esguerra, *Nature, Empire, and Nation: Explorations of the History of Science in the Iberian World* (Stanford, 2006), 112–28.

21 E. Bradford Burns, 'Concerning the Transmission and Dissemination of the Enlightenment in Brazil,' in *The Ibero-American Enlightenment*, ed. A. Owen Aldridge (Urbana, 1971), 269–70; and Francisco Betancourt, 'Enlightened Reform in Portugal and Brazil,' in *Enlightened Reform in Southern Europe and its Atlantic Colonies, c. 1750–1830*, ed. Gabriel Paquette (Burlington, Vermont, 2009), 43.

22 See Kenneth Maxwell, 'The Generation of the 1790s and the Idea of Luso-Brazilian Empire,' in *Colonial Roots of Modern Brazil*, ed. Dauril Alden (Berkeley, California, 1973), 107–44; and Neil Safier, 'A Courier between Empires: Hipólito da Costa and the Atlantic World,' in *Soundings in Atlantic History*, 263–93.

23 Safier, 'Hipólito da Costa and the Atlantic World.'

24 May, *Enlightenment in America*, 197–222; and Reid-Maroney, *Philadelphia's Enlightenment*.

25 On his life and work, see Dumas Malone, *Jefferson and his Time*, 6 vols. (Boston, 1948–81); Peter S. Onuf, *The Mind of Thomas Jefferson* (Charlottesville, 2007); Kevin J. Hayes, *The Road to Monticello: The Life and Mind of Thomas Jefferson* (Oxford, 2008); and Charles A. Miller, *Jefferson and Nature: An Interpretation* (Baltimore, 1988).

26 Médéric-Louis-Élie Moreau de Saint-Méry, *Description topographique, physique, civile, politique et historique de la partie française de l'isle Saint-Domingue*, 3 vols. (Paris, 1958 [Philadelphia, 1796]). See the discussion of Jefferson, Moreau, and Bryan Edwards in David Brion Davis, *The Problem of Slavery in the Age of Revolution, 1770–1823* (Oxford, 1999), 184–95.

27 Médéric-Louis-Élie Moreau de Saint-Méry, *Loix et contitutions des colonies françoises de l'Amérique sous le Vent*, 6 vols. (Paris, 1784–90).

28 Moreau de Saint-Méry, *Description*, 86–100. Also see Joan Dayan, *Haiti, History, and The Gods* (Berkeley and Los Angeles, 1995), 228–37; and Garraway, *Libertine Colony*, 260–75.

29 For biographical information on Moreau, see Etienne Taillemite, 'Moreau de Saint-Méry,' introduction to Moreau de Saint-Méry, *Description topographique*; and Anthony Louis Elicona, *Un colonial sous la Révolution en France et en Amérique: Moreau de Saint-Méry* (Paris, 1934).

30 Félix de Azara, *Essais sur l'histoire naturelle des quadrupeds de la province de Paraguay*, trans. Médéric-Louis-Élie Moreau de Saint-Méry, 2 vols. (Paris, Year IX [1801]).

31 Laurent Dubois, *Avengers of the New World: The Story of the Haitian Revolution* (Cambridge, Mass., 2004), 9.

32 For Hilliard's intellectual output and his status as a figure of the Enlightenment, see Gene E. Ogle, '"The Eternal Power of Reason" and "The Superiority of Whites": Hilliard d'Auberteuil's Colonial Enlightenment,' *French Colonial History* 3 (2003): 35–50; Malick Walid Ghachem, 'Sovereignty and Slavery in the Age of Revolution: Haitian Variations on a Metropolitan Theme,' (Ph.D. dissertation, Stanford University, 2001); and Malick W. Ghachem, 'Montesquieu in the Caribbean: The Colonial Enlightenment between *Code Noir* and *Code Civil*,' in Daniel Gordon, ed., *Postmodernism and the Enlightenment: New Perspectives in Eighteenth-Century French Intellectual History* (New York, 2001), 7–30; and Doris Garraway, *The Libertine Colony: Creolization in the Early French Caribbean* (Durham, North Carolina, 2005), 218–26.

33 H.D. [Michel-René Hilliard d'Auberteuil], *Considérations sur l'état présent de la colonie française de Saint-Domingue*, 2 vols. (Paris, 1776–77).

34 See Ghachem, 'Montesquieu in the Caribbean.'

35 William Max Nelson, 'Making Men: Enlightenment Ideas of Racial Engineering,' *The American Historical Review* 115, no. 5 (December 2010): 1364–94. In this article, I also discuss a plan for the racial engineering of Saint-Domingue which was written at the same time as Hilliard's by a former governor of the island, Gabriel de Bory. On Hilliard's plan, also see, Garraway, *The Libertine Colony*, 218–26.

36 On Hilliard's biography, see Ogle, 'Power of Reason.' There is additional biographical information – although some of it questionable – in Lewis Leary's introduction to Michel-René Hilliard d'Auberteuil, *Miss McCrea: A Novel of the American Revolution* (Gainesville, 1958 [1784]), 6–11.

37 On the Neufs Sœurs, see Louis Amiable, *Une loge maçonnique d'avant 1789, la R. L. Les Neufs Sœurs*, ed. Charles Porset (Paris, 1989 [1897]).

38 On Thistlewood's attempt to fashion himself as a figure of the (Atlantic) Enlightenment, see Trevor Burnard, *Mastery, Tyranny, and Desire: Thomas Thistlewood and His Slaves in the Anglo-Jamaican World* (Chapel Hill, 2004), particularly pages 101–36. Also see Douglas Hall, *In Miserable Slavery: Thomas Thistlewood in Jamaica, 1750–86* (Kingston, 1999).

39 April G. Shelford, 'Pascal in Jamaica: Or, The French Enlightenment in Translation,' *Proceedings of the Western Society for French History* 36 (2008): 53–74.

40 Shelford, 'Pascal in Jamaica,' 73–74. Thistlewood read a 1772 translation of Mercier's *Memoirs of the Year Two Thousand Five Hundred* published in Dublin. Mercier's wildly popular novel was originally published as *L'An 2440* in 1771, with many subsequent editions.

– CHAPTER 35: *The Atlantic Enlightenment* –

41 A recent notable usage (where it is epigraph, title, and point of discussion) is Dubois' excellent, *Avengers of the New World*, 57–58.

42 See Tzvetan Todorov, *On Human Diversity: Nationalism, Racism, and Exoticism in French Thought* (Cambridge, Mass., 1993); Richard H. Popkin, 'The Philosophical Basis of Eighteenth-Century Racism,' in Harold E. Pagliaro, ed., *Racism in the Eighteenth Century* (Cleveland, 1973), 245–62; and Louis Sala-Molins, *Dark Side of the Light: Slavery and the French Enlightenment* (Minneapolis, 2006).

43 This offers the opportunity to revisit questions raised by historians of Early America; see Edmund S. Morgan, 'Slavery and Freedom: The American Paradox,' *Journal of American History* 59(1) (1972): 5–29; and Davis, *The Problem of Slavery in the Age of Revolution*.

44 Joyce E. Chaplin, 'Race,' in David Armitage and Michael J. Braddick, eds., *The British Atlantic World, 1500–1800* (New York, 2002), 154. Also see Lynn Hunt, *Inventing Human Rights: A History* (New York, 2007); Rakove, *Declaring Rights*; and Eric Slauter, *The State as a Work of Art* (Chicago, 2008), 169–214.

45 See Nelson, 'Making Men;' Roxann Wheeler, *The Complexion of Race: Categories of Difference in Eighteenth-Century British Culture* (Philadelphia, 2000); Nicholas Hudson, 'From "Nation" to "Race": The Origin of Racial Classification in Eighteenth-Century Thought,' *Eighteenth-Century Studies* 29, no. 3 (1996): 247–64; Bruce Dain, *A Hideous Monster of the Mind: American Race Theory in the Early Republic* (Cambridge, Mass., 2002); Guillaume Aubert, '"The Blood of France": Race and Purity of Blood in the French Atlantic World,' *William and Mary Quarterly* 3rd ser., 61, no. 3, (2004): 439–78; Sue Peabody, *'There are No Slaves in France': The Political Culture of Race and Slavery in the Ancien Régime* (New York, 1996); Pierre H. Boulle, *Race et esclavage dans la France de l'Ancien Régime* (Paris, 2007).

46 Michel Foucault, *The History of Sexuality: Volume 1, An Introduction*, trans. Robert Hurley (New York, 1978); Ann Laura Stoler, *Race and the Education of Desire: Foucault's History of Sexuality and the Colonial Order of Things* (Durham, N. C., 1995); and Ann Laura Stoler, *Carnal Knowledge and Imperial Power: Race and the Intimate in Colonial Rule* (Berkeley and Los Angeles, 2002).

47 Nelson, 'Making Men.'

48 See Jennifer M. Spear, *Race, Sex, and Social Order in Early New Orleans* (Baltimore, 2009); Aubert, 'The Blood of France'; Joyce E. Chaplin, *Benjamin Franklin's Political Arithmetic: A Materialist View of Humanity* (Washington, D.C., 2008); Karol K. Weaver, 'The King's Midwives: The 1764 Midwife Expedition to Saint-Domingue and Why It Failed,' *Nursing History Review* 13 (2005): 5–21; Nelson, 'Making Men'; Peabody, *There are No Slaves*; Boulle, *Race et esclavage*, 85–107; Ann Twinam, 'Racial Passing: Informal and Official "Whiteness" in Colonial Spanish America,' in *New World Orders: Violence, Sanction, and Authority in the Colonial America*, ed. John Smolenski and Thomas J. Humphrey (Philadelphia, 2005), 249–72; Laurent Dubois, *A Colony of Citizens: Revolution and Slave Emancipation in the French Caribbean, 1787–1804* (Chapel Hill, 2004), 262–66; Winthrop D. Jordan, *White over Black: American Attitudes Toward the Negro, 1550–1812* (Chapel Hill, 1968); and James Sidbury, *Becoming African in America: Race and Nation in the Early Black Atlantic* (Oxford, 2007).

49 On the need for a new approach to the intellectual history of the enslaved, see Laurent Dubois, 'An Enslaved Enlightenment: Rethinking the Intellectual History of the French Atlantic,' *Social History* 31, no. 1 (February, 2006): 1–14.

50 On the 'African freemasons' in America, see James Sidbury, *Becoming African in America: Race and Nation in the Early Black Atlantic* (Oxford, 2007), 73–77, 87–88; and Bullock, *Revolutionary Brotherhood*, 158–60. On the narratives of slavery and freedom, see Audrey Fisch, ed., *The Cambridge Companion to The African American Slave Narrative* (Cambridge, 2007), 11–80. On the use of rights discourse by slave insurgents, see Laurent

Dubois, *A Colony of Citizens: Revolution and Slave Emancipation in the French Caribbean, 1787–1804* (Chapel Hill, 2004), 23–29; and Dubois, *Avengers of the New World*, 105. On the political radicalization of sailors of African descent, see Peter Linebaugh and Marcus Rediker, *The Many-Headed Hydra: Sailors, Slaves, Commoners, and the Hidden History of the Revolutionary Atlantic* (Boston, 2000). On the contributions of slaves to medical practices such as smallpox inoculation and the use of medical botanicals, see Karol K. Weaver, *Medical Revolutionaries: The Enslaved Healers of Eighteenth-Century Saint Domingue* (Chicago, 2006). On the contributions to botany, see Schiebinger and Swan, eds., *Colonial Botany*, and Londa Schiebinger, *Plants and Empire: Colonial Bioprospecting in the Atlantic World* (Cambridge, Mass., 2004).

51 Emma Rothschild, *Economic Sentiments: Adam Smith, Condorcet, and the Enlightenment* (Cambridge, Mass., 2002); Emma Rothschild, 'Global Commerce and the Question of Sovereignty in the Eighteenth-Century Provinces,' *Modern Intellectual History* 1, no. 1 (2004): 3–25; Paul Cheney, *Revolutionary Commerce: Globalization and the French Monarchy* (Cambridge, Mass., 2010); and Pernille Røge, '"La clef de Commerce": The Changing Role of Africa in France's Atlantic Empire, ca. 1760–97,' *History of European Ideas* 34, no. 4 (2008): 431–43.

52 Emma Rothschild, 'The Atlantic Worlds of David Hume,' in Bailyn and Denault, *Soundings in Atlantic History*, 405–48.

53 Robert R. Palmer, *The Age of Democratic Revolution: A Political History of Europe and America, 1760–1800* (Princeton, 1959–64); and Jacques Godechot, *France and the Atlantic Revolution of the Eighteenth Century, 1770–1799*, trans. Herbert H. Rowen (New York, 1965).

54 See Albertone and De Francesco, *Rethinking the Atlantic World*; David Armitage and Sanjay Subrahmanyan, eds., *The Age of Revolutions in Global Context, c. 1760–1840* (London, 2009); Suzanne Desan, Lynn Hunt, William Max Nelson, eds., *The French Revolution in Global Perspective* (Ithaca, 2013); Perl-Rosenthal, 'Corresponding Republics;' Jeremy Adelman, *Sovereignty and Revolution in the Iberian Atlantic* (Princeton, 2006); David Andress, *1789: The Threshold of the Modern Age* (New York, 2009); Jonathan Israel, *A Revolution of the Mind: Radical Enlightenment and the Intellectual Origins of Modern Democracy* (Princeton, 2010); David P. Geggus, ed., *The Impact of the Haitian Revolution in the Atlantic World* (Columbia, South Carolina, 2001); Ashli White, *Encountering Revolution: Haiti and the Making of the Early Republic* (Baltimore, 2010); Julia Gaffield, ed., *The Haitian Declaration of Independence* (Charlottesville, forthcoming); Wim Klooster, *Revolutions in the Atlantic World: A Comparative History* (New York, 2009); Lynn Hunt, 'The French Revolution in Global Context,' in *Age of Revolutions*; Cheney, *Revolutionary Commerce*; Laurent Dubois, 'An Atlantic Revolution,' *French Historical Studies* 32, no. 4 (Fall 2009): 655–61; Dubois, *A Colony of Citizens*; and David Armitage, *The Declaration of Independence: A Global History* (Cambridge, Mass., 2007).

INDEX

Abbasid Dynasty, 378
Abd Allah Sīdī Muhammad b., 195, 197. *See also* Muhammad
Abd Rahman, Ibrahima al-, 386–387
Abd Salam, Sabani al-, 197
Abenaki, 274
Abigail (ship), 369
Abolition Society, 139
Abu Bakr, Muhammad (Sultan), 377
Abudiente, Senior, 367
Abulafia, David, 190, 195, 216
Abu Yaqub Yusuf (sultan), 190
Acadia, 67. *See also* Nova Scotia
Acapulco, 213
Acatholic (Catholic), 122
Accompong, 609
Acosta, Jose de, *Historia natural y moral de las Indias*, 37, 39, 247
Act Concerning Religion (Calvert), 401
Act for Encouraging of Forraigne Trade, 1693 (Parliament of Scotland), 441
Act for Further Preventing the Growth of Popery (England's Act), 407. *See also* Brooke, Robert
Act for the better ordering and Governing of Negroes (Barbados), 254
Acts of Parliament, 1661 and 1662, 284
Act of Union, 365, 576
Adamastor, 104. *See also* Table Mountain
Adams, John, 132, 383, 391, 395, 408, 640, 645–646, 648
Adam, Vicente, *Lecciones de Antropologia etico politico-religiosa*, 47
Addison, 558

Admiralty, 137, 268, 548
Advent, 60
Aeneid (Virgil), 645
Afonso I (Mvemba a Nzinga), 322–323, 328, 330, 335, 338
Africa, 1, 14, 79, 85, 100, 103, 108, 151, 155, 173, 191–192, 227, 231, 238, 245, 251, 254, 256, 264–266, 269, 274, 321–322, 327, 329–330, 332, 335–339, 353, 387–389, 414, 418, 420, 424–426, 448, 450–453, 460, 481, 524, 533–534, 537, 542, 547, 549–551, 563, 601–602, 604, 606, 612, 622
African, 83, 91, 152, 254, 265, 269, 353, 387, 428, 445–446, 548
African Americans, 139, 328, 355
African Catholicism, 328–330, 339
African coast, 448, 540
African Company, 462. *See also* Mississippi Company
African east coast, 600
African Gold Coast, 308, 358, 445, 447, 449; as to Elmina, 447
African interior, 361
African Lodge No. 459, 660
African Methodist Episcopal Church, 360
African(s), 22, 79, 89, 91–92, 103, 151–152, 154–155, 181, 237–238, 250, 254–256, 326, 329, 335, 351, 353, 355, 361, 388, 426–428, 446, 450, 453, 460, 523–524, 539, 542, 551, 561, 599–606, 609–610–612
Africans and the industrial revolution in England (Inikori), 517, 526

— INDEX —

African slavery, 626
African slaves, 151, 154, 600–613
Africanus, Leo, 151
Afrikaans, 107
Afrikaners, 101, 106
age of Democratic Revolutions, 108
age of discovery, 190
Age of Revolution, 229, 605, 652
Agreeable (ship): as to owners, Barton,
    Thomas and William 523
Ahone, 13
Aiai, 219
Ailingalaplap, 212
Alawi Dynasties, 194
Alawi rule, 195
Alegre (mulatresse), 165
Alexander VI (pope), 323
Alexandria, 173
Alford, Terry, *Prince Among Slaves*, 387
Algeria, 176
Algerian economy, 181
Algerians, 174, 178
Algiers, 172, 176–177, 180–181, 197, 380
Algonquians, 26, 333
Allah, 389
Allfrey, Edward, 527
All Hallow's Parish (Maryland), 404
Almagro, Manuel y Vega, 47
Almeida, Francisco d' (Viceroy, Portuguese
    East Indies), 103
Almohad (Empire), 190, 194
Almoravid Empire, 194
Alpenvorland, Bavarian Schwabian, 117
Alps, 117
Alvaro III, king, 326
Alzate, Jose Antonio, 653–654; as to
    Gacetas de Literatura de Mexico, 654
Amar, Akhil (Professor), 291
Amaru, Tupac, 82, 84
America, 18, 21, 34, 36, 41–42, 45–50, 89,
    108, 117–123–126, 144, 252, 267,
    273–275, 281–282, 284, 286–288,
    290, 292, 327, 337, 357, 378–379,
    387, 390, 397–399, 417, 422, 427,
    447, 451, 460, 471, 477–478,
    480–481, 484, 492, 494, 500–502,
    533–534, 536, 538, 547 549, 559,
    562, 564, 575, 577–579, 583, 587,
    602, 612, 633–636, 639–641,
    643–645, 655
American Catholicism, 329

American Catholics, 332, 398–399
American Civil War, 281, 283, 291, 293
American Colonization Society, 387
American Constitution, 63, 636
American Enlightenment, 136, 650
American Independence, 641
American Indians, 3, 378. *See also* Indians
    (South American)
American in European Consciousness
    (Kupperman), 89
Americanism, 35–36, 46–47, 49; as to
    modern, 42
Americanist, 418
American Jewish historians, 417–418, 421
American Philosophical Society, 652, 655,
    657
American Republic, 644–645
American Revolution, 132, 275, 337, 353,
    360, 371, 393–395, 397, 403, 481,
    485, 492, 496, 546, 560–561,
    578–580, 605, 635–637, 640, 643,
    651–653, 657–658, 660
American(s), 35,133, 135, 145, 172, 181,
    196, 256, 273, 282, 287, 289, 291,
    380, 393–395, 427, 481, 485, 493,
    496, 546, 561, 574, 578–583, 586,
    588–589, 635, 637–640, 643, 645
American Seaman's Friend Society, 140
American southwest, 192, 361
American System, 582
American War for Independence, 132
Americas (The) 79, 83, 86, 89, 93, 104,
    120–121, 126, 143, 151, 155, 173,
    181–182, 187–188, 193, 196, 210,
    227–228, 231, 238, 245, 247–253,
    255–256, 264–265, 268–269,
    271–272, 275–276, 314, 322–328,
    330, 332, 334–336–339, 347–351,
    364, 368, 371, 378, 415, 420, 422,
    424–425, 427–428, 448, 460, 519,
    526, 547, 550–553, 560, 563, 602,
    622, 625, 639, 654
Amerindian Atlantic, 275
Amerindians, 154, 158, 165, 321, 326,
    328–330, 333, 335
Amherst, Colonel Jeffrey, 273
Amsterdam, 20, 423, 461, 474–475, 485,
    491–492, 497, 500, 513, 516, 538,
    543, 551–552, 622, 625
Andalucia, 84
Andalus, al-, 190, 197

– INDEX –

Andean(s), 82, 91, 92
Anderson, Virginia DeJohn, 25
Andes, 332
Andre (slave), 156–157
Angerstein, John Julius (Lloyds chr.), 521, 525
Anghiera, Pietro, d', 19
Anglicanism, 350, 353, 359, 403
Anglicanisation, 370
Anglican(s), 350, 354, 370–371, 404
Anglican Virginia, 407
Anglo-America, 245, 249, 252
Anglo-American(s), 83, 252
Anglo-Dutch war, 274
Anglo-French Wars, 451
Anglophone Caribbean, 426
Angola, 100, 106, 154, 188, 324, 326, 600
Angolian slaves, 154
Animals, as agents of change, 25–27; as to commercial use, 19–21; as to domesticated use, 21–26;
Anna (ship), 527
Anne Arundel County (Maryland), 404
Anne, Queen, 450, 461
Anthony the Turk (aka Anthony Jansen va Salee), 381
Anthropologie et histoire au siècle des lumieres (Anthropology and History in the Century of Enlightenment) (Duchet), 227
anti-Catholicism, 322, 324, 327, 335, 339, 394, 399–400, 404–406
antichrist, 337, 380–381
antichristians, 384
anti-Federalists, 283–284, 287–288, 292–293
Anti-Gallician Association, 576
Antigua, 358, 360, 365, 478, 480, 541
Antiguan House of Assembly, 367
Antiguo Régimen, 42. See also Carlos III
anti-Habsburg, 124
Antinomian (forbidden Maryland epithet), 401
Antilles, 152, 154–155, 230, 627
anti-Semitism, 366
Antonians, 336
Antonio, king, 329
Antwerp, 423, 474, 485, 516, 535, 548
Aotearoa/New Zealand, 209. See also New Zealand
Apaches, 83
Apostolic, 328

Appalachians, 276
Appeal to Heaven (Locke), 293
Apure (river), 41
Arabic (language), 382, 387–390
Arabic amulets, 389
Archbishop of Santa Domingo, 311
Archdiocese of Boston, 399
Archdiocese of Santo Domingo, 305
Archivo General de Indias; Historia del Nuevo Mund (Munoz), 46
Arctic Ocean, 56
Argentina, 483–484
Argentinian, 83
Aristotle, 338, 641–642; as to *Politics I*, 642
Arizona, 377
Armada de Barlovento, 312
Armesto, Felipe Fernandez, 198, 216
Arminian Enlightenment, 650
Armitage, David, 1, 24, 424; as to *The British Atlantic World*, 413
Army Bills (convertible paper money), 482
Ars Mercatoria (Hoock), 619, 621
Art and Manufactures in Britain, 584. See also Ewart, William (MP)
Articles of Confederation (US), 284, 287, 289
Article II (US Constitution), 284
Article VII of the English Bill of Rights; as to honeyed Mansfieldism, 290
Asebar Reef, 219
Ashe, Thomas, 22
Ashkenaz, 414
Ashkenazi, 420
Ashkenazification, 414
Ashkenazi Jews, 371
Ashkenazim, 371
Asia, 14, 198, 210, 217, 335, 361, 414, 420, 425, 531–536, 547, 549–551, 561, 563, 625
Asians, 93
Asian Subcontinent, 547
Asiento, 460; as to Mississippi and South Sea Bubbles, 457–458, 461, 466
Asiento de negroes, 550
Asilah, 194
Assembly (colonial Virginia), 253
assignat (banknote), 482–483
Astell, William, 460
Asti, Bernardino, d' 330
Atahuallpa, 90–91. See also Capac, Atahuallpa

669

– INDEX –

Ateneos (magazine), 47
Atkins, Samuel, *View of the Pool Below London Bridge*, 559
Atlantic Catholicism, 322, 325–326, 328, 339–340; as to Atlantic Catholic World, 332
Atlantic colonies, 347, 350, 355, 360
Atlantic commerce, 444, 446
Atlantic creoles, 602
Atlantic Enlightenment, 650–661
Atlantic Enlightenment, The (Burlington), 651
Atlantic history, 414, 421, 423–424, 634, 639; as to conceptually; circum-atlantic; conjuncto-atlantic; trans-atlantic; cis-atlantic, 1, 198, 246, 251, 256
Atlantic History: A Critical Appraisal (Greene and Morgan), 2
Atlantic islands, 7
Atlanticists, 1, 3, 413, 418
Atlantic Jewry, 423
Atlantic joint-stock commerce, 441–447
Atlantic littoral, 377, 602
Atlantic Mediterranean, 196, 216
Atlantic Ocean, 20, 34, 56–58, 62, 67, 71, 85–86, 88–89, 100, 103, 107–110, 117–118, 120, 126, 131, 133, 143–145, 153, 165, 188–190, 192–195, 197, 207, 212, 216–217, 219–220, 234, 238, 250–253, 256, 265, 266–269, 275–276, 281–282, 286,291, 338, 347–349, 351–352, 357–359, 361, 367, 376–377–382, 386–387, 390, 421, 423–424, 450, 460, 466, 485, 497, 500, 505, 531, 534–538, 540–543, 547–548–549, 554–555, 560, 581–582, 586, 603–604, 634, 639, 643
Atlantic Revolutions, 661
'Atlantic world or Atlantic/world?' (Coclanis), 533
Atlantic World, The (Benjamin), 100
Atlantic World Trade, 517–518
Atwood, Peter, 405, 407; as to *Liberty and Property, or The Beauty of Maryland Displayed*, 405–406
Auberteuil, Michel-Rene Hilliard d', 653, 655, 657; as to *Considerations sur l'etat present de la colonie francaise de Saint Domingue*, 657

Audiencia of Santa Domingo, 300, 306, 308–309, 312
Augsburg, 123–124
Augsburg Confession, 122
Augustinians, 324
Aulic Chamber (the Reichshofrat), 121
Australasia, 213, 485, 563
Australia, 110, 209
Austria, 117–118, 121–122, 125–126, 480
Austrian, 117
Austrian Empire, 118
Austrian Habsburgs, 120
Austrian Hereditary Lands, 118
Austrian Monarchy, 118, 126
Austrians, 117–118, 125–126
Avenger of the New World, 658
Ayala, Felipe Guaman Poma de, 41; *Nueva coronica y buen gobierno*, 91–92. See *also* Peru
Ayr Bank (Douglas Heron & Co.), 491–493, 495–496, 498–499, 501
Azara, Felix, 45
Azemmour, 377. *See also* Dorantes
Azzemour, 192
Azores, 84, 216, 246, 254, 268
Aztec Empire, 271

Bacon, Francis, 517
Bacon's Rebellion, 26
Badin, Stephen (of Kentucky), 398
Baepler, Paul, 178
Baghdad, 376, 378
Bahia, 389
Bailyn, Bernard, 1, 103, 424, 637; as to *A Domesday Book for the Periphery*, 427
Baker, Thomas (consul), 177
Balboa, Juan de (Governor) 304, 306–307
Balkans, 120
Baltic, 539
Baltic (region), 3, 61
Baltimore, 137, 195, 336–337; as to an Irish barony, 401
Baltimore Clippers, 143
Baltimore Harbor, 397
Banat, 117, 119–120
Banat of Temesvar, 120
Banco de San Carlos, 482–483
Banica, 310
bank note, 474, 476, 480, 482–484
Bank of Amsterdam, 625

670

– INDEX –

Bank of England, 395, 476, 482–485, 491–492, 496, 498–499, 501–502, 505, 625
Bank of France, 483
Bank of Ireland, 483
Bank of Scotland, 476
Bank of the United States, 481; as to second charter in 1816, 482, 485
banks (ocean): as to Burgeos, 57; as to Dogger, 57; as to Faroe, 57; as to Georges, 57; as to Grand, 57; as to Stellwagen, 57
Banques d'Amsterdam & de Rotterdam, 625. *See also* Savary
Baptist, 355, 357
Barbados, 253–254, 337, 355, 357, 365–368, 418, 446, 451, 480, 541, 604
Barbarian Cruelty (Troughton), 177, 181
Barbary 172, 174–175, 179, 181–182
Barbary 'pass' system, 178
Barbary pirates, 173–181
Barbary slavery, 173–183
Barbary slaves, 179–181
Barbary States, 173
Barbary States of North Africa, 173,
Barcelona, 84
Barco, Miguel del, *Historia natural y crónica de la antigua California*, and *crónica* added, 41
Barlow, Joel, 653
Barents Sea, 57–58
Baring, Alexander, 521
Barings (bank), 562
Barnard, John, 520
Barton, Benjamin Smith, 652
Barton, Thomas and William. *See Bud*
Bartram, John, 653
Bartram, William, 653
Basques, 19
Basseterre, 163–165
Batavian Republic, 109
Battle of Acoma, 379
Battle of al-Qasr al Kabir (aka Battle of Three Kings), 193
Battle of Cape Passaro, 465
Battle of New Orleans, 276
Bayaha (now Port Dauphine, Haiti), 307
Bay of Biscay, 56, 58, 61, 308
Beatriz, Dona (aka Kimpa Vita), 336
Beaufort Sea, 20

Beaver Wars, 272
Beckles, Hillary, 228
Beethoven, 117
Begin, Menachem, 414; as to Likud block, 414
Belamee, Susanes, 158, sons Charles and Jean, 158
Belgium, 484
Benedict XIV (pope), 330–331
Benezet, Anthony, 269
Bengal, 491
Benin, 323, 330
Benjamin, Thomas, *The Atlantic World*, 100
berberiscos (Muslim slave), 85
Bergen (Norway), 72
Berkeley, George, 352
Berlin, 416
Berlin Wall, 414
Bermuda, 266, 352, 357, 549
Berners, Dame Juliana, *Treatyse of Fysshynge with an Angle*, 59
Betanzos, Juan de, 90
Beta Yisrael (Ethiopian Jewry). *See also* Operation Moses
Bethel Societies, 140
Beverwijk (Albany), as to fur trade 20
Beyond Atlantic History (Coclanis), 533
Beyond the Atlantic: English globetrotters and transoceanic connections (Games), 533
beyond the line, 267
Biassou, Georges, 236–237
Bible, 354, 358
Bill for Establishing Religious Freedom, A, 1786, 383
Bill of Rights, 282, 293; as to Freedom of Religion, 418
bills of credit, 479
bill(s) of exchange, 472, 475, 477, 481, 485, 552–554, 621
Billy Budd (Melville), 131
Bingham, William, *581*
Binture, Babet, 610–611. *See also* Doussin
Birnbaum, Pierre, *Paths to Emancipation: Jews, States and Citizenship*, 418
Bishop of London, 355
Bismarck, Otto von, 416
Bismarck Archipelago, 209
Blackamoor (or blackmoor), 380
Black Atlantic, 660
Black Ball Line, 143

671

— INDEX —

Black Death, 60
Black Jacobins, The (James), 232
Black Legend, 249
Black Rock Pond, 364. *See also* Charles
   Town
Black Spartacus, 230, 232, 659
Blackstone, William, 290
Blackwell, John, 478
Blanche, Mary, 156
Blatchford, John (mariner), 133
Blenac, Count of, 160
*Bloudy Tenent of Persecution for Cause of
   Conscience, The* (Williams), 384
Boardman, Elijah, 546–547, 563
Board of Trade, 550, 586
Bogle & Scott, 497, 502
Bogle, Robert, 497–498
Bohemian crown, 118
Bohler, Peter, 359
Bohuslan, 63, 65
Bolingbroke, Viscount, 283, 636
Bolster, Jeffrey, 56
Bolton, John, Fr., 404
Bolzius, Johann Martin (pastor), 123–124
Bombay, 527
bonds, 472–473, 476–477, 479–484
Bonifacio, Jose de Andrada e Silva, 654
Bonn, 117
Book of Common Prayer, 353
Bordeaux, 231
Born, Ignaz Edler von, 125
Bory, Gabriel de, 653
Bosman, William, 605
Boston, 23, 137, 268, 287, 360, 369, 576
Boston Harbor, 492
Bostonian(s), 132, 369
Boston Tea Party 408, 559
Boswell, James, 491–492
bottomry, 518
Bourbon Reforms, 654
Bourbons, 42
Bourdain, Jean, 157
Bourdain, Marye, 157
Bourdeaux, 627
Bourne, John, 520
Boury, Jean, 160
Bowers, Newport, 137
Brabant, 63
Braudel, Fernand, 12
Braunberger, Matthias, 124
Bray, Thomas, 350. *See also* SPCK and SPG

Brazil, 85, 191, 253, 255, 267–268, 276,
   326, 364, 379, 383, 389, 478, 481,
   483–484, 531, 538–540, 542–543,
   551, 600, 609, 654
Brazil Company, 549
Brazilians (indios de Calicut), 84
Brebeuf, Jean de (Jesuit), 333
Breton, Father, 157
Breton, Raymond, 154–155
Bridgetown, (Barbados), 365
Bright, William, 584
Bristol, 231, 522, 558
Britain, 62, 100, 109–110, 120, 132, 134,
   138–140, 172, 174, 176–178, 180,
   182, 231, 267–268, 273, 275–276,
   337, 348–351, 353, 359–361, 369,
   419, 444, 450, 460, 463, 492, 494,
   496–498, 502, 505, 526, 532, 546,
   550, 552, 555–556, 559–560, 563,
   575–581, 584–585, 587–588, 627,
   639
Britain's Atlantic Colonies, 357
Britannia, Queen of the Indies, 491
British, 69, 83, 109, 134, 173, 182, 195,
   267, 268, 272, 274, 276, 287, 337,
   349, 427, 462, 466, 485, 532, 553,
   574, 587, 640
British America, 364, 368, 370, 400, 452
British American Jews, 370
British Asia and the British Atlantic (Stern),
   533
British Atlantic, 153, 286–287, 290, 293,
   369, 381, 453, 559, 563, 576
British Atlantic trade, 444
British Atlantic World, 173, 182, 281, 283,
   364, 368, 372
British Caribbean, 274
British Civil Wars and Protectorate, 176,
   337
British Colonial America, 394
British commerce, 444
British East India Company, 443, 454
British Empire, 100, 102, 110, 133, 360,
   450, 453, 466, 532–533, 546, 579
British flagged Slaver, Caribbean Arrivals,
   505
British Isles, 57, 67, 70, 110, 174, 219, 281,
   287–288, 336, 621, 624–625
British Museum, 653
British North America, 102, 273, 365, 367,
   381, 399, 401, 560–561

− INDEX −

British North American Colonies, 123
British North Americans, 576
British Parliament, *1835 Select Committee on Aborigines*, 110
British Sailors' Society, 140. *See also* Port of London Society
Britons, 173–174, 176–177, 179–182, 282, 293, 365–366, 379, 497, 546, 552, 559–560, 575, 578, 583, 590
Brodie, Adam, 368
Brooke, Robert, 407; as to his brother Thomas' lawsuit in the challenge of his father's will, 407
Brown, Simon, 501
Bruce & Co., 527
Bruges, 473, 485
Bruni, 282
Bruslons, Savary des, *Le dictionnaire universel du commerce*, 621
Brydges, James (First Duke of Chandos), 452
Bubble Act of 1720, 519, 526
Buchanan & Cunninghame partnerships, 495
Bud (ship). *See* Tryer, Captain Robert
Buenos Aires, 268, 451
Buffon, Comte de, *Histoire Naturelle*, 229, 659
Bukatatanoa, 212
Bukhara, Uzbekistan, 416
Bukowina, 118
Bulwer, Henry Lytton, 584
Burke, Edmund, 575
Burke, John, Senior, 368
Butler, Captain John, 513

Caballos, Estaban Mira, 85
Cabildo (City Council) of Santo Domingo, 307, 313
Cabildo (Town Council) of Santiago, 300–301, 311
Cabo Verde, 251
Cabot, John, 321, 535
Caciques, 88
Cadiz, 326
Cadsands (Island), 123
Caisse d'Escompte (French bank), 482
Cajamarca, 82
Cajs Nacional de Fondos de Sud America, 484
Calcutta, 527
Caldas, Jose, de, 653–654

Caledonian, 365
Caledonian Clans (opening inquiry set forth in text), 366
California, 485
Calixto, Fr., Tupak Inka de San Jose, 85–86
Calvert (family), 399
Calvert, Cecilius, 401; as to *Act Concerning Religion*, 401, 405; as to son Charles, 403; as to Charter revocation, 403
Calvert, Charles, 405
Calvin, John, 380
Calvinism, 359
Calvinist, 401, 566
Calvinist Dutch Reformed Church, 349
Calvinistic Methodism, 357
Calvinist Orthodoxy, 394
Campbell, Ian, 214
Canaan, 164
Canada, 268, 360, 395, 418, 478, 482, 485, 627
Canadian and West Greenland currents, 57
Canadian Catholics, 404
Canadian Rockies, 20
Canadian Shield, 451
Canargo, Diego Munoz, 88
Canari(es), 82, 191, 216, 246, 254–255
Canary Islands, 190–191, 196, 269
Candeler, Richard (operator of the Office of Assurances), 516–518
Canny, Nicholas, *The Origins of Empire*, 533; as to *The Oxford Handbook of the Atlantic World*, 533; *The Oxford History of the Atlantic World*, 3
Canton, 527
Canton of Berne, Switzerland, 463
capability of the Indians, 37
Capac, Atahuallpa (son of Huayna), 82. *See also* Atahuallpa
Capac, Huascar (son of Huayna), 82
Capac, Huayna (Incan), 82
Capac, Manco Inca (son of Huayna), 82
Cap Breton Canyon (ocean trench), 57
Cape Agulhas, 103
Cape Cod, 534
Cape Colony, 110
Cape Hatteras, 56
Cape of Good Hope, 100, 102–105, 110, 230, 448
Cape of Storms, 10
Cape Point, 103,
Capesterre, 156–157, 163

673

– INDEX –

Cape, The, 101–110
Cape Town, 101, 102–103, 106–109
Cape Verde Islands, 212, 216, 246
Cap François, 304, 312–313, 653, 656
Capitein, Jacobus (minister), 355
Capitol Building in Washington, D.C., 633
Cap, Le, 234
Capuchin(s), 324, 330, 336
Cap Vert, 154
Carey, Henry, 582
Caribbean, 21–22, 57, 67, 71, 80, 83–84,
  93, 151, 158–159, 165, 178, 181,
  191, 216, 221, 227–228, 230,
  232–234, 236–238, 246, 255, 265,
  267, 271, 273–274, 276, 304, 307,
  349, 353, 358, 360–361, 364, 367,
  370–371, 377–378, 390, 398, 418,
  460, 503, 531, 536–538, 540–543,
  547, 550, 563, 577, 653, 655–658,
  660
Caribbean Sea, 267
Caribs, 151, 153–159. See also Lesser
  Antilles
Caritat, Nicholas, 653
Carlos, Jose de la Puente Luna, 88
Carlos III (Spanish king), 42, 45–46. See also
  Antiguo Régimen
Carmelites, 324
Caro, Ignacio Perez, 301, 312–313
Carolina, 124, 178
Carolina low country, 252, 609
Carolinas, The, 23
Carolina Sullivan, one of the obstinate
  daughters of America, Miss (Darly),
  578
Caroline Islands, 213, 221
Carolines, 211
Carpathians, 117
Carrisolis (natives), 83
Carroll, Charles (of Annapolis), 404
Carroll, John (1st U.S. Bishop), 398
Carrollton, Charles of Carrollton, 395
Carrollton, John (priest), 395
Cartagena, 450, 548
Carteau, Felix (planter), 234–235
Carvajal, Jacinto de, 41, 46
Carvajal, Luis de (el mozo), 422
Cartwright, Peter (Methodist), 394
Casa, Bartolome de las, Bishop, 271, 322.
  See also Chiapas
Casa da India, 549

Casa de Contratacion, 40. See also Felipe II
Castaing, John, Course of the Exchange, 464
Caste War of Yucatan, 84
Castillo, 48
Castle, Elmina, 308
Castle of Public Credit, 505. See also Bank
  of England
Castor and Pollux, 328
Catalonians, 62
Catcott, Reverend Alexander, 558
Catesby, Mark, 653
Catholic, 122, 271, 321, 325, 327, 338,
  380, 394, 397–401, 403–406, 427,
  562
Catholic Africa, 339
Catholic Atlantic World, 324
Catholic Christianity, 3, 271
Catholic Church, 324, 330, 394, 397, 399,
  556
Catholic Church(es), 330, 332, 337–339,
  399–400
Catholic Encyclopedia of 1912, 621. See also
  Savary
Catholicisation(s), 329, 335
Catholic Iberians, 548
Catholicism, 282, 287, 32, 323–324,
  326–330, 332, 336–339, 347–348,
  383, 390, 394, 401, 408, 623
Catholic Mediterranean, 379
Catholic Orders of Redemption, 180
Catholics, 272, 326–330, 332–334,
  336–339, 348, 351, 381, 384, 386,
  394, 397–401, 403–408, 422
Catinquiesme, Elizabeth, 156
Cato's Letter, 283
Cavendish, Thomas, 445
Ceded Island in the Caribbean, 496
Celtic-Biscay Shelf, 57
Celtic Sea, 57
Cempoala, 88
central Africa, 237, 338
central Europe, 67, 71, 106, 117, 119, 123,
  348, 371, 414, 418
'Century of the Common Man', 125
Cercle des Philadelphes (society), 233
Ceuta, 192, 195, 246
Ceylon, 106
Chacon, Jeronimo, 308
Chachapoya, 82
Chalco-Tlamanalco, 88
Challoner, Bishop Richard, 399

674

– INDEX –

Champagne, Leger Millard, and Marguerite, 158
Champion, Richard, 580–581
Champs, Charles des, 157
Chandler, Joseph, 587
Channel Islands, 67
Charles County (Maryland), 397
Charles Ferguson & Co., 499
Charles I, king, 445, 476
Charles II, king, 283, 446; as to "King of Trade", 558
Charles V, king, 249, 338
Charles VI, king, 117, 122
Charles XII, king (Sweden), 461
Charleston, 123, 137, 365, 505
Charles Town (Charleston), 20–21, 371
Charlestown, Massachusetts, 369
Charles Town, Nevis (Metropolis or Capitol), 364; as to Pinheiro, 368
Chasseboouef, Constantin-Françoise, 653
Chauduri, K.N., 212–213
cheque, 472–474, 476–477
Chesapeake, 22, 26, 252, 550, 561
Chesapeake, Bay, 56, 138, 394
Chet, Guy, *The Ocean is a Wilderness: Atlantic Piracy and the Limits of State Authority, 1688–1856*, 2
Chevillard, Andre, 154–155
Cheyne, Andrew, 220
Chiapas, 271. *See also* Casa, Bartolome de las, (Bishop)
Chichimeca, 83
Chile, 45, 268, 387
Chilean, 83
Chimalpahin, 91
Chimayo, New Mexico, 370
China, 133, 378, 414, 466, 473–474, 527, 547, 560, 562
China Company, 462. *See also* Mississippi Company
Chinese, 466
Cholul, 80
Christ, 141, 330, 336, 352
Christendom, 199, 272, 321, 323, 340
Christian, 60, 92, 140, 327, 377
Christian Europe, 190, 417
Christianity, 36, 86, 91–92, 154, 264, 321, 323, 325, 329, 347, 351, 353, 380, 387
Christianization, 36, 352, 355
Christianized, 377
Christian Philosopher, The (Mather), 381

Christian Rome, 246
Christian(s), 154, 156, 178, 181–182, 251, 253, 321–322, 324, 367, 371, 379–384, 401, 415, 423, 427, 599
Christian Sabbath, 367
Christian Scientist, 381
Christocentric, 427
Church of England, 349–351, 355, 360, 366, 368, 370, 403–405
Church of Rome, 397
Church, the, 518
Cisalpine Movement, 400
Civilizing Process (Elias), 622
Civil War (U.S.), 485
Civil Wars, 173, 476
Clagett & Pratt (underwriters), 527
Clarke, Captain Samuel, 369
Claro, Perez, 313
classical republicanism school (U.S.), 637
Classical Tradition and the Americas, The, 634
Clavijero, Francisco Javier, 40
Clay, Henry, 586
Claypoole, James, 522
Clifford & Sons, 491
climate, 210–212
Club Massaic, 234
Clyde (river), 493
Cobden, Richard, 584
Cobo, Bernabe, *Historia del Nuevo Mundo*, 41
Coclanis, Peter, 1–3, 198 563; as to 'Atlantic world or Atlantic/world?' 533; as to 'Beyond Atlantic history', 533. *See also* Atlantic history
Cockerell, Charles Robert, 584–585
Cockpit Country, 609
Cocqui, Lay (Zapotec), 91
Code Noir (Black Code) 1685, 230–231, 236, 255, 610–611; as to Article IX, regulating slavery in the French Antilles, 159–160; as to Article XVI, with respect to slave rebellion, 61; as to proposed reform, 162; as to Article 28 regarding rights of slave to own property, 164
Code Savary (reformed French commercial code), 619
Codrington College (Barbados), 355
coin, metal, 472–473, 476–478, 480–481, 483–485

– INDEX –

Coke, Edward, *Second Part of the Institute of the Lawes of England*, 365
Colbert, Jean-Baptiste, 461, 619, 627; as Comptroller General of French finances, 627
Colden, Cadwallader, 653
Colebrooke, Sir George (Chr. EIC), 491
College of Merchants, 63
College van de Grote Visserij, 68
Collegium urbanum, 326
Collins, Edward, 143
Colloque International de Mulhouse, 619
Colombia, 483
Colombian Exchange, The (Crosby), 216
Colon, Cristobal, 85
Colonial America, 123
Colonial Assembly of Domingue, 234
Colony of New France, 9, 14
colour prejudice, 151–152, 154–165
Columbian Exchange, 197
Columbus, Christopher, 62, 84, 151, 187, 193, 246, 269, 321, 377, 415; as to 1942 Caribbean landfall, 13; as to discovery of new 'Creole' animal world, 14; as to Jewish scientists, 421
Comancheria, 83
Comanches, 83
Commander in Chief (of U.S. Military), 284
Commentaries reales (Garcilaso), 86
Commerce d'Angleterre, d'Ireland, & d'Ecosse, Du (Savary des Bruslons), 622
Commerce d'Hollande & de Flandre, Du (Savary des Bruslons), 622
Comission Cientific del Pacifico (CCP), 47–48. See also Espada, Marco Jimenez de la
Commentaries on the Constitution (Story), 291
Commentarios reales (garcilaso), 86
Commercial Treaty of Utrecht 1713, 625, 627; as to English ratification 625
Commissions of Array, 4
commodification of fish, 59–62; as to effects of commodification, 62–65
Common Council for the City of New York, 599
Commons (House of), 624
Communion, 400
Compagnie francaise des Indes occidentals (Savory), 626

Company of the East Indies, 462. *See also* Mississippi Company
Company of Merchants Trading to Guinea (aka Nicholas Crispe and Company), 445; as to Crispe's loss of control, 446
Company of Royal Adventurers Trading into Africa (CRA), 446; as to subscribers, Duke of York, Prince Rupert, 446–447; as to west coast of Africa, 446, 453
Company of Scotland tradeing to Affrica and the Indies (aka 1693 Scottish Act for Encouraging Foreign Trade), 441
Company of Senegal, 626
Company of the West, 626
Compleat Angler (Walton), 59
Concord and *Amphitrite* (ships), 523. *See also Bud*
Condamine, Charles-Marie de la, 653
Condorcet, Marquis de, 229, 653, 661; *Reflexions sur l'esclavage des Negres*, 231
Condottieri, 282
Confederacy, 291
Confederation Congress (U.S.), 284, 289
Confraternities, 330
Confraternity of Our Lady of the Rosary in Luanda, 326
Confraternity of Our Lady Star of the Negroes, 326
Congo, 600
Congregationalist, 350–351
Congregationalist Massachusetts, 407
Congregational Presbyterians, 398
Congress (U.S.), 287–288 481–482, 485, 579, 582, 586
Congress of Vienna, 275
conjuncture, 621
Connaught (Ireland), 397
Connecticut, 358, 381, 478, 480; as to Cheshire, 23
Conquistadores, 324
Considerations on the Greatness of the Romans and their Decline, (Montesquieu), 643
Considerations sur l'etat present de la colonie francaise de Saint Domingue (Hilliard), 657
Constantinople, 84
Constitution (U.S.), 283–284, 287–291, 293, 481, 636–637, 644

— INDEX —

Constitutional Convention, 636, 643

consumption, 579. *See also* Smith, *Wealth of Nations*

contagion spread, 492–493; of depravity, 139–142; of radicalism,136–139

Continental Army, 288, 397, 579

Continental Congress, 288, 481,

Continental Europe, 400–401, 408, 560

Continentals, George Washington's, 268

conversos, 255, 413, 421–422

Conway, *History of the Ship*, 55

Cook, Captain James, 213, 215, 220

Cooper, Thomas, 655

Copenhagen, 72

Cordoba, 86

Cork, 369

Cornbury, Lord, 22

Cornishmen, 176

Corn Laws, 584, 586

Cornwall, 176

Cornwallis, Charles, 268

Corpus Christi, 91

Corpus Evangelicorum, 122

Correio Braziliense (Costa), 655

Corsini, Bartholomew, 514

Costa, Hipolito Jose da, 653–655; as to *Correio Braziliense* 655

Cortes, don Martin Moctezuma Nezahualtecolotzin, 88

Cortes, Hernando, 80–81, 85–86, 91, 247, 252, 271, 322, 324; as to *Letters of Relation,* 249

Cortes, Martin (son of Hernando), 86

Cotuy, 307

Council of Martinique, 15

Council of Massachusetts, 179

Council of Reform; as to French commercial code, 619

Council of the Indies (Spain), 88, 307, 309

Councils of the Ils du Vent, 1727: as to letter of complaint, 163

Councils of the Knights of Columbus, 399

Council of Virginia, 178

Counter-Blaste to Tobacco, A (King James), 539

Counter-reformation , 324, 340

Country Party (England), 623

Course of the Exchange (Castaing), 464

Court Jews, 419–420

Court of Assurances, 517, 521

Court of Chancery, 514

Court Whigs, 283

Coutinho, Jose Joaquim de Cunha de Azerda, 654

Coya, dona Beatrice Clara, 88

Creation of the British Atlantic World, The, (Mancke and Shamm), 533

Creeks, 276. *See also* Jackson, Andrew

Creole slave, 152

Creolized Blacks, 426

Crèvecoeur, J. Hector St. John, 653

Crisp, Nicholas (member-licensee), Gynney and Bynney Company, 445–446

Croghan, George, 422

Cromwell, Oliver, 274, 284, 365

Crosby, Alfred, *The Colombian Exchange,* 216

Crowley, Sir Ambrose, 463

Cruikshank, Isaac, *French Happiness/ English Misery,* 559

Cruisers and Convoy Act, 1708, 523

crypto-Jews, 414, 422

crypto-Protestants, 122

Cuauhtemoc, 91

Cuba, 45, 49, 139, 252 305, 379, 387, 537

Cudjoe, 227

Cugoano, Quobona Ottobah, 660

Culhuacan, 88

culture clash, 35

Cunard, Samuel, 143

Curacao, 368–369, 371, 421, 425

Currency Act of 1764, 395

Curse of Ham, 164. *See also* Genesis IX, as to curse of Noah

Custom House in Paris, 625.

Cuzco, 82, 91, 332

da Gama, Vasco, 377

Dahomey, 106

Dajabon river, 311

Dale, Thomas, *Laws Divine, Moral and Martiall,* 252

Danes, 349

Daniel, Book of, 380

Danish West Indies (now U.S. Virgin Islands), 349, 484

Danse vaudoux, 656

Darien peninsula, 83

Darly, Mary, *Miss Carolina Sullivan, one of the obstinate daughters of America,* 578

Dartmouth College, 354

Dartmouth, Mayor of, 174

− INDEX −

Darwin, Charles, 48
David, Jacob, 516
Davis, Richard Beale, 633–634
Davenant, Charles (writer), 449
Davila, Pedro Franco, 45. *See also Real Gabinete de Historia Natural*
Davis, Robert C., 180
debt distribution of Port Royal and Fredericksburg stores, 502t
Declaration of February 1726; as to rights of people of colour, 162
Declaration of Independence, 132, 288, 290, 651, 655, 661
Declaration of Right, 403
Declaration of the Rights of Man, 235–236, 382, 611–612
Defoe, Daniel, 283, 558; as to government propagandist, 464, 466; as to *Robinson Crusoe*, 382
Defreeger Valley, 122
deists and *philosophes*, 635
Delabord, Jean, 157
Delaseine, Jean Baptiste, 159
Delaware, 480
Delaware Bay, 56
Delaware (river), 120
Delbourg, Madeline, 161
Deliberator, The, by the Pennsylvanian Anti-Federalist, 291
Denmark, 62–63, 65, 69, 123, 230, 348, 480
Description topographique, physique, civile, politique et historique de la partie francais de l'isle SaintDominque (Moreau), 655–656
Desmaretz (French financial reformer), 461–462
Devil's Hole (ocean trench), 57
Devil, The, 329
Devon, 176
Dewsbury, 588
Dhahabi, Al- (the golden), 187. *See also* Mansur, Ahmad al-
Diamonds and Coral (Yogev), 425
Diana (ship), 526
Dickinson, John, *Letters from a Farmer in Pennsylvania*, 640
Dictionary (Johnson), 546
Dictionary of the French Academy, The, 152, 155
dictionnaire universel du commerce, Le (Savary), 621, 625

Diderot, Denis, 230–231, 651–653. *See also Histoire des deux Indes; Supplement au Voyage de Bougainville*
Diego, Juan, 330
Dier, Andrew, 172
Dignitatis Humanae (Second Vatican Council 1965), 394
Diogenes (slave), 642
Discourse of the Contests and Dissentions Between the Nobles and the Commons in Athens and Rome (Swift), 643
Discourse on Western Planning, A (Hakluyt), 531
Discourses on the First Ten Books of Livy (Machiavelli), 64
Dixon, Jeremiah, 399
Domenico, Gio, *Il negociante*, 621
Domesday Book for the Periphery, A (Bailyn), 427
Dominica, 152, 154, 386
Dominicans, 88, 324
Dominion of New England, 478
Dona Marina, 252. *See also* Cortes
Don Carlos (ship), 606
Dorantes, Estevanico de, 377
Dorillac, Procureur General, 161
Douglass, Frederick, 138, 601
Doussin, Jean, 610
Dover (England), 123
Dowse, Jonathan, 369
dragonnades of Louis XIV, 287
Drake, Sir Frances, 193, 246, 445, 536
Dr. Watt's Psalms and Hymns, 358
Dublin, 480
Du Boisson, Sieur, 157
Dubourg, Bishop Louis William (of New Orleans), 398
Duchet, Michele, *Anthropologie et histoire au siècle des lumieres (Anthropology and History in the Century of Enlightenment)*, 227–229
du Jourdin, Michel Mollat, *Europe and the Sea*, 217
Du Lion, Governor Claude Francois, 154, 156, 158
Dupaix, Guillermo, 42, 45
Dupont, Jean, 163
DuPuis, 155
Durrnberg bei Hallein, 122
d'Urville, Dumont, 208–209

– INDEX –

Dutch, 60, 68, 71, 80, 82, 85, 103–104 106, 109, 230, 247, 267, 272, 282, 305, 340, 349, 358, 427, 447, 460, 531–536. 538–540, 542–543, 548–549, 550, 553–554, 556, 562
Dutch (language) 619
Dutch Atlantic, 532, 543–544
Dutch Batavian Republic, 100, 107
Dutch Brazil, 542
Dutch East India Company 100, 535, 549. *See also* VOC
Dutch Empire, 532–533, 627
Dutch-French Alliance, 109
Dutch Long Island, 386
Dutch Republic, 63, 106, 348, 446–447, 449, 452, 533, 561
Dutch Reformed Church, 355, 358
Dutch South Africa, 107, 484
Dutch West India Company (WIC), 21, 355, 381, 446, 448–449, 453, 478, 532, 537, 542, 549
DuTerte, Jean Baptiste, 152, 154–158
Dye, Tom, 220

east Anglian ports, 68
East Asia, 213
east coast of Africa, 103, 548, 600
Easter Duty, 165
eastern Atlantic, 199
eastern Europe, 60, 371, 418, 424
Eastern North America, 353
East Greenland Shelf, 57
East India, 123
East India Company, 103, 445–446, 466, 491–492, 526–527, 536, 538, 541, 549, 559–560. *See also* EIC
East India Trade, 534
East Indies, 100, 104–105, 107, 109, 531–532, 535–536, 539, 550, 581, 583
East Prussia, 122
East, The, 466
Ebenezer (new home in Georgia for Salzburgers), 123–124
Ecuador, 82, 38
Eddaouira, 197. *See also* Mogador
Edict of March 1724, Article VI, 162
Edict of Nantes, 349; as to Revocation, 349
Edict of 2 February 1732, 122
Edinburgh, 492, 497, 500
Edward I, king, 365

Edwards, Jonathan, 381
Egypt, 196–197, 323, 378
Egyptians, 386
EIC, 103–104, 549. *See also* East India Company
1814 Treaty, 136
1835 Select Committee on Aborigines (British Parliament), 110
Eighty Years War, 548
Eldorado (mythical better world), 119
Elias, Norbert, *Civilizing Process,* 622
el Inca (pseudonym of Garcilaso de Vega), 86
Eliot, John, 352–353
Elizabeth I, queen, 187, 192, 194, 267, 445
Ellis, William, 217–218
Elliott, J.H., 187; *Old World and the New, The,* 89
Elmina, Guinea, 542; as to Gold Coast, 447
El Niño, 210–211
Eltis, David, 182, 193
Emigrationskonsens (official sanction), 121
Empire, 118; as in Holy Roman, 118, 120
encomienda system, 37
enemy Other, 390
Engages (indentured servants), 158, 160, 255
Engels, 574
England, 20–21, 60–61, 63, 65–66, 67–68, 70, 123, 136, 173, 177–178, 187, 193–194, 196, 246, 252–254, 271–272, 274, 286, 327, 348, 355, 357, 359, 364–366, 372, 378, 381, 393, 395, 397–398, 400–401, 403–408, 447, 449, 452–453, 461, 468, 476–477–480, 483, 485, 493, 503, 516–517, 519, 521–522, 524–527, 531, 536. 541–542, 550, 556–557, 576–577, 583, 588, 619, 621–623, 626, 633–634, 638–639, 658
England, John (Bishop of Charleston), 327–328
English, 25, 60, 80, 103–104, 133, 176, 180, 19–193, 247–248, 252–253, 265, 272, 304–305, 328, 348, 378, 380, 393, 397, 401, 403–404, 407, 426, 466, 503, 505, 531, 533–543, 549–550, 562, 589, 619, 622, 625, 627, 637, 656
English (language), 379–380, 382

– INDEX –

English America, 366
English Atlantic, 217, 255, 446, 460, 533, 543–544
English Atlantic trade, 520
English Bill of Rights, 292
English Catholic, 401
English Channel, 176, 281, 522, 557
English Christians, 365
English Civil Wars, 281, 283, 286, 290
English Crown, 448
English Enlightenment, 650
English Gentleman Abroad (anon), 624
English grounde in America, 252. *See also* Chesapeake
Englishmen, 22, 176, 179, 246, 252–253, 365–366, 370, 372, 382, 393, 403, 406, 427, 609
English Navigation Acts, 550
English Restoration, 549
English Revolution, 558
English sugar imports, 504
English West Indies colonies, 367, 371
Enlightenment, 42, 228–229, 231–232, 235–236, 238, 416, 450, 653, 655, 658, 660–661
Enlightenment, Europe, 419
Enlightenment, The, 650–651, 654–656, 658–659
Eon Woerr, 212
Epictetus (slave), 642
e pluribus unum (motto of U.S.), 645
Equator, 57
Equatorial Countercurrent, 211–212
Equiano, Olaudah, 360, 601–604, 660; as to *The Interesting Narrative of Olaudah Equiano, or Gustavus, the African,* 602
Erie Canal, 394
Erle, Thomas, 291–292; *Papers of instructions for the Parliamentary meeting after the revolution,* 291
Ermenzon, (or Emmerson), Ricardo, 306
Escoto, Juan Bautista, 308
Esguerra, Jorge Canizares, *How to Write the History of the New World,* 89
Espada, Marcos Jimenez de la, 47
Estebanico the Black, 192
Ethiopa, 323
Ethiopian Jews, 419. *See also* Operation Moses
ethnic prejudices, 153

Eucharist, Sacrament of the, 400
Eurasia, 27
Euroamerican (criollos), 89
Eurocentric, 415
Europe, 1, 3, 14, 20–21, 42, 56, 60–61, 66, 71–72, 79, 83, 93, 100, 104, 107–108, 110, 120, 134, 139, 143, 151, 173, 178, 197, 228–229, 231–232, 234, 238, 245, 255–256, 264, 267, 269, 273–276, 305, 309, 312, 321, 324–327, 333–335, 339, 347–349, 355, 357–358, 360–361, 389, 397–398, 400, 414–416, 418, 421–422, 414, 424–427, 452–453, 460, 466, 473–474, 477, 481, 484, 491–492, 494, 497, 503, 505, 547, 517, 519, 531, 533–535, 537, 539, 541, 548, 550, 552, 558, 560–561, 563, 582, 588–589, 602, 619, 625, 634–635, 638–641, 643, 645, 651–652, 654, 660–661
European, 46, 84, 415, 421, 628, 640
European Americans, 426
European Atlantic, 480, 485
European Catholics, 322, 335, 348
European Catholicism, 326, 328
European Christianity, 336
Europe and the Sea (du Jourdin), 217
European Encounters with the New World (Pagden), 89
European Enlightenment, 108, 233, 654, 661
European Jewry in an Age of Mercantilism (Israel), 424
European Jews, 415–417
European Napoleonic Wars, 46
European Protestants, 349
Europeans, 13, 17–18, 27, 36, 47, 64, 67–68, 79, 82–83, 89, 91, 103–105, 125, 153–154, 156, 165, 181–182, 192, 194, 196, 213, 216, 219–220, 232, 238, 247, 249–251, 256, 264–266, 269, 276, 305–306, 322, 328–330, 332, 354, 377–380, 390, 415, 452, 460, 462, 473, 538, 541, 546, 548–549, 551, 556, 562, 600, 602–603, 605, 634–635, 638–639
Europe's America, as to Hungarian Banat, 119; as to southern Hungary, 124
Ewart, William (MP), 584

– INDEX –

Exchange Alley, 464–465
Exchange, The (London), 552
Exchequer, 476–477
Exeter, 445
Exodus, 645
Extraordinary Popular Delusions and the Madness of Crowds (Macaulay, Lord), 457
eye of Providence, 645

Fable of the Bees or, Private Vices, Public Benefits, The (Mandeville), 558
Fabra, Francisco, y Soldevila, *Filosofia de la legislacion natural fundada en la Antropologia*, 47
Faero Islands, 264, 484
Falconbridge, Alexander, 605
Familiarity of Strangers (Trivellato), 425
Faroes, 56, 62, 67, 71
Faroes Plateau, 57
Fary, Jean, 164–165
Fary, Jeanne, 164
Fatiha, 387
Fatima, 383
Fearon, Henry Bradshaw, 583
Federalist, 283–284, 644
Federalist 41, 281
Federalist Papers, 645
Federal Senate (U.S.), 644
Feijo, Joao da Silva, 654
Felipe II, 40. See also *Leyes de Indias*
Ferdinand, king, 377
Fernandez, Alvaro, 601–602
Ferrandiz, Manuel Anton, 49. *See also* Universidad Central de Madrid
Ferrantyn, Alexander, 514. *See also* Seint Anne of London
Ferreira, Alexandre Rodrigues, 654
Fes, 194, 197
Festin de Pierre, Le (Moliere), 627
Fick, Carolyn, 237
Fiji, 209, 220
Filippo Borromei & Co., 514
Filmer, Robert, *Observations upon Aristotle's Politicks*, 643
Filosofia de la legislacion natural, fundada en la Antropologia, (Fabra), 47
Finland, 64
Finnmark, 66, 71
Firmian, Leopold Freiherr von (Prince-Bishop), 122

First Maroon War, 609
First Provincial Council of Baltimore, 398
fisheries: development of, 55, 59–65
fishing, 55–59, 534
fish species, 58
Flanders, 63, 624–625
Fletcher, Andrew, 283
Fletcher, Governor Benjamin, 179
Florentine Codex (Sahagun), 89–90, 92
Florida, 21, 25, 123, 212, 308, 377, 634
Flushing Remonstrance, 386
Forbes, Sir William, 493
Ford, Richard, 174
Fordyce, Alexander, 491, 493, 498–499
Fordyce, Grant & Co., 499
Foster, Colonel, 386
Foucault, Michel, 659–660
Fouquet, Nicolas, 619
Four Moments of the Sun (Kongolese image), 330
Fourth Anglo-Dutch War, 109
Fox, George, 355, 357, 358. See also Quakers
Foxe, John, 381
Fox Wars, 274
France, 62, 63, 69, 106, 134, 138, 153, 158, 192, 194, 196, 228, 231, 234, 237–238, 255, 271, 274–275, 300, 308, 310–312, 314, 327, 333, 337, 348, 352, 398, 400, 451–452, 461, 468, 476, 478, 480, 483–485, 501, 503, 517, 532, 536, 555–556, 561, 563, 576, 578–580, 583, 585, 588, 612, 619, 621–624, 626, 651, 655–657
Franch, Alcina, 39, 42
Franciscans, 86, 88, 324
Franco-Dutch war, 308
Francophilia, 576
Franklin, Benjamin, 501, 578, 582, 645, 653, 657, 660
Franklin Institute, 587
Franks, David, 371
Franks, Jacob, 371
Franks, Rebecca, 371; as to Queen of Beauty at Meschianza, 371
Franz-Joseph, Emperor, 126
Fraserburgh, 218
Fredericksburg, 502
free burghers, 105–106, 108
Freeman, William, 521
Freemasons, 386

681

− INDEX −

free trade, 135
French, 46, 60, 68, 69, 80, 82–83, 109, 151,
    154–156, 195, 267–268, 272–274,
    282, 300–301, 304–305, 307–310,
    312–313, 328, 333, 380, 427, 496,
    562, 580, 584, 586, 612, 621–622,
    628
French (language), 619
French Acadia, 480
French America, 338
French and Indian War, 404, 481
French Antilles, 153, 159–160, 162, 164
French Army, 612
French Atlantic World, 151, 153–154, 165,
    228, 255, 460, 462, 611
French Canada, 268, 272, 339
French Caribbean Islands, 151–154, 156,
    158, 162, 164–165, 653
French Catholics, 333
French Crown, 159, 308, 314, 327, 333, 656
French East India Company, 539
French Empire, 159, 364
French Enlightenment, 229, 665
French Farmers-General, 493
French Flanders, 398
French Guadeloupe, 151. *See also*
    Guadeloupe
French Guinea, 484, 627
French Happiness/English Misery,
    (Cruikshank), 559
French Jews, 416
French Lesser Antilles, 155
French Louisiana, 161
Frenchmen, 172, 306, 609
French National Convention, 611
French Protestants, 272, 349
French Quebec, 478
French Revolution, 134, 232, 234, 237, 400,
    416, 581, 605, 611–612, 661
French Revolutionary War, 522, 655, 658
'Free Trade and Sailors' Rights', 134
Friedrich William I, king, 145
Friedman, Ellen G., 181
Frizell, James (consul), 174
Frobisher, Martin, 445
Frontier Era, 153, 156
Fundamental Constitutions of Carolina
    (Locke contributing), 653

Gabon, 524
Gacetas de Literatura de Mexico (Alzate), 654

Galacia, 62, 118, 120
Gambia Adventurers (licensee of CRA), 447
Games, Alison, 217; as to 'Beyond the
    Atlantic: English globetrotters and
    transoceanic connections', 533
Gans, Joachim (scientist), 421
Garcia, King, 328
Garcilaso de la Vega (formerly Gomez Saurez
    de Figarosa, pseudonym, el Inca), 86,
    as to *Commentarios reales,* 86
Garcilaso, Sebastian de la Vega, 86
Garraway's (London), 464
Gascoigne, Sir Bernardo, 283
*General Considerations for the Plantations
    in New England* (Winthrop), 26
Genesis (Book of), Legend of the Father, 13;
    as to Curse of Ham, Chapter IX, 164
General order of 1749; as to slaves renting
    their services, 164
Genoa, 192
Genoese, 191
Gentile(s), 364, 367, 383
George II, king, 123
George III, king, 132, 273, 290, 394
Georgia, 123–124, 350, 359, 378, 383, 390,
    481
Georgians, 466
German (language), 619
German Court Chapel, 123. *See also* St.
    James London
German Enlightenment, 650
German immigrants, 15
German Jewry, 418
German Protestants, 124
Germans, 71, 118, 584, 586
German States, 63, 68
Germany, 62, 124–125, 348, 417, 564
Gerry, Elbridge, 289
Gewaltmonopol des Staates, 289
Ghachem, Malech, 233
Gibraltar, 197, 357
Gines de Sepulveda, Juan, 322
Girard, Marie Rose, 161
Glasgow, 495, 522
Glorious Revolution, 290–291, 337,
    403–404, 476, 478
Glyn & Hallifax, 501
God, 249, 332, 333, 336, 339, 380, 382,
    384
Goddess Peace, 639
Godechot, Jacques, 661

– INDEX –

God's Gift (salmon), 63
Godwyn, Morgan, 355
Gold Coast of West Africa, 603
Golden Mountain, 68. *See also* Grosse
 Visserij
Golden Rule, 386
Gold Standard, 485
Gómara, 48
Gomes, Jesuit Diogo, 327
Gonzaga, Tomaso Antonio, 654
Good Intent (ship), 524
Gorges, Sir Fernando, 174
Gould, Seaman Roland, 144–145
gracias as sacar, 660
Granada, 86, 246, 264, 272, 474, 562
Grand Banks, 56, 212
Grand Cul-de-Sac, 161
Grand-Terre, Dominica, 154, 157, 160
Gratz, Barnard and Michael (brothers), 422
Gray's Inn, 365
Great Awakening, 351, 355
Great Britain 132, 134–135, 139–140, 142,
 145, 284, 393, 485, 517, 526, 589
Great Exhibition of 1851, 587, 589
Great Hare, 13
Great Migration, 349
Great Northern War, 461, 467
Great Recession, 618
Great Seal of the United States, 645
Great Turke, 172
Greece, 640
Greeley, Horace, 588–589
Greek(s), 638, 640
Greene, Jack, 2, 55; as to *Atlantic History: A
 Critical Appraisal*, 2
Greenland, 56, 62, 64, 264–265, 484
Greenland Seas, 57
Greenland–Scotland ridges, 56
Gregoire, Abbe Henri Baptiste, 653
Gregory XVI, pope, 327
Grenada, 496, 501, 503, 627, 657
Grenier, John, 273
Griffin, Martin (historian), 397
Gronau, Israel Christian (pastor), 123
Grotte Visserij, 68. *See also* Golden Mountain
Grundentlastung of 1949 (emigration law),
 121
Guaba, 306
Guaba valley, 311
Guadeloupe, 151–153–155, 157–165, 523,
 627, 660. *See also* French Guadeloupe

Guadeloupian Caribs, 157
Guadeloupian Sovereign Council, 157, 159
Guam, 213
Guardians of Marovo Lagoon (Hviding),
 215
Guatemala, 91, 271, 389
Guevera, Lord don Antonio de, *Relacion
 geografica or Descripcion de la cuidad
 y provincia de Tlaxcala*, 88
Guiana, 541
Guilday, Peter (historian), 397
Guiana Company, 538
Guinea, 154, 386, 542; as to Guine, 424,
 426, 602, 604
Gulf Coast, 80
Gulf of Maine, 67
Gulf of Mexico, 57
Gulf of St. Lawrence, 268
Gumilla, Jose, 41
Gutenberg, 474
Guthrie, William, *New System of Modern
 Geography*, 546
Guy, Thomas, 465, 467
Guyana, 82
Gynney and Bynney Company, 445; as to
 Nicholas Crisp (member licensee), 445
Gypsies, 365

Habsburg Empire, 120–122, 126
Habsburg Monarchy, 117–119–122
Hapsburg Trieste, Dubin and Lois' model,
 419
Hagget, William, 177
Hainaut, 63
Haiti, 137, 268, 276, 484, 612
Haitian Revolution, 137, 232, 389, 612,
 658–659, 661
Hajj, 197
Hakluyt, Richard (colonial promoter), 246;
 as to *A Discourse on Western
 Planning*, 531, 541–542
Hall, Prince, 660
Halle, 123
Hamburg, 197, 423, 461
Hamilton, Alexander, 283–284
Hamilton & Co., 501
Hamilton, Andrew (wife Abigail Franks),
 371
Hamilton-Patterson, James, 218
Hana, 219
Hannibal (ship), 603–604

– INDEX –

Hanover, 124
Harley, Lord High Treasurer, Sir, 450
Harris, William, 178
Harrington, James, 283
Hastings, Lady Betty, 464
Hart, Anne & Elizabeth, 360
Harvard University, 352
Hau'ofa, Epeli, 207; *Our Sea of Islands*, 214–216
Hausaland, 197
Hauser, Henri, *Revue de Histoire Economique et Social*, 619
Havana, 450, 458
Hawaii, 216
Hawaiian chain, 209
Hawaiian island(s), 218, 220
Hawaiians, 217–218, 220
Hawkins, John, 445, 539
Hayy ibn Yaqzan, (Ibn Tufayl), 190; as to renamed version *Philosophus Autodidactus* or *The Self Taught Philosopher*, 382
heathenism, 353–354
Hebb, David Delison, 176
Heimat, 117
Henry, Patrick, 283, 288
Henry, Prince 549. *See also* Casa da India
hereditary lands (Erblander), 117
Henry VII, king, 187
Henry VIII, king, 321
Herodotus, 151
Heron & Douglas Bank, 499
heretoch, 288
Herrnhaag, Germany, 358–359
High Court of Admiralty, 514, 517
High German (language), 621
Highlands of Scotland, 273
Hijas, 197
Hilliard d'Auberteuil, Michel-Rene, 653, 655, 657–659; as to *Considerations sur l'etat present de la colonie francaise de Saint Domingue*, 657
Hinterland, 101. *See also* southern African Highveld
Hirschman, Albert O., 619, 621
Hirshman, Elizabeth, *Jews and Muslims in British Colonial America: A Genealogical History*, 386
Hispaniola, 14, 21, 85, 269, 271, 300, 302, 304–305, 306–311, 389, 656
Historia del Nuevo Mundo (Cobo), 41

Historia del Nuevo Mundo (Munoz) 46
Historia General de las Cosas de la Neuva Espana, (Sahagun), 37
Historia natural y cronica de la antigua California (Barco), 1
Historia natural y moral de las Indias (Acosta), 37
Historia general y natural de las Indias (Oviedo), 39
Histoire des Deux Indes, L' (Raynal), 227, 230, 651–652, 657
Histoire, naturelle, Buffon, Comte de, 229
History of America (Robertson) 46
History of Lloyd's (Wright and Fayle), 519
History of Lloyd's and of Marine Insurance in Great Britain, The (Martin), 519
History of the Ship (Conway), 55
HMS *Leopard*, 134
Hoare's Bank, 463–464
Hobbes, Thomas, 643
Hogarth, William, 467, 575
Holland, 68, 123, 194, 196, 271, 274, 498, 550, 622, 624
Holland, William, 577
Holmes, Sir Robert, 447
Holofernes, 332
Holt, Arthur, 404
Holy Club (at Oxford), 357
Holy Family, 336
Holy Office, 338
Holy Land, 192
Holy Roman Empire, 117–118, 121
Holy Roman Imperial Diet in Regensburg, 122
Holyrod, John Baker, 579
Home, George, 496; as to Ayr Bank, 496
Homer, *Iliad*, 640
honeyed Mansfieldism: as to Article VII of the English Bill of Rights, 290
Hoock, Jochen 619, 621, 627–628; as to *Ars Mercatoria*, 619; as to *Innovations et Renouveaux Techniques de l'Antiquite a nos Jours*, 619, 621–622
Hottentots, 230
Houel, Sr., 164
Hough, Ebenezer, 369
House of Austria, 118
House of Burgesses, 252
House of Habsburg, 120
Howe, Kerry, 214
How to Write the History of the New World (Esguerra), 89

684

– INDEX –

Huard, Jacques Denis, 160–161
Hudson Bay, 625
Hudson Bay west coast, 451
Hudson, Henry, 535
Hudson River Valley, 26
Hudson's Bay Company (HBC), 20,
443–444, 450–454, 549
Hughes, William (of Gray's Inn), 365
Huguenots, 106, 272, 349, 361, 370, 372,
561
Hugues, Victor, 660
Hume, David, 497–498, 575, 577, 659, 661
Hundred Years' War, 217
Hungary, 117–120, 124, 125, 379. *See also*
Schwabenziige and Sachsenganger
Hunter, Governor Robert, 599
Hutcheson, Archibald, MP, 463–464. *See
also* Secret Committee
Hutchinson, Anne, 350
Hviding, Edvard, *Guardians of Marovo
Lagoon*, 215, 218

Iberia, 71, 84–85, 88–89, 193, 196, 325,
379. *See also* Spain
Iberian America, 332, 338
Iberian Atlantic World, 422, 535
Iberian Catholics, 330
Iberian Christians, 254
Iberian Conversos, 422
Iberian Crown, 329
Iberian Empire, 80, 83, 531, 535, 537, 539,
543
Iberian Inquisition, 556
Iberian Jews, 413, 421
Iberian Peninsula, 57, 190–191, 246, 264,
324, 378
Iberians, 548–549
Iberian South Atlantic, 79
Iberio-Atlantic waters, 58
Ibn Tufayl, 190; as to *Hayy ibn Yaqzan*, 382
Iceland, 56, 58, 61–63, 66–67, 71, 230, 264,
484
Icelanders, 66
Iceland Shelf, 57–58
Idrisi, al-, 190
Iliad, Homer, 640
Iles du Vent, 155, 157, 159–160, 162
Illinois, 361
impressment, 132
Inca, 80, 82–83
Inca Empire, 80, 82

Independence (U.S.), 485, 639
India, 106, 110, 414, 464, 493, 519, 522,
527, 547, 559
Indian(s), 352, 415, 426–427–428
Indian Country, 353
Indian Ocean, 103, 105–106, 109–110, 120,
207, 220, 250, 267, 378, 548–550
Indian Ocean basin, 105
Indian Ocean trade, 449
Indian Presidencies, 527
Indians (South American), 5, 45, 81, 83
Indian Wars, 273
Indies, 110, 191, 246, 306, 583
indigenist or criticist (intellectual
movement), 37
Indigenous American History, 79
indigenous peoples: as to Beothuk, 59; as to
Inuit,59; as to Mi'kmaq, 59; as to
Sami of Fennoscandia, 59, 64
Indonesia, 563
Indonesian archipelago, 106
Industrial Revolution, 471
Ines, Juana de la Cruz, 332
Inikori, Joseph, 518–527; *Africans and the
industrial revolution in England*, 517;
as to *Measuring the hazards of the
Atlantic slave trade*, 522; as to *The
Volume of the British Slave Trade
1655–1807*, 526
Innocent XI, pope 338
*Innovations et Renouveaux Techniques de
l'Antiquite a nos Jours* (Hoock), 619
*Inquiry into the Nature and Causes of the
Wealth of Nations, An* (Smith), 559
Inquiry on the Paper Credit of Great Britain
(Thornton), 492
Inquisition, The, 324, 384, 389, 421–422
Inspector General of Diamonds, 481
*Interesting Narrative of Olaudah Equiano,
or Gustavus, the African, The*
(Equiano), 602–604
Interregnum, 337
International Americanist Congress, 49
Invention of America, The (O'Gorman), 89
IOUs, 473, 474, 477–478, 480
Iraq, 414
Ireland, 120, 178, 272–273, 337, 348–349,
351, 357, 397, 401, 480, 483,
541–542, 622
Irish, 80, 82, 176, 328, 397, 428
Irish Catholics, 337

685

– INDEX –

Iroquois, 13, 275, 333, 348
Iroquois League, 272
Irwin, Geoff, 215
Isabel I, queen, 84
Isabella and Ferdinand, queen and king, 187
Ishmael, Muley, 180
Islam 3, 172, 189, 192, 199, 323, 347,
    376–384, 386, 388, 390
Islamic Antichrist, 380
Islamic North Africa, 378
Islamic West, 190
Island of Saint John (now Prince Edward
    Island), 484
Island Southeast Asia, 208–209. *See also*
    Malaysia
Israel, 415, 416; as to Ashkenazi-dominated
    Labor Party, 414
Israel, Jonathan, 417, 425; as to *European
    Jewry in an Age of Mercantilism*, 424
Israel, Solomon, 369–370
Italian, 80, 83, 180
Italian Catholics, 365
Italian states, 627
Italy, 308, 621, 624
Ixtlilxochitl, 81

Joachim, Pierre Paul François, 653
Joao I, adopted name of Nzinga a Nkuwu,
    323
Jackson, Andrew, 276. *See also* Creeks
Jacobites, 493
Jacquot, Valentin, 163
Jamaica, 22, 196, 274, 305–306, 348, 357,
    367, 383, 418, 424, 426, 446,
    450–451, 562, 606, 609, 658
Jamaicans, 658
James (ship), 524
James, C.L.R., *Black Jacobins, The*, 232
James, I, king, 397, 445; *A Counter-Blaste
    to Tobacco*, 539
James II, king, 283, 291, 403–404; as to
    ended reign, 448,
Jamestown, 266, 549
Janson, John (underwriter) 527
Japan, 209, 564
Jardin, Anne, 157
Jay Treaty, 581
Jeanneton (slave), 156
Jefferson, Thomas, 132, 290, 386, 427, 582,
    633–636, 641–642, 645, 653, 655,
    658–659; as to Aristotle, 642; as to

President, 23, 275; as to owner of a
    Qur'an, 382–384; as to *Notes on the
    State of Virginia*, 640–643
Jena (Germany), 124
Jesuited Priest (forbidden Maryland epithet),
    401
Jesuitical Catholicism, 122
Jesuit Order of Salzburg, 122
Jesuit(s), 324, 333, 337–338, 398, 405
Jesus, 401
Jesus (ship), 172–173
Jewry, 419
Jew(s), 93, 325, 335, 364–372, 383–384,
    386, 414, 421–424, 426–427, 498,
    548, 561, 611
*Jews and Muslims in British Colonial
    America: A Genealogical History*
    (Hirschman and Yates), 386
*Jews and the Expansion of Europe to the
    West, 1450–1800*, 1997 (Conference
    paper at the John Carter Brown
    Library), 419
Jewish, 414, 418, 423, 427
Jewish America, 428
Jewish Amsterdam, 420
Jewish Atlantic, 419–421, 428
Jewish Atlanticists, 420
Jewish Diaspora, 414–416, 428
Jewish Enlightenment, 650
Jewish ethnology, 423
Jewish Europe, 427
Jewish History, 413–418, 421, 423–424,
    426, 428
Jewish Naturalization Bill of 1753
    (England), 366
Jewish world, 420, 428
Jews of Recife, 366
*Jews: Social Patterns of an American Group,
    The* (a Compilation), 423
Jibaros, 41
jihad, 389
Joao I (formerly Nzinga a Nkuwu), 246, 329
Joden Savanne, 426
Johannes, Bob, *Words of the Lagoon*, 215
John Carter Brown Library Conference
    1997, *Jews and the Expansion of
    Europe to the West, 1450–1800*, 419
John IV, king, 548
John Glassford & Co., 495
John Norton & Sons, 498, 502; as to George
    Norton, 498

– INDEX –

John, Prester, 192
Johnson, Joshua, 501. *See also* Wallace Davidson & Johnson, 498
Johnson, Samuel, *Dictionary*, 546
joint stock companies, 444
joint stock trading company, 441–454
Joseph II, emperor, 121
Juan, San de Guaba, 310
Juba II, King (Mauretania), 190
Judaism, 3, 347, 368, 370, 377, 390, 419, 422–424, 426–427

Kamohoali'i, 218
Kanehunamoku, 218
Kant, Immanuel, 574, 659
Kapingamarangi Atoll, 215
Kapukaulua, 219
Karankawa Indians, 332
Karnten, 117
Katznelson, Ira, *Paths to Emancipation: Jews, States and Citizenship*, 418
Kaunitz, Wenzel Anton Graf, 119
Keith, George, 382. *See also* Society of Friends
Kelley, William, 587
Khoikhoi, 102–105, 108, 110
Kieft's War, 26, 249
Kieft, Willem, 26, 250
Kilkongo (language), 327
Kimpa Vita (aka Dona Beatriz), 332
King, Boston, 360
King David (ship), 523
kingdom of Komenda, 449
Kingdom of New Granada (Colombia), 82
Kingdom of the Kongo, 322
Kingdom of Warri, 324
King George's War, 481
King of Bohemia, 118
King of Great Britain, 284
King of Hungary, 118
King Philip's War, 93, 249, 352
King William's War, 478
Kings Bench, 514; as to Sir John Holt, Lord Chief Justice, 448
Kingston, Jamaica, 450
Kiowas, 83
Kiribati, 209
Knight, Francis, 179
Koblenz, 117
Kona, 220
Kongo, 322–326, 329–330, 336. *See also* Lukeni lua Nimi (founder)

Kongolese, 328, 336
Kongolese Catholics, 329, 332
Kongolese Catholicism, 339
Koolau, 220
Koona, 219
Kopfgeld (bonus or reward), 119
Kubary, Jan, 219
Kuenburg, Max Gandolph Graf von (Prince-Bishop), 122
Kupperman, Karen Ordal, 2; *America in European Consciousness*, 89
Ku'ula-kai, 219

Labat, 155–158
Labrador, 57, 63–64
Labrador current, 57–58
Labrador-Newfoundland Shelf, 57
Lacerda, Josee de Almeida, 654
Lacotti, Marie, 157
Lady Credit, 464. *See also* Defoe
Lafayette, Marquis de, 653
Lahontan, Baron de, 653
Lakeba, 212
Lamana, Gonzalo, 90
Lamb (ship), 523
Lamb, Samuel, 516
land banks, 477–478, 480
Ländler, 117
La Nina, 210
La Pallu Family, 610. *See also* Binture
La Rochelle, 548, 627
Las Casas, Bartolome de, 37–39
Latin, 323, 640
Latin America, 192, 306, 361, 418–419, 422, 424, 483, 562
Latrobe, Benjamin Henry, *View of the City of Richmond from the Bank of the James River*, 633
Laurens, John 579
Laval, Francois de, 327
La Vega (Haiti), 307
Lavy Seminar at Hopkins, 419
Law, John, 457, 461–462, 467, 480
Laws Divine, Moral, and Martiall (Dale), 252
Law's (John) System, 461–462, 485
lay Catholics, 325–326, 398, 400, 406
Leblond, Gabriel, 162
Lecciones de Antropologia etico politico-religiosa (Adam), 47
Lechmere, Attorney General Nicholas, 520

— INDEX —

Lee, Thomas Sim, Governor Maryland, 408
Leeward Islands, 365, 367
Legend of the Father, Book of Genesis, 13
Le Gozier, 161, 163
Le Grande Derangement, 404
Lehoula, 219
Leibniz, 107
Leinster (Ireland), 397
Leisler, Jacob, 178–179
Lenau, Nikolas (poet), 125
Lent, 60
Leon, Cieza de, 48
LeRoux, Guillaume, 161
L' Esprit des Lois: Pensees (Baron de
    Montesquieu), 230, 640, 643
Lesser Antilles, 151. *See also* Caribs
Letter on Toleration (Locke), 383, 401
Letter Patent of Denization, 367
Letters of Relation (Cortes), 249
Letters from a Farmer in Pennsylvania
    (Dickinson), 640
Letters from an American Farmer, 640. *See
    also* Jefferson
Letters Patent, 448
Levant, 176
Levant Company, 176, 549
Levenda Negra (Spanish science), 35
Levy, Nathan and Isaac, 371
Leyden, 474
Leyes de Indias, 40; in part, *Relaciones
    geograficas de Indias*, 40
Liberia, 387
*Liberty and Property, or The Beauty of
    Maryland Displayed* (Atwood), 405
Liberty of Conscience, 406
Library Company of Philadelphia, 655
Library of Congress, 655
Liburd, William, 368
Libya, 176
Lieber, Michael D., *More Than a Living*,
    215
Lienzo de Quauhquechollan, 91
Lietard, Lieutenant, 157, 159
Lima (Peru), 88
Lima, Haim Abinum de, 368; as to his
    bequests, 368
Lima, Rosa da, 332
Linnaeus, Carl, 46, 652
Lisbon, 84, 326–327, 543
Little Paris (Capetown), 109
Liverpool, 142–143, 522, 582, 584

Livorno, 425
Llanos, 41
Lloyd's, 521, 525, 527
Lloyd's List, 523–524, 552
Lobo, Pedro da Cuhna (Bishop) 335
Locke, John, 386, 558, 653; as to *Appeal to
    Heaven*, 21; as to *Essay on Human
    Understanding*; 382: as to *Letter on
    Toleration*, 383, 401; as to *Second
    Treatise*, 290; as to *Two Treatises of
    Government*, 653
Lodron, Paris Graf (prince-bishop), 122
Lofoten Islands, 66, 70
Loge des Neuf Soeurs in Paris, 657–658
*Loix et constitutions des colonies françoises
    de l'Amerique sous le Vent*, (Moreau)
    655–656
LOLR (Lender of Last Resort), 492, 506
Lom, Louis Armand d'Arce, 653
Lombard, 476
London, 109, 123, 137, 139, 142, 174, 177,
    231, 304, 350, 359–360, 366, 369,
    382, 399, 445, 457–459, 461, 464,
    467, 473, 481, 483, 485, 491–492,
    495–497, 500, 514, 516–517,
    519–522, 525, 527, 541, 547–548,
    551–552, 558, 561, 573–574,
    576–577, 581, 584, 587, 624–625,
    640, 653, 655
London Assurance Company, 519, 524, 525
Londonberry, Lord, 467
London Company, 549
Londoners, 445
London Magazine, 546, 639
London Observer, The, 587
Long Island, 26, 386, 395, 600
Longly, Richard, 156
Lopez, Francisco de Gomara, 86
Lord (The), 338, 358
Lord Baltimore, 336, 401, 403
Lord Proprietary, 401
Lords Commissioners for the Treaty for
    Commerce with France, 623
Lord's Day, 367
Lords of Trade, 403
Lords of Trade and Plantation (Barbados),
    366
Lords Lieutenant, 286, 288
Lord's Prayer, 387
Lorenzo, San de los Minas, 308
Loros (Muslim slave), 85

– INDEX –

lost tribes of Israel, 352. *See also* Native
 American Indians
Louis XIV, 287, 327, 364, 480, 550, 611; as
 to Sun King, 461
Louisiana, 162, 378, 462, 609
L'Overture, Toussaint, 232, 237, 612
Lovejovian, 281
Low Country, 250, 535
Lowestoft, 66
Loyalists, 398
Ludwell, Thomas, 26
Lukeni lua Nimi (founder). *See* Kongo
Lumbrozo, Jacob, 401
Luther, Martin, 288–289, 291, 380
Lutheran Danish National Church, 349
Lutheranism, 359
Lydia (ship), 547

Machiavelli, Niccolo, 282, 294, 298, 569,
 637, 643, 647–648; *Discourses on the
 First Ten Books of Livy,* 643
Mackay, Charles, *Extraordinary Popular
 Delusions and the Madness of
 Crowds,* 457
Madagascar, 103, 106–107, 550, 600
Madeira, 84, 172, 191, 246, 254–255,
 268–269, 369
Madison, James, 275. 281, 289, 582,
 634–635, 641, 644, 653; as to *Notes
 on Ancient and Modern
 Confederacies,* 643
Madrid, 45, 48, 88, 310, 326, 543
Maescoe, Charles, 516
Magdeleine (daughter of Marie Thomas),
 161
Magellan, 213
Maghrib, 190, 192
Maghrib, al-Aqsa-al- (the farthest West),
 188
Maghrib, Bahr al- (western sea, Atlantic),
 191
Maghribi, 195
Magreb, 414
Mahomet, 384
Mahometan (Muslim) 379–380, 382–383
Maianjor, 219
Main (river), 123
Makandal, 227
Malaspina, Alejandro, 42–44
Malaysia, 208–209. *See also* Island
 Southeast Asia

Males (from mu'allim) as revolt leaders, 389
Mali, 376
Malintzin (Cortes partner), 86
Mamachou, Marie, 159
Mama Occllo, queen (first Incan Queen),
 332
Mamluks, 378
Mammon, 546
Mancke, Elizabeth, *Creation of the British
 Atlantic World, The,* 533
Mandeville, Bernard, *The Fable of the Bees
 or, Private Vices, Public Benefits,* 558
Manhattan Island, 415
Manila Bank, 219. *See also* Oraurau-feis
Manilla, 213
Mani Vunda, religious leader, Afonso's reign
 329; as to Beatriz, 336
Mansur, Ahmad al-, Sultan of Morocco,
 187, 194, 196. *See also* Dhahabi Al-
Mapuche, 83
Marce (priest), 163
Marcus, Jacob, 370
Marguerite, La (ship), 165
Maria Theresa, empress, 117
Mariana Islands, 209, 21
market revolution, 394
maroons (fugitive slaves), 227, 274, 608–610
Marova Lagoon, 215
Marquesas Islands, 218
Marrakesh, 193
marronage, 227
Marshall Islands, 210
Marshallese, 212
Martha's Vineyard, 248
Martin, Benjamin, *Philsophical Grammar,*
 546
Martin, Frederick, *The History of Lloyd's
 and of Marine Insurance in Great
 Britain,* 519
Martineau, Harriet, 398–399
Martinican, 165
Martinique, 152–153, 162, 164–165, 255,
 389, 609–611, 627, 656, 661
Martire, d'Anghiera, Pietro, 18
Marx, Karl, 574
Maryland, 26, 336–337, 350–351, 357, 360,
 394–395, 397, 399–401, 406–407,
 446, 480–481; as to Catholics, 395,
 403–405, 408; as to Assembly and
 Delegates, 395; as to Lower House
 proposing Act of 1704 be repealed to

689

− INDEX −

defer to Act of Parliament with a Provision to prevent the Growth of Popery, 405–406–407; as to Upper House blocking the measure, 407
Maryland Constitution, 286
Maryland Farmer, 287, 290
Maryland *Gazette*, 408
Maryland Historical Society, 633
Marylandian, 406
Maryland Province of the Society of Jesus, 399
Mary Martin (ship), 173
Mascarene Islands, 109
Mascarenes, 107
Mass, 330, 333, 404
Massachusetts, 179, 248, 274, 351, 379, 382, 400, 474, 478–481
Massachusetts Bay, 349, 352, 381, 451
Massachusetts Bay Company, 445, 549
Massachusetts Constitution, 292
Mason, Charles, 365, 399
Masudi-al, 376
Mataindios (slayer of native Americans), 379
Matamoros (Muslim slayer), 379
Matar, Nabil (historian) 378
Mather, Cotton, *The Christian Philosopher*, 381–382
Maupeou revolution, 656
Mauretania, 190, 380
Maurus or moro, 380
Maurits, Johan, Governor, 478. *See also* Nassau
Mauritius, 103
Maya, 91
Mayer (Meyer), Johann Ludwig, 124
Mayne & Poyn v. De Gozi, 514
McClellan, James III, *The Black Jacobins*, 233
McCormick's Virginia Reaper, 587
Measuring the hazards of the Atlantic slave trade (Inikori), 522
Medici, 473
Mediterranean (nations), 61, 65, 191, 193, 195, 197–198, 265, 414, 418–419, 517–518, 547–548
Mediterranean Islands, 269
Mediterranean Sea, 133, 176, 191, 195, 207, 212, 378–379, 381, 539
Melanesia, 208–209, 213
Melanesians, 220
Melville, Herman, 131, 145; as to *Billy Budd*, 131; as to *Moby Dick*, 131

Menier, Sr., 1637
Menschendiebe (recruiter), 119
Mercer (ship), retaken by African King (ship)
Merchant Shipping Act of 1823, 139
merchants mappe of commerce, The (Roberts), 621
Mercier, Henri de la Riviere, 653
Mercier, Louis Sebastien, 658
Mercier, Pierre Pau de la Riviere, 661
mesalliances, 152–153, 161
Mesoamerica, 45, 80–81, 91
Mesoamericans, 82, 91
Mestizos, 85, 88–89, 92, 329–330
Metacom (aka King Philip), 248
Methodism, 359–360
Methodist(s), 355, 357, 359–360
Metternich, Clemens, 117
Mexica, 80–81, 83, 249, 377
Mexica empire, 80–81, 83
Mexican Inquisition, 380, 422
Mexicans, 271
Mexico, 14, 45, 79, 82–83, 86, 88, 252, 271, 322, 324, 380, 389, 484, 548, 634
Mexico City, 332
Mezqueta, Abraham Bueno de, 368
Michel, Jacob, 157
Micronesia, 208–209, 213, 219
mid-Atlantic, 573
mid-Atlantic Islands, 66–67, 69
Mid-Atlantic ridge, 56
Middle Ages, 265, 473
Middleburg, 474, 548
Middle Colonies, 23
Middle East, 390, 547, 563
Middle Passage 138, 387, 450, 601, 605–606, 612
migration, 117–119; as to emigration, 119–121; as to immigration, 121–125
Mikve Israel Synagogue, 368
militia controversy, 283
Militia Ordnance, 283
Mill, James, 584
Milton, John, 558; as to *Paradise Lost*, 546–547
Minas Geras, 252
Misselden, Edward, 558
missionaries, 36; as being students, 36; as being teachers, 36; as being critics, 36
Mississippi, 387
Mississippi Bubble, 457, 459, 467
Mississippi Company, 462, 626–627

– INDEX –

Mizrachi, 414
Moby Dick (Melville), 131
Mociño, José Mariano, 45
Moctezuma, 80, 88, 90, 247, 271. *See also* Cortes, don Martin Moctezuma Nezahualtecolotzin
Mogador, 197. *See also* Essaouira
Mohawk (language), 353
Mohawks, 353
Mohlen, Jorgen Thor, 477
Molière (Jean Baptiste Poquelin), *Le Festin de Pierre,* 627
Molokai, 219–220
Monarquia Indiana (Torquemada), 41
money, paper, 472–474, 476–485
Mongin, Father, 15
Mongols, 83
monograph myopia, 21
Monroe Doctrine, 276
Monsieur Colbert's Ghost (anon), 624
Montague, Lady Mary Wortley, 465
Montesquieu, Baron de, 229–230, 239, 658, 618–619, 636; as to *L'Esprit des Lois; Pensees,* 230, 641, 643; as to *Considerations on the Greatness of the Romans and their Decline,* 643
Montilla, 86
Montreal, 451
Montserrat, 365, 541
Moore, Francis, *Travels,* 546
Moor(s), 193, 325, 365, 380, 384, 387, 601
Mopox, Count of, 45
Moravia, 125
Moravianism, 358
Moravians, 355, 357, 359
Moreau, Mederic Louis-Elie de Saint-Mery, 653, 655–659; as to *Description topographique. physique, civile, politique et historique de la partie francais de l'isle Saint Dominque,* 655–656; as to *Loix et constitutions des colonies francoises de l'Amerique sous le Vent,* 655–656
Morel, Pedro de Santa Cruz, 300–302, 311–314
More Than a Living (Lieber), 215
Morgan, Philip, 2, 55, 600; *Atlantic History: A Critical Appraisal,* 2; as to *Oxford History of the Atlantic World,* 3; as to *The Oxford Handbook of the Atlantic World,* 533

Morice, Humphrey, 450
morisca, 380
moriscos, 191–193, 255, 377, 380
Mormons, 361
Mormonism, 361
Moroccanists, 189
Moroccan Jews, 196
Moroccan(s), 187, 189, 377, 387
Morocco, 172–174, 176–177, 180–181, 188–190–198, 381, 387, 448
Moros (Muslim slave), 85
Morrison, James, 584
Mosley, Joseph, Fr. 404
Mosquito Coast, 549
mortgages, 476
Mozambique, 106
Mozart, 117
MPs (Parliament), 393
Muhammad (Prophet), 380, 382,
Muhammad, Sidi b. Abd Allah 195, 197
mulatos, 92
mullatta, 380
mulatres, 154–165
Muley Ishmael, 180
Mun, Thomas, 558
Munoz, Juan Bautista, *Archivo General de Indias,* 46; *Historia del Neuvo Mundo,* 46
Munster (Ireland), 397
Murua, Martin de, 41. *See also* Peru
Musée de Paris, 657
Muscovy or Russia Company (chartered 1555), 444, 536
Museo Arqueológico Nacional, 48
Museo de America, 48
Museo Nacional de Ciencias Naturales, 48
Museo Nacional de Etnologia, 48. *See also* Velasco, Gonzales, director
muskrat, 13
Muslim(s), 192, 197, 247, 254, 365, 376–377, 381, 383–384, 386–390, 423, 427–428
Muslim Mediterranean, 193, 378
Mussulman, or Mussulmen, 380
Muthu, Sankar, 228, 230–231
Mutis, José Celestino, 45

Nadau and Marin, Monsieurs (lawyers), (Code Noir), 162
Nafi, Uqbab, 188
Nahuas (of Mexico), 79, 81

— INDEX —

Nahuatl (language), 41, 89
Napoleon, 134, 136, 265, 275, 483, 612
Napoleonic Wars, 100, 275, 485, 521–522, 581–582
Narragansett Indians, 249
Narvaez, Panfilo de, 332
Natchez, 386
National Assembly (France), 236
National Debt (Britain), 450, 457, 462
National School of Design in Birmingham, 573, 584
Native American Indians, 79–80, 84, 238, 247–250, 265, 271–273, 276, 327, 352, 379, 389, 452, 600, 609, 653
Native American Protestants, 359
Native North Americans, 15, 17, 351, 377, 599, 600–601, 610
Native Peoples of Americas: Arawak, 21, Choctaw, 21–22; Iroquois,13; Patuxent 26; Raritan, 26
Nassau. See Maurits
Navigation Acts, 367, 550, 558, 580, 587
Neale, James, Fordyce and Down, 491–498
Neapolitan Enlightenment, 650
Near Oceania, 209. See also Oceania
negociante, Il (Gio-Domenico), 621
Negroes, 601–602, 605
Negro Seamen Act, 138–139
Nemours, Pierre Samuel Dupont de, 653
Neolithic Revolution, 17; as to effect of pathogens on animals, people and fauna, 5–6
Neo-Reconquista, 192
Netherlands, 60–62, 65, 68, 247, 348–349, 351, 357, 364, 367, 425, 543, 555–556, 558–559, 561
Nueva coronica y buen gobierno (Ayala), 91–92
Nueva Granada, 45
Nevis, 364–365, 367–369, 541
Nevisians, 369
Nevis's Naval Office records, 369
New Amsterdam, 196, 274, 381, 421–422, 562
New Caledonia, 209, 220
New Canaan, 124. See also America
New Christians, 325, 548
New Continent, 41, 48
New England, 22, 58, 60, 67–68, 71, 120, 178, 248–249, 268, 272–273, 349–352, 369, 406, 478, 481, 522, 562, 573

New England Company, 352–353
New Englanders, 14, 23, 69, 349
New England Indians, 353
Newfoundland, 57–58, 60–64, 67–71, 173, 178, 212, 264–266, 321
New France, 20, 23, 327, 333, 339–340, 562–563
New Granada, 483, 654
New Guinea, 209–210
New Hampshire, 394, 480; as to Constitution, 286
New Holland, 353, 421
New Jersey, 395, 480, 640
New Jerusalem, 361
New Laws of 1542 (Native slavery ban), 85
Newman, Henry (cleric), 123
New Mexico, 82, 271, 377, 379
New Netherland(s), 17, 20, 26, 249–250, 267, 272, 274, 349, 421, 533, 535, 562
New Orleans, 386, 606
Newport, 142, 365, 367, 371
Newport, Christopher 247, 537
New South Africa, 102
New Spain, 45, 83, 85, 88–89, 312, 324, 332–333, 422, 562, 654
New Sweden, 120
New System of Modern Geography (Guthrie), 546
Newton, Isaac, 467
Newtonian Enlightenment, 558
New York, 23, 142, 178–179, 350, 357, 365, 367–369, 371, 393, 398–399, 480, 583, 644, 657
New York City (Gotham) 398, 573–574, 599–600, 612
New York Crystal Palace Exhibition of 1853, 573, 588
New Yorkers, 399
New World, 35–37, 40, 42, 46–47, 49–51, 85–86, 124, 151, 187, 191–194, 196–198, 250, 322, 324, 327–329, 336, 349, 376–378, 389, 394, 415, 419–421, 426–427, 633–634, 639, 645, 654
New Zealand, 3, 209, 563
Nightingale v. Bridges (Admiralty case 1684), 448
Nimes (temple), 633
Nine Years' War, 283, 286, 478
Nipinoukje and Pipinouke (fable), 328

692

– INDEX –

Noah, 427
'No King, No Popery' (Patriots cry, American Revolution), 394
non-Catholics, 364
non-English, 394
non-Europeans, 155–156, 165
non-Jews, 420
non-Muslims, 389
Noom, Reinier, 557
Nordland, 71
Nore, 137
Norfolk, Virginia, 134
Norgesvoldet, 72
Normandy, 627
Norse, 264
North Africa, 3, 133, 172–173–174, 177–182, 190, 192–193, 323, 377, 380–381
North African 174
North Africans, 93, 182
North America, 13, 17–19, 27, 56, 58, 67, 119–121, 123–124, 133, 143, 153, 193, 212–213, 218, 221, 248, 272–274, 276, 321, 327, 327–328, 332–333, 336, 339, 353, 355, 358, 360–361, 371, 381, 384, 386, 393, 406, 415, 419, 424, 427, 493, 503, 531, 535, 538, 540–541, 549–551, 562–563, 576, 578, 606, 633–634, 653–655
North American colonies, 132, 350
North American Enlightenment, 651
North American Great Lakes, 451
North American Indians, 353
North Americans, 378
North America's animal history, 3–5, 8
North and/or South America, 267, 271, 275–276, 378
North Atlantic, 57, 79, 93, 105, 109–110, 212, 218, 264, 268, 471, 531
North Atlantic current (Gulf Stream), 57–58
North Atlantic, physical characteristics: as to topographic factors, 56–57; as to oceanographic factors, 56–57; as to ecological factors, 56–57;
North Carolina, 17, 350, 357, 480–481
northeast North America, 59, 333
Northeastern Brazil, 82–83, 422
northeastern South America, 83
northern Africa, 246
northern Balkans, 120

northern Europe, 60, 62, 67, 144, 272, 548
northern Europeans, 304
Northern Hemisphere, 210
Northern Morocco, 190
northern South America, 85
northern Spain, 308
North Pole, 57
North Sea, 57–58, 62, 64–65, 68, 70–71, 144, 212, 534, 539, 547
Norton, George. *See* John Norton & Sons
Norton, John, 499
Norway, 56, 58, 61, 64, 66, 69, 477, 484
Norwegian, 67
Norwegian Deep (ocean trench), 57
Norwegians, 71
Norwegian Seas, 57
Norwegian Shelf, 57
Northwest Africa, 84
North West Company, 452
northwestern Europe, 105
Notes on Ancient and Modern Confederacies (Madison), 643
Notes on the State of Virginia (Jefferson), 640–642, 655
Nova Scotia, 69, 267, 273, 360, 404, 480
Nurnberg, 122
Nzinga a Nkuwu, 246, 323. *See also* Joao I

Oahu, 218
Oaths of Supremacy and Allegiance, 368
Oberhaupt, 118. *See also* House of Austria; King of Bohemia; King of Hungary
Oberösterreich, 117
Obeyesekere, Gananath, 220
Observations on the Commerce of the American States with Europe and the West Indies (Sheffield), 579
Observations upon Aristotle's Politicks (Filmer), 643
Oceania, 208–209, 213, 215, 220. *See also* Near Oceania; Remote Oceania
Ocean is a Wilderness: Atlantic Piracy and the limits of State Authority, 1688–1856, The (Guy), 2
Office of Assurances, 516–517
Official Description and Illustrated Catalogue. See Great Exhibition of 1851
O'Gorman, Edmundo, *The Invention of America*, 89
Ohio, 272

693

– INDEX –

Old and New East Indies Companies, 449
Old Calabar, 523
Old World, 35, 37, 155, 193, 198, 255, 394, 408
Old World and the New, The (Elliott), 89
O'Leary, Arthur (Franciscan priest), 397
Ontario, 353
Opechancanough, 541
Operation Moses, 414
Oran, 177
Orange, Carlos de, 310
Oraurau-feis, 219. *See also* Manila Bank
Orden de San Francisco de Neuva Espana (Torquemada), 41
Orders in Council (Britain), 134
Ordinance of November 1704: as to constraints on administrators of the French, 162
Ordinance of 1729: as to cabaret regulations, 163
Origen of Alexander, 384
Origins of Empire, The (Canny), 533
Orinoco (river), 41
Orkneys, 71
Orrery, Earl of, *A Treatise of the art of war*, 283
Osborne, Sir Edward, 172
Osnabrück Instrument of Peace, 122
Ottoman Empire, 120, 177, 193, 196, 197, 548
Ottomans, 378–379
Our Sea of Islands (Hau'ofa), 214–215
Ovid, 633–634
Oviedo, Gonzales Fernandez (cronista de Indies), 39, 48: as to *Historia general y natural de las Indias*, 39; as to *Sumario de la natural historia de las Indias*, 39
Oxford, 357
Oxford Handbook of the Atlantic World, The (Canny and Morgan), 3, 533

Pacific Coast, 82
Pacific Islands, 207–208
Pacific Islanders, 209, 212, 214, 215, 219–221, 547
Pacific Ocean, 207–214, 216, 218–219, 393
Pacific Oceanic, 42
Pacific (region), 3, 120, 213
Pacific Rim, 144, 220
Pagden, Anthony, *European Encounters with the New World*, 89

packet service, 143
Pagan, 383
Paine, Thomas, 652–653
Palatines, 349
Palau Islands, 209, 219
Palenque (Mayan ruins), 46
Palmer, Robert, 661
Panama, 211, 389, 450
Padilla, Beatriz de, 380
Papal Bull of 1493, 271
Papal Bull of 1508, 324
Papers of instructions for the Parliamentary meeting after the revolution (Erle), 291
Papillon, Thomas (MP), *365*
papists, 386, 405
Paradise Lost (Milton), 546
Paraguay, 657
Paris, 20, 231, 233–236, 457–459, 461, 467, 625, 634, 656–658
Parker, Quanah, 83
Parlement of Paris, 656
Parliament (England), 132, 137, 139, 176, 352, 366, 394, 405–407, 445, 448, 452, 476–477, 480, 481, 483, 623; as to 1566 action for seizure of Russian bound cargoes), 444
Parliamentary Committee, 584
Parliament's Currency Act of 1751, 481
Parliaments of Scotland, 441; as to *Act for Encouraging of Forraigne Trade, 1693*, 441
Parnell, Sir Henry, 584
Patagones, 41
Patagonia, 80, 84
Pater Noster and Ave Maria, 332
Paths to Emancipation: Jews, States and Citizenship (Birnbaum and Katznelson), 418
Patoulet, Jean Baptiste, 159
Patriots (American revolution), 393–394, 397–400, 578
Paul III, pope, 338
Paullu Inca, 82
Pavon, Joseph, 45
Pawnees, 83
peaceable militia, The (anonymous), 283
Peace of Nijmegen in 1678, 308. *See also* Franco-Dutch War
Pearson, David, 212
Pedro, king (Kongo), 336

– INDEX –

Peel, Sir Robert, 584
Pelleprat, Pierre, 154–155
Penal laws of England, 406
Penal Period, 406
Penn (family), 399
Penn, William, 23, 415
Pennsylvania, 119, 393, 399, 404, 480, 640
Pennsylvania Constitution, 292
Pennsylvanian Anti-Federalists, *The Deliberator*, 291
Pensees (Baron de Montesquieu), 230
Penzance, 176
Perez, Juana, 384
Perfect Merchant, The (Le parfait negociant, ou Instruction generale pour ce qui regarde le commerce des marchandises de France et des pays etrangers) (Savary), 619–621, 623, 625
Pernambuco, Brazil, 478
Peru, 41, 45, 82, 84–86, 88, 90, 92, 93, 271, 332, 389, 548, 654. *See also* Ayala and Murua, 41
Petit, Giles, 160–161
Phaedon (slave), 642
Phaedrus (slave), 642
Phelps, Thomas, 172
Phelypeaux, Governor, 610. *See also* Binture
Phénomène Savary, 621–622, 628
Philippines, 49, 209, 335
Phillips, Captain Thomas, 603–604. *See also* Hannibal
Philip II, king, 193
Pichardo, Antonio se Vinuesa, 300–301, 311–312
Philadelphia, 371, 381, 397, 587, 653, 655–657
Philadelphia Convention, 289
Philadelphienis, 284, 360, 371
Philsophical Grammar (Martin), 546
Phydiocrats, 662
Picon, Molly (film star), 424
Pimentel, Rodrigo, 305
Pina, José de, 312–313
Pinheiro, Isaac (ancestor of Moses), 368; as to wife Esther, 368–369; as to father Abraham and sisters Rachel and Sarah Goma, 369
Pinheiro, Moses, a Jew, 364; as to wife Lunah, 370; *See also* Black Rock Pond
Pinta and *Nina* (ships), 377
pirate republic (Salé), 176

Pitt, Joseph, *A True and faithful Account of the Religion and manners of the Mahommetans*, 177
Pitt the Younger (Prime Minister), 579
Pizzaro, 82, 90
Plantation Act (Parliament), 368
Pleistocene Ice Age, 13; animals and fauna before and after, 2, 11
Pliny the Elder, 151
Plymouth Colony, 349
Plymouth, Mayor of, 174
Pocahontas, 379
Pococke, Edward (Arabic first chair at Oxford), 382
Pohnpei, 210
Pointe-Noire, 157, 159, 161
Political Economy Club, 584
Politics I (Aristotle) 642
Polo, Marco, 484
Polybius, 643
Polynesia, 208–209
Polyverel, 237
Pongau, 122
Pope, 264, 384, 406
Popery, 408
popish army, 282, 287
Port-de-Paix, 312
Port Elizabeth, 109
Porter, Captain David ,134
Port Jew(s), 419–420
Port Jews: Jewish Communities in Cosmopolitan Maritime Trading Centers, 1550–1950, 419 (John Carter Brown Library Conference Paper 1997)
Portobelo, 625
Port of London Society, 140. *See also* British Sailor's Society
Port Royal (Barbados), 365, 502
Portugal, 62–63, 192, 194, 254, 267, 275–276, 326, 348, 352, 421, 478, 483–484, 532, 538, 557, 563, 654
Portuguese, 60, 82, 84, 103, 191–192, 194–195, 264–265, 269, 282, 321–322, 329, 377, 427, 447, 542–543, 548, 551, 553, 563
Portuguese Atlantic, 217, 255
Portuguese Brazil, 85
Portuguese Crown, 246, 323, 548–549
Portuguese East Indies, 103
Portuguese Empire, 384, 531, 533, 536, 654

695

— INDEX —

Portuguese littoral, 61
Postl, Karl (aka Charles Sealsfield), 125
Post-Revolutionary America, 644
Potomac River, 13
Powhatan, 247
Pragmatic Sanction, 120
Prague, 126, 421
Praying Indians, 352
Preliminary Discourse (Sale), 383
Presbyterians, 349, 351, 371; as to actions
    of Lowland Scottish, 352
Price, Richard, 653
Prideaux, Humphrey, 383; as to *The True*
    Nature of Imposture Fully Display'd
    in the Life of Mahomet, 381
Priestly, Joseph, 653, 655–656
Prince Among Slaves (Alford), 387
Prince George County (Maryland) 398
Prince of Wales (ship), 123
Prince, Mary, 601, 610
Privy Council, 174–5, 514, 516–517, 521, 580
Probanza de Meritos, (accreditation of rights
    system). *See* Felipe II
proletarianization, 144
Propaganda Fide, 326, 338
Prophet, The, 380, 382–384
Protestant anti-Catholicism, 322
Protestant Atlantic, 347–349, 351, 355,
    357–358, 361
Protestant Atlantic colonies, 348–350,
    358–359
Protestant British, 327, 337
Protestant Christians, 382
Protestant Christianity, 3, 355
Protestant English, 458
Protestant Enlightenment, 650
Protestant Episcopal Church, 360. *See also*
    Church of England
Protestant Huguenots, 561
Protestantism, 122, 286, 327, 347–349, 351,
    353–355, 357, 359–361, 370
Protestant Peasants Revolt, 122
Protestant Reformation, 272
Protestant(s), 117, 122–123, 247, 272, 290,
    327, 336, 339, 348–353, 357, 359–361,
    381, 384, 386, 399, 403–404, 427
Protten, Christian 358
Protten, Rebecca, 358
Providence, 645
Providence Colony, 384
Providence Island, 348, 549

Providence Island Company, 549
Provincial Council of Baltimore, 328
Prussia, 117, 122, 349
pseudo-Christian, 38
Pueblo Indians, 192
Puerto Rico, 49, 484, 542
Puluwat, 219
Puluwatese, 219
Puritan (forbidden Maryland epithet), 401
Puritans, 26, 349, 352
Pursburg (ship), 123

Quakers, 350–351, 357, 359, 370–372; as
    to founder Fox, 355
Quaker Pennsylvania, 407
Quasi War, 581
Quauhquecholteca, 91
Quebec, 20, 394, 478, 480, 626; as to fur
    trade, 451–453; as to Catholic
    consolidation, 327
Queen (British), 548
Queensland, 220
Qur'an, 381–383, 387, 389
Quetzalcoatl, 322

race, 151–153
racist Enlightenment, 229; *See also* Buffon,
    Count de
Radical Enlightenment, 650, 661
Raimond, Julien, 653
Raleigh, Sir Walter, 445, 541
Rall, Hieronymus Cristani von (chancellor),
    122
Randolph, Edmund, 284
Rapanui (Easter Island), 207
Raynal, Abbe, 227, 232, 653; as to
    L'Histoire des dues Indes, 227
Real Gabinete de Historia Natural, 45
    (Davila). *See also* Pedro Franco
    Davila, Director
Real Jardin Botanico, 48–49,
Recife, 364
Reck, Baron Philipp Georg Friedrich von, 123
Reconquista, 192, 246, 254, 272, 379
Red Atlantic, 79
Reddy, William; as to *Social Life of Things:*
    Commodities in a Cultural
    Perspective, 625
Rederij, 554
Red Sea, 378
Red Sea Pirates, 178

696

– INDEX –

Reducciones (closing missionary led Catholic settlements), 325
Reformation, 61, 122, 335, 340, 348, 417
Reformations, 327–328, 360
Reformers, 348
reformism: as applied to mariners, 139–142; as applied to their working wives, 141
Regensburg, 122. *See also* Holy Roman Imperial Diet
Regulating Acts of 1772, 491–492
Regulations between 1711–1715: as to prevention of slaves from selling commodities, 164
Regulation of August 1711, 16; as to slaves right to buy freedom, 164,
Regulation of 1749: as to right to work for almost free people, 164
Regulation of 1667, 15; as to powers of Gouverneur General and the Intendant, 162
Reflexions sur l'esclavage des Negres, Marquis de Condorcet, 231
Relacion geografica or *Descripcion de la cuidad y provincia de Tlaxcala,* (Guevara), 88
Remote Oceania, 209, 212, 213. *See also* Oceania
Renaissance, 421
Rensselaerwijck, 22
Repartimiento system, 269
republic, 284
Republicanism, 398
Republic of Letters, 654, 658
Republic of Texas, 484
Requerimiento, 247–248
Resolution (ship), 176
Restoration, 177, 179–180, 284, 623
Revelation, book of, 381
Revolution of 1688, 448
Revolutionary War, 287, 398–399, 640
Revue de Histoire Economique et Social (Hauser), 619
Rezio, Levy, 367
Rhine (river), 123
Rhode Island, 178, 351, 357, 384, 386, 480–481
Ricardo, David, 584
Richelieu, Cardinal, 327
Richmond, 633
Riebeeck, Jan van, 104
Roanoke, 266, 539, 541

Robben Island, 104
Roberts, Lewis, *The merchants mappe of commerce,* 621
Robertson, Robert Reverend, 365
Robertson, William, *History of America,* 46
Robinson Crusoe (Defoe), 382
Robles, Andres de, 309
Robles, Jeronimo de, 309–311
Rochefort, de, 155–156
Roman Catholic Church, 384
Roman Catholicism, 335, 611
Roman empire, 246
Romanism and rebellion (Protestant fears, Pre-American Revolutionary War), 398
Romans, 643
Rome, 322–324, 326, 338, 406, 518, 636, 640, 643–645
Rothschilds (Bank), 562
Rotterdam, 123, 622
Roundhead (forbidden Maryland epithet), 401
Rousseau, Jean-Jacques, 30, 658
Ross, Alexander, 381–382
Royal Academy, 584–585
Royal African Company (RAC), 444, 448–454, 460–461, 463, 603
Royal Bank of Scotland, 480, 495
Royalist, 446
Royal Exchange Assurance, 519, 525
Royal Mint, 476–477
Royal Navy, 132, 134, 137, 139, 267, 448, 460–461, 463, 465; as to Lord Admiral, James, Duke of York, 448
Royal Society of London, 478, 563
Rule Britannia, 286
Rupert's Land (fur trade), 451
Rush, Benjamin, 653
Russia, 20, 58, 64, 69, 424, 451, 461, 480, 564
Russian Empire, 627
Ruiz, Hipolito, 45
Ruyter, Michael de, 447

Sabbath, 600
Sabre, Angeline, 163
Sa'di Dynasty, 194–196
Safi, 190
Sahagun, Bernardino de, *Historia General de las Cosas de la Nueva Espana,* 6–7; *Florentine Codex,* 89–90
Sahara, 196

697

– INDEX –

Saharan, 195

Saharan Africa, 322–323

Sailors' rights, 135

Saint-Mery, Moreau de, 233, 655

Sala-Molins, Louis, 229–232, 236,

Salé (city), 174, 176, 178–180

Sale, George (lawyer and translator), 382; as to *Preliminary Discourse*, 383; as to half a mussulman, 383

Salee, Anthony Jansen van (aka Anthony 'the Turk'), 381

Salem, 142

Salisbury, Lord, 174

salt, 61–62

Salzburg, 117–118, 122

Salzburger Protestants, 123

Salzburgers, 118, 122–124, 349, 361

Samuel (ship), 369

San Antonio, Texas, 378

Sancho, Ignatius, 660

San Domingo, 549

Sanchez, Francisco (mayor), 307

San Juan, 548

San Lorenzo de los Minas, 308

Santa Domingo, 300–302, 304–308, 310–314

Santa Domingo (river), 41

Santa Domingo de Talavera de la Reina (monastery), 88

Sandys, George, 633–634

Santiago (Patron saint of Reconquista), 379

Santiago de los Caballeros, 300–302, 306–307, 309–312

Sao Salvador, 323, 326, 336

Sao Tome, 216, 255, 324–325, 335

Sarni, 120

Saunders, Thomas, 172

Saut Reef (Enderby bank), 219

sauvage, 155, 156, 161

Savannah, 21, 123, 365, 371

Savannah River, 123, 609

Savary, Jacques, 619–621, 623–624, 627–628; as to *Perfect Merchant, The (Le parfait negociant, ou Instruction generale pour ce qui regarde le commerce des marchandises de France et des pays etrangers)*, 619; as to *La Vie de Monsieur Savary* (preface later edition), 621

Savary, Jacques des, Bruslons, 621–622, 624–627; as to *Banques d'Amsterdam*

& de Rotterdam, 625; as to *Du Commerce d'Hollande & de Flandre*, 622; as to *Du Commerce d'Angleterre, d'Ireland, & d'Ecosse*, 622, 625; as to *Compagnie francaise des Indes occidentals*, 626; as to *Le dictionnaire universel du commerce*, 621, 625–626

Savi (Hueda), 466

Savory, Louis-Philemon, 625–627

Savoy, 123

Savoyen, Eugene von (prince), 117

Saxony, 393

Scaleby Castle (ship), 527

Scandinavia, 60, 67–68, 477

Scandinavian monarchies, 627

Scandinavians, 71

Schaitberger, Josef, 122

Schaff, Philip, Reverend, 126

Scheme of Trade, 625

School of Design in London, 586

Schopf, Johann David, 125

Schorsch, Jonathan, 415

Schwabenziige and Sachsenganger, 117. *See also* Hungary

Schwarzach, 122

Scotian Shelf, 57, 69

Scotland, 56, 68, 178, 272–273, 357, 441, 471, 479–480, 483, 485, 491–492, 499, 503, 542, 622, 651

Scots, 82, 176, 365–366, 493, 499

Scots Magazine, 497

Scottish Enlightenment, 650

Scottish Lowlanders, 349

Scottish Parliament, 443, 476

Scottish Society for Promoting Christian Knowledge, 352. *See also* Presbyterian

seafaring, 142–145

Sealsfield, Charles (formerly Karl Postl), 125

Seamen's Acts, 138

Sebastian, San, 514

Second Amendment, 282, 291–293

Second Battle of Finisterre, The, 4 October 1747 (Serres), 558–559

Second Great Awakening, 140

Second Maroon War, 609

Second Part of the Institute of the Lawes of England (Coke), 365

Second Treatise (Locke), 290

Second Vatican Council, 1965 Dignitatis Humanae, 394

Sedgwick, Robert, 274

– INDEX –

Seelenverkaufer (recruiter), 119
Seguier, 619
Seint Anne of London (ship), 514. *See also*
  Ferrantyn
Select Committee, 586
Select Committee on Aborigines, 1835, 110
Semite, 366
Senate (U.S.), 36
Senegal Adventurers, 445
Senegambia, 378, 447
Sensbach, Jon, 358
Sephardi, 414, 419–420
Sephardim, 371, 414, 417
Sermons, 358
Serpent deities, 328
Serres, Dominic, *The Second Battle of*
  Finisterrer, 4 October 1747, 558–559
Serville, Louis, 165
Sesse, Martin de y Lacasta, 45
Seven Cities of Gold, 377
Seven Years' War, 132, 275, 452, 481, 493,
  496, 554, 562, 576, 627
1764 Currency Act, 481
Sevilla (Seville), 46, 84, 85, 89, 548,
  551–552
Shaftesbury, Lord, 575
Shamm, Carole, *The Creation of the British*
  Atlantic World, 533
Sheffield Independent, The, 586
Sheffield Iron Foundry, 585
Sheffield, Lord, *Observations on the*
  Commerce of the American States
  with Europe and the West Indies,
  579–580
Shelbourne, Prime Minister Lord, 579
Shenandoah Valley, 23
Shetlanders, 66
Shetlands, 66–67, 71
Siebenburgen, 117
Sicily, 278
Siege of Tenochtitlan, 249
Siege of Vienna, 379
Sierra Leone, 139, 324, 360, 378, 445
Silva, Joaquim José da, 654
Silva, Lourenco da, 326, 338
Silva, Manuel Galvao da, 654
Simitiere, Pierre Eugene du (engraver of U.S.
  seal), 645
Simpson, Baird & Co., 501
1601 Act, 516
1648 Osnabrück Peace Treaty, 122

slave punishments, 599–607
slave rebellion in New York of 1712,
  599–600
slave rebellions, 600, 604–605
slave resistance, 601–613
slave revolt of 1737, 163
slave revolt of 1791 (Haiti), 389, 612–613
slave revolts, 600–608
slave(s): racial, 153–165, 173, 179, 181–183,
  599–601, 613; enslaved by capture by
  Barbary States of North Africa,
  172–183:
slave runaways, 606–610; as to Native
  Americans, 610
slave trading; as to asiento, 457, 459,
  460–461, 466, 550, 603–607
slavery abolition; as to Brazil, 600; as to
  Haiti 612–613
slavery, ancient, 642
slavery, 230–238, 245, 250–255, 601–613
Sloane, Hans, 653, 663
Smith, Adam, 661; as to *An Inquiry into the*
  Nature and Causes of the Wealth of
  Nations, 559, 579; as to *The Theory*
  of Moral Sentiments, 575; as to
  Wealth of Nations, 590, 618; as to
  Wealth of Nations Book II, 492–493,
  496, 581
Smith, C., 586
Smith, Captain John, 21, 379
Smith, John Jobson, 585. *See also* Sheffield
  Iron Foundry
Smith, Samuel, Rev., 404
Smith, Samuel Stanhope, 653
Smith, William, Rector; as to St. John's Fig
  Tree, Charles Town, Nevis, 364, 368
Smollett, Tobias, 577–578
Smythe, John, 514, 518
Soares, Manuel Baptista, Bishop, 326
Social Life of Things: Commodities in a
  Cultural Perspective (Reddy), 625
Sociedad Antropologica Espanola, edited
  publications, *Revista de Antropologia*
  and *Antropologia moderna* (Velasco),
  19
Society of Arts, 576
Society of Friends, 382
Society of Jesus in Europe. *See* John
  Carrollton
Society for Jewish Culture and History, 416;
  as to promoter Leopold Zunz, 416

– INDEX –

Society for Promoting Christian Knowledge (SPCK), 123
Society Royale des Science et des Arts du Cap Francois, 657
Socinian Enlightenment, 650
Solomon, 414
Solomon, Haym, 371
Solomon Islands, 209, 215
Somers, Lord, 283
Somerset, 178
Songhay Empire, 187
Son of Liberty, 288
Sonthonax, Leger Felicite, 237
Sorkin, David, 419–420
South (Colonial America), 397
South Africa, 100–102, 105, 107–108, 485
South America, 213, 321, 326, 330, 333, 390, 466, 538–539, 542, 551, 563, 606
South Asia, 144
South Atlantic, 79–80, 90, 100, 212
South Carolina, 22, 123, 137–138, 266, 350, 378, 480. *See also* Charleston.
South Carolinians, 609
south eastern North America, 378
Southeast Pacific, 207
Southel, Seth (governor), 178
southern Africa, 100–106, 107–110
southern African Highveld, 101. *See also* hinterland
southern Europe, 67, 517
southern Greenland, 264
South Sea Company (SSC), 443–444, 450–451, 453–454, 457, 460, 462–467
South Pacific, 213,
South Sea Bubble, 450, 457, 459–460, 464–468, 558
South Seas, 464
Sovereign Council (New France), 327
Sovereign Council of Guadeloupe, 159–160
Sovereignty and Liberty of the States, 289
Soyo, 324
Spain, 35, 41, 47–50, 63, 84–86, 88, 187, 188, 192, 194, 196, 254–255, 266–267, 272, 275, 304, 308, 310, 312, 314, 324–326, 337, 348, 352, 368, 378, 400, 413, 453, 457, 460, 465, 466, 471, 483–484, 517, 532, 534–539, 541–543, 548, 563, 625. *See also* Iberia

Spaniard(s), 36, 41, 46, 48, 51, 81–82, 86, 90–92, 247–249, 332, 377, 609
Spanish (language), 36, 89
Spanish, 80, 83, 89–92, 177, 195, 213, 237, 247, 249–250, 266–268, 271–272, 275, 282, 309, 333, 348, 379, 381, 427, 466, 543, 548, 562, 609
Spanish America, 84, 255, 379–380, 443, 457, 539, 551, 638, 653–654
Spanish Americanism, 42, 48, 51
Spanish Armada, 445
Spanish Atlantic, 255, 377, 533, 536–537
Spanish Catholics, 365
Spanish Crown, 47, 51, 88–89, 91, 246–247, 302, 305, 308–310, 312, 314, 324, 450, 549, 556–557
Spanish Empire, 40, 275, 384, 531, 533, 536, 661
Spanish Florida, 276
Spanish Inquisition, 324
Spanish Islamic crops, 378
Spanish Island Slaves, 13
Spanish Jesuits, 325
Spanish Main, 450, 522
Spanish Mexico, 330
Spanish New World, 377, 380
Spanish science (Levenda Negrae), 35
Spanish Town (Barbados), 365, 609
Spate, Oskar, 214
SPCK (Society for Promoting Christian Knowledge), 350, 358. *See also* Bray
Spectator, The, 589
Speightstown (Barbados), 365–366
SPG (Society for the Propagation of the Gospel in Foreign Parts), 350, 355, 358. *See also* Bray
Spithead, 137
Spread, John, 522
Springfield, Massachusetts, 383
Staatsgrundgesetz (law of 1967 granting the right to emigrate), 121
St. Amand, 157
Stamp Act of 1765, 407
Stamp Act Riots, 407–408
St. Anna Church (in Augsburg), 123
St. Anne, 332
St. Anthony (vision), 336
Staten Island, 26
Statute of Artificers, 252
St. Augustine, 308
St. Catherine (ship), 422

700

– INDEX –

St. Christopher, 152, 54
St. Domingue, 137, 153, 165, 228, 231–237, 255, 611–612, 626, 653–657, 659–660; as to Cercle des Philadelphes, 657
Steiermark, 117, 123
Stern, Philip, *British Asia and the British Atlantic*, 533
Stevens, James Wilson, 172
St. Francois, 161, 163–165
St. Helena, 103, 109, 481
Still Life with Moor and Porcelain Vessels (van Streek), 557
St. Inigoes Manor (Maryland), 397
St. James (vision), by Joao I
St. James, London, 123
St. John, Henry, 283
St. John's Fig Tree, 364. *See also* Smith, William
St. Kitts, 337, 365, 368, 525
St. Lawrence Valley, 272
St. Malo, 522
St. Mary's (Bedford), 365
St. Mary's (Maryland), 397
St. Mary's Church (German) 123. *See also* London
St. Mary's County, 397, 405
St. Mary's County Militia, 397
St. Michael's Mount, 176
Story, Joseph, 291–292; *Commentaries on the Constitution*, 291
St. Pierre, 69
Strait(s) of Gibraltar, 56, 190–191, 195–196
Streek, Jurriaen van, *Still Life with Moor and Porcelain Vessels*, 557
St. Thomas, 322, 358
Stuarts, 283
Stuyvesant, Peter, 415
St. Vincent, 154, 158
Suarez, Gomez de Figueroa, 86
Suarez, Isabel (Chimpu Ocllo, Inca Princess), 86
Suat Reef (Enderby Bank), 220
sub-Saharan Africa, 198, 265, 414
Success of London, 172
Sumario de la natural historia de las Indias (Oviedo), 39
Superior Council of Guadeloupe, 164
Superior Council of Martinique, 159, 165
Supplement au Voyage de Bougainville (Diderot), 230

Surinam, 228, 274, 367, 421, 424, 426, 481
Sutcliffe, Adam, 413–415
Swahili coast, 106
Sweden, 64–65, 120, 348, 393, 480; as to Oregund iron, 461
Swedish East India Company, 549
Swellem, Asser Levy van, 421–422
Swift, Jonathan, 464; as to *A Discourse of the Contests and Dissentions Between the Nobles and the Commons in Athens and Rome*, 643
Swiss Enlightenment, 650
Switzerland, 349
Sydney, 220
Syncretic Catholicism, 328, 332, 335; as to Kongolese, 336

Ta (Tongan concept), 221
Table Bay, 100, 103–104, 109
Table Mountain, 104. *See also* Adamastor
Tagus river, 190
Tahitian(s), 217–218, 220
Tahuantinsuyu, 82
Talleyrand, Charles Maurice de, 655
Tamaha, 218
Tamerlan (slave named for Tamberlane), 389
Tamony (pseudonymous author), 6
Tampa, 377
Tangier, 194, 196
Tantalus, 428
Tashfin, Ali b. Yusuf b., 190
Taussig, Michael, 249–250
Tenocha, 90
Tenochtitlan 80–81, 88–91. *See also* Triple Alliance
Ten-Percent Act, 449
Terence (slave), 642
Tetuan, 197
Texas, 332, 377
Texcoco, 81, 88. *See also* Triple Alliance
Thakau Lala (Empty Reef), 212
Thaouira, Francois, and children Charles and Francois, 161
Theory of Moral Sentiments, The (Smith), 575
Third Amendment (U.S. constitution), 288
Thirteen Colonies, 560
Thirty Years War, 123, 348, 417, 425
Thistlewood, Thomas, 655, 658
Thomas, Marie, mother of Magdeleine, 162

701

Thornton, Henry, *Inquiry on the Paper Credit of Great Britain*, 492
Thoughts on Slavery (Wesley), 360
Three Half Moons (ship), 173
Thucydides, 643
Timbuktu, 197
Tira de Santa Catarina Ixtepeji, 91
Tlacopan, 88, 91. *See also* Triple Alliance
Tlatelolco, 88, 90
Tlaxcala, 80, 88
Tlaxcala (city in Mexico), 88
Tlaxcalteca, 80, 90
Tobacco Imports (England and Scotland), 503f
Toby of London (ship), 173
Toland, John, 283
Tomashevsky, film star, 424
Tomil, 220
Tonga, 209, 216
Toni Malau (Saint), 336
Tonkawas, 83
Torquemada, Juan de, *Monarquia Indiana: Orden de San Francisco de Neuva Espana*, 41
Tortuga, 302, 304, 306, 308–310, 549
Trade and Navigation Acts, 497
Travels (Moore), 546
treatise of the art of war, A (Earl of Orrey), 283
Treaty of Paris, 268 17
Treaty of Ryswick, 21, 314
Treaty of Tordesillas 1494, 267, 322
Treaty of Utrecht, 451, 453, 461, 465, 523
Treatyse of Fysshynge with an Angle (Berners), 59
trekboers, 101
Trelawny Town, 609
Trelawny Town Maroons, 609
Trenchard, John, 283
Tridentine Church, 326–327
Trieste, 120, 420
Trinidad, 383
Triple Alliance (Tenochtitlan, Texcoco, and Tlacopan), 81, 88
Tripoli, 172, 174, 176, 380, 383
Trivellato, Francesca, *Familiarity of Strangers*, 425
Trois Riviere, 158
True and faithful Account of the Religion and manners of the Mahommetans, A (Pitt), 177

True Nature of Imposture Fully Display'd in the Life of Mahomet, The (Humphrey) 381
Troughton, Thomas, *Barbarian Cruelty*, 177, 181
Trouillot, Michel Rolph, 237
Trustees for Establishing the Colony of Georgia in America, 123
Tryer, Captain Robert, 523
Tunis, 174, 380
Tunisia, 176
Tupac Amaru, 274
Turgot, Anne Robert Jacques, 651, 653, 661
Turkey, 414
Turkish Janissaries, 284
Turk, 193, 380
Turks, 172, 177–178, 379, 381, 384, 386, 522
Twkakwitha, Catherine, 332
Two Treatises of Government (Locke), 653
Typhoon Alley, 221
typhoons, 210–211, 221
Tyre, 558
Tyrolian Defregger valley, 122

Ulster Protestants, 349, 397
Unanue, Hipolito, 653–654
Union of South Africa, 100
Union, The, 582
Unitarian, 655
United Kingdom, 443
United Provinces, 446, 536, 538–539
United States, 83, 102, 121, 125–126, 133–134, 136–137, 139, 141–142, 144–145, 275–276, 327, 337, 339, 360, 365, 371, 376, 383, 387, 390, 393, 398, 414–415, 418, 423–424, 471, 481–482, 484–485, 501, 526, 546, 563, 573–574, 579–583, 587–589, 633–634, 635, 638–639, 643, 645, 653, 656
United States of America, 197, 268, 563
Universidad Central de Madrid 49. *See also* Ferrandiz, Manuel Anton
University of Coimbra, 654
University of Virginia, 655
Ural Mountains, 18
Urban, Greg, 248, 250
Urlsperger, Senior Samuel, 123–124
Ursula Bonadventure (ship), 176
U.S. Constitution, 418
U.S. Continental Shelf (northeast), 57–58

– INDEX –

U.S.S. *Chesapeake*, 134
U.S. South, 137
U.S. Treasury, 481
Utrecht, 450
Utrechtean Enlightenment, 650
Uzbekistan, 414

Va (Tongan concept) 221
Vaca, Alvaro Nunez Cabeza de, 192, 332
vacuum domicilium (vacant land), 248
Valencia, Spain, 378
Valette, Jacques, 159
Valparaiso, 220
Van Dam, Rip, (governor, New York) 369
Van der Donck, Adriaen, 20
Vanderlint, Jacob, 558
Vane, Sir Henry, 283
Van Riebeeck, Jan, 6
Vassall, Samuel, 446
Vat, Jean, 123
Vaze, Manuel, 156
Velasco, Pedro Gonzalez, *Sociedad Antropologica Espanola*, 48, edited publications; *Antropologia moderna*, 48; *Revista de Antropologia moderna*, 48. *See also* Museo National de Etnologia
Venezuela, 389, 483, 538
Venice, 473
Veracruz, 313, 450, 526
Vermont, 381
Versailles, 461
Vesey, Denmark, 137
Victorian Britain, and Britons, 574
Vie de Monsieur Savary, La (Savary), 621
Vienna, 117–119, 125–126
Vierge du Bail, La (ship), 165
Vieux Fort, 159
View of the City of Richmond from the Bank of the James River (Latrobe), 633
View of the River Ij Near Amsterdam (Vroom), 557
View of the Pool Below London Bridge (Atkins), 559
Vigera, Johann Friedrich, 124
Viking Age, 71
Vikings, 264–265
Vilcabamba, 82–83
violence, 245, 249–251
Virgil, *Aeneid*, 645

Virginia, 22, 26, 178, 252–253, 254, 284, 349, 351, 353, 360, 406, 446, 478, 480–481, 494, 499, 541, 549, 633–634
Virginia Capitol building, 633, 641
Virginia Company, 352, 445, 538, 541, 633
Virginia House of Delegates, 383
Virginians, 643
Virgin of Guadalupe, 330
Virgin Islands, 349
Virgin Mary, 330,
Virgin, The, 325, 336
Visscher, Matthew, 17
Vitalist Enlightenement, 650
VOC, 100–108. *See also* Dutch East India Company
Volney, comte de, 653
Volney, Constantin Francois, 655
Voltaire (Francois Marie Arouet) 383, 657–659;
Volume of the British Slave Trade 1655–1807, The (Inikori), 526
Voortrekkers, 101
Vroom, Hendrick, *View of the River Ij Near Amsterdam*, 557

Wadi Sous, 191
Wahunsonacock (chief), 247
Waikiki, 218
Wailau, 219
Wales, 178, 485, 522
Walker tariff, 587
Wallace, Davidson & Johnson: as to Joshua Johnson, 498
Wallis, George, 573–575, 588–589
Walpole, 491, 499
Waltham System, 394
Walton, Izaak, *Compleat Angler*, 59
Wampanoag, 248–249. *See also* Metacom
Warburton, Henry, 584
Ward, Sir Patience, 623
War of Austrian Succession, 160, 275, 481
War of 1812, 135–136, 268, 276, 481, 581–582
War of Independence, 46, 525, 578, 581, 64
War of Jenkins's Ear, 275, 451
War of the League of Augsburg, 314
War of the Polish Succession, 274
War of the Spanish Succession, 21, 417, 443, 450, 461, 463, 626
Warville, Pierre Brissot de, 653

703

— INDEX —

Washington, George, 275, 383–384, 582
Wattasid dynasty, 192, 194
W. Cunninghame & Co., 499
Wealth of Nations (Smith), 618
Wealth of Nations, Book II (Smith), 492–493, 496, 579
Wedgewood, Josiah, 582
Weeloey, 220
Werber (recruiter), 119
Wesley, Charles, 359
Wesley, John, 357, 359; *Thoughts on Slavery*, 360. *See also* Holy Club
west Africa, 187–188, 196, 237, 250, 321, 355, 358, 377–378, 387, 445, 463, 547
West African Kingdom of Hueda, 466
west African(s), 192, 354, 355
west coast of Africa, 377, 444, 446
West Country (England), 6, 176
West Country Englishmen, 22
western Africa, 250, 339, 347, 425, 449, 548, 600
western Algeria, 190
Western Carolines, 219
western Europe, 42, 117, 188, 281, 414, 417–418, 547
Western Hemisphere, 274–275
Western Hispaniola, 314
western Sahara, 188
western Mediterranean, 199
western Pacific, 209, 21
west Greenland Shelf, 57
West India Company (WIC), 446–447
West India Companies, 447; as to Brandenburg, 447; as to Denmark, 447; as to Sweden, 447
West India Fashionables, 577
West Indian colonies, 12
West Indies, 23, 137, 212, 369, 523, 526, 547, 550–551, 561, 576–577, 579–580, 603, 606, 634
Westminster, 431, 579–580
West, The, 471
Wheatley, Philis (of Boston), 360, 660
Whig History, 636
Whig Junto, 283
Whitefield, George, 359
White, John (artist), 17
White Servants, 599
Whitfield, James (Archbishop of Baltimore), 327, 357–358, 398
Wigen, Karen, 208

William Alexander & Sons, 496, 501–502
William and Mary, College of, 352
William of Orange, king, 348, 403, 449
William III, 286, 403
Williamsburg, Virginia, 382
Williams, Roger, 350, 384; as to President of Providence Plantations, 386; *Wilmington Aurora*, 137; as to *The Bloudy Tenent of Persecution for Cause of Conscience*, 384
Wilson, Alexander, 655
Wine Act of 1670, 624
Winthrop, John, 21; *General Considerations for the Plantations in New England*, 26
Winthrop, John Jr, Governor, 478
Winthrop, Samuel, 478
Wissenschaft des Judentums (scientific study of Jewish history), 416; as to promoter Leopold Zunz, 416
Witherspoon, John, 653
Wolcott, Derek, 215
word of God, 141
Words of the Lagoon (Johannes), 215
World War I, 49
World War II, 208, 417
WPA, 390
Wright and Fayle, *History of Lloyd's*, 519
Wright, Frances, 583
Wyatt, Francis (governor), 21

Xerez, Franciso de, 48
Xochimilca, 90
Xhosa, 108, 110

Yap Islands, 209, 220
Yankee Doodle, 125. *See also* United States
Yates, Donald, *Jews and Muslims in British Colonial America: A Genealogical History*, 386
Yogev, Gedalia, *Diamonds and Coral*, 425
Yorkshire, 588–589
Yorktown, 268
Yucatan, 91, 271
Yucatecan Maya, 80

Zapotec, 91
Zeeland, 537
Ziegenhagen, Friedrich Michael, 123
Zuara, Gomes Eanes de, 246
Zunz, Leopold, promoter of Jewish History, 416